RONALD J. THACKER, C.P.A., Ph.D.

Professor of Accounting
University of New Orleans

ACCOUNTING PRINCIPLES

2nd edition

PRENTICE-HALL, INC., ENGLEWOOD CLIFFS, NEW JERSEY 07632

Library of Congress Cataloging in Publication Data
Thacker, Ronald James.
  Accounting principles.
    Includes bibliographical references and index.
    1. Accounting.   I. Title.
HF5635.T42 1978   657   78-10531
ISBN 0-13-002766-9

Cover Illustration by: Eric Hieber
Interior/Cover Design by: Lorraine Mullaney
Production Editor: Linda Stewart
Copyeditor: Service to Publishers
Page Makeup: York Graphic Services
Acquisitions Editor: Ron Ledwith
Manufacturing Buyer: Phil Galea

Printed in the United States of America
10 9 8 7 6 5 4 3 2 1

PRENTICE-HALL INTERNATIONAL, INC., *London*
PRENTICE-HALL OF AUSTRALIA PTY. LIMITED, *Sydney*
PRENTICE-HALL OF CANADA, LTD., *Toronto*
PRENTICE-HALL OF INDIA PRIVATE LIMITED, *New Delhi*
PRENTICE-HALL OF JAPAN, INC., *Tokyo*
PRENTICE-HALL OF SOUTHEAST ASIA PTE. LTD., *Singapore*
WHITEHALL BOOKS LIMITED, *Wellington, New Zealand*

for Martha

contents

chapter6
merchandising operations: end of period   225

3 FINANCIAL ACCOUNTING CONCEPTS AND PROCEDURES 269

 CORPORATIONS 479

chapter 21
budgets and standard cost systems and reports 799

XViii

chapter 24
income taxes and business decisions   909

UNIT 54 THE NATURE AND IMPORTANCE OF INCOME TAXES   910

UNIT 55 TAX IMPACT ON DECISIONS   928

appendix a
reversing entries   944

UNIT 56 REVERSING ENTRIES   944

preface

TO THE STUDENT   You are about to begin your study of one of the most fascinating and influential subjects in our entire social and economic sphere. Accounting is both interesting and important because it deals directly with people and how they go about forming their objectives, making decisions, and reaching their goals. Accounting is influential, indeed, because it is vitally concerned with improving the likelihood that people actually do accomplish their goals, especially those goals of an economic and social nature.

    This course should be a rewarding and pleasant experience for you. Through the use of modern learning concepts, *Accounting Principles* gives you a complete yet simple learning system to assure your mastery of this important area of knowledge. This book has been written specifically for you. The following paragraphs outline the best way for you to use this textbook in your study of accounting.

First: Read and study the text   To make it easier for you to learn accounting, the material which you will study in this textbook is divided into small manageable units. There are twenty-four chapters in the book. Each of the chapters contains either two or three units, for a total of fifty-five units. The units are arranged in a logical progression to help you completely master the essential material. Each unit includes the following elements:

1. *Objective.* The precise purpose of the unit is stated clearly and openly as the first step. Where appropriate, this section tells you how the unit relates to past material and to future material.
2. *Approach to attaining the objective.* After you learn what the unit is going to accomplish, you are briefed on how the unit's material will be covered and on the sequence of the ideas that will be presented.
3. *The text itself.* You should concentrate your major effort on this area. The material is clearly presented in a logical, step-by-step fashion to help you to learn and remember the important relationships. As a further guide, the key questions from the approach section are repeated in the text margins next to where the questions are actually discussed and answered. Charts, tables, and illustrations are included to help you to quickly and efficiently understand a particular subject.
4. *Summary of New terms.* Accounting, like most subjects you will study, has its own special language which you must learn. To help you do this, every new term is printed in color in a bold face type and is carefully defined the first time it is used in the text. In addition, a summary checklist of these new terms, with definitions, is included at the end of each unit. As a special feature of this second edition, each of

the terms listed in the *Summary of New Terms,* has a page reference number printed by it. This reference number directs you to the page in the text material where the term was first introduced and defined. Therefore, you can refer directly to the text without a loss of time in your study process. This summary will reinforce your grasp of the unit's subject matter and will also be a good place to begin a review of the unit before exams.

Second: Work the assignment material A section titled "Assignment Material" appears at the end of each unit. These questions, exercises, and problems give you a chance to apply the ideas and techniques which you have studied in the unit. You should be able to answer all the questions and work all the exercises and problems, without assistance, after you have read and studied the text. The problems marked with an asterisk (*) are particularly challenging. Your instructor may ask you to do all or part of the assignment material as homework, or perhaps some of the work will be done in class.

Working Papers, which are partially filled-in assignment forms for all of the problems, are available separately to help you in working the assignment material. The forms have the problem numbers printed on them, along with other data which will reduce your "busy work."

Third: Check your mastery of the unit A separate *Student Guide* is available for those who may want or need further assistance in the study process. The *Student Guide* includes several exercises and problems that are directly related to the subject matter of the unit. After you have worked the exercises and problems in the blank spaces and forms provided, you can check your answers with the solutions provided in the back section of the *Student Guide.* The *Student Guide* also contains a complete study program with performance objectives. These performance objectives tell you what you should be able to do when you master the content of each unit. You can use the performance objectives as another checklist of key points to be mastered in the unit.

Also available are three *Summary Cases.* Working through these summary cases (each is like an extended problem) will give you a chance to view the accounting cycle and other systems from beginning to end in one example. Each of the three independent, relatively short cases includes all the pertinent data and all the necessary accounting forms. These summary cases will help you to review and actually use the key ideas and practices developed in the units.

This three-step learning plan has proven successful in situations where there have been students with many different backgrounds. With conscientious effort, you will have success with it too.

As you can see from the above paragraphs, *Accounting Principles* has been written for the student. My main goal has been to write a text which does as much as possible to insure that the individual student's experience of accounting is successful and worthwhile. I believe that this text is the most carefully designed complete learning system for the first year of accounting available today.

Experience with the first edition has shown that an extremely high proportion of students using this text will successfully complete the first year. This is the case because of: (1) the teachability of the text; (2) the learning concepts employed in putting it together; (3) the traditional and contemporary relevance of the subject matter; and (4) the special attention given to making this text the most readable possible. There are 55 units in the second edition as compared to 75 units in the first edition. This reduction in the number of units is a result of the more intensive coverage of the basic topics. In the following paragraphs I highlight some important additional points about the text's content and organization, and the major changes that have been made in this second edition.

Content An important theme in the content of *Accounting Principles* is *balance.* There is first of all a reasonable and attractive balance between financial accounting and managerial accounting. There is also a reasonable balance between accounting procedures and accounting concepts. Finally, there is a reasonable balance between the emphasis on the different forms of business organizations.

FINANCIAL AND MANAGERIAL ACCOUNTING *Accounting Principles* provides an ideal balance between financial and managerial accounting. The recent trend is towards a strong emphasis on managerial accounting in the first course. This book recognizes this trend and treats managerial accounting as an expanding and vital topic to the first course. This book also fully treats financial accounting and thoroughly and intensively deals with financial accounting procedures and concepts before moving on to the more complex managerial areas. The second edition of *Accounting Principles* has 17 chapters that are devoted primarily to financial accounting. This comprises approximately 70% of the text material. The remaining 7 chapters, or about 30% of the chapters are devoted to managerial accounting topics. The managerial topics in the second edition are somewhat more traditional in emphasis than the first edition, concentrating on cost-flow and accumulation systems, cost-volume-profit analysis, standard costing, and similar topics. Certain less central topics to the first course, such as accounting information for marketing and pricing decisions, have been omitted from the second edition.

ACCOUNTING PROCEDURES AND ACCOUNTING CONCEPTS This book has been written with the assumption that accounting procedures and concepts are not opposing forces, but go hand in hand in the learning process. *Accounting Principles* therefore thoroughly describes and explains the accounting cycle and its bookkeeping aspects. Many teachers are convinced that accounting cannot be taught successfully without intensively dealing with the procedural aspects.

In addition, this book is concerned with why we do certain things in accounting, how the parts fit together, and how the accounting information can be used. These aspects motivate students and bring life to the study of accounting. In summary, *Accounting Principles* is neither exclusively a procedural book nor is it exclusively a conceptual book. This text is designed to give that ideal procedural-conceptual balance that the accounting teacher is looking for.

PROPRIETORSHIPS VERSUS CORPORATIONS In introducing the subject matter of accounting, this book uses the proprietorship approach. The proprietorship basis is less complex and is therefore used to introduce the student to the fundamentals of the accounting process. The first chapter, however, includes a brief discussion to let the student know about the three basic forms of business organizations. An introduction to the corporation form begins in Part II, along with merchandising operations. Gradually, the dominant form of organization, the corporation, is treated. Again, *balance* is the key. The proprietorship approach is used, but corporations are introduced after the student has a solid foundation in the accounting cycle. One important feature of this second edition is that the more difficult analytical material on corporations (corporate capital and related topics) is treated in the second half of the text, beginning with Chapter 13.

Another major improvement of the second edition is the quantity and quality of the assignment material. *Accounting Principles* now includes more assignment material than any other accounting principles text:

Exercises	233	Group B Problems	174
Group A Problems	174	Cumulative Review Problems	50

Special attention has been paid to improving the quality of the assignment material. This edition presents significantly more challenging and comprehensive problems than the first edition. *Cumulative Review Problems,* which tie the chapter units together, have now been included. To assure the accuracy of the solutions, every item of assignment material has been worked independently by two accounting professors. All solutions have been coordinated, and the problems have been improved and revised accordingly. Also, there is a brief description of the subject matter at the beginning of each problem to aid in problem selection for assignments.

Organization As you examine the table of contents, you will see that the subject matter is arranged in a logical sequence.

Part One provides an introduction to the entire field of accounting. Business events that form the basis of accounting are introduced. In a step-by-step fashion, the text guides the student through the accounting cycle. A service firm in the proprietorship form is the vehicle for this.

1. Balance-column accounts are introduced in Unit 5 and are used thereafter in the book.
2. The four-step procedure is used as the primary method for closing entries (Unit 8).
3. Material on ruling and balancing the accounts is deleted from the second edition.

Part Two builds on what the student has already learned. The entire accounting cycle is illustrated again. This time a merchandising firm is used as the example, and simple corporation accounts are introduced. Special journals are illustrated, along with subsidiary ledgers.

4. The material on special journals has been completely reworked. The special journals recording process is condensed into two units (Chapter 5) in this edition, instead of being spread over six units as in the first edition.
5. The sales returns and the purchases returns journals are not treated as basic material in the chapters. Instead, such transactions are recorded in the general journal. However, a brief illustration is given of these two journals.
6. New illustrations are given to clarify the posting process using the balance-column account.
7. Horizontal rules are included in all special journals in the second edition.
8. The treatment of inventories has been revised. See the section on adjusting the merchandise inventory account in Unit 13.
9. Detailed cost of goods sold data now appears in the income statement columns of the work sheet (Unit 13).
10. A separate appendix at the end of the text is presented for instructors who want to thoroughly and comprehensively cover *reversing* entries.

Part Three of the text continues the study of financial accounting. Special attention is given to classification and valuation concepts of assets and liabilities.

11. Unit 16 includes an expanded treatment of the voucher system.
12. The four-column bank reconciliation that was used in the first edition does not appear in the second edition. Instead, the simpler one-column reconciling form is used.
13. Unit 18 contains new material on notes, discounting, and interest.
14. Unit 19 includes a completely new treatment of perpetual inventories.
15. Unit 20 is a brief, up-to-date, coverage of the SEC requirements of disclosing current replacement prices of inventories.

16. The unit on payrolls is expanded to include material on bonus computations.
17. Unit 25 gives an especially clear explanation of present value concepts in the study of liabilities.
18. The material on partnerships is strengthened and expanded to two units.

TEXT PART *Part Four* opens the second half of the text with the study of corporate capital. This material has been expanded considerably from the first edition.

IMPORTANT CHANGES
INCLUDED IN
THE SECOND EDITION

19. In Unit 29, detailed explanations of cumulative and participating preferred provisions are presented.
20. Unit 29 includes new brief material on donated capital.
21. There is a more extensive and in depth treatment of financial statement analysis in Unit 30.
22. Current and improved treatment of extraordinary items and prior-period adjustments is included.
23. The compound interest method of accounting for bonds is used, replacing the straight-line method of the first edition.
24. Unit 37 deals with accounting principles and concepts; the sections of a sample annual report are analyzed in the text.
25. The unit on price-levels is updated and expanded to include an actual illustration (Shell Oil Company).

TEXT PART *Part Five* of the text deals with managerial accounting. First, the basic purposes and methods are treated. Then, both periodic and perpetual cost accumulation systems are covered. Standard costing and budgeting are the concluding topics.

IMPORTANT CHANGES
INCLUDED IN
THE SECOND EDITION

26. All introductory material on managerial accounting has been combined into one unit. Tools in management accounting and cost concepts are also treated in the same unit.
27. There is a new unit on end-of-period operations for a periodic manufacturing system that includes the treatment of the work sheet. This optional unit appears as an appendix at the end of the book. *Accounting Principles* has the capability of covering the *entire* accounting cycle (recording transactions through the work-sheet, closing, etc.) for all three kinds of firms—service, merchandising, and manufacturing.
28. Process cost accounting is now treated in two units rather than one. New material is added in the budgeting unit on cash budgeting.

TEXT PART *Part Six* deals with the important topics of the statement of changes in financial position, capital budgeting, and income taxes.

IMPORTANT CHANGES
INCLUDED IN
THE SECOND EDITION

29. The material on the statement of changes in financial position is entirely different from the first edition. The more traditional approach of preparing the statement from comparative balance sheets is employed.
30. The material on income taxes and business decisions has been updated and condensed to two units.

ACKNOWLEDGMENTS   An extensive set of supplementary materials accompanies the text. The items available to the student have been outlined above. Available to the instructor are: *Test Items; Transparencies;* and an extremely comprehensive *Instructor's Manual*. Details about each of these items are given in the *Instructor's Manual* and, where appropriate, in the prefatory text accompanying each item. These aids have been carefully and professionally designed to insure that the instructor's experience with this text is also successful and rewarding.

I am especially indebted to the many professors who helped make this book better than it otherwise would have been. Many of these outstanding teachers class tested the materials; others reviewed all or parts of the manuscript. They include: Thomas E. Bartlett, University of Alaska-Fairbanks; Arthur L. Hardy, San Jacinto College; Pauline Corn, Virginia Polytechnic Institute and State University; George T. Ihorn, El Paso Community College; Charles Gibson, University of Toledo; Arthur J. Kelman, Bergen Community College; O. Ronald Gray, University of Alabama in Birmingham; George Brooker, Dean Junior College; Joseph Hollis, James Madison University; Marvin J. Elkin, Erie Community College-North Campus; Axel W. Swang, David Lipscomb College; William J. Kaiser, Middlesex Community College; Bill Magers, Tarrant County Junior College; Dorothy M. Masterson, Quinsigamond Community College; Emily Miklis, Cuyahoga Community College; Raymond Stanley, Polk Community College; and Thomas H. Outlawe, C.P.A.

Special thanks go to Gordon Hosch of the University of New Orleans, who reviewed the manuscript and prepared many of the supporting materials in the package.

Thanks are also due to the many students who used the first edition and whose helpful suggestions are incorporated in this revision. Special acknowledgment is made to Ron Ledwith, Linda Stewart, and Paul Spencer of Prentice-Hall. Ron Ledwith did a superb job of evaluating the many reviews of the material and securing vital input that formed the basis for the improvements in this edition. Linda Stewart and Paul Spencer did extraordinarily fine jobs of guiding the manuscript and supplements through the production processes. The outstanding work of Designer Lorraine Mullaney is greatly appreciated.

And most important, the book could not have been written without the patience and understanding of Martha, Paul, and Stephen.

Ronald J. Thacker

PART ONE
FUNDAMENTAL
ACCOUNTING:
THE
SERVICE FIRM
AS A BASIS

chapter 1

introduction to accounting

ACCOUNTING AND BASIC BUSINESS OPERATIONS

➤ **OBJECTIVE**

One objective of this first unit is to introduce you to the subject matter of accounting by telling you something about what accounting is and why it is important. Another objective is to describe and review the basic operations of business firms in our economic system. These operations provide the setting for the information that is produced by accountants and then reported to those who choose courses of action—the decision makers—inside and outside the business firm.

➤ **APPROACH TO ATTAINING THE OBJECTIVE**

In the text to follow, these seven questions are answered:

- *What is accounting?*
- *Which individuals and groups does accounting serve?*
- *How does accounting information help people accomplish their goals?*
- *What is the accounting profession, and what does it do today?*
- *What are the kinds of business organizations, and what forms do they take?*
- *What are the basic activities of all business firms?*
- *What are assets and equities, and why are these concepts basic to all accounting?*

You can help yourself master the subject matter of this unit if you will pay particular attention to these questions as you read. When you are finished with this unit, you should be able to answer these questions thoroughly.

DEFINITIONS OF ACCOUNTING

Accounting can be defined from at least two important points of view. The definition can emphasize the uses to which accounting information is put, or it can emphasize the activities of accountants, those persons engaged in the art or process of accounting. First, we shall look at the definition that stresses use.

Emphasis on use Accounting has been defined as:

a discipline which provides . . . information essential to the efficient conduct and evaluation of the activities of any organization.
> The information which accounting provides is essential for

1. effective planning, control and decision making by management, and
2. discharging the accountability of organizations to investors, creditors, government agencies . . . and others.[1]

We can generalize from this definition to make these two points:

■ *What is accounting?*

1. The central interest, or focal point, of accounting is the organization (often the business firm). The information accounting provides is information about the organization.
2. Accounting information is vital to a business firm's activity. It is used for making decisions *inside* the organization (by **management,** the persons in charge of a business concern). It is also used for making decisions *outside* the organization (by **investors**—persons who put money in a firm in hope of a profit, by **creditors**—persons to whom the firm owes money, and by others).

Emphasis on activity In our second definition the work of the accountant is emphasized. In accounting

the . . . effects of the economic activities of an enterprise are accumulated, analyzed, quantified, classified, recorded, summarized, and reported as information. . .[2]

This statement shows that the accountant's job is a complex one involving many different activities. Basically, the accountant must:

1. Identify which data are related or relevant to the decisions to be made.

[1] American Institute of Certified Public Accountants, *By-Laws, as amended February 20, 1969* (New York, 1969), p. 40.

[2] American Institute of Certified Public Accountants, Statement of the Accounting Principles Board, No. 4, *Basic Concepts and Accounting Principles Underlying Financial Statements of Business Enterprises* (New York, 1970), p. 6.

2. Process or analyze the relevant data.

3. Transform it into information that can be used in making better decisions.

FINANCIAL AND MANAGEMENT ACCOUNTING

Accounting serves people both inside and outside the organization or business firm. Accounting is divided into two branches based on this distinction. The kind of accounting that provides information to management to aid it in operating a business is called **management accounting.** And the kind of accounting that provides information to decision makers outside the firm is called **financial accounting.** The first half of this book deals primarily with financial accounting.

Management accounting The management of a business enterprise must have a wide variety of information to reach its objectives. One major category of information is required for *planning* and *controlling* a firm's *day-to-day operations.* Management must know what is going on currently ("now"). Management also must have information to check that the business is operating smoothly to meet some desirable and acceptable goals. A second major category of information needed by management is used in *long-range planning.* Management uses this information to formulate broad policies for the firm and to make special decisions having a lasting impact on the firm.

■ *Which individuals and groups does accounting serve?*

Management accounting generally involves three functions: (1) data selection and record keeping, (2) analysis of data, and (3) preparation of reports for management use (see Illustration 1-1).

ILLUSTRATION 1-1

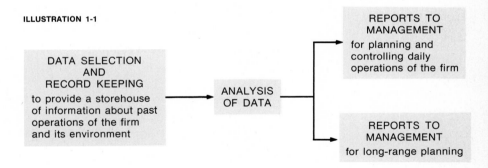

DATA SELECTION AND RECORD KEEPING
to provide a storehouse of information about past operations of the firm and its environment

ANALYSIS OF DATA

REPORTS TO MANAGEMENT
for planning and controlling daily operations of the firm

REPORTS TO MANAGEMENT
for long-range planning

Financial accounting The information financial accounting provides to outside decision makers usually takes the form of summary reports called **financial statements.** It will be a major part of your study of accounting to learn about the three primary financial statements:

1. The **income statement,** which provides information about the profitability of the operations of a firm.

2. The **balance sheet,** which provides information about the resources that a firm has acquired, including information about where these resources came from.
3. The **statement of changes in financial position,** which provides information about how the resources of a firm changed during a period of time.

Financial accounting information usually is directed toward the *common* needs of a wide variety of users. That is, each of the preceding three financial statements prepared by a firm contains information that is useful to all of these groups:

1. Owners of the firm, to help them decide whether to keep or give up their ownership interests.
2. Creditors of the firm, to help them decide whether to extend credit to the firm (let the firm obtain goods, services, or cash with postponed payment).
3. Governmental bodies, to help them review or evaluate tax returns and check that firms are following governmental rules, regulations, and laws.
4. Employees and labor unions, to help them negotiate (discuss and arrange) labor contracts or to make a wide variety of employment decisions.
5. Customers of the firm, to help them evaluate their relationship with the firm and make decisions about possible future relationships.

The information in the financial statements usually is presented in the same way from year to year. This uniformity encourages users of the statements to rely on them.

Financial accounting generally involves three functions: (1) data selection and record keeping, (2) analysis of data, and (3) preparation of reports for decision makers outside the firm (see Illustration 1-2).

ILLUSTRATION 1-2

DATA SELECTION AND RECORD KEEPING	ANALYSIS OF DATA	REPORTS TO DECISION MAKERS OUTSIDE THE FIRM
to provide a storehouse of information about past operations of the firm and its environment		1. Income statement 2. Balance sheet 3. Statement of changes in financial position

ACCOUNTING AND BUSINESS DECISIONS

Decision makers, whether inside or outside a business firm, want to make decisions (by choosing among alternative courses of action) that are *most likely* to accomplish their goals. Accounting information is created for and used by decision makers simply to make it *more likely* that the desired goals will be attained. For example, if a bank is considering lending a company $10,000, the banker (decision maker) must determine how likely it is that the company will pay back the loan according to a specific agreement. He needs detailed financial information about the company to make this judgment and accounting provides this critical information. The accounting information that the banker looks at may take the form of an income statement, a balance sheet, or a statement of changes in financial position for the company seeking the loan. In summary, before informed judgments and good decisions can be made at all levels in our economic system, information related to the decision must be selected, analyzed, reported, and then used. Accounting, both managerial and financial, is a primary source of this vital information.

■ *How does accounting information help people accomplish their goals?*

THE ACCOUNTING PROFESSION AND FIELDS OF SPECIALIZATION

The thousands of accountants in the United States today make a significant contribution to our economic and social system. There are four broad fields in which a professionally trained accountant can employ his services. These are (1) private accounting, (2) public accounting, (3) governmental accounting, and (4) accounting education. In this section we shall describe each of these fields in order to round out your introduction to the nature and significance of accounting.

Private accounting Accountants employed by individual business firms are engaged in private accounting. There are a number of different services that private accountants perform. These services include the work of (1) the controller, (2) the bookkeeper, (3) the cost accountant, (4) the internal auditor, (5) the tax specialist, and (6) accountants working on such tasks as preparing budgets.

The **controller** is the chief accounting officer of a firm. It is his job to supervise all the accounting activities of the organization. Usually he is a high-ranking officer of the company.

The roles of the **bookkeeper** and the accountant are often misunderstood today. The bookkeeper's job is to record and process the data in the accounting system. Much of the bookkeeper's job can be described as data processing. Actually, much of what a bookkeeper does in a small firm is often done by electronic computers and other machines in larger organizations. In contrast, the job of the accountant is much broader. Accounting is concerned with deciding which data are needed and are to be recorded, determining how the data are to be processed, and deciding how the reports are to be designed—how to communicate the information to the decision makers.

■ *What is the accounting profession, and what does it do today?*

Some accountants work as **cost accountants.** Usually this means that they select, process, and report information about the costs of manufacturing products. The information generated by cost accountants permits informed judgments to be made about the various costs in the manufacture and sale of the firm's goods.

Some firms, especially large ones, have an internal auditing staff. The job of the **internal auditor** is to investigate and evaluate in a systematic manner the functioning of his firm's accounting system. Internal auditors study the accounting records and make recommendations for changing the system where appropriate. In addition, the internal auditor determines to what extent the policies and requirements of management are being carried out, and thus he aids in the management process.

The **tax specialist** is the employee in charge of preparing the company's tax returns. He also advises management about the tax consequences of the various actions that management considers. In American businesses there is a wide variety of other accounting specialties, including budgeting. A **budget** is simply a plan that helps guide management; it is a stated goal against which management can compare actual performance. For example, management may budget (or plan to spend) $10 for manufacturing each of its products. The actual costs incurred can be compared to this budget as an aid to controlling the costs of current operations.

Individuals who have attained a high level of competence in management accounting may be granted the designation of CMA by the Institute of Management Accounting. To receive the *certificate in management accounting,* an individual must meet a number of requirements, including passing a comprehensive professional examination in that field.

Public accounting All the states regulate the practice of certain professions in the public interest. These professions include medicine, law, and public accountancy. Licensed professionals engaged in the practice of public accountancy are called **certified public accountants** (CPAs). A practicing CPA generally is not the employee of a business firm. He works instead for a **public accounting** firm, which performs a variety of services for business firms for a fee.

Probably the most important service performed by public accountants is *auditing.* Almost all medium-size and large business firms engage a practicing CPA to make an audit each year. An **audit** is simply an investigation and study of the financial statements and reports prepared by a firm to determine if these reports are prepared according to "generally accepted accounting principles." That is, the CPA determines if the financial statements communicate what they are supposed to, and if it is reasonable for the public, including investors and creditors, to trust the information. In the course of the audit the firm's records and accounting system are carefully analyzed by the CPA and suggestions for improvement are made to management. Of course, all CPAs are not necessarily engaged in the practice of public accounting. Some are employees of firms, some are teachers, and some work for governmental bodies.

Governmental accounting The many federal, state, and local governmental organizations have great need for the services of accountants. Some government-employed accountants help administer the tax laws and investigate income tax returns. Others design and operate accounting systems to provide governments with reports for their use in governmental decision making.

Accounting education There is a tremendous opportunity for accountants in the field of education. Colleges and universities offer advanced degrees for accountants to help prepare them to teach all aspects of accountancy.

DESCRIPTION OF BUSINESS FIRMS

The business firm is of central importance in our economic system. The many thousands of business organizations in the United States provide a framework for carrying out most of the economic activity of our country. How can we describe these thousands of firms and distinguish one from another? First, it is useful to describe them according to their output—the products and services that they produce. Second, we can examine the various forms of organization that business firms can take.

The output of firms In terms of what they produce for society, business firms can be divided into two types: (1) those that produce services, and (2) those that produce goods. Examples of **service firms** are barbershops, medical doctors, attorneys, and dry cleaning and laundering establishments. Those businesses which deal in products or goods can be either **merchandising firms** or **manufacturing firms.** A merchandising firm buys goods which are already in salable form and sells them to make a profit. Examples are grocery stores, clothing firms, and department stores. A manufacturing company obtains raw materials and supplies of various kinds and then turns these raw materials into a different finished product. Examples are automobile manufacturing companies, food processing firms, and milk processing plants. The manufacturing firm uses labor (the services of employees) and secures a variety of other services to aid it in producing and selling manufactured products. Of course, many individual business organizations produce both goods and services. An example would be a beauty shop which performs services as well as sells cosmetics and other products. Having an understanding of these various kinds of firms and the internal activities and decisions made within them is fundamental to understanding the functions of accounting information.

- *What are the kinds of business organizations, and what forms do they take?*

The form of firms Most businesses can be classified by their legal form of organization into three groups: (1) the proprietorship, (2) the partnership, and (3) the corporation. Each of these three forms has its special function in our economic system.

The simplest kind of organization, and usually the smallest, is the **proprietorship.** This is a business organization with just one owner. The objectives or goals of the proprietorship depend in large measure on the goals of the individual owner. The information needed for decisions in a proprietorship tends to focus upon those decisions concerning the owner's goals and upon the internal management of the business.

The **partnership** is a form of organization that is only slightly more complex than a proprietorship. The owners—the partners—are simply two or more individuals who combine their efforts to meet common goals. Many medical doctors, for example, establish partnerships in the practice of medicine. Partnerships usually have a written agreement among the partners which specifies the details of conducting the business. This written agreement, called the **articles of partnership,** often states:

1. The primary goals of the firm.
2. How the business will be financed.
3. How the business will be managed.
4. How the earnings and the losses of the business will be shared.
5. The conditions under which the operation of the firm will be discontinued.

As in the case of the proprietorship, the information needed for decisions in the partnership tends to focus upon those decisions concerning the owner's goals and upon the internal management of the business.

The **corporation** is the third—and the dominant—form of business organization. There are several reasons for the popularity of this form of organization, and in discussing them we will arrive at a definition of what a corporation is. First, the corporation can *acquire* **capital** (money invested by owners) *and provide for growth* in an effective manner. A corporation can be created by a state government. Therefore, the usual procedure for a group of individuals who want to begin a company is to apply to a state for a corporate **charter.** A charter is a document authorizing the creation of a corporation. The charter also includes such details as the purpose of the business and the methods (and limitations placed on the methods) of raising funds to operate the firm. The corporation issues **stock certificates** which are written evidence of the owners' (stockholders') investment or share in the company. The corporation is therefore characterized by an ownership divided into shares.

This procedure allows a large number of investor-owners to invest their money in the corporation and thereby raise capital for it. These stock certificates are readily transferable to aid in providing a market for the stock (ownership) of the company.

A second reason for the popularity of the corporate form of business is its characteristic of **limited liability.** This means that, as a separate legal entity or unit, the corporation exists independently and is responsible for all debts and other **obligations** (legal contracts or duties and binding promises) that it takes upon itself. The stockholders are not personally responsible, or liable, for the debts and obligations of the corporation. This is not the case in proprietorships and partnerships, for in them the owners are personally liable for the debts of the company. The limited liability characteristic of corporations certainly encourages the corporate form. It provides an added incentive and protection for investors who risk their capital to make more money.

TYPICAL BUSINESS OPERATIONS

Certain activities are fundamental to all business firms. The following description of these activities should give you an insight into why some economic events are especially important to report to decision makers.

The central role of resources When a business organization is formed, its management and owners must make up goals for the company. Usually these goals include producing goods or services and making a profit (earnings). A most important fact about this whole process is that *the company must gather about itself certain resources if it is to reach its goals.* Resources—or **assets,** as they are called in accounting terminology—are absolutely vital to the operation of the firm. For example, a shoe-making firm must have a factory; a barbershop must have barber equipment; a delivery service company must have delivery vehicles; and a grocery store must have groceries. Another asset which almost all businesses must have to operate is cash. And, of course, each business acquires those resources that are particularly useful to it in accomplishing its goals. Illustration 1-3 shows how acquired resources are used by the management of a firm and how certain economic events bring about changes in these assets. The diagram emphasizes the role of assets. We can conclude, then, that *information about assets* must be of central importance in reporting to management (management accounting) as well as in reporting to those decision makers outside the firm (financial accounting).

- *What are the basic activities of all business firms?*

Summary of business transactions A business transaction is an economic event that has some effect on the resources of a firm or on the sources of a firm's assets. These economic events are important and therefore must be recorded and reported to decision makers. The following list summarizes the

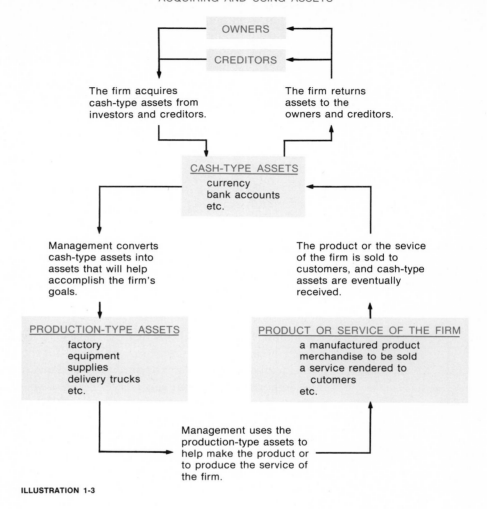

ACQUIRING AND USING ASSETS

OWNERS

CREDITORS

The firm acquires cash-type assets from investors and creditors.

The firm returns assets to the owners and creditors.

CASH-TYPE ASSETS
currency
bank accounts
etc.

Management converts cash-type assets into assets that will help accomplish the firm's goals.

The product or the sevice of the firm is sold to customers, and cash-type assets are eventually received.

PRODUCTION-TYPE ASSETS
factory
equipment
supplies
delivery trucks
etc.

PRODUCT OR SERVICE OF THE FIRM
a manufactured product
merchandise to be sold
a service rendered to
   cutomers
etc.

Management uses the production-type assets to help make the product or to produce the service of the firm.

ILLUSTRATION 1-3

business transactions that a firm might have. Observe the close relationship of these transactions to the activities described in Illustration 1-3.

1. Acquiring assets from owners (the owners invest in the firm).
2. Acquiring assets from creditors (the firm borrows money).
3. Investing resources in the kinds of assets needed to produce services or goods (the firm acquires *production-type assets*).
4. Using the resources to produce the product or service (the production-type assets are used).

5. Selling the goods or services of the firm (the firm exchanges its product or service for *cash-type assets*).
6. Returning assets to the creditors (the creditors are paid).
7. Returning assets to the owners (owners receive payment from the firm).

ASSETS AND THEIR SOURCES

One particular kind of financial statement, the balance sheet, provides information about the resources or assets that a firm has acquired, including information about the sources of these assets. Let us begin our study of financial accounting by examining a very simple balance sheet, one presented here in diagrammatic form (see Illustration 1-4). Our object is to explore what assets are and to describe their sources in more detail.

ILLUSTRATION 1-4

TOTAL ASSETS AT JUNE 1, 1978

Cash	$1,000
Building	3,000
Truck	5,000
Total assets	$9,000

Illustration 1-4 represents all the assets of a firm at a point in time. Note that at the beginning of June, 1978, this firm has assets totaling $9,000. Actually, the dollar amount of assets can be measured in a number of ways, and you will learn about this measurement process later in your study of accounting. Initially, as done here, we shall measure assets by the amount paid for the asset. In our example, the building cost $3,000 and the truck cost $5,000. Of course, the total assets of a firm will change as each day's operations take place, but here we are considering only a balance sheet and not a statement of changes in financial position.

Let us take a further look at a firm's assets, this time examining their sources. Remember that the firm described in Illustration 1-3 acquired assets from owners and from creditors (the firm or person to whom money is owed). By obtaining a share of the firm we say in accounting that these two groups acquired an *interest* in the firm. The interests of outsiders (the owners and the creditors) in the assets of a firm are called **equities**. Thus, *assets are equivalent to equities.*

Now Illustration 1-5 can help us to understand what equities are in terms of the firm examined in Illustration 1-4. This time we label the diagram to indicate what portion of the assets (the $9,000) were acquired from the

■ *What are assets and equities, and why are these concepts basic to all accounting?*

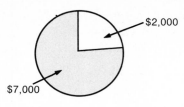

$2,000

$7,000

ILLUSTRATION 1-5

ASSETS BROKEN DOWN BY SOURCE	
Liabilities	
(owed to bank)	$2,000
Capital (owner's	
equity in the firm)	7,000
Total equities	$9,000

owners and what portion of the assets were acquired from the creditors. The illustration shows that on June 1, 1978, the firm had $9,000 of assets, that $2,000 represented a creditor's equity in the firm, and that $7,000 represented the owners' equity in the firm. Thus, we can say that *assets are also equivalent to the equity of the creditors plus the equity of the owners.*

We can describe this breakdown of assets into two kinds of equities in still another way. Creditors' equities are called **liabilities** (in our example, the $2,000 owed to the bank), and owners' equities are called **capital** (in our example, the $7,000 representing the owners' equity or interest in the firm). Thus, *assets equal liabilities plus capital.*

Providing detailed information about the resources of a firm and the sources of these assets is basic to all accounting. This relationship between assets and their sources will be an essential foundation to your progress in the study of financial accounting. We summarize it here in equation form:

$$\text{Assets} = \text{Equities}$$

or

$$\text{Assets} = \text{Equity of the creditors} + \text{Equity of the owners}$$

or

$$\text{Assets} = \text{Liabilities} \qquad + \text{Capital}$$

> **NEW TERMS**

accounting "A discipline which provides . . . information essential to the efficient conduct and evaluation of the activities of any organization."[3] [p. 4]

articles of partnership A written agreement among the partners of a partnership specifying the details of conducting the business. [p. 10]

assets Resources acquired by a firm to aid it in accomplishing its goals. [p. 11]

audit An investigation and study of the financial statements and reports prepared by the firm to determine if these reports are prepared according to "generally accepted accounting principles." [p. 8]

balance sheet A financial statement which provides information about the resources that a firm has acquired, including information about where these resources came from. [p. 6]

[3] American Institute of Certified Public Accountants, *By-Laws, as amended February 20, 1969* (New York, 1969), p. 40.

bookkeeper A person who records and processes the data in the accounting system. [p. 7]

budget A plan of action, usually in writing. [p. 8]

business transaction An economic event which has some impact on the resources of a firm or has an impact upon the sources of the firm's resources. [p. 11]

capital Refers to the equity of the owners in a firm; that portion of the total assets of a firm which represents the interest of the owners. [p. 10]

certified public accountant (CPA) A professional accountant, licensed by a state to practice public accountancy. [p. 8]

charter A document, issued by a state government, that authorizes the creation of a corporation. The charter includes details regarding the formation and operation of the corporation. [p. 10]

controller The chief accounting officer of a firm. [p. 7]

corporation A form of business organization that has the characteristics of limited liability and ownership divided into shares. [p. 10]

cost accountant A person who selects, processes, and reports of information about the costs of manufacturing products. [p. 8]

creditor A person to whom a firm owes money. [p. 4]

entity Independent existence; a corporation is a legal entity, real and distinct in itself. [p. 11]

equities The interest of outsiders in the assets of a firm. The two kinds of equities are creditors' equities (liabilities) and owners' equities (capital). [p. 13]

financial accounting That branch of accounting concerned with providing information to decision makers outside the firm. [p. 5]

financial statements Reports primarily designed for decision makers outside the firm which contain information about the financial condition of the firm, and about the amount of profit earned by the company. [p. 5]

income statement A financial statement which provides information about the profitability of the operations of a firm. [p. 5]

internal auditor An employee of a firm, an accountant, who investigates and evaluates in a systematic manner the functioning of the accounting system; he also determines to what extent the policies and requirements of management are being carried out. [p. 8]

investor A person who puts money in a firm in hope of profit. [p. 4]

liabilities The interest or equity of the creditors in a firm. [p. 14]

limited liability A characteristic of the corporate form of organization. As a separate legal entity, the corporation is responsible for all debts and other obligations it incurs; the stockholders are not personally liable. [p. 11]

management The persons in charge of a business firm. [p. 4]

management accounting That branch of accounting concerned with providing information to management to aid it in operating a business. [p. 5]

manufacturing firm A company involved in acquiring raw materials and supplies and converting these into a different finished product. [p. 9]

merchandising firm A company that buys goods which are already in salable form and sells them to produce earnings. [p. 9]

obligations Legal contracts or duties and binding promises. [p. 11]

partnership A form of business organization; an association of two or more individuals to conduct a business. [p. 10]

proprietorship A form of business organization with only one owner. [p. 10]

public accounting The independent practice of public accountancy by a licensed CPA; it includes performing audits and providing other services to business firms. [p. 8]

service firm A company whose major output is a service rendered (in contrast to a product). [p. 9]

statement of changes in financial position A financial statement which provides information about how the resources of a firm changed during a period of time. [p. 6]

stock certificate Official written evidence of an owner's investment or share in a business. [p. 10]

tax specialist A company employee in charge of preparing the company's tax returns; he also advises management about the tax consequences of the various actions that management considers. [p. 8]

QUESTIONS

Q1-1. a. Accounting can be defined from at least two important points of view. What are these points of view?
b. Give a definition of accounting that emphasizes use.
c. Give a definition of accounting that emphasizes activity.

Q1-2. Describe management accounting and financial accounting.

Q1-3. What are the two major categories of information needed by management? Distinguish between the two.

Q1-4. List and describe briefly the three major financial statements used by decision makers outside the firm.

Q1-5. Which groups are the primary users of the three financial statements discussed in the text?

Q1-6. Briefly describe how each of the groups listed in your answer to Q1-5 uses the information contained on financial statements.

Q1-7. What three functions is financial accounting said to involve?

Q1-8. Describe how accounting information leads to better decisions.

Q1-9. Briefly describe the roles of:
a. The controller.
b. The bookkeeper.
c. The cost accountant.
d. The internal auditor.
e. The tax specialist.
f. The CPA who practices public accounting.
g. The governmental accountant.

Q1-10. Contrast private accounting and public accounting.

Q1-11. Many large firms employ internal auditors, while very few small firms do so. Why do you suppose that is the case?

Q1-12. Can the work of the accountant be replaced by a computer? Can the work of a bookkeeper be replaced by a computer? In both answers, explain why or why not.

Q1-13. What is the purpose of the articles of partnership of a firm? What information is usually included in these articles?

Q1-14. What is a corporate charter? Comment.

Q1-15. What are stock certificates? What is their purpose?

Q1-16. What is limited liability? Does this concept apply to proprietorships and partnerships?

Q1-17. What are resources? What is the significance of resources in operating a business firm?

Q1-18. Which of the following would be considered assets? cash; bank accounts; liabilities; equities; manufacturing equipment; capital.

Q1-19. Compare and contrast cash-type assets and production-type assets.

Q1-20. Define a business transaction.

Q1-21. List and describe two characteristics of the corporate form of organization that have partially accounted for its popularity.

Q1-22. Explain, in a step-by-step fashion, how a business organization acquires and uses assets to accomplish its goals.

Q1-23. What are the three basic legal forms of business organizations? Briefly describe each.

EXERCISES

E1-1. For each of the six businesses listed below, indicate the primary type of output of the firm. Use these responses: (1) service firm; (2) merchandising firm; (3) manufacturing firm.

| barbershop | dentist | grocery supermarket |
| department store | attorney | pharmacy |

E1-2. The text included a list of business transactions (seven types) that a business firm could have. Refer to this list and give a specific detailed example for each of the kinds of transactions.

E1-3. At June 1, 1978, the B Company had cash amounting to $3,000. It also had a truck for which it recently had paid $4,000. The company was just formed a few days ago; the owner invested $5,000 in the firm and he had borrowed another $2,000 from First National Bank.

  a. What are the firm's total assets (resources) at June 1, 1978?
  b. What are the firm's liabilities at June 1, 1978?
  c. What is the firm's capital at June 1, 1978?
  d. In the text, this equation was given: Assets = Liabilities + Capital. Show how the dollar amounts in this exercise fit into the equation. Does the equation balance?

PROBLEMS (GROUP A)

P1-1. *Transaction analysis.* On January 1, 1978, P. J. Quick Stop Company was formed. The owner invested $10,000 cash in the business. On the same day, he borrowed another $8,000 from the local bank to provide additional assets for the business. Use a form like the one below to make the computations to answer the questions that follow.

		TOTAL ASSETS	TOTAL LIABILITIES	TOTAL CAPITAL
Jan. 1	Owner's investment	+		+
Jan. 1	Bank loan	+	+	
	Totals at Jan. 1			
Jan. 2	Purchased truck	+		
		−		
Jan. 2	Purchased office equipment	+		
		−		
Jan. 2	Bank loan	+	+	
Jan. 2	Owner's investment	+		+
	Totals at Jan. 2			

  a. At the end of the day, January 1, 1978, what is the amount of the firm's total assets?
  b. At the end of the day, January 1, 1978, what is the amount of the firm's total liabilities?
  c. At the end of the day, January 1, 1978, what is the amount of the firm's total capital?

On January 2, 1978, the company purchased a delivery truck for $5,000, paying cash. Also, office equipment was purchased for $1,000 cash. On this day, the firm borrowed another $3,000 from the bank, and the owner invested another $2,000 cash in the business.

d. At the end of the day, January 2, 1978, what is the amount of the firm's total assets?

e. At the end of the day, January 2, 1978, what is the amount of the firm's total liabilities?

f. At the end of the day, January 2, 1978, what is the amount of the firm's total capital?

P1-2. *Transaction analysis.* On March 1, 1978, M. R. Holloway invested $56,000 cash in his new business, Holloway Company. On March 3, 1978, the business borrowed $50,000 cash from the First National Bank. Store equipment was purchased on March 10, 1978, for $7,400 cash. On the same day, office supplies were purchased for $240 cash. Mr. Holloway invested another $5,000 cash in the business on March 11, 1978.

REQUIRED:

a. Set up a form similar to the one shown in P1-1, with columns for Total Assets, Total Liabilities, and Total Capital.

b. Show the effect of each of the transactions given above. Then compute the totals of the three columns at the end of March 11, 1978.

P1-3. *Transaction analysis.* A new company, Delmonico Company, was formed on June 1, 1978. The owner, James Delmonico, invested $100,000 cash in the company at that time. On June 4, the firm purchased equipment for $36,000 cash. A bank loan was made on June 10, and $60,000 cash was received from the bank. The loan will be repaid in 6 months.

The owner made a cash investment in the firm of $10,000 on June 11, 1978. A delivery truck was purchased on June 12 for $13,000 cash.

REQUIRED:

a. Set up a form similar to the one shown in P1-1, with columns for Total Assets, Total Liabilities, and Total Capital.

b. Show the effect of each of the transactions given above. Then compute the totals of the three columns at the end of June 12, 1978.

PROBLEMS (GROUP B)

P1-4. *Transaction analysis.* On January 1, 1978, Medical Enterprises Company was begun. The owner, Dr. Robert Medd, invested $21,000 cash in the business. On the same day, he borrowed another $15,000 from American State Bank to provide additional assets for the business.

a. At the end of the day, January 1, 1978, what is the amount of the firm's total assets?

b. At the end of the day, January 1, 1978, what is the amount of the firm's total liabilities?

c. At the end of the day, January 1, 1978, what is the amount of the firm's total capital?

On January 2, 1978, the firm purchased store equipment for $11,000, paying cash. Also a delivery truck was purchased for $20,000 cash. On this day, the firm borrowed another $9,000 from the bank, and the owner invested $3,000 cash in the business.

   d. At the end of the day, January 2, 1978, what is the amount of the firm's total assets?

   e. At the end of the day, January 2, 1978, what is the amount of the firm's total liabilities?

   f. At the end of the day, January 2, 1978, what is the amount of the firm's total capital?

Hint: Use a form like the following to make the computations:

		TOTAL ASSETS	TOTAL LIABILITIES	TOTAL CAPITAL
Jan. 1	Owner investment	+		+
Jan. 1	Bank loan	+	+	
	Totals at Jan. 1			
Jan. 2	Purchased store equipment	−		
		+		
Jan. 2	Purchased delivery truck	−		
		+		
Jan. 2	Bank loan	+	+	
Jan. 2	Owner investment	+		+
	Totals at Jan. 2			

P1-5. *Transaction analysis.* On April 1, 1978, Ms. Jane Johnson invested $40,000 in her new business, Johnson Products Co. On April 3, 1978, the company borrowed $5,000 cash from Second National Bank. Office equipment was purchased on April 3, 1978, for $6,500 cash. On the same day, a used truck was purchased for $8,000 cash. Ms. Johnson invested another $4,000 in the business on April 5, 1978.

REQUIRED:

   a. Set up a form similar to the one shown in P1-4, with columns for Total Assets, Total Liabilities, and Total Capital.

   b. Show the effect of each of the transactions given above. Then compute the totals of the three columns at the end of April 5, 1978.

P1-6. *Transaction analysis.* General Services Co. was formed on July 1, 1978, at which time the owner invested $59,500 cash. On July 3, 1978, the company bought equipment for $40,000 cash. A bank loan was made on July 7, 1978, for $20,000 cash. The loan will be repaid in 1 year.

      The owner made a cash investment in the firm of $8,200 on July 8, 1978. A delivery truck was purchased on July 10 for $12,000 cash.

REQUIRED:

   a. Set up a form similar to the one shown in P1-4, with columns for Total Assets, Total Liabilities, and Total Capital.

   b. Show the effect of each of the transactions given above. Then compute the totals of the three columns at the end of July 10, 1978.

UNDERSTANDING BUSINESS TRANSACTIONS

> ## OBJECTIVE

You now know what accounting is and why it is important, and you are familiar with some of a firm's basic business operations. This unit will introduce you to some of the basic accounting tools you need to analyze business operations, or transactions as they are often called. It also will show you how to report significant transactions—ones affecting a firm's assets or equities—to people who need to know something about a firm's operations.

> ## APPROACH TO ATTAINING THE OBJECTIVE

An accounting system has three necessary parts:

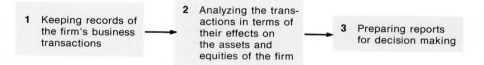

1 Keeping records of the firm's business transactions → **2** Analyzing the transactions in terms of their effects on the assets and equities of the firm → **3** Preparing reports for decision making

In studying business transactions and learning the basic tools for analyzing them, we shall answer three questions related to the three basic parts of an accounting system:

- *What is the accounting equation, and how is it used to record and analyze business transactions?*
- *What are some of the typical transactions a firm will have, and how can they be recorded and analyzed?*
- *How are financial statements put together from the various business transactions?*

THE ACCOUNTING EQUATION

In Unit 1 you saw how a firm's assets are equivalent to the interest or equity of its creditors (whose equities are called *liabilities*) plus the equity of its owners (whose equities are called *capital*). This relationship of assets, liabilities, and capital can be shown as an equation:

$$\text{Assets} = \text{Liabilities} + \text{Capital}$$

- *What is the accounting equation, and how is it used to record and analyze business transactions?*

This equation is known as the *accounting equation. It is the relationship on which all accounting is based.* Every business transaction changes this relationship in some way. The example developed in detail in the following two sections shows (1) how typical business transactions affect the equation, and (2) how financial statements are prepared.

THE BUSINESS TRANSACTIONS OF A SERVICE FIRM

Let us look at some of the transactions of a service firm called Cronin Montz Delivery Service. This company delivers packages and other items in the central section of a large city and charges its customers a fee for the service. We will start with the transactions for the company's first month of operation, June, 1978.

Acquiring assets from the owner When Mr. Montz decided to go into business for himself, he withdrew $5,000 from his personal bank account and opened another account in the name Cronin Montz Delivery Service. Because the delivery service has only one owner, it is a proprietorship. The new firm thus has $5,000 in assets, the cash in the bank, and Mr. Montz has a *claim* of $5,000 (owner's equity or capital) against the firm as a result of his investment. How does this affect the accounting equation?

- *What are some of the typical transactions a firm will have, and how can they be recorded and analyzed?*

ASSETS	=	LIABILITIES	+	CAPITAL
cash	=			**Montz, capital**
(1) Mr. Montz invests $5,000 in the business.				
+$5,000	=	–0–	+	$5,000

Acquiring assets from creditors Mr. Montz does not think that $5,000 will be enough cash to carry on his business for the first few months. He therefore applies for a loan at First National Bank, where he has already established a good credit rating in his personal dealings. Because the bank officers feel his business has a good chance to succeed, they lend him $3,000. Mr. Montz promises to pay back the $3,000 at $1,000 per month. He also agrees to an *interest charge* (payment for the use of the borrowed money). He therefore signs a *note* (a legal paper acknowledging a debt and promising to pay) with the bank, and the $3,000 is deposited in the company's checking account.

How does the loan affect the equation? The business now has an additional $3,000 in cash, but it owes First National Bank $3,000. This means that a creditor's equity, or liability, of $3,000 exists.

	ASSETS	=	LIABILITIES	+	CAPITAL
	cash	=	notes payable	+	Montz, capital
Previous balance	$5,000	=	–0–	+	$5,000
(2) The firm borrows $3,000 from the bank.	+$3,000	=	+$3,000		
New balance	$8,000	=	$3,000	+	$5,000

Investing resources in assets needed to produce the service Mr. Montz makes several decisions about how he will run his business:

1. He decides to rent—not to buy—the trucks and other vehicles he'll need to make deliveries.
2. He agrees to buy all his gasoline and have his trucks serviced at Hazel Service Station.
3. He rents a furnished office.
4. He hires part-time employees, mostly college students, to handle the deliveries.
5. He purchases $500 of supplies he needs to carry on his business from N. O. Office Supply Company on credit. He agrees to pay the $500 in 30 days, on July 1, 1978.

Of all these, the only one which has an effect on the equation at the beginning of the month is the last one, the purchase of supplies. (The other items are not business transactions because they do not affect the firm's assets or equities at this point in time.) Mr. Montz now has $500 in supplies, an additional asset, and owes N. O. Office Supply for them. What does this do to the accounting equation?

	ASSETS			=	LIABILITIES			+	CAPITAL
	cash	+	supplies	=	notes payable	+	accounts payable	+	Montz, capital
Previous balance	$8,000	+	–0–	=	$3,000	+	–0–	+	$5,000
(3) The firm buys supplies on credit.		+	$500	=		+	$500		
New balance	$8,000	+	$500	=	$3,000	+	$500	+	$5,000

Using the resources to produce the service During this first month of operation, the firm's resources—both cash and supplies—were used to help produce the delivery service. Let us look first at the use of cash. Cash was paid for these expenses:

Truck maintenance	$ 800
Truck rental	1,500
Office rent	200
Salaries	1,600
Miscellaneous expenses	100
Total cash paid	$4,200

Incurring and paying these expenses has the following effect on the accounting equation:

	ASSETS			=	LIABILITIES			+	CAPITAL
	cash	+	supplies	=	notes payable	+	accounts payable	+	Montz, capital
Previous balance	$8,000	+	$500	=	$3,000	+	$500	+	$5,000
(4) The firm pays expenses in cash as follows:									
Truck maintenance	− 800							−	800
Truck rent	− 1,500							−	1,500
Office rent	− 200							−	200
Salaries	− 1,600							−	1,600
Miscellaneous	− 100							−	100
New balance	$3,800	+	$500	=	$3,000	+	$500	+	$ 800

Before this transaction, the cash balance was $8,000. When expenses totaling $4,200 are paid, the firm's cash is reduced from $8,000 to $3,800. This expenditure of cash obviously does not create a new asset, and it does not affect the liabilities of the firm either, as can be seen in the record of transaction (4) given above. Incurring expenses, however, does have a direct effect on the capital or owner's equity of the firm: the capital is reduced. In our example, the $5,000 of capital is reduced to $800 by the $4,200 of expenses. **Expenses** thus can be defined as decreases in the owner's equity in the firm that are usually caused by spending or using assets to help produce the revenues of the firm.

In transaction (4) expenses were paid for from the asset Cash. The firm has other assets and among them are supplies. Remember that back in transaction (3) $500 of the asset Supplies were purchased. These supplies can also be used up in the production of the firm's service; that is, their use can become an expense of doing business. At the end of this month's operations, Mr. Montz determines that he has used up $300 of these supplies. This means that he still has $200 of the asset left, and that $300 of supplies have become an expense of doing business. Because they are an expense, the owner's equity is decreased by $300, as shown below:

	ASSETS			=	LIABILITIES			+	CAPITAL
	cash	+	supplies	=	notes payable	+	accounts payable	+	Montz, capital
Previous balance	$3,800	+	$500	=	$3,000	+	$500	+	$800
(5) The firm uses up supplies.		−	300					−	300
New balance	$3,800	+	$200	=	$3,000	+	$500	+	$500

Selling the services Delivery services were performed for a number of customers during the month. Cash totaling $6,000 was collected for all the services rendered. When resources like cash are received from customers in exchange for the firm's products or services, the firm is said to have produced **revenues**. The effect of these revenue collections on the equation is as follows:

	ASSETS			=	LIABILITIES			+	CAPITAL
	cash	+	supplies	=	notes payable	+	accounts payable	+	Montz, capital
Previous balance	$3,800	+	$200	=	$3,000	+	$500	+	$ 500
(6) The firm collects cash for services to customers.	+ 6,000								6,000
New balance	$9,800	+	$200	=	$3,000	+	$500	+	$6,500

As we can see from this record of transaction (6), earning fees—or revenues, as they are also called—tends to increase the assets of a company. The owner also receives the benefit of this asset growth because the owner's equity increases.

Let's summarize now what we've just learned from transactions (4), (5), and (6). **Expenses** tend to reduce the assets and the owner's equity in a firm. **Revenues,** on the other hand, tend to increase the assets of the firm and the owner's equity in those assets. Naturally a firm's profit-making goal is to have revenues substantially exceed expenses during a period of time. In our example Mr. Montz hopes that by providing services to his customers he can charge them fees and thereby cause his firm's assets *and* the owner's equity to grow. If these fees or revenues are greater than the expenses incurred to produce the revenues, then the firm makes a profit, or **net earnings,** for the period. We will examine the relationship of expenses and revenues in more detail later in this unit when we consider the income statement.

Returning assets to the creditors Mr. Montz knows that he must pay off part of the loan that he made from the First National Bank. He owes a total of $3,000 on the note payable, but he has to pay off only one-third of this amount at this time. The bank indicates that he must *remit* (submit in payment) $1,000 plus $15 in interest due on the loan. The transaction can be shown as follows:

	ASSETS			=	LIABILITIES			+	CAPITAL
	cash	+	supplies	=	notes payable	+	accounts payable	+	Montz, capital
Previous balance	$9,800	+	$200	=	$3,000	+	$500	+	$6,500
(7) The firm repays part of a loan plus interest due.	− 1,015			=	− 1,000			−	15
New balance	$8,785	+	$200	=	$2,000	+	$500	+	$6,485

This transaction is called a *compound* business transaction because it involves more than two accounts. (An **account** is the title given to a classification of information in the accounting system; examples here are the Cash, Accounts payable, and Montz, Capital accounts.) First, the asset account Cash is reduced by the amount paid the bank. Second, the creditors' equity in the firm decreases with the reduction of the liability account Notes payable from $3,000 to $2,000. Third, the $15 interest is an expense of operating the business, and it therefore reduces the owner's equity in the firm—just as all expenses reduce the capital of the owner.

Returning assets to the owner Mr. Montz decides that he needs to withdraw $600 from the business for his own personal use. The effect of this transaction on the accounting equation is:

	ASSETS			=	LIABILITIES			+	CAPITAL
	cash	+	supplies	=	notes payable	+	accounts payable	+	Montz, capital
Previous balance	$8,785	+	$200	=	$2,000	+	$500	+	$6,485
(8) The owner withdraws cash for personal use.	− 600							−	600
New balance	$8,185	+	$200	=	$2,000	+	$500	+	$5,885

The asset account Cash is reduced by $600, and because this **withdrawal** has the reverse effect of the owner investing money in the firm, Mr. Montz's equity in the firm is reduced also. The capital account Montz, Capital is thus decreased by $600.

We have looked at these eight transactions as if they occurred in some kind of well-ordered sequence. You should realize, however, that business transactions can occur in a very haphazard fashion—revenues come in and expenses are incurred continuously. The recording process we've just gone through shows how these transactions can be organized in an understandable way.

Table 2-1 shows a handy way of summarizing the transactions of the Cronin Montz Delivery Service for the month of June, 1978.

At the end of June, Mr. Montz is anxious to know whether going into business on his own has been a good idea. To do so, he should be able to answer three basic questions:

1. How well did my business do during the month? (Did I make a profit?)
2. What equity (or interest) do I have in the firm at the end of the month?
3. What is my firm's financial position at the end of the month?

From the transactions we've gone through for the month, we can prepare the reports necessary to answer these questions. These are the three different *financial statements* that we will prepare for Cronin Montz Delivery Service:

■ *How are financial statements put together from the various business transactions?*

1. The *income statement* (operating statement), which reports on the earnings of the company *during* the month.
2. The **statement of owner's capital**, which shows how the owner's equity in the firm changed during the month.
3. The *balance sheet* (position statement), which reports on the assets of the firm at the *end* of the month, along with the related equities (liabilities and owner's capital).

The income statement This statement shows the relationship between two important parts of the firm's activities: the revenues produced during the period and the expenses incurred to produce those revenues. The summary of transactions in Table 2-1 shows that the only revenues produced by the firm during June were the $6,000 in delivery fees (transaction 6). Transactions 4, 5, and 7 show all the firm's expenses during June.

An important point to note is that the withdrawal of cash by the

TABLE 2-1
TRANSACTION SUMMARY

	ASSETS		=	LIABILITIES		+	CAPITAL	
	cash	+ supplies	=	notes payable	+ accounts payable	+	Montz, capital	
(1) Mr. Montz invests $5,000 in the business.	+$5,000						+$5,000	
(2) The firm borrows $3,000 from the bank.	+$3,000			+$3,000				
(3) The firm buys supplies on credit.		+$500			+$500			
(4) The firm pays expenses in cash totaling $4,200.	−$4,200						−$ 800	Truck maintenance expense
							−$1,500	Truck rent expense
							−$ 200	Office rent expense
							−$1,600	Salaries expense
							−$ 100	Misc. expenses
(5) The firm uses up supplies.		−$300					−$ 300	Supplies expense
(6) The firm collects cash for services rendered to customers.	+$6,000						+$6,000	Delivery service revenues
(7) The firm repays part of a loan plus interest due.	−$1,015			−$1,000			−$ 15	Interest expense
(8) The owner withdraws cash for personal use.	−$ 600						−$ 600	Montz, withdrawals
End-of-month balances	$8,185 +	$200	=	$2,000 +	$500	+	$5,885	

TOTAL ASSETS $8,385	TOTAL EQUITIES $8,385

owner, Cronin Montz, does *not* affect the net earnings of the firm. With-drawals by owners are not expenses incurred to help produce revenues. They are simply the return of some of the assets to the owner. Naturally, Mr. Montz's claim on the assets (owner's equity) is reduced by his withdrawal.

A typical income statement, as Mr. Montz prepared it, is shown in Illustration 2-1. Note how Mr. Montz has figured the company's "net earn-ings" to answer his question, "Did I make a profit?" From the information in this statement we can define **net earnings** as the amount of revenues left over after the expenses of a firm for a period of time have been subtracted. For the

Cronin Montz, Delivery Service
Income Statement
For the Month Ended June 30, 1978

Revenues				
Delivery service revenue			$	6 000 00
Expenses				
Truck maintenance expense	$	800 00		
Truck rent expense		1 500 00		
Office rent expense		200 00		
Salaries expense		1 600 00		
Miscellaneous expenses		100 00		
Supplies expense		300 00		
Interest expense		15 00		
Total expenses				4 515 00
Net earnings			$	1 485 00

ILLUSTRATION 2-1

month of June Mr. Montz's net earnings were $1,485. Another name for net earnings is *net income.* Both of these terms will be used throughout this book to mean the same thing.

The statement of owner's capital This statement shows how net earnings and withdrawals by the owner affect the owner's equity in the firm. We can see from the statement of owner's capital presented in Illustration 2-2 that Mr. Montz's capital in the firm increased during June from $5,000 to $5,885. This $885 increase in capital is the amount by which net earnings exceed owner withdrawals for the period. Therefore, at the end of June Mr. Montz's equity in the firm is $5,885.

ILLUSTRATION 2-2

Cronin Montz Delivery Service
Statement of Owner's Capital
For the Month Ended June 30, 1978

Cronin Montz, Capital, June 1, 1978 (Initial investment)			$	5 000 00
Net earnings for June 1978	$	1 485 00		
Owner's withdrawals during June 1978		600 00		
Net increase in capital				885 00
Cronin Montz, Capital, June 30, 1978			$	5 885 00

Cronin Montz Delivery Service
Balance Sheet
June 30, 1978

Assets		
Cash	$ 8185 00	
Supplies	200 00	
Total assets		$ 8385 00
Equities		
Liabilities:		
Notes payable	$ 2000 00	
Accounts payable	500 00	
Total liabilities		$ 2500 00
Capital:		
Cronin Montz, Capital		5885 00
Total equities		$ 8385 00

ILLUSTRATION 2-3

The balance sheet A balance sheet made up on June 30, 1978, is shown in Illustration 2-3. Note that the end-of-month balances from Table 2-1 are repeated in a more formal way in this balance sheet. The balance sheet thus gives decision makers a summary statement of the balances of the various

ILLUSTRATION 2-4

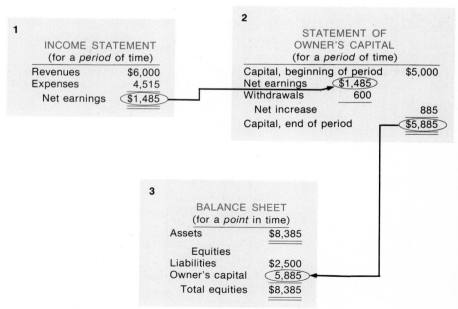

1

INCOME STATEMENT
(for a *period* of time)

Revenues	$6,000
Expenses	4,515
Net earnings	$1,485

2

STATEMENT OF
OWNER'S CAPITAL
(for a *period* of time)

Capital, beginning of period	$5,000
Net earnings	$1,485
Withdrawals	600
Net increase	885
Capital, end of period	$5,885

3

BALANCE SHEET
(for a *point* in time)

Assets	$8,385
Equities	
Liabilities	$2,500
Owner's capital	5,885
Total equities	$8,385

assets and equities at the end of a period. Mr. Montz can look at the balance sheet and tell what his firm's financial position is on June 30, 1978. A more detailed introduction to the arrangement of the accounts in a balance sheet, and the interpretation of the information itself, will be given in later chapters.

Although the three statements that we have just looked at answer different questions and contain different information, they are closely related to each other, as Illustration 2-4 shows. The net earnings from the income statement become a crucial bit of information for the statement of owner's capital, and the end-of-period capital figure becomes a crucial bit of information for the balance sheet. You also can see that *all* the information on these statements can be traced back to the summary of transactions in Table 2-1. Thus, the day-to-day transactions of a business are the raw materials of the accounting system, and the ability to analyze these business transactions is a basic technique of accounting.

❯ NEW TERMS

account The title given to a classification of information in the accounting system; examples are Supplies, Notes payable, and Capital. [p. 25]

expenses Decreases in the owner's equity in the firm, brought about usually by spending or using assets to help produce the revenues of the firm. [p. 23]

net earnings Revenues minus expenses of a firm for a period of time; the net increase in capital brought about by the earnings process; also called *net income.* [p. 25]

revenues Increases in the owner's equity in the firm, brought about usually by receiving assets from customers for the services rendered or the goods sold. [p. 24]

statement of owner's capital A financial statement which shows how the equity of the owner in the assets of the firm changed during a period of time. [p. 26]

withdrawals Decreases in the capital (owner's equity) of a proprietorship when assets of the firm are returned to the owner. [p. 26]

❯ ASSIGNMENT MATERIAL

QUESTIONS

Q2-1. What are revenues?

Q2-2. What are expenses?

Q2-3. What is the effect on the assets and the capital of a firm when the owner withdraws cash for his personal use?

Q2-4. When a company produces net earnings, what effect does it have on the total capital of a firm?

Q2-5. Does *every* business transaction change the accounting equation in some way? Explain.

Q2-6. Do owner's withdrawals reduce the net earnings of a company? Explain.

EXERCISES

E2-1. Refer to P2-1. For each of the 12 transactions, indicate the effect of the transaction on the accounting equation by choosing one of the following responses. For example, for transaction 7, using up $240 of the supplies, the effect is (d), to decrease an asset and decrease capital.
   a. This transaction increases an asset and increases capital.
   b. This transaction increases an asset and increases liabilities.
   c. This transaction increases an asset and decreases another asset.
   d. This transaction decreases an asset and decreases capital.
   e. This transaction decreases an asset and decreases liabilities.
   f. This transaction decreases an asset, decreases a liability, and decreases capital.

E2-2. Refer to P2-2. For each of the 13 transactions, indicate the effect of the transaction on the accounting equation by choosing one of the following responses:
   a. This transaction increases an asset and increases capital.
   b. This transaction increases an asset and increases liabilities.
   c. This transaction increases an asset and decreases another asset.
   d. This transaction decreases an asset and decreases capital.
   e. This transaction decreases an asset and decreases liabilities.
   f. This transaction decreases an asset, decreases a liability, and decreases capital.

E2-3. On January 1, 1978, Mr. George Robber began operating a business, Robber Enterprises. He invested $15,000 cash to start the business. During the first month of operations, he borrowed $5,000 from the bank on a 90-day loan. His expenses of operating the business for the month totaled $9,000 and the revenues produced by the company amounted to $7,500. Mr. Robber withdrew $1,000 for his personal use. What is the amount of owner's capital at the end of the first month of operations?

E2-4. Refer to P2-5. For each of the transactions, indicate the effect of the transaction on the accounting equation by choosing one of the following responses:
   a. This transaction increases an asset and increases capital.
   b. This transaction increases an asset and increases liabilities.
   c. This transaction increases an asset and decreases another asset.
   d. This transaction decreases an asset and decreases capital.
   e. This transaction decreases an asset and decreases liabilities.
   f. This transaction decreases an asset, decreases a liability, and decreases capital.

PROBLEMS (GROUP A)

P2-1. *Transactions and financial statements.* Royal Company was formed on May 1, 1978, by Jim Smith. The transactions for the first month of operations are listed below.
   1. Jim Smith invested $2,000 cash in the business.
   2. The company paid $200 for the first month's rent on the office.
   3. Collected service revenues from customers, $1,000.
   4. Purchased supplies from Ace Company for cash, $100.
   5. Purchased supplies from Jones Company on credit, $200.
   6. Collected service revenues from customers, $900.
   7. Used up $240 of the supplies.
   8. Borrowed $500 from the bank, signing a note.
   9. Paid salaries expenses, $400.
   10. Paid miscellaneous expenses, $300.
   11. Jim Smith withdrew $150 cash for his personal use.
   12. The firm paid the bank $505, which included the interest.

REQUIRED:

a. Prepare a summary transaction form similar to the one in this chapter. The equation, which forms the column headings, should include these accounts: ASSETS—Cash, Supplies; LIABILITIES—Notes payable, Accounts payable; CAPITAL—Jim Smith, Capital.

b. After you have recorded the transactions above, prepare the following financial statements:
   (1) Income statement.
   (2) Statement of owner's capital.
   (3) Balance sheet.

P2-2. *Transactions and financial statements.* Surf Company was formed on March 1, 1978, by Edward Surf. The transactions for the first month of operations are listed below.
   1. Mr. Surf invested $25,000 cash in the business.
   2. Mr. Surf borrowed $10,000 from Best National Bank to provide additional assets for operating the firm.
   3. The firm purchased supplies from Beachview Company for $700, promising to pay the amount in 30 days, on April 1.
   4. Paid the office rent, $900, cash (rent for March).
   5. Used $100 of the supplies in operating the business.
   6. Purchased $200 of additional supplies from Wilson Co., paying cash.
   7. Collected service revenues from customers, $3,100.
   8. Paid salary expenses, $450.
   9. Paid Best National Bank $1,050, which included $1,000 in repayment of the loan plus $50 interest expense for the month.
   10. Paid miscellaneous expenses totaling $800.
   11. Used $150 of supplies in operating the business.
   12. The owner withdrew $200 for personal use.
   13. Collected service revenues from customers, $1,000.

REQUIRED:

a. Prepare a summary transaction form similar to the one in this chapter. The equation, which forms the column headings, should include these accounts: ASSETS—Cash, Supplies; LIABILITIES—Notes payable, Accounts payable; CAPITAL—Edward Surf, Capital.

b. After you have recorded the transactions above, prepare the following financial statements:
   (1) Income statement.
   (2) Statement of owner's capital.
   (3) Balance sheet.

*P2-3. *Relationships among accounts.* At July 1, 1978, L. Waters Company had total liabilities of $6,000 and total assets of $12,000. At July 31, 1978, the total capital amounted to $17,000 and the total liabilities amounted to $6,000. During July, the owner withdrew $1,300 cash for his personal use. Revenues produced during July amounted to $25,000.

---

* Assignment material that has an asterisk next to the assignment number is designed to be especially challenging (and thus a bit more difficult).

a. Prepare a statement of owner's capital for the month of July, 1978.

b. What is the amount of the *total expenses* for July?

PROBLEMS (GROUP B)

P2-4. *Transactions and financial statements.* Regal Company was begun on June 1, 1978, by William Rice. Transactions for the first month of operations are listed below:

1. William Rice invested $3,000 cash in the firm.
2. Collected service revenues from customers, $3,100.
3. The company paid $300 for the first month's rent of the office.
4. Purchased supplies from Jack Co. for cash, $140.
5. Collected service revenues from customers, $1,700.
6. Purchased supplies from Smith Company on credit, $500.
7. Used up $400 of supplies.
8. Paid salaries expenses, $600.
9. Borrowed $800 from the bank, signing a note.
10. Paid miscellaneous expenses, $300.
11. The firm paid the bank $810, which included the interest.

REQUIRED:

a. Prepare a summary transaction form similar to the one in this chapter. The equation, which forms the column headings, should include these accounts: ASSETS—Cash, Supplies; LIABILITIES—Notes payable, Accounts payable; CAPITAL—William Rice, Capital.

b. After you have recorded the transactions, prepare the following financial statements:

(1) Income statement.

(2) Statement of owner's capital.

(3) Balance sheet.

P2-5. *Transactions and financial statements.* Anna Fern began operating a business on October 1, 1978. Transactions for Anna Fern Company for the first month of operations appear below:

1. Mrs. Fern invested $20,000 cash in the business.
2. Paid operating expenses in cash, $8,000.
3. Purchased supplies for $1,100 cash.
4. Purchased additional supplies from Widener Company for $900, promising to pay for them after 30 days (Accounts payable).
5. Paid $800 for employees' salaries.
6. Borrowed $6,000 from First National Bank, signing a note.
7. Used $600 of supplies in running the business.
8. Paid First National Bank $35 for the first month's interest (October). None of the loan was repaid at this time.
9. Mrs. Fern invested another $20,000 cash in the business.
10. Collected $10,000 in service revenues for the month.
11. Mrs. Fern withdrew $1,000 in cash for personal use.

REQUIRED:

a. Prepare a summary transaction form similar to the one in this chapter. The equation, which forms the column headings, should include these accounts:

ASSETS—Cash, Supplies; LIABILITIES—Notes payable, Accounts payable; CAPITAL—Anna Fern, Capital.

b. After you have recorded the transactions above, prepare the following financial statements:

(1) Income statement.

(2) Statement of owner's capital.

(3) Balance sheet.

*P2-6. *Relationships among accounts.* At June 1, 1978, Seekins Company had total assets amounting to $10,000 and total liabilities of $3,000. At June 30, 1978, the liabilities totaled $5,000 and the total capital amounted to $15,000. During the month of June, the owner withdrew $1,200 in cash for his personal use. Also, $8,000 of expenses were incurred during the month.

REQUIRED:

a. Prepare a statement of owner's capital for the month ended June 30, 1978, for Mr. J. Seekins.

b. What were the total revenues for June?

c. What is the amount of total assets at the end of June?

CUMULATIVE REVIEW PROBLEMS

P2-7. *Cumulative review problem.*

a. Match each of the following terms with its appropriate meaning.

_____ 1. balance sheet

_____ 2. cost accounting

_____ 3. controller

_____ 4. income statement

_____ 5. equities

_____ 6. management accounting

_____ 7. proprietorship

_____ 8. assets

_____ 9. creditor

_____ 10. investor

A. a financial statement that provides information about the profitability of the operations of a firm

B. the chief accounting officer of a firm

C. that branch of accounting concerned with providing information to management to aid it in operating a business

D. a financial statement that provides information about the resources that a firm has acquired including information about where these resources came from

E. resources acquired by a firm to aid it in accomplishing its goals

F. person to whom a firm owes money.

G. person who puts money in a firm in hope of profit

H. the interest of outsiders in the assets of a firm

I. the selection, processing, and reporting of information about the costs of manufacturing products

J. a form of business organization with only one owner

b. For each transaction on the next page, place a plus (+) and/or a minus (−) sign under the appropriate account title to show the effect of the transactions:

| | ASSETS | | = | LIABILITIES | + | CAPITAL |
	cash	+ supplies	= notes payable	+ accounts payable	+ capital
(1) Owner invested cash in the business.					
(2) Collected cash for services rendered.					
(3) Purchased supplies on account.					
(4) Paid office rent.					
(5) Borrowed cash from the bank signing a note.					
(6) Paid salaries expense.					
(7) Used supplies in running the business.					
(8) Repaid note plus interest.					
(9) Owner withdrew cash for personal use.					
(10) Purchased supplies for cash.					

P2-8. *Cumulative review problem.* On August 1, 1978, Don Caesar began operating a business. Transactions from Caesar Services Company are listed below and on the top of the next page.

REQUIRED:

    a. Complete the summary transaction form.

    b. From the completed transaction form, prepare an income statement, a statement of owner's capital, and a balance sheet.

| | ASSETS | | = | LIABILITIES | + | CAPITAL |
	cash	+ supplies	= notes payable	+ accounts payable	+ Caesar, capital
a. Owner invests $30,000 in the business.					
b. Owner borrows $10,000 from the bank.					
c. Paid monthly rent of $300.					

	ASSETS		=	LIABILITIES		+	CAPITAL
	cash	+ supplies	=	notes payable	+ accounts payable	+	Caesar, capital
d. Purchased supplies for $1,000 on account.							
e. Purchased supplies for cash, $500.							
f. Collected service revenues of $6,000.							
g. Paid salaries of $3,000.							
h. Owner withdrew $1,000 for personal use.							
i. Used supplies of $600.							
j. Paid interest on loan of $60.							
End-of-month balances	+	=		+		+	

TOTAL ASSETS

$ _____

TOTAL EQUITIES

$ _____

chapter 2
the accounting cycle-I

ACCOUNTS AND THEIR USES

> **OBJECTIVE**

Unit 2 covered the analysis of business transactions and the preparation of financial statements from those transactions. The accounting equation, Assets = Liabilities + Capital, was used as a framework for recording and collecting the transaction information in table form. This table technique is most useful in communicating basic ideas about financial accounting. It is a rather inefficient device, however, for processing the hundreds and thousands of transactions a firm might have in a period of time. For example, if a firm had twenty-five different assets, there would have to be twenty-five columns in the table form just to have room for the assets. You can imagine the difficulty an accountant would have handling such a form if in addition to the twenty-five assets there were also twenty liabilities and a dozen or so capital columns.

Fortunately, the business community uses many other techniques to gather accounting information. One widely used form is the *ledger account, which utilizes a debit and credit system for recording information.* The purpose of this unit is to introduce you to the *account* and to the *debit–credit system* for handling accounting information.

> **APPROACH TO ATTAINING THE OBJECTIVE**

As you study accounts and their uses, pay attention to these three questions, which the text following answers:

- *What is an account, and what is a ledger?*
- *What are the rules for entering data into accounts?*
- *How are ledger accounts related to the accounting equation?*

ACCOUNT AND LEDGER DEFINED

- *What is an account, and what is a ledger?*

An **account** is simply a class of information in an accounting system. For example, the following are asset accounts: (1) Cash, (2) Supplies, (3) Land, and (4) Trucks. The liability accounts of a firm might include (1) Notes payable and (2) Accounts payable. An example of a capital account is John Smith, Capital. In the summary transaction form that you studied in Unit 2, each of the five columns under the accounting equation represented a separate account. Also remember that each of the accounts could be increased (+) or decreased (−). The balance of an account in the example of Cronin Montz Delivery Service was the amount by which the increases in the account exceeded the decreases in the account for a period of time.

A manual (handwritten) bookkeeping system generally uses a **ledger** to classify business transactions by accounts. Each page of the ledger usually represents one account. A ledger for a company is therefore just a book containing all the company's accounts.

Illustration 3-1 presents a typical account, in this instance an asset account titled Cash. By generally accepted custom the *left* side of an account is called the **debit** side, and the *right* side is called the **credit** side. The terms debit and credit refer only to *position* with respect to a particular account and therefore do not in themselves indicate increases or decreases. These two sides actually are used to record either increases or decreases in accounts according to the rules discussed in the next section. Notice that there are spaces in the account in Illustration 3-1 to record: the date of the entry; any information needed about the entry (the Item); and a cross reference to another part of the accounting system. An account like the one illustrated would form one page in a company's ledger.

ILLUSTRATION 3-1

DATE	ITEM	REF.	DEBIT	DATE	ITEM	REF.	CREDIT

Cash   ACCOUNT NO.

RULES OF DEBIT AND CREDIT

- *What are the rules for entering data into accounts?*

In Unit 2 you learned how to analyze business transactions in terms of the accounting equation. One important fact about this system is that after each transaction, the equation was kept in balance—the assets always equaled the equities. *This central idea also lies behind the use of ledger accounts.* The balances of all the asset accounts will always equal the balances of all the equity accounts. This balance is achieved by the use of these rules of debit and credit:

To INCREASE an ASSET-type account, enter the amount on the DEBIT side.

To DECREASE an ASSET-type account, enter the amount on the CREDIT side.

Based on these rules, all asset accounts should have *debit balances* at the end of the period because increases can be expected to exceed decreases.

To INCREASE an EQUITY-type account, enter the amount on the CREDIT side.

To DECREASE an EQUITY-type account, enter the amount on the DEBIT side.

Based on these rules, all equity accounts should have *credit balances* at the end of the period because increases can be expected to exceed decreases.

In summary, when these rules are used, the total of all the debit balances of asset accounts in the ledger will equal the total of all the credit balances of equity accounts in the ledger. This balancing (assets = equities) can be referred to as a double entry system. Every business transaction entered into the accounting system must have total debits that equal total credits. Illustration 3-2 shows these relationships in a more visual way. At this point in your study of accounting you will find it extremely helpful if you will memorize these rules. You should find that after you have completed the assignment material for this unit these rules will be second nature to you.

ILLUSTRATION 3-2

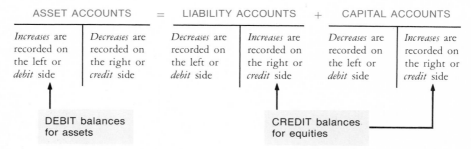

ASSET ACCOUNTS		=	LIABILITY ACCOUNTS		+	CAPITAL ACCOUNTS	
Increases are recorded on the left or *debit* side	*Decreases* are recorded on the right or *credit* side		*Decreases* are recorded on the left or *debit* side	*Increases* are recorded on the right or *credit* side		*Decreases* are recorded on the left or *debit* side	*Increases* are recorded on the right or *credit* side

DEBIT balances for assets

CREDIT balances for equities

ACCOUNTS AND THE ACCOUNTING EQUATION

■ *How are ledger accounts related to the accounting equation?*

In this section we will look at an example to see how ledger accounts can be used to carry out the same objective as the tabular form record in Unit 2. The same example used in Unit 2, with the transactions entered in table form, is shown on the next page. Directly below this example the same transaction information is entered in debit-credit fashion in a set of five ledger accounts.

Let us look at the ledger's Cash account (an asset account) more closely to see exactly how some of Cronin Montz Delivery Service transactions are recorded. In the Cash account receipts of cash during the month are

BUSINESS TRANSACTIONS RECORDED IN TABLE FORM

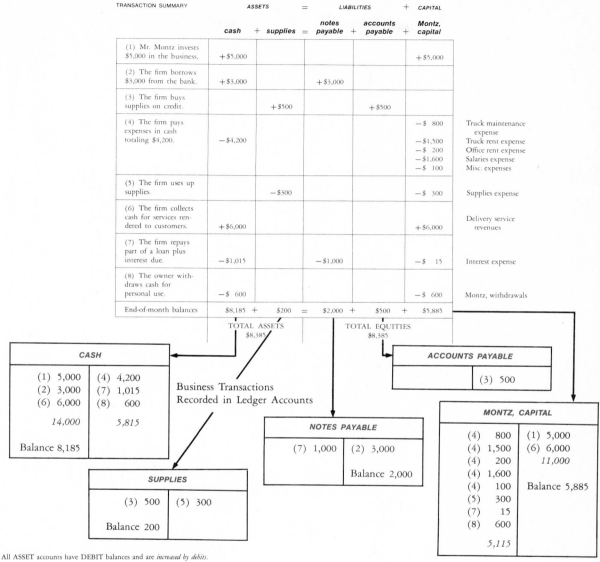

TRANSACTION SUMMARY	ASSETS		=	LIABILITIES		+	CAPITAL	
	cash	+ supplies	=	notes payable	+ accounts payable	+	Montz, capital	
(1) Mr. Montz invests $5,000 in the business.	+$5,000						+$5,000	
(2) The firm borrows $3,000 from the bank.	+$3,000			+$3,000				
(3) The firm buys supplies on credit.		+$500			+$500			
(4) The firm pays expenses in cash totaling $4,200.	−$4,200						−$ 800 −$1,500 −$ 200 −$1,600 −$ 100	Truck maintenance expense Truck rent expense Office rent expense Salaries expense Misc. expenses
(5) The firm uses up supplies.		−$300					−$ 300	Supplies expense
(6) The firm collects cash for services rendered to customers.	+$6,000						+$6,000	Delivery service revenues
(7) The firm repays part of a loan plus interest due.	−$1,015			−$1,000			−$ 15	Interest expense
(8) The owner withdraws cash for personal use.	−$ 600						−$ 600	Montz, withdrawals
End-of-month balances	$8,185 +	$200	=	$2,000 +	$500	+	$5,885	

TOTAL ASSETS $8,385 TOTAL EQUITIES $8,385

Business Transactions Recorded in Ledger Accounts

CASH

(1) 5,000	(4) 4,200
(2) 3,000	(7) 1,015
(6) 6,000	(8) 600
14,000	5,815

Balance 8,185

SUPPLIES

(3) 500	(5) 300

Balance 200

NOTES PAYABLE

(7) 1,000	(2) 3,000
	Balance 2,000

ACCOUNTS PAYABLE

	(3) 500

MONTZ, CAPITAL

(4) 800	(1) 5,000
(4) 1,500	(6) 6,000
(4) 200	11,000
(4) 1,600	
(4) 100	Balance 5,885
(5) 300	
(7) 15	
(8) 600	
5,115	

All ASSET accounts have DEBIT balances and are *increased by debits.*

Cash	$8,185
Supplies	200
	$8,385

Asset accounts are *decreased by credits.*

All EQUITY accounts have CREDIT balances and are *increased by credits.*

Notes payable	$2,000
Accounts payable	500
Montz, Capital	5,885
	$8,385

Equity accounts are *decreased by debits.* Note that revenues are recorded as credits and that expenses and withdrawals are recorded as debits.

shown on the debit side (the left side). These debits arise from transactions (1), (2), and (6). The cash payments for the month similarly are shown on the credit side (the right side) of the account. These credits arise from transactions (4), (7), and (8). The total of the cash receipts (the debits) for the period to date has been inserted below the last debit. This debit total is $14,000. The total of the cash payments (the credits) has also been entered on the credits side in the same way. This credit total is $5,815. If $5,815 is subtracted from $14,000, then we will have the amount of cash on hand, called a debit balance. In our example the debit balance is $8,185. This amount has been inserted on the debit side. If we were to make up a balance sheet at this time, the amount of cash reported on it would be the cash account's debit balance of $8,185.

Remember, however, that we have been looking at just one account on the asset side of the accounting equation. Remember, too, our basic principle that assets always equal equities. Therefore, each of the cash account's debits and credits must have a companion entry in another account. Thus, the Cash account's debits arising from transactions (1), (2), and (6) are balanced by credits in other accounts. And the Cash account's credits from transactions (4), (7), and (8) are balanced by companion debits in other accounts.

Carefully trace each of the eight transactions from one system of recording to the other. Note that each transaction recorded in the ledger accounts involves both a credit and a debit. This maintains the balance of assets and equities. You must fully understand how business transactions are recorded in ledger accounts, for this debit–credit system will be used throughout your future study in this course. The following list will help you study how the transactions are entered as debits and credits in the ledger accounts.

1. Mr. Montz invests $5,000 cash in the business.

   DEBIT Cash for $5,000
   CREDIT Montz, Capital for $5,000

2. The firm borrows $3,000 from the bank.

   DEBIT Cash for $3,000
   CREDIT Notes payable for $3,000

3. The firm buys supplies on credit.

   DEBIT Supplies for $500
   CREDIT Accounts payable for $500

4. The firm pays expenses in cash totaling $4,200.

   DEBIT Montz, Capital for each of the expenses ($800, $1,500, $200, $1,600, $100)
   CREDIT Cash for $4,200

5.	The firm uses up supplies.	DEBIT Montz, Capital for $300 CREDIT Supplies for $300
6.	The firm collects cash for services rendered to customers.	DEBIT Cash for $6,000 CREDIT Montz, Capital for $6,000
7.	The firm repays part of a loan plus interest.	DEBIT Notes payable for $1,000 DEBIT Montz, Capital for $15 CREDIT Cash for $1,015
8.	The owner withdraws cash for personal use.	DEBIT Montz, Capital for $600 CREDIT Cash for $600

» NEW TERMS

account A class of information in an accounting system; general groups of accounts are (1) asset accounts, (2) liability accounts, and (3) capital accounts. [p. 39]

credit The right side of an account; entering an amount on the credit side of an asset account represents a decrease in the asset; entering an amount on the credit side of a liability or capital account represents an increase in that equity account. [p. 39]

debit The left side of an account; entering an amount on the debit side of an asset account represents an increase in the asset; entering an amount on the debit side of a liability or capital account represents a decrease in that equity account. [p. 39]

ledger In a manual bookkeeping system, a book containing each account of a company; a separate account can be placed on each page of the ledger. [p. 39]

» ASSIGNMENT MATERIAL

QUESTIONS

Q3-1. What is an account?

Q3-2. Which side of an account is the debit side?

Q3-3. Which side of an account is the credit side?

Q3-4. Briefly state how asset accounts are increased and decreased by debits and credits.

Q3-5. Briefly state how equity accounts are increased and decreased by debits and credits.

EXERCISES

E3-1. Set up four accounts in "T" form similar to those on the next page.
  a. Enter the following six transactions in the accounts. Also indicate the transaction number in the account beside the amount.
    (1) The owner invests $14,000 cash in the firm. (This has already been entered into the accounts as a debit to Cash and a credit to Smith, Capital.)
    (2) The company collects service revenue from its customers, $4,000.
    (3) The firm borrows $1,000 from the Second National Bank.
    (4) Paid salaries of employees, $300.

CASH		TRUCKS	
(1) $14,000			

NOTES PAYABLE		SMITH, CAPITAL	
			(1) $14,000

(5) Bought a delivery truck for $4,000, paying $500 as a down payment and signing a note payable for the balance.

(6) The owner withdraws $200 for personal use.

b. After all the transactions above are recorded, compute the balance of each account and indicate whether the account has a debit balance or a credit balance. Then determine if the total of all accounts with debit balances is the same as the total of all accounts with credit balances.

E3-2. Answer the following questions by adding the word *debit* or the word *credit*.

a. The Cash account is decreased by entering a . . .

b. The Supplies account is increased by entering a . . .

c. The owner's capital is increased by entering a . . .

d. Expenses are recorded in the capital account by entering a . . .

e. Liability accounts are decreased by entering a . . .

E3-3. Answer the following questions by adding the word *debit* or the word *credit*.

a. The Nancy Froelich, Capital account is decreased by entering a . . .

b. Liability accounts are increased by entering a . . .

c. Revenues are recorded in the capital account by entering a . . .

d. The Trucks account is decreased by entering a . . .

e. Owner's withdrawals are recorded in the owner's capital account by entering a . . .

PROBLEMS (GROUP A)

P3-1. *Entering transactions in "T" accounts.* Set up five accounts in "T" form for each of the following: Cash; Supplies; Notes payable; Accounts payable; Jim Smith, Capital.

REQUIRED:

a. Record the twelve transactions of Royal Company, P2-1 (in Unit 2), in the accounts.

b. After all the transactions are recorded, compute the balance of each account and indicate whether the account has a debit balance or a credit balance. Then determine if the total of all accounts with debit balances is the same as the total of all accounts with credit balances.

P3-2. *Entering transactions in "T" accounts.* Set up five accounts in "T" form for each of the following: Cash; Supplies; Notes payable; Accounts payable; Edward Surf, Capital.

REQUIRED:

    a. Record the thirteen transactions of Surf Company, P2-2, in the accounts.

    b. After all the transactions are recorded, compute the balance of each account and indicate whether the account has a debit balance or a credit balance. Then determine if the total of all accounts with debit balances is the same as the total of all accounts with credit balances.

P3-3. *Entering transactions in "T" accounts.* Set up five accounts in "T" form for each of the following: Cash; Supplies; Notes payable; Accounts payable; Anna Fern, Capital.

REQUIRED:

    a. Record the eleven transactions of Anna Fern Company, P2-5, in the accounts.

    b. After all the transactions are recorded, compute the balance of each account and indicate whether the account has a debit balance or a credit balance. Then determine if the total of all accounts with debit balances is the same as the total of all accounts with credit balances.

PROBLEMS (GROUP B)

P3-4. *Entering transactions in "T" accounts.* Set up six accounts in "T" form for each of the following: Cash; Gardening supplies; Trucks; Accounts payable; Notes payable; G. Sheldon, Capital.

REQUIRED:

    a. Enter the following transactions for the first month of operations for Sheldon Gardening Service Co.:

        (1) The owner, G. Sheldon, invests $4,000 cash in the company.

        (2) The firm purchases gardening supplies from Taylinn Nursery Co. for $1,000, paying $200 cash and promising to pay the balance in 30 days.

        (3) Performed services for customers, collecting $2,000 in cash.

        (4) Paid the salary of an employee, amounting to $300.

        (5) Borrowed $3,000 from Lakefront Bank, signing a note.

        (6) Paid miscellaneous expenses in cash, $134.

        (7) Performed services for customers, collecting $340 in cash.

        (8) Paid $18 to Lakefront Bank for interest on the loan.

        (9) Mr. Sheldon withdrew $400 cash for personal use.

        (10) Used $700 of gardening supplies.

        (11) Purchased a truck, $5,000, paying $1,000 cash and signing a note payable for the balance.

    b. After all the transactions above are recorded, compute the balance of each account and indicate whether the account has a debit balance or a credit balance. Then determine if the total of all accounts with debit balances is the same as the total of all accounts with credit balances.

P3-5. *Entering transactions in "T" accounts.* Set up five accounts in "T" form for each of the following: Cash; Supplies; Notes payable; Accounts payable; Jack Brown, Capital.

REQUIRED:

a. Enter the following transactions for the first month of operations for Brown's Service Company:
   (1) Jack Brown invested $3,000 cash in the business.
   (2) Collected service revenues from customers, $2,000.
   (3) Paid $300 for the month's rent on the office.
   (4) Purchased supplies from Green Co. for cash, $150.
   (5) Collected service revenues from customers, $750.
   (6) Purchased supplies from Black, Inc., on credit, $400.
   (7) Used up $190 of the supplies.
   (8) Borrowed $600 from Second National Bank, signing a note.
   (9) Paid miscellaneous expenses, $410.
   (10) Paid salaries expenses, $385.
   (11) Jack Brown withdrew $200 cash for personal use.
   (12) The company paid the bank $620, which included the interest of $20.

b. After all the transactions above are recorded, compute the balance of each account and indicate whether the account has a debit balance or a credit balance. Then determine if the total of all accounts with debit balances is the same as the total of all accounts with credit balances.

P3-6. *Entering transactions in "T" accounts.* Set up five accounts in "T" form for each of the following: Cash; Supplies; Notes payable; Accounts payable; Stephen Willis, Capital.

REQUIRED:

a. Enter the following transactions for the first month of operations for Willis Service Co.:
   (1) Mr. Willis invested $31,000 cash in the business.
   (2) The owner borrowed $11,000 from the local bank to provide additional assets for operating the business.
   (3) Paid the office rent for the month, $800.
   (4) Purchased supplies from Elysian Supply Co. for $500, promising to pay for them in 30 days.
   (5) Purchased $150 of additional supplies from Royal Co., paying cash.
   (6) Used $120 of the supplies in operating the business.
   (7) Collected service revenues from customers, $4,500.
   (8) Paid the bank $2,100, which included $2,000 in repayment of the loan plus $100 interest expense for the month.
   (9) Paid salary expenses, $500.
   (10) Paid miscellaneous expenses totaling $900.
   (11) Used $200 of supplies in operating the business.
   (12) Collected $1,000 of service revenues from customers.
   (13) The owner withdrew $275 for personal use.

b. After all the transactions above are recorded, compute the balance of each account and indicate whether the account has a debit balance or a credit balance. Then determine if the total of all accounts with debit balances is the same as the total of all accounts with credit balances.

RECORDING BUSINESS TRANSACTIONS

> ## OBJECTIVE

Unit 3 introduced you to the account, to the ledger, and to rules of debit and credit for recording business transactions in modern accounting systems. This unit's first objective is to illustrate how the capital account of the business owner can be broken down into several parts or accounts to make recording and reporting easier. Remember that in Unit 3 the capital account included these entries: owner's investments as credit entries in the capital account; revenues as credit entries in the capital account; expenses as debit entries in the capital account; and withdrawals as debit entries in the capital account. Now you will learn how separate accounts can be set up to handle these elements of capital.

A second objective of this unit is to introduce the journal, its uses, and its relationship to the other elements in the manual accounting process.

> ## APPROACH TO ATTAINING THE OBJECTIVE

As you study how the capital account can be broken down into several accounts and as you study the journal and its uses, direct your attention to these four questions, which the text following answers:

- *What are the six fundamental groups of accounts used in modern accounting systems?*
- *What are the elements of the manual accounting process?*
- *What is a journal?*
- *How are business transactions recorded in a journal?*

SIX GROUPS OF ACCOUNTS

The accounting equation shows three kinds of accounts: assets, liabilities, and capital. You already have learned the rules of debit and credit for recording business transactions in these accounts. As a review of the rules, study the information in Illustration 4-1. Note particularly the examples listed below the capital accounts. These entries are the basis for breaking down the capital accounts to make recording and reporting easier.

ILLUSTRATION 4-1

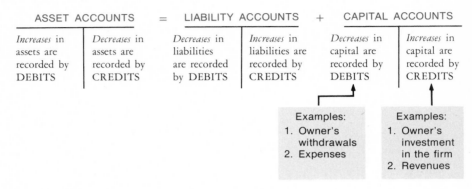

| ASSET ACCOUNTS | = | LIABILITY ACCOUNTS | + | CAPITAL ACCOUNTS |

| *Increases* in assets are recorded by DEBITS | *Decreases* in assets are recorded by CREDITS | *Decreases* in liabilities are recorded by DEBITS | *Increases* in liabilities are recorded by CREDITS | *Decreases* in capital are recorded by DEBITS | *Increases* in capital are recorded by CREDITS |

Examples:
1. Owner's withdrawals
2. Expenses

Examples:
1. Owner's investment in the firm
2. Revenues

In modern business operations, the income statement's report on the relationship of revenues and expenses is extremely important. It shows how profitable a firm's operations were during a specific period of time, and this information is especially vital to the decisions of investors and creditors. Any one firm might have several revenues and many kinds of expenses. You can see, therefore, that if just one capital account were used to record all the changes in capital, there would be a tremendous number of entries of varying kinds in an owner's capital account. For example (see Illustration 4-1), the debit side of the account would include entries for the withdrawals of the owner, as well as entries for the many expenses incurred by the firm. The credit side of the account would include entries for the investments of the owner in the firm, as well as entries for all the revenues earned during the period.

To provide a more workable system for recording and reporting, four capital-type accounts are used instead of just one. These are shown in Illustration 4-2. Observe that the accounts of a firm are now broken down to six general types:

1. Assets—ordinarily with *debit* balances.
2. Liabilities—ordinarily with *credit* balances.
3. Owner's investments—ordinarily with *credit* balances.
4. Owner's withdrawals—ordinarily with *debit* balances.

■ *What are the six fundamental groups of accounts used in modern accounting systems?*

3 Owner's CAPITAL	
	Owner's investment in the firm is recorded by CREDITS

4 Owner's WITHDRAWALS	
Owner's withdrawals are recorded by DEBITS	

| 1 ASSET accounts | = | 2 LIABILITY accounts | + |

5 REVENUE accounts	
	Revenues are recorded by CREDITS

6 EXPENSE accounts	
Expenses are recorded by DEBITS	

ILLUSTRATION 4-2

5. Revenues—ordinarily with *credit* balances.
6. Expenses—ordinarily with *debit* balances

Remember that four of these general types are capital-type accounts (owner's investments, owner's withdrawals, revenues, and expenses). Two of these capital-type accounts have credit balances, representing increases in the capital of the firm; and two of these capital-type accounts have debit balances, representing decreases in the capital of the firm.

THE ACCOUNTING CYCLE

You have learned that business transactions provide the initial information for a financial accounting system and that a system including six fundamental kinds of accounts is used to process the transactions and to serve as a basis for preparing financial statements. In this section we will examine the steps involved in a manual accounting process. These steps, which are referred to as the **accounting cycle**, are as follows:

■ *What are the elements of the manual accounting process?*

1. The transactions take place and are initially written down or recorded on a **source document.** Examples of source documents which show that a business transaction has taken place are (1) sales slips or invoices for goods sold to customers, (2) time cards or time sheets showing the details of a payroll, and (3) bills received from a supplier for merchandise purchased.

2. As transactions occur during a period they are recorded in chronological order in a book called a **journal.** The journal therefore becomes a permanent record of all the business transactions of the firm. The function and use of the journal will be described later in this learning

unit. The source documents noted above provide the information about transactions that is entered in the journal according to the rules of debit and credit.

3. Next the transactions are **posted** (transferred) from the journal to the accounts in the ledger. (This posting process will be described in Unit 5.) At the end of the period—after all transactions of the firm have been entered in the journal and posted to the proper accounts in the ledger—the balance of each account can be determined.

4. Then a list of all the accounts, with their balances, is prepared. This list, called a **trial balance,** is prepared to test the equality of the debits and credits in the ledger. This summary listing of accounts and their balances also serves as a basis for preparing the financial statements. (How a trial balance is prepared and what its function is are discussed in Unit 5.)

Illustration 4-3 summarizes these steps in the accounting cycle.

ILLUSTRATION 4-3

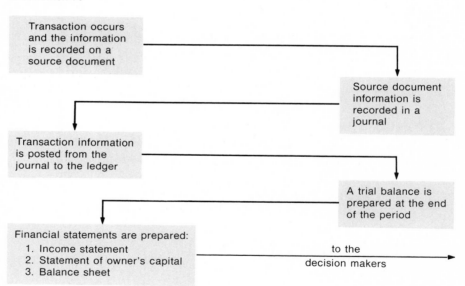

THE GENERAL JOURNAL

▪ *What is a journal?*

The function of a journal is to provide a permanent and complete record, arranged in chronological order for future reference, of all the business transactions of a firm. The manner of entering transactions in the journal displays their effects on the accounts of the firm. An example of a two-column general-purpose journal is shown in Illustration 4-4. Two business transactions have been recorded in the journal (they have been **journalized**) to illustrate

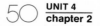

General Journal

DATE	DESCRIPTION	REF.	DEBIT	CREDIT
1978 June 15	Cash		1000000	
	C. P. Smith, Capital			1000000
	Owner invested cash in the company.			
19	Building		6000000	
	Notes payable			6000000
	Purchased a building from Z. Company; signed a 7%, 20-day note.			

(A) PAGE 6

ILLUSTRATION 4-4

the journalizing procedure. Carefully study the following description of the usual procedures for journalizing a transaction.

(A) Every page of the journal is numbered for future reference.

(B) The year is entered at the head of the date column.

(C) The date of the business transaction is entered in the date column. The name of the month need not be repeated for successive transactions during that month.

(D) The name of the account to be debited is entered against the left margin of the description column.

(E) The amount to be debited is entered in the debit amount column.

(F) The name of the account to be credited is entered on the line following the debit account entry. An indentation is made to indicate that the account is credited.

(G) The amount to be credited is entered in the credit amount column.

(H) A detailed description is entered immediately below the journal entry. This valuable information becomes a permanent record for the company.

(I) A line is usually skipped between journal entries.

(J) The reference column is provided for entering cross references to the accounts in the ledger. The posting process is explained in Unit 5.

RECORDING TRANSACTIONS IN A JOURNAL An illustration of a service firm's operations for a month is presented beginning on the next page. The transactions took place during the month of May, 1978, the first month of operations of Stevie Car Wash Company.

a. The owner invests in the firm. He contributes two assets, cash and office equipment. The two asset accounts are debited to reflect increases in these accounts. The capital account is credited to record the owner's equity in the firm. The equipment is recorded at the $800 amount to reflect the approximate value of the asset when it entered the firm.

b. The firm buys equipment to operate the car-wash service. The asset account is debited to record the increase in the asset. A debt is created by the transaction; therefore, the liability (Notes payable) is credited to show the increase in the creditor's equity in the firm.

c. Supplies to be used in washing cars are purchased on credit. The asset, Supplies, is debited to show the increase. Accounts payable, a liability, is credited to reflect the creditor's equity in the assets of the firm. The terms of the purchase are shown in the description of the journal entry.

d. The rent for the month is paid. Cash is credited to reflect the decrease in the asset Cash. Rent expense is debited; expenses are debited because they represent decreases in the owner's equity in the firm. Expenses have the effect of decreasing the profits of the company, thereby decreasing the capital.

e. The revenues earned are recorded. Revenue accounts are credited to reflect increases in the capital (owner's equity) of the firm. The Car-wash revenue account is credited for the total revenues earned of $800. Two assets are debited to show their increase. Accounts receivable, an asset account representing amounts owed to the firm, is increased by $100 to reflect amounts due from a rent-a-car company for services performed on their automobiles. Cash is debited to record the increases in that asset from collections from customers.

f. The amount due Ace Company on the May 8 purchase of supplies is paid. Cash is credited to reflect a reduction in the asset. Accounts payable is debited to reflect a decrease in the liability, the amount owed.

g. Collected cash from Roly Rent-a-Car. This is the amount owed from the May 17 transaction. Cash is debited to show the increase in the asset. Accounts receivable is credited to reflect the fact that we no longer have money owed to us; the asset Accounts receivable is being decreased to a zero balance.

DATE		DESCRIPTION	REF.	DEBIT	CREDIT
1978 *May*	1	Cash		100000	
		Office equipment		80000	
		Paul Stevie, Capital			180000
a		Owner invests cash in the business and contributes to the firm office equipment which he recently purchased for $800.			
	3	Car-wash equipment		360000	
		Notes payable			360000
b		Purchased car-wash equipment from Adele Bros. Co., signing a 120-day, 8% note.			
	8	Supplies		80000	
		Accounts payable			80000
c		Purchased car-wash supplies from Ace Company on credit; $100 payable in 10 days and the balance due in 60 days.			
d	11	Rent expense		30000	
		Cash			30000
		Paid the May rent on the building.			
	17	Accounts receivable		10000	
		Cash		70000	
		Car-wash revenue			80000
e		Revenue earned for services rendered first half of month, including cars washed on credit for Roly Rent-a-Car.			
	18	Accounts payable		10000	
f		Cash			10000
		Paid the amount due the Ace Company on the May 8 purchase.			
	27	Cash		10000	
g		Accounts receivable			10000
		Collected the amount due from Roly Rent-a-Car.			

DATE		DESCRIPTION	REF.	DEBIT	CREDIT
1978 May	31	Salaries expense		600 00	
h		Cash			600 00
		Paid employees' salaries for May.			
	31	Utilities expense		100 00	
i		Cash			100 00
		Paid utilities for May.			
	31	Accounts receivable		400 00	
		Cash		1100 00	
		Car-wash revenue			1500 00
j		Revenue earned for services			
		rendered second half of month,			
		including cars washed on credit			
		for Roly Rent-a-Car.			
	31	Paul Stevie, Withdrawals		500 00	
k		Cash			500 00
		Owner withdrew cash for			
		personal use.			

h. Salaries are paid. The expense account is debited to show the decrease in the owner's equity. The Cash account is credited to record the asset decrease.

i. Utilities are paid. As in the case of other expenses, the debit represents a decrease in capital. The asset Cash is reduced by a credit.

j. Revenues are earned. The assets are increased and the owner's equity is increased as a result of the production of revenue.

k. The owner withdraws cash for personal use. Paul Stevie, Withdrawals is a capital-type account. It is debited to reflect the decrease in the owner's equity in the firm. Cash is credited to show the decrease in the asset.

▪ How are business transactions recorded in a journal?

All the transactions for this first month are entered in a general journal. Study each of these transactions and its explanation carefully—this is a critical step in your successful mastery of accounting. This same example will provide a basis for your study in the next unit.

accounting cycle Refers to the steps involved in the manual accounting process (see Illustration 4-3). [p. 49]

journal In a manual accounting system, a book that provides a permanent and complete record, arranged in chronological order, of all the business transactions of a firm. [p. 49]

journalizing The process of recording business transactions in chronological order in a journal. [p. 50]

posting Transferring information contained in the journal entries to the ledger accounts. [p. 50]

source document A paper or other document that is created in business as a result of a business transaction. For example, a sales slip for merchandise purchased is a source document. Source documents are used as a basis for securing information about transactions before they are entered in a journal. [p. 49]

trial balance A list of all the accounts in a ledger, with their current balances. [p. 50]

> **ASSIGNMENT MATERIAL**

QUESTIONS

Q4-1. Are revenue accounts increased by debits? Explain. Are expense accounts increased by debits? Explain. Is the owner's withdrawal account increased by debits? Explain.

Q4-2. What is a source document?

Q4-3. Contrast journal, ledger, and trial balance.

Q4-4. In what order are transactions recorded in a journal?

EXERCISES

E4-1. List the steps in the accounting cycle in the order that they ordinarily are performed.

E4-2. For each of the following accounts, indicate whether the account is increased by a debit or by a credit. Also indicate whether the account usually has a debit balance or a credit balance at the end of the period.

ACCOUNT TITLE	ACCOUNT INCREASED BY	USUAL BALANCE
Example: Cash	Debits	Debit

1. John Smith, Withdrawals
2. John Smith, Capital
3. Office equipment
4. Notes payable
5. Salary expense
6. Service revenue
7. Office supplies
8. Store supplies
9. Store supplies expense
10. Rent expense
11. Accounts receivable
12. Accounts payable
13. Trucks

E4-3. In a two-column general journal, similar to the one illustrated in this unit, record the following business transactions. Be sure to use good form in journalizing and include the explanation part of each journal entry.

March 1   George Valdez, owner of Valdez Service Company, invested $6,000 cash in the business.

       4   George Valdez contributed equipment to the firm as an investment. This equipment has a value of $10,000.

       5   Additional equipment was purchased from Laura Corp. for $9,000. A down

payment of $1,000 was made, and a 6-month, 7% note was signed for the balance.

6   Purchased office supplies for $800 cash from Harry Company.

15   Paid James Company $3,000 cash. This payment is for supplies which had been purchased and recorded last month.

19   Rendered services to customers totaling $15,400. Cash was received amounting to $11,000, and the remainder is owed to the firm by the customers.

26   The owner withdrew $3,000 cash for personal use.

29   Collected $2,000 of accounts receivable.

E4-4. For each of the following accounts, indicate by a check mark whether the account is *decreased* by a debit or a credit:

	DEBIT	CREDIT
1. Cash		✓
2. Truck		✓
3. Office supplies		✓
4. Accounts payable	✓	
5. Tom Sauer, Capital	✓	
6. Salary expense		✓
7. Building		✓
8. Notes payable	✓	
9. Office equipment		✓
10. Rent expense		✓
11. Accounts receivable		✓
12. Revenue	✓	
13. Utilities expense		✓
14. Tom Sauer, Withdrawals	✓	
15. Store equipment		✓

PROBLEMS (GROUP A)

P4-1. *Journalizing.* In a two-column general journal, similar to the one illustrated in this unit, record the following business transactions. Be sure to use good form in journalizing and include the explanation part of each journal entry.

Feb. 3   Paid advertising expenses amounting to $200.

6   The owner of the firm, Mr. Q. Dryad, withdrew $400 cash to purchase items for his own use.

8   Paid the salaries of the employees, $1,000 cash.

11   Rendered services to customers, $2,000. Collected cash.

15	Purchased equipment for cash, $2,000.
18	The owner, Q. Dryad, invested $3,000 cash in the firm.
20	Rendered services to R. L. Company, which promised to pay us the amount charged, $500, in 30 days.
20	Collected $600 from Z. M. Company, who owed us that amount for services we had rendered several months ago. *Note:* You are to record the transaction for the collection, not for the rendering of the service.
25	Purchased office furniture on credit from Rockny Furniture Company, $1,400. The amount will be paid in 60 days; signed a 7% note.
28	Incurred miscellaneous expenses of operating the firm. Paid $700 cash.

P4-2. *Journalizing.* In a two-column general journal, similar to the one illustrated in this unit, record the following business transactions of Danton Hauling Service. Be sure to use good form in journalizing and include the explanation part of each journal entry.

June 1	D. R. Danton, the owner of the company, withdrew $1,000 cash for personal use.
4	Paid $650 cash for rentals of equipment used in operating the business (Equipment rent expense).
6	Incurred advertising expenses amounting to $369. Promised to pay for these expenses in 30 days.
11	D. R. Danton invested a truck in the business. The truck has a value of $6,000.
14	Rendered services to customers, $4,000. The customers promised to pay the amount in 15 days.
15	Paid salary of employees, $500.
21	Accounts receivable totaling $500 were collected.
25	Paid L. M. Salomone Co. $300, which was owed for supplies which had been purchased some time ago.
27	Rendered services to customers for $1,000 cash.

P4-3. *Journalizing.* In a two-column journal, similar to the one illustrated in this unit, record the following business transactions of Billy's Scooter Service. Be sure to use good form in journalizing the transactions and include the explanation part of each journal entry.

Dec. 1	Collected $3,140 from Becky's Sport Shop, owed to us for services we had rendered several months ago.
2	Paid $243 cash for cleaning services to Smiling K Cleaning Service.
6	Purchased supplies for the office, $413, promising to pay in 20 days.
15	Purchased equipment from Scooter Corp., $2,156, paying $156 in cash and promising to pay the balance in 90 days. A 90-day, 8% note was signed.
20	Rendered services to Becky's Sport Shop in the amount of $4,156, collecting $3,156 now. The remainder will be collected in 30 days.
24	The owner, Billy Boas, withdrew $2,100 cash for personal use.
29	Paid the salary of an employee, $400 cash.
30	Paid Williams Co. $532 cash for supplies we had purchased from them 30 days ago.

PROBLEMS (GROUP B)

P4-4. *Journalizing.* In a two-column general journal, similar to the one illustrated in this unit, record the following business transactions. Be sure to use good form in journalizing and include the explanation part of each journal entry.

March	3	The owner of the firm, Ms. Kathy Faherty, withdrew $500 cash to purchase items for her own use.
	6	Paid advertising expenses amounting to $150.
	8	Rendered services to customers, $3,500. Collected cash.
	11	Paid the salaries of the employees, $1,200 cash.
	15	Ms. Faherty invested $4,000 cash in the firm.
	18	Purchased equipment for cash, $2,500.
	20	Collected $500 from S. M. Co., which owed us that amount for services we had rendered several months ago. *Note:* You are to record the transaction for the collection, not for the rendering of the service.
	21	Rendered services to R. L. Company, which promised to pay us the amount charged, $300, in 20 days.
	25	Incurred miscellaneous expenses of operating the firm. Paid $230 cash.
	28	Purchased office furniture on credit from Gaffney Industries, $2,500. The amount will be paid in 60 days; signed a 7% note.

P4-5. *Journalizing.* In a two-column general journal, similar to the one illustrated in this unit, record the following business transactions of the Hildebrand Service Company. Be sure to use good form in journalizing and include the explanation part of each journal entry.

May	1	Dale Hildebrand, the owner of the firm, withdrew $2,000 cash for personal use.
	4	Paid $2,450 cash for rentals of equipment used in operating the business (Rent expense).
	6	Hildebrand invested equipment in the business. The equipment has a value of $5,000.
	10	Incurred advertising expenses amounting to $400. Promised to pay for these expenses in 20 days.
	14	Paid the salary of employees, $600.
	15	Rendered services to customers, $5,370. The customers promised to pay the amount in 15 days.
	20	Accounts receivable totaling $450 were collected.
	25	Paid Melody Co. $400, which was owed for supplies which had been purchased last month.
	27	Rendered services to customers for $2,800 cash.

P4-6. *Journalizing.* In a two-column journal, similar to the one illustrated in this unit, record the following business transactions of T. Morgan Service Co. Be sure to use good form in journalizing the transactions and include the explanation part of each journal entry.

Dec.	1	Paid $350 cash for cleaning services rendered by Ragland Company.
	2	Collected $4,000 from Gutchell Sports Supplies, owed to us for services we had rendered several months ago.
	6	Purchased supplies for the office, $528, promising to pay in 30 days.
	15	Purchased equipment from Services, Inc., $3,518, paying $518 in cash and promising to pay the balance in 90 days. A 90-day, 9% note was signed.
	20	The owner, T. Morgan, withdrew $3,600 cash for personal use.
	24	Rendered services to Gutchell Sports Supplies in the amount of $2,420, collecting $1,420 now. The remainder will be collected in 10 days.
	28	Paid the salary of an employee, $900 cash.
	30	Paid McDonald Co. $650 cash for supplies we had purchased from them 30 days ago.

UNIT 5

SUMMARIZING BUSINESS TRANSACTIONS

➤ **OBJECTIVE**

The objective of this unit is to introduce you to the activities in the manual accounting cycle that involve summarizing transaction information. You already have learned how to journalize the business transactions of a service firm. Now you will learn how to post these transactions from the journal to the accounts in the ledger and how to prepare a trial balance. This unit also will introduce you to the chart of accounts.

➤ **APPROACH TO ATTAINING THE OBJECTIVE**

As you study how business transactions can be summarized for reporting, pay attention to these three questions, which the text following answers:

- *How are transactions posted from the journal to the accounts in the ledger?*
- *How is the trial balance prepared, and what is its function?*
- *What is a chart of accounts and what is its function?*

**POSTING
TRANSACTIONS
TO THE ACCOUNTS**

Posting is the transfer of accounting information from a journal to a ledger. This procedure is necessary in order to gather together the effects of business transactions on each type of asset, liability, and capital account. At the end of a period of time, summary totals of this account information can be compiled for use in the preparation of a trial balance and financial statements.

- *How are transactions posted from the journal to the accounts in the ledger?*

A general journal with a single journal entry and the corresponding ledger entries are shown in Illustration 5-1. The arrows in the diagram indicate how the posting is carried out. Solid lines indicate debit posting and

ILLUSTRATION 5-1   POSTING ILLUSTRATED.

JOURNAL

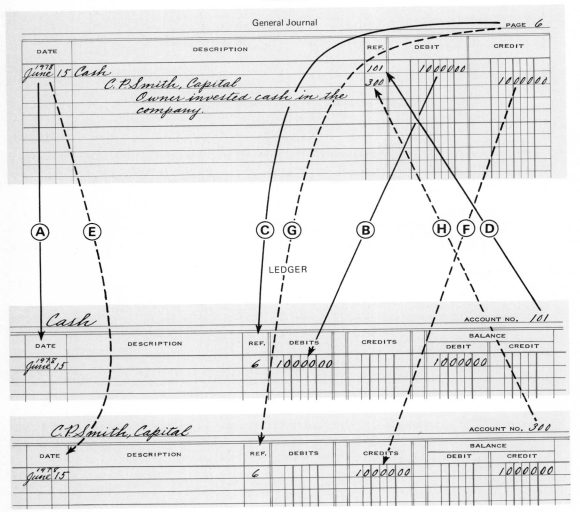

LEDGER

dashed lines note credit posting. Carefully observe the **cross-referencing** system.

Notice that the ledger accounts shown in Illustration 5-1 (Cash and C. P. Smith, Capital) are a different form from the ones illustrated in the previous unit. This form of ledger account is called the **balance-column account.** There is a column for the debit postings, a column for the credit postings, a column to show the balance of the account if it is a debit balance, and a column to show the balance of the account if it happens to be a credit balance. This form of account is widely used in business because it provides space to show the balance of the account after each transaction is posted.

Posting this journal entry with one debit and one credit involves the following:

(A) Enter the date of the journal entry in the account to be *debited* (Cash account).

(B) Enter the amount of the debit in the debit column of the account to be *debited* (Cash account).

(C) Enter the cross reference in the ledger account to show that the debit was posted from the journal (Page 6).

(D) Enter the cross reference in the *journal* to show that the debit was posted to the appropriate account (Account 101).

(E) Enter the date of the journal entry in the account to be *credited* (C. P. Smith, Capital account).

(F) Enter the amount in the credit column of the account to be *credited* (C. P. Smith, Capital account).

(G) Enter the cross reference in the ledger account to show that the credit was posted from the journal (Page 6).

(H) Enter the cross reference in the *journal* to show that the credit was posted to the appropriate account (Account 300).

An example The journal of Stevie Car Wash Company—the same illustration you studied in Unit 4—is reproduced on the next two pages. Note that now, as part of the posting process, cross references to the appropriate ledger accounts have been entered in the journal's reference column. Shown after this journal is the ledger of the company. Carefully study how each of the journal entries has been posted to the appropriate ledger accounts.

At the end of the period (a month in this case), the balance of each account is shown in the ledger. These ending balances are used in the preparation of the trial balance, which is discussed in the next section.

	General Journal				PAGE 1

DATE	DESCRIPTION	REF.	DEBIT	CREDIT
1978 May 1	Cash	101	1000 00	
	Office equipment	120	800 00	
	Paul Stevic, Capital	301		1800 00
	Owner invests cash in the business and contributes to the firm office equipment which he recently purchased for $800.			
3	Car-wash equipment	122	3600 00	
	Notes payable	202		3600 00
	Purchased car-wash equipment from Adele Bros. Co., signing a 120-day, 8% note.			
8	Supplies	103	800 00	
	Accounts payable	201		800 00
	Purchased car-wash supplies from Ace Company on credit; $100 payable in 10 days and the balance due in 60 days.			
11	Rent expense	502	300 00	
	Cash	101		300 00
	Paid the May rent on the building.			
17	Accounts receivable	102	100 00	
	Cash	101	700 00	
	Car-wash revenue	401		800 00
	Revenue earned for services rendered first half of month, including cars washed on credit for Roly Rent-a-Car.			
18	Accounts payable	201	100 00	
	Cash	101		100 00
	Paid the amount due the Ace Company on the May 8 purchase.			
27	Cash	101	100 00	
	Accounts receivable	102		100 00
	Collected the amount due from Roly Rent-a-Car.			

General Journal

DATE	DESCRIPTION	REF.	DEBIT	CREDIT
1978 May 31	Salaries expense	501	60000	
	Cash	101		60000
	Paid employees' salaries for May.			
31	Utilities expense	504	10000	
	Cash	101		10000
	Paid utilities for May.			
31	Accounts receivable	102	40000	
	Cash	101	110000	
	Car-wash revenue	401		150000
	Revenue earned for services rendered second half of month, including cars washed on credit for Roly Rent-a-Car.			
31	Paul Stevie, Withdrawals	302	50000	
	Cash	101		50000
	Owner withdrew cash for personal use.			

General Ledger

Cash — ACCOUNT NO. 101

DATE	DESCRIPTION	REF.	DEBITS	CREDITS	BALANCE DEBIT	BALANCE CREDIT
1978 May 1		1	100000		100000	
11		1		30000	70000	
17		1	70000		140000	
18		1		10000	130000	
27		1	10000		140000	
31		2		60000	80000	
31		2		10000	70000	
31		2	110000		180000	
31		2		50000	130000	

Accounts receivable — ACCOUNT NO. 102

DATE	DESCRIPTION	REF.	DEBITS	CREDITS	BALANCE DEBIT	BALANCE CREDIT
1978 May 17		1	10000		10000	
27		1		10000	0	
31		2	40000		40000	

Supplies — ACCOUNT NO. 103

DATE	DESCRIPTION	REF.	DEBITS	CREDITS	BALANCE DEBIT	BALANCE CREDIT
1978 May 8		1	80000		80000	

Office equipment — ACCOUNT NO. 120

DATE	DESCRIPTION	REF.	DEBITS	CREDITS	BALANCE DEBIT	BALANCE CREDIT
1978 May 1		1	800 00		800 00	

Car-wash equipment — ACCOUNT NO. 122

DATE	DESCRIPTION	REF.	DEBITS	CREDITS	BALANCE DEBIT	BALANCE CREDIT
1978 May 3		1	3600 00		3600 00	

Accounts payable — ACCOUNT NO. 201

DATE	DESCRIPTION	REF.	DEBITS	CREDITS	BALANCE DEBIT	BALANCE CREDIT
1978 May 8		1		800 00		800 00
18		1	100 00			700 00

Notes payable — ACCOUNT NO. 202

DATE	DESCRIPTION	REF.	DEBITS	CREDITS	BALANCE DEBIT	BALANCE CREDIT
1978 May 3		1		3600 00		3600 00

Paul Stevie, Capital — ACCOUNT NO. 301

DATE	DESCRIPTION	REF.	DEBITS	CREDITS	BALANCE DEBIT	BALANCE CREDIT
1978 May 1		1		1800 00		1800 00

Paul Stevie, Withdrawals — ACCOUNT NO. 302

DATE	DESCRIPTION	REF.	DEBITS	CREDITS	BALANCE DEBIT	BALANCE CREDIT
1978 May 31		2	500 00		500 00	

Car-wash revenue — ACCOUNT NO. 401

DATE	DESCRIPTION	REF.	DEBITS	CREDITS	BALANCE DEBIT	BALANCE CREDIT
1978 May 11		1		800 00		800 00
31		2		1500 00		2300 00

Salaries expense						ACCOUNT NO. 501	
DATE	DESCRIPTION	REF.	DEBITS	CREDITS	BALANCE		
					DEBIT	CREDIT	
1978 May 31		2	60000		60000		

Rent expense						ACCOUNT NO. 502	
DATE	DESCRIPTION	REF.	DEBITS	CREDITS	BALANCE		
					DEBIT	CREDIT	
1978 May 11		1	30000		30000		

Utilities expense						ACCOUNT NO. 504	
DATE	DESCRIPTION	REF.	DEBITS	CREDITS	BALANCE		
					DEBIT	CREDIT	
1978 May 31		2	10000		10000		

PREPARING THE TRIAL BALANCE

■ *How is the trial balance prepared, and what is its function?*

Once the balances of the individual accounts have been determined, a trial balance can be prepared. As we mentioned in Unit 4 in our discussion of the accounting cycle, a trial balance is a list of all the accounts in the ledger with their current balances. This list is prepared to test the equality of the debits and credits in the ledger at the end of a period of time. The list also is used as a basis for preparing the financial statements because it contains the information needed to prepare the income statement, the balance sheet, and the statement of owner's capital.

Illustration 5-2 presents the trial balance of Stevie Car Wash Company. Be sure to determine where each of the figures in the trial balance came from by referring to the balances in the ledger accounts in the previous section.

Occasionally, a posting error will be made and the trial balance will not balance. If a debit or credit posting is omitted, the totals in the trial balance will simply differ by the amount of the omitted posting. The journal then can be reviewed to find the error in that amount. On the other hand, if a debit or credit entry is posted on the wrong side of an account, the totals in the trial balance will differ by *twice* the amount of the error. A good procedure would be to divide the difference of the trial balance totals by two, and then refer to the journal to locate the amount of the error.

Stevie Car-Wash Company
Trial Balance
May 31, 1978

ACCT. NO.	ACCOUNT	DEBIT	CREDIT
101	Cash	1300 00	
102	Accounts receivable	400 00	
103	Supplies	800 00	
120	Office equipment	800 00	
122	Car-wash equipment	3600 00	
201	Accounts payable		700 00
202	Notes payable		3600 00
301	Paul Stevie, Capital		1800 00
302	Paul Stevie, Withdrawals	500 00	
401	Car-wash revenue		2300 00
501	Salaries expense	600 00	
502	Rent expense	300 00	
504	Utilities expense	100 00	
		8400 00	8400 00

ILLUSTRATION 5-2

You should also be aware that the trial balance can balance and still contain errors. For example, a debit of $100 to the Cash account could have been posted *in error* to the Supplies account. When the trial balance is prepared, the Cash ledger account would be *understated* by $100 and the Supplies ledger account would be *overstated* by $100. In this situation, the trial balance would balance, but the balances in two accounts (Cash and Supplies) would be incorrect. Therefore, accurate journalizing and posting is necessary if the end products of the accounting process (financial statements) are to be relied upon.

Note in Illustration 5-3 how the activities you have just studied relate to the accounting cycle.

THE CHART OF ACCOUNTS

Most firms that have manual accounting systems provide a **chart of accounts** as a reference for those engaged in bookkeeping activities. A chart of accounts is simply a list of all the accounts of the firm together with their exact titles and account numbers. All the accounts listed in a firm's chart of accounts might not be used in any one accounting period. The numbering systems for

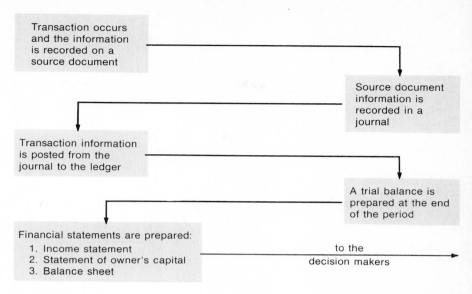

ILLUSTRATION 5-3

■ *What is a chart of accounts and what is its function?* accounts vary from company to company. The system used by Stevie Car Wash Company is listed below. The 100-level account numbers are used to represent assets; the 200s are liabilities; the 300s are capital; the 400s are revenues; and the 500s are expenses. Notice that some of the numbers are skipped to provide room in the system for adding new accounts. New accounts (such as Accumulated depreciation—Office equipment) included in the chart of accounts will be explained in the next unit.

Stevie Car Wash Company
CHART OF ACCOUNTS

Asset Accounts

101   Cash
102   Accounts receivable
103   Supplies
120   Office equipment
121   Accumulated depreciation
          —Office equipment
122   Car-wash equipment
123   Accumulated depreciation
          —Car-wash equipment

Liability Accounts

201   Accounts payable
202   Notes payable
203   Interest payable

Capital Accounts

301   Paul Stevie, Capital
302   Paul Stevie, Withdrawals

Revenue Accounts

401   Car-wash revenue

Expense Accounts

501   Salaries expense
502   Rent expense
503   Supplies expense
504   Utilities expense
505   Interest expense
506   Depreciations expense
          —Office equipment
507   Depreciation expense
          —Car-wash equipment

NEW TERMS

balance-column account A form of ledger account that includes a column to show the balance of the account after every posting. [p. 61]

chart of accounts A list of all the accounts of the firm, with their exact titles and account numbers. Used as a reference for bookkeepers and others working with the accounting system. [p. 66]

cross reference In the posting process, refers to entering the ledger account number in the journal to show where the entry was posted, and to entering the journal page in the ledger account to show the journal source of the account entry. [p. 61]

ASSIGNMENT MATERIAL

QUESTIONS

Q5-1. Make a list of the items of information that are posted *to the ledger* from the general journal (for each journal entry). *Example:* Date of journal entry.

Q5-2. What is the function of a trial balance?

Q5-3. If the trial balance totals balance, this means that there have been no errors. Do you agree? Explain your answer.

Q5-4. What is a chart of accounts? Why are some of the numbers usually skipped in preparing a chart of accounts?

Q5-5. Describe the difference between the form of ledger account used in this unit and the form of ledger account used in previous units.

EXERCISES

E5-1. If an error is made in the posting process, wherein a debit to Cash amounting to $300 is not posted (the posting is omitted in error), then the trial balance totals will differ by how much?

E5-2. If a $300 debit posting to Cash is posted in error as a *credit* to Cash, by how much will the trial balance totals differ? Explain a good procedure for finding such errors.

E5-3. For each of the transactions listed below, indicate which accounts would be debited and which accounts would be credited.

   a. Purchased supplies, paying part in cash and promising to pay for the balance in 10 days.

   b. The owner of the firm, James Bittern, contributed cash, land, and an office building to the firm as his investment.

   c. Purchased store equipment, paying part in cash and signing a note payable for the balance.

   d. The owner, James Bittern, withdrew cash from the firm for his personal use.

   e. Collected the amount due from a customer, Hubert Grimace. This was the balance owed us from a sale we made to him last month.

   f. Paid Allen Corporation the amount we owed them for a purchase of supplies that we made 2 months ago.

   g. Rendered services to a customer, A. L. Spencer, collecting part in cash and receiving his promise to pay us the balance in 30 days (Service revenue).

   h. Paid the utility bill for the month.

PROBLEMS (GROUP A)

P5-1. *Journalizing, posting, and trial balance.* On the next page are shown a chart of accounts and a list of business transactions for the first month of operations of Jackie's Barber-shop.

CHART OF ACCOUNTS

100	Cash and currency	171	Jackie Feeld, Withdrawals
102	Cash in bank	182	Revenue from services
103	Barber supplies	190	Rent expense
125	Barber equipment	191	Salaries expense
150	Accounts payable	192	Utilities expenses
151	Notes payable	193	Magazine subscriptions expense
170	Jackie Feeld, Capital	194	Miscellaneous expense

Business transactions for March, 1978:

March 2	The owner invested $400 in the business. $350 is deposited in a bank account and $50 is kept in the barbershop to make change. All cash payments made by the business are to be in the form of checks on the bank account.
3	Purchased $640 of barber equipment from BB Barber Supply Company , paying $100 in cash and signing a 7%, 3-month note for the remainder.
4	Purchased $200 of barber supplies on credit from AZ Company. The bill is to be paid in 30 days.
10	Collected $500 from customers during the last few days for services rendered. Deposited this in the bank.
12	Feeld withdrew $300 for personal use.
19	Paid salaries to employees, $200.
20	Collected $1,000 from customers and deposited this in the bank.
20	Paid the rent for the month, $175.
31	Paid salaries to employees, $300.
31	Paid magazine subscriptions, $32.
31	Paid the amount due AZ Company from March 4.
31	Collected $700 from customers and deposited this in the bank.

REQUIRED:

a. Record the business transactions in a general journal.

b. Set up a balance-column ledger account for each account appearing in the chart of accounts. Post the transactions from the journal to the ledger. Be sure to include cross references in the journal and ledger accounts.

c. Prepare a trial balance for the company at March 31. Omit from the trial balance any account that has a zero balance.

P5-2. *Journalizing, posting, and trial balance.* Below are shown a chart of accounts and a list of business transactions for the first month of operations of Ginnaged Service Company.

CHART OF ACCOUNTS

101	Cash on hand and in bank	302	M. R. Ginnaged, Withdrawals
102	Service supplies	401	Revenue from services
103	Accounts receivable	501	Salaries expense
109	Service equipment	502	Advertising expense
110	Office equipment	503	Utilities expense
201	Accounts payable	504	Rent expense
202	Notes payable	505	Maintenance expense
301	M. R. Ginnaged, Capital	506	Miscellaneous expense

Business transactions for July, 1978:

July 3   M. R. Ginnaged invested $24,000 in the business.

5   Purchased Service supplies and Service equipment from Muddog Company as follows: Service supplies, $8,000; Service equipment, $9,000. Paid $3,000 cash down on these purchases and signed a 1-year, 9% note for $14,000.

7   Rendered services to customers as follows: Services rendered for cash, $53,400; Services rendered on credit, $31,500.

17   Collected $20,000 cash from customers who owed us $31,500 from July 7. The remaining $11,500 will be collected next month.

18   Paid salaries of employees, $10,000 cash.

20   Paid utilities, $1,300.

21   M. R. Ginnaged withdrew $3,000 cash for personal use.

23   Purchased Service supplies from Muddog Company, $2,319, on credit (Accounts payable).

28   Paid advertising expenses, $1,500.

29   Paid Dust Company $1,600 for maintenance services performed for our firm.

29   Paid the monthly rent, $13,000.

30   Paid the salaries of employees, $15,400.

30   Paid miscellaneous expenses of $1,456.

30   Paid advertising expenses, $3,100 cash.

REQUIRED:

a. Record the business transactions in a general journal.

b. Set up a balance-column ledger account for each account appearing in the chart of accounts. Post the transactions from the journal to the ledger. Be sure to include cross references in the journal and ledger accounts.

c. Prepare a trial balance for the company at July 31. Omit from the trial balance any account that has a zero balance.

P5-3. *Journalizing, posting, and trial balance.* Below are shown a chart of accounts and a list of business transactions for the first month of operations of Dragon Golf Service Co.

CHART OF ACCOUNTS

101	Cash	302	H. R. Dragon, Withdrawals
102	Accounts receivable	401	Golf service revenues
104	Golf supplies	502	Salaries expense
109	Equipment	503	Rent expense
202	Accounts payable	504	Miscellaneous expense
210	Notes payable	520	Interest expense
301	H. R. Dragon, Capital		

Business transactions for February, 1978:

Feb. 1   H. R. Dragon invests $84,500 cash in the business.

2   Purchased golf supplies from Noah Co. for $8,600, payment to be made in 30 days.

4   Performed services for customers on credit, $19,000.

4   Paid rent expense, $13,500 cash.

5	Purchased equipment costing $100,000, paying $25,000 down and signing a 7%, 1-year note for the balance.
6	Performed services for customers and collected $23,000 cash.
8	Paid miscellaneous expenses, $1,240 cash.
8	Paid salaries of employees, $14,150.
9	Collected $9,000 of accounts receivable.
10	H. R. Dragon withdrew $2,100 cash for personal use.
10	Purchased additional golf supplies for $7,000 cash.
12	Paid miscellaneous expenses, $1,000 cash.
13	Performed services for customers, $10,000 on credit.
14	H. R. Dragon invested an additional $3,000 cash in the business.
15	Paid for the supplies that were purchased on Feb. 2 (Noah Co.).
27	Collected $3,000 of accounts receivable.
28	H. R. Dragon withdrew another $300 cash for personal use.
28	Paid $13,437 cash in payment of part of the note and interest as follows: Payment on note, $13,000; Interest for the month, $437.

REQUIRED:

a. Record the business transactions in a general journal.

b. Set up a balance-column ledger account for each account appearing in the chart of accounts. Post the transactions from the journal to the ledger. Be sure to include cross references in the journal and ledger accounts.

c. Prepare a trial balance for the company at February 28. Omit from the trial balance any account that has a zero balance.

PROBLEMS (GROUP B)

P5-4. *Journalizing, posting, and trial balance.* Below are a chart of accounts and a list of business transactions for the first month of operations of the Slater Garage.

101	Cash on hand and in bank
102	Office supplies
103	Accounts receivable
109	Garage equipment
201	Accounts payable
202	Notes payable
301	Steve Batey, Capital
302	Steve Batey, Withdrawals
401	Revenue from services
501	Salaries expense
502	Utilities expense
503	Rent expense
504	Interest expense

July 3	Steve Batey, owner, invests $50,000 in the business.
5	Purchased office supplies for $550 cash.
6	Purchased $5,500 in garage equipment from Purdue Equipment Company, paying $3,000 cash. The balance was on open account (Accounts payable).
7	Paid rent for July of $250.
10	Borrowed $7,000 from Shelton National Bank on a note.
12	Paid utility expense of $175.
14	Rendered services to customers as follows: Services rendered for cash, $15,200; services rendered on credit, $10,500.

17		Paid salaries to employees of $12,000.
20		Paid $1,500 to Purdue Equipment Company for equipment purchased July 6 on account.
25		Steve Batey, owner, withdrew $750 cash for personal use.
30		Paid Shelton Bank $2,000 on the principal of the note and $89 of interest.

REQUIRED:

    a. Record the business transactions in a general journal.

    b. Set up a balance-column ledger account for each account appearing in the chart of accounts. Post the transactions from the journal to the ledger. Be sure to include cross references in the journal and ledger accounts.

    c. Prepare a trial balance for the company at July 31. Omit from the trial balance any account that has a zero balance.

P5-5. *Journalizing, posting, and trial balance.* The following information is from the Alphonse Service Company's first month of operations.

CHART OF ACCOUNTS

101	Cash	301	Alphonse, Capital
102	Accounts receivable	302	Alphonse, Withdrawals
104	Office supplies	401	Service revenue
109	Equipment	501	Salary expense
202	Accounts payable	502	Rent expense
204	Notes payable	503	Advertising expense

Business transactions for June, 1978:

June	1	Mr. Alphonse, the owner, invested $20,000 in the business. He also contributed equipment worth $2,500.
	2	Rent on the building was paid for the month, $1,000.
	4	Purchased office supplies for $650 on credit.
	7	Rendered services to customers totaling $6,400. $4,000 was collected in cash, and the remainder is owed to the firm.
	8	Purchased equipment for $4,200. A down payment of $1,000 was made, and the balance is to be paid in 90 days (7%, 30-day note is signed).
	13	Collected $500 from a customer for services we had rendered on June 7.
	20	Incurred advertising expenses amounting to $250. Promised to pay the amount within 30 days.
	25	Paid employees' salaries for the month, $6,400.
	27	Paid the $650 owed for the purchase of office supplies on June 4.
	30	Paid for the advertising expense incurred on June 20.
	30	Owner withdrew $700 for personal use.

REQUIRED:

    a. Record the transactions above in a general journal.

    b. Set up a ledger account for each account appearing in the chart of accounts. Post the transactions to the accounts.

    c. Prepare a trial balance for Alphonse Service Company at June 30, 1978.

P5-6. *Journalizing, posting, and trial balance.* On the next page are presented a chart of accounts and a list of transactions for the first month of operations for Smith Dental Services Company.

ACCOUNT NO.	ACCOUNT TITLE
101	Cash
103	Accounts receivable
105	Office supplies
106	Dental supplies
120	Office equipment
121	Dental equipment
201	Accounts payable
202	Notes payable
301	J. D. Smith, Capital
302	J. D. Smith, Withdrawals
402	Dental revenue
403	Miscellaneous revenue
501	Salary expense
502	Rent expense
503	Utilities expense

1978

April 1   J. D. Smith, the owner, contributes to the firm $70,000 cash and dental equipment worth $30,000 as an investment.

3   Purchased office equipment for $18,000, paying $5,000 cash and signing a 180-day, 9% note for the balance.

7   Purchased supplies as follows:

Office supplies	$ 346
Dental supplies	900
	$1,246

Paid $500 cash for the supplies and promised to pay the balance in 10 days.

10   Rendered services as follows:

Dental services	$6,000
Miscellaneous services	2,000
	$8,000

Collected one-fourth of the amount due. The balance will be collected later.

12   Paid the monthly rent, $1,000.

17   Paid the amount due for the supplies purchased on April 7.

20   Collected $2,000 of the amount due from the April 10 transaction.

30   Paid employees' salaries, $2,000 cash.

30   Paid utility bills totaling $312.

30   Rendered services as follows:

Dental services	$3,100
Miscellaneous services	500
	$3,600

Collected half of the amount due. The balance will be collected later.

30   Mr. Smith withdrew $1,000 cash for personal use.

REQUIRED:

   a. Record the business transactions in a general journal.

   b. Set up a balance-column ledger account for each account appearing in the chart of accounts. Post the transactions from the journal to the ledger. Be sure to include cross references in the journal and ledger accounts.

   c. Prepare a trial balance for the company at April 30. Omit from the trial balance any account that has a zero balance.

CUMULATIVE REVIEW PROBLEMS

P5-7. *Cumulative review problem.* Below is presented a list of transactions for the first month of operations for the Barnard Enterprises Co.

1978

Nov. 1   Harold Barnard made the following investments in the firm:

Cash	$12,500
Service equipment	10,000
Service supplies	1,000

3   Purchased additional service supplies for $800, paying $100 in cash and promising to pay for the balance in 15 days.

4   Purchased *office* supplies for $162, promising to pay for them in 30 days.

5   Purchased service equipment for $1,700, paying $300 in cash and signing a 120-day, 8% note for $1,400.

12   Paid salaries of employees, $700.

14   Paid the rent for the month, $650.

15   Service revenue earned for the first half of the month was as follows:

Services rendered for cash	$7,350
Services rendered on credit	1300

18   Paid the amount due for the service supplies purchased on November 3.

20   Collected accounts receivable in the amount of $500.

30   Paid salaries of employees, $900.

30   Paid miscellaneous expenses, $518.

30   The owner withdrew $600 cash for his own use.

30   Service revenue earned for the last half of the month was as follows:

Services rendered for cash	$5,180
Services rendered on credit	1,500

REQUIRED:

   a. Record the transactions in a general journal.

   b. Set up ledger accounts and post the transactions to the ledger. Include appropriate cross references.

   c. Prepare a trial balance at November 30, 1978.

   d. Assume that there are no transactions for the company in November other than those listed. In that case, calculate the Net earnings for November for the firm. Also calculate the November 30 balance of the owner's capital account.

*P5-8. *Cumulative review problem.* Fill in the missing figures.

	COMPANY A	COMPANY B	COMPANY C
Total assets, beginning of month	——	90,000	——
Total assets, end of month	26,000	——	51,000
Total liabilities, beginning of month	5,000	——	10,000
Total liabilities, end of month	——	18,000	——
Total capital, beginning of month	——	40,000	35,000
Total capital, end of month	20,000	48,000	——
Total revenues during month	——	50,000	60,000
Total expenses during month	15,000	——	45,000
Net earnings for month	10,000	20,000	——
Owner's withdrawals during month	4,000	——	5,000

Hint: Assets — Liabilities = Capital at a point in time

Revenues — Expenses = Net earnings

Ending capital = Beginning capital + Net earnings — Withdrawals

chapter 3

the accounting cycle-II

ADJUSTING AND CORRECTING THE ACCOUNTS

> **OBJECTIVE**

The main products or outputs of a financial accounting system are financial statements—the balance sheet, the income statement, and the statement of owner's capital. Up to this point you have studied how to identify the inputs of the system, the business transactions; how to analyze transactions in terms of their effects on the accounting equation; and how to prepare some fairly simple financial statements from the account information recorded. This last item, preparing financial statements, generally cannot be satisfactorily completed before an additional step is performed: the adjustment of certain accounts so that up-to-date, complete amounts are reported to decision makers.

This unit therefore has two purposes. First, it will describe what the financial statements are designed to communicate and tell you why adjusting is necessary to fulfill this design. Second, it will show you how to correct or adjust the accounts so that they give back as a result or reflect what they are designed to reflect. Adjusting entries are a normal part of a manual accounting system, and three typical examples of them will be discussed in this unit.

> **APPROACH TO ATTAINING THE OBJECTIVE**

As you study adjusting entries and their function, pay attention to these three questions, which the text following answers:

- *What key information is communicated to decision makers by the financial statements?*
- *What are adjusting entries, and why are they needed?*
- *What are some examples of adjusting entries?*

THE FIRM'S FINANCIAL CONDITION

The balance sheet provides valuable information for decisions made by the higher levels of management and by investors, creditors, and others outside the business firm. Most of these decisions call for information about the assets the company has acquired to accomplish its goals and about the sources of these assets. This is exactly the financial information that the balance sheet is meant to contain.

■ *What key information is communicated to decision makers by the financial statements?*

Resources of the firm Financial statements are general-purpose reports. This means that their information is designed for use by many different individuals for various purposes. As a result, the information must be presented in a generally accepted and somewhat standardized fashion. The balance sheet, for example, is designed to provide a complete list of *all* the assets of a firm at a point in time. The user of the balance sheet, therefore, must be aware of which items are included as assets, and which are not. Assets are things that have some value to the firm as it tries to achieve its objectives. As we discussed back in Unit 1, a firm usually has cash-type assets as well as production-type assets. At the end of an accounting period, before financial statements are prepared, a determination must be made that *all* the assets of the business are in the accounts and that these assets are reported in terms of dollars according to generally agreed upon standards. The **valuation process** (determining what dollar amount to report for an asset or other account) is a most important part of accounting.

The basic idea here is that if a trial balance does not include *all* (and no more and no less than this) of a firm's assets, valued in a generally accepted way, then an adjusting journal entry must be made to correct the situation. Financial statements prepared from the adjusted trial balance will then provide the information they are designed to provide.

Sources of the resources The balance sheet also provides information about equities—the sources of the resources. You should know by now that the total assets of a company always come from two sources: from creditors (liabilities) and from the owner (capital). The liabilities listed in the trial balance at the end of a period obviously should include *all* the debts of the firm. Leaving out even one debt, or the overstatement of a debt, might be misleading to a financial statement user. Likewise, if the trial balance does not include *all* the firm's capital, valued in a generally accepted way, then an adjusting journal entry must be made to correct the situation. Examples of adjusting entries are given later in this unit.

THE FIRM'S EARNING POWER

Decision makers also customarily gather information about a firm's earning ability. The income statement is the general-purpose report on revenues and expenses that tells about earnings. Any omission or misstatement of information must be carefully avoided.

Revenues Revenues are a special kind of growth in the assets of a firm. The growth is brought about by certain sacrifices called expenses which are incurred to aid in the profit-making process. Examples of revenues are (1) the total prices charged customers for merchandise sold, (2) the amounts charged customers in a barbershop for services rendered, (3) the amount of interest earned on money lent outsiders by the firm, and (4) the rent charged tenants by a firm that owns an office building. An important point is that *all* revenues produced during a period of time must be included on the income statement, *whether they are collected in cash or not.* Failure to include all revenues or a misstatement of revenues would mislead the decision makers. Adjusting entries serve to correct or bring the revenue accounts up to date before financial statements are prepared.

Expenses Expenses generally can be defined as the use of assets to produce revenues. Examples are salaries expense, rent expense, supplies expense, and advertising and property taxes expenses. In order to measure net income properly, *all* expenses must be included on the income statement, and they must be measured according to the generally accepted standards. Adjusting entries provide a means to do these things before financial statements are prepared.

THE NEED FOR ADJUSTING ENTRIES

A manual accounting system does not always automatically provide for completeness and correctness of the accounts. This lack of completeness and up-to-date information in the accounts at the end of an accounting period is a normal situation. It is usually caused by the fact that certain source documents (such as a bill for services rendered or a payroll computation showing wages owed to employees) have simply not been prepared as of the end of the accounting period. Consequently, the transaction information has not been entered into the accounts. For example, a firm might own an asset that has not been recorded in the accounts as of the end of the period. Or a firm might have incurred an expense that has not found its way into the accounts at the balance sheet date. Or a debt which is not yet recorded might be owed. The function of **adjusting journal entries** in these instances is to correct the accounts so that the statements based on them will reveal net income and assets and equities according to generally accepted standards.

KINDS OF ADJUSTMENTS

There are two basic kinds of adjustments. The first involves situations in which a business transaction has taken place, but the information has not yet been recorded in the accounts. Consider, for example, an expense that has been incurred but not paid for. If the expense and the related liability have not been recorded, then an adjusting entry can bring the accounts up to date. Such an adjustment is illustrated below (Example 3).

■ *What are adjusting entries, and why are they needed?*

The second kind of adjustment involves a situation wherein the transaction information has already been entered in the accounts, but the balance of the account concerned needs to be corrected to reflect recent happenings. For example, supplies could have been purchased and recorded in an asset account. As of the end of the period, most of the supplies could have been used up. An adjusting entry can bring the accounts up to date. Such an adjustment is illustrated below (Example 1).

EXAMPLES OF ADJUSTING ENTRIES

The trial balance example in Unit 5 will be used here to illustrate adjusting entries. Shown in Illustration 6-1 is the trial balance of Stevie Car Wash Company at May 31, 1978, the end of the first month's operations. On May 31 the owner of the company reviewed the accounts and their balances as shown in the trial balance and made these comments:

1. "I notice that we purchased $800 of supplies. Now we've used up $200 of the supplies and have about $600 left."

ILLUSTRATION 6-1

Stevie Car Wash Company
Trial Balance
May 31, 1978

ACCT. NO.	ACCOUNT	DEBIT	CREDIT
101	Cash	1300 00	
102	Accounts receivable	400 00	
103	Supplies	800 00	
120	Office equipment	800 00	
122	Car-wash equipment	3600 00	
201	Accounts payable		700 00
202	Notes payable		3600 00
301	Paul Stevie, Capital		1800 00
302	Paul Stevie, Withdrawals	500 00	
401	Car-wash revenue		2300 00
501	Salaries expense	600 00	
502	Rent expense	300 00	
504	Utilities expense	100 00	
		8400 00	8400 00

2. "The office equipment will probably last us 6 years, and the car-wash equipment should last about 3 years. At the end of that time all the equipment will have to be discarded."

3. "We owe some interest on the note payable now."

These comments indicate that the company's accounts need to be adjusted to truly reflect the company's earnings and financial condition.

■ *What are some examples of adjusting entries?*

Example 1. Allocating cost between the asset and the expense—supplies Look at the Supplies account in the trial balance in Illustration 6-1. This balance of $800 means that an asset totaling $800 is on hand. Now trace this amount back to the journal illustrated in Unit 5. There you can see that these supplies were purchased on May 8, 1978, and were debited to an asset account.

The owner has indicated that now $200 of the supplies have been used and that $600 of supplies are still on hand. Therefore, an adjusting entry is needed in the general journal to reduce the balance of the asset account (Supplies, account 103) from $800 to $600. The same entry also must record an expense (Supplies expense, account 503). Refer to the Chart of Accounts of Stevie Car Wash Company in Unit 5. Two accounts are related to supplies: The Supplies account (103), which is to reflect this asset on the balance sheet, and the Supplies expense account (503), which is to reflect this expense (supplies used) on the income statement. The adjusting journal entry which brings these accounts up to date is shown in Illustration 6-2.

ILLUSTRATION 6-2

General Journal				PAGE *3*
DATE	DESCRIPTION	REF.	DEBIT	CREDIT
1978 May 31	Supplies expense	503	200 00	
	Supplies	103		200 00
	Adjustment to reflect supplies used during May.			

Example 2. Allocating cost between the asset and the expense—depreciation As in the case of supplies, equipment represents a cost of doing business for the firm—a sacrifice of an asset made to help produce revenue. In our example car-wash equipment was purchased on May 3 and Office equipment was acquired on May 1. Unlike supplies, however, this equipment is long-lived and is not used up on an easily measurable basis. Nevertheless, accountants have developed a way to measure this kind of use. The lessening in the value

of equipment due to use is referred to as **depreciation. Depreciation expense** is the name given to the sacrifice of equipment that the firm makes during a period of time; the asset, equipment, decreases as the asset is used in the production of revenue.

Let us explore the depreciation of the office equipment in more detail. What portion of the asset office equipment has become a depreciation expense by the end of the 1-month period? This is calculated as follows. The original cost of the office equipment on May 1 was $800. The owner has stated that this equipment will probably last 6 years. Dividing the $800 by 6 years of useful life gives an average annual cost, or sacrifice, of $133. This amounts to about $11 per month ($133 divided by 12 months). Therefore, the Depreciation expense—Office equipment is $11. This means that the firm's cost of owning and using office equipment for the month of May is $11. We say that the office equipment has depreciated $11. The value of the office equipment remaining at the end of May is therefore $789. This relationship is summarized in Illustration 6-3.

ILLUSTRATION 6-3

A similar calculation of the Depreciation expense—Car-wash equipment can be made based on the car-wash equipment's original cost of $3,600 and its useful life of 3 years. The monthly depreciation in this case is $100.

How are these depreciation expenses journalized? The journal entries in Illustration 6-4 show how the accounts are adjusted to reflect the depreciation for both the office equipment and the car-wash equipment. Let's look at the adjusting entry for office equipment more closely. Remember that the unused amount of the asset office equipment at the end of May, 1978, was valued at $789. Therefore, the net balance of the Office equipment should be reduced from $800 to $789. This is customarily done by crediting a separate asset account called **Accumulated depreciation** (see Illustration 6-4).

By using this procedure, the original cost ($800) remains in the asset account Office equipment and so this important information is preserved to be disclosed later on the balance sheet. Note that the Accumulated depreciation account reflects a credit balance as a measure of the asset used up in the operations. On the balance sheet's report on assets and equities, the credit

DATE		DESCRIPTION	REF.	DEBIT	CREDIT
1978 May	31	Depreciation expense—Office equipment	506	11 00	
		Accumulated depreciation—Office equipment	121		11 00
		Adjustment to reflect one month's			
		depreciation.			
	31	Depreciation expense—Car-wash equipment	507	100 00	
		Accumulated depreciation—Car-wash equipment	123		100 00
		Adjustment to reflect one month's			
		depreciation.			

ILLUSTRATION 6-4

balance of the Accumulated depreciation account is subtracted from the debit balance of the Office equipment account. This gives the unused amount of the asset Office equipment to be used in computing the total assets of the firm at the end of the period (see Illustration 6-5). The Accumulated depreciation account is an example of a **contra account.** A contra account is an account, the balance of which, represents a deduction from another account. Thus, the Accumulated depreciation account with its credit balance serves as a deduction from the Equipment account that has a debit balance.

Now here is one final important point to remember about the $789. This amount actually has nothing to do with what the asset is "worth" at the balance sheet date. It is not the amount the asset can be sold for. It is simply the portion of the original cost ($800) that the firm will receive benefit from in its future operations.

ILLUSTRATION 6-5

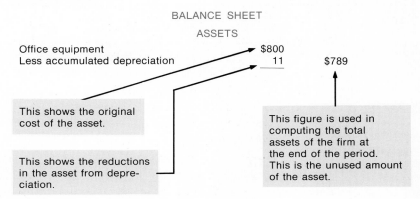

BALANCE SHEET

ASSETS

Office equipment — $800
Less accumulated depreciation — 11 — $789

This shows the original cost of the asset.

This shows the reductions in the asset from depreciation.

This figure is used in computing the total assets of the firm at the end of the period. This is the unused amount of the asset.

Example 3. Recording a debt and an expense not previously recorded—interest payable The note payable was signed on May 3, 1978; therefore, about 1 month's interest is now owed. The note was a 120-day, 8% note (these terms are from the journal in Unit 5). Interest can be computed on a daily basis, but often an approximation is good enough. The interest on the note owed for 1 month amounts to $24. This is calculated as follows:

$$\begin{array}{c}\text{Amount}\\\text{of loan}\end{array} \times \begin{array}{c}\text{Annual}\\\text{interest rate}\end{array} \times \begin{array}{c}\text{Fraction of}\\\text{year interest}\\\text{has accumulated}\end{array} = \begin{array}{c}\text{Interest}\\\text{owed}\end{array}$$

$$\$3{,}600 \times 0.08 \times 1/12 = \$24$$

The interest actually will be paid (along with the $3,600) at the end of the 120-day period. However, the $24 interest expense has been incurred and the liability has been created. The necessary adjustment to the Interest expense and Interest payable accounts is shown in the journal entry in Illustration 6-6. An **interest expense** is an expense brought about by sacrificing assets to pay others for a firm's use of their money. Thus, interest expense represents a reduction in owner's equity. **Interest payable,** a liability account, represents the amounts owed to creditors as compensation for the use of their money. As a result of the adjusting entry shown in Illustration 6-6, the company's net earnings will be reduced by the $24 expense on the income statement, and a liability for $24 will be reported on the balance sheet. Thus, fair and complete amounts will be reported to decision makers.

ILLUSTRATION 6-6

| | General Journal | | | | PAGE 3 |
DATE	DESCRIPTION	REF.	DEBIT		CREDIT
1978 May 31	Interest expense	505	24 00		
	Interest payable	203			24 00
	Adjustment to record interest				
	expense incurred on note.				

> **NEW TERMS**

accumulated depreciation An account, normally accumulating a credit balance, that represents a reduction in the corresponding asset account. For example, the *Accumulated depreciation—equipment* account credit balance represents the total reduction in the asset *Equipment* as a result of using the equipment to produce revenues. [p. 82]

adjusting journal entries Journal entries, usually prepared at the end of an accounting period in a manual accounting system, that correct the accounts so they will reveal on the statements the net income and the assets and equities according to generally accepted standards. [p. 79]

contra account A ledger account specially created to reduce another ledger account. The contra account is created so that the original balance in the related account can be preserved and disclosed on accounting reports. [p. 83]

depreciation The using-up process as applied to long-lived assets, such as plant and equipment. [p. 82]

depreciation expense That sacrifice made when resources such as equipment are used in the production of revenue; an expense (reduction in owner's equity). [p. 82]

interest expense An expense (reduction in owner's equity) brought about by sacrificing assets to pay others for the firm's use of their money. [p. 84]

interest payable A liability, appearing on the balance sheet, that indicates amounts owed to creditors as compensation for the use of their money. [p. 84]

valuation process The act of determining what dollar amount to report for an asset or other account on financial statements. [p. 78]

> **ASSIGNMENT MATERIAL**

QUESTIONS

Q6-1. What information about resources does the balance sheet provide to decision makers?

Q6-2. What information about equities does the balance sheet provide to decision makers?

Q6-3. What are revenues and expenses?

Q6-4. Why are adjusting entries needed in a manual accounting system?

Q6-5. Describe two fundamental kinds of adjusting entries.

EXERCISES

E6-1. The trial balance of Alma Sailboats Co. at December 31, 1978, showed a balance in the Office supplies account of $2,764. This amount was accumulated during the year in the Office supplies account as a result of these three purchases of office supplies: January 16, $1,000; April 30, $855; and December 14, $909. The management of the company determines that $2,000 of the supplies are still on hand at the end of the year. Make the adjusting journal entry necessary to allocate the cost between the asset and the expense. The company prepares adjusting entries and financial statements once each year at December 31.

E6-2. The trial balance of Heather Shop showed a balance in the Maintenance supplies account at May 31, 1978, of $1,240. At this date it is determined that only $250 of supplies were *used* in operating the business during the past accounting period (month of May). Prepare the necessary adjusting journal entry.

E6-3. Office equipment was purchased by Slim Company on August 1, 1978, at a cost of $6,000. The equipment is expected to have a useful life of ten years. Prepare the adjusting entry necessary at December 31, 1978, to allocate the cost between the asset and the expense. The company prepares adjusting entries and financial statements only once each year at December 31.

E6-4. Hadrian Co. borrowed $10,000 from First National Bank on December 1, 1978, signing a 90-day, 8% note for the amount. The interest will be paid (along with the $10,000) at the end of the 90-day period. Make the adjustment journal entry necessary at December 31.

E6-5. Hart Brothers Co. prepares financial statements and makes adjusting entries at the end of each month. The July 31, 1978, trial balance showed a balance of $1,800 in the asset account, Prepaid insurance. On July 1 the firm had purchased a 3-year fire insurance policy, paying $1,800 cash. Make the journal entry necessary to allocate the cost of the insurance policy between the asset (Prepaid insurance) and the expense (Insurance expense).

PROBLEMS (GROUP A)

P6-1. *Journalizing adjustments.* The trial balance of Tennessee and Wiggins Company at June 30, 1978, is given below.

Tennessee and Wiggins Company
TRIAL BALANCE
June 30, 1978

ACCOUNT NO.			
10	Cash	1,000	
50	Accounts receivable	2,000	
51	Prepaid insurance	600	
52	Supplies	200	
70	Equipment	10,000	
71	Accumulated depreciation—Equipment		400
150	Notes payable		2,000
200	T. Wiggins, Capital		8,500
201	T. Wiggins, Withdrawals	500	
300	Sales revenues		8,000
301	Salaries expenses	3,000	
302	Advertising expense	700	
303	Rent expense	800	
304	Miscellaneous expense	100	
		18,900	18,900

REQUIRED: In a general journal, make adjusting entries for each of the following:

a. The firm has used $70 of the supplies, and $130 remains on hand to be used next month.
b. On June 1, a fire insurance policy was purchased for $600. This policy will provide coverage for 1 full year. The bookkeeper debited an asset account, Prepaid insurance, on June 1 to reflect the asset or services being purchased. Make the adjusting entry to reflect 1 month's insurance expense being used.
c. The depreciation expense for the equipment for June amounts to $100.
d. Interest expense owed on the note payable amounts to $20.

Note: The answers to this problem will be used in answering P7-2 in Unit 7.

P6-2. *Journalizing adjustments, effect on account balances.* Presented on the next page is the trial balance of Newton and Franks Company at the end of a month's operations.

Newton and Franks Company
TRIAL BALANCE
June 30, 1978

Cash	$14,000	
Accounts receivable	7,000	
Prepaid insurance	3,000	
Supplies	8,500	
Equipment	5,400	
Accumulated depreciation—Equipment		600
Notes payable		4,200
L. Newton, Capital		21,000
L. Newton, Withdrawals	3,500	
Sales revenues		20,000
Salaries expense	3,000	
Advertising expense	100	
Rent expense	700	
Miscellaneous expense	600	
Depreciation expense—Equipment	–0–	
Interest expense	–0–	
Insurance expense	–0–	
Supplies expense	–0–	
	$45,800	$45,800

REQUIRED:

a. In general journal form, make adjusting entries at the end of the month's operations for each of the following:

(1) The firm used $320 of supplies in operating the business.

(2) On June 1, a fire insurance policy was purchased for $3,000. This policy provides coverage for 3 years. The bookkeeper debited an asset account, Prepaid insurance, on June 1 to reflect the asset or services being purchased. Make the adjusting entry to reflect the month's insurance expense being used.

(3) The depreciation expense for the equipment for June amounts to $250.

(4) Interest expense owed on the notes payable amounts to $35.

b. Answer the following questions.

(1) After the adjustment for supplies is made, what is the amount of supplies shown on the balance sheet?

(2) What is the amount of Insurance expense to appear on the income statement for June?

(3) What is the amount of Supplies expense on the income statement?

(4) Assume all four adjusting entries have been made and posted to the accounts. Compute the total assets to appear on the June 30 balance sheet.

(5) Assume that all four adjusting entries have been made and posted to the accounts. Compute the total liabilities to appear on the June 30 balance sheet.

(6) Assume that all four adjusting entries have been made and posted to the accounts. Compute the total expenses to appear on the June 30 balance sheet.

(7) What is the amount of the Net income for June?

P6-3. *Journalizing adjustments.* Record adjusting journal entries for the following independent situations.

a. The trial balance of a firm reflected a debit balance of $5,614 in the Store supplies account at December 31, 1978. This balance represents $600 of supplies that had been on hand the previous January 1, along with purchases of $5,014 made during 1978. A physical count of supplies at December 31, 1978, indicates that only $582 of them remain on hand.

b. At December 31, 1978, a company had a credit balance in Notes payable of $130,000, consisting of the following notes:

DATE NOTE SIGNED	AMOUNT OF NOTE	INTEREST RATE (PER YEAR)	TERM OF NOTE	TIME NOTE OUTSTANDING DURING 1978
12–1–78	$10,000	8%	90 days	1 month
12–1–78	50,000	10%	1 year	1 month
12–15–78	70,000	11%	30 days	$\frac{1}{2}$ month

c. Azy Company prepares adjusting entries and financial statements once each year at December 31. The Office equipment account at December 31, 1978 (the end of the first year of operations for the firm) showed a balance of $13,000:

DATE PURCHASED	NAME OF ITEM	EXPECTED USEFUL LIFE	COST
1–1–78	Desks	8 years	$8,000
3–1–78	Tables	10 years	3,000
10–1–78	Miscellaneous	5 years	2,000

In one entry, record the depreciation for 1978.

d. Harris Company prepares adjusting entries and financial statements once each year at December 31. The Prepaid insurance showed a balance of $2,300:

DATE POLICY PURCHASED	AMOUNT PAID	TERM OF POLICY
2–1–78	$ 500	2 years
8–1–78	800	1 year
10–1–78	1,000	1 year

Record the adjustment for insurance used (expired).

PROBLEMS (GROUP B)

P6-4. *Journalizing adjustments, analyzing effects.* The trial balance of Hankins Company at November 30, 1978, appears on the next page.

Hankins Company
TRIAL BALANCE
November 30, 1978

Cash	2,000	
Accounts receivable	4,000	
Prepaid insurance	1,200	
Supplies	400	
Equipment	20,000	
Accumulated depreciation—Equipment		800
Notes payable		4,000
R. Hankins, Capital		17,000
R. Hankins, Withdrawals	1,000	
Sales revenues		16,000
Salaries expenses	6,000	
Advertising expense	1,400	
Rent expense	1,600	
Miscellaneous expense	200	
Depreciation expense—Equipment	–0–	
Interest expense	–0–	
Insurance expense	–0–	
Supplies expense	–0–	
	37,800	37,800

REQUIRED:

a. In a general journal, make adjusting entries at the end of the month's operations for each of the following:
   (1) The firm has used $210 of the supplies in operating the business.
   (2) On November 1, a fire insurance policy was purchased for $1,200. This policy will provide coverage for 2 full years. The trial balance indicates that the bookkeeper debited an asset account, Prepaid insurance, on November 1 to reflect the asset or services being purchased. Make the adjusting entry to reflect November's insurance expense.
   (3) The depreciation expense for the equipment for November amounts to $200.
   (4) Interest expense owed on the notes payable amounts to $40.

b. After you have made the four adjusting journal entries, answer these questions:
   (1) After the adjustment for supplies is made, what is the amount of supplies to be shown in the asset section of the balance sheet?
   (2) After the adjustment for supplies is made, what is the amount of supplies expense to be shown on the November income statement?
   (3) How much is the insurance expense that appears on the November income statement?
   (4) Assume that all four adjusting entries have been made and posted to the accounts. Compute the *total assets* to appear on the November 30 balance sheet.
   (5) Assume that all four adjusting entries have been made and posted to the accounts. Compute the *total liabilities* to appear on the November 30 balance sheet.

(6) Assume that all four adjusting entries have been made and posted to the accounts. Compute the *total expenses* to appear on the November income statement.

(7) What is the amount of net income for November?

Note: The answers to this problem will be used in answering P7-5 in Unit 7.

*P6-5. *Analyzing effect of adjustments on accounts.* Below are shown (1) a trial balance of a company *before adjustments* were made, (2) an income statement, (3) a statement of owner's capital, and (4) a balance sheet.

Harrison Company
TRIAL BALANCE
December 31, 1978

Cash	9,000	
Accounts receivable	2,000	
Prepaid insurance	1,000	
Supplies	3,000	
Equipment	40,000	
Accumulated depreciation—Equipment		1,000
Notes payable		8,000
T. Harrison, Capital		28,000
T. Harrison, Withdrawals	3,000	
Service revenues		50,000
Salaries expense	11,000	
Advertising expense	2,000	
Rent expense	15,000	
Miscellaneous expense	1,000	
	87,000	87,000

Harrison Company
INCOME STATEMENT
For the Year Ended December 31, 1978

revenues		
Service revenues		$50,000
expenses		
Salaries expense	$11,000	
Advertising expense	2,000	
Rent expense	15,000	
Insurance expense	700	
Interest expense	480	
Depreciation expense—Equipment	600	
Supplies expense	1,100	
Miscellaneous expense	1,000	
Total expenses		31,880
net earnings		$18,120

Harrison Company
STATEMENT OF OWNER'S CAPITAL
For the Year Ended December 31, 1978

T. Harrison, Capital, January 1, 1978		$28,000
Net earnings for 1978	$18,120	
Less Withdrawals	3,000	
Net increase in capital		15,120
T. Harrison, Capital, December 31, 1978		$43,120

Harrison Company
BALANCE SHEET
December 31, 1978

ASSETS

Cash.		$ 9,000
Accounts receivable.		2,000
Prepaid insurance		300
Supplies.		1,900
Equipment	$40,000	
Less Accumulated depreciation.	1,600	38,400
Total assets		$51,600

EQUITIES

liabilities

Interest payable	$ 480	
Notes payable	8,000	
Total liabilities		$ 8,480

capital

T. Harrison, Capital.		43,120
Total equities		$51,600

REQUIRED: Carefully analyze the data given and prepare all the adjusting journal entries that the company must have made at December 31, 1978.

P6-6. *Journalizing adjustments.* Record adjusting journal entries for the following independent situations.

a. At December 31, 1978, a firm had the following notes payable outstanding, totaling $215,000:

DATE OF NOTE	AMOUNT OF NOTE	INTEREST RATE PER YEAR	TERM OF NOTE	TIME NOTE OUTSTANDING DURING 1978
6-1-78	$ 50,000	8%	30 months	7 months
8-1-78	10,000	10%	1 year	5 months
10-15-78	55,000	10%	2 years	$2\frac{1}{2}$ months
12-1-78	100,000	9%	90 days	1 month

Make the adjusting entry for interest, assuming that the company prepares adjusting entries and financial statements only once a year at December 31.

b. The Office supplies account of Jones Company showed a debit balance of $1,000 at March 1, 1978. During March the firm purchased $3,000 of office supplies for cash and $2,000 of office supplies on credit. At March 31, 1978, there were $1,500 of office supplies still on hand. The company prepares adjusting entries each month.

c. At April 1, 1978, the Prepaid insurance account showed a balance of $3,100, consisting of the following:

POLICY NUMBER	ORIGINAL COST	DATE PURCHASED	UNUSED INSURANCE	TERM
1	$1,200	1-1-78	$ 900	1 year
2	2,400	3-1-78	2,200	1 year
			$3,100	

On April 15, 1978, Policy No. 3 (a 2-year policy) was purchased for $1,200 cash, so the Prepaid insurance account showed a debit balance of $4,300 at April 30, 1978. Make the adjustment for insurance expense at April 30, 1978, assuming that adjusting entries are made monthly.

d. The firm prepares adjusting entries once each year at December 31. The Delivery equipment account had a balance of $41,000 at December 31, 1978, the end of the first year of operations for the company.

DATE PURCHASED	NAME OF EQUIPMENT	EXPECTED USEFUL LIFE	COST
4-1-78	Truck No. 1	4 years	$12,000
10-1-78	Truck No. 2	5 years	15,000
12-15-78	Truck No. 3	5 years	14,000

Make the adjusting entry for depreciation of delivery equipment.

THE WORK SHEET AS AN ORGANIZER

> **OBJECTIVE**

The last several units have been devoted to the accounting cycle. You have learned:

> How to identify business transactions, the input of financial accounting.
> How to record the transactions.
> How to post the transactions to ledger accounts.
> How to prepare a trial balance.
> How to record adjusting journal entries to correct the accounts.
> How to prepare financial statements.

In this unit and the next you will learn how to complete the accounting process. The specific objective of this unit is to introduce you to the work sheet and to show you how it is prepared and used.

> **APPROACH TO ATTAINING THE OBJECTIVE**

As you study the nature and purposes of the work sheet, pay particular attention to these three questions, which the text following answers:

- *What is a work sheet, and what is its purpose?*
- *How is the work sheet prepared?*
- *How is the work sheet used?*

Stevie Car Wash Company
Work Sheet
For the Month Ended May 31, 1978

ACCOUNT	TRIAL BALANCE		ADJUSTMENTS		ADJUSTED TRIAL BALANCE	
	DR.	CR.	DR.	CR.	DR.	CR.

ILLUSTRATION 7-1

DESCRIPTION AND PURPOSE OF THE WORK SHEET

- *What is a work sheet, and what is its purpose?*

A **work sheet,** sometimes called working papers, is a columnar sheet of paper that can be used in a manual accounting operation to help organize the work at the end of an accounting period. A common form of the work sheet is shown in Illustration 7-1. As we analyze a completed work sheet in this unit, we will explain the purpose and use of each of the six sets of columns shown in Illustration 7-1.

A work sheet helps the bookkeeper at the end of the period's operations because this one record shows all the key information for the financial statements. The balances of the accounts before adjusting entries, the adjustment information, and the balances of the accounts to appear on the statements are all set forth on the work sheet. The bookkeeper can complete the work of the accounting cycle by using the work sheet as a point of reference.

PREPARING THE WORK SHEET: AN EXAMPLE

- *How is the work sheet prepared?*

To illustrate the preparation of a work sheet, we will begin with the same example that we have used in previous units. Illustration 7-2 is the trial balance of Stevie Car Wash Company at the end of May's operations, before adjusting entries are recorded. Illustration 7-3, on the following page, is a completed work sheet for the month of May. Explanations of the six columns of information are given in the following paragraphs.

Trial balance information The first set of columns in the work sheet is used to prepare the trial balance at the end of the period. Note that the information in the work sheet is the same as the information in the trial balance shown in Illustration 7-2. This, then, is a first use of the work sheet—the trial balance can be prepared directly on it, and therefore a separate trial balance becomes unnecessary. The trial balance contains all the accounts with balances at the end of the period, *before* adjusting entries are recorded and posted to the accounts. Remember that the asset, expense, and withdrawal accounts all

	STATEMENT OF OWNER'S CAPITAL		BALANCE SHEET	
	DR.	CR.	DR.	

have debit balances, and that liability, capital, and revenue accounts all have credit balances.

Adjustments information The trial balance needs to be brought up to date (as you studied in Unit 6), and this is done by entering adjustment information in the second set of columns on the work sheet. The adjustments are identi-

ILLUSTRATION 7-2

Stevie Car-Wash Company
Trial Balance
May 31, 1978

ACCT. NO.	ACCOUNT	DEBIT	CREDIT
101	Cash	1300 00	
102	Accounts receivable	400 00	
103	Supplies	800 00	
120	Office equipment	800 00	
122	Car-wash equipment	3600 00	
201	Accounts payable		700 00
202	Notes payable		3600 00
301	Paul Stevie, Capital		1800 00
302	Paul Stevie, Withdrawals	500 00	
401	Car-wash revenue		2300 00
501	Salaries expense	600 00	
502	Rent expense	300 00	
504	Utilities expense	100 00	
		8400 00	8400 00

Stevie Car Wash Company
Work Sheet
For the Month Ended May 31, 1978

AC. NO.	ACCOUNT	TRIAL BALANCE DR.	TRIAL BALANCE CR.	ADJUSTMENTS DR.	ADJUSTMENTS CR.	ADJUSTED TRIAL BALANCE DR.	ADJUSTED TRIAL BALANCE CR.	INCOME STATEMENT DR.	INCOME STATEMENT CR.	STATEMENT OF OWNER'S CAPITAL DR.	STATEMENT OF OWNER'S CAPITAL CR.	BALANCE SHEET DR.	BALANCE SHEET CR.
101	Cash	130000				130000						130000	
102	Accounts receivable	40000				40000						40000	
103	Supplies	80000			(a) 20000	60000						60000	
120	Office equipment	80000				80000						80000	
122	Car wash equipment	360000				360000						360000	
201	Accounts payable		70000				70000						70000
202	Notes payable		360000				360000						360000
301	Paul Stevie, Capital		180000				180000				180000		
302	Paul Stevie, Withdrawals	50000				50000				50000			
401	Car wash revenue		230000				230000		230000				
501	Salaries expense	60000				60000		60000					
502	Rent expense	30000				30000		30000					
504	Electricity expense	10000				10000		10000					
		840000	840000										
503	Supplies expense			(a) 20000		20000		20000					
506	Depreciation expense—Office equipment			(b) 1100		1100		1100					
121	Accumulated depreciation—Office equipment				(b) 1100		1100						1100
507	Depreciation expense—Car wash equipment			(c) 10000		10000		10000					
123	Accumulated depreciation—Car wash equipment				(c) 10000		10000						10000
505	Interest expense			(d) 2400		2400		2400					
203	Interest payable				(d) 2400		2400						2400
				33500	33500	853500	853500	133500	230000				
	Net earnings (Net income)							96500			96500		
								230000	230000				
	Paul Stevie, Capital, May 31, 1978									226500			226500
										276500	276500	670000	670000

Adjustments:
(a) Supplies used during May, $200.
(b) Depreciation of office equipment, $11.
(c) Depreciation of car wash equipment, $100.
(d) Prepaid interest expense on note, $24.

ILLUSTRATION 7-3

fied and entered one by one on the appropriate account line in the adjustments column of the work sheet. The same adjustment examples that you studied in Unit 6 are used:

> *Adjustment (a)* The owner indicated that $200 of the supplies had been used and that $600 of supplies are still on hand. Therefore, Supplies expense is debited for $200; this account does not appear in the trial balance yet, so the account is shown on the next available line on the work sheet. You can find its account number (503) by looking up the firm's Chart of Accounts in Unit 5. The Supplies account is credited to reduce the balance from $800 to $600. Notice how both parts of the adjustment are keyed with (a).

> *Adjustment (b)* Depreciation expense on Office equipment is recorded for $11. Both accounts needed do not yet appear in the trial balance; therefore, the next two lines available on the work sheet are used.

> *Adjustment (c)* Depreciation expense on Car-wash equipment is recorded on the work sheet. Again two new accounts appear on the next two available lines.

> *Adjustment (d)* Unpaid interest expense on the note is recorded on the work sheet. Two new accounts, Interest expense and Interest payable, are needed to record this adjustment.

In summary, the second set of columns in the work sheet provides room for any adjustments the firm might need at the end of an accounting period.

Adjusted trial balance information The adjusted trial balance columns can now reflect all the accounts. It is these balances that will appear on the financial statements. For those accounts not affected by adjustments, the same balance is simply transferred to the adjusted trial balance columns from the trial balance columns. See the Cash account for an example with a debit balance, and see the Car-wash revenue account for an example with a credit balance.

The Supplies account was affected by an adjustment. The $800 debit balance is reduced by a $200 credit in the adjustments column, leaving a $600 debit balance to appear in the adjusted trial balance columns and on the appropriate financial statement. Also notice how the new account balances such as Supplies expense and Accumulated depreciation—Office equipment are transferred to the appropriate columns in the adjusted trial balance. Of course, the columns are totaled to check the arithmetic of the operation.

The financial statement information The adjusted trial balance now contains all the information needed to prepare the three financial statements—the income statement, the statement of owner's capital, and the balance sheet. The next step in the preparation of the work sheet is to transfer *each item on the adjusted trial balance* to the proper set of columns in the appropriate financial statement. Follow these procedures:

The debit balance of Cash appears on the balance sheet as an asset.

The debit balance of Accounts receivable appears on the balance sheet as an asset.

The debit balance of Supplies ($600) appears on the balance sheet as an asset.

The debit balance of Office equipment appears on the balance sheet as an asset.

The debit balance of Car-wash equipment appears on the balance sheet as an asset.

The credit balance of Accounts payable appears on the balance sheet as a liability.

The credit balance of Notes payable appears on the balance sheet as a liability.

The credit balance of the owner's capital account represents the beginning-of-the-month balance; therefore, it appears on the statement of the owner's capital.

The debit balance of the owner's withdrawals account appears on the statement of owner's capital.

The credit balance of Car-wash revenue appears on the income statement.

The debit balance of Salaries appears on the income statement.

The debit balance of Rent expense appears on the income statement.

The debit balance of Utilities expense appears on the income statement.

The debit balance of Supplies expense appears on the income statement.

The debit balance of Depreciation expense—Office equipment appears on the income statement.

The credit balance of Accumulated depreciation—Office equipment represents a decrease in the asset, Office equipment; therefore, it appears as a deduction from the assets on the balance sheet.

The debit balance of Depreciation expense—Car-wash equipment appears on the income statement.

The credit balance of Accumulated depreciation—Car-wash equipment represents a decrease in the asset, Car-wash equipment; therefore, it appears as a deduction from the assets on the balance sheet.

The debit balance of Interest expense appears on the income statement.

The credit balance of Interest payable is a liability and appears on the balance sheet.

Pay particular attention to the procedures above printed in solid color. After all the accounts in the adjusted trial balance are transferred to the appropriate statement, the column totals can be computed.

Income statement In the income statement columns, the credits (revenues) total $2,300 and the debits (expenses) total $1,335; therefore, the Net earnings amount to $965, the difference between revenues and expenses. This amount is entered on the next available line in the debit column just to check the arithmetic. This set of columns now contains all the information needed to prepare the actual financial statement (the income statement) to be given to management and to those people outside the firm who are interested in the earnings of the company.

Statement of owner's capital This statement contains three elements:

Owner's capital at the beginning of the period.

Net earnings for the period, which increase the capital.

Owner's withdrawals during the period, which decrease the capital.

Notice how the Net earnings figure from the income statement ($965) is moved to the credit column in the statement of owner's capital. The beginning balance of capital ($1,800) plus this increase in capital from Net earnings ($965) equals $2,765. This amount less the withdrawals ($500) is the owner's capital at the end of the period ($2,265). Note that again the columns are added to check the arithmetic. The end-of-period amount of owner's capital ($2,265) is then extended to the balance sheet columns, because the capital of the owner at the end of the period must appear on the balance sheet as an equity.

Balance sheet At this point the debits and credits in the balance sheet columns should be equal. Observe that the following items will appear on the firm's balance sheet:

Asset section of the balance sheet:
Cash
Accounts receivable
Supplies
Office equipment
Accumulated depreciation—Office equipment (as a *deduction*)

Car-wash equipment
Accumulated depreciation—Car-wash equipment (as a *deduction*)
Liability section of the balance sheet:
Accounts payable
Notes payable
Interest payable
Capital section of the balance sheet:
Paul Stevie, Capital

USES OF THE WORK SHEET

As an organizer at the end of an accounting period, the work sheet can be used as follows:

■ *How is the work sheet used?*

1. The trial balance can be entered directly on the work sheet, thus eliminating the need for a separate trial balance.
2. The adjustments can be determined and entered on the work sheet to show their effects on the accounts.
3. The accounts appearing on each of the three financial statements can be set forth in separate sets of columns.
4. The net earnings and the end-of-period balance of the owner's capital can be computed and shown on the work sheet.
5. *The financial statements can be prepared directly from the work sheet.* The income statement, statement of owner's capital, and balance sheet columns contain all the information needed to prepare each of these three statements.
6. *Adjusting journal entries can be prepared with the work sheet as a reference.* All of the adjustments, of course, appear on the work sheet.
7. *Closing journal entries can be prepared directly from the work sheet.* The next unit will explain the procedures and theory associated with closing entries.

Illustration 7-4 summarizes the manual accounting cycle that you have studied in the last several units. Examine the illustration carefully—it will help you to review and place in perspective the various steps in the cycle that have been presented thus far.

❯ NEW TERM

work sheet A columnar sheet of paper that can be used in a manual accounting operation to help organize the work at the end of an accounting period. [p. 94]

THE ACCOUNTING CYCLE

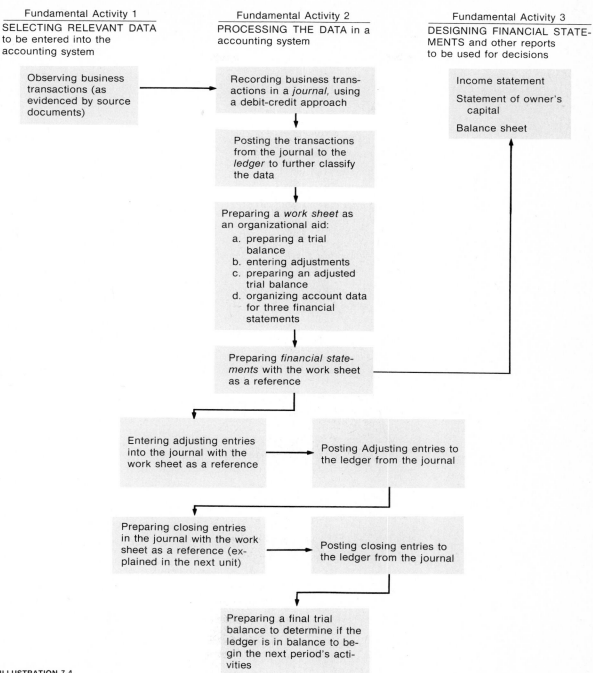

Fundamental Activity 1	Fundamental Activity 2	Fundamental Activity 3
SELECTING RELEVANT DATA to be entered into the accounting system	**PROCESSING THE DATA** in a accounting system	**DESIGNING FINANCIAL STATEMENTS** and other reports to be used for decisions

Observing business transactions (as evidenced by source documents)

Recording business transactions in a *journal,* using a debit-credit approach

Posting the transactions from the journal to the *ledger* to further classify the data

Preparing a *work sheet* as an organizational aid:
a. preparing a trial balance
b. entering adjustments
c. preparing an adjusted trial balance
d. organizing account data for three financial statements

Preparing *financial statements* with the work sheet as a reference

Income statement

Statement of owner's capital

Balance sheet

Entering adjusting entries into the journal with the work sheet as a reference

Posting Adjusting entries to the ledger from the journal

Preparing closing entries in the journal with the work sheet as a reference (explained in the next unit)

Posting closing entries to the ledger from the journal

Preparing a final trial balance to determine if the ledger is in balance to begin the next period's activities

ILLUSTRATION 7-4

QUESTIONS

Q7-1. List the six sets of columns ordinarily appearing on a work sheet. Describe the information contained in each of the sets of columns.

Q7-2. In what ways is a work sheet useful?

Q7-3. Explain how the net earnings figure appears on the work sheet.

EXERCISES

E7-1. The following is an *adjusted* trial balance for a company for the year ended December 31, 1978:

Cash	15,000	
Accounts receivable	3,000	
Prepaid insurance	4,000	
Supplies	1,000	
Furniture	20,000	
Accumulated depreciation		4,000
Accounts payable		5,000
Notes payable		16,000
B. G. Wilson, Capital		3,500
B. G. Wilson, Withdrawals	2,000	
Service revenue		40,000
Rent revenue		2,000
Miscellaneous revenue		1,000
Rent expense	5,000	
Utilities expense	1,000	
Salaries expense	11,000	
Insurance expense	2,000	
Depreciation expense	4,000	
Supplies expense	3,000	
Interest expense	1,000	
Interest payable		500
	72,000	72,000

In general journal form, make the adjusting entries that were made by the company at December 31, 1978 (depreciation, supplies, insurance, and interest). These adjustments are already reflected in the adjusted trial balance above.

E7-2. Using the information provided in E7-1, answer the following questions:

a. What was the balance of the Supplies account before the adjusting entry was made?

b. What was the balance of the Prepaid insurance account before the adjusting entry was made?

c. What is the amount of the furniture (net amount) to be included on the balance sheet of the company at December 31, 1978?

d. Why does the interest expense differ from the interest payable?

E7-3. Based on the information provided in exercise E7-1, compute the following:

a. Total revenues.

b. Total expenses.

c. Net earnings (Net income).

d. B. G. Wilson, Capital, December 31, 1978.

P7-1. *Work sheet and financial statements.* The trial balance, before adjustments, of Gayg Company at December 31, 1978, is shown below. Also shown is a chart of accounts for the firm. The firm prepares financial statements *once each year* at the end of December.

Gayg Company
TRIAL BALANCE
December 31, 1978

Cash	15,900	
Accounts receivable	1,000	
Prepaid insurance	600	
Supplies	300	
Furniture	4,000	
Equipment	9,000	
Accounts payable		1,500
Notes payable		8,000
M. R. Gayg, Capital		10,000
M. R. Gayg, Withdrawals	4,000	
Service revenue		21,000
Rent revenue		1,400
Salaries expense	5,000	
Rent expense	1,200	
Utilities expense	800	
Miscellaneous expense	100	
	41,900	41,900

Gayg Company
CHART OF ACCOUNTS

assets
101   Cash
103   Accounts receivable
105   Prepaid insurance
106   Supplies
150   Furniture
151   Accumulated depreciation
        —Furniture
160   Equipment
161   Acccumulated depreciation
        —Equipment

liabilities
201   Accounts payable
202   Interest payable
210   Notes payable

capital
301   M. R. Gayg, Capital
302   M. R. Gayg, Withdrawals

revenues
401   Service revenue
402   Rent revenue

expenses
501   Salaries expense
502   Rent expense
503   Supplies expense
504   Utilities expense
505   Interest expense
515   Depreciation expense—Furniture
516   Depreciation expense
        —Equipment
520   Insurance expense
590   Miscellaneous expense

Information for adjustments:
a. Of the $600 insurance which was purchased, only $100 has been used up this year.

b. Supplies used during the year amount to $200.
c. Depreciation expense on the furniture for the year is calculated to be $200.
d. Depreciation expense on the equipment for the year is calculated to be $500.
e. Interest expense incurred on the note, but not yet paid amounts to $50.

REQUIRED:

a. Prepare a work sheet for the firm for the year ended December 31, 1978.
b. From the work sheet, prepare an income statement, a statement of owner's capital, and a balance sheet.

P7-2. *Work sheet and financial statements.*
a. From the information provided in P6-1 (Unit 6), prepare a work sheet for the company.
b. From the work sheet, prepare an income statement, a statement of owner's capital, and a balance sheet.

P7-3. *Work sheet and financial statements.* Below are the account balances of Caldwell Company at December 31, 1978, and information for adjustments.

Caldwell Company
ACCOUNT BALANCES
December 31, 1978

101	Cash	$ 3,600
102	Accounts receivable	2,000
103	Supplies	1,500
105	Prepaid insurance	500
120	Office equipment	500
121	Delivery equipment	1,700
201	Accounts payable	1,650
202	Notes payable	1,900
301	P. Caldwell, Capital	3,000
302	P. Caldwell, Withdrawals	300
401	Sales revenue	4,600
501	Salaries expense	600
502	Rent expense	300
503	Utilities expense	150

Information for adjustments:
a. Of the $1,500 of supplies that were purchased, $600 was used.
b. Depreciation expense on office equipment amounted to $300.
c. Depreciation expense on delivery equipment amounted to $400.
d. Interest expense incurred on notes payable, but not yet paid, amounted to $65.
e. Of the $500 insurance that was purchased, only $200 has been used up this year.

REQUIRED:

a. Prepare a work sheet for the year ended December 31, 1978.
b. From the work sheet, prepare an income statement, a statement of owner's capital, and a balance sheet.

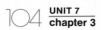

P7-4. *Work sheet and financial statements.* The trial balance, before adjustments, of Castile Moss Company at December 31, 1978, is shown below. Also shown is information for adjustments. The firm prepares financial statements once each year at the end of December.

Castile Moss Company
TRIAL BALANCE
December 31, 1978

Cash	30,000[a]
Accounts receivable	2,100
Office supplies	400
Service supplies	1,000
Office furniture	8,000
Accumulated depreciation—Office furniture	2,000
Accounts payable	3,000
Notes payable	10,000
C. Moss, Capital	5,800
C. Moss, Withdrawals	7,000
Service revenue	40,000
Rent revenue	2,500
Salaries expense	12,000
Rent expense	1,500
Utilities expense	1,000
Other expenses	300

[a] The account balances are not identified as debit or credit to provide additional practice in determining usual balances.

Information for adjustments:
a. Of the $400 of office supplies that were purchased, $150 remains on hand at the end of the year.
b. Depreciation expense on the furniture for the year amounts to $1,000.
c. Interest expense incurred on the notes payable, but not yet paid, amounts to $75.
d. Of the $1,000 of service supplies that were purchased, $800 has been used in operating the business.

REQUIRED:

a. Prepare a work sheet for the firm for the year ended December 31, 1978.
b. From the work sheet, prepare an income statement, a statement of owner's capital, and a balance sheet.

P7-5. *Work sheet and financial statements*
a. From the information provided in P6-4 (Unit 6), prepare a work sheet for the company.
b. From the work sheet, prepare an income statement, a statement of owner's capital, and a balance sheet.

*P7-6. *Working backwards on work sheet—special analysis.* Refer to P6-5 in Unit 6. From the trial balance and financial statements given, prepare a work sheet for the company.

Hint: You will have to determine the adjustments by comparing the financial statements to the unadjusted trial balance.

CLOSING THE ACCOUNTS

> **OBJECTIVE**

In this unit you will study the final procedures connected with completing the manual accounting process. You will learn about closing journal entries, about the trial balance prepared after the accounts are closed, and about preparing the accounts to begin the next accounting period.

> **APPROACH TO ATTAINING THE OBJECTIVE**

As you study the final end-of-period activities in the manual accounting process, pay particular attention to these three questions, which the text following answers:

- *How are closing entries made, and what is their purpose?*
- *What is a post-closing trial balance?*
- *What are some additional useful ideas about form in the manual accounting operation?*

Unit 7 showed you how to prepare a work sheet to help organize the end-of-period activities. You learned that one of the uses of the work sheet is as a reference in the preparation of closing entries. Here in this section we will first describe the purpose of closing entries, and then we will examine a detailed example of how these entries are made. Finally, we will look at an alternative procedure that many firms use for handling closing entries.

Purpose of closing entries At the end of an accounting period, a firm's ledger contains six types of accounts:

Asset accounts.	Owner's withdrawal account.
Liability accounts.	Revenue accounts.
Owner's capital account.	Expense accounts.

- *How are closing entries made, and what is their purpose?*

Recall the important fact that the last three of these categories (Owner's withdrawals, Revenues, and Expenses) are actually capital-type accounts. Furthermore, these three categories of accounts are *temporary* in that they represent activities measured for a *period of time* instead of a point in time. This means that every time a new accounting period is begun, the balances of these three **temporary capital accounts** must be "cleared," or closed to zero, if activities for the upcoming period are to be properly accumulated and measured. **Closing journal entries** (which are posted to the ledger accounts) perform this function.

An example of closing entries Reproduced as Illustration 8-1 is the work sheet you studied in Unit 7. This work sheet will be used here as a reference for the illustration of how closing entries are prepared.

The next step in the manual accounting process is the preparation of the closing entries in the firm's journal and then the posting of these journal entries to the proper ledger accounts. Closing entries must be made in the following manner (note that the key numbers circled in Illustration 8-1 correspond to the four closing entries in Illustration 8-2):

Step 1: *Close the revenue accounts to zero.* The revenue accounts (which are listed in the credit column of the Income Statement columns of the work sheet) must be closed to zero, so that the accounts will be ready to record the next period's revenues. Since all revenue accounts have credit balances, the revenue accounts are debited to close them and a temporary account is set up to hold their balances. This temporary account is called **Net earnings summary.**[1] This account will be used to

---

[1] This account is sometimes referred to as the *Income summary,* the *Revenue and expense summary,* or the *Profit and loss summary.*

Stevie Car Wash Company
Work Sheet
For the Month Ended May 31, 1978

AC. NO.	ACCOUNT	TRIAL BALANCE DR.	TRIAL BALANCE CR.	ADJUSTMENTS DR.	ADJUSTMENTS CR.	ADJUSTED TRIAL BALANCE DR.	ADJUSTED TRIAL BALANCE CR.	INCOME STATEMENT DR.	INCOME STATEMENT CR.	STATEMENT OF OWNER'S CAPITAL DR.	STATEMENT OF OWNER'S CAPITAL CR.	BALANCE SHEET DR.	BALANCE SHEET CR.
101	Cash	130000				130000						130000	
102	Accounts receivable	40000				40000						40000	
113	Supplies	80000			(a) 20000	60000						60000	
120	Office equipment	80000				80000						80000	
122	Car wash equipment	360000				360000						360000	
201	Accounts payable		70000				70000						70000
202	Notes payable		360000				360000						360000
301	Paul Stevie, Capital		180000				180000				180000		
302	Paul Stevie, Withdrawals	50000				50000				50000			
401	Car wash revenue		230000				230000		230000				
501	Salaries expense	60000				60000		60000					
502	Rent expense	30000				30000		30000					
504	Utilities expense	10000				10000		10000					
		840000	840000										
503	Supplies expense			(a) 20000		20000		20000					
506	Depreciation expense - Office equipment			(b) 1100		1100		1100					
121	Accumulated depreciation - Office equipment				(b) 1100		1100						1100
507	Depreciation expense - Car wash equipment			(c) 10000		10000		10000					
123	Accumulated depreciation - Car wash equipment				(c) 10000		10000						10000
505	Interest expense			(d) 2400		2400		2400					
203	Interest payable				(d) 2400		2400						2400
				33500	33500	853500	853500	133500	230000	50000	276500	670000	443500
	Net earnings (Net income)							96500			96500		
								230000	230000	226500			
	Paul Stevie, Capital, May 31, 1978									226500			226500
										276500	276500	670000	670000

Adjustments:
(a) Supplies used during May, $200.
(b) Depreciation of office equipment, $11.
(c) Depreciation of car wash equipment, $100.
(d) Unpaid interest expense on note, $24.

ILLUSTRATION 8-1

DATE	DESCRIPTION	REF.	DEBIT	CREDIT
1978 May 31	Car-wash revenue	401	2300 00	
	Net earnings summary	600		2300 00
(1)	To close the revenue account and temporarily reflect the credit balance in a summary account.			
31	Net earnings summary	600	1335 00	
	Salaries expense	501		600 00
	Rent expense	502		300 00
	Utilities expense	504		100 00
(2)	Supplies expense	503		200 00
	Depreciation expense—Office equipment	506		11 00
	Depreciation expense—Car-wash equipment	507		100 00
	Interest expense	505		24 00
	To close the expense accounts to the Net earnings summary.			
31	Net earnings summary	600	965 00	
	Paul Stevie, Capital	301		965 00
(3)	To increase the owner's capital account by the amount of the Net earnings (by the balance of the net earnings summary).			
31	Paul Stevie, Capital	301	500 00	
	Paul Stevie, Withdrawals	302		500 00
(4)	To close the withdrawals account and to reduce the owner's capital by the amount of the withdrawals.			

ILLUSTRATION 8-2

temporarily summarize all information about the earnings of the company. Now, refer to Illustration 8-2 for the first closing entry.

Step 2: *Close the expense accounts to zero.* The expense accounts (which are listed in the debit column of the Income Statement columns of the work sheet) must be closed to zero, so that the accounts will be ready to record the next period's expenses. Since all expense accounts have debit balances, the expense accounts are credited to close them to zero and a temporary account (Net earnings summary) holds their balances. Refer to Illustration 8-2 for the second closing entry.

Step 3: *Transfer the balance of net earnings (or net loss) to the owner's capital account.* After the first two closing entries above are recorded in the journal and posted to the ledger accounts, the revenue and expense accounts will have zero balances. However, the balance of the Net earnings summary account will be the amount of the net earnings (or net loss) for the period. This amount of net earnings is transferred as an increase in the owner's capital account. Refer to Illustration 8-2 for this third closing entry. This entry now closes to zero the Net earnings summary account and increases the owner's capital by the amount of the earnings for the period. (If there had been a net loss, the owner's capital account would have been debited and the Net earnings summary account would have been credited for the amount of the net loss.)

Step 4: *Close the owner's withdrawals account.* Refer to Illustration 8-2 for this last closing entry. The withdrawals account (which has a debit balance) is credited to close it to zero. The owner's capital is reduced (debited) by the amount of the withdrawals.

After the closing entries are recorded in the journal, as shown in Illustration 8-2, and then posted to the ledger accounts, *only certain accounts will have balances to begin the next period's operations:*

All asset accounts will have debit balances.
All liability accounts will have credit balances.
The owner's capital account will have a credit balance ($2,265).
The owner's withdrawals account will have a *zero* balance.
The revenue accounts will have *zero* balances.
The expense accounts will have *zero* balances.

In summary, only those accounts appearing in the Balance Sheet columns of the work sheet will have balances to begin the next operating period.

An alternative procedure for closing entries Some firms prefer to make closing entries in one summary entry, instead of using the four-step procedure described previously. In that case, the Net earnings summary account would not be used, but the effect of earnings and withdrawals would be transferred *directly* to the owner's capital account. Illustration 8-3 shows this approach. The four basic steps are referred to by the circled numbers in the illustration. However, the net effect on capital of both earnings and withdrawals are combined in the entry. Observe that both systems accomplish the same objective: to close the revenues, expenses, and withdrawals; and to show the net effect of these elements on the owner's capital account.

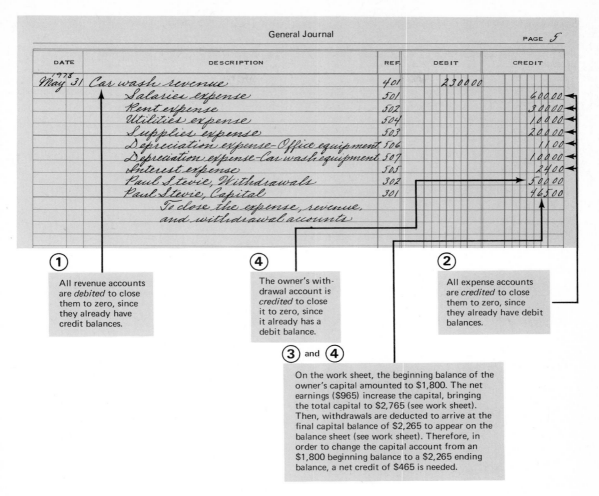

ILLUSTRATION 8-3

For purposes of working problems in this course, you are to use the four-entry approach with the Net earnings summary account—unless otherwise directed by your instructor. This alternate method is presented for comparison purposes.

The ledger illustrated The following pages contain the ledger of Stevie Car Wash Company after all business transactions, adjusting entries, and closing entries have been posted to the accounts. You may wish to compare these accounts to the way they appeared in Unit 5, before adjusting and closing entries were posted. Notice in the illustrated ledger accounts that the Net earnings summary account is included. Of course, this account would have a zero balance after all closing entries have been posted.

Cash — ACCOUNT NO. 101

DATE	DESCRIPTION	REF.	DEBITS	CREDITS	BALANCE DEBIT	BALANCE CREDIT
1978 May 1		1	100000		100000	
11		1		30000	70000	
17		1	70000		140000	
18		1		10000	130000	
27		1	10000		140000	
31		2		60000	80000	
31		2		10000	70000	
31		2	110000		180000	
31		2		50000	130000	

Accounts receivable — ACCOUNT NO. 102

DATE	DESCRIPTION	REF.	DEBITS	CREDITS	BALANCE DEBIT	BALANCE CREDIT
1978 May 17		1	10000		10000	
27		1		10000	—0—	
31		2	40000		40000	

Supplies — ACCOUNT NO. 103

DATE	DESCRIPTION	REF.	DEBITS	CREDITS	BALANCE DEBIT	BALANCE CREDIT
1978 May 8		1	80000		80000	
31	Adjustment	3		20000	60000	

Office equipment — ACCOUNT NO. 120

DATE	DESCRIPTION	REF.	DEBITS	CREDITS	BALANCE DEBIT	BALANCE CREDIT
1978 May 1		1	80000		80000	

Accumulated depreciation— Office equipment — ACCOUNT NO. 121

DATE	DESCRIPTION	REF.	DEBITS	CREDITS	BALANCE DEBIT	BALANCE CREDIT
1978 May 31	Adjustment	3		2400		2400

Car-wash equipment — ACCOUNT NO. 122

DATE	DESCRIPTION	REF.	DEBITS	CREDITS	BALANCE DEBIT	BALANCE CREDIT
1978 May 3		1	360000		360000	

Accumulated depreciation—Car-wash equipment — ACCOUNT NO. 123

DATE	DESCRIPTION	REF.	DEBITS	CREDITS	BALANCE DEBIT	BALANCE CREDIT
1978 May 31	Adjustment	3		100 00		100 00

Accounts payable — ACCOUNT NO. 201

DATE	DESCRIPTION	REF.	DEBITS	CREDITS	BALANCE DEBIT	BALANCE CREDIT
1978 May 8		1		800 00		800 00
18		1	100 00			700 00

Notes payable — ACCOUNT NO. 202

DATE	DESCRIPTION	REF.	DEBITS	CREDITS	BALANCE DEBIT	BALANCE CREDIT
1978 May 3		1		3600 00		3600 00

Interest payable — ACCOUNT NO. 203

DATE	DESCRIPTION	REF.	DEBITS	CREDITS	BALANCE DEBIT	BALANCE CREDIT
1978 May 31	Adjustment	3		24 00		24 00

Paul Stevie, Capital — ACCOUNT NO. 301

DATE	DESCRIPTION	REF.	DEBITS	CREDITS	BALANCE DEBIT	BALANCE CREDIT
1978 May 1		1		1800 00		1800 00
31	Closing—Net earnings	4		965 00		2765 00
31	Closing—Withdrawals	4	500 00			2265 00

Paul Stevie, Withdrawals — ACCOUNT NO. 302

DATE	DESCRIPTION	REF.	DEBITS	CREDITS	BALANCE DEBIT	BALANCE CREDIT
1978 May 31		2	500 00		500 00	
31	Closing	4		500 00	—0—	

Car-wash revenue — ACCOUNT NO. 401

DATE	DESCRIPTION	REF.	DEBITS	CREDITS	BALANCE DEBIT	BALANCE CREDIT
1978 May 17		1		800 00		800 00
31		2		1500 00		2300 00
31	Closing	4	2300 00			—0—

Salaries expense — ACCOUNT NO. 501

DATE	DESCRIPTION	REF.	DEBITS	CREDITS	BALANCE DEBIT	BALANCE CREDIT
1978 May 31		2	600 00		600 00	
31	Closing	4		600 00	—0—	

Rent expense — ACCOUNT NO. 502

DATE	DESCRIPTION	REF.	DEBITS	CREDITS	BALANCE DEBIT	BALANCE CREDIT
1978 May 11		1	300 00		300 00	
31	Closing	4		300 00	—0—	

Supplies expense — ACCOUNT NO. 503

DATE	DESCRIPTION	REF.	DEBITS	CREDITS	BALANCE DEBIT	BALANCE CREDIT
1978 May 31	Adjustment	3	200 00		200 00	
31	Closing	4		200 00	—0—	

Utilities expense — ACCOUNT NO. 504

DATE	DESCRIPTION	REF.	DEBITS	CREDITS	BALANCE DEBIT	BALANCE CREDIT
1978 May 31		2	100 00		100 00	
31		4		100 00	—0—	

Interest expense — ACCOUNT NO. 505

DATE	DESCRIPTION	REF.	DEBITS	CREDITS	BALANCE DEBIT	BALANCE CREDIT
1978 May 31	Adjustment	3	24 00		24 00	
31	Closing	4		24 00	—0—	

Depreciation expense — Office equipment — ACCOUNT NO. 506

DATE	DESCRIPTION	REF.	DEBITS	CREDITS	BALANCE DEBIT	BALANCE CREDIT
1978 May 31	Adjustment	3	11 00		11 00	
31	Closing	4		11 00	—0—	

Depreciation expense — Car-wash equipment — ACCOUNT NO. 507

DATE	DESCRIPTION	REF.	DEBITS	CREDITS	BALANCE DEBIT	BALANCE CREDIT
1978 May 31	Adjustment	3	100 00		100 00	
31	Closing	4		100 00	—0—	

Net earnings summary — ACCOUNT NO. 600

DATE	DESCRIPTION	REF.	DEBITS	CREDITS	BALANCE DEBIT	BALANCE CREDIT
1978 May 31	Revenue — closing	4		2300 00		2300 00
31	Expenses — closing	4	1335 00			965 00
31	Closing	4	965 00			—0—

The final end-of-period operation in a manual accounting system is to prepare a second or **post-closing trial balance.** The purpose of this is to determine if the ledger is in balance to begin the next operating period. An important fact about the post-closing trial balance is that it will include *only* asset, liability, and capital accounts because the revenues, expenses, and withdrawals have been closed.

- *What is a post-
closing trial
balance?*

If you will compare the post-closing trial balance of the Stevie Car Wash Company shown in Illustration 8-4 with the Balance Sheet columns of the work sheet in Illustration 8-1, you will see another important fact: the figures are, and should be, identical.

ILLUSTRATION 8-4

**Stevie Car Wash Company
Post-closing Trial Balance
May 31, 1978**

ACCT. NO.	ACCOUNT	DEBIT	CREDIT
101	Cash	130000	
102	Accounts receivable	40000	
103	Supplies	60000	
120	Office equipment	80000	
121	Accumulated depreciation-Office equipment		1100
122	Car-wash equipment	360000	
123	Accumulated depreciation-Car-wash equipment		10000
201	Accounts payable		70000
202	Notes payable		360000
203	Interest payable		2400
301	Paul Stevie, Capital		226500
		670000	670000

The following paragraphs contain some recommendations about common methods and procedures used in an accounting system.

- *What are some
additional useful
ideas about form in
the manual accounting
operation?*

Use of dollar signs Dollar signs usually appear in any formal report prepared for use by a decision maker. For example, dollar signs usually appear at the head (first figure) and foot (total) of every column on the balance sheet, the income statement, the statement of owner's capital, and other financial statements.

Dollar signs usually are not needed for documents in the accounting system that do not go to decision makers. These include the journal, the ledger, trial balances, and work sheets.

Use of abbreviations In order to make the financial statements going to decision makers easier to understand, it is recommended that word abbreviations not be used on them. A reasonable use of common abbreviations in the accounting system is, however, customary and useful.

Use of contra accounts A **contra account** is a separate ledger account specially created to reduce another ledger account. For example, the Accumulated depreciation—Equipment account accumulates a credit balance, which is actually a reduction in the asset account Equipment. A separate contra account is created so that the original balance in the related account (Equipment) can be preserved and disclosed on a financial statement or other report. For example, from the balance sheet information in Illustration 8-1 you can see that both the Office equipment account (with its original balance) and its contra account Accumulated depreciation—Office equipment are disclosed in this particular financial statement. Throughout this course you will study a number of contra accounts.

As a final review, restudy the diagram of the complete manual accounting cycle which appears as Illustration 7-4 in Unit 7.

❯ NEW TERMS

closing entries Journal entries made at the end of an accounting period, which serve to remove the balances from revenue accounts, from expense accounts, and from the owner's withdrawals account. In the process the owner's capital is brought up to date by reducing it by the amount of the withdrawals and increasing it by the amount of the net earnings. [p. 107]

contra account A ledger account specially created to reduce another ledger account. The contra account is created so that the original balance in the related account can be preserved and disclosed on accounting reports. [p. 116]

net earnings summary Serves to temporarily accumulate the balances of the revenue and expense accounts in the closing process; also called Income summary, Revenue and expense summary, and Profit and loss summary. [p. 107]

post-closing trial balance A second or final trial balance prepared to determine if the ledger is in balance to begin the next operating period. [p. 115]

temporary capital accounts Revenues, expenses, and owner's withdrawals. [p. 107]

QUESTIONS

Q8-1. What is the purpose of closing entries?

Q8-2. At what point in the accounting cycle are closing entries made?

Q8-3. *After closing entries are made and posted,* which groups of accounts have zero balances? Which groups of accounts have debit balances? Which groups of accounts have credit balances?

Q8-4. What is a post-closing trial balance? Why is it prepared? Which accounts are included in the post-closing trial balance?

Q8-5. Describe the customary use of dollar signs in a manual accounting and reporting system.

Q8-6. Should abbreviations be used in the accounting records? On the financial statements?

Q8-7. What is a contra account? Give one example.

EXERCISES

E8-1. A completed work sheet for the White Laundry Company for the month ended February 28, 1978, is shown on the next page. From this work sheet, prepare closing journal entries.

E8-2. Shown below are the balances appearing in the accounts of Brittany Moss Company, after adjusting journal entries have been posted to the accounts, at December 31, 1978. Prepare closing journal entries.

Cash	$30,000
Accounts receivable	2,100
Office supplies	400
Service supplies	1,000
Office furniture	8,000
Accumulated depreciation—Office furniture	2,000
Accounts payable	3,000
Interest payable	75
Notes payable	10,000
B. Moss, Capital	7,550
B. Moss, Withdrawals	7,000
Service revenue	40,000
Rent revenue	2,500
Salaries expense	12,000
Rent expense	1,500
Utilities expense	1,000
Depreciation expense—Office furniture	1,000
Interest expense	75
Office supplies expense	250
Service supplies expense	800

White Laundry Company
Work Sheet
For the Month Ended February 28, 1978

ACCOUNT	TRIAL BALANCE DR.	TRIAL BALANCE CR.	ADJUSTMENTS DR.	ADJUSTMENTS CR.	ADJUSTED TRIAL BALANCE DR.	ADJUSTED TRIAL BALANCE CR.	INCOME STATEMENT DR.	INCOME STATEMENT CR.	STATEMENT OF OWNER'S CAPITAL DR.	STATEMENT OF OWNER'S CAPITAL CR.	BALANCE SHEET DR.	BALANCE SHEET CR.
Cash	150000				150000						150000	
Accounts receivable	120000				120000						120000	
Laundry supplies	90000			(a) 30000	60000						60000	
Laundry equipment	1000000				1000000						1000000	
Accounts payable		60000		(c) 20000		80000						80000
Gay White, Capital		1280000				1280000				1280000		
Gay White, Drawings	80000				80000				80000			
Laundry revenue		310000				310000		310000				
Salaries expense	110000				110000		110000					
Rent expense	30000				30000		30000					
Other expenses	70000				70000		70000					
	1650000	1650000										
Laundry supplies expense			(a) 30000		30000		30000					
Depreciation expense—laundry equipment			(b) 10000		10000		10000					
Accumulated depreciation—laundry equipment				(b) 10000		10000						10000
Advertising expense			(c) 20000		20000		20000					
			60000	60000	1680000	1680000	270000	310000				
Net earnings							40000			40000		
							310000	310000	80000	1320000		
Gay White, Capital, February 28, 1978									1240000			1240000
									1320000	1320000	1330000	1330000

Adjustments:
(a) Laundry supplies used during February, $300.
(b) Depreciation of laundry equipment, $100.
(c) Expense (advertising) incurred but not yet paid, $200.
(Advertising expense and accounts payable)

E8-3. Presented below is an adjusted trial balance of Willy Gong Co. at May 31, 1978.

Willy Gong Co.
TRIAL BALANCE
May 31, 1978

ACCOUNT NUMBER	ACCOUNT	DEBIT	CREDIT
101	Cash	1,300.00	
201	Accounts payable		700.00
301	Willy Gong, Capital		1,800.00
401	Revenue		2,300.00
501	Salaries expense	600.00	
102	Accounts receivable	400.00	
202	Notes payable		3,600.00
302	Willy Gong, Withdrawals	500.00	
502	Rent expense	300.00	
103	Supplies	800.00	
120	Office equipment	800.00	
504	Utilities expense	100.00	
122	Other equipment	3,600.00	
		8,400.00	8,400.00

REQUIRED:

a. Prepare closing journal entries.
b. What is the amount of the owner's capital account to appear on the balance sheet at May 31?

PROBLEMS (GROUP A)

P8-1. *Closing entries.* Shown on the next page are the financial statements of Cronin Montz Delivery Service for June, 1978. Prepare closing journal entries.

Cronin Montz Delivery Service
Income Statement
For the Month Ended June 30, 1978

Revenues		
Delivery service revenue		$ 6,000.00
Expenses		
Truck maintenance expense	$ 800.00	
Truck rent expense	1,500.00	
Office rent expense	200.00	
Salaries expense	1,600.00	
Miscellaneous expenses	100.00	
Supplies expense	300.00	
Interest expense	15.00	
Total expenses		4,515.00
Net earnings		$ 1,485.00

Cronin Montz Delivery Service
Statement of Owner's Capital
For the Month Ended June 30, 1978

Cronin Montz, Capital, June 1, 1978 (initial investment)		$	5000 00
Net earnings for June 1978	$ 1485 00		
Owner's withdrawals during June 1978	600 00		
Net increase in capital			885 00
Cronin Montz, Capital, June 30, 1978		$	5885 00

Cronin Montz Delivery Service
Balance Sheet
June 30, 1978

Assets			
Cash	$ 8185 00		
Supplies	200 00		
Total assets		$	8385 00
Equities			
Liabilities:			
Notes payable	$ 2000 00		
Accounts payable	500 00		
Total liabilities		$	2500 00
Capital:			
Cronin Montz, Capital			5885 00
Total equities		$	8385 00

P8-2. *Closing entries.* Shown below are the balances appearing in the accounts of Gibson Company after adjusting journal entries have been posted to the accounts at December 31, 1978. Prepare closing journal entries.

Supplies expense	$ 1,600
Cash	55,000
Interest expense	200
Interest payable	100
Accounts receivable	4,000
Supplies	2,000
Office furniture	15,000
Depreciation expense—Office furniture	2,000
Accumulated depreciation—Office furniture	6,000
Salaries expense	25,000
Rent expense	3,000

Accounts payable	6,000
Notes payable	10,000
Service revenue	81,000
Kenneth Gibson, Capital	19,700
Kenneth Gibson, Withdrawals	15,000

P8-3. *Closing entries.* The adjusted trial balance columns of a work sheet for a company are shown below. Using this information, answer the questions that follow.

ADJUSTED TRIAL BALANCE

Cash	12,000	
Accounts receivable	21,000	
Supplies	2,800	
Prepaid insurance[a]	900	
Furniture and fixtures	78,000	
Accumulated depreciation—		
Furniture and fixtures		12,000
Accounts payable		9,000
J. E. Blake, Capital		24,800
J. E. Blake, Withdrawals	4,000	
Rent revenue		102,000
Service revenue		72,000
Wages expense	85,000	
Insurance expense	4,000	
Supplies expense	5,100	
Depreciation expense	6,000	
Interest expense	2,000	
Interest payable		1,000
	220,800	220,800

[a] Prepaid insurance is an *asset account*, representing unused insurance coverage paid for. It is not an expense.

REQUIRED:

a. Assume that you are making closing entries for the firm. List the accounts in the adjusted trial balance that would be debited.

b. Assume that you are making closing entries for the firm. List the accounts in the adjusted trial balance that would be credited.

c. What is the balance of the owner's capital account after closing entries are recorded and posted? Indicate whether the balance is a debit or a credit.

d. What is the balance of the owner's drawing account after closing entries are recorded and posted?

e. What is the balance of the Interest payable account after closing entries are recorded and posted? Indicate whether the balance is a debit or a credit.

f. What is the balance of the Rent revenue account after closing entries are recorded and posted?

PROBLEMS (GROUP B)

P8-4. *Closing entries; post-closing trial balance.* The adjusted trial balance columns of a work sheet for a company are shown on the next page.

M and R Metal Company
ADJUSTED TRIAL BALANCE
May 31, 1978

101	Cash	$1,500	
102	Accounts receivable	600	
103	Supplies	3,400	
120	Office equipment	1,750	
121	Accumulated depreciation—Office equipment		200
122	Other equipment	500	
123	Accumulated depreciation—Other equipment		100
201	Accounts payable		3,900
202	Notes payable		1,000
301	R. Melvin, Capital		1,500
302	R. Melvin, Withdrawals	500	
401	Revenue		3,150
501	Salaries expense	800	
502	Rent expense	400	
503	Utilities expense	100	
504	Depreciation expense—Office equipment	200	
505	Depreciation expense—Other equipment	100	
		$9,850	$9,850

REQUIRED:

a. Prepare closing journal entries.

b. Prepare a post-closing trial balance, using the information given. (In actual practice, the post-closing trial balance would be made from the ledger accounts to verify that the ledger is in balance to begin the next period.)

P8-5. *Closing entries; analysis of data; income statement.* The work sheet of Lettis Company showed that the December 31, 1978, ending capital balance for J. B. Lettis amounted to $93,200, which included a net increase of $18,000 from the beginning capital balance of $75,200. Revenues for the year totaled $153,000, including Service revenue of $150,000 and Miscellaneous revenue of $3,000. Expenses amounted to $128,000, including Salaries of $70,000, Utilities expense of $2,000, Rent expense of $12,000, Office supplies expense of $4,000, Depreciation expense of $8,000, Interest expense of $3,000, and Store supplies expense of $29,000.

REQUIRED:

a. From the data given, prepare closing entries.

b. Prepare an income statement for Lettis Company for the year ended December 31, 1978.

P8-6. *Closing entries prepared directly from financial statements.* Refer to P6-5 in Unit 6. From the data given, prepare closing entries for the company.

CUMULATIVE REVIEW PROBLEMS

P8-7. *Cumulative review problem.* The accounts and balances of J. Goldman Service Company at December 31, 1978, before adjustments, appear below:

Cash	27,400
Accounts receivable	20,000

Prepaid insurance	2,000
Supplies	500
Equipment	10,000
Accumulated depreciation—Equipment	2,400
Accounts payable	7,000
Notes payable	10,000
J. Goldman, Capital	36,500
J. Goldman, Withdrawals	3,000
Revenue	26,000
Salaries expense	16,000
Rent expense	2,000
Miscellaneous expense	1,000

Information for adjustments:

1. Of the $500 of supplies that were purchased, $200 remains on hand at the end of the year.
2. Depreciation expense on equipment for the year amounts to $600.
3. Interest expense incurred on the notes payable, but not yet paid, amounts to $60.
4. Of the $2,000 insurance that was purchased, only $350 has been used up this year.

REQUIRED:

a. Prepare a work sheet for the year ended December 31, 1978.
b. Journalize adjusting entries.
c. Journalize closing entries.
d. Prepare an income statement, a statement of owner's capital, and a balance sheet.

P8-8. *Cumulative review problem.* Appearing below is the *unadjusted* trial balance of B. N. Warbler Company at December 31, 1978, the end of a year's operations.

ACCOUNT NO.	ACCOUNT TITLE		
101	Cash	10,000	
102	Accounts receivable	18,000	
103	Supplies	25,000	
104	Prepaid insurance[a]	1,000	
105	Furniture and fixtures	10,000	
106	Accumulated depreciation		1,000
201	Accounts payable		2,000
202	Notes payable		5,000
301	B. N. Warbler, Capital		32,000
302	B. N. Warbler, Drawings	23,000	
401	Rent revenue		99,000
402	Service revenue		10,000
501	Salaries expense	50,000	
502	Miscellaneous expense	12,000	
		149,000	149,000

[a] An asset account.

Other accounts used by the firm are:

ACCOUNT NO.	ACCOUNT TITLE
203	Interest payable
503	Depreciation expense
504	Supplies expense
505	Insurance expense
506	Interest expense
600	Net earnings summary

Information for adjustments:
1. Depreciation expense for the year amounts to $1,000. The furniture and fixtures were purchased January 1, 1977.
2. Supplies on hand (unused) at December 31, 1978, amount to $6,000.
3. Insurance expired (used) during the year totals $800.
4. Interest owed on the note amounts to $400.

REQUIRED:

a. Prepare a work sheet for B. N. Warbler Company for the year ended December 31, 1978.
b. Set up ledger accounts for the company and enter the balances shown on the December 31, 1978, unadjusted trial balance.
c. Record adjusting entries in a journal and post them to the ledger accounts.
d. Record closing entries in a journal and post them to the ledger accounts.
e. Prepare a post-closing trial balance.

chapter 4

an overview of financial statements

THE PURPOSE AND STRUCTURE
OF THE BALANCE SHEET

▶ OBJECTIVE

You have now completed your introduction to the operation of a manual account-ing system. This unit, and the next, will place the manual accounting process into perspective. They will be concerned with relating the input of the accounting sys-tem (the business transactions) to the output of the accounting system (the finan-cial statements). More specifically, this unit will examine the balance sheet, and the next unit will deal with the income statement.

      The balance sheet is one of the most useful general-purpose financial statements that decision makers have. This unit will show you how the balance sheet, through the use of generally accepted classification and valuation con-cepts, provides information that directly helps its readers to accomplish their goals. This unit also will show you how the balance sheet is related to the account-ing cycle which you have already studied.

▶ APPROACH TO ATTAINING THE OBJECTIVE

As you study the balance sheet, its classification and valuation concepts, and its relationship to the accounting cycle, pay particular attention to these seven ques-tions, which the text following answers:

- *What is the main purpose of accounting?*
- *What kinds of decisions require accounting information?*
- *How does the accounting cycle change data into usable information for decisions?*
- *What common information about resources is needed by top management, investors, creditors, employees, and other decision makers?*
- *How is this common information communicated by the balance sheet?*
- *Why are these particular classification and valuation concepts used on the balance sheet?*
- *How is the accounting cycle related to the balance sheet?*

Accounting was defined back in Unit 1 as an information-providing activity. These two points were made:

1. The focal point of accounting is the organization (often the business firm). The information accounting provides is information about the organization.

2. Accounting information is vital to a business firm's activity. It is used for making decisions *inside* the organization (by management) and *outside* the organization (by investors, creditors, and others).

■ *What is the main purpose of accounting?*

Your study of the accounting cycle as an information-generating process has been concerned mainly with how business transactions are analyzed, recorded, summarized, and reported on financial statements. This unit will be purpose-oriented. That is, you will review the decisions that demand accounting information and see how the accounting cycle helps accomplish the main goal of accounting, which is to serve decision makers. The function of accounting in the business decision process can be summarized as follows:

Decision makers, whether inside or outside a business firm, want to make decisions (by choosing among alternative courses of action) that are *most likely* to accomplish their goals. Accounting information is created for and used by decision makers simply to make it *more likely* that the desired goals will be attained. For example, if a bank is considering lending a company $10,000, the banker (decision maker) must determine how likely it is that the company will pay back the loan according to a specific agreement. He needs detailed financial information about the company to make this judgment, and accounting provides this critical information. In summary, before informed judgments and good decisions can be made at all levels in our economic system, information related to the decision must be selected, analyzed, reported, and then used. Accounting, both managerial and financial, is a primary source of this vital information.

In serving the needs of society, accounting systems produce two fundamental kinds of reports: (1) **general-purpose financial statements,** and (2) **special-purpose reports.** The manual accounting system, which you have been studying, focuses upon general-purpose financial statements. Let us look at these first.

GENERAL-PURPOSE FINANCIAL STATEMENTS

Many different groups of decision makers in our economic system need similar kinds of information to make their decisions. Because of this common need, a single set of financial statements for a firm can be prepared, and this same set can then be used by decision makers who have differing objectives. For example, both creditors and investors can use the same financial statements because they both need similar information for their decisions.

What information is needed in common by various decision makers? It is information about the resources of the firm, information about where these resources were acquired, and information about how the resources changed and were used during a period of time. Illustration 9-1 shows how three different decision makers all require similar, specific information before informed judgments and good decisions can be made.

General-purpose financial statements have been developed so that the variety of people using them can have access to similar information. You have already been introduced to three of these statements:

The income statement.
The balance sheet.
The statement of owner's capital.

ILLUSTRATION 9-1

Decision maker	Decisions to be made (or goal to be attained)	Some factors which must be forecast (predicted) to help make the decision	Some information needed in common
INVESTOR	Whether to invest in the firm.	1. What will be the value of the investment in the future? 2. What other benefits will be received by the investor?	What resources has the firm acquired? How is the management of the firm employing the resources?
CREDITOR	Whether to lend the firm money.	1. Will the firm be able to pay its debt and interest according to the agreement? 2. Will there be any other costs or benefits for the lender?	Where did the resources come from? What are the firm's debts? How much has the firm grown through profit-making activities?
LABOR UNION	What demands to make at the next contract bargaining	1. Can the firm afford to pay its employees increased benefits? 2. What activities is the firm engaging in that might be relevant to labor negotiations?	How profitable is the firm currently? What changes in resources and earnings are likely in the future?

A fourth statement, the *statement of changes in financial position,* will be introduced later in this course. The balance sheet provides information about the assets and equities of a firm at a point in time. The statement of changes in financial position simply provides information about the *changes* in the firm's resources during a period of time. These four general-purpose statements contain the answers to the seven questions posed on the right-hand side of Illustration 9-1.

An important point to note here is that all these statements are presented according to **generally accepted accounting principles.** A generally accepted group of rules or principles for presenting the financial statement information is absolutely necessary because many different people use the same reports. These rules also provide some security for the statement users because they help make the statements dependable. For example, the term *Accounts receivable* is used on balance sheets. There must be some generally agreed upon meaning for this classification of information (Accounts receivable) if all users are to understand what the account means. Another example is the dollar value placed on an account. If the account, Land, is reported on the balance sheet at $10,000, does this mean that the land cost $10,000, that the land could be sold for $10,000, or that the firm has been offered $10,000 for the land? In other words, there must be an agreed-upon and generally accepted way of **valuing** the resources and equities—and this agreed-upon way must serve some decision purpose. In summary, two characteristics of general-purpose financial statements are their use of (1) generally accepted account classifications of information, and (2) generally accepted ways of valuing (placing a dollar amount on) accounts.

SPECIAL-PURPOSE REPORTS

Highly specialized information often needs to be reported, particularly in management accounting where reports are prepared for internal use only. This information is usually for a special, narrow purpose and need not be presented in a *generally accepted* way. For example, a foreman in a factory might want to compare the number of units of product produced by each of his four employees in the current period with the number of units each employee produced during the last period. Because this information will be used by only one decision maker (or by a closely related group), an elaborate set of generally accepted reporting rules need not be established and followed.

Accounting information and reports thus can be either special-purpose or general-purpose in nature. *The manual accounting system you studied in the last few units was concerned primarily with processing transaction information to produce general-purpose financial statements for a variety of users.* Accounting systems are usually expanded to include special-purpose information as well. Both kinds of information are vital to the functioning of our economic system.

THE IMPORTANCE OF CLASSIFICATION

▪ *How does the accounting cycle change data into usable information for decisions?*

Classification of data is a basic concept in accounting. It refers to the process of accumulating and reporting information in useful categories (accounts). Thus, you have already learned the fundamental classification processes in accounting through your study of the previous units. In the accounting cycle, the first step is to identify business transactions and to analyze these transactions in terms of their effect on the accounts. Deciding what accounts are to be used in a system and deciding what information each account will contain is exceedingly important to the decision maker. For example, information about a firm's resources could be put into two classifications: (1) cash, and (2) all other resources. This limited classification on a financial statement would not be nearly as useful as dividing (classifying) the assets into several categories such as Cash, Accounts receivable, Plant and equipment, and so on.

In the accounting system, information is classified into useful account classifications for assets, liabilities, capital, revenues, and expenses. Remember that each time a journal entry is made to record a business transaction, the classification process comes into play. If the effects of the transactions have been classified by relevant and useful groupings, the decision maker can then more readily interpret the effects the transactions have (or will have) on his current problems. The key idea here is that the classifications are *user-oriented*—the kind of classification scheme used is determined by the kinds of decisions which users have to make. In summary, designing a chart of accounts for a firm requires a good deal of thought and imagination.

The system for making journal entries must be directly related to the use to be made of the financial statements. For example, a firm might choose to have these two revenue accounts in its accounting system:

> Revenue from services.
> Revenue from sales of products.

Or this classification of the same data might be preferred:

> Revenue from services.
> Revenue from sales of product *A*.
> Revenue from sales of product *B*.

Another alternative might be:

> Revenue from geographical area *X*.
> Revenue from geographical area *Y*.
> Revenue from geographical area *Z*.

There is an almost unlimited number of classification schemes which have been used in accounting systems. In the next two units you will study the generally accepted classifications used on modern financial statements and you will see how these classifications are especially useful to decision makers.

THE IMPORTANCE OF VALUATION

In the manual accounting cycle you classified each business transaction into two accounts, and you also placed a dollar value on the transaction in the journal entry. This placing of a value on a firm's resources and equities is done because the users of the financial statements want to know something about value. The users want this information about worth or price because their goals involve changes in value. For example, the investor wants information about the possible future value of his investment, and the creditor wants information about the value of the resources he will acquire in the future if he makes a loan.

Value can be calculated in several ways. Assume that a firm purchases a delivery truck on March 1 and pays $5,500 for it. The delivery truck will be used in operating the business. At the end of the year, the company discovers that if it had to replace the truck it now would have to pay $6,000 for a new one. Further, if the truck were to be sold as a used truck, it now would bring only $3,000. Each of these figures (the $5,500 initial value, the $6,000 current-replacement value, and the $3,000 current used-truck value) is a measure of the value of the truck. But each concept of value cannot be used for the same purpose. If the company did in fact intend to sell the truck immediately, the $3,000 would be important to the decision to sell the truck. If the company was planning to continue to use the truck in the business, then perhaps another figure would be more useful for other decisions related to the firm. Accordingly, in the manual accounting cycle you learned that when an asset was purchased for use in a business the asset's *cost* was recorded and was considered a relevant concept of value.

COMMON INFORMATION NEEDED

■ *What common information about resources is needed by top management, investors, creditors, employees, and other decision makers?*

When a business organization is formed, the management and owners must decide what the objectives and goals of the company are to be. Usually these goals include producing a good or service and making a profit (earnings). A most important fact about this whole process is that the company must gather about itself certain *resources* if it is to accomplish its goals. Resources—or assets, as they are called in accounting terminology—are absolutely vital to the operation of the firm.

To know whether its goals have been achieved, a company must have certain information about its assets. The balance sheet is the general-purpose report that provides decision makers with this key information. This is the common information needed:

1. A classified list of all the resources of the firm at a point in time.
2. A measure of dollar amounts (value) of the resources.
3. Information about where the resources came from (sources of the assets).

AN OVERVIEW OF THE BALANCE SHEET

■ *How is this common information communicated by the balance sheet?*

Three modern balance sheets are illustrated on the next three pages. First, a balance sheet of a proprietorship; next, a balance sheet of the partnership form of organization; and finally, a corporation balance sheet. To simplify the example, the same figures and accounts are used on all three statements. These balance sheets have been prepared in the **report form.** That is, the assets, liabilities, and capital items are arranged vertically on the page—with assets coming first, followed by liabilities and capital below. Another arrangement (that is not illustrated in this unit) is known as the **account form.** In the account form balance sheet, the assets are shown on the left half of the page, and the equities (liabilities and capital) are shown on the right half of the page. Notice as you study the details of each balance sheet that the significant difference in presentation from one balance sheet to another appears in the capital section. The classification and valuation concepts underlying the balance sheet are our next topics.

CLASSIFICATION AND VALUATION OF ASSETS, LIABILITIES, AND CAPITAL

■ *Why are these particular classification and valuation concepts used on the balance sheet?*

The following pages also contain detailed descriptions of the classification and valuation methods used on today's balance sheets. Study this information very carefully and relate each item to the three illustrated balance sheets. *The techniques for making journal entries to implement the valuation concepts will be studied in later units.* Your goal at this point should be to understand the meaning of every classification on the balance sheet and to understand the valuation process—how a dollar amount is assigned to each category.

Like the presentation of the assets, the classification and valuation of liabilities also are described in the following pages. Relate this description to the illustrated balance sheets. Remember that liabilities represent sources of assets.

As we noted before, the capital sections of the three balance sheets differ. The form that a business organization takes calls for a special presentation of its capital. In the table that shows how capital is reported on the balance sheet, pay special attention to the owner's capital account and its counterpart in a corporation, the common stock and the retained earnings accounts.

Tim Mark Company (A Proprietorship)
BALANCE SHEET
March 31, 1978

ASSETS

current assets

Cash on hand and in banks	$ 1,000	
Marketable securities	5,000	
Accounts receivable	2,000	
Merchandise inventory	8,000	
Prepaid expenses	1,000	
Total current assets		$ 17,000

long-term investments

Stocks and bonds	$10,000	
Land	9,000	
Other investments	3,000	
Total long-term investments		22,000

plant and equipment

Store equipment	$95,000		
Less: Accumulated depreciation	5,000		
Net Store equipment		$90,000	
Buildings	$14,000		
Less: Accumulated depreciation	2,000		
Net Buildings		12,000	
Land		30,000	
Total plant and equipment			132,000

other assets

Deferred charges	$ 2,000	
Intangible assets	5,000	
Total other assets		7,000
Total assets		$178,000

LIABILITIES AND CAPITAL

liabilities

Current liabilities:

Accounts payable	$ 6,000	
Notes payable	4,000	
Expenses payable	1,000	
Total current liabilities		$ 11,000

Long-term liabilities:

Notes payable		20,000
Total liabilities		$ 31,000

capital

Tim Mark, Capital	147,000
Total equities	$178,000

Paul and Stephen Company (A Partnership)
BALANCE SHEET
March 31, 1978

ASSETS

current assets

Cash on hand and in banks	$ 1,000	
Marketable securities	5,000	
Accounts receivable	2,000	
Merchandise inventory	8,000	
Prepaid expenses	1,000	
Total current assets		$ 17,000

long-term investments

Stocks and bonds	$ 10,000	
Land	9,000	
Other investments	3,000	
Total long-term investments		22,000

plant and equipment

Store equipment	$95,000		
Less: Accumulated depreciation	5,000		
Net Store equipment		$ 90,000	
Buildings	$14,000		
Less: Accumulated depreciation	2,000		
Net Buildings		12,000	
Land		30,000	
Total plant and equipment			132,000

other assets

Deferred charges	$ 2,000	
Intangible assets	5,000	
Total other assets		7,000
Total assets		$178,000

LIABILITIES AND CAPITAL

liabilities

Current liabilities:

Accounts payable	$ 6,000	
Notes payable	4,000	
Expenses payable	1,000	
Total current liabilities		$ 11,000

Long-term liabilities:

Notes payable		20,000
Total liabilities		$ 31,000

capital

Paul Tenny, Capital	$101,000	
Stephen Wiggy, Capital	46,000	
Total capital		147,000
Total equities		$178,000

PT Corporation
BALANCE SHEET
March 31, 1978

ASSETS

current assets

Cash on hand and in banks	$ 1,000	
Marketable securities	5,000	
Accounts receivable	2,000	
Merchandise inventory	8,000	
Prepaid expenses	1,000	
Total current assets		$ 17,000

long-term investments

Stocks and bonds	$10,000	
Land	9,000	
Other investments	3,000	
Total long-term investments		22,000

plant and equipment

Store equipment	$95,000		
Less: Accumulated depreciation	5,000		
Net Store equipment		$90,000	
Buildings	$14,000		
Less: Accumulated depreciation	2,000		
Net Buildings		12,000	
Land		30,000	
Total plant and equipment			132,000

other assets

Deferred charges	$ 2,000	
Intangible assets	5,000	
Total other assets		7,000
Total assets		$178,000

LIABILITIES AND CAPITAL

liabilities

Current liabilities:

Accounts payable	$ 6,000	
Notes payable	4,000	
Expenses payable	1,000	
Total current liabilities		$ 11,000

Long-term liabilities:

Notes payable		20,000
Total liabilities		$ 31,000

capital

Capital stock	$90,000	
Retained earnings	57,000	
Total capital		147,000
Total equities		$178,000

HOW ASSETS ARE REPORTED ON THE BALANCE SHEET

asset classification	CLASSIFICATION		VALUATION		decision reasons for generally accepted rules of classification and valuation
	meaning of classification	asset valuation method generally used	meaning of valuation		
Current Assets (general category)	All those resources of the firm which are expected to be used in the *regular daily operations* of the firm during the next year.* Traditionally includes five categories: (1) Cash, (2) Marketable securities, (3) Receivables, (4) Merchandise inventory on hand, (5) Prepaid expenses.	A variety of methods, chosen to provide a measure of resources readily available in liquid or usable form (explained below).			
Cash	Currency, checks, bank accounts, and coins to be used in current regular operations during the next year.*	Face amount (the amount printed on currency or coins, or the current balance of a bank account).	Using the face amount of cash provides a measure of purchasing power available in the most liquid asset.		Decision makers need to know how much of the most liquid asset is available to be used to pay expenses and regular maturing debts in the ordinary course of running the business. If the cash is reserved or otherwise earmarked for uses other than current operations, then it cannot be classified as a current asset. (See Long-term investments below.)
Marketable Securities	Stocks, bonds, other investments expected to be converted to cash or otherwise used in current regular operations during the next year.*	Cost or market, whichever is lower.	Assume that a short-term investment in stock was made at a cost of $2,000. At the balance sheet date, the stock could be sold for $1,990. The stock is then shown on the balance sheet at the lower value, $1,990.		The lower of cost or market valuation only tells the decision maker how much the company will be able to convert the marketable securities for in the near future. If market value is higher than cost, however, the cost is used to prevent misleading the decision maker if the market is temporarily high.
Receivables	Amounts owed to the firm by outsiders in the form of regular accounts or written promissory notes to be collected during the next year.*	Amount expected to be collected.	Assume that a firm has $11,000 of Accounts receivable at the balance sheet date, but eventually expects to be able to collect only $10,900 of this because of customers who do not meet their obligations. The $10,900 would be shown on the balance sheet.		The amount expected to be collected is a measure of liquid funds flowing into the firm during the coming year to be used in running the business.

*See footnote on page 138.

Merchandise Inventory	Goods which the firm has purchased and expects to sell to customers in the future, during the next year.*	Cost or market, whichever is lower.	*Market*, in this valuation method, refers to the price that would have to be paid to replace the inventory at the balance sheet date. Assume that a firm has on hand inventory for which it had paid $6,400. Assume further that if that merchandise were to be replaced at the balance sheet date, it would cost only $6,375. Then under the cost or market, whichever is lower valuation practice, the inventory would be shown on the balance sheet at $6,375.	Decision makers are interested in knowing how many dollars management has seen fit to tie up in merchandise. Cost, therefore, is an appropriate measure to reveal this. In the event that the replacement cost has declined and the inventory is still on hand, it can be said that some of the dollars of cost represent a loss or expense, since the inventory could be replaced at a smaller amount.
Prepaid Expenses	Any expense which has been paid for in advance represents an asset. The company has purchased something of value in operating the firm that will be utilized in the next year.* Examples are: Prepaid rent, Prepaid salaries, and Supplies on hand.	Cost—that portion of the cost which is still to be used in the future.	Assume that a firm purchased a 2-year insurance policy on January 1, 1978 for $3,000. At December 31, 1978, 1 year's future value still remains. Therefore, the December 31, 1978, balance sheet would report the Prepaid insurance at $1,500.	Decision makers are interested in knowing how many dollars of expenses of the next year are already paid for. Cash will not be needed to pay these expenses in the next year.
Long-term Investments	Stocks, bonds, land, and any other investments which the firm plans to own for a number of years. These investments do not represent the firm's main source of revenue. Observe that the expected use of the investment is a factor that distinguishes Marketable securities (current) from Long-term investments.	Initially recorded at cost.	All costs associated with acquiring the long-term investment are shown on the balance sheet as the asset amount.	The company does not plan to dispose of long-term investments in the next year; therefore, the market price of the investment is not of primary concern to the decision makers. The number of dollars tied up (cost) is relevant, however, to evaluating management's use of the firm's resources.

* See footnote on page 138.

HOW ASSETS ARE REPORTED ON THE BALANCE SHEET (continued)

| asset classification | CLASSIFICATION | VALUATION | | decision reasons for generally accepted rules of classification and valuation |
	meaning of classification	asset valuation method generally used	meaning of valuation	
Plant and Equipment	Land, buildings, equipment, and other major resources which are currently being used to produce the firm's main revenues. Examples are a store building, manufacturing equipment, and furniture and fixtures. Plant and equipment are also known as **fixed assets**.	Cost—that portion of the cost which is still to be used in the future	Asset cost less accumulated depreciation.	Decision makers are interested in knowing how many dollars management has tied up in the major revenue-producing assets. Cost less depreciation is this measure of resources still to be utilized in the operations.
Other Assets	**Deferred charges** (prepaid expenses which are not expected to be used until some time further in the future than the next year, i.e., long-term prepaid expenses), **intangible assets** such as patents (the exclusive rights to use an invention), and any other noncurrent resource of the firm.	Cost—that portion of the cost which is still to be used in the future.	Assume that a firm purchased a patent for an invention for $17,000 and that the patent is expected to benefit the company for 17 years. At the end of the first year, the patent should be reported on the balance sheet at $16,000. ($17,000 cost less $1,000 expense for the first year of use).	Decision makers are interested in knowing how many dollars management has tied up in other noncurrent resources. Cost less amount utilized is a useful measure.

*In a few industries, the *operating cycle* is longer than a year. The operating cycle can be described as the process of using cash to produce or buy goods, selling the goods, and eventually converting the receivables back to cash again. In cases where the operating cycle is longer than a year, the firms use the operating cycle to determine if an asset or liability is current, instead of using the one-year rule. For example, assume a company with an operating cycle of 16 months has receivables that will be collected in 13 months from the balance sheet date. These receivables would be considered current because they will be collected during the next operating cycle. However, if a company's operating cycle is less than a year, the one-year rule is used.

HOW LIABILITIES ARE REPORTED ON THE BALANCE SHEET

| | CLASSIFICATION | | VALUATION | | |
liability classification	meaning of classification	liability valuation method generally used	meaning of valuation		decision reasons for generally accepted rules of classification and valuation
Current Liabilities	Creditors are a source of the firm's resources. Current liabilities are a measure of that portion of the firm's total assets in which short-term creditors have an interest or equity. Examples are: Salaries payable, Accounts payable, and Interest payable.	Amounts to be repaid to creditors in the next year or operating cycle.	The amount of current liabilities can be viewed in two ways: (1) as the amount to be repaid soon, and (2) as the amount of the firm's assets which has been raised through borrowing from short-term creditors.		Decision makers want to know how many dollars of resources will be needed to pay currently maturing debts in the next year and what part of the firm's assets has been acquired from short-term sources.
Long-term Liabilities	Long-term liabilities are a measure of that portion of the firm's total assets in which long-term creditors have an interest or equity. Long-term creditors are often a significant source of a company's resources.	Amounts of resources or benefits which the firm has received from long-term creditors.	Assume that a firm borrows $12,000 from a bank, and that the entire $12,000 plus all the interest due will be repaid all at once at the end of 6 years. If a balance sheet were prepared immediately after the loan, the long-term creditors' equity in the firm's assets (long-term liability) would amount to $12,000. Observe that this is a *different* amount than that to be eventually repaid at the end of 6 years.		Decision makers want to know what portion of the company's total assets was contributed by long-term creditors. Often detailed provisions of the long-term debt agreement are revealed to the decision maker on the balance sheet.

HOW CAPITAL IS REPORTED ON THE BALANCE SHEET

CLASSIFICATION		VALUATION		
capital classification	**meaning of classification**	**capital valuation method generally used**	**meaning of valuation**	**decision reasons for generally accepted rules of classification and valuation**
Proprietorship: Tim Mark, Capital	The single owner's total equity in the firm's assets.	Measured by the amounts of assets which the firm has received from the owner plus the assets generated by profit-making activities and kept in the firm.	Of all the assets of the firm, this is the amount that represents the owner's equity (Assets − Liabilities = Owner's equity). It is not the amount the owner could sell his equity in the firm for, but *it is the owner's share of the assets measured in the same way the assets were measured and reported on the balance sheet.*	Decision makers want to know what portion of the company's total assets were contributed by the owner, or were generated through earnings for the owner.
Partnership: Paul Tenny, Capital Stephen Wiggy, Capital	Same as proprietorship except equity divided among partners.	Same as proprietorship.	Same as proprietorship.	Decision makers want to know what portion of the company's total assets was contributed by each owner (partner) or was generated through earnings for each owner.
Corporation: Capital stock Retained earnings	Since a corporation ordinarily has many owners, the amounts contributed to the firm are reported in one account, Capital stock. The capital generated by the earnings process and still remaining in the firm is reported separately as **Retained earnings** and can be analyzed separately.	Same as proprietorship.	Same as proprietorship.	Decision makers want to know what portion of the company's total assets was contributed by the stockholders (owners) and what portion was generated through earnings for the benefit of all owners.

▪ *How is the accounting cycle related to the balance sheet?*

The valuation and classification concepts that you have studied in this unit are directly related to the accounting cycle and its procedures. How an asset or equity is recorded in the journal determines the classification and valuation scheme that will be used to report it on the balance sheet. For example, assume that a company buys office equipment and issues a note payable to the seller of the equipment. The company would debit the Office equipment account and credit the Notes payable account for the purchase price of the equipment, $1,250. The journal entry serves to *classify* the resource acquired by the company (Office equipment) for future reporting on the balance sheet. The journal entry also *classifies* the source of the asset, Notes payable, as a liability to be reported on the balance sheet. And, finally, the journal entry *values* an asset and liability at the cost of the equipment, and this value will be reported on the balance sheet.

A main point of this unit has been that the *needs of decision makers* are the determining factors in deciding how business transactions are entered into the accounts. You now should have a good grasp of this key idea. It lies behind much of what you will learn in the following units.

A FINAL NOTE   This unit has provided an overview of the classification and valuation concepts of the balance sheet. Many of the ideas presented will be examined in depth in later units. Examples are recording and reporting inventories, recording and reporting receivables, and recording and reporting marketable securities.

❯ NEW TERMS

account form The form of a balance sheet where assets are shown on the left half of the page, and the liabilities and capital are shown on the right half of the page. [p. 132]

classification A basic concept in accounting; refers to the process of accumulating and reporting information in useful categories (accounts). [p. 130]

current assets All those resources of the firm which are expected to be used in the regular daily operations in the firm during the next year. Traditionally includes five categories: (1) Cash, (2) Marketable securities, (3) Receivables, (4) Merchandise inventory, (5) Prepaid expenses. [p. 136]

current liabilities Debts that are to be repaid during the

next year (or during the next operating cycle, if that is longer than a year). [p. 139]

deferred charges Noncurrent assets; prepaid expenses which are not expected to be utilized until some time later than one year in the future. [p. 138]

fixed assets Another term for plant and equipment. [p. 138]

generally accepted accounting principles A group of concepts, ideas, and rules serving as a basis for preparing general-purpose financial statements. [p. 129]

general-purpose financial statements Accounting reports that are used by different groups of decision makers for different decisions; financial statements that contain common information needed for different decisions;

the balance sheet, the income statement, the statement of changes in financial position (funds statement). [p. 127]

intangible assets Assets which do not have the usual tangible (touchable) form; examples are patents, copyrights, and trademarks; reported on the balance sheet at the portion of the cost still to be utilized in the future. [p. 138]

long-term investments Stocks, bonds, land, and any other investments which the firm plans to own for a number of years. These investments do not represent the firm's main source of revenue; reported on the balance sheet at cost. [p. 137]

long-term liabilities Debts of the firm which will be settled at a date farther in the future than next year; a major method of acquiring assets for the firm is through long-term borrowings. [p. 139]

marketable securities Stocks, bonds, and other investments expected to be converted to cash or otherwise used in current regular operations during the next year; reported on the balance sheet at lower of cost or market value. [p. 136]

merchandise inventory Goods which the firm has purchased and expects to sell to customers in the next year; reported on the balance sheet at lower of cost or market, where market means the replacement price at the balance sheet date. [p. 137]

operating cycle The process of using cash to produce or buy goods, selling the goods, and eventually converting the receivables back to cash again. [p. 138]

plant and equipment Land, buildings, and other resources which are currently being used to produce the firm's main revenues; reported on the balance sheet at that portion of the cost still to be utilized in the future. [p. 138]

prepaid expenses A class of assets; any expense which has been paid for in advance and which is expected to be utilized in operating the firm during the next year; reported (valued) on the balance sheet at that portion of the cost still to be utilized in the future. [p. 137]

report form The form of a balance sheet where assets, liabilities, and capital items are arranged vertically on the page—with assets coming first followed by liabilities and capital below. [p. 132]

retained earnings Capital generated by the earnings process and which still remains in the firm; a capital account in a corporation. [p. 140]

special-purpose reports Information prepared for special decisions; the reports do not contain common information for a variety of decisions. [p. 127]

valuation A basic concept in accounting; refers to the process of placing a dollar amount (value) on the assets and equities of a firm. There is no one concept of value that is useful for all decisions. [p. 129]

> **ASSIGNMENT MATERIAL**

QUESTIONS

Q9-1. In your own words, state the purpose of accounting. Limit your answer to two or three sentences.

Q9-2. What is meant by "common information"?

Q9-3. What are generally accepted accounting principles?

Q9-4. Explain how making a journal entry involves both classification and valuation.

Q9-5. Explain how making a journal entry is related to the financial statements.

Q9-6. Describe the common information which the balance sheet presents.

Q9-7. List the five types of accounts usually classified on the balance sheet as current assets.

Q9-8. For each of the five types of current assets, indicate what valuation method is used on the balance sheet.

Q9-9. Land might be shown either as plant and equipment or as a long-term investment on the balance sheet. What factor determines where it is shown?

Q9-10. Why are long-term investments reported at their cost on the balance sheet rather than at what they are "worth"?

Q9-11. What is a deferred charge? Explain how deferred charges are valued on the balance sheet.

Q9-12. Distinguish between current liabilities and long-term liabilities.

Q9-13. How do the capital sections of balance sheets of proprietorships, partnerships, and corporations differ?

EXERCISES

E9-1. Match the terms below with the descriptions that follow.

A net earnings summary   D general-purpose
B classification   financial statements
C generally accepted   E special-purpose reports
   accounting principles   F valuation

1. information prepared for a particular decision, not containing common information for a variety of decisions
2. a basic concept in accounting, referring to the process of accumulating and reporting information in useful categories (accounts)
3. a basic concept in accounting, referring to the process of placing a dollar amount on the assets and equities of a firm
4. a group of concepts, ideas, and rules serving as a basis for preparing general-purpose financial statements
5. accounting reports which are utilized by different groups of decision makers for different decisions
6. serves to temporarily accumulate the balances of the revenue and expense accounts in the closing process

E9-2. Indicate to which balance sheet classification each of the following descriptions relates.

a. Capital which was generated by the earnings process and which still remains in the firm; a capital account in a corporation.
b. All those resources of the firm which are expected to be used in the regular daily operations of the firm during the next year. Traditionally includes five categories: (1) Cash, (2) Marketable securities, (3) Receivables, (4) Merchandise inventory, (5) Prepaid expenses.
c. Noncurrent assets; prepaid expenses which are not expected to be utilized until some time later than one year in the future.
d. Assets which do not have the usual tangible form; examples are: patents, copyrights, and trademarks; reported on the balance sheet at that portion of the cost which is still to be utilized in the future.
e. Goods which the firm has purchased and expects to sell to customers in the next year; reported on the balance sheet at lower of cost or market, where market means the replacement price at the balance sheet date.
f. Stocks, bonds, land, and any other investments which the firm plans to own for a number of years. These investments do not represent the firm's main source of revenue; reported on the balance sheet at cost.
g. Land, buildings, and other resources which are currently being used to produce the firm's main revenues; reported on the balance sheet at that portion of the cost which is still to be utilized in the future.
h. A class of assets; any expense which has been paid for in advance and which is expected to be utilized in operating the firm during the next year; reported (valued) on the balance sheet at that portion of the cost which is still to be utilized in the future.

i. Stocks, bonds, and other investments expected to be converted to cash or otherwise used in current regular operations during the next year; reported on the balance sheet at lower of cost or market value.

j. Debts of the firm which will be settled at a date further in the future than next year.

E9-3. Choose the best response for each of the following multiple-choice questions.

1. The function of accounting in the business decision process is:
   a. To report all business transactions.
   b. To serve lenders (creditors) primarily.
   c. To provide information to decision makers to aid them in choosing those alternative courses of action most likely to accomplish their goals.
   d. To provide information to decision makers to guarantee that the correct course of action will be chosen.

2. In serving the needs of society, accounting systems produce two *fundamental* kinds of reports:
   a. Income statements and statements of changes in financial position.
   b. General-purpose financial statements and special-purpose reports.
   c. Income statements and balance sheets.
   d. General-purpose financial statements and balance sheets.

3. Generally accepted accounting principles provide the foundations for preparing:
   a. Management's special-purpose reports.
   b. The income statement only.
   c. Both the income statement and the balance sheet.
   d. The trial balance.

4. The statement of changes in financial position provides information about:
   a. *Changes* in a firm's resources during a period of time.
   b. The firm's earnings.
   c. The firm's resources and equities at a point in time.
   d. The owner's capital.

5. The term *classification* refers to:
   a. The process of placing a dollar amount on the assets and equities of a firm.
   b. A group of concepts, ideas, and rules serving as a basis for preparing general-purpose financial statements.
   c. The process of accumulating and reporting information in useful categories.
   d. Special-purpose report preparation.

6. The term *valuation* refers to:
   a. The process of placing a dollar amount on the assets and equities of a firm.
   b. A group of concepts, ideas, and rules serving as a basis for preparing general-purpose financial statements.
   c. The process of accumulating and reporting information in useful categories.
   d. Special-purpose report preparation.

PROBLEMS (GROUP A)

P9-1. *Preparation of balance sheet, partnership.* The following accounts and balances appeared in the *balance sheet* columns of the work sheet of the partnership, Timmico and Sons, at December 31, 1978.

Paul Timmico, Capital	$100,000
Cash	2,000
Stephen Timmico, Capital	105,000

Marketable securities	4,000
Notes payable (due in 4 years)	31,000
Accounts receivable	3,000
Expenses payable	8,000
Merchandise inventory	110,000
Accounts payable	6,000
Notes payable (due in 3 months)	5,000
Prepaid expenses	2,000
Patents and copyrights	11,000
Investments in stocks	55,000
Deferred charges	2,000
Land (on which the store is located)	40,000
Land (held for future use)	5,000
Buildings	50,000
Accumulated depreciation—Buildings	35,000
Store equipment	10,000
Accumulated depreciation—Store equipment	4,000

REQUIRED:

a. Prepare a balance sheet in good form.

b. For each of the accounts, indicate whether the usual balance would be a debit or a credit.

P9-2. *Preparation of balance sheet, corporation.* The following accounts and balances appeared in the *balance sheet* columns of the work sheet of Wiggico Corporation at December 31, 1978.

Retained earnings	$ 65,000
Cash	10,000
Marketable securities	55,000
Capital stock	170,000
Accounts receivable	18,000
Notes payable (due in 10 years)	167,000
Notes receivable (to be collected in 4 months)	4,000
Notes payable (due in 6 months)	12,000
Accounts payable	10,000
Expenses payable	10,000
Inventories	12,000
Intangible assets	14,000
Prepaid expenses	3,000
Deferred charges	1,000
Land held for future use	147,000
Land (on which the buildings are located)	10,000
Buildings	110,000
Accumulated depreciation—Buildings	10,000
Equipment	71,000
Accumulated depreciation—Equipment	11,000

REQUIRED:

a. Prepare a balance sheet in good form.

b. For each of the accounts, indicate whether the usual balance would be a debit or a credit.

*P9-3. *Preparation of financial statements.* The following accounts and balances appeared in the *adjusted trial balance* columns of the work sheet of Stephen Wivvins Company at the end of the first year's operations, December 31, 1978.

Stephen Wivvins, Capital	$196,000
Stephen Wivvins, Withdrawals	15,000
Service revenue	60,000
Cash	2,000
Marketable securities	4,000
Notes payable (due in 4 years)	31,000
Depreciation expense—Buildings	10,000
Insurance expense	5,000
Accounts receivable	3,000
Expenses payable	8,000
Merchandise inventory	110,000
Miscellaneous expense	8,000
Interest expense	2,000
Salary expense	50,000
Depreciation expense—Equipment	1,000
Rent revenue	40,000
Accounts payable	6,000
Notes payable (due in 3 months)	5,000
Prepaid expenses	2,000
Patents and copyrights	11,000
Investments in stocks	55,000
Deferred charges	2,000
Land (on which store is located)	40,000
Land (held for future use)	5,000
Buildings	50,000
Accumulated depreciation—Buildings	35,000
Equipment	10,000
Accumulated depreciation—Equipment	4,000

REQUIRED:

a. Prepare an income statement for the year in good form.
b. Prepare a statement of owner's capital in good form.
c. Prepare a balance sheet in good form. Be sure to use the ending capital balance on the balance sheet.

**PROBLEMS
(GROUP B)**

P9-4. *Preparation of balance sheet, partnership.* The following is a list of accounts appearing on the balance sheet of Devon Brandy Co., a partnership:

B. Devon, Capital	$ 70,000
D. Brandy, Capital	30,000
L. Jones, Capital	72,000
Cash	40,000
Land	100,000
Buildings	214,000
Marketable securities	34,000
Investments in stocks and bonds	60,000
Accumulated depreciation—Buildings	100,000

Accounts receivable	20,000
Notes payable (due in 3 years)	70,000
Notes payable (due in 90 days)	10,000
Deferred charges	15,000
Merchandise inventory	31,000
Supplies	3,000
Patents	11,000
Prepaid insurance	4,000
Expenses payable	8,000
Accounts payable	12,000

All the account balances in the list are December 31, 1978 (ending), balances except the three capital accounts, which are January 1, 1978 (beginning), balances. The partnership produced net earnings totaling $300,000 during 1978. Each partner shares equally in the earnings. Personal withdrawals during 1978 were:

Devon	$70,000
Brandy	30,000
Jones	40,000

REQUIRED: Prepare a balance sheet for the partnership at December 31, 1978. You will have to compute each partner's ending capital balance from the data given: beginning capital balance plus share of net earnings, less withdrawals, equals ending capital balance.

P9-5. *Preparation of balance sheet, corporation.* The following accounts and balances appeared on the December 31, 1978, balance sheet of Intacc, Inc.

Accumulated depreciation—Equipment	$ 22,000
Accumulated depreciation—Buildings	21,000
Land (on which the buildings are located)	20,000
Deferred charges	1,000
Intangible assets	25,000
Expenses payable (taxes and interest)	21,000
Notes payable (due September 1, 1979)	15,000
Notes payable (due October 15, 1984)	150,000
Capital stock	200,000
Cash	25,000
Retained earnings	283,000
Marketable securities	100,000
Accounts receivable	18,000
Notes receivable (due March 1, 1979)	8,000
Accounts payable	15,000
Inventories	24,000
Prepaid insurance	5,000
Office supplies	1,000
Land held as an investment	150,000
Buildings	200,000
Equipment	150,000

REQUIRED:

a. Prepare a balance sheet in good form.

b. For each of the accounts, indicate whether the usual balance would be a debit or a credit.

*P9-6. *Preparation of financial statements.* The accounts in the *adjusted* trial balance of West Indies Company, a proprietorship, at the end of the first year's operations, December 31, 1978, is shown below:

Walter Montserrat, Withdrawals	$ 31,000
Cash	4,000
Notes payable (due December 1, 1982)	60,000
Insurance expense	6,000
Expenses payable	15,000
Miscellaneous expense	16,000
Salary expense	90,000
Accounts payable	10,000
Prepaid rent	4,000
Long-term investments in stocks	100,000
Land (on which the store is located)	80,000
Buildings	100,000
Equipment	30,000
Accumulated depreciation—Equipment	9,000
Accumulated depreciation—Buildings	65,000
Long-term investment in land	12,000
Deferred charges (long-term prepaid expenses)	5,000
Patents and other intangibles	25,000
Notes payable, due April 1, 1979	11,000
Rent revenue	75,000
Depreciation expense—Equipment	3,000
Interest expense	5,000
Merchandise inventory	200,000
Accounts receivable	6,000
Depreciation expense—Buildings	20,000
Marketable securities	5,000
Service revenue	100,000
Walter Montserrat, Capital	397,000

REQUIRED:

a. Prepare an income statement for the year in good form.

b. Prepare a statement of owner's capital in good form.

c. Prepare a balance sheet in good form.

THE PURPOSE AND STRUCTURE OF THE INCOME STATEMENT

➤ OBJECTIVE

The income statement is another of the most useful general-purpose financial statements that decision makers have. This unit will show you how the income statement, through the use of generally accepted classification and valuation concepts, provides information that directly helps its readers to accomplish their goals.

➤ APPROACH TO ATTAINING THE OBJECTIVE

As you study the income statement and its classification and valuation concepts, give particular attention to these three questions, which the text following answers:

- *What common information about earnings is needed by top management, investors, creditors, employees, and other decision makers?*
- *How is common information about earnings communicated by the income statement?*
- *Why are revenues and expenses reported the way they are?*

COMMON INFORMATION NEEDED

Each of the major groups of decision makers is interested in predicting something about the business firm. The investor, for example, must predict the company's future value if he is to make a good decision about whether to invest in the firm. A firm which tends to continuously make profits and accomplish its other goals tends to become more and more valuable. The investor, therefore, is quite interested in information about the earnings of the firm as a basis for predicting future activities of the company.

- *What common information about earnings is needed by top management, investors, creditors, employees, and other decision makers?*

Creditors must predict whether the company will be able to repay its loans. The profitable firm usually tends to be able to repay its debts, while the unprofitable firm sometimes does not have the ability to meet its obligations. Accordingly, creditors are quite interested in information about the earnings of the company to which they are considering lending money.

Employees and labor unions also are interested in earnings information about their company. The company's ability to meet its responsibilities to employees is in some measure tied to the company's ability to make profits. In summary, just about every group of decision makers, including the management of a firm, needs information about the earnings of the firm. This vital information is provided by the income statement which is prepared according to generally accepted accounting principles.

AN OVERVIEW OF THE INCOME STATEMENT

Shown below and on the next page are two examples of modern income statements. As you review the statements, observe the classifications of information presented.

EXAMPLE OF A PROPRIETORSHIP'S OR PARTNERSHIP'S INCOME STATEMENT

Tim Mark Company
INCOME STATEMENT
For the Year Ended December 31, 1978

- *How is common information about earnings communicated by the income statement?*

revenues

Sales of merchandise	$100,000	
Rent revenues	6,000	
Service revenues	26,000	
Total revenues		$132,000

expenses

Cost of merchandise sold	$ 60,000	
Selling expenses	18,000	
General and administrative expenses	4,000	
Interest expense	5,000	
Total expenses		$ 87,000
net earnings		$ 45,000

EXAMPLE OF A CORPORATION'S INCOME STATEMENT

ABC Corporation
INCOME STATEMENT
For the Year Ended December 31, 1978

revenues

Sales	$200,000	
Other revenues	100,000	
Total revenues		$300,000

expenses

Cost of goods sold	$120,000	
Selling expenses	40,000	
General and administrative expenses	30,000	
Interest expense	2,000	
Income taxes expense	50,000	
Total expenses		242,000

net earnings before extraordinary items $ 58,000

extraordinary gains and losses

Loss from storm	(6,000)

net earnings $ 52,000

earnings information per share of common stock[a]

Net earnings before extraordinary items	$2.90
Loss from storm	(.30)
Net earnings	$2.60

[a] 20,000 shares of common stock were outstanding during the entire year.

REVENUE CLASSIFICATION AND VALUATION

The first income statement illustrated could be that of either a proprietorship or a partnership. Whether there is one owner (proprietorship) or several (partnership), the earnings-reporting process would be the same. In a partnership, after the earnings are measured, they may be divided (allocated) among the partners according to a prearranged agreement.

■ *Why are revenues and expenses reported the way they are?*

You have already studied about revenues earned by performing a service. On the proprietorship/partnership statement illustrated, another type of revenue is shown, *Sales of merchandise.* This represents the total prices charged by the firm for merchandise (goods) sold to its customers during the period. For example, if the firm sold merchandise, which it had previously bought for $90, to customers for $110, then the revenue, *Sales of merchandise,* would be reported at $110, the total price charged. The revenue section of the income statement is designed to report *all* revenues of the firm, whether they are service revenues or revenues from sales of goods.

EXPENSE CLASSIFICATION AND VALUATION

The expense section of the income statement is designed to report all those costs (sacrifices) incurred during the period which helped (directly or indirectly) to produce revenues for the firm. The expense, **Cost of merchandise**

sold, reports the sacrifice the firm made in order to acquire the merchandise (goods) it sold to customers during the period. For example, if the firm sold merchandise, which it had previously bought for $90, to customers for $110, then the expense, Cost of merchandise sold, would be reported at $90, the cost of the goods. Accounting for transactions of merchandising firms is discussed in detail in subsequent chapters.

A company can use any categories of revenues and expenses which will clearly report the major sources of revenue earned by the firm and the major categories of sacrifices (expenses) made to produce the revenue. Two useful, common categories of expenses are (1) **Selling expenses,** and (2) **General and administrative expenses.** Selling expenses, incurred to help acquire customers and deliver the goods to them, include advertising costs, salesmen's expenses, and delivery costs. General and administrative expenses include such costs as management salaries and office expenses.

SPECIAL PROBLEMS OF CORPORATIONS

Now compare the corporation's income statement with that of the unincorporated business you just examined. Large corporations often have much more complex activities than proprietorships and partnerships; therefore, their income statements tend to differ. The major differences are in these areas:

1. Reporting income taxes.
2. Reporting extraordinary gains and losses.
3. Reporting per-share earnings information.
4. Reporting salaries of owners and managers.

Reporting income taxes A corporation is required by law to prepare an income tax return and to pay taxes when appropriate. This income tax, like any other expense, is reported on the income statement of a corporation. See our example, where **income taxes expense** is included under the expenses of ABC Corporation.

A proprietorship and partnership, on the other hand, are *not* required to pay income taxes under the laws. Instead, the earnings of these two forms of business must be reported on the owners' personal individual tax returns, even if the earnings are not taken out of the business by the owner or partners. Therefore, income tax expense would not appear on the income statements of proprietorships and partnerships.

Reporting extraordinary gains and losses Gains and losses which are not of a regular and recurring nature *and* which also do not deal with the ordinary business operations are reported in a separate section of a corporation's income statement.[1] See the example on ABC Corporation's income statement. This procedure permits the statement user to observe the earnings produced from regular business operations and to make his judgments about the firm on this basis. Then **extraordinary items** can be taken into consideration. Examples of extraordinary gains and losses are casualty losses such as major earthquakes and hurricanes where assets of the firm are damaged or lost.

Reporting per-share earnings information Corporations usually have many owners. Each owner is called a stockholder, and he is issued a stock certificate to show his number of shares of ownership (common stock) in the firm. Because each investor-owner might own a different number of shares, it becomes convenient to report information about the firm on an individual share basis.

In ABC Corporation's income statement, **per-share earnings information** is reported at the bottom of the statement. During the reported period, ABC Corporation had 20,000 shares of common stock ownership outstanding. The per-share data are:

$$\frac{\text{Per-share net earnings}}{\text{before extraordinary items}} = \frac{\$58,000}{20,000} = \$2.90$$

$$\frac{\text{Per-share loss from}}{\text{extraordinary item}} = \frac{(\$\ 6,000)}{20,000} = (\$\ .30)$$

$$\text{Per-share net earnings} = \frac{\$52,000}{20,000} = \$2.60$$

For analysis purposes, the investor can relate the price he would have to pay for a share of stock to the earnings per share of stock which the firm was able to produce during a period. In summary, three key figures on the income statement are divided by the *average number of shares of common stock outstanding during the period* to calculate per-share figures.

Reporting salaries of owners and managers When a stockholder of a corporation also is employed by the firm, any salary he is paid, like that of other employees, is reported as salary expense on the income statement.

In the case of a proprietorship or partnership, the owners usually work for the organization. When the owners are paid money, it sometimes becomes difficult to determine if the payment represents salary for services rendered to the firm or if the payment is a distribution of earnings already made (withdrawals). The usual practice followed, so that one firm can be

---

[1] Opinion 30 of the Accounting Principles Board, *Reporting the Results of Operations,* 1973, sets forth the criteria for reporting and identifying extraordinary gains and losses.

compared to another, is to treat all payments to owners as withdrawals instead of as expenses. In line with this, salaries of owners generally would not appear on the income statements of proprietorships and partnerships.

❯ NEW TERMS

cost of merchandise sold An expense, representing the cost (sacrifice) the firm made in order to acquire the merchandise it sold to customers during the period; also called cost of goods sold. [p. 151]

extraordinary items A special category of gains and losses appearing on income statements of corporations; gains or losses which are not of a regular and recurring nature and which do not deal with the ordinary business operations. [p. 153]

general and administrative expenses Costs (sacrifices) incurred in the operation and general administration of the firm; include such expenses as management salaries and office expenses. [p. 152]

income taxes expense The sacrifice or cost incurred by a corporation for federal, state, or local taxes on earnings; applies to corporate form of organization only, since proprietorships and partnerships—as firms—are not subject to income taxes. [p. 152]

per-share earnings data Information from the corporation income statement which has been converted to a per-share basis; net earnings or other figures divided by the average number of shares of common stock which was outstanding during the period. [p. 153]

selling expenses Costs (sacrifices) incurred to help acquire customers and deliver the goods to them; include such expenses as advertising and delivery costs. [p. 152]

❯ ASSIGNMENT MATERIAL

QUESTIONS

Q10-1. What are the differences in reporting income taxes in the three forms of business organizations?

Q10-2. What is an extraordinary gain or loss? How are these items shown on income statements?

Q10-3. What are the three per-share earnings figures commonly shown on income statements of corporations? How is each computed?

Q10-4. Are salaries of owners normally shown on the income statements of partnerships and proprietorships? Explain.

Q10-5. The income statement of App Company showed Income taxes expense for the year amounting to $34,000. From this information, can it be determined what the *form* of the organization is for the firm? Explain.

Q10-6. What is the usual practice for reporting payments to owners of proprietorships and partnerships?

EXERCISES

E10-1. The following information is known about Ap-ima Corporation for the year ended December 31, 1978:

Total revenues from regular operations	75,000
Total expenses from regular operations	49,000
Extraordinary gain	15,000
Number of shares of common stock outstanding during the year	10,000

Compute the three per-share earnings figures that are important to the readers of income statements.

E10-2. Assume that you are a partner in ABC Company, a partnership. During the year, the company earned $10,000, of which your share amounted to $5,000. During the year you did not withdraw any funds for personal use (no withdrawals). Does this mean that your share of the partnership earnings need not be reported on your individual income tax return? Explain.

E10-3. Assume that the net earnings per share for a corporation for the year amounted to $3.00. The extraordinary gain per share was $.10, and the per-share net earnings before extraordinary items was $2.90. During the year there were 21,500 shares of common stock outstanding. The total expenses reported on the income statement amounted to $90,000.
a. Compute the amount of the *net earnings*.
b. Compute the *total revenues*.

E10-4. A company purchased merchandise for $21,500 during the period. The same merchandise was sold a few days later (in the same year) for $31,500 cash.
a. How would the $21,500 be reported on the income statement for the year?
b. How would the $31,500 be reported on the income statement for the year?

PROBLEMS (GROUP A)

P10-1. *Preparation of corporation income statement.* From the following information on Georgi Corporation's adjusted trial balance, prepare an income statement for the year in good form. The firm had 30,000 shares of common stock outstanding during the period.

Georgi Corporation
ADJUSTED TRIAL BALANCE
December 31, 1978

Cash	9,000	
Marketable securities	6,000	
Accounts receivable	24,000	
Notes receivable	20,000	
Merchandise inventory	90,000	
Prepaid insurance	2,000	
Long-term investments	18,000	
Equipment	35,000	
Intangible assets	3,000	
Accounts payable		10,000
Notes payable		60,000
Common stock		62,000
Retained earnings		50,000
Sales of merchandise		120,000
Service revenue		60,000
Extraordinary storm damage loss	10,000	
Cost of goods sold	70,000	
Selling expenses	20,000	
General and administrative expenses	5,000	
Income tax expense	50,000	
	362,000	362,000

P10-2. *Relationships among elements of corporation financial statements.* The accounts and balances (after adjustments) of Ivan Brown Corporation at the end of 1978 are presented below:

Cash	6,000
Short-term investments	18,000
Accounts receivable	25,000
Short-term notes receivable	40,000
Inventories	123,000
Prepaid insurance	8,000
Store supplies	1,000
Investments in stocks	95,000
Investments in land	200,000
Store equipment	100,000
Accumulated depreciation—Store equipment	40,000
Office equipment	20,000
Accumulated depreciation—Office equipment	11,000
Patents	8,000
Other intangible assets	20,000
Accounts payable	31,000
Interest payable	11,000
Notes payable—Short term	100,000
Long-term notes payable	20,000
Capital stock, 30,000 shares outstanding during 1978	90,000
Retained earnings	166,000
Sales	400,000
Service revenue	80,000
Rent revenue	50,000
Cost of goods sold	119,000
Selling expenses	24,000
General expenses	30,000
Interest expense	15,000
Income taxes expense	150,000
Extraordinary gain	3,000

REQUIRED:

a. Prepare an adjusted trial balance at December 31, 1978, to prove the equality of debits and credits.

b. Showing all computations, compute the following:
   (1) Total revenues.
   (2) Net earnings before extraordinary items.
   (3) The three *per-share* figures appearing on the income statement.
   (4) Total assets at December 31, 1978.
   (5) Total liabilities at December 31, 1978.

P10-3. *Classification concepts.* For each of the accounts listed in the table on pages 158–159, indicate the financial statement on which it would appear and the section of the financial statement, by placing check marks in the appropriate boxes.

PROBLEMS (GROUP B)

P10-4. *Preparation of corporation income statement.* The adjusted trial balance of Willie Bee Corporation is presented as follows:

Willie Bee Corporation
ADJUSTED TRIAL BALANCE
December 31, 1978

Cash	15,000	
Short-term investments	10,000	
Accounts receivable	20,000	
Notes receivable (due January 14, 1979)	31,000	
Merchandise inventory	100,000	
Prepaid insurance expense	3,000	
Long-term investments	25,000	
Equipment	65,000	
Accumulated depreciation—Equipment		12,000
Copyrights	3,000	
Accounts payable		50,000
Common stock (20,000 shares outstanding during year)		80,000
Retained earnings		56,000
Sales of merchandise		203,000
Service revenues		80,000
Extraordinary loss	7,000	
Cost of goods sold	100,000	
Selling expenses	30,000	
General and administrative expenses	11,000	
Interest expense	1,000	
Income taxes expense	60,000	
	481,000	481,000

REQUIRED: Prepare an income statement for the corporation for 1978, similar to the one presented in the unit.

P10-5. *Relationships among elements of corporation financial statements.* The accounts and their adjusted balances of Victoria Company at December 31, 1978, are as follows and on the top of page 160:

Income tax expense	70,000
General expenses	12,000
Rent revenue	25,000
Service revenue	35,000
Accumulated depreciation—Office equipment	10,000
Notes receivable, due June 12, 1979	20,000
Marketable securities	15,000
Interest payable	5,000
Selling expenses	10,000
Cost of goods sold	50,000
Long-term investments (stocks)	51,000
Cash	5,000
Interest expense	9,000
Extraordinary loss	6,000
Accounts receivable	15,000
Office equipment	20,000
Notes payable, due January 1, 1990	15,000
Merchandise inventory	75,000
Intangible assets	17,000
Accounts payable	15,000

	FINANCIAL STATEMENT		SECTION									
	balance sheet	income statement	current assets	long-term investments	plant and equipment	other assets	current liabilities	long-term liabilities	capital	revenues	expenses	extra-ordinary items
Example: Cash	✓		✓									
1. Copyrights												
2. Notes payable, due in 4 months												
3. Sales of merchandise												
4. Advertising expense												
5. Marketable securities												
6. Salesmen's expenses												
7. Investment in land												
8. Expenses payable												
9. Capital stock												
10. Notes receivable, due in 16 months												
11. Interest payable												
12. Delivery expense												
13. Income taxes expense												
14. Deferred charges												

15. Office supplies												
16. Accounts payable												
17. Retained earnings												
18. Rent revenue												
19. Office salaries expense												
20. Notes receivable, due in 11 months												
21. Loss from storm damage												
22. Investment in stocks												
23. Interest expense												
24. Patents												
25. Cost of goods sold												
26. Accounts receivable												
27. Notes payable, due in 2 years												
28. Inventory												
29. Store supplies												
30. Service revenue												
31. Prepaid insurance												

Capital stock, 20,000 shares outstanding during 1978	80,000
Sales	218,000
Notes payable, short term	50,000
Accumulated depreciation—Store equipment	15,000
Store equipment	50,000
Long-term land investments	100,000
Prepaid insurance	5,000
Store supplies	1,000
Retained earnings	63,000

REQUIRED:

a. Prepare an adjusted trial balance at December 31, 1978, to prove the equality of debits and credits.

b. Showing all computations, compute the following:
   (1) Total revenues.
   (2) Net earnings before extraordinary items.
   (3) The three *per-share* figures appearing on the income statement.
   (4) Total assets at December 31, 1978.
   (5) Total liabilities at December 31, 1978.

P10-6. *Preparation of corporation income statement.* From the following information taken from the adjusted trial balance of Ima Corporation, prepare an income statement in good form for the year ended December 31, 1978.

Miscellaneous expense	3,000
Cash	15,000
Accounts receivable	21,000
Insurance expense	2,000
Supplies	4,000
Supplies expense	8,000
Prepaid insurance	1,000
Salaries expense	54,000
Cost of goods sold	100,000
Long-term investments	35,000
Common stock	132,000
Retained earnings	17,000
Sales of merchandise	200,000
Service revenue	9,000
Depreciation expense—Equipment	10,000
Equipment	90,000
Accumulated depreciation—Equipment	20,000
Intangible assets—Patents	41,000
Deferred charges	6,000
Accounts payable	35,000
Notes payable, due in 7 years	20,000
Loss from hurricane damage (extraordinary)	17,000
Income tax expense	9,000
Selling expenses	4,000
Marketable securities	13,000

There were 1,320 shares of common stock outstanding during the year. Round your per-share computations to the nearest cent.

P10-7. *Cumulative review problem.* Below are shown a chart of accounts, a list of business transactions for the first month of operations of Frank's Painting Service Co., and information for adjustments.

CHART OF ACCOUNTS

101   Cash
102   Painting supplies
103   Accounts receivable
109   Painting equipment
110   Accumulated depreciation—Painting equipment
201   Accounts payable
202   Interest payable
203   Notes payable
301   Frank Duncan, Capital
302   Frank Duncan, Withdrawals
401   Painting revenue
501   Salaries expense
502   Advertising expense
503   Depreciation expense—Painting equipment
504   Miscellaneous expense
505   Interest expense
506   Painting supplies expense
550   Net earnings summary

Business transactions for December, 1978:

Dec. 3   Frank Duncan invested $44,000 in the business.
      6   Purchased painting supplies and painting equipment from Bowers Company as follows:

          Painting supplies $16,000
          Painting equipment   12,000

          Paid $2,000 cash down on these items and signed a 1-year, 8% note for $26,000.
      8   Rendered services to customers as follows:

          Painting services rendered for cash $25,000
          Painting services rendered on credit   41,000

     10   Paid salaries of employees, $12,000 cash.
     16   Collected $35,000 cash of the amount owed to us from the December 8 customers. The remaining $6,000 will be collected next month.
     20   Paid miscellaneous expenses, $1,500.
     21   Mr. Duncan withdrew $4,000 cash for personal use.
     24   Purchased painting supplies on credit from Harriett Company, $6,500.
     28   Paid advertising expenses, $3,100.
     29   Rendered painting services for cash, $2,500.
     30   Paid salaries of employees, $32,000 cash.
     31   Paid miscellaneous expenses, $450 cash.
     31   Paid advertising expenses, $3,000 cash

Information about adjusting entries:
a. Unpaid interest on the note payable for December amounts to $173.
b. The painting equipment is expected to have a useful life of 10 years. Record 1 month's depreciation for December.
c. Painting supplies that were used up during December amount to $10,000.

REQUIRED:

a. Record the business transactions in general journal form.
b. Set up ledger accounts for each item in the chart of accounts.
c. Post the business transactions to the ledger accounts. Enter all posting references and compute the balance of each account.
d. Prepare a work sheet for the month of December.
e. Prepare an income statement, a statement of owner's capital, and a balance sheet from the work sheet.
f. Using the work sheet as a basis, record the adjusting entries in the general journal.
g. Post the adjusting entries to the ledger accounts.
h. Record closing entries in general journal form.
i. Post the closing entries to the ledger accounts.
j. Prepare a post-closing trial balance.

P10-8. *Cumulative review problem.* Refer to the example of a *corporation's* income statement (ABC Corporation) in the first part of this unit. Assume that the statement included several errors and omissions as follows:

a. The bookkeeper forgot to record depreciation on the delivery equipment amounting to $8,000 for the year. This expense is considered a Selling expense.
b. You discover that in early January, 1978, the corporation had issued another 5,000 shares of capital stock for cash investments by stockholders. Therefore, 25,000 shares were outstanding during 1978, instead of 20,000.
c. It is determined that the corporation had charged customers $210,000 during the year for merchandise it sold to them. The merchandise had cost the company $120,000. Only $200,000 was collected in cash during 1978.
d. Store supplies that had cost $7,000 were discovered to be in the warehouse. These supplies had been overlooked at December 31, 1978, when the supplies on hand were counted in preparing the adjustment for store supplies used (part of Selling expense). The adjusting entry actually was recorded as: debit Selling expense $19,000, credit Store supplies, $19,000.

REQUIRED: Prepare a corrected income statement for ABC Corporation for the year ended December 31, 1978.

PART TWO
MERCHANDISING
OPERATIONS

chapter 5

merchandising operations: recording

SPECIAL JOURNALS AND LEDGERS; SALES AND CASH RECEIPTS

> **OBJECTIVE**

You are now familiar with accounts, the debit and credit procedures, ledgers, journals, work sheets, financial statements, and the decision-making process in general. The units in Part Two (three chapters) will deal with the information-generating process and the uses of the information in a *merchandising* business. The kind of accounting system used to teach you this next phase will be an *accounting system that utilizes special journals and ledgers.*

The specific objective of this unit is to describe the types of transactions of a merchandising company and to illustrate the use of special journals and ledgers for recording cash receipts and sales of merchandise.

> **APPROACH TO ATTAINING THE OBJECTIVE**

As you study about the business transactions of a merchandising firm and about a manual accounting system using special journals and ledgers, focus your attention on these eight questions, which the text following answers:

- *What transactions are associated with a merchandising firm?*
- *Why are special journals and ledgers useful in small- and medium-size merchandising firms?*
- *What are the several elements of a manual accounting system using special journals and ledgers?*
- *What methods does a corporation use to acquire resources?*
- *How is the cash receipts journal used to record transactions?*
- *How is the sale of merchandise recorded?*
- *How is the collection of receivables recorded?*
- *How are postings made from special journals?*

Here, as a review, is a summary of the business transactions of business organizations which you studied in Unit 1.

1. Acquiring assets from owners (the owners invest in the firm).
2. Acquiring assets from creditors (the firm borrows money).
3. Investing resources in the kinds of assets needed to produce services or goods (the firm acquires production-type assets).
4. Using the resources to produce the product or service (the production-type assets are used).
5. Selling the goods or services of the firm (the firm exchanges its product or service for cash-type assets).
6. Returning assets to the creditors (the creditors are paid).
7. Returning assets to the owners (owners receive payment from the firm).

These are the kinds of transactions that any firm probably would have during a period of time. Now, within this context, let's look at some specific transactions of a merchandising firm, a firm that buys goods from suppliers and resells these goods to customers.

**THE COMMON
REPETITIVE-TYPE
TRANSACTIONS IN
MERCHANDISING**

■ *What transactions
are associated with
a merchandising
firm?*

In a merchandising operation there are six general types of transactions that tend to happen again and again. In every operating period, there will usually be a large number of each of these six transactions. This calls for an accounting system that can process many similar transactions, and a system with special journals and ledgers can serve this purpose. In the following paragraphs we will identify and briefly discuss these six repetitive-type transactions.

Purchases of merchandise The ordinary merchandising firm buys goods from many different suppliers. Some of the purchases are for cash and some are on credit; that is, they are paid for later according to some credit agreement. Often the purchasing agreement provides that if the merchandise is paid for within a certain number of days after it is purchased, then a reduction in the amount paid will be allowed. This reduction is called a **cash discount** or, more specifically, a **purchase discount**. The agreement is called the *terms* of the sale. For example, terms of a sale might be stated as follows: 2/10, n/30 (referred to as "two, ten, net, thirty"). This means that a 2% discount will be allowed if the merchandise is paid for within 10 days of the sale, and that the net amount is due at the end of 30 days after the sale. "Net amount" here refers to the total purchase price without a discount.

When merchandise is purchased, a journal entry must be made which reflects that an asset (merchandise inventory or merchandise on hand) has been acquired. If cash is paid immediately, then the asset Cash is credited to reflect the reduction. If the merchandise is to be paid for later, then the Accounts payable account would be credited to reflect the liability.

Payments of cash A merchandising firm often makes many payments of cash each day. The journal used for recording cash disbursements (payments) must provide for convenient and efficient recording of the many accounts that must be debited. For example, when cash is paid for merchandise, then the merchandise inventory account (or some other designated account) must be debited. When an accounts payable is being paid, then the liability account must be debited.

One complicating factor is the situation where a cash discount is taken when previously purchased merchandise is paid for. For example, assume that a firm purchased $100 of merchandise according to terms 3/10, n/60. The merchandise is paid for within 10 days and a 3% discount is taken. So, only $97 has to be paid. The accounts payable account, however, reflects a credit balance of $100 for the merchandise. Obviously an adjustment is needed. In Unit 12 you will learn the details of how to record and report the acquisition of merchandise, the payment for the merchandise, and the taking of a cash discount. The purpose of our discussion here is simply to describe to you the nature of the transactions and to raise questions about them.

Sales of merchandise When a firm sells merchandise that it owns, a revenue is produced. The *revenue* is the total amount charged the customer for the goods. For example, if a firm sells for $200 merchandise for which it had paid $175, then the revenue amounts to $200. Also involved is an expense of $175, which is called *cost of goods sold* or *cost of merchandise sold.* The revenue account is often labeled *Sales of merchandise,* or just simply *Sales.* Some sales are made for cash, and some are made according to credit terms similar to the terms on purchases of merchandise we discussed above. When a firm lets its customers take cash discounts, the reduction in the amount collected is called a **sales discount.**

These elements of the sales activities have been identified:

1. Making the sale and reporting the revenue.
2. Recognizing and reporting that an expense, Cost of goods sold, is involved.
3. Reporting any cash discount (sales discount) that might have been allowed customers.

Collections of cash A journal must be provided that will conveniently and efficiently take care of recording the many collections of cash. One special problem we have already mentioned is the recording and reporting of collections of receivables from sales of merchandise when a cash discount (sales discount) is allowed.

Purchases returns and allowances Another type of repetitive transaction occurs when a firm is not satisfied with the quality or some other characteristic of the goods which it has purchased. If the supplier agrees, there can be a reduction in the price of the goods purchased. Often the goods are returned to the supplier as well. The account used to reflect such reductions in cost usually is called **Purchases returns and allowances.**

Sales returns and allowances In a situation similar to that described above, a firm might allow its dissatisfied customers to reduce the amount owed to the firm. The account used to reflect such reductions in the total selling price charged customers is usually called **Sales returns and allowances.**

In summary, there are six general types of repetitive transactions which merchandising firms incur. These transactions, which you should be able to identify and describe, are (1) purchases of merchandise, (2) payments of cash (including payments for merchandise after taking a purchase discount), (3) sales of merchandise, (4) collections of cash (including collections for merchandise sold after allowing customers to deduct a sales discount), (5) purchases returns and allowances, and (6) sales returns and allowances.

ADVANTAGES OF SPECIAL JOURNALS

■ Why are special journals and ledgers useful in small and medium-size merchandising firms?

In some small and in most medium-size merchandising organizations, the number of repetitive transactions is so great that the ordinary two-column journal and general ledger is not a satisfactory system. **Special journals** are used which have features that improve the efficiency of the bookkeeping work. Two important features of special journals are:

1. Individual columns of a journal can be reserved for one kind of transaction only. This permits posting the total of the column to the ledger one time rather than posting each individual transaction which might appear in the column.
2. Each journal can be reserved for *one* kind of transaction only, thus permitting more than one bookkeeper to work on the data processing at the same time.

ADVANTAGES OF SPECIAL LEDGERS

You are already familiar with the general ledger. When special journals are used, the general ledger is still used to process the transactions in the individual accounts. It may be desirable, however, to accumulate certain other information in addition to the usual general ledger information. Listed below are two books **(special ledgers)** that a company might have in addition to a general ledger:

1. *Accounts receivable subsidiary* ledger. The function of this ledger is to provide detailed records of the amounts *owed the firm* by *each* of its customers. The accounts receivable ledger is simply a detailed analysis of the information contained in the Accounts receivable account of the general ledger.

2. *Accounts payable subsidiary* ledger. This ledger provides detailed records of the amounts *owed by the firm* to *each* of its suppliers. The accounts payable ledger is simply a detailed analysis of the information contained in the Accounts payable account of the general ledger.

Special ledgers have the important advantage of accumulating detailed information that can supplement the information contained in the general ledger.

THE ELEMENTS OF ONE MANUAL ACCOUNTING SYSTEM

This section of the unit illustrates the organization of a common type of accounting system. This particular system uses five journals and three ledgers as follows:

JOURNALS

1. Sales Journal — This journal is used only for recording *sales of merchandise made on credit* (not for cash sales). *Accounts receivable* is always involved in this journal.

2. Purchases Journal — This journal is used only for recording *purchases of merchandise and other items made on credit* (not for cash purchases). *Accounts payable* is always involved in this journal.

3. Cash Receipts Journal — This journal is used for recording *all collections of cash.*

4. Cash Payments Journal (also called Cash Disbursements Journal) — This journal is used for recording *all payments of cash.*

■ *What are the several elements of a manual accounting system using special journals and ledgers?*

5. General Journal — This general journal (the one you already have studied) is used for recording *all business transactions that will not be accommodated by one of the other four journals in the system.*

1.	General Ledger	This ledger, the main ledger, has accounts for each of the asset, liability, and capital accounts of the business.
2.	Accounts Receivable Ledger	This ledger has an account for each of the firm's customers who owes the company money, usually for merchandise. This ledger serves as a detailed breakdown of the Accounts receivable account in the general ledger.
3.	Accounts Payable Ledger	This ledger has an account for each of the firm's suppliers to whom the firm owes money, usually for merchandise purchased. This ledger serves as a detailed breakdown of the Accounts payable account in the general ledger.

Carefully review the function of each of the five journals and three ledgers just described. This perspective will be valuable to you when you are introduced to each of these elements. Also remember an important point: this particular system is just one system that can be used by a firm. There are many variations of this in actual practice.

METHODS OF ACQUIRING ASSETS IN A CORPORATION

There are three basic **sources of assets:** investments by the owners of the corporation (stockholders), loans from creditors, and resources generated through the earnings process. Let us examine each of these methods in turn.

From stockholders Unit 1, which dealt with basic business operations, introduced you to the corporate form of organization, the dominant form of business in our economy. You learned that the corporation can effectively acquire capital and provide for growth. A corporation can be created by a state government. Therefore, the usual procedure for a group of individuals who want to begin a company is to apply to a state for a corporate *charter*. A charter is a document authorizing the creation of a corporation; it also includes such details as the purpose of the business and the methods (and limitations placed on the methods) of raising funds to operate the firm.

■ *What methods does a corporation use to acquire resources?*

A corporation issues written stock certificates to evidence the owners' (stockholders') investment in the company. This procedure allows a large number of investor-owners to invest their money in the corporation and thereby raise capital for it. These stock certificates are readily transferable to aid in providing a market for the stock (ownership) of the company.

As a separate legal entity or unit, the corporation is responsible for all debts and other obligations it incurs. The stockholders are not *personally* liable for the debts and obligations of the company. This characteristic of limited liability does not apply in the case of proprietorships and partnerships, for in them the owners are personally liable for the debts of the company. The limited liability characteristic of corporations certainly encourages the corporate form. It provides an added incentive and protection for investors who risk their capital, and thus makes it easier for corporations to raise resources in order to operate.

Refer now to Unit 9, "The Purpose and Structure of the Balance Sheet," where the balance sheets of a proprietorship, a partnership, and a corporation were illustrated. As you review these balance sheets, note that the capital section of the corporation balance sheet includes two basic accounts: Capital stock and Retained earnings. Because a corporation ordinarily has many owners, the amounts contributed to the firm are reported in one account, Capital stock. The capital generated by the earnings process and still remaining in the firm is reported separately as Retained earnings and can be analyzed separately.

From creditors Like other forms of organization, the corporation borrows assets to help it operate. Often the company signs long-term *notes payable* to evidence the loan. A note spells out the due date of the loan (the maturity date), the interest rate, the names of the borrower and lender, and any other relevant details. Another form of loan involves *bonds payable*. A bond is another document (similar to a note) that is printed in advance in fixed dollar amounts to make it easier to borrow from a large number of lenders. For example, a firm might issue bonds to 100 different individuals, borrowing $1,000 from each. The printed bond certificates evidence the loan (in place of the note in the case of notes payable).

From the earnings process The third way a company acquires resources is by generating them in the earnings process, that is, through operating the business and making a profit. You learned earlier that expenses tend to reduce a firm's resources, that revenues tend to increase a firm's resources, and that making *net earnings* causes the resources of a firm to grow. When net earnings exceed the amounts returned to the owners (withdrawals),[1] then the earnings retained in the firm represent a fundamental source of resources for the company.

---

[1] Payments to owners (withdrawals) in corporations are referred to as *dividends*.

The **cash receipts journal** has two major advantages over the general journal—an ease of recording and an ease of posting. The recording process is simpler because special columns are provided in the cash receipts journal that require only the insertion of the dollar amount involved for each account. The only time an account title need be written is for those transactions involving accounts for which a special column has not been provided. If a general journal were used, a complete transaction would have to be written out each time cash was received. The posting process is simpler (see the next section) because for those accounts which have special columns, only the total need be posted.

■ *How is the cash receipts journal used to record transactions?*

A common form of a cash receipts journal is shown in Illustration 11-1. Carefully study the first three business transactions that have been entered.

The June 1 entry shows that the corporation issued 100 shares of capital stock and received investments in the firm amounting to $10,000. The amount is entered in the "Cash Debit" column and in the "General Accounts Credit" column. The function of the "General Accounts Credit" column is to provide space for recording a credit to any account for which there has not been a separate column provided in the journal. The June 2 entry shows that the firm borrowed $4,000 on a note, and the June 4 transaction involves borrowing another $70,000 cash through issuing bonds. These two amounts are entered as shown in Illustration 11-1.

The preceding entries dealt with raising cash for the firm from stockholders and from creditors. Now we will look at the process of selling the firm's product. The main business transactions of a merchandising firm that deal with selling a product are:

1. Sales made for cash.
2. Sales made on credit.
3. Sales returns and allowances.
4. Collections of sales taxes.
5. Collections of accounts receivable.

The primary revenue account traditionally used in merchandising organizations is called *Sales of merchandise,* or just simply *Sales.* The credit balance in this account at the end of an operating period is a measure of the total (gross) amounts charged the customers for goods sold to them during the period. It is customary to report the revenue on the income statement of that period in which the sale was made. You should recognize, however, that in most cases the earnings process actually spans more than one accounting period. For example, the goods may be purchased and stored in one period, the sale may

■ *How is the sale of merchandise recorded?*

CASH RECEIPTS JOURNAL

page 6

DATE		ACCOUNT CREDITED	DESCRIPTION	PR	GENERAL ACCOUNTS CREDIT	ACCOUNTS RECEIVABLE CREDIT	SALES CREDIT	SALES DISCOUNTS DEBIT	CASH DEBIT
1978 June	1	Capital stock	Issued 100 shares	301	10,000.00				10,000.00
	2	Notes payable	60-days, 6%	210	4,000.00				4,000.00
	4	Bonds payable	20-yr. 5%	220	70,000.00				70,000.00
	7	Sales	Cash sale				1,400.00		1,400.00
	8	Sales tax payable	Cash sale	205	60.00		1,000.00		1,060.00
	11	Dauphine Corp.	Collection	✓		386.00		7.72	378.28
					84,060.00	386.00	2,400.00	7.72	86,838.28
						(112)	(410)	(412)	(101)

ILLUSTRATION 11-1

SALES JOURNAL					page 72
DATE		ACCOUNT DEBITED	INVOICE NUMBER	PR	AMOUNT
1978 June	4	Dauphine Corporation 2/10, n/30	624	✓	396.00
	7	Burgundy Co. 2/10, n/30	625	✓	1,495.00
	11	Rampart, Inc. 2/10, n/30	626	✓	5,115.40
					7,006.40
					(112) (410)

ILLUSTRATION 11-2

be made in the next period, and the collection for the goods may be made in a third period. But since the making of the sale has been considered such an important event in the entire earnings process, it has become customary to reflect all the revenue in the period in which the sale is made. In a like manner, the related Cost of goods sold is shown in that same period. For example, assume that a cash sale of merchandise was made in 1978 for $100. The merchandise which was sold had cost $80 when it was purchased in 1977, the year before. According to current accounting practice, *both* the sales revenue ($100) and the expense (Cost of goods sold, $80) are reported on the 1978 income statement.

The next transaction that we will look at involves selling merchandise for cash. Refer to the cash receipts journal (Illustration 11-1) and to the June 7 transaction. Merchandise was sold to customers on that date for $1,400 cash. Notice that the entire entry is made on one line, with the debit recorded in the Cash Debit column and the credit recorded in the Sales Credit column. The *totals* of these two columns are posted to the ledger accounts at the end of the accounting period.

SALES MADE ON CREDIT Refer to the **sales journal** shown (Illustration 11-2). This journal is used for all sales of merchandise made on credit. On June 4, $396 of merchandise was sold to Dauphine Corporation on credit terms of 2/10, n/30. The amount was entered in the single column. At the end of the accounting period, the total of all sales made on credit (the total of the Amount column) is posted as a debit to Accounts receivable and as a credit to Sales. The invoice number is recorded in the sales journal for reference to the files. (An *invoice* is simply the bill or document showing the quantities, prices, and description of the merchandise sold.)

There is now a new set of procedures for you to learn here. The general ledger includes one account called Accounts receivable. This account includes *all* the amounts owed to the firm by its customers. In other words, the Accounts receivable account is a summary account. Most firms need information about *each* of their customers, not just the summary information contained in the general ledger Accounts receivable account. Therefore, a separate ledger can be kept. This ledger, called an **accounts receivable subsidiary ledger,** includes a ledger page (account) for each of the firms or persons who owes the company money. The accounts receivable subsidiary ledger is thus a detailed breakdown or analysis of the Accounts receivable account in the general ledger. Shown in Illustration 11-3 are two of the accounts appearing in the accounts receivable subsidiary ledger, those of Dauphine Corporation and Burgundy Co.

In the Dauphine Corporation account observe that the $396 debit to Accounts receivable appearing in the sales journal was posted as a debit. Note the post referencing system between the sales journal and the accounts receivable subsidiary ledger. In the sales journal a check mark is placed in the post reference (PR) column to indicate that the amount entered in the Amount column has been posted to the subsidiary ledger. In the posting

ILLUSTRATION 11-3

ACCOUNTS RECEIVABLE SUBSIDIARY LEDGER

Name Dauphine Corporation
Address 1818 March Avenue, New Orleans, LA 70122

DATE		DESCRIPTION	PR	DEBIT	CREDIT	DEBIT BALANCE	CREDIT BALANCE
1978 June	4		S72	396.00		396.00	
	6		J12		10.00	386.00	
	13		CR11		386.00	–0–	

Name Burgundy Co.
Address 2500 April Street, New Orleans, LA 70125

DATE		DESCRIPTION	PR	DEBIT	CREDIT	DEBIT BALANCE	CREDIT BALANCE
1978 June	7		S72	1,495.00		1,495.00	

reference column of the ledger account, the entry S72 is made to indicate that the entry was posted from page 72 of the sales journal (S). A similar posting procedure is illustrated for the June 7 sale to the Burgundy Co.

SALES RETURNS AND ALLOWANCES

On June 6, our firm was notified by Dauphine Corporation that some of the goods shipped to them were defective. This merchandise was returned to us and we agreed to reduce the Dauphine Corporation's account by $10. Now, refer to the general journal of the company in Illustration 11-4. The **Sales returns and allowances** account is debited and the Accounts receivable account is credited. The debit balance of the Sales returns and allowances account serves to *reduce* the gross amount of sales made (the credit balance in the Sales account).

ILLUSTRATION 11-4

GENERAL JOURNAL			page 12
1978 June	6	Sales returns and allowances	411	10.00	
		Accounts receivable/Dauphine Corporation	112/✔		10.00
		Credit memorandum 113 was issued.			

Also recorded in the general journal is the fact that **credit memorandum** 113 was issued by the firm. This source document includes all the relevant details about the merchandise that was found defective. Usually the credit memorandum takes the form shown in Illustration 11-5.

COLLECTIONS OF SALES TAXES

Most states and many local governments require that business firms collect sales taxes from customers at the time of the sale. The firms later send these sales tax collections to the appropriate governmental agency. The business firm, in these cases, is simply acting as a collection agent for the government.

Assume that a firm sold merchandise to customers for a price of $1,000. Further, assume that this sale is subject to a sales tax of 6% ($60). The company therefore must collect $1,060. The $60 becomes a liability of the firm and must be paid to the government. The gross amount of the revenue for the firm is only $1,000, even though $1,060 in cash is collected. Refer to the cash receipts journal (Illustration 11-1). The June 8 entry shows this transaction. The Cash account is debited (increased) for $1,060 in the Cash Debit column. The revenue account is credited for $1,000 in the Sales Credit

CREDIT MEMORANDUM   No. 113

HOLSTEIN COMPANY

Date: June 6, 1978

To: Dauphine Corporation,
      1818 March Avenue, New Orleans, LA 70122

WE CREDIT YOUR ACCOUNT AS FOLLOWS:

Defective merchandise from June 4 sale (stained goods) $10.00

ILLUSTRATION 11-5

column. The liability (sales tax payable) must be increased (credited) for $60; because this journal does not have a separate column for that liability, the General Accounts Credit column must be used. *In sales journals and in cash receipts journals, a special column is often used for sales tax liability.*

COLLECTIONS OF ACCOUNTS RECEIVABLE

- *How is the collection of receivables recorded?*

The next group of transactions that we will examine deals with collecting accounts receivable. Look at the cash receipts journal illustrated. The June 11 transaction is the collection of the amount owed by the Dauphine Corporation. The sales journal records that merchandise was sold to them for *$396* on June 4 with **terms of sale** of 2/10, n/30. This information also is recorded in the Dauphine Corporation account in the accounts receivable subsidiary ledger (see the example). Then, on June 6, the Dauphine Corporation returned defective goods to us for reduction of their account. Refer to both the general journal (Illustration 11-4) and the Dauphine Corporation account in the accounts receivable subsidiary ledger. After this transaction, Dauphine Corporation owes $386. If the 2% discount for paying within 10 days is allowed *on the amount owed* (0.02 × $386 = $7.72), then $7.72 must be deducted from the total amount owed ($386). So, in the cash receipts journal these things are recorded: the Accounts receivable account is credited for

$386 to reduce the asset; the Cash account is debited to show that cash is collected for $378.28; and the Sales discounts account is debited *to reflect a reduction in the gross revenues produced by the sale.* Generally, the Sales discounts account will accumulate a debit balance to evidence that discounts allowed serve to reduce the revenues and earnings.

TRADE DISCOUNTS AND CASH DISCOUNTS

At this point let us examine four terms commonly used in merchandising. These terms are: trade discounts, cash discounts, purchases discounts, and sales discounts.

Basically, there are two classes of discounts: (1) trade discounts, and (2) cash discounts. A **trade discount** is a reduction in a list price or catalog price made in determining the gross (total) amount to charge a customer. For example, a firm might print an annual catalog listing all the merchandise it sells. For each item, a list price might be printed in the catalog or price list. This list price represents the highest price that would be charged for the products. For a variety of reasons, firms sell goods to customers below the list price. One reason is that customers who buy in large quantities might be given reductions from the list price. Another reason is that cost prices may change during the year; that is, the company's own cost in buying the merchandise may change, often requiring a change in selling price. These reductions in determining the selling price are called trade discounts. Often they are stated in percentages of list prices. For example, assume merchandise which has a list price of $1,000 is sold to a customer with a 20% trade discount. The gross selling price is therefore $800. The $800 becomes the relevant amount to enter into the accounts for the sale; the $1,000 has no particular meaning for accounting purposes.

A **cash discount,** on the other hand, is a *further* reduction in the amount to be paid or collected for the goods sold. Cash discounts are often part of the terms of a sale. This encourages payments for merchandise within specified periods of time. The two classes of cash discounts, which you already have studied, are *purchases discounts* and *sales discounts.*

POSTINGS FROM SPECIAL JOURNALS

Posting from the sales journal At the end of the month, transactions that have been entered in the several special journals are posted to the general ledger and to the accounts receivable subsidiary ledger. Refer to Illustration 11-6 as you read the following discussion.

First, remember that in most firms, the journals are totaled once each month, and the appropriate totals are posted to the general ledger *monthly.* However, there is an advantage to keeping the accounts receivable subsidiary ledger posted on a *daily* basis. On any day, the management of the company should be able to determine the amount owed by any one of its customers.

- *How are postings made from special journals?*

SALES JOURNAL

DATE	ACCOUNT DEBITED	INVOICE NO.	REF.	AMOUNT
1978 June 4	Dauphine Corporation 2/10, n/30	624	✓	396 00
7	Burgundy, Co. 2/10, n/30	625	✓	1495 00
11	Rampart, Inc. 2/10, n/30	626	✓	5115 40
				7006 40
				(112) (410)

GENERAL LEDGER

Accounts receivable — ACCOUNT NO. 112

DATE	DESCRIPTION	REF.	DEBITS	CREDITS	BALANCE DEBIT	BALANCE CREDIT
1978 June 30		S72	7006 40		7006 40	
6		J12		10 00	6996 40	
30		CR6		386 00	6610 40	

Sales — ACCOUNT NO. 410

DATE	DESCRIPTION	REF.	DEBITS	CREDITS	BALANCE DEBIT	BALANCE CREDIT
1978 June 30		S72		7006 40		7006 40
30		CR6		2400 00		9406 40

ACCOUNTS RECEIVABLE LEDGER

Dauphine Corporation

DATE	DESCRIPTION	REF.	DEBITS	CREDITS	BALANCE DEBIT	BALANCE CREDIT
1978 June 4	2/10, n/30	S72	396 00		396 00	
6	Defective goods	J12		10 00	386 00	
11		CR6		386 00	—0—	

Burgundy Co.

DATE	DESCRIPTION	REF.	DEBITS	CREDITS	BALANCE DEBIT	BALANCE CREDIT
1978 June 7	2/10, n/30	S72	1495 00		1495 00	

Rampart, Inc.

DATE	DESCRIPTION	REF.	DEBITS	CREDITS	BALANCE DEBIT	BALANCE CREDIT
1978 June 11	2/10, n/30	S72	5115 40		5115 40	

ILLUSTRATION 11-6

Accordingly, most firms post to the accounts receivable subsidiary ledger daily, and post to the general ledger monthly.

Illustration 11-6 shows posting procedures from the sales journal. The total of the sales journal ($7,006.40) is posted as a debit to the Accounts receivable account in the general ledger (112). That same total ($7,006.40) is then posted as a credit to the Sales account (410). General ledger account numbers are entered at the foot of the amount column in the sales journal to show that postings were made to those accounts. The individual amounts in the sales journal are posted as debits to the accounts receivable ledger. For example, $396 is posted as a debit to Dauphine Corporation account, and $1,495 is posted as a debit to Burgundy Co. account. Check marks are made in the posting reference column of the sales journal to show that postings were made to the individual accounts receivable.

In the ledger accounts, cross references are made to the journal. For example, S72 means that the posting was made from page 72 of the sales journal.

Posting from the general journal Only one entry is shown in the general journal. Illustration 11-7 shows the posting procedure. The Sales returns and allowances account (account 411) is debited for $10 in the general ledger. This serves to reduce the revenue earned during the period by $10. The Accounts receivable account (112) in the general ledger is credited for $10. Also, the credit must be posted to Dauphine Corporation's account in the accounts receivable ledger. The check mark in the posting reference column of the journal indicates that the posting was made. In the Dauphine account, the cross reference (J12) indicates that the posting was made from page 12 of the general journal.

Posting from the cash receipts journal Refer to the cash receipts journal in Illustration 11-8. Notice how the columns are totaled. To check the accuracy of the addition, the bookkeeper usually "cross foots" the totals. That is, the total of the debit columns are added together and compared with the total of the credit columns. In this case, $84,060 plus $386 plus $2,400 equals $7.72 plus $86,838.28.

The posting procedure is as follows for the cash receipts journal. The General Accounts Credit column *is not posted as a total,* since the total represents entries in several accounts. Instead, the *individual amounts in the column* are posted to the general ledger accounts. $10,000 is posted as a credit to the Capital stock account (301), $4,000 is posted as a credit to the Notes payable account (210), and so forth. General ledger account numbers are entered in the posting reference column of the journal as the postings are made.

Next, the Accounts Receivable Credit column total is posted. The

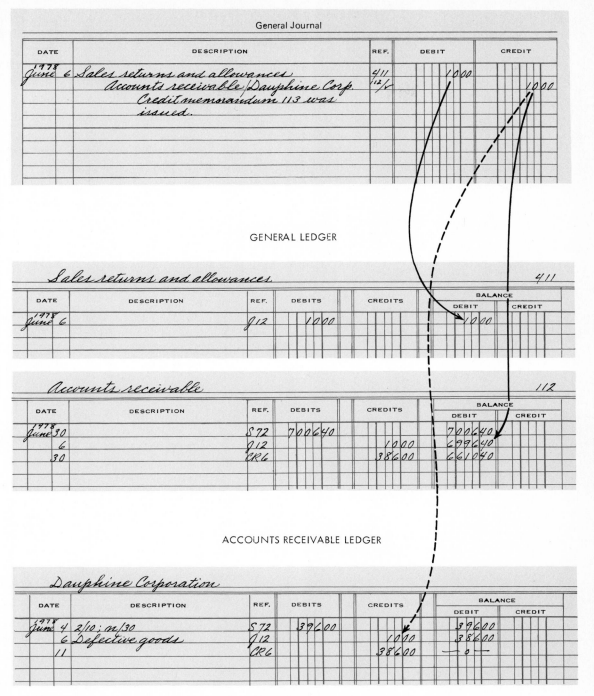

General Journal

DATE	DESCRIPTION	REF.	DEBIT	CREDIT
1978 June 6	Sales returns and allowances	411	1000	
	Accounts receivable/Dauphine Corp.	112/✓		1000
	Credit memorandum 113 was			
	issued.			

GENERAL LEDGER

Sales returns and allowances   411

DATE	DESCRIPTION	REF.	DEBITS	CREDITS	BALANCE DEBIT	BALANCE CREDIT
1978 June 6		J12	1000		1000	

Accounts receivable   112

DATE	DESCRIPTION	REF.	DEBITS	CREDITS	BALANCE DEBIT	BALANCE CREDIT
1978 June 30		S72	700640		700640	
6		J12		1000	699640	
30		CR6		38600	661040	

ACCOUNTS RECEIVABLE LEDGER

Dauphine Corporation

DATE	DESCRIPTION	REF.	DEBITS	CREDITS	BALANCE DEBIT	BALANCE CREDIT
1978 June 4	2/10; n/30	S72	39600		39600	
6	Defective goods	J12		1000	38600	
11		CR6		38600	0	

ILLUSTRATION 11-7

Cash ACCOUNT NO. 101

DATE	DESCRIPTION	REF.	DEBITS	CREDITS	BALANCE DEBIT	BALANCE CREDIT
1978 June 30		CR6	8683828		8683828	

Accounts receivable ACCOUNT NO. 112

DATE	DESCRIPTION	REF.	DEBITS	CREDITS	BALANCE DEBIT	BALANCE CREDIT
1978 June 30		S72	700640		700640	
6		J12		1000	699640	
30		CR6		38600	661040	

Sales tax payable ACCOUNT NO. 205

DATE	DESCRIPTION	REF.	DEBITS	CREDITS	BALANCE DEBIT	BALANCE CREDIT
1978 June 8		CR6		6000		6000

Notes payable ACCOUNT NO. 210

DATE	DESCRIPTION	REF.	DEBITS	CREDITS	BALANCE DEBIT	BALANCE CREDIT
1978 June 2		CR6		400000		400000

Bonds payable ACCOUNT NO. 220

DATE	DESCRIPTION	REF.	DEBITS	CREDITS	BALANCE DEBIT	BALANCE CREDIT
1978 June 4		CR6		7000000		7000000

Capital stock ACCOUNT NO. 301

DATE	DESCRIPTION	REF.	DEBITS	CREDITS	BALANCE DEBIT	BALANCE CREDIT
1978 June 1		CR6		1000000		1000000

Sales ACCOUNT NO. 410

DATE	DESCRIPTION	REF.	DEBITS	CREDITS	BALANCE DEBIT	BALANCE CREDIT
1978 June 30		S72		700640		700640
30		CR6		240000		940640

Sales discounts ACCOUNT NO. 412

DATE	DESCRIPTION	REF.	DEBITS	CREDITS	BALANCE DEBIT	BALANCE CREDIT
1978 June 30		CR6	772		772	

ILLUSTRATION 11-8

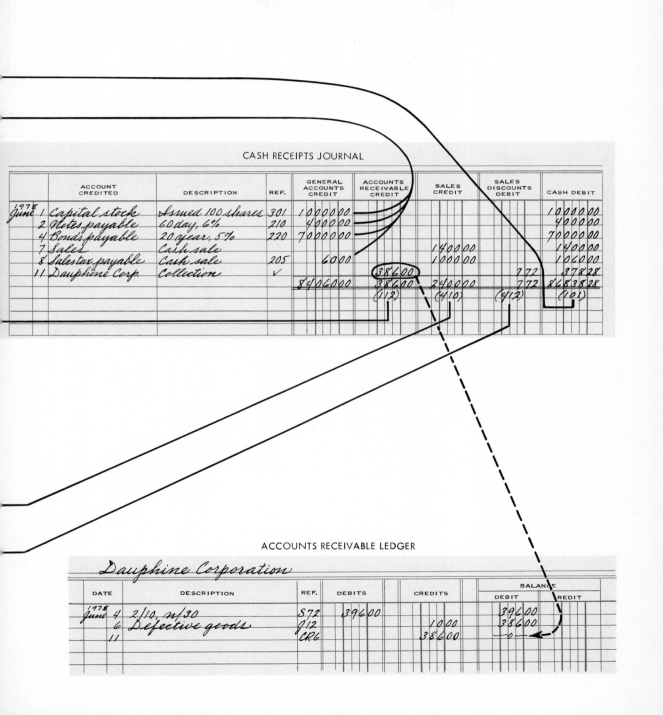

CASH RECEIPTS JOURNAL

	ACCOUNT CREDITED	DESCRIPTION	REF.	GENERAL ACCOUNTS CREDIT	ACCOUNTS RECEIVABLE CREDIT	SALES CREDIT	SALES DISCOUNTS DEBIT	CASH DEBIT
1978 June 1	Capital stock	Issued 100 shares	301	10 000 00				10 000 00
2	Notes payable	60 day, 6%	210	4 000 00				4 000 00
4	Bonds payable	20 year, 5%	220	70 000 00				70 000 00
7	Sales	Cash sale				1 400 00		1 400 00
8	Sales tax payable	Cash sale	205	60 00		1 000 00		1 060 00
11	Dauphine Corp.	Collection	✓		386 00		7 72	378 28
				84 060 00	386 00	2 400 00	7 72	86 838 28
				(112)	(410)	(412)	(101)	

ACCOUNTS RECEIVABLE LEDGER

Dauphine Corporation

	DATE	DESCRIPTION	REF.	DEBITS	CREDITS	BALANCE DEBIT	BALANCE CREDIT
1978 June	4	2/10, n/30	S72	396 00		396 00	
	6	Defective goods	J12		10 00	386 00	
	11		CR6		386 00	-0-	

column total, $386, is posted as a credit to the Accounts receivable account in the general ledger. Any individual amounts in that column (only one in this case) are posted to the appropriate accounts (Dauphine Corporation) in the accounts receivable ledger as credits. The general ledger account number for Accounts receivable (112) is entered at the foot of the column to show that the total was posted to the general ledger. Also, a check mark is placed in the posting reference column of the journal on the same line as Dauphine Corporation to show that the individual posting was made.

The Sales Credit column is posted in total only to the Sales account (410) in the general ledger. The Sales Discounts Debit column is posted in total only to the Sales discounts account (412) in the general ledger. The Cash Debit column is posted in total only to the Cash account (101) in the general ledger.

As each posting is made to the ledger accounts, the appropriate cross reference is made in the ledger account. For example, CR6 indicates that the posting was made from page 6 of the cash receipts journal.

A FINAL NOTE   Some firms choose to use a special journal (instead of the general journal) to record sales returns and allowances made on credit. This would be appropriate when a firm has many such transactions each month. Such a **sales returns and allowances journal** is shown below.

SALES RETURNS AND ALLOWANCES JOURNAL				page 12		
DATE		ACCOUNT CREDITED	CM	PR	AMOUNT
1978 June	6	Albert Company	204	✔	80.00
	10	Walter Corporation	205	✔	95.00
	24	Scott Co.	206	✔	10.00
	27	Lawrence and Co.	207	✔	8.00
					193.00

At the end of the month, the *total* of the amount column ($193) would be posted as a debit to the Sales returns and allowances account and a credit to the Accounts receivable account in the general ledger. The *individual* amounts in the journal ($80, $95, etc.) would be posted as credits to the appropriate accounts (such as Albert Company) in the accounts receivable subsidiary ledger.

accounts receivable subsidiary ledger A book containing accounts for each of the customers (accounts receivable) of a firm; the total owed by all customers as reflected by the accounts receivable ledger is the same as the amount indicated in the accounts receivable account (control) in the general ledger. [p. 175]

cash discount A reduction in the purchase price of merchandise purchased *or* a reduction in the sales price of merchandise sold if the merchandise is paid for within an agreed period of time. [p. 166]

cash receipts journal A special book, usually designed with a number of columns to facilitate posting, that provides the original entry of transactions involving the receipt of cash. [p. 172]

credit memorandum A source document that provides information about the sales returns and allowances; the credit memorandum is usually the basis for the entry made in the sales returns and allowances journal; a copy of the credit memorandum is sent to the customer as a communication device between the two companies. [p. 176]

purchase discount A cash discount taken by a firm when paying for merchandise purchased. [p. 166]

purchases returns and allowances Reductions, in the cost of purchasing merchandise, brought about by returning the unacceptable merchandise to the supplier or simply keeping the merchandise and reducing the cost (price) as agreed. [p. 168]

sales discount A cash discount allowed a customer when he pays the firm for merchandise sold to him. [p. 167]

sales journal A special book often designed with one amount column for recording sales of merchandise made on credit. [p. 174]

sales returns and allowances Reductions, in the prices charged to customers for merchandise sold, brought about by customers' returning merchandise to the firm or simply keeping the merchandise and reducing the price charged. [p. 168]

sales returns and allowances journal A special book usually designed with one column for recording sales returns and allowances in those cases where the amounts receivable is to be reduced. [p. 184]

sources of assets Acquisition of resources is one of the primary activities of the management of a corporation; major sources are (1) stockholders, (2) creditors, and (3) the earnings process. [p. 170]

special journal A journal designed to record a particular kind of transaction or transactions; it contrasts with a general journal, which can be used to record all kinds of business transactions; refer to the special journals discussed in this unit. [p. 168]

special ledger A ledger designed to accumulate detailed information that can supplement the information contained in the general ledger. [p. 169]

terms of sale The agreement between buyer and seller specifying when payment will be made and what, if any, cash discount will be allowed. [p. 177]

trade discount Reductions from a catalog or list price in determining the gross selling price to be charged a customer for merchandise; trade discounts as such do not appear in the accounts. [p. 178]

> **ASSIGNMENT MATERIAL**

QUESTIONS

Q11-1. What do the following terms of sale indicate: 4/10, n/60?

Q11-2. Differentiate among cash discounts, sales discounts, and purchase discounts.

Q11-3. What are two important advantages of special journals?

Q11-4. What is the function of a special ledger?

Q11-5. What are the six common repetitive-type transactions in merchandising firms? Briefly describe each.

Q11-6. List and explain the three major methods of acquiring resources for a corporation.

Q11-7. Explain the advantage that a cash receipts journal has over a general journal for recording certain business transactions of a business.

Q11-8. List the columns which might appear in a cash receipts journal. What is the function of each of the columns you listed? Explain the posting procedure for each of the columns.

Q11-9. Compare and contrast trade discounts and cash discounts.

Q11-10. What is a credit memorandum?

EXERCISES

E11-1. What term is given each of the following descriptions?
  a. Journal used for recording those purchases returns and allowances, when a cash refund is received for the return.
  b. Refers to reductions in the prices charged to customers for merchandise sold, brought about by customers' returning merchandise to the firm or simply keeping the merchandise and reducing the price charged.
  c. The main ledger of a company, that has accounts for each of the assets, liability, and capital accounts.
  d. A ledger with an account for each of the firm's customers.
  e. Sales discounts and purchases discounts.
  f. A cash discount taken by a firm when paying for merchandise purchased.
  g. A cash discount allowed a customer.
  h. A journal used only for recording sales of merchandise made on credit.
  i. The journal used for recording sales made for cash.
  j. The agreement between buyer and seller, specifying when payment will be made and specifying any cash discount which might be allowed.

E11-2. True or False.
  a. The terms of a sale are 2/15, n/30. This means that a 2% discount will be allowed if the merchandise is paid for within 15 days of the sale, and that the net amount (total amount without a discount) is due at the end of 30 days after the sale.
  b. All sales in merchandising businesses are made on credit.
  c. The sales journal is used for recording both sales of merchandise on credit and sales of merchandise for cash.
  d. Assume a firm sold merchandise for $300; the merchandise had cost the firm $275. The amount of *revenue* from the sale amounts to $25.
  e. Assume a firm sold merchandise for $300; the merchandise had cost the firm $275. The expense (cost of goods sold) amounts to $275.
  f. When the firm allows its customers to take cash discounts, the reduction in the amount collected is called a sales discount.
  g. When a firm returns damaged merchandise to a supplier, the reduction in the amount owed the supplier is credited to the *Purchases returns and allowances* account.
  h. When a customer returns damaged merchandise to the firm, the reduction in the amount owed the firm by the customer is debited to the *Sales returns and allowances* account.
  i. A main advantage of special journals is that many different kinds of business transactions can be recorded in the same journal.
  j. The accounts payable ledger provides detailed records of the amounts owed the firm by each of its customers.

E11-3. Refer to the section of the text, "The Elements of One Manual Accounting System." Assume that a firm is using a system with the five journals described.

Indicate for each business transaction below which journal would be used to record the transaction.

   a. Borrowed $5,000 from First National Bank, signing a 6%, 60-day, note payable.

   b. Made sales of merchandise to customers for $1,000, with terms of 2/10, n/30.

   c. Made cash sales to customers for $2,000.

   d. Purchased merchandise from Ace Company for $3,000, with terms of 3/15, n/60.

   e. Purchased merchandise from Z Company for $500, paying cash.

   f. The owner invests $20,000 cash in the business.

   g. Made the adjusting entry for supplies used, debiting Supplies expense for $300 and crediting Supplies for $300.

   h. Sales return and allowance of $10, where we reduce the amount the customer owes us.

   i. Sales return and allowance of $20, where we reimburse the customer in cash.

E11-4. Assume that a firm is using a system with the five journals described in the text. Indicate for each business transaction below which journal would be used to record the transaction.

   a. H. R. Dunn invests $84,500 in the business (cash). Mr. Dunn is the owner of the firm.

   b. Purchased office supplies from Noah Co. for $8,600, payment to be made in 30 days.

   c. Made sales of merchandise for cash, $3,000.

   d. Paid the rent expense, $500.

   e. Borrowed $10,000 from the bank on a 60-day, 7% note.

   f. Made sales of merchandise to customers, $9,000, with terms of 2/10, n/30.

   g. Paid miscellaneous expenses, $900.

   h. Returned defective merchandise to suppliers. The supplier reduces the amount we owe them by $100.

   i. Returned defective merchandise to suppliers, receiving a cash refund of $50.

   j. Made the adjusting entry for the depreciation on the office equipment.

PROBLEMS (GROUP A)

P11-1. *Recording and posting from cash receipts, sales, and general journal.* The following are selected business transactions of Pools, Inc. for the month of October, 1978.

Oct.	1	Issued 200 shares of capital stock to Mr. L. M. Jones, Jr., receiving $2,000 cash.
	2	Issued 1,000 shares of capital stock to Howard Investment Company, receiving $10,000 cash.
	4	Borrowed $14,500 from First National Bank, signing a 90-day, 7% note.
	6	Issued $75,000 of bonds (15-year, 6% interest).
	7	Sold merchandise to Banner Company for $31,400. Terms were 2/10, n/30. No sales tax was charged. Invoice 486.
	9	Sold merchandise to Boynton Co. for $10,000 cash. No sales tax was charged on this sale.
	11	Sold merchandise to Parker Company for $9,540, including sales tax of $540. Cash was collected.
	17	Collected the amount due from Banner Company from the sale of October 7.
	18	Sold merchandise to Jensen Corporation for $15,000. Terms were 2/10, n/30. No sales tax was charged. Invoice 487.

19   Jensen Corporation returned defective merchandise from the sale of October 18. We reduced their account by $1,000. Credit memorandum 174 was issued.

21   Sold merchandise to Jerico Co. for $21,000, terms 2/10, n/30. No sales tax was charged. Invoice 488.

23   Made cash sales amounting to $11,900, including sales tax of $673.

28   Collected the amount due from Jensen Corporation.

REQUIRED:

a. Set up a general journal, a cash receipts journal, and a sales journal similar to the ones illustrated in the unit. Record the business transactions.

b. Total and rule the columns of the special journals as illustrated in the text.

c. Set up general ledger accounts with account numbers as shown below and set up accounts in an accounts receivable ledger. Post from the journals to the ledgers, using appropriate posting references.

ACCOUNT NO.	GENERAL LEDGER ACCOUNTS
101	Cash
110	Accounts receivable
210	Sales taxes payable
215	Notes payable
220	Bonds payable
300	Capital stock
401	Sales
412	Sales discounts
413	Sales returns and allowances

Accounts Receivable Accounts are as follows:

Banner Company, 1911 Fourth Avenue, Norman, KS 44150
Jensen Corporation, 2315 Avenue A, Winters, FL 11390
Jerico Co., 11340 Smithton Street, Houston, TX 77013

Note: Since in this problem monthly postings are made (instead of daily posting to the accounts receivable ledger) the sequence of dates in some ledger accounts might be out of order.

P11-2. *Recording and posting from cash receipts, sales, and general journal.* The following are selected business transactions of Rivers Company for the month of January, 1978.

Jan. 2   Collected $900 from File Case Company on account.

4   Collected $980 from Tompkin Corporation. This is in payment of their $1,000 account balance (less the sales discount).

5   Issued 100 shares of capital stock to R. M. Hodges, receiving $9,000 cash.

8   Made cash sales amounting to $8,000. In addition, collected 6% sales taxes.

9   Made cash sales amounting to $18,020, which includes $1,020 in sales taxes.

11   Made sales on credit to Bill Benton, $6,400 plus sales taxes of 6%, terms 2/10, n/30 (Invoice 580).

12   Made sales on credit to William Joyce Company for $5,000, plus sales taxes of $300, terms 2/10, n/30 (Invoice 581).

15 William Joyce Company returned defective merchandise to us for credit on their account as follows (Credit memorandum 812):

Defective merchandise	$1,000
Sales tax on merchandise	60
Account credited for	$1,060

16 Issued bonds for $15,000 cash (5%, 10-year bonds).
21 Collected the amount due from Bill Benton.
22 Collected the amount due from William Joyce Company.
23 Sold merchandise to William Joyce for $1,200, plus sales taxes of 6%, terms 2/10, n/30 (Invoice 582).
24 Sold merchandise to Bill Benton, $5,000 plus 6% sales tax, terms 2/10, n/30 (Invoice 583).
25 Made cash sales totaling $14,000 plus sales taxes of 6%.

REQUIRED:

a. Set up a general journal, a cash receipts journal, and a sales journal similar to the ones illustrated in the unit. However, include an Accounts Receivable Debit column, a Sales Taxes Payable Credit column, and a Sales Credit column in the cash receipts journal. Also include a Sales Taxes Payable Credit column in the cash receipts journal. Record the business transactions.
b. Total and rule the columns of the special journals.
c. Set up general ledger accounts with account numbers as shown below and set up accounts in an accounts receivable ledger. Enter the beginning balances in the accounts of the accounts receivable ledger. Also enter a beginning balance in the Accounts receivable account in the general ledger. Post from the journals to the ledgers.

ACCOUNT NO.	ACCOUNT TITLE
101	Cash
104	Accounts receivable (beginning balance, $1,900)
200	Sales taxes payable
214	Notes payable
215	Bonds payable
310	Capital stock
400	Sales
401	Sales returns and allowances
402	Sales discounts

BALANCE	ACCOUNTS RECEIVABLE ACCOUNTS AT JANUARY 1, 1978 (BEGINNING)
–0–	Bill Benton, 545 Homer Avenue, Park, WI 78787
$ 900	File Cases Company, 5518 Washington Blvd., Arka, TX 77013
–0–	William Joyce Company, 418 West 18th, Akron, OH 45387
1,000	Tompkin Corporation, 118 South Street, Barton, MN 34715

Note: Since in this problem monthly postings are made (instead of daily posting to the accounts receivable ledger) the sequence of dates in some ledger accounts might be out of order.

P11-3. *Posting from the sales journal, the cash receipts journal, and the general journal.* Selected general ledger accounts and their account numbers are shown below:

101	Cash
110	Accounts receivable
214	Sales tax payable
240	Notes payable
245	Bonds payable
300	Capital stock
400	Sales
420	Sales returns and allowances
422	Sales discounts

Accounts receivable accounts at January 1, 1978, were as follows:

Bowers Co., 1811 Calhoun Street, New Orleans, LA 70134	$ 1,200
Crestview Corp., 230 St. Charles, Hartford, CT 55189	1,000
Darth and Co., 5324 Bates Drive, New York, NY 10021	5,000
Vantage Co., 6785 Wilshire Boulevard, Los Angeles, CA 99602	5,400
	$12,600

Set up a general ledger and an accounts receivable ledger. Enter the beginning balances of the accounts receivable accounts. Post from the following journals of the company to the appropriate ledger accounts.

Note: Since in this problem monthly postings are made (instead of daily posting to the accounts receivable ledger), the sequence of dates in some ledger accounts might be out of order.

	SALES JOURNAL						page 9

DATE		ACCOUNT	INVOICE NO.	PR	ACCOUNTS RECEIVABLE DR.	SALES TAX PAYABLE CR.	SALES CR.
1978 Jan.	2	Crestview Corp. 2/10, n/30	318		1,060.00	60.00	1,000.00
	5	Vantage Co. 2/10, n/30	319		2,597.00	147.00	2,450.00
	9	Bowers Co. 2/10, n/30	320		4,134.00	234.00	3,900.00
	11	Bowers Co. 2/10, n/30	321		5,936.00	336.00	5,600.00
	20	Darth and Co. 2/10, n/30	322		424.00	24.00	400.00
	28	Vantage Co. 2/10, n/30	323		133.56	7.56	126.00
					14,284.56	808.56	13,476.00

1978					
Jan.	6	Sales returns and allowances	400.00		
		Sales tax payable	24.00		
		Accounts receivable/Vantage Co.			424.00
		Vantage Co. returned defective			
		merchandise from Invoice 319.			
		Credit memorandum 107.			
	29	Sales returns and allowances	126.00		
		Sales tax payable	7.56		
		Accounts receivable/Vantage Co.			133.56
		Vantage Co. returned all merchan-			
		dise from Invoice 323. Wrong size.			
		Credit memorandum 108.			

PROBLEMS (GROUP B)

P11-4. *Recording and posting from cash receipts, sales, and general journal.* The following are selected business transactions for Introcorp and Co. for the month of June, 1978.

June 1 Issued 540 shares of capital stock to Howard Wheel for $5,400 cash.

       5 Sold merchandise to Brown and Sons, Inc., for $17,530. Terms were 2/20, n/60. No sales taxes were applicable. Invoice 136 was issued.

       6 Borrowed $21,000 from City National Bank. Signed a 90-day note, 8%.

       7 Sold merchandise to Greenson Company for $15,000 cash. No sales tax was charged.

       9 Sold merchandise to Blunt Company for $9,000, terms 2/10, n/30. No sales tax was applicable. Invoice 137 was issued.

     11 Allowed Brown and Sons, Inc., to return merchandise for credit on their account (from sale of June 5). Credit memorandum 143 was issued for $300.

     15 Sold merchandise to Carter Company for $1,350. Terms were 2/20, n/30. Invoice 138 was issued.

     19 Collected the amount due from Blunt Company.

     20 Sold merchandise to Percho, Inc., for $11,500 cash. This amount includes sales tax of $500.

     21 Issued 130 shares of capital stock to James Modd for $13,000 cash.

     25 Collected the amount due from Brown and Sons, Inc.

     27 Sold merchandise to Blunt Company for $1,000, terms 2/10, n/30. No sales tax was applicable. Invoice 139 was issued. No sales tax was charged.

     29 Sold merchandise to Carter Company for $3,100. Terms were 2/10, n/30. Invoice 140 was issued.

     30 Allowed Carter Company a credit of $100 on their account (Credit memorandum 144) from the June 29 sale.

REQUIRED:

a. Set up a sales journal, a cash receipts journal, and a general journal similar to the ones illustrated in the unit. Record the business transactions.

b. Total and rule the columns of the special journals as illustrated in the text.

c. Set up general ledger accounts with account numbers as shown below and set

CASH RECEIPTS JOURNAL

DATE		ACCOUNT CREDITED	DESCRIPTION	PR	GENERAL ACCOUNTS CREDIT	ACCOUNTS RECEIVABLE CREDIT	SALES CREDIT	SALES TAX PAYABLE CREDIT	SALES DISCOUNTS DEBIT	CASH DEBIT
1978 Jan.	2	Sales	Cash sale				15,000.00	900.00		15,900.00
	4	Bowers Co.	Collection			1,200.00			24.00	1,176.00
	5	Crestview Corp.	Collection			1,000.00			20.00	980.00
	6	Capital stock	500 shares		50,000.00					50,000.00
	12	Crestview Corp.	Collection			1,060.00			21.20	1,038.80
	15	Vantage Co.	Collection			2,173.00			43.46	2,129.54
	20	Bonds payable	Issuance, 6%, 10-year		100,000.00					100,000.00
	21	Sales	Cash sale				6,000.00	360.00		6,360.00
	22	Bowers Co.	Collection			4,134.00				4,134.00
	30	Darth and Co.	Collection			424.00			8.48	415.52
					150,000.00	9,991.00	21,000.00	1,260.00	117.14	182,133.86

up accounts in an accounts receivable ledger. Post from the journals to the ledgers, using appropriate posting references.

ACCOUNT NUMBER	GENERAL LEDGER ACCOUNTS
101	Cash
110	Accounts receivable
210	Sales tax payable
215	Notes payable
220	Bonds payable
300	Capital stock
401	Sales
412	Sales discounts
415	Sales returns and allowances

Accounts Receivable Accounts are as follows:

Blunt Company, 3265 West Street, Helena, MT 87659
Brown and Sons, Inc., 1500 Blanchard Avenue, New York, NY 10010
Carter Company, 32 Ibis Drive, Brown, SD 76546

Note: Since in this problem monthly postings are made (instead of daily posting to the accounts receivable ledger), the sequence of dates in some ledger accounts might be out of order.

P11-5. *Recording and posting from cash receipts, sales, and general journal.* The following are selected business transactions of Valley Company for the month of February, 1978.

Feb. 1 Collected $1,000 from Forrest Corporation on account.
2 Collected $4,410 from Glade Co. This is in payment of their account. They deducted $90 as a cash discount according to the terms of sale.
4 Borrowed $30,000 by issuing 10-year, 7% bonds.
6 Issued 390 shares of capital stock to H. Hosch Company, receiving $7,800 cash.
8 Made sales to Tom Horton for $4,318 plus 5% sales tax with terms of 2/10, n/30. Issued Invoice 346.
9 Made sales to Gary White for $5,000 plus 5% sales tax with terms of 3/10, n/30. Issued Invoice 347.
11 Made cash sales amounting to $3,000 plus 5% sales tax.
12 Sold merchandise to Don Chatham for $8,200 plus 5% sales tax. Terms were 2/10, n/30. Invoice 348 was issued.
14 Chatham returned $1,000 of merchandise for credit on his account. We credited his account for $1,050, which includes the 5% sales tax charged on the original sale of February 12. Issued credit memorandum 131.
18 Collected the amount due from Tom Horton.
21 Collected the amount due from Don Chatham.
28 Sold merchandise to Glade Co. for $3,000 plus 5% sales tax. Terms were 2/10, n/30. Invoice 349 was issued.
28 Made cash sales amounting to $3,211 plus 5% sales tax.

REQUIRED:

a. Set up a general journal, a cash receipts journal, and a sales journal similar to the ones illustrated in the unit. However, include an Accounts Receivable Debit column, a Sales Taxes Payable Credit column, and a Sales Credit column in the cash receipts journal. Also include a Sales Taxes Payable Credit column in the cash receipts journal. Record the business transactions.

b. Total and rule the columns of the special journals.

c. Set up general ledger accounts with account numbers as shown below and set up accounts in an accounts receivable ledger. Enter the beginning balances in the accounts of the accounts receivable ledger. Also enter a beginning balance in the Accounts receivable account in the general ledger. Post from the journals to the ledgers.

ACCOUNT NO.	ACCOUNT TITLE
100	Cash
104	Accounts receivable (beginning balance $5,500)
200	Sales tax payable
212	Bonds payable
300	Capital stock
401	Sales
402	Sales discounts
403	Sales returns and allowances

ACCOUNTS RECEIVABLE ACCOUNTS AT FEBRUARY 1	BALANCE
Don Chatham, Box 25, Northtown, IL 34786	–0–
Forrest Corporation, 18 Swan Street, Hisson, MI 44387	$1,000
Glade Co., 1750 Michigan Avenue, New York, NY 10010	4,500
Tom Horton, 2430 Salt Avenue, Brown, NY 00655	–0–
Gary White, P.O. Box 18, Oak Park, IL 34573	–0–

Note: Since in this problem monthly postings are made (instead of daily posting to the accounts receivable ledger), the sequence of dates in some ledger accounts might be out of order.

P11-6. *Posting from the sales journal, the cash receipts journal, and the general journal.* Selected general ledger accounts and their account numbers are shown below:

100	Cash
120	Accounts receivable
210	Sales tax payable
220	Notes payable
221	Bonds payable
301	Capital stock
401	Sales
402	Sales returns and allowances
403	Sales discounts

Accounts receivable balances at May 1, 1978, were as follows:

Gluco, Inc., 1900 Philadelphia Street, Norwich, CT 07740	$ 1,800
Holly Dresses, Inc., 677 Octavia Street, Boola, TX 77400	5,000
Smith and Branam, Inc., 1212 18th Street, Wichers, GA 25440	1,740
Tyler and Moore, 2498 Telemachus Street, Bains, GA 25904	2,000
	$10,540

Set up a general ledger and an accounts receivable ledger. Enter the beginning balances of the Accounts receivable accounts. Post from the following journals of the company to the appropriate ledger accounts.

Note: Since in this problem monthly postings are made (instead of daily posting to the accounts receivable ledger), the sequence of dates in some ledger accounts might be out of order.

	SALES JOURNAL					page 11
DATE	ACCOUNT	INVOICE NO.	PR	ACCOUNTS RECEIVABLE DR.	SALES TAX PAYABLE CR.	SALES CR.
1978 May 2	Tyler and Moore 2/10, n/30	200		1,995.00	95.00	1,900.00
6	Holly Dresses, Inc. 2/10, n/30	201		3,150.00	150.00	3,000.00
9	Gluco, Inc. 2/10, n/30	202		1,829.63	87.13	1,742.50
10	Gluco, Inc. 2/10, n/30	203		1,582.82	75.37	1,507.45
21	Smith and Branam, Inc. 2/10, n/30	204		5,260.50	250.50	5,010.00
26	Holly Dresses, Inc. 2/10, n/30	205		823.74	39.23	784.51
				14,641.69	697.23	13,944.46

	GENERAL JOURNAL			page 42
1978 May 7	Sales returns and allowances	50.00		
	Sales tax payable	2.50		
	Accounts receivable/Holly Dresses, Inc.			52.50
	Holly Dresses, Inc., returned defective merchandise from Invoice 201. Credit memorandum 759.			
27	Sales returns and allowances	100.00		
	Sales tax payable	5.00		
	Accounts receivable/Holly Dresses, Inc.			105.00
	Holly Dresses, Inc., returned part of order from Invoice 205. Credit memorandum 760.			

CASH RECEIPTS JOURNAL

DATE		ACCOUNT CREDITED	DESCRIPTION	PR	GENERAL ACCOUNTS CREDIT	ACCOUNTS RECEIVABLE CREDIT	SALES CREDIT	SALES TAX PAYABLE CREDIT	SALES DISCOUNTS DEBIT	CASH DEBIT
1978 May	1	Sales	Cash sale				21,000.00	1,050.00		22,050.00
	3	Gluco, Inc.	Collection			1,800.00			36.00	1,764.00
	4	Tyler and Moore	Collection			2,000.00			40.00	1,960.00
	5	Capital stock	1,000 shares		9,000.00					9,000.00
	12	Tyler and Moore	Collection			1,995.00			39.90	1,955.10
	13	Holly Dresses, Inc.	Collection			3,097.50			61.95	3,035.55
	20	Bonds payable	5%, 20 years		90,000.00					90,000.00
	22	Sales	Cash sales				7,000.00	350.00		7,350.00
	23	Gluco, Inc.	Collection			1,829.63				1,829.63
	31	Smith and Branam	Collection			5,260.50			105.21	5,155.29
					99,000.00	15,982.63	28,000.00	1,400.00	283.06	144,099.57

12
PURCHASES AND CASH PAYMENTS

➤ OBJECTIVE

This unit will continue to develop the example of a merchandising firm that we began in Unit 11. You have already studied how a business firm acquires assets from stockholders and creditors and how sales and collections of accounts receivable are recorded. Now you will learn how a firm invests its resources in other resources (including merchandise to be resold) and how these transactions are recorded. In this unit you will learn how to use the purchases journal and the cash payments journal.

➤ APPROACH TO ATTAINING THE OBJECTIVE

As you study about accounting for buying merchandise and cash payments, pay particular attention to these six questions, which the text following answers:

- *What business transactions involve investing the firm's resources?*
- *How is the acquisition of merchandise recorded?*
- *How is the payment of accounts payable recorded?*
- *How is the acquisition of assets other than merchandise recorded?*
- *How are dividends recorded and reported?*
- *How is the repayment of debts recorded and reported?*

BUSINESS TRANSACTIONS INVOLVING INVESTING THE FIRM'S RESOURCES

The main business transactions of a merchandising firm that deal with investing a firm's resources are:

■ *What business transactions involve investing the firm's resources?*

1. Buying merchandise for cash.
2. Paying transportation charges on purchases of merchandise.
3. Buying merchandise on credit.
4. Incurring transportation charges on credit for merchandise purchased.
5. Paying accounts payable.
6. Acquiring assets other than merchandise.

In the following sections we will discuss each of these transactions and the manner in which they are recorded.

ACQUIRING MERCHANDISE

In many merchandising firms *two* separate asset accounts are used to record information about the cost of merchandise. The first account is called **Merchandise inventory** or *Merchandise on hand. The function of this account is to record the cost of the merchandise on hand at the beginning of an accounting period.* When more merchandise is purchased during the accounting period, a second account is used. This account usually is called **Purchases of merchandise** or simply *Purchases*. At the end of the accounting period, both of these accounts (Merchandise inventory and Purchases) are used in determining the total cost of the merchandise that the firm sold.

■ *How is the acquisition of merchandise recorded?*

This method of recording the beginning inventory of merchandise in one account (Merchandise inventory) and recording additional purchases (Purchases of merchandise) in a separate account will be referred to as the **periodic method** of recording merchandise. It is called the periodic method because periodically (usually at the end of each accounting period) an actual count of the unsold merchandise on hand is made. This physical count is needed to determine the cost of the merchandise actually sold. You will study these procedures soon in some depth. The important point for you to remember now, however, is that in the system we are illustrating, the function of the Merchandise inventory account is to record the *beginning* inventory cost, and the function of the Purchases of merchandise account is to record the cost of additional purchases of merchandise made *during* the period.

Buying merchandise for cash Illustrations 12-1, 12-2, and 12-3 on the following page show two special journals: a **cash payments journal**, a **purchases journal**, and a *general journal*. You will be asked to refer back and forth among these journals as the several kinds of business transactions are discussed in this

DATE		ACCOUNT DEBITED	CK. NO.	PR	GENERAL ACCOUNTS DEBIT	ACCOUNTS PAYABLE DEBIT	PURCHASES DEBIT	PURCHASES DISCOUNTS CREDIT	CASH CREDIT
1978 June	10	Purchases of merchandise	406				6,100.00		6,100.00
	11	Transportation on purchases	407	511	100.00				100.00
	13	Jones Supply Co., Inc.	408	✔		2,000.00		40.00	1,960.00
	15	Smith Company	409	✔		70.00			70.00
	16	Ace Freight Co.	410	✔		20.00			20.00
					100.00	2,090.00	6,100.00	40.00	8,250.00
						(201)	(501)	(509)	(101)

ILLUSTRATION 12-1

unit. It will be worthwhile for you now to spend a few minutes studying the headings on each of the three journals and becoming familiar with the forms.

The first transaction that we will look at involves buying merchandise for cash. Refer to the cash payments journal (Illustration 12-1) and to the June 10 transaction. Merchandise costing $6,100 was purchased and cash was

ILLUSTRATION 12-2

DATE		ACCOUNT CREDITED	PR	ACCOUNTS PAYABLE CREDIT	PURCHASES DEBIT	general accounts debit		
						ACCOUNT DEBITED	PR	AMOUNT
1978 June	4	Jones Supply Co., Inc. 2/10, n/30	✔	2,100.00	2,100.00			
	6	Ace Freight Co., 10 days	✔	20.00		Transportation on purchases	511	20.00
	6	Smith Company, 10 days	✔	70.00	70.00			
	10	Z Company, 30 days	✔	1,000.00		Store equipment	117	1,000.00
	11	M Company, 60 days	✔	150.00		Office supplies	107	150.00
				3,340.00	2,170.00			1,170.00
				(201)	(501)			

GENERAL JOURNAL					page 12
1978 June	5	Accounts payable/Jones Supply Co., Inc. Purchases returns and allowances Debit memo 174, defective goods.	201/✔ 512	100.00	100.00

ILLUSTRATION 12-3

paid in that amount. Notice that the entire entry is made on one line, with the debit recorded in the Purchases Debit column and the credit recorded in the Cash Credit column. The *total* of each of these two columns is posted to the ledger accounts at the end of the accounting period. Notice that Check 406 was issued to pay the $6,100.

Paying transportation charges on purchases of merchandise The next entry in the cash payments journal records that on June 11, a freight bill was paid. Cash is therefore credited for $100 in the appropriate column of the journal. There is no separate column set aside in our example for the **Transportation on purchases** account; therefore, the General Accounts Debit column is used. Notice that on June 11 the Transportation on purchases account was debited for $100, Check 407 was issued, and the $100 debit was posted to account number 511—the Transportation on purchases account. The account numbers assigned to any account may differ from company to company, depending on the account-coding system used. Remember that the General Accounts Debit column *total* is *not* posted; instead, the individual entries are posted to the appropriate accounts.

Buying merchandise on credit Now refer to the purchases journal (Illustration 12-2). This journal is used for all purchases on credit. On June 4, $2,100 of merchandise was purchased from Jones Supply Co., Inc., on credit terms of 2/10, n/30. The amount was entered in the Purchases Debit column and in the Accounts Payable Credit column. The *totals* of these two columns will be posted to the appropriate accounts at the end of the accounting period. Also refer to the third entry in the purchases journal. On June 6, the firm purchased $70 of merchandise from the Smith Company, with terms of 10 days (no discount). For these two entries the General Accounts Debit column did not have to be used, because a separate column already had been set up for each account (Purchases, and Accounts Payable).

There is a new set of procedures for you to learn here. The general ledger includes one account called Accounts payable. This account includes all the amounts owed to all the creditors. In other words, the Accounts payable account is a *summary* account. Most firms need information about *each* of their creditors, not just the summary information contained in the general ledger's Accounts payable account. Therefore, a separate ledger can be kept. This ledger, called an **accounts payable subsidiary ledger,** includes a ledger page (account) for each of the firms or persons to whom the firm owes money. The accounts payable subsidiary ledger is a detailed breakdown or analysis of the Accounts payable account in the general ledger. Illustration 12-4 shows two of the accounts appearing in the accounts payable subsidiary ledger, those of Jones Supply Co., Inc., and Smith Company.

In the Jones Supply Co., Inc., account in the subsidiary ledger, observe that the $2,100 credit to accounts payable appearing in the purchases journal has been posted as a credit. Often, as in our example, the balance-column type of account is used for subsidiary ledgers so that the current balance is always available. Note the post referencing (PR) system between the purchases journal and the accounts payable subsidiary ledger. In the journal a check mark is placed in the post reference column to indicate that the amount entered in the Accounts Payable Credit column has been posted to the subsidiary ledger. In the post reference column of the subsidiary ledger

ILLUSTRATION 12-4

ACCOUNTS PAYABLE SUBSIDIARY LEDGER

Name Jones Supply Co., Inc.
Address 5518 Chatham Drive, New Orleans, LA 70122

DATE		DESCRIPTION	PR	DEBIT	CREDIT	DEBIT BALANCE	CREDIT BALANCE
1978 June	4		P18		2,100.00		2,100.00
	5		J12	100.00			2,000.00
	13		CP25	2,000.00			–0–

Name Smith Company
Address 1855 Main Boulevard, New Orleans, LA 70122

DATE		DESCRIPTION	PR	DEBIT	CREDIT	DEBIT BALANCE	CREDIT BALANCE
1978 June	6		P18		70.00		70.00
	15		CP25	70.00			–0–

account, the entry P18 is made to indicate that the entry was posted from page 18 of the purchases journal (P).

Purchases returns and allowances On June 5, the day after the firm received goods from Jones Supply Co., Inc., it was discovered that some of the goods were defective. This merchandise was returned to Jones Supply Co., Inc., and it was agreed that $100 would be reduced from the amount owed to Jones. The general journal (Illustration 12-3) is used to record this kind of transaction.

When purchased goods—an asset—are returned for some reason, adjustments must be made in the accounts where the purchase was first recorded so that these accounts will reflect true amounts. The Purchases account, normally with a debit balance, must be reduced (credited), and the Accounts payable account, a liability account normally with a credit balance, also must be reduced (debited). The credit balance of the **Purchases returns and allowances** account serves to *reduce* the cost of the purchases (the debit balance accumulated in the Purchases account).

Also recorded in the general journal is the fact that the firm issued **Debit memorandum** 174. This source document includes all the relevant details about the merchandise that was found defective. It usually takes the form shown in Illustration 12-5. A copy of the memorandum is sent to the creditor as a communication device between the two companies.

ILLUSTRATION 12-5

DEBIT MEMORANDUM	No. 174

HOLSTEIN COMPANY

Date: June 5, 1978

To: Jones Supply Co. Inc.
5518 Chatham Drive, New Orleans, LA 70122

WE DEBIT YOUR ACCOUNT AS FOLLOWS:

Defective goods from June 4 purchase _____ $100.00

Finally, notice how amounts entered in the general journal are posted to the general ledger and the accounts payable subsidiary ledger. First, the Accounts payable account (201) in the general ledger is debited for $100 (general ledger not illustrated). Also, in the accounts payable subsidiary ledger, the Jones Supply Co., Inc., account is debited for $100 (Illustration 12-4). A check mark is placed in the journal PR column to show that the posting was made. And finally, the Purchases returns and allowances account (512) in the general ledger is credited for $100 (general ledger was not illustrated).

You should recognize that at any point in time the total of all amounts owed according to the accounts payable subsidiary ledger (sum of all balances) must equal the balance of the Accounts payable account in the general ledger. For this reason an account in the general ledger which is supported by a subsidiary ledger is called a **control account.**

Special note: Some firms choose to use a special journal (instead of the general journal) to record purchases returns and allowances made on credit. This would be appropriate when a firm has many such transactions each month. Such a purchases returns and allowances journal is shown below.

PURCHASES RETURNS AND ALLOWANCES JOURNAL page 10

DATE		ACCOUNT DEBITED	DM	PR	AMOUNT
1978 June	4	James & Sons	21	✔	50.00
	9	Howard Co.	22	✔	11.00
	12	Barton, Inc.	23	✔	100.00
	19	Jantzen Corp.	24	✔	115.42
	30	Cranton & Co.	25	✔	197.58
					474.00

At the end of the month, the *total* of the amount column ($474) would be posted as a debit to the Accounts payable account and a credit to the Purchases returns and allowances account in the general ledger. The *individual* amounts in the journal would be posted as debits to the appropriate accounts in the accounts payable subsidiary ledger.

Incurring transportation charges on credit for merchandise purchased Often a firm will incur freight charges to be paid later. The Transportation on purchases account is used to record such charges if they are on merchandise *purchased.* If the freight charges are for merchandise *sold,* they are debited to a separate account called **Shipping expense** or Delivery expense. Refer to the purchases journal (Illustration 12-2). On June 6, the firm was charged $20 by the Ace Freight Co. for transportation on purchases; the terms were 10 days (no discount). Because a separate column for Transportation on purchases has not been set up, the General Accounts Debit column is used. Notice that three postings will be made. First, from the General Accounts Debit column, the Transportation on purchases account (511) is debited individually. Second, the *total* of the Accounts Payable Credit column will be posted at the end of the period. And third, the $20 will be posted as a credit to the Ace Freight Co. account in the accounts payable subsidiary ledger.

Shipping expenses for merchandise sold The preceding discussion involved freight expenses on goods *purchased.* The account Transportation on purchases is used, and this cost becomes a part of Cost of goods sold appearing on the income statement. Another kind of shipping expense involves transporting goods that have been sold to customers. These costs are *selling expenses* by their nature and must also appear on the income statement. Accounts commonly used to record this expense are *Freight out, Delivery expense,* and *Shipping expense.* Be sure you can distinguish this kind of cost (selling expense) from the Transportation on purchases.

  When freight costs on goods sold are incurred and paid for in cash, the cash payments journal is used. Cash, of course, is credited in the Cash Credit column, and Shipping expense (or Delivery expense or Freight out) is debited in the General Accounts Debit column. When these costs are incurred on credit, the purchases journal is used. Accounts payable is credited and the Shipping expense account is debited.

  Some sales agreements provide that the firm selling the merchandise will pay for the shipping and delivery costs, but that the customer will reimburse (repay) the selling company when he pays for the goods. In these cases, when the firm selling the goods prepays the freight, Cash is credited for the amount paid. *Accounts receivable would be debited at that time instead of Shipping expense, because the firm is not incurring an expense but will be reimbursed for the expenditure later.* When the customer pays his bill (including the amount for the freight), Accounts receivable will be credited.

  There are many other kinds of selling expenses in addition to the delivery expenses just mentioned. These include advertising and promotion costs, salesmen's salaries, and display and storage costs. A useful account classification system for selling expenses must be developed for each merchandising firm. As these costs are incurred in the production of earnings, they are recorded in the purchases journal or the cash payments journal in very much the same way as are other expenses and asset acquisitions.

PAYING ACCOUNTS PAYABLE

The next type of transaction that we will examine deals with paying accounts payable. Look again at the cash payments journal (Illustration 12-1). Three transactions of this type are shown, for June 13, 15, and 16. Checks 408, 409, and 410 have been issued in the amounts of $1,960, $70, and $20. Let us look at the payment to Jones Supply Co., Inc., first because this one is the most complex.

The purchases journal (Illustration 12-2) shows us that merchandise was purchased from Jones for *$2,100* on June 4 with terms of 2/10, n/30. This information also is recorded in the Jones account in the accounts payable subsidiary ledger (Illustration 12-4). Refer to that example. Remember that on June 5 we returned $100 of merchandise for a reduction (a debit) in our accounts payable. Note that this return is recorded in both the general journal and the Jones account in the accounts payable subsidiary ledger. After this transaction, a debit of $100, we owe Jones only $2,000. If we take the discount of 2% ($40) of the balance owed, we must issue a check for $1,960. So, in the cash payments journal, the Accounts payable account is debited for $2,000 to reduce the liability, the Cash account is credited to show that cash is being reduced by $1,960, and the **Purchases discounts** account is credited *to reflect a reduction in the cost of the purchases of merchandise.* Generally, the Purchases discounts account will accumulate a credit balance to evidence that discounts taken serve to *reduce* the cost of merchandise purchased.

- *How is the payment of accounts payable recorded?*

This transaction with Jones is posted as follows. The totals of each of the three columns concerned—Accounts Payable Debit, Purchases Discounts Credit, and Cash Credit—are posted to the appropriate account at the end of the period. In addition, the Jones account in the accounts payable subsidiary ledger is debited for the amount appearing in the Accounts Payable Debit column ($2,000). The two other checks written (409 and 410) did not involve discounts and did not require use of the Purchases discounts column.

ACQUIRING ASSETS OTHER THAN MERCHANDISE

If items other than merchandise are purchased, then other appropriate accounts would be debited. For example, in the purchases journal illustrated, the transactions of June 10 and 11 deal with store equipment (from the Z Company) and office supplies (from the M Company). The purchases account is *not* used for such acquisitions.

These new accounts have been illustrated in this unit:

Merchandise inventory (with a debit balance).

Purchases of merchandise (with a debit balance).

Transportation on purchases (with a debit balance).

Purchases returns and allowances (with a credit balance).

Purchases discounts (with a credit balance).

RECORDING AND REPORTING DIVIDENDS

The board of directors of a corporation, a group elected by the stockholders, makes the decisions regarding the payment of dividends. The board may choose to declare and pay dividends to stockholders occasionally or on a regular basis (quarterly, for example). Or the board of directors may choose not to pay dividends to the owners at all. The laws of the several states provide, however, that the corporation must *limit* its dividends. This limitation is for the benefit of creditors and other groups who have an interest in the company. This limitation varies from state to state, but the intent seems to be to provide for permanent retention in the firm of capital that was contributed by the stockholders. This means that dividends normally must be limited to an amount corresponding to the *capital earned* (retained earnings). As a matter of practice, however, it is most unusual for a board of directors to declare dividends equal to as much as *earnings per share* for any period. This practice makes possible the continuous increasing of retained earnings as more or less permanent capital for the firm.

■ *How are dividends recorded and reported?*

Concerning dividends, the board of directors usually specifies these three dates:

1. **Date of declaration.** This is the date that the board of directors takes action (declares that the dividends will be paid); at this point in time, the corporation has incurred a *liability* to the stockholders and the capital has decreased.

2. **Date of record.** This is the reference date for determining which stockholders will be paid the dividends; since the shares of stock of many corporations are bought and sold daily, the ownership changes from day to day.

3. **Date of payment.** This is the date that the checks are mailed to the stockholders in payment of the dividends.

A typical dividend declaration therefore might read as follows:

The board of directors of Ursulines Corporation declared the regular quarterly common stock divided on December 17, 1978, amounting to $1 per share, payable to stockholders of record December 31, 1978, and to be paid January 20, 1979.

On December 17, 1978, the declaration date, the journal entry shown in Illustration 12-6 would be made in the general journal if the Ursulines Corporation had 40,000 shares of common stock outstanding.

	GENERAL JOURNAL			page 18
DATE	ACCOUNT TITLES AND DESCRIPTION	PR	DEBIT	CREDIT
1978 Dec. 17	Dividends		40,000.00	
	Dividends payable			40,000.00
	Regular quarterly dividend of $1.00 per share of common stock; payable January 20, 1979, to stockholders of record Dec. 31, 1978.			

ILLUSTRATION 12-6

The next transaction takes place on January 20, 1979, the date of payment. The cash payments journal shown in Illustration 12-7 records the actual payment of the dividend the next year.

ILLUSTRATION 12-7

				CASH PAYMENTS JOURNAL				page 27
DATE	ACCOUNT DEBITED	CK. NO.	PR	GENERAL ACCOUNTS DEBIT	ACCOUNTS PAYABLE DEBIT	PURCHASES DEBIT	PURCHASES DISCOUNTS CREDIT	CASH CREDIT
1979 Jan. 20	Dividends payable			40,000.00				40,000.00

The **Dividends payable** account is a liability and appears on the balance sheet of the company at December 31, 1978. The Dividends account represents a reduction in Retained earnings (capital) and is closed to that account at the end of 1978.

A separate set of subsidiary records, supporting the capital stock account, is often prepared to provide the needed information about the stockholders of the firm. A ledger is usually kept containing information such as the name, address, number of shares held, and similar data related to each of the stockholders. In addition, many companies have a separate bank account to disburse (pay out) dividends to the many shareholders.

DATE		ACCOUNT CREDITED	DESCRIPTION
1978 Dec.	1	Notes payable	6%, 1 year

ILLUSTRATION 12-8

	GENERAL JOURNAL				page 18
DATE	ACCOUNT TITLES AND DESCRIPTION	PR	DEBIT	CREDIT	

DATE		ACCOUNT TITLES AND DESCRIPTION	PR	DEBIT	CREDIT
1978 Dec.	31	Interest expense		50.00	
		Interest payable			50.00
		Interest on note ($10,000 × 6% for 1 month)			

ILLUSTRATION 12-9

	CASH PAYMENTS JOURNAL								page 27

DATE		ACCOUNT DEBITED	CK. NO.	PR	GENERAL ACCOUNTS DEBIT	ACCOUNTS PAYABLE DEBIT	PURCHASES DEBIT	PURCHASES DISCOUNTS CREDIT	CASH CREDIT
1979 Dec.	1	Notes payable			10,000.00				
		Interest payable			50.00				
		Interest expense			550.00				10,600.00

ILLUSTRATION 12-10

RECORDING AND REPORTING OF DEBT REPAYMENTS

You have already studied how accounts payable are paid and recorded. When notes, bonds, and other liabilities are paid, interest is normally paid at the same time. Assume the following facts for an illustration:

The firm borrowed $10,000 cash from Quarter National Bank on December 1, 1978, to be repaid on December 1, 1979, with 6% interest.

▪ *How is the repayment of debts recorded and reported?*

Also assume that the firm prepares financial statements once each year at December 31, and closes its books at that time. The loan could be recorded in the cash receipts journal as shown in Illustration 12-8.

PR	GENERAL ACCOUNTS CREDIT	ACCOUNTS RECEIVABLE CREDIT	SALES CREDIT	SALES DISCOUNTS DEBIT	CASH DEBIT
		10,000.00			

10,000.00

At the end of the year, December 31, 1978, an adjusting journal entry would be needed to reflect the interest expense incurred for 1978 (to appear on the 1978 income statement). Also, the debt, interest payable, must be reflected on the December 31, 1978 balance sheet. The interest incurred in 1978 is computed as follows:

$$\text{principal} \times \text{rate} \times \text{time} \quad = \text{interest}$$

$$\$10,000 \times 0.06 \times 1/12 \text{ year} = \$50$$

The required adjusting entry is shown in the general journal in Illustration 12-9.

At December 1, 1979, the maturity date of the note, the total principal plus interest must be paid. This amounts to $10,600. One year's interest is $600. Remember that $50 is the interest expense for 1978, and the remaining $550 is the interest expense for 1979. The payment of the debt plus interest is shown in the cash payments journal in Illustration 12-10. The income statement for 1979 will now reflect the correct interest amount ($550), and the debt brought forward from 1978 will have a zero balance and will not appear on the December 31, 1979, balance sheet.

> **NEW TERMS**

accounts payable subsidiary ledger A book containing accounts for each of the creditors (accounts payable) of a firm; the total owed to all creditors as reflected by this ledger is the same as the amount indicated in the accounts payable (control) account in the general ledger. [p. 201]

cash payments journal A special book, usually designed with a number of columns to facilitate posting, that provides the original entry of transactions involving the disbursements of cash; also called a *cash disbursement journal*. [p. 198]

control account Any account in the general ledger that is supported by a subsidiary ledger (such as the accounts payable ledger). [p. 203]

date of declaration The date on which the board of directors acts (declares that dividends will be paid); on this date a firm has incurred a liability to the stockholders and the capital has decreased. [p. 206]

date of payment The date on which checks are mailed to stockholders in payment of dividends. [p. 206]

date of record The reference date for determining which

stockholders will be paid dividends; because the shares of stock of many corporations are bought and sold daily, the ownership changes from day to day. [p. 206]

debit memorandum A source document that provides information about the purchase return and allowance; it is usually the basis for the entry made in the purchases returns and allowances journal; a copy of it is sent to the creditor as a communication device between the two companies. [p. 202]

dividends payable A liability account, reflecting amounts owed to stockholders as a result of dividend declarations by the board of directors of the corporation. [p. 207]

merchandise inventory An asset account that in the periodic method of recording merchandise contains the balance of the merchandise on hand at the *beginning* of the accounting period. [p. 198]

periodic method An accounting method for merchandise wherein the Merchandise inventory account reflects the beginning inventory of merchandise and the Purchases of merchandise account accumulates the cost of additional purchases during the period; at the end of each period a physical count of the merchandise on hand is made to assist in determining the cost of the merchandise which was sold. [p. 198]

purchases discounts account An account, with a credit balance, that is used to accumulate reductions in the

cost of merchandise purchased through taking cash discounts. [p. 205]

purchases journal A special book, usually designed with a number of columns to facilitate posting, that provides the original entry of transactions involving acquisition of merchandise and other assets or expenses on credit (accounts payable). [p. 198]

purchases of merchandise An account, used in the periodic method of recording merchandise, that accumulates the total cost of goods purchased during a period; ordinarily accumulates a debit balance; also known as *Purchases*. [p. 198]

purchases returns and allowances journal A special book, usually designed with one column for recording purchases (merchandise) returns and allowances in those cases where the accounts payable is to be reduced. [p. 203]

shipping expense Freight costs on merchandise sold by the firm; the account accumulates a debit balance and is part of the selling expenses of the firm; not to be confused with Transportation on purchases; also called Freight out and Delivery expense. [p. 204]

transportation on purchases Freight costs on merchandise purchased by the firm; the account accumulates a debit balance; not to be confused with Shipping costs (Delivery expenses) on goods which are sold by the firm and delivered to customers. [p. 200]

❯ ASSIGNMENT MATERIAL

QUESTIONS

Q12-1. Compare and contrast the recording of freight costs on goods purchased and freight costs on goods sold.

Q12-2. Must every corporation that makes a profit declare dividends? Explain.

Q12-3. Explain the meaning of each of the following dates regarding dividends: (1) date of declaration, (2) date of record, and (3) date of payment.

Q12-4. Describe the journal entry made (if any) at each of these three dates: (1) date of declaration, (2) date of record, and (3) date of payment.

Q12-5. Describe the journal entries usually made upon the repayment of a note plus interest. Explain the exact effect of this transaction on the income statement and on the balance sheet.

EXERCISES

E12-1. Shown on the next page is a special journal (purchases journal) for a company. Using this journal as a reference, answer the following questions.

a. What, specifically, is the PR column that appears to the left of the Accounts Payable column used for?

b. To which ledger is the total of the Accounts Payable Credit column ($4,018.26) posted?
c. What posting reference is entered in the PR column for the transaction of December 20?
d. Two posting references are used for the December 8 transaction. Explain.
e. The transactions of December 8 and December 24 both deal with freight. Why are they not debited to the same account? Explain.
f. The Simpson Co. account appears in which ledger?
g. Does the transaction of December 7 *increase* the balance of Reinecke Corp. account in the subsidiary ledger?
h. How is the total of the General Accounts Debit column ($218.26) posted? Explain.
i. Will there be any account numbers (general ledger account numbers) appearing in the PR column that appears to the left of the Accounts Payable Credit column when the accounts are posted?
j. Are any postings made to the accounts receivable subsidiary ledger from the purchases journal? Explain Purchases Journal Table.

PURCHASES JOURNAL   page 20

DATE		ACCOUNT CREDITED	PR	ACCOUNTS PAYABLE CREDIT	PURCHASES DEBIT	general accounts debit		
						ACCOUNT DEBITED	PR	AMOUNT
1978 Dec.	2	Simpson Co. 2/10, n/60		700.00	700.00			
	7	Reinecke Corp. 2/10, n/30		1,000.00	1,000.00			
	8	Hall Freight, Inc. 10 days		60.00		Transportation on purchases		60.00
	15	Simpson Co. 2/10, n/60		2,000.00	2,000.00			
	20	Reinecke Corp. 2/10, n/30		100.00	100.00			
	24	Hall Freight, Inc. 10 days		74.12		Shipping expense		74.12
	25	N. O. Power Co. 10 days		84.14		General expense		84.14
				4,018.26	3,800.00			218.26

E12-2. Set up the following journals: (1) general journal, (2) cash payments journal, and (3) cash receipts journal. Record the following selected transactions in the journals.

1978

March 1   The board of directors of the company declared the regular quarterly common stock dividend on March 1, 1978, amounting to $2 per share, payable to stockholders of record March 15, 1978, and to be paid March 31, 1978. There were 50,000 shares of common stock outstanding.

     15   The firm borrowed $100,000 cash from First National Bank, to be repaid in 1 month, with 6% interest.

     31   Paid the dividends due. Check 207 was issued.

     31   Recorded the adjusting entry for interest due on the note, $\frac{1}{2}$ month.

April 12   Paid the note and interest due. Check 208 was issued.

E12-3. Here are four possible ways that the information contained in a column of a special journal might be posted:

A   The total only of the column is posted to a general ledger account.

B   The individual entries in the column are posted to the general ledger accounts; the total of the column is not posted.

C   The total of the column is posted to a general ledger account; also, the individual entries in the column are posted to a subsidiary ledger.

D   The total of the column is posted to two different general ledger accounts; also, the individual entries in the column are posted to a subsidiary ledger.

Using the letters above (A through D), indicate for each of the following columns how the column would be posted.

a. General accounts credit column of the cash receipts journal
b. Cash debit column of the cash receipts journal
c. Accounts payable credit column of the purchases journal
d. Purchases debit column of the purchases journal
e. General accounts debit column of the purchases journal
f. General accounts debit column of the cash payments journal
g. Accounts payable debit column of the cash payments journal
h. Purchases debit column of the cash payments journal
i. Purchases discounts credit column of the cash payments journal
j. Cash credit column of the cash payments journal

E12-4. For each of the following business transactions, indicate (1) the special journal to be used to record the transaction, (2) the account to be debited, and (3) the account to be credited.

Example: Purchased merchandise for cash.
          (1) Cash payments journal
          (2) Debit Purchases of merchandise
          (3) Credit Cash

a. Purchased merchandise with terms of 2/10, n/30.
b. Issued capital stock for cash.
c. Received a freight bill for merchandise purchased. The bill will be paid in 30 days.
d. Received a bill for freight on merchandise *sold* (for delivery of merchandise to customers). The bill will be paid in 30 days.
e. Borrowed cash from the bank, signing a note.
f. Paid the amount due from a purchase of merchandise, taking the appropriate cash discount.

g. Returned merchandise to a supplier. The firm's account balance was reduced by $50.

h. Purchased furniture (office) for cash.

E12-5. Below is a listing of Paley Company's accounts with their balances at December 31, 1978.

101	Cash	$50,000
102	Accounts receivable	10,000
103	Merchandise inventory	85,000
106	Office supplies	2,000
120	Office equipment	9,000
121	Accumulated depreciation—Office equipment	400
122	Land	24,000
201	Accounts payable	17,000
202	Notes payable (long-term)	22,000
301	Capital stock	41,000
302	Retained earnings	52,000
306	Dividends	5,000
401	Sales of merchandise	68,000
402	Rent revenue	10,000
501	Purchases of merchandise	15,000
502	Transportation of merchandise	100
503	Purchases discounts	450
504	Purchases returns and allowances	150
520	Advertising expense	1,700
521	Salaries expense	6,500
522	Insurance expense	2,000
523	Rent expense	500
524	Interest expense	300
525	Depreciation expense—Office equipment	400

From the information available, prepare a trial balance in good form for Paley Company at December 31, 1978.

PROBLEMS (GROUP A)

P12-1. *Recording and posting purchases and cash payments*

a. Below is a list of business transactions. Set up (1) a cash payments journal, (2) a purchases journal, and (3) a general journal similar to the ones illustrated in the text. Record each of the transactions in the appropriate journal.

1978

May 3   Purchased merchandise from ABC Company for $1,000, with terms of 3/10, n/60.

     4   Received a freight bill from MX Company for the merchandise purchased from ABC Company on May 3. The freight charges amounted to $21 and are payable in 10 days with no discount.

     6   Returned part of the merchandise to ABC Company and requested that our account balance be reduced by $50.

   11   Paid the amount due the ABC Company from the May 3 purchase, issuing Check 1897.

   12   Purchased office supplies from XYZ Company for $90, with terms of 2/10, n/30.

14 Purchased merchandise from DBA Company for $1,800 cash. Wrote Check 1898.

14 Paid the amount due MX Company from the May 4 transaction. Issued Check 1899.

b. Refer to the cash payments journal and the purchases journal used in this problem. For *each* column in *each* of the two journals, indicate the posting procedure that would be used. For example, Purchases Journal, Accounts Payable Credit column—the total is posted as a credit to the Accounts payable account in the general ledger, and the individual amounts in the column are posted as credits to the appropriate accounts in the accounts payable subsidiary ledger.

P12-2. *Recording transactions in special journals, comprehensive.* Set up the following journals: (1) purchases journal, (2) cash payments journal, (3) sales journal, (4) cash receipts journal, and (5) general journal. Record the following business transactions:

1978

July 1 A group of businessmen formed a corporation and 14,000 shares of no-par common stock were issued for $42,000 cash.

2 Purchased merchandise on credit from Wilken Company, $3,000, with terms of 2/10, n/30.

3 Borrowed $10,000 cash from First National Bank, signing a 6%, 30-day note.

5 Received a freight bill from Billy's Freight Co. on the merchandise purchased from Wilken Company on July 2. The bill amounts to $200 and will be paid in 10 days.

5 Issued bonds payable for $75,000 cash. The bonds are 20-year bonds, with an annual interest rate of 6%, with interest to be paid quarterly.

6 Returned defective merchandise to Wilken Company and issued debit memorandum 203 for $350.

7 Purchased office supplies from Horton Co. for $500, with terms of 30 days.

8 Purchased store equipment for $2,300 from Hart Corp., with terms of 30 days.

9 Purchased merchandise from Thompson, Inc., for $403 cash. Issued Check 304.

11 Paid the freight bill (Billy's Freight Co.) $200, Check 305.

11 Paid the amount due Wilken Company, Check 306.

12 Purchased a long-term investment, land, costing $15,000, signing a 2-year, 8% note payable.

13 Made sales of $14,000 to Delia Co. with terms of 2/10, n/30, Invoice 507.

14 Made cash sales of $22,000.

15 Issued Credit memorandum 718 to Delia Co. for $100 of merchandise returned.

16 Made cash sales of $20,000. Also collected an additional $600 in sales taxes.

20 Collected the amount due from Delia Co.

20 The board of directors declared dividends of 10¢ per share, payable to stockholders of record July 25, 1978, and payable in cash on July 31, 1978. 14,000 shares of common stock were outstanding.

22 Paid the amount due Hart Corp., issuing Check 307.

23 Paid a freight bill to Billy's Freight Co. for $80 for merchandise shipped to our customers. Issued Check 308.

30 Paid the dividends, issuing Check 309.

31 Paid the note and interest for the July 3 loan, issuing Check 310.

31 One-fifth of the office supplies that were purchased has been used. Make the adjusting entry.

P12-3. *Recording transactions in special journals, comprehensive.* Set up five journals as illustrated in the text. Record the following transactions. Use the letters in place of dates in the journals.

a. Issued $1,000 of bonds (10-year bonds, 7% interest payable semiannually).
b. Borrowed $15,000 from First City Bank signing a 5-year, 8% note payable.
c. Issued 2,000 shares of capital stock to P. Louie for $10,500 cash.
d. Issued 5,000 shares of capital stock to Gibson Investment Company, receiving $5.25 per share ($26,250).
e. Purchased merchandise from Sanford Supply Company for $1,050, with terms 2/10, n/30.
f. Received a freight bill from Caldwell Company for the merchandise purchased from Sanford Supply Company. The freight charges amounted to $20 and are payable in 10 days with no discount.
g. Issued $1,700 of bonds (10-year bonds, 8% interest payable semiannually).
h. Returned part of the merchandise purchased from Sanford Supply Company. We requested that our account balance be reduced by $250. Issued debit memorandum 10.
i. Paid the amount due to Sanford Supply Company, issuing Check 1107.
j. Paid the amount due to Caldwell Company for the freight bill. Issued Check 1108.
k. Purchased office supplies from Mason Company for $110, with terms of 2/10, n/30.
l. Borrowed $10,000 from First National Bank signing a 10-year, 8% note payable.
m. Purchased office supplies from Bailey Company for $180 cash. Issued Check 1109.
n. Purchased merchandise from Fairfield Company for $12,300, with terms of 3/10, n/60.
o. Received a freight bill from Harper Freight Company for merchandise purchased from Fairfield Company. The freight charges amounted to $120 and are payable in 10 days.
p. Paid the amount due Fairfield Company. Issued Check 1110.
q. Purchased merchandise from Murphy Company for $14,325 cash, issuing Check 1111.
r. Paid the amount due Harper Freight Company. Issued check 1112.
s. Made sales of merchandise to Royal Company, $5,000, with terms of 2/10, n/30. This transaction is not subject to sales taxes. Prepared Invoice 450.
t. Made cash sales amounting to $4,440. In addition, collected 6% sales taxes.
u. Made sales of merchandise to Williams Company, $1,300, with terms 3/10, n/60; issued Invoice 451. This transaction is not subject to sales taxes.
v. Williams Company returned merchandise to us for a reduction in their account amounting to $150. The merchandise was defective, and we issued Credit memorandum 325.
w. Collected the amount due from Royal Company within the discount period.
x. Paid $140 freight charges for goods shipped to our customers (Check 1113).
y. Collected the amount due from Williams Company within the discount period.
z. The board of directors declared the regular quarterly common stock dividend on April 1, 1978, amounting to $3 per share, payable in cash on April 15, 1978. 10,000 shares of common stock were outstanding.
aa. Paid the dividends due. Check 1114 was issued.

P12-4. *Recording cash receipts, cash payments, purchases, and purchases returns.* Below is a list of business transactions for Blanchard Corporation.

1978

Aug. 11   Purchased merchandise from Socola Company for $12,435, with terms of 2/10, n/30.

15   Borrowed $15,000 from First National Bank, signing a 9%, 45-day note.

18   Received a freight bill from Craig Company for the merchandise purchased on August 11 from Socola Company. The freight charges amount to $145 and are payable in 10 days.

19   Issued 350 shares of capital stock to Mary Marcus for $35,300 cash.

20   Issued 400 shares of capital stock to Sills Company for $41,000 cash.

20   Returned part of the merchandise that we had purchased from Socola Company on August 11. We requested that our account balance be reduced by $1,000, and this was done by Socola Company.

21   Paid the amount due Socola Company from the August 11 purchase. Issued Check 346.

23   Issued bonds, receiving $118,000 cash. The bonds bear 7% interest and will be repaid in 10 years.

24   Purchased office equipment from AX Office Suppliers for $1,200, with terms of 1/30 (1% discount allowed if paid within 30 days).

25   Purchased merchandise from Macking Company for $11,000 cash, issuing Check 347.

28   Paid the amount due Craig Company from the freight bill of August 18. Issued Check 348.

REQUIRED: Set up the following special journals: (1) cash receipts journal, (2) cash payments journal, (3) purchases journal, and (4) general journal. Record the transactions above in the appropriate journals.

P12-5. *Recording transactions in special journals, comprehensive.* Below is a list of some of the business transactions for Anderson Company for June, 1978.

1978

June 10   Purchased merchandise from Caveness Corporation for $15,210, with terms of 2/10, n/30.

15   Received a freight bill from Craig Freight Corporation for the merchandise purchased on June 10 from Caveness Corporation. The freight charges amount to $145 and are payable in 10 days.

18   Issued 700 shares of capital stock to Stockton Company for $2,800 cash.

19   Borrowed $20,000 from American National Bank, signing a 9%, 45-day note.

19   Returned part of the merchandise that we had purchased from Caveness Corporation on June 10. We requested that our account balance be reduced by $600, and this was done by Caveness Corporation. Issued Debit memorandum 340.

19   Paid the amount due Caveness Corporation from the June 10 purchase. Issued Check 350.

25   Issued bonds, receiving $120,000 cash. The bonds bear 7% interest and will be repaid in 10 years.

25   Paid the amount due Craig Freight Corporation from the freight bill of June 15. Issued Check 351.

28   Purchased office equipment from Barton Office Suppliers, Inc., for $2,000, with terms of 1/60 (1% discount if paid within 60 days).

29   Purchased merchandise from Monopoly, Inc., for $12,000 cash, issuing Check 352.

REQUIRED: Record the transactions in five journals similar to the ones illustrated in the chapter.

P12-6. *Recording transactions in special journals, comprehensive.* The following are selected business transactions for Caluda Co. for March, 1978:

1978

March 1   Made cash sales amounting to $2,000. In addition, collected 6% sales taxes.

2   Purchased merchandise for $1,000, with terms 2/10, n/30, from Ellzey Corp.

3   Received a freight bill for merchandise purchased from Wu Corp. The freight charges amounted to $55, to be paid in 10 days.

4   Borrowed $20,000 cash from First State Bank, signing a 7%, 60-day note.

5   The board of directors declared the regular quarterly common stock dividend amounting to $2.00 per share, payable in cash. Ten thousand shares of stock were outstanding, at $7 par value.

6   Returned defective merchandise to Ellzey Corp. Our account was reduced by $200, issuing Debit memorandum 540.

7   Made credit sales of $15,000 to Lee Corp. with terms of 3/10, n/60, Invoice 35.

8   Issued a credit memorandum no. 600 for $350 for merchandise returned from Deage Co.

9   Paid the note of $20,000 plus interest for time outstanding, issuing Check 34. We paid the note early and were charged only 5 days' interest ($20,000 × 7% × 5/360).

10   Paid the dividends, issuing Check 35.

11   Issued 2,000 shares of common stock receiving $14,000 cash.

12   Paid amount due on previous purchase of merchandise from Willman Co., $5,000, issuing Check 36.

13   Collected amount due from Deike Co., $9,950. The merchandise was sold for $10,000, and the customer was granted a $50 cash discount.

31   Recorded the adjusting entry for interest due on a note to Richter Co., of $28.

REQUIRED: Record the transactions in five journals similar to the ones illustrated in the chapter.

CUMULATIVE REVIEW PROBLEMS

P12-7. *Cumulative review problem.* Listed below are a series of business transactions for the first month of operations of Esplanade Corporation.

1978

Dec. 1   Three businessmen decided to form a corporation for the purpose of buying and selling a new, recently developed product. Application for a corporate charter was made, the charter was granted by the state, and the company began operating on December 1, 1978. Common stock was issued as follows:

SHAREHOLDER	NUMBER OF SHARES	ASSETS RECEIVED
William Barracks	1,000	$3,000 cash
John L. Burgundy	2,000	$6,000 cash
William I. Chartres	4,000	$12,000 cash

The common shares issued are called *no-par common stock;* this means that there is no par or face amount for each share.

Dec. 2   The firm decided to borrow $5,000 to aid in operating the company. A 7%, 1-month note payable was signed, and cash amounting to $5,000 was received from First National Bank.

3   Purchased merchandise on credit from St. Philip Company, $1,500, with terms of 1/15, n/60.

4   Issued bonds payable for $40,000 cash. The bonds were 15-year bonds, with an annual interest rate of 5%, with interest to be paid quarterly.

5   Received a freight bill from French Freight Co. on the merchandise purchased from St. Philip Company on December 3. The bill, to be paid in 10 days, amounts to $100.

6   Purchased office supplies from Dumaine Corporation for $200, with terms of 30 days.

7   Purchased store equipment for $1,000 from Toulouse Company, with terms of 15 days.

8   Returned defective merchandise to St. Philip Company and issued Debit memorandum 101 for $18.

9   Purchased merchandise from Conti, Inc. for $200 cash. Issued Check 101.

10   Paid the freight bill for the merchandise purchased from Conti, Inc., on December 9, $12, Check 102.

11   Paid the amount due St. Philip Company, Check 103.

12   Purchased a long-term investment, land, costing $8,000, signing a note payable for $8,000, with 8% interest, 2 years.

13   Made sales of $7,400 to Bienville Company, with terms of 2/10, n/30, Invoice 101.

14   Issued Credit memorandum 101 to Bienville Company for $300 for merchandise returned.

15   Made cash sales of $9,000.

16   Made cash sales of $10,000. Also, collected an additional $500 in sales taxes.

20   Collected the amount due from Bienville Company.

21   The board of directors declared dividends of $.15 per share, payable to stockholders of record of December 25, 1978, and payable in cash on December 30, 1978.

22   Paid the amount due Dumaine Corporation. Issued Check 104.

23   Paid a freight bill (AB Freight Company) for $40, for the shipments of December 13 to Bienville Company; Check 105.

29   Paid the dividends. Issued Check 106.

30   Paid the note and interest for the December 2 loan with Check 107.

31   One-fourth of the office supplies have been used up. The adjusting entry was made.

REQUIRED: Record the transactions in five journals similar to the ones illustrated in this chapter.

P12-8. *Cumulative review problem.* Illustrated on the following pages are seven special journals for Count Company for the month of December, 1978. All business transactions for the month have been entered in the journals, and the columns of the journals have been totaled and ruled. Notice that the company uses a sales returns and allowances journal (to record all sales returns and allowances *on credit*) and a purchases returns and allowances journal (to record all purchases returns and allowances *on credit*).

DATE		ACCOUNT CREDITED	PR	ACCOUNTS PAYABLE CREDIT	PURCHASES DEBIT	general accounts debit		
						ACCOUNT DEBITED	PR	AMOUNT
1978 Dec.	2	Simpson Co. 2/10, n/60		700.00	700.00			
	7	Reinecke Corp. 2/10, n/30		1,000.00	1,000.00			
	8	Hall Freight, Inc. 10 days		60.00		Transportation on purchases		60.00
	15	Simpson Co. 2/10, n/60		2,000.00	2,000.00			
	20	Reinecke Corp. 2/10, n/30		100.00	100.00			
	24	Hall Freight, Inc. 10 days		74.12		Shipping expense		74.12
	25	N. O. Power Co. 10 days		84.14		General expense		84.14
				4,018.26	3,800.00			218.26

DATE		ACCOUNT DEBITED		INVOICE NUMBER	PR	ACCOUNTS RECEIVABLE DEBIT	SALES TAXES PAYABLE CREDIT	SALES CREDIT
1978 Dec.	3	Pearl Company, 2/10, n/30		713		1,060.00	60.00	1,000.00
	5	Liebling, Inc.	✔	714		212.00	12.00	200.00
	6	Pearl Company	✔	715		231.50	13.10	218.40
	9	Smith Company	✔	716		106.00	6.00	100.00
	12	Brant & Brandt	✔	717		860.72	48.72	812.00
	20	Pearl Company	✔	718		2,120.00	120.00	2,000.00
	27	Smith Company	✔	719		148.40	8.40	140.00
	28	Allyn Corp.	✔	720		2,226.00	126.00	2,100.00
						6,964.62	394.22	6,570.40

SALES RETURNS AND ALLOWANCES JOURNAL page 11

DATE		ACCOUNT CREDITED	CM	PR	AMOUNT
1978 Dec.	5	Pearl Company	170		45.18
	19	Brant & Brandt	171		20.00
	26	Pearl Company	172		15.00
					80.18

PURCHASES RETURNS AND ALLOWANCES JOURNAL page 22

DATE		ACCOUNT DEBITED	DM	PR	AMOUNT
1978 Dec.	10	Reinecke Corp.	512		140.21
	17	Simpson Co.	513		21.00
	20	Simpson Co.	514		100.00
	29	Dragon Co.	515		25.50
					286.71

GENERAL JOURNAL page 25

DATE		ACCOUNT TITLES AND DESCRIPTION	PR	DEBIT	CREDIT
1978 Dec.	15	Building		20,000.00	
		Notes payable			20,000.00
		Purchased storage building; signed a 1-year, 6% note			

CASH RECEIPTS JOURNAL

DATE	ACCOUNT CREDITED	DESCRIPTION	PR	GENERAL ACCOUNTS CREDIT	ACCOUNTS RECEIVABLE CREDIT	SALES CREDIT	SALES DISCOUNTS DEBIT	CASH DEBIT
1978 Dec. 5	Pearl Company	collection of account			50.00		1.00	49.00
7	Sales	cash sales				151.00		151.00
11	Rent income			200.00				200.00
13	Pearl Company	collection of account			1,014.82		20.30	994.52
14	Sales	cash sales				750.00		795.00
	Sales taxes payable			45.00				
15	Allyn Corp.	collection of account			1,500.00			1,500.00
19	Smith Company	collecton of account			106.00		2.12	103.88
22	Brant & Brandt	collection of account			840.72	901.00	16.81	823.91
				245.00	3,511.54	901.00	40.23	4,617.31

DATE		ACCOUNT DEBITED	CK. NO.	PR	GENERAL ACCOUNTS DEBIT	ACCOUNTS PAYABLE DEBIT	PURCHASES DEBIT	PURCHASES DISCOUNTS CREDIT	CASH CREDIT
1978 Dec.	3	Simpson Co.	313			500.00		10.00	490.00
	12	General expense	314		140.00				140.00
	17	Reinecke Corp.	315			859.79		17.20	842.59
	18	Hall Freight, Inc.	316			60.00			60.00
	20	Selling expense	317		400.00				400.00
	24	Simpson Co.	318			1,979.00		39.58	1,939.42
	30	Purchases	319				2,000.00		2,000.00
					540.00	3,398.79	2,000.00	66.78	5,872.01

REQUIRED:

a. Set up a general ledger for the company and enter as the beginning balances the December 1, 1978, balances of the firm's accounts as follows:

Count Company
TRIAL BALANCE
December 1, 1978

account

101	Cash	12,000.00	
111	Marketable securities	3,000.00	
120	Accounts receivable	1,765.75	
125	Merchandise inventory	3,000.00	
130	Prepaid insurance	400.00	
131	Supplies	250.00	
157	Building	–0–	
158	Accumulated depreciation—Building		–0–
201	Accounts payable		600.00
202	Sales tax payable		–0–
210	Notes payable		5,000.00
301	Capital stock		8,000.00
302	Retained earnings		6,815.75
		20,415.75	20,415.75

Because the books were closed at November 30, 1978, there are no beginning balances in the revenue, expense, and dividends accounts.

These other accounts are used by the firm and should be included in the general ledger you set up:

303	Dividends	503	Purchases discounts
401	Sales of merchandise	504	Transportation on purchases
402	Sales returns and allowances	510	General expense
403	Sales discounts	511	Depreciation expense—Building
404	Rent income	520	Selling expense
501	Purchases of merchandise	521	Shipping expense
502	Purchases returns and allowances		

b. Set up an accounts receivable subsidiary ledger. Enter these December 1, 1978 (beginning) balances:

Count Company
SCHEDULE OF ACCOUNTS RECEIVABLE
December 1, 1978

Allyn Corp., 1900 Minest Street, New Orleans, LA 70118	$1,500.00
Brant & Brandt, 2000 Third Avenue, Los Angeles, CA 95950	–0–
Liebling, Inc., 3155 St. Agnes, Jones,TN 31209	215.75
Pearl Company, Route 50, Farmerville, OH 29500	50.00
Smith Company, 900 Delgado, Ink, LA 77015	–0–
	$1,765.75

Notice that the total of the accounts receivable accounts at December 1, 1978, is the same as the beginning balance in the Accounts receivable (control) account in the general ledger.

c. Set up an accounts payable subsidiary ledger, entering these December 1, 1978, beginning balances:

Count Company
SCHEDULE OF ACCOUNTS PAYABLE
December 1, 1978

Dragon Co., 10101 Slug Street, Marrero, LA 70150	$100.00
Hall Freight, Inc., 2518 RK Avenue, Westwego, LA 70140	–0–
N.O. Power Co., 900 Bell Street., New Orleans, LA 70115	–0–
Reinecke Corp., 218 Press Avenue, New Orleans, LA 70112	–0–
Simpson Co., 2500 D'Odin, New Orleans, LA 70122	500.00
	$600.00

Notice that the total of the accounts payable accounts at December 1, 1978, is the same as the beginning balance in the Accounts payable (control) account in the general ledger.

d. Post the information contained in the seven journals to the three ledgers you have just set up. Post the journals in the following order: purchases journal, sales journal, purchases returns and allowances journal, sales returns and allowances journal, cash receipts journal, cash payments journal, and general journal.

(In practice, the individual postings from the journals would be done daily. This practice would keep customer and creditor account balances in the subsidiary ledgers current at all times.)

e. Prepare a trial balance of the general ledger.

f. Prepare a *schedule of accounts receivable* (a listing of all the accounts and balances in the accounts receivable ledger) at December 31, 1978. See part b of this problem for an example. Be sure that the total of this schedule agrees with the Accounts receivable account in the general ledger.

g. Prepare a *schedule of accounts payable* (a listing of all the accounts and balances in the accounts payable ledger) at December 31, 1978. See part c of this problem for an example. Be sure that the total of this schedule agrees with the Accounts payable account in the general ledger.

chapter 6

merchandising operations: end of period

THE WORK SHEET AND INTERIM STATEMENTS

> **OBJECTIVE**

In this chapter you will continue your study of merchandising operations through studying (1) the work sheet and interim statements in this unit, (2) preparing financial statements in Unit 14, and (3) analyzing adjusting and closing entries in Unit 15.

One objective of this unit is to illustrate how a work sheet for a merchandising corporation is prepared. This unit will serve as a comprehensive review because the new accounts introduced in past units dealing with merchandising will be included in the example. A second objective is to illustrate how the merchandise inventory and cost of goods sold are treated at the end of an operating period. A third objective is to define and discuss interim financial statements.

> **APPROACH TO ATTAINING THE OBJECTIVE**

As you study about the work sheet, inventory, cost of goods sold, and interim statements, pay special attention to these four questions, which the text following answers:

- *What common adjusting entries are needed for a merchandising firm?*
- *How is the Merchandise inventory account corrected?*
- *How is the work sheet completed for a merchandising corporation?*
- *What are interim financial statements?*

A work sheet for Orleans Merchandising Company for the period January 1, 1978, through June 30, 1978, is presented on the next two pages. All the accounts with balances that appeared in the company's ledger are entered in the trial balance columns of the work sheet. Observe these facts:

1. The Merchandise inventory account has a debit balance of $5,000, which represents the inventory on hand at the *beginning of the period,* January 1, 1978.

2. Several accounts—in addition to the beginning inventory—are part of **Cost of goods sold** for the firm. Two of these with *debit* balances in the trial balance are: Purchases of merchandise and Transportation on purchases. Two with *credit* balances in the trial balance are: Purchases returns and allowances and Purchases discounts. Remember that all five of these accounts, as well as the ending inventory, must be considered in determining the amount of the expense, Cost of goods sold.

3. Two capital accounts are shown for the corporation: (1) Common stock, which represents the total amounts contributed by the owners (stockholders) as their investments in the firm, and (2) Retained earnings, which represents capital that was created in the past through the earnings process. The retained earnings balance of $7,000 represents this part of capital at the *beginning* of the period, January 1, 1978. Refer to Unit 9 if you feel you need a review of the nature of Retained earnings of a corporation.

4. Orleans Merchandising Company uses this account numbering system:

ACCOUNT NUMBERS	KINDS OF ACCOUNTS
100–119	Current assets
120–139	Long-term investments
140–159	Plant and equipment
200–219	Current liabilities
220–239	Long-term liabilities
300–319	Capital
400–439	Revenues
500–519	Cost of goods sold
520–539	Administrative, general, and financial expenses
540–559	Selling expenses

This scheme helps the financial statement preparer to classify accounts in the statements.

ORLEANS MERCHANDISING CORPORATION
Worksheet for the period January 1, 1978, through June 30, 1978

ACCT. NO.	ACCOUNT TITLE	TRIAL BALANCE dr.	TRIAL BALANCE cr.	ADJUSTMENTS dr.	ADJUSTMENTS cr.	ADJUSTED TRIAL BALANCE dr.	ADJUSTED TRIAL BALANCE cr.	INCOME STATEMENT dr.	INCOME STATEMENT cr.	STATEMENT OF RETAINED EARNINGS dr.	STATEMENT OF RETAINED EARNINGS cr.	BALANCE SHEET dr.	BALANCE SHEET cr.
101	Cash	10,000				10,000						10,000	
102	Marketable securities	4,000				4,000						4,000	
103	Accounts receivable	13,000				13,000						13,000	
104	Merchandise inventory	5,000		(h) 14,000	(h) 5,000	14,000						14,000	
105	Office supplies	1,000			(a) 400	600						600	
106	Store supplies	2,000			(b) 200	1,800						1,800	
121	Investments in stocks	40,000				40,000						40,000	
122	Investments in bonds	11,000				11,000						11,000	
141	Office equipment	6,000				6,000						6,000	
142	Accumulated depreciation—Office eq.		2,000		(d) 1,000		3,000						3,000
143	Store equipment	50,000				50,000						50,000	
144	Accumulated depreciation—Store eq.		10,000		(e) 2,000		12,000						12,000
145	Land	20,000				20,000						20,000	
201	Accounts payable		7,000				7,000						7,000
202	Sales taxes payable		2,000				2,000						2,000
221	Notes payable		15,000				15,000						15,000
222	Bonds payable		43,000				43,000						43,000
301	Common stock, 10,000 shares outstanding		30,000				30,000						30,000
302	Retained earnings		7,000				7,000				7,000		
303	Dividends	2,000				2,000				2,000			
401	Sales of merchandise		150,000				150,000		150,000				
402	Sales returns and allowances	3,000				3,000		3,000					
403	Sales discounts	2,000				2,000		2,000					
421	Rental income		9,000				9,000		9,000				
502	Purchases of merchandise	80,000				80,000		80,000					
503	Transportation on purchases	1,000				1,000		1,000					
504	Purchases returns and allowances		2,000				2,000		2,000				

Work sheet (partial) — year ended June 30, 1978

Acct.	Account										
505	Purchases discounts	1,000					1,000				
521	Officers and general salaries expense	9,000				9,000		9,000			
522	Insurance expense	1,000		(c) 300		700		700		700	
541	Advertising expense	6,000				6,000		6,000			
542	Sales salaries expense	12,000				12,000		12,000			
		278,000	278,000								
523	Office supplies expense			(a) 400		400		400		400	
543	Store supplies expense			(b) 200		200		200		200	
107	Prepaid insurance				(c) 300	300				300	
524	Depreciation expense—Office equipment			(d) 1,000		1,000		1,000		1,000	
544	Depreciation expense—Store equipment			(e) 2,000		2,000		2,000		2,000	
525	Interest expense			(f) 2,000		2,000		2,000		2,000	
203	Interest payable				(f) 2,000	2,000				2,000	
526	Income tax expense			(g) 5,000		5,000		5,000		5,000	
204	Income tax payable				(g) 5,000	5,000				5,000	
600	Net earnings summary			(h) 14,000	(h) 5,000	14,000	5,000	14,000	5,000		
				29,900	29,900	302,000	302,000	129,300	176,000	176,000	176,000
	Net earnings, January 1–June 30, 1978							46,700			46,700
								176,000	176,000	2,000	51,700
	Retained earnings, June 30, 1978									51,700	53,700
										53,700	53,700
										170,700	170,700

Adjustments at June 30, 1978
(a) Office supplies used
(b) Store supplies used
(c) Insurance expense expired
(d) Depreciation of office equipment
(e) Depreciation of store equipment
(f) Interest on notes and bonds
(g) Income taxes due
(h) Inventory adjustment

The work sheet illustrated shows four common types of adjustments. These are: (1) using prepaid expenses, (2) using plant and equipment, (3) incurring expenses on credit, and (4) correcting the merchandise inventory account. In this section we will examine each of these in turn.

Using prepaid expenses The first adjustment is labeled (a) on the work sheet. The firm purchased office supplies totaling $1,000 and this amount appears in the trial balance in Account 105 as a current asset. The management of the firm determined that $400 of the supplies had been used up and that $600 of the supplies remained on hand at the end of the period. Therefore, adjusting entry (a) shows a debit to the Office supplies expense account (number 523) and a credit to the asset account (105) for $400 to reduce the asset and to create an expense for the period. The purpose of this adjustment is twofold: (1) to assure that all expenses incurred in the course of the period's operations appear on the income statement, and (2) to assure that all assets (including current assets) are stated according to generally accepted accounting principles. Prepaid expenses (assets) are customarily stated at their cost, the benefit of which is to be received in the future.

- *What common adjusting entries are needed for a merchandising firm?*

Adjustment (b) is similar to (a), except that (b) deals with store supplies instead of office supplies. In this case management determines that of the $2,000 of store supplies purchased, $1,800 still remain on hand unused.

The third adjustment (c) has the same purpose, except that the bookkeeping technique of the firm is a bit different. When the insurance was paid for, the Insurance expense account (522) was debited for $1,000. In other words, when the expense was paid, the expense account was debited instead of the asset account, as in the case of the supplies. At the end of the period, the management determines that $700 of the insurance has expired (has been used up through insurance coverage) and that $300 remains unused as an asset. Adjusting entry (c) therefore corrects the accounts by setting up an asset for $300 and reducing the expense account by $300 so that its balance will be $700. An important point for you to note is that when expenses are paid for either an asset or an expense account can be debited. Then, *at the end of the period,* when it is determined how much of the expense has been used and how much is still an asset, the appropriate adjustment can be made.

Using plant and equipment You've already studied how plant and equipment are used and how their depreciation expense is recorded. Transaction (d) shows that depreciation expense of $1,000 was recorded for the use of office equipment for the period. The effect of this entry is to reduce the *net* asset, Office equipment, from $4,000 to $3,000.

Adjusting entry (e) reduces the *net* asset, Store equipment, from

$40,000 to $38,000 and sets up the appropriate expense of $2,000 for the period.

Incurring expenses on credit The next kind of common adjustment involves expenses which have been incurred but not yet recorded in the accounts. Two examples of this are illustrated in the adjustments on the work sheet. Adjustment (f) indicates that $2,000 of interest is owed on the notes and bonds. This amount will be paid in the future. Interest expense is debited to reduce the earnings of the period, and a liability, Interest payable, is credited to appear on the balance sheet.

Adjustment (g) is similar to the interest example. Management determines that about $5,000 of income taxes will be incurred as a result of earnings during the period. Therefore Income tax expense is debited for the period, and the appropriate current liability—Income tax payable (Account 204)—is credited.

In summary, all expenses related to the period must be recorded in the accounts in order to measure earnings for the period. In a like manner, all liabilities must be recorded for the proper reporting of financial condition on the balance sheet.

Adjusting the merchandise inventory account A final adjusting entry deals with correcting the Merchandise inventory account. Adjusting entry (h) as shown on the work sheet accomplishes this. The Merchandise inventory account in the trial balance reflects the *beginning* (January 1, 1978) inventory. If the balance sheet is to be prepared at the *end* of the period, then the *ending* merchandise inventory must be reported in that account. In the example it is assumed that management made a physical count of the ending merchandise and determined that the cost of the ending inventory is $14,000. The adjusting entry therefore must change the balance in the inventory account from $5,000 to $14,000. The following adjusting entries in general journal form changes the Inventory account balance:

Notice that the first entry removes the $5,000 debit balance from the inventory account by a credit. Then the second entry reinstates the inventory balance for the ending amount. The amount of inventory sold and the amount of inventory still on hand at the end of the period has a direct effect on the net earnings for the period. Therefore, the Net earnings summary account is used to reflect the impact of inventories on the profits. Later in this unit, the change in inventory will be explained in preparing the income statement.

Now, review once again adjustment (h) on the work sheet. On the Merchandise inventory line (104), the new inventory amount to appear on the ending balance sheet is $14,000 ($5,000 + $14,000 − $5,000). On the

■ *How is the Merchandise inventory account corrected?*

GENERAL JOURNAL

1978					
June	30	Net earnings summary		5,000.00	
		Merchandise inventory			5,000.00
		Adjusting entry to remove the			
		beginning balance from the			
		Merchandise inventory account.			
	30	Merchandise inventory		14,000.00	
		Net earnings summary			14,000.00
		Adjusting entry to set up the			
		ending balance in the Merchandise			
		inventory account.			

Net earnings summary line (600), both the beginning and ending inventory amounts are transferred to the adjusted trial balance, to be used later in computing the cost of goods sold for the period on the income statement. The technique we have illustrated here for adjusting the inventory account and setting up the cost of goods sold is only one of several methods that are in common use. Some firms do this by the closing entry process rather than with an adjustment.

INCOME STATEMENT CALCULATIONS

■ *How is the work sheet completed for a merchandising corporation?*

As you learned earlier when you studied the work sheet, each item appearing in the adjusted trial balance columns is extended to one of the three statements columns. In the income statement columns notice that there are several accounts that are related to the *cost of goods sold* (an expense) for the period. Here is the way to compute the cost of goods sold:

	1.	The cost of merchandise on hand at the beginning of the period
plus	**2.**	The cost of merchandise purchased during the period
equals	**3.**	The cost of the merchandise available to be sold
minus	**4.**	The cost of merchandise still on hand (unsold) at the end of the period
equals	**5.**	The cost of the merchandise that *was* sold.

By substituting accounting terminology, this becomes:

	1.	Merchandise inventory, beginning of period
plus	**2.**	**Net purchases** of merchandise
equals	**3.**	Cost of goods available for sale
minus	**4.**	Merchandise inventory, end of period
equals	**5.**	Cost of goods sold.

Now let's put some figures from the *income statement columns* of the work sheet just illustrated into an actual calculation of the cost of goods sold:

1. Merchandise inventory, January 1, 1978
   (See the Net earnings summary (600) line
   on the work sheet) .... $ 5,000
2. *Net* purchases of merchandise:
   Purchases of merchandise (502) $80,000
   Plus Transportation on purchases (503) 1,000
      Delivered cost of purchases $81,000
   Less:
      Purchases returns and allowances (504) $2,000
      Purchases discounts (505) 1,000 3,000
        Net purchases of merchandise 84,000
3. Cost of goods available for sale $89,000
4. Merchandise inventory, June 30, 1978 14,000
5. Cost of goods sold $75,000

This cost of goods sold figure ($75,000) will appear on the company's income statement when it is prepared from the work sheet. As a further note, observe that liabilities such as Interest payable (203) and Income tax payable (204) do *not* appear on the income statement; instead, their credit balances are extended to the balance sheet columns. Also, the current asset, Prepaid insurance (107), is extended to the balance sheet rather than to the income statement.

RETAINED EARNINGS CALCULATIONS

The **retained earnings** statement of a corporation is similar in form and purpose to the statement of owner's capital of a proprietorship. In our work sheet example the beginning balance of retained earnings, $7,000, is extended to the credit column. The dividends declared represent a deduction, and the net earnings for the period, $46,700, represent an increase in retained earnings. The amount of retained earnings at June 30, 1978, is calculated from the work sheet to be $51,700; this amount is extended to the balance sheet to become part of the ending capital of the corporation.

BALANCE SHEET CALCULATIONS

The final step in the preparation of the work sheet is the completion of the balance sheet columns. All asset, liability, and capital items at June 30, 1978, are extended to the proper credit or debit column. At this point the total debits and credits are equal, as you can see by examining our work sheet example.

The completed work sheet can be used for these purposes:

1. As a basis for recording adjusting entries in the appropriate journal.
2. As a basis for recording closing entries in the appropriate journal.
3. As a basis of preparing the three financial statements: the income statement, the statement of retained earnings, and the balance sheet.

INTERIM FINANCIAL STATEMENTS

Interim financial statements are financial statements that are prepared *during* an accounting period. The accounting period for most firms is the calendar year. That is, the closing entries are prepared only once each year, at December 31. These same firms, however, often prepare interim financial statements each month; this means that a work sheet would be prepared each month. The accounts need not be closed every time financial statements are prepared, nor must adjusting entries be entered in the journals and ledger. In fact, ledger accounts are usually adjusted and closed only once each year.

■ *What are interim financial statements?*

The temporary capital accounts (revenues, expenses, and dividends) accumulate balances throughout the year. To determine the amount of an expense (or revenue, or dividends) for any one month, the beginning-of-the-month balance of that account must be subtracted from the end-of-the-month balance. This procedure can be handled by setting up an additional set of columns on the work sheet. Also, appropriate adjustments are entered on the interim work sheet, but these need not be entered into the accounts monthly.

➤ NEW TERMS

cost of merchandise sold Also called *cost of goods sold;* an expense, representing the cost (sacrifice) a firm makes in order to acquire the merchandise it sells to customers during a period; calculated in the periodic inventory method as follows: (1) Merchandise inventory, beginning of period *plus* (2) *Net* purchases of merchandise *equals* (3) Cost of goods available for sale *minus* (4) Merchandise inventory, end of period *equals* (5) Cost of merchandise sold. [p. 232]

interim financial statements Financial statements prepared between ledger closings; for example, adjusting and closing entries might be made annually, but a work sheet and financial statements can be prepared quarterly. [p. 234]

net purchases The cost to the firm of *acquiring* merchan-

dise during a specific period (not to be confused with cost of goods sold); calculated as follows: (1) Purchases of merchandise *plus* (2) Transportation on purchases *less* (3) Purchases returns and allowances *less* (4) Purchases discounts *equals* (5) Net purchases. [p. 232]

retained earnings Capital generated by the earnings process and which still remains in the firm; a capital account of a corporation; *end-of-period* retained earnings (to appear on the balance sheet at the end of the accounting period) is calculated as follows: (1) Retained earnings, beginning of period (appearing in the trial balance at the end of the period) *plus* (2) Net earnings for the period according to the income statement *less* (3) Dividends declared during the period *equals* (4) Retained earnings, end of period. [p. 233]

QUESTIONS

Q13-1. Purchases of merchandise *plus* Transportation on purchases *less* Purchases returns and allowances *less* Purchases discounts *equals* what?

Q13-2. Beginning inventory *plus* Net purchases *less* Ending inventory *equals* what?

Q13-3. Under the periodic method of accounting for merchandise, which inventory appears in the trial balance of a firm at the end of a period? Beginning or ending inventory?

Q13-4. Beginning inventory *plus* Net purchases *equals* what?

Q13-5. Cost of goods available for sale *less* Ending inventory *equals* what?

Q13-6. Cost of goods available for sale *less* Cost of goods sold *equals* what?

Q13-7. On what financial statement is Cost of goods sold reported?

Q13-8. At the point in time when merchandise is purchased, is it an asset or an expense?

Q13-9. As prepaid expenses are used up, they become which, assets or expenses?

Q13-10. Ending retained earnings is computed how?

Q13-11. Explain how the adjusting entry for Merchandise inventory is made.

EXERCISES

E13-1. The following accounts and balances appeared in the trial balance (before adjustments) of Camille Company at December 31, 1978, the end of the year's operations:

Office supplies	$ 9,000
Prepaid insurance	4,000
Merchandise inventory	89,000
Equipment	40,000
Accumulated depreciation—Equipment	5,000
Sales of merchandise	99,000
Sales returns and allowances	3,000
Sales discounts	1,000
Purchases of merchandise	90,000
Purchases returns and allowances	8,000
Purchases discounts	2,000
Transportation on purchases	4,000

REQUIRED:

a. Prepare adjusting entries in general journal form, using the following information:
   (1) The cost of merchandise on hand at the end of the year, according to a physical count, amounted to $100,000.
   (2) The depreciation on the equipment for the year amounted to $5,000.
   (3) Insurance that had been used (expired) amounted to $1,000.
   (4) Office supplies on hand (unused) at December 31 amount to $2,500.
   (5) Interest incurred, but not yet paid or recorded, on the notes payable amounts to $400.

b. Compute the cost of goods sold for the year.

E13-2. a. Varied Corporation bought office supplies on December 1, 1978, for $3,000 cash. The bookkeeper for the company debited the *Office supplies* account for this amount at that time. At December 31, 1978, it was determined that all except $300 of the supplies purchased had been used in operating the business. Make the adjusting entry in general journal form to bring the accounts up to date.

b. Uniform Corporation bought office supplies on December 1, 1978, for $3,000 cash. The bookkeeper for the company debited the *Office supplies expense* account for this amount at that time. At December 31, 1978, it was determined that all except $300 of the supplies purchased had been used in operating the business. Make the adjusting entry in general journal form to bring the accounts up to date.

c. Carson Company purchased a 3-year life insurance policy on the lives of its key executives on January 1, 1978, paying $6,000 cash. The bookkeeper debited *Prepaid insurance* and credited Cash. Prepare the adjusting journal entry needed at December 31, 1978, the end of the year's operations.

d. Wilson Corporation purchased a 3-year life insurance policy on the lives of its key executives on January 1, 1978, paying $6,000 cash. The bookkeeper debited *Insurance expense* and credited Cash. Prepare the adjusting journal entry needed at December 31, 1978, the end of the year's operations.

E13-3. Below is a trial balance for a merchandising company at the end of a year's operations. A physical count of the ending inventory reveals that the goods remaining on hand had a cost of $4,000.

SM Company
TRIAL BALANCE
December 31, 1978

Cash	500	
Marketable securities	2,500	
Merchandise inventory	5,000	
Prepaid expenses	500	
Long-term investments	77,000	
Other assets	3,500	
Current liabilities		7,000
Long-term liabilities		10,500
Capital stock		40,000
Retained earnings		26,000
Dividends	2,000	
Sales of merchandise		20,500
Purchases of merchandise	7,500	
Transportation on purchases	200	
Purchases returns and allowances		400
Purchases discounts		300
Selling expenses	1,000	
General expenses	2,000	
Income taxes expense	3,000	
	104,700	104,700

REQUIRED:

a. From the data given, compute the following:
   (1) Net purchases.
   (2) Cost of goods available for sale.
   (3) Cost of goods sold.

b. Prepare the adjustments in general journal form to correct the Merchandise inventory account.

P13-1. *Work sheet; computation of cost of goods sold; adjusting entries.* Below is a trial balance of the ledger of Tammany Company at December 31, 1978, the end of the accounting year, along with information for adjustments.

Tammany Company
TRIAL BALANCE
December 31, 1978

Cash	5,000	
Marketable securities	6,000	
Accounts receivable	10,000	
Merchandise inventory	11,000	
Supplies	2,000	
Prepaid insurance	1,000	
Long-term investments	150,000	
Building	75,000	
Accumulated depreciation—Building		20,000
Accounts payable		15,000
Notes payable (long-term)		30,000
Common stock (15,000 shares outstanding)		60,000
Retained earnings		40,000
Dividends	5,000	
Sales of merchandise		247,000
Sales returns and allowances	2,000	
Sales discounts	2,000	
Purchases of merchandise	90,000	
Purchases returns and allowances		3,000
Transportation on purchases	4,000	
Purchases discounts		1,000
General expenses	31,000	
Selling expenses	22,000	
	416,000	416,000

Other information:

1. The cost of the merchandise inventory at the end of the year, according to physical count, is $9,000.
2. The supplies used during the period amount to $1,200. This company uses the Selling expenses account to record supplies used, instead of a separate Supplies expense account.
3. Depreciation on the building for the period is calculated to be $2,200.
4. Interest incurred, but not paid, on the note is $200. A separate Interest expense account is used by the company.
5. Insurance expired during the period is $900. Use the General expenses account.
6. During the period, $4,000 of maintenance expenses were paid for; this amount was debited to the General expenses account during the period. At the end of the year, it is determined that only $3,000 of these expenses were used up, and that $1,000 represents an asset to be used next year.

Note: Keep a copy of your solution to this problem—you will need it for assignments in Units 14 and 15.

REQUIRED:

    a. Prepare a work sheet for the company.

    b. Prepare adjusting entries in general journal form.

    c. Compute the cost of goods sold for 1978.

P13-2. *Work sheet; computation of cost of goods sold; adjusting entries.* Following is a listing of Weights Company's accounts with their balances at December 31, 1978.

101	Cash	28,000
102	Accounts receivable	5,000
105	Merchandise inventory	23,000
106	Office supplies	1,000
120	Office equipment	6,000
121	Accumulated depreciation—Office equipment	2,000
122	Land	45,000
123	Buildings	56,000
124	Accumulated depreciation—Buildings	8,000
201	Accounts payable	5,000
220	Notes payable	36,000
301	Capital stock (10,000 shares)	55,000
305	Retained earnings	67,000
306	Dividends	12,000
401	Sales of merchandise	113,000
404	Rent revenue	10,000
405	Interest income	4,000
406	Commission income	39,000
501	Purchases of merchandise	80,000
502	Transportation on purchases	3,000
503	Purchases discounts	1,000
504	Purchases returns and allowances	2,000
520	Advertising expense	11,000
521	Customer entertainment	3,000
522	Salesmen's salaries	24,000
523	Other selling expenses	5,000
540	Rent expense	17,000
541	General salaries	10,000
542	Office expense	8,000
543	Other expenses	3,000
550	Interest expense	2,000
551	Depreciation expense—Office equipment	–0–
552	Depreciation expense—Buildings	–0–

Information for adjustments:

1. The ending merchandise inventory amounts to $31,000.

2. Office supplies used, $400. Use the Office expense account (542).

3. Depreciation for year:

      Office equipment $1,000

      Buildings   2,000

4. Unpaid salesmen's salaries at end of year, $3,000.

Note: Keep a copy of your solution to this problem—you will need it for assignments in Units 14 and 15.

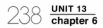

REQUIRED:

    a. Prepare a work sheet for the year.
    b. Prepare adjusting entries in general journal form.
    c. Compute the cost of goods sold for 1978.

P13-3. *Work sheet; computation of cost of goods sold; adjusting entries.* Mardi Gras Company has been operating for several years. At the end of this year's operations the book-keeper for the firm was in process of preparing a trial balance, but suddenly became ill and was unable to complete his work. You are asked to take over at that point, and you discover the following information on the desk of the bookkeeper:

LIST OF ACCOUNTS	BALANCE OF THE ACCOUNTS AT DECEMBER 31, 1978
Cash	$ 30,000
Notes receivable	110,000
Merchandise inventory	51,000
Prepaid insurance	10,000
Marketable securities	60,000
Land	15,000
Notes payable (current)	5,000
Bonds payable	75,000
Capital stock (10,000 shares)	100,000
Retained earnings	46,000
Dividends	8,000
Rent revenue	11,000
Sales	440,000
Purchases of merchandise	290,000
Purchases discounts	3,000
Purchases returns and allowances	2,000
Transportation on purchases	6,000
Salaries expense	75,000
Advertising expense	10,000
Rent expense	3,000
Entertainment expense	14,000

Additional data discovered, related to adjustments:

1. A physical count of merchandise was made and it was determined that $100,000 of merchandise is still on hand at December 31, 1978, the end of the accounting period of 1 year. The firm prepares financial statements only once each year, and the accounts include the entire year's operations.
2. Unpaid salaries at end of year, $8,000.
3. Unpaid interest on notes and bonds, $2,000.
4. Expired insurance, $3,000.

Note: Keep a copy of your solution to this problem—you will need it for assignments in Units 14 and 15.

REQUIRED:

    a. Prepare a work sheet for 1978.
    b. Prepare adjusting entries in general journal form.
    c. Compute the cost of goods sold for 1978.

P13-4. *Work sheet; computation of cost of goods sold; adjusting entries.* The trial balance of Dryad Company at December 31, 1978, the end of a year's operations, is shown below.

Dryad Company
TRIAL BALANCE
December 31, 1978

Cash on hand and in banks	16,000	
Marketable securities	11,000	
Accounts receivable	100,000	
Merchandise inventory	250,000	
Prepaid insurance	1,000	
Store supplies	1,000	
Equipment	140,000	
Accumulated depreciation—Equipment		10,000
Long-term investments	19,000	
Accounts payable		75,000
Notes payable		80,000
Common stock (15,000 shares)		200,000
Retained earnings		37,000
Dividends	15,000	
Service revenues		99,000
Sales of merchandise		400,000
Sales returns and allowances	8,000	
Sales discounts	12,000	
Purchases	300,000	
Purchases returns and allowances		10,000
Purchases discounts		3,000
Transportation on purchases	2,000	
Selling expenses	17,000	
General expenses	22,000	
	914,000	914,000

Information for adjustments:

1. The merchandise on hand at December 31, according to physical count, amounts to $275,000.
2. Unpaid salaries at December 31, amount to $3,000. This company uses the General expenses account to record salaries.
3. The equipment was purchased 2 years ago and is depreciated at the rate of $10,000 per year.
4. Interest owed on notes payable, $4,000.
5. Store supplies used during the year, $400. Use the Selling expenses account.
6. The *expired* insurance amounts to $300. Use the General expenses account.

Note: Keep a copy of your solution to this problem—you will need it for assignments in Units 14 and 15.

REQUIRED:

a. Prepare a work sheet for the year ended December 31, 1978.
b. Prepare adjusting entries in general journal form.
c. Compute the cost of goods sold for 1978.

P13-5. *Work sheet; computation of cost of goods sold; adjusting entries.* Below is a trial balance of all the accounts of Windy Company at the end of operations for 1978.

Cash	70,000	
Accounts receivable	90,000	
Merchandise inventory	100,000	
Supplies	5,000	
Office equipment	20,000	
Accumulated depreciation—Office equipment		6,000
Accounts payable		22,000
Notes payable (long-term)		44,000
Capital stock (5,000 shares)		91,000
Retained earnings		59,000
Sales		130,000
Purchases of merchandise	50,000	
Transportation on purchases	4,000	
Purchases discounts		3,000
Purchases returns and allowances		2,000
Sales commissions expense	10,000	
Maintenance expense	2,000	
Rent expense	5,000	
Interest expense	1,000	
	357,000	357,000

Information for adjustments:
1. Supplies still on hand (unused) at December 31, 1978, $1,000.
2. Depreciation on office equipment for year, $2,000.
3. Unpaid income taxes, $5,000.
4. Interest owed on notes, $3,000.
5. Ending merchandise inventory, $80,000.

Note: Keep a copy of your solution to this problem—you will need it for assignments in Units 14 and 15

REQUIRED:

    a. Prepare a work sheet for 1978.
    b. Prepare adjusting entries in general journal form.
    c. Compute the cost of goods sold for 1978.

P13-6. *Adjusting journal entries*

    a. Harrison Company has the following accounts and balances appearing in the trial balance at December 31, 1978, the end of the year's operations:

Merchandise inventory	$55,000
Purchases of merchandise	40,000
Purchases returns and allowances	2,000
Purchases discounts	1,500
Transportation on purchases	2,750

The cost of the merchandise inventory at the end of the year, according to physical count is $50,000. Make the adjusting entries in general journal form to adjust the inventory.

b. What is the amount of the cost of merchandise sold for Harrison Company in part a?

c. Unsur Corporation bought supplies on November 1, 1978, for $4,200 cash. The bookkeeper for the company debited the Supplies expense account for this amount at that time. At December 31, 1978, it was determined that all except $1,900 of the supplies purchased had been used in operating the business. Make the adjusting entry in general journal form to bring the accounts up to date.

d. Cooper Corporation purchased a 5-year fire insurance policy on January 1, 1977, paying $5,000 cash. The bookkeeper debited Prepaid insurance and credited Cash. On December 31, 1977 the correct adjusting entry was made. Make the adjusting journal entry needed at December 31, 1978, the end of the year's operations.

e. What is the balance of the Prepaid insurance account after you made the adjusting entry in part d?

f. Mason Corporation paid $2,000 of maintenance expenses during 1978. The bookkeeper debited the General expense account for this amount. At December 31, 1978, it was determined that only $1,500 of these expenses were used up. Prepare the adjusting journal entry needed at December 31, 1978.

g. The following accounts and balances appeared in the trial balance of Joseph Hanes Company at December 31, 1978, the end of the year's operations:

Office supplies	$ 10,000
Prepaid insurance	5,000
Merchandise inventory	90,000
Equipment	41,000
Accumulated depreciation—Equipment	6,000
Sales of merchandise	100,000
Sales returns and allowances	4,000
Sales discounts	2,000
Purchases of merchandise	91,000
Purchases returns and allowances	9,000
Purchases discounts	3,000
Transportation on purchases	5,000

Prepare adjusting entries in general journal form, using the following information:

1. The cost of merchandise on hand at the end of the year, according to a physical count amounted to $100,000.
2. The depreciation on the equipment for the year amounted to $2,000.
3. Insurance expired during the year is $500.
4. Office supplies on hand at December 31 amounted to $7,500.
5. Interest incurred, but not yet paid or recorded, on notes payable amounted to $175.

FINANCIAL STATEMENTS

> **OBJECTIVE**

The objective of this unit is to illustrate the major financial statements of a merchandising corporation.

> **APPROACH TO ATTAINING THE OBJECTIVE**

The information that appears on the work sheet illustrated in Unit 13 will be the basis for the financial statements illustrated and discussed here. As you study these financial statements, pay particular attention to these four questions, which the text following answers:

- *How is a detailed income statement for a merchandising corporation prepared and used?*
- *How is a summary income statement for a merchandising corporation prepared and used?*
- *How is a statement of retained earnings prepared and used?*
- *How is a balance sheet prepared and used?*

Refer to the work sheet for Orleans Merchandising Corporation presented in Unit 13. The information in the income statement columns provides the data needed to prepare the detailed income statement. Details of the composition of cost of goods sold are also contained in the income statement columns.

Shown on the next page is a detailed income statement of Orleans Merchandising Corporation prepared from the work sheet data. Let's us examine some of the entries in detail to see how the information is used.

■ *How is a detailed
income statement
for a merchandising
corporation prepared
and used?*

Net sales All three accounts which compose the net sales of a company are shown in the income statement columns of the work sheet. Net sales appears on the top of the income statement to spotlight a crucial area of activity of a merchandising firm. The top management of a company often compares net sales to each of the expenses appearing on the statement in order to determine significant changes in expense-revenue relationships.

Cost of goods sold The several elements of cost of goods sold appear in the income statement columns of the work sheet. On a detailed income statement for management's use, it is desirable to report all the elements of cost of goods sold. Be sure you trace each of these figures back to the work sheet.

Gross profit (gross margin) **Gross profit** or *gross margin* is the excess of net sales over cost of goods sold. This measure customarily gives management direct information about the relationship of prices charged for the goods to the cost of the goods. Our example indicates that the firm charged $145,000 for goods for which it had paid $69,000. This provides a gross margin of $76,000 through trading operations. The percentage relationship of cost of goods sold to net sales is a critical one for merchandising firms.

Selling expenses **Selling expenses** are all those costs incurred for the purpose of promoting, selling, and delivering the merchandise. This grouping lets management draw certain conclusions about the effectiveness of the selling and promotional program. For example, consider a firm whose selling expenses have been 18% of net sales for many months. If a new promotional and selling program is begun for the company, the change in this relationship, if any, would be important information to management.

Notice also that in this account numbering system, the numbers 540 to 559 are used to classify selling expenses. The chart of accounts and its numbering system are thus extremely useful to the bookkeeper as he prepares the financial statements.

Administrative, general, and financial expenses **General and administrative expenses** are those costs incurred for the operation of the firm. Examples are officers' salaries, office costs, certain insurance costs, and taxes. These expenses *do not* deal directly with the selling function. **Financial expenses** are those costs associated with raising funds (financing) for the company. Interest expense, of course, is a financial expense. Many firms place financial expenses in a completely separate category on the income statement. Some companies also treat income taxes expense as a separate item.

Orleans Merchandising Corporation
INCOME STATEMENT
For the period January 1, 1978, through June 30, 1978

sales of merchandise			
Gross sales		$150,000	
Less: Sales returns and allowances	$ 3,000		
Sales discounts	2,000	5,000	
Net sales			$145,000
cost of goods sold			
Merchandise inventory, January 1, 1978		$ 5,000	
Purchases of merchandise	$80,000		
Transportation on purchases	1,000		
	$81,000		
Less: Purchases returns and allowances	$2,000		
Purchases discounts	1,000	3,000	
Net purchases		78,000	
Cost of goods available for sale		$ 83,000	
Less Merchandise inventory, June 30, 1978		14,000	
Cost of goods sold			69,000
gross profit on sales of merchandise			$ 76,000
operating expenses			
Selling expenses:			
Advertising expense	$ 6,000		
Sales salaries expense	12,000		
Store supplies expense	200		
Depreciation expense—Store equipment	2,000		
Total selling expenses		$ 20,200	
Administrative, general, and financial expenses:			
Officers and general salaries expense	$ 9,000		
Insurance expense	700		
Office supplies expense	400		
Depreciation expense—Office equipment	1,000		
Interest expense	2,000		
Income tax expense	5,000		
Total administrative, general, and financial expenses		18,100	
Total operating expenses			38,300
net earnings from operations			$ 37,700
other income			
Rental income			9,000
net earnings			$ 46,700

Other income and expenses If a company has income and expenses that are not directly related to the main line of business (merchandising), a separate section of the income statement can be used. In our example rental income is treated this way.

THE SUMMARY INCOME STATEMENT FOR OUTSIDE USE

▪ *How is a summary income statement for a merchandising corporation prepared and used?*

A summary income statement for Orleans Merchandising Corporation appears below. Note that only the major categories of revenues and expenses appear on this statement. The reason for this summary, of course, is that investors, creditors, and others outside the firm only need information about the basic relationships. All the details that management needs to improve operations are not particularly relevant to outsiders, who can base their decisions on more summarized information.

Orleans Merchandising Corporation
INCOME STATEMENT
For the period January 1, 1978, through June 30, 1978

revenues		
Net sales	$145,000	
Rental income	9,000	
Total revenues		$154,000
expenses		
Cost of goods sold	$ 69,000	
Selling expenses	20,200	
Administrative, general, and financial expenses	18,100	
Total expenses		107,300
net earnings		$ 46,700
earnings per share of common stock (10,000 shares of common stock outstanding during the period)		$4.67

THE STATEMENT OF RETAINED EARNINGS

▪ *How is a statement of retained earnings prepared and used?*

The information on the statement of retained earnings (see below) appears in one set of columns on the work sheet. The retained earnings at the end of the period are determined by adding the net earnings for the period and by deducting the dividends declared during the period from the beginning retained earnings. Remember that retained earnings is one of the categories of capital for a corporation. The $51,700 balance of retained earnings at the end of the period means that this is the amount of the firm's total assets that was generated by the profit-making process.

Orleans Merchandising Corporation
STATEMENT OF RETAINED EARNINGS
For the period January 1, 1978, through June 30, 1978

Retained earnings, January 1, 1978		$ 7,000
Net earnings, January 1, 1978, through June 30, 1978	$46,700	
Dividends declared during period	2,000	
Net increase in Retained earnings		44,700
Retained earnings, June 30, 1978		$51,700

THE BALANCE SHEET

• How is a balance sheet prepared and used?

A classified balance sheet (a balance sheet with accounts arranged in useful groups) is illustrated next. The balance sheet shows the financial condition of the firm at a *point* in time (see the heading of the statement). All the other financial statements that you have studied in this unit present information about flows or *changes* during a period of time (see their headings). Study each classification on the balance sheet and trace each amount to the work sheet.

Orleans Merchandising Corporation
BALANCE SHEET
June 30, 1978

ASSETS

current assets

Cash..	$10,000	
Marketable securities...	4,000	
Accounts receivable...	13,000	
Merchandise inventory..	14,000	
Office supplies...	600	
Store supplies..	1,800	
Prepaid insurance...	300	$ 43,700

long-term investments

Investments in stocks...	$40,000	
Investments in bonds...	11,000	51,000

plant and equipment

Office equipment..	$ 6,000		
Accumulated depreciation...	3,000	$ 3,000	
Store equipment	$50,000		
Accumulated depreciation...	12,000	38,000	
Land		20,000	61,000
Total assets			$155,700

EQUITIES

liabilities

Current liabilities

Accounts payable	$ 7,000	
Sales taxes payable..	2,000	
Interest payable	2,000	
Income taxes payable...	5,000	$ 16,000

Long-term liabilities

Notes payable..	$15,000	
Bonds payable..	43,000	58,000
Total liabilities		$ 74,000

capital

Common stock..	$30,000	
Retained earnings..	51,700	
Total capital		81,700
Total equities..		$155,700

financial expenses Costs (sacrifices) associated with financing the firm (raising resources); interest expense is an example. [p. 245]

general and administrative expenses Costs (sacrifices) incurred for the operation of the firm; examples are office costs and administrative salaries; these costs are not directly associated with the selling function or cost of goods sold. [p. 244]

gross profit The excess of net sales over cost of goods sold for a period of time; also called gross margin. [p. 244]

selling expenses Costs (sacrifices) incurred for the purpose of promoting, selling, and delivering merchandise. [p. 244]

› ASSIGNMENT MATERIAL

QUESTIONS

Q14-1. What is meant by gross profit?

Q14-2. What are selling expenses? Give two examples of selling expenses.

Q14-3. What are financial expenses? Give an example of a financial expense.

Q14-4. What are general and administrative expenses? How do these differ from other expenses? Give two examples of general and administrative expenses.

EXERCISES

E14-1. The following facts are known about a company's operations:

Sales	$300,000
Sales returns and allowances	5,000
Sales discounts	3,000
Beginning inventory	50,000
Purchases of merchandise	200,000
Purchases returns and allowances	10,000
Purchases discounts	3,000
Transportation on purchases	1,000
Ending inventory	100,000
Selling expenses	50,000
General and administrative expenses	50,000

Compute the following:
a. Net sales.
b. Net purchases.
c. Cost of goods sold.
d. Gross profit.
e. Net earnings.

E14-2. The following facts are known about a company's operations:

Sales returns and allowances	$ 2,000
Sales discounts	2,000
Net sales	100,000
Beginning inventory	15,000
Purchases of merchandise	60,000
Purchases returns and allowances	2,000
Purchases discounts	2,000
Net purchases	59,000

Ending inventory	10,000
Selling expenses	3,000
Net earnings	6,000

Compute the following:

a. Sales.
b. Transportation on purchases.
c. Cost of goods sold.
d. Gross profit.
e. General and administrative expenses.

E14-3. The following facts are known about a company's operations:

Sales	$100,000
Sales returns and allowances	3,000
Net sales	95,000
Purchases of merchandise	50,000
Purchases discounts	2,000
Transportation on purchases	1,000
Net purchases	39,000
Ending inventory	10,000
Cost of goods sold	50,000
Selling expenses	5,000
General and administrative expenses	2,000

Compute the following:

a. Sales discounts.
b. Beginning inventory.
c. Purchases returns and allowances.
d. Gross profit.
e. Net earnings.

E14-4. The following facts are known about a company's operations:

Sales returns and allowances	$ 1,000
Sales discounts	2,000
Beginning inventory	10,000
Purchases returns and allowances	2,000
Purchases discounts	1,000
Transportation on purchases	8,000
Net purchases	90,000
Cost of goods sold	60,000
Gross profit	20,000
General and administrative expenses	5,000
Net earnings	3,000

Compute the following:

a. Sales.
b. Net sales.
c. Purchases of merchandise.
d. Ending inventory.
e. Selling expenses.

P14-1. *Preparation of financial statements from work sheet.* Refer to P13-1 in Unit 13. From the information contained in the completed work sheet that you prepared in that problem:
a. Prepare a *summary* income statement in good form.
b. Prepare a detailed income statement in good form.
c. Prepare a statement of retained earnings in good form.
d. Prepare a classified balance sheet in good form.

P14-2. *Preparation of financial statements from work sheet.* Refer to P13-2 in Unit 13. From the information contained in the completed work sheet that you prepared in that problem:
a. Prepare a *summary* income statement in good form.
b. Prepare a detailed income statement in good form.
c. Prepare a statement of retained earnings in good form.
d. Prepare a classified balance sheet in good form.

P14-3. *Preparation of financial statements from work sheet.* Refer to P13-3 in Unit 13. From the information contained in the completed work sheet that you prepared in that problem:
a. Prepare a *summary* income statement in good form.
b. Prepare a detailed income statement in good form.
c. Prepare a statement of retained earnings in good form.
d. Prepare a classified balance sheet in good form.

**PROBLEMS
(GROUP B)**

P14-4. *Preparation of financial statements from adjusted trial balance.* Below is the adjusted trial balance columns of the work sheet of Leafy Co. at May 31, 1978, the end of 1 month's operations.

Leafy Co.
ADJUSTED TRIAL BALANCE
May 31, 1978

Cash	21,000	
Dividends	6,000	
Marketable securities	9,000	
Merchandise inventory	25,000	
Sales of merchandise		250,000
Advertising expense	12,000	
Accounts receivable	125,000	
Miscellaneous service income		10,000
Investments in stocks and bonds	60,000	
Officers' salaries expense	20,000	
Sales returns and allowances	5,000	
Transportation on purchases	2,000	
Office equipment	60,000	
Accounts payable		15,000
Notes payable (due June 30, 1980)		55,000
Accumulated depreciation—Office equipment		15,000
Office supplies expense	1,000	
Sales salaries expense	25,000	
Insurance expense	1,000	
Sales taxes payable		2,000

Income taxes payable		10,000
Common stock		100,000
Retained earnings		37,000
Income tax expense	19,000	
Sales discounts	2,000	
Purchases of merchandise	100,000	
Purchases discounts		2,000
Purchases returns and allowances		4,000
Office supplies	1,000	
Depreciation expense—Office equipment	2,000	
Net earnings summary	29,000	25,000
	525,000	525,000

REQUIRED:

    a. Prepare a detailed income statement (the kind for management's use), including all the details of cost of goods sold, as illustrated in this unit.

    b. Prepare a summary income statement, the kind most useful to investors and creditors, as illustrated in this unit. There were 20,000 shares of common stock outstanding during the period.

    c. Prepare a statement of retained earnings.

    d. Prepare a classified balance sheet in good form.

P14-5. *Preparation of financial statements from work sheet.* Refer to P13-4 in Unit 13. From the information contained in the completed work sheet that you prepared in that problem:

    a. Prepare a *summary* income statement in good form.

    b. Prepare a detailed income statement in good form.

    c. Prepare a statement of retained earnings in good form.

    d. Prepare a classified balance sheet in good form.

P14-6. *Preparation of financial statements from work sheet.* Refer to P13-5 in Unit 13. From the information contained in the completed work sheet that you prepared in that problem:

    a. Prepare a *summary* income statement in good form.

    b. Prepare a detailed income statement in good form.

    c. Prepare a statement of retained earnings in good form.

    d. Prepare a classified balance sheet in good form.

ADJUSTING AND CLOSING

> **OBJECTIVE**

This unit will continue your study of end-of-period activities in the accounting system for a merchandising firm. Its purpose is twofold: (1) to provide you with a comprehensive review of adjusting entries and to introduce additional kinds of adjustments, and (2) to illustrate how closing entries are made for a merchandising company.

> **APPROACH TO ATTAINING THE OBJECTIVE**

As you study adjusting and closing in a merchandising corporation, pay particular attention to these three questions, which the text following answers:

- *Why are adjusting journal entries made for a merchandising firm?*
- *What kinds of adjustments do merchandising firms ordinarily have?*
- *How are closing journal entries made for a merchandising firm?*

A REVIEW OF THE PURPOSE OF ADJUSTING ENTRIES

■ *Why are adjusting journal entries made for a merchandising firm?*

A manual accounting system does not always automatically provide for *completeness* and *correctness* of the accounts. For example, a firm might have an asset that has not been recorded in the accounts as of the end of the period. Or a firm might have incurred an expense that has not found its way into the accounts at the balance sheet date. Or a debt might be owed which is not yet recorded. The function of adjusting entries in these instances and in general is to correct the accounts so that the statements based on them reveal net income and assets and equities according to generally accepted standards.

There are two basic kinds of adjustments. One involves situations in which a business transaction has taken place, but the information has not yet been recorded in the accounts. An example is the end-of-period adjustment made to record interest expense incurred on a note. The second kind of adjustment involves situations in which the information has already been entered in the accounts, but the balances of the accounts concerned need to be corrected to reflect recent happenings. An example is the adjustment made to record the using up of supplies. These basic kinds of adjustments are made so that up-to-date, complete amounts can be reported in the financial statements prepared for decision makers.

A COMPREHENSIVE CLASSIFICATION OF COMMON ADJUSTMENTS

Most adjusting entries involve at least two major categories of accounts. For example, the adjustment made to record interest expense incurred on a note involves an *expense* (interest expense) and a *liability* (interest payable). And the adjustment made to record the use of supplies involves an *expense* (supplies expense) and an *asset* (supplies). This dual involvement forms one basis for classifying and examining the various adjustments that firms must make at the end of an accounting period. Table 15-1 summarizes information about seven common adjusting entries which merchandising corporations normally make. Table 15-1 also classifies these seven adjustments on the basis of their dual effects on major account categories and thus on financial statements. Carefully study this table. Note that the details of adjustments 2d, 3, and 4 are discussed in the remainder of this section.

■ *What kinds of adjustments do merchandising firms ordinarily have?*

Receivables and bad debts Receivables are amounts owed to the firm by outsiders in the form of regular accounts or written promissory notes to be collected in the future. The customary valuation procedure for current receivables is to show the receivables on the balance sheet at the *amount expected to be collected*. This valuation method gives the reader of the balance sheet a measure of the cash expected to flow into the firm from the receivables during the coming period.

An adjusting entry is needed at the end of each accounting period to restate the receivables at their expected collectible amount. For example,

TABLE 15-1
COMMON ADJUSTING ENTRIES

ACCOUNTS AND FINANCIAL STATEMENTS AFFECTED	DESCRIPTION OF ADJUSTMENT
1. Adjustments affect *expenses* (on the income statement) and *liabilities* (on the balance sheet).	1. Expenses which have been incurred but not recorded in the accounts, and which will be paid for later; these are sometimes called *accrued expenses*. For examples, see adjustment (f) for interest and adjustment (g) for income taxes on the work sheet in Unit 13. Such adjustments normally require a debit to an expense and a credit to a liability.
2. Adjustments affect *expenses* (on the income statement) and *assets* (on the balance sheet).	2. a. *Prepaid expenses.* For examples, see adjustments (a), (b), and (c) on the work sheet in Unit 13. In adjustments (a) and (b) the asset is reduced in the adjustment to reflect the using up of the asset and the expense is recorded. Adjustment (c) is similar except that the expense account is reduced in the adjustment to reflect the amount of the cost used and the asset is created to show the future usable amount of cost.
	b. *Plant and equipment used* (*depreciation*). For examples, see adjustments (d) and (e) on the work sheet in Unit 13. The asset is used and is reduced through the adjustment, and the expense is recorded.
	c. *Inventory and Cost of goods sold.* For an example, see adjustment (h) on the work sheet in Unit 13. Review this adjustment carefully. The asset, Merchandise inventory, is stated at its future usable amount (the cost of the ending inventory), and the effect of the beginning and ending inventories on cost of goods sold is reflected in the Net earnings summary account.
	d. *Receivables and Bad debts.* This new kind of adjustment is discussed in this unit.
3. Adjustments affect *revenues* (on the income statement) and *assets* (on the balance sheet).	3. Revenues which have been earned but not recorded in the accounts, and which will be received later; these are sometimes called **accrued revenues.** This new kind of adjustment is discussed in this unit.
4. Adjustments affect *revenues* (on the income statement) and *liabilities* (on the balance sheet).	4. Amounts which have been collected but not yet earned by the company, and which will become revenues in some future period; these are sometimes called **unearned revenues.** This new kind of adjustment is discussed in this unit.

consider a firm whose trial balance at the end of the year showed these accounts and balances:

Accounts receivable	$ 10,000
Sales	100,000
Sales returns and allowances	4,000
Sales discounts	2,000

From this information we can see that the firm produced *net* sales of $94,000, and that $10,000 is the total which *potentially* can be collected from the receivables during the next period. Management now must make a study to determine the amount it *really* expects to collect from the receivables.

There are two basic ways of making the estimate. The first involves examining every account appearing in the accounts receivable subsidiary ledger and then determining the likelihood that various categories of accounts (such as past-due accounts) will be collected. This process, called *aging* of receivables, will be discussed in a future chapter.

A second procedure, which will be used in this unit, involves looking at the firm's past experience to determine the percent of sales made on credit in the past that eventually were not collected. When a firm just begins operating, such estimates might come from credit loss experience of similar firms or the industry as a whole.

Assume that in the example just given, management estimates that one-tenth of 1% (0.001, or 1/10%) of all *net* sales made on credit will not be collected. The credit losses related to this period's sales are expected to be $94, computed as follows:

$$(\$100,000 - \$4,000 - \$2,000) \times 0.001 = \$94$$

Then the following adjusting entry would be made in the firm's journal:

1978 Dec.	31	Bad debts expense	94	
		Allowance for uncollectibles		94

One effect of this adjustment is to show an expense, called a **Bad debts expense,** of $94. This expense can be viewed as an ordinary cost of making sales on credit and bearing the risk of selling to customers who do not pay their bills. The earnings for the period are reduced. The $94,000 of net sales still will be shown as the revenue for the period, but expenses will be increased by the estimated credit-loss costs. The adjustment must be made *now*—even though it is not known which specific customers will not pay their bills—so that net earnings for the period can be measured for decision-making purposes.

This adjustment also introduces a new account—the **Allowance for uncollectibles** account. This is a contra account which reduces the asset account Accounts receivable. The current asset section of the firm's balance sheet therefore would show the following after the adjustment:

Accounts receivable	$10,000	
Less Allowance for uncollectibles	94	
Net		$9,906

or

| Accounts receivable (net of allowance for uncollectibles of $94) | | $9,906 |

Remember that both accounts, Accounts receivable and Allowance for uncollectibles, are classified as assets—one with a debit balance and the other with a credit balance. The same purpose would be accomplished by crediting the $94 to the Accounts receivable account in the adjusting entry, rather than having a separate account (Allowance for uncollectibles). However, this procedure would change the balance in the Accounts receivable (control) account without changing the balances of the individual accounts in the accounts receivable subsidiary ledger. The job of preparing a schedule of accounts receivable to agree with the control account then would be made quite complicated.

A future chapter will discuss additional problems concerning receivables. These problems include entries for recognizing that a *particular* account receivable is determined to be uncollectible. Other names for the Allowance for uncollectibles account are (1) *Estimated uncollectibles,* and (2) *Allowance for bad debts.*

Accrued revenues **Accrued revenues** are revenues that have been earned in a reporting period but will be collected in the future. Such revenues and receivables must be entered into the accounts for the proper preparation of the income statement and balance sheet. Assume that a firm rents equipment to a customer for $50 per month. Further, assume that a customer has used the equipment for a month, but has not yet paid the firm. The following adjusting entry would be appropriate:

| 1978 Dec. | 31 | Rent receivable | 50.00 | |
| | | Rental income | | 50.00 |

This adjustment emphasizes that revenues need not be collected in order to be reported as earnings on the income statement. Rent receivable, of course, is a current asset on the balance sheet. Another example of an accrued receivable is interest earned, but not yet collected, on notes receivable.

Unearned revenues **Unearned revenues** are amounts that have been collected but not yet earned by a company. The amounts will become revenues in some future period. The end-of-period adjustment for unearned revenues affects both revenues and liabilities, as we shall see in the following example.

On March 3, 1978, a firm received $20,000 from customers as advance collection on fees to be earned during the coming months. At December 31, 1978, the end of the accounting year, it is determined that $15,000 of the fees have been earned and that $5,000 of the fees are to be earned in 1979. On March 3, 1978, the firm's bookkeeper made this entry:

1978				
March	3	Cash	20,000.00	
		Fees income		20,000.00

This entry increased the firm's revenues by $20,000. At the end of the year, however, because only $15,000 of the fees have been earned, this adjusting entry is necessary:

1978				
Dec.	31	Fees income	5,000.00	
		Unearned fees		5,000.00

The adjustment reduces the revenue account by $5,000, leaving a balance for the income statement of $15,000 in 1978. The Unearned fees account is a *liability* appearing on the balance sheet. Actually, the liability means that the $5,000 is an obligation to the customer until the services are rendered and until the fees are earned.

Now let's use the same example and assume that on March 3, 1978, the bookkeeper made the following entry for the collection (instead of the one illustrated above):

1978				
March	3	Cash	20,000.00	
		Unearned fees		20,000.00

If this entry had been made, then a different adjustment would be needed. Before the adjusting entry is made remember that there is no *revenue* in the accounts and a *liability* of $20,000 is recorded. Because the revenue should be $15,000 and the liability should be $5,000, the following adjustment must be made:

1978				
Dec.	31	Unearned fees	15,000.00	
		Fees income		15,000.00

Closing entries for a merchandising corporation are shown below. These entries are based on the information contained in the work sheet of Orleans Merchandising Corporation in Unit 13. Refer to the work sheet to determine the source of each account and its amount.

How are closing journal entries made for a merchandising firm?

The source of the first closing entry above is the credit side of the *income statement columns* of the work sheet (Unit 13). All four of these tempo-

1978 Dec.	31	Sales of merchandise	150,000	
		Rental income	9,000	
		Purchases returns and allowances	2,000	
		Purchases discounts	1,000	
		Net earnings summary		162,000
		To close the accounts appearing on the income statement that have credit balances.		
	31	Net earnings summary	124,300	
		Sales returns and allowances		3,000
		Sales discounts		2,000
		Purchases of merchandise		80,000
		Transportation on purchases		1,000
		Officers and general salaries expense		9,000
		Insurance expense		700
		Advertising expense		6,000
		Sales salaries expense		12,000
		Office supplies expense		400
		Store supplies expense		200
		Depreciation expense— Office equipment		1,000
		Depreciation expense— Store equipment		2,000
		Interest expense		2,000
		Income tax expense		5,000
		To close the accounts appearing on the income statement that have debit balances.		
	31	Net earnings summary	46,700	
		Retained earnings		46,700
		To close the Net earnings summary account and to increase Retained earnings by the amount of the net income for the year.		
	31	Retained earnings	2,000	
		Dividends		2,000
		To close the Dividends account and to decrease Retained earnings by the amount of the dividends.		

rary capital accounts have credit balances. Therefore, they are debited to close them out. Since these accounts all serve to *increase* the net income for the period, the Net earnings summary account is credited for their total ($162,000).

The source of the second closing entry is the debit side of the *income statement columns* of the work sheet (Unit 13). All fourteen of these temporary capital accounts have debit balances. Therefore, they are credited to close them out. Since these accounts serve to *decrease* the net income for the period, the Net earnings summary account is debited for their total ($124,300).

Next, take a look at the ledger account for the Net earnings summary account:

Net earnings summary

ACCOUNT NO. 600

DATE	DESCRIPTION	REF.	DEBITS	CREDITS	BALANCE DEBIT	BALANCE CREDIT
1978 Dec. 31	Adj.—beg. inventory	J10	500000		500000	
31	Adj.—end inventory	J10		1400000		900000
31	Closing	J11		16200000		17100000
31	Closing	J11	12430000			4670000
31	Closing	J11	4670000			0

The first two entries in this account came from the adjustment process. Remember that in Unit 13, adjusting entries were made to remove the beginning balance of the Merchandise inventory account and to set up the ending balance. Refer to page 232 for these two entries.

The third and fourth entries in the Net earnings summary account are from the closing process that we have just illustrated. Notice that after the two adjusting entries and after the first two closing entries are posted to the Net earnings summary account, the credit balance is $46,700. This is the amount of the Net earnings for 1978 (see work sheet).

Next, we are in a position to close the Net earnings summary account to zero and to increase the Retained earnings. This is done in the third closing entry. And finally, the fourth closing journal entry reduces the Retained earnings by the amount of the dividends.

❯ NEW TERMS

accrued revenues Revenues that have been earned but not recorded in the accounts; the revenues will be received later. [p. 254]

allowance for uncollectibles A current asset account, with a credit balance, which serves to reduce the amount of accounts receivable; this account is a measure of the receivables which are not expected to be collected; also called *Estimated uncollectibles* and *Allow-*

ance for bad debts. [p. 255]

bad debts expense A sacrifice (expense) incurred as a result of selling goods on credit, wherein certain customers fail to pay their accounts. [p. 255]

unearned revenues Amounts that have been collected but not yet earned by the company; the amounts will become revenues in some future period. [p. 257]

❯ ASSIGNMENT MATERIAL

QUESTIONS

Q15-1. What is the purpose of adjusting entries?

Q15-2. What adjusting entry is made at the end of each accounting period to restate the receivables at their expected collectible amount?

Q15-3. What are two basic ways of estimating credit losses?

Q15-4. How is the Allowance for uncollectibles reported on the financial statements?

Q15-5. What are accrued revenues?

Q15-6. What adjusting entry is made for accrued revenues?

Q15-7. What are unearned revenues?

Q15-8. What adjusting entry is made for unearned revenues if a liability account had been credited when the cash was received?

Q15-9. What adjusting entry is made for unearned revenues if a revenue account had been credited when the cash was received?

Q15-10. List and briefly describe the four closing entries made for a merchandising firm.

EXERCISES

E15-1. The trial balance of a firm at the end of 1978 included the following accounts and balances.

Accounts receivable	24,000
Unearned rent	9,000
Prepaid insurance	1,000
Equipment	79,000
Accumulated depreciation—Equipment	9,000
Sales salaries expense	2,000
Merchandise inventory	8,000
Purchases of merchandise	99,000
Transportation on purchases	10,000
Purchases returns and allowances	9,000
Purchases discounts	2,000
Notes receivable	14,000
Fees income	23,000
Rent expense	1,500
Sales	300,000
Sales returns and allowances	20,000
Sales discounts	6,000

Information for adjustments:

The physical count of the merchandise inventory indicates that there is inventory costing $10,000. Prepare adjusting journal entries for the following items:

a. Income taxes for the year are expected to amount to $8,000. These will be paid next year. (This is an accrued expense.)

b. $600 of the insurance has expired (been used).

c. Of the $1,500 rent expense paid, $500 represents rent payments for next year (1979).

d. The depreciation on the equipment for 1978 is estimated to be $1,000.

e. Make the adjustment for inventory.

f. One percent of net sales is not expected to be collected.

g. $65 of interest on the notes receivable has been earned but has not yet been received.

h. Of the $9,000 rent collected, only $1,500 has been earned this year.

i. Of the $23,000 fees income collected, $18,000 has been earned this year.

E15-2. Usually the building rent is paid at the beginning of each month ($600). Financial statements are prepared at the end of every month, and the accounts are closed. During May the company was running short of cash; therefore, the landlord agreed to let the payment for the May rent be made on June 3, along with the June rent. Make these entries:

a. Adjusting entry at May 31.

b. Payment for rent at June 3.

c. Adjusting entry at June 30.

E15-3. At January 1, 1978, the beginning of the year, the Estimated federal income taxes payable amounted to $1,400. During the year this amount was paid to the government. The income taxes for the year are estimated to be $1,700, of which $1,000 has been paid. These entries appeared on the books of the firm:

Jan.	15	Estimated federal income taxes payable	1,400	
		Cash		1,400
Oct.	15	Federal income taxes expense	1,000	
		Cash		1,000

Make the necessary adjusting entry at December 31, 1978.

E15-4. Elysian Fields Maintenance Service Company performs a cleaning service for customers for the fee of $50 per month. During the month, fees amounting to $3,000 were received and were credited to the Unearned service revenue account. At the end of the month, the accountant calculated that $2,200 of these fees had been earned during the month. Also he discovered that services had been rendered to Slowpay Corporation, and that we have not yet received the $50 amount due us. Make the necessary adjusting journal entries at the end of the month.

E15-5. On May 1, 1978, Wilmz, Inc., purchased a 5-year insurance policy on the lives of the key executives in the firm. The policy cost $30,000 for the 5-year period, and this amount was paid in full on May 1.

If on May 1 the Life insurance expense account was debited, what adjustment is needed at December 31, 1978?

If on May 1, the Prepaid life insurance account was debited, what adjustment is needed at December 31, 1978?

E15-6. The Big Finance Company has notes receivable on its books as follows at December 31, 1978:

NAME	AMOUNT	ANNUAL INTEREST RATE	PERIOD	DATE SIGNED
Orleans Company	$10,000	7%	90 days	12-1-78
Jefferson Company	20,000	8%	1 year	6-1-78

Prepare the adjusting journal entry to reflect the interest earned on these notes receivable during 1978.

PROBLEMS (GROUP A)

P15-1. *Adjusting journal entries.* The trial balance of a firm at the end of the accounting year (December 31, 1978) included the following accounts and balances.

Accounts receivable	$ 25,000
Unearned rent	10,000
Prepaid insurance	2,000
Equipment	80,000
Accumulated depreciation—Equipment	10,000
Sales salaries expense	3,000
Merchandise inventory	9,000
Purchases of merchandise	100,000
Transportation on purchases	11,000
Purchases returns and allowances	10,000
Purchases discounts	3,000
Notes receivable	15,000
Consulting revenue	20,000
Rent expense	1,000

It has been determined by physical count that the ending merchandise inventory amounts to $12,000. Prepare adjusting journal entries for the following items:

a. Income taxes for the year are expected to amount to $10,000. These will be paid next year. (This is an accrued expense.)
b. $700 of the insurance has expired (been used).
c. Of the $1,000 rent expense paid, $200 represents rent payments for next year (1979).
d. The depreciation on the equipment for 1978 is estimated to be $500.
e. Make the adjustment for inventory.
f. Only $24,500 of the accounts receivable are expected to be collected.
g. $35 of interest on the notes receivable has been earned but has not yet been received.
h. Of the $10,000 rent collected, only $2,000 has been earned this year.
i. Of the $20,000 consulting revenue collected, $19,000 has been earned this year.

P15-2. *Work sheet, adjusting entries, and closing entries.* The trial balance of Zee Corporation at the end of the year's operations, December 31, 1978, is shown on the next page.

Zee Corporation
TRIAL BALANCE
December 31, 1978

Cash	15,000	
Marketable securities	18,000	
Accounts receivable	22,000	
Allowance for bad debts		3,000
Merchandise inventory	30,000	
Prepaid insurance	3,000	
Office supplies	2,000	
Equipment	50,000	
Accumulated depreciation—Equipment		10,000
Long-term investments	90,000	
Accounts payable		10,000
Unearned rent		11,000
Dividends payable		8,000
Notes payable		50,000
Capital stock		100,000
Retained earnings		197,000
Dividends	15,000	
Sales		350,000
Sales discounts	4,000	
Sales returns and allowances	12,000	
Purchases of merchandise	400,000	
Purchases discounts		10,000
Purchases returns and allowances		15,000
Transportation on purchases	11,000	
Consulting revenue		40,000
Building rent expense	43,000	
Sales salaries expense	55,000	
Advertising expense	27,000	
Miscellaneous expenses	7,000	
	804,000	804,000

Information for adjustments:

a. The physical count of the merchandise inventory indicates that there is inventory costing $200,000 still on hand at December 31, 1978.

b. Income taxes for the year are expected to amount to $7,000 (accrued expense).

c. $1,000 of the insurance has expired during the year.

d. Of the $43,000 building rent expense paid, $10,000 represents payments made for next year's rent (1979).

e. The depreciation on the equipment for 1978 is $3,000.

f. Only $18,000 of the accounts receivable are expected to be collected.

g. Of the $11,000 rent collected (in the Unearned rent account), only $3,000 has been earned in 1978. The remainder will be earned in 1979.

h. $700 of office supplies remain on hand at December 31, 1978.

REQUIRED:

a. Prepare a work sheet for the company.

b. Prepare adjusting entries in general journal form.

c. Prepare closing entries in general journal form.

P15-3. *Closing entries from work sheet.* Refer to the work sheet that you prepared in P13-1 (Unit 13). Prepare closing journal entries from this work sheet.

PROBLEMS (GROUP B)

P15-4. *Closing entries, inventory adjustment, and computation of cost of goods sold and net earnings.* The following are the *adjusted trial balance* columns of the work sheet of a firm at December 31, 1978.

Cash	15,000	
Marketable securities	5,000	
Accounts receivable	50,000	
Allowance for uncollectibles		4,000
Merchandise inventory	25,000	
Prepaid insurance	1,000	
Supplies on hand	3,000	
Long-term investments	174,000	
Buildings	100,000	
Accumulated depreciation—Buildings		43,000
Accounts payable		13,000
Unearned rent		10,000
Dividends payable		14,000
Income taxes payable		10,000
Capital stock		100,000
Retained earnings		100,000
Dividends	14,000	
Sales		500,000
Sales returns and allowances	10,000	
Sales discounts	15,000	
Rent revenue		55,000
Purchases	301,000	
Transportation on purchases	7,000	
Purchases returns and allowances		11,000
Purchases discounts		2,000
Selling expenses	58,000	
Interest expense	3,000	
Rent expense	40,000	
Supplies expense	4,000	
Depreciation expense—Buildings	10,000	
Bad debts expense	1,000	
Other expenses	4,000	
Income taxes expense	17,000	
Net earnings summary	30,000	25,000
	887,000	887,000

REQUIRED:

a. Prepare closing entries in general journal form.
b. Compute the cost of goods sold.
c. Compute the net earnings.
d. Make the inventory adjusting entry that the firm must have made at December 31, 1978, in general journal form.

P15-5. *Closing entries from work sheet.* Refer to the work sheet that you prepared in P13-4 (Unit 13). Prepare closing journal entries from the work sheet.

P15-6. *Adjusting entries and closing entries.* Below is a trial balance of Landry Corporation at the end of a year's operations.

Landry Corporation
TRIAL BALANCE
December 31, 1978

Cash	213,000	
Marketable securities	16,000	
Accounts receivable	20,000	
Allowance for bad debts		2,000
Merchandise inventory	28,000	
Prepaid insurance	1,000	
Office supplies	2,000	
Equipment	48,000	
Accumulated depreciation—Equipment		8,000
Long-term investments	88,000	
Accounts payable		8,000
Unearned rent		9,000
Dividends payable		6,000
Notes payable		48,000
Capital stock		108,000
Retained earnings		195,000
Dividends	13,000	
Sales		529,000
Sales discounts	2,000	
Sales returns and allowances	10,000	
Purchases of merchandise	398,000	
Purchases discounts		8,000
Purchases returns and allowances		13,000
Transportation on purchases	9,000	
Consulting revenue		38,000
Rent expense	41,000	
Sales salaries expense	53,000	
Advertising expense	25,000	
Miscellaneous expense	5,000	
	972,000	972,000

Information for adjustments:

a. The physical count of merchandise inventory indicates that there is inventory costing $25,000 still on hand at December 31, 1978.

b. Income taxes for the year are expected to amount to $5,000 (accrued expense).

c. $750 of the insurance has expired during the year.

d. Of the $41,000 rent expense paid, $15,000 represents payments made for next year's rent (1979).

e. The depreciation on the equipment for 1978 is $2,500.

f. One-half of 1% (0.005) of *net* sales are expected to become bad debts.

g. Of the $9,000 rent collected (in the Unearned rent account), only $2,000 has been earned in 1978. The remainder will be earned in 1979.

h. $500 of office supplies remain on hand at December 31, 1978.

a. Prepare adjusting journal entries.
b. Prepare closing journal entries.

CUMULATIVE REVIEW PROBLEMS

P15-7. *Cumulative review problem.* Below is a list of account balances of the Green Acres Corporation at December 31, 1978.

Cash	25,000
Dividends	10,000
Office supplies	10,000
Marketable securities	13,000
Purchases returns and allowances	8,000
Merchandise inventory	33,000
Purchases discounts	6,000
Sales of merchandise	290,000
Purchases of merchandise	104,000
Advertising expense	16,000
Sales discounts	6,000
Accounts receivable	129,000
Income tax expense	9,000
Miscellaneous service income	14,000
Retained earnings	41,000
Investments in stocks and bonds	64,000
Common stock (10,000 shares outstanding)	104,000
Officers' salaries expense	24,000
Sales returns and allowances	9,000
Sales taxes payable	6,000
Transportation on purchases	6,000
Insurance expense	5,000
Office equipment	64,000
Sales salaries expense	29,000
Accounts payable	19,000
Notes payable (due in 1980)	59,000
Accumulated depreciation—Office equipment	9,000

Information for adjustments:
1. Merchandise inventory at December 31, 1978, amounts to $29,000.
2. $9,000 of income taxes have been paid during 1978. An additional $14,000 is owed at December 31, 1978.
3. Office supplies used during 1978 amount to $4,000.
4. Depreciation expense on office equipment during 1978, $6,000.

REQUIRED:

a. Prepare a work sheet for 1978. Arrange the accounts in the trial balance columns in this general order:
   (1) Assets.
   (2) Liabilities.
   (3) Capital and dividends.

(4) Revenues and deductions from revenues.

(5) Expenses and deductions from expenses.

b. From the work sheet, prepare adjusting entries in general journal form.

c. From the work sheet, prepare the following financial statements in good form:

(1) Summary income statement.

(2) Detailed income statement.

(3) Statement of retained earnings.

(4) Balance sheet.

P15-8. *Cumulative review problem.* The following is a trial balance of Bernard Corporation at December 31, 1978, the end of 1 year's operations.

Bernard Corporation
TRIAL BALANCE
December 31, 1978

Cash	21,000	
Marketable securities	7,000	
Accounts receivable	20,000	
Merchandise inventory	25,000	
Office supplies	2,000	
Store supplies	3,000	
Investments in stocks	70,000	
Investments in bonds	20,000	
Office equipment	9,000	
Accumulated depreciation—Office equipment		3,000
Store equipment	100,000	
Accumulated depreciation—Store equipment		10,000
Land	45,000	
Accounts payable		15,000
Sales taxes payable		5,000
Notes payable (long term)		30,000
Bonds payable		80,000
Common stock (20,000 shares outstanding)		75,000
Retained earnings		7,000
Dividends	15,000	
Sales of merchandise		307,000
Sales returns and allowances	10,000	
Sales discounts	5,000	
Rental income		21,000
Purchases	150,000	
Transportation on purchases	3,000	
Purchases returns and allowances		8,000
Purchases discounts		2,000
Officers and general salaries expense	20,000	
Insurance expense	3,000	
Advertising expense	12,000	
Sales salaries expense	23,000	
	563,000	563,000

Information for adjustments:

1. Office supplies used, $1,500.

2. Ending inventory, $17,500.

3. Store supplies still on hand (unused), $2,000.
4. Income taxes owed, $6,000.
5. Insurance expired (used), $1,200. (Notice that the Insurance expense account had been debited when payment was made for insurance.)
6. Interest owed on notes and bonds, $5,700.
7. Depreciation of office equipment, $1,000.
8. Depreciation of store equipment, $6,100.

REQUIRED:

a. Prepare a work sheet for 1978.
b. From the work sheet, prepare adjusting entries in general journal form.
c. From the work sheet, prepare the following financial statements in good form:
   (1) Summary income statement.
   (2) Detailed income statement.
   (3) Statement of retained earnings.
   (4) Classified balance sheet.

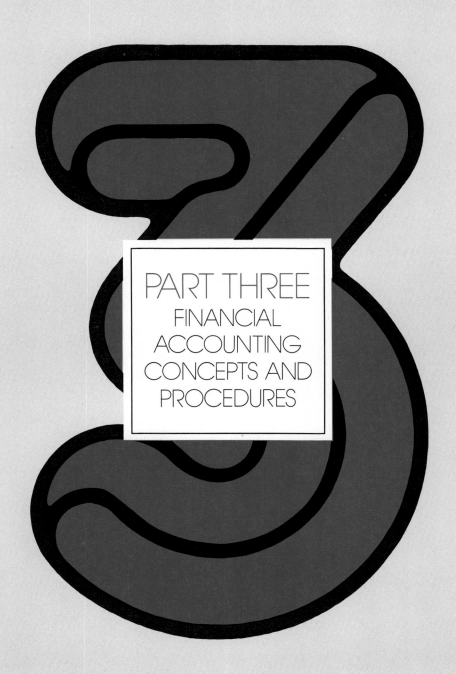

PART THREE
FINANCIAL
ACCOUNTING
CONCEPTS AND
PROCEDURES

chapter 7

cash, marketable securities, and receivables

CASH AND MARKETABLE SECURITIES

> ### ⟩ OBJECTIVE

This chapter begins a new section of this course in which additional problems and solutions in financial accounting will be introduced. You will now examine in some depth several account classifications that you have already studied. Financial accounting and some related management accounting considerations also will be covered, and special emphasis will be given to the relationships between the income statement and the balance sheet. This unit concentrates on the reporting and management of cash and marketable securities. These two highly liquid assets are usually vital to the successful operation of a business.

> ### ⟩ APPROACH TO ATTAINING THE OBJECTIVE

As you study the role of cash and marketable securities, pay special attention to these five questions, which the text following answers:

- *How are cash and marketable securities reported on financial statements?*
- *What is management's role in planning cash flows?*
- *How are cash receipts and payments controlled?*
- *How is the monthly bank statement reconciled with the accounting records?*
- *How are petty cash transactions controlled and reported?*

Classification Currency, checks, bank accounts, and coins to be used in current regular operations during the next year are customarily classified in the current asset category, Cash, on the balance sheet. This classification of cash communicates information to the decision makers about the most liquid asset management has reserved at a particular point in time for running the business. It is a general practice to *exclude* from the current asset, Cash, category any cash that has been specifically reserved for any purpose other than regular operations of the business. Such amounts are classified as noncurrent assets to provide statement readers with a meaningful picture of a firm's debt-paying ability.

■ *How are cash and marketable securities reported on financial statements?*

The current asset Marketable securities category includes stocks, bonds, and other investments that are expected to be converted into cash and used in regular operations during the coming year. These are temporary investments and can be sold on short notice to aid in running the business. If an investment is purchased and management expects to hold it for several years, it is not classified as a Marketable security in the current asset section of the balance sheet. Instead it is shown as a long-term (noncurrent) investment.

Valuation Cash is traditionally valued (reported on the financial statements) at its face amount. This valuation procedure gives the best measure of purchasing power currently tied up in the cash category. Marketable securities, on the other hand, customarily have been reported (valued) on the balance sheet at *cost or market, whichever is lower.* This example will illustrate:

A firm purchased 100 shares of ABC Company stock on December 14, 1978, to be held for a short period of time. The total cost, including brokerage commissions, was $5,143. Financial statements are to be prepared at December 31, 1978. Management determines that if the securities were sold at the balance sheet date (December 31, 1978), $5,090 would be realized. This is known as the *market value.*
These journal entries would probably appear in the firm's records:

1978			
Dec. 14	Marketable securities	5,143	
	Cash		5,143
	Adjusting entry		
1978			
Dec. 31	Loss from market declines		
	in marketable securities	53	
	Marketable securities		53[1]

[1] In actual practice, many firms credit a *contra account,* "Allowance to reduce short-term investments in equity securities to market," instead of directly reducing the Marketable securities account. This procedure allows the original cost of the securities to remain in the Marketable securities ledger account. The expense or loss account that is debited is often called "Unrealized loss on short-term investments in equity securities." Current practice is described in Financial Accounting Standards Board (FASB) Statement No. 12.

The adjusting entry reduces the current asset, Marketable securities, to the market value, $5,090. This lower value is then reported on the balance sheet. At the same time the net earnings of 1978 are reduced by $53, the loss from *holding* the securities.

If the securities were sold in 1979 for $5,112, the following entry would be made:

```
1979
Feb. 3    Cash                              5,112
               Marketable securities                5,090
               Gain on sale of marketable
                 securities                            22
```

This whole valuation procedure is a *conservative* one. That is, the procedure *guards against* reporting temporary investments at an amount greater than that which is likely to be realized in cash to be used to run the business. A substitute valuation method, which the accounting profession is considering, is to report marketable securities at their market value at the balance sheet date (rather than at the lower of cost or market). Perhaps this would give the statement reader more useful information for judging a firm's debt-paying ability.

MANAGEMENT'S PLANNING AND CONTROLLING OF CASH

Some of the important activities in management's planning and controlling of cash include (1) cash flow planning, (2) controlling cash receipts, (3) controlling cash payments, (4) the voucher system, (5) reconciling the monthly bank statement, and (6) controlling petty cash transactions. In this section we will examine some of the details of these activities.

Cash flow planning One of management's important responsibilities is to make sure that enough cash is available during the operating period to efficiently operate the business. Just as important as having enough cash is safeguarding against having an *excess* of cash on hand. Excess balances of cash must be temporarily invested so that the funds can produce earnings for the firm. Channeling excess cash balances into marketable securities is a common practice. All this implies, therefore, that management must plan and manage cash carefully.

■ *What is management's role in planning cash flows?*

The major sources of cash for a company are:

1. Cash generated by regular operations of the firm (collections from customers less cash payments for expenses are part of this concept).
2. Long-term borrowings.
3. Owners' investments in the firm.
4. Selling noncurrent assets.

The major uses of cash for a company are:

1. Payment of dividends.
2. Repaying long-term debt.
3. Purchasing noncurrent assets.

An accounting report is often prepared within a business organization to summarize the activities concerning cash for a period. This statement is called a **cash flow statement**.

Controlling receipts and payments of cash Management's responsibility regarding cash involves more than simply assuring that the right amounts of cash are on hand during the operating period. In addition, management must assure that cash is safeguarded—that only authorized payments are made and that all receipts of cash actually find their way into the firm as desired. This internal control process over cash should involve these areas, especially in larger firms:

■ *How are cash receipts and payments controlled?*

1. The **controller**'s department (the accounting department) within the firm.
2. The **treasurer**'s department within the firm.
3. Other departments within the firm.
4. The bank.

A good system for controlling cash receipts might involve the areas shown in Illustration 16-1. This suggested system involves a basic, very important idea. This idea is that the tasks associated with cash management are organized so that three *separate* individuals or groups provide control. The receipt of cash is handled by one group ("other departments"), the accounting records of cash are kept by another group (accounting department), and the cash is deposited by a third group (treasurer's department).

A good system for controlling cash payments might involve the same three groups, as shown in Illustration 16-2. Note again how three separate groups provide control.[1]

The voucher system Using these same principles of *internal control* (separation of duties within an organization to assure control), one special set of procedures for controlling cash payments is referred to as the *voucher system*. Re-

---

[1] In relatively small business firms, it may not be possible to have three separate groups to provide the necessary internal control over cash receipts and payments. In such cases, a large part of the control is accomplished by the direct involvement and participation by the owner of the business.

CONTROLLING CASH RECEIPTS

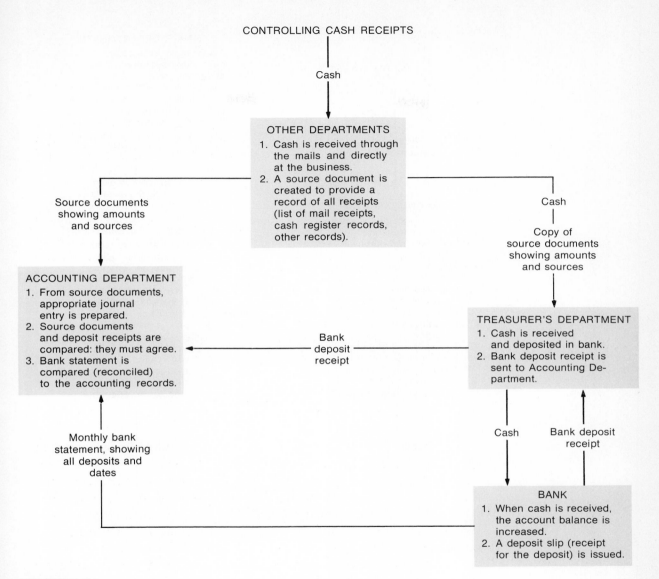

ILLUSTRATION 16-1

member that the voucher system is not used by all firms, but is simply one way of handling the control of cash payments. The main elements of the voucher system are as follows:

1. *Every* obligation that the firm incurs is recorded on a document called a **voucher.** The vouchers, which are written authorizations to issue checks, are prenumbered and are signed by the appropriate company

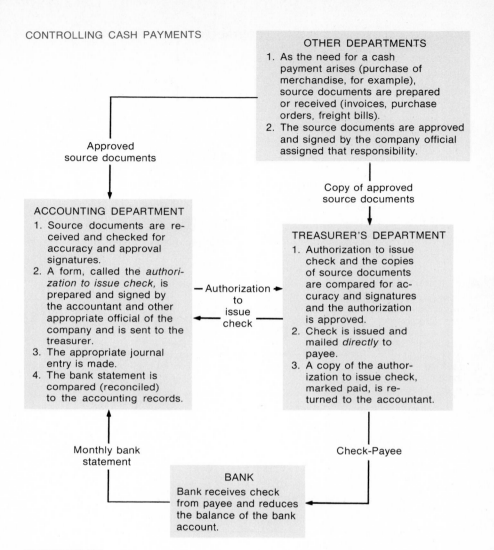

OTHER DEPARTMENTS

1. As the need for a cash payment arises (purchase of merchandise, for example), source documents are prepared or received (invoices, purchase orders, freight bills).
2. The source documents are approved and signed by the company official assigned that responsibility.

Approved source documents

Copy of approved source documents

ACCOUNTING DEPARTMENT

1. Source documents are received and checked for accuracy and approval signatures.
2. A form, called the *authorization to issue check,* is prepared and signed by the accountant and other appropriate official of the company and is sent to the treasurer.
3. The appropriate journal entry is made.
4. The bank statement is compared (reconciled) to the accounting records.

— Authorization to issue check

TREASURER'S DEPARTMENT

1. Authorization to issue check and the copies of source documents are compared for accuracy and signatures and the authorization is approved.
2. Check is issued and mailed *directly* to payee.
3. A copy of the authorization to issue check, marked paid, is returned to the accountant.

Monthly bank statement

Check-Payee

BANK

Bank receives check from payee and reduces the balance of the bank account.

ILLUSTRATION 16-2

personnel to show that the firm has received the good or service. Refer to Illustration 16-3 for an example.

2. A special journal (called a **voucher register**) is used to record all vouchers. For every voucher, the appropriate account is debited (such as Supplies, Purchases of merchandise, or Advertising expense) and the current liability account called Vouchers payable is credited. Refer to Illustration 16-4. This first entry in the voucher register (March 3) is based upon the voucher in Illustration 16-3. The Pur-

VOUCHER   No. 309

HARRIS MERCHANDISING COMPANY

Date March 3, 1978   Payee Jones, Inc.

                                    145 West 18th Street

                                    New York, NY 10010

Description	Amount
183 pounds Material 1356 Vicko Invoice 18456	$300.00

Distribution of Accounts	Approvals
Debits	
Purchases of merchandise (501) 300.00	Distribution approval *Hiram Winter*
Insurance expense (520)......	
Supplies (118).............	Controller *A.P. Jackson*
Advertising expense (531)....	
	Treasurer *Paul Thompson*
	Payment
Credit	
Vouchers payable (301) 300.00	Date paid March 10, 1978
	Check number _____ 841
	Attach all supporting documents.

ILLUSTRATION 16-3

chases of merchandise account is debited and the Vouchers payable account is credited for the $300.

3. When payment is made, another special journal is used to record *all* checks written. This journal is called a **check register** and takes the place of the cash payments journal. In this journal for *every* check that is written the Vouchers payable account is debited and the Cash in bank account is credited. Illustration 16-5 shows the check register.

4. Under the voucher system, the accounts payable subsidiary ledger is replaced by a file of unpaid vouchers. These vouchers are usually filed

VOUCHER REGISTER

page 18

DATE		VOUCHER NO.	NAME OF PAYEE	payment record CHECK NO.	payment record DATE PAID	VOUCHERS PAYABLE CREDIT	PURCHASES OF MERCHANDISE DEBIT	SELLING EXPENSES DEBIT	GENERAL EXPENSES DEBIT	OTHER ACCOUNTS	POSTING REF.	AMOUNT
1978 March	3	309	Jones, Inc.	841	3/10	300.00	300.00					
	7	310	Baltazor, Inc.			118.33				Transportation in		118.33
	11	311	Alkaline Industries			36.00			36.00			
	12	312	Bontal Company	842	3/15	1,120.42	1,120.42					
	12	313	Cole Brothers	843	3/15	50.00		50.00				
			Totals			69,518.22	41,018.20	20,956.00	1,572.40			5,971.62

ILLUSTRATION 16-4

CHECK REGISTER						page 46
DATE 1978		PAYEE	CHECK NO.	VOUCHER NO.	VOUCHERS PAYABLE DEBIT	CASH IN BANK CREDIT
		. . .				
		. . .				
March	10	Jones, Inc.	841	309	300.00	300.00
	15	Bontal Company	842	312	1,120.42	1,120.42
	15	Cole Brothers	843	313	50.00	50.00
		. . .				
		Totals			67,400.18	67,400.18

ILLUSTRATION 16-5

according to their due dates (to assure that the amounts are paid on time to receive any cash discounts allowed, and to assure that the amounts are not paid before they are due for good cash management).

Reconciling the monthly bank statement Each month, as a control procedure for cash, the accountant needs to compare the **bank statement** with the accounting records for cash. By this procedure, known as the **reconciliation** of the bank statement, the accountant can locate problems within the cash control system, investigate them, and settle them.

On pages 281 through 283 this information about the Count Company is provided in order to illustrate the reconciliation process: (1) the firm's cash receipts journal, (281) (2) the firm's cash payments journal, (282) (3) the Cash account from the firm's general ledger, (282) and (4) the bank statement from Quarter National Bank for the month of December, 1978 (283). Examine these documents carefully and then read over the table on page 284 that presents the bank statement reconciliation for Count Company at December 31, 1978. Study these points about the reconciliation illustrated in the table:

- How is the monthly bank statement reconciled with the accounting records?

1. The first half of the reconciliation form (284) serves for calculating the end-of-period cash balance ($10,740.30); the bank statement is the basis.

2. The second half of the form serves for calculating the end-of-period cash balance ($10,740.30); the accounting records are used as a basis.

3. Notice that there are four types of items that can cause the bank information to differ from the information in the accounting records:

   a. Cash received by the firm, but not yet received by the bank; this is used to adjust the *bank* balance.

   b. Payments made by the firm, but not yet recorded by the bank; this is used to adjust the *bank* balance.

   c. Cash received by the bank, but not yet recorded by the firm; this is used to adjust the *book* balance. *A journal entry is always needed in these cases to correct the accounts.* For example, if the bank collected $1,000 for the firm for rental property earnings, then this entry would be made on the firm's books (in the cash receipts journal):

Cash	1,000	
Rental property income		1,000

   d. Payments made by the bank, but not yet recorded by the firm; this is used to adjust the *book* balance. *A journal entry is always needed in these cases to correct the accounts.* For example, the $5 service charge on the bank statement would be recorded in the cash payments journal:

Bank service charge expense	5	
Cash		5

4. These steps can be used in preparing the reconciliation:

   a. On the reconciliation form, list the ending balance according to the bank statement ($14,315.81).

   b. Determine if the firm has received cash that has not yet reached the bank. This can be done by comparing the deposits recorded on the bank statement with the receipts of cash as recorded in the cash receipts journal. Compare the cash receipts journal in our example to the bank statement to determine how the $823.91 was found. More than one receipt may be combined to make a single bank deposit. Enter the amount on the reconciliation form.

   c. Determine if there have been payments made by the firm, but not yet recorded by the bank. This can be done by comparing the withdrawals recorded on the bank statement with the cash payments journal. Compare the cash payments journal in our example

CASH RECEIPTS JOURNAL

DATE		ACCOUNT CREDITED	DESCRIPTION	PR	GENERAL ACCOUNTS CREDIT	ACCOUNTS RECEIVABLE CREDIT	SALES CREDIT	SALES DISCOUNTS DEBIT	CASH DEBIT
1978 Dec.	5	Pearl Company	collection of account	✓		50.00		1.00	49.00
	7	Sales	cash sales				151.00		151.00
	11	Rent income		404	200.00				200.00
	13	Pearl Company	collection of account	✓		1,014.82		20.30	994.52
	14	Sales	cash sales				750.00		795.00
		Sales taxes payable		202	45.00				
	15	Allyn Corp	collection of account	✓		1,500.00			1,500.00
	19	Smith Company	collection of account	✓		106.00		2.12	103.88
	22	Brant & Brandt	collection of account	✓		840.72		16.81	823.91
					245.00	3,511.54	901.00	40.23	4,617.31
					(✓)	(120)	(401)	(403)	(101)

DATE		ACCOUNT DEBITED	CK. NO.	PR	GENERAL ACCOUNTS DEBIT	ACCOUNTS PAYABLE DEBIT	PURCHASES DEBIT	PURCHASES DISCOUNTS CREDIT	CASH CREDIT
1978 Dec.	3	Simpson Co.	313	✔		500.00		10.00	490.00
	12	General expense	314	510	140.00				140.00
	17	Reinecke Corp.	315	✔		859.79		17.20	842.59
	18	Hall Freight Inc.	316	✔		60.00			60.00
	20	Selling expense	317	520	400.00				400.00
	24	Simpson Co.	318	✔		1,979.00		39.58	1,939.42
	30	Purchases	319				2,000.00		2,000.00
					540.00	3,398.79	2,000.00	66.78	5,872.01
					(✔)	(201)	(501)	(503)	(101)

to the bank statement to determine how the $4,399.42 was found. Enter the amount on the reconciliation form. Also, observe that a check which may have been written in previous periods may reach the bank during the current period (a $200 check in this example). Such items do not directly affect the reconciliation.

d. Compute the corrected balance of cash.

e. On the reconciliation form, list the ending balance according to the accounting records ($10,745.30).

f. Determine if there has been cash received by the bank but not yet recorded by the firm. This can be determined by comparing the deposits on the bank statement with the cash receipts journal. Enter any amount on the reconciliation form, and *make the needed journal entry on the firm's records.*

Cash   ACCOUNT NO. 101

DATE		DESCRIPTION	REF.	DEBITS	CREDITS	BALANCE DEBIT	BALANCE CREDIT
1978 Dec.	1	Balance				12000 00	
	31		CR33	4617 31		16617 31	
	31		CP19		5872 01	10745 30	

STATEMENT OF YOUR ACCOUNT WITH

The Quarter National Bank IN NEW ORLEANS

Count Company
5518 Chatham Drive
New Orleans, LA 70122

STATEMENT DATE	ITEMS
Dec. 23, 1978	11
ACCOUNT NUMBER	PAGE
89-50-0001	1

Please notify us of any
change in your address.

CHECKS AND DEBIT ITEMS		CREDITS	DATE	BALANCE
				12,200.00
		49.00	12-6	12,249.00
200.00			12-6	12,049.00
		151.00	12-9	12,200.00
		1,194.52	12-14	13,394.52
490.00	140.00		12-15	12,764.52
		795.00	12-15	13,559.52
		1,500.00	12-16	15,059.52
842.59			12-18	14,216.93
		103.88	12-20	14,320.81
5.00S			12-23	14,315.81

BALANCE FORWARD	CREDITS		CHECKS AND DEBITS		SERVICE CHARGE	CURRENT BALANCE
	NO.	AMOUNT	NO.	AMOUNT		
12,200.00	6	3,793.40	5	1,672.59	5.00	14,315.81

SYMBOLS: D–Debit Memo L–List Post R–Returned Item S–Service Charge

"Please examine this statement promptly and immediately advise our Auditing Dept. of any errors. If no error is reported within ten days this statement will be considered correct. See reconciliation form on reverse."

g. Determine if there have been payments made by the bank, but not yet recorded by the firm. This can be done by comparing the withdrawals according to the bank statement with the cash payments journal. Enter any amount on the reconciliation form, and *make the needed journal entry on the firm's accounting records.*

Count Company
BANK STATEMENT RECONCILIATION
December 31, 1978

Balance, December 31, 1978 According to bank statement		1	4	3	15	81
Items which can cause the bank statement to differ from the accounting records:						
(1) Cash received by the firm, but not yet received by the bank:						
Deposit in transit (determined by comparing all cash receipts in the journal						
to the deposits on the bank statement)	+			8	23	91
(2) Payments made by the firm, but not yet recorded by the bank:						
Checks outstanding (determined by comparing all cash payments in the journal						
to the checks paid according to the bank statement—60.00; 400.00;						
1,939,42; 2,000.00)	−			4	39	42
Corrected balance of cash	$	1	0	7	40	30
Balance, December 31, 1978, According to Cash ledger account	$	1	0	7	45	30
Items which can cause the bank statement to differ from the accounting records:						
(3) Cash received by the bank (deposited) but not yet recorded by the firm:						
Occasionally, a bank will act as a collection agent for a company and will						
receive funds before the firm is aware of the collection. This example does						
not include such an item.	+					
(4) Payments made by the bank, but not yet recorded by the firm:						
Service charge	−				5	00
Corrected balance of cash	$	1	0	7	40	30

h. Compute the corrected balance of cash. Compare this figure for equality with the corrected cash balance computed in d above.

How are petty cash transactions controlled and reported?

Controlling petty cash transactions Most firms make all payments by check in order to further control cash disbursements. The only exception these firms make to this rule is to provide a relatively small fund of cash at the place of business. This fund, called a **petty cash** fund, is available for making the small payments required for such things as postage stamps and the miscellaneous small expenditures needed to operate an office. As control measures, these procedures are widely used:

1. One person is usually given the responsibility of operating the petty cash fund.

2. Each time an expenditure is made, a source document (called a **petty cash voucher**) is prepared to evidence the payment. The voucher is signed by the person receiving the cash and by the person in charge of the fund (petty cashier). The petty cash voucher includes the amount and purpose of the expenditure.

3. A record (usually multicolumned) is kept to record each expenditure from the petty cash fund.

4. Each time the fund is almost depleted, and also at the end of every accounting period, a check is prepared for the amounts spent and is cashed to replenish the petty cash fund. At that time cash is credited, and the appropriate expense and other accounts are debited to record all the expenditures.

Illustrated below are a petty cash record and the journal entries required to (1) set up the fund, and (2) replenish it.

	CASH PAYMENTS JOURNAL							page 25
DATE	ACCOUNT DEBITED	CK. NO.	PR	GENERAL ACCOUNTS DEBIT	ACCOUNTS PAYABLE DEBIT	PURCHASES DEBIT	PURCHASES DISCOUNTS CREDIT	CASH CREDIT
1978 Dec. 1	Petty cash	306	102	50.00				50.00
31	Postage expense	405	511	16.00				47.30
	Transportation on purchases		503	21.00				
	Office supplies		107	4.12				
	Miscellaneous expense		529	6.18				

PETTY CASH RECORD

DATE		ITEM	VOUCHER NUMBER	CASH RECEIVED	CASH PAID	accounts debited			
						POSTAGE	TRANSPORTATION ON PURCHASES	OTHER	
1978 Dec.	1	Set up fund (ck. 306)		50.00					
	2	Stamps	101		8.00	8.00			
	5	Frank's Freight Co.	102		21.00		21.00		
	7	ABC Office Co.	103		4.12			Office supplies	4.12
	15	Stamps	104		8.00	8.00			
	21	A & P (coffee)	105		6.18			Misc. expense	6.18
	31	Totals		50.00	47.30	16.00	21.00		10.30
Dec.	31	Balance			2.70				
				50.00	50.00				
Dec.	31	Balance		2.70					
	31	Reimbursement (ck. 405)		47.30					

authorization to issue check A written form or document, to be signed by the appropriate company officials, that gives permission for a check to be issued and for cash to be paid. [p. 275]

bank deposit receipt A written receipt prepared by a bank to show that a deposit has been made. [p. 275]

bank statement The written record of transactions in a bank account, showing deposits and withdrawals and beginning and ending balances of the account; usually prepared monthly by the bank and given to the owner of the account. [p. 279]

cash flow statement An accounting report, primarily for management's use, that summarizes the sources and uses of cash for a period. [p. 274]

check register A special journal similar to a cash payments journal. All cash payments made by check are recorded in this journal. In each case Vouchers payable is debited and Cash in bank is credited (used in Voucher System). [p. 277]

controller The chief accounting officer of a firm. [p. 274]

payee The person or company to receive payment, such as the person named on a check to receive payment. [p. 276]

petty cash A relatively small fund of currency and coins used at the place of business to make small expenditures. [p. 285]

petty cash voucher A written form or document prepared to show amounts and other details of a payment made out of a petty cash fund. [p. 285]

reconciliation Comparing and explaining differences; specifically, a reconciliation of a bank statement involves comparing the bank statement to the accounting records and explaining any differences. [p. 279]

treasurer An officer of a firm whose job is to act as custodian over the financial assets of the company, including the receiving and disbursing of cash, and the making of financial decisions (such as investment decisions). [p. 274]

voucher Written authorization to issue a check. [p. 275]

voucher register A special journal used to record all authorizations to issue checks (vouchers). For each entry in the voucher register, the Vouchers payable account is credited (a liability) and the appropriate account, such as Supplies or Advertising expense, is debited. [p. 276]

› **ASSIGNMENT MATERIAL**

QUESTIONS

Q16-1. On the balance sheet, under what circumstances should cash not be included in the current asset category of Cash?

Q16-2. Explain what is meant by "cost or market, whichever is lower," in reporting marketable securities.

Q16-3. Why is the practice of reporting marketable securities at cost or market, whichever is lower, considered to be a conservative practice?

Q16-4. What are the major sources of cash for a company?

Q16-5. What are the major uses of cash for a company?

Q16-6. What four areas (departments of a firm, etc.) should the control process for cash involve?

Q16-7. Why is it important to involve several persons or departments in controlling cash—rather than having *one* department handle all activities regarding cash?

EXERCISES

E16-1. At June 1, 1978, the balance of the marketable securities account of a firm was $2,319. On June 18, additional securities were purchased for $9,115 cash. On June 27, all the securities which the firm had on hand at June 1 were sold for $2,522 cash. At June 30, 1978, the balance sheet date, securities on hand had a market value of $9,050. In general journal form make all journal entries for the month, including the adjusting entry needed.

E16-2. At June 1, 1978, a check was written and cashed for $100 for the purpose of setting up a petty cash fund. At June 29, 1978, another check was written and cashed for $91, to replenish the fund. The petty cash record revealed the following expenditures for the month from the fund:

Postage	$29
Supplies	32
Transportation on purchases	17
Selling expenses	13
	$91

In general journal form, make all journal entries dealing with the petty cash fund.

E16-3. Below is shown the ledger account for Marketable securities at January 1, 1978, the beginning of the year's operations.

MARKETABLE SECURITIES

Jan. 1 Balance 10,000	

The following transactions occurred during 1978:

March 17	Purchased marketable securities for $13,000 cash.
March 25	Purchased marketable securities for $11,000 cash.
August 1	Sold the securities that were purchased on March 17 for $15,500 cash.

At December 31, 1978, the company owned marketable securities that had cost a total of $21,000. These securities had a market value of $20,300 at December 31, 1978.

REQUIRED: In general journal form make all journal entries concerning marketable securities for the year, including the adjusting entry needed.

E16-4. S. Fox Company recently set up a petty cash fund to be used for paying small bills. The fund is to contain $200 at the beginning of each month. Assume that you are the owner of the company and want to assure that this money is spent wisely and is carefully controlled.

REQUIRED: Prepare a list of procedures to assure control and reporting of the petty cash.

PROBLEMS (GROUP A)

P16-1. *Bank statement reconciliation.* Prepare a bank reconciliation form, using the following information:

a. The bank statement revealed the following:

Beginning balance	$11,000.00
Withdrawals	13,904.20
Deposits	16,500.40
Ending balance	13,596.20

b. The cash ledger account revealed the following:

Beginning balance	$11,000.00
Debits	22,700.40
Credits	22,886.34
Ending balance	10,814.06

c. Checks outstanding amounted to $9,100.14.
d. A service charge of $18 appeared on the bank statement.
e. The bank had made a collection for the company, $1,800. The company was not aware of this collection until now.
f. Deposits in transit amounted to $8,000.
g. The bank statement reveals that the company's account has been reduced by $100. It seems that the company had deposited a $100 check received from one of its customers, A. Smith, some time ago. Mr. Smith did not have funds in his account to cover the check, so his bank returned the check marked "Not Sufficient Funds" (NSF) to the company's bank, which in turn reduced our account. (The appropriate journal entry is a credit to Cash and a debit to Accounts receivable to set up the amount still due us from Smith.)

P16-2. *Bank statement reconciliation.* Prepare a bank reconciliation form, using the following information:
a. The cash ledger account revealed the following: Beginning balance of cash, $25,000; debits to the Cash account, $5,113.91; credits to the Cash account, $11,220.74.
b. The monthly bank statement revealed the following: Beginning balance of cash, $25,000; withdrawals, $9,114.72; ending balance of cash, $22,203.73.
c. A service charge of $13 appeared on the bank statement.
d. Checks outstanding totaled $2,119.02.
e. Deposits that had not reached the bank (deposits in transit) amounted to $4,000.
f. The bank had made a collection for the company of $5,204.54. This amount had not been recorded on the company's books.

P16-3. *Voucher system and petty cash.* The following selected transactions took place for a company during November, 1978:

Nov. 1   Purchased merchandise from Bandings, Inc., with terms of 10 days, $500. Voucher 916 was prepared.

       2   Issued a voucher (917) for $200 so a check could be written and cashed to set up a petty cash fund.

       3   Issued Check 174 for $200 (Cash) to set up the petty cash fund.

       5   Incurred selling expenses (Advertising) amounting to $762, Jantzen Co. Issued Voucher 918.

       5   Issued check 175 in payment of Voucher 918.

       7   Paid cash of $9.00 out of the petty cash fund for postage stamps (Petty cash Voucher B19).

     11   Issued check 176 in payment of Voucher 916.

     12   Received a freight bill for $96 from Hall Freight Company, due in 20 days. Issued Voucher 919.

     15   Issued check 177 for $713 to Howard Co. in payment of Voucher 912, which had been issued last month for office supplies.

18	Paid cash of $12 for Transportation on purchases, A Y Freight Co., from the petty cash fund (Petty cash voucher B20).
19	Purchased merchandise from Beaty Co. for cash $45 from the petty cash fund (Petty cash voucher B21).
21	Purchased merchandise from Texas Industries for $950, terms 10 days. Issued Voucher 920.
22	Issued Check 178 for $305 to Danny's Inc., in payment of Voucher 913, which had been issued last month for general expenses.
30	Issued a voucher for the amount needed to bring the petty cash fund balance up to $200, Voucher 921.
30	Issued Check 179 in payment of Voucher 921.

REQUIRED:

a. Set up the following records:
   (1) Petty cash record.
   (2) Voucher register.
   (3) Check register.
b. Record the above transactions in the appropriate records.
c. Total and rule the records at the end of the month as appropriate.
d. Assume that the transactions above were the only ones the company had during November that affected the journals and records used in this problem. Also assume that the balance of the vouchers payable at November 1, 1978, amounted to $1,018. Answer these questions:
   (1) What is the balance of the Vouchers payable account at November 30, 1978?
   (2) Prepare a list of unpaid vouchers at November 30, 1978, with voucher number and amount. Does the total of this list agree with the balance of the Vouchers payable account at November 30, 1978?

PROBLEMS (GROUP B)

P16-4. *Bank statement reconciliation.* As a firm's accountant, you recently received the company's monthly statement of its checking account from the Z National Bank. This information is revealed by the statement as of July 31, 1978.

Cash balance at July 1	$14,654.19
Cash balance at July 31	9,111.45

You compared this statement and the returned cancelled checks accompanying the statement with the records of the firm and determined the following:

a. The bank deducted from the company's account $3.62 as a service charge for the month. You immediately record this amount on the books as a cash payment (debiting Miscellaneous expenses and crediting Cash).
b. You discover that four checks, totaling $5,142.65, were written and mailed to the payees, but these checks have not yet reached the bank.
c. You discover that a deposit of $1,498.87 was mailed to the bank on July 31, but the bank had not yet reflected this amount on the bank statement for July.

REQUIRED: Compute the amount of cash that should be reported on the July 31, 1978, balance sheet of the company. Show all computations and label them carefully.

P16-5. *Bank statement reconciliation.* The following facts were gathered by the firm's accountant in connection with the monthly bank statement reconciliation at March 31, 1978:

1. Checks written during the month, according to the firm's cash payments journal, $115,007.15.
2. Deposits in transit (cash received, but not received by the bank as of March 31), $6,519.40.
3. Deposits in transit as of March 1, 1978, $5,549.78.
4. Checks outstanding at March 1, 1978, $15,395.78.
5. Checks outstanding at March 31, 1978, $15,604.12.
6. Service charge appearing on the bank statement for March (not yet recorded in books of company), $26.
7. Balance of account per bank statement at March 31, 1978, $63,419.55.
8. Balance of account per bank statement at March 1, 1978, $55,400.00.
9. Cash received according to the cash receipts journal for March, $107,500.56.
10. Cash balance according to Cash ledger account at March 1, 1978, $48,067.42.
11. Cash balance according to Cash ledger account at March 31, 1978, $40,560.83.
12. Payment made by the bank to one of our suppliers for merchandise (according to our instructions), $1,000. This payment is not yet recorded in our records.
13. Collection made by bank for us, $14,800. This collection was from a customer (Accounts receivable), and we first learned of the collection on our bank statement for March.

REQUIRED:

a. Prepare a bank statement reconciliation form at March 31, 1978.
b. Prepare the necessary entries in general journal form.

P16-6. *Internal control case.* Mena-Meadville Cafe uses these procedures:

a. Each waitress prepares a ticket when she takes the customer's order.
b. The ticket is given to the kitchen manager, who fills the order.
c. The food, along with the ticket (including total amount due) is given to the customer.
d. The customer pays at the front counter as he leaves.

The owner of the cafe has made a careful study of the costs of different types of food and the prices he charges. The income statement each period does not reflect the markup (excess of sales over cost of goods sold) which the owner believes it should. What changes could be made in the system of cash control to aid the business?

ACCOUNTS RECEIVABLE

➤ **OBJECTIVE**

The purpose of this unit is to continue your study of accounts receivable. You will be introduced here to the management of receivables and accounting for the associated credit losses. You will also study two common procedures that management uses to assess its credit and collection policies.

➤ **APPROACH TO ATTAINING THE OBJECTIVE**

As you study about receivables, pay particular attention to these four questions, which the text following answers:

- *How are receivables and bad debt losses recorded and reported?*
- *How is a specific account, which is determined to be uncollectible, written off?*
- *How is the collection of an account recorded when that account previously had been written off as uncollectible?*
- *How does management control the receivables?*

Receivables are amounts owed to the firm by outsiders in the form of regular accounts or written promissory notes to be collected in the future. The customary valuation procedure for current receivables is to show the receivables on the balance sheet at the *amount expected to be collected.* This valuation method gives the reader of the balance sheet a measure of the cash expected to flow into the firm during the coming period from the receivables.

An adjusting entry is needed at the end of each accounting period to restate the receivables at their expected collectible amount. Let's consider an example in which a firm's trial balance at the end of 1978 showed these accounts and balances:

■ *How are receivables
and bad debt losses
recorded and reported?*

Accounts receivable	$ 10,000
Sales	100,000
Sales returns and allowances	4,000
Sales discounts	2,000

We can calculate from this information that the firm produced *net* sales of $94,000 during 1978 and that $10,000 is the total that can potentially be collected from the receivables during 1979. Management now must make a study to determine the amount it really expects to collect from the receivables.

There are two basic ways of making the estimate. The first involves examining every account appearing in the accounts receivable subsidiary ledger and then determining the likelihood that various categories of accounts (such as past-due accounts) will be collected. This process, called *aging* of receivables, will be discussed later in this unit. A second procedure involves looking at the past experience of the firm to determine the percent of sales made on credit in the past that eventually were not collected. The important point here is that an estimate must be made of the amount expected to be collected. All of this assumes, of course, that firms which sell on credit will, from time to time, have uncollectible accounts.

Assume that in the example just given, management estimates that $9,900 eventually will be collected. The following adjusting entry then would be made in the firm's general journal:

1978 Dec.	31	Bad debts expense	100.00	
		Allowance for uncollectibles		100.00

The effect of the adjustment is to show in 1978 an expense of $100. This expense can be viewed as an ordinary cost of making sales on credit and bearing the risk of selling to customers who do not pay their bills. The earnings for the period are reduced. The $94,000 still will be shown as the revenue for the period, but expenses will be increased by the estimated credit-loss costs. The adjustment must be made *now*—even though it is not known which specific customers will not pay their bills—so that net earnings for *this* period can be measured for decision-making purposes.

The Allowance for uncollectibles account is a contra account that reduces the Accounts receivable. The current asset section of the firm's balance sheet would show the following after the adjustment:

Accounts receivable	$10,000	
Less Allowance for uncollectibles	100	
Net accounts receivable		$9,900

or

Accounts receivable (net of allowance for uncollectibles of $100)	$9,900

Remember that both accounts, Accounts receivable and Allowance for uncollectibles, are classified as assets—one with a debit balance and the other with a credit balance. The same purpose would be accomplished by crediting the $100 to the Accounts receivable account in the adjusting entry, rather than having a separate account (Allowance for uncollectibles). However, this procedure would change the balance in the Accounts receivable (control) account without changing the balances of the individual accounts in the accounts receivable subsidiary ledger. The job of preparing a schedule of accounts receivable to agree with the control account then would be made quite complicated.

WRITING OFF AN UNCOLLECTIBLE ACCOUNT

How is a specific account, which is determined to be uncollectible, written off?

Let us continue the example we just discussed. Only let us assume that the accounts for 1978 have been closed. The Bad debts expense account would then have a zero balance to begin 1979. However, the two current asset accounts—Accounts receivable and Allowance for uncollectibles—would have balances going into 1979.

On January 15, 1979, the manager of the firm discovers that one of his customers, X Company, who owes the firm $10, has gone into bankruptcy. He concludes that the firm will never collect the receivable of $10. Correcting the accounts to reflect this fact is called *writing off an uncollectible account*. The following general journal entry would be made:

1979					
Jan.	15	Allowance for uncollectibles		10.00	
		Accounts receivable			10.00
		To write off the X Company account which is considered uncollectible.			

Observe these facts about this journal entry:

1. The Accounts receivable balance is reduced by $10 to show that this amount is no longer part of the amount which *could be* collected. The balance of Accounts receivable is reduced from $10,000 to $9,990.

2. The Allowance for uncollectibles (credit) balance is reduced by $10 to show that, of the $9,990 receivables, a total of $90 is not expected to be collected.

3. Notice that no expense account is affected. Earnings are not changed by writing off an account receivable. This is so because the earnings were reduced previously, when the adjusting entry for the estimated uncollectibles was made.

4. Study these relationships:

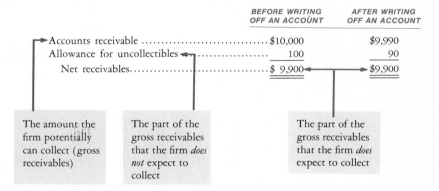

	BEFORE WRITING OFF AN ACCOUNT	AFTER WRITING OFF AN ACCOUNT
Accounts receivable	$10,000	$9,990
Allowance for uncollectibles	100	90
Net receivables	$ 9,900	$9,900

The amount the firm potentially can collect (gross receivables)

The part of the gross receivables that the firm *does not* expect to collect

The part of the gross receivables that the firm *does* expect to collect

REINSTATING AN ACCOUNT

On rare occasions, an account which has already been written off as uncollectible is eventually collected. In such cases, two entries are needed:

■ *How is the collection of an account recorded when that account previously had been written off as uncollectible?*

1979 Jan.	20	Accounts receivable	10.00	
		Allowance for uncollectibles		10.00
		To reinstate the X Company account which was previously written off as uncollectible.		
	20	Cash	10.00	
		Accounts receivable		10.00
		Collection of account, X Company		

The first entry reverses the entry that had been made when the account was written off. This corrects the records. The subsidiary accounts receivable ledger will now show that X Company has been reinstated. *This can be an important record if X Company wishes to apply to the firm for credit in the future.* The second journal entry above is simply a reflection of a collection of an accounts receivable, converting receivables to cash.

PLANNING AND CONTROL FOR RECEIVABLES

Two common procedures used by management in assessing its credit and collection policies are (1) the aging of accounts receivable, and (2) the computation of the measure called the receivables turnover. In this section is also discussed the direct write-off method of accounting for receivables.

■ *How does management control the receivables?*

Aging of accounts receivable Shown below is a work sheet for **aging of accounts receivable.** First each account is classified on the work sheet in terms of its age. Then management studies *past* records of the firm to determine what their experience has been in terms of credit losses for each major category of current and past-due accounts. These percentage loss estimates are multiplied times the balance of the receivables in each category to provide an estimate of the expected losses for the receivables. Carefully examine the work sheet and the calculation of the allowance for uncollectibles which appears below it.

WORK SHEET FOR AGING ACCOUNTS RECEIVABLE
DECEMBER 31, 1978

ACCOUNT	CURRENT (NOT PAST DUE)	1–30 DAYS PAST DUE	31–60 DAYS PAST DUE	OVER 60 DAYS PAST DUE
ABC Co.	500.00			
AX Corp.			75.00	
Baker Company		300.00		
Jones Co.	1,459.60			
⋮	⋮	⋮	⋮	⋮
Totals	91,400.60	1,655.40	700.50	200.00

CALCULATION OF ALLOWANCE FOR UNCOLLECTIBLES

AGE OF RECEIVABLES	AMOUNT	× LOSS EXPERIENCE	= EXPECTED UNCOLLECTIBLE AMOUNT
Current	$91,400.60	1.0%	$ 914.01
1–30 days past due	1,655.40	5.3%	87.74
31–60 days past due	700.50	10.9%	76.35
Over 60 days past due	200.00	70.6%	141.20
	$93,956.50		$1,219.30

Actual balance of Accounts receivable account

Recommended balance for Allowance for uncollectibles account

Assume that these are the balances in the accounts of a firm at December 31, 1978:

Accounts receivable	$93,956.50 debit balance
Allowance for uncollectibles	1,000.00 credit balance
Bad debts expense	–0–

At December 31, 1978, an adjusting entry must be made to record the bad debts expense for the year and to restate the Allowance for uncollectibles account. This entry is appropriate, assuming the balances in the accounts and the work sheet aging information:

1978 Dec.	31	Bad debts expense	219.30	
		Allowance for uncollectibles		219.30

The Allowance for uncollectibles balance is now increased from $1,000.00 to $1,219.30, which is the expected uncollectible amount of the receivables. The expense related to 1978 is estimated to be $219.30.

Remember that many estimates are required in reporting accounting information. One of these estimates involves the valuation of accounts receivable. The apparent accuracy of the $1,219.30 can be deceptive—this estimate may be incorrect by many dollars. Many firms round off these estimates, as well as other accounting information, because the cents—and sometimes hundreds of dollars—are not relevant to the decisions being made by using the information.

A second way to determine the entry for bad debts expense is to base the estimate on the *relationship of past credit losses to total sales made on credit.* For example, assume that the experience of a firm is that about 2% of all sales made on credit eventually are not collected. If a company made $100,000 of sales on credit during the period, then $2,000 would be the amount of the current expense. The $2,000 would be debited to the Bad debts expense account and would be credited to the Allowance for uncollectibles account. *The aging technique thus directly estimates the balance of the Allowance for uncollectibles account, whereas the method based upon credit sales directly estimates the bad debts expense for the period.*

Receivables turnover Another way that management often appraises its credit and collection policy is to compute a measure called the **receivables turnover.** This measure shows the relationship between the asset Accounts receivable and the credit sales made by the firm during a period:

$$\text{Receivables turnover} = \text{Net sales made on credit during the period} \div \text{Average balance of accounts receivable on hand during the period}$$

For example, if the firm made net credit sales during 1978 of $350,000, and if the *average*[1] receivables on hand during the period amounted to $10,000, then the receivables turnover is 35 times, computed as follows:

$$\frac{\$350,000}{\$10,000} = 35 \text{ times}$$

This means that, on the average, the company collected the receivables 35 times during 1978. Because uncollected accounts receivable yield no revenue, management prefers to keep the amount invested in them at a minimum. If the turnover had been 40 times during 1977, the previous year, then management probably should investigate why a relatively larger quantity of receivables, as related to net credit sales, was on hand during 1978. A decrease in the accounts receivable turnover indicates that there has been a slowing down in the collection of receivables. This may be due to some worsening in either the granting of credit or the collection practices used, or both.

Another measure to analyze the relationship between credit sales and accounts receivable is called *average collection period of receivables*. It is computed as follows:

$$\text{Average collection period of receivables} = \text{Accounts receivable at end of year} \div \text{Average sales made on credit per day during the year}$$

For example, if a firm made credit sales each day averaging $1,000, and if the firm had a receivables balance at December 31, 1978, of $12,000, then there are 12 days of sales tied up in receivables at the end of the year:

$$\frac{\$12,000}{\$1,000} = 12 \text{ days}$$

This computation can be related to the terms for which the company sells its merchandise, as well as to changes in this measure from previous periods;

---

[1] This average is often computed by adding the beginning receivables balance to the ending receivables balance and then dividing the total by 2. When monthly receivables balances are available, the balance of receivables at the beginning of the year is added to the balance of receivables at the end of *each* of the 12 months, and the total is divided by 13.

these comparisons help reveal how effectively the receivables are being managed.

Direct write-off method You have learned that the adjusting entry to record bad debts expense is necessary for two reasons: (1) so that the expense of credit losses can be reported in the measurement of earnings in the same period as the revenue from the related sales, and (2) so that the accounts receivable can be valued for decision purposes at the expected collectible amount, rather than at the gross amount. In special cases an alternative method, called the **direct write-off method,** can be used. This method is appropriate only when it is known that credit losses are not significant and only where future credit losses cannot be estimated from current sales.

Such a circumstance might arise for those businesses which sell practically all their merchandise for cash. Credit losses would be extremely rare and probably not very significant. In these situations, an adjusting entry would *not* be made in the period in which occasional credit sales are made. Instead, an entry is made only when a credit loss is actually discovered. For example:

| 1978 March | 11 | Bad debts expense | 100.00 | |
| | | Accounts receivable | | 100.00 |

This entry records the expense in the period when the loss is discovered, not in the period when the revenue was recognized from the credit sale. Remember that this clearly is *contrary* to generally accepted accounting principles because the expenses for credit losses are not reported in the same period that the revenues are reported for the sale. The method can be justified only in rare circumstances.

Continuing the same example, assume that the $100 credit loss above was later collected after all. The write-off entry above then could be reversed and the cash collection could be recorded in the usual manner if the collection were made in the same period as the write-off. If the collection were made in a different period, a problem would arise because the bad debts expense would have already been closed in the previous period. The credit in the reversal entry (to bad debts expense) would have to go to a revenue account, or perhaps to the Bad debts expense account if there were a debit balance present at that time.

aging of accounts receivable A procedure whereby each account receivable is classified according to its age (usually in terms of days past due); this classification helps in predicting bad debt losses to be incurred on the receivables. [p. 296]

direct write-off method A method of recording bad debts expense whereby the expense is recorded and reported in the period that the loss is discovered; this method is not recommended because it fails to match the revenue produced by the credit sales with the credit losses produced; the method overstates earnings in the period when the original sale was made and understates earnings in the period when the loss discovery was made. [p. 299]

receivables turnover A measure based upon the relationship of average accounts receivable on hand during the period and the net sales made on credit during the period; useful in assessing the effectiveness of receivables management. [p. 297]

> **ASSIGNMENT MATERIAL**

QUESTIONS

Q17-1. Receivables are reported on the balance sheet at the net collectible amount. This requires that an estimate of an expense (bad debts expense) be made on the income statement, and that an *estimate* of the net receivables be made on the balance sheet. What is another situation on the income statement and balance sheet where estimates are necessary and desirable if relevant information is to be reported to decision makers? Explain.

Q17-2. How is the Allowance for uncollectibles account classified on the financial statements?

Q17-3. Explain under what circumstances the Allowance for uncollectibles account balance is reduced (debited).

Q17-4. What effect does the bad debts adjusting entry have on the net receivables appearing on the balance sheet?

Q17-5. What effect does writing off an account as uncollectible have on the net receivables appearing on the balance sheet?

Q17-6. What is the effect on net earnings of the period of writing off an account as uncollectible?

Q17-7. What is meant by aging of accounts receivable?

Q17-8. What is the receivables turnover?

EXERCISES

E17-1. Martha Company had these account balances at December 31, 1978: Accounts receivable, $541,300; Allowance for bad debts, $10,912. Make entries in general journal form to record the following transactions during 1979.
   a. Sales made during the year: for cash, $121,214; on credit, $5,456,575.
   b. Collections of accounts during the year: actual cash collected, $5,381,642; discounts allowed, $130,004.
   c. Wrote off accounts as uncollectible as follows: $259.
   d. Collected an account which had previously been written off: $3,200.
   e. Made the adjusting entry for uncollectibles: bad debt losses are estimated to be 1% of total sales made on credit.
   Also, prepare the accounts receivable section of the balance sheet of Martha Company at December 31, 1979.

E17-2. a. A company prepared an aging schedule for receivables at the end of the year. The result of the aging schedule was a total estimated uncollectible amount for all receivables of $9,150. At the end of the year, before the adjusting entry, the Accounts receivable account had a balance of $900,000, the Allowance for uncollectibles account had a balance of $5,000, and the Bad debts expense account had a zero balance. Make the adjusting entry needed at the end of the year in general journal form.

b. Assume these facts about a company:

Accounts receivable, January 1, 1978	$ 100,000
Accounts receivable, December 31, 1978	$ 150,000
Cash sales made during 1978	$2,000,000
Credit sales made during 1978	$3,000,000

(1) Compute the receivables turnover.
(2) Compute the average collection period of receivables, assuming there are 360 days in the year.

E17-3. Backyard Corporation's trial balance at the beginning of 1978 revealed the following balance: Accounts receivable, $50,000. This company uses the *direct write-off method* for bad debts because its credit losses have proven to be insignificant. On March 21, 1978, the company determined that one of its customers, Slowpay, Inc., had gone out of business and that the amount owed to Backyard Corporation ($100) will probably never be collected.

REQUIRED:

a. Make the journal entry needed to write off the Slowpay, Inc., account.
b. Assume that on December 1, 1978, Backyard Corporation unexpectedly received the $100 cash that had been owed to it by Slowpay, Inc. Make the necessary entry.

E17-4. The bookkeeper of Ding's Chinese Importers prepared the following aging schedule at December 31, 1978:

AGE OF ACCOUNTS RECEIVABLE

TIME ELAPSED SINCE SALE WAS MADE	TOTAL DOLLARS OF RECEIVABLES	ESTIMATED PORTION UNCOLLECTIBLE	ALLOWANCE FOR UNCOLLECTIBLES WHICH IS REQUIRED
0–15 days	$120,000	0.5%	$ 600
16–30 days	30,000	1.0%	300
31–60 days	11,000	1.3%	143
61–120 days	4,000	2.0%	80
Over 120 days	1,000	5.0%	50
Total	$166,000		$1,173

At the same date the balance of the Accounts receivable account was $166,000, and the balance of the Allowance for bad debts account was $712. Make the adjusting journal entry necessary for bad debts expense.

P17-1. *Aging of accounts receivable; writing off an account.* The end-of-year trial balance (December 31, 1978) of Allsgood Co. reflected the following account balances:

Cash	96,518.43
Accounts receivable	62,655.78
Allowance for uncollectibles	507.50
Marketable securities	25,405.70
Bad debts expense	–0–

The accounts receivable subsidiary ledger showed these amounts:

Hampton Corporation	1,154.26	12–12–78
Janice Togs	2,519.75	11–15–78
Litton Flags Co.	11,000.00	12–9–78
Lyster and Co.	5,415.88	12–1–78
Munson Junior Co.	9,733.30	3–15–78
Patrick and Sons	5,000.00	11–16–78
Reggie and Reggie, Inc.	3,300.19	11–30–78
Scott Windows	18,750.00	12–24–78
Thompson Pecans Co.	5,000.00	12–30–78
Zander Bates and Co.	782.40	1–15–76

The dates appearing at the right of each amount above are taken from the accounts receivable subsidiary accounts. They represent the date of the oldest unpaid purchase in the account (to be used in aging accounts receivable).

Company experience related to credit losses is shown in the following table:

CATEGORY	AGE OF RECEIVABLE	EXPECTED PERCENTAGE LOSS
A	1 day to 20 days	1/5 of 1%
B	21 days to 40 days	1%
C	41 days to 60 days	2%
D	over 60 days	5%

REQUIRED:

a. Prepare an aging schedule similar to the one illustrated in the unit.

b. Prepare the adjustment for bad debts in general journal form. Base your entry on the data in the aging schedule and other data given in the accounts.

c. At December 31, the manager of the firm decided to write off the Zander Bates and Co. account as uncollectible. Make the entry in general journal form.

P17-2. *Transactions and adjustments relating to receivables.* Below are shown selected account balances of Weavil Grain Co. at January 1, 1978.

Accounts receivable	56,668.31
Allowance for bad debts	1,005.50

In summary form, transactions related to sales and collections for 1978 follow.

1. Cash sales, $100,000.

2. Sales made on credit, with terms of 2/10, n/30, $300,000.
3. Sales returns and allowances made for cash, $8,000.
4. Sales returns and allowances made on credit, $12,000.
5. Accounts written off as uncollectible during year, $1,000.
6. Collections of accounts, $314,000 cash, after allowing $6,160 in cash discounts.
7. Collection of account previously written off, $300.
8. Adjusting entry based on expected credit losses of 1% on total sales made on credit (after deducting returns, but not considering sales discounts).

REQUIRED:

a. Make general journal entries to record all the summary transactions.
b. Compute the balance of the *net* receivables after all entries are made.
c. As an alternative, assume that the company uses the direct write-off method of accounting for credit losses. Which of the eight transactions above would be recorded differently? Make the journal entries for those transactions that would be accounted for differently.

P17-3. *Managing receivables.* The ledger account for accounts receivable of Beetle Coffee Company had these balances:

DATE	BALANCE	DATE	BALANCE
1-1-78	55,000	7-1-78	70,550
2-1-78	63,018	8-1-78	63,758
3-1-78	70,500	9-1-78	90,005
4-1-78	65,600	10-1-78	73,344
5-1-78	63,400	11-1-78	69,980
6-1-78	95,199	12-1-78	91,111
		12-31-78	73,347

During 1978, monthly credit sales were:

January	75,600	July	77,000
February	84,690	August	85,000
March	78,725	September	88,000
April	75,000	October	83,975
May	90,000	November	85,235
June	84,500	December	89,568

The receivables turnover for these periods had previously been computed by management:

PERIOD	RECEIVABLES TURNOVER
1977	24.10 times
1976	24.00 times
1975	24.55 times
1974	24.63 times
1973	24.35 times

REQUIRED:

a. Compute the receivables turnover for 1978.

b. Comment in considerable detail about the meaning of the 1978 turnover as compared to the past. What can and what cannot be determined by the figures?

PROBLEMS (GROUP B)

P17-4. *Transactions related to receivables.* Data from the records of two companies are shown in the following table:

	MAGENTA COMPANY	TURQUOISE COMPANY
1. Accounts receivable balance, January 1, 1978	$100,000	$ 75,007
2. Allowance for uncollectibles balance, January 1, 1978	2,400	1,415
3. Cash sales for 1978	63,600	713,890
4. Credit sales for 1978	232,000	1,687,439
5. Collections on receivables (actual cash received)	233,000	1,489,073
6. Cash discounts allowed customers	3,000	15,245
7. Accounts written off as uncollectible during 1978	3,474	1,400
8. Accounts collected during 1978 that had previously been written off	100	376
9. Basis for bad debts adjustment	1% of net credit sales (after deducting returns and discounts)	1½% of *gross* credit sales

REQUIRED:

a. Make all entries related to the data on the books of Magenta Company.

b. Compute the December 31, 1978, *net* receivables to appear on Magenta Company's balance sheet.

c. Make all entries related to the data on the books of Turquoise Company.

d. Compute the December 31, 1978, *net* receivables to appear on Turquoise Company's balance sheet.

*P17-5. *Relationship among accounts.* Retina Sight Corporation records contained the following data:

1. Amount of *net* accounts receivable appearing on the December 31, 1978, balance sheet, $90,000.
2. Balance of the Allowance for uncollectibles at January 1, 1978, $8,000.
3. Sales made on credit during 1978, $710,000.
4. Cash sales made during 1978, $100,000.
5. Sales returns for credit on account, 1978, $10,000.
6. Amount of bad debts expense adjusting entry at December 31, 1978, $15,000.
7. Total accounts written off as uncollectible during 1978, $5,000.
8. Sales discounts allowed during 1978, $4,000.

9. Collections during 1978 of accounts that previously had been written off, $1,000.
10. Balance of Accounts receivable account at January 1, 1978, $113,000.

REQUIRED: Compute the amount of cash that the company received during the year from collection of accounts receivable (in addition to the $1,000 amount mentioned in item 9 above).

Hint: Set up the accounts related to receivables in "T" form. Fill in known data and work back to the unknown amounts.

P17-6. Analyzing errors in receivables. Assume that you were recently hired in the Accounting Department of Horrible Records Company to replace a temporary bookkeeper who had been fired. You discover the following journal entries made on the firm's records during the past month, January, 1978:

1. Cash	65,000	
Accounts receivable	250,000	
Sales		315,000
January sales.		
2. Cash	230,000	
Accounts receivable		230,000
Collections from customers, after allowing cash discounts of $4,000.		
3. Sales	18,000	
Cash		18,000
Customers were given a refund for defective merchandise.		
4. Sales	12,000	
Accounts receivable		12,000
Credit allowed customers for defective merchandise.		
5. Bad debts expense	2,000	
Accounts receivable		2,000
Account (B.J. Co.) written off as uncollectible.		
6. Cash	200	
Sales		200
Collected an account (Azy Co.) that had previously been written off as uncollectible.		

You also determine that the adjusting entry for bad debts for January had not been made. Bad debts losses are estimated to be 1% of gross sales made on credit. The balance of Accounts receivable at January 1, 1978, was $100,000, and the balance of the Allowance for uncollectibles account at that time was $3,000.

REQUIRED:

a. Prepare all the entries on the books as they should have been made.
b. Compute the balance of these accounts at January 31, 1978, as they did appear on the company's records.
   (1) Accounts receivable.
   (2) Allowance for uncollectibles.

(3) Bad debts expense.

(4) Sales.

(5) Sales returns and allowances.

(6) Sales discounts.

c. Compute the balance of the six accounts in part b as they should appear at January 31, 1978.

d. Compute the amount of overstatement or understatement of net earnings for January, 1978, as a result of the bookkeeping errors.

e. Compute the amount of overstatement or understatement of total assets at January 31, 1978, as a result of the bookkeeping errors.

NOTES, DISCOUNTING, AND INTEREST

> **OBJECTIVE**

The purpose of this unit is to present the accounting procedures and concepts related to notes receivable. You will learn how to account for and report the receiving and disposing of notes, as well as calculating, recording, and reporting the interest income earned from the notes.

> **APPROACH TO ATTAINING THE OBJECTIVE**

In the text to follow, these five questions are asked and answered:

- *How are notes receivable classified on the balance sheet?*
- *How are notes receivable recorded when they are received?*
- *How is interest calculated?*
- *What entries are made when interest is accrued and received?*
- *What is meant by discounting notes?*

CLASSIFYING NOTES

■ *How are notes receivable classified on the balance sheet?*

Notes receivable can be either long-term investments or current assets, depending upon the expected date of collection (maturity date). A note that will be collected within 1 year (or one operating cycle) of the balance sheet date would be classified as current. Such a note would appear in the current asset section of the balance sheet. In Unit 17 you learned that accounts receivable are reported at the amount expected to be collected. This is the Accounts receivable amount less the balance of the Allowance for uncollectibles account. In the case of notes receivable, if there are expected losses, a similar allowance for uncollectibles would also be set up.

A note that will be collected at a date further in the future than 1 year (or one operating cycle if the operating cycle of the business is longer than a year) from the balance sheet date is classified as long-term and would be reported on the balance sheet as a *long-term investment* or perhaps as an *other asset* (noncurrent).

RECEIVING NOTES

■ *How are notes receivable recorded when they are received?*

A company acquires notes receivable in a number of ways, including from customers and through lending money to affiliated companies and others. The following accounting entries for three situations illustrate the recording of notes.

1978					
June	17	Trade notes receivable		8,150	
		Sales			8,150
		Made sales to A. R. Jones, who signed a 90-day, 8% note in payment; face value, $8,150.			
Aug.	9	Notes receivable		100,000	
		Cash			100,000
		Lent cash to Wilson, Inc., receiving a 3-year, 7% note; face value, $100,000.			
Dec.	18	Trade notes receivable		3,000	
		Accounts receivable			3,000
		A customer, Tom Simpson, signed a 120-day, non-interest-bearing note in payment of his account; face value, $3,080.			

The June 17 entry involves the receipt of a note for sales made by the company. Such notes received in the ordinary course of business are often classified as **trade notes** to indicate that they are short-term and were received in a manner much the same as accounts receivable. They are shown as current assets on the balance sheet. At the maturity date of the note in 90 days, the note *maker* (Jones) would be expected to pay the face value of $8,150 *plus* interest at the rate of 8% per year on the 90 days. Details on the calculation of interest will follow.

The August 9 entry involves a long-term note that would be classified as a long-term investment on the balance sheet. Wilson, Inc., at the maturity date in 3 years, would be expected to pay the face value of $100,000 plus interest at the annual rate of 7% for 3 years.

The December 18 entry involves a note received from a customer in payment of his account. Notice that the note is called a "non-interest-bearing note." Of course, since money has a *time value,* there is really no such thing as a non-interest-bearing note. A so-called non-interest-bearing note simply does not identify the interest element separately from the principal or the original amount of the loan. In the December 18 example, the interest for the period of the note can be computed as follows:

Total amounts to be paid by the maker of the note (total to be received by the payee of the note)	$3,080
Less total value exchanged when note was signed	3,000
Total interest	$ 80

CALCULATING AND REPORTING INTEREST

Interest may be calculated through several basic techniques. These include a basic formula and the so-called "short-cut" method.

■ *How is interest calculated?*

Basic formula The fundamental formula for computing interest is as follows:

$$\begin{array}{c}\text{INTEREST}\\ \text{EXPENSE}\\ \text{for the period}\end{array} = \begin{array}{c}\text{Principal}\\ \text{(amount of}\\ \text{value exchanged}\\ \text{when note is}\\ \text{executed)}\end{array} \times \begin{array}{c}\text{Annual}\\ \text{interest}\\ \text{rate}\end{array} \times \begin{array}{c}\text{Fraction}\\ \text{of year}\\ \text{that note}\\ \text{is outstanding}\\ \text{this period}\end{array}$$

Simply stated, the formula is $I = PRT$.

To illustrate the calculating and reporting of interest, refer to the note of June 17 in the preceding example. *Assume that the company closes its books on December 31 each year and prepares financial statements annually.* These facts can be determined about the June 17 note:

1. The maturity date (when the note is to be paid) of the note is *September 15, 1978,* determined as follows:

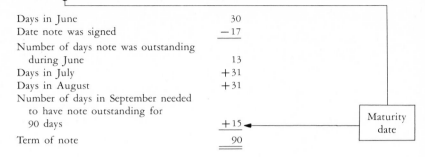

Days in June	30
Date note was signed	−17
Number of days note was outstanding during June	13
Days in July	+31
Days in August	+31
Number of days in September needed to have note outstanding for 90 days	+15
Term of note	90

2. The amount of interest on the note is $163, determined as follows:

$$I = PRT$$

$$= \$8,150 \times 0.08 \times \frac{90}{360}$$

$$= \$163$$

Notice that 360 days was used in the formula to represent a year. This is a common practice in industry, which simplifies the interest calculations. *For purposes of this course, use 360 days in your interest calculations unless otherwise stated.*

3. The journal entry at the maturity date would be:

1978				
Sept.	15	Cash	8,313	
		Interest income		163
		Trade notes receivable		8,150
		Collected the June 17 note from		
		A. R. Jones plus interest for 90 days.		

Now refer to the note that was received on August 9 in the preceding example. This long-term note will not be collected for 3 years, so there will not be a transaction involving cash until the maturity date, August 9, 1981.

At the end of 1978, before financial statements are prepared for the company, an adjusting entry must be made to reflect the interest income earned during 1978 on the note of August 9.

- *What entries are made when interest is accrued and received?*

ADJUSTING ENTRIES				
1978				
Dec.	31	Notes receivable (or Interest receivable)	2,800	
		Interest income		2,800

There are several points to observe about this adjusting entry:

1. The interest earned for the year 1978 must be recorded to be reported on the income statement.
2. This interest will be collected at the maturity date in 1981; therefore, the interest can be recorded as a noncurrent asset in the Notes receivable account. Alternatively, some firms record all accrued interest in the current asset account Interest receivable and separate the long-term portion when preparing the balance sheet.
3. Interest calculations vary considerably among companies and industries. Here are three variations of the interest calculation on the August 9 note:

Using 365 days for the year:

Interest for 1978 $= \$100,000$

$$\times\ 0.07 \times \frac{144 \text{ days*}}{365 \text{ days}}$$

$$= \$2,761.64$$

* Days note outstanding in August	
(31 − 9)	22
Days note outstanding in September	30
Days note outstanding in October	31
Days note outstanding in November	30
Days note outstanding in December	31
	144

Using 360 days for the year:

Interest for 1978 $= \$100,000 \times 0.07 \times \dfrac{144 \text{ days}}{360 \text{ days}} = \$2,800$

Rounding off to the nearest month:

Interest for 1978 $= \$100,000$

$$\times\ 0.07 \times \frac{5 \text{ months†}}{12 \text{ months}}$$

$$= \$2,916.67$$

†Note considered outstanding months of August, September, October, November, and December of 1978.

For another illustration, refer to the note of December 18 in the preceding example. This note, too, will require an adjusting entry on December 31, 1978.

ADJUSTING ENTRIES				
1978 Dec.	31	Interest receivable (or Trade notes receivable)	8.67	
		Interest income		8.67

Observe these points about the adjustment:

1. The interest earned but not yet received should be reported in a current asset account (either Interest receivable or directly in the Trade notes receivable account).

2. The total interest to be earned on the note is $80, as described on page 309. The 1978 portion of this interest can be computed as follows:

$$\$80 \times \frac{13 \text{ days*}}{120 \text{ days}} = \$8.67$$

> *31 days in December less 18 days = 13.

Short-cut method The short-cut method of computing interest is sometimes referred to as the 6% 60-day method. The method simply involves moving the decimal two places to the left in calculating interest on a 60-day, 6% note. For example, the interest on a 60-day, 6% note for $13,495.13 amounts to $134.95:

(1) Amount of note $13,495.13

(2) Amount of interest $134.95†

> †$13,495.13 × 6/100 × 60/360 = $134.95.

As a further example, compute the interest on a 6%, 30-day note for $5,000:

(1) Amount of note $5,000.
(2) Amount of interest if the note were 60 days, 6% $50
(3) Amount of interest for 30 days ($\frac{1}{2}$ the time) $25

Also, the interest on a 8%, 90-day note for $10,000 would be $200:

(1) Amount of note $10,000.
(2) Amount of interest if the note were 60-day, 6% $100
(3) Amount of interest for $\frac{1}{2}$ more time (90 days)
     ($100 + $50) $150
(4) Amount of interest for $\frac{1}{3}$ higher rate (8%)
     [$150 + (1/3 × $150) = $200] $200

Interest tables Most banks and companies dealing regularly with notes have books of interest tables for quick reference. These tables give detailed amounts of interest already calculated at varying interest rates.

DISCOUNTING NOTES RECEIVABLE

- *What is meant by discounting notes?*

When a business organization has notes receivable, it usually has the option of (1) holding the notes until their maturity dates, or (2) selling the notes at some point before maturity. If a company holds the notes receivable until maturity, the amount collected would include the face amount of the note plus any interest due. This total amount due at the maturity date (face of the note and any interest due) is known as the **maturity value** of the note.

Trade notes are usually **negotiable.** This means that the notes can be sold before the maturity date. Selling a note before its maturity date is known as **discounting** the note. To illustrate the discounting process, an example is now given:

The company received a 90-day, 8% note receivable on March 1, 1978, with a face amount of $10,000. The note is sold to First National Bank on March 30, 1978 (discounted). The **discount rate** charged by the bank is 10% (the interest rate charged by the bank).

The following series of computations relate to this note.

Maturity date The **maturity date** of the note is *May 30, 1978,* determined as follows:

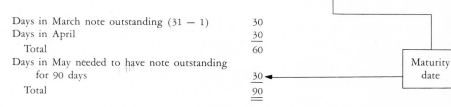

Days in March note outstanding (31 − 1)	30
Days in April	30
Total	60
Days in May needed to have note outstanding for 90 days	30
Total	90

Maturity value of note The maturity value is the total amount to be paid by the maker of the note at the maturity date.

Face amount to be paid on May 30	$10,000
Interest for 90 days:	
$10,000 × 0.08 × 90/360	200
Maturity value	$10,200

Proceeds from discounting the note The company that sells the note (discounts the note) will receive cash from the bank in an amount that is *less* than the maturity value of the note. This is the case because the bank charges a fee (interest) for the use of its money. The proceeds can be calculated as follows:

Maturity value of note (see above)	$10,200.00
Less bank charge:	
Maturity value × Discount rate × Period bank holds note	
$10,200 × 0.10 × $\dfrac{61 \text{ days}}{360 \text{ days}}$ =	172.83
Proceeds of the note	$10,027.17

Observe these facts about the computation:

1. The maturity value is customarily used when computing the interest charged by the bank (discount). Using this amount, of course, would yield a larger bank charge than if the bank used the amount lent on the loan (proceeds).
2. The bank discount rate is 10%. See facts of case.
3. The period the bank holds the note is 61 days, determined as follows:

Number of days in March that bank held note	1
Days in April	30
Days in May until maturity	30
Period note held by bank	61

4. The maker of the note is responsible for paying the bank $10,200 on May 30. If the maker **defaults,** the company that discounted the note at the bank must pay the bank the amount due. This obligation is known as a *contingent liability.*

Journal entries will now show the discounting process:

1978					
March	1	Notes receivable		10,000.00	
		Accounts receivable			10,000.00
		Received a 90-day, 8% note from			
		Horace Smith in payment of his account.			
	30	Cash		10,027.17	
		Notes receivable discounted			10,000.00
		Interest income			27.17
		Discounted the Smith note at the bank.			
May	30	Notes receivable discounted		10,000.00	
		Notes receivable			10,000.00
		Notified by the bank that Smith paid			
		his note.			

The March 1 entry shows the receipt of the note from a customer. The March 30 entry records the proceeds from discounting the note with First National Bank. The excess of the proceeds over the amount of the note on the books of the company represents interest income for the company. In the event the bank charge (discount) causes the proceeds to be less than the amount of the note on the company's books, then the difference can be *debited* to interest income (instead of credited as in the example). The effect of this is simply to reduce the interest earned for the many discounting transactions that the company might have.

Notice in the March 30 entry that a new account is introduced. The Notes receivable discounted account is a contra account that is deducted from the Notes receivable account when preparing the balance sheet of the company. Although a zero balance of *net* notes receivable is shown on the balance sheet, the contingent liability is revealed by this treatment. For example, after the note is discounted (March 30) but before the maker pays the bank at maturity (May 30), the firm's balance sheet would reveal the following:

Current assets:
. . .

Notes receivable	$10,000	
Less notes receivable discounted	10,000	
Net notes receivable		$-0-

Default by maker As a further illustration, assume that Smith, the maker of the note in the preceding example, did not pay his note when it was due on May 30. In that situation, the bank would return the note to us, and we would be required to remit the maturity value to the bank. Then we would try to collect the note from Smith. The entry upon default by Smith would be:

1978					
May	30	Accounts receivable		10,200	
		Cash			10,200
		Paid the maturity value of Smith's note to First National Bank; Smith defaulted on the note due today.			

DISCOUNTING NOTES PAYABLE The preceding discussion has dealt with notes *receivable*. Now, turn your attention to the contrasting situation when the company is borrowing money (has a liability). Assume that a firm borrows money from Republic National Bank by signing a 90-day non-interest-bearing note for $10,000, with a discount rate (interest rate) of 9%.

1978					
March	15	Cash		9,775	
		Interest expense		225	
		Notes payable			10,000
		Discounted a 90-day, 9% note payable.			

The entry above shows that the company received proceeds from the note of $9,775, after deducting interest of $225 ($10,000 × 9% × 90/360 = $225). The interest can be recorded in advance to simplify the bookkeeping. When the note is paid, this entry can be made:

| 1978 June | 13 | Notes payable | 10,000 | |
| | | Cash | | 10,000 |

Of course, if the note is still outstanding at the balance sheet date, an adjusting entry will be needed. If the amount is significant, the adjustment will reduce the Interest expense account by the amount of interest not yet incurred, and the liability (Notes payable) will be reduced by the same amount.

▶ NEW TERMS

default Failure to make payment on a note. [p. 314]

discount rate The interest rate charged by the party (bank, for example) that buys a note before its maturity; another term for interest rate. [p. 313]

discounting a note receivable Selling a note receivable before its maturity date. [p. 313]

maturity date The date on which the maker of a note is obligated to make payment. [p. 313]

maturity value The total amount due on a note at its maturity; includes the face of the note and any interest due. [p. 313]

negotiable note A note that can be sold before its maturity date. [p. 313]

notes receivable discounted A contra account that represents a deduction from the Notes receivable account; used to indicate that there is a contingent liability associated with notes that the company has discounted. Such liability exists until the maker of the discounted note makes payment at maturity. [p. 314]

trade notes Notes receivable that were received in the ordinary course of business; classified as current assets. [p. 308]

▶ ASSIGNMENT MATERIAL

QUESTIONS

Q18-1. How are notes receivable classified on the balance sheet?

Q18-2. What accounting entry is made when a trade note is received in payment of an account?

Q18-3. What adjusting entry is usually made for notes receivable on hand at the end of an accounting period?

Q18-4. What entry is usually made when notes are discounted?

Q18-5. What entry is usually made when the maker pays off a note that the company had previously discounted?

Q18-6. What entries are made when the maker of a note defaults?

Q18-7. What contingent liability would be associated with discounted notes?

E18-1. A 10%, 90-day note was dated November 21, 1978, with a face amount of $10,000.
   a. Compute the maturity date.
   b. Compute the maturity value.
   c. Compute the interest income to be reported on the lending company's income statement for 1978 from this note.
   d. Assume that the company (payee of the note) discounted the note on January 10, 1979, at a discount rate of 11%. Compute the proceeds.

E18-2. Knighton Corporation lent $30,000 cash to another company. The company signed a note, bearing 8% interest per year. All interest and principal are to be repaid in 5 years from the date of loan.
   a. How would this note be shown on Knighton's balance sheet 2 years after the loan was made?
   b. How would the note be reported on the balance sheet of the borrowing company 2 years after the loan was made?

E18-3. Hortense Corporation received a 7%, 120-day, $10,000 note receivable from a customer in payment of its account on November 14, 1978.
   a. What journal entry would be made on November 14, 1978?
   b. What adjusting journal entry would be made on December 31, 1978, assuming the company adjusts and closes its books on December 31 each year?
   c. What is the maturity date of the note?
   d. What journal entry would be made at the maturity date?

E18-4. Record the following transactions related to notes and interest. The company prepares financial statements and closes its books annually on December 31.

1978
Nov. 1   A customer signed a 90-day, non-interest-bearing note in payment of his account; face amount of note, $4,070. The customer's account balance was $4,000.
Dec. 31   Made the adjusting entry for interest on the note above.
1979
Jan. 10   Discounted the note above at First National Bank.
           The discount rate was 8%.
           The bank notified us that the note was paid at maturity.

PROBLEMS (GROUP A)

P18-1. *Receiving, discounting, and default on note receivable.* The following transactions relate to notes and interest of a company that prepares financial statements and closes its books annually on December 31:
Sold goods to Jackson Breen for $82,500. Breen signed a 120-day, 6% note in that amount on December 12, 1978, in payment. We discounted the note at the bank on March 1, 1979. The discount rate charged was 8%. Breen defaulted on the note at maturity, and we remitted the maturity value of the note to the bank. Twenty days after the maturity date of the note, Breen paid us the total amount due plus $25 as a special fee.

REQUIRED:
   a. Compute the maturity date of the note.
   b. Compute the maturity value of the note.
   c. Prepare the adjusting entry needed at December 31, 1978.
   d. Prepare the entry to record the discounting of the note on March 1, 1979.

e. Prepare the entries needed at the maturity date of the note.

f. Prepare the entry for the collection of cash from Breen.

P18-2. *Calculating maturity dates, maturity values, and proceeds from discounting.* Below are listed five separate notes.

1. 60-day, 7% note, with face amount of $10,000, dated June 16, 1978.

2. 3-year, 9% note, with face amount of $100,000, dated May 1, 1978.

3. 30-day, 10% note, with face amount of $5,000, dated December 13, 1978.

4. 90-day, 8% note, with face amount of $10,000, dated March 1, 1978.

5. 30-day, non-interest-bearing note, with face amount of $6,000, dated March 1, 1978.

REQUIRED:

a. Determine the maturity date of each of the notes.

b. Determine the maturity value of each of the notes.

c. Assume the company discounted each of the above notes receivable, after holding each note for 20 days. Compute the proceeds from each note, assuming that the bank charged a discount rate of 10%.

*P18-3. *Journal entries (transactions, adjustments, and reversals) for notes and interest.* The following are selected transactions of Work Teams, Inc., dealing with notes and interest.

1978

Dec. 2 Lent a customer, Skillets Company, $40,000 cash. We received a 1-year, 10% note with a face amount of $40,000.

12 Made sales to Wilbert Hanson for $18,000. Hanson gave us a 7%, 30-day note for the amount.

15 Received a 9%, 60-day note from Hampton Belt Works for $10,000 in payment of their account balance.

20 Made sales to Betty Green for $20,000. She signed a 10%, 60-day note in payment (face amount of $20,000).

31 Prepared adjusting entries for interest earned on the notes.

1979

Jan. 2 Prepared reversing entries as needed.

5 Received a 60-day, non-interest-bearing note with a face amount of $15,225 in payment of Harry Walsch's account. The account balance was $15,000.

12 Collected the amount due on the Hanson note (December 12, 1978).

20 Discounted the Hampton Belt Works note (December 15, 1978) at Capitol National Bank. The discount rate was 10%.

30 Discounted the Betty Green note (December 20, 1978) at Capitol National Bank. The discount rate was 11%.

REQUIRED: Prepare general journal entries. Show all computations in the explanation section of your journal entries.

PROBLEMS (GROUP B)

P18-4. *Receiving, discounting, default, and collection of note.* These data relate to notes and interest of Booray Corporation for 1978. The company closes its books annually on December 31.

1. Received a note on March 12, 1978 from Patrick Pitcher for $50,000 in payment of his account. The note was for 8% and matures in 100 days. On May 1, 1978,

we discounted this note at Blue State Bank at a discount rate of 11%. At maturity, Pitcher defaulted and we paid the bank the amount due.

2. Received a note on June 15, 1978, from Willie Walker with a face amount of $26,037.60 for sales made to him. The note was a non-interest-bearing note with a 60-day maturity. The amount of the sales made to him was $25,695. Discounted this note at First State Bank at a discount rate of 10% on July 10, 1978. Walker paid the note at maturity.

REQUIRED: Make all general journal entries associated with the notes. Show all computations in the explanation section of your journal entries.

P18-5. *Calculating maturity dates, maturity values, and proceeds from discounting.* Below are listed eight notes.

	TERM	DATE SIGNED	FACE AMOUNT	INTEREST RATE	DATE DISCOUNTED	DISCOUNT RATE
1.	30 days	1–1–78	$10,000	10%	1–20–78	11%
2.	60 days	2–20–78	$100,000	12%	3–20–78	12%
3.	120 days	3–1–78	$40,000	0%	5–1–78	10%
4.	1 year	5–12–78	$62,007	6%	12–1–78	7%
5.	3 years	6–20–78	$95,500	11%	6–20–80	10%
6.	60 days	7–1–78	$63,500	10%	8–3–78	12%
7.	90 days	8–14–78	$70,000	7%	10–10–78	11%
8.	120 days	12–21–78	$90,000	8%	2–4–79	12%

REQUIRED:

For each of the notes, determine
a. Maturity date.
b. Maturity value.
c. Proceeds from discounting.

*P18-6. *Journal entries for notes and interest.* The following table presents data about notes received.

DATE NOTE RECEIVED	TERM OF NOTE	REASON NOTE RECEIVED	FACE	INTEREST RATE	DISCOUNTED (YES OR NO)	DATE DISCOUNTED	DISCOUNT RATE	PAID AT MATURITY (YES OR NO)
3–1–78	30 days	On account	$10,000	6%	No	—	—	Yes
4–12–78	60 days	Sales	20,000	8%	Yes	5–10–78	10%	Yes
5–11–78	120 days	On account	15,000	9%	Yes	7–1–78	10%	No
5–20–78	30 days	On account	20,000	10%	No	—	—	No
6–1–78	1 year	Sales	12,000	11%	Yes	12–7–78	12%	No

REQUIRED: Treat each of the above notes as a separate case. Make general journal entries as appropriate for:

a. Receipt of note.
b. Discounting of note when applicable.
c. End of year adjustments when applicable.
d. Collection of note when applicable.
e. Payment of note by us upon default if applicable.

P18-7. *Cumulative review problem (combining bank reconciliation with note discounting procedures).* The following data were gathered in connection with the monthly bank statement reconciliation at November 30, 1978:

1. Deposits in transit as of November 30, 1978, $51,150.14.
2. Checks outstanding at November 1, 1978, $20,500.76.
3. Checks written during the month, according to the company's cash payments journal, $123,517.41.
4. Balance of cash account according to bank statement at November 1, 1978, $61,907.57.
5. Cash balance according to Cash ledger account at November 1, 1978, $51,562.11.
6. During November, our accountant mailed the following of our notes receivable to the bank. The bank discounted these notes at a discount rate of 12% and credited the proceeds directly to our bank account:
    a. 90-day note dated 10–15–78 for $20,000, bearing 10% interest.
    b. 90-day, 8% note dated 10–1–78 for $20,000.
    We have not yet recorded these collections on our books. The first note was discounted on November 10 and the second one on November 30.
7. Collection made by bank for us, $15,000. This collection was from a customer (Accounts receivable), and we first learned of the collection on our November bank statement.
8. Deposits in transit as of November 1, 1978, $6,517.22.
9. Cash received according to the cash receipts journal for November, $115,117.23.
10. Payment made by the bank to one of our suppliers for merchandise (according to our instructions), $2,055.12. This payment has not been recorded on our books.
11. Checks outstanding at November 30, 1978, $15,180.10.
12. Balance of cash account according to bank statement at November 30, 1978, $60,345.44.
13. Service charge appearing on the bank statement for November, $50. This amount has not yet been recorded on our books.

REQUIRED:

a. Prepare a bank statement reconciliation form at November 30, 1978.
b. Prepare the necessary entries in general journal form.

P18-8. *Cumulative review problem.* Below are selected summary business transactions of the Cucaracha Crepe Company for 1978.

1. Lent a customer, Ballentine Co., $21,200 cash. We received a 1-year, 10% note with a face amount of $21,200.
2. Made cash sales amounting to $60,000 and credit sales of $335,000.
3. Received a 7%, 30-day note from a customer in payment of his account, $21,000.
4. Collected cash on accounts receivable of $200,000, after allowing $6,000 of cash discounts.
5. Received a 10%, 60-day note from a customer in payment of her account, $20,000.
6. Wrote off accounts receivable as uncollectible, $3,000.

7. Discounted the note in item 1 above (Ballentine Co.) 3 months before its maturity at Second State Bank. The discount rate was 12%.
8. Collected an account receivable that previously had been written off, $156.
9. Borrowed $50,000 cash from Boston National Bank, signing a 90-day, non-interest-bearing note, with a face amount of $51,406.65.
10. Made the adjusting entry for bad debts. Uncollectibles are estimated at the rate of 1% of gross sales made on credit.
11. Collected the 7% note from item 3 above.
12. Made the adjusting entries for accrued interest. Notes had been outstanding during 1978 as follows:
    a. Ballentine Co. note had been discounted during 1978 (items 1 and 7 above)
    b. Note from item 3 above had been collected during 1978.
    c. Note from item 5 above had been outstanding for 50 days as of December 31, 1978.
    d. Note from item 9 above had been outstanding for 56 days as of December 31, 1978.

REQUIRED:

a. Prepare general journal entries.
b. Compute the balance of the following accounts at December 31, 1978, before closing entries are made:
   (1) Accounts receivable.
   (2) Allowance for uncollectibles.
   (3) Notes receivable.
   (4) Notes receivable discounted.
   (5) Interest expense.
   (6) Interest receivable.
   (7) Interest income.
   (8) Bad debts expense.

chapter 8

inventories

ERRORS; PERPETUAL METHOD; COST AND VALUATION

> **OBJECTIVE**

In this unit you will continue your study of current assets. Specifically, you will study how inventories are managed, the importance of inventories in computing net income, the perpetual method, and cost and valuation of inventories.

> **APPROACH TO ATTAINING THE OBJECTIVE**

As you study about inventories, direct your attention to these five questions, which the text following answers:

- *What is the importance of inventory reporting and the effect of errors on net income?*
- *How are basic inventory records kept?*
- *How is the perpetual method applied?*
- *How is the cost of inventories determined?*
- *How should inventories be valued?*

**EFFECT OF ERRORS
ON EARNINGS
AND FINANCIAL
CONDITION**

• *What is the
importance of
inventory reporting
and the effect of
errors on net income?*

Accurate inventory reporting is extremely important to decision makers inside the firm (management) and to decision makers outside the firm. Management is primarily concerned with such problems as deciding when to place orders for inventories (timing) and how much inventory to buy each time an order is placed (economic order quantities). This unit concentrates on the effect of inventory reporting on the financial statements, which are used by investors and creditors outside the firm.

The ideas you have already learned about the classification and valuation of merchandise inventories are directly relevant to understanding how information reported on the financial statements is used for decision making. Basically, investors, creditors, and others must have information about the earnings per share of common stock and about the resources and equities of the firm in order to make their decisions. Accurate and relevant inventory reporting is vital if useful information is to be provided on the statements.

For example, the illustration on the next page shows a set of financial statements in simplified form. For the left-hand column of figures (emphasized with color), the ending inventory has been counted and valued in terms of its cost at $10,000. For comparison purposes, the right-hand column has been calculated with the *inventory erroneously reported* at $8,000. Notice the distortion of financial information as reported in the right-hand column.

From this analysis, several generalizations can be made. Merchandise inventories which are not measured and reported on a relevant and accurate basis tend to mislead decision makers about the earnings, assets, and equities of a business. Specifically, an ending inventory which is *understated* has the effect of:

1. Overstating cost of goods sold.
2. Understating net earnings and earnings per share.
3. Understating retained earnings.
4. Understating total assets.
5. Understating total capital.

An ending inventory which is *overstated* has the reverse effect of:

1. Understating cost of goods sold.
2. Overstating net earnings and earnings per share.
3. Overstating retained earnings.
4. Overstating total assets.
5. Overstating total capital.

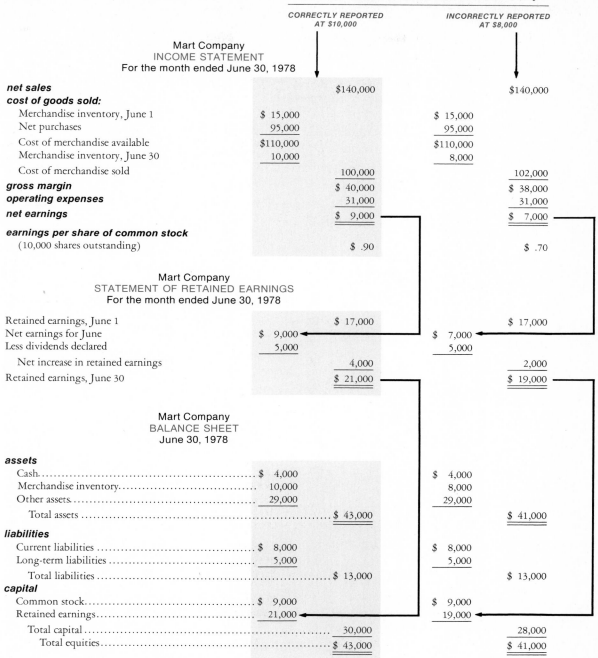

financial statements of a firm, with the inventory

	CORRECTLY REPORTED AT $10,000		INCORRECTLY REPORTED AT $8,000	

Mart Company
INCOME STATEMENT
For the month ended June 30, 1978

net sales		$140,000		$140,000
cost of goods sold:				
Merchandise inventory, June 1	$ 15,000		$ 15,000	
Net purchases	95,000		95,000	
Cost of merchandise available	$110,000		$110,000	
Merchandise inventory, June 30	10,000		8,000	
Cost of merchandise sold		100,000		102,000
gross margin		$ 40,000		$ 38,000
operating expenses		31,000		31,000
net earnings		$ 9,000		$ 7,000
earnings per share of common stock				
(10,000 shares outstanding)		$ .90		$ .70

Mart Company
STATEMENT OF RETAINED EARNINGS
For the month ended June 30, 1978

Retained earnings, June 1		$ 17,000		$ 17,000
Net earnings for June	$ 9,000		$ 7,000	
Less dividends declared	5,000		5,000	
Net increase in retained earnings		4,000		2,000
Retained earnings, June 30		$ 21,000		$ 19,000

Mart Company
BALANCE SHEET
June 30, 1978

assets				
Cash.	$ 4,000		$ 4,000	
Merchandise inventory.	10,000		8,000	
Other assets.	29,000		29,000	
Total assets		$ 43,000		$ 41,000
liabilities				
Current liabilities	$ 8,000		$ 8,000	
Long-term liabilities	5,000		5,000	
Total liabilities		$ 13,000		$ 13,000
capital				
Common stock.	$ 9,000		$ 9,000	
Retained earnings.	21,000		19,000	
Total capital		30,000		28,000
Total equities		$ 43,000		$ 41,000

INVENTORY RECORD-KEEPING SYSTEMS

To aid in the accurate and relevant reporting of the important resource of inventories, several record-keeping systems for inventories have been developed. Here we will examine two basic ones, the periodic and the perpetual methods.

■ *How are basic inventory records kept?*

Periodic method Earlier you were introduced to the periodic method. Review these elements of the method:

1. The Merchandise inventory account is used to reflect the cost of the merchandise on hand at the *beginning* of the accounting period.

2. Additional purchases of merchandise are recorded (debited) in a separate account, called Purchases of merchandise.

3. Other elements of inventory cost determination are recorded in separate accounts:

    Transportation on purchases—with a debit balance which represents additional cost of the merchandise.

    Purchases returns and allowances—with a credit balance which represents a reduction in the cost of the merchandise.

    Purchases discounts—with a credit balance which represents a reduction in the cost of merchandise.

4. At the end of the accounting period, a physical count of merchandise on hand at the end of the period is made. The cost of the ending inventory is then determined.

5. Cost of goods sold is calculated as follows:

	Beginning inventory cost
plus	Net purchases
equals	Cost of goods available for sale
minus	Cost of ending inventory
equals	Cost of goods sold

    Note that Net purchases is calculated by adding Transportation on purchases to Purchases of merchandise and deducting both Purchases returns and allowances and Purchases discounts.

6. An adjusting journal entry is made to restate the merchandise inventory at its ending amount.

■ *How is the perpetual method applied?*

Perpetual method To assure greater control over their merchandise, many firms employ the **perpetual method** of accounting for inventory and cost of goods sold. This system provides for a current and continuous running balance of merchandise inventory and cost of goods sold. At any time during the accounting period, the balance of these accounts can be determined *without* taking a physical count and preparing an adjusting journal entry.

An example will illustrate. Below is shown a general journal with selected transactions. To simplify, all the transactions deal with buying and selling one inventory item, number 1811. On the next page is shown a detailed perpetual inventory record for this item of inventory.

GENERAL JOURNAL

1978					
Jan.	10		Merchandise inventory	9,100.00	
			Accounts payable		9,100.00
			Purchased 1,000 units of item 1811 for $9.10 per unit.		
	15		Cash	13,500.00	
			Sales		13,500.00
			Sold 900 units of item 1811 for $15 per unit.		
			Cost of goods sold	8,130.00	
			Merchandise inventory		8,130.00
			Sold 900 units of item 1811:		
			$600 \times 9.00 = 5,400.00$		
			$300 \times 9.10 = \underline{2,730.00}$		
			$\underline{\underline{8,130.00}}$		
	16		Merchandise inventory	45,750.00	
			Accounts payable		45,750.00
			Purchased 5,000 units of item 1811 for $9.15 per unit.		
	29		Cash	12,000.00	
			Sales		12,000.00
			Sold 800 units of item 1811 for $15 each.		
			Cost of goods sold	7,285.00	
			Merchandise inventory		7,285.00
			Sold 800 units of item 1811:		
			$700 \times 9.10 = 6,370.00$		
			$100 \times 9.15 = \underline{915.00}$		
			$\underline{\underline{7,285.00}}$		

Now, observe these points about the journal entries and about the perpetual inventory record.

1. On January 1, there were 600 units of inventory on hand. The unit cost of these items had been $9. See the beginning balance in the inventory account illustrated, $5,400.

INVENTORY STOCK NO.	1811							BASIS	FIFO	
DESCRIPTION	Hinge							LOCATION	Bin 17	

	received			issued			balance		
DATE	UNITS	UNIT COST	TOTAL COST	UNITS	UNIT COST	TOTAL COST	UNITS	UNIT COST	TOTAL COST
1–1–78 Balance							600	9.00	5,400.00
1–10–78	1,000	9.10	9,100.00				600 1,000	9.00 9.10	5,400.00 9,100.00
1–15–78				600 300	9.00 9.10	5,400.00 2,730.00	700	9.10	6,370.00
1–16–78	5,000	9.15	45,750.00				700 5,000	9.10 9.15	6,370.00 45,750.00
1–29–78				700 100	9.10 9.15	6,370.00 915.00	4,900	9.15	44,835.00

2. On January 10, an additional 1,000 were purchased for $9.10 each. This information is recorded in the journal. In the inventory ledger, the 1,000-item purchase is recorded in the "Received" columns. Notice in the "Balance" columns that there are now 1,600 units on hand. The 600 units is jotted down separately from the 1,000 units to keep account of the difference in unit cost. The balance of the inventory account at January 10 now is $14,500, composed of the $5,400 and the $9,100.

3. On January 15, there were 900 units sold for $15 each. See the entry in the journal. The cost of these units is calculated to be $8,130 (see the journal). The method used in this example is the **FIFO method** (first-in, first-out). Since 900 units are sold on January 15, the ledger must be consulted to see the cost of those units. There are 600 units on hand with a cost of $9 each, so this amounts to $5,400. The other

300 units (to make the 900 sold) must have come from the most recent purchase (January 10) at a cost of $9.10 each. First-in, first-out simply means that the older inventory items are sold first, and the more recent purchases remain unsold in inventory.

4. The second entry in the journal for January 15 records the expense (Cost of goods sold) amounting to $8,130. Accordingly, the Merchandise inventory account is reduced, so that the balance of $6,370 will appear in that account.

5. On January 16, the company bought another 5,000 units for $9.15 each. This entry appears in the journal. Also, in the ledger account, the 5,000 units are entered in the "Received" columns and the "Balance" columns. Notice that the new balance amounts to $6,370 from the 700 units on hand *plus* the $45,750 from the recent purchase of 5,000 new units.

6. The last entry in the journal (January 29) records sales of 800 units for $15 cash each. The cost (under the FIFO method) is $7,285, consisting of 700 units at $9.10 plus 100 units from the most recent purchase at $9.15.

COST-FLOW ASSUMPTIONS

Determining the cost of the ending inventory and the cost of goods sold is a major part of financial reporting. This is true whether the periodic or perpetual method of inventory reporting is used. When the prices paid for similar inventory items vary during an accounting period, accounting for inventories can become a complex matter. In the situation where prices paid vary, firms can choose from among several methods for assigning costs to their ending inventories and to the goods they sell. In this section we will examine four different ways in which costs can be assumed to flow through a firm. For comparison purposes, our discussion of each method will make use of the basic data introduced below.

■ *How is the cost of inventories determined?*

Assume that a firm handles only one kind of product, an automobile part. The company in this example uses the *periodic* method of accounting for inventory. At January 1, 1978, the merchandise inventory on hand was as follows:

QUANTITY ON HAND	DATE PURCHASED	UNIT COST	TOTAL COST
100	11-20-77	$4.00	$ 400
1,200	12-12-77	4.10	4,920
1,300			$5,320

During the year, the firm made three purchases of parts:

QUANTITY	DATE PURCHASED	UNIT COST	TOTAL COST
3,000	3-23-78	$4.30	$12,900
2,000	7-17-78	4.20	8,400
1,000	10-11-78	4.50	4,500
6,000			$25,800

Also during the year 5,000 parts were sold at a price of $7.10 each; there were thus 2,300 parts left in the merchandise inventory at December 31, 1978. At the end of 1978, the management must take a physical inventory to determine if there are actually 2,300 units on hand.

The cost of the firm's ending inventory and the Cost of goods sold must be determined in order to prepare financial statements. A fundamental question arises: *What is the unit cost of the ending inventory and of the units sold?* Is it the most recent price—$4.50? Is it the lower price—$4.00? In order to answer these questions, some **cost-flow assumption** must be made. That is, some assumption about the order of assigning costs to the inventory and cost of goods sold must be made. Earlier in this unit you learned that this is an important point because the higher the amount at which the ending inventory is reported, the higher the earnings and earnings per share will be reported. Therefore care must be taken to choose a cost-flow assumption that reasonably measures the earnings made from buying and selling merchandise. These four cost-flow assumptions are widely used: specific identification; weighted average; first-in, first-out; and last-in, first-out. Let's examine each of them in turn.

Specific identification Assume that management, in its control and record-keeping system, identified and marked with tags each inventory item. At December 31, 1978, management then can determine how much was paid for each of the 2,300 units on hand in our example. Assume that the records revealed that the composition of the ending inventory was as follows:

ENDING MERCHANDISE INVENTORY
(Units remaining in ending inventory are specifically identified)

NUMBER OF UNITS	DATE PURCHASED	UNIT COST	TOTAL COST
400	12-12-77	$4.10	$1,640
1,000	3-23-78	4.30	4,300
900	10-11-78	4.50	4,050
2,300			$9,990

If the ending inventory is reported (valued) at $9,990, then the *cost of goods sold* can be determined:

Beginning inventory	$ 5,320
Net purchases	+ 25,800
Cost of goods available for sale	$31,120
Ending inventory	− 9,990
cost of goods sold	$21,130

Gross profit is then determined as follows:

Net sales (5,000 parts @ $7.10)	$35,500
Cost of goods sold	− 21,130
gross profit	$14,370

Most firms choose not to use the **specific identification** method for three reasons. First, the detailed record-keeping procedures are often extremely costly, especially in firms without an electronic computer. Second, if the inventory units are identical, the identification of each unit serves no useful purpose. A goal of financial accounting is to report economic information about the resources and equities of a firm—not necessarily the physical flow information about the resources. In other words, the economic and cost flows are significant; the physical flows are not. These two flows may or may not be closely related. Third, the specific identification method can lend itself to management manipulation of earnings—management simply holds back in inventory those high-cost (or low-cost) items to artificially affect earnings. Specific identification is appropriate and is used in those businesses dealing in unlike inventory items with high unit cost such as jewelry and used cars.

Weighted average Another cost-flow assumption which can be used in accounting for inventories is that all the costs incurred for the asset (inventory) are used and become expenses simultaneously. This assumption is made when depreciation on plant and equipment is recorded because this asset cannot readily be broken into units—it is purchased in one lot rather than in a series of lots as is inventory. When this method, called the **weighted average,** is used for reporting inventories, an average unit cost is determined for all the goods available for sale. This unit cost then is assumed to apply to both the cost of the inventory *and* the cost of the goods sold. The basic data introduced at the beginning of this section are used in the following illustration of the weighted average method:

$$\begin{aligned}
\text{Average unit cost of merchandise} &= \frac{\text{Cost of goods available for sale}}{\text{Total units available for sale}} \\[2mm]
&= \frac{\text{Cost of beginning inventory} + \text{Net purchases cost}}{\text{Number of units in beginning inventory} + \text{Number of units purchased}} \\[2mm]
&= \frac{\$5,320 + \$25,800}{1,300 + 6,000} \\[2mm]
&= \frac{\$31,120}{7,300} \\[2mm]
&= \$4.263
\end{aligned}$$

If the average unit cost is $4.263 and there are 2,300 units on hand at the end of the period, the value of the *ending inventory* is $4.263 multiplied by 2,300, or $9,805.

If the ending inventory is reported at $9,805, the *cost of goods sold* can be determined:

Beginning inventory	$ 5,320
Net purchases	+ 25,800
Cost of goods available for sale	$31,120
Ending inventory	− 9,805
cost of goods sold	$21,315

or

Units sold during the period	5,000
Multiplied by average unit cost	× $4.263
cost of goods sold	$21,315

Gross profit is then determined as follows:

Net sales (5,000 units @ $7.10)	$35,500
Cost of goods sold	− 21,315
gross profit	$14,185

First-in, first-out Another often-used cost-flow assumption is the first-in, first-out method, commonly called the **FIFO method.** The FIFO method (as applied in the perpetual method) was illustrated earlier in this unit. The assumption here is that the oldest purchases of inventory are sold first and become part of cost of goods sold. The most recent purchases remain in the ending inventory. Using the previous data, the FIFO calculations are as follows:

ENDING MERCHANDISE INVENTORY
(Most recent purchases are assumed
to remain in inventory)

NUMBER OF UNITS	DATE PURCHASED	UNIT COST	TOTAL COST
1,000	10-11-78	$4.50	$4,500
1,300	7-17-78	4.20	5,460
2,300			$9,960

If the ending inventory is reported at $9,960, the *cost of goods sold* can be determined:

Beginning inventory	$ 5,320
Net purchases	+ 25,800
Cost of goods available for sale	$31,120
Ending inventory	− 9,960
cost of goods sold	$21,160

or, where the oldest purchases are assumed to have been sold, the *cost of goods sold* can be determined this way:

NUMBER OF UNITS	DATE PURCHASED	UNIT COST	TOTAL COST
100	11-20-77	$4.00	$ 400
1,200	12-12-77	4.10	4,920
3,000	3-23-78	4.30	12,900
700	7-17-78	4.20	2,940
5,000			$21,160

Gross profit is then determined as follows:

Net sales (5,000 parts @ $7.10)	$35,500
Cost of goods sold	− 21,160
gross profit	$14,340

Last-in, first-out A final cost-flow assumption which is employed from time to time is the last-in, first-out method, commonly called the **LIFO method.** The assumption behind the LIFO method is that the most recent purchases of inventory are sold first and become part of cost of goods sold, and that the oldest purchases remain in the ending inventory. Again using our basic data, the calculations are as follows:

ENDING MERCHANDISE INVENTORY
(Oldest purchases are assumed
to remain in inventory)

NUMBER OF UNITS	DATE PURCHASED	UNIT COST	TOTAL COST
100	11-20-77	$4.00	$ 400
1,200	12-12-77	4.10	4,920
1,000	3-23-78	4.30	4,300
2,300			$9,620

If the ending inventory is reported at $9,620, the *cost of goods sold* can be determined:

Beginning inventory	$ 5,320
Net purchases	+ 25,800
Cost of goods available for sale	$31,120
Ending inventory	− 9,620
cost of goods sold	$21,500

or, where the most recent purchases are assumed to have been sold, the cost of goods sold can be determined this way:

NUMBER OF UNITS	DATE PURCHASED	UNIT COST	TOTAL COST
1,000	10-11-78	$4.50	$ 4,500
2,000	7-17-78	4.20	8,400
2,000	3-23-78	4.30	8,600
5,000			$21,500

Gross profit is then determined as follows:

Net sales (5,000 parts @ $7.10)	$35,500
Cost of goods sold	− 21,500
gross profit	$14,000

Assumptions compared In the preparation of meaningful financial statements, it is generally agreed that when revenues are produced, those expenses which were incurred to produce that revenue should be *matched* against the revenue to measure earnings. For example, when the 5,000 units of inventory were sold for $7.10 each, the income statement for the period the sale was made generally reports the revenues of $35,500. It is not agreed, however, as to the best method for measuring the expense of producing that revenue, that is, measuring the cost of goods sold. Our discussions above of the four cost-flow assumptions imply that earnings per share would be reported differently under each method, as shown in the accompanying table. Once a company chooses a method, that method would be expected to be used over a long period of time. This continuing use of the same method lets readers of the financial statements more readily compare the current operations of the firm with its past operations. Arbitrary changing of methods, of course, would permit manipulation of reported earnings per share and probably would mislead the statement users.

	SPECIFIC IDENTIFICATION	WEIGHTED AVERAGE	FIFO	LIFO
Net sales	$35,500	$35,500	$35,500	$35,500
Cost of goods sold	21,130	21,315	21,160	21,500
Gross profit	$14,370	$14,185	$14,340	$14,000
Operating expenses (assumed)	10,000	10,000	10,000	10,000
net earnings	$ 4,370	$ 4,185	$ 4,340	$ 4,000
net earnings per share	$2.19	$2.09	$2.17	$2.00
(2,000 shares of common stock outstanding during the period)				

Further, we can make the general statement that when the cost of inventories tends to increase consistently over time (as in our example), the FIFO method tends to report earnings in periods prior to when LIFO would report them. This is shown in the accompanying comparative table, where you can see that FIFO earnings ($4,340) clearly exceed the LIFO earnings ($4,000).

LOWER OF COST OR MARKET METHOD OF VALUING INVENTORIES

■ *How should inventories be valued?*

Our discussion has concentrated on determining the cost of the ending inventory for reporting resources at the end of the period and the cost of goods sold to appear on the income statement in the measurement of earnings. *In certain circumstances, however, reporting the ending inventory at its cost might be slightly misleading.* The American Institute of Certified Public Accountants has recommended:

A departure from the cost basis of pricing the inventory is required when the utility of the goods is no longer as great as its cost. . . The rule of *cost or market, whichever is lower* is intended to provide a means of measuring the residual usefulness of an inventory expenditure.[1]

As a result of this recommendation, it has become common practice for firms to report inventories at the lower of cost or market, where *market* means the *replacement price* of the inventory at the balance sheet date. The example below will illustrate this practice. A firm might choose, based on the calculations in the accompanying table, to compute the inventory value at $18,900, which applies the lower of cost or market rule to *each* inventory category. Most firms use this approach. This produces a lower figure, ordinarily, than applying the **lower of cost or market** rule to the total inventory ($19,200, as calculated in the example).

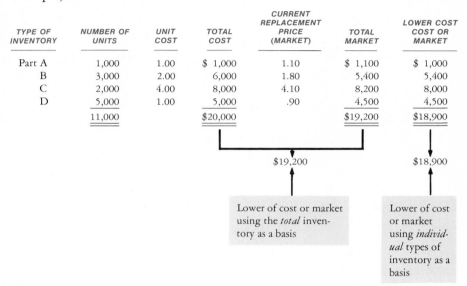

TYPE OF INVENTORY	NUMBER OF UNITS	UNIT COST	TOTAL COST	CURRENT REPLACEMENT PRICE (MARKET)	TOTAL MARKET	LOWER COST COST OR MARKET
Part A	1,000	1.00	$ 1,000	1.10	$ 1,100	$ 1,000
B	3,000	2.00	6,000	1.80	5,400	5,400
C	2,000	4.00	8,000	4.10	8,200	8,000
D	5,000	1.00	5,000	.90	4,500	4,500
	11,000		$20,000		$19,200	$18,900

$19,200

$18,900

Lower of cost or market using the *total* inventory as a basis

Lower of cost or market using *individual* types of inventory as a basis

An adjusting journal entry would be made at the end of the period to reduce the inventory from $20,000 to $18,900:

1978 Dec.	31	Expense from inventory declines	1,100.00	
		Merchandise inventory (or a contra account: Allowance for inventory declines)		1,100.00
		OR		
	31	Cost of goods sold	1,100.00	
		Merchandise inventory (or a contra account: Allowance for inventory declines)		1,100.00

[1] American Institute of Certified Public Accountants, *Accounting Research and Terminology Bulletins,* Final Edition, 1961, Chapter 4.

The effect of writing down the ending inventory is simply to reduce the current period's earnings by the amount of the adjustment. The logic is that the best measure of the utility of merchandise is the market (amount which the company and competing companies would have to pay to replace the inventory at the balance sheet date). If market is below the cost, the excess amount paid must become an expense in the period when the market declined. On the other hand, the custom has *not* been to increase the inventory amount if the market increases above cost. Such a write-up would require that earnings be recognized—and accountants have traditionally felt that earnings should not be reported until a sale of merchandise has been made.

> **NEW TERMS**

cost-flow assumption An assumption made in accounting to aid in dividing the cost of goods available for sale into two parts: (1) ending inventory and (2) cost of goods sold; costs can be assumed to flow through the firm in a number of ways, including FIFO, LIFO, and weighted average. [p. 330]

FIFO First-in, first-out technique for assigning a cost to the ending inventory and goods sold, whereby the oldest goods purchased are assumed to be sold first, and the most recent purchases are assumed to be in the ending inventory. [p. 328]

LIFO Last-in, first-out technique for assigning a cost to the ending inventory and goods sold, whereby the most-recently purchased goods are assumed to be sold first, and the oldest goods purchased are assumed to be in the ending inventory. [p. 333]

lower of cost or market A method of valuing inventories, whereby the merchandise inventory is reported on the financial statements at cost or current replacement price at the balance sheet date, whichever is lower. [p. 335]

perpetual method A record-keeping method for merchandise wherein the Merchandise inventory account is used to record all elements of merchandise cost; all changes in the inventory account are recorded currently, rather than at the end of an accounting period. [p. 326]

specific identification A technique for assigning a cost to the ending inventory and goods sold, whereby the actual physical units in the ending inventory are identified as to their original cost. [p. 330]

weighted average A technique for assigning a cost to the ending inventory and goods sold, whereby an average unit cost of the goods *available* for sale is computed and applied to the ending inventory and the goods sold. [p. 331]

> **ASSIGNMENT MATERIAL**

QUESTIONS

Q19-1. What does the American Institute of CPAs recommend regarding reporting inventories?

Q19-2. How is cost of goods sold determined?

Q19-3. Explain the effects of overstating the ending inventory on each of the following:
   a. Cost of goods sold.
   b. Net earnings.
   c. Earnings per share.
   d. Retained earnings.

e. Total assets.

f. Total liabilities.

g. Total capital.

Q19-4. Explain the effects of overstating the beginning inventory on each of the following:

a. Cost of goods sold.

b. Net earnings.

c. Earnings per share.

d. Retained earnings.

e. Total assets.

f. Total liabilities.

g. Total capital.

Q19-5. Under the perpetual method, describe the journal entry made for buying merchandise and for selling merchandise.

Q19-6. What is a cost-flow assumption?

Q19-7. Name four cost-flow assumptions and describe each.

Q19-8. Explain the lower of cost or market method of valuing inventories.

EXERCISES

E19-1. The financial statements of a firm reported the following information at the end of the year, December 31, 1978:

Net earnings per share	$1.00
Number of common shares of stock outstanding during the year	5,000
Net earnings for 1978	$5,000
Net sales	$100,000
Cost of goods sold	$60,000
Beginning inventory of merchandise	$7,000
Ending inventory of merchandise	$9,000
Retained earnings, December 31, 1978	$150,000
Total assets	$300,000
Total capital	$200,000

After the balance sheet and income statement were prepared and distributed, it was discovered that the ending merchandise inventory should have been reported at $8,000 instead of $9,000. If the statements were revised, indicate for each item in the list above the correct amount to appear on the statements.

E19-2. *Review of periodic method.* Barracks Company uses the *periodic* method of accounting for inventories.

a. Make journal entries for each of the following transactions for 1978:

May 1   Purchased merchandise from Z Company for $200 cash.

7   Purchased merchandise from X Company for $500, with terms of 2/10, n/30.

11   Paid a freight bill to M Freight Co., $80, for delivering the merchandise purchased from X Company.

17   Returned all the merchandise purchased from Z Company, because of defects. We received a check in settlement.

26 Paid the amount due X Company.

30 Sold merchandise for cash, $700.

b. Assume the company had a May 1 inventory of $4,000 and a May 31 inventory of $4,180. Compute the cost of goods sold for May.

E19-3. The following information was taken from the financial statements of R. Irene Company at December 31, 1978:

Net earnings	$ 251,000
Merchandise inventory, Jan. 1, 1978	44,300
Merchandise inventory, Dec. 31, 1978	37,000
Cost of goods sold	269,600
Retained earnings, Dec. 31, 1978	1,500,200
Total assets, December 31, 1978	4,000,900
Total liabilities, December 31, 1978	1,000,000

a. Determine the amounts each of the items above would be if the ending merchandise inventory were reported at $47,000 instead of $37,000.

b. Determine the amounts each of the items above would be if the ending merchandise inventory were reported at $32,000 instead of $37,000.

E19-4. Details concerning the ending merchandise inventory of a firm are shown below:

a. The company deals in one product only.

b. The replacement cost of the inventory at the end of the period is $4.50 per unit.

c. The goods *available* for sale consist of:

NUMBER OF UNITS	DATE OF PURCHASE	UNIT COST
1,000	11-20-78	$4.30
2,000	11-25-78	4.35
1,000	12-17-78	4.55
5,000	12-19-78	4.70
2,000	12-20-78	4.65

REQUIRED: Compute the ending inventory (consisting of 4,000 units) to be reported on financial statements, using the *lower of cost or market method:*

a. If FIFO is used to determine the cost.

b. If weighted average is used to determine the cost.

PROBLEMS (GROUP A)

P19-1. *Fifo, Lifo, Weighted average, lower of cost or market, periodic method.* The March 1, 1978, inventory of a firm, which sells two kinds of products, is as follows:

TYPE OF ITEM	NUMBER OF UNITS	UNIT COST
A	100	$8.00
B	300	7.00

Purchases made during March follow:

	TYPE OF ITEM	NUMBER OF UNITS	UNIT COST
March 7	A	100	$8.30
7	B	200	7.10
23	A	100	7.90
23	B	100	6.80

During March the firm sold 150 units of A for $11 each and sold 350 units of B for $10 each. The current replacement price (market) of inventory type A is $8 and for type B is $6.90 at the end of March.

REQUIRED:

a. For each of the two products, and then for the firm as a whole, compute the ending inventory cost. Make the computations three times, assuming the firm uses first the FIFO method, then LIFO, and then weighted average.

b. Calculate the ending inventory amount (valuation) under the lower of cost or market method, assuming FIFO is used to determine cost. Apply the lower of cost or market rule to each inventory lot and category.

c. Make the adjusting journal entry needed to write the inventory down to lower of cost or market.

P19-2. *Income statements under various cost-flow assumptions.* Zlchee Corporation deals in two products, A and B. At the beginning of 1978, the merchandise on hand was determined as follows:

PRODUCT	NUMBER OF UNITS	DATE OF PURCHASE	TOTAL INVOICE COST
A	8,400	8-10-77	$33,600
A	10,000	12-17-77	41,000
B	1,000	11-12-77	10,000

Purchases during 1978 according to the accounting records were:

DATE OF PURCHASE	NUMBER OF UNITS	PRODUCT	TOTAL INVOICE COST
1-10-78	3,000	B	$ 30,300
1-15-78	4,000	B	40,000
3-14-78	20,000	A	84,000
5-30-78	3,000	B	28,500
6-22-78	24,000	A	108,000
8-27-78	10,000	A	44,500
8-31-78	2,000	B	18,000
10-24-78	9,000	A	39,600
11-10-78	6,000	B	51,000
12-12-78	12,000	A	54,600
12-23-78	3,000	A	13,590

During 1978, 80,000 units of A were sold for $480,000 and 10,000 units of B were sold for $150,000. Expenses (in addition to Cost of goods sold) for the firm during 1978 were: Selling expenses, $6,000; Administrative and other expenses, $33,000.

REQUIRED:

a. Prepare an income statement for the company for 1978 using the first-in, first-out method of determining costs of the inventories. Show all your computations.

b. Prepare an income statement for the company for 1978, using the last-in, first-out method of determining cost of the inventories. Show all your computations.

c. Prepare an income statement for the company for 1978, using the weighted average method of determining cost of the inventories. Show all your computations.

d. Prepare an income statement for the company for 1978, using the specific identification method of determining the cost of the inventories. Show all your computations. These items were identified at the end of 1978 as being in the December 31, 1978, inventory:

PRODUCT	NUMBER OF UNITS	DATE OF PURCHASE
A	7,000	12-12-78
A	7,000	10-24-78
A	2,400	8-10-77
B	100	11-12-77
B	4,000	1-15-78
B	4,900	11-10-78

*P19-3. *Effect of changing inventory calculation methods on net income.* August and Company deals in two groups of products, Regular and Deluxe. The accountant of the firm has gathered information about the merchandise on hand at the end of the year:

	COST (FIFO)	COST (AVERAGE)	REPLACEMENT COST
Regular:			
Product 1	$ 1,000	$ 1,090	$ 1,060
Product 2	500	510	520
Product 3	750	735	740
Deluxe:			
Product 4	3,100	3,300	3,200
Product 5	5,250	5,200	5,100
	$10,600	$10,835	$10,620

Management of the company has been using the lower of cost or market method (FIFO) applied to totals in reporting inventories. The ending inventory is reported at $10,600 and the Net earnings amounted to $8,753. If the company changes inventory procedures, what will the revised Net earnings be if:

a. Lower of cost or market (Average) is applied to total inventory.
b. Lower of cost or market (Average) is applied to each of the five products.
c. Lower of cost or market (Average) is applied to each of the two types of products.
d. Lower of cost or market (FIFO) is applied to each of the five products.
e. Lower of cost or market (FIFO) is applied to each of the two types of products.

PROBLEMS (GROUP B)

P19-4. *Journal entries, perpetual method, FIFO and LIFO.* Below are selected business transactions of Harbinger Company for May, 1978.

May 9   Purchased inventory items as follows, on credit:

2,000 units of Product 111 @ $7.00 per unit

5,000 units of Product 409 @ $3.10 per unit

16   Sold products on credit as follows:

2,600 units of Product 111 for $12.00 per unit

3,650 units of Product 409 for $9.05 per unit

21   Purchased inventory items as follows, for cash:

3,000 units of Product 111 @ $7.25 per unit

3,000 units of Product 409 @ $3.50 per unit

30   Sold products for cash as follows:

2,900 units of Product 111 for $12.50 per unit

3,000 units of Product 409 for $9.50 per unit

Note: The May 1, 1978, inventory was as follows:

Product 111, 3,000 units at a cost of $6.50 per unit

Product 409, 3,000 units at a cost of $2.90 per unit

REQUIRED:

a. Prepare general journal entries for the transactions, assuming the perpetual method and assuming FIFO. Also set up and post the perpetual inventory records (ledger) for the two products.
b. Prepare general journal entries for the transactions, assuming the perpetual method and assuming LIFO. Also set up and post the perpetual inventory records (ledger) for the two products.

P19-5. *Inventory errors.* The data below were taken directly from the financial statements of Error-Prone Enterprises.

	year ending		
	12/31/77	*12/31/78*	*12/31/79*
Merchandise inventory	$ 61,592	$ 58,412	$ 63,519
Total assets	551,700	619,509	751,205
Total liabilities	401,115	412,000	455,692

	year		
	1977	1978	1979
Net earnings	$ 85,714	$ 90,506	$ 91,511
Sales	900,057	1,005,119	1,504,000
Cost of goods sold	711,123	714,519	813,736

The following errors were all discovered on February 1, 1980:
1. The January 1, 1977, inventory had been overstated by $12,000.
2. The December 31, 1978, inventory had been understated by $10,000.
3. A credit purchase had been made on December 30, 1979, for $5,000. The goods were counted and included in the December 31, 1979, inventory but the journal entry had not been made to record the purchase (periodic method).

REQUIRED:

a. Compute the corrected figures for Merchandise inventory, total assets, and total liabilities for each of the three years.
b. Compute the corrected figures for Net earnings, Sales, and Cost of goods sold for each of the three years.

P19-6. *Journal entries, perpetual method, FIFO and LIFO.* Certain transactions of Hamberg Co. for June, 1978, are included below. The company deals in three products.

1. Purchases on credit:

June	3	300 units of Product 1 @ $4.00 each
	12	500 units of Product 2 @ $6.00 each
	15	100 units of Product 1 @ $4.10 each
	18	400 units of Product 3 @ $8.09 each
	24	500 units of Product 1 @ $4.15 each
	25	100 units of Product 2 @ $6.50 each
	26	200 units of Product 2 @ $7.00 each
	29	300 units of Product 3 @ $8.10 each

2. Sales on credit:

June	5	200 units of Product 2 for $12.11 each
	8	300 units of Product 1 for $7.50 each
	14	100 units of Product 3 for $12.50 each
	20	200 units of Product 1 for $8.00 each
	27	200 units of Product 3 for $13.00 each
	30	400 units of Product 2 for $15.00 each

Note: The June 1, 1978, inventory was as follows:

PRODUCT	UNITS	UNIT COST
1	300	$3.90
2	300	5.50
3	300	8.00

REQUIRED:

a. Prepare general journal entries to record all purchases and sales under the perpetual method, assuming FIFO. Also set up perpetual inventory records (ledger pages) for the three products.

b. Prepare general journal entries to record all purchases and sales under the perpetual method, assuming LIFO. Also set up perpetual inventory records (ledger pages) for the three products.

ESTIMATING INVENTORIES;
NEW DEVELOPMENTS

➤ **OBJECTIVE**

This unit will conclude your study of inventories. Two methods of estimating cost of goods sold and inventories will be explained—the gross margin method and the retail method. Also, recent developments dealing with disclosures of inventory replacement prices will be treated.

➤ **APPROACH TO ATTAINING THE OBJECTIVE**

As you study methods of estimating cost of goods sold and inventories, pay particular attention to these three questions, which the text following answers:

- *What is meant by estimating and tentativeness in accounting?*
- *What methods can be used to estimate cost of goods sold and inventories?*
- *What are the current reporting requirements dealing with disclosure of inventory values?*

ESTIMATING AND TENTATIVENESS IN ACCOUNTING

- *What is meant by estimating and tentativeness in accounting?*

By their very nature, financial statements represent estimates; the information they provide is both inexact and tentative. Let's examine two examples to illustrate the need for estimates and the tentative nature of accounting information. First, when earnings are measured and assets are reported, you know that reporting the accounts receivable information requires a prediction about the future. Each accounting period, bad debts expense is reported on the income statement based upon an estimate of that portion of the period's credit sales which will not be collected. This estimate (which is not expected to be exact because it *does* require predicting the future) is necessary if earnings are to be measured for the current period and if receivables are to be reported to the decision makers at the expected collectible amount.

Depreciation expense and the reporting of fixed assets is another example. In order to report the depreciation expense (and thus measure the earnings) and report the asset, the expected useful life of the asset must be predicted. Such an estimate is useful, desirable, and necessary—even though the measurement is not precise.

In summary, remember that financial accounting involves allocations of costs and revenues among short periods of time (such as a year). Such allocations require predictions and make estimates necessary. The accountant, therefore, is certainly concerned with developing methods to improve the results of his estimating process. He also must be concerned with letting the users of financial statements know that the information is tentative in nature (awaiting the completion of all transactions of a firm over a long period of time) and that the information involves many estimates and judgments.

In the next two sections of this unit we will introduce two more examples of estimating in financial accounting. Both are methods of *estimating* cost of goods sold and inventories.

GROSS MARGIN METHOD

- *What methods can be used to estimate cost of goods sold and inventories?*

When the periodic method of recording cost of goods sold and inventories is used, a physical count of the ending inventory must be made before financial statements can be prepared. Taking such a physical count might be extremely costly, and if it must be taken frequently it would cost even more. For example, every 3 months many firms take the physical inventory, but financial statements might be needed monthly or even more often. The **gross margin method** of estimating the cost of goods sold and the ending inventory is used from time to time to prepare such *interim* ("in between") financial statements. With the gross margin method it is not necessary to take a physical count of ending inventory. Another reason for estimating the ending inventory might deal with casualty and fire losses. A fire might have destroyed a firm's inventory, making it impossible to take a physical inventory.

This section explains the gross margin (gross profit) method of making estimates of the cost of goods sold and inventories. Here is the method:

1. For some past period, determine the *relationship of cost of goods sold to net sales.*

$$\frac{\text{Cost of goods sold for past period}}{\text{Net sales for past period}} = x\%$$

$$\frac{\$80,000}{\$100,000} = 80\%$$

For this company this means that, in a particular past period, for every dollar of net sales made, the cost of goods sold amounted to $0.80.

2. If the same relationship of cost of goods sold to net sales holds during the current period, then *cost of goods sold* and *ending inventory* can be estimated from this past experience. Remember that in the *periodic method,* this information appears in the accounts:
   Net sales (Sales; Sales returns and allowances; Sales discounts)
   Beginning inventory
   Net purchases (Purchases; Purchases returns and allowances; Transportation on purchases; Purchases discounts)
   Remember also that in the *periodic method,* this information is *not* available in the accounts:
   Ending inventory
   Cost of goods sold

3. The estimates can be made as follows, assuming these data appeared in the accounts of the firm:

Net sales	$107,000
Beginning inventory	10,000
Net purchases	90,000

Based on the past relationship, this period's cost of goods sold is estimated to be 80% of net sales:

$$\text{Cost of goods sold} = 0.80 \times \$107,000$$
$$= \$85,600$$

From the income statement, you know that:

$$\text{Cost of goods sold} = \text{Beginning inventory} + \text{Net purchases} - \text{Ending inventory}$$

$$\$85,600 = \$10,000 + \$90,000 - \text{Ending inventory}$$

or

$$\text{Ending inventory} = \$10,000 + \$90,000 - \$85,600$$
$$= \$14,400$$

4. An income statement can be made from the estimates:

Net sales		$107,000
Cost of goods sold:		
Beginning inventory	$ 10,000	
Net purchases	90,000	
Cost of goods available for sale	$100,000	
Ending inventory	14,400	
Cost of goods sold		85,600
Gross profit		$ 21,400

Note that ending inventory is estimated as follows: Cost of goods available for sale (from the accounts, $100,000) less Cost of goods sold (estimated, 0.80 × $107,000 = $14,400).

RETAIL METHOD

The **retail method** is another commonly used way to estimate cost of goods sold and ending inventories. This procedure bases its estimate on information in the records for the *current* operating period—rather than on past relationships. In order to use this method, a dual record must be kept on all inventory items: *a record of their cost and a record of their expected selling price.* The record of selling prices (or retail) is routinely kept in businesses such as retail clothing for pricing and control purposes. When an item of inventory is purchased, the selling price is determined and recorded. The retail inventory method is as follows (the figures are assumed from the records of a firm):

1. For the current period, determine the *relationship of cost of goods available for sale to the selling price of goods available for sale.*

$$\frac{\text{Cost of goods } available \text{ for sale this period}}{\text{Selling price of goods } available \text{ for sale this period}} = x\%$$

$$\frac{\$89,000}{\$100,000} = 89\%$$

For this company this means that, *on the average,* the cost of goods sold is equal to about 89% of the selling price of the goods. This relationship holds for all goods, but for any one item of goods, the relationship might be higher or lower.

2. Cost of goods sold then can be estimated by multiplying the net sales for the period by the relationship:

$$\text{Cost of goods sold} = \text{Net sales (from the records)} \times 89\%$$
$$= \$70,000 \times 89\%$$
$$= \$62,300$$

3. Ending inventory then can be estimated as follows:

	Cost of goods available for sale (from the records)	$89,000
less	Cost of goods sold (estimated above)	62,300
equals	Ending inventory	$26,700

These same relationships can be shown in this form:

	AT COST	AT RETAIL	
Beginning inventory	$11,000	$ 13,000	
Net purchases	78,000	87,000	
Goods available	$89,000 ÷	$100,000	= 89%
Sales made during period	62,300[a]	70,000[b]	
Ending inventory	$26,700[c]	$ 30,000	
	at cost	at retail prices	

[a] Net sales times 89%: $70,000 × 0.89 = $62,300, Cost of goods sold.

[b] Net sales from the accounting records.

[c] Cost of goods available less Cost of goods sold equals Ending inventory: $89,000 − $62,300 = $26,700. *Or,* Ending inventory at retail times 0.89 equals Ending inventory at cost: $30,000 × 0.89 = $26,700.

NEW DEVELOPMENTS

■ What are the current reporting requirements dealing with disclosure of inventory values?

Unit 19 indicated that the inventories must be reported on balance sheets according to the lower of cost or market method. In many circumstances, the market (current replacement price) of the inventory is above the cost. Therefore, the inventories in perhaps most circumstances are reported on the balance sheet at their cost.

Many accountants and financial statement users have suggested throughout the years that it would be useful to disclose on the financial statements the current replacement cost of the firm's inventories and to show the amount of net earnings of the company, assuming that current replacement cost were used to value inventories.

Fairly recently, the Securities and Exchange Commission (a federal regulatory agency) required that large companies begin disclosing, through footnotes to their financial statements, these data (among others):

1. The *current replacement cost* of the firm's inventories at the end of the year.

2. The amount of the cost of goods sold if it had been calculated using the *current replacement cost* of goods when they were sold.

This disclosure provides the users of financial statements additional insights into the profitability of the firm during a period of time. For example, if the inventory costs were rapidly rising in a particular industry, such disclosure of net income calculations under both the cost basis and replacement price basis for inventories would assist in evaluating the future outlook for a firm in that industry.

› NEW TERMS

gross margin method A method for estimating cost of goods sold and ending inventory. The basis for the estimate is the relationship of cost of goods sold to net sales for some previous operating period. [p. 346]

retail method A method for estimating cost of goods sold

and ending inventory. The basis for the estimate is the relationship of cost of goods available for sale during the current period and the net selling price of the goods available for sale during the same period. [p. 348]

› ASSIGNMENT MATERIAL

QUESTIONS

Q20-1. Give two examples of estimates that are required to prepare financial statements.

Q20-2. Why are inventory estimates sometimes necessary?

Q20-3. Explain how the gross margin method of estimating inventories is applied.

Q20-4. Explain how the retail method of estimating inventories is applied.

Q20-5. Under what circumstances would the gross margin method not provide a good estimate?

Q20-6. Under what circumstances would the retail method not provide a good estimate?

Q20-7. What information does the SEC (Securities and Exchange Commission) now require large companies to disclose regarding its inventories?

EXERCISES

E20-1. Krown Corporation sells three products as follows:

PRODUCT	SELLING PRICE	COST OF GOODS SOLD PER UNIT
156	$11.95	$8.07
194	5.50	3.06
408	15.95	9.15

During November, 1978, the firm sold 3,050 units of Product 156, 5,000 units of Product 194, and 6,200 units of Product 408 at the selling prices above. The unit-cost-of-goods-sold figures above are taken from the 1977 accounting records (last year). The firm has not increased its selling prices during 1978 above those of 1977, but the cost of goods sold has increased by about 10% for Product 156 and 15% for the other two products.

Compute the total gross profit earned on each of the firm's three products for November, 1978, using the gross profit method of estimating.

E20-2. Farnsworth Company records showed these account balances on March 12, 1978:

Sales (January 1, 1978 through March 12, 1978)	$100,000
Merchandise inventory (January 1, 1978)	12,000
Purchases	59,000
Transportation on purchases	2,000
Purchases discounts	1,000
Purchases returns and allowances	3,000

On March 12, 1978, the entire inventory was destroyed by fire. The January 1, 1978, inventory was priced to sell for $28,500. And additional items bought during the period were priced to sell for $81,510.

Compute the cost of the inventory that was destroyed by fire, using the retail method.

E20-3. During the past 3 years (1974–1977), the gross margin of Farnsworth Company amounted to about 35% of net sales. Using the data given in E20-2, compute the cost of the ending inventory destroyed by fire under the gross margin method.

E20-4. Below is the 1977 income statement for Whigg Co.

Whigg Co.
INCOME STATEMENT
For the Year Ended December 31, 1977

revenues		
Sales	$900,000	
Rental income	40,000	
Total revenues		$940,000
expenses		
Cost of goods sold	$700,000	
Selling expenses	21,000	
General expenses	11,000	
Total expenses		$732,000
net income		$208,000

The accounting records for January of 1978 revealed that sales were made totaling $103,000. For that period, Selling expenses were $3,000 and General expenses were $2,000. Rental income was $1,500.

The January 1, 1978 inventory amounted to $30,000, and net purchases of merchandise of $150,000 were made during January.

a. Prepare an *income statement* for January, 1978, using the gross margin method of estimating cost of goods sold.

b. Calculate the estimated amount of inventory on hand at January 31, 1978.

P20-1. *Income statements, gross margin and retail methods.* The following information was taken from the records of Roly Company at March 14, 1978. On that date a fire destroyed the entire merchandise inventory of the firm.

1. Merchandise inventory (cost) at January 1, 1978	$ 20,000
2. Selling price of merchandise inventory at January 1, 1978	$ 25,000
3. Net purchases of merchandise (January 1, 1978, through March 14, 1978)	$100,000
4. Selling price of the above purchases	$125,000
5. Net sales of merchandise (January 1, 1978, through March 14, 1978)	$140,000
6. Operating expenses (January 1, 1978, through March 14, 1978)	$ 10,000

7. During the past several years, the cost of goods sold has been about 78% of the net sales of the company.

REQUIRED:

a. Prepare an income statement for the period January 1, 1978, through March 14, 1978. Use the gross margin method to estimate the cost of goods sold and ending inventory.

b. Prepare an income statement using the retail method of estimating the cost of goods sold and the ending inventory.

c. If you were the controller of the firm and were assisting with the preparation of the insurance claim, which of the two methods would you suggest the firm use in determining the cost of the ending inventory that was destroyed by fire? Comment.

P20-2. *Income statements, gross margin and retail methods.* The trial balance of Stephen Company at December 31, 1978, the end of the year's operations, is shown in the accompanying table. The physical count of the ending inven-

Cash	$101,200	
Accounts receivable	50,000	
Notes receivable	10,000	
Merchandise inventory	40,000	
Investments	100,000	
Accounts payable		$ 30,000
Notes payable		20,000
Common stock		200,000
Preferred stock		130,000
Retained earnings		2,700
Sales of merchandise		129,500
Sales returns and allowances	6,500	
Purchases of merchandise	200,000	
Purchases returns and allowances		18,200
Purchases discounts		5,000
Transportation on purchases	7,400	
Selling expenses	8,400	
General and administrative expenses	6,000	
Interest expense	300	
Federal income tax expense	4,100	
Dividends	2,000	
Interest income		500
	$535,900	$535,900

tory is being made. The controller of the company asks you to compute an estimate of the Cost of goods sold, and to prepare an income statement. As additional information, a condensed income statement from the previous year is shown below:

Net sales	$100,000
Cost of goods sold	$ 83,500
Selling expenses	5,000
General and administrative expenses	6,000
Federal income taxes	2,000
Total costs	$ 96,500
Net earnings	$ 3,500

Selling price of beginning inventory, $47,200; selling price of net purchases, $215,100.

REQUIRED:

a. Prepare a summary income statement, using the gross profit method.
b. Prepare a summary income statement, using the retail method.

*P20-3. *Estimating case, product lines.* Assume that you are a claim adjuster for Sparks Fire Insurance and Casualty Company. Recently you were assigned to investigate a claim of Whiz Supermarket, a policyholder. It is reported that on October 11, 1978, a fire destroyed a significant portion of the inventory of the grocery store. Your job is to determine the approximate cost of the merchandise which was destroyed by smoke or fire. You are able to gather the following data:

1. According to the balance sheet prepared at October 1, 1978, the merchandise inventory was reported as follows:

Grocery inventory	$75,100
Produce inventory	5,600
Meat market inventory	11,500
Miscellaneous inventory	9,000

2. The gross profit as a percent of net sales for each department for the preceding four months was:

	JUNE	JULY	AUGUST	SEPTEMBER
Groceries	15.1	15.6	16.1	15.9
Produce	28.0	27.3	29.1	28.5
Meats	18.9	17.1	16.5	18.8
Miscellaneous	24.3	25.0	25.1	24.7

3. Sales for the month of October until the fire amounted to the following, according to the ledger accounts:

Groceries	$55,000
Produce	4,600
Meats	10,500
Miscellaneous	8,200

4. Net purchases of merchandise during the month of October until the fire amounted to the following according to the records:

	COST	SELLING PRICES
Groceries	$11,800	$13,635
Produce	1,000	1,629
Meats	2,300	3,350
Miscellaneous	1,100	1,267

5. Through consultation with the management of the store and through your observation, the following estimates are agreed upon:
   a. 100% of the meat on hand was destroyed by fire or smoke.
   b. 100% of the produce was destroyed.
   c. 60% of the groceries was destroyed.
   d. 50% of the miscellaneous inventory was destroyed.
6. Other records reveal that the estimated selling prices of inventories at October 1, 1978, were:

Grocery inventory	$88,600
Produce inventory	7,800
Meat market inventory	13,900
Miscellaneous inventory	12,200

REQUIRED:

a. Compute the ending inventory amount that was destroyed by fire according to the gross margin method.
b. Compute the ending inventory amount that was destroyed by fire according to the retail method.
c. Which method would be most advantageous for Whiz Supermarket to use in preparing its insurance claim?

PROBLEMS (GROUP B)

P20-4. *Calculations, gross margin and retail methods.* The following information was taken from the records of Carter Company at December 31, 1978.

1. Merchandise inventory (cost) at January 1, 1978	$ 50,000
2. Selling price of merchandise inventory at January 1, 1978	55,000
3. Net purchases of merchandise for the year	130,000
4. Selling price of the above purchases	155,000
5. Net sales of merchandise for the year	200,000
6. Operating expenses for the year	16,000

7. During the past several years, the cost of goods sold has been about 82% of the net sales of the company.

REQUIRED:

a. Under the gross margin method, calculate the following for 1978:
   (1) Ending inventory.
   (2) Cost of goods sold.

(3) Gross profit.

(4) Net income.

b. Under the retail method, calculate the following for 1978:

(1) Ending inventory.

(2) Cost of goods sold.

(3) Gross profit.

(4) Net income.

P20-5. *Gross margin and retail methods, earnings per share.* Selected data from Bottom Line, Inc., records for 1978 follow.

	COST DATA	SELLING PRICE DATA
Merchandise inventory, January 1, 1978	$ 80,000	$ 96,200
Purchases	400,000	
Transportation on purchases	15,000	
Purchases returns and allowances	30,000	446,000
Purchase discounts	10,000	

Sales of merchandise during 1978 totaled $400,500.

The income statement for 1977 was as follows:

Bottom Line, Inc.
INCOME STATEMENT
For the Year Ending December 31, 1977

Sales			$580,000
Cost of goods sold:			
Beginning inventory		$ 70,000	
Purchases	$500,000		
Transportation on purchases	20,000		
	$520,000		
Less: Purchases discounts	$ 8,000		
Purchases returns and allowances	20,000	28,000	
Net purchases		492,000	
Cost of goods available for sale		$562,000	
Less Ending inventory		80,000	
Cost of goods sold			482,000
Gross margin			$ 98,000
Operating expenses			25,000
Net income			$ 73,000

Operating expenses for 1978 amounted to $20,000; also, there was a miscellaneous revenue from rental of equipment totaling $4,800 during 1978.

REQUIRED:

a. Assume that the date is December 31, 1978, and the physical count of the inventory is in process of being taken. The President of the firm asks you to prepare an estimate of this year's *earnings per share* before the inventory count is complete. You know that there were 100,000 shares of common stock outstanding during the last several years. No preferred stock is outstanding. Prepare a calculation of 1978's earnings per share, using the gross margin method. Prepare a detailed income statement for 1978 in support of your answer.

b. Compute the estimated earnings per share for 1978, using the retail method.

*P20-6. *Analysis of Methods.* The Clothing Department of Howard Discount Stores, Inc., initiated a change in pricing policy during 1978. All goods in the department are marked up 25% above their *net* cost. For example, an item that has a *net* cost of $10.00 will be sold for $12.50. However, the beginning inventory items (January 1, 1978) were not repriced. These items were marked to sell for prices ranging from 10% above cost to 30% above their cost.

Company records showed these data for 1978:

	COST	RETAIL
Beginning inventory	$114,625	$136,404
Purchases	597,821	
Transportation on purchases	15,207	
Purchases discounts	6,100	
Purchases returns and allowances	5,000	

For 1977 and prior years, the cost of goods sold amounted to about 90% of net sales. The new pricing policy was expected to decrease net sales by about 10% from the 1977 level of $600,000, but operating expenses (Selling and General) would be reduced to $40,000 for 1978.

REQUIRED:

a. Would the gross margin method give a good estimate of the ending inventory and cost of goods sold? Explain.

b. Prepare an income statement for 1978, using the gross margin method.

c. Calculate the ending inventory, using the gross margin method.

d. Would the retail method give a good estimate of the ending inventory and cost of goods sold? Explain.

e. Prepare an income statement for 1978, using the retail method.

f. Calculate the ending inventory, using the retail method.

g. The Controller of the firm suggests that the best way (in the circumstances) to calculate the estimated earnings for 1978 is to use an ending inventory as follows:

Retail value of goods available	$888,814
Less sales	540,000
Retail value of ending inventory	$348,814
$\times$	80%
Cost of ending inventory	$279,051

Do you agree? Fully explain.

*P20-7. *Cumulative review problem.* The sales and purchases of merchandise of Crudo Corporation for the first few days of January, 1978, follow.

DATE	PRODUCT	UNITS PURCHASED	UNIT COST	UNITS SOLD	SELLING PRICE
1–2–78	11A	400	$3.00		
1–2–78	12C	500	$5.50		
1–3–78	10B			300	$9.50
1–6–78	11A	500	$2.90		
1–7–78	11A			200	$5.00
1–8–78	12C			700	$6.75
1–9–78	11A			800	$5.25
1–9–78	12C			200	$7.00
1–10–78	10B	300	$5.00		

The January 1, 1978, inventory was as follows:

PRODUCT	UNITS	COST
11A	500	$2.50
12C	500	5.00
10B	500	4.50

REQUIRED:

a. Set up perpetual ledger accounts for the three products. Complete the three records, assuming the firm uses the LIFO perpetual method.

b. Compute the cost of goods sold and gross profit for each of the three products for January 1 through January 10, using the LIFO perpetual method.

c. Assume that the company uses the FIFO periodic method. Compute the cost of goods sold and gross profit for each of the three products for January 1 through January 10.

d. Assume that the company uses the FIFO periodic method (as in part c above). Also assume the lower of cost or market is applied. Compute the ending inventory for each of the three products if the current replacement cost at January 10 is as follows:

11A	$2.60
12C	$5.40
10B	$4.80

e. Assume that the company uses the weighted average periodic method. Compute the cost of goods sold and gross profit for each of the three products for January 1 through January 10.

P20-8. *Cumulative review problem.* The beginning inventory for three of a firm's products (January 1, 1978) was:

	UNITS	UNIT COST
A	500	$250
B	400	500
C	500	600

Purchases and sales during the year were:

DATE	PRODUCT	UNITS PURCHASED	UNIT COST	UNITS SOLD	SELLING PRICE
1–3–78	A	400	$270		
2–2–78	C	500	$610		
3–12–78	B			300	$1,100
4–15–78	A	500	$275		
4–20–78	A			200	$500
5–15–78	C			700	$1,500
10–1–78	A			800	$525
11–15–78	C			200	$1,300
12–30–78	B	300	$520		

During the last few years, the *gross profit as a percent of sales* has averaged as follows:

A	46%
B	51%
C	90%

REQUIRED:

a. For each product, compute the gross profit, cost of goods sold, ending inventory, and sales under the gross margin method.

b. Compute the ending inventory amount (for each product) to be shown on the balance sheet at December 31, 1978, if lower of cost or market with weighted average is applied (periodic). The current replacement prices are:

A	$250
B	$520
C	$590

chapter 9

noncurrent assets

> **OBJECTIVE**

The purpose of this unit is to show you how long-term investments are recorded and reported. You also will study their acquisition, use, and disposal.

> **APPROACH TO ATTAINING THE OBJECTIVE**

As you study about long-term investments, pay special attention to these five questions, which the text following answers:

- *Generally, how are long-term investment acquisitions recorded and reported on financial statements?*
- *How are long-term investments in bonds reported?*
- *How are long-term investments in land reported?*
- *How are long-term investments in life insurance reported?*
- *How are long-term investments in common stocks reported?*

NATURE OF LONG-TERM INVESTMENTS

Long-term investments include stocks, bonds, land, and any other investments which a firm plans to own for a number of years. These investments do *not* represent a firm's main source of revenue, but are acquired for a variety of other reasons. Common stock of another company might be purchased so that a firm can control certain actions of the other company. For example, to assure a continuing supply of a needed raw material or merchandise, a firm might buy common stock of a smaller firm which manufactures the raw material. Excess funds of a company occasionally are tied up in long-term investments. Land, for example, might be purchased with the intent of holding it for several years, then building a plant on it.

RECORDING THE ACQUISITION

■ *Generally, how are long-term investment acquisitions recorded and reported on financial statements?*

To begin your study of **long-term investments,** here are three basic points:

1. Long-term investments often include investments in bonds, common stocks, preferred stocks, land, and life insurance.
2. Long-term investments are recorded initially in the accounts and reported on the balance sheet *at their cost. This cost includes all costs associated with acquiring the long-term investment*—attorneys' fees, brokerage costs, and so on.
3. In financial statement reports to decision makers, the cost is considered a more relevant figure than the market value. Because a company does not plan to dispose of long-term investments in the next year, the market price of the investment is not of primary concern. The number of dollars tied up (cost) is relevant, however, in evaluating management's use of the firm's resources.

The following discussion will now show how each of the following common long-term investments is recorded:

1. Investments in bonds.
2. Investments in land.
3. Investments in life insurance.
4. Investments in common stocks.

INVESTMENTS IN BONDS

Study the following journal entry.

1978 Jan.	1	Investment in bonds	95,000	
		Cash		95,000
		Purchased B. Corp. 7% bonds as a long-term investment, with $100,000 face amounts, maturing in 10 years, with interest to be collected each December 31.		

Notice the investment in the bonds on January 1. The bond agreement states that the maturity (face) amount is $100,000. This means that at the maturity date (January 1, 1988) $100,000 can be collected for the investment. Each year for 10 years the investor will collect interest of 7% of the face amount of $100,000—or $7,000 per year. If the bonds are held for the 10-year period, then the total earnings on this investment are as follows:

amounts to be received from the investment in bonds:

At maturity (in 10 years)	$100,000
Cash receipts of $7,000 per year for 10 years	70,000
Total received	$170,000
amounts paid for the investment in bonds:	
Cost, including brokerage fees	95,000
TOTAL INTEREST INCOME TO BE EARNED	$ 75,000
Average interest income from the investment each of the 10 years	$ 7,500

All this information is not needed to record the $95,000 investment in bonds, *but it will be needed to record the interest as it is earned in the future.*

Refer to the journal entry in the example above, where bonds were purchased for a net cost of $95,000. From the preceding information, you know that each year during the life of the investment, the earnings of the firm will increase by $7,500, the interest earned on the investment. This journal entry describes the process for 1978:

1978 Dec.	31	Cash	7,000	
		Investment in bonds	500	
		Interest income		7,500

According to the bond agreement, the investor (our company) will receive 7% of $100,000 (the face value) each year. We calculated previously that the total of the earnings each year on the investment is $7,500. Therefore, an additional $500 has been earned that will be collected at the maturity date (10 years) as part of the $100,000 to be collected. So, at the end of the first year, December 31, 1978, the long-term investment in bonds amounts to *$95,500*. By the end of the 10-year period (December 31, 1987), the investment will reflect a balance of $100,000, which then will be converted to cash.

The entry at December 31, 1987, would be:

1987 Dec.	31	Cash	100,000	
		Investment in bonds		100,000
		Collected investment in bonds at maturity.		

Here is a summary of what you have learned about investments in bonds:

1. When bonds are purchased as an investment, they are recorded at their cost.

2. Total interest income is computed by subtracting total amounts invested from total amounts to be received from the bonds. (This can be divided by the number of years to calculate the annual interest income.)

3. Each year an entry is made to record the interest earned (income) on the investment. This interest earned may be a different amount than the cash received during the year. Cash is debited for the amount of the actual cash received; interest income is credited for the interest income (as computed in item 2 above). Any difference is either debited *or* credited to the Investment in bonds account.

4. At the maturity date, cash is received for the face of the bonds. At that time, this should also be the balance of the Investment in bonds account. Cash would be debited and Investment in bonds would be credited for the amount of the cash received.

Sometimes a firm sells its bond investment before the maturity date. In that case, Cash is debited for the amount received. The Long-term investment in bonds account is credited for its balance at the time the bonds are sold. Any difference is a *gain or loss on sale of long-term investments,* to appear on the income statement.

INVESTMENTS IN LAND The journal entries below show the acquisition of a tract of land.

1978 Jan.	24	Investment in land	100,000	
		Notes payable		100,000
		Purchased a tract of land on Harrison Road to be held for several years; issued a 7% note payable, due in 5 years.		
	26	Investment in land	6,000	
		Cash		6,000
		Paid brokerage fees, attorneys' costs, and other fees associated with purchasing the investment in land.		

The first entry shows the investment was made, signing a long-term note. Additional costs of $6,000 were incurred, and these were paid in cash. All

■ *How are long-term investments in land reported?*

costs, including brokerage fees and attorneys costs become part of the long-term investment account. This account remains in the long-term investments section of the balance sheet (at its cost) until it is sold or otherwise disposed of. The appropriate gain or loss is recorded in the period of its sale. If the land happens to be put in use for regular operations, it is no longer classified as a long-term investment. For example, if the company were to build a factory on the land, then the land would be reclassified on the balance sheet as part of plant and equipment, not long-term investments.

INVESTMENTS IN LIFE INSURANCE

■ *How are long-term investments in life insurance reported?*

It is a common practice for firms to **invest in life insurance** for the lives of its key officers and employees. If an important official dies, the life insurance proceeds will aid the company in the transition period. Some life insurance policies (called *whole* life insurance) combine two items—life insurance coverage and a long-term investment. The long-term investment is known as the *cash surrender value of life insurance,* or the amount of cash the firm could receive if the policy were canceled. Each year, as premiums are paid, part of the cost is considered an increase in the investment (cash surrender value) and part of the cost is for insurance coverage (expense).

Now refer to the journal below.

1978 Jan.	28	Investment in life insurance	1,000	
		Insurance expense	6,000	
		Cash		7,000
		Paid the 1978 premium on the life insurance policy for the firm's officers.		

The entry in our example assumes that of the $7,000 paid, $6,000 represents the insurance expense for the period, and the investment value increases by $1,000. The specific provisions of the life insurance policy would determine what part represents the insurance coverage cost and what portion is the recoverable investment.

If an insurance policy is canceled, then the investment asset is simply converted to cash—Cash is debited for the same amount that the Investment in life insurance is credited, with no gain or loss. On the other hand, in the unfortunate event that an insured person were to die, this entry would be appropriate: Cash would be debited for the amount of the settlement; Investment in life insurance would be credited for the balance of that account, which is being reduced to zero through the termination of the policy; and an account such as Net proceeds from life insurance (a revenue-type account) would be credited for the difference.

It is common practice for one company to invest in the common stock of another company, both for direct profit on the investment, and in some cases, to control the other company.

Basically, there are three types of investor-investee relationships:

1. *When the investing company owns a relatively few shares of another company.*
2. *When the investing company controls another company.*
3. *When the investing company partially controls (significantly influences) another company.*

The accounting treatment is different for each of these three types of relationships.

When the investing company owns a relatively few shares of another company
The journal below shows that the investing company bought 200 shares of common stock. This relatively small investment (in terms of all the shares of ABC Company) is initially recorded at its cost.

1978 Jan.	18	Investment in common stocks	10,462	
		Cash		10,462
		Purchased 200 shares of common stock of ABC Company for $50 per share; also paid $462 in brokerage charges and other costs.		

When they are sold, the appropriate gain or loss is recorded. In the example, if the $10,462 investment in common stocks were to be sold at a future date for $13,000 cash, then the journal entry would include a debit to Cash for $13,000, a credit to Investment in common stock for $10,462, and a credit to *Gain on sale of long-term investments* for $2,538. This gain would appear on the income statement of the period in which the sale was made, and the earnings of that period would be increased by that amount.[1]

Another point about such investments in stocks: when the board of directors (of the company whose stock a firm owns) declares a dividend, the firm must show earnings from the investment in the accounts. If, for exam-

---

[1] FASB Statement No. 12 requires that certain marketable equity securities (certain common stocks) be reported at lower of cost or market at the balance sheet date. In the case of such long-term investments in equity securities, any decline in market value is not treated as a loss on the income statement, but is reported through a special capital account. For purposes of this chapter, we will assume, unless otherwise specified, that at the balance sheet date, the market value of such investments owned is equal to or above the cost, and no adjusting entry will be required.

ple, the ABC Company (see previous example) declared a dividend of $1 per share on its common stock, then this journal entry would be made:

	Dividends receivable	200	
	Dividends income		200

An asset is created *when the board declares the dividend.* The Dividends receivable account would be reported on the balance sheet. Earnings are increased in this same period through the Dividends income account. When cash is actually collected—in this period or a future one—the receivable is reduced and the cash is increased. In other words, our earnings from investments increase in the period in which we become entitled to receive the dividend, not necessarily in the period when we collect the cash. This procedure is consistent with the accounting theory you have already studied: earnings per share are increased in periods when the net assets of the firm grow (receivable is created) from profit-making activities.

When the investing company controls another company When a company owns a sufficient number of shares of stock to *control* another company, a special relationship is created. If 50% of the common stock or more is owned, then a *parent-subsidiary* relationship exists. The company is *controlled* because more than 50% of the stockholder votes are controlled by one company (one owner).

In these cases, the parent company (investor) and subsidiary company (investee) are more-or-less considered one economic unit. So, financial statements are prepared combining *all* the resources and equities of the companies into one *economic entity.* Such combined financial statements are known as *consolidated financial statements.* They are discussed in considerable detail in Chapter 15.

When the investing company partially controls (significantly influences) another company If the investment of one company in another is not large enough for complete control but is large enough for *some degree of control,* then consolidated financial statements are *not* prepared. Instead, each of the companies (investor and investee) prepares its own financial statements in the usual fashion. In these cases, the **equity method** is used to report the long-term investment of one company in another (instead of reporting the long-term investment at cost).

Under the equity method, the *initial* investment is recorded at cost. As the company that is partially controlled (significantly influenced) produces net earnings, the long-term investment on the books of the owner company is increased for its proportionate interest in the earnings.

Accordingly, as dividends are paid by the owned company, the long-term investment account is reduced on the books of the investor company. An example follows in summary form.

		BOOKS OF COMPANY A		
1978	Investment in Company B		200,000	
	Cash			200,000
	Company A buys a 20% interest in Company B.			
1978	Investment in Company B		20,000	
	Income from Company B earnings			20,000
	Company B produced net income of $100,000 during the period (1978). Company A's share of the earnings amounts to $20,000 or 20% of $100,000.			
1978	Cash		2,400	
	Investment in Company B			2,400
	Company B paid dividends of $12,000. Company A received 20% of the dividends (20% of $12,000 = $2,400).			

To summarize reporting practice for long-term investments in common stock, there are three basic kinds of investor-investee relationships: (1) *When the investing company owns relatively few shares of another company.* In such cases, the investing company reports the long-term investment at cost (or lower of cost or market in the case of marketable equity securities according to the financial accounting standards board). (2) *When the investing company controls another company* (with 50% or more of the common shares). In such cases, consolidated financial statements are prepared for the companies. (3) *When the investing company partially controls (significantly influences) another company.* In such cases, each company prepares its own financial statements, and the owner company uses the *equity method* of reporting the long-term investment.

> **NEW TERMS**

equity method The method used for reporting long-term investments of one company in another, where one company controls the other company to some degree (not complete control); under the equity method, the initial investment is recorded at cost. As the company that is partially controlled produces net earnings, the long-term investment on the books of the owner company is increased for its proportionate interest in the earnings. As dividends are paid by the owned company, the long-term investment is reduced. [p. 366]

investment in life insurance A long-term investment which ordinarily represents the cash surrender value of a life insurance policy. [p. 364]

long-term investments Assets held on a long-term basis, in contrast to the Marketable securities in the current asset section of the balance sheet. Long-term investments are accumulated as part of a company's long-range planning process. Some of these investments produce additional earnings through dividends and interest, while others are purchased for their potential growth in market value. Resources classified as Long-term investments are *not* directly used in the production of the main revenues of the firm. Resources that are used to produce the major product or to render the major service of the company are classified as Plant and equipment. This distinction of classifications provides the user of the financial statements additional information about which of the resources are employed in which ways. [p. 361]

> ## ASSIGNMENT MATERIAL

QUESTIONS

Q21-1. Explain how brokerage fees, attorneys' costs, and so on, which are associated with purchasing long-term investments are recorded. Are they recorded as expenses or assets?

Q21-2. On which financial statement is the account, Cash surrender value of life insurance, reported? Explain.

Q21-3. Distinguish between long-term investments and fixed assets (plant and equipment).

Q21-4. What entry is made when bonds are purchased (invested in) for cash?

Q21-5. How is annual interest income computed on an investment in bonds?

Q21-6. Are the interest earned and the cash received always the same every year from an investment in bonds? Explain.

Q21-7. Does the amount reported on the balance sheet for an investment in land change as the market value of the land changes? Comment.

Q21-8. What is whole life insurance?

Q21-9. What are three basic types of investor–investee relationships dealing with common stocks?

Q21-10. Briefly discuss the reporting of common stock investments in each of the three types of relationships referred to in Q21-9.

EXERCISES

E21-1. Make accounting entries in general journal form for the following business transactions:

a. Paid the annual premium on the life insurance policy for key employees. Paid $3,000, of which $1,000 represents an increase in the cash surrender value of the life insurance policy.

b. Purchased land as a long-term investment, paying $10,000 cash and signing a 10-year, 8% note payable for $189,000. Details follow:

Land cost	$188,000
Brokerage fees	9,000
Attorneys' fees	2,000
	$199,000

c. Purchased bonds as a long-term investment from ABC Company. Details: the bonds are 10-year bonds and have a face value of $70,000; 7% interest is payable each December 31. After brokerage charges and other fees are paid, the bonds cost a total of $67,000.

d. Assume that the bonds above were purchased on January 1, 1978. Make the entry to show the collection of interest on December 31, 1978, and record the total interest earned during 1978.

E21-2. Several business transactions related to a firm's long-term investments made during 1978 are as follows:

DATE	DESCRIPTION	TOTAL COST INCLUDING BROKERAGE FEES
Jan. 14	300 shares ABA Common	$63,490
April 2	55 shares BX 5% Preferred, $80 par	5,500
June 30	100 MB 7% Bonds, $1,000 face value (interest payable July 1 and Jan. 1; maturity date, June 30, 1988)	90,000

Other events concerning the investments:

June 30   Received the semiannual dividend of BX Preferred Stock.
Sept. 1   Received the annual dividend of ABA Common, $3 per share.
Dec. 31   Received the semiannual dividend of BX Preferred Stock.

Make all accounting entries concerning long-term investments during the year. What is the total amount of long-term investments to be reported on the balance sheet at December 31?

E21-3. Blandings Corporation paid the annual premium on the life insurance policy for key employees. This $3,000 premium was paid on March 18, 1978. After the payment, the insurance company notified the firm that the cash surrender value amounted to $61,347. As a result of the March 18 payment, the cash surrender value increased by $1,213. Make the journal entry needed on March 18.

E21-4. On November 3, 1978, Wax Company purchased 200 shares of Bee Corporation common stock for $50 per share. In addition, $100 of commissions and fees were paid. On December 1, 1978, Bee Corporation declared its regular annual dividend of $1 per share, to be paid on January 11, 1979. Make all journal entries associated with the stock and dividends.

PROBLEMS (GROUP A)

P21-1. *Bond investments; bonds bought below and above face amount.*

1. On January 1, 1978, Washington Enterprises, Inc., purchased 20-year bonds of Delaware Company with face amounts totaling $20,000, bearing 7% interest, payable annually on December 31. The bonds were purchased for $18,000 cash.

2. On January 1, 1978, Jefferson, Inc., purchased 20-year bonds of Adams Corporation with face amounts totaling $20,000, bearing interest of 8%, payable semiannually on June 30 and December 31. The bonds were purchased for $23,000 cash.

REQUIRED:

a. Make all general journal entries related to the bonds during 1978 on the books of Washington Enterprises, Inc.

b. Make all general journal entries related to the bonds during 1978 on the books of Jefferson, Inc.

P21-2. *Equity method for common stock investments.*

1. City Parts Company purchased a 19% interest in Audubon Corporation for $200,000 cash (by investing in common stock). The purchase was made on January 1, 1978. During 1978, Audubon Corporation produced net earnings of $40,000. On November 30, 1978, Audubon Corporation paid dividends totaling $10,000 to its common stockholders.

2. Simmons Olde-Tyme Company uses the equity method in reporting its investment in Alma Corporation. Simmons had paid $25,000 for a 20% interest in Alma Corporation some years ago. The investment was shown on the December 31, 1978, balance sheet of Simmons at $54,300. During 1979, Alma Corporation produced net earnings of $50,000 and paid dividends totaling $40,000.

REQUIRED:

a. Assuming City Parts Company uses the equity method for reporting this investment, make all journal entries on the books of City Parts Company for the year related to this investment.

b. Prepare journal entries to reflect changes during 1979 on the books of Simmons Olde-Tyme Company.

P21-3. *Bond investment; sale before maturity.* CSS Company sold its investment in Jacksboro bonds on December 31, 1978. The company had owned 1,000 3% bonds of $1,000 face value, for which it had paid $890,000 including commissions on January 1, 1968. The bonds are to mature on January 1, 1983. Proceeds from the sale of the bonds on December 31, 1978, amounted to $990,000. The CSS Company had received the annual interest check on December 31, 1978, before the bonds were sold. The firm had not yet recorded its adjusting entries.

REQUIRED:

Record the journal entries necessary at December 31, 1978.

PROBLEMS (GROUP B)

P21-4. *Acquition of long-term investments.* Make general journal entries for the following transactions related to long-term investments:

a. Purchased 150 shares of Zimco, Inc., common stock. The $100 par value shares cost the company $110 per share plus total brokerage charges of $108. The cost basis is used for recording this investment.

b. Paid the annual premium on life insurance policies for the company's officers. The premium was $3,000. As a result of this payment, the cash surrender value increased from $20,000 to $21,340.

c. Purchased land and buildings for $90,000, of which $20,000 is considered the value of the land. Paid $4,000 cash and signed a 7% 5-year note, with a face amount of $86,000.

d. Received dividends of $1 per share from Zimco, Inc. See transaction a above.

e. Invested in 10-year bonds of Zimple Company with face amounts of $100,000. The bonds cost $92,000 cash and bear interest of 8%, payable annually at December 31. The investment was made on January 1, 1978.

f. Recorded the December 31 interest collection from the bonds in transaction e and the correct amount of interest earned for the year.

g. Made an investment in the common stock of Bilton Corporation for $100,000 cash. The purchase included 18% of the common stock of the firm, and the equity method is to be used for reporting the investment. Make the entry for the investment.

h. Bilton Corporation earned $100,000 in profits for the year (see transaction g). Make the entry needed on the books of the investing company.

i. Bilton Corporation (see transaction g) paid dividends totaling $40,000 on its common stock. Record the receipt of the dividend on the books of the investing company.

P21-5. *Analysis of transactions dealing with long-term investments.* Selected transactions from the records of Graffer Spencics, Inc., are presented.

1. Investment in Company D	50,000	
Cash		50,000
Bought 1% interest.		
2. Investment in Company E	100,000	
Common stock		100,000
Bought 20% interest.		
3. Investment in land	10,000	
Notes payable		9,000
Cash		1,000
4. Investment in Company E	5,000	
Income from Company E earnings		5,000
5. Cash	1,000	
Dividends income		1,000
Company D		
6. Cash	2,000	
Investment in Company E		2,000
7. Investment in bonds	90,000	
Cash		90,000
8%, 10-year		
8. Insurance expense	1,000	
Investment in life insurance	1,200	
Cash		2,200
9. Cash	4,000	
Investment in bonds	500	
Interest income		4,500
10. Cash	60,000	
Investment in Company D		50,000
Gain on sale of Investment in Company D		10,000

REQUIRED:

For each of the entries above describe in as much detail as you can the business transaction that led to the entry. Some of the entries are related to others. Be very specific. For example, entry 9 relates to entry 7. You should be able to determine how each of the figures and entries were derived and the time period concerned.

P21-6. *Investments: bonds; common stocks; land; life insurance.* Below is information about four investments made by Frank Imm Co.

1. On January 1, 1978, made an investment in 20-year, 8% bonds of Camm Co. with face amounts totaling $200,000. Paid $180,000 for the bonds.

2. Made an investment in 5,000 shares of Blamm Corporation common stock. Paid $100 per share cash.
3. Purchased land as an investment from Hamm Company for $90,000, signing a 3-year, 10% note for $75,000, and paying cash for the balance.
4. Paid the annual premium of $11,500 on the life insurance policy for executives. The cash surrender value at the beginning of the period was $29,650.

REQUIRED: Answer the following questions.

a. Compute the annual interest income from the bonds.
b. Compute the annual cash received from the bonds.
c. Compute the balance of the Investment in bonds to be shown on the balance sheet of the company at December 31, 1982.
d. Assume that the bonds were sold on January 1, 1983 for cash for $600 more than the amount shown on the balance sheet at December 31, 1982. Make the journal entry.
e. Assume that the common stock in item 2 above is recorded on the *cost basis* (not equity method). The Blamm Corporation earned $50,000 during the year and paid dividends totaling $40,000. The 5,000 shares owned by Frank Imm Co. represent 10% of the total common shares of Blamm Corporation. Make journal entries on the books of Frank Imm Co. for all transactions related to the investment.
f. Assume the same facts as in part e above, except that the 5,000 shares represent 60% of the shares of common stock of Blamm Corporation (instead of 10%) and the *equity method* is used. Make journal entries on the books of Frank Imm Co. for all transactions related to the investment.
g. Record the land purchase.
h. What will the balance of the Investment in land account be 4 years after the date of purchase?
i. Assume that the insurance premium was paid on December 31, 1978, and that the cash surrender value of the policy amounts to $30,100 after the premium payment. Record the payment.

PLANT AND EQUIPMENT

> ### OBJECTIVE

This unit deals with fixed assets, also known as plant and equipment. The unit will show you how plant and equipment assets are recorded and how depreciation is commonly computed and reported on financial statements. Discussed also is the accounting treatment of additional common transactions dealing with fixed assets.

> ### APPROACH TO ATTAINING THE OBJECTIVE

As you study about fixed assets, pay special attention to these five questions, which the text following answers:

- *How are plant and equipment acquisitions recorded?*
- *How is the use of plant and equipment recorded?*
- *How is plant and equipment reported on the balance sheet?*
- *What additional common transactions affect the reporting of plant and equipment?*
- *How are plant and equipment subsidiary records kept?*

Land, buildings, equipment, natural resources, land improvements, and other major *resources which are currently being used to produce the firm's main revenues* are called *plant and equipment* or *fixed assets.* Decision makers are interested in knowing how many dollars management has tied up in these major revenue-producing assets.

**RECORDING THE
ACQUISITION**

- *How are plant and
equipment acquisitions
recorded?*

Like long-term investments, **plant and equipment assets** are recorded at their full cost, including transportation and freight charges, sales taxes paid on the purchase, setup costs, and other charges related to acquiring and getting the asset ready for use. A special problem arises when both land and buildings are purchased at one price. A careful allocation between the land account and the buildings account must be made because the building has a limited life (upon which to estimate depreciation costs) and the land is considered to have an unlimited life. Such an allocation definitely would affect how the earnings of the company are measured. Let us consider the following example.

Land and buildings for use as a factory were purchased for $100,000. The company paid $10,000 cash and signed a 5-year, 6% note for the balance. The $100,000 includes all commissions, attorneys' fees, and other costs. The management also had an independent appraiser value the purchase. The land was appraised at $41,000 and the building was appraised for $65,000. Based on these facts, the general journal entry presented below could be made for the purchase of the property. Because the allocations are estimates involving much uncertainty, it might be more appropriate to round off the allocations (to the nearest thousand dollars, for example) so as not to imply accuracy that does not exist in the valuation.

Land		38,679	
Buildings		61,321	
Cash			10,000
Notes payable			90,000
Allocation made between land and			
buildings on the basis of an			
independent appraisal.			

	Appraisal	*Allocation*	
Land	$ 41,000	$41/106 \times \$100,000 =$	$ 38,679
Buildings	65,000	$65/106 \times \$100,000 =$	61,321
	$106,000		$100,000

**DEPRECIATION
METHODS**

Early in this course, you learned that a major purpose of financial accounting is to match costs against the revenues produced so that the profitability of a firm can be measured during each operating period. Fixed assets are acquired and used to help firms accomplish their goals. Since fixed assets have limited useful lives (with the exception of land), there is an expense or sacrifice associated with acquiring and using plant and equipment in the production of earnings. This expense is called *depreciation expense.* Common methods for estimating this periodic cost of using the plant and equipment include (1) the straight-line method, (2) the output or units of production method, (3) the sum-of-the-years'-digits method, and (4) the declining-balance method. In addition to these four basic techniques, group or composite approaches to the estimation of depreciation are used from time to time. These methods are described below, using the following illustrative data:

■ *How is the use of plant and equipment recorded?*

1. Purchase price of the equipment, including sales taxes — $26,000
2. Date the equipment was purchased and placed in use — March 1, 1978
3. Freight charges on delivery of the equipment — $1,000
4. Installation charges — $3,000
5. Expected useful life, in time — 5 years
6. Expected useful life, in terms of output or production — 40,000 finished products to be produced by the machine
7. Salvage or scrap value of the machine at the end of its expected useful life — $2,000
8. Number of units produced by the machine in 1978 — 10,000 units

Straight-line method The **straight-line method** allocates the expense of using the equipment to the several periods on the basis of passage of time. This method might measure earnings reasonably well in those cases where the contribution of the asset to the production of revenues is more or less the same in each operating period.

$$\text{Depreciation expense (STRAIGHT-LINE)} = \frac{\text{Total cost to become expense}}{\text{Total number of years of estimated useful life}} \times \text{Fraction of current year the asset was used}$$

$$= \frac{\$28,000}{5 \text{ years}} \times \frac{10}{12}$$

$$= \$5,600 \times \frac{10}{12}$$

$$\text{Depreciation expense (1978)} = \$4,667$$

The total cost to become expense is computed thus:

$$\$26,000 + \$1,000 + \$3,000 - \$2,000 = \$28,000$$

Notice that the scrap value *reduces* the total depreciation cost to the company; the freight and installation charges are increases.

The asset was used only 10 months in 1978 because it was put into use on March 1, 1978. Therefore, the fraction of the current year the asset was used is 10/12.

Output or units of production method The **output method** allocates the cost of the assets to the several periods on the basis of the actual production of output by the asset. The calculation, based on our illustrative data, is as follows:

$$\text{Depreciation expense (OUTPUT or PRODUCTION)} = \frac{\text{Total cost to become expense}}{} \times \frac{\text{Fraction of total expected output produced this current period}}{}$$

$$= \$28,000 \times \frac{10,000 \text{ units}}{40,000 \text{ units}}$$

$$= \$28,000 \times 1/4$$

$$\text{Depreciation expense (1978)} = \$7,000$$

The total cost to become expense is calculated the same way as in the straight-line method.

Sum-of-the-years'-digits method The **sum-of-the-years'-digits method** is one of the *accelerated depreciation* methods because the technique produces larger depreciation expense in the early years of useful life of the asset and smaller expense in the later years. It is an arbitrary formula to report a decreasing depreciation expense over time. This method has been very popular in the preparation of tax returns, since larger depreciation expenses in early years of the asset's life tend to have the effect of postponing the payment of taxes. However, in the selection of a depreciation method for the financial statements, the main consideration is to choose a method that provides for a reasonable matching of the cost (of using the fixed asset) against the revenue which is produced in the period. Here is the calculation for 1978 using the sum-of-the-years'-digits method:

$$\begin{array}{l}
\text{Depreciation expense} \\
\text{(SUM-OF-THE-} \\
\text{YEARS'-DIGITS)}
\end{array} = \begin{array}{c}\text{Total cost} \\ \text{to become} \\ \text{expense}\end{array} \times \begin{array}{c}\text{Sum-of-the-} \\ \text{years'-digits} \\ \text{factor}\end{array} \times \begin{array}{c}\text{Fraction of} \\ \text{current year} \\ \text{asset was used}\end{array}$$

$$= \$28,000 \quad \times 5/15 \quad \times 10/12$$

$$\begin{array}{l}\text{Depreciation expense} \\ \text{(1978)}\end{array} = \$7,778$$

The sum-of-the-years'-digits factor, 5/15, is determined as shown in the following table and explained below.

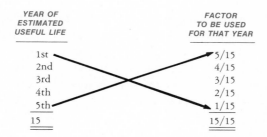

YEAR OF ESTIMATED USEFUL LIFE	FACTOR TO BE USED FOR THAT YEAR
1st	5/15
2nd	4/15
3rd	3/15
4th	2/15
5th	1/15
15	15/15

The sum of the years' digits—in this case 15—is used as the denominator of the factor for *each* year. The denominator also can be determined by the formula $(n + n^2)/2$, where n equals the number of years of useful life. The numerator of the factor is determined by *reversing* the order of the years' digits. Thus, for the first of five years the numerator is 5, for the second the numerator is 4, and so on to the fifth and last year, when the numerator is 1.

As a further explanation of the method, let's see what the depreciation expense would be for the next calendar year, 1979. Remember that as of January 1, 1979, the asset has been used previously only 10 months; therefore, two months remain in the first year of the asset's useful life. The calculation for the 12 months of 1979 therefore would involve 2 months at the 5/15 factor and 10 months at the 4/15 factor:

$$\begin{array}{l}\text{Depreciation expense} \\ \text{(1979)}\end{array} = \$28,000 \times 5/15 \times 2/12 = \$1,556$$

plus

$$\$28,000 \times 4/15 \times 10/12 = \underline{\quad 6,222\quad} \\ \underline{\underline{\$7,778}}$$

Declining-balance method The **declining-balance method** is also an accelerated depreciation method. It is appropriate in the measurement of earnings in those cases where the asset contributes to the production of earnings to a greater extent in its early life than in its later life. The method is as follows:

Depreciation expense (DECLINING BALANCE)	=	Book value at the beginning of the period	×	Declining balance factor	×	Fraction of current year asset was used
	=	$30,000	×	40%	×	10/12

$$\text{Depreciation expense (1979)} = \$10,000$$

The **book value** is defined as the balance to appear on the balance sheet, that is, the cost (asset account) less the balance of the accumulated depreciation account. The cost of this asset is $30,000. This is determined by adding the purchase price ($26,000), the freight cost ($1,000), and the installation charges ($3,000). *Notice that the salvage value is not relevant to the calculation.* Under this method, the net asset amount (Asset minus accumulated depreciation) would not be allowed to drop below the salvage value of $2,000.

The declining balance factor is an arbitrary factor. Often a factor which is equal to twice the straight-line rate is used. For example, if the asset has a useful life of 5 years, the straight-line rate is 1/5 or 20% per year. Twice the straight-line rate would be 2/5 or 40%. The 40% would be used *each* year in the computation.

Group and composite approaches Any individual firm might use a variety of depreciation methods for its several assets. The management of a company might feel that the straight-line method best measures the depreciation expense for one asset, whereas the output or units of production method might best measure depreciation on another asset. Of course, a firm would be expected to continue using the same method for an asset, once a method is chosen, in order to consistently measure earnings from period to period.

Two variations in the application of depreciation methods are the group approach and the composite approach. The **group approach** involves combining a number of more-or-less identical assets (such as typewriters) and computing the depreciation on the entire group, rather than computing depreciation for each asset separately. The **composite approach** is a variation that bases the depreciation computation on a group of similar, but not identical, assets (such as office equipment or delivery equipment). For example, all office equipment (such as typewriters, desks, filing cabinets, etc.) could be combined in determining a composite depreciation rate or basis.

The following is an illustration of a composite method:

ASSET	COST	COST TO BECOME EXPENSE (COST MINUS SALVAGE)	USEFUL LIFE	ANNUAL DEPRECIATION EXPENSE
Typewriter	$540	$500	10 years	$50
Filing cabinet	190	160	8	20
Desk	200	175	8	22
	$930			$92

The composite rate of depreciation is computed as follows for the office equipment:

$$\text{Annual rate} = \$92 \text{ divided by } \$930$$

$$\text{Annual rate} = 9.9\%$$

Therefore, each year's depreciation expense would be about 9.9% of the total cost of the office equipment group: 9.9% of $930. As new assets are added to the group, the same 9.9% can be used until it is determined that a new composite rate would be appropriate.

Objective of choosing a depreciation method The income statement and balance sheet are prepared and transmitted to investors, creditors, management, and others to aid them in their decisions relating to the firm. Therefore, choosing a depreciation method is concerned with matching costs with revenues to reflect earnings per share and with reporting the financial condition of the firm.

On the other hand, choosing a depreciation method in the preparation of the income tax return for the firm has a different purpose. This purpose is to minimize the taxes to be paid according to the tax laws or perhaps to postpone the payment of taxes, as allowed by the tax laws. Therefore, it is common for a firm to use one depreciation method on its financial statements and a different depreciation method on its tax return for the same asset. The income tax laws and their impact on business decisions will be treated in Chapter 24.

REPORTING PLANT AND EQUIPMENT ON THE BALANCE SHEET The balance sheet of a company reveals two basic items of information about the fixed assets: (1) the total cost of the assets when they were originally purchased, and (2) the remaining **service potential** of the assets (cost less the accumulated depreciation). Probably the second of these two figures is the most useful for readers of the balance sheet, because it tells them how many dollars of resources the management has committed to the plant and equipment of the company for use in the production of future earnings. And this is the figure that is added as part of the total assets of the firm on the balance sheet.

■ *How is plant and equipment reported on the balance sheet?*

Below is an example of the fixed asset section of a corporation balance sheet:

PARTIAL BALANCE SHEET

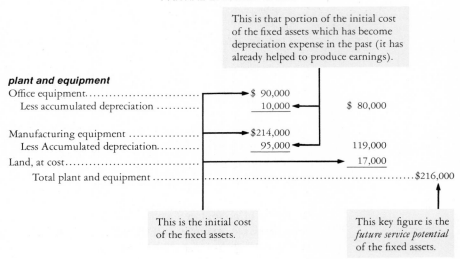

plant and equipment

Office equipment.............................	$ 90,000	
Less accumulated depreciation	10,000	$ 80,000
Manufacturing equipment	$214,000	
Less Accumulated depreciation...........	95,000	119,000
Land, at cost.................................		17,000
Total plant and equipment		$216,000

This is that portion of the initial cost of the fixed assets which has become depreciation expense in the past (it has already helped to produce earnings).

This is the initial cost of the fixed assets.

This key figure is the *future service potential* of the fixed assets.

A somewhat simpler way of showing fixed assets, and one many accountants prefer for published balance sheets, follows:

PARTIAL BALANCE SHEET

plant and equipment

Office equipment (net of accumulated depreciation of $100,000)	$ 80,000
Manufacturing equipment (net of accumulated depreciation of $95,000)	119,000
Land	17,000
Total plant and equipment	$216,000

Note that the *service potential* is given the most important position on each statement. *In corporate financial reporting it also is important to disclose either on the statements or in footnotes to the statements the depreciation method or methods used.* This lets the user of the financial statements more readily compare the earnings of a company to other companies, which may have used different methods of depreciation reporting.[1]

[1]For the current requirement for disclosure of accounting policies, see Accounting Principles Board Opinion No. 22, *Disclosure of Accounting Policies,* American Institute of Certified Public Accountants, 1972.

This section illustrates five common types of business transactions dealing with fixed assets. Understanding the accounting treatment of these transactions will help you interpret the information given by balance sheets and income statements. These common transactions involve: (1) selling fixed assets, (2) plant and equipment losses and retirements, (3) repairs and additions, and (4) use of small tools and similar equipment, and capital and revenue expenditures.

■ *What additional common transactions affect the reporting of plant and equipment?*

Selling fixed assets Plant and equipment items are purchased with the intent of using them in the production of services or goods for the organization. From time to time, however, it is desirable to dispose of an asset and to replace it. A later chapter treats this management decision process of replacing assets. The objective at this point is to show you the accounting procedures for recording sales of fixed assets.

Assume that a company had purchased a machine on January 1, 1977, for a total cost of $5,200. The machine was expected to last 4 years and was expected to have a scrap value of $400 at the end of that time. The annual depreciation on the straight-line basis is $1,200, computed as follows:

$$\frac{\$5,200 - \$400}{4 \text{ years}} = \$1,200$$

The regular depreciation entry was made at December 31, 1977. The **book value,** therefore, at the beginning of 1978 was $4,000. This is determined by subtracting the accumulated depreciation of $1,200 from the cost of $5,200. The management of the firm decides on March 1, 1978, to sell the equipment for $3,500 and to replace it with a more modern machine. The following two journal entries would be needed at March 1, 1978, to record the $200 depreciation for the first two months of 1978 and to record the sale:

1978 March	1	Depreciation expense—Equipment	200	
		Accumulated depreciation—Equipment		200
		To record depreciation for two months on equipment.		
	1	Cash	3,500	
		Accumulated depreciation—Equipment	1,400	
		Loss on sale of equipment	300	
		Equipment		5,200
		To record the sale of equipment with a book value of $3,800 cash.		

If the book value of equipment were less than the sales price of the equipment, a gain (with a credit balance) would be created in the journal entry.

The gain or the loss would be reported on the income statement of the firm for the period of the sale. The second journal entry illustrated above removes the balances of both the asset account and the accumulated depreciation account from the accounting records.

Plant and equipment losses and retirements When property is destroyed by fire or otherwise destroyed, damaged, or retired, an accounting entry must be made to show that the asset is no longer employed in the production of earnings. Two transactions are given as examples:

1. A piece of equipment with a cost of $10,000 and an accumulated depreciation balance of $7,000 is destroyed by fire. Only $1,000 is collected from insurance.
2. A piece of equipment with a cost of $5,000 and an accumulated depreciation balance of $5,000 is taken out of use and retired. There is no scrap value.

(1)	Cash	1,000	
	Fire loss (This account reduces net earnings for the period.)	2,000	
	Accumulated depreciation	7,000	
	Equipment		10,000
(2)	Accumulated depreciation	5,000	
	Equipment		5,000

Repairs and additions Repairs of plant and equipment can be classified as ordinary (expected and usual) and extraordinary. **Ordinary repairs** to fixed assets simply are debited to the appropriate expense account (such as Repairs expense) as they are incurred. The net earnings of the period when the repairs are made are then reduced. With **extraordinary repairs,** however, there is a somewhat different problem. In these cases, such as a major overhaul of a delivery truck, the benefit of the expenditure clearly extends over more than one accounting period. The total cost, therefore, must be allocated to several periods of the asset's life in order to measure earnings (match costs against revenue). This is usually accomplished by debiting the Accumulated depreciation account in the general journal as follows:

1978					
June	14	Accumulated depreciation—Trucks	1,200	
		Cash		1,200
		To record a major overhaul of the delivery truck: useful life is expected to be extended by three years.		

Notice that the asset account (Delivery trucks) is not debited for this extraordinary repair. Doing that would indicate that the *initial* cost of the trucks is $1,200 more than it actually was. Instead, the *net asset* (book value) to be depreciated is increased by the $1,200 by debiting Accumulated depreciation. This procedure allows the overhaul cost to be depreciated over the coming years.

Use of small tools and similar equipment, and capital and revenue expenditures
Often it is too expensive for a business firm to control and account for *all* its fixed assets on an item-by-item basis. For example, among some firms which use large numbers of small tools, such as wrenches and hammers, it is a common practice to periodically take a physical inventory of the tools on hand and to account for the tools in a manner similar to accounting for supplies. The beginning inventory of tools is recorded in the fixed asset account. Additional purchases are debited to that account. The ending inventory of tools determines the balance of the asset for the balance sheet, and any difference is debited to a Tools expense in an adjusting entry.

When equipment items cost so little that they are considered insignificant (not material) in relation to the firm's earnings, expenditures for them often are debited to an expense account, rather than to an asset account. The cost is reflected in one period, rather than being depreciated over several period's earnings. This procedure is justified because the transactions are not considered material and the cost of setting up the asset account and depreciation records would be excessive.

As a matter of terminology in accounting, expenditures of this kind that are debited to expense are known as **revenue expenditures** in that they have the effect of being deducted from revenue in the current period. Such expenditures that are debited to an asset account are known as **capital expenditures;** they do not reduce the capital of the firm until depreciation expenses are reported in the future. These costs are said to be *capitalized.*

CONTROLLING THE FIXED ASSETS OF A COMPANY

■ *How are plant and equipment subsidiary records kept?*

A major problem of management is to assure that fixed assets, once they are acquired, are accounted for and are physically controlled and protected from loss. A common procedure is to keep a subsidiary ledger or, in larger companies, computer records for the plant and equipment. There is thus a separate record of each asset, along with a record of the depreciation related to that asset. The form in Illustration 22-1 shows the useful information that can be recorded in a subsidiary ledger of plant and equipment. Such a ledger, of course, supports the plant and equipment and the accumulated depreciation accounts in the general ledger.

PLANT AND EQUIPMENT SUBSIDIARY LEDGER ACCOUNT

Name of asset _No. 7 Lathe_   Subsidiary ledger account _4296_

Date acquired _1/20/76_   General ledger account _$4,000_

From whom acquired _Barker_   Expected useful life _10 years_

Serial number _14692_   Estimated salvage _$2,000_

Current location _Plant 4_   Depreciation rate _10%_

Employee responsible for _Wilson_ Depreciation method _S.L._

Other information _____

Date	Ref.	Asset			Accumulated Depreciation		
		dr.	cr.	bal.	dr.	cr.	bal.
1976 Jan. 20	369	20,000		20,000			
Dec. 31	408					1,160	1,650
1977 Dec. 31	512					1,800	3,450

❯ NEW TERMS

book value The *net* figure for reporting assets on the balance sheet: cost less accumulated depreciation. [p. 381]

capital expenditure An expenditure which is treated as an asset acquisition; contrast with a revenue expenditure. [p. 383]

composite approach An approach to calculating depreciation, wherein a group of similarly used assets (such as all office furniture assets) are treated together in computing the depreciation. [p. 378]

declining-balance method A method of calculating depreciation expense; an accelerated depreciation method which allocates the expense of using the plant and equipment in greater amounts in early years of use and in lesser amounts in later years of use of the asset;

the allocation is made according to a fixed rate multiplied by the *book value* of the asset. [p. 378]

extraordinary repairs Unusual and substantial repairs of plant and equipment, the benefit of which extends over several accounting periods. Such expenditures are ordinarily debited to the Accumulated depreciation account. [p. 372]

group approach An approach to calculating depreciation, wherein a group of more-or-less identical assets are combined in the computation, rather than treating each of the assets separately. [p. 378]

ordinary repairs Usual and routine maintenance of plant and equipment, the benefit of which is assumed to be realized in the period the repairs are made. Such expenditures are ordinarily debited to an expense account. [p. 382]

output method A method of calculating depreciation expense; also called the *units of production method;* allocates the expense of using the plant and equipment to the periods of useful life on the basis of the actual production or output (use) of the asset. [p. 376]

plant and equipment subsidiary ledger A separate ledger or group of accounts to provide detailed information about a company's fixed assets; this ledger supports the general ledger accounts dealing with plant and equipment. [p. 384]

revenue expenditure An expenditure which is treated as an expense in the period of the expenditure; contrast with a capital expenditure. [p. 383]

service potential The value of an asset in helping to accomplish goals in the future; usually measured by the "book value" of an asset on the balance sheet (cost less accumulated depreciation). [p. 379]

straight-line method A method of calculating depreciation expense; allocates the expense of using the plant and equipment to the periods of useful life on the basis of the passage of time. [p. 375]

sum-of-the-years'-digits method A method of calculating depreciation expense; an accelerated depreciation method which allocates the expense of using the plant and equipment in greater amounts in early years of use and in lesser amounts in later years of use of the asset; the allocation is made according to a set of fractions. [p. 376]

» ASSIGNMENT MATERIAL

QUESTIONS

Q22-1. Contrast fixed assets and long-term investments.

Q22-2. Explain how the separate cost of land and buildings is determined when one sum is paid for land and buildings.

Q22-3. List the names of the commonly used depreciation methods.

Q22-4. Briefly describe how depreciation is computed under each of the methods in Q22-3.

Q22-5. What is meant by book value?

Q22-6. Can depreciation be different for income tax purposes than for financial statement purposes? Comment.

Q22-7. How is the service potential of fixed assets measured?

Q22-8. How are ordinary repairs accounted for?

Q22-9. How are extraordinary repairs accounted for?

Q22-10. Contrast revenue expenditures and capital expenditures.

Q22-11. What is the function of a fixed asset subsidiary ledger?

EXERCISES

E22-1. a. Assume land and buildings were purchased for a total cash price of $100,000. How would the total price ordinarily be allocated between land and buildings? Illustrate.

b. Compare and contrast the group approach and the composite approach to computing depreciation.

E22-2. Depp Company has acquired the following items of store equipment:

	COST	SALVAGE VALUE	USEFUL LIFE
Tables	$10,000	$1,000	10 years
Shelving	18,000	2,000	20 years
Cases	11,000	1,000	8 years
Cleaners	4,000	500	8 years

The company uses the *composite* method. In a fashion similar to the illustration in the text, compute the *composite rate* of depreciation that could be used each year. Round your answer to the nearest percent.

E22-3. Record the following transactions in general journal form:

   a. Added a wing to the manufacturing plant at a total cost of $23,400. A 10-year, 7% note payable was given for $15,000 and the balance was paid in cash.

   b. Purchased selling equipment (delivery trucks). Five trucks were purchased from Saluki Motors for $25,300 cash. This amount includes 4% sales taxes, $300 setup costs, and $900 freight charges.

   c. Invested in 400 shares of Gentilly, Inc., common stock. The shares cost $189.50 each. In addition, brokerage and other fees amounted to $650. Cash was paid.

   d. Carried a life insurance policy on the lives of certain of its employees. Paid the annual premium of $17,329. The increase in the cash surrender value is $2,300.

   e. Purchased a manufacturing plant and equipment from a competitor, Carrollton Company, for $294,000. Bonds payable (6%) were issued for the purchase. The Board of Directors agrees to report the acquisition in the following manner: 45% of the value purchased is to be assigned to the Land account; 45% of the value is considered the cost of the building; and the remainder is considered to be the cost of the equipment.

   f. The City Motor Company completely overhauled two of our delivery trucks. The cost, paid in cash, was $895.

   g. Repairs and maintenance charges for the fleet of trucks amounted to $653 during the year. $500 of this is paid in cash; the remainder is owed.

E22-4. Blevins Corporation purchased a machine to be used in the factory as follows:

Cost	$15,000
Delivery costs	100
Installation charges	500
Date purchased	September 1, 1978
Expected useful life	10 years
Expected useful life	20,000 hours of operating time
Salvage value expected at end of useful life	$1,500

Compute the depreciation expense for the year 1978 under each of the following methods:

   a. Straight-line method

   b. Output method, assuming that 750 hours of operating time were used in 1978.

   c. Sum-of-the-years'-digits method.

   d. Declining-balance method, assuming that twice the straight-line rate is used.

PROBLEMS (GROUP A)

P22-1. *Depreciation methods: computations.* A company purchased a machine to be used in its factory as follows:

Cost	$9,000
Delivery costs	75
Installation charges	400
Date purchased	April 1, 1978
Expected useful life	6 years
Expected useful life	10,000 hours of operating time
Salvage value expected at end of useful life	$500

Compute the depreciation expense for the year, 1978, under each of the following methods:

a. Straight-line method.

b. Output method, assuming that 1,000 hours of operating time were used in 1978.

c. Sum-of-the-years'-digits method.

d. Declining-balance method, assuming that twice the straight-line rate is used.

P22-2. *Depreciation methods; computations; book value.* Marth Company purchased a special-purpose spraying machine October 1, 1978, for $93,500 cash. This machine is expected to last about 8 years (until October 1, 1986), at the end of which time the expected scrap value is $4,000. During the 8-year period, it is estimated that 10,000,000 units of products will be sprayed with the aid of the machine.

During 1978, the machine was used to spray 500,000 products. During 1979, 2,000,000 units were sprayed; and during 1980, 2,100,000 units were sprayed.

REQUIRED: Make calculations and complete the following table:

DEPRECIATION METHOD	DEPRECIATION EXPENSE FOR 1978	DEPRECIATION EXPENSE FOR 1979	NET ASSET TO BE REPORTED ON BALANCE SHEET AT 12–31–80
Straight-line			
Production			
Sum-of-the-years'-digits			
Declining-balance (twice the straight-line rate)			

P22-3. *Journal entries, depreciation.* Habers Corporation, which closes its books annually on December 31, acquired the following equipment on September 1, 1978:

List price (catalog price)	$24,500
Less discount	1,300
Net price	$23,200
Freight	318
Installation	500
	$24,018

Scrap value, $2,000
Expected useful life, 8 years

The company bought the equipment on September 1, 1978, with a down payment of $6,000, and signing a 30-day, 7% note for the balance. On October 1, 1978, the note and interest were paid.

REQUIRED:

a. Assuming the sum-of-the-years'-digits method, prepare all entries for 1978 and 1979 (including purchase of the equipment, payment of the note and interest, and depreciation adjustments). Remember to use the 8/36 rate for the first full 12 months before switching to the 7/36 rate.

b. Prepare all entries for 1978 and 1979 under the straight-line method.

c. Prepare all entries for 1978 and 1979 under the declining-balance method, with a rate that is 150% of the straight-line rate.

d. Prepare all entries for 1978 and 1979 under the production method. The machine operated 96,400 hours during 1978 and 100,000 hours during 1979. The estimated useful life of the machine is 1 million hours.

PROBLEMS (GROUP B)

*P22-4. *Determine the missing data in the table on 389.*

P22-5. *Acquiring and using noncurrent assets.* Each of the following business transactions deals with noncurrent assets:

a. Paid routine maintenance costs on the delivery equipment, $632.

b. Purchased small tools with terms of 30 days, $113. The company accounts for these items with a fixed asset account called Small tools. An annual inventory of small tools is made to determine the adjusting entry.

c. Made *major* overhauls to two items of machinery (Machines 117 and 118), $5,114 cash.

d. Machine 209 was destroyed by fire. The fixed asset ledger showed a balance of $11,000 in the asset account and $5,000 in the accumulated depreciation account for this machine. Collected $3,200 in cash from fire insurance. Depreciation on this machine since the last adjusting entry until the time of the fire was $150.

e. Took the annual physical inventory of small tools. The beginning-of-year balance in the Small tools account was $9,214. At the end of the year, this account had a balance of $10,537. The physical inventory included tools amounting to $9,516. Make the adjustment.

f. Retired and sold for scrap Machine 827, which had a balance of $25,400 in the asset account and $25,100 in the accumulated depreciation account. Collected $190 from the scrap sale.

g. Sold Machine 246 for $22,000 cash. At the date of the last adjusting entry, this asset had a balance of $115,000, and the accumulated depreciation amounted to $90,000. Depreciation since the last adjusting entry was $5,000.

REQUIRED: Prepare all necessary journal entries.

*P22-6. *Analysis of plant and equipment changes.* The following table presents selected facts from the fixed asset ledger of Cranston Cake Company.

FIXED ASSET	AMOUNT OF ADJUSTING ENTRY FOR 1978	USEFUL LIFE	COST	SCRAP VALUE
No. 213	$11,667	8 years	$100,000	$10,000
No. 251	$400	10 years	$24,000	$1,000
No. 609	$1,074	9 years	$31,000	$2,000
No. 1519	$3,333	13 years	$60,000	$8,000
No. 2100	$47,500	7 years	$300,000	$15,000

Note: this problem continues on 390.

MACHINE	DATE OF PURCHASE	INVOICE COST	FREIGHT	INSTAL-LATION	TOTAL COST	useful life		output		DEPRECIATION METHOD	depreciation expense		BALANCE OF ACCUMULATED DEPRECIATION ACCOUNT AT 12-31-80	SCRAP VALUE
						YEARS	UNITS OF OUTPUT	1978	1979		1978	1979		
A	3-1-78	$10,000	$200	$500	$10,700	8	10,000	1,000	2,000	Straight-line	_____	_____	_____	$500
B	5-1-78	$20,000	_____	$600	$21,600	10	25,000	2,000	3,000*	Production	_____	_____	_____	$1,000
C	_____	$100,000	$2,000	$4,000	_____	10	50,000	6,000	6,000	Straight-line	$816.67	_____	_____	$8,000
D	9-1-78	_____	$3,000	$2,000	$109,000	5	50,000	6,000	6,000	_____	$14,533.33	_____	_____	$5,000
E	_____	$9,000	_____	$100	$9,500	6	10,000	1,000	2,000	_____	$2,142.86	_____	_____	$500
F	4-1-78	$10,000	$100	$300	_____	9	50,000	_____	6,000*	Production	$1,030.00	_____	_____	$100

*Output for 1980:
Machine B, 3,500 units
Machine F, 6,500 units

REQUIRED: For *each* of the five fixed assets, determine:

    a. The approximate date that the asset was bought in 1978. (All were bought during 1978). Show how you arrived at your answer.

    b. The depreciation method that was used. Each asset was depreciated a full number of months (no fraction of months).

PLANT AND EQUIPMENT TRADE-INS;
NATURAL RESOURCES; INTANGIBLE ASSETS

> **OBJECTIVE**

This unit, which completes your introductory study of noncurrent assets, has three basic objectives. First, you are introduced to the special problem of trading in fixed assets (as opposed to selling or retiring them). Second, the rules and concepts associated with accounting for and reporting natural resources are presented. And finally, the procedures and theory for reporting intangible assets are given.

> **APPROACH TO ATTAINING THE OBJECTIVE**

As you study about trade-ins, natural resources, and intangible assets, pay special attention to these five questions, which are answered in the text following:

- *What are two methods of reporting trade-ins of fixed assets?*
- *What is depletion?*
- *How are natural resources accounted for?*
- *What is amortization?*
- *How are intangible assets accounted for?*

Basically, there are two types of situations related to trading in an asset on another asset. In the first situation, an asset owned by the company is traded in on a different kind of asset. An example is trading in equipment on furniture—or trading in a delivery truck on a piece of manufacturing equipment. In such cases, the entry related to the trade-in will usually show a gain or a loss on the disposal of the asset. Since the two assets are different in nature, the gain or the loss on the asset that is disposed of (traded in) must be recognized separately from the cost of the new asset. The accounting procedure is illustrated in Case 1, which follows.

- *What are two methods
of reporting trade-ins
of fixed assets?*

CASE 1 TRADING IN AN ASSET ON A DIFFERENT KIND OF ASSET

**DESCRIPTION
OF CASE**

- *Background:*

Equipment was purchased on January 1, 1974, for $6,000 cash. Useful life was estimated to be 5 years, with a scrap value of $1,000. Straight-line depreciation was used. The balance sheet at the beginning of 1978 (January 1) showed the asset Equipment with a debit balance of $6,000 and the Accumulated depreciation—Equipment account with a credit balance of $4,000 (representing the annual depreciation of $1,000 per year for 4 years).

On *June 30, 1978,* the Equipment was traded in on *furniture.*

- *Details are:*

Actual cash value of furniture, if there were no trade-in	$ 9,400
List price of furniture	$10,000

- *Cash paid is
computed as follows:*

List price of furniture	$10,000
Less trade-in allowance given	2,275
Cash paid	$ 7,725

Now, using the facts above, we can illustrate the journal entries for the trade-in of an asset on another kind of asset.

1978					
June	30	Depreciation expense—Equipment		500	
		Accumulated depreciation—Equipment			500
		To record depreciation on equipment from beginning of the year until date it was traded in.			
	30	Furniture		9,400	
		Accumulated depreciation—Equipment		4,500	
		Cash			7,725
		Equipment			6,000
		Gain on disposal of equipment			175
		To record trade-in of equipment on furniture.			

This analysis will further explain the entries above:

1. Depreciation expense must be recorded for the first 6 months of 1978 on the Equipment for the measurement of 1978 earnings. See the first entry.

2. When an asset is disposed of, the accounting records must reflect this. Therefore, the asset (Equipment) was credited for $6,000; the Accumulated depreciation—Equipment account is reduced to zero by debiting it for $4,500. This is the January 1, 1978, balance of $4,000 plus the $500 from the first June 30 entry.

3. When an asset is acquired (Furniture), it is recorded at its *fair cash value*. This, as you learned, provides the reader of the balance sheet with a measure of all resources committed to the category.

4. A gain on the disposal of fixed assets was made in 1978, computed as follows:

Actual cash value of furniture	$9,400
Cash paid on transaction	7,725
Real trade-in allowance	$1,675
Book value of equipment ($6,000 cost less the amount utilized through use, $4,500)*	1,500
Gain	$ 175

*Equipment was used $4\frac{1}{2}$ years at a depreciation rate of $1,000 per year.

In the other situation, the asset is traded in on a similar asset—for example, a truck is traded in on another truck. In these cases, *no gain is recognized on the trade-in.* No gain is recognized because the trade-in is considered an intermediate step in the acquiring and using of the asset (the trucks in this case). The accounting procedures related to trade-ins of assets for similar assets is shown in Case 2, which follows:

CASE 2   TRADING IN AN ASSET ON A SIMILAR ASSET

DESCRIPTION OF CASE

▪ *Background:*

A truck was purchased on January 1, 1974, for $6,000 cash. Useful life was estimated to be 5 years, with a scrap value of $1,000. Straight-line depreciation was used. The balance sheet at the beginning of 1978 (January 1) showed the asset Trucks with a debit balance of $6,000 and the Accumulated depreciation—Trucks account with a credit balance of $4,000 (representing the annual depreciation of $1,000 per year for 4 years).

On *June 30, 1978,* the truck was traded in on a new truck.

■ *Details are:*

Actual cash value of new truck if there were no trade-in	$ 9,400
List price of new truck	$10,000

■ *Cash paid is computed as follows:*

List price of new truck	$10,000
Less trade-in allowance given	2,275
Cash paid	$ 7,725

Using the facts above, we can illustrate the journal entries for the trade-in of an asset on a similar asset.

1978					
June	30	Depreciation expense—Trucks		500	
		Accumulated depreciation—Trucks			500
		To record depreciation on the old truck from the beginning of the year until date it was traded in.			
	30	Trucks (new)		9,225	
		Accumulated depreciation—Trucks		4,500	
		Cash			7,725
		Trucks (old)			6,000
		To record trade-in.			

This analysis will further explain:

1. Depreciation expense must be recorded for the first 6 months of 1978 on the old truck, $500. See the first entry.

2. When an asset is disposed of, the accounting records must reflect this. Therefore the asset (Trucks) was credited for $6,000; the Accumulated depreciation—Trucks account is reduced to zero by debiting it for $4,500.

3. The new truck is recorded as follows: Cash paid ($7,725) plus book value of old truck traded in ($1,500). $7,725 + $1,500 = $9,225. The book value of $1,500 is determined by deducting the depreciation accumulated on the old truck ($4,000 plus $500 during the first 6 months of 1978) from the initial cost of $6,000.

This method just illustrated (where no gain or loss is recognized) has been referred to as the **income tax method,** because this approach has been required for income tax purposes for many trade-ins.

- *What is depletion?*

When a firm acquires natural resources, such as mining properties and oil interests, the accounting treatment is much the same as with other plant and equipment. The total initial cost is reported on the balance sheet as a noncurrent asset. The periodic usage of the asset is referred to as **depletion,** rather than as depreciation as in regular plant and equipment resources. The depletion is customarily computed on the basis of output or production. For example, assume that a firm paid $1,000,000 for mining rights. This purchase is expected to produce 2,000,000 tons of ore during the life of the resource. During the first year, 135,000 tons of ore were produced. The depletion rate is 50 cents per ton ($1,000,000 divided by 2,000,000 tons), and therefore the Depletion expense for the first year is $67,500, or 50 cents times 135,000 tons. The accounting entry is:

- *How are natural resources accounted for?*

| 1978 Dec. | 31 | Depletion expense | 67,500 | |
| | | Accumulated depletion—Mining properties | | 67,500 |

The December 31, 1978, balance sheet would report net Mining properties at $932,500, or the $1,000,000 cost less Accumulated depletion of $67,500.

This is another example of a case where the income tax laws differ from what is considered desirable for reporting information on financial statements for decision makers. The procedure just described allocates the proportion of the total cost of the mining properties that helped produce the revenue in 1978. The tax laws provide, however, that depletion be computed on an entirely different basis for different objectives. A later chapter describes the depletion concept for tax purposes. The tax concept of depletion is not directly related to the cost of the asset, as is the accounting concept of depletion.

- *What is amortization?*

Intangible assets usually are classified as a separate noncurrent category of assets on the balance sheet. They are recorded at their full cost and become expenses in a manner similar to plant and equipment items and natural resources. The using-up process for intangible assets is referred to as **amortization,** rather than as depreciation or depletion. Intangible assets simply have a different form, usually without the customary physical characteristics of other noncurrent assets. Common intangibles include patents, copyrights, trademarks, and organization costs.

Patents **Patents** are exclusive rights granted by the government to use and control inventions. These rights are issued by the United States Patent Office for a period of 17 years. If a firm purchased a patent from the inventor, the cost would be reflected on the balance sheet and would become an expense over its expected useful life, which ordinarily would be 17 years or a shorter period.

■ *How are intangible assets accounted for?*

Copyrights **Copyrights** are exclusive rights granted by the federal government to use and control literary and artistic works. Prior to 1978, these rights were granted for a period of 28 years and were renewable for another 28 years. Beginning in 1978, the federal law was changed so that copyrights are granted for the life of the creator plus 50 years (with rights going to heirs).

Like other intangible assets, the cost of copyrights are amortized (debited to expense) over their expected useful life. For example, a publishing company purchases a copyright from an author for $10,000. This acquisition, it is expected, will produce revenues for 4 years. At the date of purchase, the intangible asset account Copyrights would be debited for $10,000. At the end of each year, an expense account such as *Copyrights expense* or *Amortization of copyrights* would be debited and the Copyrights account would be credited for one-fourth of the cost.

Research and development costs Developing new products and services is vital to the growth of a business organization. These research costs tend to benefit the earnings of a number of accounting periods; therefore, many firms in the past capitalized these costs (recorded them as an asset) and amortized them over several accounting periods. Five years was a common useful life assumed for research and development intangibles. An example of a research and development cost would be expenditures for operating a laboratory to develop a new kind of chemical product. Recently, however, a ruling of the Financial Accounting Standards Board requires that such costs be treated as expenses when they are incurred. The Board believes that because of the *uncertainty* associated with any future benefits from these costs, they should not be treated as assets, but as expenses. In summary, research and development costs are recorded as **Research and development expenses.** Such costs reduce the net income in the period they are incurred, even if they are expected to benefit future periods.

Trademarks **Trademarks** are symbols or designs used to distinguish a firm's products or service. They are issued by the United States Patent Office. They are granted on a permanent basis, however, and become expenses over their expected useful life in contributing to the earnings of the firm.

Organization costs When a corporation is formed, certain costs are incurred to begin the company. These include attorneys' fees, fees paid the state in which the corporation is formed, and other costs involved with setting up the firm. Such **organization costs** are reported as assets, since these necessary costs aid in the production of earnings for much of the life of the company. Many firms arbitrarily assume that the useful life of this intangible is about 5 years, and accordingly they amortize the costs over that period.

Here is one final point about intangibles. It is not customary in modern accounting to use a contra account for intangibles. For example, there would be no account titled Accumulated amortization of patents. Instead, the asset account (Patents) would be credited *directly* in the adjusting entry, and the debit would go to a Patents expense account. The probable reason for this practice is that intangibles usually do not represent a significant portion of a company's resources; therefore, disclosure of the initial cost as well as the book value on the balance sheet does not provide vital information for the decision makers.

> **NEW TERMS**

amortization The using-up process in intangible assets; a sacrifice or expense of producing net earnings. [p. 395]

copyrights Exclusive rights granted by the federal government to use and control literary and artistic works. [p. 396]

depletion The using-up process in natural resources; a sacrifice or expense of producing earnings. [p. 395]

organization costs Cost incurred to organize and begin a corporation; an intangible asset. [p. 396]

patents Exclusive rights granted by the U.S. Patent Office to use and control inventions; granted for a period of 17 years; an intangible asset. [p. 395]

research and development costs Costs for improving or investigating some aspect of a company's operations. Charged to expense as incurred (not treated as assets). [p. 396]

trademarks Permanent rights granted by the U.S. Patent Office; an intangible asset; symbols or designs used by a firm to distinguish its products or services. [p. 396]

> **ASSIGNMENT MATERIAL**

QUESTIONS

Q23-1. What are the steps in recording the trade-in of an asset on a different kind of asset?

Q23-2. What are the steps in recording the trade-in of an asset on a similar kind of asset?

Q23-3. What is meant by the income tax method?

Q23-4. What is depletion?

Q23-5. What is amortization?

Q23-6. In general, how are intangible assets reported on financial statements?

Q23-7. Briefly identify each of the following:
    a. Patents.
    b. Copyrights.
    c. Research and development costs.
    d. Trademarks.
    e. Organization costs.

E23-1. The following accounts and balances were taken from the trial balance of Secretariat and Company at December 31, 1978, the end of the year's operations, before adjusting entries were made:

Mining properties	$300,000
Accumulated depletion—Mining properties	100,000
Small tools	18,000
Patents	12,000
Buildings	100,000
Accumulated depreciation—Buildings	10,000

Make adjusting entries for the following:

a. The mining properties are estimated to produce a total of 600,000 tons of ore during their entire useful life. During 1978, 11,000 tons were produced.

b. The patents originally had cost $17,000. Their useful life and legal life are assumed to be the same.

c. At the end of the year, small tools with a cost of $17,750 were still on hand.

d. The buildings have a useful life of 50 years, with a salvage value of $20,000. Straight-line depreciation is used.

E23-2. A computer was bought on January 1, 1974, for $75,000 cash. The useful life was estimated to be 6 years, with a salvage value of $10,000. Sum-of-the-years'-digits depreciation is used. On June 1, 1978, the computer was traded in on another computer. Details follow:

Actual cash value of new computer		$100,000
List price of new computer		$130,000
Cash paid:		
List-price	$130,000	
Trade-in allowance	50,000	
Cash paid	$ 80,000	

The company closes its books each December 31 and prepares adjusting entries annually. Prepare the accounting entries needed at June 1, 1978.

E23-3. Assume the same facts as in E23-2, except that the trade-in is on a different kind of asset. Make the necessary entries.

E23-4. Tangco, Inc., purchased patents as follows:

PATENT	DATE OF PURCHASE	COST	USEFUL LIFE
16952	1-1-78	$50,000	3 years
14318	3-1-78	$100,000	for production of 350,000 units of output
36115	12-1-78	$72,318	6 years

Patent 14318 lead to the production of 35,000 units in 1978 and 100,000 units in 1979. Prepare journal entries for the following:

a. Purchase of the patents for cash

b. Adjusting entries at December 31, 1978

c. Adjusting entries at December 31, 1979

PROBLEMS (GROUP A)

P23-1. *Plant and equipment transactions; trade-ins.* Following is a *partial* trial balance of the Elysian Corporation.

Elysian Corporation
PARTIAL TRIAL BALANCE
December 31, 1977

Delivery truck	10,000	
Accumulated depreciation—Delivery truck		6,000
Machine A	50,000	
Accumulated depreciation—Machine A		40,000
Machine B	15,000	
Accumulated depreciation—Machine B		5,000
Machine C	9,000	
Accumulated depreciation—Machine C		3,000
Machine D	11,000	
Accumulated depreciation—Machine D		10,000
Building	112,000	
Accumulated depreciation—Building		72,000
Land	50,000	
Mining properties	150,000	
Accumulated depletion—Mining properties		50,000
Patents	14,000	

Using the information above, prepare journal entries for these transactions, which occurred during 1978:

Feb. 1 Sold the delivery truck for $4,100 cash. The depreciation expense for the month of January on the truck has not been recorded yet, and amounts to $300.

March 1 Machine A was destroyed by fire. The insurance proceeds amounted to only $4,000. Depreciation expense on this item for January 1, 1978, through February 28, 1978, amounts to $400.

April 1 Traded in Machine B on a new machine (Machine E). The depreciation expense on Machine B from the first of the year until the trade-in amounts to $1,000. Machine E (new) has a cash purchase price of $20,000 and has a list or catalog price of $23,000. In addition to the trade-in, we paid $10,500 cash. Machine B and Machine E are considered *unlike* assets.

May   1 Paid $400 cash for routine repairs to the machines.

June 1 Paid $6,000 cash for a major overhaul of Machine D.

Dec. 31 Made the adjusting entry for Patent amortization. Patent expense is estimated to be 1/17 of the original cost of the patents, which was $17,000. The patents were acquired on January 1, 1975.

      31 Made the adjusting entry for depletion of mining properties, which were originally acquired for $150,000. The properties, at that time, were estimated to produce a total of 150,000 tons of ore during their useful life. During 1978, 10,000 tons of ore were produced.

P23-2. *Trade-ins.* The trial balance of a firm at December 31, 1977, after adjusting entries had been made showed the following accounts and balances:

| Lathing equipment | $17,000 |
| Accumulated depreciation—Lathing equipment | $11,000 |

On March 31, 1978 the lathing equipment was traded in on new lathing equipment. The old lathing equipment originally had a useful life of 15 years, with a salvage value of $2,000. Straight-line depreciation is used. The new lathing equipment has a catalog price of $23,000, and a cash price of $20,000. Cash amounting to $16,000 was paid with the trade-in:

Catalog price of new equipment	$23,000
Trade-in allowance	7,000
Cash paid	$16,000

REQUIRED:

a. Make all entries at March 31, 1978, assuming the trade-in is on a similar asset.
b. Make all entries at March 31, 1978, assuming the trade-in is on a different kind of asset.

P23-3. *Trade-ins.* At December 31, 1977, the Plant and equipment section of the balance sheet of MWT Company follows. At June 1, 1978, the management decided to trade in all the display equipment.

plant and equipment

Buildings (net of $1,000,000 accumulated depreciation)	$29,000,000
Manufacturing equipment (net of $1,000,000 accumulated depreciation)	11,000,000
Display equipment (net of $90,000 accumulated depreciation)	10,000

1. The list price of the new (similar) display equipment is $240,000. A trade-in allowance of $25,000 was given, leaving a balance of $215,000 before sales taxes of 5% and before installation charges of $9,000.
2. The cash price of the new equipment (excluding sales taxes and installation) is estimated by the management of MWT Company to be $220,000. The old equipment was assumed to have a 10-year useful life, with no scrap value, when it was purchased on January 1, 1969.

REQUIRED:

Record the accounting entry in general journal form to reflect the trade-in. Remember that depreciation has not yet been recorded on the old equipment during 1978.

**PROBLEMS
(GROUP B)**

P23-4. *Plant and equipment transactions.* Make journal entries for the following business transactions:

1978

March 1   Purchased manufacturing equipment for $10,700 cash, including sales taxes of $500, installation charges of $100, and freight charges of $100. Salvage value is $1,000 and useful life is 4 years, with straight-line depreciation.

April   30   Purchased land, buildings, and store equipment as follows:

Purchase price	$500,000
Legal fees and other costs	$7,000
Down payment	$100,000
7% 1-year note signed for	$407,000

Appraisals of the property were as follows:

Land	$140,000
Buildings	300,000
Store equipment	70,000
	$510,000

Round to the nearest dollar.

Dec.   1   Traded in the manufacturing equipment purchased on March 1 on new similar equipment:

Cash price of new equipment	$20,000
Less trade-in allowance	11,000
Cash paid	$ 9,000

The new equipment has a useful life of 5 years, with a scrap value of $500.

31   Made the depreciation adjusting entry for the buildings purchased on April 30. The useful life is 30 years, and the straight-line method is used. Salvage value is $1,000.

31   Made the depreciation adjusting entry for the store equipment purchased on April 30. The useful life is 8 years, and the declining-balance method is used. Salvage value is $8,000.

31   Made the depreciation adjusting entry for the manufacturing equipment acquired on December 1 (sum-of-the-years'-digits).

31   Made the adjusting entry for interest on the note signed April 30.

P23-5.   *Depletion and amortization.* These five assets appeared on the balance sheet of Brown Bread Bakers, Inc., at December 31, 1978:

ASSET	DATE ACQUIRED	COST	TOTAL PRODUCTION OR USEFUL LIFE	12–31–77 NET ASSET BALANCE	PRODUCTION DURING 1978
Patents	3–1–75	$60,000	100,000 units	$50,400	18,000 units
Copyrights	6–1–76	$100,000	5 years	$68,333	—
Mineral properties	1–1–77	$3,000,500	1,000,000 tons	$2,700,450	116,000 tons
Organization costs	4–1–74	$12,500	5 years	$3,125	—
Trademarks	7–31–77	$10,000	6 years	$9,306	—

REQUIRED:

a. Prepare an adjusting journal entry for each of the five assets at December 31, 1978, for amortization or depletion.

b. Calculate the net asset balance of each of these assets to appear on the December 31, 1978, balance sheet of the company.

*P23-6. *Plant and equipment analysis.* The fixed asset (equipment) ledger of Fall and Winter Products Company showed this information:

LEDGER NUMBER	DESCRIPTION	DATE PURCHASED	COST	USEFUL LIFE (YEARS)	SALVAGE VALUE	DEPRECIATION METHOD
1857	X-iron	3–1–74	$ 50,000	8	$1,000	Sum-of-the-years'-digits
1859	Scoop	1–31–75	12,900	10	500	Declining balance (150% of straight-line)
1865	Wedger	1–1–76	38,750	15	–0–	Straight-line
1881	Auto-Mixer	10–1–77	10,000	7	1,000	Sum-of-the-years'-digits
1892	Jolter	5–31–77	62,100	9	3,100	Declining balance (2 times straight line)
			$173,750			

At December 31, 1977, the Equipment account in the general ledger had a debit balance of $173,750. These transactions dealing with equipment took place during 1978:

Feb. 1 Purchased a Z-Baser for $9,000, signing a 6%, 60-day note for $9,000. The Z-Baser is expected to have a useful life of 7 years and a $500 salvage value. The sum-of-the-years'-digits method will be used on this equipment.

March 31 Traded in the Scoop on a new Scoop that had a cash value of $16,000. Paid cash amounting to $9,000 in addition to the old Scoop.

June 1 Sold the Jolter for $56,000 cash.

Oct. 31 Purchased a new B-Wedger for $40,000, paying $10,000 cash and signing a 9%, 90-day note for the balance. The new B-Wedger has an expected useful life of 15 years. The straight-line method is used.

Dec. 1 Traded in the old Wedger (purchased on 1–1–76) for an Automatic Screener (a different kind of asset), paying $16,250 cash. The Automatic Screener will have a useful life of 8 years (straight-line method) and a salvage value of $1,000. The Automatic Screener has a cash value of $50,000.

REQUIRED:

a. Prepare all entries related to the equipment transactions during 1978. Show all supporting calculations.

b. Prepare the adjustment for depreciation of equipment at December 31, 1978.

c. Prepare a schedule showing all equipment on hand at December 31, 1978, with the balance of the asset and the accumulated depreciation at that time.

P23-7. *Cumulative review problem.* Selected transactions dealing with long-term investments, plant and equipment, natural resources, and intangible assets follow. The company prepares adjusting entries and closes its books each December 31.

1978

Jan. 1   Purchased bonds as a long-term investment from Elysian Corporation. The bonds are 10-year bonds and have a face amount of $80,000. They bear 7% interest, payable each June 30 and December 31. Total cost of the bonds was $75,000.

March 3   Paid the annual premium on the life insurance policy for executives, $9,000. The increase in the cash surrender value of the policy is $1,500.

April 12   Bought land as an investment, paying $25,000 cash and signing a 5-year, 12% note for $75,000.

Land cost	$ 95,000
Brokerage fees	3,000
Attorneys fees	2,000
	$100,000

15   Bought 100 shares of BC common stock as an investment. Paid $9,000 cash for the shares. Cost basis is used.

May 1   Collected $95 dividends on the stock bought on April 15.

June 30   Collected interest on the bond investment.

July 3   Purchased a 20% interest in Bee Company, paying $100,000 cash for the common shares (equity method).

Oct. 12   Completely overhauled two pieces of store equipment, paying $3,000 cash.

15   Paid routine repairs on store equipment, $950.

Nov. 1   Purchased manufacturing equipment, land, and buildings for $10,000 cash and signed a 10-year, 7% note for $90,000.

appraisals

Land	$ 30,000
Buildings	50,000
Equipment	28,000
	$108,000

Dec. 31   Bee Company made a total of $30,000 in net income for 1978. See the July 3 investment.

31   Bee Company paid a total of $10,000 in dividends.

31   Made the adjustment for small tools. The 1-1-78 balance of the account was $9,720. Additional tools of $6,400 were bought during 1978. The ending inventory showed that $15,200 of tools were on hand.

31   Collected interest on the bond investment.

31   Made the needed adjusting entry for interest on the bonds.

31   Made the adjusting entry for depreciation on Type B furniture under the *composite method.* Compute the rate based on the following. The furniture had been in use all year.

ITEM	COST	SALVAGE VALUE	USEFUL LIFE
Chairs	$20,000	$2,000	8 years
Tables	11,000	1,000	10 years
Desks	50,000	4,000	7 years
Counters	4,000	500	8 years
	$85,000		

31 Recorded depletion on mineral properties that had cost $595,000 and were expected to produce 750,000 barrels of minerals. During 1978, production was 115,000 barrels.

31 Recorded amortization on a patent that had been bought $2\frac{1}{2}$ years ago for $10,000 cash. It had a useful life of 6 years.

REQUIRED: Record the transactions in general journal form.

P23-8. *Cumulative review problem.* Each of the following situations is an independent case.

1. Purchased 6% bonds on January 1, 1978, as a long-term investment, with $75,000 face amounts with interest to be collected each December 31. The bonds mature in 19 years and cost a total of $70,000, including brokerage fees of $300.

2. Purchased land, buildings, and equipment for $85,000 cash on March 1, 1978. The land was appraised at $15,000, the buildings at $50,000, and the equipment at $25,000. The equipment has a useful life of 8 years and the buildings will be depreciated over 25 years. The salvage value of the buildings is $1,000, and the salvage value of the equipment is $500. Straight-line depreciation will be used on the buildings, and the declining balance method (twice the straight-line rate) will be used for the equipment.

3. Traded in old equipment on May 1, 1978, for new equipment with a cash value of $15,000 and a list price of $18,000. The old equipment was purchased on July 31, 1976, for $10,000. It had a scrap value of $500 and a useful life of 8 years. The sum-of-the-years'-digits method is used on this type of equipment. The company prepares adjusting entries and closes its books annually on December 31. The new equipment will have a salvage value of $500 and a useful life of 8 years. $6,000 cash was paid as part of the trade-in agreement.

REQUIRED:

a. For case 1 above, record all entries associated with the bond investment for 1978 and 1979. Also, assume the bonds were sold for $100 above their book value (net amount on the books) at December 31, 1981. Prepare the entry to record the sale of the investment.

b. For case 2 above, record all entries associated with the purchase of the assets and the associated depreciation for 1978 and 1979.

c. For case 3 above, record all entries to be made dealing with the equipment for 1978 and 1979.

chapter 10
payrolls; liability concepts

> ## OBJECTIVE

The purpose of this unit is to describe and analyze the process of preparing and administering payrolls. You will be introduced here to both the financial accounting and the procedural aspects of payrolls.

> ## APPROACH TO ATTAINING THE OBJECTIVE

As you study about payrolls, give special attention to these three questions, which the text following answers:

- *What are the liabilities associated with payrolls?*
- *How are payroll transactions recorded?*
- *What special records are involved in payroll systems?*

Reporting the compensation (pay) of employees is an important part of accounting for business organizations. The two basic financial accounting goals are: (1) to accurately measure and report the expense (such as salaries and wages) on the income statement of the appropriate period, and (2) to accurately measure and report the liabilities associated with employee compensation (such as salaries payable and taxes withheld) on the balance sheet.

There are three general groups of liabilities connected with **payrolls.** They are (1) liabilities for employee compensation, (2) liabilities for payroll deductions, and (3) liabilities for the employer's payroll taxes. The following paragraphs discuss each of these three groups.

■ *What are the liabilities associated with payrolls?*

Liabilities for employee compensation As the employees of a business firm perform their services, the company (their employer) incurs an expense. Therefore, the earnings of the company are reduced in the accounting period that the services are performed. Likewise, a liability is created for the compensation owed the employees. It is important to distinguish between *employees* of a firm and others such as *independent contractors.* A firm might pay for legal services, the services of a public accountant, or the services of a painter to do maintenance work. In such cases, fees are charged for the work done by the independent contractor but no employer-employee relationship is created. And the rules related to payroll taxes and deductions do not apply.

SALARIES AND WAGES. The compensation of those employees who perform managerial and administrative tasks is often referred to as **salaries.** And the term **wages** is used to refer to the pay of employees who perform physical- or manual-type work for a company. The basis of pay for salaried employees is usually stated on a monthly or annual basis. For example, a production manager might be paid for his services at the rate of $1,200 per month. Wages, on the other hand, are often expressed in terms of an hourly rate, such as $3.75 per hour.

BONUSES. In addition to regular salaries and wages, some employees are paid bonuses. A **bonus** is an extra amount of compensation for an employee. Often the bonus is based on some special performance or contribution the employee makes. For example, a salesman's bonus might be a percent of the sales he makes, and a company's general manager might be paid as a bonus a percent of his firm's net earnings.

Here is an example of how a manager might share in a company's earnings. We will use these facts in our example:
Now, these three items—

$$B = \text{Bonus}$$

$$E = \$100,000$$

$$T = \$50,000 - 0.50B$$

will be used in the example of bonus plans in Illustration 24-1 that follows.

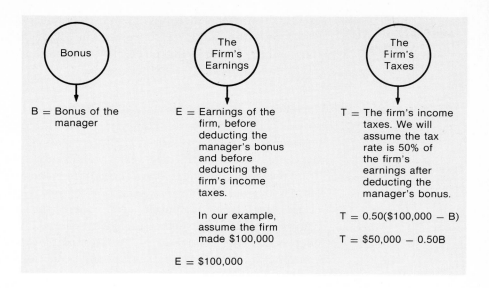

Bonus	**The Firm's Earnings**	**The Firm's Taxes**
B = Bonus of the manager	E = Earnings of the firm, before deducting the manager's bonus and before deducting the firm's income taxes.	T = The firm's income taxes. We will assume the tax rate is 50% of the firm's earnings after deducting the manager's bonus.
	In our example, assume the firm made $100,000	T = 0.50($100,000 − B)
	E = $100,000	T = $50,000 − 0.50B

OVERTIME. Some firms also include **overtime** as part of their employee compensation program. The wages for a group of employees, for example, might be $4.00 per hour, except that *time and a half* (a form of overtime pay) is paid to employees who work more than 8 hours a day or who work on Saturdays and Sundays. Assume that an employee worked during the week as follows:

	TOTAL HOURS WORKED	REGULAR TIME (HOURS)	OVERTIME (HOURS)
Monday	8	8	0
Tuesday	9	8	1
Wednesday	$8\frac{1}{2}$	8	$\frac{1}{2}$
Thursday	10	8	2
Friday	8	8	0
Saturday	4	0	4
Total	$47\frac{1}{2}$	40	$7\frac{1}{2}$

Total wages due the employee therefore would be $205, calculated as follows:

$$40 \text{ hours of regular time @ } \$4.00 = \$160.00$$
$$7\tfrac{1}{2} \text{ hours of overtime @ } \$6.00 \quad = \quad \underline{45.00}$$
$$\underline{\$205.00}$$

Liabilities for payroll deductions The tax laws in the United States require that employers deduct certain taxes from the compensation of employees and

ILLUSTRATION 24-1

EXAMPLES OF BONUS PLANS

Plan A: The manager receives a bonus of 20% of the earnings of the firm before deducting the bonus and income taxes.	*Plan B:* The manager receives a bonus of 20% of the earnings of the firm after deducting the bonus, but before deducting the income taxes.	*Plan C:* The manager receives a bonus of 20% of the earnings of the firm after deducting income taxes, but before deducting the bonus.	*Plan D:* The manager receives a bonus of 20% of the earnings of the firm after deducting both the bonus and income taxes.

Plan A:

$$B = 0.20(E)$$
$$= 0.20(\$100,000)$$
$$= \$20,000$$

Plan B:

$$B = 0.20(E - B)$$
$$= 0.20(\$100,000 - B)$$
$$= \$20,000 - 0.20B$$

$$1.20B = \$20,000$$
$$B = \$16,667$$

Plan C:

$$B = 0.20(E - T)$$
$$= 0.20[\$100,000 - (\$50,000 - 0.50B)]$$
$$= 0.20(\$100,000 - \$50,000 + 0.50B)$$
$$= \$20,000 - \$10,000 + 0.10B$$

$$0.9B = \$10,000$$
$$B = \$11,111$$

Plan D:

$$B = 0.20(E - T - B)$$
$$= 0.20[\$100,000 - (\$50,000 - 0.50B) - B]$$
$$= 0.20(\$100,000 - \$50,000 + 0.50B - B)$$
$$= \$20,000 - \$10,000 + 0.10B - 0.20B$$

$$1.10B = \$10,000$$
$$B = \$9,091$$

remit (send payment of) these taxes directly to the government. These deductions represent liabilities of the company (employer) until the amounts are sent to the governmental bodies.

In addition to tax deductions, employers and employees often agree to have other amounts deducted for such services to employees as hospitalization insurance, life insurance, and purchase of U.S. Savings Bonds.

The federal income tax laws provide that each employee fill out an **employee's withholding allowance certificate,** commonly known as a W-4 form (see Illustration 24-2). This form is filled out by the employee and given to the employer when the employee is hired. The W-4 form provides information about the payroll deductions that should be made for federal income taxes. For example, assume that an employee, John Elliot, is married and has three children. He would write on the W-4 form one allowance for himself, one for his wife, and three for his children—a total of five allowances. The employer uses this information to decide what amount to deduct (withhold) from employee's pay for federal income taxes. The government provides a series of **withholding tables** for the company to use in computing the amount of income tax to be withheld from the pay of employees. The table shown as Illustration 24-3 is an example.

Assume that John Elliot's total salary for the month amounts to $1,200. In that case, according to the withholding table illustrated, his employer must withhold income taxes amounting to $128.90 (note that this amount is circled in the table) and must remit this to the government.

Another kind of deduction that employers must withhold from the

ILLUSTRATION 24-2

| Form **W-4** (Rev. May 1977) Department of the Treasury Internal Revenue Service | **Employee's Withholding Allowance Certificate** (Use for Wages Paid After May 31, 1977) This certificate is for income tax withholding purposes only. It will remain in effect until you change it. If you claim exemption from withholding, you will have to file a new certificate on or before April 30 of next year. |

Type or print your full name
JOHN Elliot

Your social security number
461 - 50 - 0298

Home address (number and street or rural route)
2500 Westshire Boulevard

City or town, State, and ZIP code
Hammond, TX   77029

Marital Status
☐ Single   ☑ Married
☐ Married, but withhold at higher Single rate

Note: If married, but legally separated, or spouse is a nonresident alien, check the single block.

1 Total number of allowances you are claiming   5

2 Additional amount, if any, you want deducted from each pay (if your employer agrees) . . . . $

3 I claim exemption from withholding (see instructions). Enter "Exempt" . . . .

Under the penalties of perjury, I certify that the number of withholding exemptions and allowances claimed on this certificate does not exceed the number to which I am entitled. If claiming exemption from withholding, I certify that I incurred no liability for Federal income tax for last year and that I anticipate that I will incur no liability for Federal income tax for this year.

Signature ▶ John Elliot   Date ▶ 1/4 , 19 78

MARRIED Persons — MONTHLY Payroll Period

And the wages are—		And the number of withholding allowances claimed is—										
At least	But less than	0	1	2	3	4	5	6	7	8	9	10 or more
		The amount of income tax to be withheld shall be—										
$0	$208	$0	$0	$0	$0	$0	$0	$0	$0	$0	$0	$0
208	212	.30	0	0	0	0	0	0	0	0	0	0
212	216	1.00	0	0	0	0	0	0	0	0	0	0
216	220	1.60	0	0	0	0	0	0	0	0	0	(
220	224	2.30	0	0	0	0	0	0	0	0	0	0
224	228	3.00	0	0	0	0	0	0	0	0	0	0
228	232	3.70	0	0	0	0	0	0	0	0	0	0
232	236	4.40	0	0	0	0	0	0	0	0	0	0
236	240	5.00	0	0	0	0	0	0	0	0	0	(
240	248	6.10	0	0	0	0	0	0	0	0	0	0
248	256	7.40	0	0	0	0	0	0	0	0	0	0
256	264	8.80	0	0	0	0	0	0	0	0	0	0
264	272	10.10	0	0	0	0	0	0	0	0	0	0
272	280	11.50	.90	0	0	0	0	0	0	0	0	0
280	288	12.90	2.20	0	0	0	0	0	0	0	0	0
288	296	14.20	3.60	0	0	0	0	0	0	0	0	0
296	304	15.60	5.00	0	0	0	0	0	0	0	0	0
304	312	16.90	6.30	0	0	0	0	0	0	0	0	0
312	320	18.30	7.70	0	0	0	0	0	0	0	0	0
320	328	19.70	9.00	0	0	0	0	0	0	0	0	0
328	336	21.00	10.40	0	0	0	0	0	0	0	0	0
336	344	22.40	11.80	1.10	0	0	0	0	0	0	0	0
344	352	23.70	13.10	2.50	0	0	0	0	0	0	0	0
352	360	25.10	14.50	3.90	0	0	0	0	0	0	0	0
360	368	26.50	15.80	5.20	0	0	0	0	0	0	0	0
368	376	27.80	17.20	6.60	0	0	0	0	0	0	0	0
376	384	29.20	18.60	7.90	0	0	0	0	0	0	0	0
384	392	30.50	19.90	9.30	0	0	0	0	0	0	0	0
392	400	31.90	21.30	10.70	0	0	0	0	0	0	0	0
400	420	34.30	23.70	13.00	2.40	0	0	0	0	0	0	0
420	440	38.10	27.10	16.40	5.80	0	0	0	0	0	0	0
440	460	42.10	30.50	19.80	9.20	0	0	0	0	0	0	0
460	480	46.10	33.90	23.20	12.60	2.00	0	0	0	0	0	0
480	500	50.10	37.60	26.60	16.00	5.40	0	0	0	0	0	0
500	520	54.10	41.60	30.00	19.40	8.80	0	0	0	0	0	0
520	540	58.10	45.60	33.40	22.80	12.20	1.60	0	0	0	0	0
540	560	62.10	49.60	37.10	26.20	15.60	5.00	0	0	0	0	0
560	580	66.10	53.60	41.10	29.60	19.00	8.40	0	0	0	0	0
580	600	70.10	57.60	45.10	33.00	22.40	11.80	1.10	0	0	0	0
600	640	76.10	63.60	51.10	38.60	27.50	16.90	6.20	0	0	0	0
640	680	84.10	71.60	59.10	46.60	34.30	23.70	13.00	2.40	0	0	0
680	720	92.10	79.60	67.10	54.60	42.10	30.50	19.80	9.20	0	0	0
720	760	100.10	87.60	75.10	62.60	50.10	37.60	26.60	16.00	5.40	0	0
760	800	107.20	95.60	83.10	70.60	58.10	45.60	33.40	22.80	12.20	1.60	0
800	840	114.00	103.40	91.10	78.60	66.10	53.60	41.10	29.60	19.00	8.40	0
840	880	120.80	110.20	99.10	86.60	74.10	61.60	49.10	36.60	25.80	15.20	4.50
880	920	127.60	117.00	106.30	94.60	82.10	69.60	57.10	44.60	32.60	22.00	11.30
920	960	134.40	123.80	113.10	102.50	90.10	77.60	65.10	52.60	40.10	28.80	18.10
960	1,000	141.20	130.60	119.90	109.30	98.10	85.60	73.10	60.60	48.10	35.60	24.90
1,000	1,040	148.00	137.40	126.70	116.10	105.50	93.60	81.10	68.60	56.10	43.60	31.70
1,040	1,080	154.80	144.20	133.50	122.90	112.30	101.60	89.10	76.60	64.10	51.60	39.10
1,080	1,120	161.60	151.00	140.30	129.70	119.10	108.50	97.10	84.60	72.10	59.60	47.10
1,120	1,160	168.40	157.80	147.10	136.50	125.90	115.30	104.60	92.60	80.10	67.60	55.10
1,160	1,200	177.90	164.60	153.90	143.30	132.70	122.10	111.40	100.60	88.10	75.60	63.10
1,200	1,240	187.90	172.30	160.70	150.10	139.50	(128.90)	118.20	107.60	96.10	83.60	71.10
1,240	1,280	197.90	182.30	167.50	156.90	146.30	135.70	125.00	114.40	103.80	91.60	79.10
1,280	1,320	207.90	192.30	176.70	163.70	153.10	142.50	131.80	121.20	110.60	99.60	87.10
1,320	1,360	217.90	202.30	186.70	171.00	159.90	149.30	138.60	128.00	117.40	106.80	95.10
1,360	1,400	227.90	212.30	196.70	181.00	166.70	156.10	145.40	134.80	124.20	113.60	102.90
1,400	1,440	237.90	222.30	206.70	191.00	175.40	162.90	152.20	141.60	131.00	120.40	109.70

(Continued on next page)

ILLUSTRATION 24-3

MARRIED Persons — MONTHLY Payroll Period

And the wages are—		And the number of withholding allowances claimed is—										
At least	But less than	0	1	2	3	4	5	6	7	8	9	10 or more
		The amount of income tax to be withheld shall be—										
$1,440	$1,480	$247.90	$232.30	$216.70	$201.00	$185.40	$169.80	$159.00	$148.40	$137.80	$127.20	$116.50
1,480	1,520	257.90	242.30	226.70	211.00	195.40	179.80	165.80	155.20	144.60	134.00	123.30
1,520	1,560	269.10	252.30	236.70	221.00	205.40	189.80	174.20	162.00	151.40	140.80	130.10
1,560	1,600	280.30	262.80	246.70	231.00	215.40	199.80	184.20	168.80	158.20	147.60	136.90
1,600	1,640	291.50	274.00	256.70	241.00	225.40	209.80	194.20	178.50	165.00	154.40	143.70
1,640	1,680	302.70	285.20	267.70	251.00	235.40	219.80	204.20	188.50	172.90	161.20	150.50
1,680	1,720	313.90	296.40	278.90	261.40	245.40	229.80	214.20	198.50	182.90	168.00	157.30
1,720	1,760	325.10	307.60	290.10	272.60	255.40	239.80	224.20	208.50	192.90	177.30	164.10
1,760	1,800	336.30	318.80	301.30	283.80	266.30	249.80	234.20	218.50	202.90	187.30	171.70
1,800	1,840	347.50	330.00	312.50	295.00	277.50	260.00	244.20	228.50	212.90	197.30	181.70
1,840	1,880	358.70	341.20	323.70	306.20	288.70	271.20	254.20	238.50	222.90	207.30	191.70
1,880	1,920	370.90	352.40	334.90	317.40	299.90	282.40	264.90	248.50	232.90	217.30	201.70
1,920	1,960	383.70	363.70	346.10	328.60	311.10	293.60	276.10	258.60	242.90	227.30	211.70
1,960	2,000	396.50	376.50	357.30	339.80	322.30	304.80	287.30	269.80	252.90	237.30	221.70
2,000	2,040	409.30	389.30	369.30	351.00	333.50	316.00	298.50	281.00	263.50	247.30	231.70
2,040	2,080	422.10	402.10	382.10	362.20	344.70	327.20	309.70	292.20	274.70	257.30	241.70
2,080	2,120	434.90	414.90	394.90	374.90	355.90	338.40	320.90	303.40	285.90	268.40	251.70
2,120	2,160	447.70	427.70	407.70	387.70	367.70	349.60	332.10	314.60	297.10	279.60	262.10
2,160	2,200	461.10	440.50	420.50	400.50	380.50	360.80	343.30	325.80	308.30	290.80	273.30
2,200	2,240	475.50	453.30	433.30	413.30	393.30	373.30	354.50	337.00	319.50	302.00	284.50
2,240	2,280	489.90	467.40	446.10	426.10	406.10	386.10	366.10	348.20	330.70	313.20	295.70
2,280	2,320	504.30	481.80	459.30	438.90	418.90	398.90	378.90	359.40	341.90	324.40	306.90
2,320	2,360	518.70	496.20	473.70	451.70	431.70	411.70	391.70	371.70	353.10	335.60	318.10
2,360	2,400	533.10	510.60	488.10	465.60	444.50	424.50	404.50	384.50	364.50	346.80	329.30
2,400	2,440	547.50	525.00	502.50	480.00	457.50	437.30	417.30	397.30	377.30	358.00	340.50
2,440	2,480	561.90	539.40	516.90	494.40	471.90	450.10	430.10	410.10	390.10	370.10	351.70
2,480	2,520	576.30	553.80	531.30	508.80	486.30	463.80	442.90	422.90	402.90	382.90	362.90
2,520	2,560	590.70	568.20	545.70	523.20	500.70	478.20	455.70	435.70	415.70	395.70	375.70
2,560	2,600	605.10	582.60	560.10	537.60	515.10	492.60	470.10	448.50	428.50	408.50	388.50
2,600	2,640	619.50	597.00	574.50	552.00	529.50	507.00	484.50	462.00	441.30	421.30	401.30
2,640	2,680	633.90	611.40	588.90	566.40	543.90	521.40	498.90	476.40	454.10	434.10	414.10
2,680	2,720	648.30	625.80	603.30	580.80	558.30	535.80	513.30	490.80	468.30	446.90	426.90
2,720	2,760	662.70	640.20	617.70	595.20	572.70	550.20	527.70	505.20	482.70	460.20	439.70
2,760	2,800	677.10	654.60	632.10	609.60	587.10	564.60	542.10	519.60	497.10	474.60	452.50
2,800	2,840	691.50	669.00	646.50	624.00	601.50	579.00	556.50	534.00	511.50	489.00	466.50
2,840	2,880	705.90	683.40	660.90	638.40	615.90	593.40	570.90	548.40	525.90	503.40	480.90
2,880	2,920	720.30	697.80	675.30	652.80	630.30	607.80	585.30	562.80	540.30	517.80	495.30
2,920	2,960	734.70	712.20	689.70	667.20	644.70	622.20	599.70	577.20	554.70	532.20	509.70
2,960	3,000	749.10	726.60	704.10	681.60	659.10	636.60	614.10	591.60	569.10	546.60	524.10
3,000	3,040	763.50	741.00	718.50	696.00	673.50	651.00	628.50	606.00	583.50	561.00	538.50
3,040	3,080	777.90	755.40	732.90	710.40	687.90	665.40	642.90	620.40	597.90	575.40	552.90
3,080	3,120	792.30	769.80	747.30	724.80	702.30	679.80	657.30	634.80	612.30	589.80	567.30
3,120	3,160	806.70	784.20	761.70	739.20	716.70	694.20	671.70	649.20	626.70	604.20	581.70
3,160	3,200	821.10	798.60	776.10	753.60	731.10	708.60	686.10	663.60	641.10	618.60	596.10
3,200	3,240	835.50	813.00	790.50	768.00	745.50	723.00	700.50	678.00	655.50	633.00	610.50
3,240	3,280	849.90	827.40	804.90	782.40	759.90	737.40	714.90	692.40	669.90	647.40	624.90
3,280	3,320	864.30	841.80	819.30	796.80	774.30	751.80	729.30	706.80	684.30	661.80	639.30
3,320	3,360	878.70	856.20	833.70	811.20	788.70	766.20	743.70	721.20	698.70	676.20	653.70
3,360	3,400	893.10	870.60	848.10	825.60	803.10	780.60	758.10	735.60	713.10	690.60	668.10
3,400	3,440	907.50	885.00	862.50	840.00	817.50	795.00	772.50	750.00	727.50	705.00	682.50
3,440	3,480	921.90	899.40	876.90	854.40	831.90	809.40	786.90	764.40	741.90	719.40	696.90
3,480	3,520	936.30	913.80	891.30	868.80	846.30	823.80	801.30	778.80	756.30	733.80	711.30
3,520	3,560	950.70	928.20	905.70	883.20	860.70	838.20	815.70	793.20	770.70	748.20	725.70
3,560	3,600	965.10	942.60	920.10	897.60	875.10	852.60	830.10	807.60	785.10	762.60	740.10
3,600	3,640	979.50	957.00	934.50	912.00	889.50	867.00	844.50	822.00	799.50	777.00	754.50
		36 percent of the excess over $3,640 plus—										
$3,640 and over		986.70	964.20	941.70	919.20	896.70	874.20	851.70	829.20	806.70	784.20	761.70

salaries and wages of employees is the **FICA tax.** This tax, created by the Federal Insurance Contributions Act, currently amounts to 5.85% of the total annual pay of employees, up to a limit of $16,500. An employee's earnings in excess of $16,500 in any one year are not subject to the tax. The FICA tax rate has changed over the years, as has the maximum employee compensation that is subject to the tax. Therefore, *to simplify the computations for the purposes of this course, you can assume that the rate is 6% on the first $12,000 of earnings of each employee per year.* Use this information in working the problems at the end of this unit.

The FICA tax is used by the government in administering and providing benefits under the social security program. Benefits include old-age benefits, survivors benefits, old-age health programs (Medicare), and other programs.

A third group of deductions from the pay of employees might include the following:

1. Deductions for hospitalization insurance premiums.
2. Deductions for life insurance premiums.
3. Deductions for the purchase of U.S. Savings Bonds.
4. Deductions for employee retirement and pension plans.

These deductions, like those for federal income tax and FICA tax, become liabilities of the company until they are paid by the company to the appropriate party—such as to the government or to the appropriate insurance company.

Liabilities for the employer's payroll taxes Employers must pay certain taxes associated with payrolls. These taxes are expenses of the company and reduce the earnings in the period that the taxes are incurred. Likewise, a liability for the amount owed the governmental body is created when the taxes are incurred. The liability is extinguished when the government is paid. Three common employer's payroll taxes are (1) FICA tax on the employer, (2) federal unemployment compensation tax, and (3) state unemployment compensation tax.

Our earlier discussion indicated that the *employee* pays FICA tax and that this tax is withheld from his pay and remitted to the government by the employer. According to the Social Security laws, the *employer* also must pay FICA tax to help support the Social Security program. *For the purposes of this course, you can assume that the employer also pays FICA tax amounting to 6% of the first $12,000 earned by each employee every year.*

A second kind of payroll tax is the **federal unemployment compensation tax.** This tax supports a program to provide funds for employees who are unemployed (unemployment compensation benefits). The tax is paid by the *employer* only (it is not withheld from the pay of employees), and is based upon a percentage of the total pay of each employee. *For the purposes of this course, you can assume that the tax rate is 0.5% ($\frac{1}{2}$ of 1%) on the first $4,200 earned by an employee in any one year.*

A third kind of payroll tax is the **state unemployment compensation tax.** This tax supports the same unemployment insurance program as the federal unemployment compensation tax. The federal and state governments cooperate in the administration of the program. The state unemployment compensation tax is paid by the *employer* only (it is not withheld from employees), and is based upon a percentage of the total pay of each employee. *For the purposes of this course, you can assume that the rate of the tax is 2.5% of the first $4,200 earned by an employee in any one year.*

RECORDING PAYROLL TRANSACTIONS

■ *How are payroll transactions recorded?*

We will now use an example to illustrate how a payroll is prepared and how payroll transactions are recorded. To simplify the illustration, we have made three assumptions: (1) that our example firm has only three employees, (2) that the employees are paid monthly, and (3) that the firm's financial statements are prepared at the end of each month. Here are the facts of the case:

John Elliot is employed as the manager of the firm. His rate of pay is $1,200 per month. He has five withholding allowances and has earned $11,900 previously this year from the company. He has agreed to have $10 per month deducted from his pay for the United Fund.

William Jones works in the store and is paid $4 per hour and time and a half for overtime. Overtime is computed as the number of hours he works per month in excess of 165. This month, he worked 170 hours. He has three withholding allowances and has earned $4,900 previously this year from the company. He has agreed to have $3 per month deducted from his pay for the United Fund.

Thomas Wilson also works in the store and is paid $5 per hour for *all* hours worked. He has two withholding allowances and has earned $3,000 previously this year from the company. This month he worked 160 hours.

The firm's payroll would be computed as follows. First, the total pay of each employee is calculated:

1. Elliot: $1,200.
2. Jones: 165 hours $\times$ $4 = $660
             5 hours $\times$ $6 = $\underline{30}$
                                    $690
3. Wilson: 160 hours $\times$ $5 = $800.

Then, by consulting the withholding table (Illustration 24-3), the federal income tax owed by each employee is calculated:

1. Elliot: $1,200 with five allowances = $128.90
2. Jones: $690 with three allowances = $54.60
3. Wilson: $800 with two allowances = $91.10

Next, remember that we are assuming that the FICA rate is 6% on the first $12,000 of earnings of each employee per year. Therefore, the FICA tax for each employee in our example is calculated as follows:

1. Elliot: Because $11,900 had been previously earned this year, only $100 of this month's pay is subject to FICA tax: $100 × 6% = $6.
2. Jones: $690 × 6% = $41.40.
3. Wilson: $800 × 6% = $48.00.

The table below summarizes all of this information along with the United Fund deductions and the net pay calculations.

PAYROLL
Month of December, 1978

		deductions			
EMPLOYEE	TOTAL PAY	FEDERAL INCOME TAX	FICA TAX	UNITED FUND	NET PAY
1. J. Elliot	$1,200.00	$128.90	$ 6.00	$10.00	$1,055.10
2. W. Jones	690.00	54.60	41.40	3.00	591.00
3. T. Wilson	800.00	91.10	48.00	–0–	660.90
	$2,690.00	$274.60	$95.40	$13.00	$2,307.00

Based on the information summarized in this table, the payroll for the month of December can be recorded in the general journal:

1978				
Dec.	31	Administrative salaries expense	1,200.00	
		Sales salaries expense	1,490.00	
		Federal income taxes withheld		274.60
		FICA tax withheld		95.40
		Payable to United Fund		13.00
		Salaries payable		2,307.00
		To record the December payroll.		

Next, three paychecks can be written and the entries can be made in the cash payments journal:

			CASH PAYMENTS JOURNAL							page 15
DATE		ACCOUNT DEBITED	CK. NO.	PR	GENERAL ACCOUNTS DEBIT	ACCOUNTS PAYABLE DEBIT	PURCHASES DEBIT	PURCHASES DISCOUNTS CREDIT	CASH CREDIT
1978 Dec.	31	Salaries payable (J. Elliot)	294		1,055.10					1,055.10
	31	Salaries payable (W. Jones)	295		591.00					591.00
	31	Salaries payable (T. Wilson)	296		660.90					660.90

The company also must record the employer payroll taxes in the general journal. These taxes are computed as follows:

1. *FICA tax.* The tax is 6% on the first $12,000 earned by employees. This is the *same* as the amount deducted from the pay of employees: $95.40 (see payroll).
2. *Federal unemployment compensation tax.* The tax is 0.5% of the total pay of each employee on the first $4,200 earned each year. Elliot has already exceeded the $4,200, so no tax is due on his December salary (see the facts of the case). Jones also has exceeded the $4,200, so therefore no tax is due on his salary. Wilson has earned $3,000 previously, so his entire $800 is subject to the tax: $800 × 0.5% = $4. Therefore, the federal unemployment compensation tax for this entire payroll amounts to only $4.
3. *State unemployment compensation tax.* This tax is 2.5% of the total pay of each employee on the first $4,200 earned each year. Elliot and Jones both have exceeded the $4,200, so no tax is due on their salaries. Wilson has earned $3,000 previously, so the entire $800 is subject to the tax: $800 × 2.5% = $20. Therefore, the state unemployment compensation tax for this payroll amounts to $20.

Based on this information, the employer's payroll taxes for the month of December can be recorded in the general journal:

1978					
Dec.	31	Payroll taxes expense		119.40	
		Employer's FICA taxes payable			95.40
		Federal unemployment taxes payable			4.00
		State unemployment taxes payable			20.00
		To record the employer's payroll taxes			
		for December.			

Every 3 months (more often in some cases) a company must prepare the necessary reports to the governmental bodies (state and federal). A company also must submit then the amounts due from employee withholdings and from payroll taxes. At that time the appropriate liabilities are debited and cash is credited for the amounts remitted.

In summary, these liabilities have been created through payroll transactions and must be debited in the cash payments journal when the cash is credited:

Federal income taxes withheld.

FICA tax withheld.

Payable to United Fund.

Salaries payable.

Employer's FICA taxes payable.

Federal unemployment taxes payable.

State unemployment taxes payable.

Another employee deduction which is often present is the *State income taxes withheld.* In some states, the state income tax is withheld from the employee's pay and remitted to the state government.

SPECIAL PAYROLL RECORDS AND FORMS

As additional information about payrolls, three special records and forms are illustrated in this section. They are (1) the *wage and tax statement,* (2) the *employer's quarterly Federal tax return,* and (3) the *employee earnings record.*

■ *What special records are involved in payroll systems?*

Wage and tax statement The **wage and tax statement** is shown in Illustration 24-4. The federal government provides these forms. Each year the employer prepares one of these forms for each employee. Several copies of the form are prepared and given to the employee at the end of the year. The employee uses the information contained in this statement to prepare his income tax return

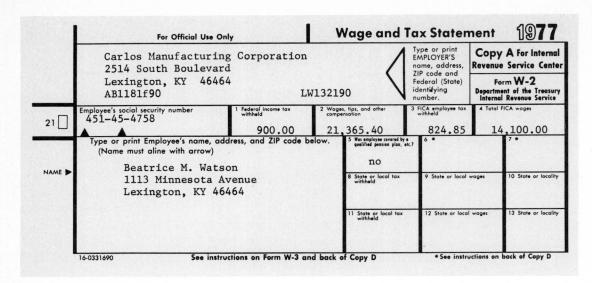

ILLUSTRATION 24-4

for the year. Note that the statement includes information about the amount of federal income tax withheld, the amount of FICA tax withheld, and the amount of total wages that were subject to income tax withholding during the year.

Employer's quarterly federal tax return The employer uses the **employer's quarterly federal tax return,** commonly called Form 941, to give the government details about the payroll of the company during each 3-month period. Information submitted on the form includes the name and Social Security number of each employee, the amount of salaries and wages of each employee, and amount of federal income tax withheld from the pay of employees. Of course, the amounts due the government are submitted with this tax return, including amounts of income tax withheld, FICA tax withheld, and FICA tax on the employer. This tax return form is shown in Illustration 24-5. The circled numbers on the illustration simply point out fourteen key areas on the form that must be filled out.

Employee earnings record Most companies keep individual records (similar to a subsidiary ledger) of payroll data for each employee, called **employee earnings records.** These records include information such as total earnings of the employee, FICA withheld, Federal income tax withheld, other deductions, and net pay. One such record is shown in Illustration 24-6.

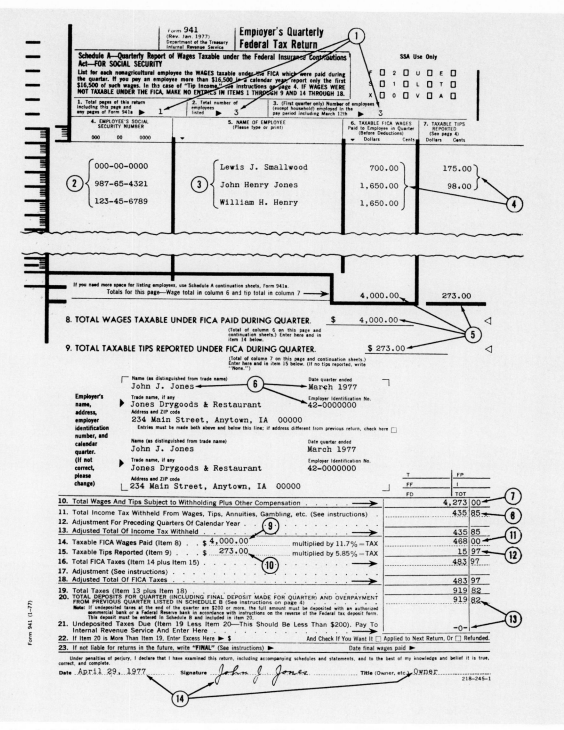

Reprinted from *Circular E, Employer's Tax Guide,* Internal Revenue Service, May, 1977, U.S. Government Printing Office, Washington, D.C., p. 11.

ILLUSTRATION 24-5

UNIT 24
chapter 10 419

EMPLOYEE EARNINGS RECORD

Name	Susan B. Derose	Number of exemptions	3
Address	5524 Charlotte Ave.	Rate of pay	$1,400/month
	New York, N.Y. 10010	Soc. Sec. No.	512-20-1154
Telephone	(212) 111-1115	Date employed	1/1/72

Date 1978	Hours Worked		Compensation			Deductions			Net Pay
	Regular	Overtime	Regular	Overtime	Total	Fed. Inc. Tax	FICA	Other	
1/31			1,400.00			191.00	84.00		1,125.00
2/28			1,400.00			191.00	84.00		1,125.00
3/31			1,400.00			191.00	84.00		1,125.00
Totals 1st. Qtr.			4,200.00			573.00	252.00		3,375.00
Totals 4th Qtr.			5,100.00			612.00	306.00		4,182.00
Totals Year			18,600.00			2,370.00	1,116.00		15,114.00

ILLUSTRATION 24-6

❯ NEW TERMS

bonus An extra amount of compensation for an employee, often based upon performance of the employee, such as a percentage of the total sales made by a salesman. [p. 407]

employee earnings record Individual records (subsidiary ledger) of the payroll information for each employee of a firm. [p. 418]

employee's withholding allowance certificate Commonly known as the W-4 form. This form is completed by the employee and given to the employer to provide information about the withholding allowances of the employee, so that the appropriate amount of income tax can be withheld from his pay. [p. 410]

employer's quarterly federal tax return Commonly known as Form 941. It is used by the employer to provide details to the government regarding the payroll of the company during each 3-month period. [p. 418]

federal unemployment compensation tax A tax levied on employers only; relates to the program which provides funds for employees who become unemployed; administered jointly with the state programs involving unemployment compensation. [p. 413]

FICA tax Tax related to the Federal Insurance Contributions Act; this tax is used by the government in administering and providing benefits in the social security program. The tax is levied on both the employee and the employer. [p. 413]

overtime The hours worked by an employee in excess of a base amount. For example, all hours worked per day in excess of 8 might be classified as overtime; overtime often carries a higher rate per hour than regular time. [p. 408]

payroll Refers to the list of employees to be paid for their services, along with details of the amounts due and the related deductions from the pay of the employees. [p. 407]

salaries The compensation of those employees who perform managerial and administrative tasks. [p. 407]

state unemployment compensation tax A tax levied on employers only; relates to the program which provides

funds to employees who become unemployed; administered jointly with the federal program involving unemployment compensation. [p. 414]

wage and tax statement Commonly known as the W-2 form. This form is completed by the employer and is given to the employee at the end of the year as a basis for preparing the employee's tax return; includes such information as the amount of federal income tax withheld, the amount of FICA tax withheld, and the total wages of the employee. [p. 417]

wages The compensation of employees who perform physical- or manual-type work. [p. 407]

withholding table A table prepared by the federal government to guide the employer in deducting income tax from the pay of employees. [p. 410]

▶ ASSIGNMENT MATERIAL

QUESTIONS

Q24-1. What are the two basic financial accounting goals regarding payrolls?

Q24-2. What are three general groups of liabilities that arise in connection with payrolls?

Q24-3. Contrast salaries and wages.

Q24-4. What is a bonus?

Q24-5. What is the function of the W-4 form?

Q24-6. List four liabilities that are created through payroll deductions.

Q24-7. Is the FICA tax paid by both employees and employers? Is the federal unemployment compensation tax paid by both employees and employers?

Q24-8. List and describe three liabilities for employer's payroll taxes.

Q24-9. What is the function of Form 941?

Q24-10. What is the function of the W-2 form?

Q24-11. What is the function of an employee earnings record?

EXERCISES

E24-1. Assume that Ruth Johnson earned $1,214 during the month of March, 1978. If she is married and has a total of four withholding allowances, how much federal income tax would be withheld from her pay in March?

E24-2. Julian Brandt, an employee of Carl Beeler and Associates, earns $4 per hour and time and a half for overtime. Overtime is any time worked in excess of 8 hours *each day*. Brandt has seven withholding allowances, and $17 of federal income taxes are to be withheld from his pay this week. The United Fund deduction amounts to $10. Brandt worked as follows this week:

Monday	8 hours
Tuesday	7 hours
Wednesday	11 hours
Thursday	8 hours
Friday	9 hours
	43

Compute Brandt's:

a. Regular pay.
b. Overtime pay.
c. Gross (total) pay.
d. FICA tax withheld.
e. Net pay (amount to be paid Brandt).

E24-3. Eunice Brown is the Executive Vice-President of Water Products, Inc. Each year, as part of her compensation, she receives a bonus of 3% of the earnings of the company after deducting both the bonus and income taxes. The company's tax rate for 1978 was 40% and the company's earnings before deducting the bonus and income taxes amounted to $200,000 for 1978. Compute Brown's bonus and the *net* earnings of the firm.

E24-4. The Board of Directors of Water Products, Inc. (see E24-3), in an attempt to build employee and executive morale, proposes that Brown's bonus (as well as certain other executives) in the future be computed on the basis of earnings after taxes, but before deducting the bonus. How much of a raise would this be for Brown, assuming the same level of company earnings and assuming the same firm income tax rate?

PROBLEMS (GROUP A)

P24-1. *Preparation of payroll; journal entries.* The following information is known about the payroll of SA Corporation for the month of December, 1978:

EMPLOYEE	PAY BASIS	TOTAL EARNINGS THIS YEAR BEFORE THIS PAYROLL	NUMBER OF WITHHOLDING ALLOWANCES	REGULAR TIME HOURS	OVERTIME HOURS
L. Abbott	$1,000 monthly	$11,400	3	—	—
J. Costello	$4 per hour[a]	2,800	6	160	10
L. Louis	$7 per hour[a]	4,100	2	160	2
H. Martin	$6 per hour[a]	2,700	2	160	-0-

[a] Time and a half is paid for overtime.

For the purposes of this problem, use the tables and rates provided in this unit

REQUIRED:

a. Prepare a payroll similar to the one illustrated in the text. Show and label all your computations. There is a deduction of $10 per month from each employee's pay for life insurance.
b. Record the payroll in general journal form.
c. Record the payment of the four employees in *general journal form* (four entries).
d. Record the employer's payroll taxes in general journal form.

*P24-2. *Analysis of payroll; entries.* The records of Bobbie Robin Co. for the year reveal that employees of the firm earned $318,490 during 1978. $25,650 of that amount was not subject to FICA taxes; $39,500 of that amount was not subject to state and federal unemployment compensation taxes. Record in general journal form the payroll taxes of the employer for the year, setting up the liabilities for the amounts due.

*P24-3. *Bonus computation.* The following table shows the profit-sharing details for three executives of Crete Operating Co., which has a current income tax rate of 42%.

NAME	BASIS OF BONUS CALCULATION
Wilton Barker, President	10% of earnings of the company after deducting both bonus and income taxes. Do not consider the bonuses of the Vice President and Production Manager when computing the President's bonus.
Bettye R. Frye, Vice-President	50% of the amount of the President's bonus.
Harry Wayne, Production Manager	50% of the amount of the President's bonus.

During 1978, the company produced earnings as shown in the following income statement.

Crete Operating Co.
INCOME STATEMENT
For the Year Ended December 31, 1978

Sales		$560,000
Other revenue		20,000
		$580,000
Cost of goods sold	$100,000	
Selling expenses	118,000	
General expenses	69,000	
Executive bonuses:		
Barker	?	
Frye	?	
Wayne	?	
Income tax expense	?	
Total expenses	?	?
Net earnings		$?

REQUIRED: Complete the income statement. Show all calculations.

P24-4. *Payroll computations.*

Part A
Edwin Veep works for Johnathan Company. He is paid at the rate of $3 per hour, with time and a half pay for hours worked in excess of 40 hours per week. Prior to this week's payroll, Veep has earned $4,050 this year with the firm. He is married and has two children, for a total of four withholding allowances. This week Edwin Veep worked 43 hours.

Answer the following questions regarding Veep's pay and related taxes for the week, using the tables and rates in the unit.

a. What is the amount of Veep's total pay for the week?
b. How much FICA tax would be deducted from his pay?
c. How much FICA tax would the *employer* owe (payroll tax) regarding Veep's salary this week?
d. How much federal unemployment compensation tax would the *employer* owe (payroll tax) regarding Veep's salary this week?
e. How much state unemployment compensation tax would the *employer* owe (payroll tax) regarding Veep's salary this week?
f. If Veep had already earned $12,200 prior to this week's payroll during the year, how much FICA tax would be withheld from this week's salary?

Part B

Jane Higgins was employed as a secretary for Higgins and Company. She earns $4.50 per hour and time and a half for overtime. Overtime is any time worked in excess of 8 hours each day. Jane has one withholding allowance, and $20 of federal income taxes are to be withheld from her pay this week. The hospitalization insurance deduction amounts to $15. Jane worked as follows this week:

Monday	8 hours
Tuesday	8 hours
Wednesday	10 hours
Thursday	7 hours
Friday	9 hours

REQUIRED: Compute Ms. Higgins':

a. Regular pay
b. Overtime pay
c. Gross (total) pay
d. FICA tax withheld
e. Net pay (amount to be paid Ms. Higgins)

P24-5. *Preparation of payroll.*

Part A

The following information is known about the payroll of Caribbean Corporation for the month of September, 1978:

EMPLOYEE	PAY BASIS	TOTAL EARNINGS THIS YEAR BEFORE THIS PAYROLL	NUMBER OF WITHHOLDING ALLOWANCES	REGULAR TIME HOURS	OVERTIME HOURS	UNITED FUND DEDUCTION	HOSPITAL- IZATION INSURANCE DEDUCTION
M. Clabert	$1,700	$11,000	3	—	—	$20	$6.34
A. Rogers	$8 per hour[a]	2,500	2	170	12	10	3.18
I. Rogers	$10 per hour[b]	9,500	2	80	3	25	3.18

[a] Time and a half for overtime.

[b] Double-time for overtime ($20 per hour for overtime).

For purposes of this problem, use the tables and rates provided in the unit.

REQUIRED:

    a. Prepare a payroll similar to the one illustrated in the text. Show and label all your computations. There is a deduction of $10 per month from each employee's pay for life insurance.

    b. Record the payroll in general journal form.

    c. Record the payment of the three employees in *general journal form* (three entries).

    d. Record the employer's payroll taxes in general journal form.

Part B

The following information is known about the payroll of Costello Corporation for the month of August, 1978.

	employee		
	J. HENDERSON	L. LANDRY	P. CASANOVA
Pay Basis	$ 1,500	$ 7.50 per hour	$10.00 per hour
Total Earnings This Year			
Before This Payroll	10,500	2,500	6,000
Number of Withholding			
Allowances	2	2	4
Regular Time Hours	—	90	135
Overtime Hours[a]	—	5	7
United Fund Deduction	30	10	20
Hospitalization Insurance			
Deduction	22.40	22.40	50.75

[a] Double-time for overtime.

For purposes of this problem, use the tables and rates provided in the unit.

REQUIRED:

    a. Compute the total pay for each employee.

    b. Compute the total deductions withheld for each employee.

    c. Compute the net pay for each employee.

    d. Record the payroll in general journal form.

    e. Record the payment of the three employees in general journal form (three entries).

*P24-6. *Bonus calculation.* Edgar Johnson is considering accepting a position as President with Nessie Industries. His pay basis would be as follows:

$$\text{Annual pay} = 10\% \text{ of the earnings of the company after deducting Johnson's pay and income taxes.}$$

Income taxes will be 40%. *Net earnings* of Nessie Industries were as follows:

1977	$296,000
1976	290,000
1975	291,000
1974	204,000
1973	211,000

The former President of Nessie Industries (who resigned on January 1, 1978) was paid a fixed salary, as follows:

1977	$30,000
1976	30,000
1975	25,000
1974	25,000
1973	20,000

REQUIRED:

a. What would the former President's salary have been for each of the 5 years, if he had been paid on the basis offered to Johnson? Show your calculations.

b. Would Johnson rather have the profit-sharing basis or a fixed salary in the circumstances? Discuss.

LIABILITY CONCEPTS

➤ **OBJECTIVE**

The purpose of this unit is to analyze the classification and valuation concepts related to liabilities in financial reporting. This unit will give you the conceptual tools you need to use the liability section of a firm's balance sheet and to understand what financial statements communicate about this important source of resources.

➤ **APPROACH TO ATTAINING THE OBJECTIVE**

As you study about liability concepts, pay special attention to these four questions, which the text following answers:

- *What are three ways of describing liabilities?*
- *How should liabilities be reported on the balance sheet?*
- *What are the common current liabilities of corporations?*
- *What are the common long-term liabilities of corporations?*

NATURE OF LIABILITIES

Liabilities on financial statements have been viewed in at least three ways: (1) as legal obligations, (2) as amounts to be paid creditors, and (3) as a measure of one source of the firm's assets. Remember that classification and valuation ideas are basic to understanding how to use financial statements. Therefore, we will now discuss these three approaches to liabilities from the point of view of classifying and valuing liabilities.

■ *What are three ways of describing liabilities?*

Liabilities as legal obligations A common notion of a debt involves the legal approach. This view holds that liabilities can be identified (classified) and measured according to some set of legal rules. All the states define these ideas through laws and court decisions. Following a legal approach to identifying a firm's liabilities is a hard concept to apply on financial statements to be used for general purposes. Among the drawbacks are that the several state laws differ on the precise meaning of a liability. In addition to identification, the *measurement* of the liability along legal lines becomes especially difficult. For example, the amount to be repaid a creditor (if it were to be repaid) during different stages in the life of a long-term liability might change and might be subject to all kinds of contingencies (chance happenings). It is generally concluded that a purely legalistic approach to classification and valuation of liabilities is not the most useful one to aid decision makers.

Liabilities as amounts to be paid creditors Many people believe that the liability section of the balance sheet measures the total amounts to be paid to creditors in the future. It does *not* do this, however, in many cases. Take notes payable, for example. Assume that a company borrows $1,000 on a 1-year, 7% note payable on June 1, 1978. You know that when the money is borrowed, Cash is debited for the $1,000 and Notes payable is credited for the $1,000. If a balance sheet were prepared right after the loan was made, the assets would have increased by $1,000 and the liabilities would have increased by the same amount.

Now, let's assume that liabilities were to be measured right after the loan by the *amounts to be paid to creditors.* If that were the case, the liability would have to be shown at $1,070, the total amount to be paid at the end of one year, including the $70 interest.

What would happen if the first concept of liabilities we studied, the legalistic one, was applied immediately after the $1,000 loan? In this case the courts might say that in order to settle the loan before maturity, some other amount (such as $1,025) would have to be paid. Users of general-purpose financial statements therefore have found that measuring liabilities as the amounts to be paid to creditors is not the most useful concept. Then what is the most useful concept, and how are liabilities reported?

Liabilities as a measure of the source of a firm's resources In modern reporting, liabilities are viewed as a source of a firm's assets. As you know, there are two basic sources—investors and creditors. The liability section of the balance sheet simply shows how much of the firm's total assets came from the creditor group.

Let us consider this illustration. At January 1, 1978, a firm's assets totaled $2,000 and its capital totaled the same $2,000. There were no liabilities. On January 1, 1978, the firm borrowed $1,000 cash, signing a 2-year, 7% note payable. These observations can be made:

1. At January 1, 1978, after the loan, the firm's assets total $3,000. The liabilities total $1,000, and the capital totals $2,000.

2. We can view liabilities as a *source* of the firm's assets: of the $3,000 assets, $1,000 were contributed by creditors and $2,000 were contributed by owners.

3. At the end of the first year, December 31, 1978, an adjusting entry would be made to debit Interest expense for $70 and to credit Interest payable for $70. This entry, as you have learned, sets up an expense to reduce earnings for 1978 by $70. This reduction in earnings, of course, reduces the *capital* of the firm. Liabilities (Interest payable) increase by $70.

4. Assume, to simplify the example, that there were no other transactions in 1978. In that case, the firm's assets would total $3,000. The firm's liabilities would now total $1,070, and the firm's capital would total $1,930. If there had been revenues, of course, the firm's assets and capital would have increased.

5. At this point we can say that the assets total $3,000, and that the *sources* of these assets are (1) the owners ($1,930), and (2) the creditors ($1,070). The firm incurred an expense of doing business ($70), and the creditor group provided the financing.

6. The existence of liabilities has this effect: the *expense* of having liabilities (borrowing money) tends to reduce the capital of the firm and tends to increase the liabilities of the firm. The liabilities are reduced by paying out assets.

DIFFERENCES IN REPORTING CURRENT AND LONG-TERM LIABILITIES

Illustration 25-1 shows how long-term liabilities are measured (valued) for reporting on balance sheets. This illustration is based on the assumption that an amount is borrowed on a note payable, and that the entire principal (amount borrowed) and interest will be paid at maturity. The diagram shows how the total liability grows each period over the life of the loan. Each balance sheet throughout the life of the loan would show a higher total

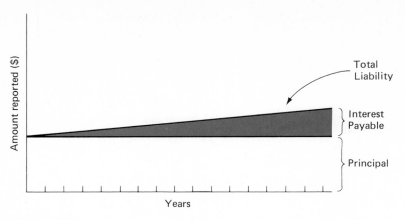

ILLUSTRATION 25-1

■ *How should liabilities be reported on the balance sheet?* liability, until the loan and interest are paid. We can conclude, therefore, that long-term liabilities are measured and reported as the *total benefits the firm has received (sources) from creditors,* as of the balance sheet date. These total benefits normally include two elements: (1) the assets (or benefits) initially received from the loan, and (2) the expenses the firm has incurred in the form of interest and which the creditors have financed for the company.

Illustration 25-1 assumes that interest is incurred on a straight-line basis. Notice how the total liability increases uniformly. In actual practice, however, interest often is computed on a compound basis. The total liability then is assumed to grow in a pattern resembling an upwardly *curved* line.

Let us now take an example to illustrate compound interest. Assume that a company borrows $3,000 cash from a bank on a note payable. Assume that the 4-year loan bears 8% interest. The amount of proceeds of the loan ($3,000) is known as the *present value.* The following table shows how the total liability for the loan grows from $3,000 to $4,081.47.

YEAR	JANUARY 1 LIABILITY (NOTE PAYABLE AND INTEREST PAYABLE)	INTEREST COMPUTATION	INTEREST FOR YEAR	DECEMBER 31 LIABILITY (NOTE PAYABLE AND INTEREST PAYABLE)
1978	$3,000.00	(0.08 × $3,000)	$240.00	$3,240.00
1979	3,240.00	(0.08 × $3,240)	259.20	3,499.20
1980	3,499.20	(0.08 × $3,499.20)	279.94	3,779.14
1981	3,779.14	(0.08 × $3,779.14)	302.33	4,081.47

Present value tables On page 431 is a *present value table* that is useful in calculating the proceeds of a loan when the amount to be paid at maturity and the interest rate are known. Refer to Table 25-1, the present value table. Given the example above, in the periods row (4 years) and in the 8% column, the present value is 0.735. This means that if the interest rate is 8% and if the

TABLE 25-1

PERIODS	4%	6%	8%	10%	12%	14%	16%	18%	20%	22%	24%	26%	28%	30%	40%
1	0.962	0.943	0.926	0.909	0.893	0.877	0.862	0.847	0.833	0.820	0.806	0.794	0.781	0.769	0.714
2	0.925	0.890	0.857	0.826	0.797	0.769	0.743	0.718	0.694	0.672	0.650	0.630	0.610	0.592	0.510
3	0.889	0.840	0.794	0.751	0.712	0.675	0.641	0.609	0.579	0.551	0.524	0.500	0.477	0.455	0.364
4	0.855	0.792	0.735	0.683	0.636	0.592	0.552	0.516	0.482	0.451	0.423	0.397	0.373	0.350	0.260
5	0.822	0.747	0.681	0.621	0.567	0.519	0.476	0.437	0.402	0.370	0.341	0.315	0.291	0.269	0.186
6	0.790	0.705	0.630	0.564	0.507	0.456	0.410	0.370	0.335	0.303	0.275	0.250	0.227	0.207	0.133
7	0.760	0.665	0.583	0.513	0.452	0.400	0.354	0.314	0.279	0.249	0.222	0.198	0.178	0.159	0.095
8	0.731	0.627	0.540	0.467	0.404	0.351	0.305	0.266	0.233	0.204	0.179	0.157	0.139	0.123	0.068
9	0.703	0.592	0.500	0.424	0.361	0.308	0.263	0.225	0.194	0.167	0.144	0.125	0.108	0.094	0.048
10	0.676	0.558	0.463	0.386	0.322	0.270	0.227	0.191	0.162	0.137	0.116	0.099	0.085	0.073	0.035
11	0.650	0.527	0.429	0.350	0.287	0.237	0.195	0.162	0.135	0.122	0.094	0.079	0.066	0.056	0.025
12	0.625	0.497	0.397	0.319	0.257	0.208	0.168	0.137	0.112	0.092	0.076	0.062	0.052	0.043	0.018
13	0.601	0.469	0.368	0.290	0.229	0.182	0.145	0.116	0.093	0.075	0.061	0.050	0.040	0.033	0.013
14	0.577	0.442	0.340	0.263	0.205	0.160	0.125	0.099	0.078	0.062	0.049	0.039	0.032	0.025	0.009
15	0.555	0.417	0.315	0.239	0.183	0.140	0.108	0.084	0.065	0.051	0.040	0.031	0.025	0.020	0.006
16	0.534	0.394	0.292	0.218	0.163	0.123	0.093	0.071	0.054	0.042	0.032	0.025	0.019	0.015	0.005
17	0.513	0.371	0.270	0.198	0.146	0.108	0.080	0.060	0.045	0.034	0.026	0.020	0.015	0.012	0.003
18	0.494	0.350	0.250	0.180	0.130	0.095	0.069	0.051	0.038	0.028	0.021	0.016	0.012	0.009	0.002
19	0.475	0.331	0.232	0.164	0.116	0.083	0.060	0.043	0.031	0.023	0.017	0.012	0.009	0.007	0.002
20	0.456	0.312	0.215	0.149	0.104	0.073	0.051	0.037	0.026	0.019	0.014	0.010	0.007	0.005	0.001
21	0.439	0.294	0.199	0.135	0.093	0.064	0.044	0.031	0.022	0.015	0.011	0.008	0.006	0.004	0.001
22	0.422	0.278	0.184	0.123	0.083	0.056	0.038	0.026	0.018	0.013	0.009	0.006	0.004	0.003	0.001
23	0.406	0.262	0.170	0.112	0.074	0.049	0.033	0.022	0.015	0.010	0.007	0.005	0.003	0.002	
24	0.390	0.247	0.158	0.102	0.066	0.043	0.028	0.019	0.013	0.008	0.006	0.004	0.003	0.002	
25	0.375	0.233	0.146	0.092	0.059	0.038	0.024	0.016	0.010	0.007	0.005	0.003	0.002	0.001	
26	0.361	0.220	0.135	0.084	0.053	0.033	0.021	0.014	0.009	0.006	0.004	0.002	0.002	0.001	
27	0.347	0.207	0.125	0.076	0.047	0.029	0.018	0.011	0.007	0.005	0.003	0.002	0.001	0.001	
28	0.333	0.196	0.116	0.069	0.042	0.026	0.016	0.010	0.006	0.004	0.002	0.002	0.001	0.001	
29	0.321	0.185	0.107	0.063	0.037	0.022	0.014	0.008	0.005	0.003	0.002	0.001	0.001	0.001	
30	0.308	0.174	0.099	0.057	0.033	0.020	0.012	0.007	0.004	0.003	0.002	0.001	0.001	0.001	
40	0.208	0.097	0.046	0.022	0.011	0.005	0.003	0.001	0.001						

time period is 4 years, then $73\frac{1}{2}$ cents can be borrowed for each $1.00 that is repaid at maturity:

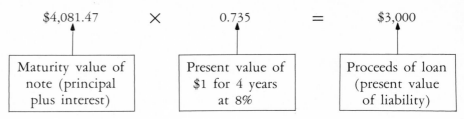

$$\$4,081.47 \qquad \times \qquad 0.735 \qquad = \qquad \$3,000$$

| Maturity value of note (principal plus interest) | Present value of $1 for 4 years at 8% | Proceeds of loan (present value of liability) |

Here are two examples using the present value table.

EXAMPLE	SOLUTION
1. The firm signs a 10%, 5-year note payable. The total amount to be repaid at maturity is $10,000. What is the amount borrowed?	1. Amount borrowed = __$6,210__ $10,000 × 0.621 = $6,210 from table 10%, 5-years

Proof:

Year	1/1	Interest	12/31
1	$6,210.00	(0.10 × $6,210) = $621.00	$ 6,831.00
2	6,831.00	(0.10 × $6,831) = $683.10	7,514.10
3	7,514.10	(0.10 × $7,514.10) = $751.41	8,265.51
4	8,265.51	(0.10 × $8,265.51) = $826.55	9,092.06
5	9,092.06	(0.10 × $9,092.06) = $909.21	10,001.27[a]

[a] Small difference of $1.27 due to rounding in table.

EXAMPLE	SOLUTION
2. The firm signed a 3-year non-interest-bearing note for $60,000. Discounted this note at the bank. There was a 12% discount (interest rate) charged by the bank. What amount of cash was borrowed?	2. Proceeds = __$42,720__ $60,000 × 0.712 = $42,720 from table 12%, 3 years

Proof:

Year	1/1	Interest	12/31
1	$42,720.00	(0.12 × $42,720) = $5,126.40	$47,846.40
2	47,846.40	(0.12 × $47,846.40) = $5,741.57	53,587.97
3	53,587.97	(0.12 × $53,587.97) = $6,430.56	60,018.53[b]

[b] Difference of $18.53 due to rounding in table.

The preceding examples involved computing the present value of a loan, when the future value (total amount due at maturity) was known. The following example involves *determining the future value* when the present value is known.

EXAMPLE	SOLUTION
A firm borrows $15,000 cash, signing a 6%, 4-year note. What is the total amount due at maturity?	Due at maturity = $18,939.39

$$\frac{\$15,000}{0.792} = \$18,939.39$$

from table
6%, 4 years

Proof:

Year	1/1	Interest	12/31
1	$15,000.00	(6% × $15,000) = $900	$15,900.00
2	15,900.00	(6% × $15,900) = $954	16,854.00
3	16,854.00	(6% × $16,854) = $1,011.24	17,865.24
4	17,865.24	(6% × $17,865.24) = $1,071.91	18,937.15[a]

[a]Off $2.24 due to rounding.

Reporting current liabilities Current liabilities are those debts that will be settled in the coming year or operating period. *They customarily are reported on the balance sheet at an amount equal to the assets (or benefits) received. This amount ordinarily is the same as the amount to be paid in cash in the coming period.* For example, if merchandise is purchased on a credit basis, then the liability, Accounts payable, is set up to equal the merchandise amount. Because the time period is so short, no interest is assumed to be associated with the current liability.

KINDS OF CURRENT LIABILITIES

Current liabilities found on corporation balance sheets include (1) accounts payable, (2) expenses payable, (3) taxes payable, (4) short-term notes, and (5) currently maturing portions of long-term obligations. Let us examine each of these briefly.

■ *What are the common current liabilities of corporations?*

Accounts payable In financial reporting, the term Accounts payable refers to short-term or current obligations that are created through the purchase of merchandise. This is the customary method of financing part of the firm's inventories.

Expenses payable This classification is reserved for operating and other expenses incurred in the routine course of business affairs. Often expenses payable are disclosed separately on financial statements in accounts such as Salaries payable, Interest payable, and Rent payable.

Taxes payable Sometimes expenses owed such as taxes payable are labeled as to the creditor. For example, a balance sheet might reveal amounts owed for Federal income taxes payable, State income taxes payable, and Employees' taxes withheld.

Short-term notes As you know, notes are written promises to pay a specified sum of money at a specified time. If the notes mature within the next year or operating period, they are classified as current on the balance sheet. *Also, if a long-term note will mature during the next year from the balance sheet date, then that liability should be reclassified from the long-term liability section to the current liability section of the balance sheet.*

Currently maturing portions of long-term obligations Some long-term obligations provide in the borrowing agreement that the loan will be paid back on an installment basis. In these situations, there is the problem of determining how much of the total liability represents a current liability and how much is long term. The liability amounts maturing in the next year are current. Therefore, the long-term liability must be split into two accounts on the balance sheet. As an example, assume that a corporation has total liability on a note payable amounting to $11,000, and that $1,000 of this total will be paid during the year following the balance sheet date. In this situation, the balance sheet should reveal current liabilities of $1,000 and long-term debt of $10,000.

KINDS OF LONG-TERM LIABILITIES

In addition to regular long-term notes, a corporation's long-term liabilities commonly include (1) bonds payable, (2) mortgages payable, (3) long-term lease obligations, (4) pension liabilities, and (5) deferred income tax liabilities. We will examine each of these in the following paragraphs.

▪ *What are the common long-term liabilities of corporations?*

Bonds payable The bonds you previously studied were viewed as long-term investments—as assets acquired by an investing company. You learned that these long-term assets are reported at their cost, and that interest is earned on the investment. In a later chapter you will study bonds from the point of view of the company which is borrowing the money. In that situation, the bonds represent long-term liabilities, which are created to acquire assets (to borrow money). Bonds are written promises to pay specified sums of money at specified times. Bonds may include many special provisions to make the bond issue more attractive to investors. Such bond agreements may include provisions regarding *call-ability, serial payments, convertibility, security,* and *sinking funds.* A bond agreement is called a **bond indenture.**

A bond is said to be **callable** if the bond agreement provides that the borrowing company may pay off (retire) the bonds before the maturity date. The amount to be paid to settle the bonds would be specified. This might be an important provision for a company if the bond agreement provided for 7% interest, and later the interest rate on similar bonds decreases to 5%. The company could pay off the old bonds and issue new ones at the lower interest cost.

Some bond issues provide for serial payments. **Serial bonds** provide that a series of payments will be made to retire the bonds, rather than the entire issue's being paid off at maturity.

Convertible bonds include the provision in the bond agreement that the bonds may be exchanged for some other security, such as the same firm's common stock or preferred stock. The provision often makes the investment more attractive to lenders because there is the possibility of their sharing in the profitability of the company (through owning stock).

Secured bonds include the provision that a certain asset or assets of the firm are specifically pledged to pay off the bonds in the event that the company is not able to otherwise settle the liability.

A **sinking fund** is a group of assets (cash and investments, usually) that can be set aside to provide funds to pay off the bonds at maturity. Many firms contribute regularly to a sinking fund, which earns interest and dividends during the life of the bond issue. Upon maturity of the bond issue, the assets are available to retire the bonds. Some bond indentures require that the company establish such a sinking fund and that it be controlled and administered by an independent party, such as a bank or other financial institution.

Mortgages payable A **mortgage payable** is a loan or note that has specific assets of the company pledged as security for repayment. It is a common practice in real estate transactions for the property which has been purchased (land and buildings, for example) to be pledged (mortgaged) to repay the loan in the event the borrower fails to do so.

Long-term lease obligations In the past few years a common practice for many companies has been to lease major items of plant and equipment on a long-term basis. The lease often runs for the entire useful life of the asset being used. Often the lease cannot be canceled. In many of these cases, the lease agreement has essentially the same effect as if the firm had borrowed the funds and then purchased the asset outright. The lease is in substance a purchase of property. In other words, a lease agreement can be a method of financing an asset. Current accounting practice treats *certain* leases of property as if the property had been purchased, even though legally it has not been. The **long-term lease liability** appears on the balance sheet to show the firm's obligation for the property.

Pension liabilities As part of a plan for compensating employees for their services, many companies set up pension agreements or plans. The pension agreement provides workers with retirement and other benefits. The cost of the pension plan becomes one of the operating expenses, similar to salary expense. Salaries are paid employees on a regular current basis, while pensions are deferred and paid to employees at a later date, such as at their retirement. The **pension liability** created is a long-term one and appears on the company's balance sheet.

Deferred income tax liabilities Income tax expense of a corporation poses a special reporting problem. In order to measure the earnings per share in a meaningful way, on each period's income statement the income tax expense must be matched against the earnings upon which that tax expense was based. This would be a relatively simple matter if all items of revenue and expense were reported on the tax return in the same period that they are reported on the income statement. Remember that the rules for reporting expenses and revenues on financial statements were developed to provide a measure of the profitability of the firm and thus to help decision makers to evaluate the company. In contrast, the rules for reporting expenses and revenues on the income tax return of a corporation are based on the tax laws. These tax laws in many cases have nothing to do with measuring earnings for decisions—or with evaluating the performance of a firm.

A very simple example will illustrate. Shown below are income statements for a corporation for two years, with a figure missing—Income tax expense. Assume that when the corporation's accountant began to prepare the income tax return for 1978, he discovered in the tax laws a provision that would allow all the revenues and expenses for 1978 to be reported on the tax return of 1979, instead of 1978. Of course, he decided to do this, because it amounted to postponing the payment of taxes. His firm also was able to invest the money in the meanwhile. All the expenses and revenues for 1978 and 1979, therefore, appeared on the 1979 income tax return (see table below). To continue our illustration, assume that the tax rate for the company is 40% of earnings (called *taxable income* on the tax return). The tax return information for 1978 and for 1979 then would be as shown in the table at the top of the next page.

INCOME STATEMENTS

	1978	1979
sales	$200,000	$300,000
expenses		
Cost of goods sold	$100,000	$160,000
Operating expenses	10,000	13,000
Income tax expense	?	?
Total expenses	?	?
net earnings	?	?
earnings per share		
(5,000 shares outstanding)	?	?

TAX RETURN INFORMATION

	1978	1979
revenues	–0–	$500,000
expenses		
Cost of goods sold	–0–	$260,000
Operating expenses	–0–	23,000
Total expenses	–0–	$283,000
taxable income	–0–	$217,000
Tax rate	40%	40%
taxes due the government	–0–	$ 86,800

The taxes to be paid in 1979 can be broken down easily into the taxes due from income generated in 1978 and 1979. Thus, the $90,000 income of 1978 ($200,000 — $100,000 — $10,000) only need be multiplied by 40% to get the deferred 1978 tax due of $36,000. And the $127,000 income of 1979 ($300,000 — $160,000 — $13,000) can be multiplied by 40% to get the 1979 tax due of $50,800. Thus:

Taxes due from income generated in 1978: $36,000
Taxes due from income generated in 1979: 50,800
$86,800   Taxes paid in 1979

The general journal entries needed to record the income tax expense for 1978 and 1979 follow:

1978 Dec.	31	Income tax expense	36,000	
		Deferred income tax liability		36,000
		To record income taxes on earnings for 1978 to be reported on a later tax return.		

1979					
Dec.	31	Income tax expense	50,800		
		Deferred income tax liability	36,000		
		Cash			86,800
		To record income taxes on 1979 earnings and to record payment of tax liability.			

These journal entries, in turn, involve reporting the income tax expense in the periods with the associated earnings. The completed income statements for 1978 and 1979 in the table that follows reflect this reporting principle.

COMPLETED INCOME STATEMENTS

	1978	1979
sales	$200,000	$300,000
expenses:		
Cost of goods sold	$100,000	$160,000
Operating expenses	10,000	13,000
INCOME TAX EXPENSE	36,000	50,800
Total expenses	$146,000	$223,800
net earnings	$ 54,000	$ 76,200
earnings per share (5,000 shares of common stock outstanding)	$10.80	$15.24

If no income tax expense had been reported in 1978, and both years' income tax expense was reported in 1979, the earnings per share would have been tremendously distorted. In that case, instead of an increase from $10.80 to $15.24, a decrease in earnings per share, from $18.00 to $8.04, would have been reported. (You can figure out these latter earnings-per-share figures on your own by using the data in the completed income statements.)

Admittedly, this is an extremely oversimplified example. It does illustrate, however, the principle that is generally followed in financial statement reporting: income tax expenses are reported in the period in which the earnings that gave rise to the taxes are reported. You also should realize from the example that the liability, Deferred income tax liability, must be reported on the balance sheet for 1978. Deferred income tax liability is usually reported as a *long-term* liability because most of the actual cases of timing differences involve several years instead of just the one year as in our example. In Chapter 24 additional complexities of reporting income taxes will be discussed.

bond indenture A written agreement related to the issuance of bonds; the agreement (indenture) includes all the provisions of the bond issue. [p. 435]

callable bonds Bonds whose bond indenture provides that the borrowing company may pay off (retire) the bonds before the maturity date. [p. 435]

convertible bonds Bonds whose bond indenture provides that the bonds may be converted into some other security. [p. 435]

deferred income tax liability A long-term liability; obligations for income taxes incurred on earnings already reported on financial statements. [p. 436]

long-term lease obligation A long-term liability; the debt created upon acquiring assets for use in the firm, when a long-term lease is used to finance the assets. [p. 436]

mortgage payable A note payable with specific pledged assets as security; a long-term liability. [p. 435]

pension liability A long-term liability; obligations to employees under a pension plan; obligations for employee compensation in the form of pensions to be paid in the future. [p. 436]

secured bonds Bonds whose bond indenture provides that certain assets of the firm are specifically pledged to pay off the bonds in the event that the company is not able to otherwise settle the liability. [p. 435]

serial bonds Bonds whose bond indenture provides that a *series* of payments will be made to retire the bonds, rather than the entire issue being paid off at maturity. [p. 435]

sinking fund A group of assets of a company set aside to provide funds to pay off bonds at maturity. [p. 435]

> **ASSIGNMENT MATERIAL**

QUESTIONS

Q25-1. List and describe in your own words three ways that liabilities have been viewed. Which of these three approaches is most significant in modern financial reporting?

Q25-2. What is the basic difference between reporting current liabilities and long-term liabilities?

Q25-3. What is the proceeds (amount borrowed) on a 15-year, 4% note payable if the total principal and interest amounts to $50,000?

Q25-4. Explain how currently maturing portions of long-term obligations are reported on the balance sheet.

Q25-5. Briefly describe each of these terms:
a. Callable bond.
b. Serial bond.
c. Convertible bond.
d. Secured bond.
e. Sinking fund.
f. Bond indenture.

Q25-6. What information does a present value table show?

EXERCISES

E25-1. Prepare the liability section of a corporation balance sheet in good form. Include both current and long-term sections, and include as many liability accounts as you have studied. Make up your own dollar amounts.

E25-2. Using the following eight codes, classify each of the following accounts to indicate in which section of the financial statements they would appear:

A   Asset section of the balance sheet
B   Current liability section of the balance sheet
C   Long-term liability section of the balance sheet
D   Capital section of the balance sheet
E   Revenues section of the income statement
F   Cost of goods sold section of the income statement
G   Selling expense section of the income statement
H   General and administrative expense section of the income statement

Accounts payable	Pension liability
Prepaid maintenance expense	Taxes payable
Buildings	Deferred income taxes payable
Allowance for uncollectibles	Mortgage payable
Purchases of merchandise	Advertising expense
Salaries payable	Long-term lease liabilities
Bonds payable	
That portion of notes payable that will be repaid during the next year	

E25-3. Fill in the blanks.

a. A group of assets that have been set aside to provide funds to pay off bonds at their maturity is known as a _____ .

b. The written agreement related to issuance of bonds is known as a _____ .

c. A liability which will be repaid at some future date further in the future than 1 year is known as a _____ liability.

d. A liability that will be repaid during the next year is known as a _____ liability.

e. Bonds that can be exchanged for some other security are known as _____ .

f. A long-term liability (note) with specific pledged assets as security is known as a _____ .

g. Bonds which include the provision that they can be paid off prior to maturity are known as _____ .

h. Bonds that are repaid in a series of installments are known as _____ .

E25-4. Answer the following true or false.

a. Users of general-purpose financial statements have found that measuring liabilities as the amounts to be paid to creditors is the most useful concept of liabilities.

b. In modern reporting, liabilities are viewed as a source of a firm's assets.

c. Accounts receivable usually are reported as current liabilities.

d. Prepaid expenses are reported on the income statement as expenses.

e. Short-term notes payable are reported as long-term liabilities on the balance sheet.

f. Currently maturing portions of long-term liabilities are reported as current liabilities on the balance sheet.

g. If a company has a total liability on a note payable of $10,000, and if $1,000 of that total will be paid during the year following the balance sheet date, then $9,000 should be reported on the balance sheet as a long-term liability.

h. Deferred income tax liability should be reported on the income statement.

i. When bonds are repaid before their maturity date, they are known as bond indentures.

j. Bonds which include the provision in the bond agreement that they may be exchanged for some other security are known as convertible bonds.

PROBLEMS (GROUP A)

P25-1. *Present value analysis.* Using the present value table in the text as needed, calculate each of the following:

a. Determine the future value (total amount due at maturity):
   (1) 6-year, 8%, note with face amount of $60,000. Proceeds, $60,000.
   (2) 20-year, 4%, note with face amount of $100,000. Proceeds, $100,000.
   (3) $10,000 non-interest-bearing note, 5 years. Discount rate, 10%.
   (4) 1 year, $6,000, 12% note. Proceeds, $6,000.

b. Determine the present value (proceeds):
   (5) 6-year, 14% note with maturity value, $91,200.
   (6) $10,000 non-interest-bearing note, 5 years. Discount rate, 10%.
   (7) 1 year, 12% note with maturity value, $893,000.
   (8) 16-year, 20% note with maturity value, $754,000.

P25-2. *Deferred income tax.* The following facts are known about the C Company:

	1978	1979
Sales	$ 90,000	$145,000
Other revenues	10,000	5,000
	$100,000	$150,000
Cost of goods sold	20,000	29,000
Selling expense	30,000	32,000
General expenses	10,000	9,000
Tax rate	40%	40%

The expenses above do not include Income tax expense. Assume that all the 1978 revenues and expenses must be reported on the 1979 tax return rather than on the 1978 tax return, according to the tax laws.

REQUIRED: Prepare income statements in good form for the company for 1978 and 1979. There were 2,000 shares of common stock outstanding during the entire time.

P25-3. *Present value concepts.*

a. Your father has indicated to you that he will give you $2,500 as a graduation present 4 years from now, when you graduate from college. He wants to deposit in a savings account at the local savings and loan association enough money to provide the $2,500 in 4 years. The expected interest rate is 6%. How much money must be deposited today to accumulate the $2,500?

b. A company will have to replace a building in 10 years, paying $750,000 cash. If the company can earn 12% on its savings, how much should the firm invest (save) today at the rate of 12% to accumulate the $750,000 in 10 years?

c. You plan to deposit $1,000 in a savings account on January 1, 1978. Each January 1 thereafter, you will deposit another $1,000. What will be the balance of the savings account at December 31, 1988, if the account earns 8% interest compounded annually?

P25-4. *Present values.*

a. Assume that you want to have $25,000 available 10 years from now. You plan to invest funds today to accumulate the $25,000, and you expect to earn 8% per year on your investments. How much money must be invested today to accumulate the $25,000?

b. Assume that you want to have $8,000 cash available to make a down payment on a house in 10 years. How much money would you have to invest today at the rate of return of 8% to have that much available at the end of 10 years?

c. Herbert W. Brunn is considering making an investment in bonds. The bond issue provides that the face amount of the bonds will be paid off in 10 years and that $600 of interest will be paid each year for the 10 years. The cash inflows from the investment in bonds will be:

First year	$600	Sixth year	$ 600
Second year	600	Seventh year	600
Third year	600	Eighth year	600
Fourth year	600	Ninth year	600
Fifth year	600	Tenth year	10,600[a]

[a] This amount includes $10,000 repayment of face amount.

Compute the amount Brunn would expect to pay for the investment in bonds if he is to earn 20% per year.

P25-5. *Income tax allocation.* Shown below are income statements for a corporation for 2 years, with the Income tax expense figure missing.

INCOME STATEMENTS

	1978	1979
sales	$100,000	$150,000
expenses		
Operating expenses and Cost of goods sold	75,000	90,000
Income tax expense	?	?
Total expenses	?	?
net earnings	?	?
earnings per share (5,000 shares outstanding)	?	?

When the accountant prepared the tax returns, he determined that $40,000 of the sales for 1978 and $25,000 of the expenses for 1978 must be reported on the tax return in 1979, as follows:

TAX RETURN INFORMATION

	1978	1979
Revenues	$60,000	$190,000
Expenses	$50,000	$115,000
Taxable income	$10,000	$ 75,000
Tax rate	40%	40%
Taxes due the government	$ 4,000	$ 30,000

REQUIRED:

a. Prepare income statements for 1978 and 1979, supplying the missing information.

b. Prepare the general journal entries related to income taxes for 1978 and 1979. Assume the amount due the government is paid each December 31.

*P25-6. *Present value and future value computations.* The following table presents data on a company's notes payable:

NOTE	TERM OF NOTE	INTEREST RATE	PROCEEDS (AMOUNT BORROWED)	MATURITY VALUE (PRINCIPAL AND INTEREST)
1	1 year	4%	_____	$90,000.00
2	5 years	_____	$10,000	$14,684.29
3	10 years	12%	_____	$100,000.00
4	3 years	16%	$128,200	_____
5	15 years	_____	$250,200	$600,000.00
6	20 years	4%	_____	$82,000.00
7	6 years	10%	$14,100	_____
8	_____	8%	$50,000	$100,000.00
9	11 years	_____	$17,725	$75,000.00
10	_____	20%	$2,790	$10,000.00

REQUIRED: Make calculations and fill in the missing figures.

CUMULATIVE REVIEW PROBLEMS

*P25-7. *Cumulative review problem.* The following information is known about the payroll of SMT Corporation for December, 1978:

EMPLOYEE	PAY BASIS	TOTAL EARNINGS THIS YEAR BEFORE THIS PAYROLL	NUMBER OF WITHHOLDING ALLOWANCES	REGULAR TIME HOURS	OVERTIME HOURS
L. Martina	$1,000 monthly	$12,100	4	—	—
B. Gregg	$6 per hour	3,000	6	160	11
L. Heidi	$7 per hour	4,150	3	160	3
X. Christina	$6 per hour	2,700	1	160	1

Hourly employees are paid time and a half for overtime. Use the tables and rates from the last unit. L. Martina, in addition to her $1,000 salary for December, is entitled to a profit-sharing bonus of 10% of earnings of the firm after deducting income taxes for the company and the bonus. The company produced earnings during 1978 of $500,000. This amount takes into consideration all revenues and expenses for the year except the December payroll and bonus. The company's tax rate is 40%.

REQUIRED:

a. Prepare all payroll and bonus computations. Martina will be issued two payroll checks for December, one for her salary and one for her annual bonus.
b. Record the payroll in general journal form.
c. Record the payment of the four employees in general journal form (five entries).
d. Record the employer's payroll taxes in general journal form.

P25-8. *Cumulative review problem.* Zane Corporation borrowed $100,000 cash on January 1, 1978, signing a 7%, 5-year note for $100,000 with no compounding of interest. On that same date Zane Corporation opened a savings account (savings certificate) that earns 7% per year compounded annually.

REQUIRED:

a. What is the amount of the liability for the note and interest on the balance sheet of Zane Corporation at December 31, 1981?
b. What is the balance in the savings account at December 31, 1982?
c. What is the maturity value of the note?
d. Draw a graph that shows two lines: (1) the balance of the liability, and (2) the balance of the savings account at each balance sheet date. The vertical axis should show dollars and the horizontal axis should show balance sheet dates as on the next page. Use a solid line for the liability and use dashed lines for the savings account balance.

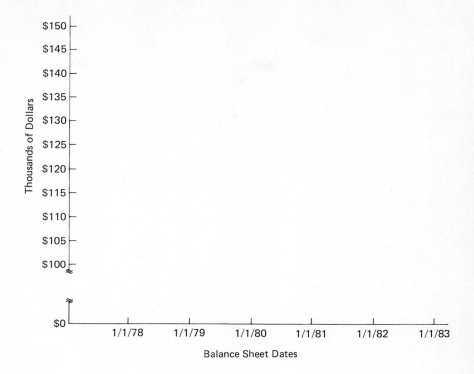

chapter 11

partnerships

PARTNERSHIPS–FORMATION AND DIVISION OF EARNINGS

» OBJECTIVE

The specific purpose of this unit is to discuss the important accounting and reporting problems associated with organizing and operating a partnership form of organization.

» APPROACH TO ATTAINING THE OBJECTIVE

As you study the reporting problems associated with partnership capital, pay special attention to these three questions, which the text following answers:

- *What are the articles of partnership?*
- *How are partners' investments recorded?*
- *How is the division of net earnings among the partners recorded and reported?*

ORGANIZING A PARTNERSHIP

The partnership form of organization is only slightly more complex than a proprietorship. The owners are simply two or more individuals who combine their efforts in a common set of goals. Many medical doctors, for example, establish partnerships in the practice of medicine. Partnerships usually have a written agreement among the partners which spells out how the business is to be run. This written agreement, called the **articles of partnership,** often states:

■ *What are the articles of partnership?*

1. The primary goals of the firm.
2. How the business will be financed.
3. How the business will be managed.
4. How the earnings and the losses of the business will be shared.
5. The conditions under which the operation of the firm will be discontinued.

■ *How are partners' investments recorded?*

To illustrate the formation of a partnership, assume that Mark Timothy and Stephen Paul agree to form one. Timothy already operates a business and will contribute some of the assets of his proprietorship in the formation of the partnership. The two men agree that the cash value of the assets contributed will be considered the investment by Timothy. The partnership also will take over the liabilities of Timothy's business:

	BALANCE OF THE ACCOUNTS IN TIMOTHY'S GENERAL LEDGER	AGREED-UPON CASH VALUE, MARKET PRICE, OR REPLACEMENT PRICE FOR PARTNERSHIP
Accounts receivable	$15,000	$15,000
Allowance for uncollectibles	500	600
Building	74,000	80,000
Accumulated depreciation—Building	10,000	
Land	45,000	50,000
Accounts payable	10,000	10,000
Notes payable	14,000	14,000

It is further agreed that Paul will contribute $150,000 cash as his investment in the partnership. The general journal entry to record the formation of the partnership and to set up the two partners' capital accounts is shown at the top of the next page.

The second journal entry emphasizes that when assets other than cash are contributed, the *agreed-upon* values are relevant for the partnership (see the right-hand column of the table above). These values usually correspond very closely to the cash value of the assets, or to their market price, or to their current replacement price (as with merchandise). The amounts appearing in the records of a former company therefore are not important.

1978				
Jan.	14	Cash	150,000	
		Stephen Paul, Capital		150,000
		To record Paul's investment in the partnership.		
	14	Accounts receivable	15,000	
		Building	80,000	
		Land	50,000	
		Allowance for uncollectibles		600
		Accounts payable		10,000
		Notes payable		14,000
		Mark Timothy, Capital		120,400
		To record Timothy's investment in the partnership.		

Notice that the agreed-upon value (expected collectible amount) of the receivables is $14,400 ($15,000 — $600). This amount is set up in the journal entry through two accounts: Accounts receivable, $15,000, and Allowance for uncollectibles, $600. An accounts receivable subsidiary ledger now could be set up to provide detailed information on the $15,000 of accounts receivable. Timothy's capital investment is computed as follows:

Accounts receivable	$ 14,400
Building	80,000
Land	50,000
Total assets contributed	$144,400
Less liabilities taken over	24,000
Total capital investment	$120,400

Once a partnership is formed, the books of record (journals and ledgers) are kept in much the same manner as a proprietorship or a corporation. A significant difference from a corporation are the partners' capital accounts.

DIVIDING EARNINGS AND PROVIDING FOR WITHDRAWALS

Partnership earnings or losses are shared as agreed by the partners. This is usually specifically stated in the articles of partnership. The agreement may provide that losses be divided differently than earnings, or perhaps in the same manner. In developing an agreement on these matters, partners often consider these two important factors:

■ *How is the division of net earnings among the partners recorded and reported?*

1. The time and effort devoted to the partnership by each partner.
2. The total investment in the partnership by each partner.

Of course, partners can agree to share profits and bear losses in any way they choose.

To illustrate accounting for division of earnings, assume these facts about a partnership agreement:

The three partners of Pearl, Allen, and Cough agree to share profits as follows:

1. Partners will be allocated salary allowances in the amounts of $10,000 for Pearl, $20,000 for Allen, and $5,000 for Cough.
2. Each partner will be allowed a 7% return on his investment during each year. During 1978 Pearl's capital account reflected an average balance of $100,000, Allen's reflected an average balance of $200,000, and Cough's reflected an average balance of $10,000.
3. After the allowances above, any remaining earnings or losses are to be shared equally.

During 1978 the net earnings of the partnership amounted to $60,000. The three partners made these cash withdrawals in 1978: Pearl, $30,000; Allen, $30,000; Cough, $10,000. Capital balances (beginning) at January 1, 1978, were Pearl $100,000; Allen $200,000; Cough $10,000.

Distribution of net earnings at the end of the year is determined according to the agreement as follows:

	TOTAL	PEARL	ALLEN	COUGH
Allowances for salaries	$35,000	$10,000	$20,000	$5,000
Allowances for return on investments (7% × average capital)	21,700	7,000	14,000	700
Total allowed under agreement	$56,700	$17,000	$34,000	$5,700
Remaining to be allocated (equally)	3,300	1,100	1,100	1,100
Distribution of earnings	$60,000	$18,100	$35,100	$6,800

Closing entries to distribute profits The allocation of the $60,000 net earnings would be accomplished in the accounting records as part of the closing entry process. Remember that as part of the process, the net earnings are allocated to the owner's capital account. In a partnership, of course, the earnings are allocated to more than one owner's capital account. Also, in the closing entries the partners' withdrawals are closed to the capital accounts. The general journal entries on the next page illustrate closing entries for the example above. The revenue and expense figures are assumed to have been taken from an end-of-period work sheet of the firm.

1978					
Dec.	31	Service revenues	200,000		
		Interest income	10,000		
		Net earnings summary			210,000
		To close the revenue accounts and temporarily reflect the credit balance in a summary account.			
	31	Net earnings summary	150,000		
		Rent expense			12,000
		Depreciation expense			20,000
		Salaries expense			90,000
		Other expenses			28,000
		To close the expense accounts to a summary account.			
	31	Net earnings summary	60,000		
		Pearl, Capital			18,100
		Allen, Capital			35,100
		Cough, Capital			6,800
		To distribute the net earnings for 1978 according to the partnership agreement. (See the preceding table on the distribution of net earnings to partners.)			
	31	Pearl, Capital	30,000		
		Allen, Capital	30,000		
		Cough, Capital	10,000		
		Pearl, Withdrawals			30,000
		Allen, Withdrawals			30,000
		Cough, Withdrawals			10,000
		To close the partners' withdrawals accounts and reduce their capital balances. (These are the actual cash withdrawals the three partners made in 1978.)			

The statement of partners' capital A financial statement, the **statement of partners' capital,** is shown below and summarizes the transactions affecting capital.

Pearl, Allen, and Cough
STATEMENT OF PARTNERS' CAPITAL
For the Year Ended December 31, 1978

	TOTAL	PEARL	ALLEN	COUGH
Capital, January 1, 1978	$310,000	$100,000	$200,000	$10,000
Net earnings for 1978	60,000	18,100	35,100	6,800
Total	$370,000	$118,100	$235,100	$16,800
Withdrawals during 1978	70,000	30,000	30,000	10,000
Capital, December 31, 1978	$300,000	$ 88,100	$205,100	$ 6,800

All resources withdrawn by owners are usually recorded in withdrawals accounts. These accounts reduce the partnership's capital. Such accounts would not appear on the *income statement* of the partnership and would not affect the earnings of the firm, since the withdrawals are distributions of net income already earned. A few partnerships, however, consider all or part of the partners' withdrawals as regular salary expenses. Such partnerships report these withdrawals on the income statement (as costs of doing business), rather than on the Statement of Partners' Capital. This practice, although not generally accepted, is useful in reflecting the net earnings when comparing the partnership to firms with the corporate form. In corporations, the salary of any stockholder, who also happens to be an employee and is paid a salary for his services, is considered an expense and reduces the earnings of the company.

An additional example of dividing net earnings Occasionally, the allowances to partners (such as interest and salaries) will exceed the net income made by the partnership. This example will illustrate.

AGREEMENT

1. Partners are allowed salaries as follows:

    Harper, $50,000

    Willis, $30,000

    Butler, $20,000

2. Partners are allowed 8% interest allowance on average capital balance during year.

3. Special allowances are given as follows:

    Harper, $3,000

    Willis, $3,000

4. Any remaining earnings or losses (deficits) are to be divided equally.

In "T" account form, the three partners' capital accounts are shown for 1978:

HARPER, CAPITAL

| 11–1–78 | Withdrawal | 30,000 | 1–1–78 | Balance | 113,000 |
| | | | 3–1–78 | Investment | 10,000 |

WILLIS, CAPITAL

		1–1–78	Balance	204,000
		10–1–78	Investment	100,000

BUTLER, CAPITAL

3–7–78	Withdrawal	11,000	1–1–78	Balance	82,000
12–1–78	Withdrawal	10,000			

Assuming the company produced net income of only $62,000 during the year, the division of profits will be as in Table 26-1.

TABLE 26-1
DIVISION OF PARTNERS' EARNINGS

	TOTAL	HARPER	WILLIS	BUTLER
Allowance for salaries	$100,000	$50,000	$30,000	$20,000
Interest on investments	33,120	9,040[a]	18,320[b]	5,760[c]
Special allowances	6,000	3,000	3,000	–0–
Total	$139,120	$62,040	$51,320	$25,760
Balance equally				
($139,120 − $62,000 = $77,120)	(77,120)	(25,706)	(25,707)	(25,707)
Distribution of earnings	$ 62,000	$36,334	$25,613	$ 53

[a] Computation of interest allowance for Harper (from Capital "T" accounts shown previously):

$$
\begin{array}{ll}
\text{2 months with a balance of } \$113,000 = & \$226,000 \\
\text{8 months with a balance of } 123,000 = & 984,000 \\
\text{2 months with a balance of } 73,000 = & 146,000 \\
\end{array}
$$

$1,356,000 ÷ 12 months = $113,000 average capital balance

$113,000 × 8% = $9,040 interest allowance

[b] Computation of interest allowance for Willis:

$$
\begin{array}{ll}
\text{9 months} \times \$204,000 = & \$1,836,000 \\
\text{3 months} \times 304,000 = & 912,000 \\
\end{array}
$$

$2,748,000 ÷ 12 = $229,000

$229,000 × 8% = $18,320

[c] Computation of interest allowance for Butler:

$$
\begin{array}{ll}
\text{2 months} \times \$82,000 = & \$164,000 \\
\text{9 months} \times 71,000 = & 639,000 \\
\text{1 month} \times 61,000 = & 61,000 \\
\end{array}
$$

$864,000 ÷ 12 = $72,000

$72,000 × 8% = $5,760

NEW TERMS

articles of partnership A written agreement among partners which spells out details such as (1) the primary goals of the firm, (2) how the business will be financed, (3) how the business will be managed, (4) how the earnings and losses of the business will be shared, and (5) the conditions under which the operation of the firm will be discontinued. [p. 448]

statement of partners' capital A financial statement of a partnership which reflects changes in the capital of the partners; similar to a statement of owner's capital in a proprietorship. [p. 451]

ASSIGNMENT MATERIAL

QUESTIONS

Q26-1. What is the name of the written agreement among the partners in a partnership? What information does this agreement often contain?

Q26-2. When assets other than cash are contributed to a partnership by one of the partners as an investment, at what value are these assets recorded on the books of the partnership?

Q26-3. In developing an agreement on profit sharing, what are two important ideas the partners usually consider?

Q26-4. Do the partners' withdrawals accounts appear on the income statement? Explain.

Q26-5. What is a statement of partners' capital?

EXERCISES

E26-1. Barton and Martin agree to form a partnership. Barton agrees to invest cash amounting to $10,000 and land with a recorded value on the books of his old company of $26,000. The land is now worth about $41,000.

Martin will contribute cash amounting to $25,000 and a building worth $100,000. This building was on Martin's books at a cost of $150,000, with accumulated depreciation of $85,000. Martin also invests accounts receivable with face amounts of $60,000. The allowance for uncollectibles on Martin's books has a credit balance of $500. It is agreed that only $59,000 of these receivables are likely to be collected. Make the journal entries on the partnership books to admit the partners.

E26-2. The partnership agreement of Wells and Towers provided for profit sharing as follows:

	WELLS	TOWERS
Interest on average capital balance	10%	10%
Salary allowance	$25,000	$31,000
Remaining earnings or losses (deficits)	$\frac{1}{3}$	$\frac{2}{3}$

During 1978, the partnership produced $100,000 of net earnings. Wells had an average capital balance of $100,000 and Towers had an average capital balance of $175,000. Calculate how the $100,000 of net earnings will be allocated between the partners.

E26-3. Refer to E26-2. Assume that the partnership had a net loss of $10,000, instead of a profit of $100,000. How would the $10,000 loss be allocated between the partners?

P26-4. *Entries for partnership formation; statement of partners' capital.* Juan Gonzales and Edward Chen agree to form a partnership (France Co.) on January 1, 1978, to operate a French restaurant. Gonzales contributes the following as his investment in the business:

1. A building that he originally paid $82,000 for; the building now has accumulated depreciation of $11,000. The building currently has an appraised value of $75,000, the amount agreed upon by the partners for the investment.
2. Land that is currently valued at $80,000 (Gonzales originally paid $10,000 for the land).

Gonzales has accounts payable amounting to $11,500. The partnership will take over these debts.

Chen will contribute the following as his investment in the business:

1. Cash amounting to $100,000.
2. Accounts receivable of $10,000. It is agreed that there should be an allowance for uncollectibles of $400.

Chen has accounts payable amounting to $20,000. The partnership will take over these debts.

The profit-sharing agreement provides that the partners will share equally in the earnings of the business, after allowing salaries of $10,000 for Chen and $12,000 for Gonzales. Both partners withdrew $5,000 cash from the business on March 31, 1978.

During the year, the restaurant produced $50,000 of net earnings.

REQUIRED:

a. Make the necessary journal entries to record the formation of the partnership.
b. Prepare a statement of partners' capital for 1978.

P26-5. *Income statement; allocation of net income; closing entries; statement of partners' capital.* The following information is known about the partnership agreement of Pierre Melancon and Sons:

1. Partners will be allocated salary allowances as follows: P. Melancon, $10,000; Q. Melancon, $21,000; L. Schwartz, $2,000.
2. Each partner will be allowed a 9% return on his investment during each year. During 1978, the current year, the average balances of capital amounted to: P. Melancon, $90,000; Q. Melancon, $100,000; L. Schwartz, $120,000.
3. After the allowances above, any remaining earnings or losses are to be shared equally.

The trial balance of Pierre Melancon and Sons at December 31, 1978, the end of the year's operations, is as follows:

Cash	10,000	
Accounts receivable	40,000	
Allowance for uncollectibles		1,000
Prepaid expenses	11,000	
a Merchandise inventory	50,000	
Plant and equipment	200,000	
Accumulated depreciation		80,000
Accounts payable		30,000
Notes payable		9,000
P. Melancon, Capital		90,000
Q. Melancon, Capital		100,000

L. Schwartz, Capital		120,000
P. Melancon, Withdrawals	21,000	
Q. Melancon, Withdrawals	70,000	
L. Schwartz, Withdrawals	1,000	
Sales		300,000
Sales returns and allowances	8,000	
Sales discounts	3,000	
Service revenue		20,000
Purchases	314,000	
Transportation on purchases	3,000	
Purchases returns and allowances		10,000
Purchases discounts		2,000
General expenses	18,000	
Selling expenses	11,000	
Other expenses	2,000	
	762,000	762,000

[a] The ending inventory amounts to $185,000.

REQUIRED:

a. Prepare an income statement for the company in good form.
b. Compute the distribution of earnings among the three partners.
c. Prepare closing journal entries for the company, similar to the illustration in the text.
d. Prepare a statement of partners' capital in good form.

P26-6. *Calculation of net income; allocation to partners; closing entries; statement of partners' capital.* The profit-sharing agreement of Koak and Wharton Co. includes the following provisions:

	KOAK	WHARTON	JOHNSON
1. Salary allowances	–0–	$21,500	$25,000
2. Interest allowance on average capital balance	9%	9%	9%
3. Remainder to be allocated	$\frac{1}{2}$	$\frac{1}{4}$	$\frac{1}{4}$

At December 31, 1978, the end of a year's operations, the adjusted trial balance is presented below.

Cash	29,000	
Marketable securities	3,000	
Accounts receivable	91,000	
Allowance for bad debts		2,000
Prepaid insurance	3,000	
Equipment	100,000	
Accumulated depreciation—Equipment		13,000
Land	110,000	
Buildings	150,000	
Accumulated depreciation—Buildings		51,000
Accounts payable		12,000

Accrued expenses		5,000
Notes payable		51,000
Koak, Capital		118,000
Wharton, Capital		131,000
Johnson, Capital		22,000
ᵃ Koak, Withdrawals	9,000	
ᵃ Wharton, Withdrawals	56,000	
ᵃ Johnson, Withdrawals	6,000	
Service revenue		314,000
Rent revenue		10,000
Interest revenue		5,000
Salaries expense	143,000	
Insurance expense	11,000	
Rent expense	5,000	
Depreciation expense—Equipment	4,000	
Depreciation expense—Buildings	9,000	
Miscellaneous expense	5,000	
	734,000	734,000

ᵃ All withdrawals were made December 1, 1978.

REQUIRED:

a. Calculate the net earnings for 1978.
b. Prepare a table showing how the net earnings will be allocated to the partners.
c. Prepare closing entries for the partnership in general journal form.
d. Prepare a statement of partners' capital for 1978.

PARTNERSHIPS–CHANGES IN OWNERSHIP; LIQUIDATION

> ### OBJECTIVE

This unit will conclude your study of partnership accounting. Specifically, accounting for ownership changes will be discussed. These include death of one of the partners, sale of one of the partner's ownership interest, admission of an additional partner, and the withdrawal of one of the partners from the business. Also, the reporting of a partnership liquidation will be treated in this unit.

> ### APPROACH TO ATTAINING THE OBJECTIVE

As you study about changes in ownership and liquidation of partnerships, pay special attention to these four questions, which the text following answers:

- *How is the sale of a partner's interest reported?*
- *How is the admission of a new partner reported?*
- *How is the withdrawal of a partner reported?*
- *How is a partnership liquidation recorded?*

OWNERSHIP CHANGES IN A PARTNERSHIP

Any change in the ownership interests of a partnership has the effect of terminating or ending the partnership. The four common ways this takes place are through (1) the death of a partner, (2) the sale of one of the partner's interest in the partnership, (3) an agreement to admit an additional partner, and (4) the withdrawal of a partner from the business. When one of these changes in ownership occurs, the business can continue simply by having the new set of partners make a new agreement for a partnership. Often the original partnership agreement specifies all the details regarding such changes in ownership.

Death of one of the partners A partnership agreement should state what is to be done if one of the partners dies. Usually the business continues to operate, but an accounting is made of the deceased partner's interest at the time of his death. The remaining partners form a new partnership and make a settlement with the estate of the deceased partner. The settlement in such cases probably would be based on the market value of the deceased partner's interest in the business. Or the partnership agreement might provide that the partnership assets be liquidated. In that case, the surviving partners would proceed as described later in this unit.

Admission of an additional partner Generally, these are the different circumstances involving admission of an additional partner:

1. An existing partner sells his partnership interest to a new partner.
2. A new partner invests in the firm—bonus to existing partners.
3. A new partner invests in the firm—bonus to new partner.
4. Goodwill is recorded for existing partners.
5. Goodwill is recorded for new partner.

Now, each of these five circumstances will be illustrated.

■ *How is the sale of a partner's interest reported?*

An existing partner sells his interest to a new partner If one of the partners sells his interest in the firm, and if the other partners agree to the admission of a new partner, then the old partner's capital is removed from the records and the new partner's capital account is set up. For example, assume that R. G. Jones purchases the partnership interest of A. J. Giorl in the XYZ Partnership. A. J. Giorl's capital balance at the time of the sale is $45,900. The agreed upon price for the interest is $75,000, and Jones pays the cash ($75,000) directly to Giorl. The general journal entry on the partnership books would be:

1978 Jan.	15	A. J. Giorl, Capital	45,900	
		R. G. Jones, Capital		45,900
		To record the sale of Giorl's interest in the firm to Jones.		

Note that the $75,000 cash did not enter the business and does not affect the accounts of the partnership.

How is the admission of a new partner reported?

A new partner invests in the firm—bonus to existing partners Very often a new partner is admitted to a very successful partnership, one that has been producing exceptional earnings. In such cases, the new partner may be willing to contribute an extra amount of investment to enter the company.

For example, the partnership of Alice, Bea, and Cathy has the following capital balances on January 1, 1978:

Alice	$20,000
Bea	20,000
Cathy	20,000
Total capital	$60,000

Diane has agreed to contribute $20,000 cash for a 20% interest in the business. Total capital of the new firm will be $80,000. Therefore, Diane has agreed to buy a 20% interest in $80,000 (which is $16,000) by contributing $20,000. Therefore, a $4,000 bonus goes to the old partners. Usually the bonus is divided among the old partners in the profit-sharing ratio. Assuming the profit-sharing ratio is $\frac{1}{3}$ for Alice, $\frac{1}{3}$ for Bea, and $\frac{1}{3}$ for Cathy, the entry to admit Diane would be as follows:

1978 Jan.	1	Cash	20,000	
		Diane, Capital		16,000
		Alice, Capital		1,333
		Bea, Capital		1,333
		Cathy, Capital		1,334

Each old partner's capital account is credited with one-third of the $4,000 bonus.

A new partner invests in the firm—bonus to new partner Occasionally, a new partner will be asked to join a partnership and will be offered a bonus situation because he is bringing something particularly desirable into the firm, such as a good reputation or special training. Assume that three partners share earnings and losses equally and have these capital balances at January 1, 1978:

Abner, Capital	$20,000
Bill, Capital	10,000
Charles, Capital	10,000
Total capital	$40,000

Duane enters the partnership on January 1, 1978. He invests $10,000 cash for a 25% interest in the business. A 25% interest in the total capital of the new partnership (25% $\times$ $50,000) would be $12,500. The entry would be:

1978					
Jan.	1	Cash		10,000	
		Abner, Capital		833	
		Bill, Capital		833	
		Charles, Capital		834	
		Duane, Capital			12,500
		To admit Duane to the partnership with a 25% interest.			

Each old partner's capital account is reduced by one-third of the $2,500 bonus that goes to the new partner.

Goodwill is recorded for existing partners Assume that Jones and Smith are partners, sharing profits equally, with capital balances of $20,000 and $30,000, respectively. Carter agrees to invest $30,000 in the partnership for a one-third interest in the firm. This implies that the new firm will be worth $90,000 (or 3 times the $30,000 investment that represents one-third of the new firm).

However, the tangible assets of the new firm total only $80,000:

Jones, Capital	$20,000
Smith, Capital	30,000
Carter, Capital	30,000
Total capital	$80,000

An intangible asset, **Goodwill,** can be recorded for the $10,000 difference.

1978 Jan.	1	Goodwill	10,000	
		Jones, Capital		5,000
		Smith, Capital		5,000
		To record goodwill for existing partners in the profit-sharing ratio.		
	1	Cash	30,000	
		Carter, Capital		30,000
		To admit Carter with a one-third interest in the firm.		

Recording goodwill in this manner is seldom recommended. Determining the amount of goodwill is highly subjective and could easily be misleading to financial statement readers.

Goodwill is recorded for new partner A new partner may be given a capital interest in the firm for a greater amount than the assets he invests. This is similar to the case of giving the bonus to the new partner.

Assume Craig invests land worth $10,000 and cash amounting to $6,000 in the partnership. It is agreed by all the partners that goodwill totaling $4,000 will be recorded.

1978 Jan.	1	Goodwill	4,000	
		Land	10,000	
		Cash	6,000	
		Craig, Capital		20,000
		To admit Craig to the partnership.		

We can now summarize the general rules for admitting a new partner to a partnership.

Whenever a new partner is admitted, certain basic things are agreed to by all the partners. These include:

1. The amount of assets that the new partner will contribute (perhaps including goodwill).
2. The amount of the new partner's capital account balance.

3. The restatement of any of the partnership assets, if this is agreed upon (perhaps including goodwill).
4. The amounts at which the old partners' capital accounts will be stated.

Because admission of a new partner is the same as beginning a new partnership, all the assets might be restated at their cash value when the new partnership is begun. All the assets of the new business will equal the total liabilities and capital of the new partnership. And all these amounts are negotiated and agreed upon by the partners.

■ *How is the withdrawal of a partner reported?*

Withdrawal of one of the partners from the business Articles of partnership usually specify what will happen if one of the partners decides to withdraw from the business for retirement or other reasons. If the other partners buy the withdrawing partner's interest directly, then the balance of the withdrawing partner's capital account is transferred to the remaining partners' capital accounts in the agreed-upon proportions. Since, technically, a new partnership is being started, the assets of the firm might be restated at their cash values or market values and the capital accounts also might be restated. Because this growth in asset values is considered part of the earnings process, the increase in assets is usually allocated to the capital accounts according to the profit-sharing agreement.

LIQUIDATION OF A PARTNERSHIP

The terms "realization" and "liquidation" are often used when the process of ending the operations of a partnership is discussed. **Realization** refers specifically to the process of selling the assets and converting them to cash. **Liquidation** refers to the whole process of selling the assets, paying the liabilities, and returning the cash to the partners for their interests in the company. The liquidation process can take several months or even several years.

■ *How is a partnership liquidation recorded?*

Two central ideas are important when a partnership is liquidated. The first is that *as the assets are converted to cash, any gain or loss (on the realization) is allocated to the partners' capital accounts according to the procedure agreed upon for sharing earnings and losses; the allocation is not made according to the balances of the partners' capital accounts.* The second idea is that *after all assets are converted to cash, and after all liabilities are paid, the partners are paid the balances of their capital accounts.* Occasionally, one of the partners will owe the partnership (the other partners) an additional sum because of the losses in the realization process. All these ideas are illustrated in the following example.

Example of realization and liquidation The ABC Partnership provides that earnings and losses are to be shared on a 2/7/1 basis as follows:

A   20%
B   70%
C   10%

The partnership began the liquidation process on June 9, 1978. At that date closing entries were made and the balances of the accounts after closing were as follows:

Cash	$ 1,000	
Merchandise inventory	3,000	
Long-term investments	10,000	
Accounts payable		$ 2,000
A, Capital		4,000
B, Capital		4,000
C, Capital		4,000
	$14,000	$14,000

During the next month, realization and liquidation took place as follows:

1. The merchandise inventory was sold for $4,000 cash.
2. The long-term investments were sold for $2,000 cash; this sale caused a substantial loss.
3. The accounts payable were paid in full.
4. Any partners owing the firm money paid the firm.
5. The partners were paid for their interests in the partnership.

The general journal entries shown below reflect these five realization and liquidation transactions. The tabular form that appears following the journal record summarizes the effects of the five transactions on the accounts of the partnership. Be sure to study both the journal and the table carefully.

    When a partnership is liquidated, there are usually many transactions that cause gains or losses on realization. In fact, there are often hundreds or thousands of individual gains or losses. It is customary in practice, therefore, to accumulate all these gains and losses in one temporary account called **Gains and losses on realization.** Then, before the partners are paid, this account is closed to the partners' capital accounts in total, according to the earnings and loss-sharing agreement. This procedure reduces the many allocations that would otherwise have to be made. If this procedure were used in the example that we just discussed, transaction (1) would show a credit of

(1)	Cash	4,000	
	Merchandise inventory		3,000
	A, Capital		200
	B, Capital		700
	C, Capital		100
	To record sale of merchandise and to distribute gain according to earnings agreement: (20%/70%/10%) × $1,000.		
(2)	Cash	2,000	
	A, Capital	1,600	
	B, Capital	5,600	
	C, Capital	800	
	Long-term investments		10,000
	To record sale of long-term investments and to distribute loss according to earnings agreement: (20%/70%/10%) × $8,000.		
(3)	Accounts payable	2,000	
	Cash		2,000
	To record payment of liabilities.		
(4)	Cash	900	
	B, Capital		900
	To record collection of cash owed to partnership by B. (See explanation in tabular form which follows on next page. *Capital account of B:* $4,000 beginning balance plus $700 in transaction (1) minus $5,600 in transaction (2) equals $900 *debit* balance.)		
(5)	A, Capital	2,600	
	C, Capital	3,300	
	Cash		5,900
	To record payment of capital balances to partners. (*Capital account of A:* $4,000 beginning balance plus $200 in transaction (1) minus $1,600 in transaction (2) equals $2,600 *credit* balance. *Capital account of C:* $4,000 beginning balance plus $100 in transaction (1) minus $800 in transaction (2) equals $3,300 *credit* balance.)		

$1,000 to the Gains and losses on realization account and transaction (2) would show a debit of $8,000 to that account. Then, in another entry, the $7,000 debit balance would be distributed to the three partners' capital accounts in the ratio of 20%, 70%, and 10%. The same final results would occur.

	CASH	MERCHANDISE INVENTORY	LONG-TERM INVESTMENTS	ACCOUNTS PAYABLE	A, CAPITAL	B, CAPITAL	C, CAPITAL
BEGINNING BALANCES (1) Sale of inventory (gain of $1,000)	$1,000 +4,000	$3,000 -3,000	$10,000	$2,000	$4,000 +200	$4,000 +700	$4,000 +100
BALANCE (2) Sale of Long-term investments (loss of $8,000)	$5,000 +2,000	-0-	$10,000 -10,000	$2,000	$4,200 -1,600	$4,700 -5,600	$4,100 -800
BALANCE (3) Liabilities are paid	$7,000 -2,000	-0-	-0-	$2,000 -2,000	$2,600	($900)[a]	$3,300
BALANCE (4) B contributes amount owed	$5,000 +900	-0-	-0-	-0-	$2,600	($900) +900	$3,300
BALANCE (5) Final liquidation of partnership	$5,900 -5,900	-0-	-0-	-0-	$2,600 -2,600	-0-	$3,300 -3,300
BALANCE	-0-	-0-	-0-	-0-	-0-	-0-	-0-

[a] The allocation of the loss creates a debit balance in B's Capital account; this means that B owes the partnership $900 if the other partners are to receive their full interests.

> ## NEW TERMS

gains and losses on realization A temporary account for accumulating the gains or losses incurred in converting the assets of a partnership to cash in the liquidation process; this account is closed to the partners' capital accounts according to the agreement for sharing earnings and losses. [p. 466]

goodwill A noncurrent (intangible) asset account used in partnership accounting to reflect the intangible resources acquired upon forming a new partnership; depending upon the situation, goodwill may be considered to be invested by a new partner, or it may be attributed to the old partners in a new partnership agreement. [p. 464]

liquidation The whole process of selling the assets, paying the liabilities, and returning the cash to the partners for their interests in the company, in the termination of a partnership. [p. 465]

realization The process of selling the assets and converting them into cash, in the termination of a partnership. [p. 465]

> ## ASSIGNMENT MATERIAL

QUESTIONS
Q27-1. What are four common ways that a partnership can end?

Q27-2. What journal entry is required when an existing partner sells his partnership interest to a new partner?

Q27-3. What journal entries are required when a new partner invests in the firm, with a bonus to the existing partners?

Q27-4. What journal entries are required when a new partner invests in the firm, with a bonus to the new partner?

Q27-5. What journal entries are required when goodwill is recorded for existing partners?

Q27-6. What journal entries are required when goodwill is recorded for a new partner?

Q27-7. What is realization, as it refers to partnerships?

Q27-8. What is liquidation, as it refers to partnerships?

Q27-9. What are the two central ideas that are important when a partnership is terminated and liquidated?

EXERCISES

E27-1. The trial balance of Kay and Baker Company at December 31, 1978, shows capital balances as follows:

Kay, Capital	$19,000
Baker, Capital	24,000

At this date, Baker sells his total interest in the partnership to Alex for $100,000 cash. Alex pays the cash directly to Baker. Make the journal entry needed to record the transaction on the books of the partnership.

E27-2. King and Smith are partners; their capital balances at December 31, 1978, are $20,000 and $30,000 respectively. They agree to admit Wilson as a partner. Wilson is to contribute $40,000 cash and is to share in the earnings and losses equally with the other partners. Before admission of Wilson, the two partners shared earnings and losses on this basis: King, $\frac{2}{3}$; Smith, $\frac{1}{3}$. The assets of the partnership are not to be revalued, since all partners agree that they are stated fairly in the records. Because of his special managerial ability and customer following, Wilson's capital account is to reflect a balance of $45,000, although he is contributing only $40,000 cash as his investment. Make the journal entry needed to admit the new partner. Goodwill is considered to go to the new partner.

E27-3. The trial balance of Lacey and Moorehouse Company, before beginning the realization and liquidation process, is shown below:

Cash	40,000	
Accounts receivable	10,000	
Allowance for uncollectibles		1,000
Merchandise inventory	17,000	
Accounts payable		20,000
L. Lacey, Capital		22,000
M. Moorehouse, Capital		24,000
	67,000	67,000

Record the following transactions in general journal form. The partners shared equally in earnings and losses.

a. Collected a total of $9,000 of the accounts receivable. The remaining receivables are expected to be collected later.

b. Accounts payable were paid in full.

c. Collected an additional $500 of accounts receivable. (At this time close the Accounts receivable and Allowance for uncollectibles account.)

d. Sold merchandise inventory for $10,000.

e. Paid the partners the amounts due for their investments.

E27-4. On March 1, 1978, the partnership of Brown and Green began the realization and liquidation process. Brown and Green shared profits as follows:

Brown	25%
Green	75%

Brown had a capital balance of $16,000 and Green had a capital balance of $26,000 at March 1, 1978. During March, all non-cash assets were sold for $80,000 cash and the liabilities, amounting to $60,000 were paid in full. Assume the cash balance before the sale of the assets was $5,000. When the final settlement was made to the partners, how much cash did each receive?

PROBLEMS (GROUP A)

P27-1. *Realization and liquidation.* The trial balance of Ace and Queen Company, before beginning the realization and liquidation process, is shown below:

Cash	9,000	
Accounts receivable	1,000	
Estimated uncollectibles		100
Equipment	11,000	
Accumulated depreciation		1,000
Accounts payable		4,000
Ace, Capital		5,900
Queen, Capital		10,000
	21,000	21,000

Record the following transactions in general journal form; use the temporary account, *Gains and losses on realization.* The partners share earnings and losses in a 2:1 ratio—Ace, $\frac{2}{3}$; Queen, $\frac{1}{3}$.

a. Collected a total of $912 cash on the receivables. The remaining $88 is assumed uncollectible.

b. Sold the equipment for $9,500 cash.

c. Paid the Accounts payable in full.

d. Paid the partners the amounts due for their investments.

P27-2. *Admission of new partner.* Below are five independent cases dealing with the admission of a new partner.

1. Richard Baux sells his entire interest in the Scott and Baux Co. partnership to Howard Brenner for $96,000 cash and land worth $60,000. The books of the partnership revealed that the capital account of Baux had a balance of $150,000 at the time of the sale.

2. The capital balances of the owners of Peanuts and Pecans Company were as follows on January 1, 1978:

		PROFIT-SHARING RATIO
David Nutt	$200,000	$\frac{1}{3}$
Bill Shell	100,000	$\frac{1}{3}$
Tom Husk	100,000	$\frac{1}{3}$
	$400,000	

John Baker agrees to buy a 16% interest in the firm for $100,000. Each of the four partners will share profits equally in the new partnership. Bonus goes to the old partners.

3. The capital balances of the owners of Breaux and Boudreaux Co. were as follows on January 1, 1978:

		PROFIT-SHARING RATIO
Horace Breaux	$200,000	$\frac{1}{3}$
Harry Conet	100,000	$\frac{1}{3}$
Don Walters	100,000	$\frac{1}{3}$
	$400,000	

Morris Harrison is given the opportunity, because of his special skills and talents, to buy a 24% interest in the partnership for $100,000. Each of the four partners will share profits equally in the new partnership. Bonus goes to the new partner.

4. The capital balances of the owners of Arts and Crafts Company on January 1, 1978, were as follows:

		PROFIT-SHARING AGREEMENT
Millard Art	$150,000	50%
Milton Art	100,000	20%
Manuel Craft	50,000	20%
Mitchell Craft	50,000	10%
	$350,000	

Mr. Johnson Carver agrees to buy a 20% interest in the firm for $100,000. Goodwill will be recorded for the existing partners.

5. The capital balances of the owners of Stanley Co. at January 1, 1978, follow:

		PROFIT-SHARING AGREEMENT
Willard Stanley	$ 70,000	$\frac{1}{10}$
Herman Livingstone	30,000	$\frac{9}{10}$
	$100,000	

John Tauzin invests a building worth $50,000 in the partnership. His interest in the partnership, it is agreed, will amount to $60,000, and goodwill will be recorded. The new profit-sharing agreement will be: Stanley, $\frac{1}{10}$; Livingstone, $\frac{7}{10}$; Tauzin, $\frac{1}{5}$.

REQUIRED: Prepare journal entries to admit the new partner for each of the five situations.

P27-3. *Realization and liquidation.* Slider Used Cars Company shares profits and losses as follows:

Jim Slider	10%
Susan Widget	20%
Bill Blight	70%

On March 18, 1978, the firm began the realization and liquidation process. At that time, the account balances were as follows:

Cash	11,000	
Marketable securities	4,000	
Accounts receivable	21,000	
Allowance for bad debts		3,000
Inventory of cars	55,000	
Equipment	20,000	
Accumulated depreciation—Equipment		12,000
Land	80,000	
Buildings	21,000	
Accumulated depreciation—Buildings		15,000
Accounts payable		31,000
Notes payable		51,000
Slider, Capital		20,000
Widget, Capital		40,000
Blight, Capital		40,000
	212,000	212,000

These events took place in March and April:
1. Receivables amounting to $15,000 were collected. No other collections are likely.
2. All the marketable securities were sold for $6,100 cash.

3. Used cars that had cost $20,000 were sold for $15,000 cash.
4. All the equipment was sold for $5,000 cash.
5. Used cars that had cost $35,000 were sold for $25,000 cash.
6. Land and buildings were sold for $81,000 cash. The land was appraised at $80,000.
7. Paid all the accounts payable.
8. Paid the note and interest, $51,700.
9. Settled with the partners.

REQUIRED:

a. Prepare a table similar to the one illustrated in the unit to show the realization and liquidation process.
b. Prepare journal entries for the realization and liquidation.

PROBLEMS (GROUP B)

P27-4. *Realization and liquidation.* George Cart, W. Horse, Mary G. Round, and P. Rabbit were partners in the firm of Festival Enterprises Company. The partnership began the liquidation process on January 1, 1978. At that date, closing entries were made and the following balances of the accounts remained:

Cash	25,000	
Accounts receivable	50,000	
Allowance for uncollectibles		2,000
Merchandise inventory	80,000	
Accounts payable		5,000
G. Cart, Capital		38,000
W. Horse, Capital		51,000
M. Round, Capital		49,000
P. Rabbit, Capital		10,000
	155,000	155,000

The partners shared earnings and losses equally. Realization and liquidation took place as follows:

Jan. 3   Accounts payable were paid in full.
     11   Sold the merchandise inventory for $20,000 cash.
     21   Collected $40,000 of the accounts receivables. The remaining receivables are expected to be collected later.
     24   Collected an additional $9,000 of accounts receivable. (At this time, close to zero the Accounts receivable account and the Allowance for uncollectibles account.)
     28   Collected any amounts due the partnership by partners.
     31   Paid the partners any amounts due them in final liquidation.

REQUIRED:

a. Prepare general journal entries for the realization and liquidation.
b. Prepare a tabular form similar to the one illustrated in the text for the realization and liquidation.

P27-5. *Admission of new partner.* Below is a list showing details of alternative ways of admitting a new partner. The existing partnership records show the following:

	CAPITAL BALANCE	SHARE OF EARNINGS
Maurice Sears	$ 61,000	30%
Montgomery Kreeger	85,000	10%
B. W. Penney	50,000	20%
Ward Benton	100,000	40%
	$296,000	100%

Alternative ways of admitting Hannibal Roebuck to the partnership:
1. Roebuck buys a 25% interest in the partnership for $96,000. Goodwill of $4,000 goes to Roebuck.
2. Roebuck buys a 25% interest in the partnership for $100,000. Goodwill of $4,000 goes to the existing partners.
3. Roebuck pays $105,000 cash directly to Benton to buy his interest in the partnership.
4. Roebuck invests $75,000 in the partnership for a 20% interest in the partnership.
5. Roebuck invests $70,000 in the partnership for a 20% interest in the partnership.

REQUIRED:

Prepare journal entries for each of the five alternatives to admit the new partner.

P27-6. *Realization and liquidation.* On January 1, 1978, the Pechulis Products Company trial balance was as follows:

Pechulis Products Company
TRIAL BALANCE
January 1, 1978

Cash	10,000	
Marketable securities	5,000	
Prepaid insurance	2,000	
Inventory	29,000	
Accounts receivable	21,000	
Allowance for bad debts		2,000
Equipment	50,000	
Accumulated depreciation—Equipment		26,000
Patents	18,000	
Accounts payable		12,000
Notes payable		10,000
Harvey, Capital		25,000
Bonn, Capital		50,000
Heidelberg, Capital		10,000
	135,000	135,000

The profit- and loss-sharing ratio is:

Harvey	30%
Bonn	30%
Heidelberg	40%

The following transactions took place during January through March:
1. Sold the patents to a competitor for $4,000.
2. Paid the accounts payable.
3. Sold the marketable securities for $5,500.
4. Sold the inventory for $31,000.
5. Collected $20,000 of the accounts receivable. The remainder is considered uncollectible.
6. Sold the equipment for $17,000 cash.
7. Canceled the insurance policy and received a $1,500 refund of premiums paid.
8. Paid the principal of the note plus $200 interest.
9. Made final settlement with the partners.

REQUIRED:

a. Prepare a table similar to the one illustrated in the unit to show the realization and liquidation process.

b. Prepare journal entries for the realization and liquidation.

CUMULATIVE REVIEW PROBLEMS

P27-7. *Cumulative review problem.* George Mills and Henrietta Lang agree to form a partnership to operate a craft shop on January 1, 1978. Lang contributes the following as her investment in the business:

1. A building that she originally paid $52,000 for; the accumulated depreciation is now $12,000. The current appraised value is $45,000, which is the amount agreed upon by the partners for the investment.
2. Land that is currently valued at $20,000.

Lang has accounts payable amounting to $5,900. The partnership will take over these debts.

Mills contributes the following as his investment in the business:

1. Cash amounting to $66,000.
2. Accounts receivable of $34,000. It is agreed that there should be an allowance for uncollectibles of $3,000.

Mills has accounts payable amounting to $20,000. The partnership will take over these debts.

The profit-sharing agreement provides that the partners will share equally in the earnings of the business.

REQUIRED:

a. Make the entries in general journal form to record the contribution of assets and liabilities to the partnership.

b. During the year, net earnings amounted to $76,000. Lang withdrew $12,000, and Mills withdrew $14,000. Make the journal entry to record the distribution of earnings to the two capital accounts.

c. Prepare a statement of owners' capital in good form for the year ended December 31, 1978.

*P27-8. *Cumulative review problem.* Records of Carson and Co. for 1978 appear below.

PARTNER	WITHDRAWALS	ADDITIONAL INVESTMENTS
Carson	$11,000	$ 2,000
Danton	25,000	50,000
Edgar	15,000	–0–

All withdrawals were made on December 1, 1978; the additional investment of Carson was made February 1, 1978; and the additional investment of Danton was made on November 1, 1978. Net earnings for the partnership were $113,500 for 1978.

Capital balances at January 1, 1978, were as follows: Carson, $96,000; Danton, $115,000; Edgar, $100,000. The profit-sharing agreement provided the following:

	CARSON	DANTON	EDGAR
1. Salary allowances	$10,000	$15,000	$20,000
2. Interest on average capital balances	8%	8%	8%
3. Balance of profit or loss (deficit)	30%	50%	20%

On January 1, 1979, the liabilities of the firm consisted of the following:

Accounts payable	$12,500
Notes payable	50,000

At that date, there were only three assets as follows:

Cash	$45,000
Accounts receivable	40,000
Allowance for uncollectibles	(4,000)
Inventories	?
Total assets	?

The partners decide to liquidate the partnership beginning January 1, 1979. It is agreed to suspend the salary and interest allowances during 1979 and to divide profits and losses on the 30:50:20 basis only. During January, these events took place:

1. Collected $35,000 of the receivables. The remainder is uncollectible.
2. Sold the inventories for 10% above their book value (cost).
3. Paid all debts.
4. Settled with the partners.

REQUIRED:

a. Prepare a schedule showing how 1978 net earnings are to be allocated to the partners.
b. Prepare closing entries to transfer the net earnings to the partners' capital accounts and to close the withdrawals accounts.
c. Prepare a table showing the realization and liquidation process.
d. Prepare general journal entries for the realization and liquidation.

PART FOUR
CORPORATIONS

chapter 12

corporations: introduction

28

CAPITAL ACQUISITION AND REPORTING

> **OBJECTIVE**

This unit describes the accounting treatment and reporting of the capital-raising process in corporations. Details about raising capital with both common and preferred stock are included.

> **APPROACH TO ATTAINING THE OBJECTIVE**

As you study about corporation capital raising, pay special attention to these three questions, which the text following answers:

- *What categories of information are revealed by the capital section of a corporation balance sheet?*
- *What technical details are important to understanding corporate capital reporting?*
- *How is the issuance of stock recorded?*

■ *What categories of
information are
revealed by the capital
section of a
corporation balance
sheet?*

Stockholders' equity usually is reported in two separate sections on a corpora-tion balance sheet. These two categories are (1) capital contributed by stock-holders, and (2) capital generated from the earnings process (retained earn-ings). This classification scheme tells the financial statement user the major *sources* of the firm's capital. Shown below is a stockholders' equity section of a balance sheet illustrating this classification. Capital contributed by stock-holders is discussed in this unit. The other major source of capital, retained earnings, is treated in Unit 29. You probably will want to refer to this exam-ple as you read the explanations in this and the next unit. After you have studied this unit, you should be able to read the stockholders' equity section of a corporation balance sheet and determine the following:

1.   The major sources of the company's capital (common stockholders, preferred stockholders, retained earnings).
2.   Details concerning each of the company's stock issues.

STOCKHOLDERS' EQUITY (CAPITAL)

capital contributed by stockholders		
Preferred stock ($100 par value 5%, 100,000 shares outstanding, 150,000 shares authorized)	$10,000,000	
Premium on preferred stock	100,000	
Preferred stock ($50 par value, 4% cumulative participating, 20,000 shares authorized and outstanding)	1,000,000	
Common stock (no par value, 2,000,000 shares authorized, 1,000,000 shares issued and outstanding)	25,000,000	
Common stock subscribed, 100,000 shares unissued	3,000,000	
Total capital contributed by stockholders		$39,100,000
retained earnings		
Appropriated:		
For general contingencies	$2,000,000	
For bonds payable	5,000,000	
Total appropriated retained earnings	$ 7,000,000	
Unappropriated retained earnings	25,419,700	
Total retained earnings		$32,419,700
Total stockholders' equity		$71,519,700

The purpose of this section is to describe for you some of the more important technical considerations dealing with stocks and stockholders' equity report-ing. These include par value and no-par-value stocks, stated values, cumulative and noncumulative preferred stocks, participating and nonparticipating preferred stocks, and convertible stocks.

■ *What technical details are important to understanding corporate capital reporting?*

Par value and no-par-value stocks Stocks (common and preferred) which have a face amount printed on them are known as *par value stocks*. Preferred stocks ordinarily have **par values,** such as $10, $50, or $100. In the case of preferred stocks, the annual dividend rate is applied to the par value to determine the dividend to be declared by the board of directors. For example, assume that you purchased 100 shares of $100 par value 5% preferred stock of the ABC Corporation for $104 per share. The annual dividend would be $5 per share, or 5% of the par value of $100 per share. The dividend is *not* based upon the $104 per share contributed to the company.

No-par-value stocks do not have a face amount printed on the stock certificates. Actually, there is no real need for stocks to have a par value. This is so because the important consideration for the company is the number of dollars the stockholders are willing to invest for each share of ownership in the company. This amount would be expected to change over time as the company becomes more or less profitable and valuable. The original par value thus would lose any meaning it might have. Even with preferred stock, the dividends could be stated on the certificate in an amount, such as $5 per share, without regard to a par amount or to a percentage rate based on par.

The custom of using par values arose in the early development of the corporate form of organization. The par value has a *legal* significance dealing with liquidating and terminating a corporation, and otherwise dealing with how much capital can be returned to the owners.

Stated values The state laws governing corporations tend to differ widely. Most state laws, however, provide that a certain amount of the capital of a corporation must remain in the corporation permanently. This amount cannot be returned to the stockholders. These laws have the effect of protecting the rights of creditors. Returning too much of the assets to stockholders (reducing the capital) can weaken the company and perhaps cause creditors to lose. The amount of a stock issue that must remain permanently in the company is known as the **legal value.** Depending upon the state, this might be an amount specified by law, or it might be the par value, or it might be a stated value. A **stated value** is an amount the board of directors designates for each share of stock. For example, the common stock of a company may be no-par stock. The board of directors could designate each share to have a stated value of $10, and this $10 amount would be shown on the balance sheet. Later in this unit you will see the journal entries for stock issues involving par value stocks, no-par-value stocks, and no-par-value stocks with a stated value.

Cumulative and noncumulative preferred stocks These provisions refer to preferred stock issues. Preferred stock may be either *cumulative* or *noncumulative* as to dividends. The **cumulative preferred stock** provision requires that the board of directors declare dividends for preferred stockholders for every year before dividends can be paid to common stockholders. In other words, preferred dividends must have been paid for every year in the past before a common stock dividend can be paid. Noncumulative preferred stock, on the other hand, provides that only *in any single year* the preferred dividends must be declared before common dividends can be declared. The cumulative provision, of course, makes the preferred stock issue more attractive to investors.

To illustrate, assume that a corporation has the following issues outstanding:

1. **Common stock:** 10,000 shares, $100 par value
2. **Preferred stock:** 1,000 shares, $100 par value, 6% *cumulative* stock

The corporation decides to declare dividends as follows:

YEAR	TOTAL AMOUNT OF DIVIDENDS (BOTH COMMON AND PREFERRED)
1976	$16,000
1977	none
1978	none
1979	$23,000

Since the preferred shares are cumulative, the dividends would be divided between preferred and common as follows:

YEAR	TOTAL DIVIDENDS	PREFERRED DIVIDENDS	COMMON DIVIDENDS
1976	$16,000	$ 6,000[a]	$10,000[b]
1977	none	none	none
1978	none	none	none
1979	$23,000	$18,000[c]	$ 5,000[d]

[a] 1,000 shares $\times$ $100 $\times$ 0.06 = $6,000 preferred dividends per year, or $6 per share.

[b] $16,000 — $6,000 = $10,000. This amounts to $1 per share ($10,000 ÷ 10,000 shares).

[c] Dividends in arrears (past due) for 1977, $6,000; plus dividends in arrears for 1978, $6,000; plus 1979 dividends of $6,000 equals $18,000.

[d] $23,000 — $18,000 = $5,000, or 50 cents per share.

Participating and nonparticipating preferred stocks These provisions also refer to preferred stock issues. Preferred stock may be **participating** or *nonparticipating* as to dividends. Assume that the preferred stock is 5% participating, $100 par value. This means that after the $5 preferred dividend is paid, and if additional dividends are paid that year, then preferred stockholders are entitled to share in the additional dividends after common stockholders have received the $5 amount. The *manner* in which the preferred stockholders share in the additional dividends is entirely dependent on the provisions of the preferred stock issue.

To illustrate, a company has the following stocks outstanding:

1. **Common stock:** 10,000 shares, $100 par value stock
2. **Preferred stock:** 1,000 shares, $100 par value, 6%, *fully participating* stock

Now, assume that the board of directors declares dividends for 1978 *totaling* $80,000. The dividends would be allocated between preferred and common as follows:

	dividends		
	PREFERRED	COMMON	TOTAL
Regular 6% preferred dividend (0.06 × 1,000 × $100)	$6,000		$ 6,000
Dividends to common at same rate as preferred (0.06 × 10,000 × $100)		$60,000	60,000
Remainder allocated on a percentage-of-par-value basis ($80,000 − $66,000 = $14,000)[a]	1,273	12,727	14,000
	$7,273	$72,727	$80,000

[a] Explanation follows.

Notice that $6,000 of regular dividends go to preferred shareholders first. Next, common shareholders are entitled to receive the same rate (6%) on their par value of $1,000,000. This amounts to $60,000. This leaves $14,000 to be distributed between common and preferred shareholders according to the participating agreement ($80,000 − $66,000 = $14,000).

The distribution is made according to the relative par values as follows:

$$\text{Participating share for preferred} = \frac{\text{Par value of preferred}}{\text{Total par value of common and preferred}} = \frac{\$100,000}{\$1,000,000 + \$100,000} = \frac{1}{11}$$

$$\frac{1}{11} \times \$14,000 = \$1,273$$

$$\begin{array}{c}\text{Participating}\\\text{share for}\\\text{common}\end{array}=\dfrac{\begin{array}{c}\text{Par value}\\\text{of common}\end{array}}{\begin{array}{c}\text{Total par value}\\\text{of common and}\\\text{preferred}\end{array}}=\dfrac{\$1,000,000}{\$1,000,000+\$100,000}=\dfrac{10}{11}$$

$$\tfrac{10}{11}\times\$14,000=\$12,727$$

Based on these figures, the *per share* dividends would amount to:

$$\text{Preferred dividends per share}=\dfrac{\$7,273}{1,000\text{ shares}}=\$7.273$$

$$\text{Common dividends per share}=\dfrac{\$72,727}{10,000\text{ shares}}=\$7.2727$$

Convertible stocks You have already studied about convertible bonds. Like convertible bonds, preferred stocks also can have a **convertible** provision. A preferred stock issue might provide that, at the option of the stockholder, each share of preferred stock could be traded for (converted to) a share of common stock. Such provisions are fairly common. They are designed to make a stock issue more attractive to investors and thus help a company acquire capital.

ISSUING STOCK FOR CASH This section illustrates the accounting entries and reporting practices related to raising capital from stockholders. The following examples all deal with common stock. Remember, however, that the entries for preferred stock would be substantially the same, except the preferred stock title would be used in the accounts in the place of common stock.

Issuing par value stock for an amount of cash equal to the par amount Assume that a firm issued 1,000 shares of $30 par value common stock for $30 per share cash. This entry would be made:

■ *How is the issuance of stock recorded?*

1978					
May	1		Cash	30,000	
			Common stock		30,000

The assets of the firm increase by $30,000; at the same time, the capital or stockholders' equity increases by $30,000.

Issuing par value stock for more cash than the par value Assume that a firm issued 1,000 shares of $30 par value common stock for $32 per share. This entry would be made:

1978					
May	5		Cash	32,000	
			Common stock		30,000
			Premium on common stock		2,000

The assets of the firm increase by $32,000; at the same time, the capital also increases by $32,000. Two separate capital accounts are used to report the issuance of stock above the par amount, although separate reporting of this information is of limited use to decision makers. The Premium on common stock account shows the capital contributed in excess of par value. Often this is called *paid in capital in excess of par value,* or simply **paid-in capital.** In a few cases, the separate reporting of the par amount might reveal something about the legal capital, or it might be an approximation of the legal capital.

The stockholders' equity section illustrated at the beginning of this unit shows the reporting practice for par value stock issued above par. See the 5% preferred stock in that illustration.

Issuing par value stock for less cash than the par value This is a rare circumstance, and in some states a corporation cannot legally issue its stock below the par value. Assume that a company issues 1,000 shares of $30 par value stock for $29 per share. This entry would be made:

1978					
May	6		Cash	29,000	
			Discount on common stock	1,000	
			Common stock		30,000

The assets of the firm increase by $29,000; at the same time, the capital increases by only $29,000. The **Discount on common stock** is a capital account with a debit balance; it serves to *reduce* the Common stock account. Remember: as a result of the transaction, the capital of the company grows by only $29,000, not by the par amount of $30,000.

Issuing no-par stock with a stated value When the board of directors gives the stock a stated value, then, for accounting and reporting purposes, the stated value is treated in the same manner as is par value. On the balance sheet, the fact that the stock has a stated value would be revealed. The Common stock account would accumulate the amount of the stated value for all of the shares issued. A Premium on common stock account might be described as *paid-in capital in excess of stated value* or, perhaps, as *capital contributed in excess of stated value*.

Issuing no-par-value stock Assume that a firm issued 1,000 shares of no-par-value common stock for $32,000 cash. This entry would be made:

1978 May	10	Cash		32,000	
		Common stock			32,000

In accounting for no-par stock, there is no basis for breaking the contributed capital into two accounts. Therefore, the total proceeds from the stock issue are credited to the stock account.

Summary *When assets are acquired by issuing stock, the firm's resources are increased by the value of the assets received. The firm's capital is increased by the same amount, although the net increase in capital may be reported in two separate accounts when there is a par or stated value.* For example, the increase in the Common stock account plus the increase in the Premium on common stock account equals the increase in total capital.

ISSUING STOCK FOR OTHER PROPERTY

Occasionally stock is issued to stockholders for property other than cash. Assume that 1,000 shares of $30 par value common stock were issued for buildings, equipment, and land. An independent appraiser had provided the following appraisals of the property:

Buildings	$15,000
Equipment	5,000
Land	11,000
	$31,000

This entry would be made:

1978 May	20	Buildings		15,000	
		Equipment		5,000	
		Land		11,000	
		Common stock			30,000
		Premium on common stock			1,000

The transaction is recorded as if the stock had been issued for cash and as if the cash had been used to purchase the property. *Note that the assets acquired are recorded at their cash value.* When an appraisal of the property contributed is not available, the value of the transaction often can be estimated by observing the current market price of the stock being issued. For example, this company's common stock could have been selling for about $31 per share, or $31,000 for 1,000 shares. The $31,000 then could be allocated among the assets acquired on some estimated basis.

STOCK SUBSCRIPTIONS

A corporation may choose to allow stockholders to purchase its stock on credit. That is, a stock subscription agreement can be designed to allow the stockholders to pay for the stock in a series of installments or to pay the whole amount at some future date. Usually the stock certificates are not actually issued until all the payments are made for the stock. These transactions will illustrate:

April 1, 1978	Stockholders subscribed to 1,000 shares of $30 par value common stock at $33 per share. On December 1, 1975, the subscribers are to pay 50% of the amount, and the remaining amount is to be paid on March 1, 1976.
Dec. 1, 1978	Received cash for 50% of the subscription price.
March 1, 1979	Received the balance of the subscriptions and issued the stock certificates.

1978					
April	1	Subscriptions receivable		33,000	
		Common stock subscribed			30,000
		Premium on common stock			3,000
Dec.	1	Cash		16,500	
		Subscriptions receivable			16,500

1979					
March	1	Cash		16,500	
		Subscriptions receivable			16,500
	1	Common stock subscribed		30,000	
		Common stock			30,000

On April 1, 1978, an asset is created — **Subscriptions receivable.** This account, like accounts receivable to be collected in the next year, would be reported on the balance sheet as a current asset. The Common stock subscribed account and the Premium on common stock account both are *capital* accounts. The word *subscribed* is included in the account title to let readers of the capital section of the balance sheet know that these shares have not yet been issued. At December 31, 1978, the balance sheet would show Subscriptions receivable as an asset in the amount of the unpaid subscriptions ($16,500).

The first entry on March 1, 1979, is similar to collecting any receivable. The second entry shows the actual issuance of common stock — the entry reclassifies the contributed capital from one category to another.

common stock Certificates (securities) issued to a corporation's main stockholders. [p. 484]

convertible stock Stock which includes the provision that the shares may be exchanged for another kind of security of the corporation. [p. 486]

cumulative preferred stock Preferred stock which includes the provision that if any regular preferred dividends are missed, the common stockholders cannot be paid dividends until the preferred stockholders receive all past dividends. [p. 484]

discount on stock A capital account with a debit balance (reduction in capital); the amount less than par value contributed to the corporation by stockholders. [p. 487]

legal value The dollar amount of a stock issue that must remain permanently in the company, according to state law. [p. 483]

paid-in capital Also called *premium on stock;* the amount in excess of par value contributed to the corporation by stockholders; a capital account. [p. 487]

par value The face value or amount printed on certain stock certificates. [p. 483]

participating preferred stock Preferred stock which includes the provision that, in any one year, after the preferred and common dividends are declared, then if there are any more dividends declared, the preferred stockholders share in those additional dividends. [p. 484]

preferred stock A type of security issued by corporations to raise permanent capital; preferred stockholders have certain preferences (advantages) over common stockholders in case of liquidation of the corporation and in the payment of dividends. [p. 484]

stated value An amount or value sometimes placed on each share of its stock by the board of directors of a corporation; when the stock has no par value, the board of directors sometimes designates a stated value. [p. 483]

subscriptions receivable An asset account, reflecting amounts owed the corporation by stockholders for shares of stock they have promised to purchase. [p. 489]

▶ **ASSIGNMENT MATERIAL**

QUESTIONS

Q28-1. What are the two main sections of the capital part of a corporation balance sheet?

Q28-2. Is the amount of the dividend on preferred stock (5%, for example) computed on the par value of the stock, the amount contributed by the stockholder, or the market value of the stock?

Q28-3. How does cumulative preferred stock differ from other preferred stock?

Q28-4. What is convertible stock?

Q28-5. What are stock subscriptions?

Q28-6. What is participating preferred stock?

EXERCISES

E28-1. The following is a list of accounts that appear on the financial statements of corporations:

Preferred stock
Premium on common stock
Premium on preferred stock
Common stock subscribed
Preferred stock subscribed
Common stock subscriptions receivable
Preferred stock subscriptions receivable

Discount on common stock

Discount on preferred stock

For each of the accounts above, indicate the usual balance of the account (debit or credit), the financial statement that it would be reported on, and the section of the statement. Use the following codes to indicate the section of the statement.

CODE	SECTION OF FINANCIAL STATEMENT
1	Revenue
2	Expenses
3	Assets
4	Liabilities
5	Contributed capital
6	Earned capital

EXAMPLE	USUAL BALANCE	STATEMENT	SECTION
Common stock	credit	Balance sheet	5

E28-2. Make journal entries for the following transactions. Each transaction is to be considered a separate case.
  a. Issued 10,000 shares of no-par-value common stock for $110 per share. 20,000 shares of this stock had been authorized.
  b. Issued 10,000 shares of no-par-value common stock for $110 per share. The board of directors assigned a stated value of $100 per share to the stock. 20,000 shares of this stock had been authorized.
  c. Issued 5,000 shares of 6%, $100 par value preferred stock for $110 per share. 10,000 shares of this stock had been authorized.

E28-3. The following transactions of the Essas Mat Company took place:
  a. Issued 17,500 shares of no-par common stock for $104.50 per share. The Board of Directors had assigned a stated value of $100 to the common shares. The charter of the company had originally authorized 125,000 shares of the common stock, and 100,000 shares were issued at stated value and were outstanding before this transaction.
  b. Issued 1,000 shares of 5% preferred stock for $115 per share. The preferred shares are cumulative, with a par value of $80 per share. The firm is authorized to issue 10,000 shares. This is the first issue.
  c. Received subscriptions for 1,000 additional shares of no-par-value common stock (see a above). The subscribers agreed to pay $105 per share during the coming year.
  Make the general journal entries for the three transactions, and prepare the capital (contributed capital) section of the balance sheet, giving effect to all the transactions, in good form.

E28-4. Prepare the necessary journal entries for each of the following transactions:
  a. A firm issued 2,000 shares of $150 par value common stock for $150 per share cash.
  b. A firm issued 2,000 shares of $150 par value common stock for $155 per share cash.

c. A firm issued 2,500 shares of $150 par value common stock for $140 per share cash.

d. A firm issued 2,500 shares of no-par value common stock for $382,500 cash.

e. A firm issued 2,500 shares of $150 par value common stock for buildings, equipment, and land. An independent appraiser had provided the following appraisals of the property:

Buildings	$100,000
Equipment	135,000
Land	115,000
	$350,000

E28-5. Prepare the necessary journal entries for each of the following transactions:

a. Stockholders subscribed to 2,500 shares of $75 par value common stock at $78 per share.

b. Received 30% of the amount due from the subscribers.

c. Received another 40% of the amount due from the subscribers.

d. Received the balance of the subscriptions and issued the stock certificates.

PROBLEMS (GROUP A)

P28-1. *Stockholders' equity transactions; balance sheet.* For the purposes of this problem, the table on page 482 is assumed to be the stockholders' equity section of a corporation balance sheet at January 1, 1978. During 1978, these transactions took place:

1978

Jan. 12 Issued 1,000 additional shares of the 5% preferred stock for $103 per share cash.

15 Issued 2,000 additional shares of the 4% preferred stock for $48 per share cash. Authorization was increased from 20,000 shares to 22,000 shares.

April 25 Issued 3,000 shares of common stock to Decatur Equipment Co. in payment for equipment purchased. The equipment has a cash price of $77,500.

June 11 Collected $1,500,000 cash from some of the common stock subscribers and issued 50,000 shares of stock.

REQUIRED:

a. Prepare accounting entries for the 1978 transactions in general journal form.

b. Prepare a stockholders' equity section in good form for the company at December 31, 1978, after giving effect to the 1978 transactions. *To simplify,* assume the retained earnings did not change during 1978.

P28-2. *Cumulative and participating preferred stocks.* TYI Corporation had the following stocks outstanding for several years:

Common stock, 20,000 shares, $100 par value

6% Preferred stock, 10,000 shares, $10 par value, cumulative, nonparticipating

Wixon Company had these stocks outstanding during that period:

Common stock, 10,000 shares, $70 par value

5% Preferred stock, 10,000 shares, $100 par value, fully participating

Dividends were declared as follows by the companies:

total dividends

	TYI	WIXON
1977	$20,000	$20,000
1978	none	none
1979	none	none
1980	$100,000	$100,000
1981	$40,000	$40,000

REQUIRED: Compute the total dividends per share declared by each company for each class of stock.

P28-3. *Stockholders' equity transactions.* Selected transactions of Transmission Repairs, Inc., for January, 1978, follow.

Jan. 4   Issued 4,000 shares of $100 par value common stock for $113 per share cash.

18   Issued 1,000 shares of the 6% $100 par cumulative preferred stock for $109 per share cash.

21   Purchased land and a building that were appraised as follows:

Land	$150,000
Building	40,000
	$190,000

In payment for the land and building, issued 1,000 shares of common stock (that have a market value of $113 per share) and signed a 2-year, 8% note payable for $77,000.

25   Received subscriptions for 500 shares of the 6% cumulative preferred stock at $111 per share.

31   Collected the full amount due on 200 of the preferred shares that were subscribed on January 25. Issued the certificates on these shares.

REQUIRED: Prepare general journal entries for the transactions.

PROBLEMS (GROUP B)

P28-4. *Stockholders' equity transactions.* The following is a list of selected transactions of Tom Terrific and Associates for October, 1978.

Oct. 3   Issued 2,000 shares of par value common stock, $80 par value, for $83 per share.

15   Issued 500 shares of the $80 par value common stock for $78 per share.

16   Purchased land and buildings from Aizo Investment Corporation. The land has an appraised value of $10,000 and the buildings have an appraised value of $72,000. The land and buildings are paid for as follows:

Issued 900 shares of common stock ($80 par value) with a market value of $82 per share	$73,800
Cash paid	8,200
	$82,000

17 Stockholders subscribed to 700 shares of $80 par value common stock at $81 per share. The amount is to be paid on October 31, and the stock certificates are to be issued.

31 Collected the amount due from the common stock subscriptions and issued the stock certificates.

REQUIRED: Prepare general journal entries for the transactions.

*P28-5. *Cumulative and participating preferred stocks.* Data about the stocks outstanding of Champignons Company follows:

6% preferred stock, noncumulative, participating, $100 par value, 5,000 shares outstanding	$ 500,000
Premium on 6% preferred stock	50,000
	550,000
5% preferred stock, cumulative, $100 par value, 5,000 shares outstanding	$ 500,000
Premium on 5% preferred stock	5,000
	$ 505,000
Common stock, $100 par value, 10,000 shares outstanding	$1,000,000
Premium on common stock	40,000
	$1,040,000

YEAR	TOTAL DIVIDENDS DECLARED	6% PREFERRED DIVIDENDS	5% PREFERRED DIVIDENDS	COMMON DIVIDENDS
1976	$55,000	$30,000	$25,000	none
1977	none	none	none	none
1978	$30,000	$20,000	$10,000	none

The company began operations on January 1, 1976. In 1979, dividends of $50,000 were declared on *common stock*. In 1980, dividends on all classes of stock totaled $200,000.

REQUIRED:

a. Compute the total minimum dividends that must have been declared during 1979 for each of the two classes of preferred stocks.

b. Compute the dividends per share that were declared during 1980 for each of the three classes of stock.

P28-6. *Stockholders' equity transactions.* Selected transactions for Julius Carter Co. for June, 1978, follow:

June 3 Issued 3,000 shares of $90 par value common stock for $91 per share.

10 Issued 1,000 shares of $90 par value common stock for $88 per share.

15 Stockholders subscribed to 900 shares of $90 par value common stock at $92 a share.

18 Purchased land, buildings, and equipment from R. C. Watson. The appraised values are:

Land	$300,000
Buildings	100,000
Equipment	50,000
	$450,000

In payment, issued 3,800 shares of common stock (with a market value of $92 a share). Signed a 6% 10-year note for the balance.

31 Collected the amount due on the common stock subscriptions and issued the certificates.

REQUIRED: Prepare general journal entries for the transactions.

DIVIDENDS AND OTHER TRANSACTIONS

> **OBJECTIVE**

This unit deals with additional business transactions involving the stockholders' equity of a corporation. The purpose of this unit is to introduce you to the nature and reporting of cash dividends, property dividends, stock dividends, stock splits, treasury stock, and to comprehensive reporting of changes in the retained earnings of a firm.

> **APPROACH TO ATTAINING THE OBJECTIVE**

As you study these other common business transactions affecting capital, pay special attention to these four questions, which the text following answers:

- *How are common transactions dealing with dividends reported, including cash dividends, property dividends, stock dividends, and stock splits?*
- *What is treasury stock, and how is it reported?*
- *What is donated capital?*
- *What is the function of the retained earnings statement?*

Many companies set up a regular dividend policy. That is, the board of directors establishes a record of declaring dividends on a regular quarterly, semiannual, or annual basis. The financial statements report the dividends, and the users of the statements can predict the dividends likely to be paid in the future by noting how the board of directors has acted in past periods.

■ *How are common transactions dealing with dividends reported, including cash dividends, property dividends, stock dividends, and stock splits?*

Although **cash dividends** are the most common, occasionally a firm might choose to pay its dividends in other property. When such **property dividends** are declared, the Dividends account is debited for the *value* of the property being given as dividends. For example, assume a board passed a dividend declaration which included these facts:

The board of directors of Royal Corporation declared a dividend on common stock on January 7, 1979. The dividend is to be paid in the preferred stock of ZZ Corporation, which is a long-term investment of Royal Corporation. One share of ZZ Corporation preferred stock is to be given as a dividend on each 100 shares of common stock of Royal Corporation outstanding. There are 100,000 shares of Royal Corporation common stock outstanding. At January 7, 1979, each share of ZZ Corporation preferred stock has a market value of $15 per share. The investment in ZZ Corporation preferred stock had cost $11 per share when it was purchased several years ago. The property dividend is to be paid January 20, 1979.

The declaration and payment of the dividend would be reported in the general journal as follows:

| 1979 Jan. | 7 | Dividends | 15,000 | |
| | | Dividends payable | | 15,000 |

1979 Jan.	20	Dividends payable	15,000	
		Long-term investments (ZZ stock)		11,000
		Gain on disposal of long-term investments		4,000

The important points for you to note about this property dividend are:

1. The capital of the firm decreases (and Dividends are debited) by the amount of the asset that is being given up (sacrificed) as dividends ($15,000, or 100,000 divided by 100 times $15).
2. A liability, Dividends payable, is created for $15,000 (100,000 divided by 100 times $15). This amount is the *market value* of the assets to be given up.
3. The second entry removes the cost of the long-term investment from the records and reflects the gain the company made from holding the

long-term investment. Its value had increased from $11,000 to $15,000.

In summary, when property other than cash is used to pay dividends (and this is only rarely), the capital of the firm decreases by the market value of the property given up by the company.

STOCK DIVIDENDS   A **stock dividend** is the issuance of a *relatively small number* of additional shares of stock to the existing stockholders. Cash is not involved in the transaction in any way. A stock dividend has about the same effect on a corporation as declaring a cash dividend and then having the stockholders immediately reinvest the amount of the cash dividend in additional shares of stock. A stock dividend, therefore, is a way for corporations to increase their *permanently* invested capital (common stock). Assume that a corporation has 5,000 shares of $20 par common stock outstanding and a total of 8,000 shares authorized. On December 1, 1978, the board of directors declares a 2% stock dividend. This means that an additional 100 shares will be mailed to existing stockholders as a dividend (2% of the 5,000 shares outstanding equals 100 shares). A stockholder who owns 1,000 shares would receive 20 shares as a dividend (2% of 1,000). Further, assume that the shares are selling on the market for $55 each at the time of the dividend. This entry would be made in the general journal:

1978 Dec.	1	Retained earnings (Dividends)	5,500	
		Common stock		2,000
		Premium on common stock		3,500

A stock dividend is relatively small compared to the total number of shares of a particular issue outstanding. It is assumed that by having the extra shares outstanding, the market price per share will stay about the same as before the dividend. Therefore, a stockholder (theoretically) could sell the additional shares he receives as a dividend; he then would be in about the same position as if a cash dividend had been paid. It also is assumed that the company could have issued these shares for $5,500 cash, and then could have used the cash for paying cash dividends; therefore the Retained earnings account is reduced by the market value of the shares issued. The Common stock account is credited for the par amount, and the Premium on common stock represents the additional permanent investment in the firm as a result of the extra shares. A stock dividend therefore involves just a *transfer* of retained earnings to contributed capital. The stock dividend has no effect on assets, total capital, or the amount of total stockholders' equity.

STOCK SPLITS

A stock split is almost identical with a stock dividend. A **stock split** is the issuance of a *relatively large number* of additional shares of stock to existing stockholders. Cash is not involved in the transaction in any way. The purpose of a stock split is to reduce the average market price per share of the company's stock. Having a smaller market value per share, it is felt by some people, increases the willingness of small investors to buy the company's stock.

Assume that a corporation has 5,000 shares of $20 par common stock outstanding and a total of 8,000 shares authorized. On December 1, 1978, the board of directors declares a four-for-one stock split. This means that an additional 15,000 shares of common stock will be mailed to stockholders. A stockholder owning one share of stock will now own four shares; and for each share previously outstanding there will be four shares outstanding after the split. The par value of the stock probably would be reduced from $20 to $5 per share, and the authorized number of shares would be increased from 8,000 to 32,000 shares. Any change in the number of shares authorized must be approved by the appropriate state authorities.

In a stock split the market price behavior of the common stock is important. Assume that before the split, there were 5,000 shares outstanding with a market value of about $55 each. Now, after the split, there are 20,000 total shares outstanding, with an approximate market value of $13.75 each (one-fourth of $55). The change in value of any one stockholder's stock is assumed to be zero as a result of the stock split.

Stock splits do not change the total capital of the firm. A journal entry is not needed, but notations must be made in the ledger accounts to reflect the new information about the common stock. The new number of shares outstanding is now 20,000 instead of 5,000; the par value is now $5 per share instead of $20; and the dollar amount of the capital originally contributed to the firm remains the same.

TREASURY STOCK

- *What is treasury stock, and how is it reported?*

Some firms purchase shares of their own stock. Such reacquired shares (when they are not canceled and retired permanently) are referred to as **treasury stock.** When a company first issues stock, the effect is to increase the assets of the firm and to increase the capital. When stock is reacquired, the reverse effect takes place. Therefore, when treasury stock is purchased, the *assets* of the firm *decrease* and the *capital* of the firm *decreases* by the same amount. Some firms purchase treasury stock and then, at a later date, reissue the stock to certain of their officers and employees as part of a compensation plan. *Stock held in the treasury has no registered owners; therefore, these shares are ignored when dividends are declared, when voting takes place, and in the event the company is liquidated.* To protect the interest of creditors and others, state laws place a limit on the amount of treasury stock a company may reacquire. Reacquiring large amounts of stock and paying out assets might weaken a firm. Two methods are in common use for reporting treasury stock on the financial statements. These are the *cost method* and the *par value method*.

Cost method of accounting for treasury stock This example will illustrate the cost method:

1. Issued 100,000 shares of common stock, $5 par value, for $6 cash per share.
2. Reacquired 1,000 shares of the common stock for $7 per share cash.
3. Reissued 600 shares of the treasury stock for $7.50 cash per share.
4. Reissued 300 shares of treasury stock for $6.50 per share.

These transactions are recorded in the general journal as follows:

(1)	Cash	600,000	
	Common stock		500,000
	Premium on common stock		100,000
(2)	Treasury stock	7,000	
	Cash		7,000
(3)	Cash	4,500	
	Treasury stock		4,200
	Paid-in capital from treasury stock transactions		300
(4)	Cash	1,950	
	Premium on common stock	150	
	Treasury stock		2,100

REACQUIRING THE SHARES. Transaction (1) records the original issuance of the common stock in the usual manner. Transaction (2) records the purchase of the treasury shares at their cost. The effect of transaction (2) is to *reduce* the assets of the firm by $7,000 and to *reduce* the capital of the firm by the same amount. If a balance sheet were prepared at this point, after transactions (1) and (2), the capital section would appear as follows:

CAPITAL

Common stock ($5 par value, 100,000 shares issued, of which 1,000 shares are held in the treasury)	$ 500,000
Premium on common stock	100,000
Total capital contributed	$ 600,000
Retained earnings (*assumed figure*)	400,000
Total	$1,000,000
Less Treasury stock, at cost, 1,000 shares	7,000
Total stockholders' equity	$993,000

REISSUING THE SHARES ABOVE COST. Transaction (3) shows that 600 of the treasury shares were reissued at $7.50 per share (600 shares times $7.50 equals $4,500). The treasury stock had cost $7 per share, so the Treasury stock account is credited for $4,200, or $7 per share times 600 shares. The net effect on the company of buying the shares for $7 and selling them for $7.50 is to *increase* the resources of the firm and the capital of the firm by $300, or 600 shares times the $0.50 difference between acquisition cost and reissue price. The contributed capital of the firm is increased permanently as a result of this transaction.

REISSUING THE SHARES BELOW COST. Transaction (4) differs from the third one in that the next 300 shares were reissued at a price *below* the acquisition cost. In this case, Cash is debited for 300 shares times the $6.50 reissue price ($1,950); and Treasury stock is credited for the cost of $7 per share ($2,100). The extra net amount of $150 (or $0.50 per share) returned permanently to stockholders reduces the contributed capital; because it reduces the amounts paid in when the stock was originally issued, the Premium on common stock account is debited.

In summary, we can make these points about accounting for treasury stock under the cost method:

1. When treasury shares are *acquired,* the assets of the firm decrease and the capital decreases by the same amount.
2. A temporary account, called Treasury stock, is set up to record the reduction in the capital of the firm. This account is shown on the balance sheet, usually at the bottom of the capital section, as a reduction in the total capital of the corporation.
3. When all the treasury shares are *reissued,* the temporary account of Treasury stock must be closed (reduced to zero).
4. If the reissue price is *above* the acquisition price, additional permanent contributed capital has been created for the firm. See transaction (3) for an example.
5. If the reissue price is *below* the acquisition price, the contributed capital of the firm has been permanently reduced. See the example in transaction (4).

Par value method of accounting for treasury stock A second major method of accounting for treasury stock is called the par value method. This method *does not* set up a temporary account to record the cost of the treasury stock and then make the final accounting for the transaction when the shares are reissued. Instead, when treasury shares are acquired, an increase or decrease in the related capital accounts is recorded immediately. It is beyond the scope of this first course to study the journal entries for the par value method, so our purpose here is simply to let you know that there is a variation in practice in accounting for and reporting treasury stock transactions. The most common method probably is the cost method.

Although it is clearly *contrary* to current accounting theory, a few firms report the Treasury stock account (with a debit balance) as an asset—just as if the firm had made an investment in the stock of another company! This is contrary to generally accepted accounting principles because the acquisition of treasury shares reduces the asset Cash and, as a result, there is less capital available in the firm. No new assets are created.

DONATED CAPITAL

- *What is donated capital?*

Occasionally a corporation will receive assets (as a contribution) from groups *other* than stockholders and creditors. For example, a city government might donate a plant site (land) to a corporation in order to have the corporation relocate in that city. This **donated capital** would be recorded by the corporation as follows:

1978					
March	31	Land		150,000	
		Contributed capital from plant site donation			150,000

The asset received (Land) is recorded at its *fair cash value* at the time of the donation. In a similar manner, permanent contributed capital (for the benefit of common stockholders) is recorded and is reported in the stockholders' equity section of the balance sheet.

COMPREHENSIVE REPORTING OF RETAINED EARNINGS

- *What is the function of the retained earnings statement?*

Shown below is a detailed statement of retained earnings, including the reporting of **appropriated retained earnings**. Some boards of directors use the retained earnings statement and the retained earnings section of the balance sheet as a device for letting stockholders, creditors, and others know some of the board's policies. Appropriating retained earnings is an example. The statement below reveals that the firm has total retained earnings at December 31, 1978, of $330,000. This represents the portion of all the assets of the firm that was generated through the earnings process in the past. Note that the board has reclassified part of the retained earnings as appropriated retained earnings. This simply means that the board is communicating these facts (refer to the statement):

1. The board, in 1976, indicated that $20,000 of the retained earnings is considered permanent capital at this time and is not available for

dividends; they did this in order to keep the company strong for plant expansion plans.

2. The board, in 1974, classified $100,000 as appropriated retained earnings for the bonds. This $100,000 of capital (owners' equity) is considered by the board at this time to be of a more-or-less permanent nature. Reductions in this capital are not planned in terms of dividends.

3. This year, 1978, the board earmarked another $60,000 for general contingencies.

Orleanian Corporation
STATEMENT OF RETAINED EARNINGS
For the year ended December 31, 1978

UNAPPROPRIATED RETAINED EARNINGS			
Balance, January 1, 1978			$142,000
additions:			
Net earnings for 1978		$98,000	
deductions:			
Cash dividends for 1978	$10,000		
2% stock dividend on common stock	20,000		
Appropriation for general contingencies	60,000	90,000	8,000
Balance, December 31, 1978			$150,000
APPROPRIATED RETAINED EARNINGS			
Balance, January 1, 1978:			
Appropriated for plant expansion (1976)		$ 20,000	
Appropriated for bond retirement (1974)		100,000	
		$120,000	
additions:			
Appropriated for general contingencies (1978)		60,000	
Balance, December 31, 1978			180,000
Total Retained Earnings, December 31, 1978			$330,000

Be sure that you are not misled by the act of reclassifying retained earnings as appropriated. *In no way* does this reserve *assets* so that contingencies can be met, or that bonds can be repaid, or that the plant can be expanded. Remember that retained earnings is a measure of the owners' equity in the firm. It tells something only about the *source* of the assets—it tells nothing about the assets themselves. The appropriation process therefore has little or no real effect except to let the readers of the financial statements know the policies of the board of directors. Appropriating retained earnings probably has no effect on the dividends to be paid. Dividends are almost always smaller than *current* net earnings, and for a profitable firm retained earnings are rarely decreased in any period.

Sometimes two accounts are kept in the general ledger: one for the unappropriated retained earnings and one for the appropriated retained earnings. Each of these accounts can have supporting records. The Orleanian Corporation's 1978 entry to appropriate $60,000 for general contingencies could be:

1978 Dec.	31	Unappropriated retained earnings Appropriated retained earnings To reclassify $60,000 of retained earnings as appropriated for general contingencies.	60,000	60,000

Any time the board chooses to reclassify appropriated retained earnings into the unappropriated category, the above entry would just be reversed.

> ## NEW TERMS

appropriated retained earnings Retained earnings which have been specially labeled or "reserved" and are not available for the declaration of dividends. [p. 502]

cash dividends Payments to stockholders; distributions of earnings, causing a decrease in Cash and a decrease in Retained earnings. [p. 497]

donated capital Contributed capital of a corporation, arising from donations to the corporation from outsiders. [p. 502]

property dividends Distributions of earnings to stockholders in the form of some asset other than cash, causing a decrease in the asset other than cash and a decrease in retained earnings for the value of the asset

at the time of the dividend. [p. 497]

stock dividends The issuance of a relatively small number of additional shares of stock to existing stockholders, causing a decrease in Retained earnings by the amount of the market value of the extra shares issued and an *increase* in the contributed capital of the firm by the same amount; assets are not affected. [p. 498]

stock splits Similar to stock dividends, except that a relatively large number of additional shares of stock are distributed to existing stockholders. No journal entry is needed to reflect the stock split. [p. 499]

treasury stock Shares of a company's own stock which it reacquires and holds for future reissuing. [p. 499]

> ## ASSIGNMENT MATERIAL

QUESTIONS

Q29-1. Differentiate between cash dividends and property dividends.

Q29-2. What is the significance of the date of declaration, the date of record, and the date of payment of dividends? What journal entry is made for cash dividends at each of these dates?

Q29-3. When a property dividend is declared, what determines the *amount* that the retained earnings account is debited?

Q29-4. Contrast stock dividends and stock splits.

Q29-5. When a stock dividend is declared, what determines the *amount* that the retained earnings account is decreased?

Q29-6. What journal entry is usually made when there is a stock split?

Q29-7. What are two methods for recording and reporting treasury stock transactions?

Q29-8. Are dividends paid on treasury shares of stock? Can the owners of treasury shares vote on corporation matters? Explain.

Q29-9. Should Treasury stock held be reported on the balance sheet as an asset? Explain.

Q29-10. What is donated capital?

Q29-11. How is donated capital recorded?

Q29-12. "The appropriation of retained earnings is a communications device." Explain.

Q29-13. "Appropriation of retained earnings is not the same as setting aside assets." Explain.

EXERCISES

E29-1. Make accounting entries in general journal form for the following transactions dealing with treasury stock. Use the cost method for recording the transactions.
   a. Issued 10,000 shares of no-par-value common stock. The stock has a stated value of $100 per share. Cash was received totaling $1,200,000.
   b. Reacquired 50 shares of the common stock, paying $125 per share cash.
   c. Reissued 25 of the shares above for $122 per share.
   d. Reissued the remaining treasury shares for $130 per share.

E29-2. Record the following business transactions in general journal form for Glade Company.

1978

April 3 The board of directors of the firm (Glade Company) declared the regular quarterly cash dividend on common stock. The dividend amounts to $1 per share, is payable to stockholders of record April 15, 1978, and is to be paid April 20, 1978. On April 3, 1978, the declaration date, there were 50,000 shares of common stock outstanding.

8 The board of directors of the firm (Glade Company) declared a special property dividend today, to be paid to common stockholders of record April 21, 1978. The dividend is to be paid on April 30, 1978. The dividend is to be paid in property (the common stock of Zebre Corporation, a long-term investment of the firm). The Glade Company had 50,000 shares of common stock outstanding. One share of Zebre Corporation common stock is to be given as a dividend on each 50 shares of Glade Company common stock outstanding. Zebre Corporation common stock has a market value of $20 per share. Zebre Corporation stock had cost Glade Company $8 per share when it was purchased several years ago.

20 Paid the cash dividend that was declared on April 3.

30 Distributed the property dividend (mailed the stock certificates) that was declared on April 8.

E29-3. The capital section of the balance sheet of Pension Company at December 31, is as follows:

Stockholders' equity:

Common stock, $100 par value, 10,000 shares authorized, 5,000 shares issued and outstanding	$500,000
Paid-in capital from common stockholders	100,000
Retained earnings	200,000
	$800,000

During January of the following year, the board of directors agreed to purchase 100 shares of the firm's own common stock on the open market; 100 shares were purchased for $110 per share.

Prepare the journal entry to record the purchase of treasury stock under the cost method. Prepare the journal entry to record the reissuance of the treasury shares for $118 per share cash.

E29-4. In the course of studying the nature of capital in Units 28 and 29, you have observed a number of business transactions that affect the reporting of capital on the balance sheet. Prepare an *all-inclusive* list of the many types of transactions that have an effect on the capital of a corporation. Before you start the list, give some thought to the organization of your answer. Which of these items on your list are of most concern to the investor who utilizes the balance sheet?

PROBLEMS (GROUP A)

P29-1. *Cash, property, and stock dividends; stock splits; capital section.* Below is shown the capital section of the balance sheet of Martha Corporation at December 31, 1977.

STOCKHOLDERS' EQUITY

Common stock (par value $50, 50,000 shares outstanding, 75,000 shares authorized)	$2,500,000	
Premium on common stock	200,000	$2,700,000
Preferred stock (6%, $100 par value, cumulative, 2,000 shares outstanding, 5,000 shares authorized)	$ 200,000	
Premium on preferred stock	20,000	220,000
Total contributed capital		$2,920,000
Retained earnings		1,000,000
Total stockholders' equity		$3,920,000

The following are business transactions during 1978:
1. Declared and paid the regular annual cash dividend on the preferred stock.
2. Declared and paid a property dividend on the common stock. One share of ABC Common Stock, an investment, will be given as a dividend for each 1,000 shares of common stock. The ABC Common Stock has a current market value of $132 per share and had cost the company $70 per share when it was purchased.
3. Declared a 1% stock dividend on the common stock. The company's common stock is selling for $55 per share on the market.
4. Declared a two-for-one stock split on the common stock and reduced the par value from $50 to $25 per share.

REQUIRED:

a. Record the transactions in general journal form.
b. Prepare the stockholders' equity section of the balance sheet after all four transactions have been recorded.

P29-2. *Cash and stock dividends; stock splits; capital section.* On May 1, 1978, the capital section of the balance sheet of Farock, Inc., included the following information:

Common stock (20,000 shares authorized, 10,000 shares outstanding, $100 par value)

Premium on common stock, $20,000

Retained earnings, $314,500

The following are business transactions of Farock, Inc., for May, 1978:

May 3   Declared a cash dividend on common stock to be paid (to stockholders of record of May 10, 1978) on May 15, 1978. The dividend amounts to $0.25 per share.

15   Paid the cash dividend that was declared on May 3.

20   The board of directors declared a 2% stock dividend on common stock. The common stock of the company is currently selling for $122 per share. Mailed the certificates to the stockholders today.

25   The board of directors declared a five-for-one stock split today. Authorization is increased from 20,000 shares to 60,000 shares, and the par value is reduced from $100 per share to $20 per share.

REQUIRED:

a. Record the necessary journal entries for the transactions.

b. Prepare the capital section of the balance sheet of the firm as it would appear on May 31, 1978, after giving effect to all the transactions.

P29-3. *Stock issuance; treasury shares.* The following are business transactions of Photo Enterprises Corporation for the month of August, 1978, the first month of operations.

Aug. 11   Issued 10,000 shares of common stock, $100 par value, for $111 per share cash. 30,000 shares were authorized.

13   Purchased a building and land. The building has an appraised value of $50,000 and the land has an appraised value of $61,000. Paid $33,300 cash and issued 700 shares of common stock in payment for the building and land.

21   Reacquired 100 shares of common stock (treasury stock), paying $115 per share.

29   Reissued 20 of the treasury shares for $116 cash per share.

31   Reissued 30 of the treasury shares for $113 per share cash.

REQUIRED:

a. Record the transactions in general journal form.

b. Prepare the capital section of the balance sheet of the firm at August 31, 1978, giving effect to all transactions. There were retained earnings amounting to $90,000 at that date.

PROBLEMS (GROUP B)

P29-4. *Retained earnings statement.* The following information is known about the retained earnings of Crestview Coffee Company:

Unappropriated retained earnings, January 1, 1978, $1,000,000

Net earnings for 1978, $300,000

Appropriated retained earnings, January 1, 1978:
  For general contingencies, $90,000
  For bond retirement, $100,000

During 1978, these events took place:
1. Cash dividends totaling $133,000 were declared. These dividends will be paid in January, 1979.
2. A stock dividend was declared. As a result of this transaction, retained earnings were reduced by $100,000.
3. The board of directors declared that the appropriation for general contingencies is to be increased from $90,000 to $150,000.

REQUIRED: Prepare a statement of retained earnings in good form, similar to the statement illustrated in this unit.

P29-5. *Dividends, appropriated retained earnings.* Record in general journal form these transactions dealing with cash dividends, property dividends, and appropriation of retained earnings:
1. Declared dividends on preferred stock, $10,000; on common stock, $25,000.
2. Paid the preferred dividends previously declared in cash. Paid $14,000 of the common dividends in cash. The remaining $11,000 represents dividends owed to the major stockholder, Burgundy Chartres, who agreed to accept a parcel of land the company owns instead of cash for his dividends. The company was running short of cash. The land had originally cost the firm $8,000 in 1952, when it was purchased, and now has a fair value of about $11,000.
3. Appropriated $5,000 of retained earnings for general contingencies, and $4,000 for retirement of bonds.

P29-6. *Stock transactions; dividends; treasury shares.*

Part A. Transactions of Company A are listed below:
1. Declared a 10% stock dividend on the common stock, par value $125. There were 2,000 shares outstanding and are selling for $130 a share. Issued the shares.
2. Declared a cash dividend of $0.50 a share on the common stock outstanding.
3. Paid the cash dividend.
4. Declared a property dividend on the common stock. One share of Nelson Common Stock, an investment, will be given as a dividend for each 2 shares of common stock. The Nelson Common Stock has a current market value of $150 per share and had cost the company $75 per share when it was purchased.
5. Paid the property dividend.

Part B. Transactions of Company B follow:
Oct. 10   Issued 20,000 shares of common stock, $50 par value, for $52 per share cash. 50,000 shares were authorized.

    15   Reacquired 100 shares of common stock (treasury stock), paying $51 per share.

    17   The board of directors declared a four-for-one stock split. Authorization is increased from 50,000 shares to 200,000 shares, and the par value is reduced from $50 per share to $12.50 per share.

    19   Declared and paid a cash dividend of $0.50 per share on the common stock outstanding.

    20   Reissued 50 of the treasury shares for $15 cash per share.

25   Declared and paid a 2% stock dividend on the common stock outstanding. The company's common stock is selling for $15 per share on the market.

REQUIRED:

a. Record the transactions of Company A in general journal form.
b. Record the transactions of Company B in general journal form. Assuming that this is the first month of operations of Company B, compute the number of shares of common stock outstanding at the end of October.

CUMULATIVE REVIEW PROBLEMS

P29-7. *Cumulative review problem.* Carter Corporation balance sheet (capital section) at December 31, 1978, follows:

Common stock, $100 par value, 10,000 shares issued and outstanding, 20,000 shares authorized	$1,000,000
Premium on common stock	150,000
Preferred stock, 6%, $50 par value, 2,500 shares issued and outstanding, fully participating	125,000
Premium on preferred stock	12,500
Retained earnings	746,000
	$2,033,500

The 1979 transactions follow.

1979
March   1   Issued 1,000 shares of common stock for $120 per share cash.
         15   Purchased 100 treasury shares, common, for $121 per share.
June   12   Declared dividends (to be divided between common and preferred according to the fully participating provision) totaling $80,000.
         30   Declared and issued a 1% stock dividend on common stock. Common stock market value is $122 per share.
Aug.   1   Sold 50 of the treasury shares for $123 cash.
Sept.   14   Appropriated $100,000 of retained earnings for general contingencies.

REQUIRED:

a. Record the transactions in general journal form.
b. Prepare the capital section of the December 31, 1979, balance sheet for the company.

P29-8. *Cumulative review problem.* Indicate the accounts to be debited and credited for each of the following transactions. Comment if appropriate.
a. No par value common stock issued for cash.
b. No par value common stock, with a stated value, issued for an amount of cash in excess of stated value.
c. Par value preferred stock issued for an amount of cash in excess of par value.
d. Cash dividends declared on common stock.
e. Cash dividends paid on common stock.
f. Property dividend declared on common stock.

g. Property dividend paid on common stock. The property given in the dividend is an investment in stock, with a book value less than the market value of the stock.

h. Purchased common treasury stock for cash (cost method).

i. Reissued common treasury stock for an amount more than the cost of treasury stock.

j. Reissued common treasury stock for an amount less than the cost of treasury stock. Stock had originally been issued at a premium.

k. Land was donated to the firm by a city.

l. Stock dividends were declared and paid on common stock. Market value per share exceeds the par value of the shares.

chapter 13

corporations: analyzing financial statements

30
ANALYZING AND USING FINANCIAL STATEMENTS

> **OBJECTIVE**

In past units you studied the classification and valuation ideas associated with general-purpose financial statements. These statements were prepared according to generally accepted accounting principles. This unit will give you some specific guidelines about how investors, creditors, and others use such financial statements in their decision-making processes.

> **APPROACH TO ATTAINING THE OBJECTIVE**

As you study how investors and creditors effectively use financial statements in making their decisions, pay special attention to these four questions, which the text following answers:

- *What major purposes do financial statements serve?*
- *What are the basic techniques available for analyzing the information in financial statements?*
- *What specific questions do decision makers commonly answer with the help of financial statements?*
- *How can graphs and charts be used in financial reporting?*

A REVIEW OF ACCOUNTING INFORMATION AND DECISIONS

■ *What major purposes do financial statements serve?*

Several different groups of decision makers in our economic system need similar kinds of information to make their decisions. Because of this common need, a single set of financial statements for a firm can be prepared. This same set can then be used by decision makers who have similar information needs but differing objectives. For example, both creditors and investors can use the same financial statements because they both need similar information for their decisions. This information needed in common concerns the resources of the firm, where these resources were acquired, and how the resources changed and were used during a period of time. Illustration 30-1 shows how three different decision makers need similar information.

Because various decision makers need the same information, general-purpose financial statements have been developed for corporations. These statements include the income statement, the balance sheet, and the statement of retained earnings—all of which you have studied in earlier units.

ILLUSTRATION 30-1

Decision maker	Decision to be made (or goal to be attained)	Some factors which must be forecast (predicted) to help make the decision	Some information needed in common
INVESTOR	Whether to invest in the firm.	1. What will be the value of the investment in the future? 2. What other benefits will be received by the investor?	What resources has the firm acquired? How is the management of the firm employing the resources?
CREDITOR	Whether to lend the firm money.	1. Will the firm be able to pay its debt and interest according to the agreement? 2. Will there be any other costs or benefits for the lender?	Where did the resources come from? What are the firm's debts? How much has the firm grown through profit-making activities?
LABOR UNION	What demands to make at the next contract bargaining	1. Can the firm afford to pay its employees increased benefits? 2. What activities is the firm engaging in that might be relevant to labor negotiations?	How profitable is the firm currently? What changes in resources and earnings are likely in the future?

■ *What are the basic
techniques available
for analyzing the
information in
financial statements?*

Financial accounting information appears on the financial statements in terms of dollars—in terms of the absolute amounts in each classification. This is the starting point for evaluating a firm. These absolute dollar amounts can be compared to some standard to make the evaluation. For example, total sales might be $100,000 for a year. The absolute amount of $100,000 is useful when compared to other figures—such as last year's sales—but expressing the information in a form other than dollars can provide additional insights into the operations of a business. Three other useful forms are percentages, ratios, and per-share amounts.

Percentages Illustrations 30-2 and 30-3 are comparative balance sheets and comparative income statements for the PT Corporation. Study these financial statements carefully. On the statements, three forms of information are shown. In the first set of columns, the absolute dollar amounts of the categories are shown for two years (1978 and 1977) so that comparisons can be made.

The next set of columns shows the absolute dollar change, the dollar increase or decrease, in each category during the year. Then the percentage change is given. For example, Marketable securities on the balance sheet decreased from $6,200 at December 31, 1977, to $5,000 at December 31, 1978. This $1,200 absolute dollar change represents a 19% decrease during the year ($1,200 divided by $6,200 equals 19%). The same analysis can be made on the income statement for the second set of columns. For example, Selling expenses were $16,000 in 1977. In 1978, Selling expenses were $22,000, which is an increase of $6,000. This increase of $6,000 is a 38% increase over the previous year ($6,000 divided by $16,000 equals 38%).

Now look at the third set of columns, which provides common-size information. **Common-size information** is simply information expressed in percentage terms for the financial statements (rather than being expressed in absolute dollar amounts). On the balance sheet, each classification (in both the asset and equity sections) is expressed as a percent of the total assets of the firm. Each classification also could be figured as a percentage of the total equities because this total is, of course, the same as total assets. For example, in 1977 the Marketable securities were 4% of the total assets ($6,200 divided by $171,300 equals 4%). In 1978, the Marketable securities were 3% of the total assets ($5,000 divided by $178,000 equals 3%).

On the income statement, common-size information is usually expressed in terms of the *net sales* of the firm. In 1977, the Cost of goods sold was 60% of the Net sales ($48,000 divided by $80,000 equals 60%). During the next year, 1978, the Cost of goods sold increased to 64% of net sales ($64,000 divided by $100,000 equals 64%).

The financial statements illustrated here combine the use of absolute

PT Corporation
BALANCE SHEET

ASSETS

	DECEMBER 31 1978	DECEMBER 31 1977	ABSOLUTE DOLLAR CHANGE DURING YEAR	PERCENTAGE CHANGE DURING YEAR	COMMON-SIZE 1978	COMMON-SIZE 1977
current assets						
Cash on hand and in banks	$ 1,000	$ 2,000	− $1,000	− 50%	1%	1%
Marketable securities	5,000	6,200	− 1,200	− 19%	3%	4%
Accounts receivable (net)	2,000	1,000	+ 1,000	+100%	1%	1%
Merchandise inventory	8,000	7,100	+ 900	+ 13%	4%	4%
Prepaid expenses	1,000	2,000	− 1,000	− 50%	1%	1%
Total current assets	$ 17,000	$ 18,300	− $1,300	− 7%	10%	11%
long-term investments						
Stocks and bonds	$ 10,000	$ 11,000	− $1,000	− 9%	5%	6%
Land	9,000	9,000	−0−	−0−	5%	5%
Other investments	3,000	3,000	−0−	−0−	2%	2%
Total long-term investments	$ 22,000	$ 23,000	− $1,000	− 4%	12%	13%
plant and equipment (net)						
Store equipment	$ 90,000	$80,000	+ $10,000	+ 13%	50%	47%
Buildings	12,000	13,000	− 1,000	− 8%	7%	7%
Land	30,000	30,000	−0−	−0−	17%	18%
Total plant and equipment	$132,000	$123,000	+ $9,000	+ 7%	74%	72%
other assets						
Deferred charges	$ 2,000	$ 1,000	+ $1,000	+100%	1%	1%
Intangible assets	5,000	6,000	− 1,000	− 17%	3%	3%
Total other assets	$ 7,000	$ 7,000	−0−	−0−	4%	4%
Total assets	$178,000	$171,300	+ $6,700	+ 4%	100%	100%

EQUITIES

	DECEMBER 31 1978	DECEMBER 31 1977	ABSOLUTE DOLLAR CHANGE DURING YEAR	PERCENTAGE CHANGE DURING YEAR	COMMON-SIZE 1978	COMMON-SIZE 1977
liabilities						
Current liabilities:						
Accounts payable	$ 6,000	$ 7,400	− $1,400	− 19%	3%	4%
Notes payable	4,000	4,000	−0−	−0−	2%	2%
Expenses payable	1,000	1,000	−0−	−0−	1%	1%
Total current liabilities	$ 11,000	$ 12,400	− $1,400	− 11%	6%	7%
Long-term liabilities:						
Notes payable	$ 20,000	$ 20,000	−0−	−0−	11%	12%
Total liabilities	$ 31,000	$ 32,400	− $1,400	− 4%	17%	19%
capital						
Common stock	$ 90,000	$ 90,000	−0−	−0−	51%	53%
Retained earnings	57,000	48,900	+ $8,100	+ 17%	32%	28%
Total capital	$147,000	$138,900	+ $8,100	+ 6%	83%	81%
Total equities	$178,000	$171,300	+ $6,700	+ 4%	100%	100%

ILLUSTRATION 30-2

PT Corporation
INCOME STATEMENT
For the Years Ended December 31

	1978	1977	ABSOLUTE DOLLAR CHANGE DURING YEAR	PERCENTAGE CHANGE DURING YEAR	COMMON-SIZE INFORMATION 1978	1977
revenues						
Net sales	$100,000	$80,000	+ $20,000	+ 25%	100%	100%
Other revenues	16,000	15,000	+ 1,000	+ 7%	16%	19%
Total revenues	$116,000	$95,000	+ $21,000	+ 22%	116%	119%
expenses						
Cost of goods sold	$ 64,000	$48,000	+ $16,000	+ 33%	64%	60%
Selling expenses	22,000	16,000	+ 6,000	+ 38%	22%	20%
General and administrative expenses	10,000	8,000	+ 2,000	+ 25%	10%	10%
Interest expense	2,000	2,000	–0–	–0–	2%	2%
Income taxes expense	5,000	7,000	– 2,000	– 29%	5%	9%
Total expenses	$103,000	$81,000	+ $22,000	+ 27%	103%	101%
net earnings before extraordinary items	$ 13,000	$14,000	– $ 1,000	– 7%	13%	18%
extraordinary gains and losses						
Loss from hurricane damage	($ 1,000)	$ –0–	(+ $1,000)	—	1%	
net earnings	$ 12,000	$14,000	– $ 2,000	– 14%	12%	18%
earnings information per share of common stock[a]						
Net earnings before extraordinary items	$ .65	$ .70	– $ .05	– 7%		
Loss from hurricane damage	(.05)	–0–	+ (.05)	—		
Net earnings	$ .60	$ .70	– $ .10	– 14%		

[a] 20,000 shares of common stock were outstanding during the entire year.

ILLUSTRATION 30-3

amounts, dollar changes, percent changes, and common-size information. Actually, in practice, any *one* published financial statement probably would not contain all this information. The decision maker, however, must be able to analyze the statements in these terms, even if only the absolute amounts are revealed by a company's statements.

Ratios A *ratio* is a proportion or fraction. Users of financial statements find that expressing certain relationships in this form is helpful. For example, one useful relationship is called the *current ratio*. It is computed as follows:

$$\text{Current ratio} = \frac{\text{Current assets}}{\text{Current liabilities}}$$

On the balance sheet illustrated, the current ratio for 1977 is $18,300 divided by $12,400, or 1.48 to 1. At December 31, 1978, the current ratio had increased to 1.55 to 1 ($17,000 divided by $11,000). This might be interpreted as good by an analyst because the relatively liquid assets have increased in relationship to the currently maturing debts. Or this might be considered bad because too many assets (more than needed) are being kept in this relatively liquid form. Perhaps these liquid assets should be invested in more profitable areas. In any event, such ratios can be useful in identifying changing areas for investigation. The ratio, by itself, cannot explain a problem or directly indicate whether a situation is good or bad. The selection and use of relevant ratios will be discussed later in this unit.

Per-share amounts Because decision makers, especially investors, are interested in buying small units of ownership (generally shares of stock), information about the earnings is especially useful to them when it is expressed in per-share terms. You have already studied how earnings per share of common stock appears on the income statement. Further explanation of the use of per-share information is given in following sections of this unit.

STANDARDS FOR EVALUATING PERFORMANCE

Using past performance as a standard for evaluation Whether the information being evaluated is expressed in absolute dollars, in percentages, as common-size information, or in ratios, there are two basic standards or goals against which the information can be evaluated. The first is the past performance of a firm. By comparing a current period's information to similar information for a series of past periods, an analyst can detect any important trends or changes for his investigation.

Using external standards for evaluation The second basis for evaluation is a standard or goal determined outside the firm. Many associations and organizations within industries regularly provide information about their firms. For example, information about retail grocery operations is available on an industrywide basis. Thus, the average current ratios of many retail grocers would be available. Other information, such as the percent that the cost of goods sold is to net sales, also would be available and is useful in evaluating a firm's operations.

In summary, two methods are widely used in evaluating a company:

1. Compare the company's information for the current period to similar information for that company in past periods;
2. Compare the company's information for the current period to information about the same industry or about competitors.

■ *What specific
questions do decision
makers commonly answer
with the help of
financial statements?*

Most decision makers who use financial statements want to answer specific questions about a company. Some important questions are:

1. How satisfactory are the current earnings?
2. What are the prospects for dividends in the future?
3. How realistic is the current market price for the company's stock?
4. Are the sources of the company's assets well balanced?
5. Is the company acquiring and managing its assets well?
6. Can the company meet all of its obligations?

The financial statement user must be able to choose the relevant information from the statements to help him answer each of these questions. Then he must compare this information to the past performance of the firm and to the standards of the industry to discover important relationships and changes.

The remaining discussion in this unit presents some of the more common ratios and relationships which can be computed from balance sheets and income statements. Remember this as you study these ratios:

1. These ratios are just a *few* of the ones commonly used. They are useful *only* when compared and evaluated in the light of some standard (such as industry standards or past performance).
2. There are many other relationships and ratios that can be computed from financial statements. The number of ratios is limited only by the number of classifications on the financial statements. The important thing is being able to ask the relevant questions about a firm and then selecting the information that is meaningful in answering those questions.

**HOW SATISFACTORY
ARE THE CURRENT
EARNINGS?**

Here are some measures computed from financial statements that help answer the question of whether current earnings are satisfactory:

1. Earnings per share $= \dfrac{\text{Net earnings} - \begin{array}{c}\text{Dividend requirements}\\ \text{on preferred stock}\end{array}}{\begin{array}{c}\text{Average number of shares of common}\\ \text{stock outstanding during the year}\end{array}}$

From the information in Illustration 30-2 and 30-3, the earnings per share for 1978 can be computed:

$$\text{Earnings per share} = \frac{\text{Net earnings} - \begin{array}{c}\text{Dividend requirements}\\\text{on preferred stock}\end{array}}{\begin{array}{c}\text{Average number of shares of common}\\\text{stock outstanding during the year}\end{array}}$$

$$= \frac{\$12,000 - \text{none}}{20,000 \text{ shares}} = \$.60$$

This measure is especially useful to investors, for it shows how much of the net earnings remains for each share of common stock after preferred dividends are paid. Unit 31 discusses this measure in detail.

2.
$$\frac{\text{Net earnings}}{\text{Net sales}} = x\%$$

This percent indicates, for each dollar of sales, how many cents of net earnings were produced during the period. It is a measure of how productive the firm was in terms of earnings. For example, a company's income statement indicated that net sales were $113,000 and net earnings amounted to $15,000:

$$\frac{\text{Net earnings}}{\text{Net sales}} = \frac{\$15,000}{\$113,000} = 13\%$$

Or, 13 cents of net income was produced for every dollar of sales made. Last year the relationship for this company happened to be 17%. Such a drop can be investigated by management and explained. For example, it could have been caused by a relative increase in cost of goods sold in relation to the prices charged for the firm's products.

3.
$$\frac{\text{Net earnings}}{\text{Total capital}} = x\%$$

This is a measure of the return on capital of the company. It indicates, for every dollar of capital invested in the firm, how many cents were produced this period in earnings. For Total capital in the equation the beginning-of-year amount is often used because this amount was invested to produce the earnings. For PT Corporation (see Illustrations 30-2 and 30-3), the return on capital for 1978 was 8.6%:

$$\text{Return on capital} = \frac{\text{Net earnings}}{\text{Total capital}} = \frac{\$12,000}{\$138,900} = 8.6\%$$

4.
$$\frac{\text{Net earnings} + \text{Interest expense}}{\text{Total assets}} = x\%$$

This measure is known as the *return on investment.* It compares (1) the total earnings made during the period before paying for any use of assets (whether borrowed or invested by owners) to (2) the total assets invested in the firm. For Total assets in the equation the beginning-of-the-year amount is often used because this amount was invested to produce the earnings. In PT Corporation (Illustrations 30-2 and 30-3), the return on investment for 1978 was 8.2%:

$$\text{Return on investment} = \frac{\text{Net earnings} + \text{Interest expense}}{\text{Total assets}}$$

$$= \frac{\$12,000 + \$2,000}{\$171,300} = 8.2\%$$

WHAT ARE THE PROSPECTS FOR DIVIDENDS IN THE FUTURE?

In order to decide to invest in a company's stock, an investor must consider several factors. One of these factors is the probable dividends that will be paid in the future. Before the profitability of an investment can be estimated, however, the cost or current market price must be known, the cash in the form of dividends to be received while holding the investment must be estimated, and the market price when the investment is sold in the future must be estimated.

Information about dividends and the dividend policy of a board of directors often can be found in a company's **annual report,** a document issued each year by most medium-size and large firms. The annual report includes all the financial statements, the statement by the independent certified public accountant that in his opinion the financial statements are presented according to generally accepted accounting principles, and other information about the past operations and the plans of the company. Much about the probability that the firm will declare future dividends can be learned from observing the record of past dividends. For example, some companies have paid a regular quarterly dividend for the past twenty-five years, with no exceptions, while other companies have never declared a dividend, although their earnings have been satisfactory. Still other firms have declared dividends irregularly.

HOW REALISTIC IS THE CURRENT MARKET PRICE FOR THE COMPANY'S STOCK?

Usually you can get the market price of a share of stock easily from a stockbroker. This market price must be evaluated in the investment decision to determine if, in the judgment of the investor, the stock is priced too high or reasonably. The measures illustrated below commonly relate the market price to the important factor of company earnings. It is generally agreed that one of the most important factors which influence the market price of stock is the current and prospective earnings of the company. Over a long period of time,

Similarly, the December 31, 1978, relationship is:

$$\text{Percent stockholders' equity is of total assets} = \frac{\text{Total capital}}{\text{Total assets}}$$

$$= \frac{\dfrac{\$2,000}{\$100,000}}{312 \text{ days}} = 6.24 \text{ days}$$

This ratio reveals what portion of the firm's assets have been financed by owners of the firm, as opposed to creditors.

3. $$\text{Percent common stockholders equity is of total assets} = \frac{\text{Total capital} - \begin{array}{c}\text{Capital related}\\\text{to preferred}\\\text{stockholders}\end{array}}{\text{Total assets}}$$

For PT Corporation, this measure is also 82.6%, since no preferred stock is outstanding. This measure deals with the long-term commitments of funds to the firm by the common stockholders. As a general rule, prospective creditors would like to see this ratio large.

IS THE COMPANY ACQUIRING AND MANAGING ITS ASSETS WELL?

Any individual asset or any group of assets can be singled out for analysis. Here are a few of the common measures used to evaluate the management of certain assets.

1. $$\text{Inventory turnover} = \frac{\text{Cost of goods sold}}{\text{Average merchandise inventory}} = x \text{ times}$$

This measure indicates how many times on the average the entire inventory was sold and replaced during the period. The PT Corporation (Illustrations 30-2 and 30-3) inventory turnover for 1978 can be computed as follows:

$$\text{Inventory turnover} = \frac{\text{Cost of goods sold}}{\text{Average merchandise inventory}}$$

$$= \frac{\$64,000}{\dfrac{\$8,000 + \$7,100}{2}} = 8.5 \text{ times}$$

The average inventory is computed by averaging the beginning and ending inventories: ($8,000 + $7,100) ÷ 2 = $7,550.

2. $$\text{Average number of days to collect the receivables} = \frac{\text{Accounts receivable (net)}}{\text{Average } \textit{daily} \text{ sales made on credit}}$$

Assume the PT Corporation does business 6 days a week, or 312 days during the year.

$$\text{Average number of days to collect the receivables} = \frac{\text{Accounts receivable (net)}}{\text{Average } \textit{daily} \text{ sales made on credit}}$$

$$= \frac{\$147,000}{\$178,000} = 82.6\%$$

3. $$\text{Relationship of net sales to total assets} = \frac{\text{Net sales}}{\text{Total assets}}$$

This measure shows how many dollars of sales were generated by each dollar of assets employed in the business. For Total assets in the equation the beginning-of-year amount is used.

4. $$\text{Plant and equipment turnover} = \frac{\text{Net sales}}{\text{Net plant and equipment (beginning of year)}}$$

$$= x \text{ times}$$

For most firms fixed assets represent one of the most significant categories of resources used in attaining the firm's objectives. Therefore, these assets are often compared to other information on the financial statements. Through these comparisons the statement user can discover important changes about the firm. This index tells how many dollars in net sales the firm was able to generate in a period for each dollar employed in fixed assets.

5. $$\text{Relationship of plant and equipment to long-term debt} = \frac{\text{Net Plant and equipment}}{\text{Long-term liabilities}} = x\%$$

This measure tells to what extent the plant and equipment is financed by long-term borrowing, rather than, for instance, by permanent owners' contributions. This is a crude index of borrowing power.

6. $$\text{Relationship of plant and equipment to total assets} = \frac{\text{Net Plant and equipment}}{\text{Total assets}} = x\%$$

This measure shows what proportion of all the firm's resources are tied up in fixed assets.

A corporation's debt-paying ability is a primary concern of its creditors and prospective creditors. These ratios and measures are often used to help assess debt-paying ability:

1. $$\text{Current ratio} = \frac{\text{Current assets}}{\text{Current liabilities}} = x \text{ times}$$

2. $$\text{Quick current ratio} = \frac{\text{Cash} + \frac{\text{Marketable}}{\text{securities}} + \frac{\text{Accounts}}{\text{receivable (net)}}}{\text{Current liabilities}}$$
$$= x \text{ times}$$

3. $$\frac{\text{Relationship of cash on}}{\text{hand to operating expenses}} = \frac{\text{Cash on hand}}{\frac{\text{Average monthly}}{\text{operating expenses}}}$$

Operating expenses are usually considered to be all expenses except Cost of merchandise sold.

4. $$\frac{\text{Relationship of the earnings}}{\frac{\text{generated by the firm}}{\text{to Interest expense.}}} = \frac{\text{Net earnings from operations}}{\frac{\text{(before deducting Interest expense)}}{\text{Interest expense}}}$$

This measure is of special interest to bondholders, for it relates the company's earnings ability to the amount of expenses related to the bonds. This measure is also referred to as the *number of times the interest is earned.*

**USING GRAPHS
AND CHARTS**

- *How can graphs and charts be used in financial reporting?*

Many corporations present supplementary financial information in their annual reports in the form of graphs and charts. Such presentations are in addition to the regular financial statements such as the income statement and balance sheet. To show how such presentations can be used, two actual examples from annual reports are now given.

Line graph showing relationship of net income to dividends Illustration 30-4 shows the dividends paid per share in relationship to the earnings per share. The difference between the two spotlights the earnings that stay in the business. This graph appeared in the 1976 annual report of United Telecommunications, Inc.

Summary table and pie diagram Illustration 30-5 appeared in the annual report of General Mills for the year ending May 29, 1977. It provides the reader with a quick summary of the operating activity and results of operations for the year.

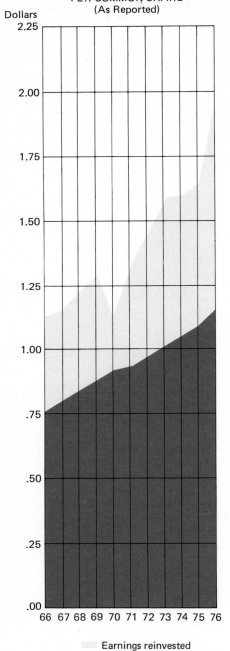

EARNINGS AND DIVIDENDS
PER COMMON SHARE
(As Reported)

Dollars

Earnings reinvested
Dividends paid

ILLUSTRATION 30-4

THE YEAR IN BRIEF
(in thousands)

	fiscal year ended		
	MAY 29, 1977 (52 WEEKS)	MAY 30, 1976 (53 WEEKS)	INCREASE
Sales	$2,909,404	$2,644,952	10.0%
Net earnings	117,034	100,538	16.4%
Earnings per dollar of sales	4.0¢	3.8¢	
Earnings per common share and common share equivalent	$ 2.36	$ 2.04	15.7%
Common stock dividends	39,083	32,391	
Net earnings after dividends	77,951	68,147	
Wages, salaries, and employee benefits	541,193	476,099	13.7%
Taxes—income, payroll, property, etc.	170,005	148,750	14.3%
—per cent of earnings before all taxes	59.3%	59.7%	

ILLUSTRATION 30-5

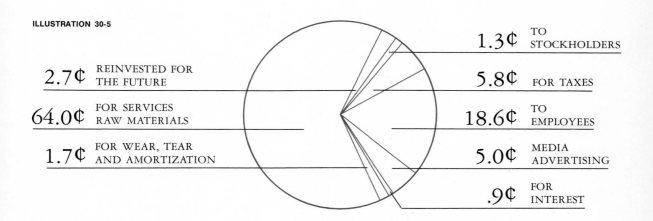

2.7¢ REINVESTED FOR THE FUTURE

64.0¢ FOR SERVICES RAW MATERIALS

1.7¢ FOR WEAR, TEAR AND AMORTIZATION

1.3¢ TO STOCKHOLDERS

5.8¢ FOR TAXES

18.6¢ TO EMPLOYEES

5.0¢ MEDIA ADVERTISING

.9¢ FOR INTEREST

HOW THE SALES DOLLAR
WAS DIVIDED

annual report A published report issued annually by medium-size and large corporations to provide information to decision makers outside the firm; annual reports usually include the financial statements, the independent certified public accountant's opinion related to the financial statements, and other information about the current operations and plans. [p. 520]

common-size financial statements Financial statements constructed so that the amounts are expressed as percentages; each item on the balance sheet can be expressed as a percent of the total assets, and each item on the income statement can be expressed as a percent of net sales. [p. 514]

▶ **ASSIGNMENT MATERIAL**

QUESTIONS

Q30-1. What are common-size financial statements, and how are they useful?

Q30-2. What specific questions do decision makers commonly answer with the help of financial statements?

Q30-3. What per-share measures are commonly used by decision makers?

Q30-4. What is a ratio?

Q30-5. What standards are used for evaluating financial information? Comment.

Q30-6. What information does the price–earnings ratio give the decision maker?

EXERCISES

E30-1. The following information was taken from the accounting records of Exid and Company for 1978:

Net earnings before extraordinary gain	$ 50,000
Extraordinary gain	10,000
Sales of merchandise	312,000
Purchases of merchandise	250,000
Sales returns and allowances	11,000
Cost of goods sold	200,000
Sales discounts	3,000
Preferred stock outstanding during the year (5%)	30,000
Dividends declared on preferred stock	1,500
Total capital at beginning of year	100,000
Interest expense	3,000
Total assets at beginning of year	400,000
Average number of common shares outstanding during the year, 10,000	

Compute as many measures as you can to help answer the question: "How satisfactory are the current earnings?"

E30-2. The following information was taken from the accounting records of Axid and Company for 1978:

Net earnings	$ 90,000
Total capital	400,000
Retained earnings	100,000
Preferred stock, 6%	30,000
Number of shares of common stock outstanding, 15,000	
Market price of common stock at end of year	60

Compute as many measures as you can to help answer the question: "How realistic is the current market price for the company's common stock?"

E30-3. The following information was taken from the accounting records of Dixe and Company for 1978:

Total assets	$100,000
Total capital	70,000
Retained earnings	10,000
Preferred stock	30,000

Compute three measures to help answer the question: "Are the sources of the company's assets well balanced?"

E30-4. Speculate as to the possible reasons for the following:
a. The current ratio of a firm increased from 3 to 1 in 1977 to 4 to 1 in 1978.
b. The inventory turnover of a firm decreased from 12 times in 1977 to 8 times in 1978.
c. The average number of days to collect the receivables increased from 10 days in 1977 to 14 days in 1978.

PROBLEMS (GROUP A)

P30-1. *Computing measures for evaluating asset management.* Using the following data, compute these measures for 1977 *and* 1978:
a. Inventory turnover
b. Average number of days to collect the receivables (assume 365 days in year)
c. Relationship of net sales to total assets

Cost of goods sold for 1977	$ 300,000
Cost of goods sold for 1978	350,000
Merchandise inventory, January 1, 1977	50,000
Merchandise inventory, January 1, 1978	60,000
Merchandise inventory, January 1, 1979	70,000
Accounts receivable, January 1, 1977	40,000
Accounts receivable, January 1, 1978	42,000
Accounts receivable, January 1, 1979	41,000
Allowance for uncollectibles, January 1, 1977	1,000
Allowance for uncollectibles, January 1, 1978	2,000
Allowance for uncollectibles, January 1, 1979	2,000
Sales for 1977 (all on credit)	400,000
Sales for 1978 (all on credit)	500,000
Total assets, January 1, 1977	1,000,000
Total assets, January 1, 1978	1,200,000
Total assets, January 1, 1979	1,210,000

P30-2. *Computing financial measures.* The following information was taken from the accounting records of the Johnson Company for 1978:

Net earnings before extraordinary gain	$ 70,000
Extraordinary gain	30,000

Sales of merchandise	332,000
Purchases of merchandise	280,000
Cost of goods sold	230,000
Sales discounts	23,000
Sales returns and allowances	31,000
Preferred stock outstanding during the year (5%)	60,000
Dividends declared on preferred stock	3,000
Total capital at beginning of year	120,000
Interest expense	23,000
Current liabilities	100,000
Total assets at beginning of year (includes $220,000 current)	420,000
Retained earnings	50,000
Average number of common shares outstanding during the year, 15,000	
Total assets on December 31, 1978 (including $230,000 current)	510,000
Total liabilities on December 31, 1978 (including $90,000 current)	310,000

REQUIRED:

a. Compute as many measures as you can to help answer the question: How satisfactory are the current earnings?

b. Compute three measures to help answer the question: Are the sources of the company's assets well balanced?

c. Compute two measures to help answer the question: Can the company meet all its obligations?

P30-3. *Income statement analysis.* Selected data from the accounting records of Virginia Fleak, Inc., for 1978 and 1977 are given below.

	1978	1977
Sales	$100,000	$85,000
Sales returns and allowances	1,000	1,000
Rental income	14,000	12,000
Income taxes expense	5,000	4,000
Sales discounts	500	600
Interest expense	2,000	2,500
Purchases of merchandise	80,000	75,000
General expenses	5,000	4,000
Purchases returns and allowances	8,000	5,000
Transportation on purchases	1,000	2,000
Selling expenses	10,000	8,000
Purchases discounts	2,000	1,000

	12-31-78	12-31-77	12-31-76
Merchandise inventory	$8,000	$6,000	$3,000
Number of shares of common stock outstanding	10,000	10,000	10,000
Market price of common stock	$22	$10	$8
Total capital	$178,000	$90,000	$80,000
Total liabilities	$90,000	$70,000	$60,000

REQUIRED:

  a. Prepare a comparative income statement for 1978 and 1977 similar to Illustration 30-3, showing dollar amounts and common-size information only.
  b. Compute as many measures as you can that help answer the question: How satisfactory are the earnings?

**PROBLEMS
(GROUP B)**

P30-4. *Common-size financial statements.* The adjusted trial balance of Orleans Merchandising Corporation showed the following accounts and balances (for the 6-month period ended June 30, 1978):

Common stock	30,000
Retained earnings	7,000
Dividends on common stock	2,000
Cash	10,000
Marketable securities	4,000
Notes payable (long-term)	15,000
Bonds payable	43,000
Accounts receivable	13,500
Allowance for uncollectibles	500
Investments in stocks	40,000
Merchandise inventory	14,000
Prepaid expenses	2,700
Investments in bonds	11,000
Equipment	56,000
Accumulated depreciation—Equipment	15,000
Accounts payable	7,000
Land	20,000
Sales taxes payable	2,000
Expenses payable	7,000
Sales	147,000
Sales returns and allowances	2,000
Rental income	9,000
Cost of goods sold	69,000
General expenses	18,100
Selling expenses	20,200

There were 10,000 shares of common stock outstanding during the period.

REQUIRED:

  a. Prepare an income statement in good form. Set up two columns for figures: (1) dollar amounts and (2) common-size information.
  b. Prepare a statement of retained earnings in good form.
  c. Prepare a classified balance sheet in good form. Set up two columns for figures: (1) dollar amounts and (2) common-size information.

*P30-5. *Preparing comparative financial statements.* The following are the adjusted trial balances (account balances) of Analytics, Inc., at the end of 1978 and 1977, before the closing entries were made.

	1978	1977
Cash	2,000	3,000
Marketable securities	11,000	12,000
Accounts receivable (net)	5,000	3,000
Inventories[a]	15,000	13,000
Prepaid expenses	2,000	4,000
Investments in securities	20,000	25,000
Land investments	78,000	15,000
Store equipment (net)	150,000	160,000
Buildings (net)	24,000	22,000
Land	61,000	61,000
Deferred charges	2,000	1,000
Patents and other intangibles	10,000	12,000
Accounts payable	12,000	14,000
Short-term notes payable	8,000	8,000
Accrued expenses payable	2,000	2,000
Long-term notes payable	30,000	30,000
Common stock	150,000	150,000
Retained earnings	127,000	100,000
Dividends	10,000	10,000
Sales	200,000	170,000
Sales returns and allowances	3,000	4,000
Sales discounts	1,000	1,000
Rent revenue	30,000	27,000
Cost of goods sold	120,000	103,000
Selling expenses	20,000	17,000
General expenses	11,000	15,000
Interest expense	4,000	5,000
Income taxes expense	10,000	15,000

[a] The company uses the perpetual inventory method.

There were 30,000 shares of common stock outstanding during 1977 and 1978. The market price of the firm's common stock at December 31, 1977, was $30; and at December 31, 1978, it was $35.

REQUIRED:

a. Prepare a comparative income statement for 1977 and 1978 similar to Illustration 30-3 in the unit, showing dollar amounts and common-size information. (Do not include absolute dollar change and percentage change data.)

b. Prepare a comparative balance sheet for December 31, 1977, and December 31, 1978, similar to Illustration 30-2, showing dollar amounts and common-size information only.

*P30-6. *Ratio analysis.* This problem is a continuation of P30-5.

REQUIRED: From the comparative financial statements that you prepared in P30-5, compute the following measures for every period or point in time that is possible with the data provided.

a. Measures dealing with how satisfactory are earnings:
   (1) Earnings per share.
   (2) Net earnings as a percent of net sales.
   (3) Return on capital.
   (4) Return on investment.
b. What can you conclude about the prospects for future dividends?
c. Measures dealing with how realistic is the current market price for the company's stock:
   (1) Price–earnings ratio.
   (2) Rate of earnings on the market price.
   (3) Book value per share of common stock.
d. Measures dealing with how well balanced are the sources of the company's assets:
   (1) Percent creditors' equity is of total assets.
   (2) Percent stockholders' equity is of total assets.
   (3) Percent common stockholders' equity is of total assets.
e. Measures dealing with asset management:
   (1) Inventory turnover. *Note:* The merchandise inventory at January 1, 1977, was $12,000.
   (2) Average number of days to collect the receivables. *Note:* All sales are made on credit; the company operates 6 days a week; use *net* sales in the computation.
   (3) Relationship of net sales to total assets.
   (4) Plant and equipment turnover.
   (5) Relationship of plant and equipment to long-term debt.
   (6) Relationship of plant and equipment to total assets.
f. Measures dealing with the ability of the company to meet its obligations:
   (1) Current ratio.
   (2) Quick current ratio.
   (3) Relationship of cash on hand to operating expenses.
   (4) Relationship of the earnings generated by the firm to interest expense.

31

EARNINGS MEASUREMENT THEORY AND PRACTICE

> ### ▶ OBJECTIVE

This unit discusses the theory underlying the measurement of earnings for corporations. The purpose of this unit is to review the theory and to illustrate the current practice surrounding reporting earnings and earnings per share on modern income statements.

> ### ▶ APPROACH TO ATTAINING THE OBJECTIVE

As you study earnings measurement theory and practice, pay special attention to these four questions, which the text following answers:

- *What are the components of net earnings?*
- *What is the form and arrangement of modern income statements?*
- *How are extraordinary gains and losses and prior-period adjustments reported?*
- *How are per-share earnings calculated?*

THE COMPONENTS OF EARNINGS

Evaluation of a company's performance in terms of its earnings involves three elements. These elements are *revenues, expenses,* and *net earnings* (net income). Net earnings, the key measure of a firm's performance, is determined in the accounting process by identifying, measuring, and matching the revenues and related expenses for a period of time.

■ *What are the components of net earnings?*

Revenue Revenue has been defined by the American Institute of Certified Public Accountants (AICPA) as follows:

Revenue—gross increases in assets or gross decreases in liabilities recognized and measured in conformity with generally accepted accounting principles that result from those types of profit-directed activities of an enterprise that can change owners' equity.[1]

As further explanation, the AICPA indicates that revenue, under current generally accepted accounting principles, comes from three general activities:

1. Selling products.
2. Rendering services and permitting others to use the firm's assets.
3. Disposing of resources other than products.

An important part of the definition of revenues above is that revenues are *gross* increases in assets. This means that revenue is the *total* price charged for products or the *total* amount charged for services rendered to customers. This total measure (revenue) is the gross output or accomplishment of the firm in a period of time. Usually revenues are revealed first (at the top) on the income statement.

Our discussion so far has focused on identifying revenues. An equally important problem is determining *in which period* revenues should be reported—in which period per-share earnings increase. According to generally accepted accounting principles, revenue is reported on financial statements in the period when the products (inventory) are sold or when the service is rendered. Many accountants think that this particular point in the earnings process is the most significant single activity in the production of earnings. Therefore, earnings per share increase in the period when the sale is made— earnings per share *do not* necessarily increase when the cash is collected or when the products are purchased or produced. The procedure for recognizing revenue when the sale is made is called **realization.**

[1] American Institute of Certified Public Accountants, *Statement of the Accounting Principles Board, No. 4,* "Basic Concepts and Accounting Principles Underlying Financial Statements of Business Enterprises," October, 1970, p. 51.

In special types of businesses, when using the realization procedure would *mislead* readers of financial statements about the earnings, other procedures for recognizing revenue have been developed. For example, a firm might be in the construction business and might work on one project for 4 years. At the end of that time, the sale is made according to a contract. The most significant part of the 4-year earnings process, however, is probably *not* the "final sale" in the fourth year; therefore, all the revenues from the project probably should *not* be reported in that one year. An alternative procedure developed for long-term construction contracts is to recognize and report part of the revenue in each of the 4 years, as the construction is taking place.

Expenses Expenses have been defined as follows:

Expenses—gross decreases in assets or gross increases in liabilities recognized and measured in conformity with generally accepted accounting principles that result from those types of profit-directed activities of an enterprise that can change owners' equity.[2]

After expenses are identified, they must be reported on the income statement and matched against the revenue. Deciding when to report expenses (that is, in which period to reduce earnings per share) is sometimes difficult. There are three general ways that expenses are assigned to periods.

In some cases, *the expense can be directly related to specific revenue.* This is the case with cost of goods sold. The products which are sold can be directly associated with the revenue they produce. Therefore, the cost of a product sold is reported in the same period and on the same income statement as is the revenue produced from selling that product.

A second procedure, *where a direct association of the expense with the revenue is not possible, involves a systematic pattern of assigning the expense to periods.* Plant and equipment and the related depreciation expense falls in this category. Depreciation methods are consistently applied to decide the timing of expense reporting. The system chosen, of course, is a determinant of how company performance and earnings per share will be reported.

A third procedure is to *immediately report the expense* on the current income statement and to reduce earnings per share immediately. An example of this might be certain advertising expenses. Management might be unable to predict with any certainty which periods this expense will benefit, so therefore the expenditure is reported immediately as expense. Other examples would be the salaries of officers of the firm. A final example could be an asset which a company owns. If it is determined that this asset has lost its usefulness and value, the asset would be reported as an expense immediately and would be reduced to zero.

[2]Ibid., pp. 51–52.

All three of the preceding procedures for recognizing expenses are presented in the publication of the AICPA cited earlier.[3]

The definitions of revenue and expense which we quoted above from the AICPA both include references to *liabilities*. Look again at the definition of revenue. An example of a revenue with a gross increase in assets would be the usual rendering of services for cash or on credit. An example of a revenue with a gross decrease in liabilities also could deal with rendering services. Assume, for example, that a company already owed a customer money from a loan. Instead of remitting cash for the services rendered to him, the customer could have reduced the amount the firm owed him.

Liabilities as well as assets also are involved with incurring expenses. A gross decrease in assets arises for expenses paid for in cash. A gross increase in liabilities arises for expenses incurred but to be paid at a later date.

AN INCOME STATEMENT ILLUSTRATED

A modern corporation's income statement is illustrated below. Examine it carefully. Three aspects of earnings reporting will be discussed in the remainder of this unit: (1) reporting extraordinary gains and losses (the statement below will be the primary example), (2) reporting prior-period adjustments, and (3) reporting earnings per share.

[3] Ibid., pp. 61–63.

■ *What is the form and arrangement of modern income statements?*

LMN Corporation
INCOME STATEMENT
For the Year Ended December 31, 1978

revenues		
Sales	$200,000	
Other revenues	100,000	
Total revenues		$300,000
expenses		
Cost of goods sold	$120,000	
Selling expenses	40,000	
General and administrative expenses	30,000	
Interest expense	2,000	
Income taxes expense	43,200	
Total expenses		235,200
net earnings before extraordinary items		$ 64,800
extraordinary gains and losses		
Loss from storm damage (net of income taxes of $4,000)		(6,000)
net earnings		$ 58,800
earnings information per share of common stock[a]		
Earnings before extraordinary items		$3.24
Loss from storm damage		(.30)
Net earnings		$2.94

[a] 20,000 shares of common stock were outstanding during the entire year.

EXTRAORDINARY GAINS AND LOSSES

■ *How are extraordinary gains and losses and prior-period adjustments reported?*

Refer to the income statement just illustrated. On the statement there are three distinct sections. The first section shows the results of the regular business operations. It shows revenues earned in the regular operations of the period, and it shows expenses associated with producing those revenues. LMN Corporation produced $300,000 of regular revenues during 1978 and incurred $235,200 of regular expenses, producing an *earnings before extraordinary items* of $64,800. This amounts to $3.24 of earnings per share before extraordinary items. These figures are extremely important in evaluating the *regular and ordinary earning power* of the company.

Extraordinary gains and losses, on the other hand, are reported in a separate section of the income statement. This is done so that the reader of the statement can differentiate between regular earnings and those earnings or losses that are not expected to happen again.

Extraordinary gains and losses are described as they are viewed in current practice:

To be classified as extraordinary, events and transactions resulting in gains and losses must be *both* unusual in nature and infrequent in occurrence:
Unusual nature—The event should possess a high degree of abnormality and be of a type clearly unrelated to, or only incidentally related to, the ordinary and typical activities of the entity, taking into account the *environment* in which the entity operates.
Infrequency of occurrence—The event should be of a type that would not reasonably be expected to recur in the foreseeable future, taking into account the *environment* in which the entity operates.
An event may be considered extraordinary for one entity, but not extraordinary for another, because of the *environments* of the two entities . . .[4]

Examples of extraordinary gains and losses which *would* be reported in the separate section of the income statement are:

1. An earthquake destroys a manufacturing plant of a company that has operations around the world.
2. Hail destroys the crops of a farm company. Hail is extremely rare in the area concerned.

An example of a loss that *would not* be treated as extraordinary is crop loss from frost of a Florida citrus farmer. In that area, frost is expected every few years.

Note that on the income statement illustrated, there is a note related

---

[4] Adapted from American Institute of Certified Public Accountants, *Opinions of the Accounting Principles Board, No. 30,* "Reporting the Results of Operations, 1973," paragraphs 19–25.

to the extraordinary loss that the loss is "net of income taxes of $4,000." Unit 32 explains both this notation and how income taxes are reported when they are associated with extraordinary items.

PRIOR-PERIOD ADJUSTMENTS

Adjustments and corrections of the earnings of **prior periods** do not appear on the current income statement because these gain and loss items are not related to the performance of the current period. Such items are very rare. Generally, they involve the correction of a error in financial statements of a prior period.[5] For example, income taxes were understated for 1976 (assume that "now" is 1978). An additional $50,000 of back taxes are now owed. This entry could be made:

1978 June	18	Retained earnings	50,000	
		Income taxes payable		50,000

This entry illustrates that actual corrections of prior periods' earnings *do not appear on the current income statement,* but instead are reported as adjustments to retained earnings.

Errors in *estimates,* such as depreciation and bad debts, are considered neither extraordinary items nor prior-period adjustments. They are treated as part of the regular recurring operations of the business.

EARNINGS PER SHARE

▪ *How are per-share earnings calculated?*

You are already basically familiar with the nature and use of earnings per share of common stock. You know that this measure applies only to shares of *common* stock because it is the common stockholders who are entitled to share in the residual earnings of the firm. The computation of earnings per share is complicated, however, when there are preferred shares outstanding. This complication arises because the dividend requirements for preferred stock tend to reduce the earnings remaining for common stockholders. The following example will illustrate.

1. The capital section of the balance sheet of a company at December 31, 1978, is presented at the top of the next page. Review it carefully.

[5] Financial Accounting Standards Board, *Statement of Financial Accounting Standards, No. 16,* "Prior Period Adjustments," June, 1977, paragraph 11.

Preferred stock (10,000 shares authorized and issued, $5 par value, 6% dividends payable semiannually)		$ 50,000
Premium on preferred stock		2,000 $ 52,000
Common stock ($5 par value, 100,000 shares issued, of which 1,000 shares are held in the treasury)	$500,000	
Premium on common stock	100,000	600,000
Total		$ 652,000
Appropriated retained earnings	$ 75,000	
Unappropriated retained earnings	500,000	575,000
Total		$1,227,000
Less Treasury stock, common, at cost, 1,000 shares		12,000
Total stockholders' equity		$1,215,000

2. The income statement for the company for 1978 reported the following:

Earnings before extraordinary items	$100,000
Extraordinary gain	40,000
Net earnings	$140,000

3. The preferred shares were outstanding during the entire year.
4. The common shares outstanding changed during 1978 as follows:

Jan. 1 90,000 shares were outstanding.
April 1 The company issued an additional 10,000 shares.
Dec. 1 The company purchased the 1,000 treasury shares.

From the information above we can compute the earnings per share figures in this form:

1.

$$\text{Per-share earnings before extraordinary items} = \frac{\left(\begin{array}{c}\text{Earnings before}\\\text{extraordinary items}\end{array}\right) - \left(\begin{array}{c}\text{Dividend requirements}\\\text{on preferred stock}\end{array}\right)}{\begin{array}{c}\text{Average number of shares of common stock}\\\text{outstanding during the year}\end{array}}$$

$$= \frac{\$100,000 - \$3,000}{97,417}$$

$$= \$.996$$

The $3,000 figure for the dividend requirement on preferred stock is determined as follows:

$$\$50,000 \times 0.06 = \$3,000$$

The number of shares outstanding during the year on the average is determined as follows:

January	90,000
February	90,000
March	90,000
April	100,000
May	100,000
June	100,000
July	100,000
August	100,000
September	100,000
October	100,000
November	100,000
December	99,000

1,169,000 ÷ 12 months = 97,417 shares outstanding on the average

2. $\text{Extraordinary gain per share} = \dfrac{\text{Extraordinary gain}}{\text{Average number of shares of common stock outstanding during the year}}$

$$= \frac{\$40,000}{97,417}$$

$$= \$.411$$

3. $\text{Net earnings per share} = \dfrac{\left(\begin{array}{c}\text{Net}\\\text{earnings}\end{array}\right) - \left(\begin{array}{c}\text{Dividend requirements}\\\text{on preferred stock}\end{array}\right)}{\text{Average number of shares of common stock outstanding during the year}}$

$$= \frac{\$140,000 - \$3,000}{97,417}$$

$$= \$1.407$$

Here is the earnings information in summary form:

Earnings before extraordinary items	$100,000
Extraordinary gain	40,000
Net earnings	$140,000
Per-share earnings before extraordinary items	$ .996
Per-share extraordinary gain	.411
Net earnings per share	$1.407

The per-share figures are based on 97,417 shares of common stock outstanding during the period. The weighted average is used for the computation so that the earnings produced will be divided by the number of shares that actually were outstanding during the period when the earnings were produced. This gives a measure of the earning power of the firm during 1978 per share of common stock that was outstanding.

> **NEW TERMS**

prior-period adjustments Corrections of earnings of a particular prior period; adjustment is made directly to the retained earnings account, rather than to an account which appears on the current income statement; such prior-period adjustments are extremely rare.

[p. 539]

realization The procedure for recognizing revenue in the period when the sale is made, rather than at any other point in the earnings process. [p. 535]

> **ASSIGNMENT MATERIAL**

QUESTIONS

Q31-1. Explain how revenue can be related to gross increases in assets.

Q31-2. Explain how revenue can be related to gross decreases in liabilities.

Q31-3. Explain how expenses can be related to gross decreases in assets.

Q31-4. Explain how expenses can be related to gross increases in liabilities.

Q31-5. Do all firms use the realization basis for recognizing revenue? Explain why or why not.

Q31-6. Explain three general ways that expenses are assigned to periods.

Q31-7. Why are extraordinary gains and losses reported in a separate section of the income statement?

Q31-8. On which financial statement are prior-period adjustments reported? Why?

Q31-9. Describe two examples of extraordinary gains and losses which are not given in the text.

EXERCISES

E31-1. Z Corporation had no extraordinary gains and losses for 1978. The net earnings amounted to $141,000. At January 1, 1978, there were 10,000 shares of common stock outstanding. At May 1, 1978, an additional 5,000 shares of common stock were issued. There were no treasury shares. The company declares and pays $30,000 of dividends on preferred stock each year. Compute the net earnings per share for 1978. Show all computations.

E31-2. Three methods are in common use for matching expenses against the revenue of periods:
A. The expense can be directly related to specific revenue.
B. It is not possible to associate the expense directly with the revenue, so a systematic pattern of assigning expenses to periods is used.

C. The expense is immediately reported as expense.

Classify each of the following expenses into one of the preceding categories.

a. Salesmen's salary expenses
b. Depreciation expense—Store equipment
c. Advertising expense
d. Utilities expense
e. Cost of goods sold

E31-3. The retained earnings statement of Braswell Company showed a January 1, 1978, balance of $12,000. During 1978, dividends totaling $3,000 were declared and paid. Also during 1978, the firm produced net earnings of $10,000. At December 31, 1978, the balance of retained earnings was $13,000. Briefly explain the kind of transaction that could have taken place during 1978 to cause the ending balance of retained earnings to be $13,000, instead of $19,000.

E31-4. From the following selected data of Elia, Inc., compute:

a. Earnings before extraordinary items (1978)
b. Net earnings per share (1978)

Data: Net income $165,000; per share loss from earthquake, $0.30; Preferred stock outstanding during entire period, 10,000 shares, $100 par value, 6%, shares originally issued for $106.

Common shares were outstanding as follows:

At 1–1–78, 30,000 shares outstanding

Issued 3–1–78, 5,000 additional shares

Purchased Treasury shares on 10–1–78, 2,000 shares

At 12–31–78, 33,000 shares outstanding

PROBLEMS (GROUP A)

P31-1. *Earnings per share computations.* Dahl Company records revealed the following:

1. The capital section of the balance sheet at December 31, 1978 included the following:

Common stock, $10 par value, 100,000 shares issued, of which 1,000 were held in the treasury	$1,000,000
Premium on common stock	75,000
Preferred stock, 5%, 5,000 shares issued and outstanding, $100 par	500,000
Premium on preferred stock	10,000
Retained earnings	2,000,000
Cost of 1,000 common treasury shares	15,000

2.

Revenues from regular operations	$7,000,000
Expenses from regular operations	4,500,000
Extraordinary gain	100,000
Prior-period adjustment	200,000

3. The preferred shares were outstanding during the entire year.
4. The common shares outstanding changed during 1978 as follows:

Jan. 1, 1978	95,000 shares were outstanding
April 1, 1978	1,000 treasury shares were purchased.
Dec. 1, 1978	5,000 additional shares were issued.

REQUIRED: Showing all computations, and rounding your answers to the nearest cent, compute:

a. Per-share earnings before extraordinary items.
b. The extraordinary gain per share.
c. The net earnings per share.

P31-2. *Income statement preparation.* On December 29, 1978, the following information was taken from the accounting records of Hobbit Corporation:

Total revenues from regular operations	$314,500
Total expenses from regular operations	200,000
Dividends on preferred stock	50,000
Dividends on common stock	20,000
Average number of shares of common stock outstanding during the year, 20,000	
Average number of shares of the preferred stock outstanding during the year, 50,000	
All revenue was produced from sales of merchandise.	
Cost of goods sold	$100,000
Selling expenses	60,000
General expenses	40,000

On December 30, 1978, two additional transactions took place. These transactions are not reflected in the information provided from the records (above):

1. There was a loss from a storm amounting to $10,000. This loss is to be treated as an *extraordinary loss.*
2. There was a correction of an error amounting to $5,000. This expense of $5,000 was considered a *prior-period adjustment* and related to 1975.

REQUIRED: Prepare an income statement for 1978 in good form, similar to the one illustrated in this unit. Show all per-share figures on the statement. For the purposes of this problem, assume that there are no income taxes.

*P31-3. *Income statement relationships.* Fill in the missing information for each of the four separate cases below. Show your computations.

	corporation			
	A	B	C	D
Total revenues (regular operations)	————	$100,000	————	$90,000
Total expenses (regular operations)	$50,000	————	$60,000	$61,000
Earnings before extraordinary items	$30,000	————	$80,000	————
Extraordinary gain (loss)	————	————	————	————
Net earnings	$40,000	$60,000	————	————
Dividends on preferred stock	$5,000	————	$10,000	————
Dividends on common stock	$1,000	$6,000	$10,000	$5,000
Average number of shares of common stock outstanding	1,000	5,000	————	26,000
Per-share earnings before extraordinary items	————	————	————	$1.00
Per-share extraordinary gain (loss)	————	$1.00	($5.00)	————
Earnings per share	————	$8.00	$9.00	$.80

P31-4. *Earnings per share.* The common stock records of Boone and Company showed outstanding balances of common stock during 1978 as follows:

	NO. OF SHARES
January 1	10,000
February 1	10,000
March 1	10,000
April 1	20,000
May 1	20,000
June 1	19,000
July 1	19,000
August 1	19,000
September 1	21,000
October 1	21,000
November 1	21,000
December 1	21,000
December 31	21,000

Transactions involving common stock were:

March 31	Issued 10,000 additional shares of common stock.
May 31	Purchased 1,000 common treasury shares.
Aug. 31	Issued 1,000 additional shares of common stock and reissued the 1,000 treasury shares.

The net earnings before extraordinary items amounted to $39,000 for the year. There was an extraordinary gain of $10,000. Preferred dividends amounting to $3,000 were declared and paid during 1978 and common dividends amounting to $4,000 were declared and paid.

REQUIRED: Showing all computations, and rounding your answers to the nearest cent, compute:

a. Per-share earnings before extraordinary items.
b. The extraordinary gain per share.
c. The net earnings per share.

P31-5. *Income statement preparation.* Selected information follows from the records of Stonehinge Tablet Company for 1978.

General expenses	$ 80,000
Sales (net)	390,000
Selling expenses	100,000
Rental income	11,000
Cost of goods sold	180,000
Total revenues	401,000
Total expenses from regular operations	360,000

Preferred stock outstanding 1,000 shares, 5%, $100 par value

Dividends on common stock $30,000

Common shares:

	NO. OF SHARES
Outstanding at January 1, 1978	12,000
Additional shares issued on April 30, 1978	+ 10,000
Additional shares issued on May 31, 1978	+ 4,000
Treasury shares acquired on December 1, 1978	− 3,000
Outstanding at December 31, 1978	23,000

These two transactions took place in 1978 (*but they are not yet reflected in the data previously given*):
1. There was an *extraordinary* storm loss amounting to $9,000.
2. There was a prior period adjustment relating to 1976 (reduction in 1976 earnings) amounting to $15,000.

REQUIRED: Prepare an income statement for 1978 in good form, similar to the one illustrated in the unit. Show all per-share figures on the income statement. For purposes of this problem, assume that there are no income taxes.

*P31-6. *Income statement relationships.* Below are data taken from the financial statements of four different corporations for 1978.

	ELMER CORPORATION	ALTA CORPORATION	KENNY CORPORATION	MAE CORPORATION
Earnings per share	$9.60	_____	$0.40	$18.00
Total revenues (regular operations)	$120,000	_____	$45,000	_____
Per-share extraordinary gain (loss)	$1.20	_____	_____	($10.00)
Total expenses (regular operations)	_____	$100,000	$30,500	$120,000
Per-share earnings before extraordinary items	_____	_____	$0.50	_____
Earnings before extraordinary items	_____	$60,000	_____	$160,000
Average number of shares of common stock outstanding	5,000	1,000	26,000	_____
Extraordinary gain (loss)	_____	_____	_____	_____
Dividends on common stock	$7,200	$2,000	$10,000	$20,000
Net earnings	$72,000	$80,000	_____	_____
Dividends on preferred stock	_____	$10,000	_____	$20,000

REQUIRED: Compute the missing figures. Show your computations.

REPORTING INCOME TAXES ON FINANCIAL STATEMENTS

➤ OBJECTIVE

The purpose of this unit is to illustrate and analyze how the income tax expense of corporations is reported on financial statements. Reporting income taxes is a special problem with which you, as a user of financial statements, should be familiar.

➤ APPROACH TO ATTAINING THE OBJECTIVE

As you study the reporting of income taxes on corporate financial statements, pay special attention to these three questions, which the text following answers:

- *How do income taxes affect internal and external decisions?*
- *What is intraperiod income tax allocation?*
- *What is interperiod income tax allocation?*

The income tax laws of our federal government provide that corporations must file income tax returns and must pay the required taxes. Proprietorships and partnerships are not subject to the income tax, so their financial statements do not have the problem of reporting these taxes. Of course, the owners of proprietorships and partnerships must prepare tax returns and pay taxes on their income, including earnings from their businesses. This unit, however, deals only with corporation financial statements.

■ *How do income taxes
affect internal and
external decisions?*

In general, the income tax laws require that a corporation compute its *taxable income* each year. Taxable income is a concept defined by the tax laws and regulations. Most revenues of corporations increase the taxable income for the year, and most expenses decrease it. However, the rules for calculating taxable income are a result of a series of laws passed over many years for many different purposes, political and otherwise. In most cases a corporation's taxable income would be expected to *differ* from its net earnings. As you know, net earnings are computed for a completely different purpose—to give decision makers information about the firm's earning ability and performance.

Here is an example of how taxable income can differ from net earnings. Assume that a corporation owns an investment in bonds of the City of Portland. During the year the corporation earns and collects $1,000 in interest income from the investment. Of course, this $1,000 is included both on the firm's income statement and in its computation of earnings. But tax laws happen to provide that certain types of income earned from municipal bonds are *not* to be included in the computation of taxable income. Therefore, the $1,000 interest income does not appear on the corporation's tax return. Taxable income and net earnings thus would differ for the year.

After taxable income is computed, the tax due is determined by multiplying the appropriate tax rate by the taxable income:

$$\begin{array}{c}\text{Income taxes}\\\text{due the}\\\text{government}\end{array} = \begin{array}{c}\textit{Taxable income}\\\textit{for the year}\end{array} \times \begin{array}{c}\text{Appropriate tax rate}\\\text{for the firm according}\\\text{to the tax laws}\end{array}$$

In this course we are concerned with two basic problems related to a corporation's income tax expense. The first is that management must consider the tax consequences of each of its decisions. A corporation's managers must realize that for each internal decision they make there may be an increase or a decrease in the amount of taxes the corporation owes to the government. Therefore, management accounting is very much involved with figuring out income taxes. Chapter 24 deals with the management accounting implications of income taxes.

The second problem deals with financial accounting, or how income taxes should be reported on financial statements. The rest of this learning unit describes how income taxes should be recorded and reported for external decision makers.

ALLOCATING INCOME TAX EXPENSE BETWEEN REGULAR OPERATIONS AND EXTRAORDINARY ITEMS

- *What is intraperiod income tax allocation?*

In Unit 31 you saw that the corporate income statement separates the ordinary regular revenues and expenses from the extraordinary gains and losses. This is done to make it easier for the decision maker to analyze a company's operations and predict the operations for the coming period. Income tax expense usually is incurred on both kinds of income—regular and extraordinary. An income statement, therefore, must allocate the expense between the two sections of the statement if a meaningful relationship between (1) per-share earnings before extraordinary items and (2) net earnings per share is to be preserved. This allocation within one period is called **intraperiod allocation of income taxes.** In this section we will examine two examples of this reporting practice. One involves an extraordinary gain and the other involves an extraordinary loss.

Intraperiod allocation, with an extraordinary gain Assume these facts about a corporation for 1978:

INFORMATION ABOUT THE EARNINGS

Revenues	$300,000
Expenses (not including income taxes)	192,000
Extraordinary gain from sale of stock (not including income taxes)	10,000

INFORMATION ABOUT THE COMPANY'S TAX RETURN

Taxable income ($300,000 − $192,000 + $10,000)	$118,000
Tax rate for the company	40%
Taxes due the government (0.40 × $118,000)	$47,200

The extraordinary gain is a major part of this example. Ordinarily, gains and losses on the sale of investments in stock are reported in the regular operating section of the income statement. In this case, however, for illustration purposes, we are assuming that for this company, this sale is *both unusual and infrequent,* so it is treated as extraordinary.

Now an income statement (see the top of next page) can be prepared in summary form from these data. Note how the income tax expense is reported in two separate sections.

ZM Corporation
INCOME STATEMENT
For the Year Ended December 31, 1978

revenues		$300,000
expenses		
Operating expenses	$192,000	
Income taxes expense	43,200[a]	
Total expenses		235,200
earnings before extraordinary gain		$ 64,800
extraordinary gain from sale of stock		
(net of income taxes of $4,000)		6,000[b]
net earnings		$ 70,800

[a] Income tax expense related to regular earnings: ($300,000 − $192,000) × 0.40 = $43,200.

[b] The gross gain on the sale of stock was $10,000 (credit balance). This $10,000 gain is taxed at the rate of 40%; therefore, the additional taxes because of the gain are $4,000. The net effect of the gain on the firm is $6,000, or the $10,000 gain less the tax impact of the gain.

The total of the income taxes due the government is $47,200 (see the information at the beginning of the example). The total income taxes expense reported on the income statement in this case also is $47,200: $43,200 reported as an expense in the regular operating section and $4,000 reported as an expense (deduction) in the extraordinary gains section.

Journal entries are shown next to illustrate the recording of the extraordinary gain and to record the income taxes for the year. The stock is assumed to have been sold for $50,000 and to have had a book value (cost) of $40,000.

1978 June	1	Cash	50,000	
		Investment in stock		40,000
		Extraordinary gain on sale of stock		10,000
		To record sale of stock for $50,000 cash; the stock had a book value of $40,000.		

1978 Dec.	31	Income taxes expense	43,200	
		Extraordinary gain on sale of stock	4,000	
		Income taxes payable		47,200
		To record the income taxes due for 1978, $47,200, including $43,200 taxes due on regular earnings and including extra taxes due on the extraordinary gain. The extra taxes reduce the net extraordinary gain.		

Intraperiod allocation of income taxes is desirable and necessary because reporting the entire taxes ($47,200) in the regular operating section of the income statement would mislead the statement readers. An extra $4,000 of income taxes would reduce earnings from operations, when actually that $4,000 was incurred because of an extraordinary event.

Intraperiod allocation, with an extraordinary loss Assume these facts about a corporation for 1978:

INFORMATION ABOUT THE EARNINGS

Revenues	$300,000
Expenses (not including income taxes)	192,000
Extraordinary loss from sale of stock (not including income taxes)	10,000

INFORMATION ABOUT THE COMPANY'S TAX RETURN

Taxable income ($300,000 − $192,000 − $10,000)	$98,000
Tax rate for the company	40%
Taxes due the government (0.40 × $98,000)	$39,200

An income statement prepared in summary form from these data is shown below. Note that the income tax expense is reported in two separate sections of the income statement.

XY Corporation
INCOME STATEMENT
For the Year Ended December 31, 1978

revenues		$300,000
expenses		
Operating expenses	$192,000	
Income taxes expense	43,200[a]	
Total expenses		235,200
earnings before extraordinary loss		$ 64,800
extraordinary loss from sale of stock (net of income taxes of $4,000)		(6,000)[b]
net earnings		$ 58,800

[a] Income tax expense related to regular earnings: ($300,000 − $192,000) × 0.40 = $43,200.

[b] The gross loss on the sale of the stock was $10,000 (debit balance). This $10,000 loss is considered a deduction on the tax return when computing taxable income. The net effect of the loss is $6,000, which is the $10,000 loss minus the tax reduction of 0.40 × $10,000.

Journal entries are shown next to illustrate the recording of the extraordinary loss and to record the income taxes for the year. The stock is assumed to have been sold for $30,000 and to have had a book value (cost) of $40,000.

1978 April	11	Cash
		Extraordinary loss on sale of stock
		  Investment in stock
		    To record sale of stock for $30,000 cash;
		    the stock had a book value of $40,000.
			30,000
			10,000
				40,000

1978 Dec.	31	Income taxes expense
		  Extraordinary loss on sale of stock
		  Income taxes payable
		    To record the income taxes due for 1978,
		    $39,200, including $43,200 taxes due on
		    regular earnings and including a
		    reduction in taxes from the extraordinary
		    loss. The extraordinary loss is reduced
		    by the tax savings of $4,000.
			43,200	4,000
				39,200

ALLOCATING THE INCOME TAX EXPENSE TO THE APPROPRIATE PERIOD

Unit 25 introduced you to the long-term liability, called Deferred income tax liability. This liability arises because in some cases, according to the tax laws, the earnings of one period need not be reported on the tax return until a later period. Even though income tax due is deferred, the taxes expense for the current period based upon current earnings still must be measured to calculate net earnings and earnings per share. The liability for income tax will be settled in the future and therefore is reported on the balance sheet as Deferred income tax liability. You will find it helpful if you review now the part of Unit 25 that provides this introduction.

■ *What is interperiod income tax allocation?*

Here we will look at two more examples of allocating income tax expense to the appropriate period's income statement. The procedure is known as **interperiod allocation of income taxes.** The first example indicates how Income tax expense can be incurred and reported *before* payment and reporting on the tax return. The second example shows how income tax expense can be incurred and reported *after* payment and reporting on the tax return.

Interperiod allocation creating a liability A series of income statements for Hosch Corporation appear below. These income statements are explained in the following list. Be sure you study carefully how the depreciation expense and the income taxes expense were determined.

1. Revenues shown in the income statements are actual operating revenues earned.

2. Operating expenses are actual operating expenses incurred during each year (not including depreciation and income taxes).

3. The Depreciation expense reported on the income statement is calculated according to the *straight-line basis*. This company believes that this method most reasonably measures the earnings of the firm and the usage of plant and equipment. The Depreciation expense amounts differ from year to year because of additional purchases and trade-ins of equipment from time to time.

Hosch Corporation
INCOME STATEMENTS
For the Years Ended December 31

	1978	1979	1980	1981	1982	TOTALS
revenues	$90,000	$125,000	$200,000	$215,000	$300,000	$930,000
expenses						
Operating expenses	$40,000	$ 56,000	$112,000	$150,000	$160,000	$518,000
Depreciation expense	11,000	13,000	13,000	20,000	20,000	77,000
Income taxes expense	15,600	22,400	30,000	18,000	48,000	134,000
Total expenses	$66,600	$ 91,400	$155,000	$188,000	$228,000	$729,000
net earnings	$23,400	$ 33,600	$ 45,000	$ 27,000	$ 72,000	$201,000
net earnings per share	$1.17	$1.68	$2.25	$1.35	$3.60	

4. The company's income tax rate is 40%. Income taxes reported on the income statement for each year would be calculated as follows: for example, for 1978, the taxes would be 40% of taxable income; taxable income is $90,000 — $40,000 — $11,000 or $39,000. Income taxes expense is $15,600, which is 40% of $39,000.

Next, refer to the data from Hosch Corporation's tax returns which follow to determine how the company's actual income tax liability is determined.

INFORMATION FROM THE INCOME TAX RETURNS OF HOSCH CORPORATION

	1978	1979	1980	1981	1982	FIVE-YEAR TOTALS
computation of taxable income						
Revenues	$90,000	$125,000	$200,000	$215,000	$300,000	$930,000
Deductions:						
Operating expenses	$40,000	$ 56,000	$112,000	$150,000	$160,000	$518,000
Depreciation expense[a]	25,000	23,000	14,000	10,000	5,000	77,000
Total deductions	$65,000	$ 79,000	$126,000	$160,000	$165,000	$595,000
Taxable income	$25,000	$ 46,000	$ 74,000	$ 55,000	$135,000	$335,000
tax rate	.40	.40	.40	.40	.40	.40
income taxes due government	$10,000	$ 18,400	$ 29,600	$ 22,000	$ 54,000	$134,000[b]

[a] The company chose to use an *accelerated depreciation method* on its tax returns. Such a method tends to postpone the payment of taxes.

[b] Note that the total of the taxes due is the same as shown in *total* on the *income statement* which is shown above. *Each year differs*, however.

Finally, study the following journal entries that record the income taxes for each of the five years. Be sure to relate each of the amounts in the entries to the preceding income statements and to the income tax return information.

1978 Dec.	31	Income taxes expense	15,600	
		Income taxes payable (current)		10,000
		Deferred income tax liability		5,600
		To record income taxes for 1978.		

1979 Dec.	31	Income taxes expense	22,400	
		Income taxes payable (current)		18,400
		Deferred income tax liability		4,000
		To record income taxes for 1979.		

1980 Dec.	31	Income taxes expense	30,000	
		Income taxes payable (current)		29,600
		Deferred income tax liability		400
		To record income taxes for 1980.		

1981 Dec.	31	Income taxes expense	18,000	
		Deferred income tax liability	4,000	
		Income taxes payable (current)		22,000
		To record income taxes for 1981.		

1982 Dec.	31	Income taxes expense	48,000	
		Deferred income tax liability	6,000	
		Income taxes payable (current)		54,000
		To record income taxes for 1982.		

These are the key conclusions about interperiod allocation of income taxes:

1. It is common practice to use different reporting methods on the income statement and on the income tax return. This difference arises because of the differing objectives of the two reports. The income statement measures performance and earnings for the company, while the tax return is prepared according to a set of somewhat arbitrary tax laws.

2. *When Income taxes expense for a period is larger than the actual taxes due,* a deferred income tax liability is created and is reported on the balance sheet.

Interperiod allocation creating an asset The preceding illustration showed that Income taxes expense for a period could be *larger* than the actual taxes due the government. Such situations give rise to a liability called **Deferred income tax liability.** In a similar manner, it is possible for the Income taxes expense for a period to be *smaller* than the actual taxes due the government for that period. In these circumstances, an asset called **Deferred income taxes (asset)** is created and reported on the balance sheet.

For example, assume that the Income taxes expense reported on an income statement for 1977 amounts to $9,000. Further, assume that the tax laws require that taxes amounting to $10,200 be paid during the year, according to the tax return. This entry would be made:

1977 Dec.	31	Income taxes expense	9,000	
		Deferred income taxes (asset)	1,200	
		Income taxes payable		10,200

Such a situation could arise in 1977 if revenue had been received in advance by a company *and*

1. If this revenue was to be earned and reported on the 1978 *income statement* of the company, and
2. If the tax laws required that the revenue be reported on the *income tax return* for *1977.*

The effect would be that taxes on the earnings would be paid in advance of reporting the earnings on the income statement, thereby creating an asset (prepaid expense or deferred charge).

In this illustration, these are the key conclusions about interperiod allocation of income taxes:

1. It is common practice to use different reporting methods on the income statement and on the income tax return. This difference arises because of the differing objectives of the two reports. The income statement measures performance and earnings for the company, while the tax return is prepared according to a set of somewhat arbitrary tax laws.
2. *When Income taxes expense for a period is smaller than the actual taxes due,* a deferred income tax (asset) is created and is reported on the balance sheet. This asset can be considered to be like prepaid expenses and deferred charges.

deferred income tax liability A long-term liability account, reflecting that portion of past income tax expenses recognized by the corporation but not yet paid by the corporation to the government. [p. 555]

deferred income taxes (asset) An asset account, similar to a deferred charge or prepaid expense, representing income taxes already paid by the government but not yet reported by the company on its income statement. [p. 555]

interperiod allocation of income taxes Dividing the income tax effects (expense) among the several account-

ing periods and income statements; interperiod allocation is required because of the differences in timing of revenue recognition and expense recognition between the corporate income statement and the corporate tax return. [p. 552]

intraperiod income tax allocation Dividing the income tax effects (expense) between the ordinary earnings section of the income statement and the extraordinary items section, all within one period's income statement. [p. 549]

▶ **ASSIGNMENT MATERIAL**

QUESTIONS

Q32-1. What is taxable income?

Q32-2. Briefly describe the purpose of intraperiod allocation of income taxes.

Q32-3. Briefly describe the purpose of interperiod allocation of income taxes.

Q32-4. Explain under what circumstances a corporation's income tax expense can be *more* than the amount owed the government for that year's taxes.

Q32-5. Explain under what circumstances a corporation's income tax expense can be *less* than the amount owed the government for that year's taxes.

Q32-6. Explain how each of the following accounts are reported on the financial statements (on which statement and in which section of the statement):
   a. Income tax expense.
   b. Deferred income tax liability.
   c. Deferred income tax (asset).

EXERCISES

E32-1. During 1978 Blad Hassel Corporation had total sales amounting to $900,000. Its cost of goods sold and operating expenses (not including income taxes) amounted to $650,000. The firm had an extraordinary gain from sale of investments of $20,000 (before considering income taxes) and an extraordinary loss from a storm of $17,000 (before considering income taxes). The company's income tax rate is 39%. Preferred dividends amounting to $15,000 were declared during 1978. There were 12,000 shares of common stock outstanding during the year. Prepare a summary income statement in good form, including per-share figures.

E32-2. The working papers of Socola, Inc., for the year ended December 31, 1978, revealed these balances:

Sales		100,000
Sales returns and allowances	2,000	
Sales discounts	4,000	
Cost of goods sold	50,000	
General expenses	10,000	
Selling expenses	12,000	
Extraordinary gain		3,000
Extraordinary loss	1,000	

Income taxes are not yet included in the preceding information. Compute (1) the Income tax expense to appear in the regular operating section of the income statement, (2) the earnings before extraordinary items, and (3) the net income. The firm's income tax rate is 40%.

E32-3. For each of the following separate situations, indicate (when interperiod tax allocation is applied) whether there would be a liability (Deferred income tax liability) or an asset (Deferred income taxes—asset).

a. The company uses straight-line depreciation on its income tax return and sum-of-the-years'-digits depreciation on its financial statements.

b. The company uses declining-balance depreciation on its income tax return and straight-line depreciation on its financial statements.

c. Revenue is reported on the income statement during the period that the sale is made, but revenue is reported on the income tax return only as cash is collected.

d. At the end of the year the company makes an adjusting entry for accrued salaries for financial statement purposes. However, salaries expense is reported on the income tax return in the period the salaries are actually paid.

E32-4. Below are entries appearing on the records of a corporation.

1. Accumulated depreciation—Building	60,000	
Accumulated depreciation—Equipment	10,000	
Extraordinary loss	50,000	
Building		100,000
Equipment		20,000
2. Income tax expense	300,000	
Extraordinary loss		20,000
Income taxes payable		280,000

(a) Explain *in detail* what events took place that led to the preceding entries.
(b) What is the company's income tax rate?
(c) What are the firm's earnings before extraordinary items?
(d) What is the *net* extraordinary loss?
(e) What is the net income of the company?

PROBLEMS (GROUP A)

P32-1. *Intraperiod income tax allocation; income statement; journal entries.* Data for MR Corporation for 1978 follow.

The revenues totaled $250,000: $200,000 represented net sales and the balance was service revenue. Cost of goods sold totaled $100,000; operating expenses (not including income taxes) amounted to $30,000. The company's tax rate is 42%. The firm made an extraordinary gain of $31,000 by disposing of a long-term investment in common stock of X Co., which had been purchased several years ago. The company sold the investment for $200,000 cash and had paid $169,000 for the investment. There were 10,000 shares of common stock outstanding at the beginning of the year. On February 1, 1978, an additional 4,000 shares were issued, and at the end of the year, 14,000 shares were outstanding. Preferred stock dividend requirements for the year amounted to $8,000. The firm's taxable income for 1978 was $151,000.

> a. Prepare an income statement.
> b. Prepare general journal entries for
>   (1) Selling the long-term investment.
>   (2) Recording the income taxes.

P32-2. *Intraperiod income tax allocation; income statement.* The accountant for Clavicle and Co. gathered the following information from the accounting records for 1978.

Net earnings (before income taxes and before extraordinary items)	$10,000
Extraordinary loss	4,000
Tax rate: 40% of taxable income	
Net sales	40,000
Service income	10,000
Operating expenses (other than income taxes)	15,000
Cost of goods sold	25,000
Taxable income ($10,000 earnings less $4,000 loss)	6,000

REQUIRED: Prepare an income statement in good form. There were 1,000 shares of common stock outstanding during the period. Dividends on preferred stock amounted to $1,000, and dividends on common stock amounted to $2,000.

*P32-3. *Interperiod income tax allocation; journal entries.* Assume the following facts about Veach Company:

Tax rate: 40%

Net earnings for 1977 (before income taxes): $100,000

Taxable income for 1977: $90,000. Salary expenses of $10,000 were deducted on the tax return for 1977; these expenses appear on the income statement for the *following year* (1978), however, because these payments were, in fact, advance salary payments.

REQUIRED: Make general journal entries:

> a. To record the payment of advance salaries on December 29, 1977 (debit Prepaid salaries).
> b. To record the income tax expense for 1977, at December 31, 1977 (creating the Deferred income tax liability).
> c. To record the payment of taxes due the government for 1977. The payment was made on January 13, 1978.
> d. To record the income tax expense at the end of 1978, December 31, 1978. (Assume that Net earnings before taxes amount to $100,000 for 1978 and the tax rate is 40%.)

PROBLEMS (GROUP B)

P32-4. *Intraperiod income tax allocation; income statement.* The accountant for Z Corporation gathered the following information from the accounting records for 1978.

Net earnings (before income taxes and before extraordinary items)	$10,000
Extraordinary gain	3,000
Tax rate: 40% of taxable income	
Net sales	40,000

Service income	10,000
Operating expenses (other than income taxes)	15,000
Cost of goods sold	25,000
Taxable income ($10,000 earnings plus $3,000 gain)	13,000

REQUIRED: Prepare an income statement in good form. There were 1,000 shares of common stock outstanding during the period. There is no preferred stock outstanding.

P32-5. *Interperiod income tax allocation; journal entries.* The income tax return of Burden Company showed that taxes due the government for 1978 amounted to $126,000. The company, which has a 42% income tax rate, uses the declining-balance method of computing depreciation on its tax return, and depreciation on its plant and equipment amounted to $90,000 for 1978. Depreciation expense on the firm's income statement was $55,000 (straight-line method). Depreciation was the firm's only item that involved interperiod allocation of income taxes. There were 25,000 shares of common stock outstanding during 1978, and the company paid preferred dividends of $15,000 for the year.

REQUIRED:

    a. Prepare the general journal entry needed to record the income taxes for 1978.

    b. Compute the earnings per share for 1978 for the company.

P32-6. *Interperiod income tax allocation; analysis.* The Patylo Company computes depreciation on its plant and equipment according to the straight-line method for its income statement. For the tax return of the firm, the sum-of-the-years'-digits method is used in order to minimize taxes paid in early years of the life of the assets. Other information about the company follows:

    1. Net earnings for the firm before Depreciation expense and before income taxes are deducted are expected to amount to $100,000 each year (1977 through 1981).

    2. The tax rate is 40%.

    3. The company is formed, and begins operations on January 1, 1977.

    4. The equipment had a total cost of $50,000 and is expected to last 5 years, with no scrap value. This is the only depreciable property owned by the company.

REQUIRED:

    a. Compute the amount of estimated *Net earnings* for each of the 5 years.

    b. Compute the amount of income taxes due the government for each of the 5 years.

    c. Compute the amount of the Income tax expense to appear on the income statement for each of the 5 years.

    d. Compute the amount of the long-term deferred income tax liability to appear on the balance sheet at the end of each of the 5 years.

    e. Prepare the general journal entry to record the income tax expense at December 31, 1977.

    f. Prepare the general journal entry to record the payment of the 1977 income taxes on January 15, 1978.

    g. Prepare the general journal entry to record the income tax expense at December 31, 1978.

P32-7. *Cumulative review problem*

Part A

On December 29, 1978, the following information was taken from the accounting records of Abernathy Corporation:

Total revenues from regular operations	$334,500
Total expenses from regular operations	260,000
Dividends on preferred stock	20,000
Dividends on common stock	40,000
Average number of shares of common stock outstanding during the year, 25,000	
Average number of shares of preferred stock outstanding during the year, 55,000	
All revenue was produced from sales of merchandise.	
Cost of goods sold	120,000
Selling expenses	80,000
General expenses	60,000

On December 30, 1978, two additional transactions took place. These transactions are not reflected in the information provided from the records (above):

1. There was a gain from the recovery of a major piece of equipment amounting to $20,000. This gain is to be treated as an extraordinary gain.
2. There was a settlement of a lawsuit in favor of the company amounting to $8,000. This gain of $8,000 was considered to be a prior-period adjustment and relates to 1973.

REQUIRED: Prepare an income statement for 1978 in good form. Show all per-share figures on the statement. For the purposes of this problem, assume that there are no income taxes.

Part B

The following information is from the 1978 accounting records of Mendez Corporation:

Revenues	$160,000
Operating expenses (other than income taxes)	40,000
Cost of goods sold	50,000
Extraordinary gain	6,000
Tax rate: 40% of taxable income	
Taxable income ($70,000 earnings plus $6,000 gain)	76,000

REQUIRED: Prepare a summary income statement in good form. There were 1,500 shares of common stock outstanding during the period. Dividends on preferred stock amounted to $2,000 and dividends on common stock amounted to $3,000.

Part C

The following information is from the 1978 accounting records of Roop Corporation:

Net earnings before extraordinary loss	$100,000
Dividends on preferred stock	15,000
Net sales	250,000
Total assets, 1-1-78	200,000
Interest expense	3,000
Market price of a share of stock	10
Total capital, 1-1-78	120,000
Current liabilities, 12-31-78	25,000
Number of shares of common stock outstanding	10,000
Current assets, 12-31-78	$ 35,000

There was an after-tax loss from the damage of a major piece of equipment amounting to $12,000. This is to be treated as an extraordinary loss.

REQUIRED:

a. (1) Earnings per share before extraordinary items.
   (2) Extraordinary loss per share.
   (3) Earnings per share.
   (4) For each dollar of net sales, how many cents of net earnings were produced?
   (5) Return on capital.
   (6) Return on investment.
   (7) Price–earnings ratio.
   (8) Current ratio.
   (9) Relationship of the earnings generated by the firm to Interest expense.
b. Prepare the journal entry to record the income taxes due, assuming a 40% tax rate.

P32-8. *Cumulative review problem*

Part A
The common stock records of Pierce and Company showed outstanding balances of common stock during 1978 as follows:

	NO. OF SHARES
January 1	20,000
February 1	20,000
March 1	25,000
April 1	25,000
May 1	25,000
June 1	24,000
July 1	27,000
August 1	20,000
September 1	20,000
October 1	20,000
November 1	24,000
December 1	24,000
December 31	24,000

Transactions involving common stock were:

Feb. 28   Issued 5,000 additional shares of common stock.
May 31   Purchased 1,000 common treasury shares.
June 30   Issued 2,000 additional shares of common stock and reissued the 1,000 treasury shares.
July 31   Purchased 7,000 common treasury shares.
Oct. 31   Reissued 4,000 of the treasury shares.

The net earnings before extraordinary items amounted to $59,000 for the year. There was an extraordinary loss of $6,000. Preferred dividends amounting to $4,000 were declared and paid during 1978 and common dividends amounting to $7,000 were declared and paid.

REQUIRED: Showing all computations, and rounding your answers to the nearest cent, compute:

a. Per-share earnings before extraordinary items.
b. The extraordinary loss per share.
c. The net earnings per share.

Part B
Three selected transactions of Arrow, Inc., are given below:
1. Office equipment was completely destroyed by a storm on June 1, 1978; the office equipment had a book value of $44,000 and was originally purchased for $62,000. This transaction will be treated as an extraordinary loss.
2. To record the income tax expense for 1978, at December 31, 1978. Facts from the firm's records follow:

Revenues	$200,000
Operating expenses (other than income taxes)	35,000
Cost of goods sold	40,000
Extraordinary loss from storm (see transaction 1 above)	44,000
Tax rate: 40% of taxable income	

3. To record the payment of taxes due the government for 1978. The payment was made on January 10, 1979.

REQUIRED: Prepare general journal entries.

chapter 14

corporations: bonds payable

UNIT 33

BONDS PAYABLE–
ACCOUNTING AND REPORTING

> **OBJECTIVE**

The purpose of this unit is to illustrate and describe how bonds payable are accounted for in modern corporations, once the decision to issue bonds has been made.

> **APPROACH TO ATTAINING THE OBJECTIVE**

As you study about bonds payable, pay special attention to these four questions, which the text following answers:

- *How are bonds that are sold at a discount reported?*
- *How are bonds that are sold at a premium reported?*
- *How is the retirement of bonds recorded?*
- *How are bond sinking funds accounted for?*

ISSUING BONDS

When a firm decides to issue bonds to raise funds for its operations, bond certificates are printed, very often in denominations (units of value) of $1,000. Many borrowing corporations turn over all of the bonds to an investment company, often called an **underwriter**. This underwriter, in turn, sells the bonds to many investors. In addition to this first sale, bonds generally can be bought and sold repeatedly and transferred to other investors. The bond certificates have printed on them such information as:

1. The face amount or maturity value.
2. The provisions for periodic cash payment to the bondholders, such as 6% annually, paid semiannually.
3. The maturity date.

▪ How are bonds that are sold at a discount reported?

When a corporation issues bonds, there are costs associated with the selling of the bonds. These issue costs must be recognized as an additional part of the cost of borrowing the funds. The following discussion describes how bonds payable are accounted for when they are issued.

Example 1 *Assume these facts about the issuance of bonds:*

1. 100 bonds issued on January 1, 1978, with maturity values of $1,000 each; the bonds mature in 10 years.
2. Annual payments ("interest") to be paid to bondholders at the rate of 6% per annum; payments to be made each December 31.
3. When the bonds were sold on January 1, 1978, it is determined that the market rate for these bonds was 8%, instead of the anticipated 6% that was printed on the face of the bonds. This simply means that the company will have to pay 8% interest per year on the money it borrows if the bonds are to be issued.

Here is the procedure usually used to accomplish this:

a. The bonds are issued according to the agreement and details originally decided upon. That is, the bonds will still mature in 10 years and the maturity amount will be $100,000. The annual payment to bondholders will still be 6% of the face amount, or $6,000 per year.
b. So that the bondholders (lenders) will receive 8% interest, however, the bonds are sold at a *discount.* That is, the company borrows less than $100,000, so the yield or effective interest amount will not be 6%, but will be 8%.

Calculating the proceeds The present value table (which you learned about in Unit 25) will provide a basis for calculating the **proceeds** (present value) of the bond issue if the interest rate is 8%. Table 33-1 illustrates.

TABLE 33-1

CALCULATION OF BOND ISSUE PROCEEDS

(1) YEAR	(2) CASH OUTFLOWS		(3) 8% PRESENT VALUE FACTOR	(4) PRESENT VALUE OF CASH OUTFLOWS
1	$ 6,000	×	0.926	$ 5,556
2	6,000	×	0.857	5,142
3	6,000	×	0.794	4,764
4	6,000	×	0.735	4,410
5	6,000	×	0.681	4,086
6	6,000	×	0.630	3,780
7	6,000	×	0.583	3,498
8	6,000	×	0.540	3,240
9	6,000	×	0.500	3,000
10	6,000	×	0.463	2,778
10	100,000	×	0.463	46,300
Proceeds of bond issue (present value)				$86,554

Columns 1 and 2 show the cash payments on the bond issue according to the bond agreement. At the end of each year for 10 years, $6,000 will be paid to the bondholders. This is 6% of the face amount of the bonds ($100,000). Also, at the maturity date (10 years), the face amount of $100,000 will be repaid the bondholders. Total cash outflows will amount to $160,000 (the total of column 2).

Column 3 shows the present value of $1 at 8% from the present value table (Table 33-2). These factors will be used to convert the several cash outflows to today's or present values. Column 2 is multiplied by column 3 to determine the present value of each cash outflow. The sum of column 4 is the amount that bondholders will be willing to invest in order to receive the $160,000 cash over the 10-year period according to the bond agreement. In other words, an investment of $86,554 today, which will produce cash of $6,000 each year for ten years and will produce $100,000 cash at the end of 10 years, will earn *exactly an 8% return*.

Calculating the interest expense Based upon the data above, the company that issues the bonds knows that it costs 8% per year to borrow the money. Interest expense, therefore, can be calculated on this basis, as illustrated in Table 33-3. This method of reporting interest expense is known as the *compound interest method* or the *scientific amortization* method.

Table 33-3 shows that the net long-term liability at January 1, 1978, when the bonds are first issued, amounts to $86,554. The Bonds payable

PRESENT VALUES OF $1

TABLE 33-2

PERIODS	4%	6%	8%	10%	12%	14%	16%	18%	20%	22%	24%	26%	28%	30%	40%
1	0.962	0.943	0.926	0.909	0.893	0.877	0.862	0.847	0.833	0.820	0.806	0.794	0.781	0.769	0.714
2	0.925	0.890	0.857	0.826	0.797	0.769	0.743	0.718	0.694	0.672	0.650	0.630	0.610	0.592	0.510
3	0.889	0.840	0.794	0.751	0.712	0.675	0.641	0.609	0.579	0.551	0.524	0.500	0.477	0.455	0.364
4	0.855	0.792	0.735	0.683	0.636	0.592	0.552	0.516	0.482	0.451	0.423	0.397	0.373	0.350	0.260
5	0.822	0.747	0.681	0.621	0.567	0.519	0.476	0.437	0.402	0.370	0.341	0.315	0.291	0.269	0.186
6	0.790	0.705	0.630	0.564	0.507	0.456	0.410	0.370	0.335	0.303	0.275	0.250	0.227	0.207	0.133
7	0.760	0.665	0.583	0.513	0.452	0.400	0.354	0.314	0.279	0.249	0.222	0.198	0.178	0.159	0.095
8	0.731	0.627	0.540	0.467	0.404	0.351	0.305	0.266	0.233	0.204	0.179	0.157	0.139	0.123	0.068
9	0.703	0.592	0.500	0.424	0.361	0.308	0.263	0.225	0.194	0.167	0.144	0.125	0.108	0.094	0.048
10	0.676	0.558	0.463	0.386	0.322	0.270	0.227	0.191	0.162	0.137	0.116	0.099	0.085	0.073	0.035
11	0.650	0.527	0.429	0.350	0.287	0.237	0.195	0.162	0.135	0.122	0.094	0.079	0.066	0.056	0.025
12	0.625	0.497	0.397	0.319	0.257	0.208	0.168	0.137	0.112	0.092	0.076	0.062	0.052	0.043	0.018
13	0.601	0.469	0.368	0.290	0.229	0.182	0.145	0.116	0.093	0.075	0.061	0.050	0.040	0.033	0.013
14	0.577	0.442	0.340	0.263	0.205	0.160	0.125	0.099	0.078	0.062	0.049	0.039	0.032	0.025	0.009
15	0.555	0.417	0.315	0.239	0.183	0.140	0.108	0.084	0.065	0.051	0.040	0.031	0.025	0.020	0.006
16	0.534	0.394	0.292	0.218	0.163	0.123	0.093	0.071	0.054	0.042	0.032	0.025	0.019	0.015	0.005
17	0.513	0.371	0.270	0.198	0.146	0.108	0.080	0.060	0.045	0.034	0.026	0.020	0.015	0.012	0.003
18	0.494	0.350	0.250	0.180	0.130	0.095	0.069	0.051	0.038	0.028	0.021	0.016	0.012	0.009	0.002
19	0.475	0.331	0.232	0.164	0.116	0.083	0.060	0.043	0.031	0.023	0.017	0.012	0.009	0.007	0.002
20	0.456	0.312	0.215	0.149	0.104	0.073	0.051	0.037	0.026	0.019	0.014	0.010	0.007	0.005	0.001
21	0.439	0.294	0.199	0.135	0.093	0.064	0.044	0.031	0.022	0.015	0.011	0.008	0.006	0.004	0.001
22	0.422	0.278	0.184	0.123	0.083	0.056	0.038	0.026	0.018	0.013	0.009	0.006	0.004	0.003	0.001
23	0.406	0.262	0.170	0.112	0.074	0.049	0.033	0.022	0.015	0.010	0.007	0.005	0.003	0.002	
24	0.390	0.247	0.158	0.102	0.066	0.043	0.028	0.019	0.013	0.008	0.006	0.004	0.003	0.002	
25	0.375	0.233	0.146	0.092	0.059	0.038	0.024	0.016	0.010	0.007	0.005	0.003	0.002	0.001	
26	0.361	0.220	0.135	0.084	0.053	0.033	0.021	0.014	0.009	0.006	0.004	0.002	0.002	0.001	
27	0.347	0.207	0.125	0.076	0.047	0.029	0.018	0.011	0.007	0.005	0.003	0.002	0.001	0.001	
28	0.333	0.196	0.116	0.069	0.042	0.026	0.016	0.010	0.006	0.004	0.002	0.002	0.001	0.001	
29	0.321	0.185	0.107	0.063	0.037	0.022	0.014	0.008	0.005	0.003	0.002	0.001	0.001	0.001	
30	0.308	0.174	0.099	0.057	0.033	0.020	0.012	0.007	0.004	0.003	0.002	0.001	0.001	0.001	
40	0.208	0.097	0.046	0.022	0.011	0.005	0.003	0.001	0.001						

TABLE 33-3
DETAILS OF THE BOND ISSUE

(1) YEAR	(2) NET LONG-TERM LIABILITY AT JANUARY 1	(3) INTEREST EXPENSE FOR YEAR (8%)	(4) CASH PAYMENT AT DECEMBER 31	(5) NET LONG-TERM LIABILITY AT DECEMBER 31	(6) AMOUNT OF BOND DISCOUNT AMORTIZATION
1 (1978)	$86,554	$ 6,924	$ 6,000	$ 87,478	$ 924
2	87,478	6,998	6,000	88,476	998
3	88,476	7,078	6,000	89,554	1,078
4 (1981)	89,554	7,164	6,000	90,718	1,164
5	90,718	7,257	6,000	91,975	1,257
6	91,975	7,358	6,000	93,333	1,358
7 (1984)	93,333	7,467	6,000	94,800	1,467
8	94,800	7,584	6,000	96,384	1,584
9	96,384	7,711	6,000	98,095	1,711
10 (1987)	98,095	7,905	6,000	100,000	1,905
		$73,446	$60,000		$13,446

account will reflect a credit balance of $100,000, and the Discount on bonds payable account will reflect a debit balance of the amount of the discount of $13,446. The net difference of $86,554 will be reported on the balance sheet as the liability.

Interest expense for the first year will be 8% of the long-term liability (8% of $86,554, or $6,924). Of this interest expense, only $6,000 is paid in cash; therefore, the net long-term liability grows by $924. The net long-term liability at December 31, 1978, is $87,478 (column 2 plus column 3 minus column 4).

Recording and reporting the bond issue In general journal form, the entries are shown for the bond issue for the first three years using the data in Table 33-3.

			GENERAL JOURNAL		
1978 Jan.	1	Cash		86,554	
		Bond discount		13,446	
		Bonds payable			100,000
		Bonds were issued to yield 8% return to bondholders.			
Dec.	31	Interest expense		6,924	
		Bond discount			924
		Cash			6,000
		To record the interest expense for 1978 (8% of $86,554); to record the cash payment to bondholders of $6,000; to amortize the bond discount.			

The first thing to observe about this first entry is that the assets of the firm increase by $86,554, the amount of the cash increase. The liabilities also increase by $86,554. The **Bond discount** account is a contra account that reduces the long-term liability, Bonds payable. Two liability accounts are set up (Bonds payable with a credit balance and Bond discount with a debit balance) so that both the maturity amount and the long-term liability (which is $86,554) can be entered in the records. If a balance sheet were prepared, the long-term liability section would appear as follows:

BALANCE SHEET AT DECEMBER 31, 1978

long-term liabilities

Bonds payable... $100,000

Less Bond discount 12,522 $87,478

At the end of the second year of the life of the bonds, this entry would be made.

GENERAL JOURNAL

1979 Dec.	31	Interest expense	6,998	
		Bond discount		998
		Cash		6,000
		To record the interest expense for 1979 (8% of $87,478); to record the cash payment to bondholders of $6,000; to amortize the bond discount.		

Notice that the interest for this year is more than for the previous year (since the liability was larger than for 1978). Trace these figures to Table 26-3.

The balance sheet at December 31, 1979, would show:

BALANCE SHEET AT DECEMBER 31, 1979

long-term liabilities

Bonds payable... $100,000

Less Bond discount 11,524 $88,476

And finally, the third year's entry and balance sheet presentation is shown on the next page.

GENERAL JOURNAL

1980					
Dec.	31	Interest expense		7,078	
		Bond discount			1,078
		Cash			6,000
		To record the interest expense for 1980 (8% of $88,476); to record the cash payment to bondholders of $6,000; to amortize the bond discount.			

BALANCE SHEET AT DECEMBER 31, 1980

long-term liabilities

Bonds payable $100,000
Less Bond discount 10,446 $89,554

The preceding example involved bonds that were sold at a *discount,* where the market rate of interest was higher (8%) than the rate in the bond agreement (6%). This next example shows how bonds can be sold at a *premium,* when the market rate of interest is less than the bond agreement rate.

■ *How are bonds that are sold at a premium reported?*

Example 2   *Assume these facts about the issuance of bonds:*

1. 100 bonds issued on January 1, 1978, with maturity values of $1,000 each; the bonds mature in 10 years.
2. Annual payments ("interest") to be paid to bondholders at the rate of 6% per annum; payment to be made each December 31.
3. The bonds are sold at a market rate of interest of 4%.

Calculating the proceeds Table 33-4 shows how the proceeds of the bond issue are determined.

TABLE 33-4
CALCULATION OF BOND ISSUE PROCEEDS

(1) YEAR	(2) CASH OUTFLOWS		(3) PRESENT VALUE FACTOR (4%)	(4) PRESENT VALUE OF CASH OUTFLOWS
1	$ 6,000	×	0.962	$ 5,772
2	6,000	×	0.925	5,550
3	6,000	×	0.889	5,334
4	6,000	×	0.855	5,130
5	6,000	×	0.822	4,932
6	6,000	×	0.790	4,740
7	6,000	×	0.760	4,560
8	6,000	×	0.731	4,386
9	6,000	×	0.703	4,218
10	6,000	×	0.676	4,056
10	100,000	×	0.676	67,600
Proceeds of bond issue (present value)				$116,278

Calculating the interest expense Since the interest cost is only 4%, the company can borrow $116,278, an amount greater than the face of the bonds. Details are given in Table 33-5.

TABLE 33-5
DETAILS OF THE BOND ISSUE

(1) YEAR	(2) NET LONG-TERM LIABILITY AT JANUARY 1	(3) INTEREST EXPENSE FOR YEAR (4%)	(4) CASH PAYMENT AT DECEMBER 31	(5) NET LONG-TERM LIABILITY AT DECEMBER 31	(6) AMOUNT OF BOND PREMIUM AMORTIZATION
1	$116,278	$ 4,651	$ 6,000	$114,929	$ 1,349
2	114,929	4,597	6,000	113,526	1,403
3	113,526	4,541	6,000	112,067	1,459
4	112,067	4,483	6,000	110,550	1,517
5	110,550	4,422	6,000	108,972	1,578
6	108,972	4,359	6,000	107,331	1,641
7	107,331	4,293	6,000	105,624	1,707
8	105,624	4,225	6,000	103,849	1,775
9	103,849	4,154	6,000	102,003	1,846
10	102,003	3,997	6,000	100,000	2,003
		$43,722	$60,000		$16,278

Recording and reporting the bond issue In general journal form, the entries are shown for the bond issue for the first 2 years using the data in Table 33-5.

GENERAL JOURNAL					

1978
Jan.
	1	Cash
		    Bonds payable
		    Bond premium
		        Bonds were issued to yield 4% return to
		        bondholders.
				116,278	100,000
					16,278

Dec.	31	Interest expense
		Bond premium
		    Cash
		        To record the interest expense for 1978
		        (4% of $116,278); to record the cash
		        payment to bondholders of $6,000;
		        to amortize the bond discount..
				4,651
				1,349
					6,000

The assets of the company increase by $116,278, the amount of the cash increase. The liabilities increase by $116,278 also. The **Bond premium** account is a liability, much the same as is the Bonds payable account. If the balance sheet were prepared at the end of the first year of the life of the bonds, the long-term liability section would appear as follows:

BALANCE SHEET AT DECEMBER 31, 1978

long-term liabilities

Bonds payable... $100,000
Add: Bond premium 14,929 $114,929

At the end of the second year of the life of the bonds, this entry would be made.

			GENERAL JOURNAL		
1979 Dec.	31		Interest expense	4,597	
			Bond premium	1,403	
			Cash		6,000
			To record the interest expense for 1979 (4% of $114,929); to record the cash payment to bondholders of $6,000; to amortize the bond premium.		

Notice that the interest for this year is less than for the previous year (since the liability was smaller than for 1978). Trace these figures to Table 33-5.

The balance sheet at December 31, 1979, would show:

BALANCE SHEET AT DECEMBER 31, 1979

long-term liabilities
Bonds payable... $100,000
Add: Bond premium 13,526 $113,526

RETIRING BONDS

▪ How is the retirement of bonds recorded?

When bonds are retired at their maturity, the amount of the net long-term liability equals the face or maturity amount. You can see this in Tables 33-3 and 33-5—at December 31, 1987, the liability amounts to exactly $100,000 in both examples. The bond discount or the bond premium at maturity would have a zero balance. When the bonds are paid off, Cash is credited for $100,000 and the Bonds payable account is debited for $100,000.

Sometimes, when the bonds have the provision that they can be called in and retired, a company chooses to retire its bonds before the maturity. The call provision might provide that the amount required to retire the bonds differs from the long-term liability amount on the company's balance sheet. For example, assume that the bonds in our Example 1 were called in and retired on December 31, 1981, for $93,000. This entry would be required to retire the bonds:

1981 Dec.	31		Bonds payable	100,000	
			Loss on retirement of bonds	2,282	
			Bond discount		9,282
			Cash		93,000

You can see from Table 33-3 that the net liability at the time the bonds were retired amounts to $90,718. The Bond discount account therefore would have to have a debit balance of $9,282 for a net liability of $90,718 (or $100,000 minus $9,282 equals $90,718). The loss on retirement of bonds ($2,282) is the difference between the amount paid to retire the bonds ($93,000) and the net liability being paid ($90,718).

Another term associated with bonds is **refunding.** It is used to refer to the process of retiring a bond issue and then immediately issuing new bonds—usually at a lower rate of interest.

REPORTING BOND SINKING FUNDS

- *How are bond sinking funds accounted for?*

Some bond indentures require that the corporation issuing the bonds set up a long-term investment called a sinking fund. This investment usually is controlled by an independent financial agent or *trustee,* who manages and invests the assets in the fund. The indenture might provide that the corporation make regular deposits of cash to the sinking fund and that the trustee invest the cash to produce earnings. The objective is to accumulate assets to pay off the bonds payable at their maturity. The following journal illustrates some of the transactions that might be associated with a sinking fund.

1978 Jan.					
	1	Bond sinking fund		10,000	
		Cash			10,000
		Annual deposit made with sinking fund trustee.			
	15	Bond sinking fund		650	
		Sinking fund income			650
		To record dividend check received by the sinking fund on its investments in common stock of AB Co.			
	25	Bond sinking fund		6,000	
		Gain on sale of sinking fund investments			6,000
		To record sale of X Co. stock for $60,000, which had cost $54,000.			

Note these points about sinking funds and the entries in the accompanying journal:

1. In many cases the trustee decides which investments will be made by the sinking fund. The trustee gives the company regular written reports showing all the transactions related to the sinking fund which have taken place during the period. The company then makes the necessary journal entries.

2. The January 1 entry shows that a current asset, Cash, is being converted to a noncurrent asset, a long-term investment.

3. As the trustee reports earnings (dividends or interest) of the fund, the company must show an increase in the long-term investment and report the earnings. The entry of January 15 assumes that the cash received from the dividends goes directly to the trustee and becomes part of the sinking fund. The Sinking fund income account appears on the income statement of the corporation in the period the earnings are made.

4. When investments in the fund are sold at a gain or loss, the trustee reports this information. A gain causes the long-term investment to grow and a loss causes it to diminish (see the January 25 transaction).

» **NEW TERMS**

bond discount The excess of the maturity amount of a bond issue over the proceeds of the bond issue. [p. 569]

bond premium The excess of the proceeds of a bond issue over the maturity amount of the issue. [p. 571]

proceeds of a bond issue The net amount of cash or other assets received by the borrowing corporation when bonds are issued. [p. 566]

refunding a bond issue Refers to retiring a bond issue and immediately issuing new bonds, usually to secure a more favorable interest rate. [p. 573]

underwriter A financial agent or institution that sells and distributes the bonds of corporations. [p. 565]

» **ASSIGNMENT MATERIAL**

QUESTIONS

Q33-1. How is the Bond discount account reported on the balance sheet?

Q33-2. How is the Bond premium account reported on the balance sheet?

Q33-3. If the market rate of interest is greater than the rate of interest in the bond agreement, will the bonds be sold at a discount? Comment.

Q33-4. If the market rate of interest is less than the rate of interest in the bond agreement, will the bonds be sold at a premium? Comment.

Q33-5. Explain how the retirement of bonds before maturity is recorded if a greater amount than book value is paid to retire the bonds.

Q33-6. Explain how the retirement of bonds before maturity is recorded if a lesser amount than book value is paid to retire the bonds.

Q33-7. What is a bond sinking fund?

Q33-8. In using a bond sinking fund, what entry is made (1) for making a deposit in the fund, (2) for showing that dividends or interest was earned and received by the fund, and (3) for showing that an investment of the sinking fund was sold at a loss.

EXERCISES

E33-1. For each of the following accounts, indicate on which financial statement the account would appear, and in what section of that financial statement:
a. Bonds payable.
b. Discount on bonds payable.

c. Premium on bonds payable.
d. Interest expense.
e. Sinking fund.
f. Sinking fund income.
g. Gain on sale of sinking fund securities.
h. Gain on retirement of bonds.

E33-2. Peter Smith, Inc., on January 1, 1978, issued bonds as follows:

Face amount of 5-year bonds, $500,000.

Semiannual interest to be paid at the rate of 6% per annum (interest is paid on June 30 and December 31 each year).

Bonds were issued for an amount to yield 8% per year to the bondholders.

Record in general journal form the following entries:
a. The issuance of the bonds (also prepare a table showing the calculation of the proceeds).
b. The cash payments at June 30 and December 31, 1978, and the recording of the year's expense.

E33-3. Santo Company set up a sinking fund to accumulate assets to pay off its bonds payable in the future. Make journal entries to record the following transactions.
a. Made the annual deposit of cash to the sinking fund, $35,000.
b. The fund received dividends and interest on the investments amounting to $2,450.
c. Sold investments in the sinking fund that had cost $15,000 for $16,000 cash.

E33-4. Rapido Calculator Company recently set up a sinking fund to accumulate assets to pay off its bonds payable in the future. Make journal entries to record the following transactions.
a. Made the annual deposit of cash to the sinking fund, $45,000.
b. Received a report from the manager of the sinking fund that the fund had recently received dividends and interest on the investments amounting to $3,432.
c. Received a report from the manager of the sinking fund that investments (in the sinking fund) that had cost $11,000 recently were sold for $11,500 cash.

E33-5. Compute the *proceeds* of a 5-year bond issue with face amounts of $200,000 issued on January 1, 1978. The rate of interest in the bond agreement is 10% payable each June 30 and December 31. Bonds were issued to have an effective interest cost of 8%.

PROBLEMS (GROUP A)

P33-1. *Bonds payable issued at discount; entries and calculations.* Assume these facts about a bond issue:

Face amounts $50,000
Date issued, January 1, 1978
Time period, 15 years
Annual interest paid each December 31
Interest rate, 8% (in bond agreement)
Effective interest rate, 12%

REQUIRED:

a. Calculate the proceeds of the bond issue.

b. Make all journal entries associated with the bond issue for 1978 and 1979. Support your entries with a table showing details of the bond issue.

c. Illustrate the long-term liability section of the December 31, *1980,* balance sheet.

P33-2. *Bonds payable issued at a discount.* A firm is interested in borrowing money through issuing bonds payable. Bonds are printed with the following provisions:

10-year bonds to be issued on January 1, 1978

Face amounts of $20,000

Stated interest rate of 4% per annum

Interest payable each December 31

Assume that the company sold the bonds on January 1, 1978. The bonds were sold at a discount, because the market rate of interest for the bonds was 6% rather than the anticipated 4%.

REQUIRED:

a. Prepare a table similar to the one in the unit to calculate the proceeds of the bond issue.

b. Prepare a table similar to the one illustrated in the unit to calculate the interest expense and other details of the bond issue. *Note:* The net long-term liability at the end of the tenth year may differ slightly from the $20,000 because of rounding in the three-digit present value table.

c. Prepare journal entries regarding the bond issue for the first 3 years of the life of the bonds.

d. Illustrate the Long-term liability section of the balance sheet of the company at December 31, *1980.*

*P33-3. *Bonds payable at premium; issued during year.* George Van, Inc., on October 1, 1978, issued bonds as follows:

Face amount of 10-year bonds, $1,000,000

Annual interest to be paid at the rate of 6% per annum (interest to be paid on October 1 each year)

Bonds were issued to yield 4%

REQUIRED:

a. Calculate the proceeds.

b. Prepare a table giving details of the bond issue.

c. Make all journal entries related to the bond issue for 1978 and 1979. *Hint:* There should be an adjusting entry at December 31, 1978, debiting Interest expense for 3 months' effective interest; debiting Bond premium; and crediting Interest payable for one-half of the semiannual payment.

PROBLEMS (GROUP B)

P33-4. *Bonds payable issued at a premium.* Assume these facts about an issue of bonds:

Date of issuance, January 1, 1978

Face amount of bonds, $300,000

Interest rate on bonds, 12%, payable each December 1

Effective interest rate, 10%

Maturity date, January 1, 1986

REQUIRED:

a. Calculate the proceeds.
b. Make all journal entries associated with the bond issue for 1978 and 1979. Support your entries with a table showing details of the bond issue.
c. Illustrate the long-term liability section of the December 31, 1980 balance sheet.

P33-5. *Bonds payable issued at a premium.* A company is interested in borrowing through the issuance of bonds payable. The bonds are printed with the following provisions:

10-year bonds to be issued on January 1, 1978

Face amounts totaling $100,000

Stated interest rate of 10% per annum

Interest payable each December 31

The company sold the bonds on January 1, 1978, at a premium. The actual market interest rate at the date of issue was 8%.

REQUIRED:

a. Prepare a table similar to the one in the unit to calculate the proceeds of the bond issue.
b. Prepare a table similar to the one illustrated in the unit to calculate the interest expense and other details of the bond issue. *Note:* The net long-term liability at the end of the tenth year may differ slightly from the $100,000 because of rounding in the three-digit present value table.
c. Prepare journal entries regarding the bond issue for the first 3 years of the life of the bonds.
d. Illustrate the Long-term liability section of the balance sheet of the company at December 31, *1980.*

*P33-6. *Bonds payable at a discount; issued during year.* D. Purdy, Inc., on July 1, 1978, issued bonds as follows:

Face amount of 8-year bonds, $10,000,000

Annual interest (July 1), 6%

Effective interest rate, 8%

REQUIRED:

a. Calculate the proceeds.
b. Prepare a table giving details of the bond issue.
c. Make all journal entries related to the bond issue for 1978 and 1979.

BONDS PAYABLE–DECISION TO ISSUE

➤ **OBJECTIVE**

This unit continues your study of bonds payable. Here we will illustrate procedures for comparing the relative impact on a company of raising capital through issuance of (1) bonds, (2) preferred stock, and (3) common stock.

➤ **APPROACH TO ATTAINING THE OBJECTIVE**

As you study about the relative impact of issuing bonds, preferred stock, and common stock, pay special attention to these four questions, which the text following answers:

- *What are the basic differences between using common stock and preferred stock as sources of capital?*
- *What procedure can be used to compare the impact of alternative sources of capital?*
- *What is financial leverage?*
- *What points should always be considered before making a financing decision?*

One of the major goals in raising capital for a corporation is to choose the source of capital which has the potential for increasing the earnings per share the greatest amount. Investors carefully study the performance of corporations in terms of changes in the earnings per share of common stock. Over a relatively long period of time, if a firm's earnings per share of common stock steadily increase, then it is likely that the price of the common stock on the market will also increase. And, of course, such an increase directly benefits the investor who owns or plans to buy the shares of common stock.

Common and preferred stocks The common stockholders are the primary owners of a corporation. They are called the *residual* stockholders because they have the rights to all the resources of the firm (the "residue") after all other obligations have been satisfied. These other obligations include obligations to bondholders and other creditors and to preferred stockholders. The rights of common stockholders are desirable for investors in growing, profitable firms because the common stockholders participate in the total (sometimes very large) growth of the corporation. The rights of common stockholders include the following:

■ *What are the basic differences between using common stock and preferred stock as sources of capital?*

1. If a corporation was discontinued (terminated), the common stockholders would have the right to share in the assets, after all other obligations were met.

2. The common stockholders have the right to vote in elections for the governing body of the corporation, the board of directors, and to vote on other major company issues. Preferred stockholders ordinarily cannot vote.

3. Common stockholders have the right to receive dividends as distributions of net earnings, providing the board of directors declares such dividends.

4. Common stockholders have the right to keep their same proportional ownership interest in the corporation if more common stock is issued. For example, if Joe Smith owns 20% of the common stock of a company, and if that company issues an additional 10,000 shares of common stock, then Joe Smith is given the opportunity to purchase an additional 2,000 shares of the new issue to keep his proportional ownership (and voting power) in the firm. This right of common stockholders is known as the **preemptive right.**

Preferred stockholders, on the other hand, have somewhat more limited rights. They are preferred in two areas. These two advantages are:

1. Their right to receive dividends, as prescribed in the stock issue, *before* common stockholders are paid dividends.

2. Their right to receive settlement for their investments in the firm *before* common stockholders, in the event the corporation were to be discontinued and liquidated. (When a corporation **liquidates,** it settles its affairs by turning its assets into cash, paying its debts, and dividing what is left among the owners.)

This unit presents a case involving two companies. Both firms are in the process of raising capital, and both firms have three potential sources of capital: (1) bonds, (2) preferred stock, and (3) common stock. Our case will illustrate that in certain circumstances, bonds should be chosen as the method of raising capital; in some other cases, preferred stock should be chosen; and in still other cases, common stock should be issued.

Company A Here are the facts about Company A:

1. If the firm *does not* raise additional capital and *does not* expand its operations, it expects to produce total revenues of $2,000,000 in 1979, the coming year. A study of its planned operations indicates that expected expenses for the year (not including income taxes) amount to $1,500,000.
2. The company's tax rate is 40% of taxable income.

■ What procedure can be used to compare the impact of alternative sources of capital?

3. The management of the company wants to raise $100,000 of additional capital. Further, management projects that if the $100,000 is raised and if a plant expansion is undertaken, the revenues during 1979 will amount to $3,000,000, instead of the $2,000,000 originally planned.
4. Also, if the expansion is undertaken, the expenses (not including income taxes and not including any interest expense if incurred) will increase to $2,450,000 from the original projection of $1,500,000.
5. The corporation management has identified three alternatives for raising the needed $100,000:

    Plan 1: *Issuance of bonds.* Ten-year bonds can be sold at face amounts of $100,000, bearing 6% interest to raise the $100,000.

    Plan 2: *Issuance of preferred stock.* 1,000 shares of $100 **par value** (face value) 6% preferred stock can be sold at par value to raise $100,000.

    Plan 3: *Issuance of common stock.* 10,000 additional shares of common stock can be sold at the current market price of $10 per share to raise the $100,000. *Before this issuance,* there were 50,000 shares outstanding.

Now we will examine the table and the computations below it on the next page. This information is an analysis of the three alternative financ-

ALTERNATIVE FINANCING METHODS

	earnings information			
	BEFORE RAISING ADDITIONAL CAPITAL	**expanding the firm by:**		
		ISSUING BONDS	**ISSUING PREFERRED STOCK**	**ISSUING COMMON STOCK**
revenues	$2,000,000	$3,000,000	$3,000,000	$3,000,000
expenses				
Expenses except interest and income taxes	$1,500,000	$2,450,000	$2,450,000	$2,450,000
Interest expense (6% × $100,000 bonds)	–0–	6,000	–0–	–0–
Income taxes (40% of taxable income)[a]	200,000	217,600	220,000	220,000
Total expenses	$1,700,000	$2,673,600	$2,670,000	$2,670,000
net earnings	$ 300,000	$ 326,400	$ 330,000	$ 330,000
Average number of shares of common stock outstanding	50,000	50,000	50,000	60,000
earnings per share of common stock[b]	$6.00	$6.53	$6.48	$5.50

In this case, issuance of BONDS will increase earnings per share the greatest amount.

[a]COMPUTATION OF INCOME TAXES EXPENSE

$$0.40 \times (\$2,000,000 - \$1,500,000) = \$200,000 \text{ before raising additional capital}$$

$$0.40 \times (\$3,000,000 - \$2,450,000 - \$6,000) = \$217,600 \text{ if bonds are issued}$$

$$0.40 \times (\$3,000,000 - \$2,450,000) = \$220,000 \text{ if preferred stock is issued}$$

$$0.40 \times (\$3,000,000 - \$2,450,000) = \$220,000 \text{ if common stock is used}$$

[b]COMPUTATION OF EARNINGS PER SHARE

$$\text{Earnings per share of common stock} = \frac{\text{Net earnings} - \text{Preferred dividend requirements}}{\text{Average number of shares of common stock outstanding during the year}}$$

$$\text{Earnings per share of common stock } \textit{before raising additional capital} = \frac{\$300,000 - \$\text{-0-}}{50,000} = \$6.00$$

$$\text{Earnings per share of common stock } \textit{if bonds are issued} = \frac{\$326,400 - \$\text{-0-}}{50,000} = \boxed{\$6.53}$$

$$\text{Earnings per share of common stock } \textit{if preferred stock is issued} = \frac{\$330,000 - \$6,000}{50,000} = \$6.48$$

$$\text{Earnings per share of common stock } \textit{if additional common stock is issued} = \frac{\$330,000 - \$\text{-0-}}{60,00} = \$5.50$$

ing methods for Company A. Four columns are set up to compare the net earnings and earnings per share of common stock for each alternative. Note that the information given is simply income statement information. Revenues, if the $100,000 is not raised, will amount to $2,000,000. In each of the three alternatives for expansion, the revenues are expected to increase to $3,000,000.

Next, notice how the expenses are predicted to increase from $1,500,000 to $2,450,000 with the expansion. The two remaining cost elements, interest expense and income taxes expense, must be studied and analyzed separately. If the bonds are issued to raise the capital, then there will be an interest expense. This expense is $6,000, because the interest rate is 6% and the bonds were issued at their face amount (0.06 × $100,000). There would be no interest expense in the other situations—if the bond alternative is not chosen.

The income taxes amount to 40% of the taxable income. The computation below the tabular analysis shows how the income taxes expense is calculated for each of the four alternatives. Taxable income is computed as follows: revenues minus regular expenses minus interest expense, if any. Notice that the income taxes expense is lower when bonds are issued than if the other two sources are chosen. This tax savings is directly attributable to the fact that the interest expense is a deductible expense according to the tax laws for computing taxable income. Dividends paid on preferred stock are *not* deductible in computing taxable income.

Now compare the four projected net earnings figures. The issuance of preferred stock or the issuance of common stock will provide the maximum net earnings. The major objective of this calculation, however, is to determine the impact on earnings per share of common stock.

The computation of earnings per share of common stock is also presented below the tabular analysis. This computation clearly indicates that the issuance of bonds will increase the earnings per share from $6.00 to $6.53. Issuance of preferred stock will produce only $6.48, and issuance of common stock will actually decrease the earnings per share from $6.00 to $5.50. In this latter situation, although the net earnings are expected to increase from $300,000 to $330,000, the average number of shares outstanding will increase from 50,000 to 60,000, thus producing a decrease in per-share earnings. In the absence of other evidence, Company A should issue the bonds to provide for the expansion of the plant.

Company B Here are the facts about Company B:

1. If the firm *does not* raise additional capital and *does not* expand its operations, it expects to produce total revenues of $200,000 in 1979, the coming year. A study of its planned operations indicates that

expected expenses for the year (not including income taxes) amount to $120,000.

2. The company's tax rate is 40% of taxable income.

3. The management of the company wants to raise additional capital amounting to $100,000. Further, management projects that if the $100,000 is raised and if a new product is introduced, the revenues during 1979 will amount to $260,000, instead of the $200,000 originally planned.

4. Also, if the expansion is undertaken, the expenses (not including income taxes and not including any interest expense if incurred) will increase to $165,000 from the original projection of $120,000.

5. The corporation management has identified three alternatives for raising the needed $100,000:

   Plan 1: *Issuance of bonds.* Twenty-year bonds can be sold to raise the $100,000 cash. The effective interest rate on the bonds will be 6%.

   Plan 2: *Issuance of preferred stock.* 1,030 shares of the company's 6% preferred stock can be sold for about $97.08 per share on the market to bring in the $100,000. The shares have face (par) amounts of $100 each and pay an annual dividend of $6 (or 6% of the face amount per year). The effective dividend cost to the company, is $6,180, or 1,030 shares times $6 per share. Therefore, the effective dividend cost to the firm is 6.18% per year ($6,180 divided by $100,000).

   Plan 3: *Issuance of common stock.* 1,000 additional shares of common stock can be sold at the current market value of $100 per share. *Before this issuance,* there were 30,000 shares outstanding.

Now let us examine the table and computations on the next page. This information is an analysis of the three alternative financing methods. The details of the computations of interest expense, income taxes expense, and earnings per share under each alternative are given below the table. This case shows that, in the absence of other considerations, the common stock should be issued. Earnings per share will increase according to the prediction from $1.60 to $1.84. Be sure to study carefully and understand how the earnings per share are computed in each of the three situations.

USING DEBT TO ADVANTAGE
Company A in the case we just examined chose to issue bonds, instead of the other alternatives, because the earnings per share increased the greatest amount through issuing bonds. This use of liabilities or debt to expand the

Company B
ALTERNATIVE FINANCING METHODS

		earnings information		
	BEFORE RAISING ADDITIONAL CAPITAL	expanding the firm by:		
		ISSUING BONDS	ISSUING PREFERRED STOCK	ISSUING COMMON STOCK
revenues	$200,000	$260,000	$260,000	$260,000
expenses				
Expenses except interest and income taxes	$120,000	$165,000	$165,000	$165,000
Interest expense[a]	–0–	6,000	–0–	–0–
Income taxes[b]	32,000	35,600	38,000	38,000
Total expenses	$152,000	$206,600	$203,000	$203,000
net earnings	$ 48,000	$ 53,400	$ 57,000	$ 57,000
Average number of shares of common stock outstanding	30,000	30,000	30,000	31,000
earnings per share of common stock[c]	$1.60	$1.78	$1.69	$1.84

In this case, issuance of COMMON STOCK will increase earnings per share the greatest amount.

[a]COMPUTATION OF INTEREST EXPENSE

$$6\% \times \$100,000 = \$6,000$$

[b]COMPUTATION OF INCOME TAXES EXPENSE

$$0.40 \times (\$200,000 - \$120,000) = \$32,000 \text{ before raising additional capital}$$

$$0.40 \times (\$260,000 - \$165,000 - \$6,000) = \$35,600 \text{ if bonds are issued}$$

$$0.40 \times (\$260,000 - \$165,000) = \$38,000 \text{ if preferred stock is issued}$$

$$0.40 \times (\$260,000 - \$165,000) = \$38,000 \text{ if common stock is issued}$$

[c]COMPUTATION OF EARNINGS PER SHARE OF COMMON STOCK

$$\frac{\$48,000 - \$-0-}{30,000} = \$1.60$$

$$\frac{\$53,400 - \$-0-}{30,000} = \$1.78$$

$$\frac{\$57,000 - \$6,180}{30,000} = \$1.69 \qquad \text{Preferred dividends} = \$6,180$$

$$\frac{\$57,000 - \$-0-}{31,000} = \boxed{\$1.84}$$

firm and to increase earnings per share by greater amounts than would be possible through other financing methods is known as **financial leverage.** Almost all corporations, as they expand and grow, at one time or another find that it is extremely advantageous to use the financial leverage offered by long-term debt. Such financing is especially attractive because the interest cost on the debt reduces taxable income and reduces the income taxes of the firm. Lower income taxes, of course, mean a higher net earnings than would otherwise be produced.

■ *What is financial leverage?*

SUMMARY OF RELEVANT FACTORS

These basic ideas have been illustrated by the cases and the discussion in this unit:

1. When any kind of expansion program is planned for a firm, the alternative sources of capital must be identified, and the estimated costs of each alternative must be determined (interest costs, dividend rates, market prices of issuance of stock, etc.).

2. The change in revenues must be estimated if the capital is raised and if the project is undertaken.

3. The change in expenses must be estimated if the capital is raised and if the project is undertaken.

■ *What points should always be considered before making a financing decision?*

4. The interest expense on debt is tax deductible and reduces the income taxes.

5. The dividends on preferred stock are *not* tax deductible.

6. In the computation of earnings per share of common stock, the preferred dividends must be deducted from the net earnings *before* dividing by the common shares outstanding during the period.

7. In the computation of earnings per share of common stock, when additional common shares are issued to raise capital, the total number of shares outstanding has increased. Such an increase in the number of shares tends to decrease the earnings per share.

8. Many of the factors mentioned above tend to change from time to time. For example: the tax rate might change; the amount of capital that can be raised through issuing each share of common stock or each share of preferred stock might change; and so on. These changes bring about differences in desirability of one alternative versus another. That is, at one point in the operations of a corporation, the issuance of bonds might be desirable; at another point in time, the issuance of common stock might produce the greatest increase in earnings per share; at another point preferred stock would be desirable.

financial leverage The use of liabilities (debt) to raise capital and to increase earnings per share by greater amounts than would be possible through other financing methods. [p. 585]

liquidation The process of settling a corporation's affairs as it is going out of business, by selling its assets, paying its debts, and dividing what is left among the owners. [p. 580]

par value The face value or amount printed on certain stock certificates. [p. 580]

preemptive right The basic right of common stockholders to keep their same proportional ownership interest in the corporation if more common stock is issued. [p. 579]

preferred stock A type of security issued by corporations to raise permanent capital; preferred stockholders have certain preferences (advantages) over common stockholders in case of liquidation of the corporation and in the payment of dividends. [p. 579]

► **ASSIGNMENT MATERIAL**

QUESTIONS

Q34-1. Which stockholders are residual stockholders? What does this mean?

Q34-2. What are the basic rights of common stockholders?

Q34-3. What are the basic rights of preferred stockholders?

Q34-4. What is financial leverage?

Q34-5. What is the preemptive right?

EXERCISES

E34-1. The management of a manufacturing company has three alternative ways of raising capital:

Alternative 1, which produces net earnings of $132,000 and earnings per share of $1.18 for the coming year.

Alternative 2, which produces net earnings of $140,000 and earnings per share of $1.25 for the coming year.

Alternative 3, which produces net earnings of $134,000 and earnings per share of $1.31 for the coming year.

In the absence of other information, which alternative would management probably choose? Explain in detail.

E34-2. Orgeron Co. has three alternatives for raising $100,000 of capital:
a. Issue 10-year bonds bearing 7% interest.
b. Issue 1,000 shares of preferred stock, with an effective dividend of 7%.
c. Issue 5,000 shares of common stock for $20 each.
The projected revenues for the coming year are $1,000,000. The projected expenses (except interest and income taxes) are $450,000. The income tax rate is 40%, and there are 100,000 shares of common stock outstanding. How should Orgeron Co. raise the $100,000? Explain.

E34-3. Set up an example, using your own figures, to illustrate that the net earnings of a company can increase from one year to another, while the earnings per share of that same company can decrease during the period.

E34-4. Fuchsia Color Company plans to borrow $100,000 by issuing 8%, 5-year bonds. These new resources will enable the firm, through entering a new market, to increase its revenues by $550,000. Expenses will increase by $500,000 (not including interest on the bonds). Evaluate this plan to the extent you can. List other data needed to make a complete analysis.

PROBLEMS (GROUP A)

P34-1. *Evaluating alternative financing methods.* Crimson Coffee Company plans to introduce a new product line and needs to raise $200,000 of additional capital. *Without* the expansion, the firm will probably produce revenues of $410,000 and will incur expenses of $250,000 during the coming year, not including income taxes. The company's tax rate is 42% of taxable income. If the capital is raised, the revenues are expected to be $550,000 and the expenses will be $350,000 instead of the $250,000 to be incurred without expansion. The management has identified three alternatives for raising the $200,000:

1. *Issuance of bonds:* Twenty-year bonds can be sold with an effective interest rate of 6.825%.
2. *Issuance of preferred stock:* 2,050 shares of 5% preferred stock can be issued for the par amount of $100 per share, producing $205,000, but the issue costs will amount to $5,000, which leaves proceeds of $200,000. Annual dividends will be $10,250.
3. *Issuance of common stock:* 2,000 additional shares of common stock can be sold for $100 per share. The common stock has a par value of $50 per share. Before the issuance, there were 30,000 shares outstanding.

REQUIRED: Prepare an analysis similar to the ones illustrated in this unit to compare the alternative ways of raising capital. Which method produces the greatest earnings per share?

P34-2. *Projected change in earnings per share through issuing bonds.* Maxcap Enterprises produced net earnings in 1978 amounting to $350,000. There were 100,000 shares of common stock outstanding during the year. Dividends on preferred stock amounted to $10,000 during 1978 and are expected to remain at this level in the future. The company's tax rate on earnings is 40%. On January 1, 1979, the company issued bonds with proceeds of $107,000. The bonds pay an effective rate of interest of 6.1056% and mature in 15 years. During 1979, the projected revenues are $1,000,000 and the projected expenses (not including interest and income taxes) are $500,000.

REQUIRED: Compute the projected *net increase* (or *net decrease*) in earnings per share of common stock from 1978 to 1979.

P34-3. *Evaluating alternative financing methods.* Fitch and Company plans to introduce plant expansion that will enable it to increase revenues by 40% over the current level of $500,000. At the same time, expenses are projected to increase from $150,000 to $220,000. To finance the expansion of the plant, $2,500,000 must be acquired. These are the alternative sources of capital:

1. Bonds: Issue 20-year bonds, bearing an interest rate of 7.96%.
2. Preferred stock: Issue preferred stock with a par value of $100 per share and with a dividend rate of 6%. The stock would be sold for its par value.
3. Common stock: Issue 12,500 shares of $100 par value common stock. The shares can be sold for $200 per share.

The company's tax rate is 40% of taxable income. There are 70,000 shares of common stock outstanding before raising the funds.

REQUIRED: Prepare an analysis similar to the one illustrated in this unit to compare the alternative ways of raising capital. Which method produces greatest earnings per share?

PROBLEMS (GROUP B)

P34-4. *Evaluating alternative financing methods.* Kaboj and Company plans a plant addition that will enable it to increase revenues by 50% over the current level of $700,000. At the same time, expenses are projected to increase from $400,000 to $460,000. To finance the addition of the plant, $1,200,000 must be acquired. These are the alternative sources of capital:

1. *Bonds:* Issue 20-year bonds with interest at the rate of 9.0833%.
2. *Preferred stock:* Issue preferred stock with a par value of $100 per share and with a dividend rate of 7%. The stock would be sold for its par value.
3. *Common stock:* Issue 6,000 shares of $100 par value common stock. The shares can be sold for $200 per share.

The company's tax rate is 42% of taxable income. There are 50,000 shares of common stock outstanding before raising the funds.

REQUIRED: Prepare an analysis similar to the ones illustrated in this unit to compare the alternative ways of raising capital. Which method produces the greatest earnings per share?

P34-5. *Evaluating alternative financing methods, bonds and preferred stock only.* These facts are known about alternatives for raising capital for Universal Products Company:

1. *Issue bonds:* Proceeds amount to $100,000; interest rate is 8.53%; 10-year bonds.
2. *Issue preferred stock:* Par value $103,000; proceeds $100,000; dividend rate, 6%; annual dividends, $6,180.
3. Projected revenues, $1,000,000.
4. Projected expenses (except interest and income taxes), $600,000.
5. Tax rate, 44%.
6. Common shares outstanding, 100,000.

REQUIRED: Prepare an analysis similar to the ones illustrated in this unit. Which of the two methods of raising the funds is preferable?

P34-6. *Alternative financing methods; bonds and preferred stock only.* These facts are known about alternatives for raising capital for Nemky and Company:

1. Issue bonds: Proceeds amount to $195,000; interest rate is 8.4615%; 10-year bonds.
2. Issue preferred stock: Par value $205,000; proceeds amount to $195,000; dividend rate, 7%; annual dividends, $205,000 $\times$ 7%.
3. Projected revenues, $2,000,000.
4. Projected expenses (except interest and income taxes), $500,000.
5. Tax rate, 42%.
6. Common shares outstanding, 100,000.

REQUIRED: Prepare an analysis similar to the ones illustrated in this unit. Which of the two methods of raising the funds is preferable?

CUMULATIVE REVIEW PROBLEMS

*P34-7. *Cumulative review problem.* Batiansila and Daughters, Inc., is considering issuing the following bond issue on January 1, 1978:

Face amounts, $500,000

Time period, 10 years

Annual interest paid each December 31

Interest rate in bond agreement, 8%

Effective interest rate, 10%

These facts are also known about the company:

Income tax rate, 40%

Common shares outstanding, 100,000

Earnings (projected for 1978) if no additional bonds or common stock are issued, $1,600,000, before income taxes

Price at which additional shares of common stock can be issued, $100

Earnings (projected for 1978) if additional bonds or common shares are issued to raise capital, $2,500,000 before interest or income taxes

On January 1, 1978, the company will take *one* of these three courses of action:

A—Issue the bonds

B—Issue additional shares of common stock at the market price of $100 per share, to raise the same amount of cash as if the bonds had been issued

C—Issue neither bonds nor common stock

REQUIRED:

    a. Prepare a table to calculate the proceeds of the bond issue, similar to the ones illustrated in Unit 33.

    b. Prepare a table showing details of the bond issue, similar to those in Unit 33.

    c. Prepare an analysis to show earnings per share under each of the three alternatives. Which alternative should be chosen?

    d. Make all journal entries associated with the bond issue for 1978 (under the assumption that the bonds were issued on January 1, 1978).

P34-8. *Cumulative review problem.* Creevy Crepes Corporation is considering opening a new retail outlet. Data gathered by management include:

    1. Income tax rate, 42%

    2. Common shares outstanding, 200,000

    3. Market price at which additional common shares can be issued, $55

    4. 1978 projected earnings, before income taxes if no additional funds are raised, $2,000,000

    5. 1978 projected earnings, before interest and income taxes if the funds are raised and the new retail outlet opened, $2,500,000

If the additional funds are raised, these are the alternatives:

A—Issue 10-year bonds with face amounts of $2,000,000, bearing annual interest (December 31) of 10%. The bonds can be sold at a market rate of 8%.

B—Issue additional shares of common stock to raise the same amount of funds that would be raised if the bonds were issued.

REQUIRED:

a. Prepare a table to calculate the proceeds of the bond issue, similar to the ones in Unit 33.

b. Prepare a table showing details of the bond issue, similar to those in Unit 33.

c. Prepare an analysis to show earnings per share under each of the two alternatives. Which alternative should be chosen?

d. Make all journal entries associated with the bond issue for 1978 (under the assumption that the bonds were issued on January 1, 1978).

chapter 15

corporations: business combinations and consolidated financial statements

BUSINESS COMBINATIONS;
CONSOLIDATED BALANCE SHEETS

> **OBJECTIVE**

This unit begins your study of business combinations and consolidated financial statements. The purpose is to explain why certain corporations purchase stock of other corporations and to describe the reporting practices when two or more corporations combine to form one entity. The unit also explains how consolidated balance sheets are constructed from the information in the accounting records of the parent and subsidiary companies. The special complications of intercompany investments, reporting earnings and dividends of the companies, and intercompany loans also will be treated.

> **APPROACH TO ATTAINING THE OBJECTIVE**

In studying about intercorporate ownership interests, business combinations, and consolidated balance sheets, direct your attention to seven questions. In the text to follow, these seven questions will be answered:

- *Why do corporations purchase stock of other corporations?*
- *What approach is used in preparing consolidated financial statements?*
- *What basic problems arise when preparing consolidated financial statements?*
- *How is the creation of the parent–subsidiary relationship reported?*
- *How are earnings and dividends of parents and subsidiaries reported?*
- *How are intercompany loans reported?*
- *What reporting problem arises when the parent invests an amount differing from book value for the subsidiary stock?*

THE LEGAL ENTITY The accounting process focuses on events as they affect an *entity,* which is a specific area of accountability. So far in this course you have studied about accounting for proprietorships, partnerships, and corporations. Each of these was considered as a separate *legal entity,* a sharply defined independent unit of activity under the law to which the accountant could relate events. The corporation financial statements that you studied, for example, were financial statements of an individual legal entity—the corporation. The statements did not include any information about any other corporation (also a legal entity).

THE ECONOMIC ENTITY As corporations grow, they often find it advantageous to associate themselves with other corporations. This section first describes some of the reasons why one corporation might buy stock of another corporation. Then the several ways that corporations can combine into one economic unit are discussed.

■ *Why do corporations purchase stock of other corporations?*

Three reasons for stock ownership among corporations A corporation might buy the stock of another corporation for a number of reasons. Most of these deal with making it easier for the firm to accomplish its goals. One reason deals with the *production* processes. A corporation may find that by owning part or all of the stock of another company, a kind of cooperation can be brought about. For example, a manufacturer of shoes could purchase a **controlling interest** (more than 50% of the common stock) of a company which produces leather, thus assuring itself of a ready supply of an important raw material. When the two corporations (both are legal entities) work together as one economic unit, an **economic entity** is said to exist.

A second reason for intercompany ownership is to gain advantages in the *selling* processes. One firm might produce a product; a second corporation might have a well-developed sales staff and distribution system. Cooperation between the two firms in the selling function can occur if one of the firms becomes the owner (or part owner) of the other firm.

A third reason for ownership interests among corporations deals with *income taxes.* In certain cases, provisions of the federal income tax laws let corporations which have related ownership interests prepare one tax return for the entire economic entity, instead of requiring that separate tax returns be prepared for each corporation or legal entity. Occasionally, this will be an advantage and will produce lower total taxes according to the tax laws. This is especially true where one of the companies is making a net loss and the other company is making net earnings. The earnings can be offset against the loss; thereby reducing the taxable income for the economic entity.

Ways of combining corporations In practice there are almost countless ways that corporations have combined—to form new legal entities as well as new economic entities. Three common ways for **business combination** are:

1. Corporation A buys all the stock of Corporation B. Corporation A continues to operate (with all the assets and liabilities of both of the original corporations), and Corporation B is discontinued. This type of business combination is often referred to as a **merger**.

2. Two separate corporations (legal entities), Corporation A and Corporation B, combine to form a third legal entity, Corporation C. Corporation A and Corporation B are then discontinued. This type of business combination is often referred to as a **consolidation**.

3. Corporation A buys a significant portion (but not all) of the stock of Corporation B. Both companies (legal entities) continue to operate as an *economic entity*. Corporation A is known as the **parent company**, and Corporation B is known as the **subsidiary company**. In this case, Corporation A owns all except a small portion of the common stock of Corporation B. The ownership interest other than Corporation A in Corporation B is known as the **minority interest**.

It is this third situation that brings up special problems of reporting to investors, creditors, and others. The investors, for example, are no longer interested in the resources, equities, and earnings of just Corporation A. Corporation B is now also a vital part of the economic entity. Therefore, financial statements must not report only information about a legal entity. Instead, the **economic entity** (including both corporations) must become the basis for the financial statements. Such financial statements which combine the accounting data of parents and subsidiaries into an economic entity are called **consolidated financial statements**, and the companies are referred to as the **consolidated group**.

CONSOLIDATED INCOME STATEMENTS

Assume that an economic entity includes two companies, the Parent Company and the Subsidiary Company. The Parent Company owns most of the common stock of the Subsidiary Company. Naturally, the financial-statement readers are interested in the operating results of the economic entity. Therefore, the revenues and expenses of the two legal entities must be combined in computing net earnings and in computing earnings per share. The general approach to preparing a consolidated income statement is shown in the table at the top of the next page.

■ *What approach is used in preparing consolidated financial statements?*

The accounting records of each of the two corporations provide information to prepare each of the two columns in this tabular analysis. It would *appear* reasonable that if the figures in each line in this analysis were

	PARENT COMPANY	SUBSIDIARY COMPANY	CONSOLIDATED INCOME STATEMENT
Net sales	$500,000	$100,000	?
Other revenues	50,000	1,000	?
Total revenues	$550,000	$101,000	?
Operating expenses:			
Cost of goods sold	$200,000	$ 40,000	?
Operating expenses	100,000	11,000	?
Total expenses	$300,000	$ 51,000	?
Earnings before extraordinary gain	$250,000	$ 50,000	?
Gain on sale of plant (net of taxes)	70,000	–0–	?
Net earnings	$320,000	$ 50,000	?

added together, the information needed to prepare the consolidated income statement would be produced. In other words, it would appear that the Net sales of the consolidated group amount to $600,000; the Cost of goods sold would appear to be $240,000; and so forth. *This is not the case, however.* The question marks are placed in the third column to point out that a consolidated income statement is *not* simply a summing of the information from the corporations in the group. Later in this unit examples will be given to illustrate and explain this point.

CONSOLIDATED BALANCE SHEETS

Let us continue the same example we just discussed, where the Parent Company owns most of the common stock of the Subsidiary Company. The consolidated balance sheet would be prepared using this general approach:

ANALYSIS FOR PREPARING
BALANCE SHEETS, DECEMBER 31, 1978

	PARENT COMPANY	SUBSIDIARY COMPANY	CONSOLIDATED BALANCE SHEET
Current assets	$ 10,000	$ 8,000	?
Plant and equipment	500,000	181,000	?
Investment in subsidiary	100,000		?
Other assets	200,000	18,000	?
Total assets	$810,000	$207,000	?
Current liabilities	$ 14,000	$ 4,000	?
Long-term liabilities	90,000	21,000	?
Preferred stock	40,000		?
Common stock	500,000	132,000	?
Premium on common stock	10,000		?
Retained earnings	156,000	50,000	?
Total equities	$810,000	$207,000	?

The accounting records of each of the two corporations provide information to prepare each of the two columns in this tabular analysis. It would *appear* reasonable to simply add the two columns horizontally to produce the figures for the consolidated balance sheet. *This is not the case, however,* for there are certain considerations which make the preparation of a consolidated balance sheet more complex than this. We will now discuss these considerations.

THE MAIN OBJECTIVE IN CONSOLIDATED REPORTING

The central purpose of consolidated financial statements is to provide information to decision makers. The information to be provided is *information about the economic entity,* not about any one of the **legal entities** in the group.

THE BASIC PROBLEMS

In analyzing information from legal entities, and in converting the information to an economic entity basis, there are several basic problems. These problems include:

- *What basic problems arise when preparing consolidated financial statements?*

1. Reporting revenues produced by transactions between two corporations in the economic entity.
2. Reporting expenses incurred by transactions between two corporations in the economic entity.
3. Reporting receivables and payables between two corporations in the economic entity.
4. Reporting the investment of one corporation in the economic entity in another corporation in the economic entity.

Let us examine each of these problems in a bit more detail.

Revenues between related companies The revenues reported on a consolidated income statement must be those revenues generated through selling goods and rendering services to persons and companies *outside* the economic entity. What happens if a parent company sells goods to a subsidiary company? Very clearly, revenue is produced in the records of the parent company. Is revenue generated through this transaction for the economic entity? The answer is *no*—because goods were simply transferred from one location in the economic entity to another location in the economic entity. The financial-statement readers would be misled if revenue between associated companies were reported on the consolidated statements. Therefore, the procedure of adding together the revenues of all the firms within the consolidated group would not be a sound one. Some of the revenue probably was produced by transactions between companies in the group. Therefore, this revenue should not be reported as earnings for the economic entity.

Expenses between related companies The consolidated income statement must report all expenses incurred by the **economic entity** in the production of revenue. Certain expenses, which arise because of transactions between the companies in the group, cannot be considered expenses of the economic entity—even though they are expenses of a legal entity in the group. For example, assume that Company A sells merchandise to Company B. Company A and Company B are in the same economic entity. Company A's records would show Cost of goods sold during the period. However, as a result of this transaction, the economic entity did not make a sale to outsiders and inventory was not converted to Cost of goods sold. Therefore, the procedure of adding together the expenses of all the firms within the consolidated group would not be a sound one. Some of the expenses probably were incurred as a result of transactions between companies in the group. Therefore, these expenses should not be reported as part of the earnings calculation for the economic entity.

Receivables and payables between related companies Certain problems arise in the reporting of assets and liabilities on consolidated balance sheets. Receivables reported on the balance sheet of the consolidated group would represent all amounts owed by outsiders to the economic entity. However, if one of the corporations in the group owed amounts to another corporation in the group, this receivable on the books of one of the companies could not be included in the assets of the economic entity. In this case no amounts are owed to the consolidated group. Similarly, there is no liability for the economic entity. The existence of such intercompany receivables and payables makes the procedure of simply adding up all the receivables and payables of the companies an undesirable practice. Instead, other measures have to be taken to make sure that the amounts reported on the consolidated balance sheet actually do represent only amounts owed to and by the economic entity to and from outsiders.

Investments between related companies A final major issue in the preparation of consolidated financial statements relates to intercompany investments. The investment of one company in another in the same group would be reflected on the financial statement of the owner company as a long-term investment. Yet, when preparing the consolidated balance sheet, it has to be recognized that the economic entity does *not* have a long-term investment. Such investments must be excluded from the assets of the group.

REPORTING THE INVESTMENT OF THE PARENT COMPANY IN THE SUBSIDIARY   In all the remaining examples in this unit, we will deal with three entities. The first is the parent company, the second is the subsidiary company, and the third is the economic entity (the parent and the subsidiary) for which the consolidated balance sheet is prepared. Assume that a corporation—Parent

Company—has been operating for several years. At January 1, 1978, its balance sheet is as follows:

■ *How is the creation of the parent–subsidiary relationship reported?*

Parent Company
BALANCE SHEET
January 1, 1978

Current assets...	$ 500,000
Other assets...	5,000,000
	$5,500,000
Current liabilities	$ 150,000
Long-term liabilities	1,000,000
Capital stock	4,000,000
Retained earnings...	350,000
	$5,500,000

On January 1, 1978, a new company—Subsidiary Company—is formed. The Parent Company agrees to buy 90% of its common stock for cash. Outsiders agree to buy the other 10%. The subsidiary issues a total of 20,000 shares of no-par common stock for $20 per share ($400,000). This includes 18,000 shares to the parent and 2,000 shares to outsiders. After this transaction, the balance sheet of the Subsidiary Company appears as follows:

Subsidiary Company
BALANCE SHEET
January 1, 1978 (after organization)

Cash...	$400,000
Common stock...	$400,000

And the balance sheet of the Parent Company, after making the investment in the Subsidiary Company, appears as follows:

Parent Company
BALANCE SHEET
January 1, 1978 (after investing in subsidiary)

Current assets..	$ 140,000
Investment in subsidiary[a]	360,000
Other assets...	5,000,000
	$5,500,000
Current liabilities	$ 150,000
Long-term liabilities	1,000,000
Capital stock	4,000,000
Retained earnings...	350,000
	$5,500,000

[a] 90% × 20,000 shares × $20 = $360,000.

Since 90% of the common stock of the subsidiary is owned by the Parent Company, outside investors would be primarily interested in reading a *consolidated* balance sheet, rather than either of the balance sheets of the individual companies (legal entities). Next is shown an analysis that converts the information appearing in the two companies' records to consolidated form. This is followed by the formal consolidated balance sheet.

WORKING PAPERS FOR CONSOLIDATED BALANCE SHEET
OF PARENT COMPANY AND SUBSIDIARY
JANUARY 1, 1978

	PARENT COMPANY	SUBSIDIARY COMPANY	adjustments		CONSOLIDATED BALANCE SHEET
			DR.	CR.	
Current assets	140,000	400,000			540,000
Investment in subsidiary	360,000	-0-		(a) 360,000	-0-
Other assets	5,000,000	-0-			5,000,000
	5,500,000	400,000			5,540,000
Current liabilities	150,000	-0-			150,000
Long-term liabilities	1,000,000	-0-			1,000,000
Capital stock	4,000,000	400,000	(a) 400,000		4,000,000
Retained earnings	350,000	-0-			350,000
	5,500,000	400,000			
Minority interest				(a) 40,000	40,000
			400,000	400,000	5,540,000

Parent Company and Subsidiary
CONSOLIDATED BALANCE SHEET
January 1, 1978

Current assets..	$ 540,000
Other assets..	5,000,000
Total assets	$5,540,000
Current liabilities	$ 150,000
Long-term liabilities	1,000,000
Capital stock	4,000,000
Minority interest..	40,000
Retained earnings...	350,000
Total equities...	$5,540,000

The working papers are begun by entering the balance sheet information from the two companies in the first two columns. Next, any needed adjustments (also called **intercompany eliminations**) are made. The only adjustment required here, labeled (a), is to adjust the long-term investment account and the capital accounts so that consolidated capital reflects only contributions by investors from outside the consolidated group. The adjustment sets up a separate *capital* account called *Minority interest.* This account on consolidated balance sheets reflects amounts invested in the subsidiary by outside investors. In this case it is $40,000, or 10% of the 20,000 shares outstanding at $20 per share. No other capital from outside the group was invested; therefore, the $400,000 of capital stock of the subsidiary must be reduced in the entry. And, finally, the third part of the adjustment is to remove the $360,000 long-term investment from the statements. There has been no long-term investment in outside investments made by the economic entity. There was simply a transfer of funds *within* the entity.

EARNINGS AND DIVIDENDS OF THE SUBSIDIARY

We will continue here with the same example used above. Assume that during 1978 the *subsidiary* produced net earnings of $30,000. To simplify the example, assume that all these earnings were produced in the form of current assets. In other words, during 1978, the Current assets of the firm increased by $30,000 and the Retained earnings increased by $30,000, after all entries were made.

- *How are earnings and dividends of parents and subsidiaries reported?*

Second, assume that the subsidiary declared and paid dividends totaling $10,000. Giving effect to both of these transactions, the balance sheet of the subsidiary at December 31, 1978, would be:

Subsidiary Company
BALANCE SHEET
December 31, 1978

Current assets ($400,000 + $30,000 − $10,000)...	$420,000
Common stock...	$400,000
Retained earnings ($30,000 − $10,000)	20,000
	$420,000

EARNINGS AND DIVIDENDS OF THE PARENT

Next, let's look at the operations of the Parent Company during 1978. The journal on the next page shows in summary form the types of journal entries that would appear *on the books of the Parent Company.* Here are comments on these entries:

1. The first entry *summarizes* the effects of the production of earnings during the year. We assume in this example that the Parent Company earned a total of $100,000 from its regular operations. The assumed effect is for both the retained earnings and the current assets to increase by the same amount.

2. The second entry shows the payment of dividends by the Parent Company; the payment is assumed to be $20,000.

3. The third entry is necessary on the Parent Company's books to show

that the Parent's investment in the subsidiary has grown. We said in the previous section that the Subsidiary Company produced $30,000 of net earnings during 1978. Since the Parent Company owns 90% of the common stock of the subsidiary, the Parent Company has a direct interest in 90% of the growth in its capital and net assets. The procedure for recording the growth in an Investment in subsidiary on the parent's books is known as the **equity method.** At this point, the long-term Investment in subsidiary would be reported at $387,000—the original cost of $360,000 plus the growth in the investment of $27,000.

4. The last journal entry records the cash received by the Parent Company from the Subsidiary Company for 90% of the dividends declared by the Subsidiary (90% of $10,000). The long-term investment account is credited because the $9,000 is viewed as a returning of part of the investment already recorded. It can be viewed as a collection of part of the $27,000 just recorded as earnings or as an increase in the retained earnings of the Parent Company.

		PARENT COMPANY—GENERAL JOURNAL		
	1978			

(1)	—	Current assets (various accounts)
		    Retained earnings
		        In summary form, to represent net
		        earnings of firm.
			100,000	100,000

(2)	Dec. 31	Retained earnings (Dividends)
		    Cash
		        To record dividends paid.
			20,000	20,000

(3)	31	Investment in subsidiary
		    Retained earnings (1978 Earnings)
		        To record Parent Company's share
		        of earnings of Subsidiary
		        (90% × $30,000).
			27,000	27,000

(4)	31	Cash
		    Investment in subsidiary
		        To record dividends received
		        from subsidiary.
			9,000	9,000

After all the preceding transactions, the Parent Company balance sheet can be prepared at December 31, 1978. Carefully examine each figure on this balance sheet (at the top of the next page) to determine its origin (beginning balance sheet plus or minus entries made during the year). The figures given in parentheses will help you trace the data.

Before you move on to the next part of this unit, be sure you can determine the origin of each figure on the December 31, 1978, balance sheet of the Subsidiary Company. Also be sure that you can determine the origin of each figure on the December 31, 1978, balance sheet of the Parent Company.

Consolidated working papers are presented next. Examine this analysis carefully to see how the information appearing in the two companies' records is converted to consolidated form.

Parent Company
BALANCE SHEET
December 31, 1978

Current assets ($140,000 + $100,000 − $20,000 + $9,000).............................	$ 229,000
Investment in subsidiary ($360,000 + $27,000 − $9,000)	378,000
Other assets...	5,000,000
Total assets	$5,607,000
Current liabilities	$ 150,000
Long-term liabilities	1,000,000
Capital stock	4,000,000
Retained earnings ($350,000 + $100,000 − $20,000 + $27,000)........................	457,000
Total equities...	$5,607,000

WORKING PAPERS FOR CONSOLIDATED BALANCE SHEET
OF PARENT COMPANY AND SUBSIDIARY
DECEMBER 31, 1978

	PARENT COMPANY	SUBSIDIARY COMPANY	adjustments DR.	adjustments CR.	CONSOLIDATED BALANCE SHEET
Current assets	229,000	420,000			649,000
Investment in subsidiary	378,000	–0–		(a) 378,000	–0–
Other assets	5,000,000	–0–			5,000,000
	5,607,000	420,000			5,649,000
Current liabilities	150,000	–0–			150,000
Long-term liabilities	1,000,000	–0–			1,000,000
Capital stock	4,000,000	400,000	(a) 400,000		4,000,000
Retained earnings	457,000	20,000	(a) 20,000		457,000
	5,607,000	420,000			
Minority interest				(a) 42,000	42,000
			420,000	420,000	5,649,000

Adjustment (a) on the working papers reduces the long-term investment in subsidiary to zero. The consolidated group actually has no long-term investment in outside companies. The only outside capital interest in the group is the minority interest, which is composed of 10% of the capital of the subsidiary (10% of $400,000 Common stock plus 10% of $20,000 Retained earnings).

The formal consolidated balance sheet is shown at the top of the next page. Examine this balance sheet carefully and compare it with the consolidated balance sheet at January 1, 1978, given earlier.

Parent Company and Subsidiary
CONSOLIDATED BALANCE SHEET
December 31, 1978

Current assets	$ 649,000
Other assets	5,000,000
Total assets	$5,649,000
Current liabilities	$ 150,000
Long-term liabilities	1,000,000
Capital stock	4,000,000
Minority interest	42,000
Retained earnings	457,000
Total equities	$5,649,000

REPORTING INTERCOMPANY LOANS

- *How are intercompany loans reported?*

The effect of intercompany loans on consolidated financial statements was discussed previously. The treatment when preparing consolidated working papers is relatively simple. Assume that at the balance sheet date, the Subsidiary Company owes the Parent Company $50,000 on a long-term note. The balance sheet of the Subsidiary Company would show $50,000 in the long-term liability section; and the balance sheet of the Parent Company would show $50,000 in the long-term investments section. An adjustment on the working papers would debit the liability and credit the receivable, simply removing the payable and the receivable from the consolidated balance sheet. This adjustment is necessary because the consolidated group has neither an asset nor a liability for this $50,000.

GOODWILL ON THE CONSOLIDATED BALANCE SHEET

- *What reporting problem arises when the parent invests an amount differing from book value for the subsidiary stock?*

In certain circumstances, a parent company is willing to pay an amount greater than the book value for the subsidiary's shares of common stock. This is especially true if the subsidiary has been operating profitably for a period of time before the parent makes the acquisition. For the basis of an illustration, refer to the "Working Papers for Consolidated Balance Sheet" for January 1, 1978, illustrated earlier in this unit. What would have been the case if the Parent Company purchased the 18,000 shares from some of the old stockholders for *$390,000?* The assumption here is that the subsidiary had originally issued the 18,000 shares to the old stockholders for $360,000. In this case then the subsidiary does not receive cash from the Parent's investment because the $390,000 goes to the old stockholders, who had originally invested $360,000 in the subsidiary (18,000 shares at $20 per share). This transaction means that the Parent Company was willing to pay an extra $30,000 above the book value in order to acquire a controlling interest in the firm. This extra payment is referred to as **Goodwill** and appears as an asset on the consolidated balance sheet.

The *adjustment* on the consolidated balance sheet working papers would be:

Goodwill	30,000	
Capital stock	400,000	
Minority interest		40,000
Investment in subsidiary		390,000

When analyzing consolidated balance sheets, decision makers must recognize that the asset, Goodwill, is created by the investment of the funds of the parent in the acquisition of a controlling interest of a subsidiary. Goodwill is the excess paid to acquire the subsidiary over the amounts reported in the subsidiary's financial statements.

> ## NEW TERMS

business combination The joining (combining) of two or more companies (usually corporations) to form a new legal entity or to form an economic entity of several corporations. [p. 594]

consolidated financial statements Financial statements prepared with the economic entity (consolidated group) as a basis, rather than with the legal entity as a basis. [p. 594]

consolidation A business combination wherein a new corporation is formed to take over the operations of two or more former corporations. [p. 594]

controlling interest A corporation (parent company) is said to have a controlling interest in another corporation (subsidiary company) if more than 50% of the common stock of the subsidiary is owned by the parent. [p. 593]

economic entity A group of corporations functioning as one entity in accomplishing its goals. [p. 593]

equity method A method of reporting the Investment in subsidiary on the financial statements of the parent company; the method reports the investment at (1) the cost, *plus* (2) the proportionate share of all earnings of the subsidiary to which the parent is entitled, *less* (3) any dividends received by the parent from the subsidiary. [p. 601]

goodwill An asset account appearing on consolidated balance sheets; the excess paid by the parent to acquire controlling interest in the subsidiary over the values reported in the financial statements of the subsidiary. [p. 604]

intercompany eliminations Adjustments on working papers for preparing consolidated financial statements; such adjustments remove transactions between the related companies in the economic entity. [p. 599]

legal entity A corporation; the accounting entity for which ordinary corporation financial statements are prepared. [p. 596]

merger A business combination wherein two or more corporations combine, with one of the original corporations taking over the assets and liabilities of the other corporation(s), which is (are) discontinued. [p. 594]

minority interest A capital account appearing on consolidated balance sheets; reflects amounts invested in a subsidiary by investors outside the economic entity. [p. 594]

parent company A corporation which owns a controlling interest in another firm, called a subsidiary company. [p. 594]

subsidiary company A corporation which is controlled by another corporation, called a parent company. [p. 594]

QUESTIONS
Q35-1. Describe three reasons for the existence of stock ownership among corporations.

Q35-2. Contrast a legal entity and an economic entity.

Q35-3. Contrast a controlling interest and a minority interest.

Q35-4. Explain in your own words the four basic problems that arise in the preparation of consolidated financial statements.

Q35-5. Briefly explain what is meant by the equity method.

Q35-6. Under what circumstances does the asset account, Goodwill, appear on consolidated balance sheets?

EXERCISES
E35-1. Pollo Corporation (the parent company) and Stepo Corporation (the subsidiary company) are considered an economic entity for consolidated reporting purposes. The net sales made by the two companies are shown below for January, 1978.

POLLO CORPORATION

DATE OF SALE	AMOUNT OF SALE	TO WHOM MERCHANDISE WAS SOLD
Jan. 18	$10,000	Wilson Mfg. Company
21	33,000	Stepo Corporation
23	11,000	Stepo Corporation
23	8,000	Magnetic Industries
29	31,000	Harvey Canals, Inc.
	$93,000	

STEPO CORPORATION

Jan. 3	$19,000	Gorden Company
4	22,000	Pollo Corporation
17	33,000	Magnetic Industries
19	3,000	Zenity and Company
25	15,000	John Smith and Sons
	$92,000	

Compute the total sales (net sales) to be shown on the consolidated income statement for the group.

E35-2. The accounting records of Wenteco, Inc., revealed that operating expenses amounted to $113,214 for 1978. Of that amount, $12,500 involved maintenance expenses that were paid to East Company, a subsidiary of Wenteco, Inc. East Company provides maintenance services to customers for a fee. The accounting records of East Company revealed that its operating expenses amounted to $33,145 for 1978. Black and Sons, Inc., is another subsidiary of Wenteco, Inc. The operating expenses of that company for 1978 amounted to $3,118.

From the information provided, compute the total amount of operating expenses that would appear on the consolidated income statement of Wenteco, Inc., and Subsidiaries (three companies).

E35-3. Gunther Corporation (the parent company) and Emery Corporation (the subsidiary company) are considered an economic entity for consolidated reporting purposes. The net sales made by the two companies are shown below for January, 1978.

GUNTHER CORPORATION

DATE OF SALE	AMOUNT OF SALE	TO WHOM MERCHANDISE WAS SOLD
Jan. 12	$20,000	Parker Company
15	10,000	Emery Corporation
20	12,000	Stiles Corporation
24	39,000	Panther Industries
	$81,000	

EMERY CORPORATION

Jan. 2	$25,000	Farmer Company
12	13,000	Country Corporation
17	7,000	Gunther Corporation
30	11,000	Driscol Company
	$56,000	

Compute the total sales (net sales) to be shown on the consolidated income statement for the group.

E35-4. Boggs, Inc., is a parent company which owns Florida, Inc. The receivables and payables of the two companies at December 31, 1978, are shown below.

BOGGS, INC.

Accounts receivable	$30,000
Notes receivable from Florida, Inc.	2,000
Notes receivable from regular customers	10,000
Notes payable to Florida, Inc.	7,000
Accounts payable	10,000
Notes payable to banks	12,000

FLORIDA, INC.

Accounts receivable	$25,000
Notes receivable from Boggs, Inc.	7,000
Notes receivable from regular customers	2,000
Notes payable to Boggs, Inc.	2,000
Accounts payable	11,000
Notes payable to banks	20,000

From the information provided:
(a) Compute the total receivables of the consolidated group to appear on the consolidated balance sheet.
(b) Compute the total payables (liabilities) to appear on the consolidated balance sheet.

P35-1. *Preparation of consolidated working papers and consolidated balance sheet.* Below are shown balance sheets of Company A (parent) and Company B (subsidiary) at December 31, 1978.

Company A
BALANCE SHEET
December 31, 1978

Current assets..	$ 82,000
Investment in subsidiary..	96,000
Loan receivable from subsidiary..	40,000
Other assets...	200,000
	$418,000
Current liabilities	$ 50,000
Long-term liabilities	100,000
Capital stock	210,000
Retained earnings...	58,000
	$418,000

Company B
BALANCE SHEET
December 31, 1978

Current assets..	$ 60,000
Other assets...	100,000
	$160,000
Loan payable to parent..	$ 40,000
Common stock (80% owned by parent).................................	100,000
Retained earnings...	20,000
	$160,000

REQUIRED:

a. Prepare consolidated working papers.

b. From the working papers, prepare a consolidated balance sheet in good form.

P35-2. *Preparation of consolidated working papers and consolidated balance sheet.* Below are shown balance sheets of G. Woods Corporation (parent) and R. Oakwood Corporation (subsidiary) at December 31, 1978.

G. Woods Corporation
BALANCE SHEET
December 31, 1978

Current assets..	$150,000
Investment in subsidiary..	210,000
Plant and equipment (net)	100,000
Other assets...	70,000
	$530,000
Accounts payable	$ 16,000
Note payable to subsidiary	20,000
Bonds payable..	200,000
Common stock..	200,000
Retained earnings...	94,000
	$530,000

R. Oakwood Corporation
BALANCE SHEET
December 31, 1978

Current assets..	$ 65,000
Note receivable from parent..	20,000
Plant and equipment (net)...	170,000
Other assets..	100,000
	$355,000
Accounts payable	$ 5,000
Bonds payable..	50,000
Common stock (70% owned by parent).................................	250,000
Retained earnings..	50,000
	$355,000

REQUIRED:

    a. Prepare consolidated working papers.

    b. From the working papers, prepare a consolidated balance sheet in good form.

P35-3. *Equity method on books of parent company.* The following relate to a parent's investment in a subsidiary. The parent owns 80% of the common stock of the subsidiary.

    a. Assume the parent company produced net earnings during 1978 amounting to $55,000. Prepare the journal entry to record the earnings (in summary form, assuming current assets increased by the amount of the earnings).

    b. The parent company declared and paid dividends on common stock amounting to $12,500 during 1978. Record the declaration and cash payment of dividends.

    c. The subsidiary declared dividends totaling $5,000 during 1978. Make the entry on the parent's books to record the receipt of the cash dividend.

    d. Make the entry necessary on the parent's books to record the growth of the parent's investment in the subsidiary as a result of subsidiary profits (parent has 80% interest in the earnings of the subsidiary). The subsidiary made net earnings of $28,000 during 1978.

PROBLEMS (GROUP B)

P35-4. *Preparation of consolidated working papers and consolidated balance sheet.* Below are shown balance sheets of Alisa Jack Enterprises (parent) and Heather Company (subsidiary) at December 31, 1978.

Alisa Jack Enterprises
BALANCE SHEET
December 31, 1978

Cash...	$ 11,000
Accounts receivable (net)	10,000
Receivable from subsidiary	90,000
Investment in subsidiary...	170,000
Plant and equipment (net)	300,000
	$581,000
Current liabilities	$ 5,000
Long-term liabilities	100,000
Common stock...	100,000
Retained earnings..	376,000
	$581,000

Heather Company
BALANCE SHEET
December 31, 1978

Cash...	$ 3,000
Accounts receivable (net)	12,000
Plant and equipment (net)	118,000
Other assets...	90,000
Long-term investments..	200,000
	$423,000
Current liabilities	$ 6,000
Long-term liabilities	127,000
Payable to Alisa Jack Enterprises......................................	90,000
Common stock (85% owned by parent).................................	140,000
Retained earnings...	60,000
	$423,000

REQUIRED:

a. Prepare consolidated working papers.

b. From the working papers, prepare a consolidated balance sheet in good form.

P35-5. *Equity method on books of parent company.* The records of a parent and subsidiary company revealed the following at December 31, 1977:

	PARENT COMPANY	SUBSIDIARY COMPANY
Current assets	75,000	21,000
Investment in subsidiary	80,000	
Plant and equipment (net)	90,000	100,000
Receivable from subsidiary	10,000	
	255,000	121,000
Current liabilities	12,000	11,000
Long-term liabilities	123,000	
Payable to parent		10,000
Common stock	100,000	80,000
Retained earnings	20,000	20,000
	255,000	121,000

The parent company owns 80% of the common stock of the subsidiary company.

REQUIRED: Make general journal entries for the following on the books of the *parent company.*

a. Assume that the parent company produced net earnings during 1978 amounting to $70,000. Prepare the journal entry to record the earnings (in summary form, assuming current assets increased by the amount of the earnings).

b. The parent company declared and paid dividends on common stock amounting to $10,000 during 1978. Record the declaration and cash payment of dividends.

c. Make the entry necessary on the parent's books to record the growth of the parent's investment in the subsidiary as a result of subsidiary profits (parent has

80% interest in the earnings of the subsidiary). The sub-subsidiary made net earnings of $20,000 during 1978.

  d. The subsidiary declared dividends *totaling* $3,000 during 1978. Make the entry on the parent's books to record the receipt of the cash dividend.

*P35-6. *Intercompany transactions.* By selecting from the following fifteen symbols, fill in the missing symbols in the seven equations that appear below. Do not repeat the same symbol *within* an equation.

Example: E = _?_   Answer: E = _A_

A   Receivables from customers and others outside the economic entity
B   Receivables from other companies within the economic entity
C   Payables to creditors and others outside the economic entity
D   Payables to other companies within the economic entity
E   Total receivables of the economic entity to be reported on the consolidated balance sheet
F   Total payables of the economic entity to be reported on the consolidated balance sheet
G   Revenues arising from transactions with customers outside the economic entity
H   Revenues arising from transactions with companies within the economic entity
I   Total revenues of the economic entity to be reported on the consolidated income statement
J   Expenses arising from transactions with companies outside the economic entity
K   Expenses arising from transactions with companies within the economic entity
L   Total expenses of the economic entity to be reported on the consolidated income statement
M   Long-term investments in other companies in the economic entity
N   Long-term investments in companies outside the economic entity
O   Total long-term investments to be reported on the consolidated balance sheet

a. A − B = _?_ − B
b. C − D = _?_ − D
c. F = _?_
d. G = _?_
e. G + H = _?_ + H
f. J = _?_
g. M + N = _?_ + M

36

CONSOLIDATED INCOME STATEMENTS

> ## ▶ OBJECTIVE

The purpose of this unit is to explain to you how consolidated income statements are constructed from the information in the accounting records of the parent and subsidiary companies.

> ## ▶ APPROACH TO ATTAINING THE OBJECTIVE

As you study about consolidated income statements, pay special attention to these three questions, which the text following answers:

- *How is a consolidated income statement prepared?*
- *What items are included on the consolidated retained earnings statement?*
- *What are other considerations when using consolidated financial statements?*

In this section you will see how a consolidated income statement is prepared from the related working papers. Shown below are the working papers for our example. Study them carefully. Note that the required adjustments on the working papers for intercompany revenues and expenses are included in the example.

▪ *How is a consolidated
income statement
prepared?*

The specific intercompany transactions during the period which dealt with revenues and expenses are as follows:

1. Subsidiary Company sold goods costing $10,000 to Parent Company for $12,000.
2. The Subsidiary Company paid the Parent Company $1,000 interest expense on an intercompany loan.
3. The Subsidiary Company rented a truck from the Parent Company and paid $2,000 rent during the year.

In the calculation of the **consolidated net earnings**—the net earnings of the consolidated group of corporations—these intercompany transactions involving expenses and revenues are excluded.

WORKING PAPERS FOR CONSOLIDATED INCOME STATEMENT
OF PARENT COMPANY AND SUBSIDIARY
FOR THE YEAR ENDED DECEMBER 31, 1978

	PARENT COMPANY	SUBSIDIARY COMPANY	adjustments DR.	adjustments CR.	CONSOLIDATED INCOME STATEMENT
Net sales	100,000	50,000	(a) 12,000		138,000
Other revenues	20,000	6,000	(b) 1,000 (c) 2,000		23,000
Total revenue	120,000	56,000			161,000
Expenses:					
Cost of goods sold	60,000	35,000		(a) 12,000	83,000
Operating expenses	19,000	12,000		(b) 1,000 (c) 2,000	28,000
Total expenses	79,000	47,000			111,000
Net earnings	41,000	9,000	15,000	15,000	
Balance					50,000
Less Minority interest in Net earnings of subsidiary (20% × $9,000)					1,800
Consolidated Net earnings					48,200

Further details in explanation of the working papers and the adjustments are as follows:

1. The first two columns include information taken directly from the income statements of the two corporations.

2. Transaction (a) requires an adjustment for the sale of goods during the period to the Parent Company from the Subsidiary Company for $12,000. To illustrate fully, assume that the subsidiary originally paid $10,000 for the goods when they were acquired from outsiders. Also assume that after the parent acquired the goods from the subsidiary for $12,000, they were sold by the parent for $15,000 to outsiders. On the *individual company records* these entries would have been made:

SUBSIDIARY COMPANY RECORDS

Inventory	10,000	
Cash		10,000
Purchase of goods from outsiders.		
Cash	12,000	
Sales revenue		12,000
Sale of goods to parent.		
Cost of goods sold	10,000	
Inventory		10,000
Cost of goods sold to parent.		

PARENT COMPANY RECORDS

Inventory	12,000	
Cash		12,000
Purchase of goods from subsidiary.		
Cash	15,000	
Sales revenue		15,000
Sale of goods to outsiders.		
Cost of goods sold	12,000	
Inventory		12,000
Cost of goods sold to outsiders.		

The special problems in consolidation occur in Cost of goods sold and Sales revenue. According to the entries above, Cost of goods totals $22,000 for the group, but actually the cost of the merchandise when it was purchased *by the economic entity* was only $10,000. Therefore, adjustment (a) reduces Cost of goods sold by $12,000. Also, the Sales revenue is overstated. The sales to outsiders amount to only $15,000, but the revenue accounts reflect $27,000 in the combined accounts. The extra $12,000 from the subsidiary's sale of goods to the parent is just a simple transfer from one location in the economic entity to another location in the same economic entity. The revenue should not be reported as earnings for the economic entity. Therefore, adjustment (a) reduces the revenue by $12,000.

3. During the period, Interest expense was paid to the parent by the subsidiary. Therefore, a correction is made to reduce the expense and the revenue (b). No revenue was produced by the economic entity through the interest transaction, and no expense was incurred.

4. Adjustment (c) on the working papers corrects the balances for the $2,000 rent that was paid to the parent by the subsidiary. No Rent expense was incurred and no Rent revenue was earned.

5. After the adjustments are made, the earnings of the economic entity total $50,000. Because 20% of the subsidiary earnings are owned by a minority interest, $1,800 (20% of $9,000) is deducted in arriving at the net earnings of $48,200 related to the majority stockholders in the economic entity.

CONSOLIDATED INCOME STATEMENT

The Parent Company and Subsidiary Consolidated Income Statement for the year is shown next. The information, of course, is taken from the consolidated working papers which we have just examined. Remember that the adjustments on consolidated working papers (for both consolidated income statements and consolidated balance sheets) *are not entered into the company accounts. The adjustments simply eliminate information that is not relevant for preparing the combined statements.*

Parent Company and Subsidiary
CONSOLIDATED INCOME STATEMENT
For the Year Ended December 31, 1978

revenues		
Net sales	$138,000	
Other revenues	23,000	
Total revenues		$161,000
expenses		
Cost of goods sold	$ 83,000	
Operating expenses	28,000	
Total expenses		111,000
net earnings from operations		$ 50,000
less share of net earnings for minority stockholders		1,800
consolidated net earnings		$ 48,200

The three elimination adjustments illustrated on the working papers were only samples of the intercompany transactions that are common in consolidated groups. Often an adjustment might involve both balance sheet accounts and income statement accounts. In these cases, consolidated working papers might be prepared to include both the income statement accounts and the balance sheet accounts on the same working papers. In this manner, adjustments could be prepared which involve a debit to an account on one of the financial statements and a credit on the other financial statement. Such a complication would arise in transaction (a) in our example above if the parent still had some of the merchandise in question on hand.

CONSOLIDATED RETAINED EARNINGS STATEMENT

- What items are included on the consolidated retained earnings statement?

A consolidated retained earnings statement is prepared in the same general form as a corporation's retained earnings statement. The difference, however, is that *consolidated* net earnings increase the retained earnings on the statement. In addition, as you observed in the preparation of the consolidated income statement, these consolidated net earnings include only earnings of the majority stockholders. The minority interest ($1,800) in the earnings was excluded. As for dividends, only dividends declared by the parent are included on the consolidated retained earnings statement. Remember also that in the preparation of the consolidated balance sheet, dividends of the subsidiary were eliminated in an adjustment. An illustration of a consolidated statement of retained earnings is presented below.

Copper Minerals Corporation and Consolidated Subsidiaries
CONSOLIDATED STATEMENT OF RETAINED EARNINGS
For the Year Ended December 31, 1978

Consolidated Retained earnings, beginning of year		$415,700
Consolidated Net earnings for 1978	$115,900	
Less Dividends of Copper Minerals Corporation (parent company), 90 cents per share of common stock	90,000	
Net increase in Consolidated Retained earnings		25,900
Consolidated Retained earnings, end of year		$441,600

USING CONSOLIDATED FINANCIAL STATEMENTS

- What are other considerations when using consolidated financial statements?

Consolidated financial statements are widely used by investors today. In fact, it is very common for large corporations to present consolidated financial statements. The annual report of the consolidated group discloses which companies are involved in the group and the manner in which each company contributes. Often a major problem with consolidated financial statements is determining what makes up the economic entity. For example, a company (A), might own only 10% of the common stock of another company (B), yet it still controls that company (B). It does so because the other 90% of B's stock is owned by a third firm (C), which happens to be controlled by A. The central accounting problem in cases of this type is identifying exactly what the economic entity is, and then reporting to decision makers the assets, equities, and earnings of that specially defined entity. You know that intercompany transactions must be eliminated when consolidated statements are prepared. In identifying the economic entity, however, it may be concluded that some of the subsidiaries are not related closely enough to be combined (consolidated). These are then referred to as **unconsolidated subsidiaries** and are reported as regular long-term investments on the consolidated statements. The **equity method** explained in Unit 35 is widely used today to value an unconsolidated subsidiary on the consolidated balance sheet.

Another problem arises when a company operates a business that is entirely different from the other companies in its group—for example, a computer manufacturer joined with a chain of restaurants. Simply combining all the assets, equities, and earnings might be misleading. Accountants and others are developing better methods of reporting by *lines of business* where the economic entity is involved in diversified activities. These methods help investors determine the main sources of a firm's earning power and strength. Below is an example of the information that might accompany the consolidated financial statements of a group which has diverse operations.

BARONNE INTERNATIONAL AND CONSOLIDATED SUBSIDIARIES
FOR THE YEAR ENDED DECEMBER 31, 1978 (000 OMITTED)

PRODUCT LINE	NET SALES OR SERVICE REVENUES		EARNINGS FROM OPERATIONS		TOTAL ASSETS EMPLOYED AT DECEMBER 31, 1978	
Auto-leasing operations	$ 100,000	5.6%	$ 10,000	3.9%	$ 170,000	2.4%
Restaurant operations	741,000	41.6%	75,000	29.4%	1,000,000	14.1%
Manufacturing operations	900,000	50.6%	145,000	56.9%	5,400,000	76.4%
Other service operations	39,000	2.2%	25,000	9.8%	500,000	7.1%
	$1,780,000	100.0%	$255,000	100.0%	$7,070,000	100.0%

▶ NEW TERMS

consolidated net earnings The net earnings of the consolidated group of corporations; computation excludes intercompany transactions involving expenses and revenues. [p. 612]

unconsolidated subsidiary A corporation partially owned by a company in a consolidated group; the ownership interest is not considered a controlling interest or the relationship is not close enough to include the subsidiary when consolidated working papers and consolidated financial statements are prepared; the investment in the unconsolidated subsidiary is reported on the consolidated balance sheet as an investment under the equity method. [p. 616]

▶ ASSIGNMENT MATERIAL

QUESTIONS Q36-1. What are consolidated net earnings?

Q36-2. What is an unconsolidated subsidiary?

Q36-3. How are investments in unconsolidated subsidiaries reported on the parent company's balance sheet?

Q36-4. How does a consolidated statement of retained earnings differ from a statement of retained earnings?

EXERCISES   E36-1. The following information was taken from the consolidated working papers of Coker Socola and Subsidiaries for the year ended December 31, 1978:

Revenue: Parent, $150,000; Subsidiary A, $100,000; Subsidiary B, $50,000.
Expenses: Parent, $100,000; Subsidiary A, $75,000; Subsidiary B, $42,000.

The parent company owns 90% of the common stock of Subsidiary A and 90% of the common stock of Subsidiary B. Subsidiary A had performed services for the parent, and charged the parent $15,000 for these services.
   a. What is the amount of the total revenue to appear on the consolidated income statement?
   b. What is the amount of the total expenses to appear on the consolidated income statement?

E36-2. For 1978, the consolidated net earnings of Cocol, Inc., and subsidiaries amounted to $75,000. Consolidated retained earnings at the beginning of the year amounted to $132,500. The parent company declared dividends amounting to $13,000 during the year. Prepare a consolidated statement of retained earnings for the year ended December 31, 1978, in good form.

E36-3. A parent company purchased merchandise from one of its subsidiaries for $25,000 cash. The subsidiary originally had paid $19,000 for the merchandise. The parent company later sold the merchandise to an outside company for $26,000.
            Make the necessary adjustment (in general journal form) that would appear on the consolidated working papers.

E36-4. A subsidiary company performed services for the parent for advertising the company's products. This entry was made on the books of the subsidiary company:

Cash	17,300	
Service revenue		17,300

The transaction was recorded by the parent as follows:

Advertising expense	17,300	
Cash		17,300

REQUIRED:

   a. Make the necessary adjustment (in general journal form) that would appear on the consolidated working papers.
   b. Compute the amount of Advertising expense that would appear on the consolidated income statement. The parent company records revealed $30,000 of Advertising expense and the subsidiary company showed $18,000 of Advertising expense.
   c. Compute the amount of Service revenue that would appear on the consolidated income statement. The parent company records revealed no Service revenue, and the subsidiary records showed $50,000 of Service revenue.

P36-1. *Preparation of consolidated working papers and consolidated income statement.* Below are shown income statements of Company A (parent) and Company B (subsidiary) for the year ended December 31, 1978.

**Company A
INCOME STATEMENT
For the Year Ended December 31, 1978**

revenues		
Net sales	$1,000,000	
Other income	100,000	
Total revenues		$1,100,000
expenses		
Cost of goods sold	$ 400,000	
Operating expenses	150,000	
Total expenses		550,000
earnings before extraordinary items		$ 550,000
Extraordinary gain (net of taxes)		200,000
net earnings		$ 750,000

**Company B
INCOME STATEMENT
For the Year Ended December 31, 1978**

revenues		
Net sales	$165,000	
Other income	10,000	
Total revenues		$175,000
expenses		
Cost of goods sold	$ 60,000	
Operating expenses	30,000	
Total expenses		90,000
net earnings		$ 85,000

Additional information:
1. During the year, the subsidiary performed maintenance services for the parent for a total cost of $7,000.
2. The subsidiary sold goods to the parent for $10,000 cash. The subsidiary had originally paid $9,000 for the goods. The parent later in the year sold the same goods for $16,000 to outsiders.
3. The subsidiary rented equipment of the parent and paid the parent $1,000 during the year for rent expense.
4. Outsiders own 5% of the subsidiary's common stock.

REQUIRED:

   a. Prepare consolidated working papers.
   b. Prepare a consolidated income statement in good form.

P36-2. *Preparation of consolidated working papers and consolidated income statement.* The records of a parent and subsidiary company revealed the following at December 31, 1978:

	PARENT COMPANY	SUBSIDIARY COMPANY
Net sales	$200,000	$64,000
Other revenues	45,000	7,000
Total revenue	$245,000	$71,000
Expenses:		
Cost of goods sold	$ 48,000	$40,000
Operating expenses	20,000	12,000
Total expenses	$ 68,000	$52,000
Net earnings	$177,000	$19,000

Additional information:

1. During the year, the subsidiary sold goods costing $21,000 to Parent Company for $25,000. These goods were sold by the Parent Company in 1978.
2. The Subsidiary Company rented equipment of the parent and paid the parent $4,000 during the year for rent expense.
3. The Subsidiary Company paid the Parent Company $600 interest expense on an intercompany loan.
4. Outsiders own 10% of the subsidiary's common stock.

REQUIRED:

a. Prepare consolidated working papers.
b. Prepare a consolidated income statement in good form.

*P36-3. *Consolidated working papers combining balance sheet and income statement accounts.* The income statements and balance sheets of a parent and subsidiary company are illustrated next:

	ROYAL COMPANY (PARENT)	DECATUR COMPANY (SUBSIDIARY)
Cash	$130,000	$ 25,000
Receivables (net)	80,000	8,000
Inventories	100,000	14,000
Investments—stock	37,000	
Investments—notes	10,000	
Fixed assets (net)	63,000	10,000
Intangibles	4,000	
	$424,000	$ 57,000
Current debt	$ 26,000	$ 2,000
Long-term debt	143,000	18,000
Common stock	200,000	30,000
Retained earnings	55,000	7,000
	$424,000	$ 57,000
Revenues	$900,000	$100,000
Cost of goods sold	$700,000	$ 89,000
Other expenses	160,000	6,000
Net earnings	$ 40,000	$ 5,000

Other facts about the consolidated group (two companies) are
1. The parent company had purchased a 100% interest in the subsidiary several years ago for $30,000 cash.
2. The subsidiary owes the parent $10,000 in long-term notes.
3. During the year the subsidiary performed advertising service for the parent company for $6,000 cash.

REQUIRED:

a. Prepare consolidated working papers. On your working papers, include both balance sheet and earnings information in the initial columns.
b. Prepare a consolidated balance sheet and a consolidated income statement in good form.

PROBLEMS GROUP B

P36-4. *Preparation of consolidated working papers and consolidated income statement.* Records of Beauregard Corporation (parent) for 1978 included the following: Net sales, $200,000; Rent revenue, $20,000; Cost of goods sold, $125,000; Selling expenses, $10,000; General expenses, $12,000. Records of Hooper Corporation (subsidiary) for 1978 included the following: Net sales, $100,000; Cost of goods sold, $65,000; Selling expenses, $10,000; General expenses, $18,000. Beauregard Corporation owns 90% of the common stock of the subsidiary, Hooper Corporation. Intercompany transactions during 1978 included the following:
1. Hooper Corporation sold goods costing $18,000 to Beauregard Corporation for $23,000 cash. Beauregard Corporation later sold these goods to outsiders.
2. The subsidiary rented equipment from the parent company, paying $18,000 cash for the rent. This amount was included in General expenses of the subsidiary and in Rent revenue of the parent.

REQUIRED:

a. Prepare working papers for the consolidated income statement for the year ended December 31, 1978.
b. Prepare a consolidated income statement in good form.

P36-5. *Preparation of consolidated working papers and consolidated income statement.* Records of two companies in a consolidated group revealed the following for 1978:

	PARENT	SUBSIDIARY
Net sales	$300,000	$100,000
Interest revenue	10,000	2,000
Other revenue	10,000	2,000
Cost of goods sold	100,000	30,000
Operating expenses	50,000	40,000

Additional information:
1. During 1978, the subsidiary sold goods, costing $20,000 to the parent company for $25,000. These goods were sold by the Parent Company in 1978.
2. The parent owns 92% of the common stock of the subsidiary.
3. During 1978, the subsidiary paid the parent $9,000 for consulting services.
4. The subsidiary paid the parent $1,000 of interest expense during 1978 on a loan.

REQUIRED:

    a. Prepare consolidated working papers.

    b. Prepare a consolidated income statement in good form.

*P36-6. *Consolidated working papers combining balance sheet and income statement accounts.* Data for working papers follow:

	1978	
	COMMUNICATIONS, INC. (PARENT)	TRANSPORTATION, INC. (SUBSIDIARY)
Cash	$ 200,000	$ 50,000
Merchandise inventory	150,000	15,000
Long-term investments (stock)	65,000	–0–
Long-term investments (notes)	15,000	–0–
Plant and equipment (net)	200,000	25,000
Intangible assets	10,000	–0–
	$ 640,000	$ 90,000
Current liabilities	$ 50,000	$ 5,000
Long-term liabilities	200,000	20,000
Common·stock	300,000	40,000
Retained earnings	90,000	25,000
	$ 640,000	$ 90,000
Revenues	$2,000,000	$200,000
Cost of goods sold	$1,000,000	$ 82,000
Operating expenses	200,000	12,000
Net income	$ 800,000	$106,000

Additional information:

1. Transportation, Inc., owes the parent $15,000 in long-term notes.
2. Communications, Inc., had purchased a 100% interest in the subsidiary several years ago.
3. During 1978, the subsidiary performed services for the parent amounting to $20,000.

REQUIRED:

    a. Prepare consolidated working papers. On your working papers, include both balance sheet and earnings information in the initial columns.

    b. Prepare a consolidated balance sheet and a consolidated income statement in good form.

CUMULATIVE REVIEW PROBLEMS

P36-7. *Cumulative review problem.* Data for 1978 follow:

	PARENT COMPANY	SUBSIDIARY COMPANY
Current assets	24,000	3,000
Receivable from subsidiary	5,000	
Receivable from parent		4,000

Investment in subsidiary	11,900	
Plant and equipment (net)	12,100	5,000
Other assets	24,000	7,000
Long-term investments	8,000	5,000
Accounts payable	20,000	3,000
Long-term liabilities	6,000	2,000
Notes payable to subsidiary	4,000	
Notes payable to parent		5,000
Common stock	11,000	4,000
Retained earnings	44,000	10,000
Net sales	20,000	10,000
Other income	12,000	4,000
Cost of goods sold	15,000	7,000
Operating expenses	6,000	5,000

Additional information:

1. During the year, the subsidiary sold goods costing $2,000 to the Parent Company for $3,000. The parent company sold these goods in 1978.
2. The Subsidiary Company rented equipment of the parent and paid the parent $4,000 during the year for rent expense.
3. The Subsidiary Company paid the Parent Company $500 interest expense on an intercompany loan.
4. Outsiders own 15% of the subsidiary's common stock.

REQUIRED:

a. Prepare working papers for a consolidated balance sheet. Also prepare a consolidated balance sheet in good form.
b. Prepare working papers for a consolidated income statement. Also prepare a consolidated income statement in good form.

P36-8. *Cumulative review problem.*

Part A

Auditco, Inc., is a parent company which owns two other firms: Taxco, Inc., and Systemsco, Inc. The receivables and payables of the three companies at December 31, 1978, are shown below.

AUDITCO, INC.

Accounts receivable	$19,000
Receivable from Taxco, Inc.	10,000
Notes receivable from regular customers	37,000
Note payable to Systemsco, Inc.	40,000
Accounts payable	13,000
Notes payable to banks	70,000

TAXCO, INC.

Accounts receivable	80,000
Notes receivable from regular customers	43,000
Note receivable from Systemsco, Inc.	11,000
Accounts payable	62,000
Notes payable to banks	90,000
Payable to Auditco, Inc.	10,000

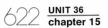

Accounts receivable	7,000
Note receivable from Auditco, Inc.	40,000
Accounts payable	4,000
Note payable to Taxco, Inc.	11,000
Notes payable to banks	8,000

REQUIRED:

a. From the information provided, compute the total receivables of the consolidated group to appear on the consolidated balance sheet.

b. From the information provided, compute the total payables (liabilities) to appear on the consolidated balance sheet.

Part B

Below are shown balance sheets of A. Dickins Corporation (parent) and L. Ennis Corporation (subsidiary) at December 31, 1978. From this information, prepare consolidated working papers.

A. Dickins Corporation
BALANCE SHEET
December 31, 1978

Current assets	$160,000
Receivable from subsidiary	18,000
Investment in subsidiary	96,000
Plant and equipment (net)	100,000
Other assets	150,000
	$524,000
Accounts payable	$ 23,000
Note payable to subsidiary	45,000
Bonds payable	92,000
Common stock	260,000
Retained earnings	104,000
	$524,000

L. Ennis Corporation
BALANCE SHEET
December 31, 1978

Current assets	$ 65,000
Notes receivable from parent	45,000
Plant and equipment (net)	35,000
Other assets	50,000
Long-term investments	47,000
	$242,000
Accounts payable	$ 79,000
Long-term liabilities	25,000
Payable to A. Dickins Corporation	18,000
Common stock (80% owned by parent)	34,000
Retained earnings	86,000
	$242,000

chapter 16

corporations: accounting principles and the changing profession

37

SOURCES OF FINANCIAL INFORMATION; PRINCIPLES AND CONCEPTS

> ## OBJECTIVE

The first objective of this unit is to describe the major sources of financial information about a corporation. One of the most important of these sources, the corporation's annual report, will be described here in detail. An example of each major section of an actual corporation's annual report will be presented.

The second objective of this unit is to present and discuss the underlying concepts and principles of financial accounting and financial reporting. The roles of several organizations in developing generally accepted accounting principles are analyzed. In addition, a checklist of basic accounting literature is presented.

> ## APPROACH TO ATTAINING THE OBJECTIVE

As you study annual reports, other sources of financial information about a company, and accounting principles and concepts, give special attention to these six questions, which the text following answers:

- *What is a corporate annual report?*
- *What are the major components of a corporate annual report?*
- *What are other sources of financial information about a corporation?*
- *What are generally accepted accounting principles?*
- *Which organizations have contributed to the development of generally accepted accounting principles?*
- *With what literature should the student of accounting be familiar?*

THE NATURE AND PURPOSE OF CORPORATE ANNUAL REPORTS

- *What is a corporate annual report?*

Most medium-size and large corporations customarily issue an **annual report** of operations and financial condition to interested parties outside the firm. This annual report is a convenient way to give a large body of relevant information to the decision makers interested in the company. Each year annual reports are mailed to all stockholders of the corporation and to others interested in the firm. In addition to this annual report, corporations whose stock is traded publicly must report detailed information to regulatory and other governmental bodies. One such body, the Securities and Exchange Commission (SEC), is a federal agency that operates primarily to protect the rights and interests of investors. For example, the information received by the SEC is also made available to decision makers. In addition, the SEC is empowered by law to regulate certain stock-trading practices in the public interest. The SEC accumulates information about corporation activities in much greater detail than is contained in annual reports. Investors, professional investment analysts, and others can use the information that is required to be reported to the SEC under the federal laws.

PARTS OF A CORPORATE ANNUAL REPORT

The customary parts of annual reports are:

1. Comments from management of the firm.
2. A financial review for the year.
3. Financial statements for the year.
4. Notes to the financial statements.
5. The opinion of the independent certified public accountants.
6. The 10-year summary.

Throughout this section of this unit, the information in our examples is taken from the *1976 Annual Report of General Mills, Inc.* Selections from this annual report are reproduced in the appendix to this unit. Be sure you examine them, as they are referred to and discussed in the following paragraphs. The assignment material at the end of this unit is designed so that you will become familiar with the location of information in annual reports.

- *What are the major components of a corporate annual report?*

Comments from the management of the firm The President and/or the Chairman of the Board of Directors usually prepare a letter or report to the stockholders to be included in the annual report. This lets the top management present outsiders with their view of the important facts about the corporation and the philosophy of management. An example of such a report appears at the beginning of our selections from the 1976 General Mills annual report. See Exhibit 37-1 in the appendix. Pay special attention to the illustration that spotlights how the sales dollar was divided for the year.

A financial review for the year Another part usually included in annual reports is the financial review for the year. In this section management spotlights the important details about the earnings and financial condition of the firm. Exhibit 37-2 is such a financial review for General Mills.

Notice how the sales increase is analyzed in terms of the three major business areas: (1) foods, (2) consumer nonfoods, and (3) specialty chemicals. The reader of the annual report can make predictions about the most important product lines of the company.

Similarly, costs and expenses for the period are analyzed. Key factors such as an increase in advertising costs are pointed out by management to explain the increases.

In summary, the financial review section of corporation annual reports concentrates (1) on giving a nutshell view of earnings and financial position, and (2) on giving reasons for the changes which occurred during the year under review.

Financial statements for the year Exhibit 37-3 contains these statements for General Mills:

1. Consolidated results of operations (income statement).
2. Earnings employed in the business (retained earnings statement).
3. Consolidated balance sheets.

Study each of these statements to review the classification and valuation concepts that you have previously learned in your study of accounting. Another statement, the consolidated statement of changes in financial position (funds statement), was included in the annual report, but it is omitted here because this statement will be introduced later in this course.

Notice that at the bottom of each of the financial statements this notation is made: "See accompanying notes to consolidated financial statements." This refers the readers of the financial statements to another important part of the annual report, the notes to the financial statements, which appear as Exhibit 37-4. The function of financial statement notes is discussed next.

Notes to the financial statements The **notes to the financial statements** are considered an *essential* part of the statements. In other words, these notes are necessary for a complete and accurate interpretation of the information on the statements. A particularly important area is the disclosure of accounting policies of the company. These policies include the basis of preparing consolidated statements, methods of valuing inventories, and methods of valuing and reporting depreciation and fixed assets. Read each note to the 1976

General Mills annual report and refer to the financial statements to observe the related reporting practices.

The opinion of the independent certified public accountants Companies whose stock is bought and sold by the public almost always submit with their financial statements an *opinion* on those financial statements made by an independent certified public accountant. One such opinion is shown in Exhibit 37-5. Most corporations whose stock is traded publicly are required by regulatory agencies to submit such an opinion.

This opinion is very significant, for it tells the investor and other decision makers that the information in the financial statements has been carefully studied and analyzed by a professional licensed accountant. As evidence of this, the accountant makes a professional judgment on the matter in written form. The accountant is not an employee of the corporation; instead, the corporation is a client of the certified public accountant who operates independently on a professional basis.

The second paragraph of the opinion illustrated indicates that, in the opinion of the licensed professional expert, the financial statements present the financial position (balance sheet) and results of operations (income statement) *fairly* according to **generally accepted accounting principles**. This means that:

1. *All* the firm's assets are *included* on the balance sheet and are *classified* and *valued* according to accepted practice (the valuation and classification concepts that you have learned in this course).
2. *All* the firm's liabilities are included on the balance sheet and are classified and valued according to accepted practice.
3. The firm's capital is reported in a generally accepted manner (with earned and contributed capital reported separately, for example).
4. The earnings for the period are measured and reported in a fair and generally accepted way (according to generally accepted concepts such as realization of revenue, reporting of expenses, and so on, as you have learned in this course).

Such an opinion and affirmation by the CPA provide an independent judgment on which the decision maker can rely.

The first paragraph in the opinion example deals with the scope of the audit examination. This statement indicates that the independent CPA followed certain practices in making his examination of the financial statements. The American Institute of Certified Public Accountants has published a series of **auditing standards** which the independent accountant uses and follows in making his examination. These standards, which you will probably study in future courses, are guidelines for the performance of the audit which give the decision maker additional assurance that the information on the financial statements actually presents a fair picture of the corporation.

The ten-year summary Many annual reports include a 10-year summary of earnings and financial position. This information lets the decision maker analyze trends for a fairly long period of the firm's history. A 10-year summary for General Mills is included in Exhibit 37-6. The items included in such a summary vary from company to company.

OTHER SOURCES OF FINANCIAL INFORMATION

■ *What are other sources of financial information about a corporation?*

In addition to the annual report, decision makers can obtain financial information about a corporation from other sources. However, much of the information gained from other sources originates on the firm's financial statements. For example, stock brokerage firms provide information to their investor-customers. Most of their data comes in the form of summary-type financial statements or from an analysis of the firm or the industry made by the analysts working for the stock brokerage firm.

You should also be aware that there are a great many publications that provide various kinds of financial information to decision makers. Among these are:

1. The *Wall Street Journal.*
2. *Forbes* magazine.
3. *Barron's* magazine.
4. *Standard and Poor's Stock Guide.*

THE NEED FOR PRINCIPLES

Early in this course you learned that financial accounting is the branch of the broad field of accounting which is concerned with reporting information about a business firm to decision makers outside the firm. You also learned that general-purpose financial statements accomplish the reporting objectives of financial accounting. As with any body of knowledge, some underlying theoretical structure must be present if a logical and useful set of practices and procedures is to be developed for reaching the goals of the field and for expanding knowledge in that field. Such a body of principles is needed as a framework to help answer new questions that arise.

THE NATURE OF GENERALLY ACCEPTED ACCOUNTING PRINCIPLES

The American Institute of Certified Public Accountants (AICPA) discusses financial accounting theory and generally accepted accounting principles as follows:

Financial statements are the product of a process in which a large volume of data about aspects of the economic activities of an enterprise are accumulated, analyzed,

■ *What are generally accepted accounting principles?*

and reported. This process should be carried out in accordance with generally accepted accounting principles. Generally accepted accounting principles incorporate the consensus at a particular time as to which economic resources and obligations should be recorded as assets and liabilities by financial accounting, which changes in assets and liabilities should be recorded, when these changes should be recorded, how the assets and liabilities and changes in them should be measured, what information should be disclosed and how it should be disclosed, and which financial statements should be prepared.

Generally accepted acounting principles therefore is a technical term in financial accounting. Generally accepted accounting principles encompass the conventions, rules, and procedures necessary to define accepted accounting practice at a particular time. The standard of "generally accepted accounting principles" includes not only broad guidelines of general application, but also detailed practices and procedures.[1]

Throughout the history of financial accounting there have been attempts to set down in writing the so-called generally accepted principles of accounting. These attempts have not been altogether successful. At the present time, there are several statements and publications, which, taken as a whole, provide written guidelines for the preparation of financial statements. Among these publications are (1) the **Accounting Research Bulletins**, published by the AICPA during the period 1939 to 1959; (2) the **Opinions of the Accounting Principles Board**, published by the AICPA during the period 1959 through 1973; and (3) **Statements of the Financial Accounting Standards Board** (FASB), published by the independent body that is now responsible for developing rules of reporting practice. These official publications give detailed guidance to independent certified public accountants (CPAs) in their job of determining whether a firm's financial statements are presented according to generally accepted principles of accounting. These publications will be discussed later in this unit.

We cannot discuss completely here all of the rules, procedures, and principles comprising generally accepted accounting principles. Instead, we can present and discuss a few basic concepts which are fundamental to financial accounting. These concepts are:

1. The business entity.
2. The business transaction.
3. Going concern.
4. Periodicity.
5. Money basis for reporting.
6. Objective verifiable evidence.

[1] American Institute of Certified Public Accountants, *Statement of the Accounting Principles Board, No. 4,* "Basic Concepts and Accounting Principles Underlying Financial Statements of Business Enterprises," October, 1970, pp. 54–55.

7. Adequate disclosure.
8. Conservatism.
9. Materiality.
10. Consistency.

The business entity Accounting information and financial statements relate to a specific entity. This entity must be identified when the accounting information is prepared and used. For example, the identification of the business (economic) entity is emphasized when consolidated financial statements are prepared.

The business transaction The business transaction is a concept that deals with the input of a financial accounting system. Reread the first paragraph of the AICPA discussion of generally accepted accounting principles that appears on pages 629 and 630. Two major problems for CPAs are deciding which changes in assets and liabilities should be recorded and how they should be recorded. The concept of what a business transaction is is basic to solving these problems. Recall that a business transaction is any economic event which affects assets or equities of the business firm, and that these business transactions are recorded in a double-entry fashion to show the effects on assets and equities.

Going concern Most business firms are organized with the purpose of operating indefinitely—not for a limited period of time. In reporting about the operations of business firms, therefore, it is assumed that they will operate indefinitely. This assumption is called the **going-concern** concept. Such an assumption is useful in accounting because it helps the CPA decide how certain types of accounting information should be reported. For example, should fixed assets be valued and reported as if they are to be liquidated (as if the firm will be discontinued)? The answer is no. Because of the going-concern assumption, they should be valued as if the firm will operate until the assets are used in the regular operations of the firm.

Periodicity **Periodicity** is a fundamental concept in accounting. It refers to the fact that accounting information, by its very nature, involves reporting activities according to relatively short *periods of time*. The usefulness of the information reported depends upon making estimates of costs and revenues and upon allocating these costs and revenues among periods in the reporting process. Waiting until the business terminates to report the information would not serve the needs of decision makers.

Money basis for reporting Because of the special role of the monetary unit in our economy, there is a close relationship between reporting financial information and the dollar or monetary unit. The dollar is a measure of value that is universally understood in our economic system. Because the measuring of value and changes in value of a firm is a primary objective of financial accounting, this monetary unit (the dollar in the United States) is used to make that measure. All the assets, equities, and changes in assets and equities therefore are measured on financial statements by their dollar equivalents.

This is not to say that other information is not included in the accounting system. Information such as descriptions of account categories, quantities of certain inventory items, and many other types of nonmonetary data might be included. But the primary information appearing on financial statements is measured in money terms to provide a universal basis for interpretation of the values.

One problem arises because the dollar is used as the measuring unit. It is a fact that the value of the dollar is not stable—it changes. Naturally the assets and equities of the firm might change, and these changes can be reported by valuing them in terms of more dollars or less dollars. But what happens if the value of the measuring unit, the dollar itself, also changes? The next unit will deal with this special problem of the changing value of the dollar. The problem is similar to measuring the length of an object in inches when the size of the inch keeps changing.

Objective verifiable evidence The information in financial statements must be based on objective verifiable evidence. This means that management must base accounting entries on actual economic events and must collect information about these economic events (transactions) which can be verified by others, including the independent CPA. For example, a debit to the Purchases of merchandise account must be supported by an invoice showing that the purchase actually was made; it must be supported by cancelled checks to show that the merchandise was paid for; and it must be supported by inventory records to show how the merchandise was used in the firm. The fact that financial statements are based upon objective verifiable evidence, and not upon the imagination or arbitrariness of management or others, gives added reason for the decision makers to rely on the information in making their decisions.

Adequate disclosure A group of standards for the disclosure of adequate information for intelligent decisions has been developed over the years. The notes to financial statements provide a basis for much of the necessary disclosure. The financial statements must reveal all important facts about the resources of the firm and about its operations. Material facts which might have a significant effect on an investment decision or on some other decision must be disclosed according to this concept. Necessarily, much judgment must be used in determining which facts are important to the decision makers and which are not. One area generally agreed to be disclosed on financial statements is information about the accounting methods used (such as the FIFO method, or the straight-line method) and information about any changes in accounting methods which the company is making. Also, basic accounting policies (such as information about preparing the consolidated statements) must be made known along with the financial statements.

Conservatism The concept of **conservatism** is of little value today, but it has had an impact on the development of accounting principles. According to this concept, if there is a reasonable choice between two methods or approaches to reporting an item, the method which produces the smaller net earnings or the smaller asset value should be chosen. Such an approach, it was believed, would guard against overstatement of earnings and assets. For example, if management believes that the sum-of-the-years'-digits method and the straight-line depreciation method are equally good for reporting purposes, then the sum-of-the-years'-digits method should be chosen because it provides for conservative reporting. It is considered more conservative than the straight-line method because it produces a lower asset value for the fixed asset and greater amounts of depreciation are charged earlier, which produces smaller net earnings during the early life of the asset.

As mentioned above, conservatism is considered today to be of little value. Accountants believe that, generally, in any one circumstance, there should be an adequate basis for choosing between alternative methods without resorting to the biased approach of conservatism. For example, choosing a depreciation method should be based upon ideas concerning the matching of costs and revenues, such as how much the assets are used each period in the production of revenues.

Materiality **Materiality** refers to how important or significant a certain item of accounting information is in relation to some other item of information. For example, assume a firm incurred an extraordinary loss of $10,000 from a storm. In deciding how to report this loss on the income statement, the management must decide if the item is material (usually in terms of the net earnings). If the net earnings amounted to $12,000 during the period, then obviously this $10,000 loss is material. The extraordinary loss, therefore, would be reported separately on the income statement. For contrast, assume that the same firm's net earnings were $100,000,000 for the year. The $10,000 loss probably would be considered immaterial and would be reported in some other category (perhaps Miscellaneous expense). Making a special category of the loss would not aid the decision makers in their decision process.

In summary, the materiality idea is used in a number of ways in financial accounting. The example above showed how an immaterial item might not be disclosed separately on financial statements. In addition, recording procedures might be built around the idea of materiality. A firm might set up the procedure that all purchases of equipment for amounts under $50 are to be considered expenses rather than assets, even if they are expected to last several years. A $10 wastebasket therefore would be reported as Office supplies expense instead of as Office equipment. Setting up records and depreciating such small items is more costly than charging them off as expenses when they are purchased. Because these items are assumed to be immaterial in terms of the company's assets and earnings, the reader of the financial statement would not be misled.

Consistency The opinion of the independent CPA indicates that the generally accepted accounting principles have been applied **consistently** (on a basis consistent with that of the preceding year). The assumption in financial statement reporting is that the same accounting rules and policies have been used from period to period (over time). All significant changes of accounting treatment must be disclosed to the readers of the financial statements; if this is not done, it is impossible to analyze a company's operations over time.

THE DEVELOPMENT OF GENERALLY ACCEPTED ACCOUNTING PRINCIPLES

Generally accepted accounting principles have developed through the aid of a number of individuals and groups. The most important organizations which have contributed include:

1. The American Institute of Certified Public Accountants.
2. The Financial Accounting Standards Board.
3. The American Accounting Association.
4. The Securities and Exchange Commission.

■ *Which organizations have contributed to the development of generally accepted accounting principles?*

The American Institute of Certified Public Accountants Founded in 1887, the AICPA has contributed continuously to the development of accounting principles. It publishes a monthly journal called the *Journal of Accountancy;* and it also prepares and administers a national *uniform certified public accountants examination.* All the states have laws which regulate the practice of public accountancy. In testing candidates for the CPA license, the states use the **uniform CPA examination** prepared by the AICPA. The examination includes four parts:

1. Accounting theory.
2. Accounting practice.
3. Auditing.
4. Commercial law.

The AICPA also developed a formal research program and staff and a number of committees and boards which aided in the development of accounting principles. Members of the AICPA must adhere to the institute's pronouncements concerning generally accepted accounting principles, which took the form of *Accounting Research Bulletins* and *Opinions of the Accounting Principles Board.*

The Financial Accounting Standards Board For a number of years the Accounting Principles Board of the AICPA was responsible for establishing accounting rules for corporate financial reporting. Recently, a new *independent* organization called the *Financial Accounting Standards Board* (FASB) was created to take over the duties of the Accounting Principles Board. This new board, which consists of seven full-time members, began functioning in 1973. The FASB is not part of the AICPA, but is governed by an independent foundation. Since its creation in 1973, it has issued several official statements on accounting principles.

The American Accounting Association The American Accounting Association (AAA) began originally as an organization of teachers of accounting. It has issued several important reports or studies on accounting principles, including *A Statement of Basic Accounting Theory* (1966). The AAA now includes many thousands of practicing accountants, teachers, and others. It publishes a quarterly scholarly journal, the *Accounting Review,* which many consider to be the leading journal dealing with topics in financial accounting theory. The AAA works closely with the AICPA and other organizations in the development of accounting principles.

The Securities and Exchange Commission This federal government body, created in 1934, exists for the protection of investors. The **Securities and Exchange Commission** prescribes reporting practices for corporations to promote sound financial reporting. Corporations under the control of the SEC (most large companies) must follow these reporting requirements. The SEC and the AICPA have cooperated in the past in deciding what reporting practices are to be recommended and required. The SEC has published *Accounting Series Releases* which summarize the minimum reporting requirements of the SEC.

A CHECKLIST OF SOME BASIC ACCOUNTING LITERATURE

This section presents a checklist of some of the important journals and other publications in the field of accounting. This list is *not* given here for you to memorize. Nor are you expected at this time to become totally familiar with all the items. Instead, the presentation is meant as a permanent reference which should be valuable to you in your future study of accounting.

Important journals

Abacus. Sydney University Press, Press Building, University of Sydney, New South Wales 2006, Australia.

Accountancy. Institute of Chartered Accountants in England and Wales, 56–66 Goswell Road, London ELIM 7AB England.

The Accountant. Gee & Co. Ltd., 151 Strand, London W.C.2, England.

Accountants' Journal. New Zealand Society of Accountants, Box 10046, Wellington, New Zealand.

The Accounting Review. American Accounting Association, 653 South Orange Avenue, Sarasota, Florida 33577.

Australian Accountant. Australian Society of Accountants, 49 Exhibition Street, Melbourne 3000, Australia.

Canadian Chartered Accountant. Canadian Institute of Chartered Accountants, 250 Bloor Street, E., Toronto 5, Ontario, Canada.

Chartered Accountants in Australia. Institute of Chartered Accountants in Australia, Box 3921, G.P.O., Sydney 2001, Australia.

The CPA Journal. New York State Society of Certified Public Accountants, 600 Third Avenue, New York, New York 10016.

Federal Accountant. Federal Government Accountants Association, 727 South 23rd Street, Arlington, Virginia 22202.

Financial Executive. Financial Executives Institute, 633 Third Avenue, New York, New York 10017.

The Internal Auditor. Institute of Internal Auditors, 170 Broadway, New York, New York 10038.

International Journal of Accounting Education and Research. Center for International Education and Research in Accounting, 320 Commerce West, University of Illinois, Urbana, Illinois 61801.

Journal of Accountancy. American Institute of Certified Public Accountants, 1211 Avenue of the Americas, New York, New York 10036.

Journal of Accounting Research. Institute of Professional Accounting, Graduate School of Business, University of Chicago, Chicago, Illinois, 60637.

Management Accounting. National Association of Accountants, 919 Third Avenue, New York, New York 10022.

The Practical Accountant. The Institute for Continuing Professional Development, 964 Third Avenue, New York, New York 10022.

The Tax Executive. Tax Executives Institute, Inc., 425 13th Street, N.W., Washington, D.C. 20004.

Taxation for Accountants. The Journal of Taxation, Ltd. 512 North Florida Ave., Tampa, Florida 33602.

The Woman CPA. American Woman's Society of Certified Public Accountants and the American Society of Women Accountants, Suite 1036, 35 E. Wacker Drive, Chicago, Illinois 60601.

"Opinions of the accounting principles board" of the AICPA These opinions were official pronouncements of the AICPA and generally must be adhered to by independent CPAs.

No. 1   *New Depreciation Guidelines and Rules,* 1962

No. 2   *Accounting for the "Investment Credit,"* 1962

No. 3   *The Statement of Sources and Application of Funds,* 1963

No. 4   *Accounting for the "Investment Credit,"* 1964

No. 5   *Reporting of Leases in Financial Statements of Lessee,* 1964

No. 6   *Status of Accounting Research Bulletins,* 1965

No. 7   *Accounting for Leases in Financial Statements of Lessors,* 1966

No. 8   *Accounting for the Cost of Pension Plans,* 1966

No. 9   *Reporting the Results of Operations,* 1966

No. 10   *Omnibus Opinion—1966,* 1966

No. 11   *Accounting for Income Taxes,* 1967

No. 12   *Omnibus Opinion—1967,* 1967

No. 13   *Amending Paragraph 6 of APB Opinion No. 9, Application to Commercial Banks,* 1969

No. 14   *Accounting for Convertible Debt Issued with Stock Purchase Warrants,* 1969

No. 15   *Earnings per Share,* 1969

No. 16   *Business Combinations,* 1970

No. 17   *Intangible Assets,* 1970

No. 18   *The Equity Method of Accounting for Investments in Common Stock,* 1971

No. 19   *Reporting Changes in Financial Position,* 1971

No. 20   *Accounting Changes,* 1971

No. 21   *Interest on Receivables and Payables,* 1971

No. 22   *Disclosure of Accounting Policies,* 1971

No. 23   *Accounting for Income Taxes—Special Areas,* 1972

No. 24   *Accounting for Income Taxes—Investments in Common Stock Accounted for by the Equity Method (Other Than Subsidiaries and Corporate Joint Ventures),* 1972

No. 25   *Accounting for Stock Issued to Employees,* 1972

No. 26	*Early Extinguishment of Debt*, 1972
No. 27	*Accounting for Lease Transactions by Manufacturer or Dealer Lessors*, 1972
No. 28	*Interim Financial Reporting*, 1973
No. 29	*Accounting for Nonmonetary Transactions*, 1973
No. 30	*Reporting the Results of Operations*, 1973
No. 31	*Disclosure of Lease Commitments by Lessees*, 1973

"Accounting research studies" made under the direction of the research division of the AICPA These research studies have no official authority, but are research efforts in important areas of financial accounting. Often these research studies led to official opinions of the AICPA.

No. 1	*The Basic Postulates of Accounting*, 1961
No. 2	*Cash Flow Analysis and the Funds Statement*, 1961
No. 3	*A Tentative Set of Broad Accounting Principles for Business Enterprises*, 1962
No. 4	*Reporting of Leases in Financial Statements*, 1962
No. 5	*A Critical Study of Accounting for Business Combinations*, 1963
No. 6	*Reporting the Financial Effects of Price-Level Changes*, 1963
No. 7	*Inventory of Generally Accepted Accounting Principles for Business Enterprises*, 1965
No. 8	*Accounting for the Cost of Pension Plans*, 1965
No. 9	*Interperiod Allocation of Corporate Income Taxes*, 1966
No. 10	*Accounting for Goodwill*, 1968
No. 11	*Financial Reporting in the Extractive Industries*, 1969
No. 12	*Reporting Foreign Operations of U.S. Companies in U.S. Dollars*, 1972
No. 13	*Accounting for Research and Development Expenditures*, 1973
No. 14	*The Accounting Basis of Inventories*, 1973
No. 15	*Stockholders' Equity*, 1973

Accounting Research Bulletins These bulletins are official and authoritative pronouncements of the AICPA. They were issued during the period 1939 to 1959, before the Accounting Principles Board was created. All these bulletins are bound together in one volume: *Accounting Research and Terminology Bulletins,* Final Edition, American Institute of Certified Public Accountants, 1961.

Statements of financial accounting standards These written statements are official and authoritative pronouncements of the FASB. Such statements, along with the "Opinions of the Accounting Principles Board" and the "Accounting Research Bulletins," provide the official guidance for financial reporting today.

No. 1   *Disclosure of Foreign Currency Translation Information,* 1973

No. 2   *Accounting for Research and Development Costs,* 1974

No. 3   *Reporting Accounting Changes in Interim Financial Statements,* 1974

No. 4   *Reporting Gains and Losses from Extinguishment of Debt,* 1975

No. 5   *Accounting for Contingencies,* 1975

No. 6   *Classification of Short-Term Obligations Expected to be Refinanced,* 1975

No. 7   *Accounting and Reporting by Development Stage Enterprises,* 1975

No. 8   *Accounting for the Translation of Foreign Currency Transactions and Foreign Currency Financial Statements,* 1975

No. 9   *Accounting for Income Taxes—Oil and Gas Producing Companies,* 1975

No. 10   *Extension of "Grandfather," Provisions for Business Combinations,* 1975

No. 11   *Accounting for Contingencies—Transition Method,* 1975

No. 12   *Accounting for Certain Marketable Securities,* 1975

No. 13   *Accounting for Leases,* 1976

No. 14   *Financial Reporting for Segments of a Business Enterprise,* 1976

No. 15   *Accounting by Debtors and Creditors or Troubled Debt Restructurings,* 1977

No. 16   *Prior Period Adjustments,* 1977

No. 17   *Applying the Lower of Cost or Market Rule in Translated Financial Statements (An Interpretation of FASB Statement No. 8),* 1977

No. 18   *Accounting for Income Taxes in Interim Periods (An Interpretation of APB Opinion No. 28)* 1977

No. 19   *Financial Accounting and Reporting by Oil and Gas Producing Companies,* 1977

No. 20   *Accounting for Forward Exchange Contracts,* 1977

No. 21   *Suspension of the Reporting of Earnings Share and Segment Information by Nonpublic Enterprises,* 1978

No. 22   *Changes in the Provisions of Lease Agreement Resulting from Refunding Tax-Exempt Debts,* 1978

Accounting Research Bulletins Official pronouncements of the AICPA on matters of financial accounting; made during the period 1939 to 1959, these bulletins provide detailed guidance to independent CPAs in their job of determining whether a firm's financial statements are presented according to generally accepted accounting principles. [p. 630]

Accounting Research Studies Research studies published by the Research Division of the AICPA; these studies have no official authority, but serve to stimulate discussion of important financial accounting issues; often they have led to official "Opinions of the Accounting Principles Board." [p. 638]

annual report A printed report containing data about a firm's operations and financial condition; issued each year, it provides information to decision makers outside the firm; customarily it includes (1) comments from management, (2) financial statements, (3) notes to financial statements, (4) CPA's opinion, and (5) 10-year summary. [p. 626]

auditing standards Guidelines for the conduct of an independent audit and for the reporting of information; standards prepared by the American Institute of Certified Public Accountants. [p. 628]

conservatism A concept in financial accounting which had some impact upon the development of accounting; it holds that if there is a reasonable choice between two methods or approaches to reporting an item, the method which produces the smaller net earnings or the smaller asset value should be chosen. [p. 633]

consistency The concept that generally accepted accounting principles must be applied in the same manner from period to period, as opposed to changing techniques and methods of reporting information from period to period. [p. 634]

generally accepted accounting principles The conventions, rules, and procedures necessary to define accepted accounting practice at a particular time. See the text for details. [p. 628]

going concern A fundamental assumption underlying financial accounting; the idea that business firms are assumed to operate indefinitely rather than for a limited period of time. [p. 631]

materiality The concept in accounting that the size (dollar amount) of an item in relation to another item should govern the reporting practice in certain circumstances. [p. 633]

notes to financial statements Additional information that accompanies corporation financial statements; an integral part of the statements necessary for the complete and accurate interpretation of the statements. [p. 627]

Opinions of the Accounting Principles Board Official pronouncements of the AICPA on matters of financial accounting; made since 1959, these opinions are similar in authority and significance to the Accounting Research Bulletins. [p. 630]

periodicity The fundamental concept in financial accounting that accounting information, by its very nature, involves reporting activities according to relatively short periods of time. [p. 631]

Securities and Exchange Commission A federal government body created in 1934 for the protection of investors; the SEC publishes *Accounting Series Releases* which govern certain accounting reporting practices of corporations. [p. 635]

uniform Certified Public Accountants examination An examination prepared by the AICPA and used by all fifty states in examining candidates to be licensed to practice public accountancy. [p. 634]

QUESTIONS

Q37-1. List and describe the six major components of a corporation annual report.

Q37-2. What are some sources of financial information for decision makers in addition to annual reports?

Q37-3. Why are generally accepted accounting principles needed?

Q37-4. Do "generally accepted accounting principles" include both broad guidelines of general application and detailed practices and procedures?

Q37-5. What are the two official publications which help to guide accountants in determining if financial statements are prepared according to generally accepted accounting principles?

Q37-6. Why is the consistency concept important in financial accounting?

Q37-7. Why is the objective verifiable evidence concept important in financial accounting?

Q37-8. What is the function of the SEC?

EXERCISES

E37-1. The following information appeared in the Interim Report to Shareholders for the three months ended January 31, 1973, of Rexnord, Inc., of Milwaukee, Wisconsin:

335TH CASH DIVIDEND

A check is enclosed for the regular quarterly dividend for each common or preferred stockholder. The common stock dividend is in the amount of 26 cents per share. This is the 335th consecutive cash dividend on the company's stock with dividends paid in each of the last 80 years, commencing in 1894. Dividends on the company's preferred stock are $62\frac{1}{2}$ cents for each share of Series A and Series C preferred stock and 59 cents per share of Series B preferred stock.

R. V. Krikorian
President

W. C. Messinger
Chairman

Explain the value of such information to decision makers.

E37-2. Go to your school library and locate a recent issue of one of the following publications: (1) *The Wall Street Journal,* (2) *Forbes,* or (3) *Barron's.* Find an article that deals with one corporation. Summarize the article and comment on how the information revealed could be useful to a prospective investor in the corporation. At the top of your paper indicate the title of the article and the date and name of the publication.

E37-3. Go to your school library and locate a recent issue of *Standard and Poor's Stock Guide.* Make a list of the kinds of information provided by this publication.

E37-4. An article in *Business Week* magazine (April 3, 1971) stated the following:

This year's crop of annual reports may be the best-read collection in business history. Since the Securities & Exchange Commission ordered companies to break down both sales and earnings for each major line of business on this year's 10-K reports—the SEC's plain-sister version of the corporate annual report—many large corporations are making the same disclosures in their annual reports to shareholders. . .

Why do you think investors and others desire such information broken down for each major line of business? Would such information be considerably more useful than summary information on sales and earnings not including breakdown by line of business?

E37-5. Go to your school library and locate a recent issue of one of the accounting journals listed in this unit. Find an article that is of some interest to you and write a one-page summary of the article. At the top of your paper, indicate the author and title of the article, the name and date of the journal, and the page numbers of the article.

E37-6. Friday Company has been operating for a number of years. The plant and equipment have been depreciated on the sum-of-the-years'-digits method throughout the history of the company. Last year the firm purchased a considerable quantity of new equipment. The net earnings for last year were not as high as previous years, so the general manager decides that all plant and equipment will be depreciated on the straight-line basis for that year's financial statements only. In future years, the company proposes to use the sum-of-the years'-digits method. By changing depreciation methods, the manager hopes to show increased earnings for the year in question. What basic accounting concept is violated by the manager's plan? Comment.

PROBLEMS (GROUP A)

P37-1. *Becoming familiar with an annual report.* Answer each of the following questions by using the annual report information of General Mills included in the appendix. Also, indicate the source of the information within that annual report.

Example: What depreciation method is used by the company on fixed assets?

ANSWER	SOURCE
Straight-line method for financial statements and accelerated methods for income tax purposes.	Notes to Financial Statements (Exhibit 37-4, Note 1.B)

a. Who are the independent auditors of the company?
b. What are the firm's three main kinds of products?
c. What was the net income made per dollar of sales?
d. How much did earnings increase this year over last year?
e. What is the amount of earnings per share?
f. What were the dividends per share of common stock?
g. How are marketable securities valued?
h. What is the firm's current ratio at the beginning and end of the year?
i. How are inventories valued?
j. How does General Mills account for intangible assets?
k. Does the company have research and development costs? How are they accounted for?
l. What subsidiaries did General Mills acquire during the year?
m. Are foreign operations significant for the company?
n. What law suits are outstanding against the firm?
o. Does the company use preferred stock to raise funds? Has it ever done so?

P37-2. *Applying principles in unfamiliar circumstances.* Here is an opportunity for you to apply generally accepted accounting principles to somewhat unfamiliar circumstances: Assume that you were recently hired as accountant for Bilson Brothers Circus. Describe how each of the following situations would be accounted for.
a. Purchase of an elephant for $4,300.
b. Payment for feed for circus animals, $3,000.
c. Payment of salaries of performers, $10,349.
d. Acquisition and use of props and other circus equipment.
e. Payment to City of Boston for use of public facilities to present the circus, $4,700.
f. One of the circus animals was killed when the truck carrying it was involved in an accident.
g. A baby elephant was born to one of the performing elephants owned by the circus.

P37-3. *Errors and financial reporting.* The *business transaction* is a concept that deals with the input of a financial accounting system.

 a. Must *all* business transactions of a business firm that take place during a period be recorded in the records of the firm? Explain your answer.

 b. Explain the effect on a company's income statement, statement of retained earnings, and balance sheet if each of the following transactions were *omitted* from the accounting records (not recorded) in error. Assume each transaction is a separate situation.

  (1) Rendered a service to a customer, $500. The customer is expected to pay for this service early next year.

  (2) The entry for depreciation of equipment, $1,200, was not recorded.

  (3) During December, the firm collected $3,000 from a customer for services to be rendered by us in January of next year. The amount was credited to Service revenue. The adjusting entry was omitted in error.

  (4) A sale of merchandise was made to a customer on credit. The cost of the merchandise was $1,000 and the selling price was $1,350. The company uses the perpetual method of accounting for merchandise. No entries were made on the company's records regarding the sale.

  (5) Incurred advertising expense this period. The amount, $1,000, will be paid next year. No entry has been made.

  (6) Purchased merchandise from a supplier for $3,000, with terms of 2/10, n/30. The merchandise has been received and is stored in the company's warehouse. The $3,000 is included in the company's ending inventory (the periodic method is used), but no entry has been made for the purchase of the merchandise.

PROBLEMS (GROUP B)

P37-4. *Accounting concepts.*

Part A

Below is a list of independent situations concerning the financial statement presentations of a company. For each of these situations, indicate whether you agree with the presentation. Comment on any basic accounting concept that is violated or that is appropriately followed.

 a. A wastebasket was purchased for $12. The wastebasket is expected to last 5 years. The $12 amount was debited to expense in the period that the purchase was made.

 b. Winston Corporation was applying for a bank loan. The personal checking account and savings account balances of the owner (President) of the firm were included as part of the assets on the balance sheet.

 c. The company purchased a tract of land for $10,000. The value of the land if it were to be sold at the balance sheet date is $23,000. The balance sheet reveals that the land is reported at $23,000.

 d. The ending inventory of the company is reported on the balance sheet at $75,000. The current replacement price of the inventory at the balance sheet date is $71,000 and the cost of the inventory was $75,000.

Part B

Imbe and Company undertook a new promotional program during 1978. Expenditures totaling $17,000 were made for introducing a new product line. Executives in the firm suggested three alternatives for reporting the $17,000 expenditure.

Suggestion 1: Treat the $17,000 as an expense for 1978.

Suggestion 2: Treat the $17,000 as an asset and write the expense off (assign the expense to periods) over a 15-year period, the expected number of years that the new product line will produce profits for the company.

Suggestion 3: Treat the $17,000 as an asset and write the expense off over a 3-year period.

REQUIRED:

a. Which of the three suggestions would give the most conservative results? Why?

b. Which of the three suggestions do you recommend? Why?

P37-5. *Comparing methods and principles.*

Part A

Generally accepted accounting principles require that revenues be reported when they are earned and that expenses be reported when they are incurred—not necessarily when *cash* is received or paid. Does this mean that readers of financial statements are not interested in cash? Explain and comment.

Part B

On January 1, 1978, Errore Corporation purchased selling equipment amounting to $193,400, *including* $1,000 of installation charges and $1,200 of freight costs. The equipment is expected to have a useful life of 10 years, with a salvage value of $11,000. The controller of the firm is trying to decide which depreciation method to use for the new equipment. A preliminary calculation indicates that earnings for the company, before deducting depreciation and before deducting income taxes, amount to $118,500. The company's income tax rate is about 30%.

REQUIRED:

a. Compute the depreciation expense for 1978, assuming the straight-line method is used.

b. Compute the depreciation expense for 1978, assuming the sum-of-the-years'-digits method is used.

c. Prepare comparative analyses of the net earnings in the following form:

	STRAIGHT-LINE METHOD	SUM-OF-THE YEARS'-DIGITS METHOD
Earnings before depreciation and income taxes		
Less Depreciaton expense		
Earnings before income taxes		
Less income taxes (30%)		
Net earnings for year		

P37-6. *Review problem: adjustments and financial statements.* The following accounts and balances appeared in the general ledger of Alowin, Inc., at December 31, 1978, the end of a year's operations, before adjusting entries were made.

Cash	3,000
Sales of merchandise	232,000
Marketable securities (at cost)	13,000
Sales returns and allowances	2,000
Accounts receivable	45,000
Sales discounts	5,000
Allowance for bad debts	1,000
Purchases of merchandise	100,000
Notes receivable (due in 4 months)	10,000
Notes receivable (due in 3 years)	50,000
Purchases returns and allowances	10,000
Merchandise inventory	15,000
Purchases discounts	3,000
Supplies	8,000
Advertising expenses	5,000
Land	83,000
Buildings	62,000
Rent expense	15,000
Service revenue	50,000
Supplies expense	–0–
Depreciation expense—Buildings	–0–
Accumulated depreciation—Buildings	10,000
Salaries expense	53,000
Salaries payable	–0–
Income taxes expense	3,000
Income taxes payable	–0–
Intangible assets	32,000
Accounts payable	4,000
Unearned service revenue	–0–
Bad debts expense	–0–
Notes payable (due in 5 years)	15,000
Dividends on common stock	3,000
Dividends on preferred stock	2,000
Retained earnings	35,000
Preferred stock	50,000
Common stock	100,000
Transportation on purchases	1,000
Loss on decline of marketable securities	–0–
Prepaid rent	–0–

REQUIRED:

a. Is Alowin, Inc., using the perpetual or periodic method of accounting for merchandise? How can you determine this?

b. The following information relates to adjusting entries needed at December 31, 1978. Prepare the necessary adjusting entries in general journal form.

 (1) Of the $8,000 of Supplies that had been purchased, only $1,000 remain on hand at the end of the year.

 (2) The ending merchandise inventory, according to physical count, had a cost of $5,000.

 (3) Salaries earned by employees, but not paid as of the end of the year, amount to $1,000.

 (4) Depreciation on the buildings is computed on the straight-line basis. The

building had an expected useful life of 50 years, cost $62,000, and has an expected scrap value of $12,000.

(5) $3,000 of the service revenue that had been collected will not be earned until 1979.

(6) Estimated income taxes for 1975 amount to $12,000. According to the records, $3,000 of this amount has already been paid in 1978. The remainder will be paid next January.

(7) Marketable securities have a market value at December 31, 1978, of $12,600. The lower of cost or market method is used by the company.

(8) $1,200 of the rent that has been paid represents rent on the equipment for *next* year.

(9) Bad debts expense amounts to $\frac{1}{2}$ of 1% of net sales.

c. Set up "T" accounts for each of the accounts listed. Enter the balances at the end of the year. Post the adjusting entries to the accounts and compute new balances.

d. Prepare an income statement in good form. There were 12,000 shares of common stock outstanding during the year. Remember to consider preferred stock dividends requirements when computing earnings per share.

e. Prepare a statement of retained earnings in good form.

f. Prepare a balance sheet in good form.

EXCERPTS FROM THE 1976 ANNUAL REPORT OF GENERAL MILLS, INC.

EXHIBIT 37-1 COMMENTS FROM MANAGEMENT OF THE FIRM

To Our Stockholders and Employees:

General Mills

August 20, 1976

Fiscal 1976 was a year of exceptional progress for General Mills. The results on the opposite page show a vitality that makes it possible to report a 10th straight year of growth in sales, a 14th successive year of improvement in earnings before extraordinary items and a 12th consecutive year of increase in dividends per share. The company made significant investments for future growth, strengthened an already sound financial position, took steps to improve use of company assets and made changes in leadership designed to assure continuing strength.

The company's performance reflects the outstanding efforts of General Mills' 51,778 employees and the strength of our diversity, our past investments and an increasingly favorable economic environment.

Operational highlights include strong sales gains over fiscal 1975 in each of the company's major business areas: 11.0 per cent for foods, 24.8 per cent for consumer non-foods and 13.4 per cent for specialty chemicals. Approximately three-fourths of this year's gain resulted from increases in physical volume, including virtually all of the 15.7 per cent sales gain in the second half. In contrast, the previous year's 15.4 per cent gain in sales came essentially as the result of inflation in selling prices. Moderating raw material costs enabled the company to reduce selling prices in a significant number of areas during the year. Inflation, for example, added only 1.6 per cent to average selling prices for domestic food products, with average prices actually 1.9 per cent lower than in the fourth quarter of fiscal 1975.

Operating profit gains over the prior year were reported by each major business area: 19.2 per cent for foods, 46.7 per cent for consumer non-foods and 5.8 per cent for specialty chemicals. Operating profits increased 25.3 per cent to $254,300,000.

General Mills' food businesses had an excellent year with record volumes in all major product categories. Operating profits for breakfast and snack items grew 21.6 per cent and accounted for one-third of the corporate gain. Fast-growing restaurant activities, with Red Lobster Inns specialty seafood restaurants expanding from 128 to 174 company-operated units during the year, had an earnings gain of 56.3 per cent. Record profitability for Gorton's seafoods, which operated at a loss the previous year, Betty Crocker desserts and baking mixes helped bring about modest gains for the product groups in which their results are reported. Impacting on food profits is a $7,000,000 pretax charge associated with

conversion of the company's Cedar Rapids plant from primarily a commercial protein facility to a package foods facility.

Consumer non-foods' substantial growth in operating profits came partially from a fifth successive year of excellent gains by worldwide craft, game and toy operations, which grew 35.9 per cent, and partially from a 65.0 per cent surge in the operating profit total for fashions, specialty retailing and furniture from the prior year's depressed level. Specialty retailing, formerly called direct marketing, saw earnings rebound strongly and above expectations as did fashions, which reported increased profitability despite a $4,020,000 pretax loss associated with the sale of the Silna Division which made doubleknit fabrics.

Specialty chemicals also finished the year strongly. After a soft first half, in line with trends in industries served, specialty chemicals experienced a strong business recovery beginning in February, 1976, which culminated in all-time high quarterly earnings in the final quarter.

Sales and earnings trends during fiscal 1976 reflected an increased level of spending for new product development and for support of existing products and services. Advertising media support increased to $111,400,000; promotional expenditures were also substantially higher than a year earlier. Advertising media costs were 4.2 per cent of sales in fiscal 1976 as compared with 3.1 per cent in the previous year and a 4.4 per cent five-year average for fiscal years 1970 through 1974. This increase in support proved effective in gaining increased volume and improving share of market for most of the company's package food lines.

Continued success in improving working capital usage and lessening inflationary pressures combined to reduce borrowing requirements and strengthen the company's financial position. Total debt at the end of fiscal 1976 was $53,331,000 under that of the fiscal 1975 year-end total, and cash and marketable securities increased by $71,861,000. The improved financial position and lower short-term interest rates, together with an increase in interest income compared with the previous year, resulted in an $8,968,000 decline in net interest expense. Gross interest expense totaled $29,400,000 as compared with $36,219,000 in fiscal 1975, a decline of 18.8 per cent.

The company's common stock was split two-for-one following shareholder approval at last year's

How the Sales Dollar was Divided

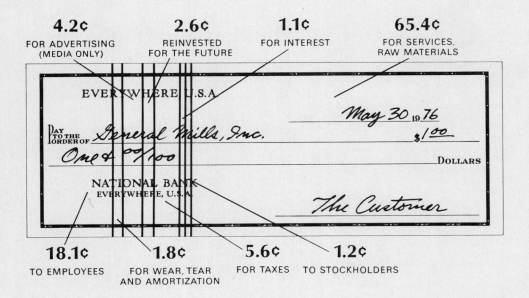

4.2¢
FOR ADVERTISING
(MEDIA ONLY)

2.6¢
REINVESTED
FOR THE FUTURE

1.1¢
FOR INTEREST

65.4¢
FOR SERVICES,
RAW MATERIALS

EVERYWHERE, U.S.A.

PAY TO THE ORDER OF *General Mills, Inc.*

May 30 19 76

$ 1 00

One & 00/100 DOLLARS

NATIONAL BANK
EVERYWHERE, U.S.A.

The Customer

18.1¢
TO EMPLOYEES

1.8¢
FOR WEAR, TEAR
AND AMORTIZATION

5.6¢
FOR TAXES

1.2¢
TO STOCKHOLDERS

(in thousands)	Fiscal Year Ended		
	May 30, 1976 (53 Weeks)	May 25, 1975 (52 Weeks)	Increase
Sales...	$2,645,000	$2,308,900	14.6%
Net earnings.......................................	100,538	76,213	31.9%
Earnings per dollar of sales...........................	3.8¢	3.3¢	
Earnings per common share and common share equivalent.....	$ 2.04	$ 1.59*	28.3%
Common stock dividends..............................	32,391	27,806	
Net earnings after dividends..........................	68,147	48,407	
Wages, salaries and employee benefits..................	479,438	402,725	19.1%
Taxes—income, payroll, property, etc....................	148,750	112,530	32.2%
—per cent of earnings before all taxes.................	59.7%	60.0%	

*Restated for two-for-one stock split in October, 1975.

Data should be read in conjunction with the financial statements on pages 23-35.

annual meeting. A two-cent increase in the quarterly dividend was declared for the payment of November 1, 1975, and again for the payment of August 1, 1976, assuring a 13th successive year of increase in dividends per share.

We remain optimistic about General Mills' future. Fiscal 1977 appears to be one of continued economic recovery worldwide, and virtually all of our operations are reporting favorable current trends and prospects.

In line with emphasis on internal growth of existing businesses, a one-third increase in gross capital expenditures to the $125,000,000 range is scheduled to continue expansion of General Mills' restaurant operations by 40 more units, to meet needs for additional food plant capacity, particularly for breakfast cereals, and to fund other projects which are essential to our growth. The entire amount of expenditures for fixed assets will be financed internally. Small acquisitions in existing areas are likely as well.

The end of fiscal 1976 marked the announcement of a new management team. President E. Robert Kinney became Chief Executive Officer on June 1,

reaches the mandatory retirement age of 65 on February 1, 1977. H. Brewster Atwater, Jr., Executive Vice President, was elected Chief Operating Officer. Other top management changes and a summary of 1976, succeeding James P. McFarland, who will continue to serve as Chairman of the Board until he changes on your Board of Directors, which includes the election of three new directors and the retirement of five who have served your company with dedication and distinction, are described in the *Business Review* of this report.

The corporate strategy of seeking consistent growth through balanced diversification with emphasis on consumer products and services remains intact. We continue to pay close attention to trends and changes in the environment which reflect consumer needs and life styles and ultimately affect the company's operations. General Mills' corporate long-term objective of increasing earnings per share at a compound rate of 10 per cent or better also remains intact. Management is confident that fiscal 1977 will bring growth consistent with our goal and our long-term record of progress.

Chairman of the Board	Vice Chairman	President

EXECUTIVE OFFICES • 9200 WAYZATA BOULEVARD • MINNEAPOLIS, MINNESOTA

Mailing Address: P.O. Box 1113, Minneapolis, Minnesota 55440 • Telephone: (612) 540-2311

EXHIBIT 37-2   A FINANCIAL REVIEW FOR THE YEAR

Management's Discussion and Analysis of Earnings

General Mills

FISCAL YEAR 1976

Sales. Strong gains over fiscal 1975 sales were attained by each of General Mills' three major business areas: 11.0 per cent for foods, 24.8 per cent for consumer non-foods and 13.4 per cent for specialty chemicals. About three-quarters of the company's overall 14.6 per cent sales gain resulted from volume increases, including virtually all of the gain in the second half, which grew at a rate of 15.7 per cent.

Costs and Expenses. Costs and expenses increased $281,424,000, or 13.0 per cent, over the prior year. This largely reflects the net effect of the following factors: 1.) growth in volume of products and services with attendant increases in raw materials, and other direct expenses, partially offset by lower average purchase prices for a number of key commodities such as wheat, sugar and shortening; 2.) substantial increases in sales promotion expenditures, including a $40,900,000 increase in media costs, which was a key factor in the overall increase of $153,853,000, or 28.5 per cent, in selling, general and administrative expenses. Continued success of the company's efforts to improve working capital turnover and lower short-term interest rates led to a decline in interest expense of $6,819,000, or 18.8 per cent. Contribution to employees' retirement funds increased $6,438,000, or 56.2 per cent (see Note 9 of notes to consolidated financial statements).

Analysis of Earnings. Net earnings reached $100,538,000, an increase of 31.9 per cent, as compared with the prior year. In addition to the above factors, earnings were affected by the unusual transactions discussed in Note 15 of notes to consolidated financial statements, which reduced net earnings by $5,800,000. A review of operating profit trends by product lines for the most recent five years appears on the opposite page. Compared with the prior year, total operating profits increased 25.3 per cent with gains reported by each of General Mills' three major business areas: 19.2 per cent for foods, 46.7 per cent for consumer non-foods and 5.8 per cent for specialty chemicals.

FISCAL YEAR 1975

Sales. Comparable rates of gain were attained by each of General Mills' three major product groups. The overall gain was essentially the result of inflation in selling prices. Sales for a number of businesses slowed in the third quarter in response to general economic conditions, out volume trends improved in the fourth quarter.

Costs and Expenses. Costs and expenses increased $313,325,000, or 16.9 per cent, over the prior year. The increase largely reflects higher costs of raw materials General Mills uses, which increased about 12 per cent in the first half beforedeclining moderately, coupled with a substantial increase in sales promotion expenditures. Interest expense increased $7,678,000, or 26.9 per cent, reflecting increased borrowings and high short-term interest rates during the first three quarters. Success of the company's efforts to improve working capital turnover reduced borrowings by year-end; the reduced borrowings and easing short-term interest rates resulted in a modest final quarter decline in interest expense.

Analysis of Earnings. Net earnings reached $76,213,000. Earnings were reduced by a change in fiscal 1975 to the LIFO method of accounting (see comment below). Operating profits for the year increased moderately in reaching $202,900,000, including the effect of the change to the LIFO method.

Change in Inventory Accounting Method. In order not to overstate reported profits as a result of inflation, the company changed its method of accounting, for a substantial portion of domestic inventories, from FIFO to LIFO basis of valuing inventories. This was necessary because of rapid increases in prices in the fiscal year, plus the expectation that inflation will continue over the long run, with inventories sold being replaced at substantially higher prices. The effect of the change was to decrease reported net earnings by $7,773,000, or 16 cents per share. This change was made to obtain better matching of current costs and revenues since current costs will be reflected in current earnings rather than being deferred in inventory valuations.

EXHIBIT 37-3 FINANCIAL STATEMENTS FOR THE YEAR

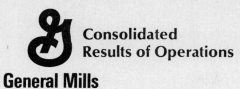

Consolidated Results of Operations

General Mills

GENERAL MILLS, INC., AND SUBSIDIARIES

	Fiscal Year Ended	
	May 30, 1976 (53 Weeks)	May 25, 1975 (52 Weeks)
	(in thousands)	
SALES.	$2,644,952	$2,308,900
COSTS AND EXPENSES:		
Costs of sales, exclusive of items shown below.	1,654,169	1,531,535
Depreciation expense (Note 1).	45,006	39,744
Amortization expense (Note 1).	1,701	2,043
Interest expense.	29,400	36,219
Contributions to employees' retirement plans (Note 9).	17,903	11,465
Profit sharing distribution (Note 10).	3,527	3,129
Selling, general and administrative expenses.	692,985	539,132
TOTAL.	2,444,691	2,163,267
EARNINGS BEFORE TAXES ON INCOME and Other Items shown below.	200,261	145,633
TAXES ON INCOME (Note 11).	(99,964)	(70,650)
OTHER ITEMS:		
Add share of net earnings of 20-50% owned companies.	1,094	1,268
Less minority interests in net earnings of consolidated subsidiaries.	(853)	(38)
NET EARNINGS.	$ 100,538	$ 76,213
EARNINGS PER COMMON SHARE AND COMMON SHARE EQUIVALENT (Notes 1 and 7)	$ 2.04	$ 1.59
Average number of common shares and common share equivalents (Note 1)	49,203	47,845

Earnings Employed in the Business

	Fiscal Year Ended	
	May 30, 1976 (53 Weeks)	May 25, 1975 (52 Weeks)
	(in thousands)	
NET EARNINGS FOR THE YEAR.	$ 100,538	$ 76,213
DIVIDENDS—Common stock ($0.66 per share—1976, and $0.58½ per share—1975) (Note 7).	(32,391)	(27,806)
NET EARNINGS AFTER DIVIDENDS.	68,147	48,407
Other adjustments.	(149)	—
NET INCREASE IN RETAINED EARNINGS.	67,998	48,407
RETAINED EARNINGS AT BEGINNING OF YEAR.	401,011	352,604
RETAINED EARNINGS AT END OF YEAR (Note 6).	$ 469,009	$ 401,011

See accompanying notes to consolidated financial statements.

Consolidated Balance Sheets

GENERAL MILLS, INC., AND SUBSIDIARIES

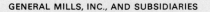

ASSETS

	May 30, 1976	May 25, 1975
CURRENT ASSETS:	*(in thousands)*	
Cash (Note 5)...	$ 4,478	$ 7,623
Marketable securities (at cost, approximates market value)................	77,351	2,345
Receivables:		
Customers...	199,966	197,062
Miscellaneous...	22,425	22,525
	222,391	219,587
Less allowance for possible losses...............................	(6,428)	(6,006)
	215,963	213,581
Inventories (Notes 1 and 4)...	353,654	345,907
Prepaid expenses.......................................	21,351	20,917
TOTAL CURRENT ASSETS................................	672,797	590,373
OTHER ASSETS:		
Land, buildings and equipment (Note 1):		
Land...	41,806	39,577
Buildings...	256,570	232,862
Equipment...	393,265	365,377
Construction in progress...................................	47,621	47,423
	739,262	685,239
Less accumulated depreciation...............................	(267,770)	(244,261)
	471,492	440,978
Miscellaneous assets:		
Investment in 20-50% owned companies (Note 1).................	11,339	12,289
Other...	23,071	15,780
	34,410	28,069
Intangible assets (Note 1):		
Excess of cost over net assets of acquired companies...............	138,802	128,658
Patents, copyrights and other intangibles.......................	10,695	17,555
TOTAL OTHER ASSETS.................................	655,399	615,260
TOTAL ASSETS...	$1,328,196	$1,205,633

See accompanying notes to consolidated financial statements.

LIABILITIES AND STOCKHOLDERS' EQUITY

	May 30, 1976	May 25, 1975
	(in thousands)	
CURRENT LIABILITIES:		
Notes payable (Note 5)	$ 24,098	$ 55,048
Current portion of long-term debt	4,405	3,637
Accounts payable and accrued expenses:		
Accounts payable—trade	194,622	147,888
Accounts payable—miscellaneous	46,671	27,284
Accrued payroll	29,933	24,557
Accrued interest	5,546	8,335
	276,772	208,064
Accrued taxes	69,045	43,301
Thrift accounts of officers and employees	3,363	3,484
TOTAL CURRENT LIABILITIES	377,683	313,534
OTHER LIABILITIES:		
Long-term debt, excluding current portion (Note 6)	281,763	304,912
Deferred Federal income taxes (Note 1)	11,231	15,338
Deferred compensation	6,442	6,346
Other liabilities and deferred credits	5,773	1,895
	305,209	328,491
TOTAL LIABILITIES	682,892	642,025
MINORITY INTERESTS	5,059	3,119
STOCKHOLDERS' EQUITY:		
Common stock (Notes 7 and 8)	172,897	161,657
Retained earnings (Note 6)	469,009	401,011
Less common stock in Treasury, at cost	(1,661)	(2,179)
TOTAL STOCKHOLDERS' EQUITY	640,245	560,489
COMMITMENTS, LITIGATION AND CLAIMS (NOTES 12, 13 AND 14)		
TOTAL LIABILITIES AND STOCKHOLDERS' EQUITY	$1,328,196	$1,205,633

EXHIBIT 37-4 NOTES TO THE FINANCIAL STATEMENTS

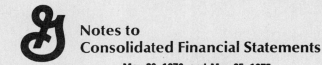

Notes to
Consolidated Financial Statements

May 30, 1976, and May 25, 1975

1. SUMMARY OF SIGNIFICANT ACCOUNTING POLICIES

Significant accounting policies used to prepare the consolidated financial statements are summarized below.

A: CONSOLIDATION

The consolidated financial statements include the following domestic and foreign operations: (1) parent company operations and 100 per cent owned subsidiaries; (2) majority-owned subsidiaries; and (3) General Mills' investment in and share of net earnings or losses of 20-50% owned companies.

All significant intercompany items have been eliminated from the consolidated financial statements.

The fiscal years of foreign operations generally end in April.

B: LAND, BUILDINGS, EQUIPMENT AND DEPRECIATION

Land, buildings and equipment are stated substantially at cost.

Part of the cost of buildings and equipment is charged against earnings each year as depreciation expense. This amount is computed primarily by the straight-line method, which means that equal amounts of depreciation expense are charged against operations each year during the useful life of an item. For tax purposes, accelerated methods of depreciation are used which provide more depreciation expense in the early years than in the later years of the life of the item. The related tax effect for accelerated depreciation is reflected in "Deferred Federal income taxes."

The useful lives employed for computing depreciation on principal classes of buildings and equipment are:

Buildings...........................	20-50 years
Machinery and equipment..........	5-25 years
Office furniture and equipment.....	5-10 years
Transportation equipment..........	3-12 years

General Mills' policy is to charge maintenance, repair and minor renewal expenses to earnings in the year incurred and to charge major improvements to buildings and equipment accounts. When major equipment items are sold or retired, the accounts are relieved of cost and the related accumulated depreciation. Gains and losses on assets sold or retired are credited or charged to results of operations.

C: INVENTORIES

Grain, family flour and bakery flour are valued at market and include adjustments for open cash trades and unfilled orders.

Raw materials, work-in-process and finished goods for a portion of the domestic food inventories, domestic crafts, games and toys inventories and certain other inventories are stated at the lower of cost, determined by the Last-in, First-out (LIFO) method, or market. Other inventories are generally stated at the cost of the most recently purchased materials (FIFO) reduced to market when lower.

D: AMORTIZATION OF INTANGIBLES

The costs of patents and copyrights are amortized evenly over their lives by charges against earnings. Most of these costs were incurred through purchases of businesses.

"Excess of cost over net assets of acquired companies" ("excess cost") is the difference between purchase prices and the values of assets of businesses acquired and accounted for under the purchase method of accounting. Any "excess cost" acquired after October, 1970, is amortized over not more than 40 years. Annually, the Audit Committee of the Board of Directors reviews these intangibles and balances are reduced if values have diminished. Because of low earnings to date and significant organizational changes in the company's travel venture, "excess cost" in the amount of $2,400,000 (both before and after taxes) was charged against earnings

General Mills

Notes to Consolidated Financial Statements (continued)

during the second quarter of fiscal 1976. At its meeting on May 24, 1976, the Board of Directors confirmed that the remaining amounts comprising the "excess cost" have continuing value.

E: RESEARCH AND DEVELOPMENT

All expenditures for research and development are charged against earnings in the year incurred. The charges for fiscal 1976 and 1975 were $25,700,000 and $22,900,000, respectively.

F: RETIREMENT EXPENSE

The company has numerous retirement plans, as described in Note 9. The annual retirement expense for the plans includes both (1) the current year's normal cost, and (2) certain prior-years costs. Prior-year costs include interest on unfunded balances, plus amortization of the unfunded balance over periods of up to 40 years.

The plans use different actuarial methods of estimating these costs. In addition, each plan's assumptions (such as turnover rates or future wage levels) may vary, according to the individual circumstances of the plan. Certain changes were made in these methods and assumptions in both fiscal 1976 and 1975. In addition, some benefit increases were made in both years, and adverse prior years' pension fund investment results were experienced. All of these factors influenced the amount of retirement expense charged to operations in each year, thereby affecting comparability. See Note 9 for additional details.

G: FOREIGN EXCHANGE

Foreign balance sheet accounts are translated into U.S. dollars at exchange rates in effect at fiscal year-end except for such accounts as land, buildings and equipment, accumulated depreciation and intangibles which are translated at exchange rates in effect when the assets were acquired. Income and expense accounts for each month are translated at the month-end exchange rates except for depreciation and amortization which are translated at the exchange rates in effect for the related assets.

Unrealized gains and losses resulting from translation procedures are credited or charged to the results of operations without deferral. The company accrues gains and losses on open forward exchange contracts based on forward contract market rates.

In fiscal 1977, the company will require only minor changes in foreign exchange accounting procedures, to conform to new rules in Standard #8 of the Financial Accounting Standards Board. Prior-year financial statements will not be restated, because the new rules do not have a material effect on such years.

H: INCOME TAXES

Investment tax credit is accounted for by the "flow-through" method; taxes on income are thus reduced by the amount of credit arising during the year.

Deferred income taxes result from timing differences between income for financial reporting purposes and tax purposes. These differences relate principally to depreciation, deferred compensation and discontinued operations.

The company's policy is to accrue appropriate U.S. income taxes on earnings of foreign subsidiary companies which are intended to be remitted to the parent company.

I: EARNINGS PER SHARE

The weighted average number of common shares outstanding and "common share equivalents" are totaled in determining "earnings per common share and common share equivalent." Common share equivalents represent potentially dilutive common shares (weighted average) as follows: (1) shares of common stock reserved for issuance upon exercise of outstanding stock options granted pursuant to company option plans (93,000 in 1976 and 81,782 in 1975); and (2) treasury shares purchased and reserved for issuance under a profit sharing plan (64,398 in 1976 and 64,296 in 1975). See Note 7 for a description of the October, 1975, stock-split, and restatement of fiscal 1975 data previously reported.

Notes to Consolidated Financial Statements (continued)

General Mills

2. ACQUISITIONS

The company made the following significant acquisitions during the past two fiscal years:

Fiscal Year 1976	Ownership	Date Acquired	Product or Major Product Group
Foot-Joy, Inc.	60%	July, 1975	Fashions
Clipper Games	100%	August, 1975	Toys
Saluto Foods Corp.	85%	March, 1976	Mixes, Family Flour, Seafoods & Other
Fiscal Year 1975			
Stevens Court, Inc.	65%	August, 1974	Corporate Unallocated
Bowers and Ruddy Galleries, Inc.	85%	October, 1974	Crafts, Games & Toys
Lord Jeff Knitting Co., Inc.	85%	December, 1974	Fashions
General Interiors	100%	April, 1975	Furniture

All of the above were accounted for by the "purchase" method. Following are the cash and common stock costs of these acquisitions, plus increased ownership in other partially owned companies and performance earnings agreements:

	Fiscal Year	
	1976	1975
Acquisitions—Cash	$2,111,000	$ 379,000
—Shares*	322,534 (a)	1,450,034 (b)
Increased ownership in partially owned companies and performance earnings agreements—Cash	$1,041,000	$3,194,000
—Shares*	13,709	—

*All share data reflect October, 1975, split.

(a) General Mills acquired 60% of the outstanding shares of Foot-Joy, Inc., in exchange for 140,680 shares of common stock and 85% of the outstanding shares of Saluto Foods Corp. for 181,854 shares of common stock. Clipper Games and all outstanding Red Lobster Restaurant franchises were purchased for cash.

(b) General Mills acquired substantially all of the assets and liabilities of General Interiors Corporation in exchange for 999,138 shares of General Mills' common stock. Two additional purchases for common stock were Bowers and Ruddy in exchange for 237,860 shares and Lord Jeff in exchange for 213,036 shares.

Sales, costs and earnings of businesses accounted for as purchases are included in results of operations from the dates of acquisition. In each of fiscal 1976 and 1975, the impact on the company's sales from these acquisitions in the year of acquisition was less than 1% of consolidated sales. Related earnings were not material.

3. FOREIGN OPERATIONS

Included in General Mills' consolidated financial statements are amounts for foreign (non-U.S.) operations, as follows:

	1976	1975
	(in thousands)	
Sales	$433,823	$386,299
Net earnings	14,991	13,462
Total assets	267,409	270,392
Net assets	135,503	131,707

The 1975 amounts have been restated from figures reported last year, in order to conform to the 1976 presentation.

Substantially all investments in 20-50% owned companies included in the consolidated balance sheets and net earnings of 20-50% owned companies included in the consolidated results of operations are for foreign operations. Significant foreign operations are primarily located in Canada and western Europe. Foreign exchange gains and losses were not material in either 1976 or 1975.

General Mills

Notes to Consolidated Financial Statements (continued)

4. INVENTORIES

Following is a comparison of year-end inventories:

	May 30, 1976	May 25, 1975
	(in thousands)	
Grain, family flour and bakery flour..............	$ 38,798	$ 29,442
Raw materials, work in process, finished goods and supplies as follows:		
Valued at LIFO..........	148,112	124,413
Valued primarily at FIFO..	166,744	192,052
Total Inventories.............	$353,654	$345,907

If the FIFO method of inventory accounting had been used throughout by the company, inventories would have been $12,496,000 and $15,884,000 higher than reported at May 30, 1976, and May 25, 1975, respectively. See Note 1 for a description of inventory valuation policies. During fiscal 1976, the domestic inventories of the Gorton Division (a seafoods operation) were changed from FIFO to LIFO. In addition, certain inventories were reduced in 1976, resulting in a liquidation of some LIFO inventory quantities, carried at costs lower than 1976 purchases. Neither of these events had a material effect on earnings.

The amounts of opening and closing inventories as used in determining costs of sales are as follows (in thousands):

May 30, 1976.........................	$353,654
May 25, 1975.........................	345,907
May 26, 1974.........................	353,311

5. SHORT-TERM BORROWINGS

The components of "notes payable" are as follows:

May 30, 1976		May 25, 1975			12-MONTH WEIGHTED AVERAGES		
Balance	Interest Rate	Balance	Interest Rate		Outstanding In Fiscal '76	Average Interest Rates	
						Fiscal '76	Fiscal '75
$22,887,000	11.2%	$32,921,000	11.3%	. . Banks (foreign)........	$21,900,000	13.1%	12.8%
—	—	—	—	. . Commercial paper (U.S.) .	9,700,000	6.6%	10.8%
—	—	20,978,000	5.6%	. . Master Notes (U.S.)....	16,500,000	6.4%	7.8%
1,211,000	5.9%	1,149,000	5.3%	. . Miscellaneous.........	1,300,000	6.5%	9.0%
$24,098,000		$55,048,000		.... Total..............	$49,400,000		

The maximum amount of notes payable outstanding at any month-end during fiscal 1976 was $118,345,000 on August 24, 1975.

The company maintains unsecured domestic credit lines to support its commercial paper, and to ensure the availability of extra funds if needed. At May 30, 1976, the company had $144,500,000 of such domestic lines available, $120,000,000 of which was paid for by fees and $24,500,000 of which was supported by 10% compensating balances (20% if the credit lines are used). The amount of the credit lines and the cost thereof are generally negotiated each year.

General Mills

Notes to Consolidated Financial Statements (continued)

6. LONG-TERM DEBT

	May 30, 1976	May 25, 1975
	(in thousands)	
4⅝% sinking fund debentures, due August 1, 1990	$ 24,695	$ 24,699
8% sinking fund debentures, due February 15, 1999.	98,528	98,465
8⅞% sinking fund debentures, due October 15, 1995.	82,993	99,176
Three 25-year 4¼% promissory notes of $10,000,000 each, due May 1, 1982, May 1, 1983, and May 1, 1984	30,000	30,000
7% sinking fund Eurodollar debentures, due November 1, 1980	12,119	12,377
8% sinking fund Eurodollar debentures, due March 1, 1986	16,040	16,638
Miscellaneous debt.	21,793	27,194
	286,168	308,549
Less amounts due within one year.	4,405	3,637
	$281,763	$304,912

The above amounts are net of unamortized bond discount ($3,180,000 in 1976 and $3,545,000 in 1975).

The sinking fund and principal payments due on long-term debt are $4,405,000, $5,782,000, $9,973,000, $16,924,000 and $18,779,000 in fiscal years ending in 1977, 1978, 1979, 1980 and 1981, respectively.

The terms of the promissory note agreements place restrictions on the payment of dividends, capital stock purchases and redemptions. At May 30, 1976, $289,992,000 of retained earnings was free of such restrictions.

7. CHANGES IN CAPITAL STOCK

The following table describes changes in capital stock from May 26, 1974, to May 30, 1976:

	Common Stock			
	$0.75 Par Value		In Treasury	
(dollars in thousands)	Shares	Value	Shares	Value
Balance at May 26, 1974.	47,301,404	$133,252	171,612	$2,418
Stock option and profit sharing plans	146,832	2,367	(18,768)	(239)
Shares issued—acquisitions	1,450,034	26,017	—	—
Other	1,062	21	—	—
Balance at May 25, 1975.	48,899,332	$161,657	152,844	$2,179
Stock option and profit sharing plans	229,926	3,788	(22,618)	(321)
Shares issued—acquisitions	322,534	7,452	(13,709)	(197)
Balance at May 30, 1976.	49,451,792	$172,897	116,517	$1,661

The shareholders also have authorized 5,000,000 shares of cumulative preference stock, no par value. None of these shares was outstanding during either fiscal 1976 or 1975. If issued, the Directors may specify a dividend rate, convertibility rights, liquidating value and voting rights at the time of issuance.

Notes to Consolidated Financial Statements (continued)

General Mills

Effective as of October 10, 1975, the shareholders voted to (1) increase the authorized common stock from 30,000,000 to 70,000,000 shares; (2) change each share of common stock, $1.50 par value, into two fully-paid and nonassessable shares of common stock, $.75 par value; and (3) eliminate the 1,000,000 shares of class B common stock previously authorized. None of the class B common was outstanding in either fiscal 1976 or 1975. Information throughout these financial statements is retroactively restated for the 2-for-1 split, to present all data on a consistent and comparable basis.

Some of the unissued shares of common stock are reserved for the following purposes:

	Number of Shares	
	May 30, 1976	May 25, 1975
Stock options outstanding......	1,323,306	1,087,298
Stock options available for grant........	714,300	43,916

8. STOCK OPTIONS

In September, 1975, the shareholders of General Mills, Inc., approved a stock option plan under which options for the purchase of 1,200,000 shares, in the aggregate, of the company's common stock may be granted to officers and key employees. The plan expires on August 31, 1980. The options under the 1975 plan may be granted subject to approval of the Compensation Committee of the Board of Directors and at a price of not less than 100% of fair market value on the date the option is granted. Options outstanding include options granted under a previous stock option plan which has expired and under which no further options may be granted. Both plans provide for termination of options at either five or 10 years after date of grant with certain exceptions due to death, disability or retirement. Information on stock options is shown in the following table.

	Shares	Average Per Share		Total Fair Market Value
		Option Price	Fair Market Value	
Granted:				
1975.................................	105,000	$24.60	$24.60	$ 2,583,000 (a)
1976.................................	485,700	30.98	30.98	15,047,000 (a)
Became exercisable:				
1975.................................	250,396	27.81	21.66	5,422,000 (b)
1976.................................	218,667	28.20	29.74	6,504,000 (b)
Exercised:				
1975.................................	146,832	16.12	23.82	3,497,000 (c)
1976.................................	229,926	16.47	29.46	6,774,000 (c)
Expired and cancelled:				
1975.................................	23,096	23.42	23.42	541,000 (a)
1976.................................	19,766	28.88	28.88	571,000 (a)
Outstanding at end of year:				
1975—to 279 officers and employees.....	1,087,298	24.85	24.85	27,015,000 (a)
1976—to 355 officers and employees.....	1,323,306	28.49	28.49	37,704,000 (a)

(a) At date of grant.   (b) At date exercisable.   (c) At date exercised.

Notes to Consolidated Financial Statements (continued)

General Mills

9. RETIREMENT PLANS

The company and many of its subsidiaries have retirement plans covering most of their domestic employees and some foreign employees. In general, the plans provide for normal retirement at age 65 with benefits computed on the basis of length of service and employee earnings. Retirement plans are reviewed and company contributions are approved by the Board of Directors, upon recommendation of the five-member Benefit Finance Committee. Two committee members are General Mills officers. The remaining three are Directors, one of whom is a member of General Mills management.

In both fiscal 1975 and 1976, various plans improved their benefits, and changed certain actuarial methods and assumptions. These changes increased fiscal 1976 costs by $3,100,000 over fiscal 1975 costs. Also, the effect of adverse retirement fund investment performance in prior years caused fiscal 1976 costs to increase by an additional $2,400,000 over fiscal 1975 costs.

By policy, the company funds all retirement costs accrued. The company's policies for accruing costs are described in Note 1. As of the latest available actuarial estimates (December 31, 1975), vested benefits approximated $192,000,000 of which $28,000,000 was unfunded. The total unfunded accrued liability (including the unfunded vested benefits) approximated $41,000,000. The comparable unfunded amounts at December 31, 1974, were $50,000,000 and $67,000,000, respectively. The decrease in unfunded liabilities was caused both by improvement in current year retirement fund investment performance, and by certain actuarial and accounting changes.

Many of the changes in U.S. retirement plans that were required by the Employees Retirement Income Security Act of 1974 (ERISA) have now been implemented. The benefit and actuarial changes described in the above paragraphs were made for reasons other than compliance with ERISA. Remaining changes for compliance with ERISA are not expected to have a material effect on retirement expense.

10. PROFIT SHARING PLANS

General Mills and certain subsidiaries have profit sharing plans covering officers and key employees who have the greatest opportunities to contribute to current earnings and the future success of their operations. The amounts to be distributed under the plans are generally determined by the relationship of net profits to predetermined profit goals. Profit sharing plans and associated payments are approved by the Board of Directors upon recommendation of the Compensation Committee. This committee consists of Directors who are not members of General Mills' management.

11. TAXES ON INCOME

The provision for income taxes is made up of the following:

	Fiscal Year	
	1976	1975
	(in thousands)	
Federal taxes	$85,313	$52,702
Foreign taxes	10,755	9,097
State and local taxes	10,298	6,906
Deferred taxes	(3,376)	4,651
U.S. investment tax credit	(3,026)	(2,706)
Total taxes on income	$99,964	$70,650

Deferred taxes result from timing differences in the recognition of revenue and expense for tax and financial statement purposes. The tax effects of these differences are as follows:

	Fiscal Year	
	1976	1975
	(in thousands)	
Depreciation	$ 393	$ 6,333
Deferred compensation	(139)	(512)
Bad debts	(121)	(231)
Discontinued operations	(2,997)	(37)
Other	(512)	(902)
Total deferred taxes	$(3,376)	$ 4,651

Notes to Consolidated Financial Statements (continued)

General Mills

The effective tax rate is different from the statutory U.S. Federal income tax rate of 48% for the following reasons:

	Fiscal Year	
	1976	1975
U.S. statutory rate..............	48.0%	48.0%
State and local income taxes, net of Federal tax benefits....	2.7	2.4
Investment tax credit..........	(1.5)	(1.9)
Other.......................	.7	—
Effective income tax rate.....	49.9%	48.5%

As of May 30, 1976, management has designated $56,917,000 of the undistributed earnings of foreign subsidiaries as permanently invested. Such earnings have already been taxed once by foreign governments. As a result, no extra U.S. taxes have been accrued on those earnings. However, extra U.S. taxes have been accrued on undistributed foreign earnings in excess of the $56,917,000, because of the policy stated in Note 1. The additional U.S. taxes so accrued were not material in either fiscal 1976 or 1975.

12. LEASE COMMITMENTS

Rent expense was $19,112,000 in fiscal 1976, and $16,523,000 in 1975. The company and its subsidiaries have a variety of noncancellable lease commitments, longer than one year in duration, for which minimum annual net rentals will total approximately $13,002,000 in fiscal 1977; $10,197,000 in 1978; $8,684,000 in 1979; $7,031,000 in 1980; $5,839,000 in 1981; $20,899,000 from 1982 to 1986; $11,015,000 from 1987 to 1991; $7,309,000 from 1992 to 1996; and $2,898,000 in all years after fiscal 1996. 92% of the commitments are for real estate. Certain leases require payment of property taxes, insurance and maintenance costs in addition to the rental payments. The company and its subsidiaries do not have any significant financing leases.

13. OTHER COMMITMENTS

At May 30, 1976, authorized but unexpended appropriations for property additions and improvements were $83,344,000.

In addition, there are options outstanding to purchase the remaining minority interests of some partially-owned companies. The options could have a maximum cost to General Mills of up to $63,000,000. In general, the option contracts provide that payments depend on actual earnings performance up to the exercise date, and would result in return on investment satisfactory to the company. The main option periods run from 1979 to 1986. The majority of such cost could be payable with shares of common stock.

14. LITIGATION AND CLAIMS

In management's opinion, all claims or litigation pending at May 30, 1976, which could have a significant effect on the consolidated financial position of General Mills, Inc., and its subsidiaries have been provided for in the accounts. The FTC complaint described below is discussed because of the significance of the company's cereals business.

In 1972 the Federal Trade Commission (FTC) issued a complaint against General Mills, Kellogg Co., General Foods Corporation and the Quaker Oats Company, alleging that the four companies share an illegal monopoly of the ready-to-eat cereal industry. The FTC seeks relief in the form of divestiture of certain cereal-producing assets, licensing of cereal brands and prohibitions of certain present practices and future acquisitions in the cereal industry. The four

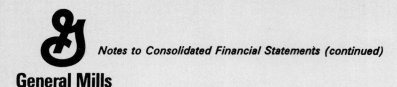

Notes to Consolidated Financial Statements (continued)

General Mills

companies have denied the allegations. An FTC "Administrative Law Judge" started hearing testimony in April, 1976.

The hearing may take over a year to complete. The Judge's findings will then be subject to review by the FTC. Any adverse decision by the FTC will then

be subject to further review in U.S. Federal courts. The company expects the matter to take several years and involve costly litigation. In the opinion of General Mills' General Counsel, the company's ready-to-eat cereal activities do not violate existing anti-trust laws. The company will continue to contest the complaint vigorously.

15. OTHER 1976 CHARGES (CREDIT)

During fiscal 1976, the company recorded the following unusual charges (credit) which were significant in total.

	Amount
Sale of Silna Division in second quarter	$2,100,000
Write-off of a portion of goodwill in travel venture in second quarter (see Note 1-D)	2,400,000
Gain from restructuring German toy operations in second quarter	(2,200,000)
Charges of $750,000 in the second quarter and $2,750,000 in the fourth quarter for converting a protein plant to package foods production	3,500,000
Total net charge (after related income taxes)	$5,800,000

Accountants' Report

PEAT, MARWICK, MITCHELL & CO.
CERTIFIED PUBLIC ACCOUNTANTS
1700 IDS CENTER
MINNEAPOLIS, MINNESOTA 55402

The Stockholders and the Board of Directors   July 23, 1976
General Mills, Inc.:

We have examined the consolidated balance sheets of General Mills, Inc. and subsidiaries as of May 30, 1976 and May 25, 1975 and the related consolidated statements of results of operations, earnings employed in the business and changes in financial position for the fiscal years then ended. Our examination was made in accordance with generally accepted auditing standards, and accordingly included such tests of the accounting records and such other auditing procedures as we considered necessary in the circumstances.

In our opinion, the aforementioned consolidated financial statements present fairly the financial position of General Mills, Inc. and subsidiaries at May 30, 1976 and May 25, 1975 and the results of their operations and the changes in their financial position for the fiscal years then ended, in conformity with generally accepted accounting principles applied on a consistent basis.

Peat, Marwick, Mitchell & Co.

EXHIBIT 37-6   THE TEN-YEAR SUMMARY

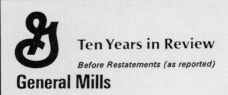

Ten Years in Review
Before Restatements (as reported)

General Mills

GENERAL MILLS, INC., AND SUBSIDIARIES

	May 30, 1976	May 25, 1975	May 26, 1974
Sales...	$ 2,645.0	2,308.9	2,000.1
Earnings before extraordinary items..	$ 100.5	76.2	75.1
Net earnings...	$ 100.5	76.2	75.1
Dividends—common stock...	$ 32.4	27.8	24.4
—preference stock	$ —	—	—
Earnings before extraordinary items and after dividends.....................	$ 68.1	48.4	50.7
Per common share and common share equivalent*			
Earnings before extraordinary items.................................	$ 2.04	1.59	1.59
Net earnings...	$ 2.04	1.59	1.59
Dividends per share*...	$ .66	.58½	.53
Common shares outstanding at year-end*................................	49,335	48,745	47,130
Preference shares outstanding at year-end..............................	—	—	—
Number of stockholders..	29,200	28,800	28,500
Market price range—common stock*...................................	$34⅛-23⅜	27¾-14⅛	33¼-23¼
—preference stock	$ —	—	107¼-85
Total assets..	$ 1,328	1,206	1,117

*Adjusted for two-for-one splits in October, 1975, and August, 1967.

dollar amounts, except per share, in millions and shares outstanding in thousands

Fiscal Year Ended

May 27, 1973	May 28, 1972	May 30, 1971	May 31, 1970	May 25, 1969	May 26, 1968	May 28, 1967
1,593.2	1,316.3	1,120.1	1,021.7	885.2	668.9	602.5
65.6	52.2	43.9	40.6	36.2	31.3	28.4
65.6	45.4	43.9	27.1	37.5	31.3	28.4
20.9	19.1	17.3	16.4	13.9	12.3	11.4
2.1	2.3	2.5	2.6	2.7	2.8	2.4
42.6	30.8	24.1	21.6	19.6	16.2	14.6
1.40	1.17	.99	.94	.89	.83	.79
1.40	1.02	.99	.63	.92	.83	.79
.50	.48	.45	.44	.40	.39⅜	.37½
42,530	40,396	39,220	37,904	35,544	32,048	30,536
1,145	1,250	1,426	1,487	1,560	1,573	1,623
29,600	31,000	32,600	32,900	32,900	30,000	29,300
33¾-24¼	26⅛-16¾	18⅛-12⅜	19⅝-11¾	21¾-15¾	21⅜-15	18⅜-13½
113-82¾	88-57	61½-42	65½-41	71½-54½	71¼-55⅝	61½-48
906	818	750	666	622	505	367

THE SPECIAL PROBLEM OF CHANGING PRICES

> ### OBJECTIVE

Unit 37 briefly mentioned reporting accounting information when the measuring unit, or dollar, changes in value. The objectives of this unit are to describe two basic kinds of price changes and to show you how the effects of these price changes on a company can be reported to decision makers.

> ### APPROACH TO ATTAINING THE OBJECTIVE

As you study about the effects of price changes, pay special attention to these four questions, which the text following answers:

- *What are specific price changes, and what are price-level changes?*
- *How are changes in the price level measured?*
- *What is the effect of a changing price level on a business firm?*
- *How can the effects of changing price levels be reported?*

CHANGES IN SPECIFIC PRICES

- *What are specific price changes, and what are price-level changes?*

The term **specific price change** refers to a change in the price for an individual good or service within the economy. For example, a raw material may have cost a firm $1 per pound last month. This month, the price may be $1.02 per pound. This change is known as a *specific* price change. Such specific price changes are important to a firm because the firm's profitability is directly related to the specific prices it pays for the goods and services it uses. Likewise, the specific prices at which the firm sells its goods and services determine the amount of revenue the firm receives. Naturally, this affects earnings.

CHANGES IN THE PRICE LEVEL

In contrast to specific price changes, there also can be changes in the *general level of prices* in the economy—**changes in the price level.** When the average prices of all goods and services in the economy tend to change, then a change in the price level occurs. For example, if prices of goods and services tend to be higher, in general, this month than they were last month, then there has been a change in the price level.

An upward change in the price level is commonly known as **inflation.** Inflation refers not to an increase in the price of a specific good or service, but rather to a *general* increase in prices. Another way of describing inflation, or a general increase in prices, is to say that *the value of the dollar has declined.* This means that each dollar will purchase *less* in terms of goods and services this period than last period.

A downward change in the general price level is referred to as **deflation.** Under circumstances of deflation, the value of the dollar is said to *increase.* Thus, the **dollar's purchasing power** increases in a time of deflation.

PRICE INDEXES

- *How are changes in the price level measured?*

It is impossible to record every individual change in the prices of goods and services in the entire economy during a period of time. Therefore, some measure is needed to estimate changes in the general price level. This is done through the construction of **price indexes.** A price index is a summary measure of the general level of prices which takes into account the changes of all the prices, but is computed on a sampling basis. The federal government regularly constructs several indexes of prices. These include:

1. The *gross national product Implicit Price Deflator.*
2. The *Consumer Price Index.*
3. The *Wholesale Price Index.*

The **gross national product Implicit Price Deflator** is an index which takes into account the prices of *all* goods and services in the economy. The **Consumer Price Index** measures price changes in goods and services ordinarily purchased by a family unit. The **Wholesale Price Index** measures changes in the prices of goods purchased by organizations on a wholesale basis for use in their production processes. Of these three indexes, the first is generally considered the best measure of general price levels; it is the one used to assess the effect of changing prices on the value of the dollar.

The following table presents the gross national product Implicit Price Deflator index for the past several years. This index is expressed in terms of the price level of 1972. This means that 1972 is taken as the base year and is given the index value of 100.

GROSS NATIONAL PRODUCT
IMPLICIT PRICE DEFLATOR
1972 = 100

YEAR	INDEX	YEAR	INDEX
1967	79.02	1972	100.00
1968	82.57	1973	105.92
1969	86.72	1974	116.20
1970	91.36	1975	127.18
1971	96.02	1976	133.88

Source: U.S. Department of Commerce, Bureau of Economic Analysis.

To help you understand the relationships shown by this price index, several questons, along with comments and explanations, are presented below.

1. What percentage did prices *increase* from 1975 to 1976?
    Answer: 5.3% increase.

$$\text{Percent change} = \frac{\text{Change in price index}}{\text{Price index at beginning}}$$

$$= \frac{133.88 - 127.18}{127.18}$$

$$= \frac{6.7}{127.18}$$

$$= 5.3\%$$

2. What percentage did prices *increase* from 1969 to 1975?
    Answer: 46.7% increase.

$$\text{Percent change} = \frac{127.18 - 86.72}{86.72}$$

$$= \frac{40.46}{86.72}$$

$$= 46.7\%$$

The preceding two questions emphasize the changes in the general level of prices. The same questions can be reworded to emphasize the *value of the dollar.*

1. What percentage did the value of the dollar (purchasing power of the dollar) *decrease* from 1975 to 1976? First, we know that as the general price level increases, the value of the dollar decreases. Therefore, there is an arithmetical relationship between the price level and the value of the dollar. This relationship is:

$$\text{Index of the value of the dollar} = \frac{100}{\text{Price level index}} \times 100$$

Using this conversion formula, the index of the value of the dollar for 1976 is:

$$\text{1976 index for the value of the dollar} = \frac{100}{133.88} \times 100$$

$$\text{1976 index for the value of the dollar} = 74.7$$

The index of the purchasing power of the dollar for the years 1967 through 1976, shown in the table below, can be computed by using the same formula.

INDEX OF THE PURCHASING
POWER OF THE DOLLAR
1972 = 100

YEAR	INDEX	YEAR	INDEX
1967	126.6	1972	100.0
1968	121.1	1973	94.4
1969	115.3	1974	86.1
1970	109.5	1975	78.6
1971	104.1	1976	74.7

Let us return now to our question: What percentage did the purchasing power of the dollar *decline* from 1975 to 1976?
    Answer: 5.0% decline.

$$\text{Percent change} = \frac{\text{Change in index}}{\text{Index at beginning}}$$

$$= \frac{78.6 - 74.7}{78.6}$$

$$= \frac{3.9}{78.6}$$

$$= 5.0\% \text{ decline}$$

2. What percentage did the purchasing power of the dollar decline from 1969 to 1975?

Answer: 31.8% decline.

$$\text{Percent change} = \frac{115.3 - 78.6}{115.3}$$

$$= \frac{36.7}{115.3}$$

$$= 31.8\% \text{ decline}$$

In summary, two concepts are fundamental to understanding the effects of changes in the general price level and the use of price indexes. These are:

1. A general price-level index, such as the gross national product Implicit Price Deflator, measures changes in prices on the average, not changes in specific prices.
2. An index of the purchasing power of the dollar is mathematically related to the price-level index. For example, when the price-level index increases, the purchasing power index decreases.

These indexes can be used to help interpret and explain the effects of changing prices on financial statements.

When price levels change (when the purchasing power of the dollar changes), there are three basic areas of direct concern to the management of a company. These are:

- *What is the effect of a changing price level on a business firm?*

1. The effect of price-level changes on money-type assets.
2. The effect of price-level changes on all other assets.
3. The effect of price-level changes on liabilities.

In the following sections we will explore each of these areas in detail.

THE EFFECT OF PRICE-LEVEL CHANGES ON MONEY-TYPE ASSETS

Money-type (or **monetary**) **assets** include Cash, Accounts receivable, Notes receivable, and Investment in bonds. Monetary assets are all those resources whose dollar amount remains fixed (usually by agreement) during their entire life. There is no change in their dollar value in the way that the value of a building or a tract of land might change in value. *During periods of inflation (increasing price levels) a business firm loses purchasing power if it owns monetary assets.*

This example will illustrate this point. Assume that a firm has $10,000 cash on hand and holds this cash for a year (from 1975 to 1976). The price index was 127.18 in 1975 and increased to 133.88 in 1976. The loss in purchasing power as a result of holding this monetary asset is computed as follows:

$$\begin{array}{c} \text{Loss in purchasing} \\ \text{power through} \\ \text{holding monetary} \\ \text{assets} \end{array} = \begin{array}{c} \text{Monetary assets at beginning} \\ \text{of period (1975), expressed} \\ \text{in terms of end-of-period} \\ \text{purchasing power (1976)} \end{array} - \begin{array}{c} \text{Monetary assets} \\ \text{at end of period} \end{array}$$

$$= \left(\frac{133.88}{127.18} \times \$10{,}000 \right) - \$10{,}000$$

$$= (1.0527 \times \$10{,}000) - \$10{,}000$$

$$= \$10{,}527 - \$10{,}000$$

$$= \$527$$

Here is further explanation of this calculation. The firm still has $10,000 cash on hand at the end of the time period (assume 1976 to be the present time). The $10,000 is expressed in terms of today's purchasing power. That same $10,000, however, had *more purchasing power* in 1975 than in 1976, because there has been inflation and the value of the dollar has declined. The first part of the formula above computes how much 1975's $10,000 would buy in terms of today's (1976) dollars. Dividing the 1975 index into the 1976 index shows that 1976 prices are 105.27% of the 1975 prices. In 1976, therefore, the firm must have $10,527 in order to buy the same thing that $10,000 would have bought in 1975. Since the firm has only $10,000, there has been a purchasing power loss of $527.

Similarly, if there is *deflation* during a period, then there is a *gain* from holding monetary assets.

THE EFFECT OF PRICE-LEVEL CHANGES ON ALL OTHER ASSETS All other assets (nonmonetary assets) are not affected by inflation in the same way as monetary assets are. An example will illustrate. Assume that a company purchased land in 1967 for $100,000 cash. The future value of the land depends on the *specific* price for that land—it is not affected by the *general* price level in the way that monetary assets are. Assume that the present time is 1976. These questions can be answered:

1. What is the value of the land today (1976)? The answer to this question depends on what buyers are willing to pay for the land if it is sold in 1976. Assume that the answer is $150,000. This specific price is not related to the *general* level of prices; therefore, a general price index is not useful here.

2. What would the company have to pay for the land in 1976 if it were to sacrifice the same purchasing power in dollars to buy the land as it

did in 1967? This is another way of asking what the cost of the land is in terms of 1976 dollars.

$$\begin{aligned}\text{Cost of the land} \atop \text{in terms of 1976 dollars} &= \frac{\text{1976 price index}}{\text{1967 price index}} \times \text{1967 Cost}\\[6pt] &= \frac{133.88}{79.02} \times \$100,000\\[6pt] &= 1.69425 \times \$100,000\\[6pt] &= \$169,425\end{aligned}$$

We can conclude that for every dollar spent in 1967, $1.69425 must be spent in 1976 to make the same sacrifice of purchasing power. The company can sell the land today for $150,000, so therefore the specific price of the land has increased less than the general level of prices.

In summary, when a firm holds nonmonetary assets, it does not gain or lose because of inflation or deflation. Instead, any gain or loss on these assets depends on the specific price changes of the asset, or perhaps on the specific use that the firm makes of the asset (such as using it up in the business).

THE EFFECT OF PRICE-LEVEL CHANGES ON LIABILITIES

A firm can *gain* purchasing power by owing liabilities during a period of inflation. In contrast, a firm can *lose* purchasing power by owing liabilities during a period of deflation. Assume that a company owed $100,000 in bonds payable for several years. The purchasing power gain from owing the bonds from 1975 to 1976 can be computed as follows:

$$\begin{aligned}\text{Purchasing power} \atop \text{gain from owing} \atop \text{bonds payable} \atop \text{from 1975 to 1976} &= \left(\frac{\text{1976 price index}}{\text{1975 price index}} \times \text{Liabilities owed during period}\right) - \text{Liabilities owed at end of period}\\[6pt] &= \left(\frac{133.88}{127.18} \times \$100,000\right) - \$100,000\\[6pt] &= (1.05268 \times \$100,000) - \$100,000\\[6pt] &= \$105,268 - \$100,000\\[6pt] &= \$5,268\end{aligned}$$

The firm gains $5,268 in purchasing power because the liabilities are monetary in nature and there has been inflation. In 1975 the company owed $100,000, which represented $105,268 of today's (1976) purchasing power. Only $100,000 is owed at 1976, so there has been a gain in purchasing power for the company.

**REPORTING THE
EFFECTS OF
PRICE-LEVEL
CHANGES**

■ *How can the effects
of changing price
levels be reported?*

To review, these are the effects on a firm when there is a general change in the price level:

1. During periods of inflation,
   a. Owning monetary assets causes a loss in purchasing power.
   b. Owing liabilities causes a gain in purchasing power.
   c. Owning nonmonetary assets has no effect on purchasing power.
2. During periods of deflation,
   a. Owning monetary assets causes a gain in purchasing power.
   b. Owing liabilities causes a loss in purchasing power.
   c. Owning nonmonetary assets has no effect on purchasing power.

The users of financial statements often want to know just how the firm has been affected by changes in the general price level. A set of financial statements can be prepared to reveal the precise effect on the firm. Such financial statements, which express the dollar amounts in terms of the current dollar value at the balance sheet date, are sometimes prepared as supplementary statements in the annual report. The AICPA has recommended use of such statements in addition to regular financial statements. Although only a minority of firms report such information regularly, it is expected that this useful information will become more and more commonly available. The exhibit on pages 674–675 shows financial information of Shell Oil Company that is adjusted for general price-level changes. Examine these statements carefully. Notice also that the report of the independent certified public accountants accompanies the information.

❯ NEW TERMS

Consumer Price Index A price-level index that takes into account the prices of goods and services ordinarily purchased by a family unit. [p. 667]

deflation The situation when the general level of prices has decreased. [p. 667]

gnp Implicit Price Deflator A price-level index that takes into account the prices of *all* goods and services in the economy. [p. 667]

inflation The situation when the general level of prices has increased. [p. 667]

monetary assets Assets whose value is fixed in money terms; this includes Cash, Accounts receivable, Notes receivable, Investment in bonds; a firm loses purchas-

ing power when it holds monetary assets during periods of inflation. [p. 667]

price index A measure of the general level of prices. [p. 667]

price-level change A shift in the general price structure within the economy when all the prices of goods and services are considered; that is, during a period of time, there has been a shift when price increases are more significant in total than price decreases (or vice versa). [p. 667]

purchasing power of the dollar Value of the dollar; the purchasing power of the dollar decreases during periods of inflation and increases during periods of deflation. [p. 667]

Supplementary Price Level Adjusted Financial Information

The high rate of inflation in recent years has materially changed the purchasing power of the dollar and caused serious distortions in the traditional measurements of income and wealth. Financial statements prepared under generally accepted accounting principles report the actual number of dollars received or expended without regard to changes in the purchasing power of the currency. Investments made over extended periods of time are added together as though the dollars involved were common units of measurement. Amortization of these prior period costs is deducted from current period revenues in calculations of net income. Since the dollar's value has changed materially, this change must be considered for a proper assessment of economic progress.

Individual business enterprises are affected differently by inflation. Holders of monetary assets, such as cash or receivables, lose purchasing power during inflationary periods since these assets will purchase fewer goods and services in time. Conversely, holders of liabilities benefit during such periods because less purchasing power will be required to satisfy their obligations. Rates of return and other financial ratios are also influenced greatly by the age of the investments and subsequent changes in the value of the dollar. For example, a capital asset acquired in 1965 for $1 is restated to $1.74 in terms of 1975 dollars for each year shown in the supplementary information, and depreciation is similarly restated. The charts below summarize the effect of inflation on Shell Oil Company during the past 10 years. As indicated, the profitability ratios are substantially lower when both income and investments are expressed in a common unit of measurement. A portion of the profits reported during this period therefore has not been a true economic gain. This is illustrated in the 1975 provision for depreciation, depletion, etc., which amounted to $597 million on the basis of the asset's original cost. However, if the cost of these assets is restated to a common unit of measurement, the current purchasing power of the dollar, the appropriate depreciation expense would be $739 million.

Long-Term Debt as a Percent of Total Capital

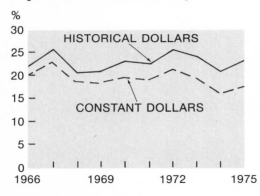

Net Income as a Percent of Total Capital

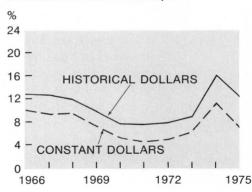

Explanatory Note

The accompanying supplementary price level adjusted financial information, expressed in terms of December 31, 1975 dollars, is based on the historical dollar financial information. Both the supplementary and historical financial information presented here should be read in conjuncton with the notes and other financial statement information in the Annual Report. The supplementary price level information reflects adjustments only for changes that have occurred in the general purchasing power of the dollar as measured by the Gross National Product Implicit Price Deflator. The amounts shown, therefore, do not purport to represent appraised value, replacement cost, or any other measure of the current value of assets. The Accounting Principles Board Statement No. 3 and a Proposed Statement of Financial Accounting Standards, which give general guidance on how to prepare and present price level financial statements, reflect deferred income taxes as non-monetary items. But for purposes of Shell's general price level restatement, such balances were classified as monetary items because Shell believes that when reversals of such tax differences take place, they give rise immediately to taxable income and to additional taxes payable in current dollars at that time. Had Shell followed the non-monetary treatment for deferred income taxes, restated net income would have been reduced by approximately 4 percent or less and restated shareholders' equity would have been reduced by about 2 percent or less in each of the last four years.

HISTORICAL DOLLARS	(Millions of dollars except per share amounts)	DOLLARS OF CURRENT PURCHASING POWER*			
1975		**1975**	**1974**	**1973**	**1972**
	Summary Statement of Income				
$8,224	Revenues	$8,414	$8,562	$6,037	$5,296
	Costs and expenses:				
597	Depreciation, depletion, etc.	739	696	667	623
706	Income, and operating taxes	723	533	315	282
	Interest & discount amortization				
71	on indebtedness	73	67	74	77
6,335	Other costs and expenses	6,493	6,722	4,709	4,113
	Income before purchasing power gain				
515	or loss on monetary items	386	544	272	201
	Purchasing power gain (loss) on:				
—	Long-term debt	68	124	88	39
—	Other monetary items	(16)	(5)	(5)	2
$ 515	Net income	$ 438	$ 663	$ 355	$ 242
	Summary Balance Sheet				
$2,475	Current assets	$2,593	$2,300	$2,078	$2,049
104	Investment & long-term receivables	123	138	117	113
4,389	Properties, plant & equipment (net)	5,828	5,476	5,221	5,238
43	Deferred charges	50	45	65	72
1,530	Current liabilities	1,530	1,354	1,167	1,185
1,202	Long-term debt	1,202	1,039	1,191	1,309
367	Deferred credits-federal income taxes	367	341	361	374
$3,192	Shareholders' equity	$5,495	$5,225	$4,762	$4,604
	Per Share Data†				
$ 7.59	Net income	$ 6.46	$ 9.84	$ 5.27	$ 3.60
$ 2.60	Cash dividends	$ 2.65	$ 2.72	$ 2.94	$ 3.10
	Ratios (see definitions on page 32)				
14.5%	Net income to shareholders' equity	8.4%	13.9%	7.7%	5.3%
12.2%	Net income to total capital	7.6%	11.7%	6.6%	5.0%
6.3%	Net income to revenues	5.2%	7.7%	5.9%	4.6%
34.2%	Dividends to net income	41.1%	27.7%	55.7%	86.1%
23.5%	Long-term debt to total capital	17.9%	16.6%	20.0%	22.1%

*Based on purchasing power dollars at December 31, 1975.
†Per weighted average share outstanding each year.

REPORT OF INDEPENDENT ACCOUNTANTS

To the Board of Directors and Shareholders of Shell Oil Company:

We have examined the financial statements of Shell Oil Company appearing in the Annual Reports to Shareholders for the years 1975, 1974, 1973 and 1972, which are covered by our reports dated February 4, 1976 and February 4, 1974. Those financial statements do not reflect the changes in the general purchasing power of the U.S. dollar from the time transactions took place. We have also examined the supplementary information for the years 1975, 1974, 1973 and 1972 restated for effects of changes in the general price level as described in the Explanatory Note on page 2. In our opinion, the supplementary Summary Statement of Income, Summary Balance Sheet and Per Share Data shown above present fairly the historical financial information restated in terms of the general purchasing power of the U.S. dollar at December 31, 1975 in accordance with guidelines, consistently applied, recommended in Accounting Principles Board Statement No. 3 and a Proposed Statement of Financial Accounting Standards, except for the treatment, with which we concur, of deferred income taxes as monetary items.

1200 Milam Street   **Price Waterhouse & Co.**
Houston, Texas 77002
February 4, 1976

The information in this exhibit appeared in the *Shell Oil Company 1975 Statistical Supplement* to the company's 1975 annual report.

specific price changes Changes in the price of an individual good or service in the economy. [p. 667]

Wholesale Price Index A price-level index that takes into account the prices of goods purchased by organizations on a wholesale basis for use in their production processes. [p. 668]

➤ ASSIGNMENT MATERIAL

QUESTIONS

Q38-1. What is meant by a specific price change?

Q38-2. What is meant by a price-level change?

Q38-3. Contrast inflation and deflation.

Q38-4. Contrast the gross national product Implicit Price Deflator and the Consumer Price Index.

Q38-5. What is the relationship of a purchasing power index to a price-level index?

EXERCISES

E38-1. a. Briefly describe the effect of price-level changes on money-type assets owned by a firm.

b. Briefly describe the effect of price-level changes on all other assets owned by a firm.

c. Briefly describe the effect of price-level changes on liabilities owned by a firm.

E38-2. Assume that at January 1, 19—, the gnp Implicit Price Deflator stood at 125 and that at December 31, 19—, it stood at 135. The following assets and equities were owned or owed during the entire period: Cash, $100,000; Accounts receivable, $40,000; Notes receivable, $30,000; Prepaid expenses, $10,000; Land and buildings, $150,000; Bonds payable, $112,000. Identify and compute all gains and losses in purchasing power.

E38-3. Assume that at January 1, 1978, the general price index stood at 104.44 and at December 31, 1978, it stood at 135.55. The following assets and equities were owned or owed during the entire period: Cash, $50,000; Accounts receivable, $36,500; Notes receivable, $24,300; Land, $49,600; Bonds payable, $125,000.

a. Compute the net loss from owning monetary assets.

b. Compute the net gain from owing the bonds.

c. Compute the total change in purchasing power.

E38-4. Matching.

_____ 1. the situation when the general level of prices has decreased

_____ 2. the situation when the general level of prices has increased

_____ 3. a measure of the general level of prices

_____ 4. value of the dollar which decreases during periods of inflation and increases during periods of deflation

_____ 5. a price-level index that takes into account the prices of goods purchased by organizations for use in their production processes

_____ 6. changes in the price of an individual good or service in the economy

A. Consumer Price Index
B. deflation
C. gnp Implicit Price Deflator
D. inflation
E. monetary assets
F. price index
G. price-level change
H. purchasing power of the dollar
I. specific price changes
J. Wholesale Price Index
K. non-monetary assets

_____ 7. a price-level index that takes into account the prices of goods and services ordinarily purchased by a family unit

_____ 8. assets whose value is fixed in money terms

_____ 9. a shift in the general price structure within the economy when all the prices of goods and services are considered

_____ 10. a price-level index that takes into account the prices of all goods and services in the economy

PROBLEMS (GROUP A)

P38-1. *Working with price indexes.* Using the two tables in this unit, answer these questions:

a. What percent did prices increase from 1967 to 1968?

b. What percent did the purchasing power of the dollar decrease from 1968 to 1971?

c. Assume a firm had Accounts receivable amounting to $1,000 from 1969 to 1970. During that period, was there a gain or loss of purchasing power? By how much?

d. Assume that a firm had liabilities totaling $10,000 from 1969 to 1970. During that period, was there a gain or loss of purchasing power? By how much?

e. What percent did prices increase from 1971 to 1976?

f. What percent did prices increase from 1971 to 1974?

g. What percent did the value of the dollar decrease from 1971 to 1976?

h. What percent did the value of the dollar decrease from 1971 to 1974?

P38-2. *Price change concepts.* Answer the following questions.

a. Assume that a firm has $50,000 cash on hand for 1 year (from 1972 to 1973). Compute the change in purchasing power experienced by the firm by holding the $50,000 cash for the year. Is the change a gain or loss?

b. A company purchased a manufacturing plant and land in 1968 for $100,000 cash. What would the company have to pay for the manufacturing plant and land in 1974 if it were to sacrifice the same purchasing power in dollars as it did in 1968?

c. Assume that a company owed $50,000 in bonds payable and other long-term liabilities for several years. Compute the change in purchasing power from 1971 to 1974 as a result of having owed the liabilities during that period of time. Is the change a gain or loss?

d. During 1973, the price of wheat increased substantially per bushel. Does this fact mean that there was inflation during 1973? Explain.

e. Assume that the gross national product Implicit Price Deflator stood at 149 on December 31, 19—. At that time what was the amount of the index for the value of the dollar?

f. Assume that at January 1, 19—, the general price index stood at 123.14 and at December 31, 19—, it stood at 131.15. The following assets and equities were owned or owed during the entire period: Cash, $40,000; Bonds payable, $90,000; Land, $70,000; Accounts receivable, $10,000.

(1) Compute the net loss from owning monetary assets.

(2) Compute the net gain from owing the bonds.

(3) Compute the total change in purchasing power.

*P38-3. *Financial-statement data conversions.* The president of Speedy Industries was requested by the board of directors to determine the effect of the recent inflation on the financial statements of the company. You have been working with him in determining the effect. Some of the information you have discovered follows.

1. The Price Index for selected periods stood at these levels:

19x4	108.1	July 19x8	121.5
19x6	113.1	August 19x8	121.9
February 19x8	119.0	September 19x8	122.2
March 19x8	119.5	October 19x8	122.9
April 19x8	119.9	November 19x8	123.4
May 19x8	120.3	December 19x8	123.7
June 19x8	120.9	January 19x9	124.1
		February 19x9	124.6

2. Equipment was purchased in 19x6 for $100,000. Depreciation expense on the equipment for the year ended December 31, 19x8, was $20,000. The accumulated depreciation account at December 31, 19x8, stood at $45,000.
3. The inventory turnover for the company is six times per year. The cost of the ending inventory (Fifo) is $10,000 (December 31, 19x8).

REQUIRED: Answer these questions:

a. What percent did prices increase from 19x6 to February 19x9?
b. How much did the equipment cost in terms of the purchasing power of the dollar in December 19x8?
c. How much was the depreciation expense in terms of December 19x8 dollars? Is this the cost of using the asset?
d. What information is needed to make a complete analysis of the effects of changing prices (specific and general prices) on the fixed assets?
e. During which months was the ending inventory purchased?
f. What was the effect of inflation on the inventory?
g. What information is needed to make a complete analysis of the effects of changing prices (specific and general prices) on the inventory?

PROBLEMS (GROUP B)

P38-4. *Financial-statement data conversions.* Selected data about plant and equipment and inventories of Inflay Co. follows:

EQUIPMENT ON HAND 12–31–76

TYPE	DATE PURCHASED	COST	ACCUMULATED DEPRECIATION
Manufacturing equipment	1970	$368,000	$150,000
Store equipment	1975	113,000	15,000
Office equipment	1973	86,000	12,000
		$567,000	$177,000

INVENTORIES ON HAND 12-31-76

TYPE	INVENTORY TURNOVER	COST
Group A	12x	$96,425
Group B	2x	11,400
Group C	4x	3,650
Group D	3x	1,955

Assumed price indexes are as follows:

12-31-76	135.20
December, 1976 average	135.07
July through December, 1976 average	129.00
October through December, 1976 average	132.40
September through December, 1976 average	130.04
1970	96.12
1973	104.15
1975	118.30

REQUIRED:

a. What percent did prices increase from 1970 to 1975?

b. What would it cost to replace the manufacturing equipment on December 31, 1976, assuming the same purchasing power sacrifice were to be made to buy the equipment?

c. The depreciation expense for 1976 on the manufacturing equipment amounted to $27,000. Compute this depreciation expense in terms of 12-31-76 dollars.

d. What would it *actually* cost to replace the store equipment on December 31, 1976? Explain.

e. Assuming the FIFO method, during what period was each of the inventory groups purchased?

f. Compute the cost of the four inventory groups in terms of current dollars (12-31-76).

P38-5. *Price-change concepts.* Using the tables in the unit, make computations.

a. What percent did the value of the dollar decrease from 1972 to 1975?

b. What percent did prices increase from 1968 to 1969?

c. What percent did the value of the dollar decrease from 1972 to 1976?

d. What percent did the purchasing power of the dollar decrease from 1969 to 1972?

e. What percent did prices increase from 1972 to 1975?

f. Assume that a company had Accounts receivable amounting to $3,000 from 1970 to 1971. During that period, was there a gain or a loss of purchasing power? By how much?

g. What percent did prices increase from 1972 to 1976?

h. Assume that a firm had liabilities totaling $25,000 from 1970 to 1971. During that period, was there a gain or a loss of purchasing power? By how much?

P38-6. *Price-change concepts.* Make computations as required.

a. At January 1, 19-1, the general price-level index stood at 125.14 and at December 31, 19-1, it stood at 132.43. The following assets and equities were owned or owed during the entire period: Cash, $63,400; Bonds payable, $214,000; Accounts receivable, $13,000; Land, $53,000. Compute (1) the net loss from owning monetary assets, (2) the net gain from owing the bonds, (3) the total change in purchasing power.

b. The gnp Implicit price deflator was as follows:

19–1   123.65
19–2   126.17
19–3   131.87

For each of the three years, compute the index for the value of the dollar.

c. The price of steel has dropped dramatically during the last 8 months. Does this indicate a situation of deflation? Explain.

d. In 1974, a company bought land that cost $124,318. Today (1976) it could buy the same land for $127,000. What amount would the company have to pay for the land today (1976), if it made the same sacrifice in purchasing power to buy the land as it did in 1974? Has the general level of prices changed in the same proportions as has the specific price of the land?

e. A firm held monetary assets totaling $347,000 during a 2-year period. The liabilities owed during that period averaged about $400,000. The index of prices increased from 133.0 to 145.8 during the 2-year period. What is the effect of inflation on the purchasing power of the company?

f. Food prices have consistently increased during the last year. Which index would measure the magnitude of this price change best: the gnp Implicit Price Deflator or the Consumer Price Index? Does an increase in the Consumer Price Index mean that there is inflation? Under what circumstances might the Consumer Price Index increase and yet there would be no inflation?

CUMULATIVE REVIEW PROBLEMS

P38-7. *Cumulative review problem (Objective and Fill-in)*
Multiple choice.

1. A printed report containing data about a firm's operations and financial condition is called
   a. Notes to financial statements.
   b. An annual report.
   c. A budget.
   d. Footnotes.

2. Guidelines for the independent audit and for the reporting of information are called
   a. Financial accounting standards.
   b. Annual reports.
   c. Budgets.
   d. Auditing standards.

3. The letter or report to the stockholders to be included in the annual report is prepared by
   a. The Chairman of the Board of Directors.
   b. The controller.
   c. The treasurer.
   d. The secretary.

4. Information included in any annual report which lets the decision maker analyze trends for a fairly long period of the firm's history is the

a. Annual report.
b. Financial statement.
c. Wall Street Journal.
d. Ten-year summary.

5. The conventions, rules, and procedures necessary to define accepted accounting practice at a particular time are called
a. Auditing standards.
b. Budgets.
c. Annual reports.
d. Generally accepted accounting principles.

6. A fundamental concept underlying financial accounting is that business firms are assumed to operate indefinitely rather than for a limited period of time. This concept is called
a. Going concern.
b. Periodicity.
c. Materiality.
d. Conservatism.

7. A fundamental concept which refers to the fact that accounting information, by its very nature, involves reporting activities according to relatively short periods of time is called
a. Materiality.
b. Periodicity.
c. Conservatism.
d. Going concern.

8. One concept holds that if there is a reasonable choice between two methods or approaches to reporting an item, the method which produces the smaller net earnings or the smaller asset value should be chosen. This concept is called
a. Materiality.
b. Conservatism.
c. Periodicity.
d. Going concern.

9. The concept which states that generally accepted accounting principles must be applied in the same manner from period to period is called
a. Materiality.
b. Going concern.
c. Consistency.
d. Conservatism.

10. The concept that the dollar amount of an item in relation to another item should govern the reporting practice in certain circumstances is called
a. Materiality.
b. Going concern.
c. Consistency.
d. Conservatism.

11. The situation when the general level of prices has decreased is called
a. Specific price changes.
b. Inflation.
c. Price-level change.
d. Deflation.

12. A measure of the general level of prices is called
a. Inflation.
b. Gnp Implicit Price Deflator.

    c. Price index.

    d. Wholesale Price Index.

13. A price-level index that takes into account the prices of goods purchased by organizations on a wholesale basis for use in their production processes is called

    a. Consumer Price Index.

    b. Gnp Implicit Price Deflator.

    c. Wholesale Price Index

    d. Price index.

14. Assets whose value is fixed in money terms are called

    a. Current assets.

    b. Monetary assets.

    c. Long-term assets.

    d. Nonmonetary assets.

15. A shift in the general price structure within the economy when all the prices of goods and services are considered is called

    a. Price-level change.

    b. Specific price change.

    c. Price index.

    d. Inflation.

16. The effect on net income in the early years of asset life of the use of the double-declining balance method of depreciation as compared to the straight-line method would be

    a. An increase.

    b. A decrease.

    c. No effect.

    d. A depreciation expense increase but no effect on net income.

Fill in the blanks.

17. The conventions, rules, and procedures necessary to define accepted accounting practice at a particular time are called _____

_____.

18. The independent body that is now responsible for developing rules of reporting practice in accounting is the _____

_____.

19. A fundamental concept that deals with the input of a financial accounting system is the _____

20. A fundamental concept underlying financial accounting is that business firms are assumed to operate indefinitely rather than for a limited period of time. This concept is called _____.

21. A fundamental concept which refers to the fact that accounting information, by its very nature, involves reporting activities according to relatively short periods of time is called _____.

22. One problem which arises because the dollar is used as the measuring unit is the fact that _____

_____.

23. Information collected by management about economic events (transactions) which can be verified is called _____ .

24. One accounting concept holds that if there is a reasonable choice between two methods or approaches to reporting an item, the method which produces the immediate smaller net earnings or the smaller asset value should be chosen.

    This concept is called _____ .

25. The concept which states that generally accepted accounting principles must be applied in the same manner from period to period is called _____ .

26. The concept that the dollar amount of an item in relation to another item should govern the reporting practice in certain circumstances is called _____ .

P38-8. *Cumulative review problem*

Part A
Accelerated depreciation (declining-balance and sum-of-the-years'-digits methods) has become exceedingly popular in the last few years for financial reporting as well as for tax calculation. State what possible impact this change in reporting practices could have on decisions made by
1. Investors
2. Labor unions
3. Creditors

Part B
On January 1, 1978, the Sagebiel Company purchased a delivery truck for $14,000. The truck is expected to have a useful life of 10 years with a salvage value of $2,000. The controller of the firm is trying to decide which depreciation method to use for the truck. A preliminary calculation indicates that earnings for the company, before deducting depreciation and before deducting income taxes, amount to $85,000. The company's income tax rate is 40%.
1. Compute the depreciation expense for 1978, assuming the straight-line method is used.
2. Compute the depreciation expense for 1978, assuming the double-declining balance method is used.
3. Prepare comparative analyses of the net earnings in the following form:

	STRAIGHT-LINE METHOD	DOUBLE-DECLINING-BALANCE METHOD
Earnings before depreciation and income taxes		
Less Depreciation expense	_____	_____
Earnings before income taxes		
Less income taxes (40%)	_____	_____
Net earnings for year	========	========

Part C

To test your ability to reason in the area of financial accounting, indicate your recommendations for reporting these special situations on the financial statements of a company:

1. A large quantity of merchandise is being shipped to the firm. It is on a train somewhere between the supplier and the company at the date of the balance sheet. The merchandise will cost $100,000.
2. The firm has agreed to purchase $2 million of goods and raw materials from Ace Supply Company during the next 2 years. No purchases have been made as of the balance sheet date.
3. A lawsuit is in process at the balance sheet date. Management figures that there is a 60% chance that the firm will lose the suit, thereby having to pay another company $200,000 in damages for patent infringement.
4. A strike is about to be called by the labor union.
5. The firm decided to discontinue all its insurance coverage. The management believes that the company is large enough and strong enough to bear its own risks.

PART FIVE
MANAGEMENT
ACCOUNTING
FUNDAMENTALS

chapter 17

objectives and methods in management accounting

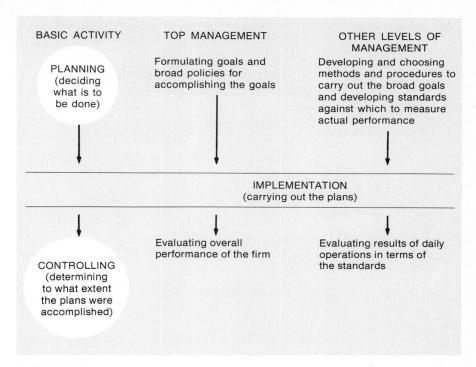

BASIC ACTIVITY	TOP MANAGEMENT	OTHER LEVELS OF MANAGEMENT
PLANNING (deciding what is to be done)	Formulating goals and broad policies for accomplishing the goals	Developing and choosing methods and procedures to carry out the broad goals and developing standards against which to measure actual performance

IMPLEMENTATION
(carrying out the plans)

	Evaluating overall performance of the firm	Evaluating results of daily operations in terms of the standards
CONTROLLING (determining to what extent the plans were accomplished)		

ILLUSTRATION 39-2

Other levels of management deal essentially with day-to-day operations of the company. These managers work within the framework of the broad policies and goals. They identify and develop alternative ways to accomplish the goals. For example, a department head in a factory is responsible for planning the activities of his department and making decisions about the best way to accomplish the departmental goals.

As part of the planning process, managers must develop *standards* against which the performance can be measured. A standard can be described as a plan, an expected outcome of some action, a goal, or an objective. Developing these standards is extremely important if the company is to determine if its goals are being attained, and if the day-to-day operations are to be guided and improved. Standards can be expressed in terms of costs, revenues, or other bases, such as hours or number of units of goods produced or sold.

Control *Control is determining to what extent the plans and goals of the firm have been accomplished.* Management is just as concerned with the control process as it is with planning. Actually, the two functions are so closely tied together that they must be considered overlapping. They are certainly interrelated. A key to understanding the relationship of planning and control is the standard. The standard, the gauge against which actual performance is measured, is formulated as part of planning. Then, upon actual performance, the standard is compared to the operations of the company. The evaluation that is made is called control.

Planning and control do not take place in simple chronological order. Instead, management is continuously involved in planning; management continuously revises its plans, seeks other ways to accomplish its goals, develops new standards of performance, and solves new problems. In addition, management is continually controlling—relating the actual happenings (actual performance) to the standards and goals that have been set. *The element that helps make possible this interaction, this continuous planning and control exchange, is the flow of management accounting information.*

Management accounting information In previous chapters you have learned the basic characteristics of the *financial* accounting system of a company. This system records and reports the business transactions, the actual economic events that are the major concern of individuals *outside* the business firm. Much of this financial accounting information also helps top management evaluate the results of the company's operations. These summary financial statements, however, do not provide the detailed information necessary for daily planning and control and for solving the special problems of running a business corporation. The management accounting information system that is required is outlined in Illustration 39-3.

As you review the description in Illustration 39-3, remember that the summary information—the summary budgets, the summary reports of actual operations, and the summary performance reports—is prepared monthly, quarterly, or annually. In contrast, the detailed reports must be prepared very frequently (daily in many cases) if management is to receive information which truly leads to changing plans and correcting undesirable actions. In the following chapters you will learn how the management accounting information described in the chart is generated and how it is used in the management of a business enterprise.

| PERFORMANCE REPORTS | A **performance report** is a management accounting statement that compares actual operations to a standard or budgeted goal. An example is the detailed daily performance report shown in Illustration 39-4. In this example, a foreman is in charge of five workers (painters), who are expected to paint 25 products per hour. There are many kinds of performance reports, but the important characteristic of this kind of report is that actual performance is compared to a standard. Management then takes corrective action based upon significant deviations from standard. Management's use of these significant deviations from standard as spurs for taking action is known as **management by the exception.** |

■ *What are performance reports?*

MANAGEMENT ACCOUNTING INFORMATION SYSTEM

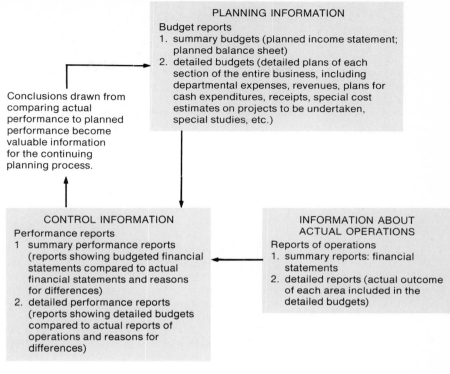

PLANNING INFORMATION

Budget reports
1. summary budgets (planned income statement; planned balance sheet)
2. detailed budgets (detailed plans of each section of the entire business, including departmental expenses, revenues, plans for cash expenditures, receipts, special cost estimates on projects to be undertaken, special studies, etc.)

Conclusions drawn from comparing actual performance to planned performance become valuable information for the continuing planning process.

CONTROL INFORMATION

Performance reports
1 summary performance reports (reports showing budgeted financial statements compared to actual financial statements and reasons for differences)
2. detailed performance reports (reports showing detailed budgets compared to actual reports of operations and reasons for differences)

INFORMATION ABOUT ACTUAL OPERATIONS

Reports of operations
1. summary reports: financial statements
2. detailed reports (actual outcome of each area included in the detailed budgets)

ILLUSTRATION 39-3

Illustration 39-5 shows a performance report in terms of revenues and expenses. When management sees that earnings for the week for Department 16 are $700 under the standard, they will take action to investigate and correct whatever is causing the deviation.

THE CONCEPT OF ORGANIZATION

- *Why is the concept of organization important to management?*

The organizing function of management is closely related to the planning and controlling functions. **Organizing** *deals with converting plans and objectives into action and desired results.* In the organizing process, management must acquire resources to carry out the objectives of the company. These resources include the various assets you have already studied—those appearing on the balance sheet. In addition to these resources, *human resources* become a vital part of management's plans. Each resource, human and other, must be given a special relationship to all other resources in carrying out the firm's plans. This set of activities can be described as *organizing*. Organizing is therefore management's process of acquiring human and other resources and setting up special relationships among the resources in order to reach the firm's goals.

DAILY LABOR PERFORMANCE REPORT

Date: Wednesday, June 19, 1978   Department: Painting

Foreman: A. M. Jones

Employee	(1) Hours Worked	(2) Standard per Hour	(3) Standard Production	(4) Actual Production	(5) Efficiency Rating
Abbott, A. B.	8.0	25	200	218	109.0
Barker, L. M.	4.0	25	100	123	123.0
Sims, J. B.	12.0	25	300	275	91.6
Tomson, L. L.	7.0	20*	140	135	96.4
Wilson, A. A.	8.5	25	212	207	97.7
Department Rating			952	958	100.6

Comments and Evaluation

*Trainee, Tomson, allowed reduced standard (20) during first week of work.

Column (1) = actual hours worked   (3) = (1) × (2)
        (2) = standard determined for painting department   (4) = actual units painted
                                                             (5) = (4) ÷ (3)

ILLUSTRATION 39-4

ILLUSTRATION 39-5

DEPARTMENTAL PERFORMANCE REPORT

Period: For week ending July 19, 1978   Department: 16

	Standard	Actual	Over (or under) standard	Explanation
Revenues	$20,000	$19,000	($1,000)	
Cost of goods sold	15,000	14,600	(400)	
Operating expenses	2,000	2,100	100	
Total expenses	$17,000	$16,700	($ 300)	
Earnings	$ 3,000	$ 2,300	($ 700)	

When the management of a company decides to assign, or allocate, a certain amount of resources to plant and equipment, this action deals with organizing resources. Further, and vitally important, when management decides to set up two or more departments with department supervisors, this also deals with organizing resources—human resources. The remainder of this unit will describe the organizational relationships often used in manufacturing corporations. Knowing these relationships will help you to understand the role of the management accounting system and the use of management accounting information.

LINE AND STAFF AUTHORITY

In studying relationships among people in an organization, the concepts of line authority and staff authority are useful. **Line authority,** in the organizational process, usually refers to authority exerted downward from a superior to a subordinate. For example, the Production Superintendent in some manufacturing companies is the direct superior over a group of department heads in a factory. Line authority exists in the relationship of the Production Superintendent to a department head. The Production Superintendent has line authority to command the department head, rather than simply to advise him.

Staff authority refers to the authority in a relationship to advise. For example, the Quality Inspector in a manufacturing plant often advises the department heads regarding the quality of the products they are producing. This staff authority might not carry the authority to command action. Of course, in actual practice there are variations of these two basic relationships to meet the needs of special circumstances in companies.

ORGANIZATION OF A MANUFACTURING CORPORATION

The organization chart presented as Illustration 39-6 shows one of the many ways that companies can be organized. The following comments on the manufacturing, sales, finance, and personnel areas should apply to most manufacturing firms, however, since every firm must provide for administration of these key areas.

- *How is a manufacturing corporation usually organized?*

Organization for manufacturing operations The key function of manufacturing in an enterprise usually is headed by a top officer, often called the vice-president of manufacturing or the vice-president of production. It is his job to oversee and manage all activities in the corporation dealing with the conversion of raw materials, labor, and other efforts (expenses) into the finished product or finished goods. Usually departments are set up in the factory, with

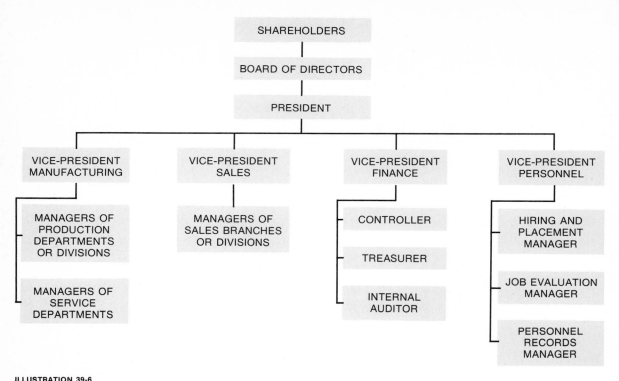

ILLUSTRATION 39-6

a manager heading each department. The production departments of a factory might include the following for one kind of manufacturing:

> Lathing Department.
> Sanding Department.
> Painting Department.
> Assembly Department I.
> Assembly Department II.

By organizing the production activities into departments, each with a department head, the costs of operating each department can be controlled more effectively. A major area of study in managerial accounting is called *cost accounting;* it deals with accumulating and reporting the costs of production on a department-by-department basis.

The vice-president of manufacturing also usually controls the service departments, each with a department head. These service departments (serving the production area) might include:

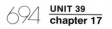

Receiving and Warehousing Department.

Purchasing Department.

Maintenance Department.

Inspection Department.

Factory Food Service Department.

Like the costs of the production departments, the costs of the service departments can be accumulated and controlled on an individual department basis.

Organization for sales operations The sales function is sometimes referred to as the marketing function. It involves determining the demand for the goods and services of the firm, selling the goods, advertising, customer relations, and similar activities. The top manager of this area is usually called the vice-president of sales or the vice-president of marketing. Some firms are organized according to divisions, and each division has a sales manager. These divisions might be set up according to geographical areas or according to groups of products.

Organization for financial operations The organization chart in Illustration 39-6 shows three major areas of responsibility for the vice-president of finance. He has line authority over the controller, the treasurer, and the internal auditor. The first area, the accounting area, is headed by the controller or chief accounting officer. The next major section of this unit explains the activities of the controller.

The treasurer is responsible for most of the financial decisions of the corporation. He evaluates alternative ways of raising capital; he is in charge of the company's banking operations; he negotiates loans for the firm; and he handles the company's investments and insurance.

The internal auditor and his staff investigate and evaluate in a systematic manner the functioning of the accounting system. Internal auditors study the accounting records and control procedures and make recommendations for changing the system where appropriate. In addition, the internal auditor helps in the management process by determining to what extent the policies and requirements of management are being carried out. It is generally recommended that the internal auditor report directly to some executive in the firm higher than the controller, so that he will be independent enough in his job to freely criticize and evaluate the systems of accounting and control that are designed and operated by the controller. In many companies, however, the internal auditor does report to the controller.

Organization for personnel operations A major problem large corporations have is to attract and hold their human resources, their employees. Often a vice-president of personnel is in charge of three major areas: (1) recruiting and placing new employees, (2) evaluating jobs within the firm (developing descriptions of jobs to aid in the recruitment and placement process), and (3) keeping personnel records.

In addition to the four vice-presidents shown in Illustration 39-6 firms might add others, such as a vice-president for research and development whose job is to oversee the development of new products and to oversee the research activities of the company.

ORGANIZATION OF THE ACCOUNTING OPERATIONS

Illustration 39-7 shows the organization for accounting which a corporation might use. The financial accounting section of the controller's office is responsible for recording all business transactions, operating the accounting records, and preparing financial statements. In many companies this section issues quarterly reports of operations to the firm's stockholders. Usually there is a separate payroll department in charge of the accumulation of information

ILLUSTRATION 39-7

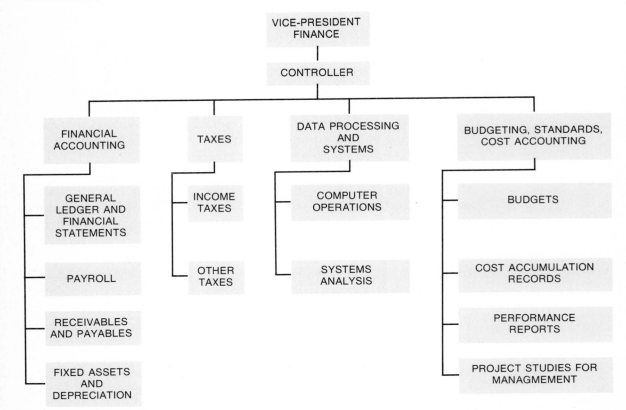

about the hours worked by all employees, the calculation of pay, the calculation of payroll deductions, and the keeping of all related records.

■ *How are the accounting operations of a corporation usually organized?*

Subsidiary records for receivables, payables, and billing are kept by one or more separate departments. Detailed records also must be maintained for the fixed assets of the company, and depreciation must be calculated periodically. A major problem of management is to assure that fixed assets, once they are acquired, are accounted for and are physically controlled and protected from loss. Some firms have thousands of fixed assets, all of which must be controlled.

The taxes department of a large corporation is often headed by a certified public accountant or an attorney who is an expert in the field of taxation. Two primary jobs of this department are:

1. The preparation of annual tax returns for the corporation.
2. Making detailed studies for management to determine the tax consequences of certain decisions (such as disposing of one of the plants and relocating in another area).

Because most large corporations use electronic computers to process the vast quantities of data needed for decisions and for communications, technical experts in the computer and systems area must be employed to design and operate the system. Systems analysts work with all other areas in the firm in designing an information processing and reporting system that will meet the needs of the decision makers at every level.

On the organization chart, the areas of budgeting, standards, and cost accounting are shown together. In practice, it is common to find them separated into two or more departments. Cost accounting involves the record-keeping system to accumulate the costs of operating the factory and related areas. Costs are usually computed and analyzed on a unit basis (average cost per unit of finished product) as well as on a departmental basis in the manufacturing process. The actual costs are compared regularly to budgets and standards, and performance records are issued to various levels of management.

Also, often within the same organizational area, certain special studies are made for management. For example, management might be thinking of buying an automatic machine to replace a semiautomatic one. A special study would be needed to determine the consequences of making the change. Other special studies must be made from time to time, and the organizational structure must accommodate such studies.

In summary, management accounting plays an extremely important role in the attainment of the firm's goals. How the firm is organized for promoting maximum benefits from the accounting operations is also important. Management accounting serves every level of management and acts as a communications link among the various areas in the firm. As a review, remember that management accounting involves these three main functions:

1. Data selection and record keeping.
2. Analysis of data.
3. Preparation of reports for management use.

> **NEW TERMS**

control The management activity concerned with determining to what extent the plans and goals of the firm have been accomplished. [p. 688]

line authority Authority exerted downward from a superior to a subordinate; the authority to command. [p. 693]

management by the exception The use by management of significant variances or deviations from standard performance as guides for taking corrective action. [p. 690]

organizing A function of management which deals with converting plans and objectives into action and desired results. [p. 691]

performance reports A management accounting statement or report that compares the actual performance of some phase of a firm's operations to the expected performance according to a standard or budget. [p. 690]

planning The management activity concerned with deciding what is to be accomplished by the organization and deciding how it is to be accomplished. [p. 688]

staff authority The authority in a relationship to advise. [p. 693]

> **ASSIGNMENT MATERIAL**

QUESTIONS

Q39-1. What are the three functions that management accounting is said to involve?

Q39-2. Explain how planning on a top management level differs from planning on the lower management levels.

Q39-3. Explain how control on a top management level differs from control on the lower management levels.

Q39-4. What is a standard?

Q39-5. What is management by the exception?

Q39-6. How is control information used in the continuous planning process? Refer to Illustration 39-3 in preparing your answer to this question.

Q39-7. Explain how the self-tests that appear at the end of each chapter in some textbooks are similar in purpose to a management accounting performance report. Be specific.

Q39-8. Define the following terms:
   a. Organizing.
   b. Line authority.
   c. Staff authority.
   d. Internal auditor.

Q39-9. Contrast production departments and service departments in a manufacturing operation.

Q39-10. List the various activities for which a controller is responsible.

Q39-11. List the various activities for which a treasurer is responsible.

Q39-12. To whom is it recommended that the internal auditor report? Why?

EXERCISES

E39-1. The packing department of Henry Kreebe, Inc., has fourteen workers. At the present time, the foreman receives only a weekly report that includes the following information: (1) number of units packed by each employee during the week, and (2) number of complaints received from customers during the preceding week for each employee's packing (a number is assigned each package to identify the packer). The foreman believes that a daily report would allow him to control the packing activities more effectively. Do you agree? Draw up a daily report that would meet the specific needs of the foreman's department. Would the complaints become part of a daily report, or would these be reported less frequently?

E39-2. A basic characteristic of performance reports is that they must contain two elements: (1) the standard of performance, and (2) actual performance. Briefly describe how performance reporting could apply to:
  a. Control of gallons of paint used in a painting department.
  b. Control of labor in the painting department of a firm.
  c. Control of number of pieces of mail sorted by a post office mail sorter employee.
  d. Control of the cost of magazine ads for a product that could be purchased by answering the magazine ad. Assume that the product is advertised and offered for sale through sixteen different magazines.

E39-3. The manager of the Blahh Cafe is concerned with the quantity of French bread that is purchased each week. He believes that almost *twice* the amount of French bread is being served than should be. He asks you to make a special study of the French bread costs, and he explains that French bread is used only for lunches numbered 1, 2, 3, and 6 on the menu. For sandwiches, regular bread is served, and this does not seem to be a problem. Make a list of the important considerations associated with your special study. If you were to prepare a special-purpose performance report for the "French bread control problem," what would be included on the report and what would be the source of the information? What broader implications does such a performance report have for possible applications to other costs?

E39-4. Complete the following statements.
  a. Organization is the management process of acquiring and providing special relationships among. . .
  b. Line authority is. . .
  c. Staff authority is. . .
  d. The negotiation of loans is usually the responsibility of the. . .
  e. The operation and supervision of the accounting activities of a firm is usually the responsibility of the. . .
  f. The organizing function of management is closely interrelated to the . . . function and the . . . function.

PROBLEMS (GROUP A)

P39-1. *Daily labor performance report.* Walton Manufacturing Company uses a daily labor performance report similar to the one illustrated in this unit. On July 13, 1978, the four employees in the lathing department worked as follows: Albert Allison, 8.0 hours; Herbert Madiz, 7.2 hours; Hennesey Ortiz, 4.0 hours; Jubilant Wyziski, 9.1 hours.

Each employee is expected to produce 34 units of product per hour according to the departmental standard. The foreman of this department, Wilbur Adamant, has been concerned because of the consistent malfunction of one of the machines used by Madiz. Some slowdown in production is expected for Madiz. Actual production for the employees is: Albert Allison, 283 units; Herbert Madiz, 200 units; Hennesey Ortiz, 139 units; Jubilant Wyziski, 350 units.

REQUIRED: Prepare a daily labor performance report similar to the one illustrated in the text.

P39-2. *Organizing a firm.* Richard Linens recently began a business which involves selling food and beverages at a local stadium during ball games. Linens plans to hire twenty employees, with about ten of them selling soft drinks and about ten of them selling hot dogs and other foods throughout the stadium. Also, there will be three other employees to assist Linens in the management of the business.

REQUIRED:

a. Draw up an organization chart for the business as you envision the operations.
b. Draw up an alternative organization chart for the business, that is, a second way that the business could be organized.
c. Comment on the reasons for differences in the two charts you have drawn.
d. Explain why the organization of a firm is so important in attaining goals.

*P39-3. *Performance report.* The Sanding Department of Axco Industries has five employees. The standard used to evaluate the employees operating the sanding machines is 50 units per hour. The only exception to this is the standard for new employees of 40 units per hour. After three weeks of experience, the standard for new employees increases to 50 units.

On December 16, 1978, the employees worked as follows:

	HOURS WORKED	ACTUAL UNITS PRODUCED
Harry Wiles	8.0 hours	410
Billy Greer	4.0 hours	190
Susan Scott	12.0 hours	620
[a] Bernice Willis	7.0 hours	275
Ken Graham	8.5 hours	430

[a] New employee.

REQUIRED:

a. In good form, prepare a daily labor performance report for the Sanding Department.
b. Assume that the average wage rate for new employees is $6 per hour and the wage for experienced employees is $8 per hour.
   (1) For each employee that performed below standard for the day, compute the approximate cost in labor to the company as a result of that employee's being below a rating of 100.0.
   (2) For each employee that performed better than standard for the day, compute the approximate labor cost savings made by that employee.

P39-4. *Daily materials performance report.* The Blipping Department of Voltaire Corporation uses one basic raw material in the manufacture of a product. Three gallons of this raw material is required to manufacture each unit of finished product. The department head, Julian Jones, has three workers who are involved with converting the raw material to the finished product. The three workers produced the following products on January 18, 1978: P. Daniel produced 34 products and used 118 gallons of raw material; A. Winto produced 37 products and used 100 gallons of raw material; L. Homberg produced 20 products and used 59 gallons of raw material.

REQUIRED:

a. Prepare a daily materials performance report for the Blipping Department using the following column headings:
   (1) Employee.
   (2) Number of finished products produced.
   (3) Number of gallons of raw materials allowed to be used according to the standard (3 gallons per unit).
   (4) Actual gallons of raw materials used.
   (5) Efficiency rating.
b. Explain how the efficiency rating should be computed.
c. Comment on any possible problems that could be brought about by one of the employees having an efficiency rating that is "too good."

P39-5. *Organization chart.* Choose a retail organization with which you are familiar, such as a retail grocery supermarket. Prepare an organization chart to describe the relationships in the firm. Comment on each basic organizational division of the company and indicate why you believe the management organized in the particular way they did.

P39-6. *Organization concepts*

a. Refer to Illustration 39-6. Which positions on the organization chart would probably have responsibility for making the following decisions and performing the following activities?
   (1) Preparing the income statement.
   (2) Evaluating the information system of the firm.
   (3) Borrowing money.
   (4) Preparing the payroll.
   (5) Developing an advertising campaign for the company.
   (6) Keeping records regarding sick leave of employees.
   (7) Training factory workers.
b. Draw an organization chart for a company, Wintergreen Manufacturing Company, that has the following managerial positions:

President	Financial Manager
Personnel Manager	Production Manager
Personnel Records Supervisor	Assembly Department Head
Sales Manager	Packing Department Head
Salesman I	Warehousing Department Head
Salesman II	Cashier
Salesman III	Accountant
Job Evaluation Supervisor	

TOOLS IN MANAGEMENT ACCOUNTING; COST CONCEPTS

> **OBJECTIVE**

The objective of this unit is to introduce you to four basic tools in management accounting. These four tools are ideas and techniques that are keys to your effectively studying and working in the field of management accounting.

> **APPROACH TO ATTAINING THE OBJECTIVE**

As you study the four basic tools that will help you to understand and use management accounting information, pay special attention to these four questions, which the text following answers:

- *How can management accounting information be structured to make it most useful?*
- *What is the function of cost classification in management accounting?*
- *How can fundamental relationships in management accounting be expressed in an equation?*
- *How can fundamental relationships in management accounting be expressed in graph form?*

■ *How can management
accounting information
be structured to make
it most useful?*

All management accounting information serves a firm in its decision-making processes and as a communication link. Because all management decisions are made to attain some goal or objective, the information provided to managers by the accounting system must be designed to help them reach their goals. This first tool, therefore, involves the recognition that management accounting information can and should be structured in terms of comparing actual events or performance with some standard, budget, or objective. When the accountant or manager masters this tool, this key idea, he recognizes that the decision process must somehow take on this structure of evaluating information against a standard before a decision can be made. Obviously, data are useless without a standard to compare them against. This tool is therefore the ability of the analyst, whether he be an accountant or a manager, to structure accounting information in terms of comparing relevant information for the decision to relevant standards or objectives for the decision.

As an example, assume that the foreman of a production department in a factory wants to control the cost of the raw materials used in the products manufactured in his department. These steps might be taken to set up a system of management accounting information reporting to control the daily usage of raw materials in his department:

1. Determine how much raw material should be used for each of the products manufactured in the department. Assume that company engineers, outside advisors, and experience in the plant indicate that three pounds of the raw material should be used for each finished product. This three pounds per product becomes the *standard,* against which performance can be measured.

2. Determine how much raw material was actually used for each of the products manufactured in the department for a period of time. This requires some kind of a record-keeping system to determine (1) how many pounds of raw material were used during the period, and (2) how many finished products were manufactured in the department during the period.

3. Design a performance report that lets the foreman evaluate the actual material usage against the material that should have been used to produce the finished goods.

In this example, assume that 200 finished products were manufactured during a particular day. Further, assume that the standard number of pounds to be used for each finished product is three. At the end of the day, the records show that 636 pounds of raw material was used to make the 200 finished products. The performance report shown at the top of the next page formally gathers and arranges these data in a usable form. Note particularly the comparison of actual information to a standard; the distance between the two is called a **variance.** The production department foreman would now have relevant information to help him make further decisions about how to control the use of raw material in his department.

PERFORMANCE REPORT
Department A
January 14, 1978

Standard usage of raw material	
(200 finished units × 3 pounds)	600 pounds
Actual usage of raw material	636 pounds
Unfavorable usage variance of raw material	36 pounds
Cost per pound of raw material	$ 7
Unfavorable cost variance for day	$252

Comments: 12 pounds was spilled and damaged by an inexperienced worker, which accounts for $84 of the cost variance.

In summary, an important tool in management accounting is the ability to design and arrange information so that it is useful in the decision-making process. This arrangement or structure takes into consideration the comparison of actual information to a standard.

In developing standards and objectives in a business organization, the standards must be set at every level—from the lower-level operating departments to the higher levels of the organization. This must be done if overall performance is to be evaluated and if the major goals are to be attained. These many lower-level subgoals must be designed so that the overall goals of the firm and top management are promoted. This idea that all the firm's subgoals must work together toward one central set of objectives is referred to as **goal congruence.**

Here is an example to illustrate goal congruence. Assume that a firm's salesmen are paid only a 3% commission on the total sales they make. The subgoal of the sales force then would tend to be to maximize sales. But it may be important for company goals for the salesmen to perform other functions in addition to selling the product—general promotion work, making contacts for other areas of the firm, doing market research to establish customer trends, and so on. The subgoals for the sales force probably should be revised to interact more effectively with the overall company goals. If the salesmen are paid *only* on the basis of their sales, they might tend to resist performing *nonsales* activities.

TOOL 2: CLASSIFYING COSTS

A second tool is the ability to classify costs. Because an important activity of management is the control of the total and many individual costs of operating a firm, the classification technique becomes especially valuable. Costs are

classified because such categorizing helps to reveal relationships among the cost data that are useful in planning and control.

■ *What is the function of cost classification in management accounting?*

One very important scheme for classifying a firm's costs is the fixed-cost and variable-cost classification. *A* **fixed cost** *is any cost that tends to remain the same total dollar amount at any level of production.* For example, assume that a company incurred $10,000 of insurance costs on a factory during a year. During the same year the firm produced 50,000 units of product in the factory. The firm could have produced 40,000, 50,000, or 60,000 units of product and the insurance expense would still have been $10,000. The insurance cost therefore is an example of a fixed cost—one that remains the same total dollar amount no matter what changes in the production level occur.

Some **costs vary**—they tend to change in total as total production changes. Assume that during one year a firm incurred raw materials costs of $10,000 and produced 5,000 units of product. The average cost of raw materials for each unit of finished product was $2. What would have happened if the firm produced 15,000 units of product instead of 5,000? How much would the raw materials cost have been? It probably would have been about $30,000, instead of the $10,000. Because production tripled (from 5,000 units to 15,000 units), the total cost of raw materials probably would triple also (from $10,000 to $30,000). Such *costs that tend to change as the level of production changes are referred to as variable costs.*

Some costs tend to behave in neither a completely fixed nor a completely variable manner. An example would be the cost of foremen's salaries in a factory. As production increases in a factory, additional foremen would be hired, but not precisely in the initial foreman-to-production ratio. The following table illustrates the partially variable, partially fixed cost of foremen's salaries.

LEVEL OF PRODUCTION (NUMBER OF FINISHED UNITS PRODUCED)	NUMBER OF FOREMEN NEEDED	SALARY PER FOREMAN	TOTAL FOREMEN SALARY COST
1,000	2	$12,000	$24,000
2,000	2	12,000	24,000
3,000	3	12,000	36,000
4,000	3	12,000	36,000
5,000	3	12,000	36,000
6,000	4	12,000	48,000
7,000	4	12,000	48,000

There are many other useful cost classification schemes, including (1) classifying costs according to manufacturing, sales, and finance; and (2) classifying costs according to average costs per unit and total costs.

A third useful tool is the ability to express cost and other management accounting information in equation form. The equation form is very useful for presenting, analyzing, and predicting accounting information, as we shall see in the following discussion of fixed and variable costs.

Equation for a fixed cost It is relatively easy to express a fixed cost in equation form. For example, where the symbol a represents fixed cost,

■ How can fundamental
relationships in
management accounting
be expressed in an
equation?

$$\text{Total fixed cost in the classification} = a$$

If we substitute a specific fixed cost in this equation (e.g., a $10,000 total insurance cost), we get this straightforward equation:

$$\text{Total insurance cost} = \$10{,}000$$

Remember that a fixed cost is a constant amount and does not change as production levels change.

Equation for a variable cost A variable cost does change with production levels. It can be expressed in equation form as follows:

$$\text{Total variable cost in the classification} = \text{Variable cost per unit of production} \times \text{Number of units of production}$$

If we let b equal the cost per unit of production and x equal the number of units of production, then we have this general equation for total variable cost:

$$\text{Total variable cost} = b \times x \qquad \text{or} \qquad bx$$

Let's consider an example involving materials cost. If we know that a factory produced 5,000 units of finished product (x) at a cost per unit of $2 ($b$), what is the total materials cost? Using our equation, we find the answer by substituting these values:

$$\text{Total materials cost} = \$2 \times 5{,}000 \text{ units}$$

$$\text{Total materials cost} = \$10{,}000$$

By using the same formula, we can estimate that if 18,000 units of product are manufactured, the total materials cost would be $36,000. This illustrates how the equation for a variable cost can be useful in predicting costs of a firm when production levels are expected to change.

Fixed and variable costs in the same equation A new example will illustrate how both fixed costs and variable costs can be built into the same equation:

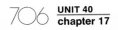

FOR OPERATING AN ENTIRE FACTORY, IT IS ESTIMATED THAT IF THE LEVEL OF PRODUCTION IS:	THEN THE TOTAL FIXED COSTS WILL AMOUNT TO	AND THE TOTAL VARIABLE COSTS WILL AMOUNT TO:
2,000 units	$6,000	$ 8,000
4,000 units	6,000	16,000
6,000 units	6,000	24,000

From these data we want to develop a general equation for the total cost of factory operation at any level of production. Such an equation would be a great help to management if they have to decide whether or not to decrease or expand production at this factory.

First, we know that the total factory costs can be expressed as follows:

Total factory costs = Total fixed costs + Total variable costs

This also can be stated in abbreviated form by substituting the equations for fixed costs and variable costs that we developed above:

$$\text{Total factory costs} = a + bx$$

From the table above we know that fixed costs are $6,000 for any level of production. And from our previous discussion we know that total variable costs are equal to the variable cost per unit of production (b) multiplied by the number of units of production (x). By dividing $8,000 by 2,000 units, or $16,000 by 4,000 units, or $24,000 by 6,000 units, we get the variable cost per unit of production, or $4 per unit. Therefore,

$$\text{Total factory costs} = \$6,000 + \$4x$$

This equation can be used to estimate the total costs of the factory at any level of production. For example, if management wanted to operate the factory at a production level of 5,500 units, what would the total costs be?

$$
\begin{aligned}
\text{Total factory costs} &= a + bx \\
&= \$6,000 + \$4x \\
&= \$6,000 + (\$4 \times 5,500) \\
&= \$6,000 + \$22,000 \\
&= \$28,000
\end{aligned}
$$

TOOL 4: EXPRESSING INFORMATION IN GRAPH FORM

A fourth useful tool is the ability to express costs and other management accounting information in another form that lends itself to analysis—the graph form. Illustration 40-1 presents the information given in the preceding example about factory costs. The graph shows the costs on the vertical axis (vertical scale). This vertical scale is sometimes referred to as the **y axis**. The costs on the graph begin at zero and go as high as $50,000. The horizontal

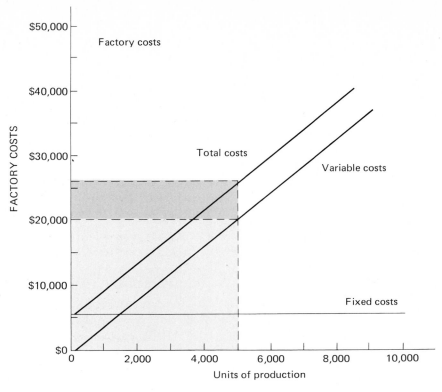

ILLUSTRATION 40-1

■ *How can fundamental*
relationships in
management accounting
be expressed in
graph form?

axis shows the levels of production for the factory, running from zero production to 10,000 units of production. This horizontal scale is sometimes
referred to as the **x axis.**

The three lines on the graph are read as follows. Every point on the
fixed-cost line represents a cost of $6,000—no matter what the level of pro-
duction is. Every point on the variable-cost line is equal to the number of
units of production (read from the x-axis value immediately below any
point) times the $4 cost per unit of production. The total-cost line represents
the sum of the fixed and variable costs. Note that the total-cost line is always
the same distance from the variable-cost line: this distance represents the
fixed cost.

In summary,

Fixed costs = $6,000 at any level of production

Variable costs = $4 × the number of units of production

Total costs = Fixed costs + Variable costs = $6,000 + $4x

where x equals the number of units of production.

Information about levels of production and factory costs can be read directly from the graph. For example, assume that the firm wants to operate at the level of 5,000 units of production in the coming year. The vertical dashed line on the graph drawn upward from 5,000 units intersects the total-cost line at $26,000. Therefore, the total costs would be $26,000, or the $6,000 fixed costs plus the $20,000 variable costs at the 5,000 level of production. Note that the vertical dashed line intersects the variable-cost line at $20,000; this point is equal to $4 times 5,000 units.

The form of the equation for total costs, $a + bx$, is referred to as the **straight-line equation,** since information expressed in this form can be shown as a straight line on a graph.

> **NEW TERMS**

fixed cost A cost that tends to remain the same total dollar amount at any level of production. [p. 704].

goal congruence The idea that all a firm's subgoals must work together toward one central set of objectives. [p. 704]

straight-line equation An equation that takes the form $a + bx$, where a is a constant amount, b is a constant amount, and x changes (x is variable). [p. 709]

variable cost A cost that tends to change directly as production changes. [p. 704]

variance The difference between a standard and actual performance; can be expressed in terms of costs or physical units, such as pounds of raw materials. [p. 704]

x axis The horizontal scale of a graph. [p. 708]

y axis The vertical scale of a graph. [p. 707]

> **ASSIGNMENT MATERIAL**

QUESTIONS

Q40-1. List and briefly describe the four tools that are useful in understanding management accounting.

Q40-2. What is goal congruence?

Q40-3. Differentiate between fixed and variable costs.

Q40-4. What is a standard?

Q40-5. Give an example of a standard.

Q40-6. What is a variance?

Q40-7. Contrast a usage variance and a cost variance.

Q40-8. What is meant by the x and y axes on a graph?

Q40-9. What is a straight-line equation?

EXERCISES

E40-1. For each of the following costs, indicate whether the cost would probably be basically fixed or basically variable.
  a. Property taxes on a plant
  b. Raw materials cost
  c. Direct labor costs to operate an assembly line
  d. Oil and grease to maintain manufacturing machinery

E40-2. a. List and describe two costs that generally behave in a variable manner.
   b. List and describe two costs that generally behave in a fixed manner.
   c. List and describe two costs that generally behave in neither a completely fixed nor a completely variable manner.

Note: In this exercise, use examples that are not included in the text.

E40-3. The following information is known about the Morton Corporation: Total fixed costs of the factory for the coming year are expected to be $240,000; the company expects to produce 12,000 units of product. Total variable costs of the factory will probably be $360,000, if the company produces 12,000 units of product.
   a. What is the straight-line equation that represents the factory costs of the company?
   b. Compute the expected total costs of the factory if 15,000 units are produced during the year.
   c. Compute the expected total costs of the factory if 10,000 units are produced during the year.
   d. What is the expected total variable cost of the factory if the company manufactures 24,000 units during the year?

E40-4. The following information is known about the Sandford Corporation: The firm plans to manufacture 4,000 units of product. At this level of production the fixed factory costs will amount to $36,000, and variable factory costs will amount to $48,000. Using this information, compute the following:
   a. Variable costs if the firm produces 8,000 units of product.
   b. Fixed costs if the firm produces 8,000 units of product.
   c. Fixed costs if the firm produces 2,000 units of product.
   d. Total costs if the firm produces 2,000 units of product.
   e. Average variable cost per unit if the firm produces 4,000 units of product.

PROBLEMS (GROUP A)

P40-1. *Straight-line equation; graph.* Assume that the straight-line equation representing the total factory costs of a company is as follows: Total costs $= a + bx$, where $a = \$10,000$ and $b = \$5$.

REQUIRED:

   a. What is the total fixed cost of the factory?
   b. What is the total variable cost of the factory if the firm operates at 20,000 units of finished goods for the period?
   c. What is the total cost (fixed and variable combined) of the factory operations if the plant produces 25,000 units of finished product during the period?
   d. Prepare a graph, in good form, showing lines for fixed costs, variable costs, and total costs. The y axis should go from zero to $160,000, and the x axis should go from zero to 30,000 units.

P40-2. *Variable and fixed costs; graph.* The following information is compiled by the management of Anole and Company: During 1978, the firm plans to manufacture 10,000 units of product. At this level of production the fixed factory costs will amount to $21,000 and the variable factory costs will amount to $42,000.

REQUIRED:

   a. Compute the variable costs if the firm produces 12,500 units of product.
   b. Compute the fixed costs if the firm produces 12,500 units of product.

c. Compute the fixed costs if the firm produces 11,300 units of product.

d. Compute the total costs if the firm produces 11,300 units of product.

e. Compute the average variable cost per unit if the firm produces 10,000 units of product.

f. Compute the average variable cost per unit if the firm produces 13,000 units of product.

g. Prepare a graph in good form showing lines for fixed costs, variable costs, and total costs. The y axis should go from zero to $120,000, and the x axis should go from zero to 20,000 units of production.

*P40-3. *Cost-behavior relationships.* Below are four independent cases. Make computations to complete the missing data.

	cases			
	A	B	C	D
Total fixed costs (1978)	$10,000	$60,000	$30,000	_____
Total variable costs (1978)	_____	_____	_____	$200,000
Unit variable costs (1978)	$3	_____	$8	$2
Number of units produced (1978)	20,000	90,000	_____	_____
Total costs (1978)	_____	$420,000	$270,000	$203,000
Total costs if production had been doubled during 1978	_____	_____	$510,000	$403,000
Total costs if production had been at 80% of the level of 1978	_____	_____	_____	_____

PROBLEMS (GROUP B)

P40-4. *Cost behavior; graph.* The following information is known about the Gecko Corporation: Total *fixed* costs of the factory for the coming year are $100,000; the company expects to produce 50,000 units of product. Total *variable* costs of the factory are $300,000 if the company produces 50,000 units of product.

REQUIRED:

a. What is the straight-line equation that represents the factory costs of the company?

b. Compute the total costs of the factory if 70,000 units are produced during the year.

c. Compute the total costs of the factory if 40,000 units are produced during the year.

d. What is the total variable cost of the factory if the company manufactures 42,500 units during the year?

e. Prepare a graph, in good form, showing lines for fixed costs, variable costs, and total costs. The y axis should go from zero to $600,000, and the x axis should go from zero to 80,000 units.

P40-5. *Fixed-, variable-cost computations; graph.* Assume that the straight-line equation representing the total factory costs of a company is as follows: Total costs = $a + bx$, where $a = $4,000$, $b = 2, and $x =$ number of units of production.

REQUIRED:

    a. Prepare a graph, in good form, showing lines for fixed costs, variable costs, and total costs. The y axis should go from zero to $25,000, and the x axis should go from zero to 10,000 units.

    b. Compute each of the following by using the straight-line equation. Then check your answers by reading the graph you have prepared.

        (1) Total costs if 8,000 units are produced.

        (2) Total costs if 7,000 units are produced.

        (3) Fixed costs if 8,000 units are produced.

        (4) Variable costs (total) if 8,000 units are produced.

        (5) Variable costs (total) if 7,000 units are produced.

        (6) Total costs if 1,000 units are produced.

P40-6. Costs under changing levels of production. During 1977, a factory produced 91,000 units of its product, with a total cost of $395,000. During the next year, 1978, production amounted to 107,000 units, with a total cost of $446,400. The fixed costs and the unit variable costs remained the same during this 2-year period.

    In planning for 1979's operations, management predicts that unit variable costs will increase by 10% and that fixed costs will increase by 15%. Production plans for 1979 are for 150,000 units to be produced.

REQUIRED:

    a. For 1977, compute the total fixed costs, total variable costs, and unit variable costs.

    b. For 1978, compute the total fixed costs, total variable costs, and unit variable costs.

    c. For 1979, compute the total fixed costs, total variable costs, and unit variable costs.

CUMULATIVE REVIEW PROBLEMS

P40-7. *Cumulative review problem*

Fill in the blanks.

1. Deciding what is to be accomplished by the organization and deciding how it is to be accomplished is called _____ .

2. Formulating goals and broad policies for accomplishing the goals is the job of _____

3. Determining to what extent the plans and goals of the firm have been accomplished is called _____ .

4. The element that helps make possible continuous planning and control exchange is the flow of _____

_____ .

5. A management accounting statement that compares actual operations to a standard or budgeted goal is called _____

_____

6. Reports showing budgeted financial statements compared to actual financial

statements and reasons for differences are called _____
_____.

7. Reports showing detailed budgets compared to actual reports of operations and reasons for differences are called _____
_____.

8. Detailed plans of each section of the entire business are called _____.
9. The use by management of significant variances or deviations from standard performances as guides for taking corrective action is called _____
_____.

10. Carrying out the plans formulated by management is called _____
_____.

11. Management's process of acquiring human and other resources and setting up special relationships among the resources in order to reach the firm's goals is called_____.

12. The authority exerted downward from a superior to a subordinate is called .

13. The authority in a relationship to advise is called _____
_____.

14. In a manufacturing operation, the job of overseeing and managing all activities dealing with the conversion of raw materials, labor, and other efforts into the finished product is the responsibility of the _____
_____.

15. A major area of study in managerial accounting dealing with accumulating and reporting the costs of production on a department-by-department basis is called_____.

16. The sales function is sometimes referred to as the _____ function.
17. Under the vice-president of finance, the head of the accounting area is the
_____.

18. The person responsible for most of the financial decisions of the corporation is the_____.

19. The person who would recommend a change in the accounting system or determine the extent to which management policies are being carried out is the_____.

20. The vice-president who recruits and places new employees is the _____
_____.

Discuss each of the following:
1. What three functions does management accounting involve?
2. What is the concept of planning?

3. What is the management activity of control?
4. What is a performance report?
5. What is management by exception?
6. Compare line authority with staff authority.
7. List the four basic tools in management accounting.

P40-8. *Cumulative review problem*

Part A

The Quaker Corporation determined the following information for the week ending March 26, 1978, for Department 8: Revenues, $20,500; Cost of goods sold, $4,250; Operating expenses, $1,500. The standard amounts set were: Revenues, $21,000; Cost of goods sold, $4,500; Operating expenses, $2,000.

REQUIRED: Prepare a departmental performance report.

Part B   True or false.

_____ 1. Organizing deals with converting plans and objectives into action and desired results.

_____ 2. Human resources need to be given a special relationship to all other resources in carrying out the firm's plans.

_____ 3. Resources of a company do not include the assets appearing on the balance sheet.

_____ 4. An example of line authority is a Quality Inspector advising the department heads regarding the quality of the products they are producing.

_____ 5. A company's internal auditor is directly under the supervision of the vice-president of personnel.

_____ 6. Organizing production activities into departments helps control costs.

_____ 7. The purchasing department would be under the direction of the vice-president of finance.

_____ 8. The treasurer is responsible for investigating and evaluating the functioning of the accounting system.

_____ 9. The taxes department makes detailed studies for management to determine the tax consequences of certain decisions.

_____ 10. Management accounting does not involve data selection or record keeping.

Part C

A firm plans in 1979 to produce 15,000 units of product for a total cost of $40,000. The previous year (1978), production costs totaled $46,000 at a unit variable cost of $2. Prepare a graph showing costs on the *y* axis and units of production on the *x* axis. Plot the lines for variable costs and total costs for the company. Identify on the graph with dashed lines the 1978 and 1979 production levels and costs.

chapter 18

cost-earnings relationships

COST-EARNINGS CONCEPTS

> **OBJECTIVE**

An objective of this unit is to introduce you to several concepts of cost. You will find that these cost concepts are useful in analyzing the behavior of a firm's costs and expenses in relation to the revenues produced.

A second objective is to introduce you to the cost–earnings model, which is often referred to as the break-even model. The model shows the relationships among a firm's revenues, fixed costs, variable costs, and net earnings. You will need to understand these relationships so that you can work with the budgeting and standard cost systems which you will study later in this course.

> **APPROACH TO ATTAINING THE OBJECTIVE**

As you study about cost concepts and the break-even model, pay special attention to these seven questions, which the text following answers:

- *What basic cost concepts are related to changes in production levels?*
- *What basic costs are components of the manufactured product?*
- *What basic cost concepts are directly involved with performance reporting?*
- *What other cost concepts are useful in management planning and control?*
- *Why is an understanding of cost behavior important?*
- *What is the basic cost–earnings model?*
- *What questions can the cost–earnings model help answer?*

COST CLASSIFICATIONS

This unit describes and classifies several different kinds of costs. Each of these classifications is useful in its own special way. However, each cost classification need not be completely separate from the others. For example, an expenditure such as cost of raw materials may be identified as several types of cost: it is a raw materials cost (this is one classification); and it also is a variable cost (another classification). This unit describes these and other costs as a foundation for your learning how cost behavior can be determined and directed.

COST CONCEPTS RELATED TO PRODUCTION LEVELS

■ *What basic cost concepts are related to changes in production levels?*

The following table lists two basic cost concepts that are related to levels of production in a factory. This fixed versus variable classification forms the structure for much of the analysis of factory operations for the purposes of planning and control. These plans are made by predicting the costs after the relationships among variable costs, fixed costs, and sales have been studied.

BASIC CONCEPT	DESCRIPTION OF THE CLASSIFICATION
1. Fixed cost	Any cost which remains about the same, in total, at any level of production in the factory. Examples might be Insurance expense for the factory and the Salary expense of the Production Superintendent.
2. Variable cost	Any cost which tends to increase in total as production levels increase and tends to decrease as production levels decrease. Examples might be Raw materials cost and Direct labor cost in the factory.

COST COMPONENTS OF THE MANUFACTURED PRODUCT

■ *What basic costs are components of the manufactured product?*

Costs of production (costs of factory operations) can be classified according to components in the manufacturing process. In this extremely useful classification every factory cost is categorized as (1) raw materials, (2) direct labor, or (3) factory overhead. These three terms are described in detail in the following table. This three-part classification of factory costs helps managers to record and control departmental operations.

BASIC CONCEPT	DESCRIPTION OF THE CLASSIFICATION
1. Raw materials cost	The cost of materials and supplies used *directly* in manufacturing the product. Examples are the rubber used in making automobile tires, the steel used in making automobiles, and the vegetables used in making canned soup. Raw materials costs are also classified as *variable costs* because the total cost of raw materials tends to increase as the total number of products manufactured increases.
2. Direct labor cost	This cost is part of the costs related to the labor force in a factory—those costs involved directly in the manufacture of the product. For example, the labor cost of men working on an assembly line would be classified as direct labor. The salary of the

3. **Factory overhead cost**
   (also referred to as *Burden* or *Manufacturing expense*)

production superintendent or the foreman would *not* be classified as direct labor, because these individuals do not work directly in producing the goods. Their cost in *indirect*. Direct labor costs are also variable costs, in that these costs (in total) increase directly as production levels increase.

This category includes *all* other factory costs besides Raw materials and Direct labor. Examples are:

Factory overhead which is variable:
   Certain kinds of supplies for maintenance of the machines
   Certain power costs
Factory overhead which is fixed:
   Depreciation on machines
   Depreciation on buildings
   Insurance and taxes
   Salaries for indirect factory labor

COSTS INVOLVED WITH PERFORMANCE REPORTING

■ *What basic cost concepts are directly involved with performance reporting?*

You know that the two elements of a performance report are (1) the actual results of operations, and (2) the standard or budgeted results of operations. Many manufacturing firms have accounting and reporting systems which accumulate and report historical costs (actual costs) *and* standard costs for each department and for each element of cost, such as raw materials, direct labor, and factory overhead. The terms historical cost and standard cost are described in detail in the following table.

BASIC CONCEPT	DESCRIPTION OF THE CLASSIFICATION
1. **Historical cost**	The term "historical cost" refers to the actual cost that was incurred. Ordinary accounting systems (financial accounting) accumulate and report historical costs.
2. **Standard cost**	This is the cost that should have been incurred in a given set of circumstances. It is the cost which is compared to historical cost in evaluating performance. For example, management determined in advance that to produce a unit of goods, 3 pounds of raw materials should be used, and that each pound of raw materials should cost $4. Therefore, the standard cost for raw materials for one unit of goods is $12. This standard cost can be compared to actual (historical) cost.

OTHER BASIC COST CONCEPTS

■ *What other cost concepts are useful in management planning and control?*

The table that follows presents several additional cost concepts that are useful to management. Familiarize yourself with these costs and refer to this table when you learn in future units how these cost concepts are used.

BASIC CONCEPT	DESCRIPTION OF THE CLASSIFICATION
1. **Replacement cost**	This is the cost to repurchase, replace, or reconstruct an asset. For example, in financial accounting, you learned that merchandise inventory is usually reported at the lower of cost or market, where market is the replacement cost at the balance sheet date.

Replacement cost of the inventory is the price that would have to be paid if the inventory were replaced at the balance sheet date. Management often uses this concept in planning. As fixed assets are used over a period of time, management must plan to replace the assets; therefore the replacement cost concept must be directly used in the decision process.

2. **Marginal cost**

This is the additional or extra cost incurred to produce one more unit of product. For example, it might cost a firm $1,000 to produce 1,200 units of product. To produce 1,201 units of product, the total cost might rise to $1,000.34. If these are the facts, then the marginal cost at the higher level of production is 34¢. Again, such a concept is useful in planning production when expansions are desired.

3. **Differential cost**

Similar to marginal cost. This is the difference between total costs when management contemplates changing from one level of production to a completely different level—or changing from one way of doing something to another way. For example, a firm might be planning to produce 1,000 units of goods at a total cost of $1,200. It has the opportunity to produce and sell another 700 units. It is determined that the total costs would rise from $1,200 to $1,356 in producing 1,700 units. The *differential cost* amounts to $156 for the extra 700 units.

4. **Sunk cost** (past costs)

When management enters a project, certain costs are incurred with the purpose of eventually increasing the firm's revenue and earnings. The term *sunk cost* is used to refer to those costs which have already been incurred and which *cannot be reduced by any management action.*

For example, assume that management has $2,000 tied up in a machine. Further assume that about $300 of this cost already has helped produce revenue—that is, the machine has been used and depreciation has been charged off in the amount of $300. The future service potential (book value) is assumed to be $1,700. Now management is seriously considering replacing that machine with a newer and more efficient machine which will increase production and revenues substantially. The old machine can be sold for only $400 cash. In making the decision whether to buy the new machine, certain past costs are considered *sunk costs* and have *no relevance for the decision to buy the new machine.* Of the book value of $1,700, only $400 can be recovered now; therefore the difference of $1,300, the sunk cost, is not related to the future decision. In summary, past costs in no way are related to a decision—only future costs are relevant.

THE FOUR ELEMENTS FOR ANALYSIS

In your study of financial accounting, you spent a lot of time on the income statement and the measurement of earnings for investors and creditors. *Management* also must evaluate the performance of the business firm. Their point of view is somewhat different from that of outsiders, however. Management is interested in more than just predicting the earnings patterns for future periods; management also must be able to direct and control the revenue and cost relationships to help produce the desired earnings. An understanding of

■ Why is an
understanding
of cost behavior
important?

cost behavior, therefore, is vital to management's job. Cost behavior—how different classifications of cost change as other elements (such as production levels) change—is the subject of the cost–earnings model we will discuss here. There are four basic elements in the cost–earnings model. These elements are:

1. Revenues.
2. Fixed costs.
3. Variable costs.
4. Net earnings.

Certain patterns of change—patterns of behavior—of these four elements can be predicted and analyzed with the use of the **break-even model.**

THE BREAK-EVEN MODEL

Let's look at a simple example to illustrate the break-even model. Kudd Company has been operating for 3 years. During the year 1978, the results of operations are as shown in the following income statement. During 1978, 10,000 units of product were manufactured and sold.

Kudd Company
INCOME STATEMENT
For the Year Ended December 31, 1978

sales (10,000) units at $10)		$100,000
expenses:		
Cost of goods sold	$50,000	
Selling expenses	27,000	
General and administrative expenses	13,000	
Total expenses		90,000
net earnings		$ 10,000

In analyzing the operations for 1978, management wants to figure out what can be done to improve the earnings. A first step in the analysis is to study the expenses to determine which expenses are fixed costs and which are variable costs. The income statement at the top of the next page shows the analysis that management made. Management studied each cost category. Those costs which were expected to remain about the same during the next year (regardless of production levels and sales levels) were classified as fixed, and those costs which were expected to change with production and sales levels during the next period were classified as variable.

Kudd Company
INCOME STATEMENT
For the Year Ended December 31, 1978

sales (10,000 units at $10)			$100,000
expenses	**variable**	**fixed**	
Cost of goods sold:			
Raw materials	$10,000		
Direct labor	20,000		
Factory overhead	5,000	$15,000	
Total cost of goods sold	$35,000	$15,000	
Selling expenses	16,000	11,000	
General and administrative expenses	9,000	4,000	
	$60,000	$30,000	90,000
net earnings			$ 10,000

Notice that in this second analysis, *every* cost was studied and classified as either fixed or variable. This question must be asked for every cost: During the next period, if the production and sales levels change, will the cost also change—or will it remain the same?

The information revealed by the second income statement also can be expressed in terms of *unit costs and revenues:*

Selling price per unit of product	$10.00
($100,000 divided by 10,000 units)	
Variable cost per unit of product	$ 6.00
($60,000 divided by 10,000 units)	
Fixed cost per unit of product	$ 3.00
($30,000 divided by 10,000 units)	
Net earnings per unit of product	$ 1.00
($10,000 divided by 10,000 units)	

Another concept useful in helping management in profit planning is the *contribution margin* per unit of product. This is the excess of the selling price over the variable costs: in our example, $10.00 minus $6.00 equals a contribution margin per unit of $4.00. This means that for each unit sold for $10.00, there remains $4.00 after all variable costs of the firm are covered. This $4.00 *contributes* toward covering the fixed costs *and* toward producing net earnings.

The *contribution margin ratio* is 40%, or $4.00 divided by $10.00. For every dollar of sales produced, 40 cents is available as a contribution to cover fixed costs and to produce net earnings—*after* variable costs of 60 cents are covered.

The break-even model in equation form The management of the Kudd Company knows that at the 10,000-unit level of production the firm earns

$10,000. The management also would like to know when their operations start to be profitable—at what point do they break even. This **break-even point** can be expressed in either units or dollars, and it will be the level of operations at which the firm makes neither a net loss nor net earnings. Total costs will *equal* total revenues at the break-even point.

Let's start with this standard equation derived from the Kudd Company's income statement:

Net earnings = Revenues — Variable expenses — Fixed expenses

These relationships also can be expressed as follows:

$$\text{Net earnings} = \begin{matrix} \text{Number of units} \\ \text{sold times} \\ \text{price per unit} \end{matrix} - \begin{matrix} \text{Number of units} \\ \text{sold times variable} \\ \text{cost per unit} \end{matrix} - \begin{matrix} \text{Fixed} \\ \text{expenses} \end{matrix}$$

We know that the price per unit is $10, the variable cost per unit is $6, and the fixed expenses are $30,000. If we let x equal the number of units sold, then for the Kudd Company this equation can be generalized to:

$$\text{Net earnings} = \$10x - \$6x - \$30,000$$
$$= \$4x - \$30,000$$

Remember now that at the break-even point net earnings are equal to zero. Therefore, if we make this substitution in our equation we have

$$0 = \$4x - \$30,000$$

This equation represents the point of zero profit. Solving for x, the number of units that Kudd Company must sell to break even (make zero profit), we get:

$$\$4x = \$30,000$$
$$x = \frac{\$30,000}{\$4}$$
$$= 7,500 \text{ units to be sold to break even}$$

This can be checked as follows:

Sales (7,500 at $10)		$75,000
Variable costs (7,500 at $6)	$45,000	
Fixed costs	30,000	75,000
Net earnings		–0–

Recall that we just calculated the break-even point in units by dividing $30,000, the firm's fixed expenses, by $4. This $4 represents the selling price per unit minus the variable cost per unit, or the **contribution margin** that we discussed earlier. Therefore, in summary, the equations above can be rearranged and stated for convenient use as follows:

$$\text{Break-even point in units} = \frac{\text{Fixed expenses}}{\text{Contribution margin per unit}}$$

$$7{,}500 \text{ units} = \frac{\$30{,}000}{\$4}$$

$$\text{Break-even point in dollars of sales and costs} = \frac{\text{Fixed expenses}}{\textbf{Contribution margin ratio}}$$

$$\$75{,}000 = \frac{\$30{,}000}{0.40}$$

The break-even model in graphic form The same relationships among revenues, fixed costs, variable costs, and net earnings that we have been discussing are presented in graph form in Illustration 41-1. Carefully examine this break-even chart and note these related points:

1. The y axis shows dollars of revenues and costs.
2. The x axis shows the number of units of production and sales.
3. The fixed costs at any level of operation are $30,000.
4. The *difference* between the total cost line and the variable cost line at *any* level of production is equal to the fixed costs ($30,000). Note that the total cost line runs parallel to the variable cost line. Therefore it is always the same amount more than the variable cost; this constant amount is the fixed cost. For example, at the 15,000-unit production level, the variable costs equal $90,000. At that level, the total costs equal $120,000. The difference is the $30,000 of fixed costs.
5. The break-even point is where the total costs line intersects (equals) the total sales line.
6. If the firm produces and sells any number of units less than the break-even point, the firm will incur a *net loss,* because total costs will be greater than total revenues.
7. If the firm produces and sells any number of units greater than the break-even point, the firm will produce *net earnings,* because total revenues will exceed total costs.
8. The contribution margin is $4 per unit. This is the $10 selling price less the $6 variable cost per unit. At the 8,000-unit level of production, the total contribution margin is $32,000. This is equal to the total revenue (sales) minus the variable costs: $80,000 minus $48,000. The $32,000 contribution margin provides $30,000 to cover

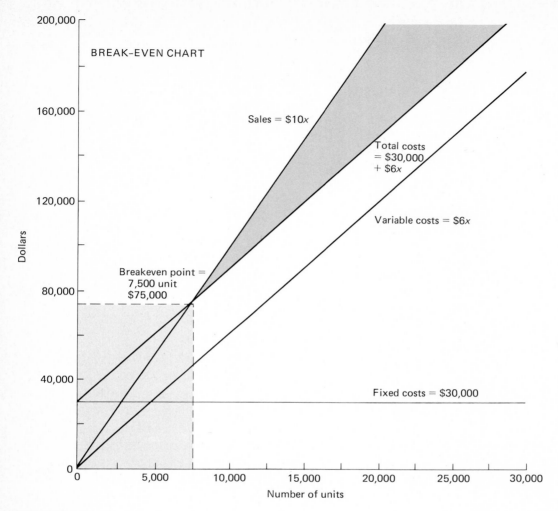

BREAK-EVEN CHART

Sales = $10x

Total costs
= $30,000
+ $6x

Variable costs = $6x

Breakeven point =
7,500 unit
$75,000

Fixed costs = $30,000

Dollars

Number of units

ILLUSTRATION 41-1

the fixed costs and $2,000 of net earnings. To continue the analysis, remember that at the break-even level of operations, the net earnings are zero—and all fixed costs have been covered, since there is no net loss. If 8,000 units are sold, then the company is operating 500 units past the break-even point. And 500 units times the contribution margin per unit of $4 equals the $2,000 net earnings. In summary:

Sales (8,000 units × $10)	$80,000
Variable costs (8,000 units × $6)	$48,000
Fixed costs	30,000
Total costs	$78,000
Net earnings	$ 2,000

9. The equations for the various items on the break-even chart in this example can be expressed as follows:

    a. Total costs = $30,000 + $6x$
    b. Variable costs = $6x$
    c. Fixed costs = $30,000
    d. Net earnings = $10x - 6x - $30,000$

USING THE BREAK-EVEN MODEL

The analysis of fixed and variable costs in relation to sales and production levels is an extremely useful planning device for a business firm. The break-even model helps management answer several important questions:

■ *What questions can the cost–earnings model help answer?*

1. If there is a change in the fixed costs of a firm, what is the effect on the net earnings? An example is an increase in the insurance costs for a firm.

2. If there is a change in the variable costs of a firm, what is the effect on the net earnings? An example is an increase in the direct labor costs per hour for a manufacturing plant.

3. If there is a change in the volume of production, what is the effect on the net earnings?

4. If there is a change in the selling price of a firm's product, what is the effect on the net earnings?

5. If there is a change in more than one of the factors (fixed costs, variable costs, production levels, price of the product), what is the effect on the net earnings?

Unit 42 provides illustrations of how the break-even model is used to answer these questions. Also, the limitations of using this model for planning are discussed.

❯ NEW TERMS

break-even model An equation or a graph showing the relationships among revenues, fixed costs, variable costs, and net earnings for a business firm. [p. 720]

break-even point The level of operations necessary for the firm to make neither a net loss nor net earnings; the point of operations at which total costs equal total revenues; can be expressed in units or dollars. [p. 722]

contribution margin The excess of the sales over variable costs for a firm; also can be expressed on a per-unit basis. [p. 722]

contribution margin ratio The percent of each sales dollar that remains after variable costs are covered. For example, if a product is sold for $20 per unit, and if the variable costs per unit amount to $15, the contribution margin per unit is $5, and the contribution margin ratio is 25%, or $5 divided by $20. [p. 723]

differential cost The difference between total costs when management contemplates changing from one level of production to another or from one way of doing something to another. [p. 719]

direct labor cost The cost related to the labor force in a factory which deals with direct manufacture of the product, as opposed to indirect labor costs (foremen and supervisors), which are considered factory overhead; direct labor cost is a variable cost. [p. 717]

factory overhead cost All factory costs except raw materials and direct labor; may be variable or fixed. [p. 718]

historical cost Actual cost that was incurred; as opposed to a standard or planned cost. [p. 718]

marginal cost The additional cost incurred to produce one more unit of product. [p. 719]

raw materials cost The cost of materials and supplies used directly in manufacturing a product; raw materials cost is a variable cost. [p. 717]

replacement cost The cost to repurchase, reconstruct, or replace an asset. [p. 718]

standard cost Cost that should have been incurred, according to some objective. [p. 718]

sunk cost A past cost which cannot be changed by management action. [p. 719]

❯ ASSIGNMENT MATERIAL

QUESTIONS

Q41-1. What two basic cost concepts are associated with performance reporting? Explain.

Q41-2. What two basic cost concepts are closely related to the level of production? Comment on the usefulness of these classifications.

Q41-3. "Each expenditure made by a company can be classified as only one particular type of cost." Do you agree? Explain.

Q41-4. Are all factory overhead costs fixed costs? Explain.

Q41-5. What is burden?

Q41-6. What are the four basic elements in the cost–earnings model?

Q41-7. What is meant by contribution margin per unit of product?

Q41-8. How is the break-even point in units computed?

Q41-9. How is the break-even point in dollars computed?

Q41-10. What important questions does the break-even analysis help answer?

EXERCISES

E41-1. Give *one example* of each of the following concepts; use your own words and your own example:

    a. Direct labor cost   f. Raw materials cost
    b. Differential cost   g. Replacement cost
    c. Factory overhead cost   h. Standard cost
    d. Historical cost   i. Sunk cost
    e. Marginal cost

E41-2. Krog Corporation's management states that the straight-line equation for their factory costs is as follows: Total factory costs $= \$10,000 + \$3x$.

    a. What is the variable cost per unit if the firm manufactures 5,000 units of product?

    b. What is the variable cost per unit if the firm manufactures 6,000 units of product?

    c. What is the fixed cost per unit if the firm manufactures 5,000 units of product?

    d. What is the fixed cost per unit if the firm manufactures 6,000 units of product?

E41-3. Match the descriptions below with the terms on the following list. Use each response only once.

A Direct labor cost   F Standard cost
B Differential cost   G Historical cost
C Raw materials cost   H Marginal cost
D Replacement cost   I Sunk cost
E Factory overhead

a. The total factory cost associated with producing 300 units of product amounts to $7,518. The total factory cost associated with producing 301 units of product amounts to $7,522. The extra $4 is what kind of cost?

b. The cost of batteries that are used in manufacturing automobiles is what kind of cost?

c. The cost actually incurred to manufacture a product amounts to $90, as opposed to the $87 which management believes should have been the cost. The $90 is what kind of cost?

d. The book value (Cost less accumulated depreciation) of a delivery truck is $1,200. The truck could be sold now for $800. The company is considering replacing the old truck with a new one. In making the decision to buy a new truck, the $400 excess of book value over market value of the old truck is what kind of cost?

e. The wages cost of employees working in the factory to directly produce the goods amounted to $7,000. What kind of cost component is this?

f. The cost actually incurred to manufacture a product amounts to $90, as opposed to the $87 which management believes should have been the cost. The $87 is referred to as what kind of cost?

g. On December 31, 1978, a company had merchandise inventory on hand which had cost $1,000. If the company were to purchase similar goods at the balance sheet date, the cost would amount to $907. The $907 is referred to as what kind of cost?

h. The cost of insurance on the factory amounts to $1,324 each year. This cost is referred to as what?

i. The total factory cost associated with producing 300 units of product amounts to $7,518. The total factory cost associated with producing 400 units of product amounts to $8,111. The extra $593 is what kind of cost?

E41-4. Complete the following:
a. Total sales divided by selling price per unit equals _____.
b. Contribution margin per unit plus variable cost per unit equals _____.
c. Selling price per unit minus variable cost per unit equals _____.
d. Selling price per unit minus variable cost per unit minus fixed cost per unit equals _____.
e. Fixed expenses divided by contribution margin per unit equals _____.
f. Break-even point in dollars equals fixed expenses divided by contribution margin _____.

PROBLEMS (GROUP A)

P41-1. *Acceptance of special order.* Yardstick Measurements, Inc., is considering manufacturing a special order of 2,000 products for one of its customers. During the year Yardstick Measurements, Inc., plans to manufacture 20,000 units of product (not including the special order of 2,000 units), for a total cost of $62,000. The production manager estimates that if the extra order is taken, the total costs of the company will increase from $62,000 to $64,200. The firm plans to sell the 20,000 units of regular production for $100,000 cash. The special customer, however, is willing to pay Yardstick only $3,000 for the extra order of 2,000 units.

a. Compute the differential cost of the special order.
b. Compute the average selling price of the regular production of 20,000 units (the average unit selling price).
c. What is the gross profit for the company if the special order is not accepted and if only 20,000 units are manufactured and sold?
d. What is the gross profit for the company if the special order is accepted and if a total of 22,000 units are sold? Assume that the special order is sold for $3,000.

P41-2. *Break-even analysis and chart.* The following facts are known about Emergency Corporation for the year ended December 31, 1978: total variable costs, when the company sold 10,000 units of product for $9 per unit, $40,000; total fixed costs, $10,000.

REQUIRED:

a. Compute the following:
   (1) Total sales.   (5) Net earnings.
   (2) Variable cost per unit.   (6) Net earnings per unit.
   (3) Fixed cost per unit.   (7) Break-even point in units.
   (4) Contribution margin per unit.   (8) Break-even point in dollars.

b. Draw a break-even chart similar to the one illustrated in this unit. The *y* axis should run from zero to $99,000; the *x* axis should run from zero to 11,000 units.

P41-3. *Break-even analysis and chart.* The management of Biloxi Company assembled the following information about the operations of the firm for the year ended December 31, 1978.

Sales (20,000 units)		$160,000
Cost of goods sold:		
Raw materials (variable)	$40,000	
Direct labor (variable)	40,000	
Factory overhead (fixed)	10,000	
Factory overhead (variable)	5,000	95,000
Selling expenses (variable)		13,000
Selling expenses (fixed)		7,000
General and other expenses (variable)		8,000
General and other expenses (fixed)		2,000

REQUIRED:

a. Compute the following amounts.
   (1) Selling price per unit of product.
   (2) Variable costs per unit of product.
   (3) Fixed costs per unit of product.
   (4) Net earnings.
   (5) Net earnings per unit of product.

(6) Break-even point in units.

(7) Break-even point in dollars of sales and costs.

(8) Contribution margin per unit of product.

b. Draw a break-even graph similar to the one illustrated in this unit. The y axis should run from zero to $200,000; the x axis should run from zero to 25,000 units.

**PROBLEMS
(GROUP B)**

P41-4. *Cost behavior.* Anogeck and Sons operates a manufacturing plant. Several of the factory costs are shown below at three possible levels of production for the coming year.

total costs

	IF 1,000 UNITS ARE PRODUCED	IF 2,000 UNITS ARE PRODUCED	IF 3,000 UNITS ARE PRODUCED
Cost A	$ 5,000	$10,000	$15,000
Cost B	500	500	500
Cost C	10,000	10,000	12,000

REQUIRED: Answer the following questions.

a. What name is usually given to costs that behave as Cost A?

b. If the firm were to produce 1,300 units, what would be the total of Cost A?

c. What is the name usually given to costs that behave as Cost B?

d. If the firm were to produce 1,300 units, what would be the total of Cost B?

e. Describe the cost behavior of Cost C.

f. Give an example of a factory cost that could behave as Cost A.

g. Give an example of a factory cost that could behave as Cost B.

h. Give an example of a factory cost that could behave as Cost C.

P41-5. *Break-even analysis.* Assume these facts about a company: total fixed costs, $10,000; total variable costs, when the firm produces and sells 15,000 units of product, $30,000; selling price of the product, $3.00 per unit.

REQUIRED:

a. Draw a break-even graph similar to the one illustrated in this unit. The y axis should run from zero to $60,000; the x axis should run from zero to 20,000 units.

b. Determine from reading the graph the number of units to be sold to break even.

c. Determine from reading the graph the net earnings or net loss produced if 15,000 units are produced and sold.

d. Compute the break-even point in units, using the formula given in this unit.

e. Compute the break-even point in dollars of sales and costs, using the formula given in this unit.

P41-6. *Break-even relationships*

a. The following information is known about the operations of Taney and Company for 1978: contribution margin per unit, $3; variable cost per unit, $5;

number of units sold during year, 50,000; fixed costs, $60,000. Compute the following:

(1) Selling price per unit
(2) Total sales
(3) Total variable costs
(4) Net earnings
(5) Break-even point in units
(6) Break-even point in dollars

b. The following information is known about the operations of Schools, Inc., for 1978: contribution margin per unit, $5; variable cost per unit, $2; Net earnings, $20,000; fixed costs, $20,000.

Compute the following:

(1) Selling price per unit
(2) Total sales
(3) Total variable costs
(4) Number of units sold during year
(5) Break-even point in units
(6) Break-even point in dollars

COST-EARNINGS APPLICATIONS

➤ OBJECTIVE

This unit has two objectives. The first is to show you how the break-even model can be used to answer questions about the effect of changes in costs, volume, and selling prices on a business firm. The second objective is to point out some basic limitations in using the break-even model.

➤ APPROACH TO ATTAINING THE OBJECTIVE

As you study about cost–earnings applications and about limitations of the break-even model, give special attention to these four questions, which the text following answers:

- *How does a change in fixed expenses affect a firm?*
- *How does a change in variable expenses affect a firm?*
- *How do changes in selling price and volume affect a firm?*
- *What are the limitations of the break-even model?*

Assume these facts about a firm:

Fixed costs	$30,000
Variable costs	$6 per unit of product
Selling price	$10 per unit of product

The firm's management has just completed a cost study and has estimated that certain fixed costs, such as insurance expense, will increase for the coming year. The total fixed expenses are expected to be $33,000 instead of the $30,000 of the previous year. In what ways does this expected change in fixed expenses affect the firm? Let's examine the break-even point first.

- **How does a change in fixed expenses affect a firm?**

Break-even point before the increase in fixed expenses The break-even point for the firm, before the increase in fixed costs, is computed as follows:

$$\text{Break-even point in units} = \frac{\text{Fixed expenses}}{\text{Contribution margin per unit}}$$

$$= \frac{\$30,000}{\$4}$$

$$= 7,500 \text{ units}$$

$$\text{Break-even point in dollars} = \frac{\text{Fixed expenses}}{\text{Contribution margin ratio}}$$

$$= \frac{\$30,000}{0.40}$$

$$= \$75,000$$

Break-even point after the increase in fixed expenses The break-even point for the firm, after the projected increase in fixed costs, is computed as follows:

$$\text{Break-even point in units} = \frac{\$33,000}{\$4}$$

$$= 8,250 \text{ units}$$

$$\text{Break-even point in dollars} = \frac{\$33,000}{0.40}$$

$$= \$82,500$$

These figures indicate that an increase in fixed costs of $3,000 for this company would increase the break-even point from 7,500 units ($75,000) to 8,250 units ($82,500). This increase of $7,500 in sales is necessary if the firm is to break even, because each additional dollar of sales contributes 60 cents to cover the variable expenses and 40 cents to cover the additional $3,000 of fixed expenses.

Increase in sales necessary to make the same earnings as last year During the last year (when fixed costs were $30,000), the firm sold 10,000 units of product. The net earnings were as follows:

Sales (10,000 × $10)		$100,000
Fixed costs	$30,000	
Variable costs (10,000 × $6)	60,000	90,000
Net earnings		$ 10,000

During the coming year, fixed costs will increase to $33,000. A question that can be answered is: How much will the firm have to *increase sales* **volume** in the next year, if net earnings are to remain at the $10,000 level? (Let x = number of units sold, the *sales volume*.)

$$\text{Net earnings} = \text{Sales} - \text{Fixed expenses} - \text{Variable expenses}$$

$$\$10,000 = \$10x - \$33,000 - \$6x$$

$$\$10,000 = \$4x - \$33,000$$

$$\$4x = \$33,000 + \$10,000 = \$43,000$$

$$x = 10,750 \text{ units}$$

This computation indicates that sales volume must be increased from 10,000 units to 10,750 units if net earnings are to remain at the $10,000 level. The extra 750 units produce a contribution margin of $4 each ($4 times 750 equals the $3,000 of extra fixed costs to be covered).

PROJECTED CHANGES IN VARIABLE EXPENSES

■ *How does a change in variable expenses affect a firm?*

To illustrate how projected changes in variable costs affect a firm, the same basic example will be used:

Fixed costs	$30,000
Variable costs	$6 per unit of product
Selling price	$10 per unit of product
Break-even point in units	7,500 units
Break-even point in dollars	$75,000
Last year's level of operations	$100,000 of sales, with $10,000 of net earnings

Break-even point after the increase in variable expenses When there is a change in the level of variable costs, the contribution margin and the contribution margin ratio change. This change has a significant effect on the company's operations. For example, assume that a new labor contract has been negotiated and that the direct labor costs are increasing next year. Total variable costs are expected to increase from $6 per unit of product to $6.50 per unit. The firm's variable-cost structure would become:

Contribution margin per unit	$3.50 (This is the $10 selling price less the variable costs per unit of $6.50.)
Contribution margin ratio	35% (This is the $3.50 divided by the $10 selling price.)

The new break-even point is computed as follows:

$$\text{Break-even point in dollars} = \frac{\$30,000}{.35}$$
$$= \$85,714 \text{ (or 8,572 units at \$10)}$$

Because of this increase in the variable cost structure, the break-even point increases by $10,714 (from $75,000 to $85,714).

Increase in sales necessary to make same earnings as last year During the last year, when the contribution margin ratio was 40%, the firm earned $10,000. This net earnings total was produced by selling 10,000 units for $100,000. During the coming year, variable costs per unit will increase in relation to the selling price of $10. A question that can be answered is: How much will the firm have to increase sales in the next year, if net earnings are to remain at the $10,000 level? (Let $x =$ the number of units sold.)

$$\text{Net earnings} = \text{Sales} - \text{Fixed expenses} - \text{Variable expenses}$$
$$\$10,000 = \$10x - \$30,000 - \$6.50x$$
$$\$10,000 = \$3.50x - \$30,000$$
$$\$3.50x = \$30,000 + \$10,000 = \$40,000$$
$$x = 11,428 \text{ units (or \$114,280 of sales)}$$

The firm will have to increase sales from $100,000 to $114,280 if the same net earnings of $10,000 are to be produced. This can be proven as follows:

Sales (11,428 × $10)		$114,280
Fixed costs	$30,000	
Variable costs (11,428 × $6.50)	74,280	104,280
Net earnings		$ 10,000

PROJECTED CHANGE IN SELLING PRICE AND VOLUME

From time to time a business firm must reevaluate its pricing policy. In this example, assume the same facts:

Fixed costs	$30,000
Variable costs	$6 per unit of product
Selling price	$10 per unit of product
Break-even point in dollars	$75,000
Break-even point in units	7,500
Last year's level of operations	$100,000 of sales, with $10,000 of net earnings

- How do changes in selling price and volume affect a firm?

The management of this firm believes that if the *selling price of the product is reduced to $9,* then a substantial additional number of units can be sold in the coming year.

Break-even point after the price reduction The break-even point with the $9 selling price is computed as follows:

$$\text{Break-even point in dollars} = \frac{\$30,000}{\text{Contribution margin ratio}}$$

The contribution margin ratio is calculated as follows. The contribution margin is $3, which is the new $9 selling price less the variable costs per unit of $6. The contribution margin ratio is therefore 0.3333, which is simply $3 divided by $9. Substituting this new ratio in our equation, we get:

$$\text{Break-even point in dollars} = \frac{\$30,000}{0.3333} = \$90,000$$

Under these conditions of the reduced selling price, the break-even point increases from $75,000 to $90,000. The new break-even point in terms of units is 10,000 ($90,000 divided by $9 equals 10,000).

Increase in sales necessary to make the same earnings as last year If the selling price is reduced to $9, the sales level needed to earn $10,000 can be computed as follows (let x = number of units sold):

$$\text{Net earnings} = \text{Sales} - \text{Fixed expenses} - \text{Variable expenses}$$

$$\$10,000 = \$9x - \$30,000 - \$6x$$

$$\$10,000 = \$3x - \$30,000$$

$$\$3x = \$30,000 + \$10,000 = \$40,000$$

$$x = 13,333 \text{ units (or } \$119,997 \text{ of sales computed as follows: 13,333 units} \times \$9 = \$119,997)$$

These figures indicate that sales must increase from $100,000 to $119,997 if the same net earnings are to be maintained. Therefore, management probably would not reduce the price from $10 to $9 unless they believed that sales could be increased by this substantial amount.

PROJECTED CHANGE IN SEVERAL FACTORS

Our last example shows how the break-even model can be used to analyze a more complex situation where several types of changes are planned. The same facts as in the previous examples will be used:

Fixed costs	$30,000
Variable costs	$6 per unit of product
Selling price	$10 per unit of product
Break-even point	$75,000
Last year's level of operations	$100,000 of sales, with $10,000 of net earnings

Management is planning these changes for the coming year:

1. The selling price will be reduced to $9.50.
2. Fixed costs will be increased to $35,000 to accommodate additional insurance and advertising.
3. Variable costs are expected to rise to $6.50 per unit of product.

These questions can now be answered:

1. What is the new break-even point for the firm in terms of units of product?
2. The management wants to increase the net earnings from $10,000 to $12,000 as a result of the new price and the advertising program. How many units must be sold to produce the $12,000 of net earnings?

The new break-even point The break-even point under the projected conditions is computed as follows:

$$\text{Break-even point in units} = \frac{\text{Fixed expenses}}{\text{Contribution margin per unit}}$$

$$= \frac{\$35,000}{\$9.50 - \$6.50}$$

$$= \frac{\$35,000}{\$3}$$

$$= 11,667 \text{ units}$$

The break-even point in dollars is 11,667 units times $9.50, or $110,836. This can also be computed:

$$\text{Break-even point in dollars} = \frac{\text{Fixed expenses}}{\text{Contribution margin ratio}}$$

$$= \frac{\$35,000}{\dfrac{\$3.00}{\$9.50}}$$

$$= \frac{\$35,000}{.3158}$$

$$= \$110,836$$

The new sales level needed to produce the increase in earnings The sales level to produce $12,000 of net earnings can be computed as follows (let x = number of units sold):

$$\text{Net earnings} = \text{Sales} - \text{Fixed expenses} - \text{Variable expenses}$$

$$\$12,000 = \$9.50x - \$35,000 - \$6.50x$$

$$\$12,000 = \$3x - \$35,000$$

$$\$3x = \$12,000 + \$35,000 = \$47,000$$

$$x = 15,667 \text{ units}$$

This represents an increase in sales of 5,667 units from the previous year's level of 10,000 units. The total sales therefore must be $148,836, or $9.50 times 15,667 units.

LIMITATIONS OF THE BREAK-EVEN MODEL

The break-even graph and the break-even equations aid in the planning process, but there are certain limitations which underlie the model. Some of the assumptions and limitations are:

■ *What are the limitations of the break-even model?*

1. *All* the expenses of the business firm must be divided into fixed and variable categories. Often this is a difficult task and estimates must be used in certain circumstances.

2. The variable expenses are assumed to remain the *same* dollar amount *per unit* of product as production increases or decreases. This assumption may not be precisely valid. For example, as production levels increase, there may be certain quantity discounts in purchasing raw materials. This situation (as well as many others) may cause the variable cost line (equation) to be slightly curved—rather than a straight line. This limitation is not as significant as it might seem,

however, because in any one period, a firm can predict production levels with good accuracy. In other words, for most firms production levels *do not* vary widely from period to period, and the variable costs would be expected to vary in a straight-line fashion in the *small* range of production levels.

3. The break-even model cannot be readily and simply adapted to firms which sell many products and are continuously changing the individual amounts of the various products that they sell.

> ### NEW TERM

volume The level of production and sales of a firm in terms of number of units. [p. 733]

> ### ASSIGNMENT MATERIAL

QUESTIONS   Q42-1. Briefly describe the effect on the break-even point of an increase in fixed expenses.

Q42-2. Briefly describe the effect on the break-even point of an increase in variable expenses.

Q42-3. Briefly explain three limitations of the break-even model.

Q42-4. What is volume?

EXERCISES   E42-1. Assume these facts about a firm:

Selling price of product per unit	$50
Fixed expenses for the firm	$100,000
Variable expenses for the firm if 60,000 units are produced and sold	$1,800,000

a. What is the break-even point for the firm in terms of dollars of sales?

b. What are the net earnings of the firm if 6,000 units are produced and sold?

c. Management anticipates that variable expenses will increase to $40 per unit of product during the coming year. How many units of product must be sold if the firm is to make $30,000 in net earnings?

E42-2. Given the following information, compute (a) total contribution margin; (b) contribution margin per unit; (c) break-even point in dollars of sales and costs; (d) increase in sales necessary to make the same earnings as last year if fixed expenses increase by $9,000; (e) increase in sales necessary to make the same earnings as last year if variable costs increase to $7 per unit.

Last year's data:

Revenues	$110,000
Variable expenses	$ 60,000
Fixed expenses	$ 45,000
Sales	10,000 units

E42-3. Indicate whether each of the following items are basically fixed costs or variable costs by placing an "F" or a "V" in each blank.

—— 1. Factory rent

—— 2. Rubber used as raw materials

—— 3. Salary of treasurer

—— 4. Sandpaper

—— 5. Fire insurance on equipment

—— 6. Depreciation—Equipment

—— 7. Shipping expenses

—— 8. Property taxes on equipment

—— 9. Glass used as raw material

—— 10. Overtime wages

E42-4. Assume these facts about a firm:

Selling price	$25 per unit of product
Variable costs	$10 per unit of product
Fixed costs	$75,000

The fixed expenses are expected to increase $15,000 next year.
a. Compute the break-even point in units and in dollars before the increase in fixed expenses.
b. Compute the break-even point in units and in dollars after the increase in fixed expenses.
c. Compute the sales volume necessary to make the same earnings as last year ($150,000) when the firm sold 15,000 units.

E42-5. Assume these facts about a firm:

Selling price	$50 per unit of product
Variable costs	$30 per unit of product
Fixed costs	$75,000

The variable cost is expected to increase from $30 to $35 per unit.
a. Compute the contribution margin per unit before the variable-cost increase.
b. Compute the contribution margin ratio before the variable-cost increase.

c. Compute the break-even point after the increase in variable expenses in units and dollars.

d. Compute the sales volume necessary to make the same earnings as last year ($225,000) when the firm sold 15,000 units.

PROBLEMS (GROUP A)

P42-1. *Changing variables, break-even analysis.* The following facts are known about a corporation:

Selling price per unit of product	$21
Variable costs per unit of product	8
Fixed costs per unit of product (*if the firm produces and sells 14,000 units*)	5
Net sales (14,000 units at $21)	$294,000

REQUIRED: Compute the following. Assume each situation below is a *separate* case.

a. Break-even point in units.
b. Break-even point in dollars.
c. Break-even point in units if the variable costs per unit are expected to increase to $9.
d. Break-even point in dollars if the fixed costs are expected to increase to $71,000.
e. The amount by which the sales of the firm must increase if net earnings are to be $112,000, and if the fixed expenses are expected to increase to $71,000.
f. The amount by which the sales of the firm must increase if net earnings are to be $112,000, and if the variable expenses are to increase to $8.50.
g. Break-even point in dollars if selling price is reduced to $19.
h. The increase in sales necessary to produce net earnings of $112,000 if the selling price is reduced to $19 per unit.

P42-2. *Cost–volume relationships, change in pricing.* Jordan Corporation's Executive Committee has outlined the following three courses of action for the company for 1979:

Plan A   (1) Set a selling price on its product of $6.95.
            (2) Hold fixed expenses at the $314,000 level.
            (3) Have variable costs per unit amounting to $3.18.

Plan B   (1) Set a selling price on its product of $5.95.
            (2) Increase fixed expenses to $350,000 (additional advertising, etc.)
            (3) Have variable costs per unit amounting to $3.18.

Plan C   (1) Set a selling price on its product of $3.95.
            (2) Increase fixed expenses to $375,000 (additional advertising, etc.)
            (3) Reduce variable costs per unit to $2.00 by modifying the manufacturing process and changing the product's design.

REQUIRED: Under each of the three plans,

a. Compute the contribution margin per unit.
b. Compute the breakeven point in dollars.
c. Compute the breakeven point in units.

d. Compute the number of units that must be sold to produce net earnings of $105,000.

*P42-3. *Break-even analysis.* Flirton and Company produced the following results during 1978:

Total sales	12,000 units
Selling price per unit	$12
Total fixed expenses	$40,000
Total variable expenses	$84,000

During 1979, the next year, the management of the company plans to slightly modify the product, reduce the raw materials cost, reduce the price, and engage in an extensive advertising campaign. These changes are expected:
1. The selling price will be reduced to $9.95 per unit.
2. The variable costs per unit will amount to $6.50.
3. The fixed expenses will increase by $10,000 for the special advertising programs.

REQUIRED:

a. What is the break-even point for the company in terms of dollars, before giving effect to the changes?
b. What is the break-even point for the company in terms of units, before giving effect to the changes?
c. What is the break-even point for the company in terms of dollars, after giving effect to the changes?
d. What is the break-even point for the company in terms of units, after giving effect to the changes?
e. Draw a break-even graph. The y axis should go from zero to $200,000; the x axis should go from zero to 20,000 units. The break-even graph should be in terms of the original data—*not giving effect to the expected changes.*
f. On the break-even graph that you prepared in e above, draw in the following, using a different color ink or pencil lead: (1) the new sales line, giving effect to the changes; (2) the new fixed cost line, giving effect to the changes; (3) the new variable cost line, giving effect to the changes; (4) the new total cost line, giving effect to the changes.

PROBLEMS (GROUP B)

P42-4. *Break-even analysis.* These facts are taken from the records and assembled by the management of Bridmann, Inc.:

Number of units sold during year	71,000
Selling price per unit	$16
Total variable expenses	$852,000
Total fixed expenses	$100,000

Management is planning these changes during the coming year:
1. The selling price will be reduced to $14 per unit.
2. Fixed costs will increase by $12,000 for additional advertising campaigns.
3. Variable expenses are expected to increase from $12 to $13 per unit as a result of a new labor contract.

REQUIRED:

  a. What is the break-even point for the company in terms of units, before giving effect to the three expected changes?
  b. What is the break-even point in terms of units, after giving effect to the three changes?
  c. Management wants to *increase* earnings by $15,000 for the coming year. How many units must be sold to attain the new earnings level?

P42-5. *Break-even analysis.* The following tabulation is from records of Beewee, Inc., for 1978:

	TOTAL	FIXED	VARIABLE
Sales (61,000 units)	$235,216		
Cost of goods sold	101,000	$31,645	
General expenses	42,000	28,500	
Selling expenses	15,400	9,620	
Other expenses	9,750	4,281	

During 1979, the basic relationships are expected to be the same as 1978, except:
1. The selling price will be increased by 5% per unit.
2. All *variable costs* (except Variable selling expenses) are expected to increase by 6%.
3. All fixed costs will not change except General expenses (fixed), which will increase to $29,000.

REQUIRED:

  a. Compute the break-even point, before giving effect to the proposed 1979 changes.
  b. Compute the break-even point, after giving effect to the 1979 changes.
  c. Compute the net earnings for 1978.
  d. Compute the net earnings for 1979, if volume of units is the same as 1978.
  e. Compute the number of units that must be sold in 1979 to produce $80,000 of net earnings.

*P42-6. *Break-even analysis.* During 1978, Janfeb, Inc., had the following results:

Sales (25,000 units)	$162,000
Cost of goods sold	80,000
Operating expenses	80,000

The firm sells only one product. Management has estimated that 80% of the cost of goods sold for 1978 were variable costs, and that 40% of the operating expenses for 1978 were variable.

During the coming year (1979), top management expects to make several significant changes in operations, including a reduction in selling price to $5.95 per unit. A new labor contract will be in effect. This and other changes will increase variable costs per unit by about 10%. Fixed costs will go up by 5%.

a. What is the break-even point for the company in terms of dollars, before giving effect to the changes?

b. What is the break-even point for the company in terms of units, before giving effect to the changes?

c. What is the break-even point for the company in terms of dollars, after giving effect to the changes?

d. What is the break-even point for the company in terms of units, after giving effect to the changes?

e. Draw a break-even graph. The break-even graph should be in terms of the original data—*not giving effect to the expected changes.*

f. On the break-even graph that you prepared in e above, draw in the following, using a different-color ink or pencil lead: (1) the new sales line, giving effect to the changes; (2) the new fixed cost line, giving effect to the changes; (3) the new variable cost line, giving effect to the changes; (4) the new total cost line, giving effect to the changes.

g. Compute the number of units that the company would have to sell in 1979 to make the same net earnings as it did in 1978.

CUMULATIVE REVIEW PROBLEMS

P42-7. *Cumulative review problem*

a. Assume that a company is contemplating an increase in production from 1,000 units to 1,250 units. It is determined that the total costs would rise from $2,500 to $3,000.

(1) Compute the differential cost for the extra 250 units.

(2) Compute the differential cost per unit.

(3) Compute the cost per unit for the present production of 1,000 units.

b. Assume that a company purchased a machine for $3,500. Two years later, management decided to replace it with a newer, more efficient machine. The old machine can be sold for $300. Compute the sunk cost assuming straight-line depreciation, 5-year useful life, and $500 salvage value.

c. The Holmes Corporation determined the following information concerning 1978 earnings:

Sales	$200,000 (10,000 units)
Raw materials	20,000
Direct labor	35,000
Factory overhead	25,000 ($15,000 variable)
Selling expenses	13,000 ($9,000 variable)
General and administrative expenses	9,000 ($6,000 variable)

(1) Prepare an income statement for 1978, classifying fixed and variable costs.

(2) Compute the contribution margin per unit of product.

(3) Compute the contribution margin ratio.

(4) Compute the break-even point in units.

(5) Compute the break-even point in dollars of sales and costs.

*P42-8. *Cumulative review problem.* Below is a comparative income statement for a firm.

	1978	1977
Sales	$600,000	$400,000
Cost of goods sold	$200,000	$150,000
Selling expenses	85,000	60,000
General expenses	132,500	95,000
Total expenses	$417,500	$305,000
Net earnings	$182,500	$ 95,000

During 1977 and 1978, the company had a selling price for its only product of $4 per unit.

Plans for 1979:
1. Reduce the selling price to $3.49 per unit.
2. Increase fixed selling expenses by $50,000 for increased advertising and general marketing.

REQUIRED:

a. By comparing 1977 and 1978 operations, and without giving effect to the 1979 plans, compute:
   (1) Breakeven point in dollars.
   (2) Breakeven point in units.
   (3) Earnings per share, assuming 30,000 shares of common stock were outstanding during 1977 and 50,000 shares were outstanding during 1978. Preferred dividends amounting to $20,000 were declared each year.
b. Giving effect to the 1979 plans, compute:
   (1) Breakeven point in dollars.
   (2) Breakeven point in units.
   (3) Number of units that must be sold in 1979 to increase the *earnings per share* by 10% over 1978.

chapter 19

manufacturing accounting;
job order systems

43

MANUFACTURING ACCOUNTING

> ### OBJECTIVE

The objective of this unit is to describe one system for recording and reporting operations in a manufacturing firm. This system uses the periodic method (as contrasted to the perpetual method) of accounting for the three manufacturing inventories—raw materials, work in process, and finished goods.

> ### APPROACH TO ATTAINING THE OBJECTIVE

As you study about manufacturing accounting under the periodic method, pay special attention to these four questions, which the text following answers:

- *What are the three inventory accounts that manufacturing businesses maintain?*
- *What recording and reporting systems are commonly used in manufacturing firms?*
- *What is a manufacturing statement?*
- *How is the manufacturing statement related to the income statement?*

You have already learned that the manufacturing costs of a firm can be classified into three general categories: (1) *raw materials* (those materials and supplies used directly in manufacturing the product), (2) *direct labor* (those labor costs associated directly with the manufactured product, as opposed to supervisory or indirect labor), and (3) *factory overhead* (all costs of the factory except raw materials and direct labor). These three cost elements of manufacturing are accumulated in inventory accounts on a firm's financial statements. The balance sheet of a manufacturing company usually reports three inventories:

■ *What are the three inventory accounts that manufacturing businesses maintain?*

1. **Raw materials inventory.** This represents the cost of direct materials and supplies which are on hand at the balance sheet date. These raw materials have not yet been used to manufacture the products of the firm.

2. **Work in process inventory.** This represents the costs incurred in working on the goods that have not been completed as of the balance sheet date. For example, a firm might have 1,000 units of product which are still on the work tables at the balance sheet date. These products will be completed during the next period. The work in process inventory usually includes all three cost elements—raw materials, direct labor, and factory overhead.

3. **Finished goods inventory.** This represents the total costs incurred to produce the units that are completed but which have not yet been sold as of the balance sheet date. The finished goods inventory usually includes all three cost elements—raw materials, direct labor, and factory overhead.

A manufacturing company, therefore, must account for three separate inventories instead of the one that a merchandising firm accounts for.

THREE SYSTEMS IN MANUFACTURING ACCOUNTING

The three popular systems of recording and reporting inventories and manufacturing processes are:

1. The periodic system.
2. The job order system, which uses perpetual methods.
3. The process cost system, which also uses perpetual methods.

Future units explain the job order system and the process cost system. This unit describes the periodic method for reporting manufacturing operations.

■ *What recording and
reporting systems are
commonly used in
manufacturing firms?*

In a periodic system, the costs of inventories are determined by a detailed listing of the inventory items on hand at the close of the accounting period. When an inventory can be determined only by such a physical count at specified intervals, the system is known as a *periodic* system. In the periodic method of reporting inventories, at the end of each period's operations physical inventories are taken of the raw materials, work in process, and finished goods inventories. Then, also at the end of the period, calculations are made for the cost of goods manufactured and then for the cost of goods actually sold. The latter cost, as you know, is a necessary bit of data for the income statement. Let's first examine a firm's manufacturing statement, which is simply a separate report on the details of the cost of the goods manufactured.

STATEMENTS AND SCHEDULES OF A MANUFACTURING CORPORATION
(Periodic Method of Recording Inventories)

**Lakefront Manufacturing Corporation
MANUFACTURING STATEMENT
For the Year Ended December 31, 1978**

Work in process, January 1, 1978			$ 18,000
Manufacturing costs incurred during 1978:			
Raw materials used			
Raw materials inventory, January 1, 1978	$ 20,000		
Purchases of raw materials	171,000		
Raw materials available for use	$191,000		
Less raw materials inventory, December 31, 1978	119,000		
Raw materials used in manufacturing		$72,000	
Direct labor costs		50,000	
Factory overhead costs		30,000	
Total manufacturing costs			152,000
Total beginning work in process and current manufacturing costs			$170,000
Less work in process, December 31, 1978			25,000
Cost of goods manufactured in 1978			$145,000

**Lakefront Manufacturing Corporation
SCHEDULE OF FACTORY OVERHEAD
For the Year ended December 31, 1978**

Indirect labor	$16,000
Electricity	1,000
Other utilities	400
Depreciation on plant and equipment	10,000
Manufacturing supplies used	600
Insurance on the factory	1,000
Other factory overhead	1,000
	$30,000

The exhibit below shows four reports of Lakefront Manufacturing Corporation which are extremely useful to its management. Let's begin our study of the periodic system by looking at the details of the firm's **manufacturing statement** for the year ended December 31, 1978. This particular report is used primarily by management. It reports the costs incurred in the factory to manufacture the firm's products during a period of time.

- *What is a manufacturing statement?*

The first item listed is the beginning work in process. The $18,000 represents the total costs that were tied up in the goods in process at January 1, 1978. This means that a total cost of $18,000 for *raw materials, direct labor, and factory overhead* was incurred during the previous year (1977) to

---

Lakefront Manufacturing Corporation
SCHEDULE OF COST OF GOODS SOLD
For the Year Ended December 31, 1978

Finished goods inventory, January 1, 1978	$ 21,000
Cost of goods manufactured in 1978	145,000
Total cost of goods available for sale	$166,000
Less finished goods inventory, December 31, 1978	53,000
Cost of goods sold	$113,000

Lakefront Manufacturing Corporation
INCOME STATEMENT
For the Year Ended December 31, 1978

Revenues	
Net sales	$200,000
Other revenues	20,000
Total revenues	$220,000
Expenses	
Cost of goods sold	$113,000
Selling expenses	40,000
General and administrative expenses	10,000
Total expenses	$163,000
Net earnings	$ 57,000
Net earnings per share	$2.85

partially complete the goods that were on hand at January 1, 1978. These goods had to be completed during 1978 and more costs had to be incurred to complete them. Also, additional new goods were probably begun and completed during 1978.

Accounting records are kept to accumulate the costs of the three cost elements in the factory. Notice that $20,000 of raw materials (inventory) were on hand at January 1, 1978. Additional purchases of raw materials amounting to $171,000 were made during 1978. In the periodic system, a separate account, Purchases of raw materials, is usually used to record these purchases. Raw materials with a total cost of $191,000 were available for use in the factory during 1978. By making a physical count of the raw materials at December 31, 1978, management determined that $119,000 of raw materials were still on hand and *unused* at the end of the year. Therefore, the cost of raw materials actually *used* in production amounted to $72,000.

A separate account is kept to record direct labor costs. During the year, $50,000 of direct labor costs were incurred. Similarly, a control account for factory overhead costs accumulates the many categories of overhead. A separate *subsidiary ledger for factory overhead* can be kept to provide detailed records for controlling the various types of overhead. A **schedule of factory overhead** is shown directly below the manufacturing statement. This schedule is prepared directly from the factory overhead subsidiary ledger. During 1978, $30,000 of factory overhead costs were incurred.

The three cost elements incurred during 1978 total $152,000. Remember that this $152,000 of manufacturing cost was used to do two things: (1) part of it was used to complete the beginning inventory of work in process, and (2) the remaining part was used to begin and complete new goods and to just begin others.

To complete the manufacturing statement the firm took a physical inventory of work in process at December 31, 1978. This inventory revealed that some goods were still in process, with costs tied up in them totaling $25,000. This ending work in process inventory is deducted from the total of the beginning work in process and the current manufacturing costs to arrive at the *cost of the goods manufactured during 1978*. Note that when work in process is completed, it becomes finished goods inventory.

THE COST OF GOODS SOLD COMPUTATION

■ *How is the manufacturing statement related to the income statement?*

Next, examine the **schedule of cost of goods sold.** This computation begins with the January 1, 1978, inventory of finished goods: $21,000. The firm knows from its manufacturing statement that an additional $145,000 of costs were incurred in producing the goods in the factory during 1978. Together these figures produce a cost of goods available for sale amounting to $166,000. Another physical inventory of the finished goods unsold and still on hand was taken at December 31, 1978. The cost of these goods was

$53,000. By deducting the ending finished goods inventory from the cost of goods available for sale, the cost of goods sold is computed to be $113,000. This figure is entered on the income statement as an expense of 1978.

OTHER PROCEDURES OF THE PERIODIC METHOD
Manufacturing firms that use the periodic method of recording factory operations have a set of end-of-period procedures similar to those you studied for merchandising firms. Illustration 43-1 on pages 752–753 diagrams the various procedures associated with a manufacturing firm that uses the periodic method. Study the cycle outlined in this diagram carefully.

A FINAL NOTE
Appendix C at the end of this book is a detailed description of how a work sheet and adjusting and closing entries for a manufacturing operation are prepared. The same company and same figures that were used in this unit are used in the work sheet example in Appendix C.

➤ NEW TERMS

cost-of-goods-sold computation In a manufacturing firm, cost of goods sold is computed as follows: beginning finished goods inventory plus cost of goods manufactured (according to the manufacturing statement) less ending finished goods inventory; also called a cost of goods sold schedule. [p. 750]

finished goods inventory A current asset consisting of the costs incurred in manufacturing the firm's products (including raw materials costs, direct labor costs, and factory overhead costs); the finished goods inventory is comprised of products which are completed, but which have not been sold as of the balance sheet date. [p. 747]

manufacturing statement A report for management use which shows the cost of the goods that were manufactured during the period; beginning work in process inventory plus manufacturing costs (raw materials used, direct labor, and factory overhead) less ending work in process inventory equals cost of the goods that were manufactured during the period. [p. 749]

raw materials inventory A current asset consisting of the supplies and direct materials to be used in manufacturing a firm's product. [p. 747]

schedule of factory overhead A report which lists all of the factory overhead accounts appearing in the subsidiary factory overhead ledger with their balances; the total of the balances of these accounts must agree with the Factory overhead (control) account in the general ledger of the company. [p. 750]

work in process inventory A current asset consisting of the raw materials costs, direct labor costs, and factory overhead costs incurred in manufacturing the products which are *uncompleted* as of the balance sheet date; also called goods in process inventory. [p. 747]

➤ ASSIGNMENT MATERIAL

QUESTIONS
Q43-1. What are the three general categories of manufacturing costs? Briefly describe each category.

Q43-2. What are the three inventories of manufacturing firms? Briefly describe each.

THE ACCOUNTING CYCLE

Fundamental Activity 1
SELECTING RELEVANT DATA
to be entered into the
accounting system

Observing business transactions
(as evidenced by source
documents)

Fundamental Activity 2
PROCESSING THE DATA in a
accounting system

Recording business
transactions in a journal, using a
debit-credit approach. These
accounts are a basis for
accumulating the manufacturing
costs: Raw materials inventory;
Purchases of raw materials;
Work in process inventory;
Direct labor costs; Factory
overhead costs; Finished goods
inventory.

Posting the transactions from
the journal to the general ledger
to further classify the data.
Usually a subsidiary factory
overhead ledger is kept to
support the Factory overhead
costs account in the general
ledger.

Preparing a work sheet as an
organizational aid:
a. preparing a trial balance
b. entering adjustments
c. preparing an adjusted trial

Fundamental Activity 3
DESIGNING FINANCIAL
STATEMENTS and other reports
to be used for decisions

Income statement (used by
management and outsiders)

Retained earnings statement
(used by management and
outsiders)

Balance sheet (used by
management and outsiders)

Manufacturing statement (used
by management only)

Computation of Cost of goods
sold (used by management
only)

Schedule of factory overhead
(used by management only)

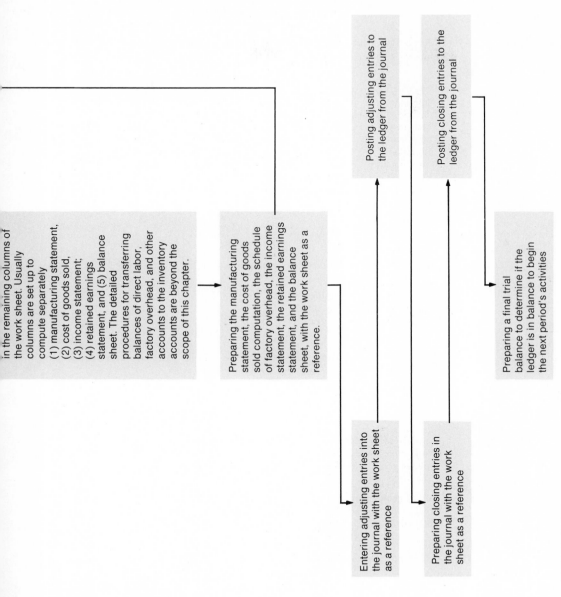

In the remaining columns of the work sheet. Usually columns are set up to compute separately (1) manufacturing statement, (2) cost of goods sold, (3) income statement; (4) retained earnings statement, and (5) balance sheet. The detailed procedures for transferring balances of direct labor, factory overhead, and other accounts to the inventory accounts are beyond the scope of this chapter.

Preparing the manufacturing statement, the cost of goods sold computation, the schedule of factory overhead, the income statement, the retained earnings statement, and the balance sheet, with the work sheet as a reference.

Entering adjusting entries into the journal with the work sheet as a reference

Preparing closing entries in the journal with the work sheet as a reference

Posting adjusting entries to the ledger from the journal

Posting closing entries to the ledger from the journal

Preparing a final trial balance to determine if the ledger is in balance to begin the next period's activities

ILLUSTRATION 43-1

Q43-3. What information is shown on a manufacturing statement?

Q43-4. How is cost of goods sold computed in a manufacturing company?

Q43-5. What is a schedule of factory overhead?

EXERCISES   E43-1. Merida Plans, Inc., trial balance (selected data) at December 31, 1978, the end of the year's operations follows:

Raw materials inventory	$ 20,000
Work in process inventory	30,000
Finished goods inventory	15,000
Purchases of raw materials	200,000
Direct labor costs	98,000
Indirect labor	63,000
Power—factory	3,000
Other utilities—factory	1,000
Depreciation—Plant and equipment	9,000
Factory insurance	2,000
Selling expenses	15,000
General expenses	12,000

The ending inventories, according to physical count at December 31, 1978, were:

Raw materials	$32,000
Work in process	36,000
Finished goods	21,000

Prepare a manufacturing statement for the firm for the year. Also calculate the amount of the cost of goods sold for 1978.

E43-2. Selected data for a year's operations are given below for Bell Company.

	BEGINNING	ENDING
Raw materials inventory	$10,000	$15,000
Work in process inventory	31,000	25,000
Finished goods inventory	50,000	51,000

Cost of goods manufactured	$200,000
Total factory overhead	20,000
Total direct labor	50,000

Calculate the total raw materials used in production.

E43-3. Complete the following statements.
   a. Beginning raw materials inventory plus purchases of raw materials less ending raw materials inventory equals. . .
   b. Cost of goods manufactured less cost of raw materials used in production less direct labor costs less beginning work in process inventory plus ending work in process inventory equals. . .

c. Cost of goods sold plus ending finished goods inventory less cost of goods manufactured equals. . .

d. Cost of goods sold plus ending finished goods inventory less beginning finished goods inventory equals. . .

E43-4. The financial statements and schedules of Barkers, Inc., reported the following amounts for 1978:

Cost of goods manufactured	$213,000
Cost of goods sold	250,000

It was discovered that all three of the inventories included errors because of inefficiencies in taking the December 31, 1978, physical inventories.

The ending raw materials inventory had been understated by $3,000.

The ending work in process inventory had been overstated by $1,000.

The ending finished goods inventory had been understated by $5,000.

Compute the correct figure that should have been reported for the Cost of goods manufactured and the Cost of goods sold.

PROBLEMS (GROUP A)

P43-1. *Relationships on manufacturing statement and income statement.* These facts are known about the manufacturing operations of a company for 1978:

Raw materials inventory, beginning	$ 50,000
Raw materials inventory, ending	40,000
Work in process, beginning	30,000
Work in process, ending	20,000
Finished goods inventory, beginning	100,000
Finished goods inventory, ending	80,000
Factory overhead	120,000
Direct labor	60,000
Purchases of raw materials	100,000
Net sales	500,000
Other revenues	10,000
Total expenses (other than cost of goods sold)	100,000
Extraordinary loss	5,000
Average number of shares of common stock outstanding during the period	10,000 shares

REQUIRED: Compute the following, showing all computations.

a. Raw materials used in production
b. Total manufacturing costs
c. Cost of goods manufactured
d. Cost of goods sold
e. Net earnings before extraordinary items
f. Net earnings per share
g. Gross profit

P43-2. *Preparation of manufacturing statement and income statement.* These facts are known about a manufacturing company for 1978:

Average number of shares of common stock outstanding during the year	20,000
Sales of finished products	$498,000
Sales returns and allowances	10,000
Sales discounts	3,000
Raw materials inventory, beginning	47,000
Raw materials inventory, ending	41,000
Work in process inventory, beginning	28,000
Work in process inventory, ending	21,000
Finished goods inventory, beginning	80,000
Finished goods inventory, ending	81,000
Factory overhead	100,000
Direct labor	55,000
Purchases of raw materials	118,000
Service revenue	21,000
Selling expenses	146,000
General, administrative, and other expenses	49,000

REQUIRED:

a. Prepare a manufacturing statement for the company (Northwest Drug Company).
b. Prepare a schedule of cost of goods sold.
c. Prepare an income statement.

P43-3. *Manufacturing statement and schedules; financial statements.* The general ledger of Auction Corporation for the year ended December 31, 1978, showed the following accounts and balances:

Cash	$ 9,000
Marketable securities	34,000
Accounts receivable	15,000
Allowance for uncollectibles	1,000
Raw materials inventory	20,000
Work in process inventory	15,000
Finished goods inventory	18,000
Prepaid insurance	2,000
Long-term investments	100,000
Plant and equipment	300,000
Accumulated depreciation	100,000
Accounts payable	31,000
Expenses payable	8,000
Federal income taxes payable	2,000
Bonds payable	130,000
Long-term notes payable	90,000
Common stock	60,000
Retained earnings	25,000
Dividends	5,000
Sales	390,000
Sales returns and allowances	11,000
Sales discounts	4,000
Rent revenue	40,000

Purchases of raw materials	150,000
Direct labor costs	45,000
Factory overhead costs	31,000
Selling expenses	30,000
General, administrative, and other expenses	88,000

Additional information: The factory overhead subsidiary ledger showed these balances: Indirect labor, $10,000; Manufacturing supplies, $300; Electricity, $1,000; Depreciation, $11,000; Insurance, $1,000; Other factory expenses, $7,700. A physical count of the inventories indicated that the December 31, 1978, balances were: Raw materials inventory, $12,000; Finished goods inventory, $60,000; Work in process inventory, $50,000. During the entire year, there were 20,000 shares of common stock outstanding.

REQUIRED:

    a. Prepare a manufacturing statement in good form.
    b. Prepare a schedule of factory overhead. Check to see if the total of the schedule agrees with the Factory overhead costs account in the general ledger.
    c. Prepare a schedule of cost of goods sold.
    d. Prepare an income statement.
    e. Prepare a balance sheet in good form. Be sure to include the *ending* inventories on the balance sheet. The ending retained earnings must be computed from the beginning balance plus net earnings less dividends.

PROBLEMS (GROUP B)

P43-4. *Preparation of manufacturing statement and income statement.* The Eastern Manufacturing Corporation accounting records included the following data for the year ended December 31, 1978.

General, administrative, and other expenses	$ 25,000
Average number of shares of common stock outstanding during the year, 20,000	
Sales of finished goods	$450,000
Sales returns and allowances	10,000
Sales discounts	1,000
Selling expenses	100,000
Raw materials inventory, beginning	25,000
Raw materials inventory, ending	20,000
Work in process inventory, beginning	14,000
Work in process inventory, ending	10,000
Finished goods inventory, beginning	46,000
Finished goods inventory, ending	29,000
Interest income	10,000
Dividends income	5,000
Factory overhead	60,000
Direct labor	40,000
Purchases of raw materials	89,000

REQUIRED:

    a. Prepare a manufacturing statement.
    b. Prepare a schedule of cost of goods sold.
    c. Prepare an income statement.

P43-5. *Manufacturing relationships.* Assume these facts concerning a manufacturing firm for 1978:

Average number of shares of common stock outstanding during the year	10,000
Sales of finished products	$175,000
Sales returns and allowances	2,000
Sales discounts	1,500
Raw materials inventory, beginning	12,000
Raw materials inventory, ending	15,000
Work in process inventory, beginning	7,000
Work in process inventory, ending	9,000
Finished goods inventory, beginning	24,000
Finished goods inventory, ending	25,000
Factory overhead	45,000
Direct labor	30,000
Purchases of raw materials	50,000
Service revenue	23,000
Selling expenses	10,000
General, administrative, and other expenses	11,000

REQUIRED:

a. From the information above, compute the following. Show all computations.
   (1) Raw materials used in production
   (2) Total manufacturing costs
   (3) Cost of goods manufactured
   (4) Cost of goods sold
   (5) Net earnings
   (6) Net earnings per share
   (7) Gross profit
b. Prepare a manufacturing statement for the company (Parker Manufacturing Company).
c. Prepare a schedule of cost of goods sold.

*P43-6. *Comprehensive manufacturing problem; statements and schedules.* Robberin, Inc., has operated a manufacturing business for several years. The accounts in the ledger at December 31, 1978, had balances as shown in the following list.

Cash	$ 15,000
General and administrative expenses	150,000
Marketable securities	60,000
Selling expenses	61,000
Accounts receivable	30,000
Factory overhead costs	65,000
Allowance for uncollectibles	2,000
Direct labor costs	59,000
Raw materials inventory	40,000
Purchases of raw materials	200,000
Work in process inventory	30,000
Rent revenue	30,000
Finished goods inventory	35,000
Sales discounts	7,000

Prepaid insurance	3,000
Sales returns and allowances	20,000
Long-term investments	200,000
Sales	800,000
Plant and equipment	700,000
Dividends	12,000
Accumulated depreciation—Plant and equipment	200,000
Retained earnings	116,000
Common stock	130,000
Accounts payable	40,000
Expenses payable	14,000
Long-term notes payable	150,000
Federal income taxes payable	5,000
Bonds payable	200,000

The factory overhead subsidiary ledger showed these balances: Indirect labor, $20,000; Manufacturing supplies used, $600; Electrical power, $2,000; Depreciation, $20,000; Insurance on factory, $3,000; Other factory overhead, $19,400.

Ending inventories were: Raw materials, $25,000; Work in process, $100,000; Finished goods, $140,000. During the entire year there were 45,000 shares of common stock outstanding.

REQUIRED:

a. Prepare a manufacturing statement in good form.
b. Prepare a schedule of factory overhead. Check to see if the total of the schedule agrees with the Factory overhead costs account in the general ledger.
c. Prepare a schedule of cost of goods sold.
d. Prepare an income statement.
e. Prepare a balance sheet in good form. Be sure to include the *ending* inventories on the balance sheet. The ending retained earnings must be computed from the beginning balance plus net earnings less dividends.

44

JOB ORDER SYSTEMS

> ### OBJECTIVE

The objective of this unit is to describe how manufacturing costs can be controlled and reported through the use of a job order cost accounting system, a system using the perpetual method of accounting for inventories.

> ### APPROACH TO ATTAINING THE OBJECTIVE

As you study job order cost accounting systems, direct your attention to these three questions, which the text following answers:

- *How does manufacturing involving mass production differ from production of individual orders?*
- *What is the structure of a cost accounting system?*
- *What journal entries and records are involved in a job order cost accounting system?*

JOB ORDER COSTING AND PROCESS COSTING

■ How does manufacturing involving mass production differ from production of individual orders?

In Unit 43 you studied manufacturing accounting in which the periodic method of reporting inventories was used. In that system, at the end of a period's operations, physical inventories were taken of the raw materials inventory, the work in process inventory, and the finished goods inventory. Then, also at the end of the period, calculations were made for the cost of goods manufactured (the manufacturing statement was prepared). Next, the cost of goods sold was calculated for the income statement. This periodic method has at least one significant limitation. The limitation is that the costs of manufacturing cannot be reported easily *during* the period's operations. Costs are determined *periodically,* not perpetually for continuous review.

The perpetual system for controlling factory costs is more popular than the periodic method because of daily cost controls possible under the perpetual system. There are two basic perpetual cost accounting systems. They are the *job order accounting system* and the *process cost accounting system.*

A **job order accounting** system is designed to control the costs for firms which produce *individual* orders or *individual* jobs. For example, a custom printing operation would probably use a job order cost accounting system. A company that builds custom-made boats also would probably use a job order cost accounting system. In such a system, individual cost records are kept for each job. The records therefore accumulate information on the costs of raw materials, direct labor, and factory overhead for *each* job. The selling price of the job can be compared to the total cost of that job; and the three cost elements of the job (raw materials, direct labor, and factory overhead) can be analyzed for control purposes and can be used as a basis for future pricing of similar jobs.

A **process cost accounting** system, on the other hand, is designed to control the costs for firms which mass-produce goods. For example, a food-processing plant might produce thousands of cans of food daily. The control emphasis in this plant would not be on the individual job or individual unit (can of food); instead emphasis would be placed on controlling the operating processes or departments within the plant. A factory that mass-produces automobile parts, as another example, might be organized into four departments: stamping department, trimming department, assembly department, and painting department. In a process cost accounting system, the cost records would be kept by departments (instead of by jobs). The three cost elements (raw materials, direct labor, and factory overhead) then could be analyzed and controlled for each separate department.

A PERPETUAL COST ACCOUNTING SYSTEM ILLUSTRATED

Whether a firm uses a job order cost accounting system or a process cost account system, certain basic procedures for accumulating cost are the same in both systems. Illustration 44-1 diagrams a basic cost accounting system which uses perpetual inventories. Note the relationships of the three perpet-

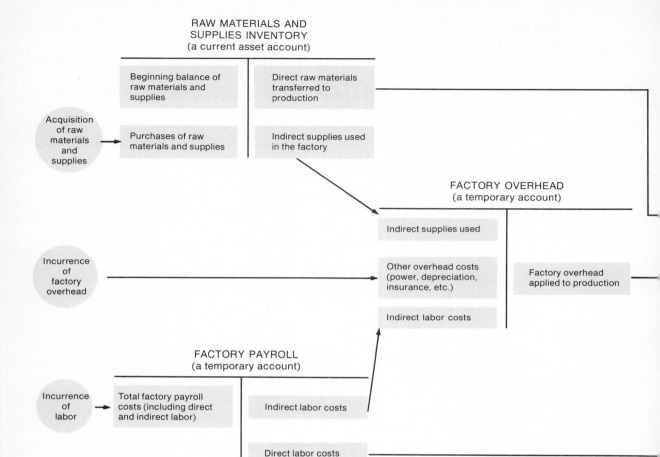

RAW MATERIALS AND
SUPPLIES INVENTORY
(a current asset account)

Acquisition of raw materials and supplies

Beginning balance of raw materials and supplies

Purchases of raw materials and supplies

Direct raw materials transferred to production

Indirect supplies used in the factory

FACTORY OVERHEAD
(a temporary account)

Indirect supplies used

Incurrence of factory overhead

Other overhead costs (power, depreciation, insurance, etc.)

Indirect labor costs

Factory overhead applied to production

FACTORY PAYROLL
(a temporary account)

Incurrence of labor

Total factory payroll costs (including direct and indirect labor)

Indirect labor costs

Direct labor costs

ILLUSTRATION 44-1

■ *What is the structure of a cost accounting system?*

ual inventories (raw materials and supplies, work in process, and finished goods) and the other accounts involved in this basic system. Carefully study this diagram and refer to it as you read the remainder of this unit.

BUSINESS TRANSACTIONS AND RECORDS

The rest of this unit describes in detail the job order variety of cost accounting. With the help of a variety of examples, we will examine the journal entries and records involved in this system.

Accounting for materials A manufacturing firm's general ledger includes an inventory account called Raw materials and supplies inventory (refer to Illustration 44-1). This current asset account usually has a debit balance at the beginning and end of each accounting period. When a firm uses many kinds

ILLUSTRATION OF A COST ACCOUNTING SYSTEM
USING PERPETUAL INVENTORIES

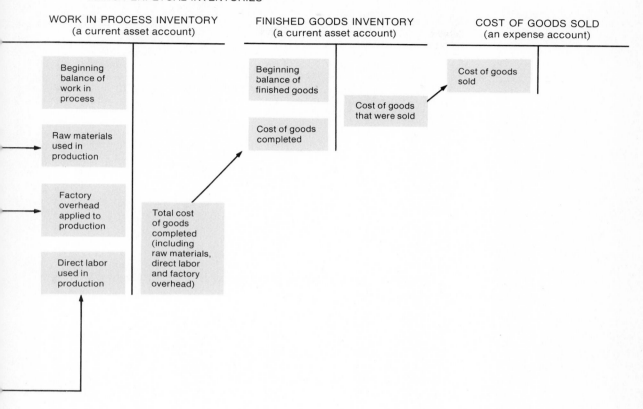

| WORK IN PROCESS INVENTORY (a current asset account) | FINISHED GOODS INVENTORY (a current asset account) | COST OF GOODS SOLD (an expense account) |

of raw materials and supplies, a subsidiary ledger can be kept to support the general ledger account. Such a ledger is usually called a *raw materials ledger* or **stores ledger.** A typical stores ledger account is shown in Illustration 44-2.

As a subsidiary record the stores ledger serves several purposes. First, the card keeps a continuous record of the quantity of each raw material on hand. Second, when the card shows that the supply has reached a certain level (the reorder point), an order can be placed to replace the stock. And third, these records provide written evidence that all raw materials purchases are actually used in production.

When the factory needs raw materials, a source document called a **materials requisition** is prepared to give the warehouse clerk authority to transfer materials to the factory. A typical materials requisition is shown in Illustration 44-3.

- *What journal entries and records are involved in a job order cost accounting system?*

STORES LEDGER CARD

Stock account no. _____

Description of item _____   Reorder point _____

Location in warehouse _____   Reorder quantity _____

Date	Ref.	Received			Issued			Balance		
		No. of Units	Unit Cost	Total Cost	No. of Units	Unit Cost	Total Cost	No. of Units	Unit Cost	Total Cost

ILLUSTRATION 44-2

The general journal that follows shows two entries dealing with raw materials and supplies.

1978 Aug.	28	Raw materials and supplies inventory	2,000	
		Accounts payable		2,000
		Purchased raw materials and supplies from Z Corp., terms 2/10, n/30.		
	30	Work in process inventory	1,000	
		Factory overhead	400	
		Raw materials and supplies inventory		1,400
		Issued raw materials and supplies to the factory: Materials requisition 904 for $1,000 and Materials requisition 905 for $400.		

The first entry illustrates the purchase of raw materials and supplies on credit. The Raw materials and supplies inventory account is debited for each purchase so that the account balance can be kept current. Every time that this account is increased, the appropriate subsidiary ledger accounts (stores cards) are increased as well. For example, if the $2,000 purchase consisted of $200 of Part 123 and $1,800 of Part 435, then the $200 would be recorded on the stores card for Part 123 as an increase (in the "Received" column) and the $1,800 would be recorded on the stores card for Part 435 in the same way. At

MATERIALS REQUISITION FORM

Requested by _____ Materials requisition no. _____
(signature)

Issued by _____ Date _____ Charge to Job No. _____
(signature)

Stock account number	Description of item	No. of Units	Unit Cost	Total Cost

ILLUSTRATION 44-3

any point in time, the total of all the balances of the stores ledger cards would equal the balance of the Raw materials and supplies inventory account in the general ledger.

The second journal entry illustrates the issuance of $1,400 of raw materials and supplies into the factory from the warehouse. The materials requisition form would be the source document supporting this entry. The entry shows that $1,000 of direct raw materials were issued to production jobs. Therefore, the Work in process inventory account is debited for that amount. When indirect materials and supplies (those not being used directly in manufacturing the product) are issued, the Factory overhead account is debited. You can trace these issuances in Illustration 44-1. Note that Factory overhead is a temporary account; its balance eventually becomes part of Work in process inventory.

Subsidiary supporting records must also be kept for the Work in process inventory account. The supporting records (subsidiary ledger) for Work in process inventory are the **job cost cards** or the job cost ledger. Illustration 44-4 presents a typical job cost card. A card (ledger page) is prepared for each job.

As the raw materials are requisitioned and transferred from the warehouse to be used on the jobs, the Work in process inventory account is debited and the Raw materials and supplies inventory account is credited (as shown in the above example). And each time the Work in process inventory is debited for materials used, the appropriate job cost cards are used to record the materials usage. The first set of columns on the job cost card shows the

```
                              JOB COST CARD

  Job no. _____   Description of job _____
  _____

  Starting date _____   Expected completion date _____   Completion date _____
```

Raw materials		Direct labor		Factory overhead	
Ref.	Amount	Ref.	Amount	Ref.	Amount

```
  Total job cost: Raw materials        _____   Comments: _____
                  Direct labor         _____   _____
                  Factory overhead     _____
                                       _____   _____
  Job selling price:                   _____   _____
```

ILLUSTRATION 44-4

dollar amount of materials used and the reference, usually the materials requisition number.

Accounting for direct labor The second cost element, direct labor, is accumulated temporarily in an account called **Factory payroll.** Refer again to Illustration 44-1. When the factory payroll is prepared, the following entry is made first:

1978				
Aug.	25	Factory payroll	5,000	
		Taxes withheld (a liability)		400
		Salaries payable		4,600

The Factory payroll account includes both direct labor costs and indirect labor costs (supervisory labor which relates to *all* jobs and is considered factory overhead). Therefore the factory payroll is further analyzed and classified into the two categories of labor. This entry is made:

1978 Aug.	25	Work in process inventory	4,000	
		Factory overhead	1,000	
		Factory payroll		5,000
		To transfer the balance of Factory		
		payroll to job cost cards (for direct		
		labor) and to Factory overhead.		

The temporary account, Factory payroll, is reduced to zero by the entry. The direct labor cost of the payroll is determined to be $4,000; therefore, this amount is debited directly to the Work in process inventory account. The indirect (supervisory) labor is debited to the Factory overhead account, which eventually also will become part of the Work in process inventory.

Each time the Work in process inventory account is debited for direct labor, the supporting job cost cards must be brought up to date. The direct labor costs are posted to the job cost cards for the jobs involved. For example, assume that the $4,000 of direct labor cost was used as follows: $1,000 of direct labor for Job 241, $500 of direct labor for Job 244, and $2,500 of direct labor for Job 600. In this case each amount would be posted to the appropriate job card.

Accounting for factory overhead As shown in Illustration 44-1, the **Factory overhead** account is a temporary account used to accumulate the overhead costs before they become part of the Work in process inventory. The Factory overhead account is debited for:

1. All indirect materials and supplies used in the factory (already illustrated).
2. All indirect labor costs (already illustrated).
3. All other factory overhead items, such as power, depreciation, factory insurance, factory taxes, etc.

As the other factory overhead items are incurred, the Factory overhead account is debited and Cash, Accounts payable, Accumulated depreciation, or some other appropriate account is credited, depending upon the circumstances. Most firms also keep a *subsidiary ledger for factory overhead.* This ledger simply has a ledger page for each type of overhead. Every time the Factory overhead account in the general ledger is debited, the appropriate subsidiary ledger account is also debited to keep a detailed record of the composition of the overhead.

Notice in Illustration 44-1 that the Factory overhead account is credited and the Work in process inventory account is debited to transfer the factory overhead costs to the Work in process. A general journal entry made to record this kind of transfer would look like this:

1978 Aug.	25	Work in process inventory Factory overhead To apply factory overhead to the jobs.	3,000	3,000

This process of transferring overhead to the work in process is usually done on an *estimated* basis because management cannot wait until the end of the period when all the overhead costs are actually incurred and recorded. The job cost cards must be kept up to date daily if the total costs are to be controlled effectively. For example, several jobs might be finished in some factories each day. The total cost of each of these jobs must be calculated then before all the overhead costs are recorded for the month (power costs, for example).

One common way of estimating the overhead to be applied to jobs can be illustrated with this example. Assume that a firm expects to incur $50,000 of direct labor costs in working on its jobs in the coming accounting period. This figure represents the best estimate that management can make. It is based on the information available about the jobs to be worked on and the cost of direct labor. Further, assume that the firm expects to incur $40,000 of factory overhead costs during the same period. This is also management's best estimate. If these estimates are reasonable, then it can be concluded that: For *every dollar of direct labor, there is estimated to be 80 cents of factory overhead.* That is, factory overhead costs are expected to total 80% of direct labor costs. In equation form:

$$\text{Overhead rate} = \frac{\text{Estimated factory overhead costs}}{\text{Estimated direct labor costs}}$$

$$= \frac{\$40,000}{\$50,000} = 80\%$$

The **factory overhead rate** can be used as the basis for transferring factory overhead to work in process and to the job cost cards. For example, if the direct labor costs for a day total $1,000, then the factory overhead is estimated to be $800 (or 80% of the $1,000). The entry would be a debit to Work in process inventory (and to the job cost cards) for $800 and a credit to the Factory overhead account. Many firms also calculate direct labor costs for jobs daily so that current cost figures can be used for control.

At the end of the accounting period, *if the estimates are correct,* the debit side of the Factory overhead account will amount to $40,000, the actual overhead incurred; and the credit side of the Factory overhead account will also be $40,000 (calculated as 80% of the $50,000 direct labor costs). Of course, the estimates would be expected to be slightly incorrect from time to time. *The next unit will explain the accounting effects of any remaining balance of the Factory overhead account at the end of the accounting period.*

Accounting for completed goods When a job is completed, the job cost card shows the total cost of the job, including raw materials, direct labor, and factory overhead. The job now becomes part of finished goods and is ready for sale. For example, assume that Job 484 has been completed with a total cost of $3,218. The entry to reflect completion of the job is:

1978 Aug.	30	Finished goods inventory	3,218	
		Work in process inventory		3,218
		Completed Job 484.		

The job cost card (no. 484) would be removed from the subsidiary records supporting the work in process inventory and filed for future reference. Finished goods subsidiary records would also be kept to support the Finished goods inventory account. The completed job cost cards could be used for this purpose.

Accounting for job sales If Job 484 were sold for $4,000, the following entry would be made:

1975 Sept.	1	Cost of goods sold	3,218	
		Finished goods inventory		3,218
		Accounts receivable	4,000	
		Sales		4,000
		Sold Job 484, costing $3,218, for $4,000 on credit.		

factory overhead A temporary account used in a cost accounting system to accumulate all factory overhead costs, including indirect labor, indirect materials and supplies, and other overhead expenses; the balance of this account is transferred each period to the Work in process inventory account. [p. 767]

factory overhead rate Often expressed as the percent that the estimated factory overhead costs are of the estimated direct labor costs; this rate is used to apply factory overhead to the jobs; Work in process inventory is debited and the Factory overhead account is credited to transfer the overhead to the individual jobs and to the work in process control account; actual factory overhead is not transferred to work in process—this is not done because the actual amounts are not known with certainty throughout the operating period. [p. 768]

factory payroll A temporary account used in a cost accounting system to accumulate all payroll costs of the manufacturing operations; the balance of the account consists of direct labor costs and indirect labor costs; the direct labor costs are transferred to the Work in process inventory account and the indirect labor costs become part of Factory overhead, which in turn becomes part of work in process. [p. 766]

job cost card The subsidiary record used to support the Work in process inventory account in a job order cost accounting system; the job cost cards are referred to as the work in process subsidiary ledger, see illustration in the text. [p. 765]

job order cost accounting A perpetual inventory system of accounting for factory costs, where individual records are kept for each job or order manufactured in the factory. [p. 761]

materials requisition Written authorization for the transfer of material from warehouse to factory; this source document provides a record of all transfers of raw materials and supplies from the warehouse (Raw materials and inventory account) to the factory (Work in process account or Factory overhead account). [p. 763]

process cost accounting A perpetual inventory accounting system, where costs are accumulated and records are kept according to departments or processes in the factory; appropriate for mass producton operations. [p. 761]

stores ledger The subsidiary ledger supporting the Raw materials and supplies account; see the stores ledger card illustrated in the text. [p. 763]

> **ASSIGNMENT MATERIAL**

QUESTIONS   Q44-1. Contrast job order and process cost accounting.

Q44-2. What entry is made in a job order cost accounting system when raw materials are purchased? when they are used on jobs?

Q44-3. How is the factory payroll recorded and then distributed?

Q44-4. What are the journal entries associated with factory overhead in a job order system?

Q44-5. For each of the general ledger accounts in a job order system listed below, indicate the name of the subsidiary ledger that is used to accumulate detailed information about the account:
a. Raw materials and supplies inventory.
b. Work in process inventory.
c. Finished goods inventory.
d. Factory overhead.

Q44-6. Describe the function of each of the following documents used in a job order cost accounting system:
a. Stores ledger card.
b. Materials requisition.
c. Job cost card.

EXERCISES

E44-1. Make accounting entries in general journal form to record the following business transactions. The firm uses a job order cost accounting system.
   a. Purchased 1,000 units of raw materials for $13,100 cash.
   b. Issued 250 units of raw materials to factory jobs, $2,000, materials requisition 200.
   c. Issued supplies with a total cost of $700 for general use in the factory, materials requisition 201.
   d. The factory payroll totaled $10,000 (direct labor totaled $7,500). FICA withheld was $50 and Federal income tax withheld was $150. Record the payroll.
   e. Transfer the balance of the Factory payroll account.

E44-2. Make accounting entries in general journal form to record the following business transactions. The firm uses a job order cost accounting system.
   a. Assume that a firm expects to incur $75,000 of factory overhead costs during the period and $100,000 of direct labor costs. Compute the overhead rate.
   b. Direct labor costs for a day totaled $2,000. Use the rate computed in part a to record the factory overhead.
   c. Assume that Job 600 has been completed, with a total cost of $7,110.
   d. Job 600 was sold for $7,500 on credit.

E44-3. Record the following transactions in general journal form. The company uses a job order cost accounting system. Use the perpetual system.
   a. Purchased raw materials for cash, $5,000.
   b. Issued raw materials to factory jobs, $2,000.
   c. Issued supplies with a total cost of $500 for general use in the factory.
   d. The factory payroll totaled $20,000 (direct labor totaled $11,000). FICA withheld was $50 and Federal income tax withheld was $150. Record the payroll.
   e. Transfer the balance of the Factory payroll account.
   f. Applied overhead at the rate of 75% of direct labor costs.
   g. Completed the job. Raw materials costs on the job totaled $300 and direct labor costs totaled $500. Transferred the job to finished goods.
   h. Sold job mentioned in part g for $2,500, with terms of 2/15, n/60.

E44-4. Ringo Corporation uses a job order cost accounting system. Make entries in general journal form to record the following business transactions:
   a. The factory payroll totaled $38,000 for the week. FICA withheld amounted to $1,700; federal income taxes withheld amounted to $4,260; state income taxes withheld amounted to $290.
   b. Transferred the balance of Factory payroll: 90% of the factory payroll was direct labor, and the remainder was indirect labor.
   c. Purchased 131,500 units of raw material A from Star Company, with terms of 2/10, n/30, $30,630.
   d. Issued materials into the production processes as follows:

[a] 141	Raw material A to be used on Job 216	$2,600
[a] 142	Raw material B to be used on Job 201	4,000
[a] 143	Supplies to be used in the factory for general purposes	1,500

[a] Materials requisition number.

   e. Applied factory overhead to work in process. The overhead rate is 62% of direct labor costs.
   f. Paid the monthly utility bill, $1,072, for the factory.

g. Paid the insurance expense for the factory, $1,000.

h. Completed Job 211. The job cost card for number 211 showed total costs as follows:

Raw materials	$10,000
Direct labor	12,000

Overhead had been applied to all jobs at the rate of 62%.

i. Sold Job 211 for $40,000 cash. See part h.

j. Sold Job 214 for $24,000, with terms of 1/10, n/30. The job cost card for Job 214 showed a total cost of $16,900, including direct labor, raw materials, and factory overhead.

PROBLEMS (GROUP A)

P44-1. *Job order entries.* Make accounting entries in general journal form to record the following business transactions. The firm uses a job order cost accounting system.

a. Purchased 10,000 units of raw material X from ABC Company on terms of 2/10, n/30. The total cost is $4,320.

b. Issued materials and supplies into the factory as follows:
 (1) Raw material X to be used on Job 241; cost, $1,000; materials requisition no. 1040.
 (2) Supplies to be used in the factory for general maintenance, $141; Materials requisition 1041.

c. The factory payroll amounted to $8,000. FICA withheld amounted to $400 and income taxes withheld amounted to $1,000.

d. Transferred the balance of Factory payroll: direct labor was $7,000 and indirect labor was $1,000.

e. Applied the factory overhead to work in process. The overhead rate is 70% of direct labor costs.

f. Paid the power bill for the factory, $700.

g. Completed Job 456. Raw materials costs on the job totaled $300 and direct labor costs totaled $900. Transferred the job to finished goods. Overhead had been applied at the 70% rate.

h. Sold Job 456 for $2,300 cash.

P44-2. *Job order entries; supporting records.* The balance sheet of the Debbit Company, a custom toy manufacturing firm, is shown below:

Debbit Company
BALANCE SHEET
January 1, 1978

ASSETS

Cash on hand and in banks	$ 87,900
Accounts receivable (net)	11,000
Raw materials inventory	4,000
Work in process—Toys	9,000
Finished toys	8,000
Investments	20,000
	$139,900

Accounts payable .... $ 6,000

Common stock.. 80,000
Retained earnings... 53,900
$139,900

Selected transactions for the month of January are shown below:

a. Paid selling expenses, $5,000.
b. Purchased raw materials on credit, $13,000.
c. Incurred direct labor and indirect labor amounting to $13,400 (payroll).
d. Transferred the balance of Factory payroll: Direct labor, $9,000; Indirect labor, $4,400.
e. Incurred overhead costs amounting to $7,000; paid cash.
f. Paid general and administrative expenses, $1,000.
g. Overhead is applied to jobs at the rate of 65% of direct labor costs.
h. Completed toys and transferred them to the finished goods storage area. The total cost of these toys (including raw materials, direct labor, and applied overhead) amounted to $25,000.
i. Sold toys which had cost $30,000 to manufacture for $50,000 cash.

REQUIRED:

a. Record the transactions in general journal form.
b. List as many supporting records (subsidiary records) as you can that would support the accounts appearing on the Debbit Company balance sheet.

*P44-3. *Job cost computations.* The following table contains data about several independent cases.

JOB NO.	TOTAL RAW MATERIALS COST OF JOB	TOTAL DIRECT LABOR COST OF JOB	FACTORY OVERHEAD RATE, BASED ON DIRECT LABOR COST	TOTAL OVERHEAD COST OF JOB	TOTAL COST OF JOB	SELLING PRICE OF JOB	GROSS PROFIT MADE ON JOB
1,496	$1,000	———	80%	———	———	$5,000	$2,000
2,150	$3,000	$9,000	70%	———	———	$25,000	———
3,506	$3,500	———	60%	———	———	$15,000	$2,000
4,111	———	$2,000	75%	———	$9,000	———	$1,000
6,543	$5,000	———	25%	———	———	$30,000	$10,000

REQUIRED: Compute the missing amounts. Show computations.

PROBLEMS (GROUP B)

P44-4. *Job order entries.* Make accounting entries in general journal form to record the following business transactions. The firm uses a job order cost accounting system.

a. Purchased 15,000 units of raw material 17 from Ace Suppliers for cash, $7,500.

b. Issued 2,000 units of raw material 17 to be used on Job 18, $1,000, Materials requisition 387.

c. Issued supplies with a total cost of $400 for general use in the factory, Materials requsition 388.

d. The factory payroll totaled $3,000 (direct labor totaled $2,300). FICA withheld was $60 and Federal income tax withheld was $150. Record the payroll.

e. Transfer the balance of the Factory payroll account.

f. Applied overhead at the rate of 75% of direct labor costs.

g. Completed Job 500. Raw materials costs on the job totaled $100 and direct labor costs totaled $300. Transferred the job to finished goods.

h. Sold Job 500 for $900, with terms of 2/15, n/60.

P44-5. *Job order entries.* Bulwark Corporation uses a job order cost accounting system. Make entries in general journal form to record the following business transactions:

a. The factory payroll totaled $19,000 for the week. FICA withheld amounted to $850; Federal income taxes withheld amounted to $2,130; State income taxes withheld amounted to $145.

b. Transferred the balance of Factory payroll: 90% of the factory payroll was direct labor, and the remainder was indirect labor.

c. Purchased 131,500 units of raw material *A* from Oscarco Company, with terms of 2/10, n/30, $15,315.

d. Issued materials into the production processes as follows (the numbers 141, 142, and 143 are materials requisition numbers):

141	Raw material A to be used on job 216	$1,300
142	Raw material B to be used on job 201	2,000
143	Supplies to be used in the factory for general purposes	750

e. Applied factory overhead to work in process. The overhead rate is 62% of direct labor costs.

f. Paid the factory's monthly utility bill, $536.

g. Paid the insurance expense for the factory, $500.

h. Completed Job 211. The job cost card for number 211 showed total costs as follows:

Raw materials	$5,000
Direct labor	6,000

Overhead had been applied to all jobs at the rate of 62%.

i. Sold Job 211 for $20,000 cash. See item h.

j. Sold Job 214 for $12,000, with terms of 1/10, n/30. The job cost card for Job 214 showed a total cost of $8,450, including direct labor, raw materials, and factory overhead.

*P44-6. *"T" account analysis; account relationships, job-order.* Assume that you have just purchased an interest in a manufacturing operation. A complete set of accounting records is not available, but you are able to gather certain bits of data from past records of last year's operations.

Beginning balance of Raw materials and supplies inventory, $10,000

Indirect supplies used in the factory, $2,000

Purchases of raw materials and supplies, $150,000

Factory overhead applied to production, $90,000

Indirect labor costs incurred, $15,000

Total factory payroll, $88,000

Beginning balance of Work in process inventory, $100,000

Total cost of goods completed and transferred to finished goods, $117,000

Ending work in process inventory, $233,000

Cost of goods sold, $100,000

Ending finished goods inventory, $57,000

One important figure that you cannot seem to locate is the *ending* balance of Raw materials and supplies inventory. This figure is needed before financial statements for the period can be completed. From the information available, determine the amount of the ending inventory of Raw materials and supplies.

Hint: Set up "T" accounts similar to the ones in Illustration 44-1. Fill in the known information, and see if you can determine the missing amounts. At the end of the period, the Factory overhead account and the Factory payroll accounts had zero balances.

CUMULATIVE REVIEW PROBLEMS

P44-7. *Cumulative review problem (periodic, manufacturing).* The general ledger of Oscar Corporation for the year ended December 31, 1978 showed the following accounts and balances:

Cash	18,000
Marketable securities	68,000
Accounts receivable	30,000
Allowance for uncollectibles	2,000
Raw materials inventory	40,000
Work in process inventory	30,000
Finished goods inventory	36,000
Prepaid insurance	4,000
Long-term investments	200,000
Plant and equipment	600,000
Accumulated depreciation	200,000
Accounts payable	62,000
Expenses payable	16,000
Federal income taxes payable	4,000
Bonds payable	260,000
Long-term notes payable	180,000
Common stock	120,000
Retained earnings	50,000
Dividends	10,000
Sales	780,000
Sales returns and allowances	22,000
Sales discounts	8,000
Rent revenue	80,000
Purchases of raw materials	300,000
Direct labor costs	90,000
Factory overhead costs	62,000
Selling expenses	60,000
General, administrative, and other expenses	176,000

Additional information: The factory overhead subsidiary ledger showed these balances—Indirect labor, $20,000; Manufacturing supplies, $600; Electricity, $2,000; Depreciation, $22,000; Insurance, $2,000; Other factory expenses, $15,400.

A physical count of the inventories indicated that the December 31, 1978 balances were:

Raw materials inventory	$ 24,000
Finished goods inventory	120,000
Work in process inventory	100,000

During the entire year, there were 20,000 shares of common stock outstanding.

REQUIRED:

a. Prepare a manufacturing statement in good form.
b. Prepare a schedule of factory overhead. Check to see if the total of the schedule agrees with the Factory overhead costs account in the general ledger.
c. Prepare a schedule of cost of goods sold.
d. Prepare an income statement.
e. Prepare a balance sheet in good form. Be sure to include the *ending* inventories on the balance sheet. The ending retained earnings must be computed from the beginning balance plus net earnings less dividends.

P44-8. *Cumulative review problem (job order)*. Make accounting entries in general journal form to record the following business transactions. The firm uses a job order cost accounting system.

a. Purchased 10,000 units of raw material X from Treasure Company, terms of 2/10, n/30. The total cost is $8,640.
b. Issued materials and supplies into the factory as follows:
   (1) Raw material X to be used on Job 241; cost, $2,000; materials requisition 1040.
   (2) Supplies to be used in the factory for general maintenance, $282; Materials requisiton 1041.
c. The factory payroll amounted to $16,000. FICA withheld amounted to $800 and income taxes withheld amounted to $2,000.
d. Transferred the balance of Factory payroll: Direct labor was $14,000 and indirect labor was $2,000.
e. Applied the factory overhead to work in process. The overhead rate is 70% of direct labor costs.
f. Paid the power bill for the factory, $1,400.
g. Completed Job 456. Raw materials cost on the job totaled $600, and direct labor costs totaled $1,800. Transferred the job to finished goods. Overhead had been applied at the 70% rate.
h. Sold Job 456 for $4,600 cash.

chapter 20

process cost accounting

PROCESS COST ACCOUNTING-COST FLOWS

➤ OBJECTIVE

The objective of this unit is to describe how manufacturing costs can be controlled and reported through the use of a process cost accounting system, a system using the perpetual method of accounting for inventories.

➤ APPROACH TO ATTAINING THE OBJECTIVE

As you study about process cost accounting systems, pay special attention to these three questions, which the text following answers:

- *How do the structure and objectives of process costing differ from job costing?*
- *What journal entries, records, and reports are involved in a process cost accounting system?*
- *How is cost accounting used to improve management's decision making?*

■ *How do the structure
and objectives of
process costing differ
from job costing?*

Illustration 44-1 in Unit 44 diagrammed the relationships among the accounts in a cost accounting system. These same basic relationships are present in *both* job order cost accounting and process cost accounting. The difference between the two systems is one of emphasis. The job order system emphasizes control of the individual jobs; therefore the Work in process inventory account is supported by job cost records. In a process cost system, the emphasis is on cost control of the processes or departments. Therefore, the work in process must be analyzed by departments through departmental records.

A common procedure is to set up in the general ledger *several* work in process inventory accounts—one for each department or process to be controlled. Thus, there would be no need for job cost records. Most of the other accounts and records as described in Unit 44 would remain the same in this system. In this unit we will examine in detail an example of process costing. These accounts in a general ledger will be used:

> Raw materials and supplies inventory
> Work in process inventory—Department A
> Finished goods inventory
> Factory payroll
> Factory overhead
> Cost of goods sold

One week's operations will be illustrated.

**A COMPREHENSIVE
EXAMPLE OF
PROCESS COST
ACCOUNTING**

A partial general ledger for our example is shown on the next page. First, note that each of the three inventory accounts has a beginning balance. Raw materials and supplies inventory has a beginning balance of $30,000. The Work in process inventory beginning balance amounts to $19,790. This figure is further broken down into the three cost elements. In a process system, records must be kept *by each department* to account for the actual physical units that are produced by the department. In this example, the $19,790 represents the costs incurred last period for partially completing 5,000 units of product. It is also known that all these units are 100% complete as to raw materials, but only 60% complete as to direct labor and 60% complete as to factory overhead. That is, more work in terms of direct labor and overhead must be added to complete the units in the coming week. The third inventory, Finished goods, has a beginning balance of $59,300; this represents 10,000 units of finished product ready for sale.

The business transactions The transactions for the week are posted to the accounts in the ledger illustrated on the next page. Let us discuss each of these transactions in turn.

PARTIAL GENERAL LEDGER

RAW MATERIALS AND SUPPLIES INVENTORY

Beginning inventory	30,000	(b)	65,000
(a)	100,000		

WORK IN PROCESS INVENTORY—DEPARTMENT A

a Beginning inventory:			c (g) Completed	252,000	
Raw materials	$5,000				
Direct labor	8,700				
Factory overhead	6,090	$ 19,790			
b {(b) Raw materials	61,000				
(d) Direct labor	115,800				
(f) Factory overhead	81,060				
	277,650				

FACTORY PAYROLL

(c)	120,800	(d)	120,800

FINISHED GOODS INVENTORY

d Beginning inventory	59,300	(h)	122,300
(g) From Dept. A	252,000		

FACTORY OVERHEAD

(b)	4,000	(f)	81,060
(d)	5,000	(i)	100
(e)	72,160		81,160
	81,160		

COST OF GOODS SOLD

(h)	122,300	
(i)	100	

a 5,000 units are in the beginning inventory: 100% complete as to raw materials and 60% complete as to direct labor and factory overhead.

b 50,000 new units were begun during the week.

c 40,000 units were completed and transferred to finished goods.

d 10,000 units 100% complete as to all three cost elements.

TRANSACTION (a). The firm purchases raw materials and supplies with a total cost of $100,000. The Raw materials and supplies inventory account is debited and an appropriate account such as Cash or Accounts payable is credited.

■ *What journal entries, records, and reports are involved in a process cost accounting system?*

TRANSACTION (b). Materials requisitions totaling $65,000 are processed during the week; therefore, the Raw materials and supplies inventory account is credited to show that the inventory is reduced. Two debits appear in the ledger for this entry: (1) The first debit is to Work in process inventory—

Department A; raw materials totaling $61,000 are used in that department. During the week 50,000 new units of product are begun, and these are the raw materials used on the new units. (2) The other debit is to the Factory overhead account for $4,000; this represents supplies used in the factory for general purposes (not exclusively for Department A).

TRANSACTION (c). The factory payroll is prepared for the week. Total labor costs amount to $120,800. Factory payroll is debited and the appropriate liabilities (Salaries payable and Accrued taxes) are credited.

TRANSACTION (d). The factory payroll of $120,800 is distributed. The labor costs associated with Department A amount to $115,800 and the indirect labor totals $5,000. Work in process—Department A is debited for the $115,800 and Factory overhead is debited for $5,000. The Factory payroll account is closed to zero by this entry.

TRANSACTION (e). Additional factory overhead costs amounting to $72,160 are incurred. The Factory overhead account is debited and the appropriate accounts such as Cash, Accounts payable, etc. are credited.

TRANSACTION (f). The factory overhead is applied to Work in process according to a predetermined rate. The rate that has been calculated for this firm is 70%. The direct labor costs for the department total $115,800; therefore the factory overhead to be applied is 0.70 times $115,800, or $81,060. The Work in process—Department A account is debited for the $81,060, and the Factory overhead account is credited for the same amount.[1]

TRANSACTION (g). During the week the department completes 40,000 units of product, and these units are transferred to the Finished goods inventory account. A major purpose of cost accounting is to determine the cost of units that are produced. A main question is: At what amount should the Finished goods inventory account be debited and the Work in process credited for the 40,000 units that are completed? Each period, a **cost of production report** is prepared to answer this question. Notice in entry (g) that the amount has been determined to be $252,000.

The entire next unit (Unit 46) will be devoted to explaining how this cost of production report is prepared. In the assignment problems in this unit, the dollar amount of the cost of goods transferred to Finished goods inventory will simply be given you [as in transaction (g).]

[1] Some firms use bases other than direct labor cost to apply overhead. For example, the relationship of total factory overhead to number of direct labor hours or machine hours of operation could be used to calculate an overhead rate. Then, for each direct labor or machine hour worked in the department, an amount of overhead could be transferred to work in process inventory.

TRANSACTION (h). During the week the company made sales as follows. The beginning Finished goods inventory, which had a cost of $59,300 (see account), was sold for $70,000 cash. Also, an additional 10,000 units that were manufactured this period were sold for $75,000 cash. For purposes of this illustration, assume that the cost of production report showed that these 10,000 units had a unit cost of $6.30, for a total cost of $63,000. In summary:

COST OF GOODS SOLD	SELLING PRICE
$ 59,300	$ 70,000
63,000	75,000
$122,300	$145,000

Transaction (h) shows the debit to Cost of goods sold and the credit to Finished goods inventory for $122,300. Also, in another entry, Cash would be debited for $145,000 and Sales would be credited for the same amount (this is not shown in the example).

Overapplied and underapplied overhead In Unit 44 we discussed the possibility that the total actual factory overhead (the debits) might be different from the overhead transferred (the credits) to the Work in process account during a period. Refer to the example in the general ledger in this unit. The actual factory overhead totaled $81,160 for the period. The overhead applied to work in process totaled $81,060. Thus less overhead was applied than was actually incurred. This is known as **underapplied overhead;** the amount in this case is $100. If more overhead is applied to work in process than is actually incurred, the situation is known as **overapplied overhead,** and a credit balance exists in the overhead account. In either case, *at least once a year,* before annual financial statements are prepared the underapplied or overapplied balance is disposed of by a journal entry.

TRANSACTION (i). This entry reduces the Factory overhead account to zero. The underapplied amount ($100) is recorded as part of cost of goods sold to show that more costs were actually incurred than were recorded in the inventory accounts.[2]

If there is a situation of overapplied overhead, Cost of goods sold can be credited and Factory overhead can be debited to correct the accounts.

COST ACCOUNTING AND DECISIONS

A cost accounting system is extremely useful to management in a number of ways. This is true whether the system is of the process type or the job order type.

[2] When the underapplied or overapplied amount is significant, some firms choose to transfer part of the amount to the inventory accounts, rather than transferring the entire balance to Cost of goods sold. This may be appropriate when a significant portion of the goods that were manufactured are still in inventory.

Marketing decisions One area in which cost accounting helps management is the setting of prices. Management can set prices much more easily and confidently when they have exact information about the cost of the jobs or units to be sold. This is just the information that cost accounting provides.

For example, a firm might have competitors on its bids for jobs. By consulting its job cost records for similar past jobs, the firm can find out details about raw materials costs, direct labor costs, and overhead costs. From these past records the firm can make more reasonable predictions of future costs and thus can submit more realistic bids.

In process operations, computations of unit costs reveal changes in cost elements which management may consider in changing selling prices and in making other decisions. If cost information for jobs or for processes is readily available, then management has a solid base for its planning activities.

■ *How is cost accounting used to improve management's decision making?*

Daily control of costs With a cost accounting system changes in the costs of the three elements (materials, labor, and overhead) can be reported on a daily basis. Through performance reports these unit costs can be compared to standards developed by management. Corrective action can be taken immediately when performance differs significantly from the goals. Periodic systems of reporting manufacturing operations do not readily provide this capability.

One example of a performance report using process cost data appears at the top of the next page. On the basis of this report, management would probably want to investigate why both direct labor and factory overhead are 10% over standard in department B. Future units will illustrate other versions of performance reports which express variances from standards in terms of total variances as well as unit variances.

WEEKLY PERFORMANCE REPORT

WEEK ENDING: June 12, 1978

	PERFORMANCE STANDARD (UNIT COST EXPECTED)	ACTUAL UNIT COST	VARIANCE
Department A			
Raw materials	$ 2.10	$ 2.11	($0.01)
Direct labor	1.90	1.95	(0.05)
Factory overhead	1.00	0.97	0.03
	$ 5.00	$ 5.03	($0.03)
Department B			
Raw materials	$ 6.00	$ 5.96	$0.04
Direct labor	5.00	5.50	(0.50)
Factory overhead	1.00	1.10	(0.10)
	$12.00	$12.56	($0.56)

cost of production report A report for management which provides a summary of activities in a manufacturing department during a period of time, including unit costs of raw materials, direct labor, and factory overhead. [p. 781]

overapplied overhead The situation wherein a greater amount of factory overhead was transferred to work in process inventory than was actually incurred during the period. [p. 782]

underapplied overhead The situation wherein a lesser amount of factory overhead was transferred to work in process inventory than was actually incurred during the period. [p. 782]

> **ASSIGNMENT MATERIAL**

QUESTIONS

Q45-1. Which of the following documents and records probably would be used in a process cost accounting system:
a. Stores ledger card.
b. Materials requisition.
c. Job cost card.
d. Cost of production report.
e. Factory overhead subsidiary ledger.

Q45-2. Explain how overapplied or underapplied overhead arises and how it is treated in the accounting records and financial statements.

Q45-3. How are raw materials recorded that are used in production in a process cost accounting system?

Q45-4. Explain how labor costs are recorded in a process cost accounting system.

Q45-5. Explain how factory overhead is recorded in a process cost accounting system.

Q45-6. What is the purpose of a cost of production report?

Q45-7. How can cost accounting improve management's decision making?

EXERCISES

E45-1. Below is the work in process account for the Painting Department of a factory.

WORK IN PROCESS—PAINTING

Beginning inventory:			Completed	$316,955
Raw materials	$11,000			
Direct labor	10,000			
Factory overhead	8,000	$ 29,000		
Raw materials		115,600		
Direct labor		208,515		
Factory overhead		166,812		

a. Make the journal entry for raw materials used in production.
b. Make the journal entry for factory overhead applied into production.
c. What is the application rate for factory overhead?
d. From the data given, can you determine the amount of factory overhead incurred during the period? Explain.
e. Make the entry to transfer out the goods completed.

E45-2. State the accounts debited and credited for each of these transactions in a process cost accounting system.
   a. Purchase of raw materials on credit.
   b. Issuing raw materials into production (Department A).
   c. Issuing supplies for general factory use.
   d. Recording the factory payroll.
   e. Distributing the factory payroll.
   f. Paying the rent on the factory.
   g. Recording depreciation on the factory equipment.
   h. Applying overhead to production.
   i. Completing goods and transferring them from Department A to finished goods.
   j. Completing goods and transferring them from Department B to Department C.
   k. Sold goods on credit.

E45-3. Below is a table showing payroll data for Modern Manufacturing Company for the week ending July 15, 1978.

| EMPLOYEE | production department | | | INDIRECT LABOR | SALES SALARIES | GENERAL SALARIES |
	A	B	C			
John Azure	146.50					
Edward Brown	65.40	65.40				
Harold Creme		314.00				
William Dusty				412.00		
Joseph Egshel			518.00			
Kerry Fawn			100.00	100.00	150.00	
Bruno Green						498.00
	211.90	379.40	618.00	512.00	150.00	498.00

Notice that some employees work in more than one area. For this payroll, withheld taxes and other deductions amount to $436.90.
   Prepare the entries to record the payroll and distribute the factory portion.

E45-4. During the week ending June 12, 1978, factory overhead was applied to the three departments as follows:

	OVERHEAD APPLIED
Cutting Department	$44,250
Sanding Department	66,670
Finishing Department	21,240

It happened that, during this period, each of the three departments had exactly $59,000 of direct labor costs. Compute the factory overhead application rate used for each department.

P45-1. *Process cost accounting, journal entries.* Make accounting entries in general journal form to record the following business transactions. The firm uses a process cost accounting system.

a. Purchased 10,000 units of raw material from ABC Company, terms 2/10, n/30. The total cost is $4,320.

b. Issued materials and supplies into the factory as follows:

   (1) Raw material X used in Department A, $1,000; Materials requisition 1040.

   (2) Raw material X used in Department B, $200; Materials requisition 1041.

   (3) Supplies to be used in the factory for general maintenance, $141; Materials requisition 1042.

c. The factory payroll amounted to $8,000. FICA withheld was $400 and income taxes withheld amounted to $1,000.

d. Tranferred the balance of factory payroll: Department A, $7,000; Department B, $1,000.

e. Applied the factory overhead to the two work in process accounts. The overhead rate is 70% of direct labor costs.

f. Paid the power bill for the factory, $700.

g. Completed units in Department B: 10,000 units were completed and transferred to finished goods. The cost of production report for the period indicated that the units had a total unit cost of $4.

h. Sold 3,000 of the above units (g) for $5.50 each, cash.

P45-2. *Process cost accounting, journal entries.* Make entries in general journal form to record the following business transactions in a process cost accounting system.

a. Purchased 5,000 units of Raw material 17 from Simmons Manufacturing Co., terms, 2/10, n/30. Total cost is $55,198.

b. Purchased factory supplies from Salamone, Inc., for $1,750 cash.

c. Issued supplies to the factory for general use. The supplies cost $57; materials requisition 75.

d. Issued 307 units of Raw material 17 to be used in the Assembly Department, $3,390; Materials requisition 76.

e. The factory payroll totaled $71,500. FICA withheld was $1,140 and Federal income taxes withheld amounted to $15,400.

f. Transferred the balance of factory payroll: Assembly Department, $18,000; Painting Department, $35,000; Finishing Department, $18,500.

g. Applied the factory overhead to the work in process accounts at the rate of 81% of direct labor costs.

h. Incurred costs as follows (paid in cash): Factory power, $500; Factory insurance, $700; Factory maintenance, $800.

i. Completed 1,000 units in the Finishing Department and transferred to finished goods. The cost of production report for the period indicated that the units had a total unit cost of $31.45 each.

j. Sold 100 units of finished product on credit for $78.45 each. The units had cost $30.15 to manufacture.

P45-3. *Process cost accounting, journal entries.* Make entries in general journal form to record the following business transactions in a process cost accounting system.

a. Issued materials and supplies into the factory as follows:

Raw material 160 used in Department A, $675; Materials requisition 25.

Raw material 161 used in Department B, $240; Materials requisition 26.

Supplies to be used for the entire factory, $530; Materials requisition 27.

b. Purchased raw materials from Pronto Products, with terms of 2/10, n/30; raw material 160, $200; raw material 161, $145.

c. The factory payroll totaled $87,430. FICA withheld was $6,220 and Federal income taxes withheld amounted to $2,210.

d. Transferred the balance of factory payroll: Department A, $34,400 and Department B, $53,030.

e. Applied the factory overhead to the two departmental work in process accounts. The overhead rate is 65% of direct labor costs.

f. Completed 4,000 units in Department A and transferred to finished goods. The cost of production report indicated that the units had a total unit cost of $5.25 each.

g. Sold 250 units of finished product on credit for $10.45 each. The units had cost $4.50 to manufacture.

PROBLEMS (GROUP B)

P45-4. *Process cost accounting, journal entries.* Make entries in general journal form to record the following business transactions. The company uses a process cost accounting system.

a. Issued materials and supplies into the factory as follows:

Raw material 2130 used in Department A, $1,200; Materials requisition 143.

Raw material 2133 used in Department B, $300; Materials requisition 144.

Supplies to be used for the entire factory, $356; Materials requisition 145.

b. Purchased raw materials from Bondy Products, with terms of 2/15, n/30: raw material 2130, $900; raw material 2133, $1,456.

c. The factory payroll amounted to $15,000. FICA tax withheld amounted to $500 and federal income taxes withheld amounted to $3,146.

d. Transferred the balance of factory payroll: Department A, $8,000 and Department B, $7,000.

e. Applied the factory overhead to the two departmental work in process accounts. The overhead rate is 60% of direct labor costs.

f. Paid factory insurance, $300.

g. Paid the electric bill for the factory, $1,200.

h. Completed units in Department B: 5,000 units were completed and transferred to finished goods. The cost of production report for the period indicated that the units had a total cost of $4.56 each.

i. Sold 4,000 units of finished product on credit for $6.00 each. The units had cost $4.56 each.

P45-5. *Process cost accounting, journal entries.* Make accounting entries in general journal form to record the following business transactions. The company uses process cost accounting.

a. The firm purchases raw materials and supplies for $65,000 cash.

b. Issued materials and supplies into the factory as follows: raw materials (Assembly Department), $17,000; supplies, $6,000.

c. The factory payroll is prepared. Total labor costs amount to $64,000. FICA withheld was $2,050 and Federal income taxes withheld amounted to $7,950.

d. The factory payroll is distributed. Labor costs amounted to $40,000 (Assembly, $25,000; Finishing, $15,000) and the indirect labor totaled $24,000.

e. Applied factory overhead to the work in process accounts at the rate of 75% of direct labor costs.

f. Completed 2,500 units in the Finishing Department and transferred to finished goods. The cost of production report for the period indicated that the units had a total unit cost of $6.20 each.

g. Sold 350 units of finished product on credit for $25.00 each. The units had cost $14.30 to manufacture.

*P45-6. *Analysis of cost flows.* Hampton Company uses a process cost accounting system. The records for the week ending May 3, 1978, have these data:

Cost of goods sold	$200,000
Total cost of goods completed in Department 114 and transferred to finished goods	234,000
Total factory payroll	176,000
Factory overhead applied to Department 114	180,000
Indirect supplies used in factory	4,000
Beginning balance of raw materials and supplies inventory	20,000
Purchases of raw materials and supplies	300,000
Indirect labor costs incurred	30,000
Beginning balance of Department 114 work in process	200,000
Ending balance of Department 114 work in process	466,000
Ending finished goods inventory	114,000

For purposes of this problem and to simplify, assume that Department 114 is the production department.

REQUIRED: By setting up the ledger accounts and analyzing the data, compute the amount of the ending Raw materials and supplies inventory.

PROCESS COST ACCOUNTING– COST OF PRODUCTION REPORT

▶ OBJECTIVE

Unit 45 provided an introduction to a process cost accounting system. In that unit you learned how to make the journal entries for the transactions in a process system. The objective of this unit is to show you how to prepare a cost of production report, which is the detailed management report that shows the unit costs of production of each of the cost elements being controlled.

▶ APPROACH TO ATTAINING THE OBJECTIVE

As you study about the cost of production report, pay attention to these four questions, which the text following answers:

- *What is the purpose of a cost of production report?*
- *What are the four basic sections of information on a cost of production report?*
- *What is meant by equivalent production and how are equivalent units computed?*
- *How is the cost of production report prepared?*

As stated in Unit 45, a **cost of production report** provides detailed information about the operations of a production department or process during a relatively short period of time. The unit costs of raw materials, direct labor, and factory overhead can be compared to the expected costs or to some standard of performance.

> Also, the cost of production report provides the basis for determining what portion of the costs in the work in process account are to be transferred to finished goods (or to another production department), and what portion of the costs are to remain in the ending inventory of work in process.

■ *What is the purpose
of a cost of
production report?*

The cost of production report for a department summarizes all activities during the period. It consists of four basic sections. The cost of production report for the department in our illustration is presented on the next page.

■ *What are the four
basic sections of
information on a cost
of production report?*

Section 1: Activity in terms of units In the first section the activity in the department *in terms of units* is accounted for. The actual units are counted to prevent losses of units during the period and to provide an accurate basis for computing unit costs. Now, this example is a continuation of the illustration of Department A in the previous unit. Refer to the work in process account on page 780 for the following figures. Five thousand units were on hand at the beginning of the week. Another 50,000 units were started during the week, so there is a total of 55,000 units for the department to account for. This 55,000 is accounted for in two ways: (1) units are completed and transferred out of the department (40,000), and (2) units are still in process (15,000).

■ *What is meant by
equivalent production
and how are equivalent
units computed?*

Section 2: Equivalent production Next, the **equivalent whole units** or *equivalent production* is calculated. To do this, it is necessary to calculate how many units of production are represented by all the costs incurred in the department; with these data the unit costs can then be computed. The unit costs are computed as follows:

$$\frac{\text{Unit cost}}{\text{of raw}} = \frac{\text{Cost of raw materials} + \text{Additional cost of raw}}{\text{in beginning inventory}} + \frac{\text{materials used during period}}{\text{Equivalent number of units that}}$$

$$\begin{array}{c}\text{Unit cost} \\ \text{of raw} \\ \text{materials}\end{array} = \frac{\begin{array}{c}\text{Cost of raw materials} \\ \text{in beginning inventory}\end{array} + \begin{array}{c}\text{Additional cost of raw} \\ \text{materials used during period}\end{array}}{\begin{array}{c}\text{Equivalent number of units that} \\ \text{were produced by these costs}\end{array}}$$

$$\begin{array}{c}\text{Unit cost} \\ \text{of direct} \\ \text{labor}\end{array} = \frac{\begin{array}{c}\text{Cost of direct labor} \\ \text{in beginning inventory}\end{array} + \begin{array}{c}\text{Additional cost of direct} \\ \text{labor used during period}\end{array}}{\begin{array}{c}\text{Equivalent number of units that} \\ \text{were produced by these costs}\end{array}}$$

Department A
COST OF PRODUCTION REPORT
For the Week Ended June 19, 1978

1. _activity in the department during week in terms of units:_[a]

Units in process, beginning (these units were 100% complete as to raw materials at beginning of week, but were only 60% complete as to direct labor and factory overhead)	5,000
New units started in production during week	50,000
Total units to account for	55,000
Units completed during week and transferred to finished goods	40,000
Units in process, ending (these units were 100% complete as to raw materials at end of week, but were only 10% complete as to direct labor and factory overhead)	15,000
Total units accounted for	55,000

2. _equivalent whole units completed during week:_

	UNITS		
	RAW MATERIALS	DIRECT LABOR	FACTORY OVERHEAD
Units completed during week	40,000	40,000	40,000
Units in ending inventory worked on this week	15,000	1,500	1,500
Equivalent whole units	55,000	41,500	41,500

3. _costs to account for during week:_

	TOTAL	RAW MATERIALS	DIRECT LABOR	FACTORY OVERHEAD
Work in process, beginning	$ 19,790	$ 5,000	$ 8,700	$ 6,090
This week's costs	257,860	61,000	115,800	81,060
Total costs	$277,650	$66,000	$124,500	$87,150
		÷	÷	÷
Equivalent whole units completed during week		55,000	41,500	41,500
Unit cost	$6.30 =	$1.20 +	$3.00 +	$2.10

4. _accounting for the costs:_

Units completed and transferred to finished goods (40,000 units at $6.30)		$252,000
Work in process at end of week:		
Raw materials (15,000 units at $1.20)	$18,000	
Direct labor (1,500 units at $3.00)	4,500	
Factory overhead (1,500 units at $2.10)	3,150	
Total work in process inventory		25,650
Total costs accounted for		$277,650

[a]Trace the figures on this report to the Work in process inventory account—Department A on page 780.

$$\text{Unit cost of factory overhead} = \frac{\text{Cost of factory overhead in beginning inventory} + \text{Additional cost of factory overhead used during period}}{\text{Equivalent number of units that were produced by these costs}}$$

Refer to the second part of the cost of production report for an example of how equivalent whole units are calculated. Forty thousand units were completed and transferred to finished goods during the week. To be transfered out of the department, the completed goods had to be 100% complete as to *all three* cost elements; therefore, 40,000 is used in all three columns of the computation.

Next the ending inventory is considered. There are 15,000 units of product in the ending inventory. Because the *raw materials* on these units are 100% complete, the *whole* 15,000 units is used in the computation. In the case of direct labor and factory overhead, it is known that the 15,000 units were only about 10% complete. Therefore, only 1,500 *equivalent whole units* of direct labor and factory overhead were produced during the week.

The report's computation thus indicates that the costs spent for raw materials in the department produced an equivalent of 55,000 units of product. The costs spent for the direct labor produced 41,500 equivalent whole units; and the costs spent for the factory overhead also produced 41,500 equivalent whole units.

■ *How is the cost of production report prepared?*

Section 3: Costs to account for The third section of the report analyzes the actual costs incurred during the week and computes the unit cost of the three cost elements. The costs are taken directly from the Work in process inventory—Department A account on page 780. In the case of raw materials, a total of $66,000 appeared in the inventory account for the week. This represents production of 55,000 units, so the unit cost for the week is $1.20, or $66,000 divided by 55,000 equivalent whole units. Direct labor unit costs are computed similarly: $124,500 divided by 41,500 units equals $3.00 per unit. The total cost of a single finished product amounts to $6.30, or the sum of the three unit costs.

Section 4: Accounting for the costs The final section of the cost of production report provides the basis for determining the cost of the 40,000 units that were transferred from work in process to finished goods inventory. Remember that this is the main question noted in our discussion of transaction (g) in Unit 45. That is, we must make a journal entry to transfer the costs of goods completed into the Finshed goods inventory account. From the data on our cost of production report, we can make the entry at the top of the next page. Notice that after this entry there is a work in process inventory balance of $25,650, or $277,650 less $252,000.

1978					
June	19	Finished goods inventory		252,000	
		Work in process inventory—Department A			252,000
		Goods completed in Department A,			
		40,000 units at $6.30.			

COST-FLOW ASSUMPTIONS

The example of a cost of production report in this unit used the *weighted average* method of computing unit costs of raw materials, direct labor, and factory overhead. In computing the unit costs, remember that the cost of the beginning inventory was added to the costs incurred this period. Then the total was divided by the equivalent production to compute the unit costs.

Some firms use other cost-flow assumptions such as the first-in, first-out method (FIFO). Under the FIFO method, unit costs are kept separate for the beginning inventory and for the current production. The beginning inventory costs involve two sets of units costs: (1) those costs incurred last period, and (2) the current costs incurred to complete the beginning inventory. For purposes of this course, we will illustrate only the weighted average method.

❯ NEW TERMS

cost of production report A report which provides a summary of activities in a manufacturing department during a period of time; usually it includes four sections: (1) activity in the department in terms of units, (2) equivalent whole units completed, (3) costs to account for, and (4) accounting for the costs. [p. 790]
equivalent whole units Also referred to as equivalent production; the number of units represented by the costs that were incurred in manufacturing; takes into consideration partially completed units in the ending inventory of work in process; computed by adding the number of units completed and transferred out to the equivalent completed portion of the ending work in process inventory. [p. 790]

❯ ASSIGNMENT MATERIAL

QUESTIONS

Q46-1. What is the purpose of a cost of production report?

Q46-2. Describe each of the four basic sections of a cost of production report.

Q46-3. How is equivalent production computed?

Q46-4. What cost-flow assumption was used in the illustration in this unit?

EXERCISES

E46-1. The Cricking Department of Inso Industries started 86,000 new units in production during the day. On the same day 81,000 units were completed and transferred to the next department.

At the beginning of the day, there were 10,000 units in process. These units were 90% complete as to raw materials and 75% complete as to direct labor and factory overhead. The units in process at the end of the day were 30% complete as to raw materials and 40% complete as to direct labor and factory overhead. Compute the equivalent whole units produced during the day for (1) raw materials, (2) direct labor, and (3) factory overhead.

E46-2. On January 1, 1978, a department had 1,000 units in production that were 80% complete as to raw materials and 60% complete as to direct labor and factory overhead. The work in process inventory for this department at January 1, 1978, had a balance of $3,400, which consisted of $1,600 of raw materials, $1,200 of direct labor, and $600 of factory overhead. Production costs for the first seven days of January, 1978, were:

Direct materials	$18,500
Direct labor	18,000
Factory overhead	9,000

10,000 new units were started in production during the week, and 7,000 units were completed and transferred out of the department.

The units on hand at the end of the week were 100% complete as to raw materials and 70% complete as to direct labor and factory overhead. The factory overhead rate is 50% of direct labor cost.

Compute the unit costs for raw materials, direct labor, and factory overhead as they would appear on the cost of production report.

E46-3. During June, 1978, there were 3,420 new units started and 5,051 units completed and transferred out of a department. There were 2,962 units in process at the beginning of June (which were 92% complete as to raw materials). The ending inventory was only 21% complete as to materials. Compute the equivalent units of materials produced during June.

E46-4. During May, 1978, these data were taken from the records of Department 17:

Beginning inventory: 11,000 units, 100% complete as to raw materials and 80% complete as to direct labor and factory overhead

Ending inventory: 8,000 units, 100% complete as to raw materials and 70% complete as to direct labor and factory overhead

Units completed and transferred out: 90,000 units

Compute the equivalent production for raw materials, direct labor, and factory overhead.

PROBLEMS (GROUP A)

P46-1. *Cost of production report.* Using the following information, prepare a cost of production report for Department C for the week ending March 13, 1978.

P46-2. *Cost of production report.* The following facts relate to Department X for a week's operations, the week ending March 20, 1978.

REQUIRED: Prepare a cost of production report for the week.

P46-3. *Cost of production report.* Using the following information, prepare a cost of production report for Department X for the week ending May 23, 1978. Round all unit costs to the nearest cent.

WORK IN PROCESS—DEPARTMENT C

a *Beginning inventory:*			c Goods completed	?
Raw materials	$20,000			
Direct labor	8,000			
Factory overhead	7,200	$ 35,200		
b *Raw materials*		200,000		
Direct labor		90,000		
Factory overhead		81,000		
		$406,200		

a 10,000 units are in the beginning inventory: 100% complete as to raw materials and 30% complete as to direct labor and factory overhead.

b 100,000 new units were begun during the week.

c 80,000 units were completed and transferred to finished goods, leaving 30,000 units in the ending inventory which were 100% complete as to raw materials and 60% complete as to direct labor and factory overhead.

WORK IN PROCESS INVENTORY—DEPARTMENT X

a *Beginning inventory:*			c Goods completed	?
Raw materials	$120,000			
Direct labor	40,000			
Factory overhead	40,000	$200,000		
b *Raw materials*		298,000		
Direct labor		113,600		
Factory overhead		113,600		
		$725,200		

a In the beginning inventory are 10,000 units: 100% complete as to raw materials and 50% complete as to direct labor and factory overhead.

b New units started during the month totaled 100,000.

c A total of 90,000 units were completed and transferred to finished goods, leaving 20,000 units in the ending inventory that were 100% complete as to raw materials and 30% complete as to direct labor and factory overhead.

WORK IN PROCESS—DEPARTMENT X

a *Beginning inventory:*			c Goods completed	?
Raw materials	20,000			
Direct labor	16,000			
Factory overhead	12,800	48,800		
b *Raw materials*		200,000		
Direct labor		120,000		
Factory overhead		72,000		
		440,800		

a Units in the beginning inventory totaled 10,000: 100% complete as to raw materials and 80% complete as to direct labor and factory overhead.

b New units begun during the week totaled 98,000.

c Units completed and transferred to finished goods totaled 58,000, leaving 50,000 units in the ending inventory that were 100% complete as to materials and 15% complete as to direct labor and factory overhead.

P46-4. *Cost of production report.* Using the following information, prepare a cost of production report for Department X for the week ending May 25, 1978. Round all unit costs to the nearest cent.

WORK IN PROCESS—DEPARTMENT X

ᵃ *Beginning inventory:*			ᶜ Goods completed		?
Raw materials	$10,000				
Direct labor	8,000				
Factory overhead	6,400	$ 24,400			
Raw materials		100,000			
ᵇ *Direct labor*		60,000			
Factory overhead		36,000			
		$220,400			

ᵃ 10,000 units are in the beginning inventory: 100% complete as to raw materials and 80% complete as to direct labor and factory overhead.

ᵇ 98,000 new units were begun during the week.

ᶜ 58,000 units were completed and transferred to finished goods, leaving 50,000 units in the ending inventory which were 100% complete as to materials and 15% complete as to direct labor and factory overhead.

P46-5. *Cost of production report, entries.* The work in process inventory account for Process 191 had a balance of $92,700 at June 7, 1978. This balance represented 20,000 units that were 90% complete as to materials and 30% complete as to direct labor and factory overhead. The $92,700 consisted of $55,800 of raw materials, $12,300 of direct labor, and $24,600 of factory overhead.

During the week (June 7–June 14), 114,800 new units were started in Process 191 and 96,200 units were completed and transferred to finished goods. Also, these costs were incurred during the week: Raw materials, $313,860; Direct labor, $195,540; Factory overhead, $391,080.

The units in process on June 14, 1978, were 70% complete as to raw materials and 20% complete as to direct labor and factory overhead.

REQUIRED:

a. Prepare a cost of production report for the week ending June 14, 1978, for Process 191.
b. Prepare the journal entry to transfer the goods completed from Process 191 to finished goods.

P46-6. *Cost of production report, entries.* During November of 1978, Department AC completed and transferred to finished goods 21,000 units of product. At the end of the month, there were 21,171 units in process. These units were 100% complete as to raw materials and 80% complete as to direct labor and factory overhead. The beginning inventory consisted of 5,916 units that were 80% complete as to raw materials and 35% complete as to direct labor and factory overhead.

November costs for Department AC were:

Raw materials	$60,376
Direct labor	86,285
Factory overhead	69,029

Beginning inventory costs were:

Raw materials	$7,098
Direct labor	4,763
Factory overhead	3,810

REQUIRED:

a. Prepare a cost of production report for the month of November, 1978, for Department AC.
b. Prepare the journal entry to transfer the goods completed from Department AC to finished goods.

CUMULATIVE REVIEW PROBLEMS

P46-7. *Cumulative review problem.* Selected data below relate to the Assembly Department of Manufco, Inc., for the month of December, 1978.
Transactions:

1. Purchased raw materials from Bonded Company for cash, $214,625.
2. Issued materials as follows:

To Assembly Department	$190,838
To Painting Department	36,500
For general factory use	696

3. The factory payroll was as follows:

Assembly Department (direct labor)	$123,160
Painting Department (direct labor)	36,955
Supervisory labor	19,500

Federal income taxes withheld amounted to $3,700 and FICA withheld totaled, $5,850.
4. Applied overhead to the Assembly Department at the rate of 75% of direct labor cost.
5. Paid factory insurance, $900.
6. Completed 49,000 units in the Assembly Department and transferred them to finished goods.
7. Sold all the units completed (transaction 6) for cash, $10 each.

Additional Information: The beginning inventory in the Assembly Department consisted of 11,600 units that were 80% complete as to raw materials ($29,696), 40% complete as to direct labor ($9,280), and 40% complete as to overhead ($6,960). During the period, 62,000 new units were started in production. The ending inventory is 70% complete as to raw materials and 30% complete as to direct labor and factory overhead.

REQUIRED:

a. Prepare a cost of production report for the Assembly Department for the month.
b. Record the business transactions given in the problem in general journal form.

P46-8. *Cumulative review problem.* Below is a partially completed work in process account for Department XO for the week ended June 19, 1978.

WORK IN PROCESS—DEPARTMENT XO

^a *Beginning inventory:*		Transferred out (200,000 units)	?
Raw materials	$186,000		
Direct labor	217,000		
Factory overhead	173,600		
Raw materials	545,600		
Direct labor	986,600		

^a 62,000 units—100% complete as to raw materials and 70% complete as to direct labor and factory overhead.

The ending inventory of 40,000 units was 90% complete as to raw materials, direct labor, and factory overhead.

REQUIRED:

a. Record these transactions in general journal form.
   (1) Issuance of the raw materials into production for the department.
   (2) Payroll for the period. Taxes withheld amounted to $7,590 and Indirect labor costs totaled $80,000.
   (3) Apply overhead to production at the same rate of direct labor cost as indicated by the beginning inventory.
   (4) Record the transfer of goods from the department to finished goods.
b. Prepare a cost of production report for the week.

chapter 21

budgets and standard cost systems and reports

STANDARDS AND THE BUDGETING PROCESS

➤ OBJECTIVE

This unit and the next two will continue your study of how a firm's manufacturing operations are reported to management. In this unit you will study the nature and purpose of budgets and how budgets are prepared.

➤ APPROACH TO ATTAINING THE OBJECTIVE

As you study about budgeting, pay special attention to these three questions, which the text following answers:

- *What is the function of budgeting and of a standard cost system?*
- *How does a firm organize for budgeting?*
- *How are budgets prepared for a manufacturing firm?*

THE NATURE OF BUDGETING

A budget is simply a written plan of operations for a firm. The budget can be a forecasted income statement or a forecasted balance sheet for a firm's entire operation; or budgets can be prepared for individual areas of activity of a firm. For example, a sales budget can concentrate on planning for revenues, and a direct labor budget can plan for this one part of the production process. There are several important aspects to the preparation and use of all budgets. Two especially important points which we will discuss here are: (1) the use of the budgeting system to make it easier to control a firm's operations, and (2) the behavioral considerations of budgeting.

■ *What is the function of budgeting and of a standard cost system?*

Budgets for planning and control A major part of management accounting is comparing actual performance to a standard to make sure that the firm's goals are being met. The budgetary system is an essential part of this planning and control. Budgets are detailed plans made by management. To make these detailed plans management must develop meaningful standards of performance in just about *every area* of the firm's operations. As examples, the standard or planned cost of raw materials must be determined, and the standard or planned cost of direct labor must be calculated. The number of units of each product expected to be sold must be forecast so that the correct number of units can be manufactured at the right times in the plant. In addition, such things as expected cash receipts and cash expenditures must be planned or budgeted.

This kind of formal planning lays the groundwork for the control process. After the firm has been operating for a period, the budgeted amounts can be compared to actual performance and corrective action can be taken where necessary.

Behavioral considerations in budgeting A second important aspect of budgeting is the *behavioral* considerations involved. How human beings in a business organization *behave* or react and respond is at the heart of the budgeting process. The budget is a written plan, so at first glance it appears to be purely impersonal and somewhat automatic. This is far from the truth. The budget is a primary means by which real people—managers and their subordinates—are evaluated. The budget serves as a standard against which human performance is judged. This fact naturally raises important behavioral problems. For instance, how are human beings motivated? How do they react to having their performance formally measured against a standard determined in large measure by others? Observe in your study of budgets and standard costs how these and other behavioral considerations become a part of the whole process of planning and control.

THE NATURE OF A STANDARD COST ACCOUNTING SYSTEM

One of the most effective ways to control manufacturing operations is to periodically compare actual costs of manufacturing with the goals or standards set by management. The budgeting process develops a series of reports called budgets, and these reports reflect the standards that management develops. When these standard (budgeted) costs are compared to actual costs, management has a powerful aid to controlling and improving manufacturing operations. An accounting system that formally uses standard costs in its journals and ledgers along with the actual costs and reports differences between actual costs and standard costs is known as a **standard cost accounting system.** The budgeting process and standard cost accounting thus work hand in hand to provide for comprehensive planning and control. This unit describes the preparation of budgets and the next two units illustrate standard cost accounting procedures and uses.

THE BUDGET COMMITTEE

■ *How does a firm organize for budgeting?*

On a purely mechanical basis, the budgets and standards for a firm could be developed and set up by one executive with the help of a staff. This procedure ordinarily is *not* used because of the human and behavioral aspects of planning and performance measurement. There are budgets and standards for every operation in the firm. The people in manufacturing certainly want to help develop the standards against which their jobs will be judged. Likewise, the people in the marketing and sales end of the business want to participate in setting sales standards. Such necessary participation can make budgeting an extremely useful device for communication within the firm. How then does a firm usually organize for budgeting?

A usual practice is the creation of a **budget committee.** The job of the budget committee in many firms is to advise the budget director and his staff on the development of standards. A budget committee would probably include representatives from each of the key areas such as manufacturing, marketing, finance, and accounting. In large firms, the **budget director** would be responsible for the actual preparation and administration of the budget. Of course, he would rely heavily on the budget committee for advice and for securing cooperation in administration of the budget. To assure participation in the budgeting process at all levels, some firms set up budget subcommittees within the major divisions or administrative units. For example, there might be a separate budget committee concerned primarily with selling prices and expected sales quantities. The work of this subcommittee would support the work of the primary committee.

The remainder of this unit describes the procedures for preparing budgets and illustrates the major budgets used by manufacturing firms.

STEP 1:
THE REVENUE
BUDGET

■ *How are budgets prepared for a manufacturing firm?*

Because budgets are plans, they are prepared before the beginning of a period's operations. A first step is to analyze the revenues to be produced in the coming period. Sales must be estimated first, because the level of operations of the factory and many other decisions are tied to the expected sales level. All kinds of revenues must be analyzed, but in our example we assume that the firm has only one kind—from sales of the company's two products, A and B.

To prepare a sales budget, these factors must be predicted and estimated:

1. Prices to be charged for each of the firm's products.
2. Number of units of each product that will be sold.

In arriving at these estimates, the budget committee and the budget director rely heavily on the budget representative from the sales or marketing area (such as the Vice President of Marketing). The marketing executives carefully study past operations of the firm as a basis for the estimates. Factors such as the amounts to be spent on advertising campaigns, selling price changes (if any), and general changes in demand for the company's products are considered. The executives in the sales area of the firm are extremely interested in making sure that a reasonable and realistic estimate becomes part of the budget, because their performance in the coming period will be judged largely by this standard. A sales budget for June, 1978, is shown below.

Beverly Company
SALES BUDGET
For the Month of June, 1978

	NUMBER OF UNITS TO BE SOLD	SELLING PRICE	TOTAL REVENUE
Product A	120,000	3.00	$360,000
Product B	50,000	4.00	200,000
Total sales budgeted			$560,000

STEP 2:
THE PRODUCTION
LEVELS BUDGET

Once the estimates of sales levels and revenues are made, an estimate of production requirements should follow. Shown on the top of the next page is a budget for determining how many units of each product should be manufactured in the period.

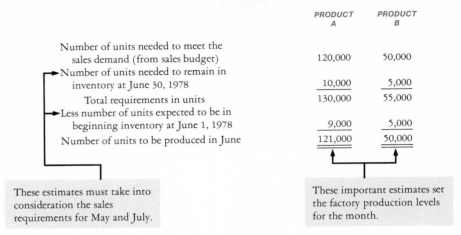

Beverly Company
PRODUCTION LEVELS BUDGET
For the Month of June, 1978

	PRODUCT A	PRODUCT B
Number of units needed to meet the sales demand (from sales budget)	120,000	50,000
Number of units needed to remain in inventory at June 30, 1978	10,000	5,000
Total requirements in units	130,000	55,000
Less number of units expected to be in beginning inventory at June 1, 1978	9,000	5,000
Number of units to be produced in June	121,000	50,000

These estimates must take into consideration the sales requirements for May and July.

These important estimates set the factory production levels for the month.

STEP 3: THE COST OF GOODS SOLD BUDGET

These separate estimates are needed before a budget for the cost of goods sold can be made:

1. Number of units and cost of each raw material to be *used.*
2. Number of units and cost of each raw material to be *purchased.*
3. Quantity and cost of direct labor to be used.
4. Expected factory overhead to be incurred.

Each of these estimates can take the form of a budget, as discussed here and on the following pages.

Raw materials usage and purchases budget Notice that the raw materials usage and purchases budget is closely tied to the production levels budget illustrated earlier. The number of units of each raw material to be used and to be purchased is directly dependent upon the production levels. Other important standards included in these budgets are: (1) the expected cost per unit of raw materials, and (2) the quantity of each kind of raw material expected to be used for each finished product.

Direct labor budget The direct labor budget (see next page) shows the total number of hours of direct labor needed for the production levels, as well as the total cost of direct labor. For the firm in this example, the standards were determined by management as follows: 1/5 hour of direct labor is needed to produce each unit of Product A, and 1/4 hour of direct labor is needed to

Beverly Company
RAW MATERIALS USAGE AND PURCHASES BUDGET
For the Month of June, 1978

	RAW MATERIAL 1	RAW MATERIAL 2
USAGE		
Product A (3 pounds of Raw material 1 and 2 pounds of Raw material 2 required)	363,000[a]	242,000[a]
Product B (9 pounds of Raw material 2 required)	–0–	450,000[a]
Total pounds of raw materials to be used in production	363,000	692,000
Expected cost of raw materials per pound	$ .21	$ .15
Expected cost of raw materials used	$ 76,230	$103,800
PURCHASES		
Production requirements in pounds of raw materials	363,000	692,000
Number of units of raw materials needed to remain in inventory at June 30, 1978	20,000	50,000
Total requirements	383,000	742,000
Less number of units expected to be in beginning inventory at June 1, 1978	14,000	65,000
Number of units to be purchased in June	369,000	677,000
Expected cost per pound	$ .21	$ .15
Expected cost of raw materials purchases	$ 77,490	$101,550

[a] See production levels budget:

121,000 units of A times 3 pounds = 363,000 pounds
121,000 units of A times 2 pounds = 242,000 pounds
50,000 units of B times 9 pounds = 450,000 pounds

produce each unit of Product B. To simplify the example, it is assumed that each hour of direct labor costs the company $3.

Beverly Company
DIRECT LABOR BUDGET
For the Month of June, 1978

	PRODUCTION LEVEL IN UNITS[a]	NUMBER OF DIRECT LABOR HOURS REQUIRED	TOTAL HOURS	COST PER HOUR	TOTAL COST
Product A	121,000	1/5 hour	24,200	$3	$ 72,600
Product B	50,000	1/4 hour	12,500	$3	37,500
Total expected direct labor hours and cost			36,700		$110,100

[a] See production levels budget.

Factory overhead budget In a cost accounting system factory overhead is allocated to work in process according to some base—such as direct labor cost or direct labor hours. This is the same procedure that you studied in job order and process cost accounting. The Beverly Company in our example uses direct labor *hours* as a base for allocating factory overhead. Look at the factory overhead budget presented below. Based upon estimates of the production departments and the budget committee, the variable overhead is expected to be $55,050 if the plant operates at 36,700 direct labor hours. This means that for each direct labor hour worked, about $1.50 of variable factory overhead is expected to be incurred. Fixed overhead of $18,350 is anticipated (at any level of production). This amounts to 50 cents per direct labor hour if 36,700 direct labor hours are worked in the factory. The $2 total overhead rate can be used in the cost accounting system to allocate factory overhead to work in process throughout the period. This allocation procedure will be illustrated in Unit 48 in a standard cost accounting system.

Beverly Company
FACTORY OVERHEAD BUDGET
For the Month of June, 1978

variable factory overhead (assuming a production level of 36,700 direct labor hours):		
Indirect labor	$46,850	
Maintenance supplies	2,000	
Electricity costs	5,500	
Other power costs	150	
Miscellaneous	550	
Total variable overhead		$55,050
fixed factory overhead		
Indirect labor—Factory management	$ 7,000	
Depreciation of plant and equipment	10,000	
Insurance	500	
Taxes	200	
Electricity costs	400	
Miscellaneous	250	
Total fixed overhead		18,350
total overhead		$73,400
Variable overhead per direct labor hour ($55,050 ÷ 36,700 hours)		$1.50
Fixed overhead per direct labor hour ($18,350 ÷ 36,700 hours)		.50
Total overhead per direct labor hour ($73,400 ÷ 36,700 hours)		$2.00

Notice in the factory overhead budget that certain costs, such as electricity costs, can appear in both the variable and fixed categories. This means that the total cost for electricity is partially fixed and partially variable. The electric bill will be $400 as a minimum *even if the plant does not operate.* As the production level in the plant increases, the electric bill will increase from the $400 in a variable fashion. At the expected level of operations (36,700

direct labor hours), the total electric bill is expected to be $5,900 (the $400 fixed portion plus the $5,500 variable portion).

The previous paragraphs and tables have outlined how the raw materials, direct labor, and factory overhead budgets are prepared. Now the cost of goods sold can be computed as shown below. Note particularly the part that the anticipated finished goods inventories play in the determination of cost of goods sold. These inventory estimates are made by management and are tied to the expected demand for the firm's products in the coming period. The computations of finished goods inventories are not included in this example.

Beverly Company
COST OF GOODS SOLD BUDGET
For the Month of June, 1978

raw materials used (from raw materials usage and purchases budget):			
Raw material 1		$ 76,230	
Raw material 2		103,800	$180,030
direct labor used (from direct labor budget)			110,100
factory overhead used (from factory overhead budget)			73,400
Total factory costs			$363,530
Finished goods inventory expected at June 1, 1978			55,300
Goods available for sale in June			$418,830
Finished goods inventory needed for June 30, 1978			82,950
cost of goods sold			$335,880

STEP 4: THE EXPENSES BUDGET

After the cost of goods sold is predicted, the operating expenses are estimated on a budget as shown below. Some companies further analyze the expenses by classifying each expense as fixed or variable.

Beverly Company
OPERATING EXPENSES BUDGET
For the Month of June, 1978

selling expenses		
Salesmen's salaries and commissions	$40,000	
Other salaries	10,000	
Advertising	4,000	
Depreciation on sales equipment	12,000	
Supplies	1,000	
Miscellaneous	3,000	$ 70,000
general and administrative expenses		
Salaries	$33,000	
Depreciation on office equipment	10,000	
Supplies	2,000	
Taxes and insurance	3,000	
Miscellaneous	2,000	50,000
Total expenses		$120,000

STEP 5: THE BUDGETED FINANCIAL STATEMENTS	The budgeted income statement (see below) can now be compiled by using the information in the other budgets. In addition, the projected June 30, 1978, balance sheet and retained earnings statement also can be prepared. These latter two statements are based mostly on information included in the budgets you have already studied. For example, the Accounts payable at June 30, 1978, which would appear on the budgeted balance sheet might be computed as follows:

Accounts payable expected to be owed at June 1, 1978	$ 11,000
Plus purchases of raw materials during June (from raw materials usage and purchases budget)	179,040
Total accounts payable	$190,040
Less cash payments expected to be made to suppliers during June	175,000
Accounts payable, June 30, 1978	$ 15,040

The procedures for constructing a budgeted balance sheet are not illustrated in this unit.

Beverly Company
BUDGETED INCOME STATEMENT
For the Month of June, 1978

budgeted sales (from sales budget)		$560,000
expenses		
Cost of goods sold (from cost of goods sold budget)	$335,880	
Operating expenses (from operating expenses budget)	120,000	
Total expenses		455,880
budgeted net earnings		$104,120

Another important part of budgeting involves cash planning. The level of factory operations is closely related to the cash receipts and cash payments to be made during the period. A budgeted cash receipts and cash payments statement would be prepared as part of the cash planning and control procedures. In summary form, the statement would include these elements:

STATEMENT OF CASH RECEIPTS AND DISBURSEMENTS

Cash balance to be on hand at June 1, 1978
Plus all anticipated cash receipts (including collections from customers)
Less all anticipated cash payments (including payments to suppliers for raw materials, payments for direct labor, factory overhead, and operating expenses)
Equals Cash balance to be on hand at June 30, 1978

Here is a detailed example of a budgeted cash receipts and disbursements statement.

Jansen Corporation
BUDGETED CASH RECEIPTS AND DISBURSEMENTS
For the Month of April, 1978

Budgeted cash balance, April 1, 1978			$ 17,692
RECEIPTS			
from customers:			
Estimated balance of Accounts receivable, April 1, 1978	$ 16,950		
Sales for April, 1978	286,900		
Total	$303,850		
Less Accounts receivable, April 30, 1978 (estimated to be 10% of April sales)	28,690	$275,160	
from rental income collections		6,000	
from interest income collections		500	
from issuance of 1,000 shares of common stock		91,000	
Total budgeted cash receipts			372,660
Total cash available			$390,352
DISBURSEMENTS			
for suppliers:			
Estimated balance of Accounts payable, April 1, 1978	$ 5,261		
Purchase requirements for April	75,205		
Total	$80,466		
Less Accounts payable, April 30, 1978 (estimated to be 15% of April purchases)	11,281	$ 69,185	
for payroll:			
Accrued salaries, April 1, 1978	$ 1,890		
Payroll for April	126,900		
Total	$128,790		
Less estimated accrued salaries, April 30, 1978 (20% of April payroll)	25,380	103,410	
for operating expenses:			
Accrued expenses, April 1, 1978	$ 5,650		
Prepaid expenses, April 30, 1978	6,950		
Estimated operating expenses for April	95,200		
Total potential payments	$107,800		
Less:			
Accrued expenses, April 30, 1978	$ 8,200		
Prepaid expenses, April 1, 1978	10,000	18,200	89,600
for new plant construction			90,000
Total budgeted disbursements			352,195
Budgeted cash balance, April 30, 1978			$ 38,157

In studying this example, look especially at these points:

1. Estimated *cash receipts from customers* are based on sales made for the month plus collections of beginning receivables, less uncollected receivables at the end of the month.

2. *Cash payments to suppliers* are based upon purchases for the month (from the purchases budget) plus payments made to settle the beginning accounts payable, less any unpaid accounts at the end of the month.

3. *The amount of the payroll* for the month differs from the cash payments to employees by the change in the accrued salaries during the month. (To simplify the example, it is assumed that taxes withheld are paid the same month they are withheld.)

4. In this example, the cash requirements for operating expenses total $89,600. This amount differs from the April operating expenses of $95,200 because of changes in accrued expenses and prepaid expenses. Notice that *beginning* accrued expenses and *ending* prepaid expenses increase the month's cash payment requirements. Likewise, the *ending* accrued expenses and *beginning* prepaid expenses *reduce* the month's cash disbursements.

> ## NEW TERMS

budget committee A committee created in a business organization to make recommendations concerning the development of standards and preparation of budgets; it usually functions in an advisory capacity to the budget executive of the firm. [p. 802]

budget director The executive in a firm whose job is to develop and administer the budgetary system. [p. 802]

standard cost accounting system An accounting system that formally uses standard costs *and* actual costs in its journals and ledgers are reports differences between actual costs and standard costs. [p. 802]

> ## ASSIGNMENT MATERIAL

QUESTIONS

Q47-1. Explain and define the function of the budget committee.

Q47-2. Explain and define the function of the budget director.

Q47-3. "The budget system is an impersonal and rather automatic process." Discuss.

Q47-4. List and briefly describe the steps in the budget preparation process.

Q47-5. How is the budgeted cash receipts from customers computed?

Q47-6. How is the budgeted cash disbursements to suppliers computed?

Q47-7. How is the budgeted cash disbursements for operating expenses computed?

E47-1. St. Andrew's Company budget records show the following data:
1. Number of units of finished goods to be produced during May, 56,000
2. Number of units of finished goods that are needed to remain in the ending inventory for May, 8,000
3. Number of units of finished goods required to meet the sales demand for May, 58,000

From the information, compute the number of units of finished goods that were expected to be available in the beginning inventory for May.

E47-2. St. Paul's Company budget records show the following data for the month of June:

1. Number of units of raw materials needed to remain in the ending inventory of raw materials, 20,000
2. Number of units of raw materials expected to be in the beginning inventory of raw materials, 10,000
3. Expected cost per unit of raw materials, 50 cents
4. Expected total cost of raw materials purchases, $35,000

From the information, compute the production requirements in terms of units of raw materials.

E47-3. Callie Gardens, Inc., expects to sell 100,000 units of product during the coming year. Experience has indicated that the sales will be distributed among the months as follows:

	%
January	5
February	5
March	7
April	8
May	8
June	5
July	5
August	8
September	10
October	9
November	9
December	21

These assumptions are made about the company: The company has a 60-day collection period, a 90-day stock turnover, a 90-day payment period, a $5 per unit selling price, and a $3 per unit cost.

For the months of July and August, compute these amounts:
a. Number of units sold.
b. Dollars of sales.
c. Cash collections from sales.
d. Number of units purchased.
e. Dollar amount of goods purchased.
f. Cash paid for purchases.
g. Net change in cash as a result of cash receipts and disbursements for goods bought and sold.

E47-4. The company closes its books on December 31, 1978. The period of time covered is 1 year.

The company manufactures and sells only one product. The expected selling price is $50 per unit and sales are projected to be 50,000 units. Finished goods on hand at the beginning of the period will be 8,000 units and it is expected that 5,000 units will remain in inventory at the end of the period.

The raw materials on hand at the beginning of the period will total 15,000 pounds and approximately 11,000 pounds should be on hand at the end of the period. The company uses only one type of raw material and it costs 50 cents per pound. Each unit of finished product contains 2 pounds of raw material.

The cost of direct labor should be $5.00 per hour and it takes 2 hours of direct labor to produce a finished unit.

Variable factory overhead at the planned level of operations is expected to amount to $282,000; fixed overhead is expected to be $188,000. Factory overhead is applied on the basis of direct labor hours.

The finished goods inventory at the beginning of the period is $168,000 and should be $105,000 at the end of the period.

Compute the following amounts:

a. Number of units to be produced during the year.
b. Budgeted cost of raw materials used in production.
c. Budgeted raw materials purchases cost.
d. Budgeted direct labor cost.
e. Budgeted variable overhead cost per direct labor hour.
f. Budgeted cost of goods sold.
g. Budgeted gross profit.

PROBLEMS (GROUP A)

P47-1. *Budget computations.* The following information has been gathered by the Budget Director of Spridle Productions, Inc.:

1. The firm manufactures and sells only one product. The selling price during the coming month will be $20 per unit. 75,000 units of finished goods are expected to be sold during the month (March). Finished goods expected to be on hand at the end of the month total 50,000 units. Finished goods expected to be on hand at the beginning of the month total 42,000 units.

2. Direct labor cost is $3 per hour. One-fourth an hour of direct labor is required to manufacture each unit of finished product.

3. Factory overhead is applied to work in process on the basis of direct labor hours. Variable factory overhead at the planned level of operations is expected to amount to $33,200; fixed overhead is expected to amount to $99,600.

4. Raw materials expected to be on hand at the beginning of the month total 5,000 gallons. Only one kind of raw material is used to produce the finished goods. One and one-half gallons of raw material are needed to manufacture each unit of finished product. Raw materials are expected to cost $.18 per gallon during the coming month. Raw materials expected to be on hand at the end of the month total 8,000 gallons.

5. The finished goods inventory at the beginning of the month amounts to $15,000; the finished goods inventory at the end of the month is $16,000.

REQUIRED: Compute the following, showing all computations:

a. Total expected dollars of sales.
b. Number of units to be produced during the month.
c. Budgeted cost of raw materials used in production.

d. Budgeted raw materials purchases cost.

e. Budgeted direct labor cost.

f. Variable overhead cost per direct labor hour.

g. Fixed overhead cost per direct labor hour.

h. Budgeted cost of goods sold.

i. Budgeted gross profit.

P47-2. *Preparation of operating budgets.* The accounting records and budget estimates of Speed and Sons, Inc., revealed the following facts concerning the month of October, 1978:

1. The company manufactures and sells only one product, Deluxe Racees. The finished goods inventory at October 1 is expected to amount to $3,000; the finished goods inventory at October 31 is expected to amount to $3,500. The company will sell its finished products for $20 per unit.

2. 80,000 units of finished goods are expected to be sold during the month.

3. Factory overhead is applied to work in process on the basis of direct labor hours.

4. Raw materials expected to be on hand at October 1 total 1,500 units. Raw materials expected to be on hand at October 31 total 1,800 units.

5. Variable factory overhead at the expected level of operations will amount to $63,000; fixed overhead is expected to be $90,000.

6. Direct labor cost is $3 per hour. Two hours of direct labor are required to produce each unit of product.

7. Raw materials are expected to cost 30 cents per unit in the coming month.

8. Only one kind of raw material is used to produce each finished good. Three units of raw materials are needed to produce each unit of finished good.

9. Beginning inventory of finished goods, 1,000 units; ending inventory of finished goods, 3,100 units.

REQUIRED: Prepare the following:

a. Sales budget.

b. Production levels budget.

c. Raw materials usage and purchases budget.

d. Direct labor budget.

e. Factory overhead budget (in summary form).

f. Cost of goods sold budget.

*P47-3. *Analysis of cash projections.* The actual sales for Finacc Corporation for the last 3 months of 1978 are shown below:

October	$118,000
November	100,000
December	156,000

Projected sales for 1979 are:

January	$112,000
February	109,000
March	110,000
April	131,000
May	120,000
June	120,000
July	115,000

August	100,000
September	104,000
October	125,000
November	120,000
December	180,000

Cost of sales for 1978 amounted to 54% of sales. During 1979, the cost of goods sold are expected to amount to 59% of sales as a result of pricing policy changes.

The company usually collects cash for all sales during the month *following* the sale. Purchases are paid for 2 months following the purchase of merchandise. Merchandise is purchased in the month preceding the sale.

At January 1, 1979, the firm had a cash balance of $85,000, and this much cash must be on hand at the end of every month to provide for regular operations.

Cash payments for operating expenses are estimated by the company each month as follows:

Cash payments required
for operating expenses = $20,000 plus (15% times Expected sales)
during the month

Other cash payments anticipated are: note and interest to be paid in August, $20,000; extraordinary repairs and overhaul of equipment to be paid in September, $14,000.

REQUIRED: Prepare a schedule to show the net change in cash for the company on a monthly basis for 1979. Indicate which months the company will need to take action to maintain the $85,000 minimum cash balance. Use these column headings for your schedule or work sheet: (1) Month, (2) Sales, (3) Cash Collections, (4) Payments for Merchandise, (5) Payments for Operating Expenses, (6) Payments for Note and Interest, (7) Payments for Repairs and Overhaul, (8) Total Payments, (9) Net Change in Cash, (10) Cash Balance.

PROBLEMS (GROUP B)

P47-4. *Preparation of operating budgets.* The following information was gathered by the budget committee of the M Company:
1. The budget period is the year ending December 31, 1978.
2. The company manufactures and sells only one product.
3. The selling price is expected to be $4 per unit.
4. 85,000 units of finished goods are expected to be sold during 1978.
5. Finished goods expected to be on hand at January 1, 1978, total 5,000 units. Finished goods expected to be on hand on December 31, 1978, total 6,000 units.
6. Raw materials expected to be on hand at January 1, 1978, total 3,000 pounds; raw materials expected to be on hand at December 31, 1978 total 7,000 pounds. Only one kind of raw material is used to produce the product. Two pounds of raw material are needed to produce each finished good.
7. Raw materials are expected to cost 35 cents per pound during the coming year.
8. Direct labor cost is $2.70 per hour. One-tenth of an hour of direct labor is required to manufacture each product.

9. Factory overhead is applied to the work in process on the basis of direct labor hours. Variable factory overhead at the expected level of operations is expected to amount to $12,900; fixed overhead is expected to be $8,600.

10. The finished goods inventory at January 1, 1978, amounts to $6,100; the finished goods inventory at December 31, 1978, amounts to $7,320.

REQUIRED: Using this information, prepare:

    a. A sales budget.
    b. A production levels budget.
    c. A raw materials usage and purchases budget.
    d. A direct labor budget.
    e. A factory overhead budget (in summary form).
    f. A cost of goods sold budget.

P47-5. *Preparation of budgeted cash receipts and disbursements statement.* Brandon Co. operates a small parts company. Actual sales for the first 3 months of 1978 and the projected sales for April and May, 1978, are shown below:

	SALES
January	$111,000
February	93,000
March	107,000
April (projected)	100,000
May (projected)	110,000

1. The average markup on cost for the company's merchandise is 80%. That is, the merchandise is sold for about 180% of the cost of the goods.

2. The company collects 60% of its sales during the month the sale is made. Twenty percent is collected during the month following the sale; and the final 20% is collected in the second month following the sale.

3. Purchases of merchandise are paid for as follows: 70% paid during the month of purchase and 30% during the month following the purchase. Merchandise is purchased in the month preceding the sale.

4. The company has a cash balance of $4,000 at March 31, 1978. There must be a cash balance of $7,500 on hand at the end of the coming month of April. Other cash payments anticipated during the month of April are: salaries and wages, $14,000; other expenses, $12,000; payment of note and installment, $20,000.

REQUIRED: Prepare a budgeted cash receipts and disbursements statement for April, 1978. Will additional financing be necessary to have the required ending cash balance of $7,500?

*P47-6. *Computing cash requirements for purchases.* For the first quarter of 1979, Gus and Hilda Enterprises prepared the following estimates of sales:

number of units to be sold

	PRODUCT A	PRODUCT B
January	10,300	50,000
February	11,000	45,000
March	15,000	49,000

The company must have a beginning inventory of each type of product that is equal to half of the upcoming month's sales in units. During April, 1979, the firm plans to sell 20,000 units of Product A and 50,000 units of Product B. During December, 1978, the company sold 12,000 units of Product A and 60,000 units of Product B.

The unit cost of the company's products amounted to $84 per unit for Product A and $50 per unit for Product B during 1978. During 1979, the unit costs are expected to increase by 10 percent.

The company pays for all purchases during the month following the purchase.

REQUIRED: Prepare a schedule (computation) that shows the *cash requirements* for merchandise purchases for the first 3 months of 1979.

UNIT 48

STANDARD COST SYSTEMS AND DECISIONS—I

▶ OBJECTIVE

This unit begins your study of standard cost accounting systems. You now know that the budgeting process (illustrated in Unit 47) consists of developing a series of planning reports and that these reports reflect the standards that management develops. When the standards are formalized in the accounting system—in journals and ledgers—the system is known as a standard cost accounting system. Such a system will be illustrated in this unit and the next. Specifically, this unit will show you how to record raw materials purchases, raw materials usage, and the factory payroll in a standard cost accounting system.

▶ APPROACH TO ATTAINING THE OBJECTIVE

As you study standard cost accounting systems, pay special attention to these four questions, which the text following answers:

- *What standards are used in a standard cost accounting system?*
- *How are transactions dealing with raw materials purchases recorded in a standard cost accounting system?*
- *How are transactions dealing with raw materials usage recorded in a standard cost accounting system?*
- *How are transactions dealing with the factory payroll recorded in a standard cost accounting system?*

817

DESCRIPTION OF THE EXAMPLE

Most of this unit and the next consist of an example of a standard cost accounting system. The data about the Beverly Company which you studied in Unit 47 will be used in this example. Unit 47 described the preparation of *budgets* and the determination of standards for raw materials, direct labor, and factory overhead. These same standards for the same company will now become part of the standard cost accounting system of Beverly Company.

UNIT STANDARDS FOR RAW MATERIALS, DIRECT LABOR, AND FACTORY OVERHEAD

- *What standards are used in a standard cost accounting system?*

A table showing the factory standards for Beverly Company on a unit basis is presented below. The information in this standard cost summary comes directly from the budgets which are prepared before the period's operations begin. One additional factory standard or goal must be recognized. This is the production level for the month. The production levels budget in the last unit indicated that factory operations would be at this level:

121,000 units of Product A and 50,000 units of Product B

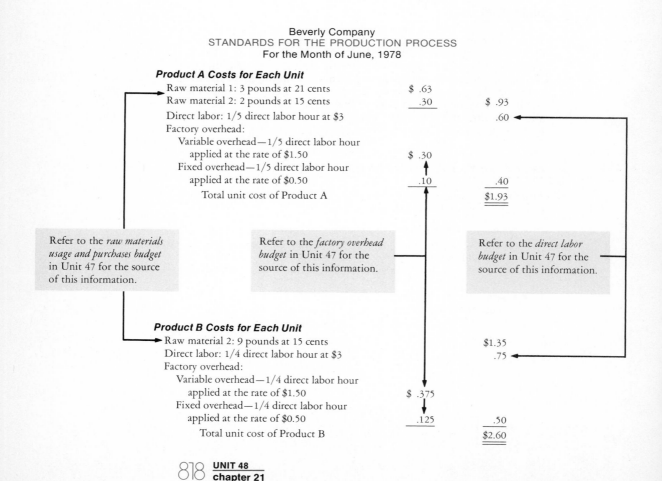

Beverly Company
STANDARDS FOR THE PRODUCTION PROCESS
For the Month of June, 1978

Product A Costs for Each Unit

Raw material 1: 3 pounds at 21 cents	$ .63	
Raw material 2: 2 pounds at 15 cents	.30	$ .93
Direct labor: 1/5 direct labor hour at $3		.60
Factory overhead:		
Variable overhead—1/5 direct labor hour applied at the rate of $1.50	$ .30	
Fixed overhead—1/5 direct labor hour applied at the rate of $0.50	.10	.40
Total unit cost of Product A		$1.93

Refer to the *raw materials usage and purchases budget* in Unit 47 for the source of this information.

Refer to the *factory overhead budget* in Unit 47 for the source of this information.

Refer to the *direct labor budget* in Unit 47 for the source of this information.

Product B Costs for Each Unit

Raw material 2: 9 pounds at 15 cents		$1.35
Direct labor: 1/4 direct labor hour at $3		.75
Factory overhead:		
Variable overhead—1/4 direct labor hour applied at the rate of $1.50	$ .375	
Fixed overhead—1/4 direct labor hour applied at the rate of $0.50	.125	.50
Total unit cost of Product B		$2.60

As a matter of convenience, this production level can be expressed in terms of direct labor hours to be worked in the factory. The direct labor budget in Unit 47 is the source for this information:

Level of operations in terms of direct labor hours:

36,700 direct labor hours

All these standards must be determined in advance; they form the basis for operation of the standard cost accounting system.

The development of unit standards is an extremely important process because the performance of departments and individuals will be judged by them. Unit standards, as you can see from the preceding table, involve both *quantity* and *price*. For example, materials standards are of two basic types. The first is the *quantity* of raw materials to be used to produce each product. This quantity standard is determined with the advice of engineering experts and quality-control experts, and from experience gained in past operations. The second type of raw materials standard is the *price*. The standard cost of each unit of raw materials must be a realistic estimate of costs if materials acquisitions are to be made in the most efficient and effective manner.

Direct labor and factory overhead standards also involve the quantity and price aspects. The number of direct labor hours allowed to produce each product is the quantity standard, and the cost of each direct labor hour is the price standard. Similarly, quantities and prices of overhead items must be controlled.

THE STRUCTURE OF A STANDARD COST ACCOUNTING SYSTEM

In this section the accounts for Beverly Company are illustrated for these three kinds of transactions:

1. Purchasing raw materials and supplies and recording the raw materials price variance.
2. Using raw materials in the factory and recording the raw materials usage variance.
3. Incurring the factory payroll and recording the direct labor rate variance and the direct labor usage variance.

■ How are transactions dealing with raw materials purchases recorded in a standard cost accounting system?

Purchasing raw materials Refer to Beverly Company's raw materials usage and purchases budget in Unit 47. According to this budget, the following purchases are anticipated for June:

369,000 pounds of raw material 1 at $.21	$ 77,490
677,000 pounds of raw material 2 at $.15	101,550
Total budgeted purchases of raw materials	$179,040

Now, assume that two purchases were *actually* made during June:

370,000 pounds of raw material 1 at \$.23	\$ 85,100	
675,000 pounds of raw material 2 at \$.14	94,500	
Total cost of actual purchases	\$179,600	

The journal entries to record the two purchases of raw materials in a standard cost accounting system would be as follows:

| 1978 June | 11 | Raw materials and supplies inventory
Raw materials price variance
    Accounts payable
        To record purchase of 370,000 pounds of
        raw material 1 for \$0.23 per pound.
        Standard cost is \$0.21 per pound.
        Unfavorable price variance is \$7,400,
        or \$0.02 × 370,000 pounds. | 77,700
7,400 | 85,100 |

| 1978 June | 15 | Raw materials and supplies inventory
    Raw materials price variance
    Accounts payable
        To record purchase of 675,000 pounds of
        raw material 2 for \$0.14 per pound.
        Standard cost is \$0.15 per pound.
        Favorable price variance is \$6,750, or
        \$0.01 × 675,000 pounds. | 101,250 | 6,750
94,500 |

In a standard cost accounting system, *the Raw materials and supplies inventory provides a record of all raw materials* (actual quantities on hand) *at their standard cost.* If this figure differs from the actual quantities at their actual cost, the difference represents either a favorable or unfavorable raw materials price variance. The difference is recorded in the **Raw materials price variance** account. The diagram at the top of the next page explains the functions of these accounts.

The Raw materials price variance account will serve as a basis for preparing reports to management at the end of the accounting period. This account shows the differences between standard prices and actual prices for all raw materials purchased during the period. Reports of the variances are illustrated in Unit 49.

RECORDING PURCHASES OF RAW MATERIALS
IN A STANDARD COST ACCOUNTING SYSTEM

ACCOUNTS   *COMPUTATIONS*

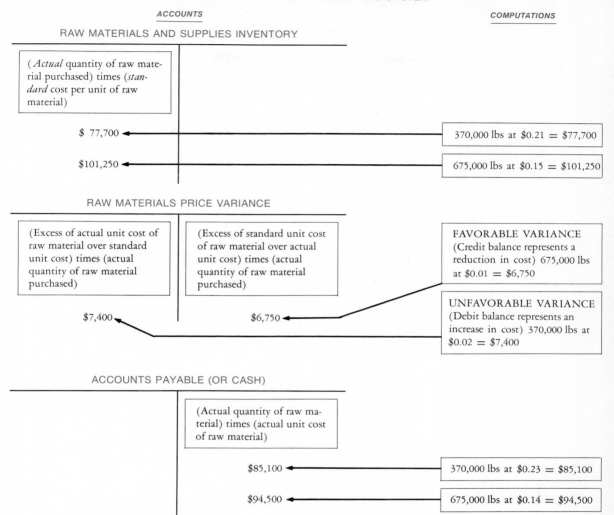

RAW MATERIALS AND SUPPLIES INVENTORY

(*Actual* quantity of raw material purchased) times (*standard* cost per unit of raw material)

$ 77,700 ◄————   370,000 lbs at $0.21 = $77,700

$101,250 ◄————   675,000 lbs at $0.15 = $101,250

RAW MATERIALS PRICE VARIANCE

(Excess of actual unit cost of raw material over standard unit cost) times (actual quantity of raw material purchased)

(Excess of standard unit cost of raw material over actual unit cost) times (actual quantity of raw material purchased)

FAVORABLE VARIANCE (Credit balance represents a reduction in cost) 675,000 lbs at $0.01 = $6,750

UNFAVORABLE VARIANCE (Debit balance represents an increase in cost) 370,000 lbs at $0.02 = $7,400

$7,400 ◄ $6,750 ◄

ACCOUNTS PAYABLE (OR CASH)

(Actual quantity of raw material) times (actual unit cost of raw material)

$85,100 ◄————   370,000 lbs at $0.23 = $85,100

$94,500 ◄————   675,000 lbs at $0.14 = $94,500

• *How are transactions dealing with raw materials usage recorded in a standard cost accounting system?*

Using raw materials Refer again to the raw materials usage and purchases budget in Unit 47. According to this budget, the production levels are expected to be: 121,000 units of Product A and 50,000 units of Product B. These finished goods are expected to require: 363,000 pounds of raw material 1 and 692,000 pounds of raw material 2.

Actual activity for the Beverly Company differed somewhat from the budget. Actual results are as follows:

	STANDARD REQUIREMENTS IN POUNDS OF RAW MATERIAL 1	STANDARD REQUIREMENTS IN POUNDS OF RAW MATERIAL 2
Actual number of units of Product A:		
120,000 units	360,000	240,000
Actual number of units of Product B:		
45,000 units	–0–	405,000
Total pounds to be used according to the standard	360,000	645,000
Actual number of pounds used in the factory	362,000	644,000
Quantity used over or under standard	2,000 over	1,000 under

This information serves as a basis for making the following general journal entries to record the issuance of raw materials into work in process.

1978 June	Work in process inventory	75,600.00	
	Raw materials usage variance	420.00	
	Raw materials and supplies inventory		76,020.00
	To record issuance of 362,000 pounds of raw material 1 into production. Standard pounds allowed are 360,000.		

1978 June	Work in process inventory	96,750.00	
	Raw materials usage variance		150.00
	Raw materials and supplies inventory		96,600.00
	To record issuance of 644,000 pounds of raw material 2 into production. Standard pounds allowed are 645,000.		

In a standard cost accounting system, the Raw materials and supplies inventory account accumulates the *standard* cost of raw materials that were purchased. Therefore this account is always debited and credited for the standard cost per unit. The Work in process inventory account, likewise, accumulates the *standard* costs of raw materials, direct labor, and factory overhead which should be incurred to manufacture the products. The diagram on the next page explains the functions of these accounts. Pay special attention to the **Raw materials usage variance** account. This account serves to accumulate the extra cost above standard (or cost savings) from quantities of raw materials used.

RECORDING USE OF RAW MATERIALS
IN A STANDARD COST ACCOUNTING SYSTEM

ACCOUNTS   *COMPUTATIONS*

RAW MATERIALS AND SUPPLIES INVENTORY

(*Actual* quantity of raw materials purchased) times (*standard* cost per unit of raw materials)	(*Actual* quantity of raw materials issued into production) times (*standard* cost per unit of raw materials)

$76,020 ◄—————— 362,000 lbs at $0.21 = $76,020

$96,600 ◄—————— 644,000 lbs at $0.15 = $96,600

WORK IN PROCESS INVENTORY

1. *Direct labor*
2. *Factory overhead*

3. *Raw materials* = (Number of units of raw materials that should have been used to produce the actual production) times (standard cost of raw materials per unit)

$75,600 ◄—————— 360,000 lbs at $0.21 = $75,600

$96,750 ◄—————— 645,000 lbs at $0.15 = $96,750

RAW MATERIALS USAGE VARIANCE

(Excess of the actual number of units of raw materials used over the standard number of units of raw materials allowed to produce the actual production) times the (standard per unit cost of raw materials)	(Excess of standard number of units of raw materials allowed to be used to produce the actual production over the actual number of units used) times the (standard per unit cost of raw materials)

$420 $150 ◄—————— (645,000 lbs — 644,000 lbs) × $0.15 = $150

(362,000 lbs — 360,000 lbs) × $0.21 = $420

■ *How are transactions dealing with the factory payroll recorded in a standard cost accounting system?*

Recording the factory payroll Refer to the direct labor budget for Beverly Company in Unit 47. According to this budget, during the month of June, 36,700 hours of direct labor are expected to cost $110,100. Next, refer to the factory overhead budget in the last unit. According to this budget for June, salaries and wages of the indirect overhead type should amount to:

Indirect labor (variable)	$46,850
Indirect labor (fixed)	7,000
	$53,850

For the month, the *actual* payroll costs are as follows:

Direct labor hours actually used in manufacturing Product A	24,100
Direct labor hours actually used in manufacturing Product B	11,200
Total actual direct labor hours	35,300
Actual cost per hour	$2.97
Actual direct labor cost	$104,841
Actual indirect labor (variable)	46,800
Actual indirect labor (fixed)	7,200
Total factory payroll	$158,841

From this information and from other payroll records of the company, the following journal entries can be made to record the payroll:

1978					
June	30	Factory payroll		158,841	
		Salaries payable			143,841
		Taxes withheld			15,000
		To record the total factory payroll and to reflect the liability for taxes withheld.			

1978					
June	30	Factory overhead		54,000	
		Work in process inventory		105,750	
		Direct labor usage variance		150	
		Direct labor rate variance			1,059
		Factory payroll			158,841
		To distribute the factory payroll to factory overhead and to work in process inventory and to record the two direct labor variances.			

The diagram on page 826 explains these journal entries and the functions of the accounts they record. Again, pay special attention to the two variance accounts: the **Direct labor usage variance** and the **Direct labor rate variance.** These accumulate the difference between actual labor costs and standard labor costs.

The diagram on page 826 explains

> **NEW TERMS**

direct labor rate variance The excess costs or cost savings caused by actual rates (costs per hour) of direct labor differing from the standard rates for direct labor; see the text for how this variance is calculated. [p. 825]

direct labor usage variance Also called *direct labor efficiency variance;* the excess costs or cost savings caused by actual quantities (hours) of direct labor used differing from the standard number of hours allowed to produce the product; see the text for how this variance is calculated. [p. 825]

raw materials price variance The excess costs or cost savings caused by actual prices of raw materials differing from standard prices; see the text for how this variance is calculated. [p. 820]

raw materials usage variance Also called *raw materials quantity variance;* the excess costs or cost savings caused by actual quantities of raw materials used differing from the standard quantities of raw materials that should have been used to produce the product; see the text for how this variance is calculated. [p. 822]

> **ASSIGNMENT MATERIAL**

QUESTIONS

Q48-1. Briefly describe how raw materials purchases are recorded in a standard cost accounting system.

Q48-2. Briefly describe how raw materials that are used in production are recorded in a standard cost accounting system.

Q48-3. Describe how payroll transactions are recorded in a standard cost accounting system.

Q48-4. Which variance represents the excess costs or cost savings caused by actual rates of direct labor differing from the standard rates?

Q48-5. Specifically state how the variance in Q48-4 (above) is computed.

Q48-6. Which variance represents the excess costs or cost savings caused by actual quantities of raw materials used differing from the standard quantities of raw materials that should have been used to manufacture the product?

Q48-7. Specifically state how the variance in Q48-6 (above) is computed.

EXERCISES

E48-1. Four purchases of raw materials were made during the week as follows:

Raw material 1098, 3,000 pounds at $3.98
Raw material 1099, 2,000 pounds at $4.19
Raw material 1099, 3,000 pounds at $4.24
Raw material 1098, 2,500 pounds at $4.00

The standard cost of Raw material 1098 is $4.00 and of Raw material 1099 is $4.20. Record in general journal form the four purchases for cash.

RECORDING FACTORY PAYROLL IN A STANDARD COST ACCOUNTING SYSTEM

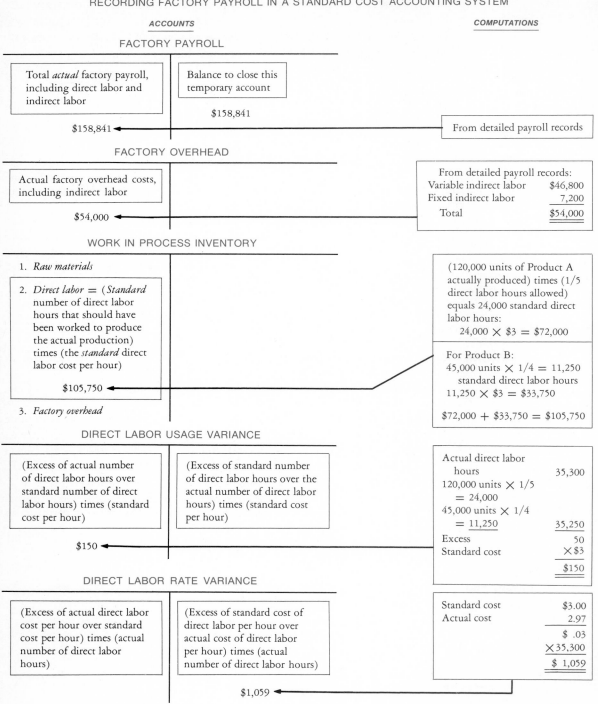

ACCOUNTS

FACTORY PAYROLL

Total *actual* factory payroll, including direct labor and indirect labor	Balance to close this temporary account
	$158,841
$158,841 ◄──	

COMPUTATIONS

From detailed payroll records

FACTORY OVERHEAD

Actual factory overhead costs, including indirect labor	
$54,000 ◄──	

From detailed payroll records:
Variable indirect labor	$46,800
Fixed indirect labor	7,200
Total	$54,000

WORK IN PROCESS INVENTORY

1. *Raw materials*

2. *Direct labor* = (*Standard* number of direct labor hours that should have been worked to produce the actual production) times (the *standard* direct labor cost per hour)

    $105,750 ◄──

3. *Factory overhead*

(120,000 units of Product A actually produced) times (1/5 direct labor hours allowed) equals 24,000 standard direct labor hours:

    24,000 × $3 = $72,000

For Product B:
    45,000 units × 1/4 = 11,250 standard direct labor hours
    11,250 × $3 = $33,750

$72,000 + $33,750 = $105,750

DIRECT LABOR USAGE VARIANCE

(Excess of actual number of direct labor hours over standard number of direct labor hours) times (standard cost per hour)	(Excess of standard number of direct labor hours over the actual number of direct labor hours) times (standard cost per hour)
$150 ◄──	

Actual direct labor hours	35,300
120,000 units × 1/5 = 24,000	
45,000 units × 1/4 = 11,250	35,250
Excess	50
Standard cost	× $3
	$150

DIRECT LABOR RATE VARIANCE

(Excess of actual direct labor cost per hour over standard cost per hour) times (actual number of direct labor hours)	(Excess of standard cost of direct labor per hour over actual cost of direct labor per hour) times (actual number of direct labor hours)

Standard cost	$3.00
Actual cost	2.97
	$ .03
	× 35,300
	$ 1,059

$1,059 ◄──

E48-2.   During the week, raw materials were used in production as follows:

Raw material 1098, 31,156 pounds
Raw material 1099, 44,918 pounds

$3\frac{1}{2}$ pounds of Raw material 1098 and 5 pounds of Raw material 1099 should be used (standard) to produce each of the 9,000 finished products produced during the week.

Record in general journal form the usage of the raw materials in production.

E48-3.   The direct labor records for the month show these data:

Direct labor hours used to produce the product	27,115
Actual direct labor cost	$113,340.70
Actual direct labor rate per hour	$4.18
Actual indirect labor cost (fixed)	$5,000.00
Actual indirect labor cost (variable)	$27,110.00

The budget for the period showed that 9,000 units were to be produced during the month, using a total of 27,000 direct labor hours (3 hours per unit). The standard direct labor rate is $4.00. The budget further showed that budgeted indirect labor cost (fixed) was $4,800 and budgeted indirect labor cost (variable) was $27,000.

Compute:

(1) The direct labor rate variance.
(2) The direct labor usage variance.

E48-4.   Using the data given in E48-3, prepare journal entries to record the factory payroll and to distribute the payroll. Taxes and other withholdings were:

Federal income taxes withheld	$10,600
FICA taxes withheld	5,900
Insurance premiums withheld	2,000
Other withholdings	3,400

PROBLEMS (GROUP A)

P48-1.   *Standard costing; raw materials and labor entries.* Assume the following facts about a company:

1. Standard costs per unit of product:

3 gallons of raw materials at $1	$ 3.00
2 hours of direct labor at $4	8.00
2 hours of direct labor used as base to apply factory overhead at the rate of $1 per hour	2.00
	$13.00

2. Actual number of finished units produced	10,000
3. Actual purchases of raw materials: 7,000 gallons at $0.99	$6,930
4. Actual raw materials used: 30,200 gallons	

5. Factory payroll:

Indirect labor costs	$500
Direct labor costs (21,940 hours at $4.10 per hour)	$89,954
Total factory payroll	$90,454

REQUIRED: Make journal entries for

   a. Purchases of raw materials and recording of raw materials price variance. Cash was paid for the purchases.

   b. Usage of raw materials in production and recording of raw materials usage variance.

   c. Factory payroll and recording of the two direct labor variances. Assume that taxes were withheld totaling $10,000 and the remainder was paid in cash.

P48-2. *Standard costing; computations and entries.* Acquarium Company produced 3,000 units of finished product during the month of June. Two raw materials are used to manufacture the product, raw material A and raw material B. Three units of raw material A and two units of raw material B are required to produce each finished product. Raw material A has a standard (budgeted) cost of $5 per unit and raw material B has a standard cost of $11 per unit.

   Direct labor cost is expected to amount to $4 per direct labor hour; 5 direct labor hours are required to manufacture each finished product. 15,500 direct labor hours were actually worked in the factory for an hourly cost of $3.97. Indirect labor amounted to $3,000.

   During June 10,000 units of raw material A were purchased at a unit cost of $4.90; and 5,000 units of raw material B were purchased during June at a unit cost of $10.00. All purchases were made on credit (2/10, n/30).

   In actual production 9,100 units of raw material A were used and 6,300 units of raw material B were used.

   Factory overhead is applied on the basis of direct labor hours. The rate of overhead application is 5 hours of overhead applied per finished unit. The overhead rate is $3 per hour.

REQUIRED:

   a. Compute the total standard cost per unit of product manufactured.

   b. Make the general journal entry to record the purchase of raw materials. Make a separate entry for each raw material.

   c. Make the general journal entry to record the usage of raw materials in production.

   d. Make the general journal entries to record the factory payroll and the two direct labor variances. Taxes withheld amount to $1,000.

*P48-3. *Materials variances; entries.* Selected data for a production department using standard costing follows.

product

	A	B	C
Raw material 18	4 oz	none	2 oz
Raw material 76	5 gal	3 gal	1 gal
Raw material 29	19 lb	21 lb	none

Costs:

	STANDARD	ACTUAL
Raw material 18	$3.47 per oz	$3.45
Raw material 76	1.20 per gal	1.24
Raw material 29	8.00 per lb	8.09

Output during period:

Product A	6,196 units
Product B	2,000 units
Product C	5,421 units

Raw materials purchased and used in production:

	A	B	C
Raw material 18 (oz)	25,000	none	10,800
Raw material 76 (gal)	30,950	6,117	5,407
Raw material 29 (lb)	117,680	41,506	none

REQUIRED:

a. Compute the raw materials price variance related to each of the three *raw materials.*

b. Compute the raw materials price variance related to producing each of the three *products.*

c. Record the purchase of raw materials (cash). Make three entries, one for each of the three raw materials.

d. Compute the raw materials usage variance related to each of the three raw materials.

e. Compute the raw materials usage variance related to each of the three products.

f. Record the usage of raw materials in production.

PROBLEMS (GROUP B)

P48-4. *Standard costing; entries for materials and labor.* The accountant for Trans-State Company gathered the following information about the factory operations for June, 1978:

1. Actual number of finished products manufactured, 20,000.

2. Actual purchases of raw materials: 15,000 units at $6.10 per unit (all purchases made on credit).

3. Standard costs per unit of finished good:

4 units of raw materials at $6	$24
3 hours of direct labor at $5	15
3 hours of direct labor used as a basis of applying overhead; overhead rate is $4 per hour	12
Total cost per unit of finished good	$51

4. Actual raw materials used in production, 80,152 units.
5. Factory payroll included indirect labor costs of $5,150. Direct labor amounted to 59,400 direct labor hours at a cost of $4.95 per hour.

REQUIRED: Make entries in general journal form for the following:

a. To record purchases of raw materials.
b. To record the usage of raw materials in production.
c. To record the factory payroll and the two direct labor variances. Federal income taxes withheld amounted to $16,000 and Social Security taxes withheld amounted to $5,570. Salaries were paid in cash.

P48-5. *Variance computations; entries for materials and labor.* The following information was taken from the standard cost accounting records of Jay P. Corporation:

1. Standard cost per unit of finished product:
   Raw materials: 3 pounds at $2.50 per pound
   Direct labor: 1/2 hour at $3.50 per hour
   Overhead: applied on the basis of direct labor hours—$2 per direct labor hour
2. Actual number of units manufactured, 10,000.
3. Actual raw materials used, 30,150 units (pounds).
4. Actual purchases of raw materials: 30,000 pounds at $2.48 per pound.
5. Indirect labor costs, $4,500.
6. Direct labor costs, 5,389 hours at $3.57 per hour.

REQUIRED:

a. Compute the following, indicating whether the variances are favorable or unfavorable.
   (1) Total standard cost per unit of product manufactured.
   (2) Raw materials price variance.
   (3) Raw materials usage variance.
   (4) Direct labor rate variance.
   (5) Direct labor usage variance.
b. Make general journal entries for the following:
   (1) To record the purchase of raw materials (for cash).
   (2) To record the usage of raw materials in production.
   (3) To record the factory payroll and the two direct labor variances (taxes withheld from the payroll total $2,500; the Salaries payable account is used).

*P48-6. *Variance analysis.* A company produces four products and uses five raw materials. All the raw materials are in terms of pounds.

Standard Quantities of Materials:

	raw material		
PRODUCTS	A	B	C
111	6	4	9
112	3	0	0
113	4	4	4

Prices of Materials:

	STANDARD	ACTUAL
A	$3.90	$3.91
B	4.00	4.10
C	1.98	1.95

Actual Production:

111	3,500
112	2,000
113	1,200

Actual Usage and Purchase of Raw Materials:

	A	B	C
111	21,106	14,100	31,100
112	6,100	none	none
113	4,810	4,800	4,850

REQUIRED:

a. Compute the raw materials price variances related to each of the three raw materials.

b. Compute the raw materials price variances related to each of the three products.

c. Record the purchase of raw materials (cash). Make three entries, one for each of the raw materials.

d. Compute the raw materials usage variance related to each of the three raw materials.

e. Compute the raw materials usage variance related to each of the three products.

f. Record the usage of raw materials in production. In your entry, show 7 usage variances.

STANDARD COST SYSTEMS AND DECISIONS–II

> **OBJECTIVE**

The objective of this unit is to show you how factory overhead transactions are recorded in a standard cost accounting system and to discuss the regular reporting of all kinds of variances to management.

> **APPROACH TO ATTAINING THE OBJECTIVE**

As you study about recording factory overhead transactions and about reporting variances, pay particular attention to these five questions, which the text following answers:

- *How are transactions dealing with factory overhead recorded in a standard cost accounting system?*
- *How are factory overhead variances analyzed?*
- *How are materials, labor, and overhead variances reported to management?*
- *How are the variance accounts closed?*
- *What is responsibility accounting?*

RECORDING ACTUAL FACTORY OVERHEAD

In a standard cost accounting system, actual factory overhead is recorded much as it is in an ordinary process or job order system. The *Factory overhead account* (a temporary account) is used to accumulate all the actual overhead costs. This account is debited for both fixed and variable overhead as it is incurred.

Refer to the factory overhead budget of Beverly Company as illustrated in Unit 47 on page 806. The company expects to incur $55,050 of variable overhead and $18,350 of fixed overhead during the month. As these overhead costs are incurred, the Factory overhead account is debited and the appropriate accounts such as Cash, Accounts payable, and Accumulated depreciation would be credited. The *actual* Factory overhead account of Beverly Company for June is shown below:

- How are transactions dealing with factory overhead recorded in a standard cost accounting system?

FACTORY OVERHEAD

Variable	52,940
Fixed	18,300
	71,240

This illustration shows the summary figures for variable and fixed overhead to simplify our example. During the month, however, the actual debit side of the account would contain many entries whose total would be the actual factory overhead. In fact, the company would probably keep a Factory overhead subsidiary ledger so that a detailed analysis could be made of the overhead at the end of the month. The factory overhead budget in Unit 47 shows the categories of variable and fixed overhead that the company anticipates.

Now compare the actual overhead in the account illustration above to the budgeted overhead in Unit 47. The differences that you see will be analyzed and explained later in this unit when we consider overhead variances.

APPLYING OVERHEAD TO WORK IN PROCESS

In a standard cost accounting system, overhead is applied on an estimated basis to work in process (just as it is in job order and process cost accounting systems). The factory overhead budget in Unit 47 shows an overhead rate for the company as follows:

Variable overhead per direct labor hour	$1.50
Fixed overhead per direct labor hour	.50
Total overhead rate	$2.00

This predetermined rate is used to transfer factory overhead to the Work in process inventory account from the Factory overhead account during the operating period.

The transfer procedure is as follows. For every direct labor hour allowed to manufacture the products, $2 of factory overhead is transferred to Work in process inventory. Remember that during June *actual* production and thus the standard direct labor hours were as follows:

120,000 units of Product A $\times$ $\frac{1}{5}$ direct labor hour allowed = 24,000
45,000 units of Product B $\times$ $\frac{1}{4}$ direct labor hour allowed = 11,250
Total standard direct labor hours[1]   35,250

Therefore, the overhead transferred to Work in process inventory would be $70,500:

$$35,250 \times \$2.00 = \$70,500$$

The general journal entry to be made during June to apply the overhead to work in process is:

1978 June	Work in process inventory Factory overhead To apply 35,250 direct labor hours allowed at the overhead rate of $2.	70,500.00	70,500.00

As a review, study the Work in process inventory account in the table on the next page ("Applying Overhead to Work in Process"). Note that three cost elements are debited to work in process during the month: raw materials, direct labor, and factory overhead. From Unit 48 you know that standard raw materials cost allowed is debited to the Work in process inventory. Also, you know that standard direct labor cost allowed is debited to Work in process inventory. And in this unit, you have just seen how factory overhead is transferred to work in process on the basis of factory overhead allowed per standard direct labor hour.

In summary, only *standard* costs are debited to the Work in process inventory account. The differences between raw materials actual costs and standard costs are recorded in these accounts:

Raw materials price variance.

Raw materials usage variance.

The differences between direct labor actual costs and standard costs are recorded in these accounts:

Direct labor rate variance.

Direct labor usage variance.

[1] See Unit 48, where standard direct labor hours are computed.

APPLYING OVERHEAD TO WORK IN PROCESS

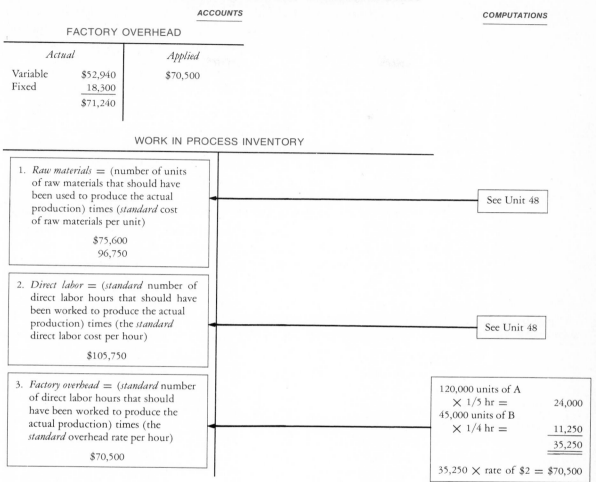

ACCOUNTS

COMPUTATIONS

FACTORY OVERHEAD

Actual		Applied
Variable	$52,940	$70,500
Fixed	18,300	
	$71,240	

WORK IN PROCESS INVENTORY

1. *Raw materials* = (number of units of raw materials that should have been used to produce the actual production) times (*standard* cost of raw materials per unit)

    $75,600
    96,750

    See Unit 48

2. *Direct labor* = (*standard* number of direct labor hours that should have been worked to produce the actual production) times (the *standard* direct labor cost per hour)

    $105,750

    See Unit 48

3. *Factory overhead* = (*standard* number of direct labor hours that should have been worked to produce the actual production) times (the *standard* overhead rate per hour)

    $70,500

    120,000 units of A
    × 1/5 hr =   24,000
    45,000 units of B
    × 1/4 hr =   11,250
                      35,250

    35,250 × rate of $2 = $70,500

     In our preceding example (the table titled "Applying Overhead to Work in Process"), the Factory overhead account has a debit balance of $740, or $71,240 minus $70,500. This end-of-period balance of the Factory overhead account can be referred to as the *overhead variance*. The next section explains how this overhead variance can be analyzed.

ANALYZING THE OVERHEAD VARIANCES

Our purpose here is to examine the $740 unfavorable overhead variance (also called underapplied overhead) in a bit more detail. In practice there are many systems for analyzing overhead. One approach analyzes the variance according to two categories: (1) the overhead budget variance, and (2) the overhead volume variance.

For example, assume that the underapplied amount—$740—was analyzed and broken down as follows:

■ *How are factory overhead variances analyzed?*

Factory overhead budget variance	$ 60 favorable
Factory overhead volume variance	800 unfavorable
Total factory overhead variance ($800 − $60 = $740)	$740 unfavorable

It is beyond the scope of this unit to describe how these two variances are computed, but we can briefly describe what they tell management.

The **factory overhead budget variance** tells management something about the actual cost of the overhead as compared to the budget. The $60 favorable overhead budget variance indicates that $60 was saved because actual overhead prices were less than the expected overhead prices.

The **factory overhead volume variance**, on the other hand, provides information about the extent to which the plant capacity was used. The $800 unfavorable overhead volume variance indicates that $800 of overhead was incurred but was not fully used because the actual level of production was lower than the capacity level of the plant.

EXAMPLE OF A VARIANCE REPORT

Below is a summary report showing all the variances that were computed for Beverly Company for the month of June, 1978. In actual practice, a number of reports would be prepared. Each would be sent to the person in the factory who is in a position to control the individual variance concerned.

■ *How are materials, labor, and overhead variances reported to management?*

Beverly Company
REPORT OF MANUFACTURING VARIANCES
For the Month of June, 1978

raw materials variances (from Unit 48)

Raw materials price variance:			
From raw material 1	$7,400 Unf.		
From raw material 2	6,750 Fav.		
Total raw materials price variance		$ 650 Unf.	
Raw materials usage variance:			
From raw material 1	$ 420 Unf.		
From raw material 2	150 Fav.		
Total raw materials usage variance		270 Unf.	
Total raw materials variances			$920 Unf.
direct labor variances (from Unit 48)			
Direct labor usage variance		$ 150 Unf.	
Direct labor rate variance		1,059 Fav.	
Total direct labor variances			909 Fav.
factory overhead variances			
Factory overhead budget variance		$ 60 Fav.	
Factory overhead volume variance		800 Unf.	
Total factory overhead variances			740 Unf.
Total factory variances			$751 Unf.

As a step in the accounting process, the several variances can be closed to zero, and their balances can be reflected in the Cost of goods sold account. The general journal entries needed to close the variance accounts are shown below.

1978					
June	30	Cost of goods sold		751.00	
		(This is the net sum of all the variances; see the report on the preceding page.)			
		Direct labor rate variance		1,059.00	
		Raw materials price variance			650.00
		Raw materials usage variance			270.00
		Direct labor usage variance			150.00
		Factory overhead			740.00
		To restate the Cost of goods sold account from standard cost to actual cost; to close each of the variance accounts and the Factory overhead accounts to zero.			

■ *How are the variance
accounts closed?*

Consider one final point. When Beverly Company's products are completed and transferred to finished goods, the Finished goods inventory account is debited for the standard cost per unit ($1.93 for Product A and $2.60 for Product B)[2] and the Work in process inventory account is credited for the same amount. All three inventory accounts in a standard cost accounting system include only standard costs; therefore, when the inventory accounts are reduced, they must be credited for the standard cost amounts. In a like manner, when the finished goods are transferred to cost of goods sold, standard costs are credited in the Finished goods inventory account and standard costs are debited in the Cost of goods sold account. These relationships are summarized in the table at the top of the next page. As noted above, the variances are closed to the Cost of goods sold account to adjust that expense from standard cost to actual cost.

**DESCRIPTION OF
RESPONSIBILITY
ACCOUNTING**

■ *What is responsibility
accounting?*

Previously, you have studied cost accumulation systems (job order and process), budgeting, and standard cost accounting. All of these areas have much in common. They are all concerned with providing information to management to aid in planning and control. In a sense, all the accounting activities just mentioned are part of **responsibility accounting.** The term responsibility accounting, however, refers specifically to those parts of accounting which emphasize the *behavioral* aspects of management planning and control— those aspects of management accounting that consider the role of individuals in accomplishing objectives. Responsibility accounting is also known as *activity accounting.*

[2]See the first illustration in Unit 48 on page 818 for the standards used for each finished unit.

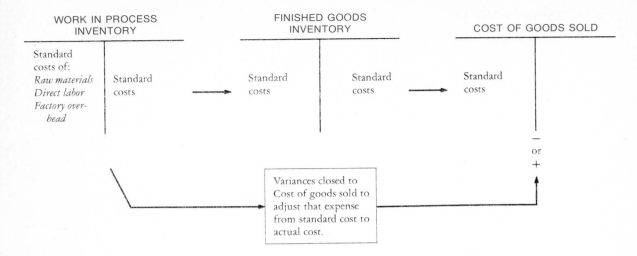

| WORK IN PROCESS INVENTORY | FINISHED GOODS INVENTORY | COST OF GOODS SOLD |

Responsibility accounting can be defined as any system of management accounting that is designed upon these fundamental concepts:

1. The standards against which performance is to be measured must be made explicit, must be communicated within the firm, and must be reasonably attainable.

2. The individuals (managers and other workers) must participate in the development of the standards against which their performance will be measured.

3. Standards should be developed for all levels of the firm, from top management to the individual factory worker level.

4. Any individual should be held accountable *only* for those areas that he can control.

5. The reporting system should emphasize only the significant deviations from standards (management by the exception).[3]

> **NEW TERMS**

overhead budget variance A comparison of the actual cost of overhead with the budgeted overhead; includes both fixed and variable overhead. [p. 836]

overhead volume variance A measure of the use of plant capacity; a fixed overhead variance. [p. 836]

responsibility accounting Also called *activity accounting;* a system of management accounting and reporting based on certain fundamental concepts or assumptions; see the last section of this unit for a list of the five concepts. [p. 837]

[3] For a detailed and thought-provoking discussion of some assumptions of responsibility accounting, see Gordon Shillinglaw, *Cost Accounting, Analysis and Control,* 3rd ed., Richard D. Irwin, Inc., Homewood, Ill., 1972, Chap. 18.

QUESTIONS

Q49-1. In a standard cost accounting system, how is actual factory overhead recorded?

Q49-2. In a standard cost accounting system, what entry is made to apply factory overhead to work in process?

Q49-3. Describe an overhead budget variance.

Q49-4. Describe an overhead volume variance.

Q49-5. What is responsibility accounting?

EXERCISES

E49-1. Refer to the list of five concepts that are fundamental to a responsibility accounting system (in this unit). For each of these five concepts, describe a situation that could exist in a business firm and be in violation of the concept.

E49-2. Go to your school library and locate the journal *Management Accounting*. Find an article that deals with the subject of responsibility accounting. Read the article and write a one-page summary. At the top of your paper, indicate the name of the author of the article, the title of the article, and the date of the journal.

E49-3. *Briefly* describe each of the following terms.

a. Performance report.
b. Responsibility accounting.
c. Standard cost accounting system.
d. Job order cost accounting system.
e. Process cost accounting system.
f. Activity accounting.
g. Budget.
h. Standard.
i. Accounting.

E49-4. Modman, Inc., records showed these variances for 1978:

Factory overhead budget variance	$ 90 unfavorable
Factory overhead volume variance	80 favorable
Direct labor usage variance	150 favorable
Direct labor rate variance	361 unfavorable
Raw materials usage variance	314 unfavorable
Raw materials price variance	115 favorable

Actual factory overhead incurred during 1978 was $9,518.

      Make the journal entry needed at December 31, 1978, to close the variance accounts.

PROBLEMS (GROUP A)

P49-1. *Recording factory overhead; report of manufacturing variances.* Assume the following facts about a company:

1. Standard costs per unit of product:

3 gallons of raw materials @ $1	$ 3.00
2 hours of direct labor @ $4	8.00
2 hours of direct labor used as a base to apply factory overhead at the rate of $1 per hour	2.00
	$ 13.00

2. Actual number of finished units produced: 10,000

3. Actual purchases of raw materials: 7,000 gallons @ $0.99 $ 6,930

4. Actual raw materials used: 30,200 gallons

5. Factory payroll:

Indirect labor costs	$ 500

Direct labor costs (21,940 hours at $4.10 per hour)	$89,954
Total factory payroll	$90,454

6. Actual factory overhead (in addition to indirect labor):

Variable overhead	$15,420
Fixed overhead	$ 5,990

7. Original factory overhead budget for the period:

Variable overhead	$18,000
Fixed overhead	$ 6,000
Number of units of product planned: 12,000	
Variable overhead per direct labor hour	$ .75
Fixed overhead per direct labor hour	$ .25
Factory overhead rate per direct labor hour	$ 1.00

REQUIRED:

a. Make general journal entries for
   (1) Recording the actual factory overhead. Assume that all factory overhead was paid in cash to simplify the example.
   (2) Recording the factory overhead applied into work in process. *Hint:* Remember that the standard direct labor hours that should have been worked to manufacture the products are used as a base.
   (3) Recording the entry to close the Factory overhead account and variance accounts to zero. Assume that the raw materials and direct labor variances were as follows:

   Raw materials price variance, $70 favorable.

   Raw materials usage variance, $200 unfavorable.

   Direct labor rate variance, $2,194 unfavorable.

   Direct labor usage variance, $7,760 unfavorable.

b. Prepare a *Report of Manufacturing Variances* similar to the one illustrated in this unit. Additional information:

   Name of company—Fair Elgotso Company

   Period of operations—Month of May, 1978

   Analysis of overhead variances—The Factory overhead volume variance amounted to $1,000 unfavorable; the remainder of the underapplied or overapplied overhead is the Factory overhead budget variance.

P49-2. *Standard costing journal entries; report of manufacturing variances.* Assume the following facts about James Irving Company at the end of operations on April 30, 1978:
   1. Standard costs per unit of product:

4 gallons of raw materials @ $2	$ 8.00
2 hours of direct labor @ $3	6.00
2 hours of direct labor used as a base to apply factory overhead at the rate of $2 per hour	4.00
	$18.00

   2. Actual number of finished units produced, 6,000
   3. Actual purchases of raw materials, 24,000 gallons at $1.98 per gallon
   4. Actual raw materials used, 24,300 gallons

5. Factory payroll:

      Indirect labor costs, $4,000

      Direct labor costs (11,980 hours at $3.10 per hour)

      Federal income taxes withheld, $2,500

      Federal social security taxes withheld, $1,300

6. Actual factory overhead, $35,000, in addition to indirect labor.

REQUIRED:

a. Make general journal entries to record:
   (1) Purchases of the raw materials (for cash).
   (2) Usage of raw materials in production.
   (3) Factory payroll. Use the Salaries payable account.
   (4) Distribution of the factory payroll.
   (5) Factory overhead incurred (for cash).
   (6) Application of the overhead to work in process.
   (7) Closing the Factory overhead account and the variance accounts to zero.

b. Prepare a *Report of Manufacturing Variances* similar to the one illustrated in this unit. The Factory overhead budget variance amounted to $56, favorable.

P49-3. *Responsibility accounting; assigning costs.* Willard Markson owns and operates a grocery store. The accompanying organization chart describes the responsibilities of the management employees.

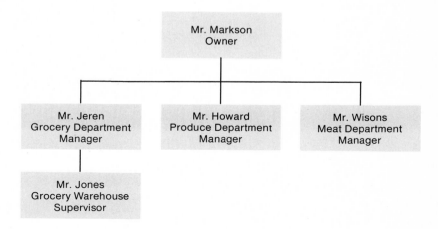

REQUIRED:

For each of the four management employees that work for Mr. Markson, prepare a list of costs for which he probably would be held responsible. Include any explanations that you consider necessary.

PROBLEMS (GROUP B)

P49-4. *Standard costing journal entries; report of manufacturing variances.* The standard cost records of Trumpets, Inc., for the month of November, 1978, included the following:

1. Standard costs per unit of product:
      6 pounds of raw materials at $1 per pound

3 hours of direct labor at $6 per hour

3 hours of direct labor used as a base to apply factory overhead at the rate of $2 per hour

2. Actual number of finished units produced, 8,000
3. Actual purchases of raw materials, 50,000 pounds at $0.98 per pound
4. Actual raw materials used, 47,900 pounds
5. Factory payroll:

Indirect labor costs, $1,000

Direct labor costs, 25,000 hours at $6.11 per hour

Federal income taxes withheld, $3,000

Federal social security taxes withheld, $6,300

6. Actual factory overhead, $50,319, in addition to indirect labor.

REQUIRED:

a. Make the journal entry to record the purchases of the raw materials (for cash).
b. Make the journal entry to record the usage of raw materials in production.
c. Make the journal entry to record the factory payroll. Use the Salaries payable account.
d. Make the journal entry to distribute the factory payroll.
e. Make the journal entry to record the factory overhead incurred (for cash).
f. Make the journal entry to apply the overhead to work in process.
g. Make the journal entry to close the Factory overhead account and the variance accounts to zero.
h. Prepare a *Report of Manufacturing Variances* similar to the one illustrated in this unit. The Factory overhead budget variance amounted to $76, unfavorable.

P49-5. *Responsibility accounting case.* The Lassyer Sales Company employs about twenty-five salesmen who call on customers throughout a three-state area. It is the responsibility of each salesman to (1) take orders for the industrial supplies that the firm sells, (2) service and clean certain equipment owned by the customers who use the industrial supplies (as a courtesy), and (3) make new contacts and call on prospective new customers.

Each salesman is paid on the following basis:

Traveling expense allowance: $300 per month
Plus: 3% of all revenues produced by the salesman

REQUIRED:

a. Comment on how motivation is involved in the pay basis for salesmen.
b. Comment on the general effect of the pay basis on the following:
   (1) Time spent and travel costs incurred to acquire *new* customers located in outlying areas of the salesman's district.
   (2) Time spent by the salesman on cleaning the equipment owned by large customers versus small customers.

P49-6. *Overhead journal entries, standard costing.* The following facts are from the accounting records of Antique Clocks Corporation for January, 1978:

Account balances at end of period:

Raw materials price variance, $5,300 credit balance

Raw materials usage variance, $4,000 debit balance

Direct labor rate variance, $3,005 debit balance

Direct labor usage variance, $4,110 credit balance

Factory overhead, $54 debit balance

During the period, $15,400 of actual overhead was incurred by the firm.

REQUIRED:

a. Make the general journal entry to record the actual overhead. Assume that cash was paid for the overhead.

b. Make the general journal entry to apply the overhead into the Work in process inventory account. The amount applied can be determined by comparing the balance of the Factory overhead account at the end of the period to the actual factory overhead incurred.

c. Make the general journal entry to close the Factory overhead account and the variance accounts to zero.

d. Prepare a *Report of Manufacturing Variances* similar to the one illustrated in this unit. The Factory overhead budget variance amounted to $100 unfavorable. The remainder of the overhead variance is the Factory overhead volume variance.

CUMULATIVE REVIEW PROBLEMS

P49-7. *Cumulative review problem*

a. Compute the number of units to be produced during the month using the inventory below:

Expected sales	50,000 units
Expected ending inventory	10,000 units
Expected beginning inventory	20,000 units

b. Compute budgeted direct labor cost. Direct labor cost is $2.00 per hour. One-half hour of direct labor is required to manufacture each unit of finished product.

c. Compute variable overhead cost per direct labor hour. Factory overhead is applied to work in process on the basis of direct labor hours. Variable factory overhead at the planned level of production is expected to amount to $30,000.

d. Compute fixed overhead cost per direct labor hour. Fixed overhead is expected to amount to $45,000.

e. Compute budgeted cost of goods sold. Budgeted cost of raw materials used in production is $20,000. Finished goods inventory at the beginning of the month amounts to $21,000. The finished goods inventory at the end of the month is $33,750. Assume FIFO.

f. Record the purchase of raw materials for cash. Actual raw materials purchased is $21,000 for 10,000 pounds. The standard costs per unit of product are the following:

1 pound of raw materials at $2	$2.00
$\frac{1}{2}$ hour of direct labor at $2	$1.00
$\frac{1}{2}$ hour of direct labor used as base to apply factory overhead at the rate of $3 per hour	$1.50
	$4.50

g. Record the usage of raw materials in production. Actual raw materials used: 41,000 pounds. Actual finished units produced: 40,000 units.

h. Record the factory payroll and the two direct labor variances.

Factory payroll:

indirect labor costs, $5,000

direct labor costs, 20,000 hours at $4.00 per hour

Federal income taxes withheld, $3,500

Federal Social Security taxes withheld, $6,000

i. Record the factory overhead incurred (for cash). Actual factory overhead, $74,000, in addition to indirect labor.

j. Record the application of the overhead to work in process.

k. Record the closing of the Factory overhead account and the variance accounts to zero.

P49-8. *Cumulative review problem (responsibility accounting, budgets).* The head of the cutting department of a manufacturing firm is paid on the following basis:

1. $500 base pay per month
2. plus $400 each month that he "makes the budget"

"Making the budget" simply means that the actual costs for the department are equal to or less than the standard (budgeted) costs. The departmental performance reports for the last four months show the following:

	BUDGETED COST	ACTUAL COST	UNDER OR [OVER] BUDGET
March			
Salaries and wages	$10,000	$10,400	
Maintenance costs	12,000	11,200	
Other costs	5,000	5,200	
	$27,000	$26,800	Made budget
April			
Salaries and wages	$10,000	$10,300	
Maintenance costs	12,000	11,500	
Other costs	5,000	5,100	
	$27,000	$26,900	Made budget
May			
Salaries and wages	$10,000	$11,000	
Maintenance costs	12,000	30,000	
Other costs	5,000	4,800	
	$27,000	$45,800	Over the budget
June			
Salaries and wages	$10,000	$11,100	
Maintenance costs	12,000	10,800	
Other costs	5,000	4,900	
	$27,000	$26,800	Made budget

REQUIRED: Answer the following questions:

  a. In what way is motivation involved in the pay plan for the head of the cutting department?
  b. Calculate four variance amounts for each of the months [the variance over or under budget for (1) salaries and wages, (2) maintenance costs, (3) other costs, and (4) total departmental budget.]
  c. Do you believe that the department head is manipulating the incurrence of costs (timing of expenses) for his own benefit? Comment.

PART SIX
ADDITIONAL
TOPICS

chapter 22

the statement of changes in financial position

WORKING CAPITAL CONCEPTS

> **OBJECTIVE**

This chapter presents a comprehensive example of the preparation of the statement of changes in financial position. This unit will lay the foundation by discussing the working capital concepts underlying the statement of changes in financial position. This financial statement is considered a fundamental statement, along with the income statement and the balance sheet.

> **APPROACH TO ATTAINING THE OBJECTIVE**

As you study working capital concepts, pay special attention to these four questions, which the text following answers:

- *What is the working capital cycle?*
- *What is meant by the* flow of funds?
- *How are working capital changes analyzed?*
- *What are the major sources and uses of funds?*

The assets on the balance sheet are not ends in themselves. Instead, they are the means through which the enterprise achieves its goals. Before the assets can be returned to the owners and the creditors, they must be in a liquid or cash form. Therefore, the assets must pass through the process of **liquidation,** that is, being converted to cash.

THE WORKING CAPITAL CYCLE

■ *What is the working capital cycle?*

The term **working capital** is a particularly apt expression for describing the continuously changing nature of the wealth of a company. The most desired form of asset for the firm is *cash*. The most desired form of asset for the customers is *inventory*. Therefore, the **working capital cycle** involves converting cash to inventories and then converting the inventories back to cash. The intervening stage of receivables identifies the current relationship between the firm and its customers. It can be concluded that all other wealth of the firm merely helps in this exchange process. Management is concerned with increasing the velocity of this flow (turnover) so that the same resources may become more productive.

Working capital is usually measured as the *excess of the current assets over the current liabilities of the company*. Illustration 50-1 shows that an increase in any current asset will increase working capital and that an increase in any current liability will decrease working capital.

COMMITTING FUNDS FOR LONG PERIODS

The land, buildings, and equipment that a firm must acquire represent the nonliquid wealth of the firm. This nonliquid wealth serves to directly produce the goods and services of the company. Such purchasing of plant and

ILLUSTRATION 50-1 WORKING CAPITAL CYCLE

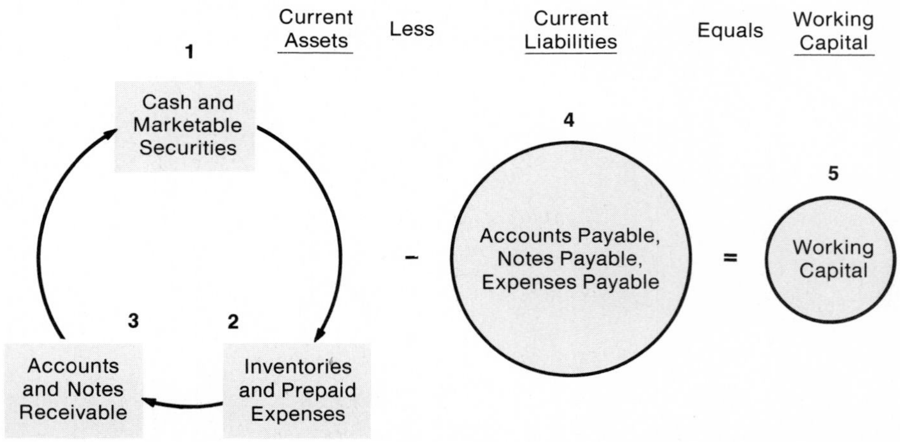

equipment (fixed assets) generally involves a one-way flow of funds. Only rarely are fixed assets sold to raise funds. Accordingly, management must recognize that such long-term commitments of funds "freeze" the use of the resources. These resources are not readily liquidated and to an extent place a special limitation on management.

THE CONCEPT OF FLOW

- *What is meant by the* flow of funds?

The **flow of funds** refers to the transfer of economic values from one asset to another (as in the purchase of a machine with cash). It also refers to the transfer of economic values from one equity to another (as in the payment of accounts payable with the proceeds of a bank loan). It refers to the transfer of economic values from an asset to an equity or vice versa (as in the distribution of dividends to stockholders).

The main objective of funds analysis is to determine for a period of time where the funds came from and what they were used for.

ANALYZING BUSINESS TRANSACTIONS

A first step in understanding the effect on financial statements of working capital changes is to **analyze business transactions.** The business transactions for the Fundz Corporation for January are shown in the list that follows. To simplify the case, the transactions are in *summary* form. For example, instead of showing the many hundreds of sales transactions that probably took place, only one summary transaction is shown for *all* the sales made during January. Study each of these 19 transactions. On a sheet of paper try to make journal entries for each transaction. Then move to the next section of this unit to check your answers.

Transaction 1: The company purchased merchandise during January totaling $190,000. Cash purchases amounted to $15,000 and purchases on credit amounted to $175,000. The perpetual inventory method is used.

Transaction 2: The company sold merchandise for $257,000 during January. Cash sales totaled $25,000 and sales made on credit totaled $232,000.

Transaction 3: The firm uses the perpetual inventory method. The cost of goods sold for all the sales totaled $150,000.

Transaction 4: The company collected $200,000 of the accounts receivable during the month. No sales discounts were allowed customers.

Transaction 5: The company paid $170,000 on the accounts payable during January. No purchase discounts were taken.

Transaction 6: Selling expenses amounting to $30,000 and General expenses amounting to $20,000 were incurred during January. Cash payments of $15,000 were made for these expenses, and the remainder of $35,000 will be paid during the coming months.

Transaction 7: The firm purchased additional supplies for cash, $4,000.

Transaction 8: The firm discovered that one of its customers unexpectedly left the country for good. The $100 amount owed to the firm (Accounts receivable) was written off as uncollectible.

Transaction 9: Additional equipment costing $7,000 was purchased. A cash down payment of $1,000 was made and a long-term note payable was signed for $6,000.

Transaction 10: The beginning balance sheet reveals that the company owns land held for future use with a cost of $13,000. The management decides to sell this land for $20,000, and cash is received for that amount. Assume that this gain is an *extraordinary gain.*

Transaction 11: The company issued 6% bonds payable to raise cash. The bonds have face amounts of $100,000. There was a bond discount of $2,000 and the cash proceeds for the company amounted to $98,000.

Transaction 12: The company issued additional preferred stock and received $30,000 cash.

Transaction 13: The board of directors declared dividends on the preferred stock totaling $3,000. These dividends will be paid in February of 1978.

Transaction 14: The board of directors declared dividends on common stock totaling $2,000. The dividends are paid in cash.

Transaction 15: The January 1, 1978, balance sheet reveals that the firm owed a $15,000 long-term note payable. This note is paid in full, along with $300 of interest due.

Transaction 16: The company sold marketable securities which had cost $9,500 for $10,000 cash.

Adjusting Entries at January 31, 1978

Transaction 17: It is estimated that the bad debts expense for January amounts to $400. The adjusting entry is made.

Transaction 18: Supplies used during the month amount to $2,100.

Transaction 19: Depreciation on the equipment is $6,000 for January and depreciation on the buildings is $2,000 for January.

Fundz Corporation
BUSINESS TRANSACTIONS IN SUMMARY FORM
Month of January, 1978

GENERAL JOURNAL

(1)	Merchandise inventory	190,000	
	Cash		15,000
	Accounts payable		175,000
	Merchandise purchases.		
(2)	Accounts receivable	232,000	
	Cash	25,000	
	Sales		257,000
	Sales of merchandise.		
(3)	Cost of goods sold	150,000	
	Merchandise inventory		150,000
	Cost of all the sales.		
(4)	Cash	200,000	
	Accounts receivable		200,000
	Collections of accounts receivable.		
(5)	Accounts payable	170,000	
	Cash		170,000
	Payments of accounts payable.		
(6)	Selling expenses	30,000	
	General expenses	20,000	
	Cash		15,000
	Expenses payable		35,000
	Incurred expenses.		
(7)	Supplies on hand	4,000	
	Cash		4,000
	Purchase of additional supplies for cash.		
(8)	Allowance for uncollectibles	100	
	Accounts receivable		100
	Wrote off an account as uncollectible.		
(9)	Equipment	7,000	
	Cash		1,000
	Notes payable (long-term)		6,000
	Purchased additional equipment, issuing		
	a long-term note and paying cash.		
(10)	Cash	20,000	
	Land held for future use		13,000
	Gain on sale of long-term investment		7,000
	Sold land held for future use for cash.		

(11)	Cash	98,000	
	Discount on bonds payable	2,000	
	Bonds payable (6%)		100,000
	Issued bonds at a discount for cash.		
(12)	Cash	30,000	
	Preferred stock		30,000
	Issued additional preferred stock for cash.		
(13)	Dividends on preferred stock	3,000	
	Dividends payable		3,000
	Declared dividends on preferred stock to be paid next month.		
(14)	Dividends on common stock	2,000	
	Cash		2,000
	Declared and paid common stock dividends.		
(15)	Notes payable	15,000	
	Interest expense	300	
	Cash		15,300
	Paid note and interest.		
(16)	Cash	10,000	
	Marketable securities		9,500
	Gain on sales of marketable securities		500
	Sold marketable securities for cash.		
(17)	Bad debts expense	400	
	Allowance for uncollectibles		400
	Adjusting entry for bad debts expense.		
(18)	Supplies expense	2,100	
	Supplies on hand		2,100
	Adjusting entry for supplies used.		
(19)	Depreciation expense—Equipment	6,000	
	Depreciation expense—Buildings	2,000	
	Accumulated depreciation—Equipment		6,000
	Accumulated depreciation—Buildings		2,000
	Adjusting entry for depreciation.		

Next, we can determine the effect on working capital of each of the nineteen transactions:

	TRANSACTION NUMBER	NET CHANGE IN WORKING CAPITAL	EXPLANATION AND ANALYSIS
■ How are working capital changes analyzed?	1	–0–	The net change in working capital is zero. The increase in the current asset Merchandise inventory increases working capital by $190,000. The decrease in the current asset Cash

		decreases working capital by $15,000. The increase in the current liability Accounts payable *decreases* working capital by $175,000. This business transaction does not change working capital.
2	+$257,000	Working capital increases by $257,000 because the current asset Accounts receivable increases by $232,000 and the current asset Cash increases by $25,000.
3	−$150,000	This transaction changes working capital. Working capital decreases by $150,000 because the current asset Merchandise inventory decreases by that amount.
4	–0–	This transaction does not change working capital on a net basis, since one part of the transaction increases working capital and the other part decreases working capital.
5	–0–	This transaction does not change working capital on a net basis, since one part of the transaction increases working capital (reducing the current liability) and the other part decreases working capital.
6	−$50,000	This transaction changes working capital. The decrease in cash decreases working capital by $15,000. The increase in the current liability decreases working capital by $35,000.
7	–0–	This transaction does not change working capital on a net basis, since one current asset is increased and another current asset is decreased.
8	–0–	This transaction does not change working capital on a net basis. The current asset Accounts receivable is decreased by the $100 credit, which decreases working capital by $100. The other part of the entry (the debit part) involves another current asset account, Allowance for uncollectibles. The effect of debiting the Allowance for uncollectibles account is to reduce it, which has the effect of *increasing* the net receivables on the balance sheet. The net effect of the transaction on working capital is zero.
9	−$1,000	This transaction decreases working capital by $1,000, since cash is the only current asset or current liability in the transaction.
10	+$20,000	This transaction increases working capital by $20,000, since the current asset Cash increases by that amount.
11	+$98,000	This transaction changes working capital by the amount of the current asset received.
12	+$30,000	This transaction increases working capital by the amount of the current asset received.
13	−$3,000	This transaction decreases working capital because the current liabilities increase.
14	−$2,000	This transaction decreases working capital because the current assets are decreased.
15	−$15,300	The company is doing two things. First, the long-term liability is being paid. Second, the current expense for interest is being paid. The payment of cash reduces the working capital.
16	+$500	The current asset Cash increases by $10,000, so therefore working capital increases by that amount. Also another current asset, Marketable securities, decreases by $9,500, which decreases working capital by that amount. The net effect is an increase in working capital of $500.
17	−$400	The current asset (net receivables) decreases by $400, since the Allowance for uncollectibles is increased.

| 18 | — $2,100 | This transaction decreases working capital since the supplies account is a current asset. |
| 19 | –0– | This transaction does not affect a current asset nor a current liability; therefore, working capital is not affected. |

Be sure to study each of the transactions to ensure that you understand under what circumstances an event will increase or decrease the working capital of a firm.

MAJOR SOURCES AND USES OF WORKING CAPITAL

- *What are the major sources and uses of funds?*

The preceding business transactions that affected working capital can be conveniently classified into categories of sources and uses of working capital. This classification will be a basis for presenting material on the **statement of changes in financial position** to be illustrated in Unit 51.

The major sources of working capital are:

1. *From current operations.* Such transactions as sales on credit and for cash *increase* working capital provided from current operations. And, in the other direction, such transactions as incurring expenses (for cash or on credit) *decrease* the working capital provided from current operations.
2. *From long-term loans.* Such transactions produce cash, inventories, or other properties.
3. *From owners' investments.*
4. *From selling noncurrent assets.*

Similarly, the major uses of working capital are:

1. *Investing in long-term commitments.* An example of this is buying plant and equipment for cash.
2. *Returning working capital to owners* (dividends declared).
3. *Repaying long-term loans.*

> ## NEW TERMS

flow of funds The transfer of economic values from one asset to another (as in the purchase of a machine with cash); from one equity to another (as in the payment of accounts payable with the proceeds of a bank loan); from an asset to an equity (as in paying cash dividends) or from an equity to an asset (as in stockholders' investments in the firm). [p. 851]

liquidation The process of converting assets to cash form. [p. 850]

statement of changes in financial position Also called a *funds flow statement;* a major financial statement that shows changes in resources and equities of a firm for a period of time. [p. 856]

transaction analysis The study of business transactions to determine their effect on the financial statements of a business enterprise. [p. 851]

working capital The excess of current assets over current liabilities. [p. 850]

working capital cycle The continuous process of converting cash to inventories and then back to cash. [p. 850]

➤ ASSIGNMENT MATERIAL

QUESTIONS

Q50-1. What are the three financial statements most useful to management?

Q50-2. What is the process of liquidation?

Q50-3. How is working capital measured?

Q50-4. What is the working capital cycle?

Q50-5. What is meant by flow of funds?

Q50-6. What are the four basic sources of working capital?

Q50-7. What are the three basic uses of working capital?

EXERCISES

E50-1. Refer to the 19 transactions used in the illustration in this unit.
  a. Which of the transactions bring about a decrease in cash?
  b. Which of the transactions bring about an increase in cash?
  c. Which of the transactions tend to decrease net earnings?
  d. Which of the transactions tend to increase net earnings?

E50-2. a. What entry is usually made to write off an account receivable?
  b. What entry is usually made to record the bad debts for a period?
  c. What entry would be made to record the selling of marketable securities for $1,000, if the company had paid $1,100 for the securities?

E50-3. What is the effect of each of the following business transactions and entries on the net working capital of the firm? Use the following responses:

  A The transaction increases net working capital.
  B The transaction decreases net working capital.
  C The transaction has no net effect on working capital.

  1. Declaration of dividends to be paid in 30 days.
  2. Payment of dividends that had previously been declared.
  3. Adjustment for depreciation expense.
  4. Payment of accounts payable.
  5. Purchase of merchandise on credit.
  6. Payment of current expenses with cash.
  7. Using supplies in operating the firm (debiting Supplies expense and crediting Supplies inventory).
  8. Adjusting entry for bad debts.
  9. Purchasing a building and issuing bonds in payment.
  10. Issuing common stock for cash.

E50-4. Indicate the *exact* effect of each of the following items on working capital:
  a. Issuing additional preferred stock.
  b. Recording bad debts expense.
  c. Purchasing equipment for cash.

d. Purchasing equipment on a short-term note.
e. Purchasing equipment on a long-term note.
f. Purchasing equipment by issuing capital stock.
g. Using up supplies on hand.
h. Declaring dividends.
i. Paying dividends that had been earlier declared.
j. Investing cash in marketable securities.
k. Returning merchandise for credit on our account.
l. Collecting an accounts receivable less the discount allowed.

PROBLEMS (GROUP A)

P50-1. *Review problem: transactions.* Caldwell Minerals Company uses the periodic method of accounting for merchandise. In summary form, selected business transactions for the company for 1978 are given below.

a. Store equipment costing $12,000 was purchased. A down payment of $2,100 was made, and a 2-year, 9% note payable was signed for the balance.
b. Cash sales amounting to $83,500 were made.
c. Insurance premiums of $3,000 were paid (fire insurance). These premiums represent insurance coverage for the next 2 years, 1979 and 1980.
d. Collected *cash* amounting to $10,950. This represents payments to the company from customers (Accounts receivable), after the customers were allowed $194 in cash discounts.
e. Purchased merchandise with terms of 2/10, n/30, $13,000.
f. The company issued 8% 10-year bonds payable. The bonds have face amounts of $120,000. The proceeds of the bond issue amounted to $124,000.
g. Recorded the adjusting entry for bad debts. The estimated credit losses related to this period's sales amount to $812.

REQUIRED: Record the business transactions in general journal form.

P50-2. *Effect of transactions on working capital.* What is the effect of each of the following business transactions on the net working capital of the firm? Use the following responses:

A The transaction increases net working capital.

B The transaction decreases net working capital.

C The transaction has no net effect on working capital.

For analysis purposes, assume that the company uses the perpetual system for reporting merchandise. That is, the Merchandise inventory account is used to record purchases of merchandise, purchases returns and allowances, transportation on purchases, and purchases discounts.

1. Purchased merchandise on credit.
2. Paid accounts payable, taking a cash discount.
3. Purchased supplies on credit.
4. Purchased supplies for cash.
5. Made the adjusting entry for supplies used.
6. Made cash sales.
7. Made the entry to record the cost of goods sold (see number 6).
8. Made sales on credit.

9. Collected accounts receivable, allowing cash discounts.
10. Paid a long-term note, along with the interest due.
11. Declared dividends on common stock.
12. Paid the dividends that were previously declared.
13. Paid general expenses in cash.
14. Incurred expenses to be paid later.
15. Sold marketable securities at a gain.
16. Sold marketable securities at a loss.
17. Sold long-term investments at a gain.
18. Sold long-term investments at a loss.

P50-3. *Preparing income statement directly from transactions; determining change in working capital.* The following are the only business transactions of Robin Company for the year ended December 31, 1978.
   a. Purchases of merchandise on credit, $200,000.
   b. Cash purchases of merchandise, $600,000.
   c. Sales of merchandise, all on credit, totaled $2,000,000; the total cost of goods sold amounted to $700,000.
   d. Collected $2,000,000 of accounts receivable, allowing no cash discounts.
   e. Paid $200,000 on accounts payable; no discounts.
   f. Incurred operating expenses totaling $100,000, of which $80,000 were paid in cash.
   g. Paid $20,000 of the taxes payable that were due at the beginning of the year.
   h. Purchased a building for $200,000 paying $30,000 cash, and issuing bonds payable for $170,000.
   i. Declared dividends on common stock, $18,000.
   j. Sold marketable securities that had cost $8,000 for $10,000.
   k. Purchased equipment for cash, $20,000.
   l. Issued common stock for cash, $100,000.
   m. Recorded depreciation, $20,000.

REQUIRED:

   a. Prepare an income statement for the firm.
   b. Calculate the net increase (or net decrease) in working capital during the year.

PROBLEMS (GROUP B)

P50-4. *Review; transactions; financial statements directly from transactions.* The business transactions for QD Corporation for the month of January, 1978, are listed below. The company uses the *perpetual* method of accounting for merchandise.
   a. Purchased merchandise for $6,000 on credit.
   b. Paid accounts payable amounting to $10,000. No purchase discounts were taken.
   c. Sold merchandise costing $5,000 for $10,000 on credit.
   d. Collected $11,000 of accounts receivable.
   e. Paid General expenses totaling $2,000.
   f. Sold Marketable securities costing $1,000 for $2,000.
   g. Purchased additional equipment for $5,000, signing a long-term note for the total amount.
   h. Issued and sold additional capital stock for $3,000.
   i. Prepaid expenses in the amount of $1,000 were used up during the month.
   j. Depreciation expense for the month amounted to $1,000.

k. Dividends of $1,000 were declared, $500 to be paid now and $500 to be paid on June 1.
l. A long-term investment that had originally cost $5,000 was sold for $7,800 cash.
m. A loan was made from First National Bank (8-year note), $10,000.
n. Purchased a storage building for $6,100 cash.
o. Paid a long-term note and interest, $5,000 plus $25 interest.
p. Recorded the unpaid interest on the notes payable, $150.

The following is the January 1, 1978, trial balance of the company.

Cash	2,000	
Marketable securities	2,000	
Accounts receivable	5,000	
Merchandise inventory	4,000	
Prepaid expenses	2,000	
Long-term investments	38,000	
Plant and equipment	61,000	
Accumulated depreciation		6,000
Other assets	6,000	
Accounts payable		7,000
Long-term notes payable		40,000
Capital stock		50,000
Retained earnings		17,000
	120,000	120,000

REQUIRED:

a. Record the transactions in general journal form. *Note:* Be sure to use the same account titles in your journal entries as those that appear in the company's trial balance. Also, when preparing the income statement, assume that the gain on sale of long-term investment is *not* an extraordinary item—that is, place the gain in the regular revenue section of the statement.

b. Prepare an income statement for January, 1978, and a balance sheet at January 31, 1978. You may use "T" accounts to accumulate the data, or you may prepare the financial statements by relating the beginning balances of the accounts directly to the transactions.

P50-5. *Effect of transactions on net working capital.* Following is a list of transactions for a company. For each of the transactions, choose one of the following responses. Also indicate the amount of the working capital change if there is one.

A   This transaction does not represent a net change in working capital.

B   This transaction *increases* the net working capital.

C   This transaction *decreases* the net working capital.

Example: Marketable securities that cost the company $1,000 are sold for $1,200 cash.

Answer: B—in the net amount of $200.

a. Purchased merchandise for $1,300 on credit.
b. Paid accounts payable amounting to $2,000.
c. Purchased additional supplies (current asset) for $300 cash.
d. Purchased additional supplies on credit, $400.

e. Made the adjusting entry to show the use of supplies on hand, $500.

f. Made cash sales, $10,000.

g. Purchased equipment for $10,000, making a down payment of $2,000, and signing a 90-day note for the balance.

h. Paid a long-term note, $14,000, along with interest due of $200, for a total cash expenditure of $14,200.

i. Declared dividends on common stock to be paid next month, $3,000.

j. Declared and paid dividends on preferred stock, $2,000.

k. Made the adjusting entry for depreciation of equipment, $1,000.

l. Purchased merchandise for cash, $12,000.

m. Collected accounts receivable, $9,000.

n. Paid general expenses, $1,000.

o. Sold a long-term investment for cash, $3,000. The cost of the investment originally was $2,000. (Extraordinary gain.)

p. Sold marketable securities which had cost $1,000 for $900 cash.

P50-6. *Journal entries; effect on working capital.* Easter and Company is a retail clothing firm. At the end of each month financial statements are prepared. During the month of August, 1978, the following business transactions took place:

Aug. 2   Purchased merchandise from HP Clothes Corporation for $73,000, terms: 3/15; n/60.

4   Received a freight bill for merchandise received from HP Clothes Corporation in the amount of $500. This bill will be paid next month.

5   Purchased merchandise for cash from PTT Company in the amount of $240,000. Also paid freight charges of $400.

8   Bought land for $90,000, paying $25,000 cash and signing a 1-year non-interest-bearing note for the balance.

10   The board of directors declared dividends totaling $11,000, payable October 31, 1978.

15   Purchased marketable securities for $5,000 cash.

16   Paid HP Clothes Corporation the amount due for the merchandise purchased on August 2.

18   Collected accounts receivable during the month as follows:

Total accounts collected	$300,000
Discounts allowed	5,500
Cash collected	$294,500

25   Paid expenses for entertaining customers of $1,000.

31   Cash sales for the month amounted to $40,000. The cost of these goods was $27,000.

31   Sales made on credit during the month were $400,000, with terms of 2/10; n/30. The cost of these goods was $291,000.

31   Paid the rent on the store for the month, $11,500.

31   Paid the employees:

Gross salaries	$5,000
Income taxes withheld	600
Other taxes withheld	200

31   Borrowed $12,000 from Mr. Z. Easter, a major stockholder in the firm, on a 60-day, 6% note.

REQUIRED:

a. For each business transaction, indicate the journal entry that would be made. The company uses the *perpetual* method of recording merchandise.

b. For each business transaction, indicate the effect on the statement of changes in financial position by choosing one of the following responses. Also, indicate the amount of the net working capital change, if there is one.

A   This transaction has no net effect on working capital.

B   This transaction *increases* the net working capital.

C   This transaction *decreases* the net working capital.

PREPARING THE STATEMENT

> **OBJECTIVE**

This unit illustrates how the statement of changes in financial position is prepared. The statement is constructed by using data revealed by the beginning and ending balance sheets and data from the income statement.

> **APPROACH TO ATTAINING THE OBJECTIVE**

As you study how the statement of changes in financial position is prepared, pay special attention to these four questions, which the text following answers:

- *What steps can be followed in preparing the statement of changes in financial position?*
- *How is the net change in working capital determined and what is a schedule of working capital changes?*
- *How are noncurrent account balance changes analyzed?*
- *How is the working capital provided from regular operations computed?*

**STEPS IN
PREPARING THE
STATEMENT OF
CHANGES IN
FINANCIAL
POSITION**

This section of the chapter will illustrate the preparation of the statement of changes in financial position. The steps in this process can be given as follows:

■ *What steps can be
followed in preparing
the statement of
changes in financial
position?*

1. Determine the *net change in working capital* during the period, and enter this amount on the statement of changes in financial position.

2. Examine the *change in each of the noncurrent asset accounts* appearing on the balance sheet. Enter these effects on the statement of changes in financial position.

3. Examine the *change in each of the noncurrent (long-term) liability accounts* on the balance sheet. Enter these effects on the statement of changes in financial position.

4. Examine the *change in each of the stockholders' equity accounts* on the balance sheet. Enter these effects on the statement of changes in financial position.

5. Determine if the amounts that you have entered on the statement reconcile to the net change in working capital.

The firm's financial statements As a basis for an example, Illustrations 51-1, 51-2, and 51-3 are the financial statements of Swingset, Inc., for 1978. Carefully review the balance sheet (Illustration 51-1), the income statement (Il-

ILLUSTRATION 51-1

Swingset, Inc.
BALANCE SHEET
December 31, 1978 and 1977

	DECEMBER 31 1978	DECEMBER 31 1977	INCREASE OR (DECREASE)
Cash	$110,000	$ 8,000	$102,000
Marketable securities	30,000	29,000	1,000
Accounts receivable (net)	80,000	83,000	(3,000)
Merchandise inventory	98,000	84,000	14,000
Prepaid expenses	2,000	2,000	–0–
Long-term investments	200,000	290,000	(90,000)
Plant and equipment (net)	90,000	85,000	5,000
Total assets	$610,000	$581,000	$ 29,000
Accounts payable	$ 30,000	$ 28,000	$ 2,000
Expenses payable	4,000	9,000	(5,000)
Notes payable (long-term)	20,000	10,000	10,000
Bonds payable (long-term)	100,000	111,000	(11,000)
Preferred stock	50,000	35,000	15,000
Common stock	200,000	200,000	–0–
Retained earnings	206,000	188,000	18,000
Total equities	$610,000	$581,000	$ 29,000

lustration 51-2), and the statement of retained earnings (Illustration 51-3). Information from these three financial statements will be used to prepare the statement of changes in financial position (Illustration 51-4).

ILLUSTRATION 51-2

Swingset, Inc.
INCOME STATEMENT
For the Year Ended December 31, 1978

Revenues and gains		
Sales	$200,000	
Rent income	5,000	
Gain on sale of marketable securities	2,000	$207,000
Expenses and losses		
Cost of goods sold	$ 70,000	
Operating expenses	83,000	
Depreciation expense	15,000	
Loss on sale of long-term investment	7,000	175,000
Net earnings		$ 32,000

ILLUSTRATION 51-3

Swingset, Inc.
STATEMENT OF RETAINED EARNINGS
For the Year Ended December 31, 1978

Retained earnings, January 1, 1978			$188,000
Net earnings for 1978		$32,000	
Dividends—Common	$10,000		
Preferred	4,000	14,000	
Net increase in Retained earnings			18,000
Retained earnings, December 31, 1978			$206,000

ILLUSTRATION 51-4

Swingset, Inc.
STATEMENT OF CHANGES IN FINANCIAL POSITION
For the Year Ended December 31, 1978

Sources of Funds		
Regular current operations	$54,000	
Sale of long-term investments	83,000	
Issuance of notes payable	10,000	
Issuance of preferred stock	15,000	
Total sources		$162,000
Uses of Funds		
Purchase of plant and equipment	$20,000	
Repayment of bonds payable	11,000	
Declaration of dividends	14,000	
Total uses		45,000
Net increase in working capital		$117,000

Step 1: Determine the net change in working capital The net change in working capital for the year can be determined by reviewing the comparative balance sheets of the company in Illustration 51-1. The following schedule, called a schedule of working capital, lists the *current assets* and *current liabilities* of the company and shows the net change that took place.

■ *How is the net change in working capital determined and what is a schedule of working capital changes?*

SCHEDULE OF WORKING CAPITAL CHANGES—1978

| | DECEMBER 31 | | |
	1978	1977	CHANGE
Cash	$110,000	$ 8,000	$102,000
Marketable securities	30,000	29,000	1,000
Accounts receivable (net)	80,000	83,000	(3,000)
Merchandise inventory	97,000	83,000	14,000
Prepaid expenses	3,000	3,000	–0–
Total current assets	$320,000	$206,000	$114,000
Accounts payable	$ 30,000	$ 28,000	$ 2,000
Expenses payable	4,000	9,000	(5,000)
Total current liabilities	$ 34,000	$ 37,000	$ (3,000)
Working capital (current assets minus current liabilities)	$286,000	$169,000	$117,000

This net *increase* in working capital, $117,000 is a key figure in evaluating the change in financial position of the company. Now refer to Illustration 51-4. Notice that the $117,000 is entered as the last item on the statement—and it is this figure that the statement of changes in financial position analyzes in detail.

Step 2: Analyze noncurrent asset changes In this second step, we go back to the comparative balance sheets in Illustration 51-1. There are two noncurrent assets: long-term investments and plant and equipment.

■ *How are noncurrent account balance changes analyzed?*

LONG-TERM INVESTMENTS. Illustration 51-1 reveals that long-term investments *decreased* by $90,000. We can conclude that investments must have been sold during the period. Was there a gain or loss on the sale of these long-term investments? The income statement should show any gain or loss. Illustration 51-2 indicates that there was a loss on sale of long-term investments amounting to $7,000. Based upon this information, the following transaction must have taken place during 1978:

1978	Cash	83,000	
	Loss on sale of long-term investments	7,000	
	Long-term investments		90,000

Through this analysis, we have determined that cash amounting to $83,000 was received—the firm sold investments with a book value of $90,000 (Illustration 51-1) and incurred a loss of $7,000 (Illustration 51-2); $90,000 minus $7,000 equals $83,000.

We now proceed to enter the $83,000 increase in working capital from this transaction on the statement of changes in financial position. Refer to Illustration 51-4 and observe the source of funds for this amount.

PLANT AND EQUIPMENT. The second noncurrent asset on the balance sheet is plant and equipment. Illustration 51-1 shows that there was a net increase in plant and equipment amounting to $5,000, perhaps implying a purchase during the period. We next must ask the question: Was plant and equipment sold? Since there is no gain or loss from sale of plant and equipment on the income statement (Illustration 51-2), we can assume that the company sold no plant and equipment during 1978.

Remember, however, that the recording of depreciation each year has the effect of *decreasing* the net plant and equipment on the balance sheet. During 1978, depreciation amounted to $15,000 (see Illustration 51-2). Recording depreciation caused the plant and equipment to decrease by $15,000—yet the balance sheet reveals that there was a *net* increase of $5,000 during the year. Our conclusion must be that the firm purchased an additional $20,000 of equipment during 1978:

PROOF

January 1, net plant and equipment (Illustration 51-1)		$85,000
Additional purchases of equipment	$20,000	
Less depreciation charged off	15,000	
Net increase in plant and equipment (from Illustration 51-1)		5,000
December 31, net plant and equipment (Illustration 51-1)		$90,000

So, we now enter the $20,000 on Illustration 51-4, the statement of changes in financial position, as a use of funds for the purchase of plant and equipment, $20,000. Trace this amount to Illustration 51-4.

Step 3: Analyze long-term liability changes The balance sheet shows that the company has two long-term liabilities, notes payable and bonds payable. Changes in each of these accounts can affect the financial position of the company.

NOTES PAYABLE. The notes payable increased by $10,000. This means that the firm borrowed an additional $10,000. Borrowing represents a source of funds for the company. Notice in Illustration 51-4 that the $10,000 is entered accordingly.

BONDS PAYABLE. The bonds payable account decreased from $111,000 to $100,000 during 1978. From this information, we know that the company paid off the long-term debt in the amount of $11,000. Now refer to Illustration 51-4 to see how this $11,000 becomes a use of **funds** for the company.

Step 4: Analyze stockholders' equity changes There are three stockholders' equity accounts on the balance sheet: preferred stock, common stock, and retained earnings. Changes in each of these accounts bring about a change in financial position.

PREFERRED STOCK. There was an increase in preferred stock of $15,000. This implies that the company raised funds by issuing additional preferred stock. The statement of changes in financial position shows this amount as a source of funds (Illustration 51-4).

COMMON STOCK. The common stock account did not change during the year (see Illustration 51-1). Therefore, no indication of activity in common stock appears on the statement of changes in financial position.

RETAINED EARNINGS. The retained earnings statement provides a detailed analysis of the changes in this account. One change, the dividends, amounted to $14,000. This is a use of working capital, as shown in Illustration 51-4.

The last change in retained earnings deals with the net earnings produced by the firm during 1978, $32,000. We know by examining the income statement (Illustration 51-2) that some working capital must have been produced from regular current operations of the company. For example, producing revenues would be expected to increase working capital; and incurring expenses would generally decrease working capital. So, our job is to calculate the amount of *working capital provided by regular current operations.* We can do this in two ways as illustrated in the following pages:

Observe these points about the calculation:

1. The net working capital provided by operations, $54,000, is entered on the statement of changes in financial position (Illustration 51-4) as a source of funds.
2. Depreciation expense is omitted from this calculation. Remember that depreciation had already been considered when we analyzed the

Method 1 (*data from income statement, Illustration 51-2*)

■ How is the working capital provided from regular operations computed?

revenues that increased working capital:

Sales (both cash and credit sales increase working capital, since both cash and accounts receivable are current assets)	$200,000	
Rent income (usually a cash increase)	5,000	
Gain on sale of marketable securities (this gain is a growth in the current assets)	2,000	
Total		$207,000

less expenses that decreased working capital:

Cost of goods sold (inventory is reduced when the goods are sold)	$ 70,000	
Operating expenses (include expenses paid in cash, prepaid expenses used up, and expenses to be paid later—in all these cases, working capital decreases through a decrease in a current asset or in an increase in a current liability)	83,000	
Total		153,000
working capital provided from regular operations		$ 54,000

change in the Plant and equipment account. Depreciation expense *does not* require a use of working capital like other expenses. The entry that includes a debit to depreciation expense and a credit to the asset plant and equipment (Accumulated depreciation) *does not* affect the working capital of the company.

3. Another item on the income statement, the loss on sale of long-term investments, was not included in this computation. Also, it was considered earlier when the long-term investment account was being analyzed.

Method 2 (*data from income statement, Illustration 51-2*)

net earnings (from income statement)	$32,000
plus those items of expense did not actually require the use of working capital or were considered in earlier computations (Depreciation expense and Loss on sale of long-term investments in this case)	+ 15,000
	+ 7,000
less those items appearing in the revenue section of the income statement that *did not* actually bring in working capital or were considered in earlier computations (none in this case; an example would be rent income earned where a long-term note receivable was accepted in payment)	–0–
working capital provided by regular operations	$54,000

Step 5: Reconcile the changes The last step in preparing the statement of changes in financial position is to reconcile the changes to determine if the difference between the sources and uses of working capital actually equals the net change in working capital. The statement (Illustration 51-4) indicates

that total sources amount to $162,000, that uses amount to $45,000, and that there is a net increase of $117,000, the difference between the two.

NONWORKING CAPITAL CHANGES ON THE STATEMENT. Occasionally, a company will have an important financial transaction that does not directly affect the working capital of the company, yet that should be reported on the statement of changes in financial position. Here are two examples:

1. A building is acquired and bonds payable are issued in payment.
2. Bonds payable are retired by issuing common stock to the bondholders.

Notice that in these examples, net working capital of the company does not change. Such transactions, of course, directly affect the financial position of the company and should be reported on the statement of changes in financial position. In each such case, both a source and a use of funds would be reported on the statement.

Below is a partial statement of changes in financial position showing two transactions as above:

SOURCES

From bonds payable (issued to pay for buildings)	100,000
From common stock (issued to retire bonds payable)	40,000

USES

Purchased building (issuing bonds in payment)	100,000
Retired bonds payable (issuing common stock in payment)	40,000

DECISIONS AND THE FLOW OF FUNDS

An opinion of the Accounting Principles Board of the American Institute of Certified Public Accountants included this statement:

The Board concludes that information concerning the financing and investing activities of a business enterprise and the changes in its financial position for a period is essential for financial statement users, particularly owners and creditors, in making economic decisions. When financial statements purporting to present both financial position (balance sheet) and results of operations (statement of income and retained earnings) are issued, a statement summarizing changes in financial position should also be presented as a basic financial statement for each period for which an income statement is presented.[1]

---

[1] American Institute of Certified Public Accountants, *Opinions of the Accounting Principles Board No. 19,* "Reporting Changes in Financial Position," March, 1971, p. 373.

The statement of changes in financial position provides additional insight into the relationships between the income statement and the balance sheets at the beginning and end of an operating period. In other terms, the statement provides information for a particular kind of decision. The decision deals with proper management of a firm's assets. One of the basic activities of management is to plan and control the acquisition of assets necessary to operate a business and to plan and control the use of these assets.

These fundamental questions are answered by the statement of changes in financial position:

1. How much working capital was generated by current operations?
2. What were the other sources and amounts of working capital flowing into the business?
3. What were the major uses and amounts of working capital flowing out of the business?

By using the answers to the preceding questions as a base, and by comparing the answers with information from previous periods and with information about similar firms, you can more readily estimate and plan flows of resources for the coming operating periods. Also, investors and creditors can use the information to evaluate the debt-paying ability of the firm and the general effectiveness of management in the acquisition and use of resources.

> **NEW TERM**

funds Commonly refers to any one of the following groups of assets: (1) cash, (2) working capital (current assets minus current liabilities), (3) all resources. In accounting terminology, however, "funds" very often refers to working capital. [p. 868]

> **ASSIGNMENT MATERIAL**

QUESTIONS   Q51-1. What are the major sources of resources for a business firm?

Q51-2. What are the major uses of resources for a business firm?

Q51-3. What is working capital provided by regular current operations? How is this figure computed?

Q51-4. What fundamental questions can a statement of changes in financial position answer?

Q51-5. Is the statement of changes in financial position considered by the American Institute of Certified Public Accountants to be a basic financial statement that *must* accompany the balance sheet and income statement of companies?

E51-1. What is the effect of each of the following journal entries on *working capital provided by operations?*

a. Depreciation adjusting entry.

b. Supplies used adjusting entry.

c. Purchase of merchandise on credit.

d. Purchase of merchandise for cash.

e. Payment of an accounts payable.

f. Adjusting entry to restate inventory and set up cost of goods sold.

g. Declared dividends.

E51-2. The following information was taken from the accounting records:

General, administrative and selling expenses	$ 8,000
Sales of merchandise	250,000
Accounts receivable, January 1	75,000
Accounts receivable, December 31	40,000
Prepaid expenses, January 1	4,000
Prepaid expenses, December 31	6,000
Depreciation expense	12,000
Cash purchases of merchandise	160,000
Credit purchases of merchandise	100,000
Inventory, January 1	11,000
Inventory, December 31	120,000
Accounts payable, January 1	40,000
Accounts payable, December 31	35,000

Compute the working capital provided by regular current operations.

E51-3. For many companies, the working capital provided by operations increases consistently, period after period, by a greater amount than the Net earnings of a company. How can this be explained, and what does it mean? Is it possible for working capital to increase as earnings are decreasing?

E51-4. You have been hired to set up an accounting system for a new drugstore that will begin operations next month. Write a report to the owner of the store; this report should convince him that, in addition to the regular financial statements (balance sheet and income statement), a budgeted statement of changes in financial position should be prepared at the beginning of each month and that this should be compared with actual resource flows each month. Also include in your report recommendations concerning the preparation of a budgeted resource flow statement to cover the entire first year's operations. Your report should be comprehensive and persuasive.

PROBLEMS (GROUP A)

P51-1. *Preparing a statement of changes in financial position.* Balance sheets of Chathamm, Inc., follow.

	DECEMBER 31	
	1978	1977
Cash	$ 50,000	$ 8,000
Accounts receivable (net)	40,000	30,000
Merchandise inventory	71,000	30,000
Plant and equipment (net)	154,000	165,000
Investments	20,000	5,000
	$335,000	$238,000

Accounts payable	$ 26,000	$ 29,000
Accrued expenses payable	3,000	4,000
Bonds payable	50,000	30,000
Capital stock	200,000	150,000
Retained earnings	56,000	25,000
	$335,000	$238,000

Additional information: Dividends of $8,000 were declared during the year. No additional purchases or disposals of equipment were made during the year. No long-term investments were sold.

REQUIRED: From the information above, prepare a statement of changes in financial position.

P51-2. *Preparing a statement of changes in financial position.* Following are the comparative balance sheets for a company, along with the income statement for the year. The company declared dividends on common stock of $400,000 and dividends on preferred stock of $176,000 during the year.

Run Corporation
COMPARATIVE BALANCE SHEETS

	DECEMBER 31, 1978	JANUARY 1, 1978	NET INCREASE OR (DECREASE)
Cash...	$ 317,400	$ 20,000	+$ 297,400
Accounts receivable (net)	280,000	80,000	+ 200,000
Marketable securities........................	20,000	100,000	— 80,000
Inventories	400,000	200,000	+ 200,000
Prepaid expenses	10,000	10,000	-0-
Long-term investments......................	160,000	150,000	+ 10,000
Plant and equipment (net)	2,400,000	200,000	+ 2,200,000
	$3,587,400	$760,000	+$2,827,400
Accounts payable	$ 86,000	$ 82,000	+$ 4,000
Taxes payable................................	20,000	20,000	-0-
Expenses payable............................	5,000	10,000	— 5,000
Bonds payable...............................	414,400	240,000	+ 174,400
Preferred stock	120,000	100,000	+ 20,000
Common stock...............................	310,000	200,000	+ 110,000
Retained earnings...........................	2,632,000	108,000	+ 2,524,000
	$3,587,400	$760,000	+$2,827,400

Run Corporation
INCOME STATEMENT
For the Year Ended December 31, 1978

Sales		$6,000,000
Cost of goods sold	$2,000,000	
Operating expenses	400,000	
Depreciation expense	500,000	2,900,000
Net earnings		$3,100,000

REQUIRED: Prepare a statement of changes in financial position.

P51-3. *Analyzing transactions.* Following is a list of transactions for a company. For each of the transactions, choose one of the following responses. Also indicate the amount of the working capital change.

A   This transaction does not represent a net change in working capital.

B   This transaction *increases* the working capital provided by regular operations.

C   This transaction *decreases* the working capital provided by regular operations.

D   This transaction is a separate source (increase) in working capital (not from regular operations).

E   This transaction is a separate use (decrease) of working capital (not from regular operations).

Example: The company declared dividends on common stock totaling $10,000. $2,000 of the dividends are to be paid now and the remainder in 3 months.

EFFECT	AMOUNT
E	$10,000

1. Sold equipment for $3,000 cash. The equipment had cost the company $10,000 and the balance of the Accumulated depreciation account at the time of the sale was $8,000.

2. Purchased marketable securities for $2,000 cash. The company hopes to sell these securities next month for about $2,100 cash to provide funds at that time.

3. Purchased an investment in land for $19,000, making a down payment of $1,000 and signing a 3-year, 5% note for the balance.

4. Incurred selling expenses amounting to $2,000, of which $300 was paid in cash. The remainder will be paid later this year.

5. Made sales amounting to $9,000. $3,000 of the sales were cash sales and the remainder were sold on terms of 2/10; n/60.

6. Made the adjusting entry for bad debts expense, $2,000. The balance of the Allowance for bad debts account before the adjusting entry was $1,000.

7. Paid income taxes due from last year, $4,000. This transaction represents the payment of a current liability, Income taxes payable.

8. Paid $300 for prepaid insurance, a current asset.

9. Made the adjusting entry to record the use of Supplies on hand, $400. The balance of Supplies on hand, after the reduction of $400, was $900.

10. Issued bonds payable with face amounts of $10,000. The bonds were sold at a premium of $1,000, providing proceeds of $11,000.

PROBLEMS (GROUP B)

P51-4. *Preparing a statement of changes in financial position.* Following are the comparative balance sheets for Roll Corporation, along with the income statement for the year. *Additional data:* The company declared $88,000 of preferred dividends during the year and $200,000 of common dividends during the year.

Roll Corporation
COMPARATIVE BALANCE SHEETS

	DECEMBER 31, 1978	JANUARY 1, 1978	NET INCREASE OR (DECREASE)
Cash..	$ 158,700	$ 10,000	+$ 148,700
Accounts receivable (net)	140,000	40,000	+ 100,000
Marketable securities........................	10,000	50,000	— 40,000
Inventories	200,000	100,000	+ 100,000
Prepaid expenses	5,000	5,000	–0–
Long-term investments	80,000	75,000	+ 5,000
Plant and equipment (net)	1,200,000	100,000	+ 1,100,000
	$1,793,700	$380,000	+$1,413,700
Accounts payable	$ 43,000	$ 41,000	+$ 2,000
Taxes payable...............................	10,000	10,000	–0–
Expenses payable............................	2,500	5,000	— 2,500
Bonds payable...............................	207,200	120,000	+ 87,200
Preferred stock	60,000	50,000	+ 10,000
Common stock...............................	155,000	100,000	+ 55,000
Retained earnings...........................	1,316,000	54,000	+ 1,262,000
	$1,793,700	$380,000	+$1,413,700

Roll Corporation
INCOME STATEMENT
For the Year Ended December 31, 1978

Sales		$3,000,000
Cost of goods sold	$1,000,000	
Operating expenses	200,000	
Depreciation expense	250,000	1,450,000
Net earnings		$1,550,000

REQUIRED:

a. Compute the net increase in working capital for the year.

b. Compute the working capital provided by regular operations.

c. Prepare a statement of changes in financial position in good form.

P51-5. *Preparing a statement of changes in financial position.* Balance sheets of Blap, Inc. follow.

> *Additional information:* Dividends on preferred stock declared during the year amounted to $1,000; dividends on common stock amounted to $8,000. No buildings were purchased or sold. Equipment was purchased for cash, $88,000. No equipment was sold. Purchased a patent for $4,000 during the year.

	DECEMBER 31	
	1977	1978
Cash	$ 45,000	$ 30,000
Marketable securities	10,000	12,000
Accounts receivable	40,000	42,000
Allowance for bad debts	(1,000)	(2,000)
Merchandise inventory	100,000	90,000
Prepaid insurance	1,000	2,000
Long-term investments	200,000	210,000
Land	8,000	8,000
Buildings and equipment	312,000	400,000
Accumulated depreciation—Buildings and equipment	(45,000)	(51,000)
Intangible assets	3,000	7,000
	$673,000	$748,000
Accounts payable	$ 9,000	$ 11,000
Short-term notes payable	50,000	40,000
Accrued expenses payable	3,000	5,000
Long-term notes payable	100,000	150,000
Bonds payable	100,000	40,000
Preferred stock	20,000	27,000
Common stock	100,000	105,000
Retained earnings	291,000	370,000
	$673,000	$748,000

REQUIRED:

a. Prepare a schedule of working capital.

b. Prepare a statement of changes in financial position.

*P51-6. *Multiple choice*

1. The three most useful general-purpose financial statements for *management* are the
   (1) Income statement, statement of retained earnings, and balance sheet.
   (2) Income statement, balance sheet, and statement of changes in financial position.
   (3) Income statement, statement of retained earnings, and statement of changes in financial position.
   (4) Statement of retained earnings, balance sheet, and statement of changes in financial position.

2. Which one of the following is not one of the four basic managerial needs for funds flow analysis?
   (1) To determine the financial consequences of operations.

(2) To determine the urgency of problems.

(3) To determine important personnel policies.

(4) To aid in securing new financing.

3. A statement of changes in financial position is also called a

    (1) Schedule of changes in working capital.

    (2) Balance sheet.

    (3) Working capital cycle.

    (4) Funds statement (funds flow statement).

4. Working capital is computed by subtracting current liabilities from

    (1) Current assets.

    (2) Total assets.

    (3) Total capital.

    (4) Fixed assets.

5. The following journal entry has what effect on net working capital?

Retained earnings	5,000	
Dividends payable		5,000

    (1) Increases net working capital.

    (2) Decreases net working capital.

    (3) Has no net effect on working capital.

    (4) Only rarely changes working capital.

6. The term *flow of funds* refers to the

    (1) Economic values of a firm.

    (2) Asset transfers to other assets only.

    (3) Selling assets.

    (4) Transfer of economic values.

7. The following may be regarded as a source of funds, when analyzing balance sheet account changes (comparative balance sheets):

    (1) Asset increases.

    (2) Asset decreases.

    (3) Liability decreases.

    (4) Capital decreases.

8. The following journal entry has what effect on net working capital?

Patent amortization expense	1,000	
Patents		1,000

    (1) Increases net working capital.

    (2) Decreases net working capital.

    (3) Has no net effect on working capital.

    (4) Only rarely changes working capital.

9. The following journal entry has what effect on net working capital?

Depreciation expense	600	
Accumulated depreciation		600

    (1) Increases net working capital.

    (2) Decreases net working capital.

(3) Has no net effect on working capital.

(4) Only rarely changes working capital.

10. These facts are determined by studying the comparative balance sheets of a firm:

	ENDING	BEGINNING
Equipment	$13,000	$10,000
Accumulated depreciation—Equipment	3,000	1,900

The depreciation on equipment for the year amounted to $2,000. Calculate the amount to be shown on the statement of changes in financial position as a use of funds for buying equipment.

(1) $1,900

(2) $2,100

(3) $3,000

(4) $3,900

P51-7. *Cumulative review problem.* The trial balance of ZZ Company at June 1, 1978, the beginning of the month, is as follows:

Cash	$ 2,000	
Marketable securities	2,000	
Accounts receivable (net)	5,000	
Merchandise inventory	4,000	
Prepaid expenses	2,000	
Investments	38,000	
Plant and equipment (net)	55,000	
Other assets	6,000	
Accounts payable		$ 7,000
Long-term notes payable		40,000
Capital stock		50,000
Retained earnings		17,000
	$114,000	$114,000

Business transactions for June are:

a. Purchased merchandise for $6,200 on credit.

b. Paid accounts payable amounting to $10,000.

c. Sold merchandise costing $5,000 for $14,000 on credit.

d. Collected $11,100 of accounts receivable.

e. Paid general expenses totaling $1,900.

f. Sold marketable securities costing $1,400 for $1,350 cash.

g. Purchased additional equipment for $5,000, signing a long-term note for the total amount.

h. Issued additional capital stock for $2,800 cash.

i. Prepaid expenses at the end of the month totaled $2,300. This adjustment was made: Prepaid expenses were debited for $300, and General expenses were credited for $300.

j. Depreciation expense for month is $1,200.

k. Dividends of $1,500 were declared; $1,000 to be paid now, and the balance to be paid in three months.
l. Bad debts expense for the month amounts to $100.
m. Purchased a building for $70,000 issuing Capital stock in payment for the total amount.

REQUIRED:

1. For each business transaction, indicate the journal entry that would be made. The company uses the *perpetual* method of recording merchandise.
2. For each business transaction, indicate the effect on the statement of changes in financial position by choosing one of the following responses:

A   This transaction *increases* the working capital provided by regular operations.

B   This transaction *decreases* the working capital provided by regular operations.

C   This transaction *increases* working capital from selling noncurrent assets.

D   This transaction *increases* working capital from long-term borrowings.

E   This transaction *increases* working capital from owners' investments in the firm.

F   This transaction *decreases* working capital from purchasing noncurrent assets.

G   This transaction *decreases* working capital from paying long-term liabilities.

H   This transaction *decreases* working capital from declaring dividends.

I   This transaction has no net effect on working capital.

*P51-8. *Cumulative review problem* (case analysis of cash and working capital). Financial statements for Toddler Bonnet Company, Inc., are presented in Illustrations 1 and 2. The creation of a bank overdraft had caused considerable concern and embarrassment on the part of Mrs. Service, the manager-owner of the company, and she is anxious to be informed of the circumstances that gave rise to such a condition. Equipment in the form of sewing and cutting machines was sold during the year for $1,200, having cost $3,200.

ILLUSTRATION 1

Toddler Bonnet Company, Inc.
COMPARATIVE BALANCE SHEET

ASSETS		NOVEMBER 30, 1977		NOVEMBER 30, 1978
Cash..		$ 3,286		$ (124)
Accounts receivable (net)		8,773		10,496
Inventories		12,396		20,746
Prepaid property taxes.........................		210		230
Unexpired insurance............................		1,283		921
Machinery and equipment.....................	$10,605		$7,405	
Less: Accumulated depreciation............	4,678	5,927	4,573	2,832
Organization Expense		970		470
Total assets		$32,845		$35,571

Accounts payable	$ 3,043	$ 4,503
Notes payable to banks	18,000	15,000
Accrued expenses	1,292	2,863
Loans from owner...............................	1,500	3,000
Capital stock	10,000	10,000
Retained earnings	(990)	205
Total Equities	$32,845	$35,571

ILLUSTRATION 2

Toddler Bonnet Company, Inc.
INCOME STATEMENT AND SUMMARY OF RETAINED EARNINGS
Year Ended November 30, 1978

Sales		$141,668
Cost of sales (including $1,275 depreciation of machinery)		102,580
Gross profit		$ 39,088
Operating expenses		35,898
Net profit from operations		$ 3,190
Deduct:		
Loss on sale of machinery	$620	
Provision for income taxes	875	1,495
Net profit to retained earnings		$ 1.695
Add: Beginning retained earnings		(990)
		$ 705
Deduct; Write-off of organization expense		500
Ending retained earnings		$ 205

REQUIRED: Prepare a statement of changes in financial position, together with an appropriate explanation to satisfy Mrs. Service's anxiety regarding the circumstances that produced a bank overdraft in spite of profitable operations for the year.

Note: The financial statements provided in this problem were prepared by the company and do not necessarily reflect current generally accepted accounting principles.

chapter 23

capital budgeting and long-range planning

INTRODUCTION TO CAPITAL BUDGETING

❯ OBJECTIVE

The objective of this unit is to introduce you to the aspect of management's long-range planning called capital budgeting. This unit will describe two methods of making capital budgeting decisions: (1) the payback method, and (2) the return on average investment method.

❯ APPROACH TO ATTAINING THE OBJECTIVE

As you study about capital budgeting, pay special attention to these four basic questions, which the text following answers:

- *What is capital budgeting?*
- *What methods are used for selecting projects?*
- *What is the payback method?*
- *What is the return on average investment method?*

DESCRIPTION OF CAPITAL BUDGETING

Capital budgeting is one aspect of management's long-range planning process. It deals with selecting which major projects a company should commit resources to. Capital budgeting essentially deals with choosing projects and deciding how the company should finance those projects. Management also must determine which projects are available (such as investing in a new plant or buying a new machine) and must compare the relative profitability of the projects in making the selections (choosing among the alternatives). As a general rule, the more profitable projects are chosen over the less profitable ones. Several capital budgeting methods have been developed to compare the relative profitability of projects.

- *What is capital budgeting?*

CAPITAL BUDGETING METHODS IN CURRENT USE

In some cases, management makes capital budgeting decisions on an intuitive basis. That is, very little thought goes into the decision. For example, when a delivery truck breaks down, the manager decides to have a major overhaul or perhaps to replace the truck. Or when a machine is completely worn out and cannot be repaired, it is replaced. This intuitive approach to capital budgeting very clearly fails to lead the firm toward a maximization of net earnings. In almost all cases where projects are chosen in this way, it can be shown that planning for replacement and planning for the selection of alternative projects will save the company money.

- *What methods are used for selecting projects?*

Commonly used capital budgeting methods (in addition to the unacceptable intuitive approach) include:

1. The payback method.
2. The return on average investment method.
3. The present value method.

The remainder of this unit will explain the payback method and the rate of return on average investment method. The third method will be explained in Unit 53. These are not the only methods used in practice, but they are representative of current capital budgeting techniques.

THE PAYBACK METHOD

A case will be used to explain the capital budgeting methods. Assume these facts:

- *What is the payback method?*

A firm is considering the purchase of a special-purpose machine to use in its manufacturing operations. The production manager and the purchasing agent gather this information about the prospective investment:

1. The initial cost of the machine will be $12,000.
2. The machine will have a useful life of about 10 years, with a salvage value at the end of its useful life of about $1,000.

3. This new machine will speed up the assembly line considerably. Each year for the 10 years the labor and other factory costs will be cut by about $2,000 per year. These cost savings can be viewed as *cash inflows,* because by purchasing and using this machine, cash payments for expenses will be reduced by $2,000 per year.

The **payback method** is simply a computation to determine how many years it will take the firm to recover its original investment of $12,000. The formula for computing the payback period is:

$$\frac{\text{Payback period}}{\text{in terms of years}} = \frac{\text{Initial investment (initial cash outflow)}}{\text{Average annual cost savings (annual cash inflow)}}$$

Based upon the facts of the case, the payback period is computed as follows:

$$\text{Payback period} = \frac{\$12,000}{\$2,000} = 6 \text{ years}$$

This computation tells the management of the firm that if $12,000 are spent on the project, it will take about six years before this initial outlay of cash is recovered. Any additional (above $12,000) cash inflows will contribute to the overall profit of the project.

Some firms set up a general rule for certain types of capital investments. The rule might be that no project will be considered for investment unless the payback period is 5 years or less. This procedure would tend to reject certain projects which are not expected to provide earnings in a relatively short period of time.

There are several basic objections to using the payback method in the capital budgeting process. The most important of the faults of this method is that the payback period does not directly measure the *profitability* of the project. And profitability is the major consideration in capital budgeting. For example, assume there are two possible projects to select from:

Project A: Initial cost $1,000
Useful life, 5 years
Annual cost savings, $200
Salvage value, none

Project B: Initial cost, $1,000
Useful life, 10 years
Annual cost savings, $200
Salvage value, none

According to the payback formula, both of these projects would have a payback period of 5 years. In each case, the computation would be to divide the initial cost of $1,000 by the annual cash inflows of $200 to get the payback period of 5 years. Obviously, however, Project B is far superior to Project A in terms of profitability. Project A is expected to produce *no net earnings:*

PROJECT A

Annual cost savings	$200
Annual depreciation expense	200
Average annual increase in net earnings	–0–

If Machine A is purchased, the savings in annual costs would increase earnings by $200. But the depreciation expense would be $200 per year on the machine, and this would reduce the net earnings. It is assumed that the company uses the straight-line method to compute the annual depreciation expense. The initial cost of $1,000 (with no scrap value) divided by 5 years equals $200 of annual depreciation.

Machine B, on the other hand, has a longer useful life, and the $200 annual cash inflows will continue a longer period of time. The annual net earnings for Machine B can be computed as follows:

PROJECT B

Annual cost savings	$200
Annual depreciation expense	100
Average annual increase in net earnings	$100

In summary, the payback method measures the period of time it will take to recover the initial investment. This does not directly provide information about whether a project should be accepted (invested in) or rejected. In spite of this significant limitation, some companies use the payback method as their major means of deciding which projects to accept or reject.

Payback period with uneven annual cash inflows The formula given to compute the payback period was:

$$\text{Payback period} = \frac{\text{Initial investment}}{\text{Average annual cash inflow}}$$

In some circumstances, however, the cash inflows will *not* be the same for each of the years—and the "average annual cash inflow" becomes somewhat meaningless in the formula. For example, assume these facts:

1. Initial cost, $12,000.
2. Useful life of 10 years, with a salvage value of $1,000.
3. *Average annual* cost savings of the machine, $2,000, but the savings are expected to be greater in early years as follows:

YEAR	CASH SAVINGS
1	$4,000
2	$4,000
3	$3,000
4	$2,000
5	$2,000
6	$1,000
7	$1,000
8	$1,000
9	$1,000
10	$1,000

$20,000 ÷ 10 years = $2,000 average

How many years will it take the company to recover its $12,000 initial investment? This is the payback period. The answer is about $3\frac{1}{2}$ years.

First year	$4,000
Second year	4,000
Third year	3,000
	$11,000 recovered at beginning of 4th year
Fourth year	1,000 ($\frac{1}{2}$ of the 4th year's inflows)
	$12,000

In summary, when there are uneven cash inflows, the actual inflows must be counted, year by year, to determine the payback period.

RETURN ON AVERAGE INVESTMENT METHOD

A second capital budgeting method, the **rate of return using the average investment,** will be illustrated with the same data:

1. The initial cost of the machine will be $12,000.
2. The machine will have a useful life of about 10 years, with a salvage value of $1,000.
3. The annual cost savings (cash inflows) will be about $2,000 per year.

The rate of return is the percent that the increase in net earnings from the project is expected to be of the investment that the firm has in the project. The formula to compute the rate of return is:

$$\text{Rate of return} = \frac{\text{Average annual increase in net earnings from the project}}{\text{Average investment in the project}}$$

This can be stated in other terms:

$$\text{Rate of return} = \frac{\text{Annual cash savings} - \text{Depreciation expense}}{\dfrac{\text{Initial cost of the project}}{2}}$$

And, applying the facts of the case, the rate of return is:

$$\text{Rate of return} = \frac{\$2,000 - \$1,100}{\dfrac{\$12,000}{2}} = \frac{\$900}{\$6,000} = 15\%$$

Now let's examine in more detail the elements making up these equations.

Average annual increase in net earnings from the project The average annual increase in net earnings from the project is computed by deducting the increase in the firm's annual depreciation expense from the annual cash savings. The depreciation expense will amount to $1,100 per year if the straight line method is used ($12,000 minus scrap value of $1,000 equals the total amount—$11,000—to be depreciated over 10 years). If this project is undertaken, the net earnings will probably increase each year by about $900. This increase in profits for the company can now be compared to the amount of assets tied up in the project during the period of time, 10 years.

Average investment in the project The initial investment to undertake the project is $12,000. Each year, the company has a net cash savings or cash inflow of $2,000. This $2,000 cash savings represents the recovering of part of the $12,000 investment as well as a collection of some of the earnings from the project. The point is that as each year passes, the company has *less and less* invested in the project. Each year, some of the initial investment is returned to the business through the cash savings. At the beginning of the 10-year period the company has $12,000 invested. At the end of the 10-year period, the company has no investment in the project. As a general rule, it can be said that the *average* amount invested in a project during its useful life is about *half* of the amount of the initial investment. Therefore, the initial investment can be divided by *two* to estimate the average investment that produces the $900 per year increase in net earnings.

Accepting or rejecting the project The management of a company must determine its *minimum desired rate of return* in order to use the rate of return method. For example, the company in our case may have decided that all projects undertaken must promise an average annual rate of return of at least 18%. If this is the minimum desired rate of return, then the project above would not be invested in. This minimum rate is determined by management after careful study of its past operations and after careful study of the cost of securing its capital. The rate chosen must be high enough to assure that the firm continues to produce earnings at levels of the past when the earnings are compared to the total capital invested in the firm. The minimum desired rate of return is also known as the **cost of capital.**

Limitations of the return on average investment method The basic objection to this method is that the computation does not take into consideration the *timing of the cash flows.* As a result, the rate of return is only a crude estimate, and is not the actual rate of return for the project.

To illustrate the problem of timing of cash flows, assume that a firm is considering two projects:

Project C: Initial cost, $1,000
Useful life, 5 years
Annual cost savings, $300 each year of useful life
Salvage value, none

Project D: Initial cost, $1,000
Useful life, 5 years
Annual cost savings as follows:

1st year	$1,300
2nd year	50
3rd year	50
4th year	50
5th year	50
	$1,500

Both projects require an initial cost of $1,000. And both projects have a useful life of 5 years. Both projects also will produce total cash inflows of $1,500. The only difference in the two projects is the *timing* of the cash savings. The inflow of cash is sooner in Project D than in Project C. Many factors can cause the cash savings to vary from year to year in a project. For example, maintenance costs for a project may change from year to year.

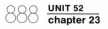

Now let us compare the rates of return using the average investment method for the two projects:

$$\text{Rate of return on Project C} = \frac{\$300 - \$200}{\dfrac{\$1,000}{2}} = \frac{\$100}{\$500} = 20\%$$

$$\text{Rate of return on Project D} = \frac{\$300 - \$200}{\dfrac{\$1,000}{2}} = \frac{\$100}{\$500} = 20\%$$

The profitability of the two projects appears to be identical according to the method. The *average annual cash inflows* for the two projects are identical, although the timing of the cash inflows differs.

The point being illustrated here is that this method indicates that the two projects are identical in profitability. In actuality, *they are not.* Project D definitely is *more profitable* than Project C. The reason for this is the *time value of money.* If Project D is chosen in preference to C, then the large cash inflows of Project D in the first year will be available to the company for additional investments. This extra available cash can be invested to increase profits.

To illustrate the time value of money, assume that a friend offers to give you a present of $1,000 cash. He gives you two options: (1) you can have the $1,000 today, or (2) you can have the $1,000 exactly 1 year from today. Which option do you choose? Which option is the most valuable gift? Of course, the preferable one is the gift today. If you receive the $1,000 today, you could immediately invest the cash in a savings account (or other investment). If the interest earned amounted to 6%, then at the end of 1 year your investment would be worth $1,000 plus 6% in interest or another $60. It can be stated that the gift today is worth more than the same gift one year from now because of the *time value of money.*

Unit 53 explains in detail the concepts underlying the time value of money and presents a method that considers the time value of money in making capital budgeting decisions. This method is the *present value method.*

> **NEW TERMS**

capital budgeting The part of management's long-range planning process that deals with selecting projects or making investments. [p. 883]

cost of capital The minimum desired rate of return that a firm has for accepting projects. [p. 888]

payback method A method used in capital budgeting which provides information about how many years it will take a firm to recover its initial investment from a project; the payback period in terms of years is computed by dividing the initial investment in a project by the average annual cost savings (cash inflows). [p. 884]

return on average investment method A method used in capital budgeting which estimates the profitability or rate of return on the average investment that a firm has in a project; the rate of return is computed by dividing the average annual increase in net earnings by the average investment in the project; this method does not take into consideration the timing of cash flows. [p. 886]

> **ASSIGNMENT MATERIAL**

QUESTIONS

Q52-1. Define capital budgeting.

Q52-2. What are cost savings?

Q52-3. What are cash inflows?

Q52-4. What are three methods commonly used in capital budgeting?

Q52-5. What is the major limitation of the payback method?

Q52-6. What is the major limitation of the return on average investment method?

EXERCISES

E52-1. The following facts are known about a project:

Initial cost of the machine, $15,000

Useful life, 5 years

Cost savings, $4,000 per year for each year of useful life

Salvage value, $2,000

a. Using the above data, compute the payback period for the project. Round your answer to the nearest tenth of a year.

b. Compute the rate of return on average investment for the project. Round your answer to the nearest whole percent.

E52-2. A firm is comparing two projects for investment. All characteristics of the two projects are the same except the timing of the cash savings.

cash savings

	PROJECT A	PROJECT B
First year	$ 3,000	$ 6,000
Second year	4,000	5,000
Third year	5,000	4,000
Fourth year	6,000	3,000
Total inflows	$18,000	$18,000

Which of the two projects is more profitable? Why?

E52-3. Molla Company gathers the following facts about several projects it is considering undertaking:

project

	A	B	C	D
Initial cost of the project	$12,000	$87,000	$90,000	$13,000
Useful life	5 years	13 years	9 years	6 years
Cost savings each year of useful life	$ 5,000	$10,000	$11,000	$ 3,000
Salvage value	$ 500	$ 7,000	none	$ 200

a. Compute the payback period for each project. Round your answers to the nearest tenth of a year.

b. Compute the rate of return on the average investment for each project. Round your answers to the nearest whole percent.

E52-4. A company is considering investing in a machine that costs $30,000. The useful life is 5 years, and the annual total cost savings will amount to $8,000. The salvage value is expected to amount to $4,000.

a. Compute the payback period.

b. Compute the rate of return on average investment.

**PROBLEMS
(GROUP A)**

P52-1. *Comparing payback method and average rate of return, uneven cash inflows.* Wolla Corporation is considering investing in the following projects:

cash savings

	PROJECT A	PROJECT B
First year	$ 6,000	$ 7,500
Second year	7,000	7,500
Third year	8,000	7,500
Fourth year	9,000	7,500
	$30,000	$30,000

Each of the two projects has a useful life of 4 years and a scrap value of $1,000. Each project will initially cost $20,000.

REQUIRED:

a. Compute the payback period for each project. Round your answers to the nearest tenth of a year.

b. Compute the rate of return on the average investment for each project. Round your answers to the nearest whole percent.

c. Which project should be chosen according to the payback method, assuming only one of the two can be undertaken? Which project should be chosen according to the rate of return on average investment, assuming only one of the two can be undertaken?

d. Which of the two projects is actually more profitable? Explain.

P52-2. *Payback period; return on average investment.* Darensbourg Corporation gathers the following facts about three projects it is considering undertaking.

project

	A	B	C
Initial cost of the project	$15,000	$20,000	$25,000
Useful life	5 years	6 years	7 years
Cost savings each year of useful life	$ 4,000	$ 6,000	$10,000
Salvage value	$ 300	none	$ 500

REQUIRED:

    a. Compute the payback period for each project. Round your answers to the nearest tenth of a year.

    b. Compute the rate of return on the average investment for each project. Round your answers to the nearest whole percent.

P52-3. *Alternative investments.* Lou-Fights, Inc., is considering the following alternative investments:

project (brand name)

	TURNPP	CARTT	POTAY	PEPPER	BLAN
Initial cost of project	$50,000	$39,000	$53,000	$82,000	$80,000
Expected useful life and savings	a	b	c	d	e
Salvage value	$ 1,000	$ 2,000	$ 900	$ 5,000	$ 5,000

^a Annual cash savings of $6,000 for 10 years.

^c Annual cash savings of $10,000 for 8 years.

^d Annual cash savings of $10,000 for 10 years.

^e Annual cash savings of $10,000 for 12 years.

^b Cash savings as follows:

First year	$ 5,000
Second year	8,000
Third year	8,000
Fourth year	8,000
Fifth year	8,000
Sixth year	8,000
Seventh year	8,000
	$53,000

REQUIRED:

    a. Compute the payback period for each project. Round your answers to the nearest tenth of a year.

    b. Compute the rate of return on the average investment for each project. Round your answers to the nearest whole percent.

    c. Which project is the best project under the payback method (assuming the shortest payback is the best)?

    d. Which project is the best project under the rate of return on average investment?

PROBLEMS (GROUP B)

P52-4. *Payback period; return on average investment.* Compute the payback period and the rate of return on average investment on each of the following projects:

project

	1	2	3	4
Investment required	$20,000	$80,000	$90,000	$10,000
Useful life	6 years	13 years	9 years	5 years
Annual cost savings (after taxes)	$ 5,000	$10,000	$11,000	$ 4,000
Salvage value	$ 500	$ 8,000	none	none

P52-5. *Payback period; rate of return on average investment.* Sveum Company is considering investing in the following projects:

cash savings

	PROJECT A	PROJECT B
First year	$12,000	$10,000
Second year	17,000	10,000
Third year	19,000	10,000
Fourth year	–0–	10,000
Fifth year	–0–	8,000
	$48,000	$48,000

Project A has a useful life of 3 years and Project B has a useful life of 5 years. Each project has a scrap value of $2,000. Project A will initially cost $25,000, and Project B will cost $30,000.

REQUIRED:

a. Compute the payback period for each project. Round your answers to the nearest tenth of a year.

b. Compute the rate of return on the average investment for each project. Round your answers to the nearest whole percent.

c. Which project should be chosen according to the payback method, assuming only one of the two can be undertaken?

d. Which project should be chosen according to the rate of return on average investment, assuming only one of the two can be undertaken?

P52-6. *Alternative investments (similar to P52-3).* Harris Promoters, Inc., is evaluating five projects as follows:

project

	BAKER	KRESS	PIKE	TAYLOR	WOLF
Initial cost of project	$100,000	$78,000	$106,000	$164,000	$160,000
Expected useful life and savings	a	b	c	d	e
Salvage value	$ 2,000	$ 4,000	$ 1,800	$ 10,000	$ 10,000

[a] Annual cash savings of $12,000 for 10 years.

[b] Cash savings as follows:

First year	$ 10,000
Second year	16,000
Third year	16,000
Fourth year	16,000
Fifth year	16,000
Sixth year	16,000
Seventh year	16,000
	$106,000

[c] Annual cash savings of $20,000 for 8 years.

[d] Annual cash savings of $20,000 for 10 years.

[e] Annual cash savings of $20,000 for 12 years.

REQUIRED:

a. Compute the payback period for each project. Which project is best?

b. Compute the rate of return on average investment on each project. Which project has the highest rate of return?

53

CAPITAL BUDGETING APPLICATIONS

➤ OBJECTIVE

The purpose of this unit is to illustrate a capital budgeting application using the present value method.

➤ APPROACH TO ATTAINING THE OBJECTIVE

As you study about the present value method of selecting projects, pay special attention to these seven questions, which the text following answers:

- *What is the time value of money?*
- *What is present value?*
- *What is a present value table?*
- *What information can be determined from a present value table?*
- *What is the present value method?*
- *What are examples of applying this method?*
- *What is the impact of income taxes on the selection of projects?*

THE TIME VALUE OF MONEY

- What is the time value of money?

An example was presented at the end of Unit 52 to explain the concept that a gift (or cash inflow) today has a *greater* value than does the same gift (cash inflow) a year from today. This concept is called the **time value of money.** This situation implies that the *timing* of cash inflows and cash outflows associated with an investment project has a direct bearing on the *profitability* of the project. This difference in value based upon timing differences in cash flows can be measured, as will be shown next.

THE PRESENT VALUE OF CASH INFLOWS

- What is present value?

In comparing two situations (such as the two gifts), some basis is needed to make the comparison. The concept used to make a comparison is known as the **present value.** Follow this example:

Gift 1: $1,000 in cash will be given to you today.

Gift 2: $1,000 in cash will be given to you one year from today.

We concluded in Unit 52 that Gift 1 would be accepted in preference to Gift 2 because of the time value of money. The $1,000 could be invested at once, and at the end of one year, the earnings on the investment would exceed the amount of Gift 2.

Another way of precisely measuring the relative values of the two gifts is to express both gifts in terms of their *present values*—in terms of today's values.

	AMOUNT OF CASH INFLOW	TIME OF CASH INFLOW	PRESENT VALUE OF CASH INFLOW
Gift 1	$1,000	Today	$1,000
Gift 2	$1,000	One year from today	943[a]
Greater value of Gift 1 over Gift 2			$ 57

[a] The calculation of this figure and the selection of an interest rate are explained later in this unit.

The *present value* of Gift 1 is $1,000 because this amount of cash is available for investment or use today. The present value of Gift 2 is *less* than $1,000, however, because the money will not be received until later. What is the present value, then, of the second gift? The answer to this question can be approached from at least two ways. First, the question can be asked: *How much money must be invested today in order to have an investment of $1,000 at the end of 1 year?* A gift of that amount of money (which happens to be $943 if the interest rate is 6%) would be *equivalent* to the second gift of $1,000 at the end of one year.

Another way of examining the present value of the second gift is as follows. Assume Gift 1 was accepted. *Part* of that money could be invested at 6% interest now to provide a total amount of $1,000 after 1 year. *Of the $1,000 received from Gift 1 today, $943 could be invested for the year at 6% to provide $1,000 at the end of a year.* There would still be $57 available today from the first gift. Therefore, the first gift is worth (has a present value) $57 more than the second gift.

But how was the $943 present value of Gift 2 determined? This question is answered next.

PRESENT VALUE TABLES

■ *What is a present value table?*

On the next page is a table which shows amounts for the present values of $1. This table represents calculations, at various rates of interest (rates of return), of the present values of investments. For example, refer to the 6% column and the 1 period (1 year) row. The present value amount shown in the table is 0.943. This means that for each $94\frac{3}{10}$ cents which are invested today at 6% interest, $1 will have accumulated at the end of 1 year. If you are dealing with $1,000 instead of $1, then simply multiply the amounts in the table by 1,000. Gift 2 in the previous example therefore has a present value of $943, which is computed by multiplying the 0.943 by 1,000. The table indicates, therefore, that if $943 were invested at 6%, then the investment would be worth $1,000 at the end of 1 year.

Present value tables are expressed in terms of $1 so that the present values can readily be converted to any amount of dollars by simply multiplying the amount in the table by the number of dollars. The meaning and use of the present value table will be further explained through a series of examples in the next section of this unit. Also notice that this is the same present value table you used in computing proceeds of a bond issue (Unit 33).

DETERMINING INFORMATION FROM THE TABLE

■ *What information can be determined from a present value table?*

Here are two examples that make use of present value concepts. Refer to the present value table as necessary to answer the questions.

Example 1 Your father has said that he will give you $2,500 as a graduation present 4 years from now, when you graduate from college. He wants to deposit in his savings account at the local savings and loan association enough money to provide the $2,500 in 4 years. The expected interest rate is 6%. How much money must he deposit today to accumulate the $2,500?

Refer to the present value table. Look at the intersection of the 6% column and the 4-year row. The present value of $1 is 0.792. This means that just over 79 cents must be deposited now for each dollar to be available in 4 years. If you multiply 0.792 times $2,500, you get a present value of $1,980. This means that if $1,980 is invested in the savings and loan at 6% annual

PRESENT VALUES OF $1

PERIODS	4%	6%	8%	10%	12%	14%	16%	18%	20%	22%	24%	26%	28%	30%	40%
1	0.962	0.943	0.926	0.909	0.893	0.877	0.862	0.847	0.833	0.820	0.806	0.794	0.781	0.769	0.714
2	0.925	0.890	0.857	0.826	0.797	0.769	0.743	0.718	0.694	0.672	0.650	0.630	0.610	0.592	0.510
3	0.889	0.840	0.794	0.751	0.712	0.675	0.641	0.609	0.579	0.551	0.524	0.500	0.477	0.455	0.364
4	0.855	0.792	0.735	0.683	0.636	0.592	0.552	0.516	0.482	0.451	0.423	0.397	0.373	0.350	0.260
5	0.822	0.747	0.681	0.621	0.567	0.519	0.476	0.437	0.402	0.370	0.341	0.315	0.291	0.269	0.186
6	0.790	0.705	0.630	0.564	0.507	0.456	0.410	0.370	0.335	0.303	0.275	0.250	0.227	0.207	0.133
7	0.760	0.665	0.583	0.513	0.452	0.400	0.354	0.314	0.279	0.249	0.222	0.198	0.178	0.159	0.095
8	0.731	0.627	0.540	0.467	0.404	0.351	0.305	0.266	0.233	0.204	0.179	0.157	0.139	0.123	0.068
9	0.703	0.592	0.500	0.424	0.361	0.308	0.263	0.225	0.194	0.167	0.144	0.125	0.108	0.094	0.048
10	0.676	0.558	0.463	0.386	0.322	0.270	0.227	0.191	0.162	0.137	0.116	0.099	0.085	0.073	0.035
11	0.650	0.527	0.429	0.350	0.287	0.237	0.195	0.162	0.135	0.112	0.094	0.079	0.066	0.056	0.025
12	0.625	0.497	0.397	0.319	0.257	0.208	0.168	0.137	0.112	0.092	0.076	0.062	0.052	0.043	0.018
13	0.601	0.469	0.368	0.290	0.229	0.182	0.145	0.116	0.093	0.075	0.061	0.050	0.040	0.033	0.013
14	0.577	0.442	0.340	0.263	0.205	0.160	0.125	0.099	0.078	0.062	0.049	0.039	0.032	0.025	0.009
15	0.555	0.417	0.315	0.239	0.183	0.140	0.108	0.084	0.065	0.051	0.040	0.031	0.025	0.020	0.006
16	0.534	0.394	0.292	0.218	0.163	0.123	0.093	0.071	0.054	0.042	0.032	0.025	0.019	0.015	0.005
17	0.513	0.371	0.270	0.198	0.146	0.108	0.080	0.060	0.045	0.034	0.026	0.020	0.015	0.012	0.003
18	0.494	0.350	0.250	0.180	0.130	0.095	0.069	0.051	0.038	0.028	0.021	0.016	0.012	0.009	0.002
19	0.475	0.331	0.232	0.164	0.116	0.083	0.060	0.043	0.031	0.023	0.017	0.012	0.009	0.007	0.002
20	0.456	0.312	0.215	0.149	0.104	0.073	0.051	0.037	0.026	0.019	0.014	0.010	0.007	0.005	0.001
21	0.439	0.294	0.199	0.135	0.093	0.064	0.044	0.031	0.022	0.015	0.011	0.008	0.006	0.004	0.001
22	0.422	0.278	0.184	0.123	0.083	0.056	0.038	0.026	0.018	0.013	0.009	0.006	0.004	0.003	0.001
23	0.406	0.262	0.170	0.112	0.074	0.049	0.033	0.022	0.015	0.010	0.007	0.005	0.003	0.002	
24	0.390	0.247	0.158	0.102	0.066	0.043	0.028	0.019	0.013	0.008	0.006	0.004	0.003	0.002	
25	0.375	0.233	0.146	0.092	0.059	0.038	0.024	0.016	0.010	0.007	0.005	0.003	0.002	0.001	
26	0.361	0.220	0.135	0.084	0.053	0.033	0.021	0.014	0.009	0.006	0.004	0.002	0.002	0.001	
27	0.347	0.207	0.125	0.076	0.047	0.029	0.018	0.011	0.007	0.005	0.003	0.002	0.001	0.001	
28	0.333	0.196	0.116	0.069	0.042	0.026	0.016	0.010	0.006	0.004	0.002	0.002	0.001	0.001	
29	0.321	0.185	0.107	0.063	0.037	0.022	0.014	0.008	0.005	0.003	0.002	0.001	0.001	0.001	
30	0.308	0.174	0.099	0.057	0.033	0.020	0.012	0.007	0.004	0.003	0.002	0.001	0.001	0.001	
40	0.208	0.097	0.046	0.022	0.011	0.005	0.003	0.001	0.001						

interest, there will be $2,500 available in 4 years. This can be demonstrated as follows:

	BEGINNING OF YEAR VALUE OF INVESTMENT	INTEREST COMPUTATION	INTEREST FOR YEAR	END OF YEAR VALUE OF INVESTMENT
First year	$1,980	(0.06 × $1,980)	$119	$2,099
Second year	2,099	(0.06 × $2,099)	126	2,225
Third year	2,225	(0.06 × $2,225)	134	2,359
Fourth year	2,359	(0.06 × $2,359)	141	2,500

Example 2 Assume that a company is considering buying a machine that will provide cash savings for the firm for 3 years. This machine will save the company $1,000 in operating costs each year for the 3 years. Further, assume that the firm ordinarily expects to get a rate of return on all its investments of at least 18%. *How much could the company pay for this machine to get an 18% return on its investment?*

Refer to the present value table in the 18% column. The present value amount for 1 year is 0.847, for the second year it is 0.718, and for the third year it is 0.609. A dollar received at the end of the first year has a present value of 84.7 cents; a dollar received at the end of the second year has a present value of 71.8 cents; and a dollar received at the end of the third year has a present value of 60.9 cents. Applying these facts to the case, this table can be constructed:

	AMOUNT OF CASH INFLOWS	PRESENT VALUE OF EACH DOLLAR	PRESENT VALUE OF THE INFLOW
First year	$1,000	0.847	$ 847
Second year	1,000	0.718	718
Third year	1,000	0.609	609
Present value (today's value) of all the cash inflows			$2,174

This calculation indicates that if the firm invests $2,174 in the machine, and if an 18% return is produced on the investment, the cash inflows will be $1,000 for each year for 3 years. If the company selling the machine is asking more than $2,174 for the machine, the profit on the project would be less than 18% and the firm would not accept the investment.

DESCRIPTION OF THE PRESENT VALUE METHOD

The **present value method** of capital budgeting is a technique for selecting projects that attempts to overcome the limitations of the payback method and the return on average investment method. Basically, the present value method takes into consideration the time value of money. As a capital budgeting method, it compares the present value of the cash inflows of a project to the present value of the cash outflows of the project. If the present value of the cash inflows exceeds the present value of the cash outflows, the project is accepted. The method can be described through the flow diagram shown in Illustration 53-1. Study this diagram carefully before you go on to the next section of this unit.

ILLUSTRATION 53-1

FLOW CHART OF THE PRESENT-VALUE METHOD
OF SELECTING PROJECTS

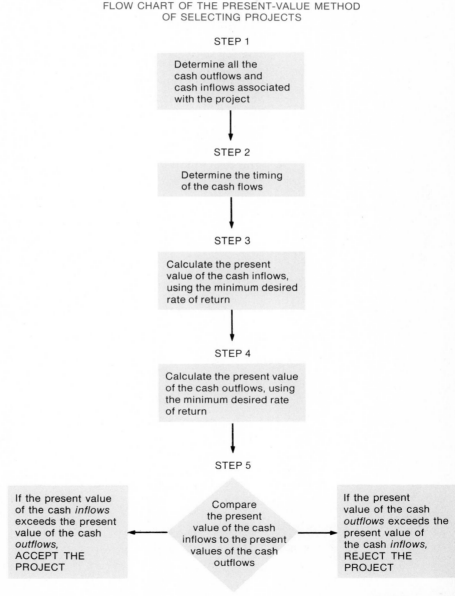

STEP 1

Determine all the
cash outflows and
cash inflows associated
with the project

STEP 2

Determine the timing
of the cash flows

STEP 3

Calculate the present
value of the cash inflows,
using the minimum desired
rate of return

STEP 4

Calculate the present value
of the cash outflows, using
the minimum desired rate
of return

STEP 5

If the present value
of the cash *inflows*
exceeds the present
value of the cash
outflows,
ACCEPT THE
PROJECT

Compare
the present
value of the cash
inflows to the present
values of the cash
outflows

If the present
value of the cash
outflows exceeds the
present value of
the cash *inflows,*
REJECT THE
PROJECT

We will use two case examples to illustrate the use of the present value method in making capital budgeting decisions. A work sheet can be prepared to organize the data called for in the flow diagram (Illustration 53-1).

■ *What are examples of applying this method?*

Case 1 Assume the following facts about an investment. A firm is considering the purchase of a special-purpose machine to use in its manufacturing operations. The production manager and the purchasing agent gather this information about the prospective investment:

1. The initial cost of the machine will be $12,000.
2. The machine will have a useful life of about 10 years, with a salvage value at the end of its useful life of about $1,000.
3. This new machine will speed up the assembly line considerably. Each year for the 10 years the labor and other factory costs will be cut by about $2,000 per year. These cost savings are cash inflows, because by purchasing and using this machine, cash payments for expenses will be reduced by $2,000 per year.
4. The desired minimum rate of return is 12%.

The data are organized on the work sheet shown below. The following comments will explain the details.

Work Sheet
PRESENT VALUE METHOD

	AMOUNT OF CASH INFLOW (OUTFLOW)	TIMING OF CASH FLOWS	12% PRESENT VALUE FACTOR	TOTAL PRESENT VALUE OF INFLOWS	TOTAL PRESENT VALUE OF OUTFLOWS
1. Initial investment	($12,000)	Present	1.000		$12,000
2. Annual cash savings	$ 2,000	1st year	0.893	$ 1,786	
	2,000	2nd year	0.797	1,594	
	2,000	3rd year	0.712	1,424	
	2,000	4th year	0.636	1,272	
	2,000	5th year	0.567	1,134	
	2,000	6th year	0.507	1,014	
	2,000	7th year	0.452	904	
	2,000	8th year	0.404	808	
	2,000	9th year	0.361	722	
	2,000	10th year	0.322	644	
3. Salvage value	1,000	10th year	0.322	322	
4. Total present value				$11,624	$12,000
5. Net disadvantage of taking on the project ($12,000 — $11,624)				376	
				$12,000	$12,000

Initial investment The initial investment of $12,000 is a cash outflow. In the first column of the work sheet, cash outflows are enclosed in parentheses and cash inflows do not have parentheses. This initial payment of $12,000 is made at the present time; therefore, the present value factor would be 1, or 100%, as shown in the third column. Because this payment is the only outflow, the present value of all outflows associated with the project is $12,000, as shown in the column total (last column on the work sheet).

Annual cash savings The cash savings (inflows) for this project happen to be the same each year. The present value factors are taken from the present value table (12% column). Trace each of these figures to that table to be sure you understand the source. The present value of each of the ten inflows is computed by multiplying the factor from the table by the inflow ($2,000). Notice how the present value decreases as the inflows become farther and farther away from the present time.

Salvage value The firm plans to sell the machine at the end of its ten-year life for $1,000 cash. This $1,000 is another cash inflow and must be considered when computing the present value of all the inflows. The factor from the table is from the 12% column and the 10-year row. The present value of the $1,000 scrap value amounts to $322.

Comparing the present values of inflows with outflows The present value of all cash inflows totals $11,624. This means that if the firm invests $11,624 today at a 12% rate of return, the investment would produce the same cash flows associated with the project (it would produce $2,000 per year for 10 years plus the inflow of $1,000 from the salvage). If the firm has to pay *more* than $11,624 for the investment, then the project becomes *less* profitable than 12%. If the firm can purchase the investment for *less* than $11,624, then the project will produce earnings greater than 12%. In this case, the project would *not* be accepted, because there is a net disadvantage of $376 in making investment.

Case 2 Our second application will illustrate a project with cash inflows that are not the same each year. Here are the facts of the case:

Initial cost, $11,950

Cash savings: First year $5,000
            Second year   3,000
            Third year   7,000

Useful life, 3 years

Salvage value, $2,000

Minimum desired rate of return, 14%

The work sheet shown below organizes the data as called for in the flow diagram in Illustration 53-1.

In this case, the total present value of the cash inflows amounts to $12,767. This means that the firm can pay $12,767 for the investment and will have a return of 14% on its investment. The price of the investment is only $11,950, so therefore the investment would be made. The net present value advantage of investing in the project is $817. The net earnings of the firm will increase by $817 above the regular expected earnings (14%) during the course of the project.

Work Sheet
PRESENT VALUE METHOD

	AMOUNT OF CASH INFLOW (OUTFLOW)	TIMING OF CASH FLOWS	14% PRESENT VALUE FACTOR	TOTAL PRESENT VALUE OF INFLOWS	TOTAL PRESENT VALUE OF OUTFLOWS
1. Initial investment	($11,950)	Present	1.000		$11,950
2. Annual cash savings	$ 5,000	1st year	0.877	$ 4,385	
	3,000	2nd year	0.769	2,307	
	7,000	3rd year	0.675	4,725	
3. Salvage value	2,000	3rd year	0.675	1,350	
4. Total present value				$12,767	$11,950
5. Net advantage of investing in the project					817
				$12,767	$12,767

CONSIDERING INCOME TAXES IN CAPITAL BUDGETING

The purpose of this brief discussion is to indicate that the income taxes of corporations definitely have an effect on the cash inflows associated with a project, and accordingly they have an effect on the present value and profitability of the investment. For example, assume that on a project a firm expects in one of the years to have cash savings of $1,000. The effect of the cash savings is to increase the earnings of the firm by $1,000 for that year. Greater earnings in turn tend to increase the taxable income of the company. If the tax rate for the company happens to be 40%, there will be additional taxes amounting to 40% of the $1,000 cash savings. Therefore, the cash savings for the year will be the $1,000 *less* the amount of *extra* taxes associated with the cash savings.

- *What is the impact of income taxes on the selection of projects?*

Another complicating tax factor is that when an investment is made, there is additional depreciation expense. This expense *decreases* the taxable income and therefore *decreases* the income taxes. Thus, the tax reduction from the extra depreciation must be taken into consideration when computing the cash inflows from a project. The tabulation at the top of the next page will illustrate the points about taxes.

The $680 would be the amount of the cash inflow for the year to be used in making the capital budgeting analysis under the present value method. The purpose of this discussion is to indicate that when there are cash savings from a project, there are also extra income taxes associated with the project. This fact must be considered when computing cash inflows.

1. *Total cash savings for the year*		$1,000
2. *Less extra taxes to be paid because of the cash savings:*		
Increase in taxable income from the cash savings	$1,000	
Decrease in taxable income from the depreciation expense on the project (figure assumed)	− 200	
Net increase in taxable income	$ 800	
Tax rate	× 40%	
Extra taxes		320
3. *Net cash inflow for the year*		$ 680

> ## NEW TERMS

present value The equivalent of today's value of a cash inflow or outflow which is expected to take place at some time in the future; the present value is the equivalent investment needed today to produce the desired future cash amount at the appropriate interest rate. [p. 895]

present value method A capital budgeting method that compares the present value of the cash inflows of a project to the present value of the cash outflows of the project; if the present value of the cash inflows exceeds the present value of the cash outflows, the project is accepted. [p. 898]

present value table A table showing the present value of one dollar at various rates of return for various periods of time. [p. 896]

time value of money The concept that a dollar received today is worth more to a business or an individual than a dollar to be received sometime in the future; the dollar received in the present could be invested immediately to earn a return which when added to the original dollar would be greater than the dollar to be received in the future. [p. 895]

> ## ASSIGNMENT MATERIAL

QUESTIONS

Q53-1. Explain the impact of income taxes on the computation of cash inflows from a project.

Q53-2. Assume that you want to have $25,000 available 10 years from now. You plan to invest funds today to accumulate the $25,000, and you expect to earn 8% per year on your investments. How much money must be invested today to accumulate the $25,000?

Q53-3. What is meant by the time value of money?

Q53-4. Describe the present value method of capital budgeting.

E53-1. These facts are known about an investment that a company is considering: the initial cost of the investment is $5,000; the expected cash inflows from the investment are:

First year	$1,000
Second year	3,000
Third year	5,000

The firm has decided that it must earn at least 20% on investments of this nature.
a. Determine the amount that the company can afford to pay for this investment if it is to earn the 20% rate of return.
b. Should the firm make the investment for the price of $5,000?

E53-2. The following facts are known about an investment that Printsco, Incorporated is considering: the initial cost of the investment is $14,500; the expected cash inflows from the investment are: first year, $4,500; second year, $6,500; third year, $10,000; fourth year, $3,000. The firm must earn at least 22% on investments of this nature. Should the company make the investment? Explain and show all calculations.

E53-3. Your father has indicated that he will give you a choice of gifts as follows:

Gift A: He will give you $4,000 now.

Gift B: He will give you three payments of $2,000 each, the first payment at the end of 2 years, the second payment at the end of 4 years, and the third payment at the end of 6 years.

Gift C: He will give you $5,000 at the end of 3 years.

a. Compute the present value of each of the three gifts. Assume that you plan to invest at the rate of 6%.
b. Which gift would you choose, assuming you want the most valuable gift? (at the 6% rate)
c. Compute the present value of each of the three gifts. Assume that you plan to invest at the rate of 20%.
d. Which gift would you choose, assuming you want the most valuable gift? (at the 20% rate)

E53-4. a. Assume that you want to have $8,000 cash available to make a down payment on a house in 10 years. How much money would you have to invest today at the rate of return of 8% to have that much available at the end of 10 years?
        These facts are known about an investment that a company is considering: the initial cost of the investment is $10,000; the expected cash inflows from the investment are: first year, $3,000; second year, $8,000; third year, $4,000; fourth year, $2,000. The firm has decided that it must earn at least 12% on the investment.
b. What is the present value of the cash inflow for the first year?
c. What is the present value of the cash inflow for the second year?
d. What is the present value of the cash inflow for the third year?
e. What is the present value of the cash inflow for the fourth year?
f. How much can the company pay for the investment and make the 12% rate of return?
g. Should the company pay the $10,000 amount for the investment?

P53-1. *Present value method, selecting projects.* Compto and Company is considering investing in one of the following three projects. These data are gathered about the projects:

PROJECT ZIPP		PROJECT HIPP	
Initial cost	$20,000	Initial cost	$17,000
Useful life	4 years	Useful life	4 years
Cash savings:		Cash savings:	
First year	$ 9,000	First year	$ 3,000
Second year	8,000	Second year	5,000
Third year	3,000	Third year	9,000
Fourth year	6,000	Fourth year	9,000
Salvage value	none	Salvage value	none

PROJECT BLIPP

Initial cost	$13,000
Useful life	4 years
Cash savings:	
First year	$10,000
Second year	2,000
Third year	2,000
Fourth year	2,000
Salvage value	none

The company expects to earn an annual rate of return on all projects amounting to 16%.

REQUIRED:

a. Determine the amount that the company can afford to pay for each project to earn the 16% annual return.
b. Based on the facts given, which project should be selected?

P53-2. *Present value method, selecting projects, tax consequences.* The following facts are known about an investment that a company is considering. The initial cost is $6,000; the expected cash inflows are:

First year	$2,000 cash savings
Second year	3,000 cash savings
Third year	5,000 cash savings
Third year	500 salvage value

The minimum desired rate of return is 20%.

REQUIRED:

a. Prepare a work sheet similar to the one illustrated in the text to apply the present value method. Indicate whether the project should be accepted or rejected. Ignore income tax consequences for this part of the problem.
b. Assume the company has a 45% tax rate. Compute the net cash inflows for each of the 3 years, giving effect to the taxes. The company uses straight-line depreciation.

*P53-3. *Present value method, selecting projects, tax consequences.* Tanny Corporation management is considering investing in a new piece of manufacturing equipment as follows:

Initial cost: $175,432.19
Expected cash inflows: $20,000 per year for 13 years
Salvage value: $7,500
Minimum desired rate of return: 14%

REQUIRED:

a. Prepare a work sheet to apply the present value method. Should the project be accepted? Ignore income tax consequences.
b. Work the problem, except give consideration to income tax consequences when computing the annual cash savings. The company's tax rate is 40%. Straight-line depreciation is used.

PROBLEMS (GROUP B)

P53-4. *Present value computations.* Herbert W. Brunn is considering making an investment in bonds. The bond issue provides that the face amount of the bonds will be paid off in 10 years and that $600 of interest will be paid each year for the 10 years. The cash inflows from the investment in bonds will be:

First year	$600	Sixth year	$ 600
Second year	600	Seventh year	600
Third year	600	Eighth year	600
Fourth year	600	Ninth year	600
Fifth year	600	Tenth year	10,600[a]

[a] This amount includes $10,000 repayment of face amount.

REQUIRED:

a. Compute the amount Brunn would expect to pay for the investment in bonds if he is to earn 20% per year.
b. Compute the amount Brunn would expect to pay for the investment in bonds if he is to earn 18% per year.
c. Compute the amount Brunn would expect to pay for the investment in bonds if he is to earn 6% per year.

*P53-5. *Present value method, selecting projects, alternative rates, tax consequences.* Brandcorp Enterprises is evaluating two projects, with plans to invest in one of the two.

MACHINE A		MACHINE B	
Initial cost	$18,000	Initial cost	$18,000
Expected cash inflows:		Expected cash inflows:	
First year	$10,000	First year	$ 6,000
Second year	4,000	Second year	6,000
Third year	8,000	Third year	6,000
Fourth year	4,000	Fourth year	6,000
Fifth year	4,000	Fifth year	6,000
Salvage value	$ 1,000	Salvage value	$ 1,000

REQUIRED:

   a. Prepare a work sheet similar to the one illustrated in the text to apply the present value method to each of the investments. Ignore income tax consequences. Which of the two projects is preferable? Assume that the company has a desired minimum rate of return of 20%.

   b. Work the problem, except assume that the minimum desired rate of return is 12% instead of 20%. Which of the two projects is preferable?

   c. Work the problem, except give consideration to income tax consequences when computing the annual cash savings. The company's tax rate is 42%. The desired minimum rate of return is 20% and the firm uses the straight-line depreciation method.

P53-6. *Present value method, selecting projects.* Two investments in machines are being considered. Assume a company's minimum desired rate of return is 14%.

	A	B
Initial investment	$12,000	$12,000
Annual cash inflows:		
First year	3,000	4,000
Second year	6,000	6,000
Third year	12,000	10,000
Salvage value	1,000	2,000

REQUIRED: Which investment is preferable? Prepare a work sheet similar to the one illustrated in the text to apply the present value method to each of the investments. Ignore income taxes.

CUMULATIVE REVIEW PROBLEMS

P53-7. *Cumulative review problem*

   a. Assume that you want to have $10,000 available 4 years from now. You plan to invest funds today to accumulate the $10,000, and you expect to earn 8% per year on your investments. How much money must be invested today to accumulate the $10,000?

   b. How much money must be invested today at 10% interest in order to accumulate $30,000 10 years from now?

   c. How much money must be invested today at 6% interest in order to accumulate $5,000 5 years from now?

   d. How much money must be invested today at 12% interest in order to accumulate $15,000 8 years from now?

   e. How much money must be invested today if you expect to earn 16% per year on your investment and want to have $20,000 available 20 years from now?

   f. The following facts are known about an investment that Walker Company is considering: the initial cost of the investment is $24,500; the expected cash inflows from the investment are: first year, $4,000; second year, $5,000; third year, $7,500; fourth year, $4,000. The firm must earn at least 18% on investments of this nature. Should the company make the investment? Explain and show all calculations.

P53-8. *Cumulative review problem*

Part A

The following facts are known about an investment that a company is considering. The initial cost is $10,000; the expected cash inflows are:

First year	$5,000 cash savings
Second year	6,000 cash savings
Third year	7,000 cash savings
Third year	1,000 salvage value

The minimum desired rate of return is 16%.

REQUIRED: Prepare a work sheet similar to the one illustrated in the text to apply the present value method. Indicate whether the project should be accepted or rejected. Ignore income tax consequences for this problem.

Part B

Richter Corporation management is considering investing in a new piece of manufacturing equipment as follows:

Initial cost: $35,000

Expected cash inflows: $4,000 per year for 12 years

Salvage value: $6,000

Minimum desired rate of return: 14%

REQUIRED: Prepare a work sheet to apply the present value method. Should the project be accepted? Ignore income tax consequences.

chapter 24

income taxes and business decisions

THE NATURE AND IMPORTANCE OF INCOME TAXES

> ## OBJECTIVE

This final chapter deals with income taxes and business decisions. We have considered income taxes before, and here they will be discussed in terms of their extremely important impact on a variety of business decisions. The decision maker must be aware of the tax impact on his many decisions. This chapter therefore outlines the more important provisions of the tax laws and relates these provisions to specific business decisions. The objective of this first unit is to discuss the nature and importance of income taxes.

> ## APPROACH TO ATTAINING THE OBJECTIVE

As you study about the nature and importance of income taxes, pay special attention to these four questions, which the text following answers:

- *How important are income taxes to federal and state governments?*
- *What is the legal background of the federal tax laws?*
- *How are federal income taxes on individuals computed?*
- *How are federal income taxes on corporations computed?*

INCOME TAXES AT THE FEDERAL AND STATE LEVELS

■ *How important are income taxes to federal and state governments?*

Income taxes are a tremendously important source of revenue for both federal and state governments in the United States. In recent years, *corporation* income taxes have provided about 20% of the total revenues of the federal government. Income taxes on *individuals* have provided about 45% of the total revenues of the federal government. Therefore, about two-thirds of the federal revenues can be associated with the federal income tax laws.

State and local governmental bodies also make use of income taxes as a source of revenues. More than forty states have enacted state income tax laws which tax individuals, corporations, or both. Many of these laws are similar to the federal tax laws. The income taxes are said to provide the second most significant source of revenue for the state governments in the United States, with the state sales taxes providing the greatest revenues. Local governmental bodies also have taxed the incomes of individuals and corporations. Local income taxes have been used as a source of revenue in about one-fifth of the states. We can conclude that income taxes are extremely important as a source of revenues on both the federal and state levels, and that these taxes are considered vital for providing services by governments.

BACKGROUND OF THE FEDERAL TAX LAWS

■ *What is the legal background of the federal tax laws?*

There are four aspects to the legal background of the federal tax laws. These are (1) the United States Constitution, (2) the Internal Revenue Code, (3) the income tax regulations, and (4) the decisions of the courts. Let us examine each of these in turn.

The constitution The United States Constitution as originally written gave the federal government the power to collect taxes. This power was limited by the Constitution, however. The Constitution provided that "No . . . tax, shall be laid, unless in proportion to a census or enumeration. . ."[1] An income tax, of course, would be in proportion to the *income* of individuals and businesses—not in proportion to the population. Therefore, the income tax as we know it today was prohibited by the Constitution.

In 1913, the Sixteenth Amendment to the Constitution was adopted. This amendment provided Congress with the power to lay and collect income taxes—without regard to the population or census of the several states. This amendment began the continuing process of developing the income tax laws as we know them today.

The code The original income tax law was passed by Congress in 1913. Since that time the Congress has enacted laws dealing with the federal income tax in almost every one of its sessions. The **Internal Revenue Code** is simply a compilation of all the current federal income tax laws. This code provides the

---

[1] Constitution of the United States, Article I.

legal basis and includes the details of the individual and corporation income tax laws.

The regulations The income tax laws authorize the Treasury Department of the federal government to administer the tax laws. The Commissioner of Internal Revenue is the executive who is primarily in charge of administration. The Commissioner is responsible for providing a set of regulations which interpret the Internal Revenue Code and prescribe specific operating procedures for administration of the law. These **income tax regulations** are extremely important to the functioning of the income tax structure.

The court decisions In some circumstances there may be a disagreement between the Treasury Department (Internal Revenue Commissioner) and a taxpayer. Such disagreements often center around how the income tax laws (Internal Revenue Code) should be interpreted in a specific case. The courts regularly handle such disputes, and the court decisions then become important in interpreting similar cases in the future.

In summary, the four important aspects of the legal background of the income tax laws are the Constitution of the United States, the Internal Revenue Code, the income tax regulations, and the court decisions. Each has its place in the functioning of the income tax system.

INCOME TAXES ON INDIVIDUALS

We will now summarize the structure for computing the federal income taxes for individuals. Illustration 54-1 shows the computation as a series of five steps. Each of these steps is discussed in more detail in the following paragraphs.

■ *How are federal income taxes on individuals computed?*

Step 1: Determine the taxpayer's total income This is the starting point for computing the federal income tax liability of an individual for a year. All revenues and gains of the taxpayer that are recognized during the year must be determined. This includes salaries and wages earned, gains on sale of assets, interest income, rent income, dividends income, and any *net* earnings from a business, trade, or profession.

The federal income tax laws provide that certain kinds of revenues and gains can be *excluded* from the computation of income which is to be taxed. Here are a few of the items which are excluded:

1. Gifts received.
2. Certain scholarships and fellowships.
3. Social Security benefits.

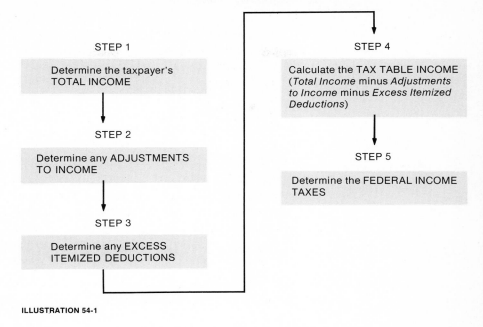

COMPUTATION OF
INDIVIDUAL FEDERAL INCOME TAX LIABILITY

STEP 1

Determine the taxpayer's
TOTAL INCOME

STEP 2

Determine any ADJUSTMENTS
TO INCOME

STEP 3

Determine any EXCESS
ITEMIZED DEDUCTIONS

STEP 4

Calculate the TAX TABLE INCOME
(*Total Income* minus *Adjustments
to Income* minus *Excess Itemized
Deductions*)

STEP 5

Determine the FEDERAL INCOME
TAXES

ILLUSTRATION 54-1

4. Interest on municipal bonds and state bonds.
5. Life insurance proceeds.

Another important **exclusion** allowed by the income tax laws is the first $100 of dividends income received by the taxpayer each year. On a joint return (prepared by husband and wife together as one income tax return), both parties can exclude $100, for a total of $200.

Step 2: Determine any adjustments to income According to the federal income tax laws, there are certain reductions, or adjustments to income, that can be made. Some of these are:

1. Certain moving expenses.
2. Certain employee business expenses.
3. Certain payments made to retirement programs.
4. Alimony payments.

There are detailed restrictions as to the extent to which such expenditures of the taxpayer can be deducted.

Step 3: Determine any excess itemized deductions These kinds of deductions are included in itemized deductions:

1. Interest expense.
2. State and local taxes.
3. Charitable contributions.
4. Medical and dental expenses.
5. Casualty losses.
6. Other miscellaneous deductions.

The tax laws specifically indicate under which circumstances the expenses listed above qualify as itemized deductions. *There are certain limitations to each of the categories above.* For example, medical expenses are deductible only to the extent by which they exceed 3% of the taxpayer's total income after deducting adjustments to income.

Remember that this third step is concerned with determining the *excess* **itemized deductions.** These procedures are used:

Excess
Itemized Deductions $=$ Itemized Deductions $-$ Standard Deduction

Currently, the tax laws provide that the standard deduction is:

$1,600 for a married taxpayer filing a separate income tax return
$2,200 for a single individual or an unmarried **head of household** (to be explained later)
$3,200 for married taxpayers filing a joint income tax return

For example, assume a taxpayer is married and files a joint income tax return with his wife. Itemized deductions (including interest, state income taxes, charitable contributions, etc.) total $5,500. Then the excess itemized deductions would amount to $2,300, or $5,500 minus $3,200.

Step 4: Calculate the tax table income The tax table income is computed by deducting the *adjustments to income* and the *excess itemized deductions* from the *total income.*

Step 5: Determine the federal income taxes Next, the taxpayer's income taxes can be determined by referring to the tax tables provided by the government. Refer to Illustration 54-2 for a sample of the tables.

The federal income tax liability for the year is computed by applying the appropriate tax rate to the tax table income. Shown on the following pages are four tax tables. The first table (Table A) is for use by taxpayers who are single (unmarried). Table B is for married taxpayers. The laws provide that married individuals can file a joint income tax return (including incomes of both husband and wife on the same tax return), or they can file separate tax returns (Table C). There is also a special category of taxpayers called *heads of households*. These unmarried individuals who operate households do not qualify for the rates allowed married taxpayers, but they do qualify for the rates shown in Table D. Note that the rates differ for each of the four types of taxpayers.

To illustrate the computation of the tax, assume that Joseph Smith, a single taxpayer, has *tax table income* during the year amounting to $10,760. Table A is used. His federal income tax liability would amount to $1,392. This amount appears in the column under "1" exemption, opposite the $10,750–$10,800 row.

A taxpayer is allowed a deduction (reduction in taxes) for each *personal exemption*. For example, if a taxpayer and his wife have three children, five personal exemptions are allowed. The taxpayer would use the "5" exemptions column of Table B to determine his tax. If his tax table income were $25,375, the total taxes would amount to $3,759 according to Table B.

INCOME TAXES ON CORPORATIONS

We will now summarize the structure for computing the federal income taxes for corporations. Illustration 54-3 on page 922 shows the computations as a series of six steps. Each of these steps is discussed in more detail in the following paragraphs.

■ *How are federal income taxes on corporations computed?*

Step 1: Determine the corporation's TOTAL REVENUES As in the case of individual income taxes, determining the corporation's total revenues is the starting point for computing the income tax liability. All revenues and gains of the corporation that are recognized during the year must be determined. These include sales of products, service revenues, gains on sales of assets, interest income, rent income, and any other kind of revenue or gain.

Step 2: Determine the EXCLUSIONS Certain revenues and gains are excluded by the corporation tax laws. Remember, however, that the corporation tax laws may differ in certain circumstances from the tax laws for individuals.

Step 3: Calculate the GROSS INCOME This is the amount determined in step 1 minus the amount determined in step 2.

Step 4: Determine the DEDUCTIONS FROM GROSS INCOME As in the case of individuals, the law provides for certain specified deductions from the gross

1977 Tax Table A—SINGLE (Box 1)

(For single persons with tax table income of $20,000 or less who claim fewer than 4 exemptions)

To find your tax: Read down the left income column until you find your income as shown on line 34 of Form 1040. Read across to the column headed by the total number of exemptions claimed on line 7 of Form 1040. The amount shown at the point where the two lines meet is your tax. Enter on Form 1040, line 35.

The $2,200 zero bracket amount, your deduction for exemptions and the general tax credit have been taken into account in figuring the tax shown in this table. **Do not take a separate deduction for them.**

Caution: *If you can be claimed as a dependent on your parent's return AND you have unearned income (interest, dividends, etc.) of $750 or more AND your earned income is less than $2,200, you must first use Schedule TC (Form 1040), Part II.*

If line 34, Form 1040 is— Over	But not over	1	2	3
If $3,200 or less your tax is 0				
3,200	3,250	4	0	0
3,250	3,300	11	0	0
3,300	3,350	18	0	0
3,350	3,400	25	0	0
3,400	3,450	32	0	0
3,450	3,500	39	0	0
3,500	3,550	46	0	0
3,550	3,600	54	0	0
3,600	3,650	61	0	0
3,650	3,700	69	0	0
3,700	3,750	76	0	0
3,750	3,800	84	0	0
3,800	3,850	91	0	0
3,850	3,900	99	0	0
3,900	3,950	106	0	0
3,950	4,000	114	0	0
4,000	4,050	122	0	0
4,050	4,100	130	0	0
4,100	4,150	138	0	0
4,150	4,200	146	0	0
4,200	4,250	154	4	0
4,250	4,300	162	11	0
4,300	4,350	170	19	0
4,350	4,400	178	26	0
4,400	4,450	186	34	0
4,450	4,500	194	41	0
4,500	4,550	203	49	0
4,550	4,600	211	56	0
4,600	4,650	220	64	0
4,650	4,700	228	71	0
4,700	4,750	236	79	0
4,750	4,800	244	87	0
4,800	4,850	251	95	0
4,850	4,900	259	103	0
4,900	4,950	266	111	0
4,950	5,000	274	119	0
5,000	5,050	283	127	0
5,050	5,100	291	135	0
5,100	5,150	300	143	0
5,150	5,200	308	151	0
5,200	5,250	317	159	6
5,250	5,300	325	168	14
5,300	5,350	334	176	21
5,350	5,400	342	185	29
5,400	5,450	351	193	36
5,450	5,500	359	202	44
5,500	5,550	368	210	52
5,550	5,600	376	219	60
5,600	5,650	385	227	68
5,650	5,700	393	236	76
5,700	5,750	402	245	84
5,750	5,800	410	254	92

Continued next column

If line 34, Form 1040 is— Over	But not over	1	2	3
5,800	5,850	419	264	100
5,850	5,900	427	273	108
5,900	5,950	436	283	116
5,950	6,000	444	292	124
6,000	6,050	453	302	133
6,050	6,100	461	311	141
6,100	6,150	470	321	150
6,150	6,200	478	330	158
6,200	6,250	487	340	167
6,250	6,300	495	349	175
6,300	6,350	504	359	184
6,350	6,400	512	368	192
6,400	6,450	521	378	201
6,450	6,500	529	387	210
6,500	6,550	538	397	219
6,550	6,600	546	406	229
6,600	6,650	555	416	238
6,650	6,700	563	425	248
6,700	6,750	572	435	257
6,750	6,800	580	444	267
6,800	6,850	589	454	276
6,850	6,900	597	463	286
6,900	6,950	606	473	295
6,950	7,000	615	482	305
7,000	7,050	624	492	314
7,050	7,100	634	501	324
7,100	7,150	643	511	333
7,150	7,200	653	520	343
7,200	7,250	662	529	352
7,250	7,300	672	538	362
7,300	7,350	681	546	371
7,350	7,400	691	555	381
7,400	7,450	700	563	390
7,450	7,500	710	572	400
7,500	7,550	719	580	409
7,550	7,600	729	589	419
7,600	7,650	738	597	428
7,650	7,700	748	606	438
7,700	7,750	757	615	447
7,750	7,800	767	624	457
7,800	7,850	776	634	466
7,850	7,900	786	643	476
7,900	7,950	795	653	485
7,950	8,000	805	662	495
8,000	8,050	814	672	504
8,050	8,100	824	681	514
8,100	8,150	833	691	523
8,150	8,200	843	700	533
8,200	8,250	852	710	542
8,250	8,300	862	719	552
8,300	8,350	871	729	561
8,350	8,400	881	738	571

Continued next column

If line 34, Form 1040 is— Over	But not over	1	2	3
8,400	8,450	890	748	580
8,450	8,500	900	757	590
8,500	8,550	909	767	601
8,550	8,600	919	776	611
8,600	8,650	928	786	622
8,650	8,700	938	795	632
8,700	8,750	947	805	643
8,750	8,800	957	814	653
8,800	8,850	966	824	664
8,850	8,900	976	833	674
8,900	8,950	985	843	685
8,950	9,000	996	852	695
9,000	9,050	1,007	862	706
9,050	9,100	1,018	871	716
9,100	9,150	1,029	881	727
9,150	9,200	1,040	890	737
9,200	9,250	1,051	900	748
9,250	9,300	1,062	909	758
9,300	9,350	1,073	919	769
9,350	9,400	1,084	928	779
9,400	9,450	1,095	938	790
9,450	9,500	1,106	947	800
9,500	9,550	1,117	957	811
9,550	9,600	1,128	966	821
9,600	9,650	1,139	976	832
9,650	9,700	1,150	985	842
9,700	9,750	1,161	996	852
9,750	9,800	1,172	1,007	862
9,800	9,850	1,183	1,018	871
9,850	9,900	1,194	1,029	881
9,900	9,950	1,205	1,040	890
9,950	10,000	1,216	1,051	900
10,000	10,050	1,227	1,062	909
10,050	10,100	1,238	1,073	919
10,100	10,150	1,249	1,084	928
10,150	10,200	1,260	1,095	938
10,200	10,250	1,271	1,106	947
10,250	10,300	1,282	1,117	957
10,300	10,350	1,293	1,128	966
10,350	10,400	1,304	1,139	976
10,400	10,450	1,315	1,150	985
10,450	10,500	1,326	1,161	996
10,500	10,550	1,337	1,172	1,007
10,550	10,600	1,348	1,183	1,018
10,600	10,650	1,359	1,194	1,029
10,650	10,700	1,370	1,205	1,040
10,700	10,750	1,381	1,216	1,051
10,750	10,800	1,392	1,227	1,062
10,800	10,850	1,403	1,238	1,073
10,850	10,900	1,414	1,249	1,084
10,900	10,950	1,425	1,260	1,095
10,950	11,000	1,436	1,271	1,106

Continued on next page

ILLUSTRATION 54-2

(If your income or exemptions are not covered, use Schedule TC (Form 1040), Part I to figure your tax)

If line 34, Form 1040 is— Over	But not over	And the total number of exemptions claimed on line 7 is— 2	3	4	5	6	7	8	9	If line 34, Form 1040 is— Over	But not over	And the total number of exemptions claimed on line 7 is— 2	3	4	5	6	7	8	9
					Your tax is—										Your tax is—				
18,800	18,850	2,611	2,424	2,236	2,053	1,858	1,658	1,458	1,258	22,400	22,450	3,563	3,353	3,143	2,949	2,731	2,509	2,286	2,064
18,850	18,900	2,624	2,436	2,249	2,064	1,869	1,669	1,469	1,269	22,450	22,500	3,577	3,367	3,157	2,961	2,744	2,521	2,299	2,076
18,900	18,950	2,636	2,449	2,261	2,075	1,880	1,680	1,480	1,280	22,500	22,550	3,591	3,381	3,171	2,974	2,756	2,534	2,311	2,089
18,950	19,000	2,649	2,461	2,274	2,086	1,891	1,691	1,491	1,291	22,550	22,600	3,605	3,395	3,185	2,986	2,769	2,546	2,324	2,101
19,000	19,050	2,661	2,474	2,286	2,099	1,902	1,702	1,502	1,302	22,600	22,650	3,619	3,409	3,199	2,999	2,781	2,559	2,336	2,114
19,050	19,100	2,674	2,486	2,299	2,111	1,913	1,713	1,513	1,313	22,650	22,700	3,633	3,423	3,213	3,011	2,794	2,571	2,349	2,126
19,100	19,150	2,686	2,499	2,311	2,124	1,924	1,724	1,524	1,324	22,700	22,750	3,647	3,437	3,227	3,024	2,806	2,584	2,361	2,139
19,150	19,200	2,699	2,511	2,324	2,136	1,935	1,735	1,535	1,335	22,750	22,800	3,661	3,451	3,241	3,036	2,819	2,596	2,374	2,151
19,200	19,250	2,711	2,524	2,336	2,149	1,946	1,746	1,546	1,346	22,800	22,850	3,675	3,465	3,255	3,049	2,831	2,609	2,386	2,164
19,250	19,300	2,724	2,536	2,349	2,161	1,957	1,757	1,557	1,357	22,850	22,900	3,689	3,479	3,269	3,061	2,844	2,621	2,399	2,176
19,300	19,350	2,736	2,549	2,361	2,174	1,968	1,768	1,568	1,368	22,900	22,950	3,703	3,493	3,283	3,074	2,856	2,634	2,411	2,189
19,350	19,400	2,749	2,561	2,374	2,186	1,979	1,779	1,579	1,379	22,950	23,000	3,717	3,507	3,297	3,087	2,869	2,646	2,424	2,201
19,400	19,450	2,761	2,574	2,386	2,199	1,990	1,790	1,590	1,390	23,000	23,050	3,731	3,521	3,311	3,101	2,881	2,659	2,436	2,214
19,450	19,500	2,774	2,586	2,399	2,211	2,001	1,801	1,601	1,401	23,050	23,100	3,745	3,535	3,325	3,115	2,894	2,671	2,449	2,226
19,500	19,550	2,786	2,599	2,411	2,224	2,012	1,812	1,612	1,412	23,100	23,150	3,759	3,549	3,339	3,129	2,906	2,684	2,461	2,239
19,550	19,600	2,799	2,611	2,424	2,236	2,023	1,823	1,623	1,423	23,150	23,200	3,773	3,563	3,353	3,143	2,919	2,696	2,474	2,251
19,600	19,650	2,811	2,624	2,436	2,249	2,034	1,834	1,634	1,434	23,200	23,250	3,787	3,577	3,367	3,157	2,931	2,709	2,486	2,264
19,650	19,700	2,824	2,636	2,449	2,261	2,045	1,845	1,645	1,445	23,250	23,300	3,801	3,591	3,381	3,171	2,944	2,721	2,499	2,276
19,700	19,750	2,836	2,649	2,461	2,274	2,056	1,856	1,656	1,456	23,300	23,350	3,815	3,605	3,395	3,185	2,956	2,734	2,511	2,289
19,750	19,800	2,849	2,661	2,474	2,286	2,069	1,867	1,667	1,467	23,350	23,400	3,829	3,619	3,409	3,199	2,969	2,746	2,524	2,301
19,800	19,850	2,861	2,674	2,486	2,299	2,081	1,878	1,678	1,478	23,400	23,450	3,843	3,633	3,423	3,213	2,981	2,759	2,536	2,314
19,850	19,900	2,874	2,686	2,499	2,311	2,094	1,889	1,689	1,489	23,450	23,500	3,857	3,647	3,437	3,227	2,994	2,771	2,549	2,326
19,900	19,950	2,886	2,699	2,511	2,324	2,106	1,900	1,700	1,500	23,500	23,550	3,871	3,661	3,451	3,241	3,006	2,784	2,561	2,339
19,950	20,000	2,899	2,711	2,524	2,336	2,119	1,911	1,711	1,511	23,550	23,600	3,885	3,675	3,465	3,255	3,019	2,796	2,574	2,351
20,000	20,050	2,911	2,724	2,536	2,349	2,131	1,922	1,722	1,522	23,600	23,650	3,899	3,689	3,479	3,269	3,031	2,809	2,586	2,364
20,050	20,100	2,924	2,736	2,549	2,361	2,144	1,933	1,733	1,533	23,650	23,700	3,913	3,703	3,493	3,283	3,044	2,821	2,599	2,376
20,100	20,150	2,936	2,749	2,561	2,374	2,156	1,944	1,744	1,544	23,700	23,750	3,927	3,717	3,507	3,297	3,057	2,834	2,611	2,389
20,150	20,200	2,949	2,761	2,574	2,386	2,169	1,955	1,755	1,555	23,750	23,800	3,941	3,731	3,521	3,311	3,069	2,846	2,624	2,401
20,200	20,250	2,961	2,774	2,586	2,399	2,181	1,966	1,766	1,566	23,800	23,850	3,955	3,745	3,535	3,325	3,085	2,859	2,636	2,414
20,250	20,300	2,974	2,786	2,599	2,411	2,194	1,977	1,777	1,577	23,850	23,900	3,969	3,759	3,549	3,339	3,099	2,871	2,649	2,426
20,300	20,350	2,986	2,799	2,611	2,424	2,206	1,988	1,788	1,588	23,900	23,950	3,983	3,773	3,563	3,353	3,113	2,884	2,661	2,439
20,350	20,400	2,999	2,811	2,624	2,436	2,219	1,999	1,799	1,599	23,950	24,000	3,997	3,787	3,577	3,367	3,127	2,896	2,674	2,451
20,400	20,450	3,011	2,824	2,636	2,449	2,231	2,010	1,810	1,610	24,000	24,050	4,011	3,801	3,591	3,381	3,141	2,909	2,686	2,464
20,450	20,500	3,024	2,836	2,649	2,461	2,244	2,021	1,821	1,621	24,050	24,100	4,025	3,815	3,605	3,395	3,155	2,921	2,699	2,476
20,500	20,550	3,036	2,849	2,661	2,474	2,256	2,034	1,832	1,632	24,100	24,150	4,039	3,829	3,619	3,409	3,169	2,934	2,711	2,489
20,550	20,600	3,049	2,861	2,674	2,486	2,269	2,046	1,843	1,643	24,150	24,200	4,053	3,843	3,633	3,423	3,183	2,946	2,724	2,501
20,600	20,650	3,061	2,874	2,686	2,499	2,281	2,059	1,854	1,654	24,200	24,250	4,067	3,857	3,647	3,437	3,197	2,959	2,736	2,514
20,650	20,700	3,074	2,886	2,699	2,511	2,294	2,071	1,865	1,665	24,250	24,300	4,081	3,871	3,661	3,451	3,211	2,971	2,749	2,526
20,700	20,750	3,087	2,899	2,711	2,524	2,306	2,084	1,876	1,676	24,300	24,350	4,095	3,885	3,675	3,465	3,225	2,984	2,761	2,539
20,750	20,800	3,101	2,911	2,724	2,536	2,319	2,096	1,887	1,687	24,350	24,400	4,109	3,899	3,689	3,479	3,239	2,996	2,774	2,551
20,800	20,850	3,115	2,924	2,736	2,549	2,331	2,109	1,898	1,698	24,400	24,450	4,123	3,913	3,703	3,493	3,253	3,009	2,786	2,564
20,850	20,900	3,129	2,936	2,749	2,561	2,344	2,121	1,909	1,709	24,450	24,500	4,137	3,927	3,717	3,507	3,267	3,022	2,799	2,576
20,900	20,950	3,143	2,949	2,761	2,574	2,356	2,134	1,920	1,720	24,500	24,550	4,151	3,941	3,731	3,521	3,281	3,036	2,811	2,589
20,950	21,000	3,157	2,961	2,774	2,586	2,369	2,146	1,931	1,731	24,550	24,600	4,165	3,955	3,745	3,535	3,295	3,050	2,824	2,601
21,000	21,050	3,171	2,974	2,786	2,599	2,381	2,159	1,942	1,742	24,600	24,650	4,179	3,969	3,759	3,549	3,309	3,064	2,836	2,614
21,050	21,100	3,185	2,986	2,799	2,611	2,394	2,171	1,953	1,753	24,650	24,700	4,193	3,983	3,773	3,563	3,323	3,078	2,849	2,626
21,100	21,150	3,199	2,999	2,811	2,624	2,406	2,184	1,964	1,764	24,700	24,750	4,208	3,997	3,787	3,577	3,337	3,092	2,861	2,639
21,150	21,200	3,213	3,011	2,824	2,636	2,419	2,196	1,975	1,775	24,750	24,800	4,224	4,011	3,801	3,591	3,351	3,106	2,874	2,651
21,200	21,250	3,227	3,024	2,836	2,649	2,431	2,209	1,986	1,786	24,800	24,850	4,240	4,025	3,815	3,605	3,365	3,120	2,886	2,664
21,250	21,300	3,241	3,036	2,849	2,661	2,444	2,221	1,999	1,797	24,850	24,900	4,256	4,039	3,829	3,619	3,379	3,134	2,899	2,676
21,300	21,350	3,255	3,049	2,861	2,674	2,456	2,234	2,011	1,808	24,900	24,950	4,272	4,053	3,843	3,633	3,393	3,148	2,911	2,689
21,350	21,400	3,269	3,061	2,874	2,686	2,469	2,246	2,024	1,819	24,950	25,000	4,288	4,067	3,857	3,647	3,407	3,162	2,924	2,701
21,400	21,450	3,283	3,074	2,886	2,699	2,481	2,259	2,036	1,830	25,000	25,050	4,304	4,081	3,871	3,661	3,421	3,176	2,936	2,714
21,450	21,500	3,297	3,087	2,899	2,711	2,494	2,271	2,049	1,841	25,050	25,100	4,320	4,095	3,885	3,675	3,435	3,190	2,949	2,726
21,500	21,550	3,311	3,101	2,911	2,724	2,506	2,284	2,061	1,852	25,100	25,150	4,336	4,109	3,899	3,689	3,449	3,204	2,961	2,739
21,550	21,600	3,325	3,115	2,924	2,736	2,519	2,296	2,074	1,863	25,150	25,200	4,352	4,123	3,913	3,703	3,463	3,218	2,974	2,751
21,600	21,650	3,339	3,129	2,936	2,749	2,531	2,309	2,086	1,874	25,200	25,250	4,368	4,137	3,927	3,717	3,477	3,232	2,987	2,764
21,650	21,700	3,353	3,143	2,949	2,761	2,544	2,321	2,099	1,885	25,250	25,300	4,384	4,151	3,941	3,731	3,491	3,246	3,001	2,776
21,700	21,750	3,367	3,157	2,961	2,774	2,556	2,334	2,111	1,896	25,300	25,350	4,400	4,165	3,955	3,745	3,505	3,260	3,015	2,789
21,750	21,800	3,381	3,171	2,974	2,786	2,569	2,346	2,124	1,907	25,350	25,400	4,416	4,179	3,969	3,759	3,519	3,274	3,029	2,801
21,800	21,850	3,395	3,185	2,986	2,799	2,581	2,359	2,136	1,918	25,400	25,450	4,432	4,193	3,983	3,773	3,533	3,288	3,043	2,814
21,850	21,900	3,409	3,199	2,999	2,811	2,594	2,371	2,149	1,929	25,450	25,500	4,448	4,208	3,997	3,787	3,547	3,302	3,057	2,826
21,900	21,950	3,423	3,213	3,011	2,824	2,606	2,384	2,161	1,940	25,500	25,550	4,464	4,224	4,011	3,801	3,561	3,316	3,071	2,839
21,950	22,000	3,437	3,227	3,024	2,836	2,619	2,396	2,174	1,951	25,550	25,600	4,480	4,240	4,025	3,815	3,575	3,330	3,085	2,851
22,000	22,050	3,451	3,241	3,036	2,849	2,631	2,409	2,186	1,964	25,600	25,650	4,496	4,256	4,039	3,829	3,589	3,344	3,099	2,864
22,050	22,100	3,465	3,255	3,049	2,861	2,644	2,421	2,199	1,976	25,650	25,700	4,512	4,272	4,053	3,843	3,603	3,358	3,113	2,876
22,100	22,150	3,479	3,269	3,061	2,874	2,656	2,434	2,211	1,989	25,700	25,750	4,528	4,288	4,067	3,857	3,617	3,372	3,127	2,889
22,150	22,200	3,493	3,283	3,074	2,886	2,669	2,446	2,224	2,001	25,750	25,800	4,544	4,304	4,081	3,871	3,631	3,386	3,141	2,901
22,200	22,250	3,507	3,297	3,087	2,899	2,681	2,459	2,236	2,014	25,800	25,850	4,560	4,320	4,095	3,885	3,645	3,400	3,155	2,914
22,250	22,300	3,521	3,311	3,101	2,911	2,694	2,471	2,249	2,026	25,850	25,900	4,576	4,336	4,109	3,899	3,659	3,414	3,169	2,926
22,300	22,350	3,535	3,325	3,115	2,924	2,706	2,484	2,261	2,039	25,900	25,950	4,592	4,352	4,123	3,913	3,673	3,428	3,183	2,939
22,350	22,400	3,549	3,339	3,129	2,936	2,719	2,496	2,274	2,051	25,950	26,000	4,608	4,368	4,137	3,927	3,687	3,442	3,197	2,952

Continued next column

Continued on next page

1977 Tax Table B—MARRIED FILING JOINTLY (Box 2) and QUALIFYING WIDOW(ER)S (Box 5)

(Continued)

(If your income or exemptions are not covered, use Schedule TC (Form 1040), Part I to figure your tax)

If line 34, Form 1040 is—		And the total number of exemptions claimed on line 7 is—							
Over	But not over	2	3	4	5	6	7	8	9
		Your tax is—							
26,000	26,050	4,624	4,384	4,151	3,941	3,701	3,456	3,211	2,966
26,050	26,100	4,640	4,400	4,165	3,955	3,715	3,470	3,225	2,980
26,100	26,150	4,656	4,416	4,179	3,969	3,729	3,484	3,239	2,994
26,150	26,200	4,672	4,432	4,193	3,983	3,743	3,498	3,253	3,008
26,200	26,250	4,688	4,448	4,208	3,997	3,757	3,512	3,267	3,022
26,250	26,300	4,704	4,464	4,224	4,011	3,771	3,526	3,281	3,036
26,300	26,350	4,720	4,480	4,240	4,025	3,785	3,540	3,295	3,050
26,350	26,400	4,736	4,496	4,256	4,039	3,799	3,554	3,309	3,064
26,400	26,450	4,752	4,512	4,272	4,053	3,813	3,568	3,323	3,078
26,450	26,500	4,768	4,528	4,288	4,067	3,827	3,582	3,337	3,092
26,500	26,550	4,784	4,544	4,304	4,081	3,841	3,596	3,351	3,106
26,550	26,600	4,800	4,560	4,320	4,095	3,855	3,610	3,365	3,120
26,600	26,650	4,816	4,576	4,336	4,109	3,869	3,624	3,379	3,134
26,650	26,700	4,832	4,592	4,352	4,123	3,883	3,638	3,393	3,148
26,700	26,750	4,848	4,608	4,368	4,137	3,897	3,652	3,407	3,162
26,750	26,800	4,864	4,624	4,384	4,151	3,911	3,666	3,421	3,176
26,800	26,850	4,880	4,640	4,400	4,165	3,925	3,680	3,435	3,190
26,850	26,900	4,896	4,656	4,416	4,179	3,939	3,694	3,449	3,204
26,900	26,950	4,912	4,672	4,432	4,193	3,953	3,708	3,463	3,218
26,950	27,000	4,928	4,688	4,448	4,208	3,967	3,722	3,477	3,232
27,000	27,050	4,944	4,704	4,464	4,224	3,981	3,736	3,491	3,246
27,050	27,100	4,960	4,720	4,480	4,240	3,995	3,750	3,505	3,260
27,100	27,150	4,976	4,736	4,496	4,256	4,009	3,764	3,519	3,274
27,150	27,200	4,992	4,752	4,512	4,272	4,023	3,778	3,533	3,288
27,200	27,250	5,008	4,768	4,528	4,288	4,037	3,792	3,547	3,302
27,250	27,300	5,024	4,784	4,544	4,304	4,051	3,806	3,561	3,316
27,300	27,350	5,040	4,800	4,560	4,320	4,065	3,820	3,575	3,330
27,350	27,400	5,056	4,816	4,576	4,336	4,079	3,834	3,589	3,344
27,400	27,450	5,072	4,832	4,592	4,352	4,093	3,848	3,603	3,358
27,450	27,500	5,088	4,848	4,608	4,368	4,107	3,862	3,617	3,372
27,500	27,550	5,104	4,864	4,624	4,384	4,121	3,876	3,631	3,386
27,550	27,600	5,120	4,880	4,640	4,400	4,135	3,890	3,645	3,400
27,600	27,650	5,136	4,896	4,656	4,416	4,149	3,904	3,659	3,414
27,650	27,700	5,152	4,912	4,672	4,432	4,163	3,918	3,673	3,428
27,700	27,750	5,168	4,928	4,688	4,448	4,178	3,932	3,687	3,442
27,750	27,800	5,184	4,944	4,704	4,464	4,194	3,946	3,701	3,456
27,800	27,850	5,200	4,960	4,720	4,480	4,210	3,960	3,715	3,470
27,850	27,900	5,216	4,976	4,736	4,496	4,226	3,974	3,729	3,484
27,900	27,950	5,232	4,992	4,752	4,512	4,242	3,988	3,743	3,498
27,950	28,000	5,248	5,008	4,768	4,528	4,258	4,002	3,757	3,512
28,000	28,050	5,264	5,024	4,784	4,544	4,274	4,016	3,771	3,526
28,050	28,100	5,280	5,040	4,800	4,560	4,290	4,030	3,785	3,540
28,100	28,150	5,296	5,056	4,816	4,576	4,306	4,044	3,799	3,554
28,150	28,200	5,312	5,072	4,832	4,592	4,322	4,058	3,813	3,568
28,200	28,250	5,328	5,088	4,848	4,608	4,338	4,072	3,827	3,582
28,250	28,300	5,344	5,104	4,864	4,624	4,354	4,086	3,841	3,596
28,300	28,350	5,360	5,120	4,880	4,640	4,370	4,100	3,855	3,610
28,350	28,400	5,376	5,136	4,896	4,656	4,386	4,114	3,869	3,624
28,400	28,450	5,392	5,152	4,912	4,672	4,402	4,128	3,883	3,638
28,450	28,500	5,408	5,168	4,928	4,688	4,418	4,143	3,897	3,652
28,500	28,550	5,424	5,184	4,944	4,704	4,434	4,159	3,911	3,666
28,550	28,600	5,440	5,200	4,960	4,720	4,450	4,175	3,925	3,680
28,600	28,650	5,456	5,216	4,976	4,736	4,466	4,191	3,939	3,694
28,650	28,700	5,472	5,232	4,992	4,752	4,482	4,207	3,953	3,708
28,700	28,750	5,489	5,248	5,008	4,768	4,498	4,223	3,967	3,722
28,750	28,800	5,507	5,264	5,024	4,784	4,514	4,239	3,981	3,736
28,800	28,850	5,525	5,280	5,040	4,800	4,530	4,255	3,995	3,750
28,850	28,900	5,543	5,296	5,056	4,816	4,546	4,271	4,009	3,764
28,900	28,950	5,561	5,312	5,072	4,832	4,562	4,287	4,023	3,778
28,950	29,000	5,579	5,328	5,088	4,848	4,578	4,303	4,037	3,792
29,000	29,050	5,597	5,344	5,104	4,864	4,594	4,319	4,051	3,806
29,050	29,100	5,615	5,360	5,120	4,880	4,610	4,335	4,065	3,820
29,100	29,150	5,633	5,376	5,136	4,896	4,626	4,351	4,079	3,834
29,150	29,200	5,651	5,392	5,152	4,912	4,642	4,367	4,093	3,848
29,200	29,250	5,669	5,408	5,168	4,928	4,658	4,383	4,108	3,862
29,250	29,300	5,687	5,424	5,184	4,944	4,674	4,399	4,124	3,876
29,300	29,350	5,705	5,440	5,200	4,960	4,690	4,415	4,140	3,890
29,350	29,400	5,723	5,456	5,216	4,976	4,706	4,431	4,156	3,904
29,400	29,450	5,741	5,472	5,232	4,992	4,722	4,447	4,172	3,918
29,450	29,500	5,759	5,489	5,248	5,008	4,738	4,463	4,188	3,932
29,500	29,550	5,777	5,507	5,264	5,024	4,754	4,479	4,204	3,946
29,550	29,600	5,795	5,525	5,280	5,040	4,770	4,495	4,220	3,960

Continued next column

If line 34, Form 1040 is—		And the total number of exemptions claimed on line 7 is—							
Over	But not over	2	3	4	5	6	7	8	9
		Your tax is—							
29,600	29,650	5,813	5,543	5,296	5,056	4,786	4,511	4,236	3,974
29,650	29,700	5,831	5,561	5,312	5,072	4,802	4,527	4,252	3,988
29,700	29,750	5,849	5,579	5,328	5,088	4,818	4,543	4,268	4,002
29,750	29,800	5,867	5,597	5,344	5,104	4,834	4,559	4,284	4,016
29,800	29,850	5,885	5,615	5,360	5,120	4,850	4,575	4,300	4,030
29,850	29,900	5,903	5,633	5,376	5,136	4,866	4,591	4,316	4,044
29,900	29,950	5,921	5,651	5,392	5,152	4,882	4,607	4,332	4,058
29,950	30,000	5,939	5,669	5,408	5,168	4,898	4,623	4,348	4,073
30,000	30,050	5,957	5,687	5,424	5,184	4,914	4,639	4,364	4,089
30,050	30,100	5,975	5,705	5,440	5,200	4,930	4,655	4,380	4,105
30,100	30,150	5,993	5,723	5,456	5,216	4,946	4,671	4,396	4,121
30,150	30,200	6,011	5,741	5,472	5,232	4,962	4,687	4,412	4,137
30,200	30,250	6,029	5,759	5,489	5,248	4,978	4,703	4,428	4,153
30,250	30,300	6,047	5,777	5,507	5,264	4,994	4,719	4,444	4,169
30,300	30,350	6,065	5,795	5,525	5,280	5,010	4,735	4,460	4,185
30,350	30,400	6,083	5,813	5,543	5,296	5,026	4,751	4,476	4,201
30,400	30,450	6,101	5,831	5,561	5,312	5,042	4,767	4,492	4,217
30,450	30,500	6,119	5,849	5,579	5,328	5,058	4,783	4,508	4,233
30,500	30,550	6,137	5,867	5,597	5,344	5,074	4,799	4,524	4,249
30,550	30,600	6,155	5,885	5,615	5,360	5,090	4,815	4,540	4,265
30,600	30,650	6,173	5,903	5,633	5,376	5,106	4,831	4,556	4,281
30,650	30,700	6,191	5,921	5,651	5,392	5,122	4,847	4,572	4,297
30,700	30,750	6,209	5,939	5,669	5,408	5,138	4,863	4,588	4,313
30,750	30,800	6,227	5,957	5,687	5,424	5,154	4,879	4,604	4,329
30,800	30,850	6,245	5,975	5,705	5,440	5,170	4,895	4,620	4,345
30,850	30,900	6,263	5,993	5,723	5,456	5,186	4,911	4,636	4,361
30,900	30,950	6,281	6,011	5,741	5,472	5,202	4,927	4,652	4,377
30,950	31,000	6,299	6,029	5,759	5,489	5,218	4,943	4,668	4,393
31,000	31,050	6,317	6,047	5,777	5,507	5,234	4,959	4,684	4,409
31,050	31,100	6,335	6,065	5,795	5,525	5,250	4,975	4,700	4,425
31,100	31,150	6,353	6,083	5,813	5,543	5,266	4,991	4,716	4,441
31,150	31,200	6,371	6,101	5,831	5,561	5,282	5,007	4,732	4,457
31,200	31,250	6,389	6,119	5,849	5,579	5,298	5,023	4,748	4 473
31,250	31,300	6,407	6,137	5,867	5,597	5,314	5,039	4,764	4,489
31,300	31,350	6,425	6,155	5,885	5,615	5,330	5,055	4,780	4,505
31,350	31,400	6,443	6,173	5,903	5,633	5,346	5,071	4,796	4,521
31,400	31,450	6,461	6,191	5,921	5,651	5,362	5,087	4,812	4,537
31,450	31,500	6,479	6,209	5,939	5,669	5,378	5,103	4,828	4,553
31,500	31,550	6,497	6,227	5,957	5,687	5,394	5,119	4,844	4,569
31,550	31,600	6,515	6,245	5,975	5,705	5,410	5,135	4,860	4,585
31,600	31,650	6,533	6,263	5,993	5,723	5,426	5,151	4,876	4,601
31,650	31,700	6,551	6,281	6,011	5,741	5,442	5,167	4,892	4,617
31,700	31,750	6,569	6,299	6,029	5,759	5,459	5,183	4,908	4,633
31,750	31,800	6,587	6,317	6,047	5,777	5,477	5,199	4,924	4,649
31,800	31,850	6,605	6,335	6,065	5,795	5,495	5,215	4,940	4,665
31,850	31,900	6,623	6,353	6,083	5,813	5,513	5,231	4,956	4,681
31,900	31,950	6,641	6,371	6,101	5,831	5,531	5,247	4,972	4,697
31,950	32,000	6,659	6,389	6,119	5,849	5,549	5,263	4,988	4,713
32,000	32,050	6,677	6,407	6,137	5,867	5,567	5,279	5,004	4,729
32,050	32,100	6,695	6,425	6,155	5,885	5,585	5,295	5,020	4,745
32,100	32,150	6,713	6,443	6,173	5,903	5,603	5,311	5,036	4,761
32,150	32,200	6,731	6,461	6,191	5,921	5,621	5,327	5,052	4,777
32,200	32,250	6,749	6,479	6,209	5,939	5,639	5,343	5,068	4,793
32,250	32,300	6,767	6,497	6,227	5,957	5,657	5,359	5,084	4,809
32,300	32,350	6,785	6,515	6,245	5,975	5,675	5,375	5,100	4,825
32,350	32,400	6,803	6,533	6,263	5,993	5,693	5,391	5,116	4,841
32,400	32,450	6,821	6,551	6,281	6,011	5,711	5,407	5,132	4,857
32,450	32,500	6,839	6,569	6,299	6,029	5,729	5,424	5,148	4,873
32,500	32,550	6,857	6,587	6,317	6,047	5,747	5,442	5,164	4,889
32,550	32,600	6,875	6,605	6,335	6,065	5,765	5,460	5,180	4,905
32,600	32,650	6,893	6,623	6,353	6,083	5,783	5,478	5,196	4,921
32,650	32,700	6,911	6,641	6,371	6,101	5,801	5,496	5,212	4,937
32,700	32,750	6,930	6,659	6,389	6,119	5,819	5,514	5,228	4,953
32,750	32,800	6,949	6,677	6,407	6,137	5,837	5,532	5,244	4,969
32,800	32,850	6,969	6,695	6,425	6,155	5,855	5,550	5,260	4,985
32,850	32,900	6,988	6,713	6,443	6,173	5,873	5,568	5,276	5,001
32,900	32,950	7,008	6,731	6,461	6,191	5,891	5,586	5,292	5,017
32,950	33,000	7,027	6,749	6,479	6,209	5,909	5,604	5,308	5,033
33,000	33,050	7,047	6,767	6,497	6,227	5,927	5,622	5,324	5,049
33,050	33,100	7,066	6,785	6,515	6,245	5,945	5,640	5,340	5,065
33,100	33,150	7,086	6,803	6,533	6,263	5,963	5,658	5,356	5,081
33,150	33,200	7,105	6,821	6,551	6,281	5,981	5,676	5,372	5,097

Continued on next page

1977 Tax Table B—MARRIED FILING JOINTLY (Box 2) and QUALIFYING WIDOW(ER)S (Box 5)

(Continued)

(If your income or exemptions are not covered, use Schedule TC (Form 1040), Part I to figure your tax)

If line 34, Form 1040 is— Over	But not over	2	3	4	5	6	7	8	9
33,200	33,250	7,125	6,839	6,569	6,299	5,999	5,694	5,389	5,113
33,250	33,300	7,144	6,857	6,587	6,317	6,017	5,712	5,407	5,129
33,300	33,350	7,164	6,875	6,605	6,335	6,035	5,730	5,425	5,145
33,350	33,400	7,183	6,893	6,623	6,353	6,053	5,748	5,443	5,161
33,400	33,450	7,203	6,911	6,641	6,371	6,071	5,766	5,461	5,177
33,450	33,500	7,222	6,930	6,659	6,389	6,089	5,784	5,479	5,193
33,500	33,550	7,242	6,949	6,677	6,407	6,107	5,802	5,497	5,209
33,550	33,600	7,261	6,969	6,695	6,425	6,125	5,820	5,515	5,225
33,600	33,650	7,281	6,988	6,713	6,443	6,143	5,838	5,533	5,241
33,650	33,700	7,300	7,008	6,731	6,461	6,161	5,856	5,551	5,257
33,700	33,750	7,320	7,027	6,749	6,479	6,179	5,874	5,569	5,273
33,750	33,800	7,339	7,047	6,767	6,497	6,197	5,892	5,587	5,289
33,800	33,850	7,359	7,066	6,785	6,515	6,215	5,910	5,605	5,305
33,850	33,900	7,378	7,086	6,803	6,533	6,233	5,928	5,623	5,321
33,900	33,950	7,398	7,105	6,821	6,551	6,251	5,946	5,641	5,337
33,950	34,000	7,417	7,125	6,839	6,569	6,269	5,964	5,659	5,354
34,000	34,050	7,437	7,144	6,857	6,587	6,287	5,982	5,677	5,372
34,050	34,100	7,456	7,164	6,875	6,605	6,305	6,000	5,695	5,390
34,100	34,150	7,476	7,183	6,893	6,623	6,323	6,018	5,713	5,408
34,150	34,200	7,495	7,203	6,911	6,641	6,341	6,036	5,731	5,426
34,200	34,250	7,515	7,222	6,930	6,659	6,359	6,054	5,749	5,444
34,250	34,300	7,534	7,242	6,949	6,677	6,377	6,072	5,767	5,462
34,300	34,350	7,554	7,261	6,969	6,695	6,395	6,090	5,785	5,480
34,350	34,400	7,573	7,281	6,988	6,713	6,413	6,108	5,803	5,498
34,400	34,450	7,593	7,300	7,008	6,731	6,431	6,126	5,821	5,516
34,450	34,500	7,612	7,320	7,027	6,749	6,449	6,144	5,839	5,534
34,500	34,550	7,632	7,339	7,047	6,767	6,467	6,162	5,857	5,552
34,550	34,600	7,651	7,359	7,066	6,785	6,485	6,180	5,875	5,570
34,600	34,650	7,671	7,378	7,086	6,803	6,503	6,198	5,893	5,588
34,650	34,700	7,690	7,398	7,105	6,821	6,521	6,216	5,911	5,606
34,700	34,750	7,710	7,417	7,125	6,839	6,539	6,234	5,929	5,624
34,750	34,800	7,729	7,437	7,144	6,857	6,557	6,252	5,947	5,642
34,800	34,850	7,749	7,456	7,164	6,875	6,575	6,270	5,965	5,660
34,850	34,900	7,768	7,476	7,183	6,893	6,593	6,288	5,983	5,678
34,900	34,950	7,788	7,495	7,203	6,911	6,611	6,306	6,001	5,696
34,950	35,000	7,807	7,515	7,222	6,930	6,629	6,324	6,019	5,714
35,000	35,050	7,827	7,534	7,242	6,949	6,647	6,342	6,037	5,732
35,050	35,100	7,846	7,554	7,261	6,969	6,665	6,360	6,055	5,750
35,100	35,150	7,866	7,573	7,281	6,988	6,683	6,378	6,073	5,768
35,150	35,200	7,885	7,593	7,300	7,008	6,701	6,396	6,091	5,786
35,200	35,250	7,905	7,612	7,320	7,027	6,719	6,414	6,109	5,804
35,250	35,300	7,924	7,632	7,339	7,047	6,737	6,432	6,127	5,822
35,300	35,350	7,944	7,651	7,359	7,066	6,755	6,450	6,145	5,840
35,350	35,400	7,963	7,671	7,378	7,086	6,773	6,468	6,163	5,858
35,400	35,450	7,983	7,690	7,398	7,105	6,791	6,486	6,181	5,876
35,450	35,500	8,002	7,710	7,417	7,125	6,809	6,504	6,199	5,894
35,500	35,550	8,022	7,729	7,437	7,144	6,827	6,522	6,217	5,912
35,550	35,600	8,041	7,749	7,456	7,164	6,845	6,540	6,235	5,930
35,600	35,650	8,061	7,768	7,476	7,183	6,863	6,558	6,253	5,948
35,650	35,700	8,080	7,788	7,495	7,203	6,881	6,576	6,271	5,966
35,700	35,750	8,100	7,807	7,515	7,222	6,900	6,594	6,289	5,984
35,750	35,800	8,119	7,827	7,534	7,242	6,919	6,612	6,307	6,002
35,800	35,850	8,139	7,846	7,554	7,261	6,939	6,630	6,325	6,020
35,850	35,900	8,158	7,866	7,573	7,281	6,958	6,648	6,343	6,038
35,900	35,950	8,178	7,885	7,593	7,300	6,978	6,666	6,361	6,056
35,950	36,000	8,197	7,905	7,612	7,320	6,997	6,684	6,379	6,074
36,000	36,050	8,217	7,924	7,632	7,339	7,017	6,702	6,397	6,092
36,050	36,100	8,236	7,944	7,651	7,359	7,036	6,720	6,415	6,110
36,100	36,150	8,256	7,963	7,671	7,378	7,056	6,738	6,433	6,128
36,150	36,200	8,275	7,983	7,690	7,398	7,075	6,756	6,451	6,146
36,200	36,250	8,295	8,002	7,710	7,417	7,095	6,774	6,469	6,164
36,250	36,300	8,314	8,022	7,729	7,437	7,114	6,792	6,487	6,182
36,300	36,350	8,334	8,041	7,749	7,456	7,134	6,810	6,505	6,200
36,350	36,400	8,353	8,061	7,768	7,476	7,153	6,828	6,523	6,218
36,400	36,450	8,373	8,080	7,788	7,495	7,173	6,846	6,541	6,236
36,450	36,500	8,392	8,100	7,807	7,515	7,192	6,865	6,559	6,254
36,500	36,550	8,412	8,119	7,827	7,534	7,212	6,884	6,577	6,272
36,550	36,600	8,431	8,139	7,846	7,554	7,231	6,904	6,595	6,290

If line 34, Form 1040 is— Over	But not over	2	3	4	5	6	7	8	9
36,600	36,650	8,451	8,158	7,866	7,573	7,251	6,923	6,613	6,308
36,650	36,700	8,470	8,178	7,885	7,593	7,270	6,943	6,631	6,326
36,700	36,750	8,491	8,197	7,905	7,612	7,290	6,962	6,649	6,344
36,750	36,800	8,512	8,217	7,924	7,632	7,309	6,982	6,667	6,362
36,800	36,850	8,533	8,236	7,944	7,651	7,329	7,001	6,685	6,380
36,850	36,900	8,554	8,256	7,963	7,671	7,348	7,021	6,703	6,398
36,900	36,950	8,575	8,275	7,983	7,690	7,368	7,040	6,721	6,416
36,950	37,000	8,596	8,295	8,002	7,710	7,387	7,060	6,739	6,434
37,000	37,050	8,617	8,314	8,022	7,729	7,407	7,079	6,757	6,452
37,050	37,100	8,638	8,334	8,041	7,749	7,426	7,099	6,775	6,470
37,100	37,150	8,659	8,353	8,061	7,768	7,446	7,118	6,793	6,488
37,150	37,200	8,680	8,373	8,080	7,788	7,465	7,138	6,811	6,506
37,200	37,250	8,701	8,392	8,100	7,807	7,485	7,157	6,830	6,524
37,250	37,300	8,722	8,412	8,119	7,827	7,504	7,177	6,849	6,542
37,300	37,350	8,743	8,431	8,139	7,846	7,524	7,196	6,869	6,560
37,350	37,400	8,764	8,451	8,158	7,866	7,543	7,216	6,888	6,578
37,400	37,450	8,785	8,470	8,178	7,885	7,563	7,235	6,908	6,596
37,450	37,500	8,806	8,491	8,197	7,905	7,582	7,255	6,927	6,614
37,500	37,550	8,827	8,512	8,217	7,924	7,602	7,274	6,947	6,632
37,550	37,600	8,848	8,533	8,236	7,944	7,621	7,294	6,966	6,650
37,600	37,650	8,869	8,554	8,256	7,963	7,641	7,313	6,986	6,668
37,650	37,700	8,890	8,575	8,275	7,983	7,660	7,333	7,005	6,686
37,700	37,750	8,911	8,596	8,295	8,002	7,680	7,352	7,025	6,704
37,750	37,800	8,932	8,617	8,314	8,022	7,699	7,372	7,044	6,722
37,800	37,850	8,953	8,638	8,334	8,041	7,719	7,391	7,064	6,740
37,850	37,900	8,974	8,659	8,353	8,061	7,738	7,411	7,083	6,758
37,900	37,950	8,995	8,680	8,373	8,080	7,758	7,430	7,103	6,776
37,950	38,000	9,016	8,701	8,392	8,100	7,777	7,450	7,122	6,795
38,000	38,050	9,037	8,722	8,412	8,119	7,797	7,469	7,142	6,814
38,050	38,100	9,058	8,743	8,431	8,139	7,816	7,489	7,161	6,834
38,100	38,150	9,079	8,764	8,451	8,158	7,836	7,508	7,181	6,853
38,150	38,200	9,100	8,785	8,470	8,178	7,855	7,528	7,200	6,873
38,200	38,250	9,121	8,806	8,491	8,197	7,875	7,547	7,220	6,892
38,250	38,300	9,142	8,827	8,512	8,217	7,894	7,567	7,239	6,912
38,300	38,350	9,163	8,848	8,533	8,236	7,914	7,586	7,259	6,931
38,350	38,400	9,184	8,869	8,554	8,256	7,933	7,606	7,278	6,951
38,400	38,450	9,205	8,890	8,575	8,275	7,953	7,625	7,298	6,970
38,450	38,500	9,226	8,911	8,596	8,295	7,972	7,645	7,317	6,990
38,500	38,550	9,247	8,932	8,617	8,314	7,992	7,664	7,337	7,009
38,550	38,600	9,268	8,953	8,638	8,334	8,011	7,684	7,356	7,029
38,600	38,650	9,289	8,974	8,659	8,353	8,031	7,703	7,376	7,048
38,650	38,700	9,310	8,995	8,680	8,373	8,050	7,723	7,395	7,068
38,700	38,750	9,331	9,016	8,701	8,392	8,070	7,742	7,415	7,087
38,750	38,800	9,352	9,037	8,722	8,412	8,089	7,762	7,434	7,107
38,800	38,850	9,373	9,058	8,743	8,431	8,109	7,781	7,454	7,126
38,850	38,900	9,394	9,079	8,764	8,451	8,128	7,801	7,473	7,146
38,900	38,950	9,415	9,100	8,785	8,470	8,148	7,820	7,493	7,165
38,950	39,000	9,436	9,121	8,806	8,491	8,167	7,840	7,512	7,185
39,000	39,050	9,457	9,142	8,827	8,512	8,187	7,859	7,532	7,204
39,050	39,100	9,478	9,163	8,848	8,533	8,206	7,879	7,551	7,224
39,100	39,150	9,499	9,184	8,869	8,554	8,226	7,898	7,571	7,243
39,150	39,200	9,520	9,205	8,890	8,575	8,245	7,918	7,590	7,263
39,200	39,250	9,541	9,226	8,911	8,596	8,265	7,937	7,610	7,282
39,250	39,300	9,562	9,247	8,932	8,617	8,284	7,957	7,629	7,302
39,300	39,350	9,583	9,268	8,953	8,638	8,304	7,976	7,649	7,321
39,350	39,400	9,604	9,289	8,974	8,659	8,323	7,996	7,668	7,341
39,400	39,450	9,625	9,310	8,995	8,680	8,343	8,015	7,688	7,360
39,450	39,500	9,646	9,331	9,016	8,701	8,362	8,035	7,707	7,380
39,500	39,550	9,667	9,352	9,037	8,722	8,382	8,054	7,727	7,399
39,550	39,600	9,688	9,373	9,058	8,743	8,401	8,074	7,746	7,419
39,600	39,650	9,709	9,394	9,079	8,764	8,421	8,093	7,766	7,438
39,650	39,700	9,730	9,415	9,100	8,785	8,440	8,113	7,785	7,458
39,700	39,750	9,751	9,436	9,121	8,806	8,461	8,132	7,805	7,477
39,750	39,800	9,772	9,457	9,142	8,827	8,482	8,152	7,824	7,497
39,800	39,850	9,793	9,478	9,163	8,848	8,503	8,171	7,844	7,516
39,850	39,900	9,814	9,499	9,184	8,869	8,524	8,191	7,863	7,536
39,900	39,950	9,835	9,520	9,205	8,890	8,545	8,210	7,883	7,555
39,950	40,000	9,856	9,541	9,226	8,911	8,566	8,230	7,902	7,575

Continued next column

1977 Tax Table C—MARRIED FILING SEPARATELY (Box 3)

(For married persons filing separate returns with tax table income of $20,000 or less who claim fewer than 4 exemptions)

To find your tax: Read down the left income column until you find your income as shown on line 34 of Form 1040. Read across to the column headed by the total number of exemptions claimed on line 7 of Form 1040. The amount shown at the point where the two lines meet is your tax. Enter on Form 1040, line 35.

The $1,600 zero bracket amount, your deduction for exemptions and the general tax credit have been taken into account in figuring the tax shown in this table. **Do not take a separate deduction for them.**

Caution: If you or your spouse itemize deductions, or if you can be claimed as a dependent on your parent's return AND you have unearned income (interests, dividends, etc.) of $750 or more AND your earned income is less than $1,600 you must first use Schedule TC (Form 1040), Part II.

If line 34, Form 1040 is— Over	But not over	1	2	3
If $2,600 or less your tax is 0				
2,600	2,625	2	0	0
2,625	2,650	5	0	0
2,650	2,675	9	0	0
2,675	2,700	12	0	0
2,700	2,725	16	0	0
2,725	2,750	19	0	0
2,750	2,775	23	0	0
2,775	2,800	26	0	0
2,800	2,825	30	0	0
2,825	2,850	33	0	0
2,850	2,875	37	0	0
2,875	2,900	41	0	0
2,900	2,925	44	0	0
2,925	2,950	48	0	0
2,950	2,975	52	0	0
2,975	3,000	56	0	0
3,000	3,050	61	0	0
3,050	3,100	69	0	0
3,100	3,150	76	0	0
3,150	3,200	84	0	0
3,200	3,250	91	0	0
3,250	3,300	99	0	0
3,300	3,350	106	0	0
3,350	3,400	114	0	0
3,400	3,450	122	0	0
3,450	3,500	130	0	0
3,500	3,550	138	0	0
3,550	3,600	146	0	0
3,600	3,650	154	4	0
3,650	3,700	162	11	0
3,700	3,750	170	19	0
3,750	3,800	178	26	0
3,800	3,850	186	34	0
3,850	3,900	194	41	0
3,900	3,950	203	49	0
3,950	4,000	211	56	0
4,000	4,050	220	64	0
4,050	4,100	228	71	0
4,100	4,150	237	79	0
4,150	4,200	245	87	0
4,200	4,250	254	95	0
4,250	4,300	262	103	0
4,300	4,350	271	111	0
4,350	4,400	280	119	0
4,400	4,450	289	127	0
4,450	4,500	299	135	0
4,500	4,550	308	143	0
4,550	4,600	318	151	0
4,600	4,650	327	159	6
4,650	4,700	337	168	14
4,700	4,750	346	176	21
4,750	4,800	356	185	29
4,800	4,850	365	193	36
4,850	4,900	375	202	44
4,900	4,950	384	210	52
4,950	5,000	394	219	60

Continued next column

If line 34, Form 1040 is— Over	But not over	1	2	3
5,000	5,050	403	227	68
5,050	5,100	413	236	76
5,100	5,150	422	245	84
5,150	5,200	432	254	92
5,200	5,250	441	264	100
5,250	5,300	451	273	108
5,300	5,350	460	283	116
5,350	5,400	470	292	124
5,400	5,450	479	302	133
5,450	5,500	489	311	141
5,500	5,550	498	321	150
5,550	5,600	508	330	158
5,600	5,650	517	340	167
5,650	5,700	527	349	175
5,700	5,750	536	359	184
5,750	5,800	546	368	192
5,800	5,850	555	378	201
5,850	5,900	565	387	210
5,900	5,950	574	397	219
5,950	6,000	584	406	229
6,000	6,050	593	416	238
6,050	6,100	603	425	248
6,100	6,150	612	435	257
6,150	6,200	622	444	267
6,200	6,250	631	454	276
6,250	6,300	641	463	286
6,300	6,350	650	473	295
6,350	6,400	661	482	305
6,400	6,450	672	492	314
6,450	6,500	683	501	324
6,500	6,550	694	511	333
6,550	6,600	705	520	343
6,600	6,650	716	530	352
6,650	6,700	727	539	362
6,700	6,750	738	549	371
6,750	6,800	749	558	381
6,800	6,850	760	568	390
6,850	6,900	771	577	400
6,900	6,950	782	587	409
6,950	7,000	793	596	419
7,000	7,050	804	606	428
7,050	7,100	815	615	438
7,100	7,150	826	626	447
7,150	7,200	837	637	457
7,200	7,250	848	648	466
7,250	7,300	859	659	476
7,300	7,350	870	670	485
7,350	7,400	881	681	495
7,400	7,450	892	692	504
7,450	7,500	903	703	514
7,500	7,550	914	714	523
7,550	7,600	925	725	533
7,600	7,650	936	736	542
7,650	7,700	947	747	552
7,700	7,750	958	758	561
7,750	7,800	969	769	571

Continued next column

If line 34, Form 1040 is— Over	But not over	1	2	3
7,800	7,850	980	780	580
7,850	7,900	991	791	591
7,900	7,950	1,002	802	602
7,950	8,000	1,013	813	613
8,000	8,050	1,024	824	624
8,050	8,100	1,035	835	635
8,100	8,150	1,046	846	646
8,150	8,200	1,057	857	657
8,200	8,250	1,068	868	668
8,250	8,300	1,079	879	679
8,300	8,350	1,090	890	690
8,350	8,400	1,101	901	701
8,400	8,450	1,114	912	712
8,450	8,500	1,126	923	723
8,500	8,550	1,139	934	734
8,550	8,600	1,151	945	745
8,600	8,650	1,164	956	756
8,650	8,700	1,176	967	767
8,700	8,750	1,189	978	778
8,750	8,800	1,201	989	789
8,800	8,850	1,214	1,000	800
8,850	8,900	1,226	1,011	811
8,900	8,950	1,239	1,022	822
8,950	9,000	1,251	1,033	833
9,000	9,050	1,264	1,044	844
9,050	9,100	1,276	1,055	855
9,100	9,150	1,289	1,066	866
9,150	9,200	1,301	1,079	877
9,200	9,250	1,314	1,091	888
9,250	9,300	1,326	1,104	899
9,300	9,350	1,339	1,116	910
9,350	9,400	1,351	1,129	921
9,400	9,450	1,364	1,141	932
9,450	9,500	1,376	1,154	943
9,500	9,550	1,389	1,166	954
9,550	9,600	1,401	1,179	965
9,600	9,650	1,414	1,191	976
9,650	9,700	1,426	1,204	987
9,700	9,750	1,439	1,216	998
9,750	9,800	1,451	1,229	1,009
9,800	9,850	1,464	1,241	1,020
9,850	9,900	1,476	1,254	1,031
9,900	9,950	1,489	1,266	1,044
9,950	10,000	1,501	1,279	1,056
10,000	10,050	1,514	1,291	1,069
10,050	10,100	1,526	1,304	1,081
10,100	10,150	1,539	1,316	1,094
10,150	10,200	1,551	1,329	1,106
10,200	10,250	1,564	1,341	1,119
10,250	10,300	1,576	1,354	1,131
10,300	10,350	1,589	1,366	1,144
10,350	10,400	1,602	1,379	1,156
10,400	10,450	1,616	1,391	1,169
10,450	10,500	1,630	1,404	1,181
10,500	10,550	1,644	1,416	1,194
10,550	10,600	1,658	1,429	1,206

Continued on next page

1977 Tax Table D—HEAD OF HOUSEHOLD (Box 4)

(Continued)

(If your income or exemptions are not covered, use Schedule TC (Form 1040), Part I to figure your tax)

If line 34, Form 1040 is— Over	But not over	And the total number of exemptions claimed on line 7 is— 1	2	3	4	5	6	7	8
		Your tax is—							
8,800	8,850	899	771	626	453	283	113	0	0
8,850	8,900	907	780	636	462	292	122	0	0
8,900	8,950	916	788	645	471	301	131	0	0
8,950	9,000	925	797	655	480	310	140	0	0
9,000	9,050	935	805	664	489	319	149	0	0
9,050	9,100	945	814	674	498	328	158	0	0
9,100	9,150	955	822	683	507	337	167	3	0
9,150	9,200	965	831	693	516	346	176	11	0
9,200	9,250	975	839	702	525	355	185	19	0
9,250	9,300	985	848	712	534	364	194	27	0
9,300	9,350	995	856	721	544	373	203	35	0
9,350	9,400	1,005	865	731	553	382	212	43	0
9,400	9,450	1,015	873	740	563	391	221	51	0
9,450	9,500	1,025	882	750	572	400	230	60	0
9,500	9,550	1,035	890	759	582	409	239	69	0
9,550	9,600	1,045	899	769	591	418	248	78	0
9,600	9,650	1,055	907	778	601	427	257	87	0
9,650	9,700	1,065	916	788	610	436	266	96	0
9,700	9,750	1,075	925	797	620	445	275	105	0
9,750	9,800	1,085	935	805	629	454	284	114	0
9,800	9,850	1,095	945	814	639	463	293	123	0
9,850	9,900	1,105	955	822	648	472	302	132	0
9,900	9,950	1,115	965	831	658	481	311	141	0
9,950	10,000	1,125	975	839	667	490	320	150	0
10,000	10,050	1,135	985	848	677	499	329	159	0
10,050	10,100	1,145	995	856	686	509	338	168	0
10,100	10,150	1,155	1,005	865	696	518	347	177	8
10,150	10,200	1,165	1,015	873	705	528	356	186	16
10,200	10,250	1,175	1,025	882	715	537	365	195	25
10,250	10,300	1,185	1,035	890	724	547	374	204	34
10,300	10,350	1,195	1,045	899	734	556	383	213	43
10,350	10,400	1,205	1,055	907	743	566	392	222	52
10,400	10,450	1,215	1,065	916	753	575	401	231	61
10,450	10,500	1,225	1,075	925	762	585	410	240	70
10,500	10,550	1,235	1,085	935	772	594	419	249	79
10,550	10,600	1,245	1,095	945	781	604	428	258	88
10,600	10,650	1,255	1,105	955	791	613	437	267	97
10,650	10,700	1,265	1,115	965	800	623	446	276	106
10,700	10,750	1,275	1,125	975	810	632	455	285	115
10,750	10,800	1,285	1,135	985	819	642	464	294	124
10,800	10,850	1,295	1,145	995	829	651	474	303	133
10,850	10,900	1,305	1,155	1,005	838	661	483	312	142
10,900	10,950	1,315	1,165	1,015	848	670	493	321	151
10,950	11,000	1,325	1,175	1,025	857	680	502	330	160
11,000	11,050	1,336	1,185	1,035	867	689	512	339	169
11,050	11,100	1,346	1,195	1,045	876	699	521	348	178
11,100	11,150	1,357	1,205	1,055	886	708	531	357	187
11,150	11,200	1,367	1,215	1,065	895	718	540	366	196
11,200	11,250	1,378	1,225	1,075	906	727	550	375	205
11,250	11,300	1,388	1,235	1,085	917	737	559	384	214
11,300	11,350	1,399	1,245	1,095	928	746	569	393	223
11,350	11,400	1,409	1,255	1,105	939	756	578	402	232
11,400	11,450	1,420	1,265	1,115	950	765	588	411	241
11,450	11,500	1,430	1,275	1,125	961	775	597	420	250
11,500	11,550	1,441	1,285	1,135	972	784	607	429	259
11,550	11,600	1,451	1,295	1,145	983	794	616	439	268

Continued next column

If line 34, Form 1040 is— Over	But not over	And the total number of exemptions claimed on line 7 is— 1	2	3	4	5	6	7	8
		Your tax is—							
11,600	11,650	1,462	1,305	1,155	994	803	626	448	277
11,650	11,700	1,472	1,315	1,165	1,005	813	635	458	286
11,700	11,750	1,483	1,325	1,175	1,016	822	645	467	295
11,750	11,800	1,493	1,336	1,185	1,027	832	654	477	304
11,800	11,850	1,504	1,346	1,195	1,038	841	664	486	313
11,850	11,900	1,514	1,357	1,205	1,049	851	673	496	322
11,900	11,950	1,525	1,367	1,215	1,060	860	683	505	331
11,950	12,000	1,536	1,378	1,225	1,071	871	692	515	340
12,000	12,050	1,547	1,388	1,235	1,082	882	702	524	349
12,050	12,100	1,559	1,399	1,245	1,093	893	711	534	358
12,100	12,150	1,570	1,409	1,255	1,104	904	721	543	367
12,150	12,200	1,582	1,420	1,265	1,115	915	730	553	376
12,200	12,250	1,593	1,430	1,275	1,125	926	740	562	385
12,250	12,300	1,605	1,441	1,285	1,135	937	749	572	394
12,300	12,350	1,616	1,451	1,295	1,145	948	759	581	404
12,350	12,400	1,628	1,462	1,305	1,155	959	768	591	413
12,400	12,450	1,639	1,472	1,315	1,165	970	778	600	423
12,450	12,500	1,651	1,483	1,325	1,175	981	787	610	432
12,500	12,550	1,662	1,493	1,336	1,185	992	797	619	442
12,550	12,600	1,674	1,504	1,346	1,195	1,003	806	629	451
12,600	12,650	1,685	1,514	1,357	1,205	1,014	816	638	461
12,650	12,700	1,697	1,525	1,367	1,215	1,025	825	648	470
12,700	12,750	1,708	1,536	1,378	1,225	1,036	836	657	480
12,750	12,800	1,720	1,547	1,388	1,235	1,047	847	667	489
12,800	12,850	1,731	1,559	1,399	1,245	1,058	858	676	499
12,850	12,900	1,743	1,570	1,409	1,255	1,069	869	686	508
12,900	12,950	1,754	1,582	1,420	1,265	1,080	880	695	518
12,950	13,000	1,766	1,593	1,430	1,275	1,091	891	705	527
13,000	13,050	1,779	1,605	1,441	1,285	1,102	902	714	537
13,050	13,100	1,791	1,616	1,451	1,295	1,113	913	724	546
13,100	13,150	1,804	1,628	1,462	1,305	1,124	924	733	556
13,150	13,200	1,816	1,639	1,472	1,315	1,135	935	743	565
13,200	13,250	1,829	1,651	1,483	1,325	1,146	946	752	575
13,250	13,300	1,841	1,662	1,493	1,336	1,157	957	762	584
13,300	13,350	1,854	1,674	1,504	1,346	1,168	968	771	594
13,350	13,400	1,866	1,685	1,514	1,357	1,179	979	781	603
13,400	13,450	1,879	1,697	1,525	1,367	1,190	990	790	613
13,450	13,500	1,891	1,708	1,536	1,378	1,201	1,001	801	622
13,500	13,550	1,904	1,720	1,547	1,388	1,212	1,012	812	632
13,550	13,600	1,916	1,731	1,559	1,399	1,223	1,023	823	641
13,600	13,650	1,929	1,743	1,570	1,409	1,234	1,034	834	651
13,650	13,700	1,941	1,754	1,582	1,420	1,245	1,045	845	660
13,700	13,750	1,954	1,766	1,593	1,430	1,256	1,056	856	670
13,750	13,800	1,966	1,779	1,605	1,441	1,267	1,067	867	679
13,800	13,850	1,979	1,791	1,616	1,451	1,278	1,078	878	689
13,850	13,900	1,991	1,804	1,628	1,462	1,289	1,089	889	698
13,900	13,950	2,004	1,816	1,639	1,472	1,300	1,100	900	708
13,950	14,000	2,016	1,829	1,651	1,483	1,311	1,111	911	717
14,000	14,050	2,029	1,841	1,662	1,493	1,322	1,122	922	727
14,050	14,100	2,041	1,854	1,674	1,504	1,334	1,133	933	736
14,100	14,150	2,054	1,866	1,685	1,514	1,345	1,144	944	746
14,150	14,200	2,066	1,879	1,697	1,525	1,357	1,155	955	755
14,200	14,250	2,079	1,891	1,708	1,536	1,368	1,166	966	766
14,250	14,300	2,091	1,904	1,720	1,547	1,380	1,177	977	777
14,300	14,350	2,104	1,916	1,731	1,559	1,391	1,188	988	788
14,350	14,400	2,116	1,929	1,743	1,570	1,403	1,199	999	799

Continued on next page

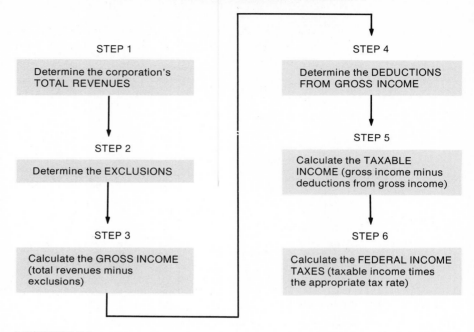

COMPUTATION OF
CORPORATION FEDERAL INCOME TAX LIABILITY

STEP 1

Determine the corporation's
TOTAL REVENUES

STEP 2

Determine the EXCLUSIONS

STEP 3

Calculate the GROSS INCOME
(total revenues minus
exclusions)

STEP 4

Determine the DEDUCTIONS
FROM GROSS INCOME

STEP 5

Calculate the TAXABLE
INCOME (gross income minus
deductions from gross income)

STEP 6

Calculate the FEDERAL INCOME
TAXES (taxable income times
the appropriate tax rate)

ILLUSTRATION 54-3

income. These include:

1. Expenses of operating the corporation, such as cost of goods sold, selling expenses, general and administrative expenses, and depreciation on plant and equipment.
2. Deductions associated with long-term capital gains (to be discussed in Unit 55).
3. A number of other special deductions.

Step 5: Calculate the TAXABLE INCOME The taxable income can now be computed by subtracting the *deductions from gross income* from the *gross income.* Notice that the diagram for corporations differs from the diagram presented earlier for individuals.

Step 6: Calculate the FEDERAL INCOME TAXES The federal income tax liability for the year is computed by applying the appropriate tax rate to the taxable income of the corporation. There are two steps to applying the tax rate to the taxable income. The normal tax rate of corporations is 22% of taxable income. In addition, there is a tax called a **surtax,** which is an additional amount of tax on that taxable income exceeding $25,000 for the year. The surtax rate is 26%. Here is how the tax is computed:

Assume a corporation has taxable income of $27,000 for the year. The 22% tax rate applies to the taxable income. The excess of taxable income over $25,000 is taxed at an additional 26%:

Normal tax (22% × $27,000)	$5,940
Surtax [26% × ($27,000 − $25,000)]	520
Total corporation income tax liability	$6,460

❯ NEW TERMS

exclusion As provided by the federal income tax laws, certain revenues and gains can be excluded in the computation of taxable income; certain exclusions are allowed for individuals and certain exclusions are allowed for corporations. [p. 913]

head of household A special category of individual income taxpayer; unmarried individuals who operate households and otherwise qualify may use a special table of tax rates, which generally provides lower tax rates than the tables for single individuals. [p. 914]

income tax regulations The set of regulations and prescribed operating procedures for the administration of the federal income tax laws, as determined by the Commissioner of Internal Revenue of the Treasury Department. [p. 912]

Internal Revenue Code A compilation of all current federal income tax laws. [p. 911]

itemized deductions Personal deductions allowed under the individual income tax laws; they are composed of expenditures for interest expense, state and local taxes, charitable contributions, medical and dental expenses, casualty losses, and other miscellaneous deductions; certain limitations apply to these deductions. [p. 914]

surtax An additional amount of tax on that portion of a corporation's taxable income exceeding $25,000 for a year. [p. 922].

❯ ASSIGNMENT MATERIAL

QUESTIONS

Q54-1. About what percent of total federal revenues comes from income taxes?

Q54-2. Do all the states have state income taxes?

Q54-3. Do some local governmental units use the income tax as a source of revenues?

Q54-4. List and briefly describe the four aspects of the legal background of the federal tax laws.

Q54-5. Explain these terms as they relate to individual federal income taxes:
a. Total income.
b. Adjustments to income.
c. Itemized deductions.
d. Excess itemized deductions.
e. Tax table income.

Q54-6. Why would a taxpayer rather be classified as a head of household instead of a single individual, if he had the option?

E54-1. For each of the following independent situations, determine the amount of individual income taxes:

NAME	NUMBER OF EXEMPTIONS	TAX TABLE INCOME	TYPE OF RETURN
James M. Carteen	1	$10,462	single
Susan P. Allerson	3	$13,804	head of household
Walter and Joan Small	7	$24,960	joint
Betty and William Green	5	$30,000	joint

E54-2. Compute the corporation federal income taxes for each of the corporations listed below:

CORPORATION	TAXABLE INCOME
Halligren Corp.	$ 69,518.24
Gregory, Inc.	$119,600.00
Banister and Co., Inc.	$ 16,215.25

E54-3. Wallace Burgoyne and his wife earned salaries as follows:

NAME	SALARY	INCOME TAXES WITHHELD DURING YEAR
Wallace Burgoyne	$15,500	$2,500
Bess Burgoyne	13,600	3,100

Other earnings were:

Dividends	$ 500
Interest (corporate bonds)	400
Interest (savings account)	300
Interest (municipal bonds)	200
Share of net earnings of an investment in a partnership	5,500

Compute the *total income* for the Burgoynes (step 1 in the diagram in the unit).

E54-4. The Burgoynes (E54-3) had only one adjustment to income, which was $1,400 of employee business expenses. Their total itemized deductions were $3,354. Compute the amount of income taxes due the government (or refund due) for the year.

PROBLEMS (GROUP A)

P54-1. *Individual income taxes.* Horace Winchester earned $12,000 from his job at a factory. Other earnings of the Winchesters included dividends of $700 and interest income of $300 from corporation bonds and $600 interest income from municipal bonds. Winchester is married and lives with his wife and five children.

During the year, Winchester had no adjustments to income. Mrs. Winchester earned $14,000 in salary income from her job. Itemized deductions were as follows:

Interest expense	$1,675
State and local taxes	1,000
Charitable contributions	3,000
	$5,675

Federal income taxes were withheld from salaries as follows:

Mrs. Winchester	$1,318
Mr. Winchester	1,295

REQUIRED: Calculate the following:

    a. Total income.

    b. Adjustments to income.

    c. Excess itemized deductions.

    d. Tax table income.

    e. Federal income taxes.

    f. Amount still owed to the government (or refund due).

P54-2. *Individual income taxes.* Walter M. Suggs is in process of preparing his individual federal income tax return. He will prepare a joint return. He gathers the following information from his personal records:

    1. Mr. Suggs is an employee of Ace Corporation and earned $12,193.45 during the year.

    2. His wife earned $18,500 as an employee of Kings Company during the year.

    3. The Suggs have four children and will claim them as dependents on the tax return.

    4. Income in addition to salaries includes:

        Interest on bank accounts, $1,300.19

        Interest on municipal bonds, $1,000.00

        Gifts from relatives, $200.00

        Rental income, $5,000.00

    5. Deductible expenses associated with the rental income, $3,924.75.

    6. The itemized deductions of Mr. and Mrs. Suggs total $3,286.58.

REQUIRED: Compute the federal income taxes. Label all computations. Follow the steps given in the unit.

P54-3. *Corporate federal income taxes.* Avocat Corporation records showed the following information for the year:

Sales of merchandise	$250,000	
Other income (rent and interest)	40,000	
Total revenues		$290,000
Cost of goods sold	$135,000	
Selling expenses	20,000	
General expenses	5,000	
Other expenses	2,000	
Total expenses		162,000
		$128,000

All the revenues of the company are taxable and all the expenses are deductible for the year. There are no exclusions.

REQUIRED:

    a. Calculate the following, labeling all calculations:

      (1) Total revenues.

    (2) Exclusions.

    (3) Gross income.

    (4) Deductions from gross income.

    (5) Taxable income.

    (6) Federal income taxes.

  b. What is the amount of *net earnings* for the corporation for the year?

PROBLEMS (GROUP B)

P54-4. *Individual income taxes.* Michelle Hatamall qualifies as a head of household under the federal tax laws. She lives with two dependents in her own home and therefore is entitled to three personal exemptions. Ms. Hatamall earned $8,597.87 as an employee of Uno Brothers, Inc., during the year. She earned interest on bank accounts amounting to $305; and she earned interest on her account at the First Savings and Loan Association totaling $418. She also received a cash gift from her uncle amounting to $5,300. Her other income consisted of $1,500 in fees which she charged clients for part-time secretarial services that she performed. Itemized deductions included: interest paid, $1,300; state and local taxes, $250; charitable contributions, $1,100.

REQUIRED: Compute the federal income taxes for the year.

P54-5. *Individual income taxes.* Sarah and James Scott gathered the following data in regard to their federal income tax return:

1. Salaries:

NAME	SALARY	INCOME TAX WITHHELD
Sarah Scott	$12,000	$2,000
James Scott	10,000	1,500

2. The Scotts have two children, who are counted as exemptions.

3. Other earnings:

Interest on savings accounts	$ 318
Interest on bonds of City of New York	412
Revenue from consulting (James)	615
Dividends (Common stock)	1,000

4. Expenditures included:

Church contributions	$536
State and local taxes	400
United Fund	50
Interest on house mortgage	900
Other interest	150

5. A joint return is to be prepared.

REQUIRED: Calculate the following:

  a. Total income.

  b. Adjustments to income.

  c. Excess itemized deductions.

d. Tax table income.

e. Federal income taxes.

f. Amount still owed to the government (or refund due).

*P54-6. *Corporate federal income taxes.* A partially completed income statement for 1977 is shown below for Tacks, Inc.

Tacks, Inc.
INCOME STATEMENT
For the Year Ended December 31, 1977

revenues

Sales (net)	$600,000	
Rental income	50,000	
Interest income	6,000	$656,000

expenses

Cost of sales	$315,000	
Selling expenses	100,000	
General expenses	114,000	
Income tax expense	?	?

net earnings ?

earnings per share ?

Additional Information:

1. At January 1, 1977, there were 5,000 shares of common stock outstanding. On October 1, 1977, an additional 1,000 shares were issued for cash.

2. $20,000 of the rental income for 1977 is taxable in 1978 and $30,000 is taxable in 1977.

REQUIRED:

a. Compute the federal income taxes due the government for 1977.

b. Compute the 1977 income tax expense to appear on the 1977 income statement. This involves interperiod tax allocation.

c. Compute the 1977 earnings per share.

TAX IMPACT ON DECISIONS

> **OBJECTIVE**

This unit continues our study of income taxes. It explains how the income tax laws affect organizing a business, raising capital, distributing earnings to the owners, investing the firm's resources, and producing and selling the product of the company.

> **APPROACH TO ATTAINING THE OBJECTIVE**

As you study about the tax impact on capital-raising and earnings distribution activities, pay special attention to these eight questions, which the text following answers:

- *Are different types of firms taxed in different ways?*
- *How do income taxes affect the choice of financing methods?*
- *How is the distribution of earnings affected by the income tax laws?*
- *What is the investment tax credit provision?*
- *Which investments produce tax-free earnings?*
- *What is the capital gains provision?*
- *How important is the timing of expenses?*
- *What special treatment is given the extractive industries?*

- *Are different types
  of firms taxed in
  different ways?*

Unit 1 described the three common forms of business organizations: the proprietorship, the partnership, and the corporation. When a business is organized, one of the main factors to consider is the impact of taxes on the earnings of the company.

The table below represents information about how a firm is taxed and about how its owners are taxed for each of the three basic forms of business organization. In summary, proprietorships and partnerships *do not* pay income taxes, but corporations do pay income taxes. As *individuals,* owners (proprietors, partners, and shareholders) of businesses pay income taxes on (1) their earnings from proprietorships, (2) their share of earnings from partnerships, (3) dividends received from corporations, and (4) salaries received from corporations.

It would appear that since corporate earnings are taxed *when the earnings are produced,* and since dividends are taxed to individuals *when they are received,* then this **double taxation** would be a significant disadvantage of the corporate form of organization. Several other factors, however, must be considered in order to properly assess the impact of the form of organization on the taxes. These other factors include:

1. The tax rates of the individual proprietors, partners, or shareholders.
2. The corporation tax rates.

TYPE OF BUSINESS	HOW THE FIRM IS TAXED	HOW THE OWNERS ARE TAXED
CORPORATION	Corporations must pay income taxes on their earnings. Each year, the corporation prepares a corporate tax return, following the steps indicated in the previous unit. The normal corporation tax rate is 22% of taxable income, and the surtax rate is 26% of the taxable income of the company exceeding $25,000.	The shareholders of a corporation do not pay taxes on the earnings of the corporation. However, if the corporation declares a dividend, the amount of the dividend received by the shareholder from the corporation becomes part of the income of the shareholder and must be reported on his *individual* income tax return and is taxed accordingly. A second way that a shareholder can be taxed is if he happens to also be an employee of the corporation. In that case, his salary becomes part of the income of the shareholders and must be reported on his individual income tax return.
PARTNERSHIP	Partnerships *do not* pay income taxes. However, each year a partnership *information* return is prepared. This return reveals to the government the amount of earnings the firm produced and how the earnings are to be shared by the partners.	Each partner in a partnership files his individual income tax return. The partner's share of the partnership earnings becomes part of his income on his individual income tax return and is taxed accordingly.
PROPRIETORSHIP	Proprietorships *do not* pay income taxes. The earnings of the proprietorship are considered individual earnings of the owner.	The owner of a proprietorship prepares an individual tax return each year. This tax return includes as income the earnings from the proprietorship and is taxed accordingly.

3. Expected level of business net earnings each year.
4. The expectation of distributing earnings to owners.

CHOICE OF FINANCING METHOD

You have already studied the tax impact on securing additional resources. Unit 34 illustrated the effect on earnings per share of issuing common stock, issuing preferred stock, and issuing bonds to finance an expansion program. Another significant factor in the financing decision is the tax effect on a business brought about by payment of interest.

- *How do income taxes affect the choice of financing methods?*

In the corporate form of organization, the interest expense incurred on debts (bonds, for example) *reduces* taxable income. This makes the use of debt advantageous in many circumstances. For example, if the interest expense of a corporation is $100,000, and if the tax rate is 56%, the effective cost of borrowing might be computed as follows:

Interest cost	$100,000
Tax savings through deducting interest expense in computing taxable income (56% of $100,000)	56,000
Net cost of interest	$ 44,000

Similarly, interest expense can be deducted in computing the taxable income of individuals. If a partnership incurs interest expense, then this expense is deducted before computing the earnings to be divided among the partners.

In summary, the tax laws encourage the use of borrowing in financing a business because interest expense reduces taxable income and income taxes of corporations or individuals.

DIVIDENDS AND TAXES

Dividends declared by a corporation have no effect on the taxes of that corporation. Dividends do increase the taxable income of the shareholders, however. Withdrawals of owners from a proprietorship or partnership have no effect on the individual taxes of the owners. All these facts must be considered when a business firm is comparing methods of financing, such as securing investments from the owners to expand the business or borrowing the needed funds from creditors.

- *How is the distribution of earnings affected by the income tax laws?*

THE INVESTMENT TAX CREDIT PROVISION

The **investment tax credit** is a special provision of the federal tax laws. The provision is designed to stimulate the economy by encouraging businesses to invest their resources in additional plant and equipment and other investments. The investment tax credit has not been a permanent provision of the tax laws, though it has been in effect during several periods in past years. The Revenue Act of 1971 restored the current investment tax credit provision.

Briefly, the law provides that taxpayers (individuals and corporations) will be allowed a direct credit (reduction) against their income taxes when they make a certain type of investment. The current provision is that the taxpayer is allowed a reduction in his taxes amounting to 10% of the cost of new investments he makes. To qualify, the investment generally must be property used in business which is to be depreciated. There are a number of specific requirements in the tax law which must be satisfied before the investment can qualify for the tax credit.

Here is an example of the investment tax credit. A firm purchased a new machine to use in its factory. The machine is expected to have a useful life of eight years and the initial cost is $10,000. Assuming the machine qualifies under the law, the investment tax credit would be $1,000, or 10% of the cost of $10,000. When the company computes its income taxes due based upon its taxable income, $1,000 can be deducted directly from the amount due. If the income taxes for the company amount to $12,000 before considering the investment tax credit, the net amount due the government will be $11,000, which is the $12,000 minus the $1,000 investment tax credit.

The investment tax provision is extremely important to businesses. The effect of this provision is to reduce the cost of certain types of investments. For example, a machine with a cash price of $10,000 would only cost the firm $9,000 after the investment tax credit is considered.

TAX-FREE EARNINGS ON CERTAIN INVESTMENTS

Another set of provisions of the tax laws allows the earnings from certain kinds of investments to be excluded from taxable income. The most popular of the exclusions allowed are the earnings on municipal and state bonds. A company or individual can invest in municipal bonds and the interest income from the bonds is considered tax-free by the tax laws. This makes these special investments especially advantageous to taxpayers who have relatively high tax rates.

To illustrate, assume that a taxpayer is considering investing $10,000 in securities. He can purchase the City of Newshore bonds which will pay interest of 5% per year, or he can invest in the bonds of Jones Corporation which will produce interest of 7% per year. The investor considers that both investments are safe and otherwise meet the investment requirements. The table at the top of the next page shows the relative attractiveness of the two kinds of bonds for three taxpayers with different tax rates.

The corporation bonds produce $700 per year for each investor, before taxes. This is the 7% interest rate times the investment of $10,000. The $700 per year interest income on the corporation bonds becomes part of the taxable income of the investor and is subject to income taxes at the taxpayer's tax rate.

The corporate tax rate is assumed to be 56%; therefore, the taxes on

	(1) GROSS AMOUNT OF INTEREST RECEIVED FROM CORPORATION BONDS BEFORE PAYING INCOME TAXES	(2) INCOME TAXES ON EARNINGS OF CORPORATION BONDS	(1) minus (2) NET AMOUNT RECEIVED FROM CORPORATION BONDS AFTER PAYING INCOME TAXES	INTEREST RECEIVED FROM MUNICIPAL BONDS (NO TAXES APPLICABLE)
Assuming the investor is a corporation with a tax rate of 56%	$700	$392	$308	$500
Assuming the investor is an individual with a tax rate of 22%	$700	$154	$546	$500
Assuming the investor is an individual with a tax rate of 69%	$700	$483	$217	$500

the earnings from the corporate bonds amount to $392. This leaves earnings after taxes from the investment of only $308. Therefore, the investment in these corporation bonds is less desirable than receiving $500 of tax-free interest from the municipal bonds.

The second investor shown in the table has a tax rate of only 22%. His taxes are lower ($154) on the $700 of corporation bonds interest. The corporation bond investment is therefore more desirable for him than the tax-free investment.

The third investor has a high tax rate. It is considerably better for him to invest in the municipal bonds. As a general rule, investments in municipal and state bonds and in other tax-free investments become more and more desirable as the tax rate of the investor increases.

CAPITAL GAINS AND LOSSES

- *What is the capital gains provision?*

The capital gains and losses provisions of the income tax laws have been in effect for many years. The tax law classifies certain assets of individuals and corporations as capital assets. Gains and losses made on these capital assets receive special treatment in the computation of income taxes. A **capital asset** is roughly defined as being *any asset except the following:* business inventories, accounts and notes receivable, plant and equipment used in business, certain intangible assets such as copyrights and artistic compositions, and certain short-term municipal, state, and federal notes and bonds. Almost all kinds of long-term investments such as investments in stocks and bonds are considered capital assets. The following discussion shows the capital gains and losses treatment in computing income taxes of individuals; the provisions in the law differ somewhat for corporations.

All capital gains and losses classified as short-term or long-term The first step in determining the tax treatment is to classify each **capital gain** or **capital loss** as short-term or long-term. A capital gain or loss which arises from holding a capital asset for *1 year or less* is classified as a **short-term capital gain** or a **short-term capital loss**. A capital gain or loss which arises from holding a capital asset for *more than 1 year* is classified as a **long-term capital gain** or a **long-term capital loss**. The treatment under the tax laws for short-term capital gains and losses is different from the treatment of long-term capital gains and losses.

The net capital gains and losses As the next step, all short-term capital gains and short-term capital losses of the taxpayer are combined. The resulting figure is the *net short-term capital gain* or the *net short-term capital loss*.

Then all long-term capital gains and long-term capital losses of the taxpayer are combined. The resulting figure is the *net long-term capital gain* or the *net long-term capital loss*.

After the procedures above, the net short-term capital gain or loss and the net long-term capital gain or loss of the taxpayer are combined to determine the *net capital gain* or the *net capital loss*.

Treatment if there is a net capital loss If the individual taxpayer has a net capital loss, this loss may be deducted from his taxable income before computing the income taxes. In any one year, however, the deduction cannot exceed $3,000. Any excess not deducted can be carried forward to future years to be deducted, however, within certain limitations. Corporations are not allowed to deduct net capital losses from their taxable income.

Treatment if there is a net capital gain The treatment of net capital gains is of special importance to investors. Net capital gains must be included in taxable income, but a special deduction is allowed in certain circumstances. *This special deduction is 50% of the excess of the taxpayer's net long-term capital gain over net short-term capital loss.* There are many special limitations and provisions of the capital gains treatment. The description above is designed to give you a general understanding of the structure, not to provide you with a precise interpretation of the law.

An illustration The following illustration will apply the computational procedures just described. Assume that a taxpayer had the following transactions dealing with capital assets during the year:

1. Sold an investment in ABC Common stock for $89,000 cash on December 1, 1978. The investment had been purchased on October 18, 1978, for $93,500.

2. Sold an investment in XY Bonds for $10,000 cash on April 1, 1978. The investment had been purchased March 5, 1978, for $9,500.

3. Sold an investment in BC Preferred stock for $100,000 on June 3, 1978. The investment had been purchased on May 10, 1970, for $25,000.

4. Sold an investment in ZZ Common stock for $118,000 on October 1, 1978. The investment had been purchased on June 19, 1976, for $119,000.

The first two transactions above would be classified as short-term because the investments were held 1 year or less. The last two transactions above would be classified as long-term because the investments were held more than 1 year.

The capital gains and losses are computed as follows:

Transaction 1: Short-term capital loss ($4,500)

Transaction 2: Short-term capital gain $500

Transaction 3: Long-term capital gain $75,000

Transaction 4: Long-term capital loss ($1,000)

The information above indicates that there is a:

1. *Net* short-term capital loss of $4,000 (which is $4,500 minus $500).
2. *Net* long-term capital gain of $74,000 (which is $75,000 minus $1,000).
3. *Net* capital gain of $70,000 (which is $74,000 minus $4,000).

The taxable income of the taxpayer will be increased by the net capital gain ($70,000) less the capital gains deduction allowed of 50% of the excess of the net long-term capital gain over the net short-term capital loss. This excess is $70,000, or $74,000 minus $4,000. And 50% of the excess is $35,000. Therefore, the increase in taxable income as a result of all four transactions is only $35,000, which is the $70,000 net capital gain less the capital gains deduction of $35,000.

Here is another illustration that includes both a net short-term capital gain and a net long-term capital gain. The taxpayer had four transactions as follows: (1) a short-term capital gain of $1,000, (2) a short-term capital loss of $400, (3) a long-term capital gain of $10,000, and (4) a long-term capital loss of $3,000.

The transactions above would be analyzed as:

1. *Net* short-term capital gain of $600 (which is $1,000 minus $400).

2. *Net* long-term capital gain of $7,000 (which is $10,000 minus $3,000).

3. *Net* capital gain of $7,600 (which is $600 plus $7,000).

The taxable income of the taxpayer will be increased by the net capital gain ($7,600) less the capital gains deduction allowed of 50% of the excess of the long-term capital gain over the net short-term capital loss. This excess is $7,000 or $7,000 minus zero since there is no net short-term capital loss. And 50% of the excess is $3,500. Therefore, the increase in taxable income as a result of all four transactions is $4,100, which is the $7,600 net capital gain less the capital gains deduction of $3,500.

The importance of the capital gains provisions centers around the 50% deduction allowed on long-term capital gains. Taxpayers who make investments and wait at least 1 year to sell the investments are able to reduce their taxes on the capital gains by about half because of the 50% deduction allowed under the law. The capital gains provisions described apply to individuals. A similar, but different in several respects, set of rules apply to corporations.

THE TIMING OF EXPENSES

Another factor which the managers of businesses and individual taxpayers must consider in making their decisions is the timing of expenses and deductions. Income taxes often can be postponed by careful *timing* of certain transactions. Major areas that lend themselves to controlled timing are:

- *How important is the timing of expenses?*

1. Choice of depreciation methods.
2. Timing of expenses and deductions.
3. Choice of methods of computing cost of goods sold and inventories.

Choice of depreciation methods Businesses can use a variety of depreciation methods in their computation of depreciation expense. For example, any one of the following methods may be used for income tax purposes: straight-line method, sum-of-the-years'-digits method, and declining-balance method. Choosing an *accelerated* depreciation method, such as the declining-balance method, has the effect of postponing the payment of income taxes. Under an accelerated depreciation method, more depreciation expense is calculated for the early years of the asset's useful life. This greater depreciation in early years reduces the taxable income and accordingly reduces the income taxes that would be paid in the early years. Of course, less depreciation is taken in later years, thereby increasing the income taxes of those years. The net effect is to *postpone* the payment of taxes when an accelerated depreciation method is used as opposed to the straight-line method. The postponing of taxes is ordinarily highly advantageous to taxpayers. It is advantageous because the amount of assets that ordinarily would be used to pay taxes in early years can be invested in other assets, such as investments. These investments will produce revenues in the meanwhile and thus increase the net earnings.

Timing of expenses and deductions Assume that a company is considering performing some routine maintenance on its plant. This maintenance expense will amount to about $10,000. The management plans to have the work done in January of 1979. Instead, it is decided that incurring the expense in December of 1978 will serve to postpone the payment of taxes. The company's taxable income will be reduced in 1978 by $10,000 if the expense is incurred early (in December rather than in January). If the tax rate is 56% for the corporation, then taxes in 1978 will be reduced by $5,600. This $5,600 tax savings can be invested during the next year to produce additional earnings. If the expense for the maintenance is incurred in January, 1979, the $5,600 will not be available for investment.

Generally, incurring expenses in an earlier year rather than in a later year serves to postpone taxes. Likewise, an individual taxpayer can pay for some of his itemized deductions in earlier years, thereby postponing taxes. Assume an individual is considering contributing $1,000 to his church during 1979 and expects to treat the $1,000 as part of his itemized deductions in computing his taxable income. If the taxpayer makes all or part of the contribution to the church during the last part of 1978, as opposed to 1979, then the deduction for the 1978 contribution will reduce his 1978 taxes. This postponement of taxes provides the taxpayer with usable funds that he would not ordinarily have.

Choice of methods of computing cost of goods sold A company has a choice of methods for computing cost of goods sold and inventories. The common cost-flow methods (which you have already studied) are specific identification, first-in first-out, last-in first-out, and weighted average. You have also studied the lower of cost or market method of valuing inventories and cost of goods sold. Each of these methods produces its special effect on the net earnings of the firm.

The purpose behind choosing a method for *financial statement* preparation is to measure net earnings and to indicate the financial condition of the firm through the inventory amount. The purpose of a method for *income tax purposes* is to minimize or postpone the taxes. Because the purposes are different, the inventory methods need not be the same for financial statement purposes and for income tax calculation purposes.[1]

The LIFO method has been used for tax purposes by many firms because this method tends to postpone income taxes during periods in which

[1] The only exception to this according to the federal income tax laws is LIFO.

the cost of the inventories is increasing. For example, assume that the cost of a firm's inventory tends to increase month after month. The LIFO method requires that the most recent costs (higher costs) become part of cost of goods sold first. Then the older (lower) costs become part of this expense later. The overall effect is for the more recent higher costs to become expenses (cost of goods sold) in earlier periods, thereby reducing the taxable income of earlier periods.

SPECIAL TREATMENT FOR THE EXTRACTIVE INDUSTRIES

■ What special treatment is given the extractive industries?

Certain companies which extract natural resources, such as oil- and gas-producing and mining firms, are given special tax treatment. This special treatment was originally instituted because of the extra risks and uncertainty that the extractive industries have.

When a mining company prepares its income statement, one of its major expenses is the *Depletion expense.* This expense, which is similar to depreciation, is part of the *cost* of the natural resources which are being used up. The tax laws provide that such companies may compute their Depletion expense in a special manner—rather than limiting this expense to a fraction of the cost of the properties. The **depletion allowance,** which reduces taxable income on the income tax return of the company, is calculated by multiplying a fixed percent (as determined by law) by the *revenues* produced by the property.

To illustrate, assume that a small oil-producing company had revenues of $1,000,000 during the year. The tax laws have allowed that company to deduct as Depletion expense 22% of the revenues, or $220,000, although the Depletion expense based upon cost may have been only $100,000. The percentage depletion rates are different for different natural resources. For example, gravel producers have been allowed a 5% of revenues depletion deduction, while silver producers have been allowed 15%.

In recent years, the income tax laws have been changed regarding depletion allowances for oil and gas producing companies. At the present time, depletion allowances are permitted only for certain gas wells and for small oil and gas producers and royalty owners.

❯ NEW TERMS

capital asset According to the federal tax laws, any asset except business inventories, accounts and notes receivable, plant and equipment used in business, certain intangible assets, and certain short-term municipal, state, and federal notes and bonds. [p. 932]

capital gains and losses Gains and losses from assets

classified under the federal tax laws as capital assets; capital assets ordinarily include investments in stocks and bonds and other property; special treatment is given capital gains and losses under the laws, as described in the text. [p. 933]

depletion allowance A special deduction allowed certain

firms in the extractive industries in computing their taxable income; the depletion allowance is computed by multiplying a fixed percent (determined by law for the kind of natural resources concerned) by the total revenues from the operation. [p. 937]

double taxation Refers to the fact that corporations pay corporate income taxes on their earnings, and then the shareholders pay individual income taxes on the dividends that they receive from the corporation. [p. 929]

investment tax credit A provision in the federal income tax laws that allows a direct credit (reduction in taxes) against the taxes due equal to 10% of the cost of certain property purchased during the period. [p. 930]

long-term capital gain or loss A gain or loss on a capital asset that was held more that 1 year. [p. 933]

short-term capital gain or loss A gain or loss on a capital asset that was held 1 year or less. [p. 933]

> **ASSIGNMENT MATERIAL**

QUESTIONS

Q55-1. What is the purpose of the investment tax credit provision?

Q55-2. Describe how the investment tax credit is calculated.

Q55-3. Which investments produce tax-free earnings?

Q55-4. Are investments in municipal bonds generally more attractive to taxpayers with high tax rates than to taxpayers with low tax rates? Explain.

Q55-5. Define a capital asset.

Q55-6. Contrast short-term capital gains or losses with long-term capital gains or losses.

Q55-7. State how the special capital gains deduction (of 50%) is computed and applied.

Q55-8. What are three major areas that lend themselves to controlled timing?

Q55-9. In terms of the tax effects, compare the straight-line method and the declining-balance method of computing depreciation.

Q55-10. Describe how the special depletion allowance is applied in the oil- and gas-producing industry for income tax computation purposes.

EXERCISES

E55-1. Assume a company purchased a machine during the year that qualifies under the law for the investment tax credit. The machine cost $50,000, has a useful life of 10 years, with an expected scrap value of $5,000. The taxable income of the company is $100,000 for the year. Assuming that the normal tax rate is 22% and the surtax rate is 26%, compute the amount of taxes due the government for the year.

E55-2. Assume that your individual tax rate is 60%. You are considering purchasing one of the following investments:
a. Corporate bonds, costing $100,000 that will produce interest of $6,000 each year.
b. Municipal bonds, costing $100,000 that will produce interest of $3,000 each year.
Which investment would you prefer? Make an analysis similar to the table in the text.

E55-3. An individual taxpayer had the following transactions during the year dealing with capital assets:
a. Sold an investment that he had held for 13 months for $10,000 cash. The cost of the investment was $6,000.
b. Sold an investment that he had held for 4 months for $3,000 cash. The cost of the investment was $3,100.
c. Sold an investment that he had held for 3 months for $1,000 cash. The cost of the investment was $700.

REQUIRED: Compute the following:

   a. Net short-term capital gain (or loss).
   b. Net long-term capital gain (or loss).
   c. Net capital gain (or loss).
   d. What is the increase in taxable income as a result of all three transactions, after considering the 50% deduction allowed?

E55-4. Which method of computing inventory cost (FIFO, LIFO, weighted average) will result in the greatest postponement of taxes, assuming the cost of inventories is continuously rising? Explain.

E55-5. Chargeport Minerals Company is in the business of exploring for and producing oil and gas. During the year, the company produced total oil and gas revenues of $24,325,400. The oil and gas properties owned by the company had cost the company a total of $50,000,000. Operating expenses for the company (not including depletion) for the year amounted to $8,500,000. The depletion allowance rate for income tax purposes amounts to 22%.

REQUIRED: Compute the maximum depletion allowance the company could claim for federal income tax purposes.

E55-6. One of the objectives of the management of a company is to maximize net earnings. One factor in this process is to minimize the income tax costs of the firm. Prepare a report which lists the ten most important provisions (in your opinion) of the tax laws with which every businessman should be familiar. Also indicate the possible consequences of a manager's not being familiar with each provision.

PROBLEMS (GROUP A)

P55-1. *Individual and corporate income taxes.* Joe Good is an employee of Good Corporation. He is the President of the company and owns 70% of the common stock of the corporation. Joe was paid a salary for his job as President during the year amounting to $30,000.

The corporation had earnings before income taxes of $200,000 during the year and declared dividends totaling $40,000. Joe received dividends from his corporation amounting to $28,000, which is 70% of the total dividends declared. Joe has *other* taxable income totaling $15,000. His itemized deductions totaled $4,795. A joint return will be filed.

REQUIRED:

   a. Using the above information and using the tax rates in Unit 54, compute the income taxes to be paid by the corporation.
   b. Using the above information, compute the tax table income for the Goods.
   c. Assume the business is a partnership instead of a corporation. Compute the tax table income of Good for the year. Joe is to share 70% of the earnings of the partnership.

Hint: The total earnings of the partnership would be $200,000 plus $30,000 owner's salary, since payments to a partner are considered withdrawals—not expenses.

P55-2. *Individual and corporate income taxes.* Bill H. Blue, an employee of Archer Corporation, earned a salary of $18,950 during the year. His wife earned $12,043 during the year as an employee of Wilson, Incorporated. Mr. and Mrs. Blue have five children and claim them as dependents on their joint income tax return. The income of the Blues in addition to salaries includes:

Interest on bank accounts, $904

Interest on municipal bonds, $1,100

Gifts from relatives, $300

Rental income, $4,324
   (deductible expenses associated with the rental income amount to $4,000, leaving a profit of $324)

Dividends from Walker Corporation, $543

Dividends from Archer Corporation

Dividends from Wilson, Incorporated

Archer Corporation declared total dividends on common stock during the year amounting to $20,000; Wilson, Incorporated declared dividends on common stock totaling $100,000. Mr. Blue owns 25% of the common stock of Archer Corporation and 2% of the common stock of Wilson, Incorporated. Itemized deductions for Mr. and Mrs. Blue include interest paid amounting to $1,000, state and local taxes of $800, and charitable contributions of $100. Archer Corporation earned $50,000 before income taxes during the year; and Wilson, Incorporated, earned $200,000 before income taxes.

REQUIRED:

    a. For Mr. and Mrs. Blue's joint income tax return, calculate the following:
        (1) Total income.
        (2) Adjustments to income.
        (3) Excess itemized deductions.
        (4) Tax table income.
        (5) Federal income taxes.
    b. Calculate the income taxes to be paid by Archer Corporation for the year.
    c. Calculate the income taxes to be paid by Wilson, Incorporated, for the year.

P55-3. *Capital gains and losses.* Joe Verde had the following business transactions that deal with capital assets during the year:
    a. Sold an investment in ABC common stock for $204,000 on June 3, 1978. The investment had been purchased on May 1, 1970, for $185,600.
    b. Sold an investment in Carpo, Inc., preferred stock on December 30, 1978, for $3,260. The investment had been purchased on February 11, 1976, for $3,000.
    c. Sold an investment in ARC Enterprises common stock for $50,000 on December 15, 1978. The investment had been purchased on October 1, 1978, for $57,000.
    d. Purchased 100 shares of common stock of Zeeco, Inc., on December 20, 1978, for $9,000 cash.
    e. Sold an investment in Banter Bonds for $15,000 cash on April 1, 1978. The investment had been purchased March 1, 1978, for $14,000.
    f. Sold an investment in Spring Day Company common stock for $100,000 on October 15, 1978. The investment had been purchased on June 1, 1965, for $35,000.

REQUIRED: Compute the following:

a. Net short-term capital gain or loss.
b. Net long-term capital gain or loss.
c. Net capital gain or loss.
d. How much is the increase in taxable income as a result of all transactions, after considering the 50% deduction allowed?

PROBLEMS (GROUP B)

P55-4. *Individual and corporate income taxes.* Andrew Nicole, a single person, is employed by Nicole and Sons, Inc. He also owns 45% of the common stock of the company. During the year, he was paid a salary of $25,000. The corporation produced earnings before income taxes of $214,500 and declared dividends on common stock totaling $100,000. Mr. Nicole had other income totaling $12,000 and itemized deductions totaling $6,455.

REQUIRED:

a. Compute the tax table income for Mr. Nicole.
b. Compute the federal income taxes for Nicole and Sons, Inc.
c. Assume that the business is a partnership instead of a corporation. Compute the individual tax table income of Mr. Nicole, assuming he is to have 45% of the earnngs of the partnership. Remember that Mr. Nicole's salary of $25,000 would be considered a withdrawal, not an expense.

P55-5. *Individual and corporate income taxes.* Grad Council is married and has three young children. He and his wife file a joint federal income tax return each year. The Councils have interests in three businesses as follows:

10% interest in Curricula Company (a partnership).

12% interest in Winters Corporation, owning 1,200 of the 10,000 shares of common stock of the company.

20% interest in Summerco, Inc., owning 100 of the 500 shares of common stock of the company.

During the year the three companies produced earnings before income taxes as follows:

Curricula Company	$100,000
Winters Corporation	200,000
Summerco, Inc.	58,500

Mr. Council received a salary of $10,000 from each of the three companies for services rendered. The $10,000 that he received from Curricula Company is recorded as a "withdrawal" on the books of the firm. During the year, Winters Corporation declared dividends amounting to $5 per share of common stock, and Summerco, Inc. declared common dividends of $10 per share. Income of the Councils other than that mentioned included:

Interest on bank accounts, $1,000
Gifts from friend, $5,000

Interest income (from loan to business associate), $3,000

Itemized deductions for Mr. and Mrs. Council total $1,875.

REQUIRED:

a. Compute the tax table income for the Councils.

b. Compute the income taxes to be paid by Winters Corporation for the year.

c. Calculate the income taxes to be paid by Summerco, Inc., for the year.

P55-6. *Depletion allowance; income statement and tax return.* The Resources Corporation purchased certain oil and gas properties for $3,000,000 several years ago. During 1978 the company extracted oil and gas as indicated by the following income statements:

Resources Corporation
INCOME STATEMENT
For the Year Ended December 31, 1978

Revenues from oil and gas production		$9,000,000
Miscellaneous revenues		200,000
Total		$9,200,000
Depletion allowance (22%)	$1,980,000	
Other costs and expenses	6,000,000	
Total		7,980,000
		$1,220,000
Federal income taxes		579,100
Net earnings		$ 640,900
Earnings per share of common stock		$6.41

Resources Corporation
INCOME STATEMENT
For the Year Ended December 31, 1978

Revenues from oil and gas production		$9,000,000
Miscellaneous revenues		200,000
Total		$9,200,000
Depletion expense	$ 750,000	
Other costs and expenses	6,000,000	
Total		6,750,000
Net earnings before income taxes		$2,450,000
Federal income taxes		579,100
Net earnings		$1,870,900
Earnings per share of common stock		$18.71

REQUIRED:

a. Which of the two income statements should be included in the annual report of the firm?

b. Explain the difference in the two statements. Is one of the statements misleading and incorrect?

*P55-7. *Cumulative review problem.* Val Baldini, Ed Farbes, and B. Herman plan to form a business to manufacture and sell a product recently invented by Baldini. The taxable earnings of the new firm are expected to be about $100,000 per year for each of the first five years. The three promoters of the business would share equally in the earnings. Each of the three men has other income. Baldini is convinced that the group should form a partnership. On the other hand, Farbes and Herman indicate that the only form of organization they will consider is the corporation. Herman is especially interested in determining the dividend policy of the corporation before the company is organized. As their accountant, you have been called on to prepare a report that sets forth the consequences of choosing a form of business organization. Be specific in indicating precisely how one form of organization may be preferable to one of the men, while another form would be better for another.

*P55-8. *Cumulative review problem.* Atchafalaya and Company, in a plant expansion program, recently spent $2,000,000 for new equipment. The accountant for the company advised the management before the expenditure was made that a 10% investment tax credit would be allowed. That is, the tax bill of the company for this year would be reduced by 10% of the $2,000,000 expenditure, $200,000. You investigate the matter and determine that two methods of reporting this transaction on the company's financial statements are acceptable:

Method 1
Reflect the asset on the balance sheet at $2,000,000, the amount paid for the asset. Reflect the Income tax expense at the actual amount paid for the year.

Method 2
Reflect the asset at the net cost, $1,800,00, the net outlay for the equipment. This is the $2,000,000 spent for the equipment, less the $200,000 refund or subsidy allowed by the government to help stimulate the economy. Reflect the Income tax expense this year at the amount of the tax liability before considering the investment tax credit. The $200,000 is reported on the balance sheet as a liability, which will be written off and will reduce future income tax expense, because the real reduction in Income tax expense comes in future years when the equipment actually helps produce revenues and not when the equipment happened to be purchased.

REQUIRED: Comment in detail on the implications of the two treatments for users of the balance sheet and income statement.

appendix a

reversing entries

56

REVERSING ENTRIES

❯ OBJECTIVE

This unit explains the accounting procedure called reversing entries. Reversing entries are accounting entries that are made at the beginning of every accounting period by some firms to prepare the way for recording other entries later in the period. This unit will tell why this optional procedure is useful to some companies and why some companies do not use reversing entries at all.

❯ APPROACH TO ATTAINING THE OBJECTIVE

As you study about reversing entries, pay special attention to these three questions, which the text following answers:

- *What are reversing entries?*
- *Why are reversing entries optional?*
- *What are the four basic kinds of adjusting entries that can be reversed?*

Reversing entries are accounting entries that are made at the *beginning* of an accounting period, before the regular business transactions are recorded. These reversing entries are simply the same as certain adjusting entries that were made at the end of the previous period—*except that they are reversed.* For example, assume that at December 31, 1977, this adjusting entry was made:

| 1977 Dec. | 31 | Salaries expense | | 500 | |
| | | Salaries payable | | | 500 |

The $500 is the amount of salaries owed employees for the last few days of the year—for work since the last payroll in December. Remember that the Salaries expense account would be closed out at December 31, but the Salaries payable (liability) would be carried forward to 1978.

If the next payroll is January 10, 1978, for $1,200, then this entry could be made:

1978 Jan.	10	Salaries payable		500	
		Salaries expense		700	
		Cash (Taxes withheld, etc.)			1,200
		January 10 payroll.			

To make the entry above, the bookkeeper had to remember that $500 of the January 10 payroll was for December salaries and that the liability account (Salaries payable) had to be reduced.

The example above assumed that the company *did not* use reversing entries. Now, look at the journal of a firm that *does* use the reversing procedure:

1977 Dec.	31	Salaries expense		500	
		Salaries payable			500
		Adjustment for accrued salaries at end of 1977.			

—Closing entries also made at December 31, 1977—

1978 Jan.	1	Salaries payable		500	
		Salaries expense			500
		To reverse adjustment for accrued salaries.			
	10	Salaries expense		1,200	
		Cash (Taxes withheld, etc.)			1,200
		January 10 payroll.			

A closer look below at the Salaries expense and Salaries payable ledger accounts shows the effect of reversing entries. To simplify, it is assumed that 1977 salaries, before the adjustment at December 31, amounted to $10,700.

Salaries expense   ACCOUNT NO. 510

DATE	DESCRIPTION	REF.	DEBITS	CREDITS	BALANCE DEBIT	BALANCE CREDIT
1977 Dec. 31	Balance (year)				10 700 00	
31	Adjustment	G10	500 00		11 200 00	
31	Closing	G11		11 200 00	-0-	
1978 Jan. 1	Reversal	G12		500 00		500 00
10	Payroll	G15	1 200 00		700 00	

Salaries payable   ACCOUNT NO. 225

DATE	DESCRIPTION	REF.	DEBITS	CREDITS	BALANCE DEBIT	BALANCE CREDIT
1977 Dec. 31	Adjustment	G10		500 00		500 00
1978 Jan. 1	Reversal	G12	500 00			-0-

The adjustment brought 1977 Salaries expense to a balance of $11,200. This amount was closed out at the end of 1977. The reversing entry at January 1 set up a credit balance in the Salaries expense account of $500. Finally, the January 10 payroll entry of $1,200 brought the Salaries expense account balance up to $700, the actual 1978 salary expense. The reversing entry simply allows the bookkeeping department to debit salaries expense for *all payrolls,* without considering previous accruals.

Now, observe the Salaries payable account. The adjusting entry sets up a credit balance of $500. The subsequent reversal clears the balance of this account automatically, so the bookkeeper does not have to remember to clear it later.

OPTIONAL NATURE OF REVERSING ENTRIES

■ *Why are reversing entries optional?*

The example above showed two ways to accomplish the same objective. In the first situation illustrated, no reversing entry was made. In that case, the bookkeeper had to remember to debit the Salaries payable account for $500 when the January 10 payroll was recorded. In the other case, when a reversing entry had been made on January 1, the bookkeeping department did not have to remember to debit a liability. Instead, the Salaries expense account could be routinely debited for all payrolls—including the first one of the year.

From this situation we can say that reversing entries are optional. Those companies that use them find that it simplifies the recording of subsequent transactions. This unit will now explain the four basic kinds of adjusting entries that can be reversed.

KINDS OF ADJUSTMENTS THAT NEED REVERSING

- *What are the four basic kinds of adjusting entries that can be reversed?*

Basically, there are four kinds of *adjusting* entries that need to be reversed. These are:

1. Accrued expenses.
2. Prepaid expenses, when an *expense* account had been debited upon paying for the expense.
3. Accrued revenues.
4. Unearned revenues, when a *revenue* account had been credited upon collecting the cash.

An example of each will now be shown.

The reversing entry for accrued expenses The previous illustration of salaries was such an example. For review, let's take a similar one.

1977					
March	15	Equipment rent expense		575	
		Cash			575
		Cash payment for equipment 1977 rentals.			
Oct.	19	Equipment rent expense		615	
		Cash			615
		Cash payment for 1977 rentals.			
Dec.	31	Equipment rent expense		300	
		Equipment rent payable			300
		Adjustment for rent owed at end of 1977.			

—1977 CLOSING ENTRIES MADE HERE—

1978					
Jan.	1	Equipment rent payable		300	
		Equipment rent expense			300
		Reversing entry.			
March	6	Equipment rent expense		950	
		Cash			950
		Cash payment for rent, including $300 of 1977 rent and $650 of 1978 rent.			

Study the preceding entries carefully. Observe that the Equipment rent expense account will show a debit balance of $1,490 for 1977. The 1978 balance of Equipment rent expense, as of March 6, is $650.

The reversing entry for prepaid expenses In your study of adjustments in Unit 15 you learned that when an expense is paid (such as for supplies), *either* an asset account or an expense account could be debited.

When the expense account had originally been debited, a reversing entry is needed. When the asset (Prepaid expense) account had been debited, a reversing entry is not needed.

Here is an example:

	COMPANY A ASSET ORIGINALLY DEBITED			COMPANY B EXPENSE ORIGINALLY DEBITED		
1977						
May 4	Supplies	1,000		Supplies expense	1,000	
	Cash		1,000	Cash		1,000
	Purchased supplies.			Purchased supplies.		
Dec. 31	Supplies expense	800		Supplies	200	
	Supplies		800	Supplies expense		200
	Adjustment for $800 of supplies used, and $200 on hand.			Adjustment for $800 of supplies used, and $200 on hand.		

—CLOSING ENTRIES MADE HERE—

	COMPANY A ASSET ORIGINALLY DEBITED			COMPANY B EXPENSE ORIGINALLY DEBITED		
1978						
Jan. 1	No reversing entry needed.			Supplies expense	200	
				Supplies		200
				Reversal of adjustment.		
Feb. 12	Supplies	300		Supplies expense	300	
	Cash		300	Cash		300
	Purchased supplies.			Purchased supplies.		

This illustration shows that Company A records its supplies in an *asset* account during the year and transfers the used portion to an expense through an adjustment. No reversing entry is needed because the $200 is already in the asset account to begin the next year.

Company B, on the other hand, keeps its supplies cost in an *expense* account during the year, and sets up an asset at the end of the year for the unused portion ($200). The reversing entry is needed to transfer the $200 from the asset account to the *expense* account (which is used to record supplies throughout the year).

Reversing entry for accrued revenues We will use the case of interest to show how reversing entries are made for accrued revenues.

1977					
Oct.	1	Notes receivable		10,000	
		Cash			10,000
		Lent a customer $10,000 cash on a 6%, 4-month note.			
Dec.	31	Interest receivable		150	
		Interest income			150
		Adjustment for accrued revenue ($10,000 × 6% × 3/12 = $150) for 3 months.			

—CLOSING ENTRIES MADE HERE—

1978					
Jan.	1	Interest income		150	
		Interest receivable			150
		Reversing entry			
Feb.	1	Cash		10,200	
		Notes receivable			10,000
		Interest income			200
		Collection of note and interest.			

The adjustment at December 31, 1978, serves to report interest income of $150 during 1978 (3 months). The reversing entry in 1978 sets up a debit balance of $150 in the Interest income account and closes out the Interest receivable account. When the $200 is credited to the Interest income account on February 1, the balance of the Interest income changes from the debit balance of $150 to a credit balance of $50. The amount of interest earned during 1978 is $50, or 1 month's interest.

Reversing entry for unearned revenues In your study of adjustments in Unit 15, you learned that when a revenue is collected (such as Fees income) either a liability or a revenue account could be credited.

When the revenue account had originally been credited, a reversing entry is needed. When the liability account (Unearned fees) had been credited, a reversing entry is not needed.

Here is an example:

	COMPANY A LIABILITY ORIGINALLY CREDITED			COMPANY B REVENUE ORIGINALLY CREDITED		
1977						
June 12	Cash	50,000		Cash	50,000	
	Unearned fees		50,000	Fees income		50,000
	Collected			Collected		
	fees.			fees.		
Dec. 31	Unearned fees	40,000		Fees income	10,000	
	Fees income		40,000	Unearned fees		10,000
	Adjustment			Adjustment		
	to record			to record		
	$40,000 of			$40,000 of		
	fees earned,			fees earned,		
	leaving			leaving		
	$10,000			$10,000		
	unearned.			unearned.		

—CLOSING ENTRIES MADE HERE—

	COMPANY A LIABILITY ORIGINALLY CREDITED			COMPANY B REVENUE ORIGINALLY CREDITED		
1978						
Jan. 1	No reversing			Unearned fees	10,000	
	entry needed.			Fees income		10,000
				Reversal of		
				adjustment.		
Mar. 8	Cash	31,000		Cash	31,000	
	Unearned fees		31,000	Fees income		31,000
	Collected			Collected		
	fees.			fees.		

This illustration shows that Company A records its fees in a *liability* account during the year and transfers the earned portion to a revenue account through an adjustment. No reversing entry is needed because the $10,000 is already in the liability account to begin the next year.

Company B, on the other hand, keeps its fees in a *revenue* account during the year and sets up a liability at the end of the year for the unearned portion ($10,000). The reversing entry is needed to transfer the $10,000 from the liability account to the *revenue* account (which is used to record the fees throughout the year).

OTHER ADJUSTMENTS Adjustments other than those previously discussed in this unit ordinarily do not require reversing entries. In summary, the following table indicates which adjusting entries would be reversed when a firm uses reversing entries:

		reversing entry needed	
ADJUSTING ENTRY		*YES*	*NO*
1. Accrued expenses adjustment		✔	
2. Accrued revenues adjustment		✔	
3. Prepaid expenses adjustment when the original debit was to an asset account			✔
4. Prepaid expenses adjustment when the original debit was to an expense account		✔	
5. Unearned revenue adjustment when the original credit was to a liability account			✔
6. Unearned revenue adjustment when the original credit was to a revenue account		✔	
7. Bad debts adjustment			✔
8. Depreciation adjustment			✔
9. Merchandise inventory adjustment			✔

» NEW TERM

reversing entries Optional accounting entries made at the *beginning* of an accounting period. Reversing entries are simply the reverse of certain adjusting entries to make the work of the bookkeeper easier in recording subsequent transactions. [p. 946]

» ASSIGNMENT MATERIAL

QUESTIONS

Q56-1. When are reversing entries made?

Q56-2. What is meant by the statement that reversing entries are optional?

Q56-3. List the four basic kinds of adjusting entries that should be reversed when the company prepares its reversing entries.

Q56-4. List five basic kinds of adjusting entries that should not be reversed when a company prepares its reversing entries.

Q56-5. In what way does the use of reversing entries make the work of the bookkeeper easier?

EXERCISES

E56-1. At December 31, 1977, before adjusting entries were made, the Salary expense account of a company showed a balance of $5,167. It is determined that salaries owed employees for the last few days of the year amount to $432. On January 8, 1978, the first payroll for the year was prepared and it totaled $875, including the $432 owed from the previous year.

a. Prepare the adjusting journal entry at December 31, 1977.

b. Prepare the reversing entry if one is needed at January 1, 1978.

c. What is the balance of the Salary expense account at January 8, 1978, after all postings are made?

d. What is the balance of the Salaries payable account at January 8, 1978, after all postings are made?

E56-2. Refer to E15-1 (Unit 15). Assume the company follows the procedure of making reversing entries each year. Prepare the necessary reversing entries at January 1, 1979.

E56-3. Refer to E15-2 (Unit 15). Assume that the company follows the procedure of making closing entries and reversing entries monthly. Using the data given, and assuming the firm originally debits all rent payments to the *expense* account,

a. Prepare the adjusting entry at May 31.

b. Prepare the reversing entry (if needed) at June 1.

c. Prepare the entry to record payment on June 3.

d. Prepare the adjusting entry (if needed) at June 30.

PROBLEMS (GROUP A)

P56-1. *Reversing entries.* Using the data in P15-1 (Unit 15) and assuming the firm prepares reversing entries where appropriate, prepare the reversing entries needed at January 1, 1979.

P56-2. *Reversing entries.* Using the data in P15-2 (Unit 15) and assuming the firm prepares reversing entries where appropriate, prepare the reversing entries needed at January 1, 1979.

P56-3. *Adjusting and reversing entries.* Consider the information for adjustments below. Each case is independent from the other cases.

1. At December 31, 1978, before adjustments, the Prepaid insurance account shows a balance of $6,000. This represents 30 months of insurance coverage beginning January 1, 1978.

2. The company has earned rent of $2,000. This amount is both uncollected and unrecorded at December 31, 1978.

3. The beginning inventory amounted to $10,000 and the ending inventory cost is $15,000.

4. The firm estimates bad debts to be 1% of credit sales. Total sales are $174,000, of which $110,000 were made on credit.

5. Unearned subscriptions showed a balance of $12,000 at the end of 1978. The actual amount still unearned at December 31, 1978, was $8,000.

6. The Supplies account had a balance of $3,000 at December 31, 1978. The supplies on hand at December 31, 1978, amounted to $1,000.

7. The Insurance expense account had a balance of $3,000 at December 31, 1978. This represents payment for a 30-month policy, beginning on January 1, 1978.

8. The Supplies expense account showed a balance of $800 at December 31, 1978. Supplies used during 1978 totaled $700.

9. The Equipment account had a balance of $20,000 at December 31, 1978. At that same date, the Accumulated depreciation—Equipment totaled $9,000. Expense for this year totals $1,000.

10. The Subscriptions revenue account had an unadjusted balance of $5,000 at December 31, 1978. Of this amount $3,000 has been earned.

11. The Subscriptions revenue account had an unadjusted balance of $8,000 at December 31, 1978. Of this amount, $4,200 is still unearned.

12. Income taxes owed but unpaid and unrecorded at December 31, 1978, total $20,000.
13. Accrued salaries at December 31, 1978, are $9,000.

REQUIRED:

    a. Prepare adjusting entries for each of the independent cases.
    b. Prepare reversing entries where appropriate.

PROBLEMS (GROUP B)

P56-4. *Adjusting and reversing entries.* Listed below are data for adjustments at December 31, 1978. Each case is considered independent from the others.

1. Subscriptions revenue has a credit balance of $6,000. The unearned portion of this balance is $1,000.
2. The Supplies expense account has a debit balance of $800. Supplies on hand at December 31 total $500.
3. Rent earned but uncollected and unrecorded at the year end totals $4,000.
4. The Unearned subscriptions revenue account has an unadjusted credit balance of $7,000. The actual unearned amount at December 31 is $5,500.
5. The Supplies account has a balance of $4,000. Supplies on hand amount to $3,000.
6. The Insurance expense account has a $4,000 balance. This was for a 20-month policy effective on January 1, 1978.
7. Income taxes incurred but unrecorded total $5,675.
8. The Subscriptions revenue account has a balance of $5,470, of which $500 has been earned.
9. Merchandise inventory at January 1, 1978, was $5,000, and the ending inventory was $4,500.
10. Depreciation expense for the year on the buildings was calculated to be $15,400.
11. Credit sales of merchandise amounting to $700,000 were made in 1978. Bad debt losses are estimated by management to be $\frac{1}{2}$ of 1% of credit sales.
12. Prepaid insurance has a balance at the end of the year of $3,600. This represents payment for a 3-year policy effective March 1, 1978.

REQUIRED:

    a. Prepare adjusting entries for each of the independent cases.
    b. Prepare reversing entries where appropriate.

P56-5. *Reversing entries.* Using the data in P15-6 (Unit 15) and assuming the firm prepares reversing entries where appropriate, prepare the reversing entries needed at January 1, 1979.

P56-6. *Adjusting and reversing entries.* On pages 955 and 956 are presented data for adjustments for several independent cases for the end of a year's operations.

REQUIRED:

    a. Prepare adjusting journal entries.
    b. Prepare reversing entries where appropriate.

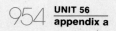

	BALANCE OF LEDGER ACCOUNT AT DECEMBER 31, 1978	OTHER DATA
1. Supplies Supplies expense	$900 –0–	Supplies on hand at December 31, 1978, $200
2. Supplies Supplies expense	–0– $700	Supplies on hand at December 31, 1978, $200
3. Supplies Supplies expense	$500 –0–	Supplies used during 1978, $300
4. Supplies Supplies expense	–0– $1,000	Supplies used during 1978, $900
5. Salaries expense Salaries payable	$7,000 –0–	Salaries owed at December 31, 1978, $1,000
6. Income tax expense Income tax payable	$8,000 1,000	During the year $8,000 of taxes were paid, including $1,000 of 1977 taxes and $7,000 of this year's taxes. Income taxes owed at December 31, 1978, amount to $4,200

7. Bad debts expense
   Accounts receivable
   Sales made on credit
   Allowance for bad debts
	–0–
	$ 10,000
	100,000
	300
		Credit losses are estimated to be $\frac{1}{4}$ of 1% of sales made on credit

8. Equipment
   Accumulated depreciation—Equipment
   Depreciation expense—Equipment
	$60,000
	10,000
	–0–
		Depreciation expense for 1978 is $1,000

9. Unearned service revenue Service revenue	$50,000 –0–	Service revenue earned during 1978, $10,000
10. Unearned service revenue Service revenue	$70,000 –0–	Service revenue unearned at December 31, 1978, $8,000
11. Unearned service revenue Service revenue	–0– $100,000	Service revenue earned during 1978, $85,000

	BALANCE OF LEDGER ACCOUNT AT DECEMBER 31, 1978	OTHER DATA
12. Unearned service revenue Service revenue	–0– $80,000	Service revenue unearned at December 31, 1978, $8,000
13. Interest receivable Interest income Notes receivable	–0– $ 6,000 200,000	Interest earned but not yet recorded, $3,000
14. Merchandise inventory	$20,000	Merchandise inventory at December 31, 1978, amounts to $18,000

CUMULATIVE REVIEW PROBLEMS

P56-7. *Cumulative review problem (related to P56-8).* Below are presented (1) a trial balance at January 1, 1978, the beginning of a year's operations, (2) summary transactions for 1978, and (3) data for adjustments. Some transactions were not accounted for consistently during the year; therefore, special care should be given when analyzing adjustments.

Beisbol Corporation
TRIAL BALANCE
January 1, 1978

Cash	30,000	
Accounts receivable	10,000	
Allowance for uncollectibles		300
Other receivables	–0–	
Merchandise inventory	20,000	
Prepaid insurance	2,000	
Prepaid rent	1,600	
Supplies	2,000	
Equipment	31,000	
Accumulated depreciation—Equipment		11,000
Accounts payable		5,000
Other payables		–0–
Unearned service revenue		–0–
Notes payable		–0–
Capital stock		50,000
Retained earnings		30,300
Service revenue		–0–
Sales		–0–
Purchases	–0–	
Purchases returns and allowances		–0–
Transportation on purchases	–0–	
Bad debts expense	–0–	
Depreciation expense—Equipment	–0–	
Insurance expense	–0–	
Operating expenses	–0–	
Rent expense	–0–	
Supplies expense	–0–	
Interest expense	–0–	
	96,600	96,600

Business transactions for 1978 in summary form:

1. Sales for the year on credit $80,000; for cash $15,000.
2. Merchandise purchases on credit, $55,000.
3. Paid transportation on purchases, $1,000.
4. Collected service revenue, $5,000 (use the *liability* account).
5. Returned $2,000 of defective merchandise to suppliers and received credit on our account.
6. Paid cash for operating expenses, $6,000.
7. Collected $67,000 cash from customers in payment of their accounts.
8. Paid $8,000 for rent, debiting the *expense* account. This is for 20 months, beginning May 1, 1978.
9. Paid accounts payable totaling $57,000 cash.
10. Borrowed $10,000 from First National Bank, signing a 90-day, 10% note on December 1, 1978.
11. Paid $3,600 for an 18-month insurance policy, debiting the *expense* account. The policy is effective August 1, 1978.
12. Bought supplies for $3,000 cash, debiting the *asset* account.

Information for adjustments:

a. Operating expenses owed but unrecorded at December 31, 1978, amount to $500.
b. Earned $2,000 of the service revenue during the year that was collected in advance.
c. Recorded interest expense on the note. Round to nearest dollar.
d. Recorded depreciation expense, $2,000.
e. Recorded additional accrued service revenue, $500.
f. The ending inventory amounted to $35,000.
g. Supplies on hand amounted to $500.
h. Bad debts are estimated to be $\frac{1}{2}$ of 1% of credit sales.
i. The beginning balance of Prepaid insurance of $2,000 represents 20 months of insurance, beginning January 1, 1978. Also refer to transaction 11.
j. The beginning balance of Prepaid rent ($1,600) represented four months rent beginning January 1, 1978. Also refer to transaction 8.

REQUIRED:

a. Record the year's transactions in *general* journal form.
b. Record adjusting entries in general journal form.

P56-8. *Cumulative review problem (related to P56-7).* Refer to P56-7.

REQUIRED:

a. Set up "T"-type accounts for all the accounts in the trial balance of the company. Enter the beginning balances.
b. Record the year's transactions *directly* in the "T" accounts. Compute the ending balance of each account.
c. Prepare a work sheet for the company, using the data given.
d. Prepare closing entries in general journal form.

appendix b

systems fundamentals and automated data processing

57

SYSTEMS FUNDAMENTALS AND AUTOMATED DATA PROCESSING

> ### OBJECTIVE

So far you have studied the accounting operation from the reference point of (1) the business transaction serving as the input into the system, (2) the manual journal and ledger as the processing mechanism, and (3) the financial statements as the output of the system to be used in business decisions. It is now time for you to take a broader view of this whole process of generating and using information for decisions. The purpose of this unit is to introduce you to fundamental concepts in the area of systems, to relate these concepts to what you have already studied, and to point the way for further study of accounting activities and uses.

This unit also will give you an overview of the more complex machine- and computer-based information and accounting systems now in operation. After you have read this description you should be able to put into perspective the manual system you have already studied.

> ### APPROACH TO ATTAINING THE OBJECTIVE

As you study about systems, direct your attention to these six questions, which the text following answers:

- *What is a system?*
- *What are the characteristics of an information system?*
- *What kinds of systems are involved with accounting?*
- *What elements are common to all information systems?*
- *How are data selected and entered into the system?*
- *How does the computer process the data and prepare the output?*

DEFINITION OF A SYSTEM

- *What is a system?*

In its simplest form a **system** can be defined as a set of components or elements which are put together in a particular way to attain a goal. Determining what the goals are to be for an activity, identifying the elements of the system, and determining how the elements are to be combined to provide a workable system are challenges that man faces continuously. For example, in your study of the manual accounting operation for a service firm, you have already analyzed one kind of system. The output of manual accounting (a kind of *information* system) was the information about the earnings and financial position of a firm—the income statement and balance sheet. The elements of that system included the people involved, the general journal, the ledger and accounts, the source documents, the financial statements, and a number of other components and relationships. Other examples of systems are traffic-control systems, manufacturing systems, and food preparation systems.

DESCRIPTION OF AN INFORMATION SYSTEM

- *What are the characteristics of an information system?*

As just mentioned, there are many kinds of systems, each with its own kind of output. The accountant, however, is mostly concerned with one kind of output—information for decisions. Therefore, he is concerned with **information systems.** Let's examine three fundamental points about information systems.

First, since there is an almost unlimited amount of information that might be related to a group of decisions, the accountant must select only that information which is relevant to the decision to be made. In the accounting system you have already studied, the business transaction was identified as the relevant input for that system.

Second, the cost of providing the information must be considered. That is, for an information system to function effectively, its users must be able to relate the cost of providing a certain kind of information to the benefit received from the information in the form of improved decisions.

Third, the fact that human beings are involved in the functioning of information systems must not be ignored. Information of various kinds and in various forms very definitely affects human behavior: it affects people's motivations and thus, in turn, has an impact on society. Because of these effects the accuracy and soundness of information systems in our society become highly important.

FORMS OF INFORMATION SYSTEMS

There are at least three general forms of information systems operating in business firms today. These are (1) systems using completely manual handwritten journals and ledgers, (2) systems using mechanical and electrically operated machines in place of handwritten journals and ledgers, including

■ *What kinds of systems are involved with accounting?*

punched-card equipment, and (3) systems using electronic computers. Let us look at each of these systems in turn.

Manual systems The manual accounting system for a service firm which you studied involved a two-column journal for recording all business transactions. This system effectively communicated to you the basic ideas about financial accounting. In actual business firms, however, this exact form of journal and ledger is rarely used. The reason for this is that in businesses the number of transactions to be recorded each accounting period might be in the hundreds or thousands. It would be just too expensive and time-consuming to record each of the many hundreds of transactions in that way.

As an improvement on the system you studied, a series of *special journals and ledgers* can be developed. These special journals and ledgers can process more efficiently the many business transactions a firm might have each month. In other words, a firm might use several journals, instead of just one general journal, to record its transactions. Each journal would be used to record a special kind or group of transactions. Special-purpose ledgers could be set up as well.

Electrically operated machine systems As a business firm grows and as its operations become more complex, it soon becomes apparent that a handwritten accounting system cannot rapidly and accurately process the vast quantities of data needed for decisions inside and outside the firm. Most firms turn to machines to help perform the function of data processing. There are countless types of machines designed to perform more or less automatically the function performed by the journal and ledger in a manual system. The important point to remember is that each transaction still must be analyzed in terms of its effect on the accounts before it is entered into the system, whether the system is a manual or machine-assisted one.

Electronic computer-based systems A third, and most advanced, kind of information system centers around an electronic computer. The electronic computer has the important advantages of speed, accuracy, and flexibility. The potential of the electronic computer is so vast in terms of information processing that computer-based information systems can be designed which combine the functions of providing information for a wide variety of decisions both inside and outside the firm. For example, the manual system you have studied was generally limited to financial accounting information in the form of the balance sheet and the income statement. But computer-based systems are often designed which are broad enough to accomodate financial accounting, managerial accounting, income tax accounting and records, forecasting, and many other decision uses.

All information systems—from the smallest manual bookkeeping system to the most complex information system of a giant corporation—have certain common elements. These elements are shown in Illustration 57-1. In the following sections each of these elements is explained and related to manual and computer operations.

ILLUSTRATION 57-1

■ *What elements are
common to all
information systems?*

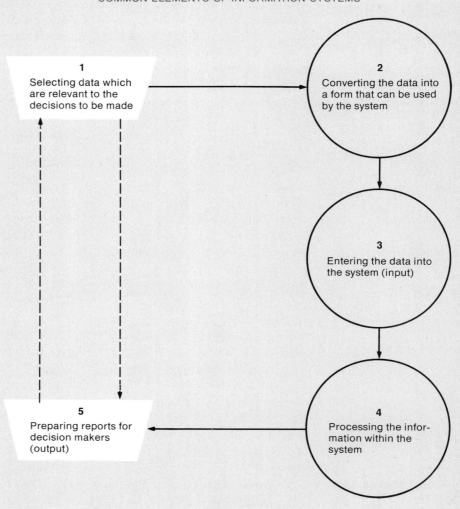

COMMON ELEMENTS OF INFORMATION SYSTEMS

1 Selecting data which are relevant to the decisions to be made

2 Converting the data into a form that can be used by the system

3 Entering the data into the system (input)

4 Processing the infor-mation within the system

5 Preparing reports for decision makers (output)

**DATA SELECTION
AND INPUT**

The first step in providing information to decision makers is to select data that are related to the decisions to be made and that can be converted into information that will lead to better decisions. Correctly selected data will

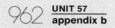

improve the likelihood that the decisions made are the right decisions, based upon the objectives of the decision maker.

■ How are data selected and entered into the system?

Illustration 57-1 shows dashed lines between *selecting data* and *preparing reports.* These lines are meant to emphasize the fact that knowing what kind of data to select depends on the kind of decisions to be made. The input data and the output reports must be viewed as part of the same function, information for decisions. *One cannot be determined without reference to the other.*

Source documents Some orderly procedure must be established if all relevant data are to be identified and entered into an information system. In the case of financial accounting systems, the first written evidence of relevant data is called a **source document.** The business transaction is the economic event that becomes the input for financial accounting systems, and the source document is the written evidence that a business transaction has taken place. Because there are many kinds of business transactions (payment of expenses and collection of revenues, for example), there are many kinds of source documents.

Shown in Illustrations 57-2 and 57-3 are two examples of common source documents that provide a first written record of a business transaction. The **invoice** is the source document commonly used to provide detailed information about a sale of goods or services. The **purchase order** is the source document commonly used to provide detailed information about goods or services ordered by a firm. Information from source documents such as these becomes part of the accounting system.

Our previous examples dealt with a financial accounting system in which business transaction information was the basic input. *Remember that some information systems are broader in scope than financial accounting; the data selected for input therefore may include many other things beside business transactions.* For example, information about economic conditions, detailed data concerning running a factory, and detailed data about the sales force of a firm might become part of the input.

Input procedures The variety of machines used in modern accounting and data processing systems is almost limitless. There also are a great many ways that machines are built to receive data for processing. For example, an electric adding machine uses a keyboard in the input process. Each time the "8" key is depressed, the quantity (eight) is entered into the machine. If you were to add up a group of business transactions, then the information from the source documents would be changed into a different form (through the keyboard of the adding machine) for use by the machine.

With many thousands of transactions and other items to enter into an accounting system, a machine with more advantages than an adding machine must be used. Among the input devices that have been developed

INVOICE

Telephone 834-9485

epc   *Esquire Printing Company*
INCORPORATED

3847 AIRLINE HIGHWAY / METAIRIE, LOUISIANA 70001

Sold To:

JOB NUMBER	YOUR ORDER NUMBER	DATE DELIVERED	INVOICE DATE

QUANTITY	DESCRIPTION	AMOUNT

RECEIVED BY		SALES TAX
		TOTAL

ILLUSTRATION 57-2 AN INVOICE.

for more advanced machines are *punched cards, punched paper tapes,* and *magnetic tapes.*

A commonly used kind of **punched card** is shown in Illustration 57-4. Remember that the punched card is simply an input device for a machine. Information can be placed in the card in a form that can be used by a specially built machine, much as the adding machine can use information entered into it via its keyboard. The first step is that information from source documents (both alphabetic and numeric information) is punched into the card. A machine called a **keypunch machine,** with a keyboard similar to that of a typewriter, and with a human operator, types (punches) the holes in the cards. Notice in the punched card shown in Illustration 57-4 that the nu-

PURCHASE ORDER

Telephone 834-9485

P. O. NO. _____

INVOICES AND PACKING LIST
MUST SHOW P. O. NUMBER

Esquire Printing Company
INCORPORATED

TERMS: _____

3847 AIRLINE HIGHWAY / METAIRIE, LOUISIANA 70001

TO: _____

Date of Order: _____

_____

Freight Terms: _____

_____

Cancel Date: _____

QUANTITY	DESCRIPTION	UNIT PRICE	AMOUNT	CHARGE TO

_____ Ordered By

ILLUSTRATION 57-3   A PURCHASE ORDER.

ILLUSTRATION 57-4

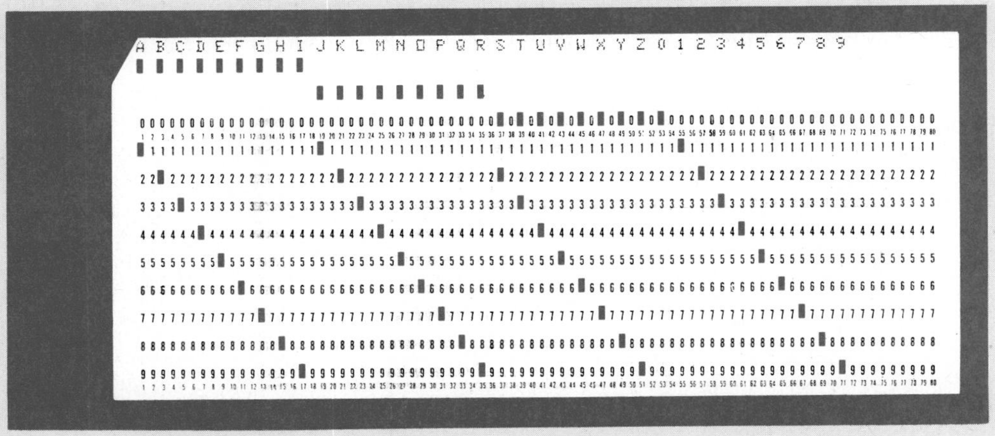

meric information is represented by one hole in a column, while the alphabetic information is represented by two holes in a column. The keypunch machine automatically punches holes in the correct columns when the keys of its keyboard are depressed. The locations of the holes in the rows and columns of the card represent the information to be used by another data processing machine.

This second machine, whether it be an electronic computer or some other machine, is constructed so that it can "read" the information from the punched cards fed into it. This "reading" process can be compared again to an adding machine. Running a card with holes in it through a machine is very much like depressing keys on a keyboard. When the adding machine keys are depressed, the information is entered into the wheels and other internal mechanisms of the adding machine. The computer or other machine can sense (through electric circuits) where the holes are located on the cards and can enter that information internally.

An important fact about punched cards as input devices is that they can enter much greater quantities of information into a system than manual methods—and in much less time. Also, once information is punched into cards, the cards can be stored in convenient form for later use.

Punched paper tapes are also used as input devices in modern machines. The same principle applies as is used in punched cards, except that holes are punched in *channels* along a continuous length of tape to represent the numeric and alphabetic information. The tape was developed to improve the speed of input; a continuous length of punched paper tape can be fed into a machine quite rapidly.

Magnetic tapes have come into widespread use in recent years in connection with electronic computer applications. Even greater quantities of information can be stored in a small space on the magnetic tape, which is usually a metal-coated plastic material. The magnetic tape does not use holes to represent information; instead, tiny magnetic spots on the tape, according to their positions, represent the information. Special machines are built to sense and "read" the location of the magnetic spots.

In addition to keyboards, punched cards, punched paper tapes, and magnetic tapes, a number of other input devices are used. Often a specially built input device will serve a firm's needs. For example, many department stores have set up direct connections between the cash registers in their store and an electronic computer. As sales are made in the store, the information is automatically entered into the accounting system. In this case, the keyboard of the cash register serves as the input to the computer.

INTERNAL PROCESSING AND OUTPUT

Because you are already familiar with a manual accounting operation, the other widely used system will be described here: the electronic computer system.

Electronic computer system **Electronic computers** differ from other machines in that the calculations are made through the use of electronic circuits, rather than through the movement of wheels and levers as in some adding machines and calculators. Since there are no moving parts in the calculation process, the arithmetic is performed almost at the speed of light. Electronic computers came into commercial use during the 1950s, and today they are common in business organizations. Electronic computers can be built to accomodate a wide variety of input devices, including punched cards, punched paper tapes, and magnetic tapes. Since the internal calculations are performed so rapidly, the input and the output operations are the only major obstacles to speed. High-speed input and output devices have been developed to assist firms in operating large-scale information systems.

■ *How does the computer process the data and prepare the output?*

Another characteristic of electronic computers (in addition to their great speed) is that they can store internally vast quantities of information. This information then can be recalled by the computer for use in a variety of problems it might be solving. This storage, or *memory,* can hold two kinds of data: (1) it can store instructions to the computer that tell it what operations to perform and in what sequence to perform them, such as add and subtract, or print a particular figure on a report; and (2) it can store the data on which the operations will be performed.

The **central processing unit** of a computer has three parts: (1) the control unit, (2) the arithmetic unit, and (3) the storage unit. The **control unit** acts as a monitor or switchboard in the execution of the instructions that are given to the machine. It assures that the predetermined set of instructions, called a **program,** is performed in the proper sequence. Further, it coordinates the activities of the input equipment and the output equipment of the computer installation.

The **arithmetic unit** is the part of the central processing unit that actually performs the adding, subtracting, multiplying and dividing. Remember that these operations are handled by electronic circuits instead of by wheels or other mechanical devices.

The **storage unit** or memory section of the central processing unit includes many storage areas called *locations.* Stored in these memory cells are the steps of the program (instructions), as well as the data on which the instructions are to be performed. The control unit activates the program, helps select the instructions and data from the memory, assures the performance of the prescribed arithmetic, and activates the output and input equipment when necessary. Illustration 57-5 summarizes the computer operation.

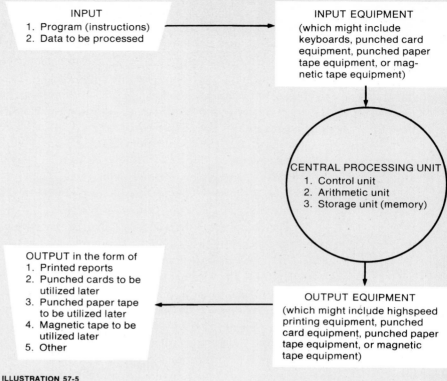

INPUT
1. Program (instructions)
2. Data to be processed

INPUT EQUIPMENT
(which might include keyboards, punched card equipment, punched paper tape equipment, or magnetic tape equipment)

CENTRAL PROCESSING UNIT
1. Control unit
2. Arithmetic unit
3. Storage unit (memory)

OUTPUT in the form of
1. Printed reports
2. Punched cards to be utilized later
3. Punched paper tape to be utilized later
4. Magnetic tape to be utilized later
5. Other

OUTPUT EQUIPMENT
(which might include highspeed printing equipment, punched card equipment, punched paper tape equipment, or magnetic tape equipment)

ILLUSTRATION 57-5

» NEW TERMS

arithmetic unit One of the three major sections of the central processing unit of an electronic computer; it performs the adding, subtracting, multiplying, and dividing. [p. 967]

central processing unit The main section of an electronic computer, containing the control unit, the arithmetic unit, and the storage unit (memory). [p. 967]

control unit One of the three major sections of the central processing unit of an electronic computer; it acts as a monitor or switchboard for execution of the program. [p. 967]

electronic computer A machine which performs arithmetic and other functions through the use of electronic circuits. [p. 967]

information system A system whose primary output is information to be used by decision makers. [p. 960]

invoice A source document commonly used to provide detailed information about a sale of goods or services. [p. 963]

keypunch machine A machine with a keyboard similar to that of a typewriter; it punches holes in cards to transfer information to a form usable by other machines. [p. 964]

magnetic tape Metal-coated plastic tape on which information can be stored in the form of magnetic spots; an input device. [p. 966]

program The step-by-step set of instructions which is given to an electronic computer. [p. 967]

punched card An input device that utilizes holes in columns and rows to represent numeric and alphabetic information. [p. 964]

punched paper tape An input device that utilizes holes in channels on the tape to represent numeric and alphabetic information. [p. 966]

purchase order A source document commonly used to provide detailed information about goods or services ordered by a firm. [p. 963]

source document Written evidence that a business trans-

action has taken place; examples include invoices, bills, monthly statements, and sales slips. [p. 963]

storage unit One of the three major sections of the central processing unit of an electronic computer; the memory area which contains locations to store information. [p. 967]

system A set of components or elements which are put together in a particular way to attain a goal or set of goals. [p. 960]

➤ ASSIGNMENT MATERIAL

QUESTIONS

Q57-1. What is a system?

Q57-2. What is an information system?

Q57-3. List three basic characteristics of an information system.

Q57-4. A financial accounting system has a somewhat more limited purpose than some information systems. Discuss.

Q57-5. List and describe three general forms of information systems operating in our economy today.

Q57-6. List and briefly discuss each of the elements that are common to all information systems.

Q57-7. Refer to Illustration 57-1, the summary of common elements of information systems. Explain the significance of the dashed lines on the diagram.

Q57-8. Explain why the data selection function is of such importance in information systems.

Q57-9. What is the function of source documents?

Q57-10. List two source documents that are used in businesses and that were not mentioned in the unit.

Q57-11. List and describe the input devices introduced in this chapter. Which of these has the advantage of greatest speed?

Q57-12. Describe the three major parts of the central processing unit of an electronic computer and their functions.

Q57-13. What form can the input and the output of an electronic computer take?

Q57-14. What is the characteristic which fundamentally differentiates an electronic computer from other machines?

EXERCISES

E57-1. Briefly describe the kind of *information* needed by each of the following individuals:
   a. The manager of a small short-order cafe.
   b. The minister of a church.
   c. An electrician working for a large company.
   d. A bus driver for a municipal transit company.
   e. A barber who owns a barbershop.
   f. A college teacher.

E57-2. Given below are a series of descriptions. For each description, state the term that best summarizes the description.

Example:—metal coated plastic tape used as an input device in a computer system   *Term:* magnetic tape

    a. The step-by-step set of instructions for an electronic computer.

    b. The section of the electronic computer that contains the memory, the arithmetic unit, and the control unit.

    c. A machine containing electronic circuits that can perform arithmetic.

    d. A machine that punches holes in cards.

    e. That section of the central processing unit that performs the arithmetic.

    f. The memory of a computer.

    g. An input device that utilizes holes punched in channels.

    h. An input device that utilizes holes punched in columns.

    i. That activity in an information system involving preparation of reports for decision makers.

E57-3. True or False.

    a. Selecting data that are relevant to the decisions to be made in an element common to all information systems.

    b. All electronic computers utilize punched cards as input devices.

    c. Knowing what kind of data to select as input is dependent upon the kind of decisions to be made.

    d. Source documents are generally the output of information systems.

    e. The source document is the written evidence that a business transaction has taken place.

    f. Journals and ledgers are examples of source documents.

    g. The source document commonly used to provide detailed information about a sale of goods and services is known as an invoice.

    h. There is no information system that is broader in scope than financial accounting.

    i. Punched cards can contain numeric *and* alphabetic information.

    j. Electrically operated punched card systems came into use in the early 1900s.

E57-4. 1. A set of components or elements which are put together in a particular way to attain a goal is a _____.

    2. A system whose primary output is information to be used by decision makers is a (an) _____.

    3. Name three examples of systems in our economy today.

        a. _____

        b. _____

        c. _____

    4. Name three general forms of information systems operating in business firms today.

        a. _____

        b. _____

        c. _____

    5. Which type of system have you studied involving a two-column journal for recording all business transactions? _____

6. Which type of system can handle several types of accounting as well as fore-casting?_____

7. The accountant is most concerned with one kind of output which is ___
_____.

8. How do the users of an information system justify its cost?

_____

_____

9. The three important advantages of electronic computers are

_____, _____, and
_____.

10. Name three elements of the manual accounting information system.

a. _____

b. _____

c. _____

PROBLEMS (GROUP A)

P57-1. *Analysis of reporting system.* Assume you were recently hired as general manager of the Modern Drug Stores Company. This company has four medium-size retail drug stores, located in East Harrison, California. The stores have been operating successfully for about 10 years.
   a. Prepare a list of the general kinds of information that you would probably need as general manager of the company. Give some thought to this and try to develop a list which covers most of the kinds of decisions that you think you would be involved with.
   b. What *form* would the information system of the company probably take?
   c. As general manager, would you be particularly interested in the nature of the firm's information system? Why or why not?

P57-2. *Analysis of information system—case.* A large and very well known chain of motels, Holiday Inns, uses an electronic computer in providing information about room reservations at each of the many motels. The information system can provide information about vacancies at any Holiday Inn. For example, assume you live in Miami and want to make a room reservation in Memphis for the next night. You call the central reservations office and the reservations employee inquires of the computer if there are vacancies in the Memphis motel; if so, a reservation can be made.

Based only on the information above, work up your own answers to the questions that follow. The purpose of this problem is *not* to determine exactly how the Holiday Inn system works; rather, the purpose is to give you a chance to think about the elements common to *all* information systems.
   a. The first element of an information system involves selection of data that are relevant to the decisions to be made. Describe or list the kinds of decisions that would be made with the use of information from a reservations system. Who needs the information (who are the decision makers)?

b. What kind of data would be entered into the system? What would be the source of these data? Make a list of the kinds of inputs.

c. Make a list of the kinds and forms of the output from this information system. Be sure that the output is consistent with the decisions you described in (a) above.

P57-3. *Input–output; chart of accounts.* The Terrier Hardware Company is owned by Ed Walton and Joe Thompson. The firm operates two retail hardware stores. The Uptown Management Services and Computer Company has offered to handle the accounting records for the stores for a monthly fee. You have been hired to help plan the system.

REQUIRED:

a. Make a list of all the possible kinds of business transactions that the hardware stores are likely to encounter.

b. For each of these types of business transactions, design (draw an example) of a source document that would probably form the main basis for recording the transaction.

c. Construct a chart of accounts with account code numbers.

d. Each month the computer operator will pick up from the hardware stores the necessary input information. What kind of data will this input be? What form will it be in?

PROBLEMS (GROUP B)

P57-4. *Systems review*

Part A

Describe the form of information system that would *most likely* be used by each of the following firms:

a. Small cafe.
b. IBM.
c. Walter Reed Hospital.
d. Local insurance company.
e. Pet store.
f. University of 20,000 students.
g. Eastern Airlines.
h. An independent grocery store.

Part B

Place the following terms under the correct headings:
(Some may be used twice.)

a. Source documents:

(1) _____

(2) _____

b. Input devices:

(1) _____

(2) _____

(3) _____

(4) _____

Keyboards
Punched card equipment
Purchase order
Magnetic tapes
Storage unit
Invoice
High-speed printing equipment
Punched paper tapes

c. Input equipment:

    (1) _____

    (2) _____

    (3) _____

    (4) _____

Punched paper tape equipment
Arithmetic unit
Punched cards
Control unit
Magnetic tape equipment

d. Output equipment:

    (1) _____

    (2) _____

    (3) _____

    (4) _____

Part C

Matching.

_____ 1. storage unit

_____ 2. source document

_____ 3. punched paper tape

_____ 4. purchase order

_____ 5. program

_____ 6. invoice

_____ 7. control unit

_____ 8. punched card

_____ 9. electronic computer

_____ 10. central processing unit

a. the first written evidence of relevant data

b. the source document commonly used to provide detailed information about a sale of goods or services

c. the source document commonly used to provide detailed information about goods or services ordered by a firm

d. an input device that utilizes holes in columns and rows to represent numeric and alphabetic information

e. the main section of an electronic computer, containing the control unit, the arithmetic unit, and the storage unit (memory)

f. one section of the central processing unit which acts as a monitor or switchboard for execution of the program

g. a machine which performs arithmetic and other functions through the use of electronic circuits

h. a machine with a keyboard similar to that of a typewriter which punches holes in cards to transfer information to a form usable by other machines

i. metal-coated plastic tape on which information can be stored in the form of magnetic spots

j. the step-by-step set of instructions which is given to an electronic computer

k. an input device that utilizes holes in channels on tape to represent numeric and alphabetic information

l. a section of the central processing unit which is the memory area containing locations to store information

P57-5. *Systems and computers*

Part A
Matching.

_____ 1. information system

_____ 2. control unit

_____ 3. invoice

_____ 4. source document

_____ 5. program

_____ 6. punched paper tape

_____ 7. electronic computer

_____ 8. purchase order

_____ 9. cash discount

_____ 10. special ledger

A. one of the major sections of the central processing unit of an electronic computer which acts as a monitor or switchboard for execution of the program

B. written evidence that a business transaction has taken place

C. a reduction in the purchase price of merchandise purchased or a reduction in sales price if the merchandise is paid for within an agreed period of time

D. a ledger designed to accumulate detailed information that can supplement the information contained in the general ledger

E. a system whose primary output is information to be used by decision makers

F. a machine which performs arithmetic and other functions through the use of electronic circuits

G. a source document commonly used to provide detailed information about a sale of goods or services

H. the step-by-step set of instructions which is given to an electronic computer

I. a source document commonly used to provide detailed information about goods or services ordered by a firm

J. the memory area of an electronic computer

K. an input device that utilizes holes in columns and rows to represent numeric and alphabetic information

L. an input device that utilizes holes in channels on tape to represent numeric and alphabetic information

Part B
Assume a firm uses special journals. Indicate for each business transaction below which journal would probably be used to record the transaction.

_____ 1. Made sales of merchandise for cash.

_____ 2. Borrowed money from a bank signing a note payable.

_____ 3. Purchased merchandise for cash.

_____ 4. Owner invests cash in the business.

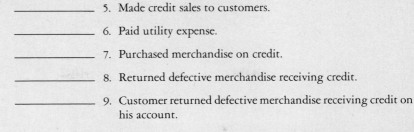

_____ 5. Made credit sales to customers.

_____ 6. Paid utility expense.

_____ 7. Purchased merchandise on credit.

_____ 8. Returned defective merchandise receiving credit.

_____ 9. Customer returned defective merchandise receiving credit on his account.

_____ 10. Made the adjusting entry for the depreciation on equipment.

P57-6. *Computer-prepared accounting reports.* A major department store in your city recently has installed an electronic computer. The financial statements are prepared by the computer at the end of each month. The controller has observed that the computer is not being used to its full capacity and hires you to make an investigation of other possible uses for the computer. The store is organized in the following manner:

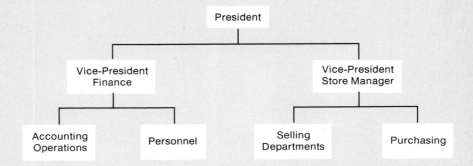

REQUIRED:

Outline the accounting reports that the computer could aid in preparing. To whom would these reports be directed? What is the nature of these reports?

appendix C
end-of-period manufacturing operations

58

END-OF-PERIOD MANUFACTURING OPERATIONS

➤ OBJECTIVE

This appendix will explain how to prepare the work sheet for an enterprise that is engaged in manufacturing operations. Unit 43 introduced you to the manufacturing statement under the periodic method of recording inventories. This appendix uses the same example that was given in that unit, Lakefront Manufacturing Corporation. Also, this appendix shows how adjusting and closing entries are made from the manufacturing work sheet.

➤ APPROACH TO ATTAINING THE OBJECTIVE

As you study about end of period activities in a manufacturing operation, pay special attention to these three questions, which the text following answers:

- *How is the work sheet prepared for a manufacturing firm?*
- *How are adjusting entries recorded for a manufacturing firm?*
- *How are closing entries recorded for a manufacturing firm?*

**PREPARING THE
WORK SHEET**

▪ *How is the work
sheet prepared for a
manufacturing firm?*

Refer to Illustration 58-1 on pages 980 and 981. This is an illustration of a work sheet prepared for Lakefront Manufacturing Corporation. Each set of columns will now be discussed to show you how such a work sheet differs from the work sheet of a merchandising firm (with which you are already familiar).

Trial balance columns The trial balance columns simply list the ledger accounts and their balances at the end of the year. Especially notice the account numbering system used by this firm:

100's	assets
200's	liabilities
300's	capital
400's	revenues
500's	accounts related to manufacturing operations
600's	selling expenses
700's	general expenses
800's	net earnings summary

Also, pay special attention to the fact that the three inventory accounts (105, 106, 107) appearing in the trial balance columns are the *beginning* inventories, under the periodic method.

Adjustments columns The firm had five adjustments as discussed below.

(a) The first adjustment is for depreciation of the factory plant and equipment. It is assumed that the depreciation amounts to $10,000. This amount is debited to a factory overhead account (506) and credited to the accumulated depreciation account (121).

(b) Adjustment (b) for manufacturing supplies used reduces the asset (prepaid expense) for $600 and sets up an overhead item (507) for that amount. Notice that the remaining supplies on hand of $8,400 (based on physical count) appears in the adjusted trial balance columns.

(c) This adjustment is for $1,000 of expired insurance on the factory.

(d) Pay special attention to this inventory adjustment. According to physical count, the ending Raw materials inventory amounts to $119,000. This amount is debited to account 105. On that same line of the work sheet, the beginning inventory of $20,000 is credited to remove the old balance from the inventory account. Now look near the bottom of the adjustments columns for the **Manufacturing summary** account (550). To complete the entry, these same inventory amounts ($119,000 and $20,000) are entered temporarily in a summary account, since the Raw materials inventory changes will affect the cost of goods manufactured.

Similarly, the new balance of Work in process inventory (according to physical count) of $25,000 is debited to account 106. The old balance of $18,000 is credited. And, again these two amounts are debited and credited to the Manufacturing summary account (550) to complete the adjustment.

(e) The final adjustment is the Finished goods inventory (e). The physical count of $53,000 is entered as a debit in account 107. The old balance of $21,000 is credited to the Finished goods inventory account. Likewise, the two amounts are recorded temporarily in the Net earnings summary account (801), to be used later in computing Net income.

Adjusted trial balance columns As in the case of merchandising firm, the adjusted balances of the accounts appear in this set of columns. Observe that the three inventory accounts (105, 106, 107) show their correct ending balances. The temporary Manufacturing summary account and the temporary Net earnings summary account show both beginning and ending inventories for later use.

Manufacturing statement columns This set of columns contains all the information needed to prepare the manufacturing statement. Only two inventories are used in the computation of the cost of goods manufactured. As a study aid, refer directly to the manufacturing statement of Lakefront Manufacturing Corporation as shown on page 748 of Unit 43. This statement was prepared from the manufacturing statement columns of the work sheet of Illustration 58-1. Trace each figure from the work sheet to the manufacturing statement.

On the work sheet, pay special attention to the fact that the Cost of goods manufactured is entered in the credit column as a *balancing* figure (since the cost is a debit). Then this amount ($145,000) is transferred as a cost to the debit column of the income statement columns of the work sheet.

Income statement columns The income statement that you studied in Unit 43 on page 749 was prepared from this work sheet. Trace every figure appearing on the work sheet to the income statement. Notice how the finished goods inventory is used in computing the cost of goods sold, which, in turn, appears on the income statement.

Balance sheet columns To simplify the example, the work sheet illustrated does not include columns for the statement of retained earnings. Instead, all accounts involving retained earnings (beginning retained earnings, dividends, and net earnings) are entered in the balance sheet columns. The

ILLUSTRATION 58-1

Lakefront Manufacturing Corporation
MANUFACTURING WORK SHEET
For the Year Ended December 31, 1978

ACCOUNT NUMBERS		TRIAL BALANCE dr.	TRIAL BALANCE cr.	ADJUSTMENTS dr.	ADJUSTMENTS cr.	ADJUSTED TRIAL BALANCE dr.	ADJUSTED TRIAL BALANCE cr.	MANUFACTURING STATEMENT dr.	MANUFACTURING STATEMENT cr.	INCOME STATEMENT dr.	INCOME STATEMENT cr.	BALANCE SHEET dr.	BALANCE SHEET cr.
101	Cash	12,000				12,000						12,000	
102	Marketable securities	80,000				80,000						80,000	
105	Raw materials inventory	20,000		(d) 119,000	(d) 20,000	119,000						119,000	
106	Work in process inventory	18,000		(d) 25,000	(d) 18,000	25,000						25,000	
107	Finished goods inventory	21,000		(e) 53,000	(e) 21,000	53,000						53,000	
110	Manufacturing supplies	9,000			(b) 600	8,400						8,400	
111	Prepaid insurance	5,000			(c) 1,000	4,000						4,000	
120	Plant and equipment	210,000				210,000						210,000	
121	Accumulated depreciation		80,000		(a) 10,000		90,000						90,000
125	Land	75,000				75,000						75,000	
201	Accounts payable		10,000				10,000						10,000
210	Notes payable		30,000				30,000						30,000
301	Common stock		125,000				125,000						125,000
302	Retained earnings		275,400				275,400						275,400
303	Dividends	1,000				1,000						1,000	

Worksheet (manufacturing)

Acct No.	Account	Trial Balance Dr	Trial Balance Cr	Adjustments Dr	Adjustments Cr	Adjusted Trial Balance Dr	Adjusted Trial Balance Cr	Cost of Goods Manufactured Dr	Cost of Goods Manufactured Cr	Income Statement Dr	Income Statement Cr	Balance Sheet Dr	Balance Sheet Cr
401	Sales		200,000				200,000				200,000		200,000
402	Other revenues		20,000				20,000				20,000		20,000
501	Purchases of raw materials	171,000				171,000		171,000					
502	Direct labor costs	50,000				50,000		50,000					
503	Indirect labor	16,000				16,000		16,000					
504	Electricity	1,000				1,000		1,000					
505	Other utilities	400				400		400					
520	Other factory overhead	1,000				1,000		1,000					
601	Selling expenses	40,000				40,000				40,000			
701	General and administrative expenses	10,000				10,000				10,000			
		740,400	740,400										
506	Depreciation on plant and equipment			(a) 10,000		10,000		10,000					
507	Manufacturing supplies used			(b) 600		600		600					
508	Insurance on the factory			(c) 1,000 (d) 20,000	(d) 119,000	20,000	119,000	20,000	119,000				
550	Manufacturing summary			(d) 18,000	(d) 25,000	18,000	25,000	18,000	25,000 144,000				
801	Net earnings summary			(e) 21,000	(e) 53,000	21,000	53,000	21,000	53,000	21,000	53,000		53,000
				267,600	267,600	947,400	947,400						
	Cost of goods manufactured								145,000 289,000	145,000			
								289,000	289,000	216,000	273,000		587,400
	Net income									57,000			57,000
										273,000	273,000	587,400	587,400

balance sheet of the company can be prepared directly from this set of columns.

ADJUSTING ENTRIES

The general journal that follows shows the adjusting journal entries for the company. These adjustments are taken from the adjustments columns of the work sheet.

■ *How are adjusting entries recorded for a manufacturing firm?*

ADJUSTING ENTRIES

1978					
(a) Dec.	31	Depreciation on plant and equipment		10,000	
		Accumulated depreciation			10,000
		To record 1978 depreciation on factory plant and equipment.			
(b)	31	Manufacturing supplies used		600	
		Manufacturing supplies			600
		To record supplies used in factory.			
(c)	31	Insurance on the factory		1,000	
		Prepaid insurance			1,000
		To record expired insurance.			
(d)	31	Raw materials inventory		119,000	
		Work in process inventory		25,000	
		Manufacturing summary			119,000
		Manufacturing summary			25,000
		To record *ending* inventories according to physical count.			
(d)	31	Manufacturing summary		20,000	
		Manufacturing summary		18,000	
		Raw materials inventory			20,000
		Work in process inventory			18,000
		To remove the *beginning* inventories from the accounts.			
(e)	31	Finished goods inventory		53,000	
		Net earnings summary			53,000
		To record the *ending* Finished goods inventory.			
(f)	31	Net earnings summary		21,000	
		Finished goods inventory			21,000
		To remove the beginning Finished goods inventory from the accounts.			

CLOSING ENTRIES

The five-step procedure for recording closing entries is shown in the following journal.

■ *How are closing entries recorded for a manufacturing firm?*

1978					
Dec.	31	Manufacturing summary	251,000	
		Purchases of raw materials		171,000
		Direct labor costs		50,000
		Indirect labor		16,000
		Electricity		1,000
		Other utilities		400
		Other factory overhead		1,000
		Depreciation on plant and equipment		10,000
		Manufacturing supplies used		600
		Insurance on the factory		1,000
		To close all accounts related to the manufacturing statement and temporarily place their balances in the Manufacturing summary account.		
	31	Sales	200,000	
		Other revenues	20,000	
		Net earnings summary		220,000
		To close the revenue accounts.		
	31	Net earnings summary	195,000	
		Selling expenses		40,000
		General and administrative expenses		10,000
		Manufacturing summary		145,000
		To close the expenses.		
	31	Net earnings summary	57,000	
		Retained earnings		57,000
		To transfer the net income for 1978 to the Retained earnings account.		
	31	Retained earnings	1,000	
		Dividends		1,000
		To close the Dividends account and to reduce the retained earnings.		

As a final explanation, the two temporary summary accounts are shown below:

MANUFACTURING SUMMARY

(d) ADJUSTMENT for beginning raw materials		20,000	(d) ADJUSTMENT for ending raw materials		119,000
(d) ADJUSTMENT for beginning work in process		18,000	(d) ADJUSTMENT for ending work in process		25,000
12/31 CLOSING ENTRY (Manufacturing costs)		251,000	12/31 CLOSING ENTRY		145,000
		289,000			289,000

(e) ADJUSTMENT for beginning finished goods	21,000	(e) ADJUSTMENT for ending finished goods	53,000
12/31 CLOSING ENTRY (Expenses)	195,000	12/31 CLOSING ENTRY (Revenues)	220,000
12/31 CLOSING ENTRY (Net income)	57,000		
	273,000		273,000

Each of the entries above can be traced to the adjusting and closing entries in the journals shown.

> **NEW TERM**

manufacturing summary A temporary account used to accumulate the cost of goods manufactured for a period. [p. 978]

> **ASSIGNMENT MATERIAL**

QUESTIONS

Q58-1. How do the columns used in a work sheet for a manufacturing firm differ from the columns used in a work sheet for a merchandising firm?

Q58-2. Explain how the adjusting entry is made for the Raw materials inventory.

Q58-3. Explain how the adjusting entry is made for the Work in process inventory.

Q58-4. Explain how the adjusting entry is made for the Finished goods inventory.

Q58-5. What is the purpose of the Manufacturing summary account?

EXERCISES

E58-1. Prepare the adjusting entries related to the three inventories from the following data:

	1978	
	BEGINNING	ENDING
Raw materials inventory	$ 6,000	$ 7,000
Work in process inventory	13,000	9,000
Finished goods inventory	10,000	12,000

E58-2. Using the information given in E43-1 (Merida Plans, Inc.),
a. Prepare adjusting entries for inventories.
b. Prepare the closing entry that summarizes the manufacturing costs in the Manufacturing summary account.

E58-3. Using the data from E43-2 (Bell Company), prepare adjusting entries for the inventories at the end of the year.

E58-4. Below are *selected* adjusting and closing entries from the journal of a firm:

1978 Dec.	31	Manufacturing summary	6,000	
		Raw materials inventory		6,000
	31	Manufacturing summary	60,000	
		Factory overhead		20,000
		Purchases of raw materials		23,000
		Direct labor		17,000
	31	Finished goods inventory	12,000	
		Net earnings summary		12,000
	31	Retained earnings	18,000	
		Net earnings summary		18,000

Give a detailed explanation of each of the preceding entries.

PROBLEMS (GROUP A)

P58-1. *Inventory adjustments, closing entries, manufacturing.* Below are end-of-period account balances of Southern Drug Company at December 31, 1978.

Sales	$498,000
Sales returns and allowances	10,000
Sales discounts	2,000
Raw materials inventory	47,000
Work in process inventory	28,000
Finished goods inventory	80,000
Factory overhead	100,000
Direct labor	56,000
Raw materials purchases	120,000
Service revenue	20,000
Selling expenses	145,000
General expenses	50,000

REQUIRED:

a. Prepare adjusting entries for the inventories. The physical count at the end of the year follows:

Raw materials	$40,000
Work in process	21,000
Finished goods	78,000

b. Prepare closing entries for the firm. Dividends declared on common stock totaled $30,000.

P58-2. *Preparing entries, manufacturing.* Prepare closing entries for the Eastern Manufacturing Corporation from the data appearing in P43-4 in Unit 43.

P58-3. *Work sheet, closing entries, manufacturing.* The general ledger of Rotation Corporation for the year ended December 31, 1978, showed the following accounts and balances:

Cash	$ 9,000
Marketable securities	34,000
Accounts receivable	15,000
Allowance for uncollectibles	1,000
Raw materials inventory	20,000
Work in process inventory	15,000
Finished goods inventory	18,000
Prepaid insurance	2,000
Long-term investments	100,000
Plant and equipment	300,000
Accumulated depreciation	100,000
Accounts payable	31,000
Expenses payable	8,000
Federal income taxes payable	2,000
Bonds payable	130,000
Long-term notes payable	90,000
Common stock	60,000
Retained earnings	25,000
Dividends	5,000
Sales	400,000
Sales returns and allowances	11,000
Sales discounts	4,000
Rent revenue	40,000
Purchases of raw materials	150,000
Direct labor costs	55,000
Factory overhead costs	31,000
Selling expenses	30,000
General, administrative, and other expenses	88,000

Additional Information: The factory overhead subsidiary ledger showed these balances: Indirect labor, $10,000; Manufacturing supplies, $300; Electricity, $1,000; Depreciation, $11,000; Insurance, $1,000; Other factory expenses, $7,700. A physical count of the inventories indicated that the December 31, 1978, balances were: Raw materials inventory, $12,000; Finished goods inventory, $60,000; Work in process inventory, $50,000. During the entire year, there were 20,000 shares of common stock outstanding.

REQUIRED:

a. Prepare a work sheet for the company.
b. Prepare closing entries for the company.

PROBLEMS (GROUP B)

P58-4. *Inventory adjustments, closing entries, manufacturing.* Refer to P43-5 in Unit 43.

REQUIRED:

a. Prepare adjusting journal entries for the inventories.

b. Prepare closing journal entries. There were $5,000 of common stock dividends during the year.

P58-5. *Closing entries, manufacturing.* Refer to P43-6 in Unit 43.

REQUIRED: Prepare closing entries in general journal form.

P58-6. *Work sheet, manufacturing.* Use the data in P43-6 in Unit 43 for this problem.

REQUIRED: Prepare a work sheet for the company for the year ended December 31, 1978.

index

B

Bad debts, 253, 255, 260
  adjustment, 293
  direct write-off method, 299, 300
Balance sheet, 6
  account form, 132, 141
  capital section, 482
  consolidated, 595
  corporation:
    illustrated, 135
  defined, 14
  illustrated, 247
  partnership:
    illustrated, 134
  proprietorship:
    illustrated, 133
  report form, 132, 142
Bank deposit receipt, 275, 287
Bank statement, 279, 287
  reconciliation, 279
Behavioral considerations, 801
Bond discount, 569, 574
Bond indenture, 435, 439
Bond premium, 571, 574
Bonds, 434
  callable, 435, 439
  convertible, 435, 439
  discount, 569, 574
  investments, 361
  issuing, 565
  premium, 571, 574
  proceeds, 566, 574
  refunding, 573, 574
  retiring, 572
  secured, 435, 439
  serial, 435, 439
  sinking fund, 435, 439
  underwriter, 565, 574
Bonus, 407, 420
Book value, 378, 381, 384
  per share, 521
Bookkeeper, 7, 15
Break-even:
  analysis, 732–37
  chart, 724
  equation, 721
  model, 720, 725
    limitations, 737
  point, 722, 725
Budget, 8, 15
  cash receipts and disbursements, 809

Budget (*cont.*)
  cost of goods sold, 807
  direct labor, 804, 805
  factory overhead, 805, 806
  operating expenses, 807
  production levels, 803–804
  raw materials, 804, 805
  revenue, 803
Budget committee, 802, 810
Budget director, 802, 810
Budgeting:
  nature, 801
Business combination, 594, 604
Business decisions, 7
Business entity, 631
Business firm, 4
  description, 9
  manufacturing, 9, 15
  merchandising, 9, 15
  service, 9, 15
Business transaction, 11, 15, 631
  common, 166

C

Callable bonds, 435, 439
Capital, 10, 14, 15, 482
  on balance sheets of different organi-
    zation forms, 140
  donated, 502, 504
Capital asset, 932, 937
Capital budgeting, 883, 889
Capital expenditure, 383, 384
Capital gains provisions, 932–34, 937–
  38
Cash, 136
  classification, 272
  planning, 273
  valuation, 272
Cash discount, 166, 178, 185
Cash dividend, 497, 504
Cash flow statement, 274, 287
Cash payments journal, 198, 209
Cash receipts and disbursements state-
    ment:
  budgeted, 809
Cash receipts journal, 172, 185
Cash surrender value, 364, 368
Cash-type assets, 12
Central processing unit, 967, 968
Certificate in Management Accounting,
  8

Certified public accountant, 8, 15
Chart of accounts, 66, 68
Charter, 10, 15, 170
Check register, 277, 287
Classification, 130, 141
Classifying costs, 704
Closing entries, 107, 116
  illustrated, 109
  manufacturing firm, 982
  merchandising firm:
    illustrated, 258
  partnership, 450
    illustrated, 451
CMA Examination, 8
Code:
  Internal Revenue, 911, 923
Collection period of receivables, 298
Common-size information, 514, 528
Common stockholders:
  rights, 579, 586
  preemptive, 579, 586
Common stocks, 365
Composite approach to depreciation,
  378, 384
Compound interest method, 566
Computer (*see* Electronic computer)
Concepts, 630–34
Conservatism, 633, 640
Consistency, 634, 640
Consolidated financial statements, 594,
  604
  using, 615
Consolidated group, 594
Consolidated net earnings, 612, 616
Consolidation, 594, 604
Constitution of United States, 911
Consumer Price Index, 667, 673
Contra account, 83, 85, 116
Contribution margin, 722, 725
  ratio, 723, 725
Control, 688, 698
Control account, 203, 209
Control unit, 967, 968
Controller, 7, 15, 274, 287
Controlling, 5
Controlling interest, 593, 604
Convertible bonds, 435, 439
Convertible preferred stock, 486, 490
Copyrights, 396, 397
Corporate charter, 170
Corporation, 10, 15
  balance sheet:
    illustrated, 135
  charter, 10, 15

F

Factory overhead, 718, 726, 767, 770
  applying, 833
  budget variance, 836, 838
  overapplied, 782, 784
  rate, 768, 770
  schedule, 748, 750, 751
  underapplied, 782, 784
  volume variance, 836, 838
Factory payroll, 766, 770
FASB (see Financial Accounting Standards Board)
Federal unemployment compensation tax, 413, 420
FICA tax, 413, 420
FIFO method, 328, 332, 337
Financial accounting, 15
Financial Accounting Standards Board, 272, 365, 396, 635
Financial expenses, 245
Financial leverage, 585, 586
Financial statements, 5, 15, 127 (see also Balance sheet, Income statement, Retained earnings statement, Statement of changes in financial position, Statement of owner's capital, Statement of partners' capital)
  analysis, 517–25
  budgeted, 808
  consolidated, 594, 604
    using, 615
  interim, 234, 346
  price-level adjusted, 674–75
  statement of changes in financial position, 856
Financing methods, 581
  tax effects, 930
Finished goods inventory, 747, 751
Fire loss, 382
Firm, 4
Fixed assets, 141 (see also Plant and equipment)
Fixed cost, 705, 709, 717
Flow diagram:
  capital budgeting, 899
  income tax, 913, 922
Flow of funds, 851, 856
Footnotes to financial statements, 349, 627, 640
Form 941, 419, 420
Form of organization:
  choosing, 929

Funds, 868, 871
  flow, 851, 856
Funds statement (see Statement of changes in financial position)

G

Gain on sale of long-term investments, 365
Gain on sale of marketable securities, 273
Gains and losses on realization, 466, 468
General and administrative expenses, 152, 154
General expenses, 244
General Mills, Inc., 626
General price change, 667, 673
Generally accepted accounting principles, 129, 141, 535, 628, 640
  nature, 629
  need for, 629
Goal congruence, 704, 709
Goals, 11
Going concern, 631, 640
Goodwill:
  on consolidated balance sheet, 603–4
  partnerships, 463–64, 468
Governmental accounting, 9
Graph for costs, 708
Gross margin, 244
Gross margin method, 346, 350
Gross national product Implicit Price Deflator, 667, 673
Gross profit (see Gross margin)
Group approach to depreciation, 378, 384

H

Head of household, 914, 923
Historical cost, 718, 726

I

Income statement, 5, 15
  consolidated, 594

Income statement (cont.)
  corporation:
    illustrated, 163
  illustrated, 537
  merchandising firm:
    illustrated, 245
  proprietorship:
    illustrated, 150
  summary, 246
Income tax:
  and capital budgeting, 902
  court decisions, 912
  deferred, 436, 439
  interperiod allocation, 552, 556
  intraperiod allocation, 549, 556
  tables, 916–21
Income tax expense, 152, 154
Income tax method, 395
Income tax regulations, 912, 923
Independent contractor, 407
Index of prices, 667, 673
Inflation, 667, 673
Information:
  creditors, 513
  investors, 513
  labor unions, 513
  relationship to decisions, 513
Information system, 960, 968
  elements, 962
Input, 962
Institute of Management Accounting, 8
Intangible assets, 138, 142
Intercompany eliminations, 599, 604
Intercompany loans, 603
Interest:
  bonds, 362
  calculating, 208, 309
    bonds, 566
    short-cut method, 312
    6%, 60-day method, 312
  compound, 430
  number of times earned, 525
  tables, 312
Interest expense, 21, 84, 85
Interest payable, 84, 85
Interim financial statements, 234, 346
Internal auditor, 8, 16
Internal control, 274
Internal Revenue Code, 911, 923
Interperiod allocation of income taxes, 552, 556
Intraperiod allocation of income taxes, 549, 556
Inventory, 137, 142 (see also Merchandise inventory)